MW01196378

Dao Companions to Chinese Philosophy

Volume 19

Series Editor

Yong Huang, Department of Philosophy
The Chinese University of Hong Kong
Shatin, New Territories, Hong Kong

Editorial Board

Stephen Angle, Wesleyan University
Middletown, USA

Shirley Chan, Faculty of Arts
Macquarie University
Sydney, NSW, Australia

Paul R. Goldin, University of Pennsylvania
Philadelphia, PA, USA

Chenyang Li, Nanyang Technological University
Singapore, Singapore

Jana Rosker, University of Ljubljana
Šalovci, Slovenia

Amy Olberding, Department of Philosophy
University of Oklahoma
Norman, OK, USA

While "philosophy" is a Western term, philosophy is not something exclusively Western. In this increasingly globalized world, the importance of non-Western philosophy is becoming more and more obvious. Among all the non-Western traditions, Chinese philosophy is certainly one of the richest. In a history of more than 2500 years, many extremely important classics, philosophers, and schools have emerged. As China is becoming an economic power today, it is only natural that more and more people are interested in learning about the cultural traditions, including the philosophical tradition, of China.

The Dao Companions to Chinese Philosophy series aims to provide the most comprehensive and most up-to-date introduction to various aspects of Chinese philosophy as well as philosophical traditions heavily influenced by it. Each volume in this series focuses on an individual school, text, or person.

All books to be published in this Series will be fully peer-reviewed before final acceptance.

Yuri Pines

Editor

Dao Companion to China's *fa* Tradition

The Philosophy of Governance by Impartial Standards

 Springer

Editor
Yuri Pines (ID)
Hebrew University of Jerusalem
Jerusalem, Israel

ISSN 2211-0275   ISSN 2542-8780   (electronic)
Dao Companions to Chinese Philosophy
ISBN 978-3-031-53629-8   ISBN 978-3-031-53630-4   (eBook)
https://doi.org/10.1007/978-3-031-53630-4

© The Editor(s) (if applicable) and The Author(s), under exclusive license to Springer Nature Switzerland AG 2024
This work is subject to copyright. All rights are solely and exclusively licensed by the Publisher, whether the whole or part of the material is concerned, specifically the rights of translation, reprinting, reuse of illustrations, recitation, broadcasting, reproduction on microfilms or in any other physical way, and transmission or information storage and retrieval, electronic adaptation, computer software, or by similar or dissimilar methodology now known or hereafter developed.
The use of general descriptive names, registered names, trademarks, service marks, etc. in this publication does not imply, even in the absence of a specific statement, that such names are exempt from the relevant protective laws and regulations and therefore free for general use.
The publisher, the authors, and the editors are safe to assume that the advice and information in this book are believed to be true and accurate at the date of publication. Neither the publisher nor the authors or the editors give a warranty, expressed or implied, with respect to the material contained herein or for any errors or omissions that may have been made. The publisher remains neutral with regard to jurisdictional claims in published maps and institutional affiliations.

This Springer imprint is published by the registered company Springer Nature Switzerland AG
The registered company address is: Gewerbestrasse 11, 6330 Cham, Switzerland

Paper in this product is recyclable.

Preface

The work on this volume started in the middle of COVID pandemic which mercilessly exposed weaknesses of every single government and political system in dealing with a major crisis. It continued when my motherland, Ukraine, became the victim of a vicious attack by what was normally perceived a fraternal state. And I write this preface at the time when my country of citizenship, Israel, is enmeshed in a new, bloodiest ever, round of its endless conflict with neighboring Palestinians. The three crises (and others, which evolve around us, even with less media attention) differ very much in their nature, background, and potential outcomes. They have only one thing in common: they expose inadequacy of political leaders, whose shortsightedness, narrowmindedness, impulsiveness, and dependence on inept aids and PR-advisors lead their countries into abyss. And these crises also demonstrate that all too often the leaders' lofty discourse of moral superiority conceals nothing but meanness of their actions.

It is against this backdrop that I ponder about the potential relevance of the millennia-old *fa* tradition (often dubbed Legalism), which prioritized impartial norms over personalized decision-making, proposed dissociating politics from moralizing discourse, and pitilessly exposed selfishness of any political actor. The texts associated with this tradition are not easy to read: they abound with provocative and outright appalling statements, and I suspect that should their authors come alive, myself and most of this volume's contributors would find ourselves in an opposing camp. However, their emotionless and realistic approach to politics has a certain allure. Besides, the practicality of their advice was valued by political leaders throughout much of China's history, even though few would openly acknowledge this.

This lack of open endorsement is not surprising. The *fa* thinkers' notorious harshness and authoritarian stance, and especially their assault on fellow intellectuals, gave rise to strong anti-*fa* sentiments which hindered studies of these texts in the past, and which discourage scholars in China and abroad from dealing with them even today. The neglect is unfortunate and self-defeating, though. Whereas few if any of us will be converted to the *fa* texts' approach, the readers will benefit immensely from understanding their rationale, their strength and weaknesses, their intellectual and political context, and their short- and long-term impact. Introducing these topics is the goal of this volume.

Originally, this volume had two editors. Whereas my friend, Paul R. Goldin, decided to stop his involvement with the volume, his help at the initial stages of production was immense and I am deeply indebted to him. I am grateful to the contributors who continued to work on their papers even during the apex of COVID crisis and who were overwhelmingly cooperative and tolerant to editorial quibbles. And special thanks to the dedicated assistant, Dr. Avital Rom, who had not just helped in translating and revising the Chinese-language submissions, but also offered considerable editorial assistance.

This research was supported by the ISF Research Grant 568/19 and Michael W. Lipson chair in Chinese studies, the Hebrew University of Jerusalem.

November 2023, Beijing   Yuri Pines

Contents

Introduction: The *fa* Tradition in Chinese Philosophy

Yuri Pines

The intellectual tradition that is called in Chinese "The School of *fa*" (*fajia* 法家) and in English is best known as "Legalism" gained prominence in the latter half of the Warring States period (Zhanguo 戰國, 453–221 BCE). Adherents of the *fa* tradition (as we prefer to call it henceforth) were political realists who sought to attain a "rich state and a powerful army" (*fuguo qiangbing* 富國强兵) and to ensure domestic stability in the age marked by intense inter- and intra-state competition. They believed that human beings—commoners and elites alike—will forever remain selfish and covetous of riches and fame, and one should not expect them to behave morally. Rather, a viable sociopolitical system should allow individuals to pursue their selfish interests exclusively in the ways that benefit the state, namely agriculture and warfare; and a proper administrative system should allow officials to benefit from ranks and emoluments, but also prevent them from illicitly enriching themselves or subverting the ruler's power. Both systems should remain unconcerned with individual morality of the rulers and the ruled; rather they should be based on impersonal norms and standards most commonly identified as *fa* 法— laws, administrative regulations, clearly defined rules of promotion and demotion, and the like. These recommendations were duly implemented in many of the competing polities, most notably the state of Qin 秦, which successfully unified the Chinese world and established the first imperial dynasty in 221 BCE.

Qin's success marked the zenith of the *fa* tradition's influence; but it also became one of the major reasons for its subsequent denigration. Qin's assault on private

This research was supported by the Israel Science Foundation (grant No. 568/19) and by the Michael William Lipson Chair in Chinese Studies. I am grateful to the volume's contributors, especially to Romain Graziani, for their comments on this introduction.

Y. Pines (✉)
Hebrew University of Jerusalem, Jerusalem, Israel
e-mail: yuri.pines@mail.huji.ac.il

© The Author(s), under exclusive license to Springer Nature Switzerland AG 2024
Y. Pines (ed.), *Dao Companion to China's* fa *Tradition*, Dao Companions to Chinese Philosophy 19, https://doi.org/10.1007/978-3-031-53630-4_1

learning which peaked with the notorious book burning in 213 BCE made this dynasty singularly hated in the eyes of the imperial literati for millennia to come (Barbieri-Low 2022: 157–85). The short-lived Qin dynasty (it collapsed in 207 BCE) was reimagined as an epitome of cruelty, oppressiveness, senseless autocracy—in short, all that went wrong with the unified empire (Pines 2014). The *fa* tradition was identified as the major reason for Qin's malfunction and swift collapse. Whereas many of its practical recipes remained in use throughout imperial history and beyond, leading some scholars to depict imperial China as a "Confucian-Legalist state" (e.g., Zhao 2015), the intellectual tradition itself lost an aura of legitimacy and its vitality. Beginning in the second century of the Han dynasty 漢 (206/202 BCE–220 CE), open endorsement of the *fa* legacy was no longer politically acceptable (Song, Chap. 16, this volume). Even in the twentieth century, despite partial rehabilitation of the *fa* ideology, it remained hugely controversial. Not a few scholars in China and abroad viewed (and continue to view it) as an unpleasant fact of China's history, a kind of historical aberration that merits scanty attention if at all. Only recently the ideological tensions surrounding the study of *fa* texts began receding, allowing scholars to take a fresh look at this fascinating—even if not necessarily morally attractive—tradition.

1 Defining the *fa* Tradition

The *fa* tradition is best known in European languages as the "School of Law" or "Legalist school." As Paul R. Goldin (2011) has demonstrated, this designation suffers from two problems. First, the term *fa* does not necessarily mean "law." Whereas this translation is surely correct in many contexts (see Lau and Lüdke, Chap. 8, this volume), it can as often refer to "standards," "models," "norms," "methods," and the like; sometimes it refers to the entirety of political institutions designed to maintain the proper functioning of the state.[1] Second, viewing *fajia* as a "school" is misleading also because there was no self-aware and organized intellectual current of *fa* adherents on a par with the followers of Confucius 孔子 (551–479 BCE) or Mozi 墨子 (ca. 460–390 BCE).[2] Throughout millennia, this term was used primarily as a

---

[1] See the observation of Zhang Binglin 章炳麟 (a.k.a. Zhang Taiyan 章太炎, 1869–1936): "*Fa* is the grand name for the political system" 法者，制度之大名 (Zhang [1900] 2000, 35: 565).

[2] This does not mean that the *fa* thinkers did not have devoted disciples. Suffice it to mention that the composition of the *Book of Lord Shang* (*Shangjunshu* 商君書) was performed not by Shang Yang 商鞅 (d. 338 BCE) alone but by his anonymous followers, whom Zheng Liangshu (1989) dubs "Shang Yang's school" 商鞅學派. It is highly likely that the preservation and circulation (and possibly redaction) of the text of *Han Feizi* 韓非子 was similarly performed by Han Fei's 韓非 (d. 233 BCE) disciples and followers. Note furthermore that *Han Feizi* refers once to Shang Yang and Shen Buhai 申不害 (d. 337 BCE) not as persons but as *jia* 家 (a term that from the Han dynasty onward referred to a "school" or "scholastic lineage") (*Han Feizi* 43.1.1; Chen 2000: 957; for an assertion that *jia* here refers to persons only, see Petersen 1995: 3). All this suggests that some "proto-*fajia*" groups could have existed back in the Warring States period. It is clear, nonetheless,

bibliographic category under which intellectually related texts were catalogized in the imperial libraries. As such the *fajia* designation is heuristically useful; but to avoid the impression of a coherent "school" or "scholastic lineage," most of the contributors to this volume opted for a more neutral term *fa* tradition.[3]

The Han and later librarians' categorization of certain texts under the *fajia* label was not entirely arbitrary. The seeds of grouping several thinkers as belonging to the same intellectual current can be traced already to Han Fei 韓非 (d. 233 BCE), who is often considered the most significant representative of the *fa* tradition. In chapter 43 of *Han Feizi* 韓非子, "Defining the Standards" ("Ding fa" 定法), the thinker presents himself as the synthesizer and improver of the ideas of two of his predecessors, Shang Yang 商鞅 (d. 338 BCE) and Shen Buhai 申不害 (d. 337 BCE). Pairing Shen Buhai and Shang Yang, and adding Han Fei himself to them became common from the early Han dynasty (see, e.g., *Huainanzi* 6: 230, 11: 423, 20: 833). The historian Sima Qian 司馬遷 (ca. 145–90 BCE) identified these three thinkers as adherents of the teaching of "performance and title" (*xingming* 刑名) (*Shiji* 62: 2146, 68: 2227), the term which remained a secondary designation of the *fa* tradition thereafter.[4] The fourth thinker identified in the Han imperial catalog as belonging to *fajia*—Shen Dao 慎到 (fourth century BCE)—also figures prominently in *Han Feizi*, where a whole chapter (40, "Objection to Positional Power" ["Nan shi" 難勢]) is dedicated to the defense and improvement of Shen's ideas (Pines 2020). These four thinkers (or, more precisely, the texts associated with them) form the core of the *fa* tradition.

The term *fajia* was coined by Sima Qian's father, Sima Tan 司馬談 (d. 110 BCE) in his essay "On the Essentials of the Six Schools of Thought" 六家之要指 (*Shiji* 130: 3289–91). It was first employed as a bibliographical category by the Han librarian, Liu Xiang 劉向 (77–6 BCE), whose catalog was later incorporated into the "Treatise on Arts and Letters" ("Yiwenzhi" 藝文志) chapter of *Hanshu* 漢書 (The Han History) by Ban Gu 班固 (32–92). The "Treatise on Arts and Letters" identifies ten texts as belonging to *fajia*. Four—*Lord Shang* 商君 (later known as the *Book of Lord Shang* [*Shanjunshu* 商君書], *Shēnzi* 申子, *Shènzi* 慎子 and *Han*

---

that these groups were much less cohesive and less visible than the Confucians and Mohists, for example. For more about the complexity of using the term *jia* as "scholastic lineage," see Smith 2003 and Csikszentmihalyi and Nylan 2003.

[3] Among alternative designations contemplated by the contributors, one can note Vogelsang's (Chap. 12) "Political Realists" (defended also in Vogelsang 2016: 39–45; for an earlier example, see Waley 1939). Vogelsang borrows the designation from Hans Morgenthau, who defined Political Realism as an approach that "sets politics as an autonomous sphere of action and understanding apart from other spheres, such as economics, ethics, aesthetics, or religion" (Morgenthau 1978: 5). It should be noted that this definition does not imply that the Political Realists' rivals were mere idealists, which would be an unfair judgement; yet because such an impression may be inadvertently created nonetheless, the author of this introduction prefers to eschew the Political Realists label.

[4] See for instance, *Qingding siku quanshu zongmu tiyao* 101: 1; I borrow translation of *xingming* from Goldin 2020: 13; see more about the term in Wang and Indraccolo; Chaps. 20 and 14 in this volume.

Feizi—are attributed to the thinkers mentioned above. In addition, there are also *Lizi* 李子, attributed to Li Kui 李悝, a minister and legislator in the court of Marquis Wen of Wei 魏文侯 (r. 445–396 BCE); *Chao Cuo* 鼂錯 by an eponymous Han minister (d. 154 BCE); and four other works the authors and dates of which are no longer identifiable (*Hanshu* 30: 1735). *Lizi* was lost relatively early; the works of Shen Buhai and Chao Cuo were still listed in the imperial catalog of the Liang dynasty 梁 (502–557), but were considered lost by the time of Sui 隋 (581–618; *Suishu* 34: 1003–4); they reappeared in the Tang 唐 (618–907) imperial catalog (*Jiu Tangshu* 47: 2031) and were lost again thereafter. The Sui bibliographers had also reclassified another pre-Qin text, *Guanzi* 管子 (originally classified under the "Daoist" 道家 section) as belonging to *fajia*, and this identification was followed by most later bibliographers.[5] Our selection of texts and thinkers for the following discussion broadly follows these early bibliographical lists for the reasons outlined below.

It should be immediately recalled that bibliographical classification is not rocket science, and its usefulness diminishes once we face composite texts that comprise chapters with heterogeneous ideological content, such as *Guanzi* (Sato, Chap. 5, this volume). The heuristic advantage of school labels further diminishes once these labels are reified and turned into a major analytical device. This was particularly the case in the early 1970s, when the term *fajia* became deeply politicized in the People's Republic of China (PRC), and this politicization impacted studies of *fajia* elsewhere (Pines, Chap. 17, this volume). Back then, many thinkers, from Xunzi 荀子 (d. after 238 BCE) to Zhang Binglin 章炳麟 (a.k.a. Zhang Taiyan 章太炎, 1869–1936) were classified in PRC as *fajia*, leading to their political and scholarly endorsement (Chen 2019). By contrast, such an eminent scholar as Herrlee G. Creel (1905–1994) dedicated back then a lengthy discussion to emphatically dissociate Shen Buhai from the "Legalists" (Creel 1974: 137–62). From today's perspective, such discussions are largely pointless. Bibliographic classifications do not pretend to be precise. They do reflect certain commonalities among the texts grouped together in terms of their ideas, terminology, or argumentative patterns; but these commonalities neither mean uniformity nor do they imply strict separation of a certain group of texts from those classified under a different label. The traditional bibliographers' observations should never be allowed to determine the nature of our research; they, however, can serve as a convenient starting point for a discussion, as is done in this volume.

The *fa* tradition that we discuss in this volume is emphatically not a single-keyword tradition. Nor does it possess any monopoly on advocacy of *fa*. The term *fa* was employed in a variety of texts of other traditions—starting from the *Yellow*

---

[5] In addition to *Guanzi*, *Shangzi* 商子 (i.e., the *Book of Lord Shang*), *Shenzi* 慎子, and *Hanzi* 韓子 (i.e. *Han Feizi*), the Sui bibliographers classified two other works under the *fajia* category: *On Correctness* (*Zhenglun* 正論, should be *On Administration*, *Zhenglun* 政論) by Cui Shi 崔寔 (ca. 103–170 CE), and *Essentials for our Age* (*Shiyaolun* 世要論) by Huan Fan 桓範 (d. 249 CE). Judging from the currently preserved textual remnants of both treatises, this identification is disputable; both Cui and Huan clearly viewed themselves as belonging to the Confucian tradition.

Thearch Manuscripts (*Huangdi shu* 黃帝書), unearthed in 1973 from Tomb 3, Mawangdui (Wang, Chap. 20, this volume) and ending with such a definitely non-*fajia* text as *Mengzi* 孟子 (*Mengzi* 7.1). Nor is *fa* the only keyword appropriate for the discussion of the rule by impersonal standards. In certain texts, this function can be performed by a "Confucian" concept such as ritual (*li* 禮). One of the most notable examples is the *Gongyang Commentary* on the *Springs and Autumns Annals* (*Gongyang zhuan* 公羊傳), which de-emphasizes personal cultivation and prioritizes institutional solutions to political turmoil; these solutions are usually referred to as "ritual," but notably also as "King Wen's *fa* and measures" 文王之法度.[6] Should we decide to incorporate some of the above texts in our discussion, it would be more appropriate to speak of *fa* traditions rather than a single tradition.

Despite this attractive possibility to discuss the usages of *fa* in early Chinese thought in general, we opted for a narrower focus on a relatively small group of texts identified by traditional bibliographers as belonging to *fajia*. The primary unifying thread of these texts is the insistence on the superiority of impersonal standards and institutional designs over reliance on the personal qualities of rulers and ministers, or, in modern parlance, the superiority of the rule of *fa* (*fazhi* 法治) over the "rule of men" (*renzhi* 人治).[7] There are further points of agreement among the texts discussed in this volume. Thus, they display uniform commitment to safeguarding the ruler's authority vis-à-vis his ministers, who are more often than not identified as the ruler's rivals. They dismiss the past models as irrelevant and insist that as "times changed," so the sociopolitical system should be altered as well (Vogelsang, Chap. 12). They are generally dismissive of self-serving intellectuals and of their moralizing discourse (Pines, Chap. 18), although this does not necessarily means advocating "amoral" statecraft (McLeod Chap. 15 *pace* Graham 1989: 267–91). They are skeptical about the possibility that humans can overcome their innate quest for riches and fame (or social status, *ming* 名) through moral self-cultivation, and prefer to treat the people as they are and not as they should be (Harris, Chap. 10). These points can be considered the common foundations of the *fa* tradition.

These commonalities do not imply, for sure, uniformity among the texts discussed, nor even within some of these texts. The different emphases of the *fa* texts had been duly exposed already in *Han Feizi*'s "Defining the Standards" chapter. Sometimes we encounter implicit polemics between two chapters of the same text: chapter 15, "Attracting the People" ("Lai min" 徠民) of the *Book of Lord Shang*, for example, polemicizes with chapter 6, "Calculating the Land" ("Suan di" 算地).[8] Different chapters of the *fa* texts present at times contradictory perspectives on such

---

[6] *Gongyang zhuan*, Wen 9.1 (Liu 2011: 301); more in Gentz 2015. For more about early meaning of *li*, when it was still dissociated from personal cultivation and was aimed to serve as a panacea to the entirety of sociopolitical problems, see Pines 2000.

[7] The terms *fazhi* and *renzhi* have been popularized in the early twentieth century, most notably through the endorsement by China's most outstanding intellectual then, Liang Qichao 梁啓超 (1873–1929); see Hong 2018: 19–39.

[8] See Yoshinami 1985 and Pines, Forthcoming; or see Queen 2013 for differences between two chapters of *Han Feizi* that focus on the exegesis of *Laozi* 老子.

ideas as, e.g., the qualities expected of a sovereign (cf. Lewis, Chap. 11 vs. Pines 2013 and Graziani 2015); they diverge in their modes of argumentation, in their philosophical sophistication, in the degree of their willingness to assault the moralizing discourse of their opponents, and so on. But similarities are pronounced enough to justify speaking of a single intellectual tradition. We hope that our discussion will outline the intellectual contours of this tradition and allow further investigation about the relation of other texts, which share some of the *fa* tradition's ideas and vocabulary, to this intellectual current.

2   The *fa* Texts and Studies of Chinese Philosophy

The *fa* tradition had an odd destiny in imperial China. On the one hand, many of its tenets, such as the usage of objective and quantifiable standards in assessing the officials' performance, were duly adopted by the empire's leaders (see Korolkov, Chap. 7, this volume; cf. Creel 1974: 233–93). On the other hand, some of the *fa* thinkers' basic recommendations proved untenable for the unified empire. For instance, the discontinuation of universal military service in the Han dynasty (Lewis 2000) caused a gradual atrophy of the system of ranks of merit advocated by Shang Yang, turning the crux of his social engineering program irrelevant to imperial-era statesmen (Pines 2016: 29–31). Even more consequentially, the emergence of powerful local elites early in the Han dynasty eroded another pillar of *fa* thought, the insistence on the state as the sole provider of material and social benefits. As the political and intellectual power of these elites increased, more and more ideas of the *fa* thinkers were sidelined. Such prominent tenets of *fa* thought as the evolutionary view of history, the dismissive attitude toward self-cultivation, the derision of moralizing discourse, the denigration of independent intellectuals and the like, largely disappeared from the imperial-era political texts.

The most visible development of the imperial era was rapid loss of prestige of *fa* thinkers and texts. When the Imperial Counsellor Sang Hongyang 桑弘羊 (152–80 BCE) defended Shang Yang, Shen Buhai, and Han Fei during the so-called Salt and Iron Debates of 81 BCE, this was the last major occasion in imperial China's history that a leading statesman had openly identified himself with these thinkers and proudly positioned himself as their heir.[9] Thenceforth, manifold supporters of "a rich state and a strong army" policy would usually prefer to distance themselves from Shang Yang or Han Fei, even if admiring their deeds. The image of the *fa* thinkers was too tarnished to merit open identification. These thinkers, were viewed, following Sima Tan, as "strict and having little kindness" 嚴而少恩 (*Shiji* 130: 3289), as advocates of cruel laws and merciless punishments, and as proponents of the policies that were diametrically opposite to the cherished "educational

---

[9] See particularly chapters 7 ("Fei Yang" 非鞅) and 56 ("Shen Han" 申韓) of *Yantielun* 鹽鐵論 (the text that purportedly records the 81 BCE debates; see more in Polnarov 2018).

transformation" (*jiaohua* 教化). One of the imperial China's most brilliant intellectuals, Su Shi 蘇軾 (literary name Dongpo 東坡, 1036–1101) remarked, derisively, "From the Han onward, scholars have been ashamed to speak about Shang Yang and Sang Hongyang" 自漢以來，學者恥言商鞅、桑弘羊 (*Dongpo quanji* 105: 14). Indeed, a few sympathetic voices notwithstanding, the overwhelming majority of the imperial-era literati preferred to distance themselves from the *fa* tradition even when applying its ideas in practice (Song, Chap. 16, this volume).

The immediate consequence of this negative image was the decline of interest in *fa* texts and their limited circulation. Of the texts classified as *fajia* in the Han, Sui, and Tang imperial catalogs, only one—*Han Feizi*, prized for its superior literary qualities—had survived the vicissitudes of time more or less intact. Two other texts—the *Book of Lord Shang* and *Guanzi* (which, recall, is only partly related to the *fa* tradition)—survived in a tolerably readable shape, albeit with many chapters having been lost or corrupted by unprofessional copyists. Two other preimperial *fajia* texts—*Shēnzi* 申子 and *Shènzi* 慎子—survived only in fragments (see Creel 1974 for the former; Thompson 1979 and Xu 2013 for the latter).

Seeds of rediscovery of these texts were sown in the late Qing 清 (1636/1644–1912) era thanks to the attention from the "evidential research" (*kaozheng* 考證) scholars. Their efforts in restoring the readability of the *Book of Lord Shang* and reassembling *Shènzi* 慎子 and *Shēnzi* 申子 fragments are invaluable, and so are advances in the textual analysis of *Han Feizi* that were simultaneously made in Japan (Sato 2013). However, *kaozheng* scholars paid little if any interest to the *fa* thought as such. It was only on the eve of the collapse of the Qing dynasty and of the imperial order itself, when, amid massive reevaluation of the past, scholars started paying attention to the long-sidelined *fa* tradition. We witness a robust interest, from the beginning of the twentieth century, in the *fa* texts, which attracted scholars because of the resonance of their ideas with aspects of modern Western thought, be it the evolutionary view of history or the idea of *fazhi*, viewed by many as compatible with the Western "rule of law." However, as Pines shows in this volume (Chap. 17), the twentieth-century rediscovery remained somewhat abortive due to the lingering political dislike of the authoritarian aspects of the *fa* tradition, as well as mere scholarly inertia. Even the odd outburst of adoration of *fa* thinkers during the 1973–1975 campaign "Reappraise the *fa* thinkers, criticize Confucians" 評法批儒 did not result in major breakthroughs. Once the campaign ended, the interest in the *fa* tradition in mainland China receded anew, whereas elsewhere the bizarre endorsement of *fa* thinkers by Maoist radicals had actually discouraged in-depth engagement with their texts.

This legacy of lackluster interest in the *fa* tradition is still well recognizable in modern research, especially in the aftermath of Maoist "Reappraise the *fa* thinkers" campaign.[10] It is most transparent in the subfield of "Chinese philosophy" in the

---

[10] Before the mid-1970s, several Western scholars paid due attention to the *fa* texts. Most notable is Léon Vandermeersch's *La formation du Légisme* (1965); but see also Arthur Waley's *Three Ways of Thought in Ancient China* (1939). For the Soviet engagement with the *fa* tradition (overwhelmingly focused on the *Book of Lord Shang*), see Pines, Chap. 17, this volume.

West. Even a brief survey of major introductory-level studies of Chinese philosophy through the last decades of the twentieth century and into the first decade of the twenty-first suffices to demonstrate the ongoing sidelining of the *fa* tradition. In these studies, the *fa* texts usually merit just between 5% and 10% of total space dedicated to China's preimperial thinkers.[11] Most of the *fa* texts are habitually ignored altogether, with attention is given only to *Han Feizi* (actually just to five–ten chapters of the *Han Feizi* corpus; other chapters—especially those based on historical argumentation—attract no scholarly attention whatsoever). Similarly, until the second decade of the twenty-first century, the *fa* thinkers merited little if any attention in major Anglophone scholarly journals that deal with Chinese philosophy, such as *Dao, The Journal of Chinese Philosophy*, and *Philosophy East and West*.

The reasons for this neglect are complex. One is an understandable dislike of the ideology which was portrayed for centuries (not entirely undeservedly) as supportive of authoritarianism, oppressiveness, and anti-intellectualism. Second is the bad state of preservation of most *fa* texts and their low literary appeal (with *Han Feizi* being a major exception to this rule). Third is the self-perpetuating conviction that insofar as Han Fei synthesized his predecessors' ideas, it sufficed to study his thought as a good introduction to the *fa* tradition as a whole. And fourth, a subtler but possibly more important reason for the philosophers' dislike of the *fa* texts was the overwhelmingly practical orientation of the *fa* tradition, which makes it look less philosophically engaging.

With regard to the latter problem recall the ongoing uphill battle fought by scholars of Chinese philosophy to get recognition from their peers from "general" (i.e., Euro-American) philosophy departments (Van Norden 1996; Defoort 2001, 2006, 2020; Jiang 2021: 26–34). It seems that many colleagues are still haunted by Hegel's derisive judgment of Confucius as "only a man who has a certain amount of practical and worldly wisdom—one with whom there is no speculative philosophy" (Hegel 2009: 107). It may be in an implicit reply to this derision that not a few scholars of Chinese philosophy tend to prefer discussions of abstract and "speculative" matters in early Chinese thought to the engagement with practical and this-worldly issues (Pines 2015: 7–12). The *fa* tradition with its clearly pronounced preference of practical solutions to needless speculations may appear to many colleagues as something that would hinder rather than bolster the much-sought recognition of Chinese thought as "philosophy."

---

[11] For instance, in Benjamin I. Schwartz's *The World of Thought in Ancient China* (1985), the "Legalism" chapter comprises 29 of the book's net 460 pages; in Angus C. Graham's *Disputers of the Tao* (1989), it is 26 of 440 pages; in Anne Cheng's *Histoire de la pensée chinoise* (1997), it is 15 of 292 pages dedicated to pre-Han philosophers; in Wolfgang Bauer's *Geschichte der chinesischen Philosophie* (2001), the "Legalists and the End of the Philosopher's Era" chapter occupies only 8 of 117 pre-Han pages. Later introductory-level studies eschew earlier *fa* thinkers and focus on *Han Feizi* 韓非子 alone. In Bryan W. Van Norden's *Introduction to Classical Chinese Philosophy* (2011), *Han Feizi* merits 15 of 200 pages dedicated to pre-Qin thought. Only in Karyn Lai's, *An Introduction to Chinese Philosophy* (2008) and Paul R. Goldin's *The Art of Chinese Philosophy* (2020) do the "Legalists" and *Han Feizi* break, even if slightly, the glass ceiling of 10% of the relevant text.

These headwinds notwithstanding, since the second decade of the twenty-first century one can note a clear change. This decade witnessed a translation cum study of the *Shenzi Fragments* (Harris 2016); two translations cum study of the *Book of Lord Shang* (Vogelsang 2017; Pines 2017); publication of the *Dao Companion to the Philosophy of Han Fei* (Goldin 2013); a special issue on *fajia* (more precisely, Han Fei's) philosophy in the *Journal of Chinese Philosophy* (issue 38.1 [2011]; see Cheng 2011), and more relevant articles than were written in the previous half-century. One of the best testimonies to the ongoing change is the recent magnum opus by Tao Jiang, *Origins of Moral-Political Philosophy in Early China* (2021), in which almost one quarter of the text is dedicated to the *fa* thinkers. This increasing interest in the *fa* tradition is paralleled in China, where the topic had been largely de-politicized (as for 2023), and where a scholarly society for studies of *fajia* was formed in 2015. Overall, these new trends are conducive for in-depth engagement with the *fa* tradition. This is precisely the goal of our volume.

3 The Structure of This Volume

The 24 chapters of this volume are divided into four sections. The first introduces the major thinkers and texts associated with the *fa* tradition. Chapter 1 (Yuri Pines) deals with Shang Yang and the *Book of Lord Shang* focusing on the comprehensiveness of the text's vision and its unwavering commitment to the idea of a "total state" as the only way to ensure proper political order. In Chap. 2, Yu Zhong analyzes Shen Buhai and *Shēnzi* 申子 fragments to show that Shen decidedly belonged to the *fa* tradition, with *fa* being the pivotal term of his thought (*pace* Creel 1974). In Chap. 3, Eirik Harris analyzes the tensions between morality and politics in the *Shènzi* 慎子 fragments, concluding that the state consequentialism advocated by Shen Dao had no moral foundation; rather that was "a state consequentialism predicated on the assumption that the ruler wishes to rule over a strong and stable state." In Chap. 4, Pines discusses tensions in *Han Feizi* thought and argues that despite different emphases among the text's chapters, Han Fei's insistence on humans' perennial self-interest as the foundational factor that shapes the political sphere remains the unifying thread of *Han Feizi*.[12] In Chap. 5, Sato Masayuki analyzes multiple usages of *fa* in *Guanzi* and presents a new hypothesis about the evolution of *fa* thought in the text. In Chap. 6, Christian Schwermann focuses on the economic thought of Chao Cuo, showing that despite his aura of pragmatism, Chao could be bookish and insufficiently understanding the realities on the ground: he was "more of a social engineer and a visionary than an economist."

Part II, the largest in the book, focuses on specific ideas of the *fa* thinkers. Given the practical orientation of the *fa* ideology the section duly starts by introducing the

---

[12] There is considerable resonance between Pines's observations and those of Goldin (2005: 58–65), but Pines questions Goldin's assertion (2005: 65) that Han Fei "reduces the Way to the Way of the ruler."

impact of *fa* ideas on early imperial administration. As Maxim Korolkov shows (Chap. 7), the idea of the rule by impartial standards, far from being a wishful thought, was duly applied in running the empire, especially in running the bureaucratic apparatus itself. However, in the long term, overreliance on quantifiable criteria in assessing the officials' performance proved to be less suitable to the empire's needs. The shift from impersonal standards to personalized ("Confucian") methods of personnel evaluation in the Han dynasty marked the end of robust experimentation with the *fa* ideas.

Ulrich Lau and Michael Lüdke's Chap. 8 tackles the volume's major keyword, *fa* 法. The precise meaning of this term, and in particular its relation to the concept of "the law" had been discussed both by scholars of Chinese philosophy (Creel 1974: 144–51; Goldin 2011: 91–93) and those dealing with early Chinese legal texts (Brown and Sanft 2011). Lau and Lüdke's analysis of the latter documents brings them to the conclusion that *fa* often does mean "the law," and that it is "intimately connected to notions of impartial and consistent application of the law throughout society." This discussion is an important contribution to the ongoing exploration of *fa*. Whether or not this concept is an outgrowth of *fa* thought, or is "the prerequisite for the new schools of thought" remains, however, an open question.

In Chap. 9, Song Hongbing focuses on the tension between the rule of *fa* (*fazhi* 法治), which implies impartiality, fairness, and universal applicability of common game rules (which indeed strengthens the parallels between the rule of *fa* and the Occidental "rule of law"), and the more problematic aspect of the *fa* tradition, to wit, the advocacy of political trickery, secrecy, and manipulativeness, usually associated with the term *shu* 術 (techniques of rule). Song avers that the shadowy nature of *shu* is not accidental: rather it reflects the *fa* thinkers' sober realization of the nature of politics as the struggle for power which cannot be completely subsumed within fair and impartial game rules. Song further asserts how the *fa* thinkers wholehearted commitment to the defense of the ruler's authority was a double-edged sword, which in due time weakened the political position of the *fa* adherents and the appeal of their ideas.

In Chap. 10, Harris analyzes the *fa* thinkers' views of human motivation, often identified as "human nature" (*xing* 性) or "dispositions" (*qing* 情), and its impact on policy making. Having surveyed the views of three major *fa* texts (the *Shènzi* fragments, the *Book of Lord Shang*, and *Han Feizi*), Harris concludes that all three "contend that, from the perspective of creating and maintaining political order, the most effective method is for the state to employ the already existing motivations of those over whom it rules. Once human motivations are understood, it becomes a relatively simple task to channel those motivations to get people to act in ways that the state wishes." Whereas the surveyed texts differ in their emphases and degrees of the discussion's sophistication, their bottom line is the same: the state should not alter the subjects' motivations (e.g., through "educational transformation") but simply utilize them.

In Chap. 11, Mark E. Lewis presents the complexity of the *fa* (especially *Han Feizi*'s) views of rulership. The magnitude of the ruler's tasks in the state envisioned by the *fa* thinkers is unparalleled; but how can one ensure that the sovereign will be able to perform his legislative, administrative, and supervisory functions adequately? Lewis concludes that Han Fei's solution is subjecting the ruler to "rigorous intellectual self-cultivation." He situates Han Fei's views in a broader context of the Warring States-period texts which aimed at "creating a higher form of person (or embodied self)." These texts are further placed in a broader comparative context in which the "recurring interplay between the elaboration of new forms of rulership and new models of personhood can be understood as a reflection of the range of ideas embraced in the term 'power,' from the capacity for effective action in the world (necessary to creating person or self) to the essence of political organization, as embodied in the monarch."

In Chap. 12, Kai Vogelsang analyzes the surprisingly modern-looking historical outlook in the *Book of Lord Shang* and *Han Feizi*. He shows how their understanding that "times change"—an understanding shared by a great variety of Warring States-period texts—brought about the paradigmatic shift from "exemplary history" based "on the assumption that despite the difference between past and present there remains a fundamental correspondence between them" to "sequential history" in which radical departures from earlier sociopolitical patterns were justified. However, unlike supporters of historical progress in the Occident, the *fa* thinkers (whom Vogelsang calls Political Realists) never developed a philosophy of history, nor the idea of its *telos*. Their historical outlook remained just a tool in political polemics, and once their ideas "fell into disrepute," the notion of sequential history was "easily replaced by another mode of history that supported another political program."

In Chap. 13, Romain Graziani explores the connection between the concept of *fa* and that of "tools and measurement devices whose didactic images became part of the semantic vocabulary of political power." The idea of objective measurements that supersede individual qualities of merchants and artisans was applied to the political sphere resulting in the new political architecture, which "sidelined the vision of the state as a family and replaced it with the image of a complex administrative machine that extended uniformly across the territory. In this territory, no personality is indispensable in itself, including that of the sovereign, whose power and authority lie exclusively in his shrewd use of tools, techniques and methods to control his agents and his people." Graziani shows the limitations of this ideal of an objective polity, because complete depersonalization of the agents, most notably the sovereign himself, was impossible. The discussion highlights both the intellectual boldness of the *fa* tradition and the problem of the ultimate inapplicability of its recipes.

In Chap. 14, Lisa Indraccolo shifts the focus to the philosophy of language of the *fa* texts—a topic that has not been systematically discussed heretofore. As Indraccolo demonstrates, "the discourse about the more or less deliberate mis-use of language and the dangers it entails—not only posing a potential life-threatening risk to an advisor or minister at court, but endangering the stability of the whole government, and even the organic functioning of the state at large—plays a cardinal role in *fǎ* thinking." The *fa* thinkers were well aware of both the importance and the danger of rhetorical skills, and tried to limit their abuse, in particular through engaging in broader debates about "the urgent necessity to 'rectify names' (*zhèngmíng* 正名),

i.e. to re-establish clear, univocal correspondences between names (of titles, official positions, but in *fǎ* texts also occasionally punishments and legal forms of action) and their corresponding realities." The article also explores the complexity of the term *xíngmíng* (刑名 or 形名) in the *fa* tradition's texts.

In Chap. 15, the final chapter of Part II, Alexus McLeod discusses the role of morality in the ideology of *fa* texts. McLeod disagrees with a fashionable depiction of the *fa* thought as "amoral." This view "overlooks the ways in which moral concerns were worked into *fa* tradition texts, as well as the ways in which *fa* tradition thinkers took morality to be a necessary and useful component of human life (and even, in certain rare conditions, of the ruler's political toolkit), even if they did not take it to play the same role Confucians argued it should." What we observe in the "*fa* tradition texts is not a rejection of morality, but an insistence on making a distinction between politics and morality, and a severing of the necessary link between the two that the Confucians insist on."

Part III comprises only two chapters, which trace the ups and downs in the views of the *fa* tradition throughout the imperial period (Song, Chap. 16), and in the modern era (Pines, Chap. 17). Since both chapters have been extensively referenced in the first parts of this introduction, I shall shift here immediately to Part IV, which analyzes the *fa* ideology from a comparative perspective. This section comprises five chapters: three that juxtapose the *fa* tradition with major intellectual currents of the Warring States era, and two that compare *fa* ideas with aspects of Occidental political thought.

In Chap. 18, Pines explores commonalities and differences between two major intellectual currents in Chinese political thought—the *fa* tradition and Confucianism. Both shared common orientations of traditional Chinese political thought, such as "the quest for political stability which both traditions associated with political unification under the aegis of a single omnipotent monarch; the support for meritocratic principle of rule, the paternalistic view of the people," and so forth. However, Pines focuses on their disagreements, the most dramatic of which concerned the views of the proper relation between the educated elite and the state. Whereas Confucians wanted to preserve autonomy and dignity of the intellectuals, the *fa* thinkers considered this detrimental to political order. These conflicting approaches shaped two radically different models of meritocracy—the top-down one in which objective criteria are used to select and monitor appointees, and the bottom-up one, in which peer opinion matters most. As Pines shows, each of the models had clear advantages and disadvantages, understanding which is relevant not only for studying early China but also for understanding the strengths and weaknesses of current meritocratic discourses.

In Chap. 19, Tao Jiang shifts attention to the often-neglected links between the *fa* texts and *Mozi*. He argues that "*fajia* thinkers were indebted to the Mohists for the moral-political norm of impartiality as well as the central notion of *fa* (law, standard) in the *fajia* theories." Jiang identifies Mohism "as a form of universal state consequentialism that promotes a statist approach to maximize wealth, order, and population." He then considers "the *fajia* project as a way to operationalize the Mohist project, attempting to work out in granular details how to institute the Mohist principle of impartiality through state bureaucracy and enforcement of a uniform standard, i.e., legal and administrative codes." By analyzing the *fa* tradition's indebtedness to the Mohists, Jiang not only highlights interrelationships between two major non-Confucian currents, but also turns attention to the pivotal role of impartiality in *fa* thought. Jiang also explains why the *fa* thinkers failed to realize their ideals through statist means.

In Chap. 20, Wang Pei focuses on the somewhat paradoxical relationships between the *fa* tradition and *Laozi* and related texts. The *Laozi*'s avowed minimalism contrasts with the advocacy of state activism in *fa* texts; but the *fa* thinkers' indebtedness to *Laozi* is easily discernible, especially on the level of the texts' vocabulary. The connection is often not direct but is maintained through the intermediary texts which are usually identified as belonging to the so-called Huang-Lao 黃老 tradition. The commonality is most easily observable in the importance of the term *xingming* 刑名 in both groups of texts. Even so, common vocabulary does not mean identical ideas. Thus, whereas in Huang-Lao texts the theory of *xingming* was "based on the desire to discover the Way of Heaven," in the *fa* texts it "has morphed into the technique of supervising the ministers." Wang concludes that fundamentally, both currents differ in their understanding of the relations between *fa* and the Way.

Two last chapters of Part IV shift attention to cross-cultural comparison. In Chap. 21, Jason P. Blahuta compares the ideas in the *Book of Lord Shang* and *Han Feizi* with those of Niccolò Machiavelli (1469–1527). Both the *fa* thinkers and Machiavelli sought ways of coping with sociopolitical crisis in their polities, and the remedy offered by the *fa* ideologues was "shockingly effective." However, their unwavering advocacy of *fa* as the absolute determinant of political action fares badly in Blahuta's eyes in comparison to a more flexible approach advocated by Machiavelli. The latter is not burdened by an unwavering belief in the monarchic form of rule as singularly acceptable; nor does he "resort to state control of all aspects of life." By contrast, "the *fa* tradition sponsors a vision of society that is disturbingly close to some aspects of Hannah Arendt's analysis of totalitarianism," which is not the case with Machiavelli.

The issue of whether or not the totalitarian label for the *fa* thinkers is justified is tackled in Chap. 22 by Alexandre Schiele. Schiele shows the problematic nature of the term "totalitarianism," which he calls "a label of questionable value." He highlights major differences between Shang Yang (whose vision of a total state makes him in the eyes of many a perfect candidate for being China's earliest "totalitarian") and that of Fascist thinkers, such as Giovanni Gentile (1875–1944) or Ernst Jünger (1895–1997). The difference is not just in the absence of ideological fervor in the *Book of Lord Shang* but also in the fact that the text "is predicated on establishing a stable and predictable order that the [modern totalitarians] utterly reject." Schiele finds more useful parallels not between Shang Yang and modern totalitarians but between the former and the modern advocates of "rational-legal authority," most notably Max Weber (1864–1920).

The disagreement between Blahuta and Schiele about the applicability of "totalitarian" label to the *fa* thinkers is one of many examples of disagreements among the contributors. These disagreements are expectable: the contributors differ in their disciplinary background (historians, philosophers, political scientists), in their local scholarly tradition (they come from a great variety of countries from East Asia, Europe, Middle East, and North America), in their political beliefs, and in their degree of sympathy (or antipathy) toward the *fa* tradition. What unifies all of us is an unwavering adherence to the texts: each of the discussants' arguments is based on her or his reading of the *fa* texts rather than viewing the *fa* tradition through the prism of one's political likes and dislikes. Our common goal is to understand and interpret the textual evidence instead of imposing our individual views on it.

This observation brings us to the epilogue to this volume, which tackles a question that is raised only implicitly in other chapters. What is the relevance, if any, of the *fa* tradition to present-day China and to the broader world? This question has recently gained additional importance in light of the 20th Congress of the Communist Party of China (CPC) in October 2022. At this Congress, CPC had formally adopted, albeit without much fanfare, a clause that places "China's fine traditional culture" (more accurately translatable as "fine aspects of Chinese traditional culture" 中華優秀傳統文化) as one of the pillars of the Party's ideology.[13] But which aspects of traditional culture should be considered "fine" and which are redundant and moribund? And which ideas from the repertoire of the *fa* tradition fit the designation of "fine" (i.e. applicable) aspects of the past?

It would be foolhardy to try to answer this immensely complex question in a systematic fashion, but as a courtesy to our readers we offer one article that proposes a few tentative answers. In the last chapter of the volume, Bai Tongdong analyzes the advantages of Han Fei's ideas and their potential applicability in the present. Bai's interest in Han Fei's relevance is not confined to China (although China remains the focus of his discussion, when, for instance, he prioritizes Han Fei's ideology over Maoist practices). Yet Bai's broader goal is "to defend the soundness and the relevance of Han Fei's philosophy against a comparative background, among schools within the realm of Chinese philosophy, between Chinese and Western philosophy, and between the ancients and moderns." The point is not to advocate wholesale adoption of Han Fei's ideas (the weaknesses of which Bai, like most of the contributors to this volume readily recognizes). The point is to remind the readers: "Even if we wish to have a more complicated society with Confucian morality or contemporary Western liberal values (justice, dignity, and etc.), we still need to have a functioning polity that can bring about minimal peace and prosperity." Building a hybrid system that ensures "minimal peace and prosperity" on the

---

[13] The original passage in the official English translation says: "Chinese Communists are keenly aware that only by integrating the basic tenets of Marxism with China's specific realities and fine traditional culture and only by applying dialectical and historical materialism can we provide correct answers to the major questions presented by the times and discovered through practice and can we ensure that Marxism always retains its vigor and vitality." The Chinese text (in simplified characters) is: 中国共产党人深刻认识到，只有把马克思主义基本原理同中国具体实际相结合、同中华优秀传统文化相结合，坚持运用辩证唯物主义和历史唯物主义，才能正确回答时代和实践提出的重大问题，才能始终保持马克思主义的蓬勃生机和旺盛活力。(Xi 2022, section II).

one hand and morality and justice on the other is the task for our contemporary political thinkers. If our volume offers them some food for contemplation, then our goal had been realized.

4   Appendix: Major Critical Editions and European-Languages Translations of *fa* Texts

The brief summary below does not pretend to present systematically and comprehensively the textual history of the major *fa* texts. Instead, we briefly introduce the most convenient modern editions to help the students who want to deepen their understanding of these texts. In addition, we provide a brief summary of major translations of the *fa* texts into European languages.

4.1   **Shangjunshu** 商君書 *(The Book of Lord Shang)*

Currently, three major editions of the *Book of Lord Shang* can be considered adequate for the study of the text. The most easily accessible is that by Jiang Lihong 蔣禮鴻, *Pointing an Awl at the Book of Lord Shang* 商君書錐指, prepared in 1944 and published in 1986 as part of the prestigious series, *Newly Compiled Compendium of the Masters* 新編諸子集成 by Zhonghua shuju publishers. This edition, however, suffers from many inaccuracies and is superseded by Gao Heng's 高亨 (1900–1986) *The Book of Lord Shang, Commented and Translated* (商君書注譯, 1974). Gao's is one of the finest studies produced under the duress of the Cultural Revolution (1966–1976). His edition, however, is less appropriate for critical study of the text because of its use of simplified characters.

Among more recent editions, the most notable is that by Zhang Jue 張覺, *The Book of Lord Shang, Collated with Subcommentaries* 商君書校疏 (2012). The edition excels in consulting ten different recensions from the Ming and Qing period and recording all cases of textual discrepancies among various recensions. The text also collects most of earlier commentaries, and thus is immensely helpful for researchers. Its usefulness, however, is somewhat impaired by Zhang's refusal to engage modern studies of the text (aside from Gao Heng with whom Zhang repeatedly polemicizes) and by Zhang's rigid rejection of the vast majority of textual amendments offered by the scholars beginning in the nineteenth century. Zhang also regrettably ignores recent paleographic discoveries, which, as had been demonstrated, e.g., by Li Ling (1991), are important for resolving some of the difficult textual problems of the *Book of Lord Shang*.

The *Book of Lord Shang* merited more translations into European languages than other *fa* texts. Two earliest are the English translation cum study by Jan J. L. Duyvendak's ([1928] 1963) and the Russian translation cum study by Leonard

S. Perelomov (1968, rev. ed. in 1993). Both are excellent works and among the finest Sinological products of their times, even though the translations were somewhat impaired by the absence back then of truly good critical editions of the text. A French translation by Jean Lévi (1981; rev. ed. 2005) was directed at a broader public and was less rigorous academically. In 2017 two simultaneous translations cum studies of the text have been published: into German (Vogelsang 2017) and into English (Pines 2017). Both benefitted from the existent critical editions and from the recent scholarship of the text in European and Asian languages.

4.2   Shēnzi 申子 *(Shen Buhai's* 申不害*) Fragments*

The poor state of preservation of Shen Buhai's fragments (of which only around 1500 characters remain) explains why no critical edition of this text was published. Currently English translation cum textual study by Herrlee G. Creel (1974) remains unsurpassed.

4.3   Shènzi 慎子 *(Shen Dao's* 慎到*) Fragments*

The most systematic attempt to trace the reliability of the existent *Shènzi* fragments is that by P. M. Thompson (1979). His critical edition of the text served the foundation for its only translation into a European language—the English translation by Eirik Harris (2016). In Chinese, the *Newly Compiled Compendium of the Masters* series opted for the recent study by Xu Fuhong (2013). Note that Xu's study includes several fragments of *Shènzi*, the authenticity of which was rejected by Thompson and Harris.

4.4   Han Feizi 韓非子

The most easily accessible edition of *Han Feizi* is that by Wang Xianshen 王先慎 (1859–1922), published in 1998 in the *Newly Compiled Compendium of the Masters* series. The edition suffers from not a few problems in both punctuation and insufficient or inaccurate annotation. It is generally superseded by Chen Qiyou's *Han Feizi, Newly Collated and Annotated* 韓非子新校注 (2000). Zhang Jue's *Han Feizi, Collated with Subcommentaries* 韓非子校疏 (2010) is convenient in terms of improved textual accuracy (it is based on the collation of seven premodern editions and a few modern ones), but is less systematic than Zhang's study of the *Book of Lord Shang*. Zhang's glosses, especially on historical narratives in *Han Feizi*, are also wanting.

The earliest translation of *Han Feizi* into a European language, by the Russian Sinologist Alexey Ivanov (1912), remained largely forgotten in the aftermath of World War I and the Russian revolution. The only full translation into English (Liao 1939–1959) is by now fairly outdated. Jean Lévi's translation into French (1999) shares the advantages and disadvantages of Lévi's translation of the *Book of Lord Shang*. In its accessibility it is paralleled by partial English translation of the text by Burton Watson ([1964] 2003). A new full translation by Christoph Harbsmeier (forthcoming) will hopefully increase the text's accessibility to the Anglophone audience.

4.5 *Guanzi* 管子

Guanzi merited considerable scholarly attention through much of the twentieth century, although more studies were dedicated to the text's economic chapters and those that deal with the art of self-cultivation that to the chapters more directly relevant to the *fa* thought. The best accessible edition is that by Li Xiangfeng (2004), selected for the *Newly Compiled Compendium of the Masters* series. It does not supersede, however, an earlier and more comprehensive study by Guo Moruo et al. (1956). The only full translation of the text is the opus magnum by W. Allyn Rickett (1985 and 1998; the revised edition of the first volume was published in 2001).

References

Barbieri-Low, Anthony J. 2022. *The Many Lives of the First Emperor of China*. Seattle: University of Washington Press.

Bauer, Wolfgang. 2001. In *Geschichte der chinesischen Philosophie: Konfuzianismus, Daoismus, Buddhismus*, ed. Hans van Ess. Munich: C.H. Beck.

Brown, Miranda, and Charles Sanft. 2011. Categories and Legal Reasoning in Early Imperial China: The Meaning of *Fa* in Recovered Texts. *Oriens extremus* 50: 283–306.

Chen, Qiyou 陳奇猷 (1917–2006). 2000. *Han Feizi, Newly Collated and Annotated* 韓非子新校注. Shanghai: Shanghai guji chubanshe.

Chen, Chuang 陳闖. 2019. *Studies of Ancient Texts During the Movement 'Reappraise the fa Thinkers, Criticize Confucians'* "評法批儒"運動時期的古典學術研究. PhD. Dissertation, Shandong University.

Cheng, Anne. 1997. *Histoire de la pensée chinoise*. Paris: Éditions due Seuil.

Cheng, Chung-Ying. 2011. Preface: Understanding Legalism in Chinese Philosophy. *Journal of Chinese Philosophy* 38 (1): 1–3.

Creel, Herrlee G. 1974. *Shen Pu-hai: A Chinese Political Philosopher of the Fourth Century B.C.* Chicago/London: University of Chicago Press.

Csikszentmihalyi, Mark and Michael Nylan. 2003. Constructing Lineages and Inventing Traditions through Exemplary Figures in Early China. *T'oung Pao* 89 (1–3): 59–99.

Defoort, Carine. 2001. Is There Such a Thing as Chinese Philosophy? Arguments of an Implicit Debate. *Philosophy East and West* 51 (3): 393–413.

————. 2006. Is 'Chinese Philosophy' a Proper Name? A Response to Rein Raud. *Philosophy East and West* 56 (4): 625–660.

————. 2020. The Exclusion of Chinese Philosophy: 'Ten Don'ts,' 'Three Represents,' and 'Eight Musts'. *Philosophy East and West* 70 (1): 214–225.

Dongpo quanji 東坡全集 (Collected Writings of [Su] Dongpo). N.d. By Su, Shi 蘇軾 (1036–1101). E-*Siku quanshu* edition.

Duyvendak, Jan J.-L., trans. [1928] 1963. *The Book of Lord Shang: A Classic of the Chinese School of Law*. Rpt. Chicago: University of Chicago Press.

Gao, Heng 高亨. 1974. *The Book of Lord Shang, with Commentaries and Translation* 商君書注譯. Beijing: Zhonghua shuju.

Gentz, Joachim. 2015. Long Live The King! The Ideology of Power between Ritual and Morality in the *Gongyang zhuan* 公羊傳. In *Ideology of Power and Power of Ideology in Early China*, ed. Yuri Pines, Paul R. Goldin and Martin Kern, 69–117. Leiden: Brill.

Goldin, Paul R. 2011. Persistent Misconceptions about Chinese 'Legalism'. *Journal of Chinese Philosophy* 38 (1): 64–80.

————., ed. 2013. *Dao Companion to the Philosophy of Han Fei*. Dordrecht: Springer.

————. 2020. *The Art of Chinese Philosophy: Eight Classical Texts and How to Read Them*. Princeton: Princeton University Press.

Graham, Angus C. 1989. *Disputers of the Tao: Philosophical Argument in Ancient China*. La Salle: Open Court.

Graziani, Romain. 2015. Monarch and Minister: The Problematic Partnership in the Building of Absolute Monarchy in the *Han Feizi* 韓非子. In *Ideology of Power and Power of Ideology in Early China*, ed. Yuri Pines, Paul R. Goldin, and Martin Kern, 155–180. Leiden: Brill.

Guo, Moruo 郭沫若, Wen Yiduo 聞一多 and Xu Weiyu 許維遹, eds. 1956. *The Collection of Guanzi Commentaries* 管子集校. Beijing: Kexue chubanshe.

Han Feizi. See Harbsmeier, forthcoming.

Hanshu 漢書 (*History of the [Former] Han Dynasty*). 1997. By Ban, Gu 班固 (32–92) *et al.* Ed. Yan, Shigu 顏師古 (581–645). Beijing: Zhonghua shuju.

Harbsmeier, Christoph, trans. Forthcoming. *Han Feizi, A Complete Translation: The Art of Statecraft in Early China*. Ed. Jens Østergaard Petersen and Yuri Pines. Leiden: Brill.

Harris, Eirik Lang. 2016. *The Shenzi Fragments: A Philosophical Analysis and Translation*. New York: Columbia University Press.

Hegel, Georg W. F. 2009. *Lectures on the History of Philosophy, 1825–6*. Vol. 1, *Introduction and Oriental Philosophy*. Edited by Robert F. Brown. Translated by Robert F. Brown and J. M. Stewart with the assistance of H. S. Harris. Oxford: Oxford University Press.

Hong, Tao 洪濤. 2018. The Concept of the Rule of *fa* and the *fa* Tradition's Thought in the 20th Century (A) 20 世紀中國的法治概念與法家思想(上). *History of Political Thought* 政治思想史 9 (1): 13–45.

Huainanzi. See Major et al. 2010.

Ivanov, Alexey I. (Иванов Алексей И.). 1912. *Материалы по китайской философии. Школа Фа. Хань Фэй-цзы* (Sources of Chinese Philosopy; the *fa* school. Han Feizi). St. Petersburg. Electronic reprint: http://librams.ru/book-16869.html (downloaded Oct 1, 2023).

Jiang, Lihong 蔣禮鴻, ed. 1986. *Pointing an Awl at the Book of Lord Shang* 商君書錐指. Beijing: Zhonghua shuju.

Jiang, Tao. 2021. *Origins of Moral-Political Philosophy in Early China: Contestation of Humaneness, Justice, and Personal Freedom*. Oxford: Oxford University Press.

Lai, Karyn. 2008. *An Introduction to Chinese Philosophy*. Cambridge: Cambridge University Press.

Lévi, Jean, trans. 1981. *Le livre du prince Shang*. Paris: Flammarion.

————, trans. 1999. *Han-Fei-tse ou Le Tao du Prince*. Paris: Editions du Seuil.

————, trans. 2005. *Le livre du prince Shang*. 2nd ed., with an updated introduction. Paris: Flammarion.

Lewis, Mark E. 2000. The Han Abolition of Universal Military Service. In: *Warfare in Chinese History*, ed. Hans Van de Ven, 33–76. Leiden: Brill.

Li, Ling 李零. 1991. *Shangjunshu* zhong de tudi renkou zhengce yu juezhi 《商君書》中的土地人口政策與爵制. *Guji zhengli yu yanjiu* 古籍整理與研究 6:23–30.

Li, Xiangfeng 黎翔鳳, ed. 2004. Guanzi, *Collated and Annotated* 管子校注, collated by Liang, Yunhua 梁運華. Beijing: Zhonghua shuju.

Liao, W.K., trans. 1939–1959. *The Complete Works of Han Fei tzu: A Classic of Legalism*. 2 volumes, 25–26. London: Probsthain's Oriental Series.

Liu, Shangci 劉尚慈, ed. 2011. *The Springs-and-Autumns Annals with Gongyang Commentary, Translated and Annotated* 春秋公羊傳譯注. Beijing: Zhonghua shuju.

Major, John S. et al., trans. and ed. 2010. *The Huainanzi: A Guide to the Theory and Practice of Government in Early China*. New York: Columbia University Press.

Mengzi yizhu 孟子譯注 (*Mengzi*, Translated and Annotated). 1992. Ed. Yang Bojun 楊伯峻. Beijing: Zhonghua shuju.

Morgenthau, Hans Joachim. 1978. *Politics Among Nations: The Struggle for Power and Peace*. 5th ed. New York: Knopf.

Perelomov, Leonard S. (Переломов, Леонард С.). 1968. *Книга правителя области Шан (Шан цзюнь шу)* (*The Book of Lord Shang*). Moscow: Nauka.

———. (Переломов, Леонард С.). 1993. *Книга правителя области Шан (Шан цзюнь шу)* (*The Book of Lord Shang*). With a new afterword. Moscow: Ladomir.

Petersen, Jens Østergård. 1995. Which Books Did the First Emperor of Ch'in Burn? On the Meaning of *Pai Chia* in Early Chinese Sources. *Monumenta Serica* 43: 1–52.

Pines, Yuri. 2000. Disputers of the *Li*: Breakthroughs in the Concept of Ritual in Pre- imperial China. *Asia Major* (Third Series) 13 (1): 1–41.

———. 2013. Submerged by Absolute Power: The Ruler's Predicament in the *Han Feizi*. In *Dao Companion to the Philosophy of Han Fei*, ed. Paul R. Goldin, 67–86. Dordrecht: Springer.

———. 2014. Introduction to Part III: The First Emperor and his Image. In: *Birth of an Empire: The State of Qin Revisited*, ed. Yuri Pines, Lothar von Falkenhausen, Gideon Shelach and Robin D.S. Yates, 227–238. Berkeley: University of California Press.

———. 2015. Introduction: Ideology and Power in Early China. In *Ideology of Power and Power of Ideology in Early China*, ed. Yuri Pines, Paul R. Goldin, and Martin Kern, 1–28. Leiden: Brill.

———. 2016. Social Engineering in Early China: The Ideology of the *Shangjunshu* (*Book of Lord Shang*) Revisited. *Oriens Extremus* 55: 1–37.

———, trans. and ed. 2017. *The Book of Lord Shang: Apologetics of State Power in Early China*. New York: Columbia University Press.

———. 2020. Worth vs. Power: Han Fei's 'Objection to Positional Power' Revisited. *Asiatische Studien/Études Asiatiques* 74 (3): 687–710.

———. Forthcoming (2023). Waging a Demographic War: Chapter 15 ('Attracting the People') of the *Book of Lord Shang* Revisited. *Bochumer Jahrbuch zur Ostasienforschung* 46.

Polnarov, Anatoly. 2018. Looking Beyond Dichotomies: Hidden Diversity of Voices in the *Yantielun* 鹽鐵論. *T'oung Pao* 104: 465–495.

Qingding siku quanshu zongmu tiyao 欽定四庫全書總目提要 (Summary of the Catalogue of the Imperially Approved *Complete books of the Four Storehouses*). 1772. By Ji, Yun 紀昀 (1724–1807) *et al.* Accessed through https://ctext.org/library.pl?if=gb&res=5932.

Queen, Sarah. 2013. *Han Feizi* and the Old Master: A Comparative Analysis and Translation of *Han Feizi* Chapter 20, 'Jie Lao' and Chapter 21, 'Yu Lao'. In *Dao Companion to the Philosophy of Han Fei*, ed. Paul R. Goldin, 197–256. Dordrecht: Springer.

Rickett, W. Allyn, trans. and ed. 1985 and 1998. *Guanzi: Political, Economic, and Philosophical Essays from Early China* (volumes 1–2). Princeton: Princeton University Press. (The revised edition of volume 1 republished in Boston: Cheng and Tsui).

Sato, Masayuki. 2013. Studies of *Han Feizi* in China, Taiwan, and Japan. In *Dao Companion to the Philosophy of Han Fei*, ed. Paul R. Goldin, 257–281. Dordrecht: Springer.

Schwartz, Benjamin I. 1985. *The World of Thought in Ancient China*. Rev. ed. Cambridge, MA: The Belknap Press of Harvard University Press.

Shiji 史記 (*Records of the Historian*). 1997. By Sima, Qian 司馬遷 (ca. 145–90 BCE) *et al.* Ed. Zhang Shoujie 張守節, Sima, Zhen 司馬貞, and Pei, Yin 裴駰. Beijing: Zhonghua shuju.

Smith, Kidder. 2003. Sima Tan and the Invention of Daoism, 'Legalism,' *et cetera. Journal of Asian Studies* 62 (1): 129–156.

Suishu 隋書 (History of the Sui dynasty). 1997. By Wei, Zheng 魏徵 (580–643) et al. Beijing: Zhonghua shuju.

Jiu Tangshu 舊唐書 (Old History of the Tang Dynasty). By Liu, Xu 劉昫 (888–947) et al. Beijing: Zhonghua shuju.

Thompson, P.M. 1979. *The Shen Tzu Fragments*. Oxford: Oxford University Press.

Van Norden, Bryan W. 1996. What Should Western Philosophy Learn from Chinese Philosophy? In *Chinese Language, Thought, and Culture: Nivison and His Critics*, ed. Philip J. Ivanhoe, 224–249. Chicago: Open Court.

———. 2011. *Introduction to Classical Chinese Philosophy*. Indianapolis and Cambridge: Hackett.

Vandermeersch, Léon. 1965. *La formation du Légisme: Recherche sur la constitution d'une philosophie politique caractéristique de la Chine ancienne*. Paris: Publications de l'Ecole Française d'Extrême-Orient 56.

Vogelsang, Kai. 2016. Getting the Terms Right: Political Realism, Politics, and the State in Ancient China. *Oriens Extremus* 55: 39–72.

———, trans. 2017. *Shangjun shu: Schriften des Fürsten von Shang*. Stuttgart: Alfred Kröner.

Waley, Arthur. 1939. *Three Ways of Thought in Ancient China*. London: George Allen & Unwin.

Wang, Xianshen 王先慎 (1859–1922), ed. 1998. *Han Feizi, With Collected Explanations* 韩非子集解. Collated by Zhong, Zhe 鍾哲. Beijing: Zhonghua shuju.

Watson, Burton. 2003. *Han Feizi: Basic Writings*. New York: Columbia University Press. [The original in Wade-Giles romanization published in 1964]

Xi, Jinping 習近平. 2022. Full text of the Report to the 20th National Congress of the Communist Party of China (October 16). Downloaded from Xinhua site (https://english.news.cn/20221025/8eb6f5239f984f01a2bc45b5db0c51/c.html), October 28, 2022. (Chinese text on http://www.gov.cn/xinwen/2022-10/25/content_5721685.htm).

Xu, Fuhong 許富宏, ed. 2013. *Shenzi, with Collected Collations and Commentary* 慎子集校集注. Beijing: Zhonghua shuju.

Yantielun jiaozhu 鹽鐵論校注 (*Salt and Iron Debates*, Collated and Annotated). 1996. Compiled by Huan, Kuan 桓寬 (first century BCE). Ed. Wang Liqi 王利器. Beijing: Zhonghua shuju.

Yoshinami, Takashi 好井隆司. 1985. Analyzing the Process of Formation of Qin Dynasty's Power on the Basis of 'Attracting the People' and 'Calculating the Land' Chapters of the *Book of Lord Shang* 商君書徠民、算地兩篇よりみた 秦朝權力の形成過程. *Journal of Oriental Research* 東洋史研究 44 (1): 1–22.

Zhang, Binglin 章炳麟. 1900 [2000]. *Forceful Book with Detailed Glosses* 訄書詳注. Ed. Xu Fu 徐復. Shanghai: Shanghai guji chubanshe.

Zhang, Jue 張覺, ed. 2010. *Han Feizi, Collated with Subcommentaries* 韓非子校疏. Shanghai: Shanghai guji chubanshe.

——— 張覺. 2012. *The Book of Lord Shang, Collated with Subcommentaries* 商君書校疏. Beijing: Zhishi chanquan chubanshe.

Zhao, Dingxin. 2015. *The Confucian-Legalist State: A New Theory of Chinese History*. Oxford: Oxford University Press.

Zheng, Liangshu 鄭良樹. 1989. *Shang Yang and his School* 商鞅及其學派. Shanghai: Shanghai guji chubanshe.

Part I
Major Texts and Thinkers

Chapter 1
Shang Yang and *The Book of Lord Shang*

Yuri Pines

Shang Yang 商鞅 (also known as Gongsun Yang 公孫鞅, or Lord of Shang 商君, d. 338 BCE) is one of the best known—and most controversial—statesmen in China's long history. He is renowned primarily as the major reformer whose policies propelled the state of Qin from relative marginality early in the Warring States period (Zhanguo 戰國, 453–221 BCE) to center stage of the Chinese world, setting it on course to eventual unification of "All-under-Heaven" (*tianxia* 天下). At the same time, Shang Yang is also infamous as a ruthless and cynical politician, the author of a series of appalling statements and of oppressive policies. A millennium-old verdict of Su Shi 蘇軾 (1036–1101), "from the Han 漢 [206/202 BCE–220 CE] onward, scholars have been ashamed to speak about Shang Yang" 自漢以來，學者恥言商鞅 (*Dongpo quanji* 105: 14), remains to a certain extent valid nowadays. The thinker and the text associated with him—the *Book of Lord Shang* (*Shangjunshu* 商君書)—continue to ignite strong emotions (see Pines, Chap. 17, this volume). Recently, the situation started changing, as scholars are more eager to look at the text not as a foil in current ideological struggles but as repository of novel and engaging, even if at

This research was supported by the Israel Science Foundation (grant No. 568/19) and by the Michael William Lipson Chair in Chinese Studies.

Y. Pines (✉)
Hebrew University of Jerusalem, Jerusalem, Israel
e-mail: yuri.pines@mail.huji.ac.il

© The Author(s), under exclusive license to Springer Nature Switzerland AG 2024
Y. Pines (ed.), *Dao Companion to China's* fa *Tradition*, Dao Companions
to Chinese Philosophy 19, https://doi.org/10.1007/978-3-031-53630-4_2

times controversial or even appalling ideas.[1] In the context of the current volume, this book is valuable as the foundational text for studying the concept of the rule by impartial standards (*fa* 法).

1   Shang Yang: The Reformer

Shang Yang, the alleged author of the *Book of Lord Shang*, is arguably the most famous and most influential statesman of the Warring States period. His biography is narrated in chapter 68 of *Records of the Historian* (*Shiji* 史記) by Sima Qian 司馬遷 (ca. 145–ca. 90 BCE); other chapters provide additional details about Shang Yang's career. The biography itself is not entirely reliable: it contains many literary embellishments and the admixture of later legends; many of the stories told by Sima Qian (or by the authors of his primary sources) should be read *cum grano salis* (Yoshimoto 2000; Jiang Chongyue 2021: 1–5). Nonetheless, the biography is not pure fiction, either; some of its details can now be corroborated thanks to new paleographic discoveries (Tong 2013: 311–19). It can therefore be conveniently utilized to reconstruct the factual skeleton of Shang Yang's career.

Gongsun Yang (the future Shang Yang) was a scion of the ducal house of the tiny state of Wei 衛. He looked for employment in the neighboring state of Wei 魏, the major power of his time. Having failed to advance there, he turned westward to the court of Qin, where the newly ascendant Lord Xiao 秦孝公 (r. 361–338 BCE) invited foreign advisors to come and propose ways of strengthening the state and restoring its erstwhile glory. Gongsun Yang succeeded in impressing his new employer; in 359 BCE, he overpowered his conservative opponents in court debates that are purportedly reproduced in the first chapter ("Revising the Laws" 更法) of the *Book of Lord Shang*, and gained the lord's confidence. He was appointed to the position of chief minister and launched two series of reforms, which profoundly reshaped Qin's entire sociopolitical structure. Following a successful 20-year career—which also included diplomatic and military achievements—Gongsun Yang was granted a fief at the location named Shang, and henceforth he was known as the Lord of Shang or Shang Yang (Pines 2017: 7–24).

The range of reforms attributed to Shang Yang in Sima Qian's biography is extraordinarily broad. They encompass almost every important aspect of life in the state—from the penal code to taxation, from unification of weights and measures to changes in land allocation, from administrative centralization to reform of the

---

[1]On the dearth of studies of the *Book of Lord Shang*, especially in the West, see Pines 2017: 251–52, notes 3–5. Among signs of renewed interest in the *Book of Lord Shang*, see two simultaneous translations cum studies of the text (Pines 2017; Vogelsang 2017) and a forthcoming special issue of *Bochumer Jahrbuch zur Ostasienforschung* 46 (2023). Tao Jiang's recent monograph (2021: 243–67) is the first major study of early Chinese philosophy in which Shang Yang's thought is systematically discussed. Interest in the *Book of Lord Shang* increases in mainland China as well (see, e.g. Jiang Chongyue 2021 and 2022).

regional administration. It is highly likely that some of the reforms started before Shang Yang's arrival and many matured only after his death (Lewis 1999: 603–04), but there is no doubt that many real reforms were initiated by Shang Yang. The boldest and most consequential of these was the introduction of the system of ranks of merit which replaced the erstwhile aristocratic ranks. Ranks of merit became the major positive incentive through which the population was directed toward two tasks deemed by Shang Yang as essential, namely, agriculture and warfare. This system, which profoundly reshaped Qin's society, may be considered one of the boldest experiments in social engineering worldwide (Pines 2016b).

The new system was based on twenty (initially fewer) ranks of merit for which most males were eligible regardless of pedigree or economic status. The eight lowest ranks were distributed in exchange for military achievements, in particular the decapitation of enemy soldiers, or could be purchased by wealthy individuals in exchange for grain. Successful rank holders could be incorporated into the military or civilian administration and thereafter be promoted up the social ladder. Each rank granted its holder economic, social, legal, and sumptuary privileges, such as the right to cultivate a certain amount of land, the right to be given slaves to assist in its cultivation, the right to redeem certain punishments, and so forth. From the unearthed Qin and early Han legal and administrative materials, we know that the ranks were not fully inheritable; under normal circumstances, a man could designate one heir to his rank, but the heir received a rank one or two positions lower than his father, and the decrease was sharper for the holders of higher ranks (except for the one or two highest ones). The system therefore generated a much higher degree of social mobility than had prevailed in the aristocratic age.[2]

The system of ranks of merit effectively transformed society from one based on pedigree, in which the individual's position was determined primarily by his or her lineage affiliation, into a more open one in which individual merit, especially military merit, for the most part determined social position. This system dramatically increased the motivation of Qin's soldiers to fight and attain merit on the battlefield, which contributed to Qin's army becoming one of the most formidable war machines in China's history. Besides, the system had far-reaching sociopolitical consequences. First, it broke the monopoly of the hereditary aristocracy on power and effectively abolished this stratum or at the very least radically weakened it. Second, it empowered the state, which henceforth gained unprecedented control over determining an individual's social and economic status. And third, it brought about a radical change in the composition of the elite and even its cultural outlook. This change, which is most clearly observable from the changing mortuary customs

---

[2] The earliest systematic introduction to the system of ranks of merit in English comes from Michael Loewe (1960), updated in Loewe 2010. For other magisterial studies, see Nishijima 2004, Zhu 2008, and Korolkov 2010: 101–12. For the most detailed attempt to apprehend the impact of Shang Yang's reforms on Qin's social structure, see Du 1985. Many insightful observations about the system's functioning are scattered throughout Barbieri-Low and Yates 2015; see especially pp. 872–76 and pp. 437–38n130, q.v. for further references. See also Yang 2021 for important observations about the system's transformation from Shang Yang's times into the early Han era.

of Qin elites after Shang Yang's reforms (Shelach and Pines 2006), demonstrates the reform's depth, comprehensiveness, and ultimate success.

His successes notwithstanding, Shang Yang met a tragic end. Soon after the death of his patron, Lord Xiao, Shang Yang was accused of plotting rebellion and summarily executed. The details of his clash with the son and heir of his patron are too mired in later legend to allow reliable reconstruction (Pines 2017: 22–23). What matters is that Shang Yang's reform program was not abandoned. The state of Qin, reinvigorated by Shang Yang's reforms, continued its steady expansion for over a century until it finally unified the Chinese world in 221 BCE.

2   The Text: Dating and Style

The *Book of Lord Shang* survived the vicissitudes of history better than most other texts associated by early Han bibliographers with the "school of *fa*," but it still was badly battered due to centuries of neglect. The text has suffered the loss of five out of an original twenty-nine chapters and considerable corruption in some of the remaining chapters. Serious studies of the text—such as parsing it into paragraphs and sentences (*zhangju* 章句), providing it with adequate glosses, and analyzing the dates of its composition—started in earnest only in the late nineteenth century and only recently can be said to have reached a relatively advanced level (Pines 2017: 26–31). This bad state of preservation—aside from ideological biases mentioned above—is one of the reasons for the dearth of studies of the *Book of Lord Shang* in the modern era.

Two additional factors that hindered engagement with the *Book of Lord Shang* are the text's low literary quality and its perceived inauthenticity. Zhou Duanchao 周端朝 (1172–1234) was probably the first to note that the text, full as it is of "redundant and excessive words" 汎濫淫辭, is inadequate as an introduction to Shang Yang's ideas; instead, one would be better off reading the biography in the *Records of the Historian* (*Wenxian tongkao* 212: 7). Slightly later Huang Zhen 黃震 (1213–1280) also noted the low literary quality of the text and claimed that the book is too "disordered" 煩亂 to have been produced by a "gifted law official" such as Shang Yang: "its authenticity is doubtful and cannot be verified" 真偽殆未可知 (*Huangshi richao* 55: 30). These comments did not inspire further studies of the text. Indeed, well into the twentieth century the overwhelming majority of discussions about Shang Yang were based on his biography penned by Sima Qian rather than on the *Book of Lord Shang*. Even today, Shang Yang's image in the *Records of the Historian* casts a long shadow over studies of Shang Yang and his intellectual legacy (Pines, Chap. 17, this volume).

Throughout much of the twentieth century, the question of authenticity of the *Book of Lord Shang* was particularly contestable. Since some of the book's chapters, most notably chapter 15, "Attracting the People" ("Lai min" 徠民), contains information that postdates Shang Yang's death by almost 80 years (Tong 2016; Pines 2023), it is clear that at the very least some of the book is not related to the historical Shang Yang. These instances of belated information prompted many scholars, especially in the first half of the twentieth century, to conclude that the book as a whole is "inauthentic," which, in turn discouraged in-depth engagement with the text (Pines, Chap. 17, this volume). Only gradually a more nuanced view of the *Book of Lord Shang* as a composite text gained prominence. This approach was most productively utilized by Zheng Liangshu (1989). Zheng averred that the book is a collective product of "Shang Yang's school" (*Shang Yang xuepai* 商鞅學派): its production started with Shang Yang and continued by his disciples and followers through more than a century after his death. Whereas some of Zheng's conclusions are debatable, his overall approach can be validated. First, the *Book of Lord Shang* is not a mishmash of unrelated chapters (such as, e.g., *Guanzi* 管子) but rather a product of a relatively close group of thinkers; hence the text is highly coherent in terms of its style, lexicon, and basic ideas. Second, this coherence notwithstanding, one may observe subtle dialogue among different chapters, which indeed may reflect intellectual evolution within "Shang Yang's school" (for a few examples, see Pines 2012, Yoshinami 1985, and Pines 2023). And third, whereas it is pointless to speculate which of the chapters were penned by Shang Yang personally, or try to date each of the chapters with any precision, we can at the very least conclude that most of the datable chapters were composed either during Shang Yang's lifetime or in a generation or so after his death. As such the bulk (but by no means all) of the text reflects the realities of the first decades of Shang Yang's reforms in Qin (Pines 2017: 36–54).

Speaking of the text's style, it is true that the *Book of Lord Shang* is not a literary masterpiece. In terms of sophistication of its arguments and literary richness, it fares badly in comparison with texts by many other preimperial masters, most notably with the ideologically close *Han Feizi* 韓非子 (for which see, e.g., Goldin 2020: 218). This is especially true of its early chapters, the language of which is dull and devoid of such literary embellishments such as metaphors, parables, and the like. The authors' individual voices are rarely heard, and we know next to nothing of their aspirations or frustrations. Although the text is bitterly polemical, the opponents remain nameless, as is the case in most other texts from the first half of the Warring States period. The style of many chapters resembles, even if superficially, the style of *Laozi* 老子, as William Baxter summarizes it: "It is entirely free of narration, in the sense that its statements are general and not anchored to any particular persons, times, or places. There is no indication of who is speaking, no direct reference to historical events. This contrasts strikingly with Confucian discourse" (Baxter 1998: 240).

Baxter's observations are applicable to most of the *Book of Lord Shang*'s chapters. They, too, are free of narration; the statements are not anchored to particular persons, times, or places; the authors remain nameless; and historical events are referred to only in a couple of demonstrably late chapters (e.g., 15, 17). The book's style is plain and straightforward. The authors seek neither religious nor metaphysical justifications for their proposals; philosophical digressions in the text are few and far between (although when they do occur, they are highly insightful, as discussed below). This ostensible simplicity is most appropriate for a book that repeatedly derides "argumentativeness and cleverness" 辯慧 (*Book of Lord Shang* 3.4, 3.5, 4.3, 5.1, 25.4; Zhang 2012: 42, 46, 62, 74, 275).[3] In some of the chapters, most notably 4, "Eliminating the Strong" ("Qu qiang" 去強), minimalism and straightforwardness are brought to their extremes. The chapter, which may have been designed as the text's "canon" (Pines 2017: 141–42), consists of short and energetic sentences. Everything—including grammatical particles—is sacrificed for the sake of brevity (even the ubiquitous particle *ye* 也 is present only once). The text's messages are clarified in an almost sloganlike fashion; one may dislike them, but one cannot miss them. A correct policy will make the state strong (*qiang* 強) and turn its leader into the True Monarch (*wang* 王)[4]; a wrong choice will cause the state's collapse (*wang* 亡). These are one's policy choices: take it or leave it.

The style of chapter 4 is reflective, to a certain extent, of the bulk of the *Book of Lord Shang*. For instance, most of the chapters similarly (even if less radically) reduce the usage of particles (the so-called empty words, *xuci* 虛詞) to an absolute minimum, as is appropriate for a text that deals with "substantial" (*shi* 實) matters.[5] Not all "empty words" are excluded, though. Some are hugely popular with the authors, in particular the words that create an impression of logicality and the absolute correctness of their proposals. One of their favorite terms is *bi* 必 (surely, inevitably): it recurs no fewer than 186 times in the *Book of Lord Shang* (in comparison, in the much longer *Mengzi* this particle is used 100 times). Even more popular are illative expressions meaning "hence" or "therefore," such as *gu* 故 (252 times), *shigu* 是故 (15 times), and *shiyi* 是以 (16 times), and especially a related term for indicating the policy's outcome, *ze* 則, "then" (more than 500 times).[6]

Another interesting feature of the *Book of Lord Shang* is the number of chapters—no fewer than seven—that use the first-person pronoun *chen* 臣, literally meaning "I, your subject/your minister." It is conceivable that these chapters derived from court memorials submitted by Shang Yang and his successors to Qin rulers. It may be significant, though, that the editors who collected these memorials preferred to retain *chen* rather than a common first-person pronoun such as *wu* 吾. Perhaps they were hinting that an appropriate mode of intellectual activity is that directed exclusively from a minister toward the ruler rather than being directed at fellow intellectuals. This being said, it is clear that by circulating these memorials, the editors did hope to engage a much broader audience than the ruler alone. Despite the text's derision of "argumentativeness and cleverness," it is fully engaged in polemics with members of the educated elite. This polemical perspective explains the selection of

---

[3] Hereafter, all the references to the *Book of Lord Shang* are to the paragraphs as adopted in Pines 2017 (without adding the book's title); Chinese references are to Zhang's 2012 edition.

[4] The True Monarch (a notion associated with the verbal usage of *wang* 王) refers not to the self-proclaimed kings of the Warring States, but to the one who acts as appropriate to the Monarch, that is able to unify All-under-Heaven. In most texts (but not in the *Book of Lord Shang*), the True Monarch is also identified as a moral paragon (Pines 2014: 259–63).

[5] For insightful observations about the interrelation between the style and the content of early Chinese texts, see Gentz and Meyer 2015: 13.

[6] My calculations are based on Miao and Wu 1998.

the topics covered. The *Book of Lord Shang* is not—and was never designed to be—a comprehensive introduction to Shang Yang's reforms. Rather, its focus is providing the reforms' rationale and defending some of their more controversial aspects.

3 Beyond "Alienating Rhetoric": The Goal of Self-Strengthening

Perceptions of the *Book of Lord Shang* were largely shaped by Shang Yang's portrait in *Records of the Historian*. Sima Qian's verdict that Shang Yang "was a man of little kindness" 少恩 (*Shiji* 68: 2237) determined the image of Qin's statesman for millennia to come (Song, Chap. 16, this volume). The *Book of Lord Shang* itself amply contributes to this image. Take for instance, "When penalties are heavy and rewards are light, then superiors love the people, and the people are [ready] to die for their superiors" 重罰輕賞，則上愛民，民死上 (4.4; Zhang 2012: 64 ["Qu qiang"]). One does not need additional negative PR as an advocate of merciless punishments.

Sima Qian's portrait of Shang Yang aside, the unfavorable image of the Qin thinker and the book attributed to him are strongly influenced by a series of provocative and fairly appalling pronouncements that permeate the *Book of Lord Shang*. The book derides fundamental moral norms, such as benevolence, righteousness, filiality, fraternal duty, trustworthiness, and honesty, as "parasites" (or "lice," *shi* 虱; see 13.4 ["Jin ling" 靳令], 3.5 ["Nong zhan" 農戰], and 4.3 ["Qu qiang"]; Zhang 2012: 158, 47, 62); calls for the creation of a regime in which "villains … rule [the] good" 以姦民治善民, and advocates military victory by performing "whatever the enemy is ashamed of" 事興敵所羞為 (4.3 and 4.1; Zhang 2012: 62 and 57 ["Qu qiang"]). Appalling as they are, however, these statements are not the core message of the book. They are concentrated primarily in a few early chapters, whereas in later ones, they are moderated, qualifying the amoral image proudly adopted by the author of the early chapters (Pines 2012). Notably, however, the editors who moderated the abusive pronouncements of early chapters did not eradicate them completely. Perhaps the appalling statements were considered by then a hallmark of Shang Yang's message, a feature that signified the text's novelty, a source of attraction to certain elite followers disgusted with the dominant moralizing discourse of their days. Anyhow, we should look beyond the smokescreen of the text's alienating rhetoric, and discern its more fundamental and by far more sophisticated messages.

The overarching commitment of the *Book of Lord Shang* (and, arguably, of historical Shang Yang) is to create "a rich country and a strong army" (*fu guo qiang bing* 富國强兵, a stock phrase whose earliest usage is documented precisely in the *Book of Lord Shang* 8.2; Zhang 2012: 122 ["Yi yan" 壹言]). This is viewed as the first crucial step toward the ultimate goal of unifying All-under-Heaven and establishing the "fourth" dynasty after the Xia 夏, Shang 商 and Zhou 周 (see the next passage). All the rest—the rule through impartial standards, advocacy of harsh

punishments, and, more broadly, the idea of "social engineering" (Sect. 5 below)—
are secondary to the immediate objective of the state's enrichment and empowerment; these are just useful tools. Ditto for the rest of the authors' concrete proposals.
Shang Yang and other contributors to "his" text are dealing with the concrete problem of the state's survival and ultimate victory in the bitter competition with its
rivals. The value of their proposals should be judged vis-à-vis this goal.

The authors perceive the world as being enmeshed in a zero-sum game:
"Nowadays… every state of ten thousand chariots is engaged in [offensive] war, and
every state of one thousand chariots is engaged in defense" 今世……萬乘莫不
戰，千乘莫不守. This is the basic premise: the only solution is to commit the state
to warfare. Alas, the rulers continue to follow the ways of the former paragon monarchs, which are no longer appropriate. "These ways [of the former paragons] have
been blocked for a long time, but contemporary rulers are unable to discard them;
hence, the Three Dynasties lack the fourth" 此道之塞久矣，而世主莫之能廢
也，故三代不四 (7.3; Zhang 2012: 111 ["Kai sai"]).

War is essential, but its outcome is not decided on the battlefield alone. Rather,
full granaries are an equally important precondition for success. This requires comprehensive utilization of the country's natural resources, the most important of
which is land. The toughest task is to maintain a balance between agricultural development (without which the army cannot be fed) and waging war. One who is able to
maintain the balance will emerge victorious: "Hence, when an army is dispatched,
provisions are ample, and resources are abundant; when the army is at rest, the
people are working, and the accumulated [surplus] suffices for a long time. This
is what is called the standard of utilizing territory and being ready for battle" 故
兵出，糧給而財有餘；兵休，民作而畜長足。此所謂任地待役之律也 (6.2;
Zhang 2012: 89 ["Suan di" 算地]).

Shang Yang's quest for the state's enrichment and empowerment should be
understood against the backdrop of dramatic changes in economic and military life
during the Warring States period. The first of these was the formation of an agro-
managerial state, aimed at maximizing its grain surplus by expanding cultivated
lands and increasing agricultural yields. This new type of the state activism was
evidently related to the widespread introduction of iron utensils, which revolutionized agriculture, accelerated demographic growth and contributed toward urbanization and commercialization in the economy (Wagner 1993; Yang 1998: 42–57). One
of the major policy goals outlined in the *Book of Lord Shang* is to encourage an
unwilling population to engage in wasteland cultivation rather than to move into
burgeoning non-agricultural economic sectors.

Parallel to the "iron revolution" in agriculture another revolution occurred on the
battlefields. The introduction of the crossbow and concurrent developments in other
military technologies prompted the replacement of aristocratic chariot-based armies
with mass infantry armies staffed by peasant conscripts. Military campaigns became
longer, more devastating, and crueler. At home, administrators had to learn how to
mobilize, train, and motivate the entire male population and how to ensure adequate
supplies. In the army, commanders had to ensure the conscripts' loyalty, to turn
them into valiant fighters, or, at a minimum, prevent them from deserting (Lewis

1990: 53–96 and 1999: 620–30; Yates 1999: 25–30). It is in this respect that the *Book of Lord Shang* presents a set of radical and arguably highly efficient solutions that had far-reaching consequences for the military prowess of the state of Qin.

The desire of Qin rulers to direct the population to agriculture and warfare was not exceptional. To a significant extent, this was a common vector of development of the competing Warring States. Questions of agricultural policy and mass conscription were addressed by most of the thinkers of this age. While their specific answers differed, the need to maintain large standing armies and have granaries full was broadly approved across the spectrum of ideological divides. The achievement of historical Shang Yang and the *Book of Lord Shang*'s authors was in providing highly compelling—albeit often morally dubious—answers to the questions of common concern.

4 Philosophical Foundations: History, the State, and Human Nature

The *Book of Lord Shang* advocates a variety of novel departures in social, political, and economic life. Predictably, this novelty aroused considerable opposition; and many chapters of the text are focused on providing justifications for the radical alteration of established patterns. These justifications amount to what may be the major and best-known contribution of the *Book of Lord Shang* to early Chinese philosophy: the idea that sociopolitical system should be modified to adapt to ever changing circumstances. This point is vividly elucidated in the book's first chapter, "Revising the Laws" ("Geng fa" 更法). During an alleged discussion in front of Lord Xiao of Qin, Gongsun Yang, a newcomer to the court of Qin, rebuffed his conservative opponents, who claimed that "one who imitates antiquity does not err" (法古無過):

> 前世不同教，何古之法?帝王不相復，何禮之循?伏羲神農教而不誅，黃帝堯舜誅而不怒(→拏)，及至文武，各當時而立法，因事而制禮。禮、法以時而定，制、令各順其宜，兵甲器備各便其用。臣故曰:「治世不一道，便國不必法古。」
>
> Former generations did not adopt the same teaching: So which antiquity should one imitate? Thearchs and Monarchs did not repeat one another: So which rituals should one conform to? Fuxi and Shennong taught but did not punish; the Yellow Thearch, Yao, and Shun punished but did not implicate [the criminals'] families; and Kings Wen and Wu both established laws appropriate to the times and regulated rituals according to their undertakings. Rituals and laws are fixed according to the times; regulations and orders are all expedient; weapons, armor, utensils, and equipment, all are used according to their utility. Hence, I, your subject, say, "there is no single way to order the generation; to benefit the state, one need not imitate antiquity." (1.4; Zhang 2012: 11)

This statement encapsulates the essentials of Shang Yang's message. Antiquity and its paragons are not disparaged, but their model was appropriate for their time only and cannot be followed today. Simply put, there can be no unified model of the past. The lesson to be learned from the paragons' successes—if there is one—is to be flexible and adaptive. This idea permeates the *Book of Lord Shang*: the ruler should never confine himself to established patterns but rather do whatever is expedient. Responding to "the times" and modifying one's methods of rule constitute the book's major recipes for political success.

The idea of "changing with the times" was not controversial in itself; rather, as Martin Kern argues, it was advocated in a great variety of preimperial and early imperial texts (Kern 2000: 170–74). Unlike these texts, however, the *Book of Lord Shang* put forward a new vision of history, which curiously resembles the notion of historical evolution (cf. Vogelsang, Chap. 12, this volume). This novel vision is presented with utmost clarity in those sections of the *Book of Lord Shang* that explore the origins of the state, most notably the opening section of chapter 7, "Opening the Blocked" ("Kai sai" 開塞). This chapter starts with the following observation:

天地設，而民生之。當此之時也，民知其母而不知其父，其道親親而愛私。親親則別，愛私則險。民眾而以別、險為務，則有亂。當此時也，民務勝而力征。

When Heaven and Earth were formed, the people were born. At that time, the people knew their mothers but not their fathers; their way was one of attachment to relatives and of selfishness. Attachment to relatives results in particularity; selfishness results in malignity. The people multiplied, and as they were engaged in particularity and malignity, there was turmoil. At that time, the people began seeking victories and forcefully seizing [each other's property]. (7.1; Zhang 2012: 107)

From the first phrases we can see the distinctiveness of Shang Yang's approach. The majority of preimperial narratives of state formation depicted primeval society as plagued by intrinsic turmoil; by contrast, a minority view, evident in some chapters of *Zhuangzi* 莊子, considered the prepolitical age as an era of harmony and peace (Pines and Shelach 2005; Pines 2013: 27–31). "Opening the Blocked" combines both approaches: turmoil is not intrinsic to a stateless society, but it evolves eventually because of population pressure. Elsewhere, the text states with greater clarity that when "the people were few, but trees and animals plenty" (人民少而木獸多), there were indeed no reasons for social conflict; hence, "neither punishments nor administrative [means] were used, yet there was order" (刑政不用而治; *Book of Lord Shang* 18.1; Zhang 2012: 207). That primeval harmony was unsustainable, however. As "Opening the Blocked" chapter explains, when "the people multiplied," their intrinsic selfishness began endangering social order. As the weaknesses of stateless society became evident, it had to be reformed:

務勝則爭，力征則訟（→爭），訟而無正，則莫得其性也。故賢者立中正，設無私，而民說仁。當此時也，親親廢，上賢立矣。

Seeking victories results in struggles; forceful seizure results in quarrels. When there are quarrels but no proper [norms], no one attains his natural life span. Therefore, the worthies established impartiality and propriety and instituted selflessness; and the people began rejoicing in benevolence. At that time, attachment to relatives declined, and elevation of the worthy was established. (7.1; Zhang 2012: 107)

The promiscuous (or matriarchal?) kin-based order, which fostered selfishness, proved inadequate for coping with population pressure and the resulting struggles; hence, unidentified "worthies" (*xianzhe* 賢者) intervened, replacing that order with the incipient stratified society based on "elevation of the worthy." It was at this stage that morality was first taught to the populace, apparently calming the struggles and the forceful mutual seizure of property of the earlier age. We witness, then, profound social, ideological, and political change. However, morality and social stratification alone could not resolve the fundamental problem of human selfishness, which, after a new cycle of population increase, became equally damaging to the new social order:

凡仁者以愛利為務，而賢者以相出為道。民眾而無制，久而相出為道，則有（→又）亂。故聖人承之，作為土地、貨財、男女之分。分定而無制，不可，故立禁。禁立而莫之司，不可，故立官。官設而莫之一，不可，故立君。既立君，則上賢廢而貴貴立矣。

In general, the benevolent are devoted to the love of benefit, whereas the worthy view overcoming one another as the [proper] Way. The people multiplied yet lacked regulations; for a long time they viewed overcoming one another as the [proper] Way, and hence there again was turmoil. Therefore, the sages took responsibility. They created distinctions among lands, property, men, and women. When distinctions were fixed but regulations were still lacking, this was unacceptable; hence, they established prohibitions. When prohibitions were established but none supervised [their implementation], this was unacceptable; hence they established officials. When officials were instituted but not unified, this was unacceptable; hence, they established the ruler. When the ruler was established, the elevation of the worthy declined, and the esteem of nobility was established. (7.1; Zhang 2012: 107)

Once again, the population increase and the resultant turmoil caused profound change in social, political, and even ethical norms: this time the result was dispensing with the morality-based order run by the worthies and its replacement with a powerful bureaucratic polity. The text's insistence on the correlation between the human's objective conditions and the sociopolitical and moral order curiously resembles Karl Marx's (1818–1883) famous thesis that "it is not the consciousness of men that determines their existence, but their social existence that determines their consciousness" (Marx [1859] 2010: 263). The text brings the reader to the conclusion that nothing is permanent. Kinship structures, morality, social regulations—everything is prone to change once new economic situation prompted by the struggle for limited resources ensues. This, view allows unprecedented dynamism to the degree unencountered in other premodern Chinese texts with the possible exception of *Han Feizi* (for which see Chap. 4, Sect. 2.2, this volume).

This dynamism permeates the entire narrative of the state formation. The state was not established by the sages' fiat, as argued in a great majority of other texts (including in chapter 23 of the *Book of Lord Shang* itself), nor was it intrinsic to human society from its inception, as argued, for example, in *Xunzi* 荀子.[7] Rather, its formation was a result of a lengthy process of increasing political complexity. Society evolved from an egalitarian, promiscuous, kin-based order to an incipient stratified order and then to a mature political organization based on property

---

[7] See *Xunzi* 9:164–65 ("Wang zhi" 王制). For the state as the creation of the sages, see *Guanzi* 31:568–69 ("Junchen xia" 君臣下), *Book of Lord Shang* 23.1 (Zhang 2012: 258 ["Jun chen" 君臣]), and *Zhuangzi* 29: 778 ("Dao Zhi" 盜跖) (where the sages are depicted as malevolent beings who destroyed the primeval idyll).

distinctions, prohibitions, and officials. This process was crowned with the establishment of a ruler, and it is only then that we can speak of a fully formed state. In the earlier stages of human history, kinship ties and moral upbringing could provide effective substitutes to the powerful bureaucratic entity. However, in the current situation of fierce competition for limited resources, the situation in which "the generation is knowledgeable" and "extra crafty," the only effective means of preserving order is enforcing it from above (see *Book of Lord Shang* 6.7 ["Suan di"] and 7.2 ["Kai sai"]; Zhang 2012: 97 and 110). The political system based on laws, regulations, and prohibitions and run by officials under the unifying aegis of the supreme sovereign provides the singularly effective remedy for social turmoil.

Enforcement of order is the must; but it is not sufficient to make the state truly effective. Real success will come when the leaders learn how to channel the subjects' aspirations into directions deemed necessary for the state's success. This brings us to the second (and much less noted) pillar of the *Book of Lord Shang*'s ideology—the view of human nature (*xing* 性, or "disposition," *qing* 情).[8] Humans are intrinsically selfish (*si* 私) and covetous of material and social benefits. This selfishness may endanger social order; as the authors note "The people's disposition is to be ruled well; but their activities bring about turmoil" (民之情也治，其事也亂; 5.4; Zhang 2012: 78 ["Shuo min" 說民]). Namely, unrestricted desire to satisfy one's interests may undermine the foundations of orderly rule, without which the people will not be able to satisfy their basic needs. For a clever ruler, however, the fact that humans are selfish is also a source of opportunity. The text explains:

民之於利也，若水於下也，四旁無擇也。民徒可以得利而為之者，上與之也。

The people follow after benefit as water flows downward: it has no preference among the four directions. The people do only whatever brings them benefit; and the benefit is granted by superiors. (23.3; Zhang 2012: 260 ["Jun chen" 君臣])

It is impossible to prevent the people from seeking benefit. What is required is just to allow them pursue personal benefit only in the ways that serve the common (*gong* 公) good. The authors explain how to achieve this in chapter 6, "Calculating the Land" ("Suan di" 算地):

民之性：饑而求食，勞而求佚，苦則索樂，辱則求榮，此民之情也。民之求利，失禮之法；求名，失性之常。奚以論其然也？今夫盜賊，上犯君上之所禁，而下失臣民之禮，故名辱而身危，猶不止者，利也。其上世之士，衣不煖膚，食不滿腸，苦其志意，勞其四肢，傷其五臟，而益裕廣耳，非性之常，而為之者，名也。故曰名利之所湊，則民道之。

The nature of the people is to seek food when they are hungry, to seek respite when they are belabored, to seek joy when they are embittered, to seek glory when they are humiliated: this is the people's disposition. In seeking benefit, the people lose the standard of ritual,[9] in

---

[8] Although the *Book of Lord Shang* is one of the earliest texts in China to systematically base its political vision on the views of human nature (or, as Harris, Chap. 10, this volume, prefers, "human motivations"), this point is only rarely acknowledged in research. For laudable exceptions, see Xiao 2006, Sato 2013a: 155–57 and 2013b: 249–50, Jiang 2021: 253–55, and Harris, Chap. 10, this volume.

[9] The combination *li zhi fa* 禮之法 (the "standard of ritual") is peculiar to the *Book of Lord Shang*; it probably implies here the essential norms of behavior embedded in the broader concept of ritual (for which see Pines 2000).

seeking a name (repute), they lose the constant of their nature. [10] How can I demonstrate this? Now, criminals violate the prohibitions of rulers and superiors above and lose the ritual of subjects below; hence, their name is dishonored and their body endangered, but they still do not stop: this is because of benefit. In the generations of old, there were men of service (*shi* 士) who did not have enough clothes to warm their skin or enough food to fill their bowels. They exerted their four limbs and injured their five internal organs above, but they behaved ever more broad-heartedly. This was not the constant of their nature, yet they did it: this was because of the name. Hence, it is said: wherever the name and benefit meet, the people will go in this direction. (6.4; Zhang 2012: 94)

This discussion is one of the earliest systematic analyses of human nature in Chinese history.[11] Two major factors influencing human behavior are the quest for riches and for a name. The first does not require much discussion, as it is a commonplace in most early Chinese texts which normally take for granted the importance of material benefits for the people. But the authors add here the second motivation, the quest for a name (*ming* 名). The term *ming* in the above passage refers primarily to one's reputation, but more commonly throughout the text it refers to high social status, which—just like fine reputation—could be passed on to posterity. The quest for a good name was identified from the early Warring States period as one of the chief motivators of the actions of elite members, the men of service (*shi* 士) (Pines 2020; cf. Lewis 2021). In contrast to earlier texts, such as *Lunyu* 論語 and *Mozi* 墨子, however, the *Book of Lord Shang* implies that this quest is shared by everybody and not just by the elite members. This observation is central to the authors' political recommendations.

The authors are aware of the potential negative implications of the quest for riches and name, and even of a certain contradiction between these two desires. The quest for material benefits causes people to transgress against moral and legal norms and even to sacrifice their fine name, which becomes "dishonored." The quest for a name, on the other hand, may not only cause them to reject material benefits, but it even transcends their quest for life. If unchecked, these two desires may jeopardize the social order. Yet these desires are innate and cannot be altered: "The people's desire for riches and nobility stops only when one's coffin is sealed" (民之欲富貴也，共闔棺而後止。17.4; Zhang 2012: 203 ["Shang xing" 賞刑]). What, then, is to be done? The solution is to understand the people's basic disposition and then to manipulate it to attain the state's goals. The text explains:

夫農，民之所苦；而戰，民之所危也。犯其所苦、行其所危者，計也。故民生則計利，死則慮名。名利之所出，不可不審也。利出於地，則民盡力；名出於戰，則民致死。

Farming is what the people consider bitter; war is what the people consider dangerous. Yet they brave what they consider bitter and perform what they consider dangerous because of calculation [of a name and benefit]. Thus, in [ordinary] life, the people calculate benefits; [facing] death, they think of a name (repute). One cannot but investigate whence the name

---

[10] The "constant of one's nature" (*xing zhi chang* 性之常) refers here to the fear of death. In seeking fame, the people are ready to sacrifice their lives.

[11] The chapter "Calculating the Land" was composed no later than ca. 330 BCE (see Pines 2017: 39–40).

and benefit come. When benefits come from land, the people fully utilize their strength; when the name comes from war, the people are ready to die. (6.5; Zhang 2012: 95 ["Suan di"])

The solution is simple: One's quest for riches should be realized exclusively through farming, while high social status (the "name") should be attainable only by those who excel at war. When such a system is built, the population can be directed to the "bitter and dangerous" pursuits of agriculture and warfare simply because of the desire to realize one's personal aspirations. The people will till, fight, and benefit the state not out of high moral commitment but out of selfish considerations: By benefitting the state, they benefit themselves, and vice versa. The establishment of the system that realized this insight was Shang Yang's major achievement as a reformer.

5 Social Engineering: Rewards and Punishments

Frequent pronouncements in the *Book of Lord Shang* that advocate enforcing the order on the people through heavy punishments create an impression that the authors' vision is confined to creation of a coercive and suppressive regime. This impression is not entirely wrong, but it obscures a much more radical aspect of Shang Yang's program, namely proactively channeling social forces toward desirable social and political ends. This approach, which curiously resembles modern ideas of social engineering,[12] is the hallmark of Shang Yang's boldness. It is based not on coercion alone but rather on a combination of positive and negative incentives that will direct the people to engage in the "bitter and dangerous" tasks of agriculture and warfare. The rationale is explained in the following passage:

人君(→生)而有好惡，故民可治也。人君不可以不審好惡。好惡者，賞罰之本也。夫人情好爵祿而惡刑罰，人君設二者以御民之志，而立所欲焉。夫民力盡而爵隨之，功立而賞隨之，人君能使其民信於此明如日月，則兵無敵矣。

Human beings have likes and dislikes; hence the people can be ruled. The ruler must investigate likes and dislikes. Likes and dislikes are the root of rewards and penalties. The disposition of the people is to like ranks and emoluments and to dislike punishments and penalties. The ruler sets up the two in order to guide the people's will and to establish whatever he desires. When ranks come only after the people have fully used their force, when rewards come only after their merits are established, when the ruler is able to let his people trust these [two] as [unequivocally] as they visualize the sun and moon—then the army has no rivals. (9.3; Zhang 2012: 131 ["Cuo fa" 錯法])

The recommendation is clear: To properly motivate the people, the ruler should employ a combination of positive (rewards, ranks, emoluments) and negative (punishments, penalties) incentives. A clear, fair, and unequivocal implementation of these two will direct the people to the pursuits desired by the ruler (in this passage referring primarily to military pursuits, which are elsewhere supplemented by farming). The entire sociopolitical system advocated in the *Book of Lord Shang* can be seen as the realization of this recommendation.

---

[12] For the concept of "social engineering," see Alexander 1996, and Podgórecki 1996.

5.1 Punishments

Let us start with the negative incentives. The most (in)famous of these are harsh punishments which are repeatedly proclaimed in the book to be the primary means of causing the people to comply with the ruler's orders. Individual chapters differ with regard to the appropriate mix of rewards and punishments. Some insist on their balanced application (17.1-3; Zhang 2012: 190–97 ["Shang xing"]); some favor nine punishments for a single reward (4.4; Zhang 2012: 64 ["Qu qiang"]); and some—albeit very few—insist that rewards should not be bestowed at all (18.4; Zhang 2012: 214 ["Hua ce"]).[13] Their discrepancies notwithstanding, the authors of different chapters agree that only harsh and ineluctable punishments will effectively deter the people's transgressions. This is explained for instance in chapter 7, "Opening the Blocked":

> 夫民憂則思，思則出度；樂則淫，淫則生佚。故以刑治，則民威；民威，則無姦；無姦，則民安其所樂。以義教，則民縱；民縱，則亂，亂則民傷其所惡。吾所謂刑[14]者，義之本也；而世所謂義者，暴之道也。夫正民者，以其所惡，必終其所好；以其所好，必敗其所惡。
>
> When the people worry, they become thoughtful; when they are thoughtful they generate [proper] measures. When the people are happy, they are licentious; when they are licentious they give birth to laxity. Hence, if you order them through punishments, the people are overawed; when they are overawed, there is no depravity; when there is no depravity, the people reside in peace doing what they like. If you instruct them through righteousness, the people indulge themselves; when the people indulge, there is turmoil; when there is turmoil, the people will be hurt by what they detest. What I call "punishments" is the root of righteousness, while what our generation calls righteousness is the way of violence. Hence, if you order the people through what they detest, they will surely end in what they like; if you do it through what they like, they will surely be defeated by what they detest. (7.4; Zhang 2012: 113)

Overawing the people is the principal way of directing them to socially and politically acceptable behavior. Once the people realize that the evildoer will inevitably be denounced, apprehended, and penalized mercilessly for even a minor or "about to be committed transgression" (將過)—they will submit to laws, allowing for a blessed situation of "returning to virtue" (反於德, 7.5; Zhang 2012: 117). These recommendations are further specified in chapter 17, "Rewards and Punishments" ("Shang xing" 賞刑):

---

[13] Zheng (1989) used these divergent viewpoints as reflective of different dates of origin of individual chapters, arguing that the differences reflect an evolution of views within "Shang Yang's school." I doubt, however, that these differences actually reflect a neat evolution: even a single author may alter his specific recommendations when facing different audience or circumstances. Besides, the chapters differ in their understanding of rewards: some focus on rewarding the denouncement of crimes, while other—the majority—discuss rewards for valiant fighters. This is another source of their difference re the balance between rewards and punishments.

[14] Most recensions have *li* 利 ("benefit") instead of *xing* 刑 ("punishments"); Zhang Jue (2012: 114n8) follows Yan Kejun's amendment and restores *xing*.

所謂壹刑者，刑無等級。自卿相、將軍以至大夫、庶人，有不從王令，犯國禁，亂上制者，罪死不赦。有功於前，有敗於後，不為損刑。有善於前，有過於後，不為虧法。忠臣孝子有過，必以其數斷。守法守職之吏有不行王法者，罪死不赦，刑及三族。周官之人，知而訐之上者，自免於罪。無貴賤，尸襲其官長之官爵田祿。故曰：「重刑連其罪，則民不敢試。」民不敢試，故無刑也。夫先王之禁：刺殺，斷人之足，黥人之面，非求傷民也，以禁姦止過也。故禁姦止過，莫若重刑。刑重而必得，則民不敢試，故國無刑民。國無刑民，故曰：「明刑不戮。」

What is called unifying punishments means imposing punishments without regard for one's status. From chief ministers, chancellors, and generals down to nobles and commoners: Whoever disobeys the king's orders, violates the state's prohibitions, or wreaks havoc on the regulations of one's superior should be executed without pardon. If he had merits before but failed thereafter, this should neither reduce the punishment, nor diminish the law. When loyal ministers and filial sons transgress, their cases should be decided according to the rules.

When an official responsible for safeguarding the royal law does not implement it, he should be executed without pardon. Moreover, the punishments should extend to the three degrees of his family members. When his colleagues know of [his crime] and denounce it to the superiors, they avoid punishment; and, whether noble or base, they inherit their superior's office, rank, fields, and emoluments. Hence, it is said: "When punishments are heavy and criminals are mutually responsible, the people dare not try [to break the law]." When the people dare not try, there are no punishments.

Hence, the prohibitions of the former kings, such as [carrying out] executions, cutting off feet, or branding the face, were imposed not because they sought to harm the people but only to prohibit depravity and to stop transgressions. Hence, to prohibit depravity and to stop transgressions nothing is better than to make punishments heavy. When punishments are heavy and [criminals] are inevitably captured, then the people dare not try [to break the law]. Hence, there are no penalized people in the state. When there are no penalized people in the state, it is said: "Clarifying punishments [means] no executions." (17.3; Zhang 2012: 196)

This passage presents the text's three main postulates with regard to punishments. First, there is equality before the law: Every transgressor should be punished, his background notwithstanding (note that in practice, the Qin law allowed rank holders to redeem certain punishments). Second, the system of mutual responsibility—including within the ruling apparatus—should ensure the culprit's inevitable apprehension. Third, the notorious severity of punishments—e.g., a variety of mutilations and outright execution of the transgressor—is essential to preserve the law's deterrence. In combination, these premises are expected to bring about the blessed situation of "eradicating punishments through punishments," which is the authors' ultimate goal.

5.2 Making the People Fight

As noted above, the repeated advocacy of harsh punishments in the *Book of Lord Shang* often obscures other positive and negative incentives advocated throughout the text to direct the population toward desirable ends. Positive incentives, i.e. "rewards," are especially important. The predominant meaning of "rewards" in the *Book of Lord Shang* refers to granting ranks of merit and related social, economic, and legal benefits to those who excel at war. These are the major means of motivating the peasant conscripts to fight valiantly. The text reiterates: "The way of using soldiers is to commit oneself to unifying rewards" 用兵之道，務在一賞; "Ranks and emoluments are the essence of the army" 爵祿者，兵之實也; "Rule through punishments; make war through rewards" 以刑治，以賞戰 (6.1 ["Suan di"], 9.1 ["Cuo fa"], 13.1 ["Jin ling"]; Zhang 2012: 92, 128, 153). Elsewhere, the authors explain their point in more detail:

> 聖人之為國也，壹賞、壹刑、壹教。壹賞，則兵無敵。……所謂壹賞者，利祿官爵，摶出於兵，無有異施也。夫固知愚、貴賤、勇怯、賢不肖，皆盡其胸臆之知，竭其股肱之力，出死而為上用也。天下豪傑賢良從之如流水；是故兵無敵，而令行於天下。
>
> When the sage rules the state, he unifies rewards, unifies punishments, and unifies teaching. When rewards are unified, the army has no rivals. . . . What is called "unifying rewards" means that benefits, emoluments, official position, and rank uniformly derive from military [attainments] and that there are no other ways to dispense them. Therefore, the knowledgeable and the ignorant, the noble and the base, the courageous and cowardly, the worthy and unworthy—all fully utilize their innermost wisdom and fully exhaust the power of their limbs, going forth to die in the service of their superiors. The bravos and the worthies from All-under-Heaven will follow [the ruler] just as water flows downward. Hence, his troops will have no rivals, and his orders will be implemented throughout All-under-Heaven. (17.1–2; Zhang 2012: 190–91 ["Shang xing"])

The only reason the conscripts will be ready "to die in the service of their superiors" is that they will be able to obtain "benefits, emoluments, official position, and rank." The ranks are singularly important for the reasons outlined above (pp. 25–26). They mattered not just because of the accompanying social, material, and political benefits, but also because soldiers killed in action could bequeath their rank in full (i.e., without reduction) onto the heir. This made the ranks an attractive compensation for the risk the soldier faced on the battlefield. This was also the realization of one's quest for a transcendent "name." Once granted, the rank—much like one's reputation—could outlive its mortal bearer and benefit one's descendants. As such, ranks became a reasonable compensation for death in the service of the lord of Qin.[15]

Ranks aside, the *Book of Lord Shang* recognizes other means of encouraging soldiers to fight. Whereas the above passage reduces the problem of motivation to the need to reward meritorious soldiers and officers with enhanced socioeconomic status, this policy is supplemented elsewhere by negative incentives. In particular, inflicting swift and ineluctable punishments on deserters from the battlefield is essential to deterring timid soldiers. "Use punishments to handle cowards: they will surely become brave. Use rewards to handle the brave: they will [be ready to] die" 怯民使以刑必勇，勇民使以賞則死 (4.4; Zhang 2012: 64 ["Qu qiang"]). The text clarifies:

> 凡戰者，民之所惡也；能使民樂戰者，王。強國之民，父遺其子，兄遺其弟，妻遺其夫，皆曰：「不得，無返！」又曰：「失法離令，若死，我死。鄉治之，行間無所

---

[15] One of the earliest chapters of the *Book of Lord Shang*, 19, "Within the Borders" ("Jing nei" 境內) contains several important hints about practical implementation of the ranks system during military campaigns. See detailed discussion in Pines 2016a: 119–25.

逃，遷徙無所入。」行間之治，連以五，辨之以章，束之以令。拙(→ 趉)無所處，
罷無所生。是以三軍之眾，從令如流，死而不旋踵。

> As for war, it is something the people hate. He who is able to make the people delight in war is the [True] Monarch. Among the people of a powerful state, fathers send off their sons, older brothers send off their younger brothers, wives send off their husbands, and all say: "Do not come back without achievements!" They also say: "If you violate the [military] law and disobey orders, you will die, and I shall die. Under the canton's control,[16] there is no place to flee from the army ranks, and migrants can find no refuge."
>
> To order the army ranks, link them into five-men squads, distinguish them with badges, and bind them with orders. Then there will be no place to flee, and defeat will never ensue. Thus, the multitudes of the three armies will follow the orders as [water] flows [downward], and even facing death they will not turn back. (18.3; Zhang 2012: 211–12 ["Hua ce" 畫策])

The discussion here is more sophisticated than the previous references to ranks and emoluments as the sole means of enhancing martial valor. Rewards, even if substantial, are insufficient for creating a powerful army. Equally important are strict military discipline and the rule of terror against deserters and other transgressors. The inevitability of punishment—thanks in part to the system of mutual responsibility, which causes family members (and neighbors and superiors) to be implicated in case of a major crime—is the guarantee of compliance.[17] Then, the combination of positive and negative incentives brings about a profound internalization of military values—that is, a militarization of culture (see more below, pp. 49–51). Soldiers will fight to the death not out of an abstract commitment to the ruler and the state. Even if they continue to hate war, they will know that it is their only chance to not just survive, but to advance socially and economically.

5.3 Making the People Till

The combination of positive and negative incentives also figures prominently in the authors' second goal of directing the population to farming. Here, however, the balance between the two types of incentives changes. Whereas the text does speak intermittently of granting ranks in exchange for high grain yields (4.11 ["Qu qiang"], 20.3 ["Ruo min" 弱民]; Zhang 2012: 72 and 240) or selling ranks to the rich (8.2; Zhang 2012: 122 ["Yi yan"]), it never specifies how the system is supposed to work. It seems that unlike the military-based bestowal of ranks, which could rest on uniform and quantifiable criteria, such as cutting off the enemy's heads, it was impossible to fix a ratio of yield per rank in the field of agriculture because of its fluctuating productivity. This may explain why in encouraging agricultural pursuits the authors' focus shifts from positive to negative incentives, reducing the attractiveness of non-agricultural occupations.

The aim of discouraging non-agricultural occupations is particularly noticeable in chapter 2, "Orders to Cultivate Wastelands" ("Ken ling" 墾令). It is arguably the

---

[16] A canton (xiang 鄉) was a sub-county unit.

[17] For the functioning of the system of mutual responsibility in practice, see Barbieri-Low and Yates 2015: 786.

dullest and least sophisticated chapter in the entire *Book of Lord Shang* (and probably one of the earliest; Pines 2021: 87–91). The chapter presents twenty short recommendations about how to push the population toward farming. Each one briefly introduces the desired policies, summarizes their social effects, and concludes with the uniform desideratum "then wastelands will surely be cultivated" (則草必墾矣). In marked difference from what we know of Qin's practical measures for expanding arable lands, such as distributing iron tools and draft animals, initiating irrigation projects, and even granting ranks of merit to the new settlers, the chapter focuses exclusively on discriminatory measures against those who do not engage in agriculture. Three groups figure prominently in the text as targets for discrimination. The first are members of the high elite, nobles, and officials, whose lavish lifestyle (2.4, 2.6, 2.7; Zhang 2012: 20, 22) and social advancement due to "broad learning" (2.14; Zhang 2012: 30) spoil the people's *mores* and distract them from farming. Moreover, members of the elite protect their dependents, who thereby escape agricultural labor. These dependents—composed of a variety of members of the lower elite and sub-elite—are the second group targeted by the text (2.4, 2.7, 2.8, 2.11, 2.13, 2.16, 2.20; Zhang 2012: 20, 22–24, 26, 28, 32, 37). In restricting their ability to enjoy elite patronage, the state will direct these people toward agricultural production. The third targeted group is merchants. They should be squeezed of their profits, humiliated, and discriminated against to make their occupation exceedingly unattractive (2.5, 2.6, 2.10, 2.15, 2.17, 2.19; Zhang 2012: 21, 22, 25, 31, 34, 36). The chapter's argument is exemplified in the following passage:

祿厚而稅多，食口眾者，敗農者也。則以其食口之數賤(→賦)而重使之，則僻淫、游惰之民無所於食。無所於食，則必農；農，則草必墾矣。

  If emoluments are bountiful and taxes abundant, then too many people rely on their mouths to eat, and agriculture is devastated.[18] So impose [on rich households] levies according to the number of mouths in their households and double their conscript obligations.[19] Then deviant, floating, and idle people will have nothing to rely upon for sustenance; if they have nothing to rely upon for sustenance, they will have to be engaged in agriculture, and should they be engaged in agriculture, then wastelands will surely be cultivated. (2.4; Zhang 2012: 20)

From this passage, it seems that in pre-reform Qin society elite members could shield some of their dependents from levies and conscript obligations, which allowed the "deviant, floating and drifting people" to enter into the nobles' service and avoid agricultural work. By closing this loophole, the authors hoped to steer this undesirable social element back to farming. This idea permeates chapter 2 of the *Book of Lord Shang*.

---

[18] This hints at the pre-reform situation, in which the nobles' income derived directly from the subordinate population of their allotments (*cai yi* 采邑), whose tax quotas could be adjusted by the master (Zhu 1990: 544–55). Hence, rich emoluments meant increase in taxation. This is how the authors of *Comprehensive History of China's Economy* interpret the sentence (Zhou 2007: 1143–44); see also Zhang 2012: 20n1.

[19] From the context, it seems that those "who rely on their mouths" are the retainers of officers and nobles whose bountiful emoluments allowed them to sustain many dependents.

This somewhat simplistic approach of chapter 2 with regard to agricultural activities is balanced out by later chapters of the *Book of Lord Shang*, which present a more sophisticated view of the ways to expand arable lands and maximize the state's profits (Pines 2021). One topic, however, remains consistent throughout most of the text: the authors' belief that squeezing merchants of their profits is the best way to encourage agricultural prosperity. Chapter 22, "External and Internal" ("Wai nei" 外內), specifies:

> 苟能令商賈技巧之人無繁，則欲國之無富，不可得也。故曰：欲農富其國者，境內之食必貴，而不農之徵必多，市利之租必重，則民不得無田。無田，不得不易其食；食貴則田者利，田者利則事者眾。食貴，糴食不利，而又加重徵，則民不得無去其商賈、技巧，而事地利矣。故民之力盡在於地利矣。

> If you can cause merchants and peddlers and crafty and tricky people not to prosper, then even if you do not want to enrich the state, you will not but attain that. Hence, it is said: "He who wants the farmers to enrich his state makes food within the borders expensive. He must impose multiple taxes on those who do not farm and heavy levies on profits from the markets." Then the people will have to work in the fields. Those who do not work in the fields will have to exchange [their products] for food; when food is expensive, those who work in the fields benefit. When working in the fields brings benefit, then those who engage in it are many. When food is expensive, and purchasing it is not profitable, and in addition [it] is heavily taxed, then the people will have to cast away [the occupations of] merchants and peddlers and crafty and tricky people and engage in profiting from the soil. Thus, the people's strength is fully committed to the soil alone. (22.2; Zhang 2012: 255)

The discussion encapsulates the recommendations in the *Book of Lord Shang*, which are detailed in chapter 2 and elsewhere. A series of discriminatory measures against merchants and "crafty and tricky" artisans are supposed to discourage the people from engaging in these professions. As a result, they will ultimately have no alternative but to shift to agriculture. As Roel Sterckx (2015) has noted, this advocacy of clear anti-merchant policies distinguishes the *Book of Lord Shang* from other pre-imperial texts (see also Ochi 1993: 182–88). The authors' excessive dislike of merchants—who should be humiliated, suppressed, and see their profits diminished—demonstrates their insufficient understanding of the positive aspects of a market economy.[20] Their view of artisans as exclusively engaged in parasitic "skillful arts" (*jiyi* 技藝) (3.2, 3.3; Zhang 2012: 40, 43) is equally odd: The authors seem to be unaware of—or unwilling to acknowledge—the artisans' huge contribution to the Qin economy (Barbieri-Low 2007). Yet insofar as the authors' avowed goal is to direct the entire population toward farming, their recommendations are understandable (cf. Bai, Chap. 23, this volume). To turn "the bitter task" of tilling into an attractive occupation, the policy makers had to discourage any alternative.

---

[20] The Warring States period witnessed rapid marketization of economy (von Falkenhausen Forthcoming); but Qin apparently lagged behind its eastern peers in the pace of its transition to market; thus, coinage was introduced to it only after Shang Yang's death, in 337 BCE, centuries after it spread in the Zhou royal domain and the adjacent areas (*Shiji* 6: 289; for archeological evidence of Qin coinage's belatedness, see Chen 2006: 222–24). For examples of more sophisticated understandings of the market laws than those demonstrated in the *Book of Lord Shang*, see articles in Levi Sabattini and Schwermann 2021.

Although unsound over the long term, the policy was clearly effective in the short term. One passage summarizes:

> 故吾教令：民之欲利者，非耕不得；避害者，非戰不免。境內之民莫不先務耕戰而得其所樂。故地少粟多，民少兵強。能行二者於境內，則霸王之道畢矣。
>
> Hence, my teaching causes those among the people who seek benefits to gain them nowhere else but in tilling and those who want to avoid harm to escape nowhere but to war. Within the borders, everyone among the people first devotes himself to tilling and warfare and only then obtains whatever pleases him. Hence, though the territory is small, grain is plenty, and though the people are few, the army is powerful. He who is able to implement these two within the borders will accomplish the way of Hegemon and Monarch. (25.5; Zhang 2012: 277 ["Shen fa" 慎法])

6 Safeguarding Impersonal Standards

The vision of a universal system of positive and negative incentives centered on the ranks of merit promulgated in the *Book of Lord Shang* is the core of the book's concept of the rule by *fa* 法. The term *fa* in the text at times refers squarely to laws, including codified legal regulations (see, e.g., chapter 26, "Fixing Divisions" ["Ming fen" 明分]), but equally often the referent are broader norms and standards governing all aspects of social, political, and legal life. *Fa* is the major keyword denoting impersonal standards; rarely it is supplemented by such terms as *du* 度, "gauges" or "measures," *shù* 數, "methods," and *shù* 術, "techniques." The two latter terms can refer to the governing of the administrative apparatus, but this usage in the *Book of Lord Shang* is much less frequent than in *Han Feizi*. The real focus of *fa* and related concepts is employment of uniform standards of promotion and demotion and of conferring ranks and offices.

To be efficient, the system of impartial rules should be clear and fair. The emphasis on the clarity (*ming* 明) of laws, regulations, and promotion procedures permeates the *Book of Lord Shang*. "He who excels at ruling the state, his methods of appointing officials are clear; hence, he does not rely on knowledge and deliberations" 善為國者，官法明，故不任智慮; "The people participate in [military and agricultural] undertakings and die for the sake of regulations because the superiors are clear in establishing glorious names and doling out rewards and penalties" 夫民之從事死制也，以上之設榮名，置賞罰之明也; "Hence, when the ruler bestows ranks and emoluments, the way [they are distributed] should be clear. When the way is clear, the state daily grows stronger; when the way is obscure, the state daily approaches dismemberment" (是故人君之出爵祿也，道明；道明，則國日強；道幽，則國日削 (3.4 ["Nong zhan"], 8.1 ["Yi yan"], 9.1 ["Cuo fa"]; Zhang 2012: 46, 120, 128). Transparency of regulations is the *sine qua non* for ensuring the people's compliance with the state's rules.

Nevertheless, even the most transparent regulations and laws will remain a dead letter if they are whimsically circumvented by power holders. The need to fairly and impartially adhere to *fa* is the second source of the authors' concern. Laws and norms can be distorted by unscrupulous ministers who may sell official positions to their cronies (3.3; Zhang 2012: 42–43 ["Nong zhan"]), but the major threat to the impartiality of *fa* comes from the ruler himself. Time and again, the text urges the sovereign to observe standards (laws) and not to give in to his personal predilections, especially when determining promotions and demotions. It clarifies:

> 今上論材能知慧而任之，則知慧之人希（晞）主好惡，使官制物，以適主心。是以官無常，國亂而不壹，辯說之人而無法也。如此，則民務焉得無多，而地焉得無荒？
>
> Now, if the ruler appoints [the people] only after considering their talents, abilities, knowledge, and cleverness, then the knowledgeable and the clever will observe the sovereign's likes and dislikes and how he employs officials to manage affairs so as to conform to the sovereign's mind. Therefore, [the appointment of] officials will lack constant [norms], the state will be in turmoil and not engaged in the One (i.e., agriculture cum warfare), and argumentative persuaders will not [be reined in by] the law. In this case, how can the people's pursuits not be numerous; how can land not be laid to waste? (3.5; Zhang 2012: 47 ["Nong zhan"])

The ruler's over-reliance on his personal skills in determining who is worthy to serve and who is not is doubly damaging. First, it undermines his authority, allowing scheming ministers to dupe the sovereign and shift the power to their own hands (see also 3.3 ["Nong zhan"], 14.3 ["Xiu quan" 修權], 25.1-2 ["Shen fa"]; Zhang 2012: 42–43, 168, 271–73). Second, it wreaks havoc on the norms of promotion and demotion, causing the people to abandon the One—agriculture-cum-warfare—for the sake of easier routes of individual advancement. The criticism of the ruler, whose fondness of personal appointees jeopardizes the meritocratic system of government service, culminates in chapter 14, "Cultivation of Authority" ("Xiu quan" 修權):

> 世之為治者，多釋法而任私議，此國之所以亂也。……不以法論智、能、賢、不肖者，惟堯；而世不盡為堯。是故先王知自議譽私之不可任也，故立法明分，中程者賞之，毀公者誅之。賞誅之法，不失其議，故民不爭。
>
> Rulers of our age frequently cast away standards and rely on private deliberations: this is why their states are in turmoil. [...] Only [the sage thearch] Yao 堯 was able to discuss one's wisdom, ability, worthiness, or unworthiness without resorting to standards; yet the world does not consist only of the likes of Yao. Therefore, the former kings knew that they could not rely on their own deliberations and private appointments; hence, they established standards and clarified divisions so that those who were within the norms were rewarded, and those who damaged the common [interests] were prosecuted. The standards of rewards and prosecutions did not lose their appropriateness; hence, the people did not struggle. (14.2; Zhang 2012: 166)

> 今亂世之君、臣，區區然皆擅一國之利，而當一官之重，以便其私，此國之所以危也。故公私之交，存亡之本也。
>
> Now all rulers and ministers of [this] calamitous age act in a petty way, monopolizing the benefits of a single state and appropriating the authority of their office so as to benefit their private [interests]. This is the reason why the state is endangered. Hence, the interrelationship between the common and the private is the root of survival or ruin. (14.4; Zhang 2012: 170)

The ruler should represent the common (*gong* 公, also meaning "duke") interests of the polity. However, like any other individual, he may, due to private (*si* 私) motives, promote favorites and obstruct those from whom he is estranged.[21] If this were to happen, the system would stop working, because becoming the ruler's (or a high minister's) favorite would open an easier way upwards than engagement in fighting and tilling. Here, we find the seeds of the ruler's depersonalization that are fully observable in the *Han Feizi* (see Chap. 4, Sect. 3.3, this volume). While the sovereign is supposed to be the major beneficiary of a properly functioning sociopolitical system, he should nevertheless sacrifice his personal predilections for the sake of the system's success.

This brings us to the touchy question: the relation between the ruler and the laws. On the one hand, it is clear that the ruler is the sole law-giver and law-changer. The first chapter, "Changing the Laws," focuses precisely on the crucial role of Lord Xiao of Qin who decided "to change the laws so as to attain orderly rule" 變法以治 (1.2; Zhang 2012: 7 ["Geng fa"]). On the other hand, once the laws were enacted, they should not be changed whimsically. The enigmatic sentence "The sovereign values multiple changes; the state values minimal changes" 主貴多變，國貴少變 (4.1; Zhang 2012: 57 ["Qu qiang"]) is explained in the text's internal exegesis as follows: standards (or laws) should be constant; policies, on the other hand, should be flexible (20.5; Zhang 2012: 242 ["Ruo min"]). The importance of the laws' stability is reflected in the frequent use of the adjective *chang* 常 (constant) throughout the text (3.3–3.5 ["Nong zhan"]; 5.9 ["Shuo min"], 17.4 ["Shang xing"], 18.8 ["Hua ce"]; Zhang 2012: 42–47; 84; 202; 220).

Then, if the state is run as a perfect mechanism, what is the ruler's role in maintaining this mechanism? The answer—surprising in light of the staunchly authoritarian image of the "school of *fa*"—is that the ruler should not interfere much in policy making. This point was well noted by the editors of the *Book of Lord Shang*. The first chapter is the only one in which Lord Xiao of Qin makes a meaningful appearance: he outlines his plans to alter the existent laws, then listens to the advisors' opinions, and finally approves Shang Yang's proposal to institute radical reforms. Henceforth, the lord disappears from the text entirely except for the final chapter in which he asks a single question how to let the officials internalize laws and regulations and remains silent thereafter. Perhaps for the book's editors this was the desirable degree of the ruler's activism: to outline his plans, to listen to his ministers' arguments, then to make the decision and cease intervening in everyday running of the state.

7   Intellectuals and Elites in the Total State

One of the most notable features of the *Book of Lord Shang* is its perceived anti-intellectualism. The book derides intellectuals as "peripatetic eaters" 游食者 (*Book of Lord Shang* 3.6, 3.10 ["Nong zhan"], 22.2 ["Wai nei"], 23.3 ["Jun chen"]; Zhang

---

[21] For more about the meanings of *gong* and its relation to the ruler's interests, see the Chap. 4, p. 116.

2012: 49, 55, 255, 259) and "caterpillars" 螟螣蚵蠋 (3.6; Zhang 2012: 49 ["Nong zhan"]); dismisses traditional culture and advocacy of moral values as state-ruining "parasites" (蝨; 13.4; cf. 3.5, 4.3; Zhang 2012: 158, 47, 62); warns against allowing the peasants to become "knowledgeable" 知 and "fond of learning" 好學問 (2.14; Zhang 2012: 30 ["Ken ling"]), and the like. This anti-intellectual stance is perplexing. Not only that it could not endear the author(s) to the vast majority of educated elite, but it also was to a certain extent self-defeating. After all, the contributors to the *Book of Lord Shang* did not rise in ranks as peasants and soldiers. Nor were they necessarily shy of demonstrating their intellectual expertise and even superiority over the rulers (the topic is hinted at in chapters 1, 6, 7, and 15, among others). As such they clearly partake in the common ethos of intellectually active men-of-service of the Warring States period, who positioned themselves as society's and the rulers' guides (Pines 2009: 123–31). Why then the authors adopted the self-damaging anti-intellectual stance?

A possible explanation will take us back to the concept of the rule by impersonal standards. The efficiency of the system of ranks of merit promulgated by Shang Yang depended not only on its transparency and fairness but also on its exclusivity. Namely, to make this system fully effective, the state had to cut off any alternative routes of social, economic, and political advancement. The authors duly warn, "If the ruler advances flatterers and those who request audiences yet degrades the meritorious and strong, then even if ranks are bestowed, the army remains weak. If the people can get benefits and emoluments without having to risk their lives in the face of difficulty, then emoluments are issued, but the state remains poor" (人君者先便請謁，而後功力，則爵行而兵弱矣。民不死犯難，而利祿可致也，則祿行而國貧矣; 9.4; Zhang 2012: 132 ["Cuo fa"]). Opening outlets for social and political advancement outside the system of ranks of merit inevitably causes the people to seek better routes for improving their economic and social status than engagement in the "bitter and dangerous" pursuit of agriculture cum warfare.

This insight explains the authors' repeated assaults on groups that sought advancing outside the "single outlet" (*yi kong* 壹空) of tilling and fighting. In particular, the authors reserve their ire for travelling scholars on the one hand and for merchants and artisans on the other:

善為國者，其教民也，皆從壹而得官爵。是故{不作壹，}[22]不官無爵。國去言，則民樸；民樸，則不淫。民見上利之從壹空出也，則作壹，作壹則民不偷營。民不偷營，則多力；多力，則國強。今境內之民，皆曰：「農戰可避，而官爵可得也。」是故豪傑皆可變業，務學《詩》、《書》，隨從外權，上可以得顯，下可以求官爵；要靡事商賈，為技藝：皆以避農戰。具備，國之危也。民以此為教者，其國必削。

He who excels at ruling the state teaches the people to engage exclusively in the One (i.e., agriculture-cum-warfare) in order to attain offices and ranks. Hence, {those who are not engaged in the One} will have neither offices nor ranks. When the state eliminates [superfluous] talk, the people will be simple; if they are simple, they will not be licentious. If the people see that the benefits above come from a single outlet, they will engage in the One. If they engage in the One, the people will not recklessly demand [riches]. If the people

---

[22] The addition in figure brackets follows Gao Heng's suggestion (1974: 32n5).

do not make reckless demands, they will have abundant force; when force is abundant, the state will be powerful. Yet nowadays all the people within the borders say: "One can escape from agriculture and war and still get offices and ranks." Therefore, the powerful and eminent are able to change their occupation: they diligently study *Poems* and *Documents* and then follow foreign powers.[23] At best, they attain renown, and at the least they are able to seek after offices and emoluments. As for the petty and insignificant: they become merchants and peddlers, engage in skillful arts, and all escape agriculture and warfare. In such a situation, the state is endangered. If the people consider this a [proper] teaching, the state will be dismembered. (3.2; Zhang 2012: 40 ["Nong zhan"])

Travelling scholars, who excel in learning and "superfluous talk," acquire official positions that should be granted exclusively to those who excel at war. For their part, merchants, peddlers, and skillful artisans attain a decent livelihood without having to engage in agriculture. The authors' vehement attacks on these segments of the population reflect not just ideological dislike of the scholars' proposals or a misguided rejection of the merchants and artisans' economic usefulness but rather the idea of these groups' social undesirability. Scholars, merchants, and artisans should be suppressed because their very existence creates alternative means of individuals' empowerment and enrichment and undermines the system of ranks of merit. This conclusion is summarized in chapter 18, "Charting the Policies":

不作而食，不戰而榮，無爵而尊，無祿而富，無官而長，此之謂姦民。

Those who do not work but eat, who do not fight but attain glory, who have no rank but are respected, who have no emolument but are rich, who have no office but lead—these are called "villains." (18.6; Zhang 2012: 216 ["Hua ce"])

Behind this short and robust statement, one can discern the authors' bold idea: to prevent those outside the system of ranks from possessing political, social, and economic power. The state is to exclusively grant this power; it is up to the government to decide who should enjoy food, glory, respect, riches, and leadership. Those identified in the text as "villains" are actually remnants of autonomous social and economic elites, who, in the authors' eyes, have no right to exist. Whether Shang Yang's reforms succeeded in eliminating these elites is debatable, yet it needs be mentioned here that the currently available Qin paleographic sources give no indications of their later existence.[24] This means that the ranks granted by the state became the exclusive, or at the very least the primary, means of enhancing one's status.

This understanding sheds a new light on the reasons for the immense dislike of Shang Yang among the vast majority of educated elite members throughout Chinese history. His vision was of the total state that controls social, economic, and to a certain degree also intellectual and cultural life, so as to maximize the utilization of its material and human resources. This total state left no place either for the elite's

---

[23] "Foreign powers" evidently refers to foreign states, which often meddled in the domestic affairs of their rivals by fostering ties with powerful statesmen.

[24] For a survey of paleographic materials from pre-imperial and imperial Qin, see Pines et al. 2014: 8–11. One needs to exercise particular caution in dealing with these materials, which overwhelmingly reflect the viewpoint of Qin administrators; yet it is important to note that from the currently available materials, there is no evidence for the existence of independent elites in late Warring States-era Qin, nor even lineages as notable social units.

power, or for the intellectuals' autonomy. Even the very dignity of the educated elite—the hallmark of Confucius's legacy (Pines, Chap. 18, this volume)—was viewed by the authors of the *Book of Lord Shang* with deep suspicion. That the intellectuals reciprocated in kind comes as no surprise.

8   The State and Its People: The Limits of Indoctrination

Shang Yang is often perceived as "people-basher," or a leader of "little kindness" 少恩 (*Shiji* 68: 2237). Many of the *Book of Lord Shang's* statements support this impression:

> 昔之能制天下者，必先制其民者也；能勝強敵者，必先勝其民者也。故勝民之本在制民，若冶於金、陶於土也。本不堅，則民如飛鳥走獸，其孰能制之？　民本，法也。故善治者，塞民以法，而名地作矣。
>
> In the past, those who were able to regulate All-under-Heaven first had to regulate their own people; those who were able to overcome the enemy had first to overcome their own people. The root of overcoming the people is controlling the people as the metalworker controls metal and the potter clay. When the roots are not firm, the people will be like flying birds and running animals: Who will then be able to regulate them? The root of the people is law. Hence, those who excel at orderly rule block the people with law; then a [good] name and lands can be attained. (18.2; Zhang 2012: 210 ["Hua ce"])

The people are equated with the state's enemy; they are potentially unruly "like flying birds and running animals"; they should be controlled "as the metalworker controls metal and the potter clay." These similes alone suffice to demonstrate the authors' overt pejorative attitude toward the people (cf. Graziani, Chap. 13, this volume). Elsewhere, the text plainly summarizes, "When the people are weak, the state is strong; when the people are strong, the state is weak" 民弱國強，民強國弱 (20.1; Zhang 2012: 238 ["Ruo min"]). These pronouncements fully support the image of Shang Yang as "people-basher."

And yet this conclusion would be premature. The authors insist throughout the book that the ultimate goal of the political system is to benefit the people. By over-awing them and preventing them from misbehaving, the rulers actually demonstrate their "care" or "love" for the people 愛民 (1.2 ["Geng fa"], 4.4 ["Qu qiang"], 5.4 ["Shuo min"], 13.5 ["Jin ling"]; Zhang 2012: 7, 64, 78, 161). Moreover, the political and legal system should also be attentive to the people's sentiments. Laws in particular should be adopted only after taking careful account of the people's disposition:

> 故聖人之為國也，觀俗立法則治，察國事本則宜。不觀時俗，不察國本，則其法立而民亂，事劇而功寡。此臣之所謂過也。
>
> Hence, in ruling the state, the sage establishes laws after observing customs and then attains orderly rule; he inspects the roots of the state's affairs and then acts appropriately. Without the observation of current customs and without the inspection of the roots of the state, laws can be established, but the people will be in turmoil; undertakings will be numerous, but achievements few. This is what I, your minister, call "to err." (6.9; Zhang 2012: 100 ["Suan di"])

Why should laws be established only after observing the people's customs? The authors explain that such observation is a precondition for the commoners' full internalization of and compliance with the laws. Some statements in the text sound surprisingly "democratic," e.g., "The well-ordered state values decisions made below" (治國貴下斷; 5.9; Zhang 2012: 84 ["Shuo min"]). Of course, this does not mean blindly following public opinion. Rather, the authors envision a dialectic relation between the laws and the people. Laws should be based on an understanding of the people's disposition (i.e., their intrinsic quest for rewards and fear of punishments) and should accord with their customs. Then, strict enforcement of the laws will cause the people not just to comply with but also to internalize the laws, making the laws fully efficient (Wu and Lin 2016).

The text's complex attitude to the people is reflected also in its views of their intellectual capabilities. On the one hand, the *Book of Lord Shang* echoes *Laozi*, valorizing the people's simplicity (*pu* 樸) and even ignorance (*yu* 愚).[25] "Knowledgeable" peasants are considered a malady (2.14; Zhang 2012: 30 ["Ken ling"]). The authors insist that "when [the people] are committed to farming, they are simple; when they are simple, they fear orders" 屬於農則樸，樸則畏令 (6.3; Zhang 2012: 92 ["Suan di"]). Simultaneously, however, they recognize that this simplicity may not be attainable any longer: the generation is said to be knowledgeable 知 and crafty 巧 (6.7 ["Suan di"], 7.2, 7.4 ["Kai sai"]; Zhang 2012: 97, 110, 113). As specified in Sect. 5 above, these knowledgeable people should be coerced to obey the rulers. But what about more efficient means employed by the modern advocates of the "total" (totalitarian) state? Should the state imbue the people with the desirable values? Should it brainwash them?

The answer is quite surprising. In a single passage that deals with "teaching" (or "indoctrination," *jiao* 教) as a positive goal, the authors outline a simpler way for making the people internalize the norms. This will be done in a very fair and transparent way: let the people understand where their benefit lies and whence the danger comes, so that they comply with the state's demands out of sheer self-interest. Chapter 17, "Rewards and Punishments," clarifies:

所謂壹教者，博聞、辯慧、信廉、禮樂、修行、羣黨、任譽、清濁(→請謁)，不可以富貴，不可以評刑，不可獨立私議以陳其上。……雖曰聖智、巧佞、厚樸，則不能以非功罔上利。然富貴之門，要存戰而已矣。彼能戰者，踐富貴之門；強梗焉，有常刑而不赦。是父兄、昆弟、知識、婚姻、合同者，皆曰：「務之所加，存戰而已矣。」夫故當壯者務於戰，老弱者務於守；死者不悔，生者務勸。此臣之所謂壹教也。民之欲富貴也，共闔棺而後止。而富貴之門，必出於兵。是故民聞戰而相賀也；起居飲食所歌謠者，戰也。此臣之所謂「明教之猶至於無教也。」

What is called "unification of teaching" is that none of these—the broadly educated, the argumentative, the knowledgeable, the trustworthy, the honest, those skilled at ritual and music, those who cultivate their conduct, those who establish cliques, or those who are

---

[25] For *Laozi*'s valorization of the people's ignorance, see, e.g., stanza 3 (*Boshu Laozi* 237). In the short text of the *Laozi*, statements in favor of the people's simplicity (*pu* 樸) recur thrice (stanzas 19, 33, 57). In the *Book of Lord Shang*, the term *pu* is used no less than seventeen times to depict the desirable condition of the people—more than in the entire corpus of preimperial philosophical texts combined.

appointed due to their reputation or [after] having requested an audience—will be allowed to become rich and noble, to criticize punishments, or to establish their private opinions independently and submit them to superiors. ... Even if one is sagacious and knowledgeable, crafty and glib-tongued, generous or simple, he should not be able to seek benefits from superiors unless he has merit. Thus, the gates of riches and nobility are exclusively in the field of war. He who is able to [distinguish himself at] war will pass through the gates of riches and nobility; he who is stubborn and tenacious will meet with constant punishments and will not be pardoned.

Therefore, fathers and elder brothers, minor brothers, acquaintances, relatives by marriage, and colleagues all say: "What we should be devoted to is only war and that is all." Hence, the able-bodied are devoted to war, the elderly and infirm are devoted to defense; the dead have nothing to regret; the living are ever more devoted and encouraged. This is what I, your minister, call the "unification of teaching."

The people's desire for riches and nobility stops only when their coffin is sealed. And [entering] the gates of riches and nobility must be through military [service]. Therefore, when they hear about war, the people congratulate each other; whenever they move or rest, drink or eat, they sing and chant only about war. This is why I, your minister, say: "Clarifying teaching is like arriving at no teaching." (17.4; Zhang 2012: 202–203)

This passage is fascinating. From the first phrases, the authors dissociate the "Confucian-sounding" term *jiao* from any kind of educational activity, which they perceive as actually detrimental to *jiao*. What is called "unification of teaching" here refers to a recurring topic in the *Book of Lord Shang*: strict adherence to the system of the exclusive distribution of ranks and honor through military service. When this system functions, it causes the people to understand that the only way to satisfy their desires for riches and glory is to engage in war; hence, war becomes the focus of the people's aspirations. We have encountered the same war-oriented mentality in passage 18.3, quoted earlier (pp. 40–41). There, too, the adoration of war comes purely from egoistic motives: first, war is the only way to enhance one's status; and, second, fighting is also the only way to avoid a deserter's due punishment. When the inevitability and desirability of war are internalized, the people no longer need to be encouraged to go to the front: they will eagerly volunteer to do it.

It is important to note here that, fundamentally, the *Book of Lord Shang* does not envision any more sophisticated military indoctrination. Any person knowledgeable of the history of mass armies in the West may be perplexed: Why did the authors not promote any positive means of encouraging the people's commitment to war? Why do we never encounter in this text (or any other) the adoration of the martial spirit akin, for example, to the Romans' maxim "*Dulce et decorum est pro patria mori*" (It is sweet and glorious to die for the fatherland); the dehumanization of the enemy; the identification of martiality with masculinity; the presentation of war as the only way to ensure the people's security; or any other device employed worldwide to encourage men to fight? The answer perhaps has to do with the authors' fundamental mistrust of any education and indoctrination. Rather than being brainwashed to sacrifice themselves for the state out of abstract commitment, the people should be directed to do so according to their intrinsic and immutable selfishness. Fighting to the death in order to attain rank or just to avoid the inevitable punishment inflicted on deserters and their kin is preferable to fighting for the sake of some chimera. Instead of cheating the people with hollow ideological constructs, the authors prefer to clarify substantial gains and losses from engagement in war or evading it, respectively, and then let the people's basic "disposition" direct them to the ends desired by the state.

In the final reckoning, the *Book of Lord Shang* does not propose an ideological superstructure that should bind the people together or that should somehow influence their actions. Indoctrination is envisioned primarily as a negative action, which should prevent the corrosive impact of moralizing discourse from distracting the people from agriculture and warfare. The authors, however, do not put forward any alternative set of messages to replace this discourse. Similarly, whenever they talk of "teaching" or of "transforming" (*hua* 化) and unifying the people's customs (8.1 ["Yi yan"], 17.1 ["Shang xing"]; Zhang 2012: 120, 190), they do not imply any active dissemination of ideas or ideals among the populace. A perfect state should manipulate its subjects exclusively through the combination of rewards and punishments: clearly outlined rules that explicate personal gains and losses for compliance or transgression. Any ideological incentives then become redundant. Thus, the text's lack of interest in brainwashing makes it insufficiently "totalitarian."[26]

9 Epilogue: Immoral Means and Moral Ends?

The *Book of Lord Shang*, full as it is with harsh and provocative pronouncements is often identified as representative of the "amoral science of statecraft" (Graham 1989: 267–85). More radical critics place it squarely among the anti-utopias (e.g., Lévi 2005: 38–42; Zhang 2016) or identify it with "antihumanistic" spirit (Huang 2010). But to understand the text, one should look beyond its "alienating rhetoric" (Pines 2012). Actually, as noted above, the authors frequently identify the oppressive measures they advocate as a necessary means toward attaining laudable moral ends (cf. McLeod, Chap. 15, this volume). For instance, chapter 18 summarizes its brief narrative of state formation in the past and its relevance to the present as follows: "Therefore, in order to eradicate war with war, even waging war is permissible; to eradicate murder with murder, even murdering is permissible; to eradicate punishments with punishments, even making punishments heavy is permissible" 故以戰去戰，雖戰可也；以殺去殺，雖殺可也；以刑去刑，雖重刑可也 (18.1; Zhang 2012: 208 ["Hua ce"]). The same idea is echoed elsewhere (4.8 ["Qu qiang"], 5.7 ["Shuo min"]; Zhang 2012: 69, 81). Once the text promises that implementation of its ideas would eventually restore "the utmost virtue" 至德 in All-under-Heaven (7.5; Zhang 2012: 116 ["Kai sai"]). And on one occasion it promotes an even loftier moral ideal:

> 聖君知物之要，故其治民有至要。故執賞罰以壹輔。……聖君之治人也，必得其心，故能用力。力生強，強生威，威生德，德生於力。聖君獨有之，故能述仁義於天下。

---

[26] For a different analysis of the unfitness of "totalitarian" label to the *Book of Lord Shang*, see Schiele, Chap. 22, this volume

> The sage ruler understands the essentials of things. Hence, in ordering the people, he possesses the most essential; thus, he firmly holds the rewards and punishments to support the One. … The sage ruler, in ordering others, should first attain their hearts; hence, he is able to employ force. Force gives birth to strength; strength gives birth to awesomeness; awesomeness gives birth to virtue; virtue is born of force. The sage ruler alone possesses it; hence, he is able to implement benevolence and righteousness in All-under-Heaven. (13.6; Zhang 2012: 162 ["Jin ling"])

How should we understand this passage about "implementing benevolence and righteousness in All-under-Heaven," coming as it is from the chapter that identified "benevolence and righteousness" as "parasites" (13.4; Zhang 2012: 158)? Is it a later addition aimed to alleviate the alienating impact of the rest of the chapter? Without ruling out this possibility, we may entertain another option: namely, that the passage above (and a few other "moralizing" passages scattered throughout the text) speak not of the present but of the future. Currently, in the age of bitter warfare, the goal is to create "a rich state and a strong army." This requires full mobilization of human and material resources which cannot be achieved without coercion. Hence the text dispenses with the misleading moralizing discourse, and advocates employing whatever means available to empower the state. In the long term, however, perhaps after the establishment of the "fourth dynasty" (p. 30 above), morality will prevail. In the unspecified future, as laws and regulations are fully internalized, even the coercive state will wither and the people will attain the blessed situation of "self-governance" 自治 (26.6; Zhang 2012: 288 ["Ding fen"]).

It is tempting to discuss here the dialectical spirit of the *Book of Lord Shang*. Rather than the wishful thinking of Mengzi 孟子 (d. ca. 304 BCE) and his ilk, according to whom moral ends, such as unification of All-under-Heaven, should be attained by moral means only (*Mengzi* 1.6), the authors of the *Book of Lord Shang* are ready to accommodate harsh and cruel means that will serve the same moral ends (cf. McLeod, Chap. 15, this volume). Once peace and tranquility are attained, there will be no need in excessive coercion, and morality (perhaps even moralizing discourse itself) will be legitimate again. These utopian goals are only rarely outlined in the text, though. The authors' focus is on the here and now, and insofar as moralizing discourse in the here and now is practiced by self-serving peripatetic advisors who distract the people from agriculture and warfare, it should be silenced. In the final account this became the hallmark of Shang Yang's ideas, turning the thinker into an odious figure of whom "scholars are ashamed to speak."

References

Alexander, Jon, and Joachim K.H.W. Schmidt. 1996. Social Engineering: Genealogy of a Concept. In *Social Engineering*, ed. Adam Podgórecki, Jon Alexander, and Rob Shields, 1–20. Ottawa: Carleton University Press.

Barbieri-Low, Anthony J. 2007. *Artisans in Early Imperial China*. Seattle: University of Washington Press.

1 Shang Yang and *The Book of Lord Shang*   53

Barbieri-Low, Anthony J. and Robin D. S. Yates. 2015. *Law, State, and Society in Early Imperial China: A Study with Critical Edition and Translation of the Legal Texts from Zhangjiashan Tomb No. 247*. Leiden: Brill.

Baxter, William H. 1998. Situating the Language of the *Lao-tzu*: The Probable Date of the *Tao-te-ching*. In *Lao-tzu and the Tao-te-ching*, ed. Livia Kohn and Michael LaFargue, 231–253. Albany: State University of New York Press.

Book of Lord Shang. See Pines 2017.

Boshu Laozi jiaozhu 帛書老子校注 (Silk Manuscript *Laozi*, Collated and Annotated). 1996. Ed. Gao, Ming 高明. Beijing: Zhonghua shuju.

Chen, Longwen 陳隆文. 2006. *A Study of the Monetary Geography of the Spring and Autumn and Warring States Periods*春秋戰國貨幣制度研究. Beijing: Renmin chubanshe.

Dongpo quanji 東坡全集 (Collected Works of Su Dongpo). n.d. By Su, Shi 蘇軾 (1036–1101). E-*Siku quanshu* edition.

Du, Zhengsheng 杜正勝. 1985. "Analyzing Society Formed by Shang Yang's Reforms Through the Prism of the System of Ranks" 從爵制論商鞅變法所形成的社會. *Bulletin of the Institute of History and Philology, Academia Sinica* 中央研究院歷史語言研究所集刊 56. 3: 485–544.

Falkenhausen, Lothar von. Forthcoming. *Economic Trends in China During the Age of Confucius (1050–250 BC): The Archeological Evidence*. Los Angeles: Cotsen Institute of Archaeology at UCLA.

Gao, Heng 高亨. 1974. *The Book of Lord Shang, Annotated and Translated*商君書注譯. Beijing: Zhonghua shuju. (A very good study and annotations of the text despite being produced under the duress of the Cultural Revolution)

Gentz, Joachim, and Dirk Meyer. 2015. Introduction: Literary Forms of Argument in Early China. In *Literary Forms of Argument in Early China*, ed. Joachim Gentz and Dirk Meyer, 1–36. Leiden: Brill.

Goldin, Paul R. 2020. *The Art of Chinese Philosophy: Eight Classical Texts and How to Read Them*. Princeton NJ: Princeton University Press.

Graham, Angus C. 1989. *Disputers of the Tao: Philosophical Argument in Ancient China*. La Salle, Ill.: Open Court.

Guanzi jiaozhu 管子校注 (*Guanzi*, Collated and Annotated). 2004. Ed. Li, Xiangfeng 黎翔鳳. Beijing: Zhonghua shuju.

Huang, Shaomei 黃紹梅. 2010. *Study of Shang Yang's Anti-Humanism* 商鞅反人文觀研究. Yonghe (Taipei County): Hua Mulan chubanshe.

Huangshi richao 黃氏日抄 (Mr. Huang's Daily Transcriptions). n.d. By Huang, Zhen 黃震 (1213–1280). E-*Siku quanshu* edition.

Jiang, Tao. 2021. *Origins of Moral-Political Philosophy in Early China: Contestation of Humaneness, Justice, and Personal Freedom*. Oxford: Oxford University Press.

Jiang Chongyue 蔣重躍. 2021. "Re-reading Shang Yang and the *Book of Lord Shang*" 重讀商鞅和《商君書》. *Bohai University Journal* 渤海大學學報 3: 1–13.

——— 蔣重躍. 2022. *The Book of Lord Shang* 商君書. (From "A Hundred Classics in China's Traditional Culture" 中華傳統文化百部經典 series). Beijing: Guojia tushuguan chubanshe. (A useful introductory-level edition)

Kern, Martin. 2000. *The Stele Inscriptions of Ch'in Shih-huang: Text and Ritual in Early Chinese Imperial Representation*. New Haven, CT: American Oriental Society.

Korolkov, Maxim [Корольков, Максим]. 2010. "Земельное законодательство и контроль над землей в эпоху Чжаньго и в начале раннеимперской эпохи (по данным обнаруженных законодательных текстов.") [Land Law and Land Control in the Zhanguo Era and Early Imperial Era (According to Discovered Legal Texts)]. Ph.D. thesis. Russian Academy of Sciences, Institute of Oriental Studies.

Laozi. See *Boshu Laozi jiaozhu*.

Lévi, Jean, trans. 2005. *Le livre du prince Shang*. 2nd ed., with an updated introduction. Paris: Flammarion.

Lewis, Mark E. 1990. *Sanctioned Violence in Early China*. Albany: State University of New York Press.

———. 1999. Warring States: Political History. In *The Cambridge History of Ancient China: From the Origins of Civilization to 221 B.C*, ed. Michael Loewe and Edward L. Shaughnessy, 587–650. Cambridge: Cambridge University Press.

———. 2021. *Honor and Shame in Early China*. Cambridge: Cambridge University Press.

Loewe, Michael. 1960. The Orders of Aristocratic Rank of Han China. *T'oung Pao* 48 (1–3): 97–174.

———. 2010. Social Distinctions, Groups, and Privileges. In *China's Early Empires: A Reappraisal*, ed. Michael Nylan and Michael Loewe, 296–307. Cambridge: Cambridge University Press.

Marx, Karl. [1859] 2010. "A Contribution to the Critique of Political Economy, Part One." Trans. Yuri Sdobnikov. Rpt. in Karl Marx and Friedrich Engels, *Collected Works*, vol. 29, 257–419. Lawrence & Wishart, Electric Books.

Mengzi yizhu 孟子譯注 (*Mengzi*, Translated and annotated). 1992. Ed. Yang, Bojun 楊伯峻. Beijing: Zhonghua shuju.

Miao, Ruosu 苗若素 and Wu, Shiqi 吳世琪. 1998. *Dictionary of the* Book of Lord Shang 商君書詞典. In *Dictionaries of Major Pre-Qin Texts (Liezi, the Book of Lord Shang, the Gongyang Commentary on the Springs-and-Autumns Annals)* 先秦要籍詞典 (列子·商君書·春秋公羊傳), ed. Wang Shishun 王世舜, 65–96. Beijing: Xueyuan chubanshe.

Nishijima, Sadao 西嶋定生. 2004. *The Formation of Ancient China's Empire and its Structure: Study of the Twenty-Ranks System* 中國古代帝國的形成與結構: 二十等爵制研究., trans. Wu Shangqing 吳尚清. Beijing: Zhonghua shuju.

Ochi, Shigeaki 越智重明. 1993. *Studies in the History of the Warring States, Qin, and Han* 戰國秦漢史研究. Vol. 2. Fukuoka: Chūgoku Shoten.

Pines, Yuri. 2000. Disputers of the *Li*: Breakthroughs in the Concept of Ritual in Pre-imperial China. *Asia Major (Third Series)* 13 (1): 1–41.

———. 2009. *Envisioning Eternal Empire: Chinese Political Thought of the Warring States Era*. Honolulu: University of Hawai'i Press.

———. 2012. Alienating Rhetoric in the *Book of Lord Shang* and its Moderation. *Extrême-Orient, Extrême-Occident* 34: 79–110.

———. 2013. From Historical Evolution to the End of History: Past, Present and Future from Shang Yang to the First Emperor. In *Dao Companion to the Philosophy of Han Fei*, ed. Paul R. Goldin, 25–45. Dordrecht: Springer.

———. 2014. The Messianic Emperor: A New Look at Qin's Place in China's History. In *Birth of an Empire: The State of Qin Revisited*, ed. Yuri Pines, Lothar von Falkenhausen, Gideon Shelach, and Robin D.S. Yates, 258–279. Berkeley: University of California Press.

———. 2016a. A 'Total War'? Rethinking Military Ideology in the *Book of Lord Shang*. *Journal of Chinese Military History* 5 (2): 97–134.

———. 2016b. Social Engineering in Early China: The Ideology of the *Shangjunshu* (*Book of Lord Shang*) Revisited. *Oriens Extremus* 55: 1–37.

———. 2017, trans. and ed. *The Book of Lord Shang: Apologetics of State Power in Early China*. New York: Columbia University Press. (Major recent translation cum study of the *Book of Lord Shang*)

———. 2020. 'To Die for the Sanctity of the Name': Name (*ming* 名) as Prime-mover of Political Action in Early China. In *Keywords in Chinese Culture*, ed. Li Wai-yee and Yuri Pines, 169–218. Hong Kong: The Chinese University Press.

———. 2021. "Agriculturalism and Beyond: Economic Thought of the *Book of Lord Shang*." In: *Between Command and Market: Economic Thought and Practice in Early China*, ed. Elisa Levi Sabattini and Christian Schwermann, 76–111. Leiden: Brill.

———. 2023 (forthcoming). "Waging a Demographic War: Chapter 15 ('Attracting the People') of the *Book of Lord Shang* Revisited," *Bochumer Jahrbuch zur Ostasienforschung* 46.

Pines, Yuri, and Gideon Shelach. 2005. 'Using the Past to Serve the Present': Comparative Perspectives on Chinese and Western Theories of the Origins of the State. In *Genesis and Regeneration: Essays on Conceptions of Origins*, ed. Shaul Shaked, 127–163. Jerusalem: Israel Academy of Science and Humanities.

Pines, Yuri, and with Lothar von Falkenhausen, Gideon Shelach, and Robin D. S. Yates. 2014. General Introduction: Qin History Revisited. In *Birth of an Empire: The State of Qin Revisited*, ed. Yuri Pines, Lothar von Falkenhausen, Gideon Shelach, and Robin D.S. Yates, 1–36. Berkeley: University of California Press.

Podgórecki, Adam. 1996. Sociotechnics: Basic Concepts and Issues. In *Social Engineering*, ed. Adam Podgórecki, Jon Alexander, and Rob Shields, 21–62. Ottawa: Carleton University Press.

Sabattini, Elisa Levi, and Christian Schwermann, eds. 2021. *Between Command and Market: Economic Thought and Practice in Early China*. Leiden: Brill.

Sato, Masayuki. 2013a. Did Xunzi's Theory of Human Nature Provide the Foundation for the Political Thought of Han Fei? In *Dao Companion to the Philosophy of Han Fei*, ed. Paul R. Goldin, 147–165. Dordrecht: Springer.

———— 佐藤將之. 2013b. *Origins of Xunzi's Idea of the Rule by Ritual and Study of the Warring States-Period Masters*荀子禮治思想的淵源與戰國諸子之研究. Taida zhexue congshu 臺大哲學叢書 8. Taipei: Taida chuban zhongxin.

Shelach, Gideon, and Yuri Pines. 2006. Secondary State Formation and the Development of Local Identity: Change and Continuity in the State of Qin (770–221 B.C.). In *Archaeology of Asia*, ed. Miriam T. Stark, 202–230. Malden, Mass: Blackwell.

Shiji 史記 (*Records of the Historian*). 1997. By Sima Qian 司馬遷 (ca. 145–90 BCE) et al. Annotated by Zhang Shoujie 張守節, Sima Zhen 司馬貞, and Pei Yin 裴駰. Beijing: Zhonghua shuju.

Sterckx, Roel. 2015. Ideologies of the Peasant and Merchant in Warring States China. In *Ideology of Power and Power of Ideology in Early China*, ed. Yuri Pines, Paul R. Goldin, and Martin Kern, 211–248. Leiden: Brill.

Tong, Weimin 仝衛敏. 2013. *Integrative Study of the* Book of Lord Shang *and Unearthed Documents*出土文獻與《商君書》綜合研究. Vols. 16–17 of *Series of Studies of Classical Texts* 古典文獻研究輯刊, ed. Pan Meiyue 潘美月 and Du Jiexiang 杜潔祥. Yonghe (Taipei County): Hua Mulan chubanshe. (A good study of the *Book of Lord Shang* in the context of recently unearthed paleographic documents)

————. 2016. "A New Exploration of the Dates of the 'Attracting the People' chapter of the *Book of Lord Shang*." Trans. Yuri Pines. *Contemporary Chinese Thought* 47.2: 138–151.

Vogelsang, Kai, trans. 2017. *Shangjun shu: Schriften des Fürsten von Shang*. Stuttgart: Alfred Kröner.

Wagner, Donald B. 1993. *Iron and Steel in Ancient China*. Leiden: Brill.

Wenxian tongkao 文獻通考 (Comprehensive Examination of Authoritative Sources and Later Interpretations). n.d. (1319). By Ma, Duanlin 馬端臨 (1254–1332). E-*Siku quanshu* edition.

Wu, Baoping 吳保平 and Lin, Cunguang 林存光. 2016. "Reflections on the Concept of 'Law' of Shang Yang from the Perspective of Political Philosophy: Function, Value and Sprit of the 'Rule of Law,'" trans. Yuri Pines. *Contemporary Chinese Thought* 47.2: 125–137.

Xiao, Yang. 2006. When Political Philosophy Meets Moral Psychology: Expressivism in the *Mencius*. Dao 5 (2): 257–271.

Xunzi jijie 荀子集解 (*Xunzi*, with Collected Glosses). 1992. Ed. Wang, Xianqian 王先謙 (1842–1917), Shen, Xiaohuan 沈嘯寰, and Wang, Xingxian 王星賢. Beijing: Zhonghua shuju.

Yang, Kuan 楊寬. 1998. *History of the Warring States* 戰國史. Rev. ed. Shanghai: Renmin chubanshe.

Yang, Zhenghong 楊振紅. 2021. "Analyzing the Origins of the System of Twenty Ranks, Their Subsequent Stratification and Its Basic Principles as Seen from the Newly Unearthed Bamboo and Wooden Manuscripts" 從新出簡牘看二十等爵制的起源、分層發展及其原理. *Journal of Historical Science* 史學月刊 1: 34–52.

Yates, Robin D.S. 1999. Early China. In *War and Society in the Ancient and Medieval Worlds: Asia, the Mediterranean, Europe, and Mesoamerica*, ed. Kurt Raaflaub and Nathan Rosenstein, 7–45. Cambridge, Mass: Center for Hellenic Studies.

Yoshimoto, Michimasa 吉本道雅. 2000. "Introductory Study to Shang Yang's Reforms" 商君變法研究序說. *Journal of History* 史林 83–84: 1–29.

Yoshinami, Takashi 好并隆司. 1985. "Analyzing the Process of Formation of Qin Dynasty's Power on the Basis of 'Attracting the People' and 'Calculating the Land' Chapters of the *Book of Lord Shang*" 商君書徠民、算地兩篇よりみた 秦朝權力の形成過程. *Journal of Oriental Research* 東洋史研究 44.1: 1–22.

Zhang, Jue 張覺. 2012. *The Book of Lord Shang, Collated with Subcommentaries* 商君書校疏. Beijing: Zhishi chanquan chubanshe. (The most systematic textual study of the *Book of Lord Shang*)

Zhang, Linxiang 張林祥. 2016. "Progress or Change? Rethinking the Historical Outlook of the *Book of Lord Shang*." Trans. Yuri Pines. *Contemporary Chinese Thought* 47.2: 90–111.

Zheng, Liangshu 鄭良樹. 1989. *Shang Yang and his School* 商鞅及其學派. Shanghai: Shanghai guji chubanshe. (An engaging attempt to trace intellectual evolution of "Shang Yang's school" through the chapters of the *Book of Lord Shang*)

Zhou, Ziqiang 周自強. 2007. *Comprehensive History of China's Economy: The Pre-Qin Economy Volume* 中國經濟通史: 先秦經濟卷. Beijing: Zhongguo shehuikexue chubanshe.

Zhu, Fenghan 朱鳳瀚. 1990. *A Study of Family Formations in the Shang and Zhou* 商周家族形態研究. Tianjin: Tianjin guji chubanshe.

Zhu, Shaohou 朱紹侯. 2008. *Investigating the System of Ranks for Military Merits* 軍功爵制考論. Beijing: Shangwu yinshuguan.

Zhuangzi jinzhu jinyi 莊子今注今譯 (*Zhuangzi*, with New Glosses and New Translation). 1994. Ed. Chen, Guying 陳鼓應. Beijing: Zhonghua shuju.

Chapter 2
On Shen Buhai's Legal Thought

Zhong Yu 喻中

Allusions in early Chinese philosophical discourses to the thought of "Shen-Shang" 申商 or "Shen-Han" 申韓 indicate that, in traditional China, the thought of Shen Buhai 申不害 (d. 337 BCE) enjoyed an ideological status comparable to that of Shang Yang 商鞅 (d. 338 BCE) and Han Fei 韓非 (d. 233 BCE). However, despite Shen Buhai's fame, only a handful of scholarly works are dedicated to the study of his ideas. In most cases, scholars only briefly refer to him (for example, a brief analysis by Guo Moruo in his "Critique of Early *Fa* Thinkers" 前期法家的批判; see Guo 2012: 254–62). Only few academic works focus on Shen Buhai, the most prominent of which being Herrlee G. Creel's monograph (1974).

One reason for the paucity of studies on Shen Buhai is that most of his work has long since been lost. The "Treatise on Arts and Letters" ("Yiwenzhi" 藝文志) of the *Hanshu* 漢書 (History of the Former Han Dynasty) mentions a *Shenzi* 申子 in six chapters (*pian* 篇) among the ten texts in 217 *pian* in its *fa* section (*Hanshu* 30: 1735). However, the current *Shenzi* consists of only the fragments of several passages. The "Da ti" 大體 chapter of *Shenzi* collected in the *Qunshu zhiyao* 群書治要 (Essentials of orderly rule from multiple books) compendium assembled in 631, is only about 600 characters length, which constitute the main body of Shen Buhai's surviving works. A few fragments of Shen Buhai's writings are scattered in such works as *Han Feizi* 韓非子, *Zhanguo ce* 戰國策, and *Lüshi chunqiu* 呂氏春秋; a few more survive in later compendia such as *Yiwen leiju* 藝文類聚 (Anthology of

Translated: Avital Rom
This article is adapted from Yu 2021.

Z. Yu 喻中 (✉)
China University of Political Science and Law, Beijing, China

© The Author(s), under exclusive license to Springer Nature Switzerland AG 2024
Y. Pines (ed.), *Dao Companion to China's fa Tradition*, Dao Companions to Chinese Philosophy 19, https://doi.org/10.1007/978-3-031-53630-4_3

literary excerpts arranged by category, compiled in 624), *Taiping yulan* 太平御覽 (Imperial readings from the Taiping era, compiled 983), and so forth (see more in Creel 1974: 295–336). Many fragments were collected by Yan Kejun 嚴可均 (ca. 1762–1843) in his *Quan shanggu Sandai Qin Han Sanguo Liuchao wen* 全上古三 代秦漢三國六朝文 (Complete prose from the highest antiquity to the Three Dynasties, Qin, Han, the Three Kingdoms and the Six Dynasties, hereafter *Sandai*). Although these enable us to outline the thought of Shen Buhai, the surviving fragments are merely the tip of a now-lost iceberg. The fact that so little of Shen Buhai's writings has been handed down to us may affect scholars' enthusiasm to study this thinker.

Another, more subjective, cause for the lack of scholarly attraction towards studying Shen Buhai lies in the tendency to categorize Shen's work as focusing on the concept of *shu* 術. *Shu*, largely speaking, refers to strategies and techniques for rulership, a topic deemed by some as unworthy of academic focus. For example, Zhang Shunhui (2005: 15) argues that "if the essence of the ruler's actions is 'deceit' (as implied in the common interpretation of *shu*), then the essence of the Way of the ruler is no more than 'pretense'. We can use the popular expression 'playing dumb' (*zhuang hutu* 裝糊塗) to expose the so-called mystery at the core of the strategies of rulership as implied in 'facing south and employing *shu*.'" Given that *shu* is devalued as "pretense" and "deceit," one can understand why the labeling of Shen Buhai's ideology as concentrated on *shu* affected its status throughout Chinese history.

However, the usage of "pretense" and "deceit" to depict the thought of Shen Buhai is a blunt oversimplification. In what follows, I shall try to demonstrate that the common categorization of Shen Buhai's work as "discourses of *shu*" (*shulun* 術論) or "rule by *shu*" (*shuzhi* 術治) is unsuitable. A common thread running through the thought of pre-Qin Masters is that of *zhi* 治, or orderly rule. As argued by Sima Tan 司馬談 (d. 110 BCE): "As for the [schools] of *yin-yang*, Ru [Confucians], Mohists, *fa*, and Dao and *de* [the Way and virtue]—all are committed to orderly rule" 夫陰 陽、儒、墨、名、法、道德，此務為治者也 (*Shiji* 130: 3288–89). Shen Buhai being no exception, his theories promoted a particular "Way of orderly rule" 治道. How, then, can Shen's "Way of orderly rule" be summarized? To this, different disciplines will doubtlessly suggest different approaches and methods; and different scholars provide different answers. The present essay sets out to explicate the ideological identity of Shen Buhai through the prism of legal thought.

1 "To Speak of *shu*" Is "to Speak of *fa*": A New Explanation of "Shen Buhai Spoke of *shu*"

The labeling of Shen Buhai's intellectual thought as *shu* is a commonly accepted identification that can be traced to Han Fei's highly influential chapter, "Ding fa" (定法, Fixing laws or Defining standards). The chapter focuses on a comparative examination of Shen Buhai and Shang Yang. It is comprised of three dialogues. In the first, Han Fei's interlocutor asks: "As for Shen Buhai and Gongsun Yang (i.e., Shang Yang), which of these two thinkers' doctrines is more urgent for the state?"

申不害、公孫鞅，此二家之言孰急於國? To this question, the respondent (presumably Han Fei) provides the following answer:

是不可程也。人不食，十日則死；大寒之隆，不衣亦死。謂之衣食孰急於人，則是不可一無也，皆養生之具也。今申不害言術而公孫鞅為法。術者，因任而授官，循名而責實，操殺生之柄，課群臣之能者也。此人主之所執也。法者，憲令著於官府，刑罰必於民心，賞存乎慎法，而罰加乎奸令者也。此臣之所師也。君無術則弊於上，臣無法則亂於下，此不可一無，皆帝王之具也。

　　Such things cannot be compared. If a man does not eat for ten days, he will die; if a great cold occurs and he is not well clothed, he will also die. When one asks whether clothes or food are more urgent to men, then the point is that you cannot be without either one— they are all the tools of nourishing life. Now, Shen Buhai spoke of *shu*, and Gongsun Yang enacted *fa*. As for *shu*—it means bestowing office on the basis of concrete responsibilities, demanding performance on the basis of titles, wielding the levers of life and death, and examining the capacities of the ministers. These are the things the ruler of men is to hold on to. As for *fa*, it means that regulations and ordinances are displayed in the official archives, that punishments and fines appear inevitable to the people's minds, and that rewards are meted on those who are cautious in regard to the laws, and punishments are applied to those who offend against ordinances. This is what the ministers take as their guiding authority. If the ruler is without *shu*, he will be in the dark above; if the ministers are without *fa*, chaos ensues below—this, too, is a case where 'you cannot be without either one': both are the tools of thearchs and monarchs. (*Han Feizi* 43.1; Chen 2000: 957 ["Ding fa" 定法])[1]

It is here that we find the origin of the saying "Shen Buhai spoke of *shu*." Within the context of *Han Feizi* "Shen Buhai spoke of *shu*" comes hand in hand with the notion that "Gongsun Yang enacted *fa*."

　　According to the definition of *Han Feizi*, two key features characterize *shu*. First, *shu* is in the hands of the ruler, which is contrasted by *fa* being adhered to by senior ministers. Second, in practice, *shu* comprises of the following components: the ruler appoints ministers according to their abilities and expertise, each office has concrete responsibilities according to its title and status, the ruler has control over issues of life and death, and the ruler regularly assesses the skills and abilities of his ministers. These features demonstrate that *shu* in its core is an institutionalized system through which the ruler manages his ministers. They imply that *shu* is what nowadays would be seen as a meritocratic system, with regular job assessments resulting in punitive or rewarding measures. As such, it cannot be dismissed as "pretense" or "deceit." Rather, it is a set of specifications and norms regulating the ruler's management of his ministers and officials. The corresponding *fa*, promulgated by the officials in government, is similarly a system of regulatory norms and specifications, primarily comprised of rewards and punishments. Those who abide by the law should be rewarded, and those who defy the law should be punished. This reward and punishment system in turn should conform to the psychological expectations of the masses. Therefore, the so-called *fa* refers mainly to the basis upon which ministers rely in dealing with government affairs and the basis for rewarding and punishing various management objects.

---

[1] Translations of *Han Feizi* are modified from Harbsmeier, Forthcoming. We adopt Harbsmeier's division of *Han Feizi* into chapters and paragraphs (borrowed from Zhang 2010).

According to *Han Feizi*'s dualistic division of *shu* and *fa*, the former is a system for the use of a ruler managing his ministers, while the latter is the system for the use of ministers in managing the polity. Both have their scope for adjustment, but both are tools for governing the state. The discussion in *Han Feizi* displays no order of priority either between *shu* and *fa*, or between Shen Buhai, who emphasizes *shu*, and Gongsun Yang, who emphasizes *fa*.

However, *shu* and *fa* differ in function. The difference between the two is explained in the third dialogue of the "Ding fa" chapter. A speaker inquires: "If the sovereign uses the techniques of Master Shen and the officials implement the laws of Lord Shang, would that work?" (主用申子之術，而官行商君之法，可乎?). To this, Han Fei replies:

申子未盡於術，商君未盡於法也。申子言:「治不逾官，雖知弗言。」治不逾官，謂之守職也可; 知而弗言，是不謂過也。人主以一國目視，故視莫明焉; 以一國耳聽，故聽莫聰焉。今知而弗言，則人主尚安假借矣?商君之法曰:「斬一首者爵一級，欲為官者為五十石之官; 斬二首者爵二級，欲為官者為百石之官。」官爵之遷與斬首之功相稱也。今有法曰:「斬首者令為醫、匠。」則屋不成而病不已。夫匠者手巧也，而醫者齊藥也，而以斬首之功為之，則不當其能。今治官者，智能也; 今斬首者，勇力之所加也。以勇力之所加而治者智能之官，是以斬首之功為醫、匠也。故曰:二子之於法術，皆未盡善也。

Master Shen did not fully grasp *shu* and Lord Shang did not fully grasp *fa*. Master Shen said: "In government you should not go beyond your official duty. Even if you know something [outside your duties], you should not speak up." "In government not to go beyond your official duty" that can be called to attend to one's duties; but "to know [of something] and not speak up," that is not calling out transgression. The sovereign sees through the eyes of the whole state; hence nobody's vision is clearer than his. He hears through the ears of the whole state; hence nobody's hearing is keener than his. Now, if one knows something but does not speak up, how would the ruler stay informed?

The *fa* of Lord Shang says, "He who has cut off one head, his rank should rise one degree. If he wishes to take office, it must be an office with a salary of fifty bushels. He who has cut off two heads, his rank should rise by two degrees. If he wishes to take office, it must be an office with a salary of one hundred bushels." The promotion in office and rank corresponded to the heads cut off. Now, if there were to be a rule saying: "those who cut off a head should become doctors or carpenters," then houses would not be built, and illnesses not cured. Carpenters are skillful with their hands, doctors mix medicines. Should they be appointed on the basis of the ability to cut off heads, the appointment would not suit their abilities. Now, managing an official post requires intellect and ability. Now, in cutting off heads, it is boldness and strength that are deployed. To take people who deploy boldness and strength and set them to administer offices requiring intellect and ability is like taking success in cutting off heads as basis for making people doctors or carpenters. Thus, I say: both masters' grasp of *fa* and *shu* was still imperfect (*Han Feizi* 43.3; Chen 2000: 962–63).

According to this passage, *Han Feizi* differentiates between *shu* and *fa* on the basis of their function. What Han Fei aims to emphasize is that neither Shen Buhai's *shu* nor Shang Yang's *fa* is perfect—both of them can be improved. What, then, are the shortcomings of Shen Buhai's *shu*? According to *Han Feizi*'s quote attributed to Shen Buhai, officials are not to interfere with matters beyond their scope of authority. They may have knowledge of something beyond their appointed role, but even if they do, they are not to speak up. This view is reminiscent of modern-day ideas pertaining to the legal power of statutory authorities. According to contemporary legal thought, when it comes to public authority, no power can be exercised without specific authorization in the law.[2] That one cannot exceed their statutory authority is a basic principle in present day concepts of the rule of law, and is also a leading principle in Shen Buhai's thought. This much is not challenged by Han Fei. What he does critique is Shen's second statement, namely that officials should not speak of issues beyond the premise of their appointment, even if they do possess relevant knowledge. Therein lies the difference between the thought of *Han Feizi* and that of Shen Buhai. According to *Han Feizi,* ministers are obliged to report to the sovereign on all issues, even if outside their area of authority. Unlike Shen Buhai, Han Fei expects that ministers act as the ears and eyes of the ruler. As far as Shen Buhai is concerned, if a minister is charged with the duty of gathering information, he should report all that he knows to the sovereign. However, if the law or his official tasks do not require him to perform such a duty, he is under no duty to report all affairs. Han Fei's criticism on the imperfection of Shen Buhai's *shu* in fact highlights the concept of statutory power embedded in Shen's legal thought.

Let us now continue to the second dialogue included in the "Ding fa" chapter, in which an inquirer asks: "To follow the *shu* without *fa*, or to follow *fa* without *shu*—what is wrong with that?" 徒術而無法，徒法而無術，其不可何哉? The reply is as follows:

申不害，韓昭侯之佐也。韓者，晉之別國也。晉之故法未息，而韓之新法又生；先君之令未收，而後君之令又下。申不害不擅其法，不一其憲令，則姦多。故利在故法前令則道之，利在新法後令則道之，利在故新相反，前後相勃，則申不害雖十使昭侯用術，而姦臣猶有所譎其辭矣。故托萬乘之勁韓，十七年而不至於霸王者，雖用術於上，法不勤飾於官之患也。

Shen Buhai was an aide to Marquis Zhao of Han. Han was a state created by the partition of Jin. Before the old laws of Jin were discontinued, the new laws of Han came into effect. Before the ordinances of the former rulers had been rescinded, the ordinances of the new rulers have already been issued. Shen Buhai neither consolidated the laws, nor did he unify the regulations and ordinances, and hence wickedness was rampant. Thus, if one benefitted from the old laws and earlier ordinances, he would follow them; if one benefitted from the new laws and latter ordinances, he would follow them. Since benefit was to be found in the opposition between the old and new, and the contradiction between former and latter, then, even if Shen Buhai made a tenfold effort to have Marquis Zhao utilize *shu,* treacherous ministers still would have distorted his words. Thus, although the powerful ten-thousand-chariots-strong Han was entrusted to him for seventeen years, it failed to achieve the position of hegemonic king. This was because despite utilizing [the methods of] *shu* with the ruler, there was the trouble of no orderly *fa* amongst the officials. (*Han Feizi* 43.2; Chen 2000: 959).

I omit Han Fei's criticism of the weaknesses of Shang Yang's system; let us focus on his assertion that Shen Buhai's *shu* was insufficiently effective. This assertion is based on the argument that Shen Buhai did not clear up the legal chaos in the state of Han in which the old laws, inherited from the Han ancestral state of Jin 晉 were not completely abolished, whereas new laws had been promulgated already. Although Han Fei deems it as "lacking *fa*," this does not imply the complete absence of *fa,* but rather refers to the problem of mixing old and new laws without ordering

[2] "The simple proposition that a public authority may not act outside its powers (ultra vires) might fitly be called the central principle of administrative law" (Wade and Forsyth 2009: 27).

them properly. The coexistence of two legal systems created multiple loopholes utilized by unscrupulous individuals, which jeopardized orderly rule. In *Han Feizi*'s view, by failing to eliminate this legal disorder, Shen Buhai did not fully implement his responsibilities in serving his master, Marquis Zhao of Han韓昭侯 (r. 362–333 BCE) and thus failed to achieve hegemony to his ruler. This is where Shen was negligent, hence he is described as "following *shu* and lacking *fa*." This conduct of "following *shu* without having *fa*" had obvious negative consequences, which are the reason for Han Fei's criticism of Shen Buhai.

Let me suggest three objections to *Han Feizi's* criticism of Shen Buhai's thought. First, there is the question of whether Shen Buhai, to begin with, was indeed responsible for the Han failure to attain hegemony. I would argue that he was not. Following the partition of Jin 晉 into the states of Zhao 趙, Wei 魏, and Han 韓 between 453–403 BCE, none of the newly formed states was as strong as Jin used to be. Of the three, Han was arguably the weakest. True, it is hailed in *Zhanguo ce* 戰國策 (Stratagems of the Warring States) as possessing "the territory of a thousand *li* squared and hundreds of thousands of armored soldiers. All of the strong bows and sturdy crossbows under Heaven originate in the state of Han" 地方千里，帶甲數十萬。天下之強弓勁弩，皆自韓出 (*Zhanguo ce* 1991: 26.5: 967 ["Han 韓 1"]). However, from "The Hereditary House of Han" chapter in *Shiji* 史記 (Records of the Historian) we learn of Han's perennial weakness prior to and following the reign of Marquis Zhao:

懿侯二年，魏敗我馬陵。五年，與魏惠王會宅陽。九年，魏敗我澮。十二年，懿侯卒，子昭侯立。昭侯元年，秦取我西山。二年，宋取我黃池。魏取朱。六年，伐東周，取陵觀、邢丘。八年，申不害相韓，修術行道，國內以治，諸侯不來侵伐。

In the second year to the reign of Marquis Yi (369 BCE), the army of Wei defeated Han at Maling. In the fifth year, [Marquis Yi] met King Hui of Wei in Zhaiyang. In the ninth year, Wei defeated us at Kuai. In the twelfth year, Marquis Yi died and his son Marquis Zhao ascended the throne. On the first year of Marquis Zhao's reign (358 BCE), Qin defeated us at the Western Mountain. In the second year, Song seized our Huangchi, and Wei seized Zhu. In the sixth year, Han invaded Eastern Zhou[3] and seized Lingguan and Xingqiu. In the eighth year, Shen Buhai was appointed prime-minister of Han. He rectified the state's *shu* and implemented the Way. The country was well-governed within, and regional lords did not dare attack (*Shiji* 45: 1868–69).

Prior to Shen Buhai's appointment, during the time of Marquis Yi 懿侯 and the early years of Marquis Zhao, the state of Han had suffered repeated assaults by Wei, Qin, and Song. Yet after Shen Buhai became the prime minister, this situation had changed. This change is reflected also in Shen Buhai's section in "The arrayed biography of Laozi and Han Fei" (老子韓非列傳) in *Shiji*:

內修政教，外應諸侯，十五年。終申子之身，國治兵強，無侵韓者。

[Shen Buhai] reformed government and teaching within, and reacted to regional lords from without. He [stayed in office] for fifteen years. Up until the death of Master Shen, the state was well-governed, its army strong, and none invaded Han (*Shiji* 63: 2146).

---

[3] This is one of the two tiny principalities into which the royal domain was split in the fourth century BCE.

The two excerpts from *Shiji* express the view that as a result of Shen Buhai's governance, the power of the state of Han had increased significantly, and its status among
the regional lords was greatly raised. In critiquing Shen Buhai for not achieving a
hegemonic position for the state of Han, Han Fei displays an unrealistic expectation.
Only several decades after Shen's death, by the time of Han Fei himself, the status
of the state of Han had plummeted. A member of the royal clan of Han, and himself
unable to restore the state's power, Han Fei unjustly cast the blame on the previous
century's Shen Buhai. Put differently, although Han Fei's wish for a Han hegemony
in its earlier days is understandable, it is inappropriate for him to blame Shen Buhai
for failing to achieve hegemony after the state "was entrusted to him for seventeen
years." What Han Fei did not seem to realize is that his portrayal of "the powerful
ten-thousand-chariots-strong Han" reflects the achievements of Shen Buhai's
administration, rather than its shortcomings. Comparing the different evaluations of
Shen Buhai's achievements by Sima Qian and Han Fei, one can conclude that Han
Fei's personal anxiety concerning the state of Han had affected his ability to fairly
evaluate Shen Buhai. Conversely, Sima Qian, a couple of centuries later, provides a
more balanced perspective in evaluating Shen Buhai's political achievements.

Second, in spite of Han Fei's high expectations that led to his critique of Shen
Buhai's achievements, he did not favor either the thought of Shen Buhai, or that of
Gongsun Yang (Shang Yang). Rather, he assessed the two as being of equal importance; as far as concerns the governance of the state or the structuring of rulership,
he regarded Shen Buhai's *shu* and Gongsun Yang's *fa* as two interdependent and
mutually complementing (rather than contrasting) ideas. The governing of a state
required both *shu* and *fa*. Nonetheless, on the institutional level, Han Fei believed,
both ideas needed to be much improved. For the time being, we shall not discuss
here the extent to which Han Feizi's ideas of "improvement" were correct or
accurate.

Third, although *Han Feizi* presents "speaking of *shu*" and "enacting *fa*" as representing the difference between Shen Buhai and Shang Yang, the text also implies
that the two concepts have much in common. Both *shu* and *fa* refer to laws, institutions, and standards. As mentioned above, *shu* refers mainly to the systems of selection, assessment, and reward or punishment conferred upon officials. Underlying
these systems are principles of law and order. As for *fa*, it is a system of rewards and
punishments that is promulgated by the officials toward society at large, which is
enacted after considering the people's sentiments. As institutional regulatory systems, *shu* and *fa* are similar. There are, of course, differences between the two: *shu*
predominantly provides standards for the ruler in his management of officials; while
fa mainly provides standards for the officials in their management of the people.
That is, in terms of their concrete implementation, *shu* and *fa* are different, each
having its own use and scope for adjustment.[4]

---

[4] Another difference is outlined in *Han Feizi*: "*Fa* must be as clear as possible, but you do not want
your *shu* to be seen" 法莫如顯，而術不欲見 (*Han Feizi* 38.8.2; Chen 2000: 922 ["Nan 3" 難三]).
However, this idea is not found in existent Shen Buhai's fragments. Perhaps this is *Han Feizi*'s
viewpoint that does not represent that of Shen Buhai.

The above analysis demonstrates that Shen Buhai's "speaking of *shu*" is, in essence, equivalent to speaking of *fa*, as both *shu* and *fa* refer to laws, institutions, and standards. This understanding may be supported by the statement in the "Shen Han" 申韓 chapter of *Yantie lun* 鹽鐵論 (Debates on salt and iron): "Shen [Buhai] and Shang [Yang] used *fa* to strengthen the states of Qin and Han" 申、商以法強秦、韓 (*Yantie lun* 56: 579). This succinct statement defines Shen Buhai's political tool in his empowerment of the state of Han as *fa*. However, the *shu* (or *fa*) of which Shen Buhai speaks is that of the ruler towards his ministers; while that of Shang Yang is that of the ministers towards the people: people who accomplished highly in farming and warfare were rewarded in accordance with *fa*, and those who, on the contrary, failed to achieve results were punished in accordance with *fa*. According to Shang Yang's *fa*, "from chief ministers, chancellors, and generals down to nobles and commoners, whoever disobeys the king's orders, violates the state's prohibitions, or wreaks havoc on the regulations of one's superior should be executed without pardon" (自卿相、將軍以至大夫、庶人，有不從王令、犯國禁、亂上制者，罪死不赦 *Book of Lord Shang* 17.3; Zhang 2012: 196 ["Shang xing" 賞刑]).[5] Unlike Shen Buhai's *shu*, which focuses on the ruler's control over his ministers, Shang Yang's *fa* at its core concerns all the people, regardless of status and rank.

Han Fei's definition of the regulatory system that allowed the ruler to manage and control his officials as *shu* in fact reflects aspects of the legal system during his own time. The Springs-and-Autumns (Chunqiu 春秋, 770–453 BCE) and the Warring States (Zhanguo 戰國, 453–221 BCE) periods were marked by the decline of the Zhou power and the incessant competition among rival states for supremacy in the fragmented Zhou world. Back then, the state's success was determined by its "strength" (*li* 力), as reflected in Han Fei's recommendation: "A clear-sighted ruler commits himself to strength" 明君務力 (*Han Feizi* 50.7; Chen 2000: 1141 ["Xian xue" 顯學]). "Strength" here and elsewhere refers primarily to the state's military prowess. This strength was undermined, however, by the traditional system of power dispersal, in which old aristocratic lineages controlled autonomous allotments (*caiyi* 采邑), weakening therewith the state's ability to be governed in an orderly manner and to fully utilize its material assets and manpower.[6] The road to success in bitter interstate competition was, therefore, through the centralization of power, which was the precondition for full mobilization of the state's resources. The goal of Han Fei's theory which synthesizes *fa*, *shu*, and *shi* 勢 (positional power) is to help the ruler to consolidate his power, without which attaining a strong state would be a pipe dream. This consolidation of power requires precisely what Han Fei calls *shu*. But strengthening the ruler through *shu* is not a standalone goal. It is subordinate to the broader concern of strengthening the state, a notion which is often associated with the concept of *fa*.

---

[5] All references to the *Book of Lord Shang* are to translations in Pines 2017 and to Zhang 2012 edition.

[6] For the power of aristocratic lineages, especially during the Springs-and-Autumns period, see Zhu 1990: 450–594; for the allotments, see Lü 2006.

The legal system and the notion of the "rule of *fa*" (often translated, somewhat problematically, as the "rule of law") of Shen Buhai and Han Fei's age had two basic components. First, it served to regulate the relationships between rulers and ministers. Second, it served to regulate the relationships between the officials and the people. The legal system of that age concerned three categories of political actors: the ruler, the officials, and the people. It had to adjust two types of relationships: one is between the ruler and his ministers, and the second is between the ministers (in their capacity as officials) and the people. As for the ruler and the people, there was no need for a direct relationship between them, because the ruler managed the people through the intermediaries—his officials and important ministers. Within the legal relationships that comprise the categories of ruler, ministers, and the people, Shen Buhai's focus, called by Han Fei *shu*, was on the ruler-minister relations. This was indeed different from Shang Yang's focus on the state-society relations (i.e., those between the officials and the people).

Notably, the term *shu* does not appear in the surviving fragments of *Shenzi*. The notion that "Shen Buhai spoke of *shu*" emanates from *Han Feizi*. For more than two thousand years, Han Fei's description of Shen Buhai as "speaking of *shu*" has been passed down, becoming the common understanding of Shen Buhai's ideology (see more in the conclusion to this chapter). In fact, the *shu* of which Shen speaks is itself a form of *fa*, but one that bears a specific meaning: it refers to the laws, rules, and regulations intended for adjusting the relationship between the ruler and his officials. It is on the basis of this understanding that we are able to remove the layers of academic fog, and deepen our understanding of the legal thought of Shen Buhai.

2   Rationalization, Systematization, and Legalization of the Ruler-Minister Relationship

In contemporary legal thought, and in particular in public law theory, the relationship between the state and the people forms a conceptual axis of a sort. A core topic of discussion is that of handling the relationship between state-power on one hand, and civil-rights on the other (for Chinese scholarly debates on this topic, see Yu 2019: 197). At the time of Shen Buhai, the modern concept of citizenship did not exist, and regional states were inherently different from the modern-day nation-state. Within the context of the Springs-and-Autumns and the early Warring States periods, *Shenzi*'s legal philosophy centered on the relationship between the ruler and the ministers, which was perceived by him as the most significant type of political-legal relationship. The process of Jin's demise and its partition was the strongest manifestation of the negative consequences of the increasing ministerial power and the decrease in the ruler's authority. The disorder and instability of the ruler-minister relationship was the main cause for the decline of that powerful state.

Similar processes occurred across the Springs-and-Autumns period world.[7] An orderly delimitation of the ruler-minister relationship was therefore an essential departure point in the improvement of the potency of state governance. It is within this context that the focal points of Shen Buhai's thought lay in rationalizing, standardizing, and legalizing the relationship between the ruler and his ministers, which meant creating a rational system of legal relationship between the ruler and the ministers. Through the "Da ti" chapter and other fragments of *Shenzi*, we may outline the objectives of the construction of this relationship.

The fundamental problem underlying the ruler-minister relationship in the time of Shen Buhai was that the ruler's power could be usurped by ministers. This was a source of great concern for contemporaneous rulers. In fact, both the collapse of Jin and the birth of the state of Han were products of this problem. *Shenzi*'s "Da ti" depicts the problem bluntly:

今人君之所以高為城郭，而謹門閭之閉者，為寇戎盜賊之至也。今夫弒君而取國者，非必逾城郭之險而犯門閭之閉也。蔽君之明，塞君之聽，奪之政而專其令，有其民而取其國矣。

Now the reason why a ruler builds lofty inner walls and outer walls, looks carefully to the barring of doors and gates, is [to prepare against] the coming of invaders and bandits. But one who murders the ruler and takes his state does not necessarily climb over difficult walls and batter in barred doors and gates. [He may be one of the ministers, who] by limiting what the ruler sees and restricting what the ruler hears, seizes his government and monopolizes his commands, possesses his people and takes his state (Creel 1974: 344).[8]

The greatest threat to the ruler therefore comes not from external foes but from members of his closest entourage, the ministers who, by cutting off his sources of information, made the ruler "lose sight and hearing." Those ministers will eventually become the potential replacers of the ruler in power. The extent to which the sovereign is endangered is clear from another passage in the text:

今使烏獲、彭祖負千鈞之重，而懷琬琰之美；令孟賁、成荊帶幹將之劍衛之，行乎幽道，則盜猶偷之矣。今人君之力，非賢乎烏獲、彭祖，而勇非賢乎孟賁、成荊也。其所守者，非特琬琰之美，千金之重也，而欲勿失，其可得耶？

Now suppose that Wu Huo and Pengzu were each to bear a burden of a thousand *jun* and carry precious jade on his person. Let them be guarded by Meng Ben and Cheng Jing, who carry Gan Jiang swords.[9] If they travel by a deserted road, robbers will still plunder them. Now, the strength of the ruler is not superior to that of Wu Huo and Pengzu, and he is not braver than Meng Pen and Cheng Jing. That which is in his keeping is not merely of the

---

[7] For the process of ministerial empowerment in the Springs-and-Autumns period and its political ramifications, see, e.g., Zhu 1990: 567–594.

[8] All "Da ti" references henceforth are from *Qunshu zhiyao* 36: 445–446; translations of all *Shenzi* extracts are modified from Creel 1974.

[9] Wu Huo (d. 306 BCE) was a renowned strongman from the state of Qin. His mention in the chapter attributed to Shen Buhai (who died, recall, in 337 BCE) raises the suspicion that the attribution is wrong. Pengzu, a legendary paragon of longevity, is never paired with Wu Huo or associated with exceptional strength. Meng Ben (fl. 310 BCE) and Cheng Jing (?) are paragons of courage; again, Meng Ben's life time postdates that of Shen Buhai. Gan Jiang is the name of a legendary swordsmith. (Editor)

value of precious jades or of the weight of a thousand *jun*. Though he wishes not to lose it, can he [avoid doing so]? (Creel 1974: 345–346)

This, of course, is merely a metaphor. Power is more attractive than jade; and there are far more people who covet power than people trying to steal jade. Under such circumstances, being unable to manage the ruler-minister relationship constitutes a great danger for the ruler—indeed, much greater than the danger facing Wu Huo and Pengzu carrying the jade. This is the political and historical context against which the thought of Shen Buhai grew. Later generations became accustomed to criticizing Shen Buhai as an advocate of the sovereign's autocratic rule. Little did these critics realize the magnitude of the danger lurking for the rulers of that era, both from within their realm and from outside. Facing the danger of being annexed by external foes on the one hand and the threat of domestic usurpation on the other, the rulers of the pre-Shen Buhai age had little means of safeguarding their position.[10] Within most polities, the relations between the ruler and his senior ministers—who often were affiliated to the ruling lineage—were maintained according to the ritual norms that preserved the hierarchy between the lineage's trunk and branch lines.[11] Alas, these means were not effective from the ruler's point of view. For instance, the sovereign could not, at his own will, deprive ministers of their political and economic positions. The history of the Springs-and-Autumns period demonstrated time and again the weakness of the sovereigns and their inability to protect their own authority. The example of the dissolution of the state of Jin is too well known. In Shen Buhai's natal state of Zheng 鄭 the situation was arguably even worse: for almost two centuries, from the first half of the sixth century BCE to the very end of the Zheng polity in 375 BCE, the power in the state belonged to ministerial lineages, which rotated chief positions among themselves, whereas the rulers were completely eclipsed (Zhu 1990: 577–82). This is the problem that Shen Buhai sought to resolve; and it is within the political context of this era that we must understand the thought of Shen Buhai.

---

[10] For the pace of annexations, suffice it to recall that the *Chunqiu* 春秋 (Springs-and-Autumns Annals) and its commentaries mention well over one hundred polities, of which less than two dozen survived by the Warring States period (and only seven or eight remained by the eve of Qin unification of 221 BCE); the rest were annexed. *Chunqiu* and the commentaries also enumerate dozens of cases of the rulers' assassinations by their kin or ministers. Sima Qian states: "*Chunqiu* mentions thirty-six cases of the ruler's assassination, fifty-two cases of the state's annihilation, whereas the number of the regional lords who had to flee unable to protect their altars of soil and grain is uncountable" 春秋之中，弒君三十六，亡國五十二，諸侯奔走不得保其社稷者不可勝數 (*Shiji* 130: 3297). Actually, the number is even higher, if we consider assassination of incumbent rulers who were murdered before their official enthronement (which was scheduled to the first day of the new lunar year following the death of the previous sovereign). Counting only major states, such as Jin, Qin, Chu 楚, Qi 齊, Wu 吳, Lu 魯, Zheng, Wei 衛, Chen 陳, Cai 蔡, and Song we have over sixty cases of the ruler's assassination; and the number will be even higher if minor polities be added to this account (Yin 1987).

[11] See more on the proximity of kinship and political structures in the Springs-and-Autumns period in Zhu 1990: 450–594; Tian and Zang 1998: 242–313.

Shen Buhai's major breakthrough was his reframing of the legal relationship between the ruler and the minister. The ruler-minister relationship, according to the "Da ti" chapter, is in its core a "root-branch" (*benmo* 本末) type of relationship:

明君如身，臣如手；君若號，臣如響。君設其本，臣操其末；君治其要，臣行其詳；君操其柄，臣事其常。為人臣者，操契以責其名。名者，天地之綱，聖人之符。張天地之綱，用聖人之符，則萬物之情無所逃之矣。

The clear-sighted ruler is like the torso; [his] ministers are like hands. The ruler is like a shout; his ministers are like an echo. The ruler plants the root; the ministers hold up the branches. The ruler orders the essentials; the ministers carry out the details. The ruler holds the levers; the ministers carry on everyday affairs. One who is a minister holds the [debtor's portion of a] contract, which demonstrates the obligations of his name [i.e. of his official entitlement]. 'A name' is the cord of Heaven and Earth's [net]; it is the tally of the sages. He who strings the cord of Heaven and Earth, and utilizes the sages' tallies, then no aspect of the myriad things can elude him. (Creel 1974: 347–48)

The comparison of the ruler to the body, which commands the hands, or the shout, which gives rise to an echo, provides a clear message: the ruler is the "root" (*ben* 本), whereas the minsters are the "branches" (*mo* 末). The branches have no existence without the root; and the root precedes the branches. The framing of ruler-minister relationship within the root-branch analogy serves to highlight the subordinate status of the ministers. Yet both rulers and ministers have a proper place in this relationship: the ruler should deal with "the essentials," namely the guiding principles of action; whereas the ministers should focus on the "details," i.e. routine conduct of government affairs.

The packaging of the ruler-minister relationship within the root-branch metaphor would be self-evident for persons of later ages; but in Shen Buhai's time, this was a novel departure. In the preceding aristocratic age, the relationship between regional lords and their officials was primarily framed within the system of kinship relations. Most ministers back then belonged to the branch lineages of the ruling lineage; most possessed highly autonomous power base (the so-called "allotments"; see above p. 64); and in terms of economic and military power they were the ruler's peers rather than subordinates. It was only around Shen Buhai's lifetime that the ruler-minister relations were transformed into a bureaucratic relationship, as is duly reflected in *Shenzi* fragments.

An insightful comment attributed to Shen Buhai states that "[Those whose] intelligence is equal, cannot command each other; [those whose] strength is equal cannot overcome each other" 智均不相使，力均不相勝 (*Sandai* 4: 32; Creel 1974: 360). It is possible that this reference to the similarity in intelligence and strength between two political actors refers to the situation of near equality between the ruler and chief ministers, characteristic of the aristocratic age. From Shen Buhai's point of view, this was an intolerable situation. To restore the sovereign's power, the ministers should no longer occupy the position of the ruler's peers but rather be relegated to that of his servitors (*chen* 臣). A significant difference between the sovereign and such ministers was that only the sovereign could independently act on his own will. The ministers were obliged to follow the ruler's orders, just like the hand follows the orders of the body. Thus, Shen Buhai's statement that "The name is the cord of Heaven and Earth's [net]" can be interpreted also as referring to the "names" (designations, titles) of a ruler and the ministers. Ministers are the ruler's servitors; and insofar as they act according to their title, the political system will function well. In this context the idea that "then no aspect of the myriad things can elude him [the ruler]" can be interpreted as pertaining to the fact that each political actor would act strictly within the framework of his position without overstepping the limits of his personal authority. To achieve this, it is important to imbue the ministers with the "ministerial [i.e., servitor's] mindset" (in modern parlance, 人臣意識).

Defining the ruler-minister relationship through the "root and branches" paradigm is not just a way to warn the ministers against overstepping their authority, but, more importantly, an admonition to the ruler. The ministers should develop "the ministerial mindset," while the ruler needs to have "the ruler's mindset." The latter comprises three primary aspects: avoiding favoritism, "demonstrating non-action," and using "correct names." Let us see know how the three principles are implemented.

2.1 Avoiding Favoritism

The "Da ti" chapter says:

夫一婦擅夫，眾婦皆亂；一臣專君，群臣皆蔽。故妒妻不難破家也，而群臣不難破國也。是以明君使其臣並進輻湊，莫得專君。

When one wife gains exclusive influence with the husband, all the wives are thrown into disorder; when one minister monopolizes the ruler's [trust], all the ministers are confused. Thus, a jealous wife can easily break a family, and an unruly minister can easily break a state. Therefore, the clear-sighted ruler causes his ministers to advance together converging like the spokes of the wheel, so that none monopolizes the ruler's [trust]. (Creel 1974: 343–44)

Shen Buhai requires that the ruler "causes his ministers to advance together converging like the spokes of the wheel." The ruler is required to keep all his ministers at an equal distance, enabling them to surround their sovereign (who therefore forms a type of axis). In reality, the ruler must have had ministers with whom he was in closer terms and those who were more distant, as is the nature of men. However, Shen Buhai issues a specific warning aimed at the sovereign lest he exaggerates in displaying fondness towards any specific minister, which would dangerously allow "one minister to monopolize the ruler's [trust]." The ruler should restrain his emotional preferences and approach his relationship with the ministers in a rationalized, standardized, and systematized manner. The relationship between the sovereign and his ministers should therefore be determined not by the sovereign's personal likes and dislikes, but by the institutionalized "root-branch" (or axis-spokes) relationship. Only when the ministers are reduced to acting as the wheel's spokes and are firmly controlled by the ruler, shall the institutions of the state be guided by the ruler effectively and orderly.

2.2 *"Demonstrating Non-action"*

The "Da ti" chapter says:

故善為主者，倚於愚，立於不盈，設于不敢，藏於無事，竄端匿疏，示天下無為。
是以近者親之，遠者懷之。示人有餘者，人奪之；示人不足者，人與之。剛者折，
危者覆，動者搖，靜者安，名自正也，事自定也。是以有道者，自名而正之，隨事
而定之也。鼓不與於五音，而為五音主；有道者，不為五官之事，而為治主。君知
其道也，官知其事也。十言十當、百為百當者，人臣之事也，非君人之道也。

Therefore, he who excels at being a master, relies on [an appearance of] stupidity, establishes himself in insufficiency, places himself in timidity, conceals himself in having no
undertakings, hides his motives, and covers up his track. He demonstrates non-action to All
under Heaven. Therefore, those who are near are intimate with him, whereas those who are
distant think longingly of him. One who shows men that he has a surplus, men rob him,
whereas one who shows men that he has not enough, men give him. The sturdy are cut
down, the endangered are protected; the active are shaken, the tranquil are at peace. Names
rectify themselves, undertakings settle themselves. Hence, he who possesses the Way, starts
from names and lets them be rectified, then proceeds toward undertakings and lets them be
settled.

The sound of the drum is not one of the five notes, and yet it is their master. He who
possesses the Way does not perform the tasks of the five officials, and yet he is the master
of orderly rule. The ruler should understand his Way; the officials should understand their
tasks. To speak ten times and ten times be right; to act a hundred times and a hundred times
succeed—this is the task of a minister and not the Way of the ruler. (Creel 1974: 348–50)

This passage contains elements of the so-called Huang-lao Daoist thinking. Because
of these elements, some scholars argued, "Shen Buhai's teaching distantly succeeds
the *Laozi* and more closely inherits the Huang-Lao teaching from the Jixia academy.
This is an important stage in the development of Daoist strategic thought" (Jiang
1988). Indeed, the Huang-Lao connections of Shen Buhai were recognized long
ago, as argued by Sima Qian, "The teaching of Shenzi was rooted in Huang-Lao and
prioritized *xingming*" 申子之學本于黃老而主刑名 (*Shiji* 63: 2146; see also Wang
Pei, Chap. 20, this volume). However, even if *Shenzi* does absorb Daoist ideas, it is
still in essence a representative example of *fa* thought. At their foundation, there is
a crucial difference between the *fa* ideas and Daoism as exemplified by *Laozi* and
Zhuangzi. Although the latter ideas can be translated into practical political and
legal theories, Daoist thinkers tended to act as bystanders to practical politics,
whereas figures who we identify with *fa* thought are avid political activists.
Doubtlessly, Shen Buhai falls into the latter category.

Daoism advocates the idea of non-action (*wu wei* 無為), and so does Shen Buhai.
However, the focus of Shen Buhai's recommendation is not "non-action" as such,
but rather "demonstrating" (*shi* 示) non-action. The principle of non-action refers to
the ruler's appearance. The reasons for this display of non-action are discussed in
another quotation of Shen Buhai that appears in *Han Feizi*:

申子曰:上明見，人備之；其不明見，人惑之。其知見，人飾之；不知見，人匿
之。其無欲見，人司之；其有欲見，人餌之。故曰:吾無從知之，惟無為可以規之。
　一曰: 申子曰: 慎而言也，人且知女；慎而行也，人且隨女。而有知見也，人且
匿女；而無知見也，人且意女。女有知也，人且臧女；女無知也，人且行女。故
曰:惟無為可以規之。

Shenzi said: "When the ruler's clear-sightedness is apparent, then people will take precautions against it; if a lack of clear-sightedness is apparent, then people will lead him astray. If the ruler's understanding is apparent, then people will put on elaborate shows; when his lack of understanding is apparent, people will keep him in the dark. If the ruler's lack of desires is apparent, then people will spy after him; if his desires are apparent, then people will bait him with [what he desires]. So it is said: 'You have no way of understanding them [your underlings], only through non-action can you scrutinize them.'"

An alternative source says: Shenzi said: "Be cautious when speaking, lest people come to know you; be cautious with your demeanor, lest people follow you. If your understanding is apparent, then people will keep you in the dark; if your lack of understanding is apparent, people are going to guess at your plans. If you have understanding, then people will hide from you; if you lack understanding, then people are going to take over your actions. So it is said: 'Only through non-action can you scrutinize them'" (*Han Feizi* forthcoming: 34.2.1–2.2; Chen 2000: 775 ["Wai chu shuo you shang" 外儲說右上]).

As is apparent in the passage above, *Shenzi*'s conceptualization of "non-action" refers to the ruler's design of his own public image. It is a means to protect the ruler's authority hijacked by the underlings. The ruler should be inscrutable or else his cunning ministers would mislead him. Hence, the "Da ti" chapter's section cited at the beginning of this subsection focuses not on the ruler's real state of affairs but on his image. This refers not just to "non-action" but also to the ruler's "having not enough" (*buzu* 不足): the focus is not on the reality of lacking resources but on the ruler being careful about his public display. Shen Buhai reminds the ruler that "the active are shaken, the tranquil are at peace." Being "tranquil" 靜 is an essential precaution against becoming vulnerable. Elsewhere, the *Shenzi* fragments explain the latter point:

天道無私，是以恆正。天道常正，是以清明。地道不作，是以常靜。地道常靜，是以正方。舉事為之，乃有恆常之靜者，符信受令必行也。

The Way of Heaven has no selfishness, hence it is always correct. The Way of Heaven is constantly correct, hence it is clear and bright. The Way of Earth is not to create; hence it is constantly tranquil. The Way of Earth is constantly tranquil, hence it is correctly foursquare. In maintaining undertakings, [the ruler] acts, but he still maintains constant tranquility. It is because his tallies are reliable and the one who receives the command will inevitably implement it. (*Sandai* 4: 33; Creel 1974: 359).

This short passage is not easy to understand; Creel considers its second part as referring to the minister rather than to the ruler (he follows the idea that the minister parallels Earth, whereas the ruler should parallel only Heaven; see Creel 1974: 359–360n4). In my view, "tranquility" is not applied to the minister but to the ruler. Recall, first, that patterning the ruler's behavior after Heaven and Earth alike is common in the so-called Huang-Lao texts.[12] Recall, second, that the notion of tranquility as pertinent to the ruler's functioning is advocated in many of the Warring States-period texts. For instance, *Xunzi* recommends: "A clear-sighted ruler hastens to obtain [appropriate] persons, whereas a deluded ruler hastens to obtain positional

---

[12] Take for instance *Guanzi* 管子: "Be like Earth, be like Heaven,//What partiality or favoritism [have they]? Be like the moon, be like the sun, //These are the norms of the ruler." 如地如天, 何私何親? 如月如日, 唯君之節 (*Guanzi* 1.17 ["Mu min" 牧民]; translation modified from Rickett 1998: 56).

power" 明主急得其人，而暗主急得其執 (*Xunzi* 12: 230 ["Jun dao" 君道]; trans. modified from Hutton 2014: 117). Xunzi suggests then, that having obtained a worthy minister, the ruler could relegate him his power and reside in blessed tranquility: "Hence the ruler works hard in looking for [proper officials] and is at rest when employing them" (*Xunzi* 11: 223–24 ["Wang ba" 王霸], trans. cf. Hutton 2014: 113).

This ideal of a tranquil ruler became deeply entrenched in the notion of "non-action," which proliferated in the latter half of the Warring States period. The philosophical aspects of the idea of "non-action" (or, as Slingerland [2003] renders it, "effortless action") had been discussed extensively, but here we should focus on its political aspect, especially its relation to the views of rulership. Shen Buhai may well be among the earliest voices to integrate the idea of non-action and the mode of the ruler's functioning. As the extract cited at the beginning of Sect. 2.3 below clarifies: the ruler "has no undertakings, yet All under Heaven by itself reaches the apex [of orderly rule]." Shen Buhai's concept of the ruler's non-action is not merely an echo of *Laozi*'s popular concept, but has a deeper underlying administrative insight. The ruler should hold the levers of power, whereas everyday routine managerial duties should be relegated to the ministers. The ruler's primary task is to supervise and control his underlings. For early *fa* thinkers, such as Shen Buhai and Shen Dao 慎到, this concept of inactive rulership was a reasonable solution to the tension between the limited abilities of an individual sovereign and the immense magnitude of his tasks (see also Pines 2009: 92–93).

Tranquility is therefore the ruler's asset. Aside from safeguarding his power as mentioned in *Han Feizi* section above, the maintenance of tranquility by the sovereign reflects the advantages of a well-functioning government system based on the reliability of the tallies and binding implementation of the ruler's commands. In this system, the sovereign's personal activism is not required. Tranquility and ostensible inaction are part of the fundamental distinctions between the affairs of official and the Way of the ruler. This Way of the ruler as advocated by *Shenzi* would eventually become a source of inspiration for *Han Feizi*.

2.3 Correct Names

The "Da ti" chapter says:

昔者堯之治天下也以名。其名正則天下治。桀之治天下也亦以名，其名倚而天下亂。是以聖人貴名之正也。主處其大，臣處其細，以其名聽之，以其名視之，以其名命之。鏡設精，無為而美惡自備；衡設平，無為而輕重自得。凡因之道，身與公無事，無事而天下自極也。

In the past, Yao ruled All under Heaven by means of names. His names were correct; hence All under Heaven was ordered. Jie also ruled All under Heaven by means of names. His names were perverse and All under Heaven was in turmoil. Therefore, the sage values correctness of the names. The sovereign handles large [issues], the minister handles the fine points. [The sovereign] listens [to affairs] according to their names, looks into them according to their names, commands them according to their names. He is like a mirror that reflects the light—it does nothing and yet beauty and ugliness present themselves. He is like a scale that establishes equilibrium—it does nothing and yet the light and the heavy discover themselves. In general, the Way of responding means that [the ruler] personally has no undertakings. He has no undertakings, yet All under Heaven by itself reaches the apex [of orderly rule]. (Creel 1974: 352)

Both Emperor Yao and tyrant Jie resorted to "names" in their governance; yet whereas Yao's names were correct, those of Jie were perverse resulting in great turmoil. The "correctness" of the names is primarily reflected in the proper positions occupied by the sovereign and his ministers. The term *ming* 名 (name) refers to both social status and political position. Underlying the concept of *ming* are various concrete, specific titles. In terms of status, the most important division is between the ruler (the root) and the minister (the branches). The ruler is singular; the ministers are a cohort. Within the cohort of ministers, each further has his specific title, his *ming*. The sovereign should judge a minister according to the duties specific to his particular position, and require that his achievements correspond to that position. This is what is called in later texts "to assign responsibilities according to the titles" (or "demand that reality accords the name," *xunming zeshi* 循名責實).[13]

   The notions of "a mirror that reflects the light" or "a scale that establishes equilibrium" reflect the idea of dispelling interpersonal relations and assessing officials in accordance with their position and the duties their position entails. This is precisely "to assign responsibilities according to the titles." Beauty and ugliness reveal themselves in the face of a polished mirror; the light and the heavy can be clearly determined when weighed on a right scale. This is the rationale behind the ruler-minister relationship as developed by Shen Buhai, which also constitutes the core element of his legal philosophy. His essential aim is to weaken the influence of kinship or other personalized relations between the ruler and his ministers, and establish a rationalized, legalized relationship in their stead. Personalized relationship will remain elastic and ambiguous; it is forever negotiable and ever-changing, which might be politically and economically costly. It may allow ministerial abuses of power or, worse, subversion of the sovereign's authority. A regime based on personalized relationships at the top is at the very least an inefficient one, and in worse cases a dangerous and unstable one. It is for this reason that Shen Buhai asks of the ruler to model himself after Yao and rule by means of "correct names," that is, establish a ruler-minister relationship which is rationalized, institutionalized, and legalized. Only in this way can one establish an efficient mechanism of governance.

---

[13] See *Huainanzi* 9: 301 ("Zhu shu" 主術).

3 Three Principles of Rule by *fa*: Clear *fa*, Relying on *fa*, and Implementing *fa*

As is made clear by the analysis above, arguing that "Shen Buhai spoke of *shu*" is, in practice, the same as saying "Shen Buhai spoke of *fa*." If we speak of the *fa* enacted by Shang Yang as primarily focusing on the relationship between officials and the people, then the *fa* discussed by Shen Buhai is primarily concerned with the relationship between the ruler and the ministers. The core problem with which Shen Buhai dealt was that of systematizing and legalizing the ruler-minister relationship. The "Da ti" chapter metaphorizes this relationship using the "root-branch" paradigm. It further takes "correct names" as its point of departure, thus constructing the rationale underpinning the legal relationship between the ruler and the ministers.

A statement of Shen Buhai cited in *Yiwen leiju* compendium exposes his ideas further:

申子曰，君必有明法正義，若懸權衡以正輕重，所以一群臣也。又曰，堯之治也，善明法察令而已。聖君任法而不任智，任數而不任說。黃帝之治天下，置法而不變，使民{而安不}[14]安樂其法也。

Master Shen said, "The ruler must have clear *fa* (standards, laws) and correct principles, just as one suspends a scale and balance-beam to weigh lightness and heaviness. Therewith his ministers are unified." He also said, "Yao's orderly rule was being good at clarifying *fa* and being scrupulous in issuing commands, and that is all. The sage ruler relies on *fa* and not on intelligence; he relies on methods (*shu* 數) and not on persuasions. When the Yellow Thearch ruled All under Heaven in an orderly fashion: he established *fa* and did not alter it; he caused the people to be secure and pleased by his *fa*." (*Yiwen leiju* 54: 967; Creel 1974: 353, 357)

This passage corresponds with the "Da ti" in that it focuses on the ruler-minister relationship. Where it differs from the "Da ti" is in the particular emphasis it places on the legal thought of Shen Buhai. Building on this, and utilizing additional sources, let us elaborate below on the three legal principles embedded in Shen Buhai's thought.

3.1 *Clear* fa

Shen Buhai first and foremost emphasizes the idea of "clear *fa* and correct principles" (*mingfa zhengyi* 明法正義). This is the first element in Shen Buhai's legal thought. Just like a scale and balance-beam accurately measure the weight of things, "clear *fa* and correct principles" can accurately measure the officials' performance. These tools allow the ruler to objectively assess officials and therewith guide the officials' actions and even unify their values. One can imagine all the ministers gazing up towards a scale reflecting their status, accomplishments, rewards and

---

[14] Following Creel (1974: 357n6) and the variant citation in *Taiping yulan* ("Lüling xia" 律令下), we consider the characters 而安不 before 安 as redundant. (Editor)

punishments; surely this would increase their dedication to the job. Therein lies the analogy drawn by Shen Buhai.

Generally speaking, the compound *ming fa* 明法 can be understood in two ways. First it refers to the need for laws or standards to be public and made available for all to see. This principle of legal transparency is strongly pronounced in other texts of the *fa* tradition, such as the *Book of Lord Shang* and *Han Feizi*. Secondly, the term "clarity" (*ming* 明) refers also to the ruler's clear-sightedness. Shen Buhai explains: "Being able to see independently is called clear-sightedness (*ming* 明); being able to hear independently is called sharpness of hearing. He who is able to make decisions independently becomes therewith the master of All under Heaven" 獨視者謂明，獨聽者為聰。能獨斷者，故可以為天下主. [15] Therefore, clear *fa* refers not only to the laws' publicity but also, perhaps foremost, to the clear-sightedness of the ruler in his vision of laws and standards. The ruler should establish laws and standards on the basis of the natural course of things rather than opt for an individualistic and capricious establishment of selfish laws. This is what is meant by *ming fa*.

As for "correct principles" (or righteousness/dutifulness, *zhengyi* 正義), one can understand the meaning from the following quotation of Shen Buhai:

明君治國，而晦晦，而行行，而止止。三寸之機運而天下定，方寸之基正而天下治，故一言正而天下定，一言倚而天下靡。

A clear-sighted ruler in ordering his state dims what should be dimmed, implements what should be implemented, stops when he should stop. The pivot of three inches length moves and All under Heaven is stabilized. When the foundation of just one inch squared is correct, All under Heaven is ruled well. Therefore, one word is correct and All under Heaven is stabilized; one word is perverse and All under Heaven topples. (*Sandai* 4: 32; cf. translation in Creel 1974: 353–355)

Only with a correct mindset can the ruler be correct in his speech. The correct or impartial speech (*zheng yan* 正言), is contrasted with perverse or biased (*yi* 倚) speech. Recall Shen Buhai's statement cited above (p. 71): "The Way of Heaven has no selfishness, hence it is always correct. The Way of Heaven is constantly correct, hence it is clear and bright." Correctness refers to being unselfish, dispelling with self-interest (*si* 私). In the context of the ruler-minister relationship, this means primary avoiding personal favoritism. Taken from this perspective, the compound "correct principles" (*zhengyi*) appears close to its modern meaning as "justice."

To summarize, Shen Buhai's "clear *fa* and correct principles" should be understood as objective, neutral, open and transparent laws, and as justice free of favoritism. Akin to a just scale, it provides a code of conduct for all ministers to follow. This is what Shen Buhai means when he argues that "Yao's orderly rule was being good at clarifying *fa* and being scrupulous in issuing commands and that is all." Yao's advantage was impartiality and transparency. This is the foundation of the ruler's orderly governance in All under Heaven.

---

[15] Cited from *Han Feizi* 34.2.13; Chen 2000: 783 ("Wai chu shuo you shang"). The nuance of *du* 獨 is complex here: the word means "independent" as well as "alone, the only one." The point is the ruler's exclusive decision-making, not allowing the ministers to usurp the right of the final say.

3.2 *Relying on* fa

On the basis of "clear *fa* and correct principles," Shen Buhai put forward the notion that "the sage ruler relies on *fa* and not on intelligence; he relies on methods (*shu* 數) and not on persuasions." Reliance on *fa*, in this context, means the utilization and appliance of laws and standards. It is contrasted with "relying on intelligence" (*ren zhi* 任智). The ruler should not trust his personal wisdom, but rather prioritize impartial set of standards and regulations. Similarly, he should not trust external persuasions (*shui* 說). The above statement from *Shenzi* also appears in the opening lines of "Reliance on *fa*" ("Ren fa" 任法) chapter of *Guanzi* (*Guanzi* 45: 900; Rickett 1998: 144). In both cases, *fa* and *shu* are used in tandem as complementary segments of the system of impartial standards that should be prioritized over both the ruler's personal experience or the persuaders' talk.

The point that the ruler should not trust persuaders' talk is too obvious to be discussed in detail here. Recall that Shen Buhai postulates a perennial contest between the ruler and his aides; for sure skillful persuaders could mislead the ruler, or, worse, advance their private interests by making proposals that fit the ruler's mood. In fact, an anecdote told in both *Han Feizi* and *Zhanguo ce* presents Shen Buhai himself as precisely the latter type of manipulator: having observed the ruler's inclinations, Shen Buhai is said to have made a proposal that left Marquis Zhao feeling "greatly pleased" (*Han Feizi* 30.3.4; Chen 2000: 602 ["Nei chu shuo shang" 內儲說上]; *Zhanguo ce* 26.3: 965 ["Han 韓 1"]). The story, ironically, uses the figure of Shen Buhai as a negative example to caution the rulers—heeding persuaders' talks is imprudent and potentially dangerous.

Shen Buhai's more essential point in demanding "reliance on *fa*" is that reliance on the individual abilities of the ruler is fundamentally wrong. *Han Feizi* contains several anecdotes which show Shen Buhai's employer, Marquis Zhao, using various tricks to impress his officials with exceptional personal sagacity (e.g., *Han Feizi* 30.6.2; Chen 2000: 610 ["Nei chu shuo shang"]; *Han Feizi* 31.4.2; Chen 2000: 639 ["Nei chu shuo xia"]). From Shen Buhai's point of view, though, this was a waste of time. This point is exemplified in the following anecdote preserved in the "Relying on methods" ("Ren shu" 任數) chapter of *Lüshi chunqiu*:

> 且夫耳目知巧固不足恃，惟修其數、行其理為可。韓昭釐侯視所以祠廟之牲，其豕小，昭釐侯令官更之。官以是豕來也，昭釐侯曰：「是非向者之豕邪?」官無以對。命吏罪之。從者曰：「君王何以知之?」君曰：「吾以其耳也。」申不害聞之，曰：「何以知其聾?以其耳之聰也。何以知其盲?以其目之明也。何以知其狂?以其言之當也。故曰去聽無以聞則聰，去視無以見則明，去智無以知則公。去三者不任則治，三者任則亂。」以此言耳目心智之不足恃也。耳目心智，其所以知識甚闕，其所以聞見甚淺。以淺闕博居天下，安殊俗，治萬民，其說固不行。

> (Furthermore), the ears, eyes, intelligence, and skillfulness are for sure not sufficient to be depended on. Only cultivating proper methods and implementing proper principles is acceptable. When Marquis Zhaoxi [i.e., Marquis Zhao] of Han looked over the sacrificial animals to be used at the ancestral temple, the pig was too small, so the marquis ordered an official to substitute another. The official brought back the same pig. The marquis asked: "Is it not the same pig that was here just before?" When the official had no response, the

marquis ordered an officer to punish him. His followers asked, "How you, our lord, recognize that it was the same pig?" The lord answered, "By its ears."

When Shen Buhai heard about this incident, he said: "By what do we recognize that he is deaf?—By the keenness of his ears. By what do we recognize that he is blind? —By the clarity of his vision. By what do we recognize that he is mad?—By the appropriateness of his words. Hence, it is said: If a person excludes listening and has no other means of hearing, then his hearing will be keen; if he excludes looking and has no other means of watching, then he will see clearly; and if he eliminates intelligence and has no other means of recognizing, then he will be impartial. If these three faculties are dismissed and not employed, there is order. If they are employed, there is turmoil."

This contends that the ear, eyes, heart, and intelligence, are not sufficient to be depended on by themselves. In the case of the ear, eye, heart, and intelligence, their means of understanding are extremely deficient, and their means of hearing and seeing are extremely shallow. He who occupies a broad place in All-under-Heaven but uses what is deficient and shallow to pacify diverse customs and govern the myriad people—such an approach will definitely not work (*Lüshi chunqiu* 17.3; translation modified from Knoblock and Riegel 2000: 415–16).

Shen Buhai did not approve of the governing method displayed by Marquis Zhaoxi (i.e., Marquis Zhao) on this occasion. Marquis Zhao utilized his personal wisdom to expose the official's petty tricks. For Shen Buhai, such a resort to the ruler's ears, eyes, heart, and intelligence was an insufficiently reliable method. Even if one discerns the details of a little pig's ear, this method cannot be applied when it comes to more substantial matters of the state. The personal senses of the ruler have a limited scope of function. Beyond this scope, the ruler becomes powerless.

3.3 Implementing **fa**

The ruler must bear in mind not just the need to "rely on *fa*," but also to "implement *fa*" (*xingfa* 行法). The latter means giving force to laws and standards, rather than merely having them exist in the void. Only if laws and decrees are strictly enforced does a ruler merit respect. Shen Buhai asserts: "The reason why the ruler is honored is [that he has the power to] command. [But if] commands are not carried out, this amounts to having no ruler. Therefore, a clear-sighted ruler is careful about commands" 君之所以尊者，令。令不行，是無君也，故明君慎令 (*Yiwen leiju* 54: 968). Whereas this quote refers to the ruler's individual commands, the implementation and enforcement of law in general is even more important. This point is clarified in an anecdote about Shen Buhai told in *Han Feizi*:

韓昭侯謂申子曰：「法度甚不易行也。」申子曰：「法者，見功而與賞，因能而受官。今君設法度而聽左右之請，此所以難行也。」昭侯曰：「吾自今以來知行法矣，寡人奚聽矣。」一日，申子請仕其從兄官。昭侯曰：「非所學於子也。聽子之謁，敗子之道乎，亡其用子之謁?」申子辟舍請罪。

Marquis Zhao of Han told Master Shen: "Standards and measures are very hard to implement." Shenzi said: "Standard (*fa*) means meting out rewards according to actual merits, conferring appointments according to one's abilities. Now you have established standards and measures but you heed to personal requests from your entourage. This is why you find it hard to implement standards." Marquis Zhao said: "Henceforth I know how to implement standards. I shall certainly not listen to special requests anymore."

One day, Master Shen made a special request to give his half-brother an office. Marquis Zhao said: "That would not be what I learnt from you, Sir. Should I listen to your proposal and offend against your teachings? Or should I not act in accordance with your proposal?" Master Shen moved out of his dwelling and pleaded guilty (*Han Feizi* 32.5.11; Chen 2000: 708 ["Wai chushuo zuo shang" 外儲說左上]).

The same anecdote is narrated also in *Zhanguo ce* (26.4: 966 ["Han 韓 1"]). Its focus is on an important point: the need not just to adopt standards and laws (*fa*), but also to strictly implement and enforce them. The difficulty of implementing *fa* lies in the ruler, who, if he listens to the personal requests of his advisors, metes out rewards, grants, and official positions in a way external to this system of laws and standards. Shen Buhai reckons that in order to resolve the problem, the ruler should firmly refuse all requests coming from his officials, strictly adhering to impartial regulations that allow meting out rewards and official positions only in accordance with merit. As for Shen Buhai's request for an official position for his brother, Guo Moruo commented, "this shows that for Shenzi himself, talk did not guarantee action. Beautiful words came out of his mouth, but when it came to doing, it was a different thing altogether" (Guo 2012: 260). An alternative explanation, presenting Shen Buhai in a more positive light, would be that he tested Marquis Zhao. In refusing Shen's personal request, the marquis passed the test and met Shen Buhai's expectations. These two explanations are nicely elucidated in two different endings of the anecdote. According to *Han Feizi*, "Master Shen moved out of his dwelling and pleaded guilty," acknowledging his own wrongdoing. Contrastingly, in the *Zhanguo ce*'s narration of the same anecdote, the story ends with Shen Buhai's praise of the ruler: "My lord is really the appropriate man!" 君真其人也! (*Zhanguo ce* 26.4: 966). The latter implies that Marquis Zhao was tested by Shen Buhai and had passed the test posed in response to the problem of "the standards and measures being very hard to implement."

Yet another anecdote in *Han Feizi* may show that Marquis Zhao had followed Shen Buhai's advice:

韓昭侯使人藏弊褲，侍者曰：「君亦不仁矣，弊褲不以賜左右而藏之。」昭侯曰：「非子之所知也。吾聞明主之愛一嚬一笑，嚬有為嚬，而笑有為笑。今夫褲，豈特嚬笑哉！褲之與嚬笑相去遠矣。吾必待有功者，故收藏之未有予也。」

Marquis Zhao of Han ordered people to store up his worn-out trousers. An attendant said: "Surely you are not kind-hearted. Your used trousers you are not giving to your entourage, but you have them stored up." Marquis Zhao said: "This is not something you understand. I have learnt that when the enlightened ruler is sparing with his every frown and his every smile, when he frowns he has a reason for frowning, and if he smiles he has a reason for smiling. Now, trousers are surely not just frowns and smiles! Trousers are very different form frowns and smiles. I am bound to wait for someone with achievements to his credit, so that is why I store them up and do not give them away" (*Han Feizi* 30.3.8; Chen 2000: 600 ["Nei chu shuo shang"]).

This passage shows that Marquis Zhao had fully complied with Shen Buhai's recommendation to "reward in accordance with their merit," and that even when the reward was merely an old pair of trousers, he could still not bestow it in vain. It was only to a person of the appropriate merit that he could hand his trousers. This is the concept of "implementing *fa*" in action.

4 Conclusion

The discussion above has demonstrated, so I hope, that the statement "Shen Buhai spoke of *shu*" is, in essence, the same as saying "Shen Buhai spoke of *fa*." This understanding allows us to rethink Creel's following suggestion:

> For two thousand years Shen Buhai has been called a member of the *fajia* 法家. Western Sinologists, with only a few exceptions, have translated *fajia* as "Legalist school." … In fact, Shen Buhai was not a legalist. This does not mean that he did not believe that law has a place in the administration of government… (Creel 1974: 135; modifying the citation to *pinyin*).

Putting aside the quibbles about the definition of *fajia*, we may argue that Creel's exclusion of Shen Buhai from this intellectual current is inaccurate. Not only did Shen Buhai believe "that law has a place in the administration of government"; but further, he was a *fa* thinker of the highest theoretical caliber. His legal thought was focused on the ruler-minister relationship. He sought to depersonalize these relations and maintain them within the rationalized, institutionalized legal system. With this as his foundation, Shen put forwards the set of three legal principles, namely adhering to "clear *fa*," "relying on *fa*," and "implementing *fa*." These three demonstrate sophistication and maturity of Shen Buhai's legal thought. Therewith, Shen Buhai contributed to the development of the Warring States-period legal thought and left his imprint on China's institutional history in general, as is correctly discussed by Creel.

Scholars all too often tend to identify Shen Buhai narrowly as a single-minded advocate of "techniques of rule" (*shu* 術). For example, Liang Qichao 梁啟超 (1873–1929) defined the "Shenzi school" 申子一派 as "the doctrine of ruling with *shu*" (術治主義) (Liang 1999: 3671). The same observation was echoed by many other scholars, such as Feng Youlan 馮友蘭 (1895–1990) (Feng 2010: 183), Xiao Gongquan 蕭公權 (1987–1981) (Xiao 2005: 150), Qian Mu 錢穆 (1895–1990) (Qian 2011: 250), Guo Moruo (Guo 2012: 254) and so forth. All these observations can be traced back to Han Fei's insistence that "Shenzi spoke of *shu*." However, as the discussion above has shown, the term *shu* in the theory of Shen Buhai is (in and of itself) nothing other than *fa*. In the surviving fragments from *Shenzi*, the character *shu* is nowhere to be seen. Although the fragments contain some characters closely related to *shu*, the core of Shen Buhai's discussions evolve not around *shu*, but around *fa*.

One of the persistent labels associated with Shen Buhai is his initial status as "a lowly minister." Sima Qian observed that Shen was "a lowly minister from the old state of Zheng" 故鄭之賤臣 (*Shiji* 63: 2146). Many scholars considered Shen's low status to be an important source of inspiration for his theories. For instance, Qian Mu opined "Shenzi entered the court as a lowly minister, and his *shu* was predominantly used to quietly observe what his superior liked, and to speak and act on that basis" (Qian 2011: 250). This observation, which is based on both Sima Qian's assertion and *Han Feizi*'s and *Zhanguo ce*'s anecdotes that present Shen Buhai as a skillful manipulator, implies that due to his humble background, Shen Buhai unscrupulously acted with the aim of climbing the social ladder, to the extent that he "catered to his superior's every liking" in every possible way. *Shu* as promoted by this "lowly minister" was subsequently seen as merely a tool for acquiring personal power and influence. This view is misleading in my opinion.

Shen Buhai's identification as a "lowly minister" may well correctly reflect his relatively humble background, but the question remains how this background influenced his political views. I would argue that Shen's position as an outsider in the Han court, dominated as it was by the members of the ruling lineage, could have enabled Shen to see more clearly the shortcomings of the kin-based political system. It is from this viewpoint that Shen arrived at the conclusion that the political system must be depersonalized, and it is from this viewpoint that he sought the rationalization, systematization, and legalization of the ruler-minister relations. His aim was not to flatter the ruler but rather to enhance his ability to govern the state, and subsequently strengthen political order.

Eventually, Shen Buhai's efforts bore fruit. *Zhanguo ce* cites an anonymous persuader: "Marquis Zhaoxi (i.e., Marquis Zhao) was a clear-sighted ruler of the type that appears only once in a generation; Shen Buhai was a man of worth of the type that appears only once in a generation" 昭釐侯，一世之明君也；申不害，一世之賢士也 (*Zhanguo ce* 28.5: 1051 ["Han 3"]). Sima Qian, as cited above, admitted that "up until the death of Master Shen, the state was well-governed, its army strong, and none invaded Han." This rare period of stability and strength, which is hardly ever seen in the history of the state of Han, was in all likelihood the result of applying the legal thought of Shen Buhai. Behind "the state was well-governed and its army strong" stood an architect of legal thought who knew how to analyze power relations and how to marry theory with practice. This was Shen Buhai.

References

Book of Lord Shang. See Pines 2017.
Chen, Qiyou 陳奇猷, ed. 2000. *Han Feizi, Newly Collated and Annotated* 韓非子新校注. Shanghai: Shanghai guji chubanshe.
Creel, Herrlee G. 1974. *Shen Pu-hai, A Chinese Philosopher of the Fourth Century B. C.* Chicago IL: The University of Chicago Press.
Feng, Youlan 馮友蘭. 2010. *A History of Chinese Philosophy* 中國哲學史 (Volume 1). Shanghai: Huadong shifan daxue chubanshe.
Guanzi jiaozhu 管子校注 (*Guanzi*, collated and annotated). 2004. Compiled by Li, Xiangfeng 黎翔鳳. Beijing: Zhonghua shuju.
Guo, Moruo 郭沫若. 1945 (2012). "Critique of the Early *Fa* Thinkers" 前期法家的批判. Rpt. in Guo, Moruo, *Shi pipan shu* 十批判書, 227–249. Beijing: Zhongguo huaqiao chubanshe.
Han Feizi. See Harbsmeier, forthcoming, and Chen Qiyou 2000.
Hanshu 漢書 (History of the Former Han Dynasty). 1997. By Ban, Gu 班固 (32–92) et al. Annotated by Yan, Shigu 顏師古 (581–645). Beijing: Zhonghua shuju.
Harbsmeier, Christoph, trans. Forthcoming. *Han Feizi, A Complete Translation: The Art of Statecraft in Early China*. Ed. Jens Østergaard Petersen and Yuri Pines. Leiden: Brill.

Huainanzi 淮南子=*Collected Glosses to the Grand Illumination from Huainan* 淮南鴻烈集解.
   1997. Ed. Liu, Wendian 劉文典 (1889–1958), Feng, Yi 馮逸, and Qiao, Hua 喬華. Beijing:
   Zhonghua shuju.

Hutton, Eric L., tr. 2014. *Xunzi: The Complete Text*. Princeton NJ: Princeton University Press.

Jiang, Chongyue 蔣重躍. 1988. "Arguing that Shen Buhai is not a Legalist" "申子非法家辨".
   Texts 文獻 03: 81–93.

Knoblock, John and Jeffrey Riegel, trans. 2000. *The Annals of Lü Buwei: A Complete Translation
   and Study*. Stanford: Stanford University Press.

Liang, Qichao 梁啟超 (1873–1929). 1999. *The Complete Works of Liang Qichao* 梁啟超全集.
   Beijing: Beijing chubanshe.

Lü, Wenyu 呂文鬱. 2006. *Zhoudai caiyi zhidu* 周代的采邑制度. Beijing: Shehui kexue wenxian
   chubanshe.

Lüshi chunqiu jiaoshi 呂氏春秋新校釋. 1995. Ed. Chen, Qiyou 陳奇猷. Shanghai: Shanghai guji
   chubanshe.

Pines, Yuri. 2009. *Envisioning Eternal Empire: Chinese Political Thought of the Warring States
   Era*. Honolulu: University of Hawai'i Press.

———, trans. and ed. 2017. The Book of Lord Shang: *Apologetics of State Power in Early China*.
   New York: Columbia University Press.

Qian, Mu 錢穆. 2011. *Chronology of Pre-Qin Masters* 先秦諸子系年. Beijing: Jiuzhov chubanshe.

Quan shanggu Sandai Qin Han Sanguo Liuchao wen 全上古三代秦漢三國六朝文 (Complete
   prose from the highest antiquity to the Three Dynasties, Qin, Han, the Three Kingdoms and
   the Six Dynasties). 1958. Compiled by Yan, Kejun 嚴可均 (ca. 1762–1843). Rpt. Beijing:
   Zhonghua shuju.

Qunshu zhiyao 群書治要 (Essentials of orderly rule from multiple books). 2014. Compiled by Wei
   Zheng 魏徵 (580–643), ed. Shen, Xilin 沈錫麟. Beijing: Zhonghua shuju.

Rickett, W. Allyn, trans. 1998. *Guanzi: Political, Economic, and Philosophical Essays from Early
   China*. Princeton: Princeton University Press.

Shiji 史記 (Records of the Historian). By Sima, Qian 司馬遷 (ca. 145–90 BCE) et al. Annotated by
   Zhang, Shoujie 張守節, Sima, Zhen 司馬貞, and Pei, Yin 裴駰. Beijing: Zhonghua shuju, 1997.

Slingerland, Edward. 2003. *Effortless Action: Wu-wei as Conceptual Metaphor and Spiritual Ideal
   in Early China*. Oxford: Oxford University Press.

Taiping yulan 太平御覽 (Imperial readings from the Taiping era). 2000. Ed. Li, Fang 李昉
   (925–996). Beijing: Zhonghua shuju.

Tian, Changwu 田昌五 and Zang, Zhifei 臧知非. 1998. *Study of Zhou and Qin social structure* 周
   秦社會結構研究. Xian: Xibei daxue chubanshe.

Wade, H.W.R., and C.F. Forsyth. 2009. *Administrative Law*. 10th ed. Oxford: Oxford University
   Press.

Xiao, Gongquan 蕭公權. 2005. *A History of Chinese Political Thought* 中國政治思想史. Beijing:
   Xinxing chubanshe.

Xunzi jijie 荀子集解 (*Xunzi*, with collected explanations). 1992. Ed. Wang, Xianqian 王先謙
   (1842–1917), Shen, Xiaohuan 沈嘯寰, Wang, Xingxian 王星賢. Beijing: Zhonghua shuju.

Yantielun jiaozhu 鹽鐵論校注. 1996. Compiled by Huan, Kuan 桓寬 (first cent. BCE). Annotated
   by Wang, Liqi 王利器. Beijing: Zhonghua shuju.

Yin, Zhenhuan 尹振環. 1987. "Using Instances of Royal Succession and Regicide to Analyze
   the Advance of Authoritarian Dictatorship" 從王位繼承和弒君看君主專制理論的逐步形成.
   Chinese History 中國史研究 4: 17–24.

Yiwen leiju 藝文類聚 (Anthology of literary excerpts arranged by category). 1982. Compiled
   by Ouyang, Xun 歐陽詢 (557–641), ed. Wang, Shaoying 汪紹楹. Shanghai: Shanghai guji
   chubanshe.

Yu, Zhong 喻中. 2019. *On China's Spirit of* fa 論中國法的精神. Xian: Shaanxi renmin chubanshe. (A study that investigates the *fa* thought in the context of China's past, present, and future).

——— 喻中. 2021. "On Shen Buhai's Legal Philosophy" 論申不害的法理學說. *Journal of
   Nanjing Normal University (social sciences)* 南京師大學報 (社會科學版) 6: 101–109.

Zhang, Shunhui 張舜徽. 2005. *In-depth Analysis of Debates about the Way during the Zhou to Qin Era* 周秦道論發微. Beijing: Shifan daxue chubanshe.

Zhang, Jue 張覺, ed. 2010. *Han Feizi, Collated with Subcommentaries* 韓非子校疏. Shanghai: Shanghai guji chubanshe.

——— 張覺, ed. 2012. The Book of Lord Shang, Collated with Subcommentaries 商君書校疏. Beijing: Zhishi chanquan chubanshe.

Zhanguo ce zhushi 戰國策注釋 (*Stratagems of the Warring States*, with glosses and explanations). 1991. Annotated by He, Jianzhang 何建章. Beijing: Zhonghua shuju.

Zhu, Fenghan 朱鳳瀚. 1990. *Study of the Family Morphology in Shang and Zhou* 商周家族形態研究. Tianjin: Tianjin guji chubanshe.

Chapter 3
Morality vs. Impartial Standards in the *Shenzi Fragments*

Eirik Lang Harris

In this chapter, I wish to take the opportunity to lay out certain aspects of the political philosophy found within the *Shenzi Fragments* 慎子逸文 by investigating the question of the relationship between morality and politics described within those fragments. The *Shenzi* is a relatively piecemeal collection of short paragraphs and phrases traditionally attributed to Shen Dao 慎到. Not much is known of Shen Dao, however. According to *The Grand Scribe's Records* (*Shiji* 史記), he was a member of the Jixia 稷下 Academy, an intellectual center that flourished under the patronage of King Xuan of Qi 齊宣王, and he seems to have been active in the latter half of the fourth century BCE and the first part of the third.[1]

The fragments as they currently exist come from a wide variety of sources, and there has been no direct transmission of the purported book bearing Shen Dao's name. The most complete existing source is the *Essentials of Governing from Multiple Books* 群書治要 (Wei 2011), a text compiled in 631 CE as a distillation of views on governance for the emperor. Additionally, a range of fragments attributed to Shen Dao have been found in a wide variety of other sources, and it is a collection of these sources that makes up what we today call the *Shenzi Fragments*.[2]

The fact that all we have are fragments encompassing a mere 3,000 or so Chinese characters, ostensibly pulled from a substantially larger text, means that even if

---

[1] See Nienhauser Jr. 1994: 183–84; Thompson 1979: 127–28.

[2] Extensive discussions of these sources can be found in Thompson 1979 and Xu 2013.

I wish to thank Thai Dang, Paul R. Goldin, Philip J. Ivanhoe, and the students of my 2021 graduate seminar in Chinese Political Philosophy at Colorado State University for useful discussions and comments on the ideas presented herein

---

E. L. Harris (✉)
Department of Philosophy, Colorado State University, Fort Collins, CO, USA
e-mail: eiriklangharris@gmail.com

© The Author(s), under exclusive license to Springer Nature Switzerland AG 2024
Y. Pines (ed.), *Dao Companion to China's fa Tradition*, Dao Companions to Chinese Philosophy 19, https://doi.org/10.1007/978-3-031-53630-4_4

we think that we have discerned a particular political vision from these fragments, we must always be aware that the fuller context of the original, were it available to us, might push us toward a different interpretation.[3] Our material is sketchy, with numerous fragments not directly linked to one another, and often absent a direct political context. Nonetheless, it may be possible to build up a coherent political philosophy from these fragments.

Elsewhere, I have attempted to do just this and argued that the *Shenzi Fragments* builds up a political philosophy that openly questions the tight connection between ethics and politics that is found in a range of early Chinese political philosophers. In particular, I see these fragments as working to divorce politics from morality and developing what A.C. Graham calls an "amoral science of statecraft" (Harris 2016; Graham 1989: 267).[4] I stand by such an interpretation, but also feel that deeper analysis may be useful, particularly since I also attribute to the fragments a political theory that some have called "state consequentialism" (Ivanhoe 2000: 15). Since consequentialism is traditionally viewed as a moral theory, such a claim potentially sits at odds with claims about the amorality of Shen Dao's political theory.

To expand upon and clarify my interpretation of the political philosophy of the *Shenzi*, I will look at three overlapping ways in which one might think that morality is maintained in these fragments and examine what exactly falls out of these three views. To presage my conclusion, I will argue that insofar as any morality remains, it is a morality that is so different, not only in scope but in kind, as to be perhaps better thought of under a different term. In doing so, this paper expands on a line of argument sketched in Harris 2016, and claims that insofar as there is a vision of what is "good" to be found in the *Shenzi*, this vision is based on political success criteria rather than on what is good either for any individual or for any group of individuals.

1   Ruling the State by Following "Conventional Virtues"

While we do see attacks in the *Shenzi* against using certain traditionally praised virtues such as loyalty (忠) and filial piety (孝) (*Shenzi* 46–51), at the same time, there are passages that seem to indicate that that potency (德), often translated as 'virtue' in other texts, is an essential quality for the ruler (*Shenzi* 1–6, 16, 25, 84) and that such a ruler should employ the worthy (*Shenzi* 54, 86) and utilize rituals (*Shenzi* 25, 73, 74, 111, 113) in ordering the state.[5] Claims like these might lead one to conclude that, even if there are important differences between the *Shenzi*

---

[3] Memoir 14 of *The Grand Scribe's Records* 史記, compiled before 90 BCE, claims that Shen Dao wrote twelve discourses (Sima 1982: 2347–48). There is also a record in *The History of the Former Han* 漢書 that indicates that before the end of the first century BCE, there existed a work of some 42 bundles of bamboo slips attributed to Shen Dao (Ban 1962: 1735).

[4] Broad studies of the *Shenzi Fragments* include Thompson 1979; Chen 2001; and Xu 2013.

[5] The numbering of the *Shenzi* is based on Thompson 1979, which also forms the basis for the numbering in Harris 2016.

Fragments and texts that more obviously work to base their political theories on moral foundations, such as the *Mengzi* 孟子 or the *Xunzi* 荀子, the *Shenzi* has not fully untethered itself from a moral grounding.

Let us begin by examining how the *Shenzi* talks about rituals (禮), a term that those familiar with the *Mengzi* and *Xunzi* may take to refer to a particular 'virtue'.[6] 'Ritual' appears in five of the fragments, and does so in a favorable light in each. *Shenzi* 111 seems to imply that the ruler ought to accord with ritual in his own actions:

111. 昔者，天子手能衣而宰夫設服，足能行而相者導進，口能言而行人稱辭；故無失言失禮也。

In the past, the Son of Heaven could dress himself, but his chamberlains arrayed his robes. His feet were capable of walking, but his Chancellor led him forward. His mouth could speak, but his intermediaries announced his words. Therefore he was without error in speech and without error in ritual (禮). (Xu 2013: 70)

A very similar passage occurs in the beginning of Chapter 24, "Noble man" ("Junzi" 君子) of the *Xunzi* (Wang 1992: 450), and these similarities might lead one to think that the *Shenzi* is recalling the cultivated rulers of the past, implying that contemporary rulers as well should cultivate their ritual propriety. On the *Xunzi's* account, rituals serve a range of purposes throughout society. One of the most basic purposes is to restrict the actions of individuals within the state. Indeed, the *Xunzi* takes rituals to have been created by the sage kings of the past because the distinctions, divisions, and actions required of those particular rituals have good consequences. They allow for the establishment of order, the nourishment of the people, and the satisfaction of desires.[7] These rituals are seen to provide an optimal solution to social organization. However, they do not provide this ideal solution simply by providing a set of standards to accord with, resulting in human flourishing. Rituals cannot be fully efficacious if one simply accords with them in order to avoid punishment, sanctions, or something else unpleasant as a result of violating them. Rather, what makes rituals so powerful is that they can be used as a tool for moral cultivation, for modifying individuals' desires and motivations.

As the *Xunzi* conceives it, it is possible to come to understand not merely what the rituals dictate, but why they so dictate. The process of moral cultivation, via rituals, leads one to reshape one's values, gaining moral, rather than merely self-interested, reasons for according with the rituals. Once this process is completed, one has developed internal reasons for following the rituals – one is now acting from an understanding of and belief in the way of life that underlies the rituals rather than merely acting in accordance with the rituals.[8] This has implications both moral and political. Morally, it provides access to a way of life unavailable to any who have not

---

[6] Confucian texts such as the *Analects*, *Mengzi*, and *Xunzi* use this term not simply to a particular set of social guidelines but to a particular virtue that arises when one comes to understand why particular social guidelines are (or ought to be) in place. For an enlightening article pointing out that this 'virtue' interpretation was not shared throughout the early Chinese corpus, see Pines 2000.

[7] See the opening lines of Chapter 19 of the *Xunzi*.

[8] For more on this aspect of the *Xunzi's* thought, see Kline III 2004; Harris 2013; Ivanhoe 2014; Stalnaker 2016.

so cultivated themselves. And from the perspective of political organization, it provides an additional set of reasons to follow the rituals. They are not followed merely because they are prescribed; rather, they are followed because it is understood that what they prescribe is good. This additional reason for action makes them an even more efficacious political force since they will be followed by such individuals even in the absence of punishments, sanctions, or other unpleasant consequences.

None of this, however, seems to be present in the *Shenzi*. Rather, insofar as rituals are effective tools, they are so merely because they re-align what it is in someone's interest to do. As we see in *Shenzi* 73,

> 73. 書契，所以立公信也；度量，所以立公審也；法制禮籍，所以立公義也。凡立
> 公，所以棄私也。
>
> …. Documents and contracts are how trust is established publicly. Standardized measurements are how length and volume are determined publicly. Laws, institutions, rituals (禮), and documents are how norms are set up publicly. In all these cases, establishing public standards is the means by which private interests are discarded. (Xu 2013: 18)

Documents, contracts, standardized measurements, laws, institutions, and rituals all serve the same purpose – discarding private interests. Or, more accurately, what they all do is change what it is in an individual's interest to do, preventing them from taking unsanctioned advantage of others. In general, as the *Shenzi* notes, people act in their own interests, and it is necessary for the ruler to accord with this fact in governing.[9] What documents and contacts do is to spell out what individuals have agreed to, and thus to eliminate cheating or deviously taking advantage of others by making it no longer in one's self-interest to do so. Standardized measurements also serve this purpose. It is not that those in the marketplace no longer wish to take advantage of their customers. However, with standardized weights, their customers know exactly how much they are getting, eliminating one avenue sellers previously had to take advantage of customers. And the same is the case with laws, institutions, and rituals. These all serve to clearly articulate and lay out what is permissible and what is impermissible. But importantly, as is stressed elsewhere, it is not that laws or rituals in and of themselves change behaviors. Rather, it is because there are negative sanctions attached to their violation – sanctions that individuals fear more than they desire to engage in the actions that these laws and rituals proscribe.

Thus, as the *Shenzi* says, private interests are discarded. Previously, it may have been in my interest to renege on an oral agreement, to cheat customers over lengths or weights in the marketplace, to steal from others, or to engage in any of a variety of anti-social activities that brought profit to me. However, with the implementation of contracts, weights and standards, laws, and rituals, I can no longer pursue my private interests in the same way, for it is no longer in my interest to do so. Yet there is no indication here that this results in a change of desires, values, or beliefs. There is no cultivation going on. Rather, all of these tools work precisely because they make use of already existing human motivations rather than developing new motivations. So, insofar as the *Shenzi* makes use of rituals, it does so in a markedly

---

[9] See, for example, *Shenzi* 28–32 (Xu 2013: 24–28).

different way from texts such as the *Xunzi*, ignoring those aspects of ritual that could lead it to be conceived of as a virtue.

Shenzi 113 may also be seen as driving this message home, though it is admittedly less than fully clear:

113. 國有貴賤之禮，無賢不肖之禮；有長幼之禮，無勇怯之禮；有親疏之禮，無愛惡之禮也。

States [should] have rituals (禮) governing the treatment of the honored and the lowly but [should] lack rituals (禮) governing the treatment of the worthy and the unworthy. They [should] have rituals (禮) governing the treatment of the old and young but [should] lack rituals (禮) governing the treatment of the courageous and the timid. They [should] have rituals (禮) governing the treatment of close and distant relatives but [should] lack rituals (禮) governing the treatment of those cared about and those loathed. (Xu 2013: 63)

Whatever this fragment means, it seems to advocate the usage of rituals in ways that are importantly different from how they are used in the Confucian tradition.[10] Rituals should regulate the treatment of the honored and the lowly, young and old, close and distant relatives. But they are not tools that should be used to regulate worthy and unworthy, courageous and timid, cared about and loathed. What might be the difference between these two groupings? Here is one possibility: the former are recognized social distinctions while the latter are not. Rules and regulations delineate the social status of honored and lowly, make clear distinctions between age groups, and mandate how different groups of relatives are to be treated. These are all objective distinctions that can be encoded in these rules and regulations. On the other hand, worthiness, bravery, and likeability may be conceived of as being subjectively determined. And, in particular, they are subjective determinations that rulers often make that lead them to treat certain people better than others. Rulers that make the subjective determination that someone possesses the virtues of worthiness or bravery, and act based on this endanger their rule and the state itself. Such subjective determinations on the part of the ruler are problematic for a variety of reasons: they may incorrectly identify these traits, praising those with these traits is not necessarily conducive to a strong and stable state, and doing so may engender resentment in the hearts of those not so praised.

On such a reading, the point of this fragment would be that in assessing individuals, rituals should work based on clearly understood, recognized, and recognizable standards rather than by trying to pick out the predilections of the individuals involved. Rituals can help divide people into objective categories but cannot make determinations about who actually possesses moral characteristics. Hence, the *Shenzi* seems to be arguing that there should be no ritual distinctions based on moral cultivation or lack thereof. Again, the point seems to be that insofar as rituals are effective tools, they are effective because they function in the way that laws and

---

[10] While I focus on what I see as a distinction between subjectively determined relations of the sort advocated in the *Lunyu* and *Mengzi*, among other Confucian texts, on the one hand and objectively determined relations of the sort advocated by the *Shenzi*, this is not to claim that the *Shenzi* is not reacting to other currents of Chinese thought on this issue.

other rules and regulations function – by identifying and regulating actions rather than motives.

This interpretation may be further supported by examining what the *Shenzi* has to say about worthiness more broadly. As we saw above, the traditionally moral virtue of worthiness is not something that is to be ritually defined, because it is subjectively determined. There may be additional reasons to ignore worthiness in governing the state, however, and these reasons may further our understanding of why we cannot conceive of the *Shenzi's* political philosophy as being grounded in morality. However, these attacks on the inefficaciousness of worthiness as a political tool need to be reconciled with those places where the *Shenzi* seems to see a place for worthiness within the state.

Looking at *Shenzi* 53–54 may help us:

> 53–54. 亡國之君，非一人之罪也；治國之君，非一人之力也。將治亂在乎賢使任職，而不在於忠也。
>
> Being lord of a failed state is not the fault of a single person. Being lord of a well-ordered state is not due to the strength of a single person. Bringing order to disorder rests in worthy officials' holding governmental positions and does not rest in loyalty. (Xu 2013, 44)

This seems to indicate that worthy individuals can benefit the *Shenzi's* ideal political organization. However, there are a few things to note. First, while worthiness appears in a positive light, it is not the real subject or focus. The focus of *Shenzi* 53–54 is that single individuals do not lead to the success or failure of a state, and thus, this mention of worthiness actually comports with later mentions that are much less positive. What is central here is not that a worthy individual be in a position of power but rather that appropriately skilled individuals be placed in appropriate bureaucratic positions within the state. As *Shenzi* 56 continues,

> 56. 故廊廟之材，蓋非一木之枝也；狐白之裘，蓋非一狐之皮也。治亂安危存亡榮辱之施，非一人之力也。
>
> Hence, the timber for the imperial court does not all come from the branches of a single tree, and a white fur coat does not come from the pelt of a single fox. The conferring of order or disorder, security or danger, survival or destruction, glory or dishonor are not due to the strength of a single person. (Xu 2013: 44–45)

This seems to be a clear attack on the idea that so long as a virtuous ruler or prime minister is in place, the state will be well-ordered and secure. To take a modern example, just as a cuckoo clock can accurately tell the time only when all its gears are arranged appropriately, so too can a state function well only when its bureaucratic machinery – including all its people – are arranged appropriately. No matter how awesome the cuckoo bird in the former case or the ruler/minister in the latter, the appropriate gears must be in the correct place and working properly.

None of this means that there is no place for those who are worthy. However, it is to say that success does not come from the moral quality of worthiness itself. Indeed, there is no indication that those who are being described as 'worthy' here are those who have particular *moral* qualities rather than having those task specific skills and talents that allow them appropriately to fulfill the duties of their office. Furthermore, at the same time that this passage wishes to rely upon the 'worthy,' it wishes to make clear that the moral quality of 'loyalty' is useless. One could, perhaps, read this as arguing over what virtues are important in the political realm. However, given that we see no such argument elsewhere in the *Shenzi*, along with the fact that, as we shall soon see, 'worthiness' is denigrated in many passages of the *Shenzi*, such a path may not be fruitful. Rather, I suggest that in this passage, 'worthiness' simply refers to the quality of having those task-specific capacities allowing one to fulfill the duties of one's office.

Additionally, there are several passages indicating that worthiness is at best irrelevant. As we see in *Shenzi* 70:

70. 折券契，屬符節，賢不肖由之；物以此得而不託於信也。
   As for breaking contracts into halves and joining together the halves of tallies, both the worthy and the unworthy follow these [procedures]. Things can be obtained in this manner without relying upon trust. (Xu 2013: 73)

This passage seems to quite clearly indicate that worthiness is irrelevant if one has the appropriate rules and regulations in place. One need not be worthy (or, relatedly, trustworthy) if rules and regulations are in place that identify and sanction those who do not uphold their end of a bargain. Under such a system, if I make a contract with someone, I need not care about whether they are morally good individuals who have internal reasons to fulfil their part of the bargain. Rather, I can simply rely upon the legal and bureaucratic standards of the state to ensure that that person does not violate their contract, regardless of internal motivations.

Indeed, in a passage that recalls a similar set of ideas in the *Laozi* 老子 38, *Shenzi* 19–20 laments:

19–20. 今也，國無常道，官無常法，是以國家日繆。教雖成，官不足；官不足則道理匱；道理匱則慕賢智；慕賢智則國家之政要在一人之心矣。
   Today, the state lacks a constant Way, and offices lack constant models. Because of this, the state is deteriorating day by day. Even if they have been well educated, [competent] officials will be insufficient [in number]. When officials are insufficient, the patterns of the Way will languish. When the patterns of the Way languish, there will be a yearning for the worthy and the wise. When there is a yearning for the worthy and the wise, the most crucial elements for governing the entire state will depend on the mind of a single person. (Xu 2013: 13)

In a fashion similar to the *Laozi* 38's contention that a desire to recover the moral qualities so prized by the Confucians arises only when we have drifted from the Way, and this pursuit only leads us further astray, the *Shenzi* argues that it is only when no overarching bureaucratic structure is in place to ensure that the state is well regulated that a desire for personal qualities such as worthiness and wisdom arises. This desire is born from a recognition that the state is not well-ordered, that it is not serving its people, and that they, and the state itself, are in danger. However, this desire leads to a mis-diagnosis of the problem. The problem is not that morally cultivated individuals are not in positions of power. Rather, it is that a well-regulated bureaucratic and legal system whose design is based on an understanding of patterns of the natural world and of human beings is not in place (Harris 2015).

While the *Shenzi* does not evince the same distain for moral qualities that we see in texts such as the *Han Feizi*, and never explicitly identifies those possessing such qualities as a danger to the state (see Harris, Chap. 10, Sect. 3, this volume), there is no indication that the possession of such qualities allows one to be more effective in public service. As we see in *Shenzi* 77:

> 77. 故有道之國，法立則私善不行，君立則賢者不尊；民一於君，事斷於法，國之大道也。
>
> Therefore, in states that have the Way, when the law is established, private goodness will not be pursued. When a lord is established, worthies will not be revered. People are united under the lord and affairs are decided by the law—this is the great Way of the state. (Xu 2013: 64)

It is not that morally cultivated individuals have no place in the state – so long as they have relevant task-specific talents and abilities. Rather, it is that these moral qualities are not seen – by the state or its people – as central to success. Political success is to be found in a system, not an individual.

2 Political Success Comes from According With the Way (道 *Dao*)

Insofar as what it means to base the political on the moral is to rely upon those who have a range of moral qualities to govern, it does not appear that the *Shenzi* provides us with a political morality. However, this is not the only way that we might think that political order has a moral foundation. Rather, a range of texts as diverse as the *Xunzi* and *Laozi* derive a conception of normativity from their understanding of the *Dao*, the overarching Way. Such texts believe that coming to a deeper understanding of the Way tells us how we should act, both as individuals and as parts of broader communities. Indeed, the Way tells us what those communities ought to look like, how they should be structured, and how this contributes to the flourishing of their constituent parts.

We might, then, think that insofar as a deeper understanding of the overarching Way conveys information about how we ought to behave, it encodes a moral order to be followed. If this is the case, it would seem to imply that if the *Shenzi* advocates following the Way in its political provisions, even if its understanding of the Way differs dramatically from that of other texts, its politics is similarly based on morality. And, it is undeniable that the *Shenzi* does advocate according with the Way. For example, *Shenzi* 28 tells the ruler that, "The Way of heaven is such that if you 'follow' then you will be great, while if you alter then you will be insignificant" (天道，因則大，化則細) (Xu 2013: 24). Does this then mean that its political prescriptions are, at their core, moral in nature?

The *Shenzi* advocates according with the Way, and believes that a deeper understanding of this Way will allow for the development of a normativity – a set of 'oughts' for how to structure society. So, at a certain level, what the *Shenzi* is trying to do is to examine the natural world and its overarching Way in order to determine what should be done. However, the reason for discerning the Way and according with it is not because this is what best allows human beings to cultivate themselves and live full, enriching, and flourishing lives in which they have tapped into new sources of values that would otherwise not be available to them. Rather, for the *Shenzi*, the reason to accord with the Way is because doing so allows for the greatest political order. A deeper understanding and following of the Way is seen not as a method for the moral cultivation of the individual or for creating a morally good society, but, rather, for creating the strongest, most stable political organization possible. From a deeper understanding of the Way, including the dispositions of human beings, it is possible to determine a political normativity – that is, to develop a set of 'oughts' aimed at maximizing the consequences to the state, in particular, stability, strength, and order.[11]

While the *Shenzi* is not explicit about why this is the ultimate goal, given the context of the Spring and Autumn and Warring States periods, when life was precarious and the overthrow of rulers often led to the decimation of their states and substantial loss of life among the populace, it should not be too surprising that order and stability were of paramount concern. And, while the *Shenzi* does not begin with an imagined scenario of the state of nature as did Thomas Hobbes, it is possible that a similar set of concerns motivated him – how is it possible to move from a situation of conflict, chaos, and insecurity to a situation of peace, order, and security?[12] However, unlike Hobbes, the fundamental justification was the well-ordered state, rather than maximizing the individual's possibility of pursuing their desires. The well-ordered state was a goal in and of itself.[13]

Therefore, the goal underlying a deeper understanding of the Way, including the fundamental dispositions of human beings, was an engineering one – how is it possible to take the material available and create the strongest, most stable state possible? As I have argued elsewhere, within the *Shenzi*, we see a range of claims that lead to its preferred political solution: 1) The natural world follows a set of regular patterns, 2) human beings also follow a set of natural patterns (based on their fundamentally self-interested dispositions), and 3) it is thus possible to replicate in the political realm the same sort of fixed and regular patterns observed in the natural world (Harris 2016).

Given the fundamental role of self-interest in motivating human actions, laws are going to be central to ensuring that people act in ways that are beneficial to the state when they are otherwise not inclined.[14] As we see in *Shenzi* 75–77:

---

[11] Importantly, this political normativity does not assume that the good of the individual and the good of the state go together. The assumption that they do go together is a feature of many (perhaps most) ancient political thinkers, both East and West. Note, that there is also much agreement between the *Shenzi* and the *Laozi* on this point, though they pull apart in their understandings of exactly what the natural world actually tells us (Harris 2021).

[12] Note, again, however, that this would be an extrapolation as the remaining fragments simply do not concretely address this issue.

[13] And, of course, the echoes of this are still heard throughout East Asia today.

[14] For more extended discussions of the law in the *Shenzi*, see Yang 2011, 2013.

75–77. 法之功，莫大使私不行；君之功；莫大於使民不爭。今立法而行私，是私與法爭；其亂甚於無法。立君而尊賢，是賢與君爭；其亂甚於無君。故有道之國，法立則私善不行，君立則賢者不尊；民一於 君，事斷於法，國之大道也。

> Among the achievements of the law, none is greater than causing private interests not to be pursued. Among the achievements of the lord, none is greater than causing the people not to quarrel. Now, establishing the law and yet still pursuing private interests leads to conflict between the private and the law, and the chaos of this is greater than if there were no laws at all. Establishing a lord and yet still revering the worthies leads to conflict between worthies and lords, and the chaos of this is greater than if there were no lord at all. Therefore, in states that have the Way, when the law is established, private goodness will not be pursued. When a lord is established, worthies will not be revered. People are united under the lord and affairs are decided by the law—this is the great Way of the state. (Xu 2013: 64)

The law, and indeed the entire bureaucratic system, including the ruler, once established, is able to bring order to chaos. Indeed, the power of the law at creating order out of chaos is so central that, as we see in *Shenzi* 23, "Even if the law is not good, it is still better than having no law at all" (法雖不善，猶愈於無法) (Xu 2013: 18). Why might the *Shenzi* think this? A legal apparatus that establishes laws, identifies those who violate them, and unfailingly implements the prescribed punishment for such violations, provides a structure that ensures greater predictability of human action and a decrease in resentment arising from different treatment for similar actions (Harris 2016: 31–36). This increase in stability and reduction of resentment arising from the mere implementation of a legal system, regardless of its content will, in and of itself, increase the strength and stability of the state. We can turn to *Shenzi* 82 to investigate this reasoning further:

82.   一兔走街，百人逐之；非一兔足為百人分也，由未定分也。分未定，堯且屈力而況眾人乎?積兔滿市，過者不顧；非不欲兔也，分已定矣。分已定，人雖鄙不爭。故治天下及國，在乎定分而已矣。

> If a rabbit runs through the streets, a hundred people will pursue it. This is not because a single rabbit is sufficient to be divided among a hundred people but rather because its allotment has not yet been determined. When allotment has not yet been determined, even Yao would exhaust his strength [to attain it], and even the more so the masses. If piles of rabbits fill the market, and people pass by without turning their heads, it is not because they do not desire rabbits [but rather because] the allotment has already been decided. When allotment has already been decided, then people, even if they are base, will not contend with one another. Therefore, governing all under heaven and the state rests in making allotments and that is all. (Xu 2013: 79)

While this passage does not explicitly discuss law, it is certainly implied. The allotments referenced are allotments established by the law and upheld by threat of sanction. Were this not the case, then, given the *Shenzi's* conception of human dispositions, the mere fact that one person had been allotted a pile of rabbits would not prevent another person from taking the rabbits from person X. After all, person Y still desires rabbits, so if they do not act on that desire, it must be because of a fear of losing something that they value more than the rabbits.

The mere establishment of divisions and allotments, then, in and of itself increases order within the state. And, importantly for the *Shenzi's* purposes, it does so regardless of how rabbits, or, indeed, anything else is allotted. However, this does not mean that the *Shenzi* is unconcerned with the content of the law, for it certainly is – a point that comes across quite clearly in *Shenzi* 78–79:

78–79. 故治國，無其法則亂；守法而不變則衰；有法而行私，謂之不法。以力役法者，百姓也；以死守法者，有司也；以道變法者，君長也。

Thus, if in ordering a state, one were to do away with its laws, then there would be chaos; if its laws were to be preserved and not modified, then it would decline; if it were to have its laws but allow private interests to manifest themselves, then this is called not abiding by the law. Those who are willing to exert themselves to serve the law are those of the hundred surnames. Those who are willing to lay down their lives in service of the law are the officials. Those who change the laws in accordance with the Way are the lords and leaders. (Xu 2013: 78)

This passage brings us back to a fundamental theme in the *Shenzi* – that the chances for strength, security, and order are maximized if the legal system bases its particular laws on a deeper understanding of the Way. And here, the Way encompasses not only the regularities of the natural world but also the dispositions of human beings. The idea is that some laws will be more effective than others at maximizing the strength, security, and order of the state. Which laws are these? It is those that are established based on a deep understanding of the particularities of the world around us insofar as they are relevant to human action along with an understanding of what actually motivates human beings. By understanding these things, it is possible to set up a system ensuring that human beings are motivated to engage in those actions that, given the current situation, will lead to order.

However, this passage also evinces an understanding of the fact that circumstances will change over time, and, as circumstances change, it is necessary to change the content of the laws to ensure that this content continues to accord with the Way. The problem here is not that the Way itself has changed. Rather, at different times and in different conditions, different aspects of the patterns of the Way become more relevant.

If we pull back and examine the thinking that may underlie such a view, we can think of the case of drought and flooding. Such events do not indicate that the natural processes regulating the world have changed – they are simply the result of different aspects of the complex patterns of the natural world revealing themselves. And the same can be said of long-term human population growth – it does not violate natural patterns – it arises because of them.

While population growth, drought, flooding, or indeed, long term climate change, are all natural processes, they do require that laws regulating human activity change as well. If human population growth leads to an insufficiency of water resources in a particular area, then this may require that laws be established in response to this. These laws are not established because people have changed or because the world has changed. People have always wanted water. However, when there are few people and lots of water, then the worries of *Shenzi* 82 do not arise, since people can satisfy their desire for water without coming into conflict. When population increases lead to an insufficiency of water, then, absent allotment, the worries of *Shenzi* 82 arise again.

Therefore, while any bureaucratic and legal system would reduce conflict and increase order within the state, maximizing this order requires understanding the realities of a particular time and place and what these realities imply about how to respond to the overarching Way.

3 State Consequentialism as a Form of Moral Normativity?

So far, we have seen that the *Shenzi* sees no role for conventional virtues or moral cultivation in its politics, and so its political philosophy cannot be seen as under-girded by morality in this sense. Additionally, we have seen that while the *Shenzi* does advocate according with the Way, it does not do so for moral reasons. Rather, doing so maximizes the strength, security, and stability of the state and is justified for these reasons. This, then leads us to the state consequentialism of the *Shenzi*. As we have seen, what this text thinks *ought* to be done is whatever will lead to the strongest, most stable, and most well-ordered state. Whatever does this is justified. Whatever detracts from this is not.

But, one might counter, we still have a normativity here, and there is a sense in which it is a moral normativity. After all, the *Shenzi* does seem to think that a well-ordered state is one in which people have the greatest chance of survival. On such an understanding, state consequentialism benefits the people. This may lead to the conclusion that is has a moral basis. However, the *Shenzi* never claims that the fundamental aim of the ruler should be to help the people. As we see in *Shenzi* 22, "The [position of lord] was established in order to serve the state" (立國君以為國也) (Xu 2013: 16). While the state may be thought of as a collective including both ruler and ruled, the establishment of the lord was not envisioned as having as its direct aim maximally benefitting the people of the state.

Furthermore, there is no categorical claim made in the *Shenzi* that under all circumstances the ruler ought to have the goal of maximizing order within the state. And, insofar as this is the ruler's goal, it is not because it is the right or good thing to do. It is not because creating this order will maximize the collective welfare of the people within the state. While there is a relationship between the two and while the *Shenzi* would claim that a well-ordered state is in the best interests of those living in that state, this is not what justifies the well-ordered state.[15] Instead, it takes as its starting point the assumption that the ruler does have such a goal. Therefore, its advice is hypothetical in nature. Insofar as there is a normativity in the *Shenzi*'s advice to the ruler, it is on a par with the normativity inherent in the claims I regularly make to my students that, if they want to do well in my classes, they ought to

---

[15] Developing ideas from Brindley 2013, Jiang 2021: 281–282, 452 reads *fa* texts such as the *Shenzi* and the *Han Feizi* as developing a conception of universal justice arising from a concern with the public (*gong* 公) over the private (*si* 私). While the normativity of the public is clear, a question remains about whether this normativity appropriately construed as including a conception of moral justice.

do the assigned readings, come to class prepared to discuss them, and submit all assignments on time. The point is not that the students have a moral obligation to do these things, and it is certainly not that people in general have a moral obligation to do these things. Rather, the point is that if you wish to achieve some thing, in this case, doing well in my classes, then engaging in a particular set of actions, which here involves doing the assigned readings, coming to class prepared to discuss them, and submitting all assignments on time, is appropriate.

Therefore, if one wishes to create and sustain a strong, stable, and well-ordered state that will survive and not be endangered, then the appropriate thing to do – the thing that the ruler 'ought' to do, is follow the advice of the *Shenzi*. And, in doing so, the ruler may very well maximize the collective welfare of those within the state. But this is not *why* the ruler is following the advice of the *Shenzi*. Rulers who follow the advice of the *Shenzi* do so because they value order. And order, while seen as instrumentally valuable, is not seen as being in the service of some greater, deeper intrinsic value. Nothing is intrinsically valuable. Rather the state is valuable simply because rulers value the state. Order is valuable simply because rulers value order as a tool that maintains the state. Rulers, as a matter of fact, desire to rule over strong, stable, and prosperous states, and political order is a tool that allows this goal to be achieved.[16]

4   Conclusion

Throughout this chapter, we have examined a variety of interpretations of the *Shenzi Fragments* that might lead one to think that there is some sort of morality underlying its political philosophy. We began by examining the positive references to a range of what we might think of as "conventional virtues" – traits such as worthiness, ritual propriety, and virtue/potency itself. However, in each instance, we saw that insofar as these traits are advocated, they are stripped for their moral connotations. We then examined whether we might think that there is a morality undergirding the *Shenzi's* political philosophy insofar as it advocates according with the overarching Way. However, again, we saw that this advocacy is based on practical, rather than moral, reasons. Finally, we examined whether the state consequentialism of the *Shenzi* implied some sort of moral normativity. And again, we could find no such moral

---

[16] This also points both to a formal similarity to Machiavelli and to a fundamental difference. If asked why one should follow his prescription, the *Shenzi* (and later the *Han Feizi*) would respond by saying that doing so allows for the realization of a strong and stable state. The Machiavelli of *The Prince*, on the other hand would say that doing so maximizes the glory of the prince. Following Machiavelli's prescription allows the prince to enjoy and revel in glory, an importantly different goal (toward which end the state will be instrumentally valuable). For both of them, however, the people are important, but only instrumentally so. Should the rulers' actions lead to a decimation of the population, then the rulers would be incapable of realizing their goals – irrespective of the content of those goals. (For a different take about Machiavelli and possible comparisons between his and the *fa* thinkers' views, see Blahuta, Chap. 21, this volume).

foundation. Rather, it is a state consequentialism predicated on the assumption that the ruler wishes to rule over a strong and stable state. If this does not happen to be the case, then it has nothing to say.

We lamentably lack the full text from which these brief fragments may have been drawn, and thus lack the fuller context within which the fragments that have reached us were first recorded. As such, we must be aware of the possibility that these brief and scattered fragments may not provide us with a full exposure to the ideas of the text from which they originated. However, what we do have in these brief fragments is a political normativity – a hypothetical imperative to put it in Kantian terms – that has as its goal nothing further than the establishment and maintenance of a strong and stable state. And the reason it has that goal is simple – that is actually what rulers desire, nothing more.

References

Ban, Gu 班固 (32–92). 1962. *History of the Former Han* 漢書. Beijing: Zhonghua shuju.
Brindley, Erica Fox. 2013. The Polarization of the Concepts *Si* (Private Interest) and *Gong* (Public Interest) in Early Chinese Thought. *Asia Major* 26 (2): 1–31.
Chen, Fu 陳復. 2001. *Shenzi's Thought* 慎子的思想. Taibei: Tangshan chubanshe. (Expansive study of Shen Dao's thought, focusing on his "objective viewpoint.")
Graham, Angus C. 1989. *Disputers of the Tao: Philosophical Argument in Ancient China*. La Salle: Open Court.
Harris, Eirik Lang. 2013. The Role of Virtue in Xunzi's 荀子 Political Philosophy. *Dao: A Journal of Comparative Philosophy* 12 (1): 93–110.
———. 2015. Aspects of Shen Dao's Political Philosophy. *History of Philosophy Quarterly* 32 (3): 217–234.
———. 2016. *The Shenzi Fragments: A Philosophical Analysis and Translation*. New York: Columbia University Press. (Complete, annotated English language translation cum study of the *Shenzi*).
———. 2021. Harmony and Nature: Thoughts from Laozi and Shen Dao. In *Harmony in Chinese Thought: A Philosophical Introduction*, ed. Chenyang Li, Sai Hang Kwok, and Dascha Düring, 193–209. Lanham: Rowman & Littlefield.
Ivanhoe, Philip J. 2000. *Confucian Moral Self Cultivation*. 2nd ed. Indianapolis: Hackett Publishing.
———. 2014. A Happy Symmetry: Xunzi's Ecological Ethic. In *Ritual and Religion in the Xunzi*, ed. T.C. Kline III and Justin Tiwald, 63–87. Albany: State University of New York Press.
Jiang, Tao. 2021. *Origins of Moral-Political Philosophy in Early China: Contestation of Humaneness, Justice, and Personal Freedom*. Oxford: Oxford University Press.
Kline, T.C., III. 2004. Moral Cultivation Through Ritual Participation: Xunzi's Philosophy of Ritual. In *Thinking Through Rituals: Philosophical Perspectives*, ed. Kevin Schilbrack, 188–206. New York: Routledge.
Nienhauser, William H., Jr., ed. 1994. *The Grand Scribe's Records, Volume 7: The Memoirs of Pre-Han China*. Bloomington: Indiana University Press.
Pines, Yuri. 2000. Disputers of the *Li*: Breakthroughs in the Concept of Ritual in Preimperial China. *Asia Major (Third Series)* 13 (1): 1–41.
Sima, Qian 司馬遷 (ca. 145–ca. 90 BCE). 1982. *Records of the Grand Historian* 史記. Beijing: Zhonghua shuju.

Stalnaker, Aaron. 2016. Xunzi on Self-Cultivation. In *Dao Companion to the Philosophy of Xunzi*, ed. Eric L. Hutton, 35–66. New York: Springer.

Thompson, P.M. 1979. *The Shen Tzu Fragments*. Oxford: Oxford University Press.

Wang, Xianqian 王先謙 (1842–1917). 1992. *Xunzi, with collected explanations* 荀子集解. 1992. Ed. Shen Xiaohuan 沈嘯寰, Wang Xingxian 王星賢. Beijing: Zhonghua shuju.

Wei, Zheng 魏徵 (580–643). 2011. *Essentials of Governing from Multiple Books* 群書治要. Taibei: Shijie shuju.

Xu, Fuhong 許富宏. 2013. *Shenzi, with Collected Collations and Commentary* 慎子集校集注. Beijing: Zhonghua shuju.(Most recent critical edition of the *Shenzi Fragments*, including a wider variety of fragments that have variously been attributed to Shen Dao than those included in Harris: 2016).

Yang, Soon-ja. 2011. "Shen Dao's Own Voice in the *Shenzi Fragments*." *Dao: A Journal of Comparative Philosophy* 10.2: 187–207.

———. 2013. Shen Dao's Theory of *fa* and His Influence on Han Fei. In *Dao Companion to the Philosophy of Han Fei*, ed. Paul R. Goldin, 47–63. New York: Springer.

Chapter 4
Han Feizi: The World Driven by Self-Interest

Yuri Pines

Han Fei 韓非 (d. 233 BCE) is often considered "the great synthesizer of Legalism" (Graham 1989: 268; cf. Schwartz 1985: 339; Feng 2001: 746–50). This assessment reflects to a certain extent Han Fei's own self-presentation. In one chapter ("Defining Standards" or "Fixing Laws" [43, "Ding fa" 定法]), the author positions himself as the synthesizer and improver of two major traditions that were later associated with the "school of *fa*": that of Shang Yang 商鞅 (d. 338 BCE) and of Shen Buhai 申不害 (d. 337 BCE). Elsewhere (chapter 40, "Objections to Positional Power" ["Nan shi" 難勢]), *Han Feizi* proposes a sophisticated defense and improvement of Shen Dao's 慎到 views. Insofar as Shang Yang, Shen Buhai, and Shen Dao were all considered by the Han dynasty as quintessential representatives of the "school of *fa*" (see Introduction, this volume), Han Fei's position at the apex of this school's development seems to be justified.

Speaking beyond the "school of *fa*," one can immediately note parallels between Han Fei's intellectual breadth and that of his alleged teacher, Xunzi 荀子 (d. after 238 BCE). Much like Xunzi, Han Fei was eager to engage ideas across the spectrum of contemporaneous political thought. Both thinkers, the "titans at the end of an age" (Goldin 2020), crowned generations of vibrant intellectual activism. Both were less concerned with effecting new breakthroughs but rather with refining their predecessors' ideas, overcoming their shortcomings, providing more sophisticated and compelling argumentation in favor of the views they supported, and of course refuting the ideas of manifold opponents. Here the parallels end, though. In contrast to Xunzi, Han Fei was less concerned with creating a compelling philosophical

This research was supported by the Israel Science Foundation (grant No. 568/19) and by the Michael William Lipson Chair in Chinese Studies.

Y. Pines (✉)
Hebrew University of Jerusalem, Jerusalem, Israel
e-mail: yuri.pines@mail.huji.ac.il

© The Author(s), under exclusive license to Springer Nature Switzerland AG 2024
Y. Pines (ed.), *Dao Companion to China's* fa *Tradition*, Dao Companions
to Chinese Philosophy 19, https://doi.org/10.1007/978-3-031-53630-4_5

system. Rather the text that bears his name is renowned for its inquisitive analysis of the opponents' ideas, its cynicism, audacity, and merciless exposure of the fallacy of commonly accepted truths. All of these make *Han Feizi* a truly rewarding reading.

1 Han Fei and *Han Feizi*

1.1 Biography

The major source of information about Han Fei's life is the chapter "Arrayed Biographies of Laozi and Han Fei" 老子韓非列傳 in Sima Qian's 司馬遷 (ca. 145–90 BCE) *Records of the Historian* (*Shiji* 63: 2146–55). This source is somewhat disappointing, though. Most of Han Fei's biography comprises citations from *Han Feizi* (one chapter—"The Difficulties of Persuasion" [12, "Shui nan" 說難]—is reproduced in its entirety). Other biographic information is reduced to absolute minimum. We are told that Han Fei was a scion of the ruling house of the state of Hán 韓 (not to be confused with the Hàn 漢 dynasty), that he studied with Xunzi and was envied by the fellow student and future chancellor of the Qin empire, Li Si 李斯 (d. 208 BCE). We also learn that Han Fei was a stutterer, which made him a weak persuader but an avid writer. Han Fei was reportedly frustrated with his home state, Hán, and remained unemployed there. When, finally, the king of Hán dispatched Han Fei as a messenger to King Zheng of Qin 秦王政 (the would be First Emperor), the results were tragic. Although King Zheng admired Han Fei's writings, he was persuaded by Li Si and another Qin minister, Yao Jia 姚賈,[1] that Han Fei should not be trusted. Han Fei was arrested and Li Si masterminded his elimination in the jail shortly before King Zheng regretted his decision.

The dearth of details in Han Fei's biography suggests that Sima Qian had few clues about Han Fei's life aside from those that can be inferred from the text of *Han Feizi* (cf. Kern 2015). Except for the identification of Han Fei as Xunzi's disciple and the story of Han Fei's death in Qin custody, the information seems to derive from the text itself. Even the story of Han Fei's stuttering may be an intelligent guess based on the fact that *Han Feizi* is one of a very few Masters' texts that contains just a single dialogue between the putative author and his contemporary (in chapter 42, "Asking Tian" ["Wen Tian" 問田]). Han Fei's failure to find an adequate employer may also be an inference from numerous chapters that express frustration with benighted rulers and their selfish advisors who block talented outsiders. Even Sima Qian's account about Han Fei's final mission to Qin could be a conjecture based on chapter 2, "Preserving Han" (2, "Cun Han" 存韓), which contains Han

---

[1]Yao Jia's role as Han Fei's nemesis is suggested in an anecdote preserved in the *Stratagems of the Warring States* (*Zhanguoce* 戰國策). There it is told of Han Fei's attempt to slander Qin's gifted diplomat, Yao Jia; but Yao Jia excelled in defending himself, causing the King of Qin to execute Han Fei instead (*Zhanguoce* 7.8: 476–78 ["Qin 秦 5"]). Note that in this version of the story, Li Si is not involved in Han Fei's death.

Fei's memorial delivered to King Zheng so as to save his native state. The memorial itself is duly followed by Li Si's refutation of its arguments, which could have convinced Sima Qian of Li Si's perennial rivalry with Han Fei.

"Preserving Han" is the single segment of *Han Feizi* that provides clear clues about the thinker's activities (Han Fei is directly identified in Li Si's reply). In the current version of *Han Feizi*, this chapter is preceded by another memorial-based chapter, "First Audience in Qin" (1, "Chu jian Qin" 初見秦), which presents a very different set of arguments. The chapter (which is ignored in *Records of the Historian*) outlines the way for Qin to speedily subjugate "All-under-Heaven" (*tianxia* 天下). Notably, ruining the state of Han is due to be among the first steps toward attaining this goal (*Han Feizi* 1.5; Chen 2000: 24).[2] How to reconcile the contradictory message of the two memorials? One possibility, endorsed by no less an authority than Sima Guang 司馬光 (1019–1086) is a cynical reading: Han Fei had brazenly suggested eliminating his natal state so as to ingratiate himself with the king of Qin (*Zizhi tongjian* 6: 222). Alternatively, many scholars argued that the memorial was penned not by Han Fei, but by one of Qin leaders, such as the famous diplomat Zhang Yi 張儀 (d. 307 BCE), to whom the memorial is (erroneously) attributed in the *Stratagems of the Warring States* (*Zhanguoce* 戰國策), or chief minister Fan Sui 范雎 (d. 255 BCE), or Fan's replacement Cai Ze 蔡澤.[3] Yet another solution is implied in the chapter's name, "First Audience in Qin": namely, the memorial was presented during Han Fei's earlier visit to Qin and is unrelated to the second visit, during which "Preserving Han" was submitted. Insofar as rich historical data in chapter 1 suggest that it was penned ca. 255–250 BCE, the latter inference is plausible, even if the authorship itself remains unverifiable.[4]

1.2   The Text: Authorship and Dating

The controversy about the first chapter of *Han Feizi* is indicative of the problems faced by scholars of the text in general. The text is not consistent in its arguments. Thus, in one chapter ("Eminent Teachings" [50, "Xian xue" 顯學]), it ridicules those who call upon the ruler "to attain the people's heart" 得民之心, whereas elsewhere ("Merit and Fame" [28, "Gong ming" 功名]) it considers attaining the people's heart an essential precondition for the ruler's success (*Han Feizi* 50.11 vs. 28.1; Chen 2000: 1147 vs. 551). In one chapter ("The Five Vermin" [49, "Wu du"

---

[2] All citations from *Han Feizi* follow the divisions adopted in Harbsmeier (forthcoming) borrowed from Zhang 2010. My translations borrow from those of Harbsmeier and, when appropriate, from Goldin (2020: 201–28).

[3] See respectively *Zhanguoce* 3.5: 171–75 ("Qin 1"); *Han yiwenzhi kaozheng* 6: 230; Dou 2019. Zhang Yi's authorship is surely wrong: the memorial addresses many events that occurred decades after Zhang's death.

[4] See more in Zheng 1993: 11–15; Jiang 2000: 14–25; Song 2010: 9–13; Dou 2019. For the historical context of that memorial, see Pines Forthcoming.

五蠹]), filiality is dismissed as politically subversive, whereas elsewhere ("Loyalty and Filiality" [51, "Zhong xiao" 忠孝]) it is hailed as a foundational political virtue (*Han Feizi* 49.9 vs. 51.1; Chen 2000: 1104 vs. 1151). Legacy of the former kings is routinely dismissed as irrelevant, but sometimes is invoked as a positive example to be followed, most notably in two chapters which are likely to be based on Han Fei's memorials: "Having Standards" ("You du" 有度) and "Wiping away Deviance" ("Shi xie").[5] Many chapters warn the ruler against skillful persuaders, but chapter 12, "The Difficulties of Persuasion," positions the author himself as a cynical manipulator of the ruler for the sake of personal advancement (see more in Hunter 2013). Yet on another occasion ("Asking Tian") the author suddenly presents himself as a heroic martyr, eager to sacrifice himself for the sake of his principles (*Han Feizi* 12.1 vs. 42.1: Chen 2000: 254 vs. 955).

Individual chapters of *Han Feizi* differ considerably also in the basic mode of their argumentation. A few chapters, evidently inspired by *Laozi* 老子, seem to be interested in metaphysical stipulations of the political order, whereas most other ignore metaphysics altogether. The first two chapters employ the argumentation current among the travelling persuaders, although these persuaders and their glib talk are routinely attacked elsewhere in *Han Feizi*. Several chapters (e.g., "Ten Missteps" [10, "Shi guo" 十過]) base the entire argumentation on a series of historical exempla, as was common in the Warring States-period texts, whereas elsewhere the author(s) either problematizes the usage of the exempla, or dismisses historical arguments altogether (see below). And when historical exempla are invoked, the degree of accuracy differs dramatically: some stories contain brazen anachronisms,[6] whereas other are based on what appears as meticulous reading of earlier historical texts, such as *Zuozhuan* 左傳 (*Zuo Tradition* or *Zuo Commentary*) (Pines 2022). How can we reconcile these differences and contrasts?

The three possible solutions to the heterogeneity of *Han Feizi* chapters are those outlined in the debates about chapter 1 (cf. Goldin 2020: 225–26). First, it is possible that different chapters were penned by different authors. Second, the chapters can reflect different stages in Han Fei's intellectual maturation: at certain points of time, the thinker could endorse one view or adopt a certain mode of argumentation, whereas later he could modify it or even abandon it altogether (this explanation is most notable in Zheng 1993). And third, there is Paul R. Goldin's suggestion: "Han Fei's avowed opinion simply changes with his audience. Now he may excoriate duplicitous ministers; now he may explain how to gull a king. It is impossible to say which is the 'real' Han Fei, because in neither authorial mode does Han Fei disclose his personal views" (Goldin 2020: 222). Most possibly all three answers are correct at times.

---

[5] *Han Feizi* 6.3, 19.2 and 19.8; in addition, see also 25.2 ("An wei" 安危) Chen 2000: 100, 344, 367, 526)

[6] For a few examples, see Wang Yinglin's 王應麟 (1223–1296) *Kunxue jiwen* 困學紀聞 10: 1265–75; Pines 2020a: 263nn.80–81.

In the nineteenth and especially the twentieth century, considerable effort was invested in distinguishing the authorship and dating of each of the text's chapters (for the most systematic studies, see Lundahl 1992 and Zheng 1993; see also Jiang 2000: 3–48). In light of the above observations, it is clear that in most cases, a definitive answer is impossible. Incidentally, we may say with a high degree of confidence that two chapters, which display considerable ideological, lexical, and stylistic differences—such as the two exegetical chapters dedicated to *Laozi* (20, "Explicating Lao" ["Jie Lao" 解老], and 21, "Illustrating Lao" ["Yu Lao" 喻老])—may have been penned by different authors (Queen 2013). One chapter (53, "Adjusting Orders" ["Chi ling" 飭令]) is probably an alternative version of chapter 13, "Making Orders Strict" ("Jin ling" 靳令) of the *Book of Lord Shang* (*Shangjunshu* 商君書), which was inadvertently incorporated into *Han Feizi* (Mozawa 1991). Yet it is also possible to read it as a part of a cluster of chapters (53–55) that adopt the *Book of Lord Shang's* diction and revolve around the ideas that dominate the latter (how to rule the people efficiently, how to accord the government with their basic dispositions, how to use properly rewards and punishments, and the like). Whether these three chapters are part of the corpus from which the *Book of Lord Shang* was created, or, rather, are Han Fei's attempt to engage Shang Yang's legacy is impossible to verify. As for the bulk of *Han Feizi*, the authorship of most chapters will remain contestable. Yet insofar as no chapter seems to evince knowledge of the imperial unification of 221 BCE, it is likely that they do not postdate Han Fei's lifetime. Even if not necessarily written by Han Fei, they may be a reliable source for the ideas of Han Fei and his disciples, followers, or like-minded thinkers who contributed to the eponymous text.

1.3 The Text's Allure

Argumentative heterogeneity notwithstanding, most of *Han Feizi* chapters display a consistent philosophical outlook based on the premise that human self-interest cannot be reined in by ethical and moral norms, and that selfishness characterizes every social actor—both the leaders and the led. Political implications of this idea will be addressed below. Here it should be noted that the text's cynicism may also explain its lasting appeal even among the imperial literati who rejected its ideas. *Han Feizi's* incisive analysis of human behavior, merciless exposition of hidden motivations behind ostensibly noble conduct and words, black humor, provocativeness, and immense richness of its literary language make it comparable to *Zhuangzi* 莊子. These features allow the reader to tolerate some of *Han Feizi's* appalling statements, reading these *cum grano salis*. Take for instance the following cautioning to the rulers in chapter 17, "Precautions against the Entourage" ("Bei nei" 備內)

> 且萬乘之主，千乘之君，后妃、夫人、適子為太子者，或有欲其君之蚤死者。何以知其然?夫妻者，非有骨肉之恩也，愛則親，不愛則疏。語曰:「其母好者其子抱。」然則其為之反也，其母惡者其子釋。丈夫年五十而好色未解也，婦人年三十而美色衰矣。以衰美之婦人事好色之丈夫，則身見疏賤，而子疑不為後。此後妃、夫人

之所以冀其君之死者也。唯母為后而子為主，則令無不行，禁無不止，男女之樂不
減於先君，而擅萬乘不疑，此鳩毒扼昧之所以用也。故《桃左春秋》曰：「人主道
疾死者不能處半。」人主弗知，則亂多資。故曰：「利君死者眾，則人主危。」

Whether one is the sovereign of ten-thousand-chariots (a large state) or the ruler of one-thousand-chariots (a medium-sized state), among one's consorts, wives, and the son chosen to be the Crown Prince, there are those who desire the early death of their ruler. How do I know this to be so? Between husband and wife, there is not the kindness of a relationship of flesh and bone. If he loves her, he is intimate with her; if he does not love her, she is estranged. There is a saying: "If the mother is favored, her son will be embraced." If this is the case, the inverse is: If the mother is disliked, her son will be disowned. The lust of a man of fifty has not yet dissipated, whereas the beauty and allure of a woman of thirty have faded. If a woman whose beauty has faded serves a man who still lusts, she will be estranged and disesteemed; her son will be viewed with suspicion and will not succeed to the throne. This is why consorts and wives hope for the ruler's death. But if the mother becomes a dowager and her son becomes the sovereign, then all her commands will be carried out, all her prohibitions observed. Her pleasures with males and females will be no less than with her former lord, and she may arrogate to herself power over the ten thousand chariots without suspicion. Such is the use of poison, strangling, and knifing. Thus is it said in the *Springs and Autumns of Tao Zuo*: "Less than half of all rulers die of illness." If the ruler of men is unaware of this, disorders will be manifold and unrestrained. Hence it is said: "when those who benefit from the ruler's death are plenty, the sovereign is endangered." (*Han Feizi* 17.2; Chen 2000: 322)

Han Fei's cynicism surely appalled traditional readers as it does many modern ones, but it also contributed to the text's allure. Whereas few would reject outright a possibility of true love and affection in human relations, most would acknowledge that Han Fei's observations cannot be easily dismissed. The higher the stakes in one's race toward riches and power, the higher is the possibility that one will trample moral and social norms. History—especially the history of ruling houses worldwide—provides ample examples to validate Han Fei's warnings.

Han Fei's career failure and personal tragedy was another, even if somewhat paradoxical, reason for the text's lasting appeal. In contrast to the *Book of Lord Shang*, many of whose chapters derive from ministerial memorials, and which often discusses quotidian affairs of economic and military management, *Han Feizi* is the text of an outsider. Only a few of its chapters (1–4, 6, 19, and 51) appear to originate from the thinker's memorials to the ruler (as identified by the first-person pronoun *chen* 臣 [I, your subject]). Even fewer are occasions in which the text focuses on practical policies. What further distinguishes it from the *Book of Lord Shang*, are several chapters, such as "Solitary Frustration" (11, "Gu fen" 孤憤) that lament the fate of a gifted and devoted man of service who is blocked by malevolent political heavyweights from fulfilling his aspirations. This incidental adoption of a markedly ministerial stance as opposed to the common focus on the ruler's interests may have endeared *Han Feizi* to some of Confucian-minded readers.

The text of *Han Feizi* fared much better than other texts from the "school of *fa*" section of the Han imperial catalogue. All of its 55 chapters outlined in that catalog survived, and most of them did not suffer considerable textual corruption. The text's lasting popularity is suggested also by the fact that it is the source no less than 77 "set phrases" (*chengyu* 成語) in Modern Chinese (Li and Chen 2009: 46). The text attracted considerable interest of scholars not just in China but notably in Tokugawa and Meiji Japan (Sato 2013b). Overall, despite the predominantly negative view of Han Fei's ideas on the part of both traditional and modern scholars (Song 2013 and Chap. 16, this volume), the text of *Han Feizi* attracted and continues to attract considerable scholarly attention, past and present.

2 Philosophical Foundations

Han Feizi is commonly regarded as philosophically the most sophisticated text of the *fa* tradition. In the only English-language monograph dedicated to its philosophy, the authors, Wang Hsiao-po and Leo S. Chang plainly state that other *fa* personalities were "men of action" who "probably did not possess the philosophical bent of mind to work out an integrated theoretical foundation for *fajia*." Han Fei, by contrast is hailed as "the most systematic and theoretically sophisticated synthesizer of the various strains of *fajia* thought" (Wang and Chang 1986: 6–7). Putting aside for the time being the dismissive attitude toward Han Fei's predecessors, one can easily understand Wang and Chang's enthusiasm. At the very least on the level of philosophical argumentation, *Han Feizi* is remarkably sophisticated. Some of its chapters employ historical arguments; other present metaphysical stipulations of political order, and other make forays into logical argumentation or even invoke philological observations to bolster their conclusions.[7] This richness is indeed unparalleled in the texts of the *fa* tradition. Nonetheless, Paul R. Goldin averred (with regard to most of *Han Feizi* chapters), "Han Fei would rank as an outstanding writer, but a somewhat derivative thinker" (Goldin 2020: 218). How can Goldin's verdict be reconciled with that of Wang and Chang? Let us start with the ideas explored by Wang and Chang and then move to other philosophical foundations of Han Fei's theory.

2.1 The Way

Wang and Chang (1986: 6) claim that Han Fei's "theoretical sophistication is nurtured by his imaginative interpretation and adoption of the philosophical Daoism of Laozi." Indeed, the proximity of certain chapters of *Han Feizi* to *Laozi* is striking. Aside from two exegetical chapters, mentioned above (p. 103), the text comprises at least three other chapters (5, "The way of the Sovereign" ["Zhu dao" 主道], 8, "Extolling Authority" ["Yang quan" 揚權] and 29, "The Great Body" ["Da ti" 大

---

[7] Historical and metaphysical ideas are discussed below in the text. For logical arguments, see, e.g., the "contradiction" (*maodun* 矛楯) concept (*Han Feizi* 40.3.1; Chen 2000: 945 ["Nan shi"]) and the derivative arguments in 50.2 (Chen 2000: 1129 ["Xian xue"]); for the arguments based on philological (more accurately, graphological) observations, see 49.10 (Chen 2000: 1105 ["Wu du"]).

體]) which borrow much of *Laozi*'s vocabulary and poetic cum enigmatic style. Not incidentally, Sima Qian paired Han Fei's biography with that of Laozi and, moreover, opined that the ideas of Han Fei "originated from the meaning of the Way and its virtue" 原於道德之意 (*Shiji* 63: 2156) and that "in the end his [Han Fei's] roots were in Huang-Lao" 而歸本於黃老 (*Shiji* 63: 2146). We shall turn to the notion of Huang-Lao later. Here suffice it to say that Sima Qian's somewhat counterintuitive observation—after all *Laozi*'s renowned minimalism contrasts sharply with the assertive state endorsed by Han Fei and other *fa* thinkers—continues to perplex scholars (cf. Graham 1989: 285–89; Goldin 2020: 224–28; T. Jiang 2021: 406–10; Wang Pei, Chap. 20, this volume). To understand the role of what Goldin (2020: 226) dubs "*Laozi* diction" in *Han Feizi*, it is appropriate to start with the chapter "The Great Body," which, arguably, presents the most sophisticated blend of Han Fei's and *Laozi*-related ideas:

> 古之全大體者：望天地，觀江海，因山谷……不以智累心，不以私累己；寄治亂於法術，託是非於賞罰，屬輕重於權衡。不逆天理，不傷情性……守成理，因自然；禍福生乎道法，而不出乎愛惡。
>
> Those in ancient times who preserved the Great Body intact, gazed out across Heaven and Earth, observed the rivers and the sea, and adapted to the mountains and valleys. … They neither encumbered their minds with intellect, nor encumbered themselves with self-ishness. They consigned matters of order and chaos to laws and techniques, entrusted matters of right and wrong to rewards and punishments, and deputed questions of light and heavy to the scales and weights. They neither acted contrarily to Heaven's patterns, nor harmed their nature… They kept to the established pattern and adapted to what was so by itself. People's bad or good fortune originated in the law (or standard, *fa*) of the Way, and did not emerge from the ruler's love or hatred. (*Han Feizi* 29.1; Chen 2000: 555)

This extraordinarily beautiful passage presents *Han Feizi*'s common recommendation to entrust the governance to "laws and techniques" (*fashu* 法術) and rewards and punishments, avoiding overreliance on the ruler's intelligence and limiting the impact of his selfish inclinations. This recommendation, however, is encapsulated in the vocabulary which immediately reminds one of the *Laozi* and of the ideas that are commonly dubbed "Huang-Lao." The latter term was vaguely used in the Han dynasty to depict a variety of cosmological, philosophical and political ideas that borrowed the names of Huang Di 黃帝 (Yellow Thearch) and *Laozi*. With the discovery of the so-called *Huang Di manuscripts* (*Huangdi shu* 黃帝書) from Tomb 3, Mawangdui, Changsha 長沙馬王堆 (Hunan), the content of Huang-Lao ideas as perceived in Han Fei's own time became clearer. At the core of Huang-Lao thought stands what Randall P. Pereenboom dubs "foundational naturalism," meaning that "the cosmic natural order serves as the basis, the foundation, for construction of human order" (Peerenboom 1993: 27). This idea is precisely what appears in the above extract. The ancient sages who preserved the "Great Body" (viz. the supreme natural and political order) intact, did it by observing natural patterns and acting accordingly. In the latter part of the chapter the ruler is explicitly called upon "to adapt to Heaven's decree" 因天命 (which in this context refers to the natural course of affairs rather than the Western Zhou-type "Mandate of Heaven") and to pattern himself (*ze* 則) after Heaven and Earth (*Han Feizi* 29.2 and 29.3; Chen 2000: 555

and 559). Furthermore, the term "the law (or the standard) of the Way" (*Dao fa* 道法)—a relatively rare compound in the received texts[8]—unmistakably connects "The Great Body" chapter to the *Huang Di manuscripts*, which actually start with the "Dao fa" chapter that proclaims: "The Way generated the law" 道生法 (*Huangdi shu* 1.1:1).

In "The Great Body" chapter, the patterning of the political realm after "Heaven's patterns" (*tianli* 天理) should lead to a state of ultimate tranquility and peace:

> 故至安之世，法如朝露，純樸不散；心無結怨，口無煩言。故車馬不疲弊於遠路，旌旗不亂於大澤，萬民不失命於寇戎，雄駿不創壽於旗幢；豪傑不著名於圖書，不錄功於盤盂，記年之牒空虛。故曰：利莫長於簡，福莫久於安。
>
> Hence in the age of the perfect peace, laws were like morning dew—pure, simple and not diluted. Hearts were without resentment, mouths without superfluous words. Hence cart horses were not exhausted on lengthy roads, banners were not mixed chaotically at great marshes, the myriad people did not lose their predestined life at the hands of invaders and belligerents, outstanding men did not impair their longevity under flags and standards, bravos were neither incising their names on maps and documents nor recording their merit on [bronze] *pan* and *yu* [vessels]; and the wooden planks for the yearly records remained blank.[9] Hence it is said: There is no more lasting benefit than simplicity; there is no more enduring good fortune than peace. (*Han Feizi* 29.1; Chen 2000: 555)

This state of affairs of ultimate simplicity, tranquility, and peace, where no military undertakings occur, unmistakably resembles *Laozi*'s views (cf. *Laozi* 30, 31, 80), and contrasts with *Han Feizi*'s habitual advocacy of an assertive state dedicated to agriculture and warfare. This does not necessarily imply, however, that the chapter was not penned by Han Fei; after all much of its vocabulary, and, most notably the idea of the superiority of impartial laws and regulations over human abilities are distinctively related to *Han Feizi*.[10] Acclaim of tranquility and quietude recurs in another of *Han Feizi*'s chapters that employs "*Laozi* diction," namely "The Way of the Sovereign," but there the goal is primarily to direct the ruler toward non-interference in quotidian political affairs (see Sect. 3.3). Elsewhere, "*Laozi* diction"

---

[8] The compound *daofa* (which can be translated either as the Way and the law, or, as I prefer above and as is clearly appropriate in the light of the *Huang Di manuscripts*, "the law/standard of the Way") appears in two more chapters of *Han Feizi* (19.6 and 44.6; Chen 2000: 359 and 973 ["Shi xie" 飾邪 and "Shuo yi" 說疑]). Aside from *Han Feizi* it is attested to thrice in *Xunzi* and in two chapters of *Guanzi* ("The ruler and the minister A" ["Jun chen shang" 君臣上] and "Reliance on Law" ["Ren fa" 任法]).

[9] Blank seasonal records (in which only the season's first month is nominated) appear in the *Springs-and-Autumns Annals* (*Chunqiu* 春秋), when no events during the season were considered significant enough to be recorded (Chen Minzhen 2023).

[10] "The Great Body" is part of a cluster of chapters (24–29), which are very close to each other in terms of ideas, lexicon, and modes of argumentation. The ostensible proximity of these chapters to Confucian ideas and to *Laozi* caused considerable debates about their authorship. Yet, as many scholars observed, differences of argumentation aside, the chapters present the ideas that overall are aligned with the rest of *Han Feizi*, except that they lack the aura of cynicism which is prominent elsewhere in the text. Some scholars speculated that these chapters may have been produced by Han Fei at an early stage of his intellectual career. See more in Lundahl 1992: 241–60 and Zheng 1993: 262–377.

provides philosophical stipulations for the ruler's authority. In the chapter "Extolling Authority," Han Fei directly links the unifying power of the sovereign with that of the Way:

夫道者，弘大而無形。德者，覈理而普至。至於羣生，斟酌用之，萬物皆盛，而不與其寧。道者，下周於事，因稽而(→天)[11]命，與時生死。

As for the Way, it is vast and formless; as for virtue, it investigates the patterns, reaching everywhere. As it arrives at all the living; as for virtue, it investigates the patterns, reaching everywhere. As it arrives at all the living, if you use it properly, the myriad things will all prosper; but [the Way] will not participate in their serenity. As for the Way, it is involved in undertakings below, on the basis of which it coordinates Heaven's decree, giving [the things] time for life and death. (*Han Feizi* 8.5; Chen 2000: 152)

The discussion begins with sophisticated elaboration on the nature of the Way and virtue (or potency, *de* 德). The Way is a highly abstract cosmic force, but, surprisingly, it is also engaged "in undertakings below"; it is the source of the life and death of myriad things. Yet after this short preface the author immediately focuses on what matters to him—the principles of rulership:

參名異事，通一同情。故曰：道不同於萬物，德不同於陰陽，衡不同於輕重，繩不同於出入，和不同於燥溼，君不同於羣臣。凡此六者，道之出也。道無雙，故曰一。是故明君貴獨道之容。君臣不同道。下以名禱，君操其名，臣效其形。形名參同，上下和調也。

Sort out names, distinguish between undertakings, penetrate oneness, and align with the [things'] essence. Hence it is said: The Way is not identical with the myriad things; virtue is not identical with *yin* and *yang*; scales are not identical with light and heavy; an ink-line is not identical with the degree of deviation [of what is measured]; a tuning instrument is not identical with the dry or wet [state of the strings]; the ruler is not identical with the ministers. All these six are products of the Way. The Way has no counterpart; hence, it is named "the One." Therefore, the clear-sighted ruler revers the demeanor of the solitary Way. The ruler and the ministers do not follow the same Way. The underlings are appraised according to the titles (names [*ming* 名]): the ruler embraces the title, the minister provides his performance (form [*xing* 形]); when the performance and the title match each other, the superior and the inferior are well attuned. (*Han Feizi* 8.5; Chen 2000: 152)

The concept that the ruler's position derives from the cosmic way is common in "Huang-Lao" and similar texts that invoke cosmological patterns as a means of bolstering the ruler's authority (Pines 2009: 38–44). Yet what matters to Han Fei are not theoretical explorations but rather concrete recommendations for the ruler how to manage his ministers through the employment of the "titles and performance" technique (of which see Sect. 3.2 below). A similar rapid shift from "*Laozi* diction" to practical advice to the sovereign recurs in "The Way of the Sovereign" chapter (see below p. 126). It is clear that practical issues matter to Han Fei and other contributors to *Han Feizi* more than philosophical abstractions. The question to be asked now is what is the place of these abstractions in Han Fei's political theory in general?

The answer is uncertain. Wang and Chang (1986) consider *Han Feizi*'s invocations of the Way and its virtue as "the philosophical foundations of Han Fei's political theory." The importance of the chapters that employ "*Laozi* diction" in the overall structure of *Han Feizi* is accepted by some of the contributors to this volume,

---

[11] For reading 而 as 天, see Tao Hongqing's 陶鴻慶 (1859–1918) gloss, cited in Chen 2000: 153n4.

most notably Mark E. Lewis (Chap. 11). This said, one can note that cosmological speculations occupy a minor place in the text as a whole. Except for the chapter "The Great Body," which is fully absorbed in the Huang-Lao thought, other chapters do not demonstrate a similar attempt to systematically blend cosmology and Han Fei's political recommendations. Two exegetical chapters of the *Laozi* (especially the philosophically more sophisticated chapter 20) are less attuned to Han Fei's political theory. Two other chapters—"The Way of the Sovereign" and "Extolling Authority"—can be identified as core ideological chapters of the text; but in both "*Laozi* diction" is employed only briefly, with attention immediately shifting to political matters. In the overwhelming number of other chapters, the Way, Heaven and Earth dyad, or other cosmological digressions are not present at all.[12] Evidently, the author(s) did not consider these arguments compelling enough or important enough to be constantly utilized.

The reasons for the presence of "*Laozi* diction" in several of *Han Feizi* chapters have been discussed by Paul R. Goldin (2020: 225–28). Following his analysis, I may offer mine conclusion. The popularity of *Laozi* and related texts in the intellectual milieu of the late Warring States period is undeniable. Han Fei might have toyed with borrowing ideas, terms, and even poetic style of these texts so as to bolster his own ideas of rulership and ruler-minister relations. Yet this embrace of "*Laozi* diction" does not appear as intellectually consequential for Han Fei. What mattered to him were not the cosmic patterns but human affairs. For any single invocation of the Way and its virtue, one can find dozens of references to the affairs of remote and recent past through which Han Fei explicates the cruel nature of human politics. History and observation of human mores matter to Han Fei incomparably more than Heaven and Earth.

2.2   Lessons from the Past

One of the most notable features of *Han Feizi* is its peculiar historical outlook (recently discussed in Pines 2013a; Bai 2020; Vogelsang, Chap. 12, this volume). Much like the *Book of Lord Shang*, the text endorses what Kai Vogelsang (Chap. 12, this volume) dubs "sequential history." Namely, as time passes human society changes and sociopolitical regulations should be altered accordingly. The ruler who heeds Confucian and Mohist exhortations to follow the patterns of the former kings is as stupid as a peasant who watches by the stump for another rabbit to break its neck near the stump, as it happened once in the past (*Han Feizi* 49.1; Chen 2000: 1085 ["Wu du"]). History does not repeat itself; what was valid once is not necessarily valid nowadays.

---

[12] There are a few exceptions, of course, insofar as several sentences in other chapters can also be related to the "*Laozi* diction." See, for instance, chapter 28, "Merit and Fame," which recommends the ruler to "preserve the Way of so-by-itself" 守自然之道 (*Han Feizi* 28.1; Chen 2000: 551).

Han Fei's sequential view of history is exposed most systematically in chapter 49, "Five Vermin." The chapter starts with the depiction of human society's transformation from primeval "high antiquity" 上古, when rulership was given to the most knowledgeable—those who taught the people to make nests and obtain fire by drilling woods—through the "middle antiquity" 中古 of fighting the floods, down to the "recent antiquity" 近古, when the righteous leaders of the Shang and Zhou dynasties eliminated the tyrants by launching punitive expeditions. Each of these fitted the conditions of their age. Han Fei concludes:

> 今有搆木鑽燧於夏后氏之世者，必為鯀、禹笑矣；有決瀆於殷、周之世者，必為湯、武笑矣。然則今有美堯、舜、湯、武、禹之道於當今之世者，必為新聖笑矣。是以聖人不期脩古，不法常可，論世之事，因為之備。

> Now, suppose that there had been someone who had made nests of wood or drilled firewood during the times of the Xia—they would certainly be laughed at by [the flood fighters] Gun and Yu. Suppose that there had been someone who dug drainage canals during the times of the Yin (Shang) and Zhou—they would certainly be laughed at by [the Shang and Zhou founders,] Tang and Wu. So, if people praise the way of Yao, Shun, Tang, Wu, and Yu in our own time, then they will certainly be laughed at by the new sage. Thus, the sages are not committed to cultivating antiquity and do not take something constantly acceptable as their standard. They judge the current affairs of their age and take the appropriate measures for them. (*Han Feizi* 49.1; Chen 2000: 1085).

The story of the human society's development from "high" to "middle" to "recent" antiquity has prompted considerable debates about whether it can be considered an example of an evolutionary view of history (Song 2010: 14–15). Putting these debates aside, the bottom line is clear: "the sages are not committed to cultivating antiquity and do not take something constantly acceptable as their standard." Every era demands its own means of coping with problems; every age requires new sages. The new sage, whose coming Han Fei evidently anticipates (i.e. the new universal ruler) would have to employ a different set of norms from his predecessors. A prudent statesman should focus on the current affairs and act accordingly.[13]

The idea that policies should be adjusted to specific circumstances was not controversial in the Warring States-period thought, when the understanding of profound changes and the need to adapt to them was shared by thinkers of different intellectual affiliations (Vogelsang 2023 and Chap. 12, this volume; cf. Kern 2000: 170–74). But Han Fei's approach is by far more sophisticated than just recommending simple adaptation:

> 古者丈夫不耕，草木之實足食也；婦人不織，禽獸之皮足衣也。不事力而養足，人民少而財有餘，故民不爭。是以厚賞不行、重罰不用而民自治。今人有五子不為多，子又有五子，大父未死而有二十五孫；是以人民眾而貨財寡，事力勞而供養薄，故民爭。雖倍賞累罰而不免於亂。

> In ancient times, men did not plow, [because] fruits of herbs and trees sufficed for food; women did not weave, [because] the skins of birds and beasts sufficed for clothes. Without wasting their force, they had enough to nourish themselves; the people were few while

---

[13] For infrequent positive invocations of the legacy of the former kings in *Han Feizi*, see Sect. 1.2 above (p. 102).

goods were plenty; hence people did not compete. Therefore, no rich rewards were bestowed, no severe punishments used, but the people were ordered by themselves. Nowadays, five children are not considered too many, and each child also has five children; the grandfather is still alive, and he already has twenty-five grandchildren. Therefore, the people are plenty while commodities and goods are few; people work laboriously, but provisions are scanty; hence the people compete. Even if [the ruler] multiplies rewards and piles on punishments, he will not avoid calamity. (*Han Feizi* 49.2; Chen 2000: 1087–88)

Han Fei introduces here the crucial impact of economic conditions on social mores. Primeval idyll was possible in an underpopulated society, when a favorable land-man ratio ensured affluence without much effort. Yet in the current situation of extreme overpopulation—from which Han Fei's home country of Han suffered more than most of its neighbors (Pines Forthcoming)—the resultant dearth of commodities generated struggles and contest that could not be reined in without coercion from above. Moral behavior was, therefore, not intrinsic to humans but was influenced primarily by their material conditions. Ancient paragons of magnanimity such as Yao 堯, who allegedly yielded his power to Shun 舜, or Yu 禹, who personally toiled to subdue the floods, behaved selflessly because in their age the position of rulership was not associated with prestige or benefits. But this is not the case any longer:

輕辭天子，非高也，勢薄也；爭土橐，[14]非下也，權重也。

People relinquished the position of the Son of Heaven not because they were high-minded, but because the advantages [of this position] were light; [now] people struggle for sinecures in the government not because they are low-minded, but because the power [of this position] is weighty. (*Han Feizi* 49.3; Chen 2000: 1088–89)

Much like in the case of the *Book of Lord Shang* (Chap. 1, pp. 32–34, this volume) Han Fei's understanding of the interrelations between human morality and economic conditions curiously resembles Karl Marx's famous dictum, "It is not the consciousness of men that determines their existence, but their social existence that determines their consciousness" (Marx [1859] 2010: 263). This understanding has immediate implications. Moral means of rule were appropriate to the ages of relevant affluence and limited social contest, but they are no longer suitable: "benevolence and righteousness had its use in antiquity but are not useful in our times" 仁義用於古不用於今也 (*Han Feizi* 49.4; Chen 2000: 1092). Han Fei concludes:

上古競於道德，中世逐於智謀，當今爭於氣力。

In high antiquity people were competing in the Way and virtue, in mid-antiquity they were vying with one another in intelligence and strategies, and in our times they contest in fighting spirit and force. (*Han Feizi* 49.4; Chen 2000: 1092)

Han Fei's insistence on the priority of the present over the past could easily discourage interest in history, but this is patently not the case. To the contrary, no single thinker of the Warring States era equals Han Fei in mastery of the past and the multiplicity of its usages in the thinker's ideological constructs. Unlike many opponents

---

[14]Amending 土橐 to 仕托 following Wang 1998: 444.

of the moralizing discourse—such as the authors of *Laozi* and the *Book of Lord Shang*—Han Fei does not eschew exemplary history, which, throughout the Warring States period was primarily an intellectual weapon of moralizing thinkers, viz. the followers of Confucius and Mozi (Pines 2022: 343–44). Instead, in a remarkable display of intellectual audacity and analytical sophistication, Han Fei turns historical lessons upside down. Rather than illustrating the just deserts principle and validating intellectual and moral superiority of paragon rulers and ministers from the past, history teaches precisely what Han Fei wants it to teach: to wit, that everybody is self-interested, that lofty pronouncements cannot be trusted, and that morally upright behavior of today maybe a guise for usurpation of power of tomorrow. These *exempla* permeate numerous chapters of *Han Feizi*, some of which (most notably, 10, 21–23, 30–35) are nothing but collection of historical anecdotes narrated so as to validate Han Fei's ideological needs.

Han Fei's resort to historical *exempla* is not exceptional by itself; actually, it was fairly common in the Warring States-period philosophical writings (Schaberg 2011; Vogelsang 2007: 223–63; Goldin 2008). What distinguishes *Han Feizi* from his opponents, though, aside from the huge number of these *exempla*, are two points. One is his readiness to question the commonly accepted didactic bottom line of well-known historical anecdotes. In the four "Objections" or "Problematizing" ("Nan" 難) chapters (36–39), the author narrates 28 anecdotes, following which he questions the anecdote's commonly accepted didactic message and presents a different interpretation of the lesson that could be gleaned from the narrated story. This questioning, which is highly unusual in the anecdotal genre as a whole,[15] demonstrates that any historical narrative can be understood in more than one fashion and there is no single ready didactic conclusion from the past. As noted by David Schaberg, "This work's treatment of anecdotes is […] both the pinnacle of historical argumentation and, in a sense, the undoing of it" (Schaberg 2011: 405). Han Fei's sophistication peaks in the fourth of the "Objections" chapter, in which he demonstrates superb knowledge of *Zuozhuan* and its complex narratives. There the questioning of the common didactic message is based on discussing long-term historical developments that commonly eschew the attention of the anecdotes' protagonists or later observers. The chapter, which may be dubbed the earliest example of *Zuozhuan* exegesis (Pines 2022), is the testimony to Han Fei's position as, arguably, China's earliest historical critic.[16]

The second peculiarity of Han Fei's engagement with the past is the frequent employment of ironic or manipulative history, which places Han Fei closer to *Zhuangzi* 莊子 than to later historical exegetes. The background for this playful

---

[15] Normally, debates about the anecdote's lesson were conducted subtly, by retelling an anecdote with new emphases rather than openly questioning its bottom line. See examples in Van Els and Queen 2017.

[16] For the emergence of historical criticism in early China, see Vogelsang 2007: 264–90. In later publications (e.g., in Chap. 12, this volume), Vogelsang changed his designation from "critical" to "sequential" history.

engagement with the past is Han Fei's awareness that Confucians and Mohists' resort to historical arguments is itself manipulative:

孔子、墨子俱道堯、舜，而取舍不同，皆自謂真堯、舜，堯、舜不復生，將誰使定儒、墨之誠乎？……今乃欲審堯、舜之道於三千歲之前，意者其不可必乎！無參驗而必之者，愚也；弗能必而據之者，誣也。故明據先王，必定堯、舜者，非愚則誣也。

    [Followers] of Confucius and Mozi all speak about Yao and Shun, but they differ in what they accept and what they reject; yet each of them claims himself to be a real follower of Yao and Shun. But Yao and Shun cannot come back to life, so who would settle who is right: Confucians or Mohists? .... Now, if we are to examine the three-thousand-year-old way of Yao and Shun, we understand that it is impossible to determine it indubitably. He who claims certain knowledge without examining the issue is a fool; he who relies on things which are impossible to ascertain is an impostor. Thus, those who openly adduce the former monarchs as evidence and claim they can determine indubitably [the way of] Yao and Shun, are either fools or impostors. (*Han Feizi* 50.1; Chen 2000: 1124–25 ["Xian xue"])

Having dismissed the possibility to ascertain the ways of the former kings, Han Fei at times opts to ridicule his opponents by inventing counternarratives that question the paragons' morality. Suffice it to demonstrate this by a short story.

湯以伐桀，而恐天下言己為貪也，因乃讓天下於務光。而恐務光之受之也，乃使人說務光曰：「湯殺君而欲傳惡聲于子，故讓天下於子。」務光因自投於河。

    [Shang's founder,] Tang, because he attacked [the Xia tyrant,] Jie, was afraid that All under Heaven would say that he was greedy for power, so he yielded All under Heaven to Wuguang. But then he was afraid that Wuguang would accept the offer, so he sent an emissary to Wuguang, advising him: "Tang has killed the ruler and wants to pass on the bad reputation to you. That is why he yielded All under Heaven to you." Wuguang thereupon threw himself into the [Yellow] River. (*Han Feizi* 22.1; Chen 2000: 461 ["Shui lin shang" 說林上])

In just a few phrases Han Fei succeeds in ridiculing everybody. The righteous founder of the Shang, Tang the Successful 成湯, is a greedy power seeker. An abdication gesture—hailed in many other texts as an epitome of the paragons' selflessness (Pines 2005; cf. Allan 2016)—is nothing but a cynical manipulation. And a purist who commits suicide just to prevent his reputation from being sullied appears doubly ridiculous. The story, which resembles similarly cynical manipulations of the past in *Zhuangzi* (e.g. in the chapter "Yielding Kingship" ["Rang wang" 讓王], analyzed in Pines 2005: 284–85), was either outright invented or at the very least dramatically revised by Han Fei to fit his agenda. Its reliability does not matter: just as moralizers invent stories about, e.g. Shun's filiality and Tang's righteousness,[17] so counter-moralizers can invent the stories of their own. The bottom line is that all historical narratives about remote past are "fake histories" and should not be trusted.

---

[17] The clearest example of this creativity with regard to the life details of the paragons are the stories scattered throughout *Mengzi*. It is possible that segments of *Han Feizi*'s historical criticism (especially in chapter 51, "Loyalty and filiality") are directed specifically against Mengzi; yet detailed discussion will await another study.

2.3 Human Nature

History constantly evolves and requires adaption to changing circumstances; but there are also some constant factors that should be taken into consideration. The most notable of these is perennial human covetousness for riches and fame. Whereas this covetousness does not necessarily lead to violent competition (see the discussion of primeval idyll on pp. 110–111), in Han Fei's contemporary world, this is the major factor that should be considered by policymakers.

Han Fei's views of human nature (or, more precisely, human motivations) has been discussed in the past (e.g., Jiang 2000: 127–72; Sato 2013a) and is analyzed by Harris (Chap. 10, this volume); hence I shall be brief here. In a nutshell, *Han Feizi* echoes the *Book of Lord Shang* and *Shenzi* 慎子 fragments first, in asserting that humans are self-interested and, second, that this self-interest is not inimical to political order but, rather, should serve as its foundation:

> 好利惡害，夫人之所有也。賞厚而信，人輕敵矣；刑重而必，人不北矣。長行徇上，數百不一人。喜利畏罪，人莫不然。
>
> Liking benefit and disliking harm is something that all humans have in common. If rewards are generous and reliable, then people will think little of the enemy. If punishments are heavy and ineluctable, then the people will not flee. As for dying for their superior on an extended march, there is not one among a hundred [who has such a motivation]. Yet being fond of benefits and fearful of incurring criminal guilt—everybody will do so. (*Han Feizi* forthcoming: 37.7.2; Chen 2000: 893 ["Nan er" 難二])

The point is clear. Humans think only of personal wellbeing. In the above citation their focus is on seeking benefits; but elsewhere, as in the *Book of Lord Shang*, the quest for a good name (meaning both reputation and enhanced social status; Pines 2020c) is considered as equally important (see pp. 133–134 below). The state is supposed to use this self-interest as a lever to direct the people toward the desired behavior (in the above case, participation in military campaigns). The entire legal and administrative system should be based on human dispositions:

> 人情莫不出其死力以致其所欲；而好惡者，上之所制也。民者好利祿而惡刑罰。
>
> The human disposition is such that they will all do their utmost in order to achieve what they desire. As for their likes and dislikes, these are controlled by the ruler. The people like benefits and emoluments and detest punishments and penalties. (*Han Feizi* 55.1; Chen 2000: 1184 ["Zhi fen" 制分])

This intrinsic link between humans' self-interest and the political system leads Han Fei to odd—and highly provocative—claims against moral purists. The text admits that a few exceptional individuals can transcend their self-interest and behave loftily, but considers this a socially negative phenomenon: "These are called people who cannot be made to follow orders" 此之謂不令之民也 (*Han Feizi* 44.3; Chen 2000: 969 ["Shuo yi" 說疑]).[18] In one of the most provocative anecdotes in the entire text, Han Fei tells approvingly how the sagacious founder of the state of Qi,

---

[18] Note that the compound *bu ling* 不令 has a second meaning of "not good"; Han Fei clearly plays on both meanings.

Grand Duke Wang 太公望, executed two lofty recluses who were neither seeking benefits nor social status, and sought disengagement from the state: "These two call themselves the worthy *shi* (士, men of service) of our generation, but they are of no use to their ruler" 已自謂以為世之賢士而不為主用; they are like thoroughbreds that cannot be steered left or right. "That is why I executed them" 是以誅之 (*Han Feizi* 34.1.7; Chen 2000: 770 ["Wai chushuo you shang" 外儲說右上]). The state is not in need of exceptionalities, but rather of regular self-interested subjects.

Scholars often discuss Han Fei's view of human dispositions in the context of the influence of his putative teacher, Xunzi. As Sato (2013a) and Harris (Chap. 10, this volume) demonstrate, this discussion may be misleading: Han Fei's views are much more indebted to earlier *fa* scholars than to Xunzi. Yet it is useful to juxtapose Han Fei and Xunzi so as to highlight the single most important difference between them (and by extension between the *fa* tradition and Confucianism as a whole). Whatever Confucians thought about humans' innate dispositions, they all agreed that human morality can be improved through self-cultivation and that morally upright and cultivated "noble men" (*junzi* 君子) should form the state's sociopolitical elite. Han Fei could not disagree more. Elite members, be these high ministers, members of the ruler's entourage, or loftily speaking "noble men"—all are motivated by self-interest only. The universal selfishness (*si* 私) is the quintessential feature of political life. There are exceptions, to be sure, but they are too rare to be considered for the functioning political system. The fundamental premise of the ruler should be that he is surrounded not by loyal servants but by mortal enemies. Han Fei explains:

> 千金之家，其子不仁，人之急利甚也。桓公，五伯之上也，爭國而殺其兄，其利大也。臣主之間，非兄弟之親也。劫殺之功，制萬乘而享大利，則羣臣孰非陽虎也?
>
> If, in a house with a thousand pieces of gold, the sons are not benevolent [to each other], that is because man's urge for profit is extremely strong. Lord Huan of Qi (r. 685–643 BCE) was the supreme among the Five Hegemons, but when struggling for control in the state, he killed his elder brother. That was because the profit involved was large. Between a minister and a ruler, there is not a relation as close as that between elder and younger brother. When the thing achieved through murder and arrogation of power is to command ten thousand chariots-large [state] and enjoy huge profit, then of all the ministers who is not a [notorious usurper] Yang Hu? (*Han Feizi* 39.2.2; Chen 2000: 928 ["Nan si" 難四])

Once again, the cynicism is astounding (cf. pp. 103–104 above). The quest for profit outweighs anything—be it kinship ties or ministerial obligations. The ruler is surrounded by manipulators and traitors. Every minister is a potential usurper. Elsewhere Han Fei clarifies: every powerful family wants to amass more power; every official seeks benefit for himself; any lofty advice can be a disguise for a carefully planned usurpation.[19] Therefore, Han Fei speaks approvingly of an irreverent ancient saying, "The leper feels pity for the king" 厲憐王 (*Han Feizi* 14.8; Chen 2000: 297). This explains Goldin's summary of Han Feizi's political stance: "one might imagine a counselor speaking before a newly crowned king. 'You are the king!' he says. 'Congratulations—everyone wants to kill you now. Listen to me, and

---

[19] See, e.g., *Han Feizi* 6.2 and 7.1; Chen 2000: 91–92 and 120–21 ("You du" and "Er bing" 二柄).

you might survive'" (Goldin 2020: 202). It is time now to shift our attention to how the ruler should be rescued from the plotters and how should the polity prosper under these gloomy conditions.

3 Political Recommendations

The question of how to manage a society torn apart by conflicting interests is no less relevant today than it was in Han Fei's times. For *Han Feizi* the answer is clear—it is reducing personal impact on policy making by relegating everything to impartial standards and norms. Only this can ensure that the polity's common interests (*gong* 公) are served, whereas selfishness and private interests (*si* 私) of major political actors are reined in. Impartiality (also defined as *gong*) can be considered the supreme moral value for Han Fei and his fellow *fa* thinkers (T. Jiang 2021: 267 ff.). It is also the only practical means to ensure the success and very survival of the ruler and the polity.

The term *gong* is controversial. Liu Zehua (2003: 332–73) and Paul R. Goldin (2020: 204–05) both noted that normally the term refers to the ruler ("duke, lord"), from which one can infer that the "common" interests of the polity are actually coterminous to the personal interests of the ruler. This is a correct observation but it should be qualified. In principle, the interests of the sovereign and the polity are indeed identical; Han Fei shared the common conviction of contemporaneous think-ers that without a powerful ruler, the polity will simply fall apart (Liu 2000; Pines 2009: 13–111). This does not mean however, slavishly catering to the ruler's per-sonal interests. Han Fei—perhaps more than any other thinker—was painstakingly aware that the ruler is not the most brilliant individual. His shortsightedness, intem-perate behavior, personal favoritism, and intellectual limitations—all may lead him astray, causing his own selfish or private (*si*) inclinations to ruin the common (*gong*) interests. Hence, the calls to impose impartial standards and norms were aimed not only at reining in malevolent ministers and unruly subjects but also to monitor the ruler himself. As we shall see below, the ruler remained the weakest link in Han Fei's political construct.

3.1 Rule by Impartial Standards

The appeals to the priority of impartial standards over individual abilities of politi-cal actors permeate *Han Feizi*. The text uses several terms to depict these standards, including "gauges and measures" (*duliang* 度量), "scales and weights" (*quanheng* 權衡), "ink-line" (*sheng* 繩) and the like (Graziani, Chap. 13, this volume). Yet by far the most important *terminus technicus* is *fa* 法. This is a notoriously polysemic term. In *Han Feizi*, it can refer to the cosmic patterns of the Way (as in the extract cited on p. 106 above), but also to minute legal regulations the reading of which puts a ruler to sleep (*Han Feizi* 32.5.7; Chen 2000: 706 ["Wai chushuo zuo shang 外儲 說左上]). It can refer to laws, standards, methods, models, and political institutions. *Fa* can be established (*li fa* 立法) by the ruler (*Han Feizi* 19.7; Chen 2000: 362 ["Shi xie" 飭邪]), but also by outstanding ministers (*Han Feizi* 34.3.4; Chen 2000: 789 ["Wai chushuo you shang"]), including by Han Fei himself (*Han Feizi* 42.2.1; Chen 2000: 955 ["Wen Tian"]); elsewhere, *fa* is directly associated with such "law-giving" (or institutions-reforming) ministers as Guan Zhong 管仲 (d. 645 BCE) and Shang Yang (*Han Feizi* 49.12; Chen 2000: 1111 ["Wu du"]). This heterogeneity should be taken into consideration once we analyze the usages of *fa* in *Han Feizi*: quite often the text plays between two or three meanings of the term, making any attempt to fix a uniform translation untenable (cf. Liu 2020: 1–24). This said, a few passages offer a good introduction for the primary meanings of *fa* in *Han Feizi*:

申子曰：「法者，見功而與賞，因能而受官。……」
　　Shenzi [i.e., Shen Buhai] said: "As for *fa*, it means bestowing rewards according to actual merits, conferring appointments according to one's abilities. …" (*Han Feizi* 32.5.11; Chen 2000: 708 ["Wai chushuo zuo shang"])

法者，編著之圖籍，設之於官府，而布之於百姓者也。……是以明主言法，則境內 卑賤莫不聞知也。
　　As for *fa*, it is compiled and written down on charts and documents, deposited in the repositories of the offices and promulgated to the hundred clans. … Therefore, when the clear-sighted ruler speaks of *fa*, everyone within his frontiers, including the lowly and base, will hear and understand it. (*Han Feizi* 38.8.2; Chen 2000: 922–23 ["Nan san" 難三])

法者，憲令著於官府，刑罰必於民心，賞存乎慎法，而罰加乎姦令者 也。此臣之所師也。
　　As for *fa*, it means that regulations and ordinances are displayed in the official archives, that punishments and fines appear inevitable to the people's minds, that rewards are meted on those who are cautious in regard to the laws, and punishments are applied to those who offend against ordinances. This is what the ministers take as their guiding authority. (*Han Feizi* 43.1; Chen 2000: 957 ["Ding fa"])

In the first of these citations, the definition of *fa* offered by Shen Buhai is relatively narrow and focuses on administrative regulations, what Goldin defines as "impersonal administrative technique of determining rewards and punishments in accordance with a subject's true merit" (Goldin 2011: 92; cf. Creel 1974: 135–62). Two other cases speak of *fa* as something much broader—laws that regulate the life of the "hundred clans" and are related to the broad array of "regulations and ordinances" and "rewards and punishments." These laws should be transparent and well understood by the masses. The point of the laws' transparency, including the importance of official archives as a means to ensure broad legal knowledge of the population unmistakably relates these two statements to the discussion in chapter 26 ("Fixing Divisions" ["Ding fen" 定分]) of the *Book of Lord Shang* (that chapter is an all likelihood contemporaneous with *Han Feizi*; Pines 243–44). That legal knowledge was broadly promulgated in the state of Qin (and probably throughout the

Warring States-period world) can be confirmed from other sources (Korolkov 2011; Sanft 2014: 140–142). In this context, therefore, the meaning of *fa* can be translated as "legal rules as a whole" or "the law" (cf. Lau and Lüdke, Chap. 8, this volume). It can be surmised that *fa* refers primarily to transparent and impartial norms that should regulate sociopolitical life in the state in general and within the administrative apparatus in particular. As such, in Han Fei's eyes it becomes a panacea for all social ills:

故矯上之失，詰下之邪，治亂決繆，絀羨齊非，一民之軌，莫如法。

For correcting the oversights of superiors, for prosecuting the wickedness of subordinates, for bringing order to chaos and sorting out tangles, for removing the superfluous and evening out the wrong, and for uniting the tracks of the people, nothing is as good as *fa*. (*Han Feizi* 6.5, Chen 2000: 111 ["You du"])

故治民無常，唯治為法。法與時轉則治，治與世宜則有功。

Thus there is no constant [way] to order the people—only through laws (*fa*) can they be ordered. When laws are modified according to the changing times, then there is orderly rule; when orderly rule fits to the current generation then there is success. (*Han Feizi* 54.2; Chen 2000: 1178 ["Xin du" 心度])

Why *fa* is so important? It is because this is the best alternative to the habitual appeal to the incumbents' personal abilities and moral qualities as advocated by Confucians. This appeal is naïve at best, or, worse, is outright manipulative. First, those who call upon having moral people at the top do not understand the nature of political authority. This authority is determined primarily by one's "positional power" (*shi* 勢) rather than by one's intelligence and morality. Han Fei famously contrasts the failure of Confucius—"the sage under Heaven" 天下聖人—to attract many followers with the success of Confucius's mediocre employer, Lord Ai of Lu 魯哀公 (r. 494–468 BCE), who "when he sat facing south [as appropriate to the sovereign] and ruled over his state, nobody within the borders dared not be his servant" 南面君國，境內之民莫敢不臣. Here and elsewhere Han Fei reiterates: "The people surely submit to positional power" 民者固服於勢 and to it alone (*Han Feizi* 49.6; Chen 2000: 1096 ["Wu du"]).[20]

The second reason for dismissing the Confucian focus on the appointees' qualities was outlined above. In society driven by self-interest, reliance on loyal and selfless ministers is self-deluding. As Han Fei explains:

今貞信之士不盈於十，而境內之官以百數，必任貞信之士，則人不足官。……故明主之道，一法而不求智，固術而不慕信，故法不敗，而羣官無姦詐矣。

Today, there are no more than ten honest and trustworthy men of service, but there are hundreds of offices within the boundaries. If you insist on exclusively appointing honest and faithful men of service, then there will be not enough people for the official positions. … Thus, the Way of the clear-sighted sovereign is to unify *fa* and not to seek the intelligent; to solidify techniques of rule and not to esteem the trustworthy. As a result, *fa* will not be violated, and there will be neither vile nor deceit among the officials. (*Han Feizi* 49.11; Chen 2000: 1109 ["Wu du"])

---

[20] The point is elaborated in full in chapter 40, "Objections to positional power" ("Nan shi" 難勢) (Pines 2020b).

In the above extract, the focus on *fa* and techniques of rule (*shu* 術) is relatively narrow: it refers primarily to the employment and control of officials. Insofar as these officials (with a few exceptions) are committed *en masse* to serving their private interests, the ruler should avoid placing trust in them. Nor should he trust his own abilities. The third reason for prioritizing impartial norms is that they compensate for the ruler's personal inadequacy. This inadequacy is a given: having limited mental abilities and limited access to information, the ruler would never be able to overcome the tricks of his underlings unless he relies on *fa*:

> 夫為人主而身察百官，則日不足，力不給。且上用目，則下飾觀；上用耳，則下飾聲；上用慮，則下繁辭。先王以三者為不足，故舍己能而因法數，審賞罰。先王之所守要，故法省而不侵。……故治不足而日有餘，上之任勢使然也。
>
> If the sovereign personally inspects his hundred officials, the whole day will not be enough; his strength will not suffice. Moreover, when the superior uses his eyesight, the underlings embellish what he sees; when he uses his hearing, the underlings embellish what he hears; when he uses his contemplation, the underlings elaborate their words. The former kings considered these three [methods] as insufficient: hence they cast away personal abilities and relied on *fa* and [administrative] methods, examining rewards and punishments. The former kings preserved the essentials [of rule]; hence the laws (*fa*) were clearly understood and not violated. … Thus, there was more than enough daytime to achieve orderly rule: it was because the superior relied on their positional power. (*Han Feizi* 6.4; Chen 2000: 107 ["You du"])

The ruler's positional power allows him to employ the full plethora of laws or standards (*fa*), methods (*shu* 數) and techniques of rule (*shu* 術) that will thwart the underlings' machinations and ease the sovereign's life. This system of impartial norms also relieves him of an unbearable personal burden and reduces (if not annuls) the need for individual perspicacity. Against this backdrop it becomes clear why Han Fei believes in impartial standards and laws as the best means to safeguard the ruler's authority and ensure political stability in general.

One final point that clarifies the advantages of impartial norms is that, even if not ideal, they are predicated on average human beings and hence are broadly applicable. Han Fei clarifies:

> 立法，非所以備曾、史也，所以使庸主能止盜跖也；為符，非所以豫尾生也，所以使眾人不相謾也。不獨恃比干之死節，不幸亂臣之無詐也；恃怯之所能服，握庸主之所易守。
>
> *Fa* is established not to prepare for [moral paragons like] Zengzi and Scribe [Yu], but to enable a mediocre sovereign to stop the likes of [the ultimate villain,] Robber Zhi. Tallies are introduced not to prepare for the likes of [a proverbially faithful man,] Wei Sheng, but to cause the masses not to cheat each other. Do not simply rely on [the righteous martyr] Bigan's dying for his probity; do not succumb to thinking wishfully that rebellious ministers are without deceit. Rely on what a meek man can tame; hold fast to what a mediocre sovereign easily protects. (*Han Feizi* 26.4; Chen 2000: 536 ["Shou dao" 守道])

This is one of notable instances in which *Han Feizi* openly discusses the ruler's expected mediocrity (see more in Sect. 3.3 below). The passage also clarifies with much candor the ultimate advantage of the system of rule by impartial standards and laws. This system may not be fitting to outstanding personalities, but it is applicable to average leaders and average subjects; it is based on something that "ordinary men and women will understand clearly" 夫婦所明知 (*Han Feizi* 49.11; Chen 2000: 1109 ["Wu du"]). A good system should be predicated neither on capable rulers, nor on morally upright ministers, nor on valiant and devoted subjects. It should be functional under mediocrities and that is why it will be sustainable.

3.2 The Ruler and his Ministers

The chapter "Defining Standards" (or "Fixing Laws") of *Han Feizi* juxtaposes the ideas of Shang Yang and Shen Buhai. Famously, it asserts that Shang Yang was too focused on *fa*, whereas Shen Buhai was too preoccupied with techniques of rule, *shu* 術. Although Han Fei's summary is not necessarily accurate (as Yu Zhong, Chap. 2 in this volume demonstrates, Shen Buhai was concerned primarily with *fa*), it encapsulates correctly the major difference between Han Fei's two famous predecessors. Shang Yang's ideas were conducive to the establishment of the state's control over society and directing the populace to agriculture cum warfare, but he (and other contributors to the *Book of Lord Shang*) paid only a scanty interest to the problems of governing the political apparatus. This was the major contribution of Shen Buhai, and also may be considered Han Fei's own major input into the *fa* theory. Han Fei's observation, "the sage orders the officials, not the people" 聖人治吏不治民 (*Han Feizi* 35.4.1; Chen 2000: 829 ["Wai chushuo you xia" 外儲說右下]) can be considered a real breakthrough. No problem can be dealt with adequately unless the ruler possesses an efficient and responsive bureaucratic apparatus.

Dealing with the bureaucrats poses two problems. First, Han Fei notes that the officials will normally do whatever possible to cater to their selfish needs, bringing about dereliction of duty, corruption, and the resultant weakening of governability. Second, and more peculiar to *Han Feizi*, the text repeatedly warns that the real problem with the officials is not just that of corruption and inefficiency. Rather, powerful officials are bent on subverting the sovereign's power and even outright usurping the throne. A prudent ruler should adequately deal with both—indirect and direct—threats. To do so, he must pay utmost attention to the "techniques of rule" (*shu* 術). The term *shu* is explained as follows:

七術：一曰、眾端參觀，二曰、必罰明威，三曰、信賞盡能，四曰、一聽責下，五曰、疑詔詭使，六曰、挾知而問，七曰、倒言反事。此七者，主之所用也。

The seven techniques are: First: survey and compare all the various views on a matter; second: make punishments ineluctable and majestic authority clear; third: make rewards reliable and make people use their abilities to the full; four: listen to proposals one by one, and hold the subordinates responsible [for proposals]; five: issue confusing edicts and make wily dispositions; six: keep your knowledge to yourself and ask advice; seven: say the opposite of what you mean and do the opposite of what you intend. These seven are what the ruler should use. (*Han Feizi* 30.0.0; Chen 2000: 560; ["Nei chushuo shang" 內儲說上])

The seven techniques can be divided into two groups. The first four present a series of bureaucratic devices aimed at monitoring the officials' performance. Of primary importance in this context is the ruler's control of rewards and punishments, which are identified in chapter 7 as the "Two Levers" ("Er bing" 二柄) through which the ruler regulates his underlings. These first four techniques resonate with another definition of *shu* in *Han Feizi*: "Technique is bestowing office on the basis of concrete responsibilities, demanding performance on the basis of titles, wielding the levers of life and death, and examining the abilities of the ministers" 術者，因任而授官，循名而責實，操殺生之柄，課羣臣之能者也 (*Han Feizi* 43.1.2; Chen 2000: 957 ["Ding fa"]). The latter definition adds two more dimensions to *shu*, namely the ruler's control over appointments and examination of the ministers' abilities. Taken together, these six aspects of *shu* are all reasonable devices that can be adequately utilized in modern management. Nonetheless, even these ostensibly innocent bureaucratic means can serve sinister needs. Before we go into the last three of the "seven techniques," let us focus on one of Han Fei's more detailed discussions about the ruler's control over the bureaucracy. The chapter "Two Levers" explains:

> 人主將欲禁姦，則審合刑名；刑名者，言異事也。為人臣者陳而言，君以其言授之事，專以其事責其功。功當其事，事當其言，則賞；功不當其事，事不當其言，則罰。……故明主之畜臣，臣不得越官而有功，不得陳言而不當。越官則死，不當則罪。[21] 則羣臣不得朋黨相為矣。
>
> A sovereign who wants to suppress treachery must examine and match performance (the form, *xing* 形) and title (the name, *ming* 名). Performance and title refer to the difference between the proposal and the task. The minister lays out his proposal; the ruler assigns him the task according to his proposal, and solely on the basis of the task determines [the minister's] merit. When the merit matches the task, and the task matches the proposal, [the minister] is rewarded; when the merit does not match the task and the task does not match the proposal, he is penalized. … Thus, when the clear-sighted sovereign nourishes his ministers, the minister should not claim merit by overstepping [the duties of] his office, nor should he present the proposal that does not match [his task]. One who oversteps his office's [duties] dies; one who[se proposal] does not match [the task] is punished; then ministers are unable to form cabals and cliques. (*Han Feizi* 7.2; Chen 2000 126–27)

This is one of several sections of *Han Feizi* that elucidates the principle of "performance and titles" (*xingming* 形名)—one of the crucial elements in Han Fei's administrative thought (cf. Wang Pei and Indracollo, Chaps. 20 and 14, this volume). Goldin (2020: 214) compares this principle to the modern call for bids. A minister makes the proposal on the basis of his official duties; his actual performance is then matched against his proposal and the result (reward or punishment) is determined accordingly. Whether or not one accepts the logic of this management style, it is safe to say that in principle it is not controversial. However, it is framed above within the context of the ruler's struggle against ministerial treachery and against cabals and cliques. This brings us to the second part of Han Fei's "seven techniques" cited above. Techniques five to seven—"issue confusing edicts and make wily

---

[21] Following Chen Qiyou's gloss (Chen 2000: 129–30), I omit a sentence here that appears to be an old gloss misplaced into the text.

dispositions; keep your knowledge to yourself and ask advice; say the opposite of what you mean and do the opposite of what you intend"—do not make good bureaucratic sense. Surely none of us would welcome these techniques employed in our company or university. Why does Han Fei recommend these cunning methods? Why does he insist that in contrast to the transparency of *fa*, the techniques of rule should be secret? See the follows:

術者，藏之於胸中，以偶眾端而潛禦群臣者也。故法莫如顯，而術不欲見。

As for techniques of rule, they are hidden in the breast. It is that through which you match up all the various ends and from your secret place steer the ministers. Therefore, laws are best when they are clear, whereas techniques should not be seen. (*Han Feizi* 38.8.2; Chen 2000: 922–23 ["Nan 3"])

The reason behind this secrecy is that the techniques of rule serve not just to help the ruler perfect the bureaucratic mechanism, but, more urgently, to safeguard him against closest aides. Here comes one of the most controversial segments of *Han Feizi* thought. No other text is so adamant in its repeated warnings to the ruler: beware of everybody; especially of your ministers. For instance, "Extolling Authority" chapter postulates:

黃帝有言曰：「上下一日百戰。」下匿其私，用試其上；上操度量，以割其下。故度量之立，主之寶也；黨與之具，臣之寶也。臣之所不弒其君者，黨與不具也。故上失扶寸，下得尋常。有國之君，不大其都；有道之臣，不貴其家。有道之君，不貴其臣；貴之富之，彼將代之。

The Yellow Thearch said: "A hundred battles a day are fought between the superior and his underlings." The underlings conceal their selfish [interests], trying to test their superior; the superior employs gauges and measures to restrict the underlings. Hence when gauges and measures are established, they are the sovereign's treasure; when the cliques and cabals are formed, they are the ministers' treasure. If a minister does not murder his ruler, this is because the cliques and cabals are not formed yet. Hence, when the superior loses half-inches and inches, the underlings gain yards and double-yards. The ruler who possesses the capital does not enlarge secondary cities;[22] the minister who possesses the Way does not esteem his kin; the ruler who possesses the Way does not ennoble his ministers. If he ennobles and enriches them, they will replace him. (*Han Feizi* 8.8; Chen 2000: 170 ["Yang quan"])

Han Fei's conclusion is amazing, on a par with the observation cited above that every minister is a potential usurper (p. 115). The ministers are by definition the ruler's mortal enemies. If they did not carry out the assassination, it is only because they did not prepare adequately, or, as Han Fei explains elsewhere, because the ruler was prudent enough to outwit them through the proper application of the techniques of rule (see, e.g., *Han Feizi* 33.2.3; Chen 2000: 730 "Wai chushuo zuo xia" 外儲說左下). Elsewhere the text identifies ministers as tigers who are ready to devour the sovereign the moment his vigilance fades (*Han Feizi* 8.7 and 5.2; Chen 2000: 164

[22]The potential of a secondary city to rival the capital and become the base for a rebellion was recognized already in *Zuozhuan*, which contains several warnings about that (e.g., *Zuozhuan*, Yin 1.4a; Huan 18.3; Zhao 11.10).

and 74–75 ["Yang quan" and "Zhu dao"]).[23] This is not a consistent view in *Han Feizi*; a few chapters laud the model ministers, such as Shang Yang, who were able to transcend their selfishness and committed themselves fully to the strengthening of the state. These model ministers are part of a broader group of "men of service skilled in laws and techniques of rule" (*fashu zhi shi* 法術之士) with whom Han Fei probably identified himself (Pines 2013b: 82–84). Yet these loyal and committed ministers appear just in a few chapters of the text (mostly, 11, 13, and 14), whereas the topos of plotting and scheming ministers permeates the text in its entirety and may well serve as its leitmotif.

The assumption of perennial enmity between the rulers and their ministers explains some of the most questionable aspects of Han Fei's recommendations to the ruler, such as "issue confusing edicts" or "say the opposite of what you mean." At times Han Fei is carried out by his own rhetoric, proposing even more deplorable ways of dealing with the ruler's rivals:

生害事，死傷名，則行飲食；不然，而與其讎；此謂除陰姦也。

    If leaving them alive harms your undertakings, yet killing them ruins your reputation, then do it with [poisoned] food and drink. Otherwise, hand them over to their enemies. This is called removing the treacherous. (*Han Feizi* 48.3; Chen 2000: 1054 ["Ba jing" 八經])

This is one of the most appalling statements even in *Han Feizi*, which does not eschew provocation (see more in Song, Chap. 9, this volume). But readers should be reminded that it does not represent the crux of Han Fei's recommendations. Reining in the ministers is normally done in a more acceptable way. Thus, having compared the ministers to the ruler-devouring tigers, Han Fei explains: "when the application of laws and the punishments is reliable, the tigers will be transformed into humans, reverting to their true state" 法刑苟信，虎化為人，復反其真 (*Han Feizi* 8.7; Chen 2000: 164 ["Yang quan"]). In the final account, ministers are human beings, and they can even serve the ruler well. All that is needed is to remember that the ruler-minister relations are based not on devotion and loyalty but on pure calculation of benefit:

且臣盡死力以與君市，君垂爵祿以與臣市。君臣之際，非父子之親也，計數之所出也。君有道，則臣盡力而姦不生；無道，則臣上塞主明而下成私。

    A minister brings to the rulers' market [his ability] to exhaust his force to the point of death; a ruler brings to the ministers' market [his power] to bestow ranks and emoluments. Ruler-minister relations are based not on the intimacy of father and child, but on the calculation [of benefits]. When the ruler possesses the Way, the ministers exert their force, and the treachery is not born; when he lacks the Way, the ministers impede the ruler's clear-sightedness above, and accomplish their private [interests] below. (*Han Feizi* 36.3.2; Chen 2000: 851–52 "Nan 難 1")

In society driven by self-interest, the ruler and the ministers can find their modus vivendi. Insofar as the ruler relies on techniques of rule and utilizes the benefits of

---

[23] What is really surprising about these statements is that they can be contrasted with the rarity of ministerial usurpations and assassinations of the rulers in a century and a half that preceded Han Fei's time (Yin 1987: 21; Pines 2013b: 75).

his positional power, in particular his control over rewards and punishments, the ministers will serve him faithfully. They will do it not because they are morally committed to the sovereign or the polity, but as a result of a simple calculation of personal benefit. This is yet another manifestation of the advantage of the rule by impartial standards.

3.3 The Ruler

Han Fei's unequivocal siding with the ruler against the ministers (i.e., the members of Han Fei's own stratum) explains why this thinker was condemned as the defender of "monarchic despotism" and "absolute authoritarianism" (Hsiao 1979: 386, 417). That said, not everybody accepts this verdict. A.C. Graham, for instance, opined that Han Fei's system makes sense only "if seen from the viewpoint of the bureaucrat rather than the man at the top" (Graham 1989: 290–292). The paradoxes of Han Fei's views of rulership have attracted considerable attention in recent years (cf. Pines 2013b; Galvany 2013: 101–05; Graziani 2015; Lewis, Chap. 11, this volume). As noted by many scholars, the ruler figures in *Han Feizi* both as the pivot of the political system whose power should be resolutely defended and as its weakest link. How to explain this paradox?

A possible solution is to distinguish between two levels of the ruler-related discussions in *Han Feizi*. These two levels are present in the vast majority of the Warring States-period political texts, all of which shared the basic ideology of monarchism (for which see Liu 2000; Pines 2009: 25–107). On one level, the ruler's singularity epitomized the idea of political unity, first within a single polity, and, ultimately, in All-under-Heaven. The ruler's undivided authority should guarantee political stability; hence institutional limitations on his power were unanimously rejected. As symbol of unity and stability, the ruler was imagined to be omnipotent, omniscient, omnipresent—in short all but divine. Han Fei's presentation of the ruler as an earthly counterpart of the Way (above, pp. 107–108), or equation of ruler with Heaven (*Han Feizi* 48.1; Chen 2000: 1045 ["Ba jing"])—all belong to this line of argumentation. On a second level, however, the ruler was tacitly understood to be less than perfect human being, who should be guided and corrected so as to prevent him from jeopardizing the political order over which he presided. How to reconcile between these "two bodies" of the ruler (to borrow from Kantorowicz 1957) became the challenging issue not just for the Warring States-period thinkers but for traditional Chinese political culture in general (Pines 2012: 44–75). And nowhere does this tragic contradiction between an abstract and a concrete ruler appears stronger than in *Han Feizi*.

Han Fei's unwavering commitment to the principle of monarchism was elucidated above and does not require further elaboration. Yet as we have already noted, Han Fei at times refers to an average ruler as mediocrity (pp. 119–120). This is not a slip of a brush. Having rejected in principle the idea of non-hereditary power transfer (see more below, Sect. 4, pp. 130–131), Han Fei—as other thinkers of his age—had to acquiesce to the situation in which the top executive, the single most important political actor, was determined by birthright alone. Han Fei is "therefore obliged to integrate the unavoidable fact of absolute submission to an individual who is more often than not totally unqualified for the exercise of supreme command" (Graziani 2015: 162).

Han Fei outlines the problem with utmost clarity in one of the text's most fascinating chapters, 40, "Objections to Positional Power" (Pines 2020b). The chapter starts with presenting Shen Dao's views, according to which the ruler's qualities do not impact his authority; only positional power matters. Then a Confucian-minded objector intervenes. He argues, first, that the ruler's qualities do matter a lot: just as the speed of the chariot is determined not just by the horses' quality, but also by the charioteer's skills, so the functioning of the state is determined by the sovereign's moral and intellectual abilities. Second, he cautions against Shen Dao's sidelining of the rulership's moral aspects. If positional power is granted to bloodthirsty tyrants like Jie 桀 of the Xia dynasty and Zhòu 紂 (d. ca. 1046 BCE) of the Shang, it is like "adding wings to a tiger" 為虎傅翼. "Positional power is what nourishes the heart of a wolf or a tiger, and [allows them to] accomplish the deeds of violence and turmoil. It is the great disaster of All-under-Heaven" 勢者，養虎狼之心，而成暴亂之事者也。此天下之大患也 (*Han Feizi* 40.2.2; Chen 2000: 942).

After this attack comes the response of the counter-objector (presumably, Han Fei himself). The counter-objector admits that positional power can be abused by tyrants, and that its import is less evident in the case of moral paragons such as Yao and Shun. But then comes the major point:

> 且夫堯、舜、桀、紂千世而一出，是比肩隨踵而生也。世之治者不絕於中，吾所以為言勢者，中也。中者，上不及堯、舜，而下亦不為桀、紂。抱法處勢，則治；背法去勢，則亂。
>
> Besides, if Yao and Shun or Jie and Zhòu appear even once in a thousand generations, this is like being born shoulder to shoulder and being treading on each other's heels. [Yet] the average [rulers] cannot be cut out of the generations of orderly rule. The positional power of which I am talking is about the average [rulers]. The average is he who does not reach Yao or Shun above, but also does not behave like Jie or Zhòu below. When one embraces *fa* and acts according to the positional power, there is orderly rule; when one turns his back on *fa* and dismisses positional power, there is turmoil. (*Han Feizi* 40.3.2; Chen 2000: 945)

The author clarifies with utmost candor: his political theory is not designed for exceptionally good or bad individuals but, rather for average rulers. These rulers are not good charioteers, but a well-functioning political system will allow them to attain excellent results.

> 夫良馬固車，五十里而一置，使中手御之，追速致遠，可以及也，而千里可日致也，何必待古之王良乎?
>
> Now good horses and solid vehicles can go fifty *li* before they are given a single rest at a relay station. Even if you make a mediocre person steer them when you pursue someone going fast or is trying to cover a long distance, you can achieve your objective. Why must you wait for [a paragon charioteer] Wang Liang of antiquity? (*Han Feizi* 40.3.3; Chen 2000: 946)

Even a mediocrity can function well if the system is designed accordingly. And most rulers are mediocrities. This observation ostensibly contradicts Han Fei's periodic appeals to the idea of a sage monarch and his much more frequent invocations of the image of a "clear-sighted sovereign" (*ming zhu* 明主). The latter is surely a desideratum. But as an astute observer of history, Han Fei seems to realize that this desideratum is normally unattainable. Not accidentally, most of historical anecdotes scattered throughout *Han Feizi* repeatedly tell about short-sighted and intemperate rulers who dismissed good advice of their aides and brought about disaster on themselves and their states (Graziani 2015). These anecdotes problematize, if not outright subvert the text's habitual sidelining with the ruler against his ministers. They may reflect Han Fei's frustration with his own political construct. How to ensure that the ruler—the absolute focus of political authority—does not misuse or abuse his enormous power?

The answer is again surprising. Having postulated that the ruler should consistently monitor his officials and preserve the levers of rewards and punishments firmly in his hands, the text tries to limit the ruler's impact on quotidian government affairs. The ruler should eschew any expression of personal emotions, cast away personal desires and avoid manifestations of favoritism. The proposed reasons for this self-abnegation vary from one passage to other. Sometimes it is presented as a means to protect the ruler from scheming ministers who would observe his emotions and try to dupe him (see citation on p. 119 above). Alternatively, in the chapter "The Way of the Sovereign," the ruler's depersonalized stance is regarded as fitting the impartial norms of the Way (*Han Feizi* 5.1; Chen 2000: 66). Yet in the same chapter Han Fei immediately turns to a more sinister explanation of the desirability of the ruler's passivity:

明君之道，使智者盡其慮，而君因以斷事，故君不窮於智；賢者敕其材，君因而任之，故君不窮於能；有功則君有其賢，有過則臣任其罪，故君不窮於名。是故不賢而為賢者師，不智而為智者正。臣有其勞，君有其成功，此之謂賢主之經也。

The way of a clear-sighted ruler: Let the wise completely exhaust their contemplations and rely on them to decide on matters—then the ruler is not depleted of wisdom. Let the worthy utilize[24] their talents and rely on them and assign task accordingly—then the ruler is not depleted of abilities. When there is success, the ruler possesses a worthy [name]; when there is failure, the minister bears the responsibility. Thus the ruler is not depleted of a [good] name. Hence, being unworthy, he is the master of the worthies; being unwise, he is the corrector of the wise. The minister works, while the ruler possesses the achievements: this is called the foundations of the worthy sovereign. (*Han Feizi* forthcoming: 5.1; Chen 2000: 67)

This passage is somewhat ironic. Whereas the ruler is referred to as "clear-sighted," he is also presumed to be potentially unworthy and unwise. By dispensing with any manifestation of personal inclinations and abilities, the ruler benefits twice. First, he avoids the traps of scheming ministers; and second, he is able to manipulate them and achieve undeserved glory and fame. The latter promise—an unabashed appeal

---

[24] Following Lu Wenchao 盧文弨 (1712–1799), I emend *chi* 敕 to *xiao* 效 (Chen 2000: 73n25).

to the ruler's selfishness[25]—should lure him into adopting Han Fei's views. Hinting at the possibility that the sovereign, albeit unworthy and unwise, will become the teacher and corrector of his worthy subjects, Han Fei again discloses his ultimately low expectations of the monarch's morality and wisdom. This qualifies the text's constant invocations of a "clear-sighted sovereign."

And yet Han Fei remains unsettled about the ruler's proper functioning. The dismissive attitude in some passages is contrasted with others, in which Han Fei promotes "the idea of the ruler's creation of a supremely potent self through rigorous intellectual self-cultivation" (Lewis, Chap. 11, this volume, p. 315). Calls for the ruler to refrain from activism suit well the notion that a few devoted ministers may run the state in the ruler's stead (Pines 2013b), but are contradicted elsewhere, when Han Fei insists that the ruler, who must constantly keep vigilance against his ministers, cannot function through non-action: "He retains ministers according to performance and title, and regulates them with gauges and measures. He must never omit doing this, so how can he relax?" 以刑名收臣，以度量準下，此不可釋也，君人者焉佚哉?(*Han Feizi* 37.5.2; Chen 2000: 882 ["Nan 2"]). These contradictions permeate the text. Perhaps they are irresolvable. With his unparalleled clarity of mind, Han Fei may have understood more than his contemporaries the perennial weakness of the system in which a single—potentially inept—individual plays the superhuman role. That this sober understanding came from a thinker dubbed "the most sophisticated theoretician of autocracy" (Wang and Chang 1986:12) deserves utmost attention.

3.4 The People

Hsiao Kung-chuan 蕭公權 (1897–1981), who called Han Fei the defender of monarchic despotism, averred that in Han Fei's political system "the ruler in his own person became the ultimate objective of politics and its sole standard" (Hsiao 1979: 385–86). By contrast, Wang and Chang (1986: 117–31) marshaled impressive evidence that the ultimate goal of Han Fei's system was to benefit the people (*li min* 利民). Indeed, it is not difficult to find statements that support the latter observation in *Han Feizi*. The text reiterates: the people at large are the ultimate beneficiaries of the political system. Actually, the assault on powerful ministers is justified at times in terms of protecting the people below from the powerholders' abuse (*Han Feizi* 17.3; Chen 2000: 323 ["Bei nei" 備內]). Thus, Han Fei depicts the rule of the sage monarch as follows:

聖人者，審於是非之實，察於治亂之情也。故其治國也，正明法，陳嚴刑，將以救群生之亂，去天下之禍，使強不陵弱，眾不暴寡，耆老得遂，幼孤得長，邊境不侵，君臣相親，父子相保，而無死亡係虜之患，此亦功之至厚者也！愚人不知，顧以為暴。

---

[25] For a very similar point, see *Han Feizi* 48.2; Chen 2000: 1049 ("Ba jing" 八經).

The sage investigates the substance of right and wrong, examines the conditions of order and calamity. Hence, when ordering his state, he corrects and clarifies the laws, and lays out strict punishments. He intends therewith to save all the living creatures from calamity, to eradicate the disasters of All-under-Heaven, to prevent the strong from lording it over the weak and the many from impinging on the few. [He lets] the old follow [their predestined course of life], the young and the orphans grow up. The borders are not invaded; the ruler and ministers are intimate; fathers and sons protect each other; there are no worries of [premature] death and [enemy's] captivity: this is the greatest of the merits. Yet stupid people do not understand this and consider him oppressive. (*Han Feizi* 14.5; Chen 2000: 287)

The list of the sage's achievements can easily be transposed into any other contemporaneous text of whatever ideological current. The idea that the people at large ("All-under-Heaven") are the ultimate beneficiaries of the sage's rule and that their well-being is the ultimate goal of the sage's concern is among the foundational features of traditional Chinese political thought in general (Pines 2009: 187–211; Song 2010: 135–56). What distinguishes *Han Feizi*, though, is the bottom line of the above extract—the complaint that the people consider a good monarch "oppressive." To understand why they do so is not difficult. When Han Fei speaks about orderly rule, he repeatedly echoes Shang Yang's ideas that coercion is the only viable means of ruling the people:

今有不才之子，父母怒之弗為改，鄉人譙之弗為動，師長教之弗為變。夫以父母之愛、鄉人之行、師長之智，三美加焉，而終不動，其脛毛不改。州部之吏，操官兵，推公法，而求索姦人，然後恐懼，變其節，易其行矣。故父母之愛不足以教子，必待州部之嚴刑者，民固驕於愛、聽於威矣。

Suppose there is a son of no talent: his parents scold him but he will not reform himself, his neighbors berate him but he will not budge, his teachers and seniors educate him but he will not change. Now, the love of his parents, the proper conduct of his neighbours, the intelligence of his teachers and seniors, these three excellent influences are brought to bear on him, but he refuses to budge and he does not change as much as a hair on his shin. But when the local official, wielding weapons from the state arsenal, exercises the impartial law and seeks to tie up the villains, only then he becomes terrified, changes his standards, and reforms his behavior. Thus parental love is not enough to educate children, and you have to rely on severe punishments by local officials. The people certainly are arrogant towards love but obedient to awe-inspiring majesty. (*Han Feizi* 49.7; Chen 2000: 1099 ["Wu du"])

The bottom line is clear. Moral suasion does not suffice to deter villains; only coercion based on impartial law (*gong fa* 公法; i.e., common rules that have no room for private sentiments) works. This understanding does not apply to villains only. The people at large will submit to force alone. As is explained in the chapter "Measures of Heart" (54, "Xin du" 心度), laws are the only way to protect the people against themselves:

聖人之治民，度於本，不從其欲，期於利民而已。故其與之刑，非所以惡民，愛之本也。刑勝而民靜，賞繁而姦生。故治民者，刑勝，治之首也；賞繁，亂之本也。夫民之性，喜其亂而不親其法。

When the sage rules the people, he measures from the root and does not follow their desires. His aspiration is to benefit the people, that is all. Thus when he metes out punishments on them, this is not because he dislikes the people—it is the very root of love. When punishments prevail, the people are tranquil; when rewards are abundant, villainy arises. Thus if the people are well-governed, it is because punishments prevail; this is the starting point of orderly rule. If rewards are abundant, this is the root of turmoil. It is in the nature of the people that they delight in turmoil and are not devoted to the law. (*Han Feizi* 54.1; Chen 2000: 1176–77)

This passage, which strongly resembles the argumentation in the *Book of Lord Shang* (e.g., *Book of Lord Shang* 7.4 ["Kai sai"; Zhang 2012: 113]; see also McLeod, Chap. 15, this volume), provides the common rationale for the *fa* thinkers' emphasis on the advantages of coercive methods. By their very nature, the people are unruly; hence, the benevolent sage should overawe them so as to attain tranquility.[26] Why the people's nature is such? It is because their intelligence is lacking: "The intelligence of the people cannot be used, because it is just like the mind of an infant 民智之不可用，猶嬰兒之心也" (*Han Feizi* 50.11; Chen 2000: 1147 ["Xian xue"]). The infant detests unpleasant medical treatment because it does not understand the long-term benefits. Ditto for the people. The government should lead them resolutely toward the brave new world of universal stability by suppressing their turmoil-oriented inclinations.

By comparing the people to a toddler, Han Fei employs the common paternalistic simile which permeates the texts of the Warring States period (Flavel and Hall 2020). In the context of *Han Feizi*, the paternalistic paradigm is employed primarily to highlight the fallacy of the frequent calls for the rulers "to attain the hearts of the people" 得民之心. Han Fei shrewdly utilizes another common viewpoint of competing thinkers—that the commoners *en masse* are morally and intellectually inferior to the elites (Pines 2009: 210–14; Song 2010: 145–49)—to ridicule appeals to the people's hearts/mind. Han Fei reminds the readers:

欲得民之心而可以為治，則是伊尹、管仲無所用也，將聽民而已矣。 ⋯⋯夫求聖通之士者，為民知之不足師用。⋯⋯故舉士而求賢智。

Should attaining the people's hearts bring about orderly rule, then there would be no use for [the model ministers] Yi Yin and Guan Zhong: it would be enough just to listen to the people and that is all.... One seeks sagacious and all-penetrating *shi* (士, men of service) because the people's knowledge is considered insufficient to be guided by. ... Hence the *shi* are elevated, and the worthy and knowledgeable are sought after. (*Han Feizi* 50.11; Chen 2000: 1147 ["Xian xue"])

Here we can observe Han Fei's rhetorical brilliance. If the people's voices are to be heeded, then the need for meritocratic government may disappear. Han Fei cannily addresses *shi* fears for their positions at courts, manipulating them against the people-oriented discourse. He reminds the audience that the very idea of elevating "the worthy and knowledgeable" men of service contradicts the populist (or quasi-democratic?) idea of seeking "the people's hearts."[27] Han Fei shrewdly notes the

---

[26] Elsewhere, Han Fei summarizes this point eloquently: "Thus it is the Way of the law to be bitter first, and in the long run advantageous; and it is the Way of benevolence to be self-indulgent and lead to impoverishment" 故法之為道，前苦而長利；仁之為道，偷樂而後窮 (*Han Feizi* 46.6; Chen 2000: 1011 ["Liu fan" 六反]).

[27] This is not the place to discuss the contradictions between meritocracy and democracy (for which, see, e.g., Bell 2015). But at least on one point Han Fei was prescient. The moment the

contradiction between the broadly proclaimed idea of "listening to the people" and the self-interest of the intellectuals. And he is sure that the latter will prevail: once reminded that in a people-based political system they will lose their sociopolitical advantages, the intellectuals will abandon this discourse entirely. The *yin* of selfishness will forever overcome the *yang* of public commitment.

4 A Class Traitor? Han Fei and the Intellectuals

Han Fei delights in polemics. Much like his supposed teacher, Xunzi, he engages a broad variety of intellectual traditions of his age—from supporters of reclusion to admirers of the sword-wielding bravoes (*xia* 俠), from advocates of the horizontal and vertical alliances to debaters of whether a white horse is a horse. Yet the bulk of Han Fei's polemical zeal is directed against those whom he dubs "scholars" (*xuezhe* 學者 or *xueshi* 學士), "students of texts" (*wenxue* 文學), "Confucians" (Ru 儒), or "Confucians and Mohists" (Ru-Mo 儒墨), a term which in some cases should better be translated as "moralizers" (Lee 2014). He is merciless in exposing the shallowness of their discourse, be this the call to "attain the people's hearts" (Sect. 3.4, p. 129 above) or endorsement of the revered virtue of filiality (*xiao* 孝). With regard to the latter, Han Fei reminds that the Confucian prioritization of family values allows sons to conceal their father's crimes, and, worse, legitimates the soldiers' desertion from the battlefield to take care of an aging parent. Han Fei concludes: "a filial son to a father is an absconding subject to the ruler" (夫父之孝子，君之背臣也; *Han Feizi* 49.9; Chen 2000: 1104 ["Wu du"]).

Han Fei's incisiveness peaks in chapter 51, "Loyalty and Filiality," where the author resorts to the moralizers' cherished values in order to assault their revered paragons—such as selfless abdicators Yao and Shun and the founders of the Shang and Zhou dynasties, kings Tang and Wu. The chapter (which evidently originated as a memorial to an unidentified king), reminds the reader that both abdication, associated with Yao and Shun, and dynastic rebellion, associated with Tang and Wu, mean subverting the inviolable norms of hereditary succession:

> 堯、舜、湯、武，或反君臣之義，亂後世之教者也。堯為人君而君其臣，舜為人臣而臣其君，湯、武為人臣而弒其主、刑其尸，而天下譽之，此天下所以至今不治者也。……今堯自以為明而不能以畜舜，舜自以為賢而不能以戴堯，湯、武自以為義而弒其君長，此明君且常與，而賢臣且常取也。故至今為人子者有取其父之家，為人臣者有取其君之國者矣。父而讓子，君而讓臣，此非所以定位一教之道也。
>
> Yao and Shun, [kings] Tang and Wu: each of them opposed the propriety of ruler and minister, wreaking havoc in the teachings for future generations. Yao was a ruler who turned his minister into a ruler; Shun was a minister who turned his ruler into a minister; Tang and Wu were ministers who murdered their masters and defamed their bodies; but All-under-Heaven praise them—therefore, All-under-Heaven has not been ruled well. … Now, Yao

considered himself clear-sighted but was unable to feed Shun,[28] Shun considered himself worthy but was unable to support Yao, Tang and Wu considered themselves righteous but murdered their rulers and superiors. This means that a "clear-sighted" ruler should constantly give, whereas a "worthy" minister—constantly take. Hence until now there are sons who take their father's house, and ministers who take their ruler's state. When a father yields to a son, and a ruler yields to a minister—this is not the way of fixing the positions and unifying the teaching. (*Han Feizi* 51.1; Chen 2000: 1151)

The chapter continues with vicious criticism of the paragons, including accusing Shun—the single most admired personality among the men of service of the Warring States era—of not only making his father a servant but also making his mother a bondwoman (*qie* 妾), a term which, scandalously, may also refer to a concubine (Goldin 2017). Yet the point is not just to ridicule the paragons. Han Fei shows that the very discourse that lauds those paragons (who are paired elsewhere in the chapter with lofty-minded "zealous men of service" [*lie shi* 烈士])—is subversive by its nature:

夫為人子而常譽他人之親曰：「某子之親，夜寢早起，強力生財以養子孫臣妾」，是誹謗其親者也。為人臣常譽先王之德厚而願之，是誹謗其君者也。非其親者知謂之不孝，而非其君者天下皆賢之，此所以亂也。故人臣毋稱堯、舜之賢，毋譽湯、武之伐，毋言烈士之高，盡力守法、專心於事主者為忠臣。

Now, if a son always praises other people's parents, saying "Such-and-such a son's parents get to sleep late and get up early. With all their might they produce wealth in order to keep their offspring, their male and female servants"—that would be to malign his own parents. If a minister always praises the bountiful virtue of the former kings, turning his hopes toward it—that is to malign his ruler. He who rejects his parents is called unfilial; but he who rejects his ruler is considered worthy throughout All-under-Heaven. That is why [All-under-Heaven] is in turmoil.

Thus, one's subject should not praise the worthiness of Yao and Shun, should not extol the punitive expeditions of Tang and Wu, should not talk about the loftiness of zealous men of service. [Only] he who dedicates all his force to safeguard the standards (or laws, *fa*) and focuses whole-heartedly on serving the sovereign is the loyal minister. (*Han Feizi* 51.5; Chen 2000:1155)

Here we discover a darker side of Han Fei's criticism of his opponents. He is not engaged just in intellectual polemics, as is common, e.g., in *Zhuangzi*. Rather, he shows how an ostensibly innocent praise of former paragons can serve as a cunning ploy to subvert the ruler's power and then calls upon the cessation of this subversive discourse. Recall that this recommendation appears in what purports to be Han Fei's memorial to the ruler. This is then a call for action—a call for instant suppression of subversive intellectual activity.

This brings us to the final, and arguably, the most problematic aspect of Han Fei's legacy: his open assault on fellow intellectuals.[29] This assault develops along several lines. First, echoing the *Book of Lord Shang* (Chap. 1, Sect. 7, this volume),

---

[28] Referring to Shun's humble position under Yao's rule before his sudden elevation, see *Han Feizi* 36.2; Chen 2000: 845–847 ("Nan yi").

[29] I use the term "intellectual" for an intellectually active segment of men of service. For a broader equation of the Warring States-period *shi* as a whole with "intellectuals," see Yu 2003: 3–76, esp. pp. 3–4.

Han Fei cautions against patronizing talkative men of service at the expense of tillers and soldiers: "Those whom [the state] benefits are not those whom it uses; those
whom it uses are not those whom it benefits" 所利非所用，所用非所利 (*Han
Feizi* 49.10 ["Wu du"] and 50.4 ["Xian xue"]; Chen 2000: 1105 and 1135). The
scholars' uselessness derives from the very nature of their discourse, e.g., their
abuse of "subtle and mysterious words that even the most intelligent find hard to
understand" (微妙之言，上智之所難知也; *Han Feizi* 49.11; Chen 2000:1109
["Wu du"]). Worse, the ideological cleavages among the moralizers and their conflicting interpretations of the former paragons' legacy make their ideas intrinsically
impracticable. Han Fei ridicules the rulers who admire the eloquence of the scholars' arguments and patronize proponents of contradictory doctrines without checking the applicability of their recommendations:

> 夫冰炭不同器而久，寒暑不兼時而至，雜反之學不兩立而治。今兼聽雜學繆行同異
> 之辭，安得無亂乎？
>
>   Yet ice and [burning] coals cannot coexist in the same vessel for a long time, cold and
> hot weather do not come at the same season. You cannot establish simultaneously motley
> and contradictory teachings and attain orderly rule. Now, if you listen to the similar and
> dissimilar words of motley teachings and misguided behaviors how can you fail to end up
> in turmoil? (*Han Feizi* 50.2; Chen 2000:1130 ["Xian xue"])

Han Fei's criticism of the uselessness of the moralizer's doctrines was not much
controversial; we can find ready parallels not only in Shang Yang's diatribes but also
in Xunzi's dismissal of rival philosophers.[30] What distinguishes Han Fei from his
predecessors though is the second line of his criticism, viz. his readiness to identify
unrestrained selfishness behind the moralizers' lofty pronouncements. With his
inquisitive mind, Han Fei notes how his opponents' laudation of principled intellectuals is just a means to ensure the ruler's patronage to themselves and their ilk. In
particular, Han Fei identify the meritocratic discourse of his age as detrimental to
real meritocracy.[31] Those who hail high-minded men of letters as "worthies" subvert
the true meritocracy, because their definition of "worthiness" has nothing to do with
one's real contribution to the state. In the chapter "Eight Explanations" (47, "Ba
shuo" 八說), the author enumerates different manifestations of selfish conduct, each
of which is lavishly praised by the adherents of "textual studies" 文學 and their ilk,
and reminds: "These eight are the selfish praises of the ordinary men, and the great
defeat for the sovereign" 此八者，匹夫之私譽，人主之大敗也 (*Han Feizi* 47.1;
Chen 2000: 1023). The chapter explains further:

> 匹夫有私便，人主有公利。不作而養足，不仕而名顯，此私便也。息文學而明法
> 度，塞私便而一功勞，此公利也。
>
>   Ordinary men have their (selfish) interests but the sovereign is concerned with common
> benefit. Not to work but to have enough to sustain oneself, not to serve but to have one's
> name illustrious—these are private interests. Stopping textual studies and publishing the

---

[30] See, e.g., chapter 6, "Against the Twelve Masters" ("Fei shier zi" 非十二子) of *Xunzi*, and more
discussion in Chap. 18, Sect. 4, this volume.

[31] For contextualization of Han Fei's views of meritocracy in the Warring States-period discourse,
see Pines 2013c; see also Yuan 2005 and Pines, Chap. 18, this volume.

laws and gauges, blocking private interests and unifying merits and toils [on agriculture and warfare]—that is the common benefit. (*Han Feizi* 47.3; Chen 2000: 1027)

Adherents of "textual studies" do not deserve the proud designation of *shi*; rather they are "ordinary men" or "commoners" (*pifu* 匹夫). Their goal is to avoid bitter toil or government service and yet enjoy material and social benefits. To advance this selfish goal, scholars create favorable reputation for their peers as an alternative to the state-sponsored system of the ranks of merit. That worthless talkers are promoted is bad enough; but Han Fei notes that the danger of the moralizers' discourse is even higher. It amounts to the promotion of an alternative hierarchy of values in which lofty intellectuals are placed at the top at the expense of all the rest, the rulers included.[32] And this alternative hierarchy erodes the very foundations of the sociopolitical order:

民之重名與其重賞也均。賞者有誹焉，不足以勸；罰者有譽焉，不足以禁。……明主之道，賞必出乎公利，名必在乎為上。

The people attach the same importance to reputation (the name, *ming* 名) and rewards. If some of those who are rewarded are also blamed, then [the rewards] will not suffice to encourage them; if some of those who are punished are also praised, then [the punishments] will not suffice to prohibit [transgressions]. ... The Way of the clear-sighted sovereign is such that rewards inevitably derive from benefitting the common interest, and reputation inevitably come from acting for the superiors. (*Han Feizi* 48.7; Chen 2000: 1079 ["Ba jing" 八經])

Han Fei correctly identifies the quest for a good reputation as one of the primary motivational forces in human behavior (see more in Pines 2020c; Lewis 2021). Because of their importance, praise and blame should never be determined by the adherents of textual studies or by Confucian "noble men." They should be controlled by the state and the state alone. The system of ranks of merit, introduced by Shang Yang, will be functionable only insofar as it is not undermined by any alternative system of values. If intellectuals are allowed to promote such values independently, broader rejection of the rules imposed by the state will ensue. This is the third line of Han Fei's attack against the intellectuals. Their discourse is not just useless and self-serving, it is actually subversive of the entire political order. This point is clarified, for instance, in chapter 45, "Deluded Assignments" ("Gui shi" 詭使), which cautions against fake reputations created by the self-declared "sages," the "knowledgeable," and the "worthy":

上無其道，則智者有私詞，賢者有私意。上有私惠，下有私欲。聖智成羣，造言作辭，以非法措於上。上不禁塞，又從而尊之，是教下不聽上、不從法也。是以賢者顯名而居，姦人賴賞而富。賢者顯名而居，姦人賴賞而富，是以上不勝下也。

When the superior lacks the Way, the knowledgeable have selfish (private) words, and the worthies have selfish aspirations. When the superior has private generosity, the underlings have private (selfish) desires. "Sages" and "knowledgeable" multiply; they produce speeches and create statements in order to attack the standards (or laws, *fa*) being implemented from above. When the superior, instead of prohibiting and blocking them, follows and respects them, this is to teach the underlings neither to heed the superior, nor to follow

---

[32] For this alternative hierarchy, see more in Pines 2009: 123–35; see also Chap. 18, Sects. 2 and 3, this volume.

the standards. Therefore, the "worthies" will rest on their illustrious reputation, and the villains will rely on rewards to become rich. When the "worthies" rest on their illustrious reputation, and the villains rely on rewards to become rich, this means that the superior cannot overcome his underlings. (*Han Feizi* 45.6; Chen 2000: 998)

This extract can serve as an excellent summary of Han Fei's views. The intellectuals are useless, but they yearn for the ruler's support. In order to maintain high sociopolitical position without contributing anything practical to the state, they promote an alternative system of values in which the reputation generated by the men of learning competes with the state-ordained system of ranks of merit. Dangerously, they succeed at convincing the ruler of the attractiveness of their values, which results in the erosion of the state's power. The intrinsic selfishness of these intellectuals coupled with the sophistication of their discourse that deludes the ruler and the ruled creates grave results. It benefits not just useless "worthies," but also allows "villains" 姦人 to advance economically, jeopardizing the sociopolitical order in its entirety. Hence Han Fei concludes:

故明主之國，無書簡之文，以法為教；無先王之語，以吏為師；無私劍之捍，以斬首為勇。

Accordingly, in the country of a clear-sighted sovereign there are no texts written in books and on bamboo strips, but the law is the teaching; there are no discourses of the former monarchs, but officials are the teachers; there is no private wielding of swords, but beheading [enemies] is the valor. (*Han Feizi* forthcoming: 49.13; Chen 2000: 1112 ["Wu du"])

Here Han Fei moves from disallowing "discourses of the former monarchs" (probably collections of historical anecdotes about the former worthies; see Petersen 1995) to complete sociopolitical subjugation of the intellectuals, who should be incorporated into officialdom and cease to exist as an autonomous group. In the ideal political order, teaching and learning should be maintained by officials and for officials. Independent, free-floating intellectuals of the Warring States era have no place in this order. Han Fei, himself a brilliant independently-minded intellectual, commits here an act of class betrayal. He places the interest of the state and the ruler—the apex of impartiality—above the interest of his stratum and, indirectly, of himself.

As is well known, Han Fei's views were heeded. Soon after the thinker's tragic death in Qin's custody, his ideological ally, possibly a fellow student, and, reportedly, his nemesis—Li Si—made the crucial step toward realizing Han Fei's program. Qin's notorious biblioclasm of 213 BCE was not designed by Han Fei but it can fairly be considered the realization of his proposals.[33]

This brings me to the final point of the chapter. Whereas the designation of *fa* thinkers as "totalitarians" is methodologically problematic (Schiele, Chap. 22, this volume), Han Fei's fight against independently minded intellectuals (much like Shang Yang's ideal of a total state discussed in chapter 1) had the potential of moving into totalitarian direction. It is appropriate here to use Tao Jiang's astute summary:

---

[33] For the biblioclasm, see more in Petersen 1995; Kern 2000: 183–96; Pines 2009: 180–82.

Left to its own device, the impartialist state, conceived of by Han Feizi and other *fajia* thinkers, was totalitarian in its monopoly of values under Heaven since no alternative source of values was allowed under such a system. … This totalitarian orientation toward impartiality articulated and defended in the *fajia* project exposed a dark side to a single-perspective, monistic notion of justice, especially when it is enforced by an all-powerful state, if that idea is untampered or unbalanced by other norms like humaneness or personal freedom (T. Jiang 2021: 457).

Jiang's suggestion that hampering an all-powerful state with such norms as "humaneness or personal freedom" could modify its excesses is interesting from our modern point of view. But for Han Fei it would be a non-starter. He remained fully committed to the idea of an impartial state that will not be hampered by anything. For this state, he was ready to sacrifice his stratum; and for this state he eventually sacrificed his life. But Han Fei as a political analyst—a function in which he excelled more than that of a political theorist—had also realized well that such an impartial state would never function smoothly because in the final account it will more often than not be run by mediocre, selfish, and overall inadequate individuals. Alas, with all his brilliance, Han Fei succeeded only in identifying the problem but not in solving it. Herein lies his tragedy.

References

Allan, Sarah. 2016. *The Heir and the Sage: Dynastic Legend in Early China* (rev. ed.). Albany: State University of New York Press.

Bai, Tongdong 白彤東. 2020. "Han Feizi's Account of the Transition from 'Antiquity' to 'Modernity'" 韓非子對古今之變的論説. *Fudan Journal (Social Sciences)* 復旦學報(社會科學版)5: 37–46.

Bell, Daniel. 2015. *The China Model: Political Meritocracy and the Limits of Democracy*. Princeton NJ: Princeton University Press.

Book of Lord Shang. See Pines 2017.

Chen, Qiyou 陳奇猷 (1917–2006). 2000. *Han Feizi, Newly Collated and Annotated* 韓非子新校注. Shanghai: Shanghai guji chubanshe. (One of the best current editions of *Han Feizi*)

Chen, Minzhen. 2023. How to Understand "Empty" Records: On the Format and Compilation of *Chunqiu* from the Perspective of Bamboo Manuscripts. In *Zuozhuan and Early Chinese Historiography*, ed. Yuri Pines, Martin Kern, and Nino Luraghi, 63–88. Leiden: Brill.

Creel, Herrlee G. 1974. *Shen Pu-hai, A Chinese Philosopher of the Fourth Century B.C.* Chicago IL: The University of Chicago Press.

Dou, Zhaorui 竇兆鋭. 2019. "Investigating the Authorship of the 'First Audience in Qin' Chapter of *Han Feizi*" 《韓非子·初見秦》篇作者考. *Journal of Historical Science* 史學月刊 9: 13–22.

Durrant, Stephen W., Wai-yee Li, and David Schaberg. 2016. *Zuo Tradition / Zuozhuan Commentary on the "Spring and Autumn Annals"*. Seattle: University of Washington Press.

Feng, Youlan 馮友蘭 (1895–1990). 2001. *Newly Edited History of Chinese Philosophy* (*Volume A*) 中國哲學史新編(上卷). Beijing: Renmin chubanshe.

Flavel, Sarah, and Brad Hall. 2020. Exemplary Paternalism: A Consideration of Confucian Models of Moral Oversight. *Culture and Dialogue* 8 (2): 220–250.

Galvany, Albert. 2013. Beyond the Rule of Rules: The Foundations of Sovereign Power in the *Han Feizi*. In *Dao Companion to the Philosophy of Han Fei*, ed. Paul R. Goldin, 87–106. Dordrecht: Springer.

Goldin, Paul R. 2008. Appeals to History in Early Chinese Philosophy and Rhetoric. *Journal of Chinese Philosophy* 35 (1): 79–96.

———. 2011. Persistent Misconceptions about Chinese 'Legalism'. *Journal of Chinese Philosophy* 38 (1): 64–80.

———. 2017. Copulating with One's Stepmother—Or Birth Mother? In *Behaving Badly in Early and Medieval China*, ed. N. Harry Rothschild and Leslie V. Wallace, 56–69. Honolulu: University of Hawai'i Press.

———. 2020. *The Art of Chinese Philosophy: Eight Classical Texts and How to Read Them*. Princeton NJ: Princeton University Press.

Graham, Angus C. 1989. *Disputers of the Tao: Philosophical Argument in Ancient China*. La Salle, IL: Open Court.

Graziani, Romain. 2015. Monarch and Minister: The Problematic Partnership in the Building of Absolute Monarchy in the *Han Feizi* 韓非子. In *Ideology of Power and Power of Ideology in Early China*, ed. Yuri Pines, Paul R. Goldin, and Martin Kern, 155–180. Leiden: Brill.

Guanzi jiaozhu 管子校注 (*Guanzi*, Collated and Annotated). 2004. Ed. Li, Xiangfeng 黎翔鳳. Beijing: Zhonghua shuju.

Han Feizi. See Harbsmeier, forthcoming.

Han yiwenzhi kaozheng 漢藝文志考證 (Textual Study of the "Treatise on Arts and Letters" from the *History of the Former Han Dynasty*). 2011. By Wang, Yinglin 王應麟 (1223–1296). Rpt. In Wang, Yinglin, *Investigation of the Han Dynasty Institutions* 漢制考 and *Textual Study of the "Treatise on Arts and Letters" from the History of the Former Han Dynasty* 漢藝文志考證. Collated by Zhang, Sanxi 張三夕 and Yang, Yi 楊毅. Beijing: Zhonghua shuju.

Harbsmeier, Christoph, trans. Forthcoming. Han Feizi, *A Complete Translation: The Art of Statecraft in Early China*. Ed. Jens Østergaard Petersen and Yuri Pines. Leiden: Brill.

Hsiao, Kung-Chuan (Xiao Gongquan 蕭公權). 1979. *A History of Chinese Political Thought. Volume One: From the Beginnings to the Sixth Century A.D.*, translated by Frederick W. Mote. Princeton NJ: Princeton University Press.

Huangdi shu: Mawangdui Han mu boshu Huang Di shu jianzheng 馬王堆漢墓帛書《黃帝書》箋證 (*The Book of the Yellow Thearch, a Silk Text from a Han Tomb at Mawangdui, with Commentary*). 2004. Ed. Wei, Qipeng 魏啓鵬. Beijing: Zhonghua shuju.

Hunter, Michael. 2013. The Difficutly with the 'Difficulties of Persuasion' ('Shui nan' 說難). In *Dao Companion to the Philosophy of Han Fei*, ed. Paul R. Goldin, 169–196. Dordrecht: Springer.

Jiang, Chongyue 蔣重躍. 2000. *Political Thought of Han Feizi* 韓非子的政治思想. Beijing: Beijing shifan daxue chubanshe. (One of the best studies of *Han Feizi* political thought)

Jiang, Tao. 2021. *Origins of Political-Moral Philosophy in Early China: Contestation of Humaneness, Justice, and Personal Freedom*. Oxford: Oxford University Press.

Kantorowicz, Ernst H. 1957. *The King's Two Bodies: A Study in Mediaeval Political Theology*. Princeton: Princeton University Press.

Kern, Martin. 2000. *The Stele Inscriptions of Ch'in Shih-huang: Text and Ritual in Early Chinese Imperial Representation*. New Haven, CT: American Oriental Society.

———. 2015. The 'Masters' in the *Shiji*. *T'oung Pao* 101 (4–5): 335–362.

Korolkov, Maxim. 2011. Arguing About Law: Interrogation Procedure Under the Qin and Former Han Dynasties. *Études Chinoises* 30: 37–71.

Kunxue jiwen 困學紀聞 (Observations of Assiduous Studies). 2008. By Wang, Yinglin 王應麟 (1223–1296). Ed. Weng, Yuanqi 翁元圻 (1751–1826), Yue, Baoqun 樂保群, Tian, Songqing 田松青, and Lü, Zongli 呂宗力. Shanghai: Shanghai guji chubanshe.

Lee, Ting-mien. 2014. When 'Ru-Mo' May Not Be 'Confucians and Mohists': The Meaning of 'Ru-Mo' and Early Intellectual Taxonomy. *Oriens Extremus* 53: 111–138.

Lewis, Mark Edward. 2021. *Honor and Shame in Early China*. Cambridge: Cambridge University Press.

Li, Linhao 李林浩 and Chen, Sufang 陳蘇方. 2009. "Attempting to Analyze Proverbs that originated from *Han Feizi*" 試析源自《韓非子》的成語. *Journal of Mudanjiang University* 牡丹江大學學報 18.10: 46–48.

Liu, Zehua 劉澤華. 2000. *China's Monarchism* 中國的王權主義. Shanghai: Renmin chubanshe. (A major study of traditional Chinese political thought)

———. 劉澤華. 2003. *Draft of the Studies from 'Washing the Ears Studio'* 洗耳齋文稿. Beijing: Zhonghua shuju.

Liu, Sixuan 劉斯玄. 2020. *My Shallow Understanding of Han Feizi Thought* 韓非子思想蠡測. Taipei: Wanjuan lou. (A short but useful analysis of the usage of certain keywords in *Han Feizi*)

Lundahl, Bertil. 1992. *Han Fei Zi: The Man and the Work*. Stockholm: Institute of Oriental Languages, Stockholm University.

Marx, Karl. [1859] 2010. "A Contribution to the Critique of Political Economy, Part One," trans. Yuri Sdobnikov. Rpt. in Karl Marx and Friedrich Engels, *Collected Works*, vol. 29, 257–419. Lawrence & Wishart, Electric Books.

Mozawa, Michinao 茂澤方尚. 1991. "Which of the Chapters Was Composed Earlier— 'Adjusting Orders' of *Han Feizi* or 'Making Orders Strict' of the *Book of Lord Shang*" 『韓非子』「飭令」篇と『商君書』「靳令」篇——両篇の前後関係について. *Komazawa Historiogaphy* 駒澤史學 43: 1–23.

Peerenboom, Randall P. 1993. *Law and Morality in Ancient China: The Silk Manuscripts of Huang-Lao*. Albany: State University of New York Press.

Petersen, Jens Østergård. 1995. Which Books Did the First Emperor of Ch'in Burn? On the Meaning of *Pai Chia* in Early Chinese Sources. *Monumenta Serica* 43: 1–52.

Pines, Yuri. 2005. Disputers of Abdication: Zhanguo Egalitarianism and the Sovereign's Power. *T'oung Pao* 91 (4–5): 243–300.

———. 2009. *Envisioning Eternal Empire: Chinese Political Thought of the Warring States Era*. Honolulu: University of Hawai'i Press.

———. 2012. *The Everlasting Empire: The Political Culture of Ancient China and Its Imperial Legacy*. Princeton NJ: Princeton University Press.

———. 2013a. From Historical Evolution to the End of History: Past, Present and Future from Shang Yang to the First Emperor. In *Dao Companion to the Philosophy of Han Fei*, ed. Paul R. Goldin, 25–45. Dordrecht: Springer.

———. 2013b. Submerged by Absolute Power: The Ruler's Predicament in the *Han Feizi*. In *Dao Companion to the Philosophy of Han Fei*, ed. Paul R. Goldin, 67–86. Dordrecht: Springer.

———. 2013c. Between Merit and Pedigree: Evolution of the Concept of 'Elevating the Worthy' in Pre-imperial China. In *The Idea of Political Meritocracy: Confucian Politics in Contemporary Context*, ed. Daniel Bell and Li Chenyang, 161–202. Cambridge: Cambridge University Press.

———. 2017. *The Book of Lord Shang: Apologetics of State Power in Early China*. trans. and ed. New York: Columbia University Press.

———. 2020a. *Zhou History Unearthed: The Bamboo Manuscript Xinian and Early Chinese Historiography*. New York: Columbia University Press.

———. 2020b. Worth vs. Power: Han Fei's 'Objection to Positional Power' Revisited. *Asiatische Studien/Études Asiatiques* 74 (3): 687–710.

———. 2020c. 'To Die for the Sanctity of the Name': Name (*ming* 名) as Prime-Mover of Political Action in Early China. In *Keywords in Chinese Culture*, ed. Li Wai-yee and Yuri Pines, 169–218. Hong Kong: The Chinese University Press.

———. 2022. *Han Feizi* and the Earliest Exegesis of *Zuo zhuan*. *Monumenta Serica* 70 (2): 341–365.

———. Forthcoming (2023). "Waging a Demographic War: Chapter 15 ('Attracting the People') of the *Book of Lord Shang* Revisited," *Bochumer Jahrbuch zur Ostasienforschung* 46.

Queen, Sarah. 2013. *Han Feizi* and the Old Master: A Comparative Analysis and Translation of *Han Feizi* Chapter 20, 'Jie Lao' and Chapter 21, 'Yu Lao'. In *Dao Companion to the Philosophy of Han Fei*, ed. Paul R. Goldin, 197–256. Dordrecht: Springer.

Sanft, Charles. 2014. *Communication and Cooperation in Early Imperial China*. Albany: State University of New York Press.

Sato, Masayuki. 2013a. Did Xunzi's Theory of Human Nature Provide the Foundation for the Political Thought of Han Fei? In *Dao Companion to the Philosophy of Han Fei*, ed. Paul R. Goldin, 147–165. Dordrecht: Springer.

———. 2013b. "Studies of *Han Feizi* in China, Taiwan, and Japan" In *Dao Companion to the Philosophy of Han Fei*, ed. Paul R. Goldin, 257–281. Dordrecht: Springer.

Schaberg, David. 2011. Chinese History and Philosophy. In *The Oxford History of Historical Writing, Volume 1: Beginnings to AD 600*, ed. Andrew Feldherr and Grant Hardy, 394–414. Oxford: Oxford University Press.

Schwarcz, Vera. 1985. *The Chinese Enlightenment: Intellectuals and the Legacy of the May Fourth Movement of 1919*. Berkeley: University of California Press.

Schwartz, Benjamin I. 1985. *The World of Thought in Ancient China*. Cambridge, Mass: Harvard University Press.

Shiji 史記 (Records of the Historian). 1997. By Sima, Qian 司馬遷 (ca. 145–90 BCE) et al. Annotated by Zhang, Shoujie 張守節, Sima, Zhen 司馬貞, and Pei, Yin 裴駰. Beijing: Zhonghua shuju.

Song, Hongbing 宋洪兵. 2010. *A New Study on Political Thought of Han Feizi* 韓非子政治思想再研究. Beijing: Zhongguo renmin daxue chubanshe. (The most systematic study of *Han Feizi* in the broad context of the Warring States-period political thought)

———. 2013. "Studies of *Han Feizi* during the Republican Period" 民國時期之"韓非學"研究. *National Studies Journal* 國學學刊 4: 91–103.

Van Els, Paul, and Sarah Queen, eds. 2017. *Between Philosophy and History: Rhetorical Uses of Anecdotes in Early China*. Albany: State University of New York Press.

Vogelsang, Kai. 2007. *Geschichte als Problem: Entstehung, Formen und Funktionen von Geschichtsschreibung im Alten China*. Wiesbaden: Harrassowitz.

———. 2023. 'Times have Changed': History beyond the *Zuozhuan*. In *Zuozhuan and Early Chinese Historiography*, ed. Yuri Pines, Martin Kern, and Nino Luraghi, 289–324. Leiden: Brill.

Wang, Xianshen 王先慎 (1859–1922), ed. 1998. *Han Feizi, With Collected Explanations* 韩非子集解. Collated by Zhong, Zhe 鍾哲. Beijing: Zhonghua shuju. (A convenient, even if somewhat inaccurate and outdated edition)

Wang, Hsiao-po, and Leo S. Chang. 1986. *The Philosophical Foundations of Han Fei's Political Theory*. Honolulu: University of Hawai'i Press.

Xunzi jijie 荀子集解 (*Xunzi*, with collected explanations). 1992. Ed. Wang, Xianqian 王先謙 (1842–1917), Shen, Xiaohuan 沈嘯寰, Wang, Xingxian 王星賢. Beijing: Zhonghua shuju.

Yang, Bojun 楊伯峻. 1990. *The Springs-and-Autumns Annals and the Zuo Tradition, Annotated* 春秋左傳注. Beijing: Zhonghua shuju.

Yin, Zhenhuan 尹振環. 1987. "Using Instances of Royal Succession and Regicide to Analyze the Advance of Authoritarian Dictatorship" 從王位繼承和弒君看君主專制理論的逐步形成. *Chinese History* 中國史研究 4: 17–24.

Yu, Yingshi 余英時. 2003. *Shi and Chinese Culture* 士與中國文化. Shanghai: Shanghai renmin chubanshe.

Yuan, Lihua 袁禮華. 2005. "Respecting the Worthies but not Elevating the Worthies; Employing the Worthies and yet Guarding against the Worthies: Initial Discussion of Han Fei's Meritocratic Views" 重賢不尚賢，用賢且防賢—韓非賢能觀初探, *Journal of Nanchang University (Humanities and Social Sciences)* 南昌大學學報(人文社會科學版) 1: 59–63.

Zhang, Jue 張覺, ed. 2010. *Han Feizi, Collated with Subcommentaries* 韓非子校疏. Shanghai: Shanghai guji chubanshe. (A convenient collation, but less good in terms of its commentaries)

——— 張覺. 2012. *The Book of Lord Shang, Collated with Subcommentaries* 商君書校疏. Beijing: Zhishi chanquan chubanshe.

Zhanguoce zhushi 戰國策注釋 (*Stratagems of the Warring States with Commentaries and Explanations*). 1991. Ed. He, Jianzhang 何建章. Beijing: Zhonghua shuju.

Zheng, Liangshu 鄭良樹. 1993. *Composition and Thought of Han Feizi* 韓非之著書及思想. Taipei: Xuesheng shuju. (A major, even if not entirely convincing attempt to study the dates of each of *Han Feizi*'s chapters)

Zhuangzi jinzhu jinyi 莊子今注今譯 (*Zhuangzi*, with New Glosses and New Translation). 1994. Ed. Chen, Guying 陳鼓應. Beijing: Zhonghua shuju.

Zizhi tongjian 資治通鑒 (*Comprehensive Mirror to Aid the Government*). 1992. By Sima, Guang 司馬光 (1019–1086). Annotated by Hu, Sanxing 胡三省 (1230–1302). Beijing: Zhonghua shuju.

Zuozhuan: see Durrant, Li, and Schaberg 2016 and Yang 1990.

Chapter 5
The Concept of *fa* in *Guanzi* and Its Evolution

Masayuki Sato 佐藤將之

Note on Translation

Translating key terms of early Chinese political and ethical discourse is always tough and doubly so when we deal with a composite text such as *Guanzi*. For instance, the key term of this chapter, *fa* 法, may refer to "law," "standard," "method," "model," "principle," and so forth. In this case I prefer not to translate. In other cases, such as *yi* 儀, which can refer to proper demeanor, standard, decorum, or authoritative norms, I adopt different translations and renderings of this term in my discussion, depending on the context. The terms *yi* 義 and *li* 禮 are even tougher. For *yi*, which means "righteousness," "propriety," "morality," or "duty" among others, I opted for "righteousness" in most cases, but for "duty" in a few other contexts. For *li*, I believe that the most accurate translation in the context of *Guanzi* will be "ritual and social norms," but for the sake of brevity in translated passages I often opt for "ritual" only. The solution for these and a few other terms is far from ideal, but it allows me to strike balance between consistency and accuracy.

Introduction

This chapter analyzes the concept of *fa* in *Guanzi* from the perspective of conceptual history and explores the significance of this concept's evolution in the text. Previous discussions on the topic were influenced primarily by two points: (1) the mention of the "*fa* of Guan Zhong" in the "Five vermin" ("Wudu" 五蠹) chapter of *Han Feizi*, and (2) the classification of *Guanzi* as belonging to the "School of *fa*" (*fajia* 法家) in Chinese imperial catalogues starting with the "Treatise on classics and other texts" 經籍志 of *Sui History* (*Suishu* 隋書) (636) to the *Essentials of the*

I wish to thank Justin Wu 吳君健 for his help in translating and editing the present chapter.

M. Sato 佐藤將之 (✉)
National Taiwan University, Taipei, Taiwan
e-mail: msato@ntu.edu.tw

© The Author(s), under exclusive license to Springer Nature Switzerland AG 2024
Y. Pines (ed.), *Dao Companion to China's* fa *Tradition*, Dao Companions to Chinese Philosophy 19, https://doi.org/10.1007/978-3-031-53630-4_6

Catalogue of the Comprehensive Library in Four Sections (*Siku quanshu zongmu tiyao* 四庫全書總目提要) (1798). This classification could have encouraged systematic research on *Guanzi*'s place within the *fa* tradition, but this did not happen. One of the reasons that may have discouraged scholars from dealing with the topic is the fact that despite abundant occurrences of *fa* in *Guanzi*, only a few chapters focus on the term specifically. Besides, most of the studies of *Guanzi* ever since the twentieth century focused on its economic thought, whereas the term *fa* in the text attracted little attention. With the discovery of the so-called *Yellow Emperor Manuscripts* (*Huangdi shu* 黃帝書) from the early Han Tomb 3, Mawangdui, Changsha (Hunan) 長沙馬王堆 in 1973, scholars noticed similarities between the idea of "the Way and the Law" or "*fa* of the Way" (*Dao fa* 道法) in those manuscripts and in certain *Guanzi* chapters. This encouraged explorations of *Guanzi*'s views of *fa*; yet the discussion heretofore had focused either on similarities between the *fa* thought in *Guanzi* and that in *Han Feizi* 韓非子 and the *Book of Lord Shang* (*Shangjunshu* 商君書), or, alternatively on Confucian elements in *Guanzi*'s thought. A systematic study of the evolution of the view of *fa* in *Guanzi* itself is still lacking.

In this chapter, I shall explore all the usages of the term *fa* in *Guanzi*, analyze different layers of its meaning, and check how the concept of *fa* is connected to other key concepts and topics in the text. On the basis of this discussion I hope to make further inferences about the text's ideas and also about the relative importance of *fa* for the authors of different chapters and textual segments. I shall start with surveying how the twentieth century scholars understood the discourse on *fa* in *Guanzi*. Then I summarize major usages of *fa* in the text, and move to in-depth analysis. In Sect. 3, I outline three aspects of *fa* in *Guanzi*, which are related to (1) Searching for an ideal ethical order, which can be expressed by the term "ritual and social norms" (*li* 禮); (2) *fa* in a metaphysical context; (3) *fa* as related to the juxtaposition of "common" or "impartial" (*gong* 公) and "selfish" (*si* 私). This analysis will lead me to explore different semantic strata of the term *fa* in *Guanzi*. I shall continue with discussing the possibility that these strata may reflect the development of the concept of *fa*. In Sect. 3.4, I focus on the discussions of *fa* in the chapters "Seven *fa*" ("Qifa" 七法), "Conforming to *fa*" ("Fafa" 法法), and "Relying on *fa*" ("Renfa" 任法). From the analysis of these three chapters, each of which focuses on *fa*, we can infer that the *fa* discourse of *Guanzi* evolved from "Seven *fa*" to "Conforming to *fa*" and then to "Relying on *fa*." In my conclusion, I shall argue that insofar as the discussion of *fa* in "Relying on *fa*" chapter pertains to other important topics in *Guanzi*, such as the discourse of "common/ impartial vs. selfish," and insofar as *fa* plays a supreme value in this chapter, the term *fa* can indeed be said to be one of those fundamental components of *Guanzi*'s thought. This in turn justifies the classification of *Guanzi* in general as representative of the Warring States period *fa* tradition.

1 *Guanzi* as a Repository of *fa* Thought

Guanzi is a composite text that was formed through a long period of accretion. I share a dominant scholarly opinion, summarized by Allyn W. Rickett, according to which *Guanzi* has little to do with the historical Guan Zhong 管仲 (d. 645 BCE), except that Guan Zhong's name was borrowed because of his fame as a political leader (Rickett 1985: 16–17). In my eyes, the text of *Guanzi* fundamentally reflects intellectual, cultural, political, economic, and social realities in the Warring States-period (Zhanguo 戰國, 453–221 BCE) state of Qi 齊. I disagree with Rickett's (and a few other scholars') attempts to date many of the *Guanzi* chapters to the Qin 秦 (221–207 BCE) and Han 漢 (206/202 BCE–220 CE) periods. It is likely that the text as a whole was produced in the Warring States period, incorporating perhaps a certain number of anecdotes, maxims, and narratives from the earlier Springs-and-Autumns (Chunqiu 春秋, 770–453 BCE) era. The earliest layer of the text is represented by the chapters assembled in the so-called "Canonical Statements" 經言 section (see more in note 14 below). These chapters were composed no later than the middle Warring States period. The latest layer is the chapters identified as "Explanations of *Guanzi*" 管子解 section, which may have been completed around the time of Qin unification of the Chinese world. Other chapters were probably composed during the last century of the Warring States period (i.e., ca. 320–220 BCE).

The ideological affiliation of the text was a source of many controversies. Scholars continue to debate on "what is the leading theme in *Guanzi*?" The text's diversity is reflected in debates about its classification as belonging to one of the schools of thought (see below). Modern scholars provided a few idiosyncratic categories for *Guanzi*'s ideological affiliation, such as "Huang-Lao Daoism" 黄老道家, "*Fa* School of Qi" 齊法家, "Tian-Qi[1] Reformers" 田齊變法, "Jixia[2] scholars" 稷下學者, "the school of Guanzi" 管子學派, and so on.[3] This indecisiveness surrounding its categorization shows how broad is the scope of *fa* thought in the text.

The relation between *Guanzi* and the *fa* tradition was proposed already in the late Warring States period. In the "Five vermin" chapter, Han Fei 韓非 (d. 233 BCE) states: "There are many fiefdoms and noble families which possess *fa* of Shang

---

[1] The term Tian-Qi is utilized in research for the post-386 BCE state of Qi ruled by the Tian lineage.

[2] Jixia refers to the so-called Jixia Academy 稷下學宮, a major think tank maintained by the Tian rulers of Qi between the fourth and third centuries BCE. Concerning the origin, evolution, and characteristics of thought of the Jixia Academy, see Sato (2003: 72–84, 108–62). Weingarten (2015) has elucidated how the Warring States thinkers constructed and proposed their advice about contemporary political issues in the form of their (both in real and fictitious) dialogues, mainly with Qi rulers. However, Weingarten pays little attention to the possibility that the inquiries into *fa*-related issues occupied one of the major topics in their intellectual discourse.

[3] The naming of "Huang-Lao Daoism" as a characterization of the *Guanzi*'s thought has become prevalent following the observation of similarity of thought between the *Guanzi*, and *Yellow Emperor Manuscripts* in the 1980s. The term "*Fa* School of Qi" has been maintained by Zhang Dainian (1982). The "Tian-Qi Reformers" label was coined by Hu Jiacong (1995). "The school of Guanzi" is favored by Kanaya Osamu (1995). See more below in this section.

[Yang] and Guan [Zhong]" 藏商、管之法者家有之 (*Han Feizi* 49: 451; translation is my own). Here, the "*fa* of Guanzi" (管子之法) seems to be a popular idea among the nobles of the Warring States period interested in ruling methods or laws.[4] Han Fei's comment also indicates broad readership of *Guanzi*-related texts. This popularity remains intact well into the end of the Western Han 西漢 (206/202 BCE–9 CE) period. When Liu Xiang 劉向 (ca. 77–6 BCE) collated the texts from the imperial library, there were as many as 564 bundles ("chapters," *pian* 篇) of the text associated with *Guanzi*.[5]

What then is referred to as the "*fa* of Guanzi" in the "Five vermin" chapter? The context suggests a text focused on achieving orderly rule (*zhi* 治). However, *Han Feizi* laments the situation in which, despite wide popularity of "*fa* of Shang and Guan," the "state becomes poorer" 國愈貧 (*Han Feizi* 49: 451; trans. Liao 1959: 290). Clearly, in Han Fei's eyes, texts dedicated to *fa* are not enough to enrich the state. Maybe this pessimistic view encouraged Western Han thinkers to dissociate *Guanzi* from *fa*. Thus, the summarizing chapter "Outline of the essentials" ("Yaolüe" 要略) of *Huainanzi* 淮南子 (composed ca. 140 BCE) proposes the following backdrop for the formation of *Guanzi*:

> 桓公憂中國之患，苦夷狄之亂，欲以存亡繼絕，崇天子之位，廣文、武之業。
> Lord Huan of Qi (r. 685-643 BCE) worried about the Central States suffering from the turmoil caused by the Yi and Di [savages]. He wanted to preserve the perished [states] and continue the cut off [sacrifices],[6] to venerate the position of the Son of Heaven and to expand the enterprise of [kings] Wen (d. ca. 1047 BCE) and Wu (d. ca. 1042 BCE) of Zhou. (*Huainanzi* 1998: 21:1460; trans. modified from Major et al. 2010: 865)

The authors of this chapter believe that *Guanzi* was written in order to re-establish political order when the Zhou civilization faced an existential threat. Notably, they do not associate the text with the notion of *fa*. Nor does this association transpire in Guan Zhong's biography in Sima Qian's 司馬遷 (ca. 145–90 BCE), *Records of the Historian* (*Shiji* 史記). In his summary of the "Biographies of Guan Zhong and Yan Ying" (管晏列傳) Sima Qian mentions: "I have read Mr. Guan's 'On Shepherding the People,' 'On Mountains That Are High,' 'On Military Taxes,' 'Light and Heavy,' and 'Nine Treasuries'" 吾讀管氏牧民、山高、乘馬、輕重、九府 (*Shiji* 62; Takigawa 1932–1934: 62–9; trans. Rickett 1998: 346). Evidently, Sima Qian considered these five chapters—rather than those dealing with *fa*—as representative of Guan Zhong's book. Elsewhere, Sima Qian cites the text of one chapter, "On Shepherding the People" ("Mu min" 牧民):

> 倉廩實則知禮節，衣食足則知榮辱，上服度則六親固。···四維不張，國乃滅亡。

---

[4] It seems that *fa* in the "Five Vermin" chapter does not refer to concrete laws but to a variety of policies aimed at enriching the nation. In any case, it is clear that for Han Fei the principal content of the *Guanzi* was concerned with *fa*.

[5] Liu Xiang collated these 564 texts into 86 chapters (*pian*) of *Guanzi*, divided into 24 scrolls (*juan* 卷), of which ten had been subsequently lost (see more in Rickett 1985: 7).

[6] "Preserving the perished [states] and continuing the cut off [sacrifices]" refers to the peculiar policy of Lord Huan of Qi who restored two major polities (Wei 衛 and Xing 邢) extinguished by the Di 狄 incursions.

> When the granaries are full, they will know ritual and moderation; when their clothing and food is adequate, they will know [the distinction between] honor and shame; when the sovereign complies with [proper] measures, the six relationships will be secure. [...] If the four cardinal virtues do not prevail, the state will perish. (*Guanzi* 1: 2–3; translation modified from Rickett 1985: 52)[7]

The citation suggests that Sima Qian viewed this statement as representative of *Guanzi*'s thought. The key terms here are "ritual [and social norms]" (*li* 禮)[8] and "complying with [proper] measures" (*fudu* 服度), both of which refer to guiding norms and order. For Sima Qian, the core of *Guanzi*'s ideology was promoting normative order in the state. Once again, the term *fa* is absent.

This lack of interest in the *fa* of *Guanzi* continues with the Han archivist, Liu Xiang, who, as noted above, was responsible for collating and editing the text. For Liu Xiang, the text's core content was promoting order in the state. Liu Xiang also prepared the catalog of the imperial library, which was later incorporated (with certain modifications) into the "Treatise on Arts and Letters" ("Yiwenzhi" 藝文志) chapter of *Hanshu* (漢書 *The Han History*) by Ban Gu 班固 (32–92). In that text, "*Guanzi* in 86 chapters" 筦子八十六篇 was classified under the Daoist 道家 section. Only with the "Treatise on Classics and Other Texts" of *Sui History* did this classification change. Thereafter, *Guanzi* appears under the *fa* school 法家 section in all major bibliographic catalogues.

The heterogeneity of classifications of *Guanzi* in traditional scholarship is echoed in the multiplicity of approaches toward this text in modern times. Many scholars were attracted to *Guanzi*'s economic thought as represented in particular in its "Light and Heavy" (*qingzhong* 輕重) chapters.[9] Other scholars focused on the so-called "Four chapters," which have strong resonance with the so-called Daoist

---

[7] All my translations from *Guanzi* are modified from Rickett (volume 1, 1985 and volume 2, 1998); references to Rickett are included hereafter alongside translated passages from the text. I also modify translations of other texts to which I refer in what follows (e.g., Pines 2017 for the *Book of Lord Shang* and Harris 2016 for *Shenzi Fragments*).

[8] *Li* 禮 is also one of the core terms employed in *Guanzi*'s political, social, and ethical discussions (Sato 2003: 225–33; 2013: 111–75). In particular, *li* is treated as the embodiment of the ideal order in the way that is reminiscent of *Xunzi*. Whereas its primary meaning in *Guanzi* is that of peace and political order, it also refers to the sense of moral duty and social norms rather than merely ritual or ceremonies. Thus, I prefer to translate it as "ritual and social norms."

[9] These are Chapters 80–86 of the text. The interest in them started with Liang Qichao's *Biography of Guanzi* (1909; discussed below in the text); Liang's frequent use of such terms as "economy" (*jingjixue* 經濟學), "national economy" (*guomin jingji* 國民經濟), "state economy" (*guojia jingji* 國家經濟) shifted the focus of research to modern social science away from traditional philological occupation. Liang's lead was followed by later scholars, e.g., Huang Han 黃漢 (?-?), *Guanzi's Economic Thought* (1935); Yu Huancheng 俞寰澄 (1881–1967), *Guanzi's [Theory of] Controlled Economy* (1946); Ma Feibai's 馬非白 (1896–1984), "New Exposition of 'Light and Heavy' chapters of the *Guanzi*" (1979), and so forth. For a recent treatment of these chapters in English, see van Ess 2021.

thought.[10] The *fa* affiliation of *Guanzi* remained marginal in the eyes of many. For instance, Luo Genze 羅根澤 (1900–1960) in his *Search for Guanzi's Origin* 管子探源 (Luo 1931) assigned *Guanzi*'s chapters to different schools, and only five of them were labeled belonging to the *fa* school.[11] Kimura Eiichi 木村英一 (1906–1981), the leading Japanese scholar on pre-Qin *fa* thought, did not even discuss *Guanzi* in the context of pre-Qin *fa* school (Kimura 1944).

Among the twentieth-century scholars who paid attention to the concept of *fa* in *Guanzi* and to its affiliation with the *fa* school, the most notable are Liang Qichao 梁啟超 (1873–1929), and, later, Zhang Dainian 張岱年 (1909–2004), Kanaya Osamu 金谷治 (1920–2006), Hu Jiacong 胡家聰 (1921–2000), and Yokoyama Yutaka (橫山裕). Among them, Liang is notable for his search of similarities between *Guanzi* and modern constitutionalism; Zhang and Hu focused on *Guanzi* as representative of the so-called "*Fa* school of Qi"; whereas Kanaya and Yokoyama were more interested in the perspective of *Guanzi* as an evolving text through which one can trace the evolution of the views of *fa* from the Warring States to the Qin and Han dynasty. In what follows, I shall summarize their views before moving to the twenty-first century scholarship.

Liang Qichao, arguably the most influential intellectual in early twentieth century China, penned his *Biography of Guanzi* 管子傳 in 1909, in the waning years of the Qing 清 (1636/1644–1912) rule (Liang [1909] 1989). His book was not a pure academic enterprise, but rather an attempt to project his ideal of a constitutional state through the explication of *Guanzi*'s thought. Liang considered *Guanzi* as representing Guan Zhong's own thoughts and argued that the text represents the ideas of constitutionalism and the rule of law (*fazhi* 法治) that China needs. Arguably, Liang's study of *Guanzi* was a projection of his own ideals. Nonetheless, Liang should be credited for paying attention to the importance of the concept of *fa* in *Guanzi*. His analysis of *Guanzi*'s *fa* from the comparative perspectives of the Western political philosophy and the Occidental idea of the rule of law was a major step toward attracting attention to the centrality of *fa* in the text.

---

[10] The so-called "Four chapters" consists of the two chapters of "Art of the mind" ("Xinshu" 心術), as well as "Purifying the mind" ("Baixin" 白心), and "Inner training" ("Neiye" 內業). An association of the *Guanzi*'s thought with the Daoist tenet was raised by an inquiry into these chapter's authors, especially by Guo Moruo's 郭沫若 (1892–1978) (Guo 1982 [1951]). Guo Moruo was also the core compiler of the study Guanzi *with Collected Commentaries* (管子集校), renowned as the best commentary work in the modern *Guanzi* scholarship ever since its publication (Guo et al. 1956). Akatsuka Kiyoshi 赤塚忠 (1913–1983) in his detailed research of the "Four Chapters" (1968), argued that the thought in the "Four Chapters" preserves passages indicative of a religious origin of the Warring States-period Daoist thought. More recently, Chen Guying 陳鼓應 suggested that "Four Chapters" is a representative work of the Warring States-period philosophy (Chen 2003).

[11] Luo classified "*Fa* and prohibitions" ("Fajin" 法禁) and "Conforming to *fa*" as belonging to the "Warring States *fa* school"; "Relying on *fa*" and "Clarifying *fa*" ("Mingfa" 明法) as belonging to the "*Fa* school from the second half of the Warring States period," and "Cardinal sayings" ("Shuyan" 樞言) as the "late Warring States work of *fa* school related to Daoism" (Luo 1931).

Liang suggested dividing contemporaneous theories of governing the country into two categories: *laissez-faire* (放任主義) and interventionism (干涉主義). Taking the examples of Germany and Japan during the nineteenth century, he argued that "interventionism" is more suitable to attain "a rich state and a strong army" (*fuguo qiangbing* 富國强兵). Liang associated the *fa* tradition as representing the state "interventionism" in traditional Chinese political thought (Liang [1909] 1989: 16–17). As for *Guanzi*, its advantages in Liang's eyes were not just in its interventionist ideas but also in its notion of the rule of *fa* which was close to the modern Western notion of the "rule of law." The point it that both the ruler and the people should be subjected to *fa* (Liang [1909] 1989: 18). *Fa* in *Guanzi* allows neither abuse of power nor suppressing the people's activities. Liang moreover, identifies in two extracts from *Guanzi* antecedents of modern parliamentary politics. The chapter "Nine Things to be Preserved" ("Jiushou" 九守) says:

以天下之目視，則無不見也。以天下之耳聽，則無不聞也。以天下之心慮，則無不知也。

If one takes the eyes of the world to see, there is nothing that will not be seen. If one takes the ears of the world to hear, there is nothing that will not be heard. If one takes the mind of the world to think, there is nothing that will not become known. (*Guanzi* 55: 1041; Rickett 1985: 234)

"The Ruler and Ministers I" ("Junchen shang" 君臣上) chapter also maintains:

夫民別而聽之則愚，合而聽之則聖。[...] 是以明君順人心，安情性，而發於眾心之所聚。

Now, when the people are listened to individually, they are stupid. However, when they are listened to collectively, they are sagelike... Hence, the enlightened prince accords with the hearts of the people, is at ease with their natures, and proceeds from a consensus of the masses. (*Guanzi* 30: 565; Rickett 1985: 410)

These two extracts strengthen Liang's view of *Guanzi* as a text that "laid a blueprint for constitutional parliamentary monarchy" (Liang 1989[1909]: 25), suitable for China as a modern state. Needless to say, this subordination of an early text to modern needs results in serious research flaws, but the novelty of Liang's approaches cannot be denied. Liang's interpretation of *Guanzi* through the prism of the rule of law remained influential well through the second half of the twentieth century, as several studies published in Taiwan testify (e.g., Mei 1954; Dai 1985; Xu 1990).[12]

Among later scholars who focused on *fa* as the central idea of *Guanzi* the most notable is Zhang Dainian. In his *Studies on the Sources of the History of Chinese Philosophy* 中國哲學史史料學 (1982), Zhang dedicated a chapter to *Guanzi*, in which he characterized *Guanzi*'s thought as follows:

Most of *Guanzi* was written in the Warring States period, yet there is a guiding idea throughout its chapters. This idea is that of *fa* thought. I believe that most of *Guanzi* was produced by *fa* thinkers from Qi, who admired Guan Zhong. These *fa* thinkers, the admirers of Guan Zhong, have their peculiarities. They emphasize the legal system on the one hand, and yet

---

[12] Among these scholars, Dai is a legal scholar. In Japan, among scholars who based their studies of pre-Qin *li* and *fa* on modern legal theories, the notable one is Ishikawa 1989; yet this book does not address *Guanzi*'s *fa* specifically.

on the other they affirm the importance of transformation through moral education; they give equal importance to ritual (*li*) and law (*fa*). This is different from the *fa* thought of Shang Yang and Han Fei, who emphasized the legal system alone. I think that although *Guanzi* ostensibly appears as an "eclectic" school (*zajia* 雜家), in reality his core chapters may be considered as a school in its own right (Zhang Dainian 1982: 47).

Zhang clearly identified *fa* as the principal idea in *Guanzi*. However, his analysis of the *fa* thought in *Guanzi* did not go beyond the observation that "they affirm the importance of transformation through moral education; they give equal importance to ritual (*li*) and law (*fa*)." In a later article, "The Historical Value of Qi Scholarly Tradition" (1989), Zhang slightly modified his previous view. There, he defined *Guanzi* as a "systematic synthetic work." Nonetheless, he also affirmed that *fa* is the core idea of *Guanzi*. *Guanzi* "clearly has its own core doctrine. This doctrine is the unification of *fa* (law) and *jiao* (education), or equally emphasis on law and education" (Zhang 1989: 9).

In the 1990s, Hu Jiacong, who was inspired by Zhang's view, published a monograph titled *A New Study of the* Guanzi (管子新探) (1995). This book provided arguably the most detailed examination and analysis of *Guanzi*'s *fa* available theretofore. Hu analyzed intellectual contents of each of *Guanzi*'s chapters, and from this tried to evaluate the peculiarities of the text's *fa* thought. Yet the book's major achievement is not just that but also that it provides a historical context to *Guanzi*'s thought. Why *fa* ideas stand at the text's core? Hu paid close attention to the political situation at Qi in the early to middle Warring States period. He showed that *Guanzi*'s thought as a whole "is guided by the *fa* ideology of Qi. The reforms by the Tian 田 rulers promoted the *fa*-school politics based on the rule of *fa*." Therefore, Hu concluded that a third of the currently existing 76 chapters of *Guanzi* were penned by the scholars whom he identified as "members of the *fa* school from Qi" 齊法家 (Hu 1995: 21–22).

In Japan, the key major contribution to the studies of *Guanzi* was Kanaya Osamu's monograph *Study of* Guanzi 管子の研究 (1987).[13] In this book, Kanaya asserted the importance of *fa* in *Guanzi*'s system of thought, and allocated a chapter to the discussion of the text's "*fa* thought." According to Kanaya, the discourse of *fa* in *Guanzi* can be divided into three types: (1) the simple discourse of *fa* in the chapters that belong to the so-called "Canonical statements" ("Jingyan" 經言, Chapters 1–9).[14] *Fa* in these chapters refer to simple actualization of political demands, and

---

[13] Especially notable is the fourth section of chapter four, which deals with *fa* thought in *Guanzi* (Kanaya 1987: 176–198).

[14] The chapters of *Guanzi* are grouped into eight larger sections called "statements" (*yan* 言). These are (1) "Canonical statements" ("Jingyan" 經言, chapters 1–9), (2) "External statements" ("Waiyan 外言, 10–17), (3) "Inner statement" ("Neiyan" 內言, 18–26), (4) "Short discourse" ("Duanyu" 短語, 27–44), (5) "Minor statements" ("Quyan" 區言, 45–49), (6) "Miscellaneous chapters" ("Zapian" 雜篇, 50–62), (7) "Explanation of the *Guanzi*" ("Guanzi jie" 管子解, 63–67) and (8) "Light and heavy" ("Qing Zhong" 輕重, 68–86). The exact time and reasons for such grouping are not known. Kanaya hypothesized that the grouping was adopted immediately upon the establishment of *Guanzi*'s 86 chapters (Kanaya 1987: 41). The English translation of the section names follows Rickett 1985: 5.

its major content is that of "ineluctable commands" 必行令. (2) In the "External statements" chapters ("Waiyan 外言, 10–17), such as "Conforming to *fa*," one encounters a self-reflective view of *fa* based "the eclectic synthesis of the Way and *fa*" 道法折衷. (3) In chapters such as "Clarifying *fa*" in the "Minor statements" ("Quyan" 區言, 46–49) section,[15] the objective nature of *fa* is emphasized, much as it is done in Han Fei's advocacy of the absolute supremacy of *fa*. Based on this threefold division, Kanaya explained the evolution of *Guanzi*'s political thought. According to Kanaya, *fa* in *Guanzi* originally referred to practical issues, moving then to the synthetic view of *fa* and the Way, and finally to the more sophisticated view of *fa* which evolved under the impact of Han Fei. Kanaya also opined that the synthesis between *fa* and the Way in *Guanzi* has been formed in relation to the thought of Shen Dao (on whom see Harris, Chap. 3, this volume). Recall that Shen Dao as one of the Jixia masters could have exerted considerable influence on the development of the *fa* discourse in *Guanzi*.[16]

Yokoyama Yutaka followed Kanaya's research, publishing three articles about the *fa* discourse in *Guanzi* and the evolution of *Guanzi*'s *fa* thought (Yokoyama 1990a, b, 1993). Whereas Yokoyama followed Kanaya's analysis, his study focused less on *Guanzi*'s historical background and more on the inner logic of its views of *fa*. Compared to the scholars reviewed above, the most prominent characteristic of Yokoyama's studies is his focus on commentarial chapters ("Jie" 解) that are attached to a few of *Guanzi*'s chapters. For instance, Yokoyama focused on the structure of arguments in the chapter "Explanation on 'Clarifying *fa*'" ("Mingfa jie" 明法解), which revolves around *fa*. Yokoyama quite successfully explained the inner development of the *fa* discourse in the commentarial chapters in the *Guanzi*. His view can be summarized in the following three points: (1) The understanding of *fa* in the parts of "Canonical statements" and "External statements" of *Guanzi* is basically coherent. (2) However, in "Canonical statements," the necessity of *fa* is "induced" (as Yokoyama calls it) by the need to enrich the country's economy, whereas in "External Statements," the necessity of *fa* is presupposed, and the discussion of *fa* is "deduced" from this presupposition. (3) The discourse of *fa* in the commentarial chapters is a reconstructed discourse combining both the older discourse focused more on practical utility and the "Daoist" structure of "Heaven and Earth." More specifically, the *fa* in the commentarial chapters is based on the content of the chapter "Clarifying *fa*," but at the same time it incorporates the *fa* concept from the chapter "Relying on *fa*," which emphasizes the view of *fa* that is more aligned to the concept of "natural law."

Among more recent publications, several studies reflect ongoing interest in *Guanzi*'s *fa* discourse. In particular, studies by Zhang Guye 張固也 (2006), Yanaka

---

[15] The translation of *qu* 區 as "minor" follows Rickett 1985: 5. Kanaya summarizes several opinions about the meaning of the character *qu* and why this group of chapters came to be called "Quyan" (Kanaya 1987: 60).

[16] Kanaya believed that Shen Dao was active in Qi between the end of King Xuan's 齊宣王 to King Min's 齊閔王 reign, i.e. ca. 310–284 BCE. He also argued that Shen Dao promoted a kind of *fa* similar to "natural law" (Kanaya 1987: 95–96).

Shin'ichi 谷中信一 (2010) and Guo Lihua 郭梨華 (2019) are worth mentioning. Zhang's *Study of* Guanzi 《管子》研究 evolved from the earlier studies by Hu Jiacong and Kanaya. Zhang outlined the development of the "*Fa* School in Qi" as reflected in the changes from the "Canonical statements" section of *Guanzi* through "External statements," "Miscellaneous chapters" ("Zapian" 雜篇, Chapters 50–62), and "Minor statements" to the "Explanations of *Guanzi*" ("Guanzi iie" 管子解) section. In particular, Zhang regards the discourse of *fa* in the chapter "Explanations on 'Clarifying *fa*'" as the synthesis of the Warring States' Confucianism and the *fa* tradition. Zhang also suggests that the ideas in the "Explanations of *Guanzi*" section were formed in the process of interaction with Xunzi's thought (Zhang 2006: 369). Yanaka's study of Qi's intellectual tradition includes a chapter on *Guanzi*, in which he analyzes the evolution of *fa* thought in the text. Yanaka divides it into "Early *Guanzi* school" and "Later *Guanzi* school" (Yanaka 2010: 337–87). As for Guo Lihua, his research has convincingly demonstrated that *Guanzi*'s discourse on socio-political order contains the double structure of *fa* and *li* ("ritual and social norms") (Guo 2019).[17]

At the end of this survey, let me clarify a few issues that distinguish my research from that of my predecessors. First, I am not inclined to follow Liang Qichao's approach and try to correlate *Guanzi*'s ideas of *fa* with the Western notion of the "rule of law." Whereas such comparison was an interesting new departure back in the early twentieth century, and whereas it may still be of some value for scholars interested in the applicability of China's traditional thought in the present, I think it is not a good perspective through which to start exploration of *fa* thought in early texts in general and in *Guanzi* in particular. At the very least one should avoid simplistic subordination of the reading of early texts to current political needs. In my eyes, for example, it is doubtful that Liang Qichao himself believed in *Guanzi* as a precursor of China's parliamentarism.[18]

Second, I believe that there is a problem with these scholars' discussions of the "School of *fa*" (*fajia*) as an analytical category. All too often we read statements such as "certain ideas in *Guanzi* show characteristics of the School of *fa*," but what is meant by that? Is it the "School of *fa*" of which *Han Feizi* is representative? Or is it the one described by Sima Tan 司馬談 (d. 110 BCE) in his "Essentials of the Six Schools of Thought (論六家要旨) (*Shiji* 130: 3289–91)? Whatever is the answer, in the time period during which the *fa* thought in *Guanzi* was evolving, it is doubtful that either Han Fei's "School of *fa*" or Sima Tan's "School of *fa*" existed. In other words, *Guanzi*'s discourse on *fa* could well be earlier than the writings of Han Fei, let alone Sima Tan.

To avoid these methodological pitfalls, I shall proceed in a different way. My goal is to thoroughly clarify the meaning of *fa* in *Guanzi* and its role in *Guanzi*'s

---

[17] Among recent studies of *Guanzi*'s political thought, one should mention also Guo Yingzhe (2018), but this study does not discuss the content of *Guanzi*'s *fa*.

[18] For a recent discussion of China's twentieth century debates about the "rule of law" and its relevance to the *fa* tradition, see Hong Tao 2018 (pp. 19–39 for specific discussion of Liang Qichao).

political thought in general. Only after accomplishing this, further comparative endeavors will be possible. In my reading, I shall relate *Guanzi*'s ideas of *fa* with other key concepts in the texts, such as "ritual and social norms" (*li*), and the juxtaposition of impartiality or common interests (*gong*) to selfishness (*si*). Understanding the role played by *fa* in *Guanzi* is more important than debating whether or not the text should be labeled as belonging to the "School of *fa*." This said, I still hope that a thorough and systematic discussion of the concept of *fa* in this article will enable me to present more or less a helpful observation on this issue.

Moreover, I shall demonstrate that the concept of *fa* has different meanings and roles in different chapters of *Guanzi*. This diversity is one of the reasons that inhibit understanding of *Guanzi*'s views of *fa*. In the present study I shall apply the method of *begriffsgeschichte* ("conceptual history") to analyze all the usages of *fa* and closely related terms such as *ling* 令 (decree, command, order) and *du* 度 (standards and regulations) in *Guanzi*. Based on this analysis, I shall investigate different facets of *fa* in *Guanzi* and the evolution of this term, as well as its role in *Guanzi*'s thought in general. I hope to demonstrate that the usage of *fa* in *Guanzi* evolved under the impact of three different intellectual traditions. I shall finish with observations about the role of *Guanzi*'s *fa* thought in the broader picture of the middle to late Warring States-period political thought.

2   Usages of *fa* in *Guanzi*

One can easily understand why *Guanzi* was classified under the "*Fa* School" in the imperial catalogues ever since the *Sui History*. The text not just contains many references to *fa*, but also has the highest number of chapters with the term *fa* in their titles. The current *Guanzi* contains 76 chapters (10 were lost). Excluding the chapter titles, the character *fa* appears 424 times in 42 chapters.[19] In addition, *fa* appears in nine chapter titles of *Guanzi*.[20] Among the Masters' texts, only in *Han Feizi* is the number of *fa* occurrences higher (446 times in the text and once in a chapter title). In the much shorter *Book of Lord Shang*, *fa* appears 234 times in the text and four times in chapter titles. As for *Guanzi*, it should be mentioned that aside from the chapters that contain *fa* in their title, a few others focus on *fa*-related topics and propose important ideas about the conceptualization of *fa*. These chapters include

---

[19] The usage is highly uneven. 107 occurrences are in a single chap. 67, "Explanations on 'Clarifying *fa*'"; 37 of these are in the repeated phrase "'Clarifying *fa*' chapter says" 明法曰. Actually, in "Clarifying *fa*" chapter itself, the term *fa* appears only ten times. The second most frequent occurrence is in chap. 45, "Relying on *fa*," with 47 usages. Thus, the three chapters ("Clarifying *fa*", "Explanation on 'Clarifying *fa*'" and "Relying on *fa*") combined contain 164 occurrences of *fa*, that is over one third of all the term's occurrences in *Guanzi*. See also Appendix 1

[20] These are "Seven *fa*," "*Fa* of inscribed tables" ("Banfa" 版法), "*Fa* and prohibitions," "Conforming to *fa*," "*Fa* of Warfare" ("Bingfa" 兵法), "Relying on *fa*," "Clarifying *fa*," and two "Explanations": "Explanation on '*Fa* of inscribed tables'" ("Banfa jie" 版法解) and "Explanations on 'Clarifying *fa*.'"

Chart 1 *Fa*-related compounds in *Guanzi* and Pre-Qin Texts

Compound	*Guanzi*	*Han Feizi*	*Book of Lord Shang*	Additional occurrences
Fazhi 法制	20	4	7	1 each in *Shenzi* 慎子 and *Liji* 禮記; 2 in *Lüshi chunqiu* 呂氏春秋
Faling 法令	19	19	38	1 each in *Liji*, *Xunzi* 荀子, and *Lüshi chunqiu*
Fadu 法度	15 (+ 1 *dufa* 度法)	10	3	1 each in *Lunyu* 論語 and *Shenzi*; 2 in the *Book of Documents* 尚書; 9 in *Xunzi*; 6 in *Zhuangzi* 莊子
falü 法律	3	1	–	1 each in *Zhuangzi* and *Lüshi chunqiu*
Fazheng 法政	3	–	–	1 in *Liji*; 12 法正 in the *Xunzi*
Fadao 法道	2	–	–	
Gongfa 公法	11	7	–	1 in *Yinwenzi* 尹文子; 2 in *Lüshi chunqiu*
Xingfa 刑法	3	2	–	1 in *Zuozhuan* 左傳; 3 in *Guoyu* 國語; 2 in *Liji*; 4 in *Xunzi*; 3 in *Mozi* 墨子
Yifa 儀法	3	–	–	3 in *Mozi*
Fayi 法儀	3	–	–	1 in *Xunzi*; 2 in *Mozi* ("Fayi" chapter)
Fashu 法術	4	37	1	

"The five aids" ("Wufu" 五輔), "Ruler and ministers I," "Seven ministers and seven rulers" ("Qichen qizhu" 七臣七主), and "Maintaining restraint" ("Jin cang" 禁藏) among others. For the distribution of the term *fa* across the chapters, see Appendix 1.

How is *fa* used in *Guanzi*? First, we should distinguish between its appearances as standalone concept and as part of the compounds. Chart 1 below summarizes the usages of major *fa*-related compounds in *Guanzi* and in two major texts of the *fa* tradition, *Han Feizi* and the *Book of Lord Shang*. Several compounds—"institutions designated by law" (*fazhi* 法制), "law and orders" (*faling* 法令) and "law and restrictive regulations" (*fadu* 法度)—appear frequently in all the three texts. By contrast, "impartial law" (*gongfa* 公法, i.e., law that everybody obeys equally) appears in *Guanzi* and *Han Feizi*, but never in the *Book of Lord Shang*. "The method of ruling by law and standard" (*fashu* 法術) appears both in *Guanzi* and *Han Feizi*,[21] but in the latter the frequency is much higher, which shows that this term may be primarily associated with Han Fei. Interestingly and somewhat counterintuitively, "penal law" (*xingfa* 刑法) appears only very infrequently in *Guanzi* and *Han Feizi* and never in the *Book of Lord Shang*.

---

[21] It should be noted that there is a salient contrast or difference in the meaning of the compound *fashu* in *Guanzi* and *Han Feizi*. In *Guanzi*, it invariably refers to the method of ruling by law and standard, which must be implemented by the morally motivated loyal ministers, not the ruler. Here, there is no implication that *shu* should be monopolized by the ruler to rein in his ministers as implied in *Han Feizi* (see Pines and Song, chapters 4 and 9, this volume). This peculiarity of the usage of certain keywords in *Guanzi* explains my choice of translations that deviate from the commonly used translations, employed in most chapters of this volume.

2.1 Defining **fa**

In analyzing the content of *fa* in *Guanzi* we may benefit from a variety of statements in the text that try to clarify the meaning of this term or of related compounds. I have identified four primary ways through which *Guanzi* authors delineate the meaning of *fa*. First, and the most common, are the statements "*fa* is X" (*fazhe* 法者X也). This formula appears in 15 cases, the most notable of which are the following pronouncements:

1. 法者，將立朝廷者也。 *Fa* [is created] to establish [the authority of] the court.
2. 法者，將用民力者也。 *Fa* [is created] to make use of the people's strength.
3. 法者，將用民能者也。 *Fa* [is created] to make use of the people's abilities.
4. 法者，將用民之死命者也。 *Fa* [is created] to make use of [the power of] life and death over the people.[22]
5. 法者，所以同出，不得不然者也。 *Fa* is the means by which conformity is produced so that people will have to act as they should. (*Guanzi* 36: 770; Rickett 1998: 78 ["Xinshu shang" 心術上])
6. 法者，上之所以一民使下也。 *Fa* is the means by which the sovereign unifies his people and employs his subjects.[23] (*Guanzi* 45: 905; Rickett 1998: 146 ["Renfa"])
7. 法令者，君臣之所共立也。 *Fa* and orders are things the ruler and his ministers establish jointly. (*Guanzi* 52: 998; Rickett 1998: 210 ["Qichen qizhu"])[24]

It is interesting to note parallels, and even implicit dialog between the passages of *Guanzi* and those in other *fa* texts that employ the same "*fa* is X" formula. For

---

[22] Citations 1–4 are from *Guanzi* 3: 57–58; Rickett 1985: 98 ("Quanxiu" 權修).

[23] This passage is paired with another one which says: "Selfishness is the means by which subordinates encroach upon *fa* and create disorder for the ruler" (私者，下之所以侵法亂主也).

[24] The other usages of "*fa* is X" formula are (8) 法者，天下之至道也。 *Fa* is the supreme way of the world. (*Guanzi* 45: 906; Rickett 1998: 147 ["Renfa"]); (9) 法者，不可[不]恆也。 *Fa* must remain constant. (*Guanzi* 45: 902; Rickett 1998: 146 ["Renfa"]) (10) 法者，所以興功懼暴也。 *Fa* is the means to elevate the meritorious and frighten the cruel. (*Guanzi* 52: 998; Rickett 1998: 210 ["Qichen qizhu"]);(11) 法律政令者，吏民規矩繩墨也。 *Fa*, statutes, and administrative ordinances, are the compass, square, and the ink-line for the officials and the people. (*Guanzi* 52: 998; Rickett 1998: 210 ["Qichen qizhu"]); (12) 法者，天下之儀也，所以決疑而明是非也，百姓所縣命也。 *Fa* is the standard of All-under-Heaven, the means to resolve doubts and clarify right and wrong. It is that on which the fate of the hundred clans depends. (*Guanzi* 53: 1008; Rickett 1998: 217 ["Jin cang"]); (13) 法度者，萬民之儀表也。禮義者，尊卑之儀表也。 *Fa* and regulations set the standards of good form for the myriad people. Ritual and righteousness set the standards of good form between honored and lowly. (*Guanzi* 64: 1181; Rickett 1985: 79 ["Xingshi jie" 形勢解]); (14) 法者，天下之程式也，萬事之儀表也。 *Fa* sets the pattern for the world and the standards for all undertakings. (*Guanzi* 67: 1213; Rickett 1998: 160 ["Mingfa jie" 明法解]); and (15) 度法者，量人力而舉功。禁繆者，非往而戒來。 Regulating *fa* takes into account the strength of the people and promote their achievements. Instituting proper restraints involves criticizing the past as a warning for the future. (*Guanzi* 75: 1314; Rickett 1998: 403 ["Shanquanshu" 山權數]).

instance, in *Han Feizi* this formula is used five times; *fa* denotes the method or standard for deciding rewards and penalties[25]; it must be preserved in administrative offices so its contents can be clearly known by all who are ruled.[26] In the *Book of Lord Shang*, the same formula is used thrice: *fa* is the means for caring for the people[27]; and it is noted that *fa* should be established jointly by ruler and ministers.[28] In *Shenzi Fragments*, the same formula appears in the following passage: "As for *fa*, it is the means of synchronizing the motion in the world, the system of attaining absolute impartiality and great stability" 法者，所以齊天下之動，至公大定之制也 (Xu Fuhong 2013: 108; this passage is not included in Harris's translation)." Elsewhere, Shen Dao explains different ways of *fa* interaction with rulers, government officials, and commoners.[29] For Shen Dao, *fa* also enables rulers to systematically control the flow of political events, and thus to establish the principle of fairness for all his subjects (Sato 2003: 133–38).

The passages with "*fa* is X" formula show immense interest of *fa* thinkers in defining the term *fa*, ascertaining its overall importance, and determining which sociopolitical group bears primary responsibility for upholding it. These discussions have clear parallels with *Guanzi* and may belong to the same discursive pattern. Note also the appearance of theoretical terms such as "the Way" (*dao* 道) "absolute impartiality" (*zhigong* 至公), both from *Shenzi Fragments*. The parallels between these theoretical explorations of *fa* and those in *Guanzi* will be discussed in Sect. 3.

Three other formulae employed in *Guanzi* to explain *fa* are peculiar to this text reflecting the authors' intention to add clarity to *fa*'s functions and significance. The second formula is "X is called" (*weizhi* 謂之) or "is named" (*yue* 曰) *fa*. There are

---

[25] "As for *fa*, it means bestowing rewards according to actual merits, conferring appointments according to one's abilities" 法者見功而與賞，因能而受官 (*Han Feizi* 32. 285 ["Wai chushuo zuo shang" 外儲說左上], citing Shen Buhai 申不害).

[26] "As for *fa*, it is compiled and written down on charts and documents, deposited in the repositories of the offices and promulgated to the hundred clans" 法者，編著之圖籍，設之於官府，而布之於百姓者也 (*Han Feizi* 38. 380 ["Nan san" 難三]); "As for *fa*, it means that regulations and ordinances are displayed in the official archives, that punishments and fines appear inevitable to the people's minds" 法者，憲令著於官府，刑罰必於民心 (*Han Feizi* 43. 397 ["Ding fa" 定法]). Other two references to "*fa* is X" are: 法者，王之者[本]也。"As for *fa*, it is the root of [becoming] the True Monarch" (*Han Feizi* 54. 474 ["Xin du" 心度]); and 法者所以敬宗廟，尊社稷。"As for *fa*, it is a means to ensure reverence for the ancestral temple and respect for the altars of soil and grain." (*Han Feizi* 34. 324 ["Wai chushuo you shang" 外儲說右上])

[27] 法者，所以愛民也。*Fa* is [the means by which] to care for the people. (*Shangjunshu* 1:3; Pines 2017: 121 ["Geng fa" 更法]).

[28] 法者，君臣之所共操也。*Fa* is what the ruler and minsters jointly establish. (*Shangjunshu* 14: 82; Pines 2017: 194 ["Xiu quan" 修權]). The same chapter also states: 法者，國之權衡也。*Fa* is the scale and weight of the state. (*Shangjunshu* 14: 83; Pines 2017: 195).

[29] 以力役法者，百姓也；以死守法者，有司也；以道變法者，君長也。Those who are willing to exert themselves to serve *fa* are those of the hundred surnames. Those who are willing to lay down their lives in service of *fa* are the officials. Those who change *fa* in accordance with the Way are the lords and chiefs. (Xu Fuhong 2013: 78; Harris 2016: 124)

three such usages.[30] The third is the phrase "law/method (*fa*) for X" (X *zhi fa* /X之法), which specifies the content or attributes of *fa*; such a formula appears seven or eight times.[31] And the fourth way is explicating *fa* through its component items. There are two such occurrences.[32] Overall, there is clear that *Guanzi* authors were very much interested in defining what *fa* is.

Now, let us take a closer look at the various meanings of *fa* in *Guanzi*. For the sake of convenience, I outline four primary semantic layers of *fa*: (1) *fa* as law or government regulations, (2) *fa* as paired with "demeanor" or "standard" (*yibiao* 儀表), which denotes proper verbal and behavioral expressions of lord and ministers at the court, (3) *fa* as measuring scales/standard, and (4) *fa* as the "principle of order" of the natural world and the cosmos. It should be mentioned immediately that this is not a rigid division and that in quite a few cases the precise content of the term *fa* remains complicated and can absorb aspects of each of these four meanings simultaneously. These complexities will be discussed in Sect. 3.

---

[30] These are as follows: (16) 尺寸也、繩墨也、規矩也、衡石也、斗斛也、角量也、謂之法。 Measuring rod, ink-line, compass and square, beam and weight, peck and bushel, and grain leveler are called standards [of measurement] (*fa*). (*Guanzi* 6: 106; Rickett 1985: 128 ["Qifa" 七法]); (17) 如四時之不貸，如星辰之不變，如宵如晝，如陰如陽，如日月之明，曰法。 Like the constancy of the four seasons, like the immutability of the stars and planets, like night, like day, like *yin*, like *yang*, like the radiance of the sun and moon—this is said to be [the essence of] *fa*. (*Guanzi* 43: 893; Rickett 1998: 137 ["Zheng" 正]); (18) 當故不改，曰法；愛民無私，曰德。 What accords with precedents and does not change is called *fa*. Loving the people and being unselfish is called virtue. (Guanzi 43: 893; Rickett 1998: 138 ["Zheng"]).

[31] *Guanzi* contains the following eight usages: (1) 錯繆之法 (*Fa* for stocking the supply of faggots; *Guanzi* 59: 1154; Rickett 1998: 290 ["Dizi zhi" 弟子職]); (2) 古之法 (*Fa* of ancient times; *Guanzi* 45: 902; Rickett 1998: 146 ["Renfa"]); (3) 君之法 (The ruler's *fa*; *Guanzi* 57: 1064; Rickett 1998: 252 ["Du di" 度地]); (4) 主之法令 (The sovereign's *fa* and ordinances; *Guanzi* 67: 1208; Rickett 1998: 155 ["Mingfa jie"]); (5) 奉主之法 (To uphold the sovereign's *fa*; *Guanzi* 67: 1218; Rickett 1998: 166 ["Mingfa jie"]); (6) 臣之法 (The minister [in taking his ruler as] a model (*fa*); *Guanzi* 67: 1221; Rickett 1998: 169 ["Mingfa jie"]); (7) 輕重之法 (*Fa* for making economic priorities; *Guanzi* 78: 1374; Rickett 1998: 432 ["Kuidu" 揆度]); (8) 穀之法 (Grain's price; *Guanzi* 78: 1388; Rickett 1998: 442 ["Kuidu"]; Rickett [p.442, note 67] emends 法 to 沽 in this passage).

[32] The first is in the chapter "The Five aids," which elaborates "five duties dictated by *fa*" 法有五務 (*Guanzi* 10: 194; Rickett 1985: 195). These "five duties" are: "the ruler selects ministers to take charge of offices" 君擇臣而任官, "grandees take charge of offices and handle state affairs" 大夫任官辯事, "the heads of offices take charge of affairs and attend to their responsibilities" 官長任事守職, "men of service cultivate themselves and perfect their talents" 士修身功材, and "the common people engage in agriculture and horticulture" 庶人耕農樹藝 (*Guanzi* 10: 198–199; Rickett 1985: 198). In short, every social stratum has a fixed role to fulfill. The second relevant passage is from "*Fa* and prohibitions" ("Fajin" 法禁) chapter, which says: "when these three have been preserved in government offices, they will be implemented as *fa*" 三者藏於官則為法, meaning first, "the legal system (or institutions designated by the law) is not open to discussion" 法制不議, second, "there is no pardoning of punishments and executions" 刑殺毋赦, and third, "the awarding of ranks and salaries is not above what officers actually attained" 爵祿毋假 (*Guanzi* 14: 273; Rickett 1985: 235).

2.2 Fa *as "Law" or "Government Regulations"*

This is the most common usage of *fa* in *Guanzi*. This meaning dominates the usage of *fa* in compounds such as "institutions designated by the law" (*fazhi* 法制), "law and orders" (*faling* 法令), "law and restrictive regulations" (*fadu* 法度), "law and legal statutes" (or, *falü* 法律), "law and administration" (法政 *fazheng*), "impartial laws" (or "laws that everybody obeys equally") (*gongfa* 公法), and "punishment and law" or "penal law" (*xingfa* 刑法). The idea that both the ruler and the ministers are bound to obey *fa* permeates the text. It recurs in discussions that stress the importance of *fa* and in manifold warnings, such as "If the ruler abandons *fa*, the state will be disordered."

Speaking of more concrete meanings of *fa* in the political context, these concern first of all administration of appointments, promotions, and demotions. "The ruler selects the worthy, assesses the talented, and treats them according to *fa*" 選賢論材 而待之以法 (*Guanzi* 30: 554; Rickett 1985: 405 ["Junchen shang"]). In selecting the prime minister, the ruler should "examine his merits and clarify this by *fa*" 論勞 而昭之以法 (*Guanzi* 31: 586; Rickett 1985: 421 ["Junchen xia"]). Simultaneously, the punitive aspects of *fa* are duly emphasized: "*Fa* is the means to elevate the meritorious and frighten the cruel" 法者，所以興功懼暴也 (*Guanzi* 52: 998; Rickett 1998: 210 ["Qi chen qi zhu"]). In some chapters, the punitive aspects gain more prominence: "What determines execution, extermination, prohibition, or punishment for even the smallest of things that are not at one with the Way is called *fa*" 簡 物小未一道，殺僇禁誅謂之法 (*Guanzi* 36: 759; Rickett 1998: 73 ["Xin shu shang"]). These aspects are duly integrated in the chapter "Explanations on 'Clarifying *fa*'":

> 當於法者賞之，違於法者誅之，故以法誅罪，則民就死而不怨。以法量功，則 民受賞而無德也。
>
> Reward those who accord with *fa*, execute those who violate it. Hence when you execute the guilty according to *fa*, then people are killed but there is no resentment; when you measure merit and mete rewards according to *fa*, then people are rewarded but there is no sense of gratitude. (*Guanzi* 67: 1213; Rickett 1998: 160).

Concerning the realm of *fa* application, the "The All-embracing unity" ("Zhouhe" 宙合) chapter says: "The countryside has its customs; the state has its *fa*" 鄉有俗， 國有法 (*Guanzi* 11: 235; Rickett 1985: 213). This suggests that *fa* is to be promoted on the state level, whereas customs may have a parallel role on the communal level. Moreover, *fa* is also mentioned as "the standard for All-under-Heaven" 天下之儀 (*Guanzi* 53: 1008; Rickett 1998: 217 ["Jin cang"]), implying that its applicability is broader than that on the level of an individual state.

It is worth noting that when explaining the necessity and importance of *fa*, the authors tend to emphasize two reasons for its implementation. First, it is required because "human hearts are cruel" 人之心悍 (*Guanzi* 12: 246; Rickett 1985: 219); and second it is useful as "the means by which the sovereign unifies his people and employs his subjects" 上之所以一民使下 (*Guanzi* 45: 905; Rickett 1998: 146 ["Ren fa"]). In both cases, the authors eschew ethical argumentation in favor of *fa*.

However, this does not mean that the concept of *fa* in the thought of *Guanzi* excludes ethical aspects. In Sects. 3.1 and 3.2, I shall turn to the relation between *fa* and morality.

2.3 Fa *as Paired with Proper Demeanor (Yibiao* 儀表*)*

One of the curious aspects of the *fa* discourse in *Guanzi* is *fa*'s proximity to the notion of proper demeanor, standard, or decorum (*yi* 儀 or *yibiao* 儀表, meaning proper verbal and behavioral expressions of lord and ministers at the court). *Yi* and *fa* can form compound words, such as *fayi* (thrice) and *yifa* (also thrice; see Chart 1 above). Interestingly, these compounds appear neither in the *Book of Lord Shang* nor in *Han Feizi*, the fragments of Shen Dao and Shen Buhai's writings, nor in the *Yellow Emperor Manuscripts*. Nor do those texts display any interest in the concept of *yi* 儀 as such. By contrast, the term *yi* and related compounds recur frequently (14 times) in the chapter "On standards and rules" ("Fayi" 法儀) of *Mozi*. Overall, the combination of the concepts of *fa* and *yi* is an important peculiarity of the discourse of *fa* in *Guanzi*.

Concerning the relationship between *yi* and *fa* in *Guanzi*, we can discern three aspects. First, *yi* can be a component of *fa*, as in the following: "The court has fixed measures and proper rules of demeanor (*yi*) to uphold the honor of the sovereign's position. His clothing, including mourning caps, are completely covered by *fa* and regulation" 朝有定度衡儀以尊主位。衣服絤綷盡有法度 (*Guanzi* 30: 559; Rickett 1985: 407 ["Junchen shang"]). Here, the "clothing, including mourning caps" should belong to the category of *yi*, but they are regulated by "*fa* and regulations" (*fadu*).[33] *Yi* is submerged within *fa*. The second type of relations between the concepts can be formulated as such: if the ruler and the ministers maintains proper demeanor (*yi*), then *fa* can be promoted, e.g.: "the moment the ruler establishes rules of demeanor (*yi*), the various offices will enforce his laws (*fa*)" 君壹置則儀，則百官守其法; or, alternatively, "If the ruler is not consistent in establishing rules of demeanor, then many of his subordinates will turn their backs on *fa* and replace it private reasoning" 君之置其儀也不一，則下之倍法而立私理者必多矣 (*Guanzi* 14: 273; Rickett 1985: 235 ["Jin cang"]). The third possibility is elevating both *yi* and *fa* to a higher level of equally important supreme principles of governance. The chapter "Relying on *fa*" says:

法者，不可[不][34]恆也。存亡治亂之所從出，聖君所以為天下大儀也。

---

[33] Compare to the chapter "Ruler and Ministers II" which uses the term *fazhi* "institutions designated by law" to depict rules of marital connections between regional lords which are usually covered by the term "ritual and social norms" (*Guanzi* 31: 585; Rickett 1985: 420–21).

[34] Since this sentence directly follows the argument in which the *fa*'s consistency is embraced by the author, many commentators suggest adding *bu* 不 after *ke* 可 (Guo 1956: 756). Rickett's translation also follows this emendation.

Law (*fa*) must remain constant. It is the determining factor as to whether one survives or perishes, has order or chaos. It is the great standard (*yi*) by which the sage ruler fashions the world. (*Guanzi* 45: 902; Rickett 1998: 146)

Since the ruler is addressed here as the "sage ruler" (*shengjun* 聖君), the author probably realized that this is an ideal state of affairs that an ordinary ruler cannot attain. In the above text, *yi* can be seen as a synonym of *fa*. This notion is echoed elsewhere "*Fa* is the standard (*yi*) of All-under-Heaven" 法者，天下之儀也 (*Guanzi* 53: 1008; Rickett 1998: 217 ["Jin cang"]).

When we explore the relations between *fa* and *yi*, we may note that there are also important interrelationships between *yi* and orders, commands, or ordinances (*ling* 令). The "Youguan" 幼官 chapter says:

定宗廟，育男女，官四分，則可以立威行德，制法儀，出號令。
　　Secure the ancestral temples. Provide for the men and women. Control the four classes. Then you may establish your majestic power, implement virtue, regulate *fa* and demeanor (*yi*), and issue orders and commands."[35] (*Guanzi* 8: 177; Rickett 1985: 191)

In this context it is difficult to determine whether or not there is any cause-effect relationship between "regulating *fa* and demeanor" and "issuing orders and commands." But elsewhere the relation is clearer:

衣冠不正則賓者不肅，進退無儀則政令不行。
　　If clothing and caps are not worn correctly, guests will not be respectful; if advancing and retiring do not accord proper demeanor, governmental commands will not be carried out. (*Guanzi* 2: 37; Rickett 1985: 79 ["Xingshi" 形勢])

Here, the use of the "if-then" formula clearly signifies proper demeanor as the precondition for carrying out "governmental commands." Note that elsewhere conforming to *fa* is set as the precondition of the implementation of commands (or orders).[36] From this we can infer that in *Guanzi* the three concepts *yi*, *fa*, and *ling* form a causal relationship that changes depending on context.

This brings us to the question: why is *yi* so highly emphasized in *Guanzi*? Concerning this question, the chapter "Explanation on 'Conditions and circumstances'" ("Xingshi jie") offers the most detailed explanation in its exegesis on the above citation from "Conditions and circumstances":

儀者，萬物之程式也。法度者，萬民之儀表也。禮義者，尊卑之儀表也。故動有儀則令行，無儀則令不行；故曰：「進退無儀，則政令不行。」
　　Demeanor is what sets the pattern of conduct for the myriad things. *Fa* and regulations are the standards of demeanor for the myriad people. Ritual and righteousness are the standards of demeanor for the noble and the base. Hence, when in one's actions demeanor is observed, his commands are carried out; if there is no demeanor, commands are not carried out. Hence it is said "if advancing and retiring do not accord proper demeanor, governmental commands will not be carried out." (*Guanzi* 64: 1181; Rickett 1985: 79)

---

[35] This phrase is repeated in "Youguantu" 幼官圖 chapter.

[36] E.g., "if [the ruler] conforms to what is unlawful, his orders will not be carried out. If orders are issued yet are not carried out, it is because the orders do not conform to the law" 法不法則令不行，令而不行，則令不法也 (*Guanzi* 16: 293; Rickett 1985: 251 ["Fa fa"]); cf. *Guanzi* 30: 559 ["Junchen shang"]).

Here demeanor (*yi*) is elevated to the position of supreme principle, which encompasses both *fa* (laws) and regulations, as well as ritual and propriety. This point is reiterated in the opening phrases of the "Explanation on 'Conditions and circumstances'" chapter: "If (the ruler's) speech is trustworthy, his movements sedate, and his clothing and cap are worn correctly, ministers and subordinate officials will be respectful" 言辭信，動作莊，衣冠正，則臣下肅 (*Guanzi* 64: 1181; Rickett 1985: 79). This point is related to the idea from the chapter "Conforming to *fa*," which argues that since the ruler's behavior influences that of his subjects, he must "establish demeanor to ensure his own correctness" 立儀以自正也 (*Guanzi* 16: 312; Rickett 1985: 263). This notion of self-correction probably also signifies the solemn attitude in words, actions and dress.

This observation brings us to consider the relation between *fa*, *yi*, and the concept of "ritual and social norms" (*li* 禮). As we have seen above, *li* and *yi* can be directly connected. This point is reiterated elsewhere: "rules of ritual and demeanor are sufficient to distinguish the noble from the base" 禮儀足以別貴賤 (*Guanzi* 53: 1012; Rickett 1998: 219 ["Jin cang"]). In Sect. 3.1, I shall discuss further how *yi* 儀 (demeanor, or authoritative norms), *fa*, orders and ordinances (*ling*), and "ritual and social norms" interact in *Guanzi*.

2.4   Fa *as Weights and Measures*

This usage is relatively rare in *Guanzi*. Putting aside two possibly relevant occurrences in "Calculations and measures" ("Kuidu" 揆度) chapter, the usage of *fa* as weights and measures can be divided into three sub-types. First, weights and measures are the content of *fa* (cf. Graziani, Chap. 13, this volume). The clearest example is in the "Seven *fa*" chapter: "Measuring rod, ink-line, compass and square, beam and weight, peck and bushel, and grain leveler are called standards [of measurement] (*fa*)" 尺寸也、繩墨也、規矩也、衡石也、斗斛也、角量也、謂之法。(*Guanzi* 6: 106; Rickett 1985: 128). The "Seven *fa*" further explains, "Hoping to govern the people well and unite the masses while remaining ignorant of standards for measurement is like attempting to write with the left hand while holding it in check with the right" 不明於法，而欲治民一眾，猶左書而右息之 (*Guanzi* 6: 106; Rickett 1985: 129). Second, weights and measures are used as parallel to *fa* in referring to proper policies, e.g. "involving laws (*fa*) and punishments or weights and measures" 論法辟(→刑)[37]衡權斗斛 (*Guanzi* 30: 546; Rickett 1985: 402 ["Junchen shang"]). Third, and most commonly, weights and measures are used as a metaphor that elucidates *fa*'s role in ruling the state:

---

[37] Reading 辟 as punishments (刑) following Yin Zhizhang's 尹知常 gloss (Li Xiangfeng 2004: 546).

雖有明智高行，倍法而治，是廢規矩而正方圜。

Even though one may have a clever eye and a skillful hand, if one turns his back to *fa* and tries to attain order, it is like abandoning compass and T-square and trying to determine the square and the round. (*Guanzi* 16: 308; Rickett 1985: 262 ["Ren fa"])

法律政令者，吏民規矩繩墨也。

Laws, administrative statutes, and official orders, are the compass, T-square, and ink-line of government functionaries and the people. (*Guanzi* 52: 998; Rickett 1998: 210 ["Qichen qizhu"])

夫繩扶撥以為正，准壞險以為平，鉤入枉而出直，此言聖君賢佐之制舉也。……國猶是國也，民猶是民也；桀紂以亂亡，湯武以治昌。章道以教，明法以期，民之興善也如化。

The ink-line assists in making the crooked straight. The level reduces rough places to make them smooth. The bevel-compass is inserted into the uneven to produce a concentric (curve). This refers to the sagely ruler's selecting worthy assistants through (appropriate) institutions... The state was the same state, the people were the same people; but Jie and Zhòu lost them by causing disorder, whereas Tang and Wu[38] brought them prosperity by creating good order. The latter manifested the Way through their teachings and clarified their laws (*fa*) through their expectations. It was due to the merits of Tang and Wu that the people became so prosperous and good. (*Guanzi* 11: 213; Rickett 1985: 205 ["Zhouhe" 宙合])

Note a subtle difference between the first two and the third case. In the first two, the compass and T-square are clearly equivalent to *fa* as the fundamental principle of governing. In the third case, however, it is emphasized that norms and institutions did not change between the "disorder of Jie and Zhòu" and the "good order of Tang and Wu"; hence when the sage kings "clarified their laws (*fa*)" the parallel with instruments of measurement is lost. Besides, in the third citation, *fa* is not seen as an instrument to secure political power or achieve order, but rather is directed at appointing the good people.

2.5   Fa *as the Guiding Principles of the Natural World*

This usage too is relatively rare in *Guanzi*. It appears most prominently in the chapter "*Fa* of inscribed tables" ("Banfa" 版法), which says:

法天合德，象地無親。參於日月，佐於四時。

Model (*fa*) yourself on Heaven, unifying your virtue. Imitate the Earth by being impartial. Form a trinity with the sun and moon and a quintuplet with the four seasons. (*Guanzi* 7: 128; Rickett 1985: 144)

This is the only time the term *fa* appears in the chapter "*Fa* of inscribed tables." It is used as a verb, and it is unlikely that the chapter considers *fa* as the principle of the natural world. In the chapter titled "Rectification" ("Zheng" 正), however (item 17,

---

[38] Jie and Zhòu were vicious tyrants of the Xia and Shang dynasties, who were replaced, respectively, by the righteous contenders for power, kings Tang and Wu.

note 30 above), *fa* is used as a noun in the context of cosmic patterns; for details see Sect. 3.2 below. There is another important connection, that is between *fa* and the Way (*Dao* 道). This relation appears, e.g., in the chapter "Conforming to *fa*": "when an enlightened monarch is on the throne, the Way of *fa* is carried out throughout the country" 明王在上，法道行於國 (*Guanzi* 16: 302; Rickett 1985: 257). Although we cannot determine whether the compound "*fadao* 法道" here means "*fa* and *dao*" or "the *dao* of *fa*," suffice it to note that *fadao* is promoted by the "enlightened monarch," which suggests that it is not purely the principle of the natural world. This dissociation between the Way and the natural world is implied in the "Cardinal saying" chapter:

> 法出于禮，禮出于治。治、禮，道也。
> Laws emanate from ritual, ritual emanates from orderly rule. Orderly rule and ritual constitute the Way. (*Guanzi* 12: 246; Rickett 1985: 219)

Here, *fa* is associated to the Way through ritual (*li* 禮) and orderly rule (*zhi* 治). These terms are associated with the human Way rather with that of the natural world. As such, the metaphysical associations of *fa* are difficult to determine with certainty. However, the terminology employed here does relate *Guanzi* to the vocabulary of the *Yellow Emperor Manuscripts*. This connection will be discussed it Sect. 3.2.

Let me summarize the discussion heretofore. It is clear that *fa* in *Guanzi* has multiple meanings, which sometimes coexist even within a single chapter. This precludes any possibility to determine a single unified meaning of *fa* in the text. This complexity reflects the nature of *Guanzi* as an evolving text written by different authors and in different periods of time. From analyzing how *fa* was conceptualized by the authors of different chapters or paragraphs we can trace how the *fa* ideal emerged in their discourse.

3 The *fa* Discourse in *Guanzi*

In this section, I shift the attention to the content and intellectual significance of the *fa* discourse in *Guanzi*. There are two issues that I want to explore. First, to which extent did the concept of *fa* become a major topic of political discourse? For instance, in the "Canonical statements" section, the term *fa* does appear intermittently but it never figures as a topic of the chapter's concern. By contrast, *fa* becomes a relatively important topic in several chapters of the "External statements" and "Minor statements" sections, and the major topic of one chapter, "Relying on *fa*," the first chapter of the latter section. Second, I want to assert the principal axis of *fa* discourse in those chapters that focus on this concept. What are the reasons for the importance of *fa* in the eyes of different authors?

Despite the immense diversity of usages of *fa* in *Guanzi*, we can distinguish three major topics that permeate most of the *fa*-related discourse in the chapters that attach importance to this concept. First, *fa* is a method to realize the ideal ethical order. In *Guanzi*, this ideal order is primarily achieved through ritual and social norms (*li*), whereas *fa* in this context is a tool that is subordinate to *li* 禮 and to *yi* 儀. Second, when *fa* appears as subordinate to metaphysical concepts such as the Way (*dao* 道) and its potency (*de* 德), its role is to preserve the uniformity and immutability of policies. Third, *fa* is used as a means to ensure "impartiality" (*gong* 公) and overcome "selfishness" (*si* 私), especially when the ruler deals with apportioning offices or meting out rewards and punishments. In what follows, I shall analyze each of these three strands separately and then investigate their mutual impact. I hope to illustrate therewith how the more synthetic and theoretically sophisticated *fa* discourse emerged in *Guanzi*.

3.1 Fa *and the Ideal Ethical Order* (fa *Versus "Ritual and Social Norms"*)

In most of the *Guanzi* chapters, whenever the need to create an ethical order in the state is discussed, the dominant term is not *fa* but *li* 禮.[39] This is most clear in the "Canonical statements" section. For instance, Chap. 1, "Shepherding the people" ("Mumin" 牧民) argues that without the "four cardinal virtues" (*siwei* 四維) the state is doomed to perish; these virtues are "ritual and social norms, righteousness, integrity, and the sense of shame 禮義廉恥 (*Guanzi* 1: 11; Rickett 1998: 53). *Fa* is notably absent from that list. But when *fa* and *li* are mentioned together, how are they related? Given the paucity of joint appearances, this question is not easy to answer. However, there are three situations in which *fa* is used in the context of attaining the same ethical order that is normally attained through *li*.

In the first situation, the subtle hierarchy between *li* and *fa* is suggested by the order of their invocation. For instance, "The Five Aids" chapter enumerates the essentials of proper governance (*zheng* 政): these are "virtue" (*de* 德), "righteousness" (or duty) (*yi* 義), "ritual and social norms" (*li* 禮), *fa*, and, finally, authority (*quan* 權). The order of these virtues from *de* downward is explicated through the interconnected phrases, e.g.: "once the people understand virtue but still do not understand righteousness…" (民知德矣，而未知義……*Guanzi* 10: 197; Rickett 1998: 196). "The Five Aids" chapter claims that *li* includes the following "eight cardinal roles" (*bajing* 八經): "righteousness of the superior and inferior, distinctions between the noble and base, gradations for old and young, measures for poor and rich" 上下有義，貴賤有分，長幼有等，貧富有度 (*Guanzi* 10: 198; Rickett 1998: 197). As for *fa*, it is focused on "five duties" (*wuwu* 五務):

> 君擇臣而任官，大夫任官辯事，官長任事守職，士修身功材，庶人耕農樹藝藪。
> The prince selects ministers to take charge of offices. Grandees take charge of offices and discuss affairs. The heads of offices take charge of affairs and attend to their

---

[39] My own research on the concept of "ritual and social norms" in *Guanzi* shows the proximity of its idea of the overarching importance of *li* with that of *Xunzi*. See Sato 2013: 111–175.

responsibilities. The men of service discipline themselves and perfect their talents. The common people engage in agriculture and horticulture. (*Guanzi* 10: 198; Rickett 1985: 198)

Even though the author does not state which is more important, *fa*'s five duties or *li*'s eight cardinal roles, from the fact that *de* is placed at the beginning of the sequence, one can infer that the virtues mentioned early in the passage are more important that those that appear later, which in turn places *li* above *fa*. The same sequence in which *li* precedes *fa* and both act in the same direction recurs in the chapter "Zhong kuang" 中匡:

> 遠(→內)⁴⁰舉賢人，慈愛百姓，外存亡國，繼絕世，起諸孤，薄稅斂，輕刑罰，此為國之大禮也。法行而不苛，刑廉而不赦，有司寬而不凌，菀瘺困滯，皆法度不亡，往行不來而民游世矣，此為天下也。
>
> Internally, elevate worthies and compassionately care for the hundred surnames. Externally, preserve ruined states and continue cut-off sacrifices. Raise up the orphans, lessen taxes, lighten punishments. Such is the great ritual and social norms (*li*) of the state. Laws (*fa*) should be executed without cruelty. Punishments should be scrupulously correct with no pardons. Officers should be generous and not harsh. Laws and procedures (*fadu*) should not ignore those who are friendless and childless, troubled and depressed. Do not impose returning on those who left the country, so the people may travel freely. Such is managing of All-under-Heaven. (*Guanzi* 19: 386; Rickett 1985: 316)

This is a difficult text that perplexes commentators, and some details may be lost due to textual corruption, but the general principle is still clear. "The great ritual and social norms" (*dali* 大禮) clearly has a priority over "laws and procedures" (*fadu* 法度), although both are aligned: the first is the basic principle of ruling the state, whereas the second is the practical method. This pattern of hierarchy between *li* and *fa* is observable also in the chapter "Ruler and ministers I," which starts with asserting "Heaven has its constant images, earth has its constant shapes, humans have their constant ritual and social norms; once established they are not changed —this is called three constants" 天有常象，地有常形，人有常禮，一設而不更，此謂三常; only much later the chapter mentions that the ruler "makes himself clear when issuing laws (*fa*) and instituting procedures" 所出法制度明 (*Guanzi* 30: 550; Rickett 1985: 402). This may be called a sequence-based hierarchic pattern between *li* and *fa*.

The second situation in which *li* and *fa* are aligned but *li* is still superior to *fa* is in the chapter "Cardinal sayings," which postulates that *fa* originates from *li*:

> 人故相憎也。人之心悍，故為之法。法出于禮，禮出于治，治、禮，道也，萬物待治、禮而後定。
>
> Men in ancient times were hostile to each other, and their hearts were cruel. Therefore, laws (*fa*) were made for them. The laws emanated from ritual and social norms, ritual and social norms emanated from orderly rule. Orderly rule and ritual and social norms constitute the Way. The myriad creatures await orderly rule and ritual and social norms, and then become fixed. (*Guanzi* 12: 245–46; Rickett 1985: 219)

---

⁴⁰Guo Songtao 郭嵩燾 (1818–1891) suggested amending *yuan* 遠 to *nei* 內 (Guo Moruo 1956: 304). Rickett follows this suggestion.

The "A emanates from B, B emanates from C" style of argumentation is common in early Chinese intellectual discourse. Here, the author argues that *fa* emanates from ritual and social norms, with the latter clearly having the priority.[41] Evidently, *li* stands above *fa* and encompasses the latter.

The third case of interrelationships between *li* and *fa* is of different nature: here the importance of *li* is invoked to clarify the points that are elsewhere explicated through the term *fa*. The case is the paired chapters "*Fa* of inscribed tables" and the "Explanation on the '*Fa* of inscribed tables.'" The first is a short chapter from the "Canonical statements" section. Despite the appearance of the term *fa* in its title, the chapter refers to *fa* only twice: once as a verb "to model,"[42] and once in the meaning of laws: "Rectify the laws (*fa*), straighten out the regulations (*du*), and there will be no [need to] pardon the execution of criminals" 正法直度，罪殺不赦 (*Guanzi* 7:127; Rickett 1985: 142). *Li* is never mentioned in the "*Fa* of inscribed tables." By contrast, in the explanatory chapter both *fa* and *li* figure prominently. Here I would like to focus on the latter:

> 慶勉敦敬以顯之，富祿有功以勸之，爵貴有名以休之
>
> Commend and encourage those whom you respect to give them prominence. Enrich and grant emoluments to those who have merit to inspire them. Award ranks and nobility to those who have achieved fame to make them happy (*Guanzi* 7: 127; Rickett 1985: 140)

The term *fa* is not invoked here, but the guiding norms of rewarding the meritorious as outlined in this extract fall under the rubric of *fa* in many of *Guanzi* chapters and elsewhere. Notably, the commentary in the chapter "Explanation on the '*Fa* of inscribed tables'" resorts to "ritual and righteousness" (*liyi* 禮義) to explain the above passage:

> 凡人君者，欲民之有禮義也；夫民無禮義，則上下亂而貴賤爭。
>
> The ruler of men always desires his people to exhibit ritual and righteousness. Now, if the people lack ritual and propriety, there will be turmoil between superiors and inferiors, and contention between the noble and the base." (*Guanzi* 66: 1199; Rickett 1985: 140)

"Ritual and righteousness" recur elsewhere in the explanatory chapter: in its comment on the recommendation "summoning the distant is through cultivating the near" 召遠在修近 (*Guanzi* 7: 128; Rickett 1985: 145) the "Explanation on the '*Fa* of inscribed tables'" clarifies that the ultimate goal of "cultivating the near" is to have "ritual and righteousness manifested" 禮義章明 (*Guanzi* 66: 1204; Rickett 1985: 145). It may be inferred that for the authors of the "Explanation on the '*Fa* of inscribed tables'" *li* and *fa* are equally important tools of attaining the ideal ethical order.

---

[41] This reminds of the proposition in the *Yellow Emperor Manuscripts* according to which "The Way gave birth to *fa*" 道生法 (*Huangdi shu* 1.1:1 ["Dao fa" 道法]).

[42] Model yourself after Heaven, unify your virtue 法天合德 (*Guanzi* 7: 128; Rickett 1985: 144).

3.2 Fa *and Metaphysical Concepts*

The metaphysical context of *fa* is less common in *Guanzi* than the connection of *fa* to the notion of ideal ethical order, but it is present in three of the text's chapters. In these chapters, *fa* appears as subordinate to such metaphysical concepts as the Way and its potency; and the goal of its mention in metaphysical context is usually to emphasize *fa*'s immutability, uniformity, and perpetuity. The first example comes from the chapter "Rectification." When this chapter enumerates virtues, it mentions "the Way," "potency," *fa*, "governance" (*zheng* 政), and "punishments" (*xing* 刑), whereas the terms that are common elsewhere in *Guanzi*, such as "righteousness" and "ritual and social norms" are absent. As for *fa*, the mode of its depiction in "Rectification" resembles that of the Way:

> 如四時之不貣，如星辰之不變，如宵如畫，如陰如陽，如日月之明，曰法。
> Like the constancy of the four seasons, like the immutability of the stars and planets, like night, like day, like *yin*, like *yang*, like the radiance of the sun and moon—this is said to be [the essence of] *fa*. (*Guanzi* 43: 893; Rickett 1998: 137)

This relation of *fa* to natural phenomena, which curiously resembles the "Lun" 論 section of the "Canon: Law" ("Jing fa" 經法) chapter of the *Yellow Emperor Manuscripts*,[43] emphasizes the constancy and immutability of *fa*. This point recurs elsewhere, e.g., in the chapter "Purifying the mind," which says: "Heaven does not alter its seasons for anything; similarly, enlightened rulers and sages do not bend his laws for anyone" 天不為一物枉其時；明君聖人，亦不為一人枉其法 (*Guanzi* 38: 789; Rickett 1998: 86). Like the change of Heavenly seasons, *fa* is constant and predictable.

The second chapter that puts *fa* in the metaphysical context is "The art of mind I." That chapter is divided into the canonical and the explanatory parts, with the term *fa* appearing in both. An example of *fa* in the canonical parts is the discussion about "the five aids." There, *fa* is explained as follows: "what determines execution, extermination, prohibition, or punishment for even the smallest of things that are not at one with the Way is called *fa*" 簡物小未一道，殺僇禁誅謂之法 (*Guanzi* 36: 759; Rickett 1998: 73). *Fa* is listed alongside the Way, potency, righteousness, and "ritual and social norms" as the last of the virtues of governance, which may hint at its lesser importance compared to other virtues. However, a closer look yields a more interesting feature, once we resort to the explanatory part, which explains *fa* as follows:

---

[43] The section enumerates seven attributes of Heaven as follows: "Luminous and correct is the Way of Heaven. To be fitting is the measure of Heaven. To be faithful is the timing of Heaven. Having climaxed to reverse is the nature of Heaven. To be of necessity is the decree of Heaven. [...] is what Heaven decrees to the myriad things. These are called the seven *fa*" 明以正者，天之道也；適者，天度也；信者，天之期也；極而反者，天之生(性)也；必者，天之命也；[....]者，天之所以為物命也:此之謂七法 (*Huangdi sijing* 1.6: 57; Sawada 2006: 86; trans from Chang and Feng 1998: 129–30).

法者所以同出，不得不然者也。故殺僇禁誅以一之也。故事督乎法，法出乎權，權出乎道。

    Fa is the means by which conformity is produced so that [people] will have to act as they should. Therefore execution, extermination, prohibition, and punishment are used to unify [people's conduct]. Affairs are supervised by *fa*. *Fa* derives from authority (*quan* 權), authority derives from the Way. (*Guanzi* 36: 770; Rickett 1998: 77–78).

In this passage, the author maintains that the *fa* should derive from authority (or scales, weights *quan* 權),[44] which in turn derives directly from the Way. *Fa* (which in this context clearly refers to punitive laws) is the means to stabilize the political realm, unify the people's action, and supervise human undertakings.

    What stands out is that, while the author(s) of "The art of mind I" in both canonical and explanatory parts maintain the main function of *fa* is ordering a country, both parts seem to relate *fa*'s foundation to the Way. The canonical part relates *fa* to ethical values such as ritual and duty, and the explanatory part relates *fa* to a political concept *quan* (authority).[45] In other words, *fa* in "The art of mind I" chapter can be considered either as a step down to earth from more abstract virtues enumerated before it or as an essential political device to stabilize the metaphysically-inspired order.

    The third example of metaphysical connection of *fa* comes from the chapter "Ruler and ministers I." The term *fa* recurs 23 times in that chapter, and in particular, there are two passages which contain the compound "the Way and *fa*" or "the *fa* of the Way" (*daofa* 道法).[46] This compound highlights special features of *fa* in *Guanzi*. The first passage goes as follows:

是故天子有善，讓德於天。諸侯有善，慶之於天子。大夫有善，納之於君。民有善，本於父，慶之於長老。此道法之所從來，是治本也。

    Thus, whatever his goodness, the Son of Heaven concedes his virtue to Heaven. Whatever their goodness, the regional lords offer it to the Son of Heaven. Whatever their goodness, the grandees present it to their rulers. Whatever their goodness, the people consider it to have come from their fathers and offer it to their elders. This is the source the Way and *fa*, the root of orderly rule. (*Guanzi* 30: 559; Rickett 1985: 408)

This passage explains the interaction of people of different ranks with their superiors. If those of lower ranks do good things, they will be repaid by their superiors.

---

[44] In Griet Vankeerberghen's extensive study of the early concept of *quan* 權, she observes that in *Guanzi*, *quan* primarily means "weight" (Vankeerberghen 2005–2006: 58). However, as is the case of the term *weiquan* 威權 (awe-inspiring *quan* = authority) in the chapter "Conforming to *fa*," in many cases the term refers directly to political power rather than associating it with "weighing."

[45] In this explanatory paragraph, the concept of principle/pattern (*li* 理) appears six times, suggesting that it is the core idea of this passage. Here, we can observe an inclination of the authors of "The art of mind I" chapter to use metaphysical principles. For the role of *Guanzi* in the late Warring States-period discourse about the concept of *li* 理, see Tang Kwok Kwong (Deng Guoguang 鄧國光) 2007: 269–318, and Sato's response in Sato 2013: 180–81.

[46] *Dao* and *fa* appear together twice also in the chapter "Relying on *fa*," but there *dao* is used as a verb "to be guided by," e.g., "if the people are not guided by *fa*" 民道法 (*Guanzi* 45: 902; Rickett 1998: 145) and "the hundred surnames united in harmony, obey orders, are guided by *fa*" 百姓輯睦聽令道法 (*Guanzi* 45: 906; Rickett 1998: 147). In the chapter "Conforming to *fa*," the compound *fadao* 法道 appears twice (see Sect. 2.5, p. 159).

What remains unclear is how this pattern of subordination and reward is connected to the compound *daofa* 道法. We may speculate that this compound is related to the "On standards and rules" ("Fayi" 法儀) chapter in *Mozi*, which says: "Nothing is better than modeling (*fa*) oneself after Heaven. Heaven's conduct is expansive and impartial" 莫若法天，天之行廣而無私.[47] Indeed, other *Mozi* chapters such as "Conforming with superiors" ("Shangtong" 尚同) and the "The Will of Heaven" ("Tianzhi" 天志) also emphasize Heaven's superiority over the Son of Heaven. Such an argumentative framework resembles that of the passage quoted above from the "Ruler and ministers I" chapter. Here, the concept of *daofa* can also be related to modelling oneself after the superior entity (only that, in this case, the Way replaces Heaven). This interpretation may be supported by a passage from the chapter "Explanation on 'Conditions and circumstances'" which recommends: "The enlightened ruler patterns himself on the way of Heaven" 明主法象天道 (*Guanzi* 64: 1182; Rickett 1985: 81).

The second passage which includes the term *daofa* is less clearly related to metaphysical concerns. In one of its opening sentences, the passage says: "There is a constant way for ruling the people, and there are constant methods (*fa*) for producing wealth" 治民有常道，而生財有常法 (*Guanzi* 30: 563; Rickett 1985: 409). This implies that the Way focuses on ruling the people, whereas *fa* is concerned more narrowly with producing wealth. Nevertheless, since producing wealth by extracting resources from the natural world is usually regarded as an accomplishment of the following the Way, the author of this chapter may find in *fa*, too, a similar means of following the Way, i.e., producing wealth mainly by exploiting natural resources. It is not exactly a metaphysical *fa* but still a term that is strongly related to human interaction with the natural world. The passage ends with the following statement:

> 民治財育，其福歸於上，是以知明君之重道法而輕其國也。
> When people are well ruled and wealth is cultivated, prosperity accrues to the sovereign. From this we understand that the enlightened ruler emphasizes the Way [of administering the people] and the methods [for producing wealth] while deemphasizing [the power of] the state. (*Guanzi* 30: 563; Rickett 1985: 409)

From this statement we may infer that for the chapter's author, ruling the state refers primarily to ruling the people and producing wealth. This point fits well to the overall emphasis in *Guanzi* on producing wealth on the one hand and administering the people in the way that makes them fit ethical norms on the other. If so, then the compound *daofa* in the "Ruler and ministers I" encapsulates the major objective of *Guanzi*'s political thought. That said, it should be recalled here that the core concept for the chapter "Ruler and ministers I" is not *fa* but "ritual and social norms" (see more in Sato 2013: 147–75). Think of the phrase cited in Sect. 3.1 above: "Heaven has its constant images, earth has its constant shapes, humans have their constant ritual and social norms; once established they are not changed—this is called three constants" 天有常象，地有常形，人有常禮，一設而不更，此謂三常 (*Guanzi* 30: 550; Rickett 1985: 402). Here "ritual and social norms" appears as the highest

---

[47] See *Mozi* 4 (Wang 2005: 75); trans. modified from Standaert 2013: 243.

order in the human world, standing above *fa*. It may be concluded then that despite the importance of the compound *daofa*, the notion of *fa* in the chapter "Ruler and ministers I" remains of limited importance in comparison to the Way and to ritual and social norms. At this stage of *fa* discourse in *Guanzi*, *fa* was still not elevated to the position of a core value. That latter development came only in the chapter "Relying on *fa*" discussed in Sect. 3.4.3 below.

3.3 Fa *within the Framework of "Impartiality-Selfishness" Discourse*

Unlike the relatively muted discussion of *fa* in the context of ideal ethical order (see Sect. 3.1 above), the term *fa* figures prominently in the discussions of "impartiality vs. selfishness" (*gong-si* 公私). Surprisingly, only a few scholars of *Guanzi* paid attention to the juxtaposition between impartiality and selfishness in that text. To my best knowledge the only exception is Noguchi Tetsuya's 2016 article. Noguchi analyzed the usages of "impartiality," "selfishness," and "unselfishness" (*wusi* 無私) in *Guanzi*, exposing the importance of these concepts in the text's argumentative framework. Noguchi further opined that the "impartiality-selfishness" discussions in *Xunzi* and *Han Feizi* may derive from those in *Guanzi* (Noguchi 2016: 264). In what follows I shall utilize Noguchi's ideas, shifting the focus to the relation of the "impartiality-selfishness" dichotomy to the discourse of *fa*. In this context, I want to highlight three points:

First, the *fa* discourse in *Guanzi* often develops within the framework of "counter-selfishness." Namely, the importance of *fa* is emphasized because of its effectiveness in stemming the corrosive impact of selfishness on political life. For instance, the chapter "Ruler and ministers I" argues that selfishness is manifested through "the accumulation of evil intentions" 姦心之積; it can bring about the "disasters of infringement upon, coercing, and murdering the ruler" 侵偪殺上, "chaos of partisanship and internal struggles" 比周內爭之亂, and the like. To stem this "accumulation of evil intentions," the ruler must "be adept in establishing clear laws (*fa*) and not violate them selfishly" 善明設法，而不以私防 (*Guanzi* 30: 558; Rickett 1985: 406). This view is echoed in the chapter "Relying on *fa*":

> 夫法者，上之所以一民使下也。私者，下之所以侵法亂主也。
> *Fa* is the means by which the superior unifies his people and employs his subjects. Selfishness is the means by which [the subjects] encroach upon *fa* and create disorder for the sovereign. (*Guanzi* 45: 905; Rickett 1998: 146)

It is worth noting that for the authors of "Relying on *fa*," the opposite of "selfishness" or "self-interest" is not "impartiality" or "common interest" (*gong*), but rather *fa* (see more in Sect. 3.4.3 below). The same pattern is observable in the chapter "*Fa* and prohibitions," which cautions the ruler who "is inconsistent in establishing the standards of demeanor" 君之置其儀也不一 that "his subordinates who turn their backs on *fa* and replace it with establishing selfish patterns are bound to be plenty"

下之倍法而立私理者必多 (*Guanzi* 14: 273; Rickett 1985: 236).[48] Thus, whenever *Guanzi* expresses opposition to selfish interests, even if the term "impartiality" does not transpire, *fa* as the opposite of selfishness is duly emphasized.

Second, on many occasions the concept of *fa* and that of "impartiality" are linked together. The clearest case is that of the compound "impartial laws (*fa*)" (*gongfa* 公法; this term can be translated as "laws that everybody obeys equally"). This compound appears ten times in four different chapters of *Guanzi*, invariably in the context of counter-selfishness discussions. Despite slight differences in their argumentations, the authors of different chapters generally agree that upholding "impartial laws" is necessary for the state's survival. Thus, the "Five aids" chapter claims: "if impartial laws are ignored whereas selfish crookedness prevails" 公法廢而私曲行, then "at the very least your armies will be crushed and lands pared away; and at worst you will die and the state will be destroyed" 小者兵挫而地削，大者身死而國亡 (*Guanzi* 10: 192; Rickett 1985: 195). The chapter "Eight observations" ("Ba guan" 八觀) cautions: "when selfish dispositions are carried out, the impartial laws are damaged" 私情行而公法毀; this is one of the three conditions that lead "the state to destroy itself" 國居而自毀 (*Guanzi* 13: 272; Rickett 1985: 234). In the chapter "Relying on *fa*," *gongfa* is mentioned four times and in each of these cases it plays a central role. When the ruler "turns his back on impartial laws" 倍其公法, states the text, he will be "an endangered sovereign" 危主 (*Guanzi* 45: 908; Rickett 1998: 148). In another passage, in which *gongfa* appears thrice, the author explains that "selfishness is the way [for the ruler] to be kept in ignorance and lose one's position" 夫私者，壅蔽失位之道也 (*Guanzi* 45: 911; Rickett 1998: 150). Time and again the chapter's authors caution that selfishness will cause the state to be "cast away" 舍, "be in turmoil" 亂, and "be daily reduced" 日損.[49]

This frequent recurrence of *gongfa* compound distinguishes *Guanzi* from other pre-Qin texts. The only other Warring States-period text in which this compound appears is *Han Feizi*, where it is mentioned six times. Four of these are in Chap. 6, "Having standards" ("Youdu" 有度)," which bears many similarities with the chapter "Clarifying *fa*" of *Guanzi*.[50] In "Having standards," the term "impartial laws" is mentioned in the context of "counter-selfishness" discourse, which resembles *Guanzi*. There is a subtle difference, though: in *Guanzi* the one who should uphold the "impartial laws" is invariably the ruler, whereas in *Han Feizi* these are the ministers and the people (*Han Feizi* 6: 36). Two other usages are in the chapters "Solitary frustration" ("Gufen" 孤憤) and "Five vermin." In the first of these cases, Han Fei

---

[48] Note also the relation between *yi* (demeanor, standard) and *fa* in this chapter.

[49] One other chapter of *Guanzi* where *gongfa* appears—"Explanation on 'Clarifying *fa*'"—does not mention the term *si* directly in relation to *gongfa* compound. However, the chapter's "counter-selfishness" discourse is hinted at by such phrases as "if those who praise them are numerous, he rewards them" 譽眾者則賞之 and "if people who are given commissions are worthless..." 寄託之人不肖 (*Guanzi* 67: 1214–15; Rickett 1998: 162). In both cases the ruler is criticized for making selfish (rather than impartial) appointments.

[50] Note that in the chapter "Clarifying *fa*," the compound *gongfa* does not appear. We may infer that this chapter was composed earlier, whereas two related discourses that use the compound *gongfa*—namely, the chapter "Having standards" of *Han Feizi* and "Explanations on 'Clarifying *fa*'" of *Guanzi* were composed later.

laments the fate of the "men of service skilled in *fa* and techniques of rule" 法術之
士 (*Han Feizi* 11: 80) who will "be executed through the usage of impartial law" 公
法而誅 (*Han Feizi* 11: 81). Ironically, thus, in "Solitary frustration," *gongfa* does
not appear to play a positive function (as it can be manipulated to kill innocent and
devoted men of service). By contrast, in the "Five vermin" chapter, "impartial law"
is a positive means to scare and rectify "a child of no talent" 不才之子 (*Han Feizi*
49: 447). From these contradictory usages we may infer that by Han Fei's life-time
(the end of the Warring States period), the term *gongfa* was applied to depict the
publicly known laws and ordinances. If so, this compound is not Han Fei's invention.

Third, we should note the combination of *fa* and the compound *wusi* 無私 (unselfishness) as one of the basic characteristics of the *fa* thought in *Guanzi*. The term *wusi*
appears 32 times in *Guanzi*, and the scope of its application is very broad. Authors of
several chapters emphasize the importance of unselfishness. This is the recurrent pattern in different sections of the text. Take for instance the "Canonical statements" section: "the unselfish may be placed (in charge of) administration" 無私者，可置以為
政 (*Guanzi* 1: 17; Rickett 1985: 57 ["Mumin"]); "Remain trustworthy through both
profit and loss, be unselfish" 信利害而無私 (*Guanzi* 9: 182; Rickett 1985: 180
["Youguantu" 幼官圖]). In "External statements" section we have: "Honest, correct
and unselfish" 中正而無私 (*Guanzi* 10: 198; Rickett 1985: 197 ["Wufu"]); "the [True]
Monarch unselfishly provides his people with living goods" 王施而無私 (*Guanzi* 11:
211 ["Zhouhe"]; my translation here diverges much from Rickett 1985: 204). The
appearances of the concept of unselfishness in the (presumably early) "Canonical statements" section suggest that it evolved in the early stages of *Guanzi* formation. Although
there are only a few cases in which the terms "unselfishness" and *fa* are mentioned
together, the impact of the idea of "unselfishness" on the discourse of *fa* in *Guanzi*
should not be ignored. Take, for instance, the chapter "Relying on *fa*":

> 以法制行之，如天地之無私也，是以官無私論，士無私議，民無私說，皆
> 虛其匈以聽於上。
>
> If [the ruler] implements this through the institutions designated by the law (*fa*), he
> becomes unselfish like Heaven and Earth. Therefore, his officials present no selfish argu-
> ments, men of service offer no selfish advice, and the people have no selfish talk. All open
> their hearts to heed superiors. (*Guanzi* 45: 911; Rickett 1998: 150)

The author of the chapter proposes that the goal of the "institutions designated by
the law" (*fazhi* 法制) is to achieve "unselfishness." This idea is echoed in the chapter "Explanations on 'Clarifying *fa*'": "the ordinary officials in maintaining their
tasks implement the law (*fa*) and are unselfish" 平吏之治官也，行法而無私
(*Guanzi* 67: 1215; Rickett 1998: 163).[51] If the sections "Canonical statements" and
"External statements" belong to the early layers of *Guanzi*, whereas the chapters
"Relying on *fa*" and "Explanations on 'Clarifying *fa*'" belong to the later layer,[52]

---

[51] This phrase explains the one from the chapter "Clarifying *fa*": "thus men who delight in reward
and hate punishment abandon the impartial way and indulge in selfish schemes" 喜賞惡罰之人，
離公道而行私術矣 (*Guanzi* 46: 916; Rickett 1998: 162).

[52] Since the "Explanations on 'Clarifying *fa*'" chapter comments on an earlier chapter, it obviously
belongs to a relatively late stage of *Guanzi* formation. For the possible dates of "Relying on *fa*,"
see Sect. 3.4.3; see also Rickett 1998: 143–44.

then we may observe the following pattern. The concept of "unselfishness" as essential for governance evolved at the early stages of *Guanzi* formation; it was intrinsically connected to the term "impartiality" (*gong* 公), was often associated with Heaven and Earth, and was demanded of the ruler. Originally, this discourse of unselfishness was not related to that of *fa*; but this changed with the formation of the mature discourse of *fa* in "Relying on *fa*" chapter (Sect. 3.4.3 below) as well as in the section "Explanations of *Guanzi*." There, the two discourses of unselfishness and *fa* became integrated, and the unselfish conduct was demanded thenceforth of officials (in the "Explanations on 'Clarifying *fa*'") or even of the ruled people in general (in "Relying on *fa*"). Moreover, the chapter "Explanations on 'Clarifying *fa*'" in the above citation integrates "implementing the law (*fa*)" and "unselfishness" as the necessary conditions through which the ruler maintains the "impartial way" (*gongdao* 公道) in distributing rewards and punishments. From here, we can see that the chapter's author establishes the notions of "unselfishness" and "impartiality" upon the foundations of the *fa* discourse.

3.4   The Evolution of the fa Discourse in Guanzi

In the previous sections I have not only outlined the three strands of the *fa* discourse in *Guanzi* but also have highlighted a possible evolution of this discourse during the 100 odd years from the middle to the late Warring States period. Here, I want to zoom in on this evolution by analyzing views of *fa* in three chapters—"Seven *fa*," "Conforming to *fa*," and "Relying on *fa*." The first belongs to the "Canonical statements" section, which is believed to be the earliest layer of the text; the second belongs to "External statements," and the third—to "Minor statements." Whereas this categorization does not suffice to prove the chapters' dating, my working hypothesis is that these chapters reflect different stages in the evolution of the *fa* discourse in *Guanzi*, as I hope to demonstrate below. The commonalities and differences among these three chapters allow us to trace how *fa* in *Guanzi* evolved from being just one of the tools to rule the state, to the core concept of comprehensively ordering the political realm.

"Seven fa"

The chapter "Seven *fa*" comprises discussions on three different topics.[53] It starts with the section "seven *fa*" (*qifa* 七法), which outlines seven standards or principles of running the state; then discusses four kinds of actions by which the ruler harms the state (*sishang* 四傷); and finally focuses on what is required to attain military success (*weibing zhi shu* 為兵之術). It is possible that these three segments were

---

[53] There are different proposed divisions of the chapter; e.g. both Li Xiangfeng (*Guanzi* 6: 105–15) and Rickett (1985: 128–35) divide it into four sections. I consider the two last sections as one.

originally independent texts, later being grouped into one. The term *fa*, aside from appearing in the chapter's title, recurs throughout the chapter and has different semantic meanings. It seems that the chapter's author or editor combined different usages of *fa* to bolster the importance of this term; as such, the chapter "Seven *fa*" may reflect the earliest attempt in *Guanzi* to provide a comprehensive discussion of *fa*.

In the first section, *fa* is defined as the standards of measurements (see the citation at the beginning of Sect. 2.4). Then, in the "four harms" section, the dangers of damaging *fa* are exposed.[54] That section refers to the "laws for regulating offices" (*guanfa* 官法) and "penal laws" (*xingfa* 刑法), which means that the meaning of *fa* shifts from standards of measurement to administrative and penal regulations. The author of the latter passage warns that damaging *fa* will result in such problems as "commodities flowing upwards (as bribes)" 貨上流 and "robbers and brigands prevailing" 盜賊勝 (*Guanzi* 6: 111; Rickett 1985: 131). However, even though *fa* is portrayed as an important political instrument, it is never presented as the core concept of running the state.

The last section of the chapter seems to strengthen the importance of *fa*. In discussing military success, it states first, "[The sovereign] rules [the people] as one body, hence he is able to issue orders and commands and clarify fundamental laws" 有一體之治，故能出號令，明憲法矣. Shortly thereafter, the chapter concludes: "only after [the ruler] has instituted standards of demeanor and laws and issued orders and commands, will he be able to rule the people well and unite the masses" 制儀法、出號令，然後可以治民一眾矣 (*Guanzi* 6: 121; Rickett 1985: 135). Ruling the people as one body (which is the prerequisite of military success) requires clarification of "fundamental laws" (*xianfa* 憲法) and institutionalization of the "standards of demeanor and laws" (*yifa* 儀法). The term *fa* is prominent here, but note also its close proximity to the standards of demeanor in the final sentence of the chapter. Overall, this chapter reflects the mindset in which the standards of demeanor or "ritual and social norms" (*li* 禮), the term that figures prominently elsewhere in the chapter) are still considered the core for attaining political order. The fact that "Seven *fa*" does not discuss *fa* in the context of "impartiality-selfishness" dichotomy also suggests that it belongs to a relatively early stage of *Guanzi*'s *fa* thought.

"Conforming to *fa*"

The chapter "Conforming to *fa*" is relatively long. It can be divided into 22 segments, some of which deal with *fa*, whereas other address other topics, such as elevating the worthy, rectifying the people, opposing to selfishness, opposing to

---

[54] The other three types of "harms" (*shang* 傷) discussed are harms to the majesty of the sovereign (*shangwei* 上威); harms to customary teachings (*sujiao* 俗教); and harms to the country's masses (*guozhong* 國眾).

lenience, the ruler's virtue, his positional power (*shi* 勢), and so forth.[55] What, then, is the role of *fa* in this multi-dimensional chapter?

I want to propose three characteristics of *fa* in the chapter "Conforming to *fa*." First, the presence of the term *fa* in the chapter's title suggests that the author or the editor of the chapter considered *fa* as the unifying thread of all the discussions, including even the segments that do not address *fa* directly. The importance of *fa* is furthermore asserted at the beginning and in the summary of the chapter. The chapter starts with the following statement:

> 不法法則事毋常，法不法則令不行，令而不行，則令不法也。法而不行，則修令者不審也。
>
> If [the ruler] does not conform to *fa*, government affairs will lack a constant [standard]. If he conforms to what is unlawful (not *fa*), his orders will not be carried out. If orders are issued yet are not carried out, it is because the orders do not conform to *fa*. If they conform to *fa* yet are not carried out, it is because those who issue the orders are not discerning in their judgment. (*Guanzi* 16: 293; Rickett 1985: 250–51)

This point of centrality of *fa* is repeated in the final statement: "[the ruler] does not neglect his laws (*fa*) because of his love for the people. The laws are more to be loved than the people" 不為愛民虧其法，法愛於民 (*Guanzi* 16: 316; Rickett 1985: 266). These statements that frame the entire chapter unmistakably show the centrality of *fa* for its general design.

Second, throughout the chapter *fa* is used primarily in two ways: as related to measuring standards and as guiding norms to run the state. The first usage appears in segment 15: "a skillful person is able to produce a compass and T-square but is unable to make correct squares and circles without them" 巧者能生規矩，不能廢規矩而正方圓; similarly, "even the sage, though able to produce laws, is unable to put the state in order without them" 雖聖人能生法，不能廢法而治國 (*Guanzi* 16: 308; Rickett 1985: 261–62). This is reminiscent of the opening phrases of the "The Way and the laws" ("Dao fa") chapter of the *Yellow Emperor Manuscripts*:

> 道生法。法者，引得失以繩，而明曲直者也。故執道者，生法而弗敢犯也，法立而弗敢廢也。
>
> The Way gives birth to the laws. These laws, prescribed according to calculus of gains and losses, are yardsticks to measure and to distinguish what is correct from what is crooked. Therefore, he who has holds the Way gives birth to laws but dares not violate them, establishes laws but dares not discard them. (*Huangdi sijing* 1; Sawada 2006: 6; trans. modified from Chang and Feng 1998: 100)

---

[55] The 22 themes are: (1) promote *fa*, (2) elevate the worthy, (3) strict punishments, (4) the ruler's self-constrain, (5) oppose selfishness, (6) oppose lenience, (7) law as the "people's parent," (8) frugality, (9) rectify the people (avoid whimsical change of orders and commands, of rewards and punishments), (10) importance of *fa* in making use of the people, (11) to care for the people, avoid damaging *fa*, (12) the ruler's virtue, (13) positional power, (14) rectification, (15) the ruler issues the laws but cannot discard the law, (16) orders are the great treasure of the state, (17) establish standards of demeanor to rectify oneself (18) elevate the worthy, (19) rectify the people (elevate the worthy), (20) be careful in using the military, (21) elevate the worthy and oppose ministerial cabals, (22) promote *fa*. This division into segments is mine (different editors proposed other divisions). Mine closely parallels the one adopted on ctext.org website.

The resemblance of argumentation may imply an ideological connection between the two chapters. However, as we have seen above, the link between *fa* and standards of measurement was outlined already in the chapter "Seven *fa*," which, however, did not carry on the simile to emphasize the ruler's need to observe his own laws. In "Conforming to *fa*" chapter, this usage becomes central.

As for the role of *fa* in governing the state, "Conforming to *fa*" chapter emphasizes the following points. First, *fa* can prevent evil people from engaging in their iniquities, e.g. its implementation will "stop the violent" 暴人止 (*Guanzi* 16: 303; Rickett 1985: 258). Second, laws (*fa*) facilitate "employing the masses" 民之用者眾 (*Guanzi* 16: 302; Rickett 1985: 257). Third, through *fa*, the ruler can make "all the people to set aside what they like and perform what they detest" 民皆舍所好而行所惡; hence, "the superior's orders are completely carried out and his prohibitions are completely effective" 上令盡行，禁盡止 (*Guanzi* 16: 302–03; Rickett 1985: 257). The three points combined show the pivotal role of *fa* in ruling the state. Recall, furthermore, that "Conforming to *fa*" chapter also engages in discussion of positional power (*shi* 勢), echoing the views of Shen Dao and Han Fei.[56] Thus, aside from glossing over the topic of "techniques of rule" (*shu* 術), the *fa* discourse in "Conforming to *fa*" chapter appears to be very mature. Possibly, this discourse evolved parallel to that of the *Book of Lord Shang*, absorbing ideas of *fa* from *Han Feizi* and related texts. Should we then label the chapter "Conforming to *fa*" as representative of the *fa* tradition's ideology in general? Before answering this question, let us consider the third point of the *fa* discourse in this chapter.

The third point is that despite the importance attached to *fa* in "Conforming to *fa*" chapter, many of the chapter's segments demonstrate that *fa* is less central to it than what first impression may suggest. For instance, the chapter never discusses *fa* in the context of opposing selfishness (a topic which figures prominently—unrelated to *fa*—in segment 5). From this, we may infer that the *fa* discourse still did not take the central place in the entirety of the chapter's arguments. Furthermore, whereas in a few of the chapter's segments (e.g., 10 and 11) *fa* is indeed assigned with the pivotal role in governing the state, elsewhere it appears in a more subordinate position, for instance to the concept of rectification. Thus, in segment 14 it is noted: "violation of laws (*fa*) derives from being non-rectified" 法之侵也，生於不正 (*Guanzi* 16: 308; Rickett 1985: 261). The segment further emphasizes the importance of rectification to make "the speech fit the tasks" 言必中務 and "in action think of what is good" 行必思善 (*Guanzi* 16: 308; Rickett 1985: 261). To the extent that the phrase "to think of what is good" reminds readers of the importance of the moral excellence of a ruler, the validity of the implementation of *fa* in this

---

[56] The *locus classicus* for discussing the term *shi* 勢 is Chap. 40 of *Han Feizi*, "Objections to positional power" ("Nanshi" 難勢). The chapter introduces Shen Dao's view of positional power, followed by a Confucian refutation and then the author's own counter-refutation (see, e.g., Pines 2020). For comparing the usage of *shi* in this and other contemporaneous texts, see, e.g., Ames 1994: 72–94.

discussion is predicated on whether or not a ruler can excel morally.[57] Similarly, in segment 17, the proposal "establish laws (*fa*) to order yourself" 置法以自治 goes hand in hand with "establish standards of demeanor to rectify yourself" 立儀以自正也; these are the preconditions for "making laws implementable and correcting the institutions" 行法修制 (*Guanzi* 16: 312; Rickett 1985: 263). This prioritizing of self-rectification as the primary means for ensuring the implementation of laws distinguishes "Conforming to *fa*" chapter from other major works of the *fa* tradition discussed in this volume. Further differences are observable in other segments of the chapter, e.g., the repeated emphasis on elevating the worthy, the insistence on frugality, and so forth.

To summarize, it is clear that the editor of "Conforming to *fa*" chapter wanted to emphasize the importance of *fa*, which is reflected from the chapter's title and from its framing of the argument between the two passages which focus overwhelmingly on *fa*. However, in many of the chapter's other segments *fa* appears as an important but far from central element in ensuring proper political order. In light of this observation, I believe that "Conforming to *fa*" chapter represents a transitive stage in the development of *fa* thought in *Guanzi*. It is time now to move to the apex of the *fa* discourse in *Guanzi*, viz. "Relying on *fa*" chapter.

"Relying on *fa*"

In "Relying on *fa*" chapter, *fa* is undoubtedly the core concept, as reflected in the chapter's title, its structure, and in its content. For heuristic convenience, I propose to divide the chapter into nine segments (again, similar to the division adopted by the ctext.org platform). Just like the chapter "Conforming to *fa*," "Relying on *fa*" is framed by the passages which emphasize the importance of *fa*. But it is not just the chapter's title and framing passages that matter: each of the passages in the chapter deals with *fa*. The entire chapter is designed to demonstrate the importance of *fa* in ordering a single state and even All-under-Heaven (*tianxia* 天下). We cannot assess for sure which of the chapters—"Relying on *fa*" or "Conforming to *fa*"—was composed earlier, but at the very least in terms of the development of *fa* discourse, the views that transpire throughout "Relying on *fa*" are consistent with those of the framing passages of "Conforming to *fa*" chapter, namely they buttress the overarching importance of *fa*. Arguably, the chapter "Relying on *fa*" displays higher theoretical sophistication in its discussion of *fa* from what is observable in "Conforming to *fa*" chapter. This difference is evident from the opening phrases of the former chapter:

> 聖君任法而不任智，任數而不任說，任公而不任私，任大道而不任小物，然後身佚而天下治。

---

[57] For moral argumentation in the Warring States' political discourse, see Sato 2003: 84–108 and 237–77. For *Guanzi*'s focus on the moralization of the people and the role of ritual, see Sato 2013: 111–46.

> The sage ruler relies on *fa*, not on intelligence; on statistical methods, not on empty talk; on impartiality, not on selfishness; on the Great Way, not on petty matters. Afterward, he may be at ease, yet All-under-Heaven will be well governed. (*Guanzi* 45: 900; Rickett 1998: 144)

This short passage encapsulates some of the most important ideas of the *fa* tradition: priority of impersonal laws and standards (*fa*) over individual abilities, discard of "empty talk," the emphasis on the impartiality-selfishness dichotomy, and identification of *fa* with the Great Way. In this theoretical framework, *fa* enables a ruler to attain effortlessly a perfect state of order of All-under-Heaven. Such an image of the orderly rule by an inactive sovereign can be observed in *Han Feizi* (Pines 2013) and also in a variety of other texts, including those in the *fa* tradition.

Let us move now to the main characteristics of *fa* in "Relying on *fa*" chapter. First, how is *fa* related to other central concepts and topics? In "Relying on *fa*" chapter we do encounter the topics that were prominent in, e.g. "Conforming to *fa*," such as elevating the worthy, thriftiness, opposing to selfishness, positional power, the ruler's virtue, rectification, and so forth. Yet, in "Relying on *fa*" each of these topics is subordinated to *fa*. For instance, segment 6 advocates that the ruler preserves the "six handles": "to give life or kill, to enrich or impoverish, to ennoble or debase" 生之殺之；富之貧之；貴之賤之. Then the author cautions: "laws (*fa*) being inequitable and orders being incomplete are also ways to be stripped of one's handles on power and to lose one's position" 法不平，令不全，是亦奪柄失位之道也 (*Guanzi* 45: 909; Rickett 1998: 148). *Fa* appears as standing above the "six handles." Or take segment 3: "*Fa* must remain constant. It is the determining factor as to whether one survives or perishes, has order or chaos. It is the great standard (*yi* 儀) by which the sage ruler fashions the world" 法者，不可[不]恆也。存亡治亂之所從出，聖君所以為天下大儀也 (*Guanzi* 45: 902; Rickett 1998: 146). Here we encounter the term *yi* (standard, demeanor, authoritative norms) which is usually given precedence over *fa*, but in this segment it is equivalent to *fa*. One could further look at the term "standards of demeanor and laws" (*yifa*), which we encountered in the chapter "Seven *fa*." This term recurs in segment 6 of "Relying on *fa*" (the "six handles" segment), but it is completely subordinate to *fa* there. This contrasts with the independent paramount importance of the notion of standards of demeanor (or authoritative norms) elsewhere in *Guanzi* (especially in the section "Canonical statements"). Like other important terms, the notion of *yi* 儀 in the chapter "Relying on *fa*" chapter is skillfully absorbed into the discourse of *fa*.

The author of "Relying on *fa*" invested considerable effort in integrating the *fa* discourse with the "counter-selfishness" debate. No less than seven of the chapter's nine segments (1, 3, 4, 5, 6, 8, and 9) employ the "counter-selfishness" argument.[58] Aside from these, segment 7 also cautions the ruler against "close associates who crowd around, expressing their affection and making known their desires to the sovereign" 近者以偪近親愛有求其主 (*Guanzi* 45: 911; Rickett 1998: 149), an

---

[58] See *Guanzi* 45: 900; 905; 906; 908; 909; 911; 913; Rickett 1998: 144, 146, 147, 148, 149, 150, 151.

argument that can also be categorized as belonging to the "counter-selfishness" discourse. Therefore, aside from segment 2, which provides historical argumentation in favor of adopting the rule by *fa*, all segments address the problem of selfishness and the need to combat it. Consider also the chapter's last sentence: "if [the ministers and the hundred clans] act with selfish minds, the *fa* system will be damaged and orders will not be carried out" 以其私心舉措，則法制毀而令不行矣 (*Guanzi* 45: 913; Rickett 1998: 151). This ending suggests that the author of the chapter tried to use the *fa* discourse to establish anti-selfish political principles.

The above example demonstrates how the chapter "Relying on *fa*" succeeds in integrating the ideas, which are unrelated to *fa* elsewhere in *Guanzi*—either positional power, standards of demeanor, or "counter-selfishness"—into an overarching discursive framework that prioritizes *fa* above all. The same pattern can be observed with regard to other keywords as well. For instance, segment 3 argues "what is called benevolence, righteousness, ritual and music all emanate from *fa*. These are the means by which the former sages united their people" 所謂仁義禮樂者皆出於法，此先聖之所以一民者也 (*Guanzi* 45: 902; Rickett 1998: 145). This statement appears to be a reply to the following statement of the chapter "Cardinal saying": "Laws (*fa*) emanate from ritual, ritual emanates from orderly rule. Orderly rule and ritual constitute the Way. 法出于禮，禮出于治，治、禮，道也 (*Guanzi* 12: 246; Rickett 1998: 219). In that latter statement, as elsewhere in *Guanzi*,[59] *fa* is seen as subordinate to the moral order in which "ritual and social norms" or the Way play a superior role. By contrast, in the chapter "Relying on *fa*," it is *fa* that is considered the origin of "benevolence," "righteousness," "ritual and social norms," and music. Nor does *fa* derive from the Way. Evidently, it has an entirely independent value.

Additional argumentative patterns serve to further strengthen the importance of *fa* in "Relying on *fa*." For instance, segment 2 argues that "the orderly rule of the Yellow Emperor" 黃帝之治 was superior to that of Yao because Yao was just "skilled in clarifying laws (*fa*), prohibitions, and orders" 善明法禁之令, whereas the Yellow Emperor excelled in "establishing laws and not changing them, making his people feel at ease with his laws" 置法而不變，使民安其法者 (*Guanzi* 45: 901; Rickett 1998: 145). What makes the Yellow Emperor superior is the ability to "establish" and not just "clarify" permanent laws. Notably, in this comparison the term "the Way" which is often associated with the paragon thearchs of the past is not used at all; apparently *fa* itself is of supreme value in determining one's success or failure.

A final notable point in this eulogy to *fa* is the emphasis on its applicability to the entire subcelestial world, All-under-Heaven. The chapter itself had been composed in the Warring States period, as is evident from an occasional mention of "regional lords of neighboring states" 鄰國諸侯 (*Guanzi* 45: 906; Rickett 1998: 147). However, the ultimate goal of *fa* application is All-under-Heaven rather than an

---

[59] For instance, the chapter "The art of mind I" maintains: "laws emanate from political authority, and political authority emanates from the Way" 法出乎權，權出乎道 (*Guanzi* 36: 770; Rickett 1998: 78).

individual state. This is evident not just in the discussion of early thearchs, such as the Yellow Emperor or Yao, but also in the discussions directed at the ideal sovereign of the current (or future) era. For instance, segment 8 says: "superiors take impartiality as the basis for conducting inquiries, make judgement according to the *fa* system; therefore, being entrusted with All-under-Heaven is not an onerous task" 上以公正論，以法制斷，故任天下而不重也 (*Guanzi* 45: 911; Rickett 1998: 150). Elsewhere, the chapter depicts the sage ruler as who can "be at ease, yet All-under-Heaven will be well governed" 身佚而天下治; and "let his robes fall and fold his hands, yet All-under-Heaven will be well governed" 垂拱而天下治 (*Guanzi* 45: 900; Rickett 1998: 144–45). Clearly, the scope of *fa* implementation is the entire realm and not just a single state.

To summarize, the chapter "Relying on *fa*" elevates the efficiency of ruling by *fa* to a new level. *Fa* is superior to moral concepts such as benevolence, righteousness, ritual and social norms, and music; it overshadows such concepts as the Way (see also Rickett 1998: 143). Its efficiency is manifested on multiple levels. It is the means to prevent ministerial conspiracies or internal strife induced by everybody's selfishness; it is the apex of impartiality—ruling by *fa* means being "like Heaven and Earth in having no selfishness" 如天地之無私 (*Guanzi* 45: 911; Rickett 1998: 150). It represents fairness, as implied, among other things, from the frequent usage of the compound "impartial laws" (*gongfa* 公法) throughout the chapter.[60] The chapter elevates *fa* to the new level of supreme principle through which the "impartiality-selfishness" dichotomy should be maintained. And in addition, the scope of *fa*'s implementation expands from a single state to All-under-Heaven. This chapter marks the culmination of the *fa* discourse and of the elaboration of the idea of the rule by *fa* in *Guanzi*.

4 Conclusion

The above discussion has demonstrated the multiplicity of meanings of *fa* in *Guanzi* and highlighted considerable differences in the usage of *fa* in different chapters of the text. *Fa*—which can refer to such things as measurement standards, laws, ordering principles of the cosmos, or even proper demeanor—appears as an extraordinary rich term. It has ethical and metaphysical dimensions, and is a particularly potent means of dealing with the "impartiality-selfishness" dichotomy. This richness of meanings and usages reflects a lengthy process of evolution of *fa* discourse. I have attempted to trace aspects of this evolution through comparing the usage of *fa* in three chapters—"Seven *fa*," "Conforming to *fa*" and "Relying on *fa*." Of the three, the most notable is the latter, in which *fa* becomes an overarching principle that encompasses political, moral, and even metaphysical aspects. In this chapter, *fa* is presented as the panacea to the entirety of sociopolitical ills.

---

[60] Four of the eleven usages of this compound in *Guanzi* is in the chapter "Relying on *fa*."

This discussion allows us to situate the *fa* discourse of *Guanzi* within a broader pattern of the Warring States-period *fa* tradition. In this context, particularly noteworthy is the supremacy of *fa* in the chapter "Relying on *fa*." The chapter places *fa* at the apex of value system no less than in such texts as the *Book of Lord Shang*, the *Yellow Emperor Manuscripts*, the *Shenzi Fragments*, or even *Han Feizi*. The *fa* discourse throughout that chapter integrates several Warring States-period political theories within the *fa* framework. This discourse reaches a high level of theoretical depth. Therefore, at least insofar as this specific chapter is concerned, it can be categorized as belonging to the *fa* tradition. As such, it can justify the inclusion of *Guanzi* within the "School of *fa*" category starting with the "Treatise on Classics and Other Texts" of the *Sui History*.

Appendix 1 Distribution of the term *fa* in *Guanzi* chapters

Chapter number	Section	Chapter's name	Occurrences	Comment
1	經言	牧民	1	
2	經言	形勢	5	
3	經言	權修	2	
6	經言	七法	11	
7	經言	版法	3	
8	經言	幼官	3	
9	經言	幼官圖	3	
10	外言	五輔	5	
11	外言	宙合	5	
12	外言	樞言	2	
13	外言	八觀	8	
14	外言	法禁	11	
15	外言	重令	2	
16	外言	法法	31	
17	外言	兵法	4	
19	內言	中匡	4	
20	內言	小匡	4	
24	內言	問	1	
26	內言	戒	1	
30	短語	君臣上	23	
31	短語	君臣下	7	
33	短語	四稱	1	
35	短語	侈靡	7	
36	短語	心術上	5	
38	短語	白心	4	
43	短語	正	3	
45	區言	任法	55	

(continued)

Appendix 1 (continued)

Chapter number	Section	Chapter's name	Occurrences	Comment
46	區言	明法	10	
47	區言	正世	6	
48	區言	治國	1	
52	雜篇	七臣七主	25	
53	雜篇	禁藏	12	
56	雜篇	桓公問	1	
57	雜篇	度地	3	
59	雜篇	弟子職	1	
64	管子解	形勢解	11	
66	管子解	版法解	17	
67	管子解	明法解	109	37 times in the formula 明法曰
73	輕重	國蓄	1	
75	輕重	山權數	3	
76	輕重	山至數	1	
78	輕重	揆度	5	
80	輕重	輕重甲	1	

References

Akatsuka, Kiyoshi 赤塚忠. 1968 (1987). "The Original Form of Daoist Thought" 道家思想の原初の形態. Rpt. in Akatsuka, *A Study of the Thoughts of the Warring States Masters* 諸子思想の研究, 71–145. Tokyo: Kenbunsha.

Ames, Roger T. 1994. *The Art of Rulership: A Study of Ancient Chinese Political Thought*. Albany: State University of New York Press.

Chen, Guying (Guu-ying) 陳鼓應. 2003. *Annotations on Four Chapters of Guanzi: A Representative Text of Jixia Daoists* 管子四篇詮釋：稷下道家代表作. Taipei: Sanmin shuju.

Chang, Leo S., and Yu Feng, trans. and ed. 1998. *The Four Political Treatises of the Yellow Emperor: Original Mawangdui Texts with Complete English Translations and an Introduction*. Honolulu: University of Hawaii Press.

Dai, Dongxiong 戴東雄. 1985. *Legal Thought of Guanzi* 管子的法律思想. Taipei: Zhongyang wenwu gongyingshe.

Guanzi. See Li, Xiangfeng 2004.

Guo, Lihua (Kuo, Li-Hua) 郭梨華. 2019. "The 'Rule of *fa*' Thought Manifested in Jixia Academy: With the Focus on *Guanzi*" 稷下學宮所彰顯的法治思想——以《管子》為主的研究. *Guanzi Journal* 管子學刊2: 29–35.

Guo, Moruo 郭沫若. [1951] 1982. "A Study of Remnants of the Works of Song Xing and Yin Wen" 宋鈃尹文遺著考 Rpt. in *Complete Work of Guo Moruo: History Section* 郭沫若全集·歷史編. vol. 1. Beijing: Renmin wenxue chubanshe, 547–572.

Guo, Moruo 郭沫若. Wen Yiduo 聞一多 and Xu Weiyu 許維遹, eds. 1956. *The Collection of Guanzi Commentaries* 管子集校. Beijing: Kexue chubanshe. [The most important work on textual collation of modern *Guanzi* studies].

Guo, Yingzhe 郭應哲. 2018. "Guanzi's New Theory of the State: The Social Ontology of Power Concentration" 《管子》新國家理論的務實思維:權力集中並尊重社會本體, *Taiwan Journal of Political Science* 政治科學論叢 76: 31–60.

Harris, Eirik Lang. 2016. trans. and ed. *The Shen Tzu Fragments: A Philosophical Analysis and Translation*. New York: Columbia University Press.

Hong, Tao 洪濤. 2018. "The Concept of the Rule of *fa* and the *fa* Tradition's Thought in the 20th Century" (A) 20世紀中國的法治概念與法家思想(上). *History of Political Thought* 政治思想史 9.1: 13–45.

Hu, Jiacong 胡家聰. 1995. *A New Study of the* Guanzi 管子新探. Beijing: Zhongguo shehui kexue chubanshe. [A representative work in mainland China which includes a comparative analysis with Mawandui texts.]

Huainanzi jishi 淮南子集釋 (*Huainanzi*, with collected explanations). 1998. Ed. He Ning 何寧. Beijing: Zhonghua shuju.

Huang, Han 黃漢. 1935. *The Guanzi's Economic Thoguht* 管子經濟思想. Shanghai: Shangwu yinshuguan.

Ishikawa, Hideaki 石川英昭. 1989. *A Study of the Ritual and Legal Thought in Early China* 中國古代禮法思想の研究. Tokyo: Sōbunsha.

Jiang, Lihong 蔣禮鴻. 1986. *Pointing an Awl at the Book of Lord Shang* 商君書錐指. Beijing: Zhonghua shuju.

Kanaya, Osamu 金谷治. 1987. *Study of Guanzi* 管子の研究. Tokyo: Iwanami shoten. [The most important work on textual formation and thought in Japanese *Guanzi* studies.]

Kimura, Eiichi 木村英一. 1944. *A Study of the fa school* 法家思想の研究. Tokyo: Kōbundo.

Ma, Feibai 馬非白. 1979. *A New Interpretation of Guanzi's 'Light and Heavy' Chapters* 管子輕重新詮. Beijing: Zhonghua shuju.

Li, Xiangfeng 黎翔鳳, ed. 2004. Guanzi, *Collated and Annotated* 管子校注, collated by Liang, Yunhua 梁運華. Beijing: Zhonghua shuju.

Liang, Qichao 梁啟超. [1909] 1989. *Biography of Master Guan* 管子傳. Rpt. Taipei: Taiwan Zhonghua shuju (edition based on volume 28 of *A Selected Work of Liang Qichao* 飲冰室專集 [Beijing: Zhonghua shuju], 1936).

Liao, W. K. 廖文奎. 1959. *Han Fei Tzu: Works from Chinese*. London: Arthur Probsthain.

Luo, Genze 羅根澤 1931. *A Serach for Guanzi's Origin* 管子探源. Shanghai: Zhonghua shuju. [A pioneering work of modern *Guanzi* studies on the text and its thought.]

Major, John S., Sarah A. Queen, Andrew Seth Meyer, and Harold D. Roth, trans. and ed. 2010. *The Huainanzi: A Guide to the Theory and Practice of Government in Early China*. New York: Columbia University Press.

Mei, Zhongxic 梅仲協. 1954. Guanzi's Legal Thought and the Principle of Rule of Law 管子的法律思想與法治主義. In *Collected Articles on China's Political Thought and Institutions* 中國政治思想與制度論集. ed. Zhang Qiyun 張其昀, et al. Taipei: Zhonghua wenhua chuban shiye weiyuan hui.

Mozi. See Wang Huanbiao.

Noguchi, Tetsuya 野口哲哉. 2016. "*Guanzi's* Discourse on Impartial-Selfish: The Origin of the Impartial-Selfish Discourse" 管子の公私論——公私論の淵源, in Noguchi, *The "Impartial-Selfish" Discourse in Ancient China* 中國古代の「公・私」論, 203–265. Nagoya: V2 Solution.

Pines, Yuri. 2013. Submerged by Absolute Power: The Ruler's Predicament in the *Han Feizi*. In *Dao Companion to the Philosophy of Han Fei*, ed. Paul R. Goldin, 67–86. Dordrecht: Springer.

———, trans. and ed. 2017. *The Book of Lord Shang: Apologetics of State Power in Early China*. New York: Columbia University Press.

———. 2020. Worth vs. Power: Han Fei's 'Objection to Positional Power' Revisited. *Asiatische Studien/Études Asiatiques* 74(3): 687–710.

Rickett, W. Allyn, trans. and ed. 1985/1998. *Guanzi: Political, Economic, and Philosophical Essays from Early China* (volumes 1–2). Princeton: Princeton University Press. [A pioneering and the most comprehensive work on *Guanzi* ever in modern Anglo-American scholarship.]

Sato, Masayuki. 2003. *The Confucian Quest for Order: The Origin and Formation of the Political Thought of Xun Zi*. Leiden: Brill Academic Publishers.

——— 佐藤將之. 2013. *A Study of the Origin of Xunzi's Thought of Ritual and Social Norms and the Hundred School Masters* 荀子禮治思想的淵源與戰國諸子之研究. Taipei: National Taiwan University Press. [A study which has elucidated the importance of the idea of ritual and social norms in *Guanzi*.]

Sawada, Takio 澤田多喜男, trans and ed. 2006. *The Yellow Emperor's Four Canons* 黃帝四經. Tokyo: Chisen shokan.

Shangjunshu. See Jiang Lihong 1986.

Shenzi. See Xu Fuhong 2013.

Shiji. See Takigawa, Kametarō.

Standaert, Nicolas. 2013. Heaven as a Standard. In *The Mozi as an Evolving Text: Different Voices in Early Chinese Thought*, ed. Defoort Carine and Nicolas Standaert, 237–269. Leiden: Brill.

Takigawa, Kametarō. 瀧川龜太郎 1932–1934. ed. *A Study of Collected Collations and Commentaries on the* Shiji 史記會注考證. Tokyo: Tōhō bunka gakuin tōkyō kenkyūjo.

Van Ess, Hans. 2021. Situating the 'Qingzhong' 輕重 Chapters of the *Guanzi* 管子. In *Between Command and Market: Economic Thought and Practice in Early China*, ed. Elisa Levi Sabattini and Christian Schwermann, 114–144. Leiden: Brill.

Vankeerberghen, Griet. 2005–2006. Choosing Balance: Weighing (*quan*) as a Metaphor for Action in Early Chinese Texts. *Early China* 30: 47–89.

Wang, Huanbiao 王煥鑣. 2005 *A Collected Commentaries of* Mozi 墨子集詁. Shanghai: Shanghai guji.

Weingarten, Oliver. 2015. Debates around Jixia: Argument and Intertextuality in Warring States Writings Associated with Qi. *Journal of the American Oriental Society* 135 (2): 283–307.

Xu, Fuhong 許富宏, ed. 2013. *A Collected Collations and Commentaries of* Shenzi 慎子集校集注. Beijing: Zhonghua shuju.

Xu, Hanchang 徐漢昌. 1990. *A Study of* Guanzi's *Thoguht* 管子思想研究. Taipei: Xuesheng shuju. [A representative work of the text and thought of *Guanzi* in modern Taiwan scholarship.]

Yanaka, Shin'ichi 谷中信一. 2010. *The Development of the Thought and Culture in the Qi Region and the Formation of Ancient China* 齊地の思想文化の展開と古代中國の形成. Tokyo: Kyūko shoin.

Yokoyama, Yutaka 橫山裕. 1990a. "A Study of the Legal Thought in the "Jingyan" Part of *Guanzi*『管子』經言類の法思想について". *Studies in Chinese Philosophy* (Kyūshū University) 中國哲學論集 16:37–53.

——— 橫山裕. 1990b. "A Study of the Legal Thought in the 'Waiyan' Part of the *Book of Guanzi*]. *Chūgoku tetsugaku ronshū*『管子』外言類の法思想について". *Studies in Chinese Philosophy* (Kyūshū University) 中國哲學論集 17: 18–34.

——— 橫山裕. 1993. "A Study of the Thought of the Group Discussing *Fa* in the Book of Guanzi——With Close Focus on the Formation of its Central Idea"『管子』法グループの思想について——その中心思想の成立を中心に. *Studies in Chinese Language, Literature and Philosophy* 九州中國學會報 31:1–21.

Yu, Huancheng 俞寰澄. 1946. *The* Guanzi's *Theory to Control Ecomony* 管子之統制經濟. Wenzhou: Zhonghua zhuzi zhiban yinshuachang.

Zhang, Dainian 張岱年. 1982. *Study of the Source Materials of the History of Chinese Phiosophy* 中國哲學史史料學. Beijing: Sanlian.

——— 張岱年. 1989. "The Historical Value of Qi Scholarly Tradition" 齊學的歷史價值. *Knowledge of Literature and History* 文史知識 3: 8–10.

Zhang, Guye 張固也. 2006. *Study of* Guanzi《管子》研究. Jinan: Qilu xueshe.

Chapter 6
The Ideology of Chao Cuo

Christian Schwermann

"A fool!" (*yu* 愚), was all that Yang Xiong 揚雄 (54 BCE – 18 CE), one of the most eminent Confucian scholars of the late Western Han 西漢 (206/202 BCE – 9 CE), had to say according to his *Fayan* 法言 (Exemplary Sayings) when asked by a student about Chao Cuo 鼂錯 (d. 154 BCE).[1] This judgment is not at all as clear as some would seem to suggest.[2] Did Yang Xiong mean that Chao Cuo was "morally obtuse," "either because he was a cruel official or because he failed to see the enmity his policies were engendering," as Michael Nylan surmises in her translation of the *Fayan* (Nylan 2013: 195, 246)? Or did he rather refer to the fact that Chao Cuo sacrificed his life in order to bring about the reduction of the titular kings *(wang* 王*)* and to strengthen the imperial house and the central government?[3]

---

[1] See *Fayan yishu* (1987. 11. 460) ("Yuan Qian" 淵騫). More often than not Chao Cuo's family name is incorrectly given as 晁 in early Chinese texts (Loewe 2000: 27).

[2] See, for example, Marc Nürnberger in a note to his translation of the parallel lives of Yuan Ang 袁盎 (d. 148 BCE) and Chao Cuo (Nürnberger 2008: 351).

[3] The titular kings, who were entrusted with the administration of the eastern half of the empire at the beginning of the Western Han dynasty, stayed at the imperial court only occasionally and otherwise resided in their sub-dominions. When the imperial house tried to curtail the power of the titular kings and place their territories under central administration, partly on the initiative of Chao Cuo, seven of them revolted in what is known as the Rebellion of the Seven Kings in 154 BCE. At first, they were only concerned with maintaining the status quo and their privileges, such as the monopoly on the use of force, the right to mint coins and levy taxes. But eventually their leader wanted to crown himself emperor, which led to the destruction of the titular kingdoms in the second half of the second century BCE. For details, see the comprehensive study by Reinhard Emmerich (2002).

C. Schwermann (✉)
Ruhr-Universität Bochum, Bochum, Germany

© The Author(s), under exclusive license to Springer Nature Switzerland AG 2024
Y. Pines (ed.), *Dao Companion to China's* fa *Tradition*, Dao Companions
to Chinese Philosophy 19, https://doi.org/10.1007/978-3-031-53630-4_7

Whatever political differences there may have been, self-effacement of a minister was foolish from the Confucian point of view, even when it was offered for a good cause. "To bring destruction upon himself is what a humane man does not do" 身亡者，仁人所不為也, is what Liu Xiang 劉向 (79–8 BCE), an even more eminent Confucian scholar, decreed on this issue in his *Shuoyuan* 說苑 a quarter of a century before Yang Xiong.[4] On the other hand, Chao Cuo is portrayed quite positively by adherents of the *fa* 法 tradition. For example, in the eponymous chapter of the *Yantielun* 鹽鐵論 (Debates on Salt and Iron), the Imperial Councilor (*yushi dafu* 御史大夫), Sang Hongyang 桑弘羊 (152–80 BCE), presents him as a reformer following in the footsteps of Shang Yang 商鞅 (d. 338 BCE) and even insinuates that it was the emperor who was responsible for Chao's "murder" (*sha* 殺) (*Yantielun jiaozhu* 1992: 8: 113 ["Chao Cuo" 晁錯]). Obviously, the diverging historical judgements regarding Chao Cuo in received texts are due to the different ideological positions of the respective judges involved. While the authors of *Shiji* 史記 (Records of the Scribes, a.k.a. Records of the Historian) and *Hanshu* 漢書 (Documents of the Han, a.k.a. History of the [Former] Han Dynasty) characterize him as a harsh official or, as Michael Loewe puts it, as "a man of an unyielding and hard frame of mind" 錯為人陗直刻深 (Loewe 2000: 27; cf. *Shiji* 101: 2745, and *Hanshu* 1962: 49: 2277), the Imperial Councilor of the *Yantielun* praises his achievements on behalf of the imperial house.

Indeed, in addition to his role in crushing the titular kingdoms, Chao Cuo's contributions to border defense in the northwest and military policy toward the Xiongnu 匈奴 deserve special mention.[5] During Emperor Wen's 文帝 reign (i.e. Liu Heng 劉恆, r. 180–157 BCE), the Xiongnu had raided Han territory several times. Chao Cuo not only emphasized that border security depended on the election of suitably qualified generals, but also proposed using foreign peoples who had defected to the Han as auxiliaries in defense. Moreover, he developed an entirely new concept of sustainable border defense that was not based on short-term military service of one year, and proposed establishing permanent *Wehrbauern* colonies, that is, defense farming colonies, in the northwest, which would later be called *tuntian* 屯田. Families from the interior were to be lured there with the prospect of being awarded ranks of merit and supplied with land and goods. On the one hand, the colonists were to farm and cultivate the borderland, on the other, they were to protect it against Xiongnu raids and therefore to be assigned to military units and given training in arms. These proposals, which Emperor Wen agreed to, had a far-reaching influence on the further development of border defenses in the northwest.[6]

---

[4] *Shuoyuan jiaozheng* (1987: 9: 206) (Zheng jian" 正諫). Compare Schwermann (2017a: 157).

[5] For the following and for additional biographical details, see the brief account of Chao Cuo's life by Michael Loewe (Loewe 2000: 27–29).

[6] For the origins and early history of the *tuntian*-system see Liu 1988; Zhu 2012.

In view of these outstanding achievements and the partially contradicting judgments about Chao Cuo, the question of which ideological camp he actually belonged to becomes all the more pressing. With a reference to the much-invoked early Han syncretism one would neither be able to do justice to him nor to find an answer to the question as to which paths his thinking ran along.[7]

1 Was Chao Cuo a Philanthropist?

Chao Cuo's identification as a representative of the *fa* tradition has a long pedigree. *Shiji* mentions that he had studied the writings of Shang Yang and Shen Buhai 申不害 (d. 337 BCE) in his youth (*Shiji* 101: 2745; cf. *Hanshu* 49: 2276). The "Treatise on Arts and Letters" ("Yiwenzhi" 藝文志) chapter of *Hanshu* records an item "Chao Cuo" in 31 chapters (*pian* 篇) under the *fajia* 法家, "School of *fa*," section (*Hanshu* 30: 1735).[8] Nonetheless, Western scholars of early China tend to interpret his support of welfare policy as a Confucian stance.[9] Can we clarify better his ideological position? Was he a supporter of a strong monarchy that would govern the country centrally with the help of impartial standards (*fa*)? Did he believe that government action should be guided by the needs of the time rather than by moral values and time-honored precedents? In other words, did he think in terms of progress rather than tradition, and did he conceive of the future as something that could be shaped or even planned?[10]

Possibly the role he played in curtailing the titular kingdoms and putting down the Rebellion of the Seven Kings points to the latter stance. Unfortunately, as Marc Nürnberger notes, the details of his advice on this matter, for example memorials to the throne on the reduction of the titular kings, have not been handed down (Nürnberger 2008: 351). However, two memorials – or at least excerpts from these – on questions of economic policies have been transmitted in the first chapter on "Food and Money," i.e., the economy (*shihuo* 食貨), in the *Hanshu*. Since they deal with central questions of government, are concerned with the future development of the empire, and because they are written from a reformist point of view and thus implicitly assume that the political, social and economic future can be shaped or

---

[7] For a convenient survey of research of what has been referred to as "Han syncretism" see McLeod 2022.

[8] The "Treatise on Classics and Other Texts" 經籍志 of *Suishu* 隋書 (Documents of the Sui, 636) mentions "New Documents by Mr. Chao" 朝氏新書 by Chao Cuo that were preserved in the imperial archives of the Liang 梁 dynasty (502–552) but had been lost by the time of Sui 隋 (581–618). See *Suishu* (34: 1003): 梁有朝氏新書三卷，漢御史大夫鼂錯撰，亡。

[9] See, for example, Kroll (1978–1979: 14–15), Nishijima Sadao (1986: 577–78), and Loewe (2000: 27–29).

[10] For incipient concepts of futures of planning and preservation in ancient Chinese economic thought see Schwermann (2018: 69–98).

even planned in certain ways, they will be the focus of the following analysis and be examined with regard to possible influences of the *fa* tradition.[11]

In fact, Chao Cuo, who was sacrificed by Emperor Jing 景帝 (i.e. Liu Qi 劉啟, r. 157–141 BCE) in a vain attempt to pacify the Rebellion of the Seven Kings and executed in 154 BCE, is renowned not only for his policy to reduce the power of the titular kings but also for his proposals for economic reform, especially for his call to "take away where there is abundance and to supplement what is not enough" 損有 餘補不足.[12] As the two above-mentioned memorials show, his basic economic tenets, which are epitomized in this verbal parallel to chapter 77 of the received *Laozi* 老子 (Master Lao), include the ideas to

(1) increase demand for grain and price of grain by selling ranks to peasants and pardoning their crimes in exchange for grain,
(2) accordingly deplete the granaries of rich merchants and fill those of the state,
(3) temporarily reduce or remit taxes, and
(4) even, by implication, introduce commodity monies in the form of grain and bolts of textiles in order to promote agriculture.

As has been indicated above, the scholarly consensus among Western scholars of early China regards Chao Cuo as a representative of Confucian-type welfare policy and holds that his proposals aimed at the elimination of economic inequality and redistribution of surplus wealth so as to help those in need.[13] Moreover, in his influential paper on the economic views of Sang Hongyang, Jurij L. Kroll postulated that the economic idea to "take away where there is abundance and to supplement what is not enough" must not be divorced from its larger cultural context (Kroll 1978–1979: 15–16). Considering this saying as a quotation from chapter 77 of the received *Laozi*, and basing his interpretation of Chao Cuo's proposals on the context in the received *Laozi*, Kroll argued that Chao Cuo's admonition should be seen as an aspect of the more fundamental cultural notion that the ideal ruler in dealing with the "myriad people" (*wan min* 萬民) ought to imitate the universalistic attitude of Heaven (*tian* 天) towards the "myriad beings" (*wan wu* 萬物). However, Kroll

---

[11] See *Hanshu* (24A: 1130–1135). As Swann points out, the second text seems to be an excerpt from an originally longer memorial, and a slightly revised version of the first document can be found in Xun Yue's 荀悅 (148–209) *Hanji* 漢紀, an officially commissioned annalistic abridged version of the *Hanshu* (Swann 1950: 158, n. 102). Compare *Qian Hanji* (7: 4a–5a). For further memorials by Chao Cuo see *Hanshu* (49: 2277–99). They all date from the reign of Emperor Wen and deal with topics such as the duties of the monarch and the qualities required of him, the appointment of capable officials, questions of military strategy and border defense, in particular against the incursions of the Xiongnu, and the establishment of permanent frontier settlements in the north (Loewe 2000: 27–29).

[12] See *Hanshu* (24A: 1133). Compare *Laozi* 老子 77 (Boshu Laozi jiaozhu 203): 天之道，損有餘 而補不足。("The Way of Heaven is to take away where there is abundance and to supplement what is not enough.")

[13] See note 9 above. Note, however, that this assessment of Chao Cuo has lately been sporadically questioned in the Chinese academia. Thus, Chao Cuo has been classified as a "neo-*fa*-thinker" (*xin fajia* 新法家) in two studies by Gong Liuzhu (2014 and 2016).

appears to have overemphasized the philosophical context in *Laozi* 77 at the expense of Chao Cuo's social and economic thought. The notion of "taking away where there is abundance and supplementing what is not enough" was in wide circulation in Warring States and early imperial literature. It was rather a proverb than a quotation from the *Laozi* and was applied not only to economic thought but also to topics as diverse as self-cultivation or the treatment of certain diseases in early Chinese medicine.[14]

What will be attempted in the following is to both transcend the culturalist approach *and* to show that Chao Cuo was not an advocate of Confucian-type social welfarism.[15] Admittedly, when reading his two extant memorials on how to "respect the peasants" (*zun nongfu* 尊農夫) and generate "profit for the people" (*min li* 民利) (*Hanshu* 24A: 1133), one cannot help feeling reminded of Anthony F.P. Hulsewé's suggestive question as to whether Han China may have been a "proto 'welfare state'" (Hulsewé 1987: 265–85). However, when analyzed with regard to their ideological background and hidden statist agenda, these two memorials do not seem to bespeak an ideal of philanthropism or a primary interest in the well-being of the subjects. As "a man of an unyielding and hard frame of mind" and as a pragmatic *Realpolitiker*, who is said to have studied the teachings of Shang Yang and Shen Buhai (see the beginning of this section above), Chao Cuo could hardly have argued otherwise than that the state's vital interest lay in the maximum exploitation of the rural population. To test this thesis, the first step is to examine Chao Cuo's view of the common people and his concept of "social engineering."[16] Secondly, the various economic measures that he proposed against the background of his statist thought will be analyzed. Finally, it will be attempted to evaluate these, also taking into account the historical background and the question as to in how far they may have been put into practice in the first half of the second century BCE.

2 Shepherding the People

In the opening section of his first memorial, which was submitted in 178 BCE (Swann 1950: 158), Chao Cuo contrasts the situation of the common people under the sage kings of the past with their condition under early Han rule. He comes to the conclusion that whereas under Yao 堯, Yu 禹 and Tang 湯 the people had plenty of supplies, they now suffered need. According to Chao Cuo, this was because

---

[14] For instance, as a quick search in the database of the *Thesaurus Linguae Sericae* (*TLS* 2020, last accessed September 23, 2022) shows, variants of this proverbial wisdom can even be found in early medical literature, for example in the "Lingshu jing" 靈樞經 (Canon of the Spiritual Pivot) section of the *Huangdi neijing* 黃帝內經 (The Inner Canon of the Yellow Emperor) dating to the first century BCE, see *Huangdi Suwen Lingshu jing* (5: 3b): 損有餘益不足。

[15] Compare my analysis of concepts of economic justice and of distribution policies in early Chinese texts (Schwermann 2017b: 63–73).

[16] I borrow the concept of "social engineering" from Yuri Pines (Pines 2016).

wastelands were not fully cultivated, the manpower of the people was not fully utilized, and many of them had not settled down and wandered idly around in the
country instead of applying themselves to farming:

> 地有遺利，民有餘力，生穀之土未盡墾，山澤之利未盡出也，游食之民未盡歸農
> 也。民貧，則姦邪生。貧生於不足，不足生於不農，不農則不地著，不地著則離鄉
> 輕家，民如鳥獸，雖有高城深池，嚴法重刑，猶不能禁也。(*Hanshu* 24A: 1130–1131)
>
> [This is because] the land has neglected benefits; the people have unused manpower;
> lands [suitable] to grow grain are not all yet opened for cultivation; the benefits of moun-
> tains and marshes have not been fully extracted, and peripatetic eaters have not wholly
> returned to farming. When the people are poor, crime and depravity are born. Poverty is
> born of insufficiency; insufficiency is born of not farming; not farming means that [the
> people] are not settled on the land; not settling down on the land [means] that [the people]
> desert their [native] townships, and neglect their families. [Such] people are like birds and
> beasts, they cannot be restrained by prohibitions, even though there are high walls and deep
> moats, strict laws and severe punishments. (translation modified from Swann 1950: 159)

These are arguments that are typical for representatives of the *fa* tradition, feature
prominently in the *Shangjunshu* 商君書 (Documents Pertaining to the Lord of Shang,
a.k.a. *The Book of Lord Shang*) and are virtually spread throughout this book:[17] agriculture should be promoted, wastelands should be developed, the state's rural population should be fully exploited, and the farmers should be sedentary and tied to the land
that they are expected to be tilling, so as to prevent mobility and waste of agricultural
workforce.[18] The borrowings go so far that in places the author even adopts the specific terminology of the *Shangjunshu*, using, for example, the expression *youshi zhi
min* 游食之民, "peripatetic eaters," and thus modifying the terms *youshi* 游食 and
youshi zhe 游食者 that recur there.[19] Note that criticism of an excessive geographic
mobility of the commoners pervades large parts of the *Shangjunshu*. Compare, for
example, the following section from the sixth chapter, "Suan di" 算地 (Calculating
the Land), which explains the reasons for such mobility and the means to remedy it:

> 今則不然。世主之所以加務者，皆非國之急也。身有堯、舜之行，而功不及湯、武
> 之略者，此執柄之罪也。臣請語其過。夫治國舍勢而任說說，則身修而功寡。故事
> 《詩》、《書》談說之士，則民游而輕其上；事處上，則民遠而非其上；事勇士，

---

[17] Note that I translate the title of this text as literally as possible so as to indicate that it is not a book
written by an individual author, namely the historical Shang Yang, but a convolute of writings
produced by many different authors, who either referred to Shang Yang as the founder of their
school of thought or were later subsumed under this author figure, and dating from different periods of the fourth and third centuries BCE. For the dating of the individual chapters and the composition of the text see Pines (2017: 25–58). A concept of individual authorship does not seem to have
emerged before the late second century BCE (Schwermann 2014: 30–37).

[18] See Yuri Pines' summary of what he calls the "ideology of the total state" (Pines 2017: 59–99).
Compare Kai Vogelsang's account of what he calls "political realism" (*Politischer Realismus*)
(Vogelsang 2017: 22–79).

[19] See *Shangjunshu jiaoshu* (3.6: 49; 3.9: 55) ("Nong zhan" 農戰), (22.2: 255) ("Wai nei" 外內),
(23.4: 260) ("Jun chen" 君臣). As a search in the database of the *Thesaurus Linguae Sericae* (*TLS*
2020, last accessed September 23, 2022) shows, they occur six times in the *Shangjunshu*, more
often than in any other early Chinese text, including four times in the chapter "Nong zhan," which
Yuri Pines dates to the first half of the fourth century BCE (Pines 2017: 52). It was probably from
there that they were adopted one to two hundred years later by the authors of the *Xunzi* 荀子
(Master Xun), *Han Feizi* 韓非子 (Master Han Fei), and *Guanzi* 管子 (Master Guan).

則民競而輕其禁；技藝之士用，則民剽而易徙；商賈之士佚且利，則民緣而議其
上。故五民加於國用，則田荒而兵弱。談說之士資在於口，處士資在於意，勇士資
在於氣，技藝之士資在於手，商賈之士資在於身。故天下一宅，而圍身資。民資重
於身，而偏託勢於外。挾重資，歸偏僻家，堯、舜之所難也。故湯、武禁之，則功立
而名成。（*Shangjunshu jiaoshu* 6.6: 97）

But now things are different. The sovereigns of our age are devoted exclusively to matters that are of no urgency to the state. They behave as if they are Yao or Shun, but their
merits do not compare with those of Tang and Wu: this is the fault of power holders. I, your
subject, would like to discuss their errors:

In ruling the state, if you discard the power of authority and rely on the persuaders' talk,
then you personally will be cultivated but will have meager achievements. Thus, when you
employ the *shi* engaged in *Poems*, *Documents*, and persuaders' talk, the people will wander
and disregard their ruler; if you employ reclusive *shi*, then the people will be estranged and
reject their superiors; if you employ brave *shi*, then the people will be quarrelsome and
disregard the prohibitions; if you employ *shi* who are skilled artisans, then the people will
be volatile and easily migrate; when the *shi* who are merchants and peddlers are at ease and
yet reap benefits, then the people follow their lead and question their superiors. Hence,
when these five types of people join the ranks of state employees, the fields are covered by
weeds, and the army is weak.

The capital of persuading *shi* is their mouth; the capital of reclusive *shi* is their mind; the
capital of brave *shi* is their [fighting] spirit; the capital of skillful artisan *shi* is their hands;
the capital of merchant and peddler *shi* is their bodies. Hence, for them, All-under-Heaven
is just one home, and they move across it with their bodies as their capital. The people's
capital is accumulated in their bodies, and they can empower themselves anywhere abroad;
carrying their accumulated capital, they flock to any place as if to their home: even for Yao
and Shun it would be difficult [to make this situation orderly]. Hence, [kings] Tang and Wu
prohibited it; thereby they established their achievements and accomplished [a good] name.
(Pines 2017: 161–62)

Here "peripatetic eaters" are described more precisely as "five types of people"—
scholars, recluses, bravoes, artisans, and travelling merchants—who wander around
in the country or even move across "All-under Heaven" (*tianxia* 天下) and, through
the success of their careers, encourage others to also become itinerant. According to
this section (6.6), the most important way for a ruler to prevent people from "carrying their accumulated capital" and "flocking to any place as if to their home" is to
wield his power (*shi* 勢) and prohibit geographical mobility. Note that Chao Cuo, in
his memorial quoted above, argues that itinerant people "are like birds and beasts"
and "cannot be restrained by prohibitions, even though there are high walls and
deep moats, strict laws and severe punishments." Thus, he seems to distance himself
from *Shangjunshu* on this point, reflecting a perhaps more mature political experience on the side of Chao Cuo in comparison to the Qin reformers.

However, disincentives are not all that can be used to make people farm according to the *Shangjunshu*. Section 6.7 there reiterates the argument advanced in sections 6.4 and 6.5 of the text (*Shangjunshu jiaoshu* 94–95) that the people can also
be guided by capitalizing on their quest for a good name and for profit:

民之性：度而取長，稱而取重，權而索利。明君慎觀三者，則國治可立，而民能可
得。（*Shangjunshu jiaoshu* 6.7: 100）

The nature of the people is such that when measuring, they take what is longer; when
weighing, they take what is heavier; when using scales, they seek profits. The clear-sighted
ruler carefully observes these three [behaviors]; only then can he establish orderly rule in
the state and attain the people's abilities. (Pines 2017: 163)

In a similar vein, Chao Cuo describes the sovereign as a shepherd (*mu* 牧) of the people who does not force his subjects to engage in farming but rather manipulates them to do so by appealing to their greed for profit:

夫腹飢不得食，膚寒不得衣，雖慈母不能保其子，君安能以有其民哉！明主知其然也，故務民於農桑，薄賦斂，廣畜積，以實倉廩，備水旱，故民可得而有也。民者，在上所以牧之，趨利如水走下，四方亡擇也。(*Hanshu* 24A: 1131)

    When hunger gnaws at the stomach and one cannot obtain food, when cold bites the skin and one cannot obtain clothes, [under such conditions] even a loving mother is unable to protect her child, and how can a ruler be able to hold [the allegiance of] his people? A clear-sighted sovereign understands that. He, therefore, strives to keep his people at agriculture and sericulture, lightens the poll tax and other government levies, and increases the stores [of grains] in order to fill [government] granaries and storehouses, in preparedness against floods and droughts, so that his people may be held [in allegiance]. [The attitude of] the people depends upon the methods by which the ruler shepherds them, for they hasten after benefits just as water runs downwards, and they do not have any [definite] preferences into which of the four directions [they go]. (translation modified from Swann 1950: 160–61)

While Chao Cuo's warning that peasants cannot be forced to engage in farming, just like his call for lowering taxes and other levies, clearly deviates from *Shangjunshu*, his suggestion that the sovereign should manipulate his subjects into doing so by appealing to their greed is plainly derived from it.[20] As mentioned above, according to this work, the ideal ruler should utilize the universal human trait to strive for a good name and profit to encourage farming.[21] This is exactly what is meant when Chao Cuo says that people "hasten after benefits just as water runs downwards" and accordingly proposes the selling of ranks and pardoning of crimes in exchange for grain. Once again, note the verbal parallel to chapter 23 of the *Shangjunshu*, "Jun chen" 君臣 (Ruler and Ministers):

民之於利也，若水於下也，四旁無擇也。民徒可以得利而為之者，上與之也。(*Shangjunshu jiaoshu* 23.4: 260)

    The people follow after benefit as water flows downward: it has no preference among the four directions. The people do only whatever brings them benefit, and the benefit is granted by superiors. (Pines 2017: 233)[22]

---

[20] See, for example *Shangjunshu jiaoshu* (3.1–3.2: 39–40) ("Nong zhan"), (2012: 6.4–6.5: 94–95) ("Suan di"); (compare *Shangjunshu zhuizhi* [3: 20, 6: 46]). Compare Pines (2021: 78–113), to whom I owe the references.

[21] See Pines (2021: 80–87) on strategies of "making the people farm" in the *Shangjunshu*.

[22] See also the verbal parallel to chapter 64 of the *Guanzi* 管子 (Master Guan), "Xingshi jie" 形勢解, *Guanzi jiaozhu* (64: 1175), which according to Rickett (1985: 61) does not date to before 122 BCE and thus was probably written more than thirty years after Chao Cuo's death: 民，利之則來，害之則去。民之從利也，如水之走下，於四方無擇也。故欲來民者，先起其利，雖不召而民自至。設其所惡，雖召之而民不來也。Compare the translation by W. Allyn Rickett (Rickett 1985: 71): "When people are benefited, they come; when they are harmed, they leave. People follow after benefits just as water runs downhill. It has no preference among the four directions. Therefore those who wish to make the people come must first initiate benefits for them. Then, even though not summoned, the people will arrive by themselves. [On the other hand] if what is harmful to them is instituted, the people will not come, even though they are summoned."

Quite obviously, Chao Cuo shared the conviction of earlier representatives of the *fa* tradition who argued that human nature was covetous but could be put to good use by being manipulated. The above-quoted passages show that Chao Cuo conceived of the rural population when being unsettled as beasts that had to be domesticated, and when being settled as livestock that had to be shepherded (*mu* 牧) to make sure that farmers fully devote themselves to their primary occupation.

The importance of the political metaphor of "shepherding the people" (*mu min* 牧民) within the *fa* tradition is evident from the fact that it forms the title of the eponymous first chapter of *Guanzi* 管子 (Master Guan).[23] From the perspective of those early Han political thinkers who were under the influence of this tradition the monarch was, as it were, a "human resource manager" who was supposed to extract maximum productivity from his subjects.[24] Moreover, he was expected to "tranquillize the people" (*an min* 安民) by keeping them busy and engaging them in farming so as to prevent the peasant uprisings which had led to the downfall of the Qin 秦 (Sabattini 2012). Of course, Chao Cuo also describes the hardships of the peasants, for example when he criticizes oppressive government measures, which only lead to the result that "in many cases fields and dwellings are sold, children and grandchildren are vended, in order to pay debts" 有賣田宅鬻子孫以償責者 (*Hanshu* 1962: 24A: 1132; Swann 1950: 164). But he only does so in order to lend more weight to his proposals for economic reform.

3 Suppressing Commerce and Promoting Farming

Chao Cuo's proposals are motivated by the fear that rich merchants, who are characterized as parasites feeding on the toil of the farmers, might take advantage of their wealth to form alliances with titular kings and marquises (*wang hou* 王侯) (*Hanshu* 24A: 1132; Swann 1950: 165). Contrasting their lives of luxury with the fate of poor peasants, who even have to sell their children and grandchildren to eke out a living (*Hanshu* 24A: 1132), Chao Cuo portrays tradespeople as follows:

而商賈大者積貯倍息，小者坐列販賣，操其奇贏，日游都市，乘上之急，所賣必倍。故其男不耕耘，女不蠶織，衣必文采，食必〔粱〕〔粱〕肉；亡農夫之苦，有仟伯之得。因其富厚，交通王侯，力過吏勢，以利相傾；千里游敖，冠蓋相望，乘堅策肥，履絲曳縞。此商人所以兼并農人，農人所以流亡者也。(*Hanshu* 24A: 1132)

As for traveling traders and resident merchants, large ones hoard stocks [of commodities in order to get] one hundred per cent profit; small ones sit in rows in market stalls to buy and sell. Those possessing a superabundance [of wealth obtained by trade in] rare [articles]

[23] See *Guanzi jiaozhu* (1: 1–20). Compare Schwermann 2017b. Note that the metaphor is used throughout the *Guanzi* and is also employed in the above-quoted chapter 64 (*Guanzi jiaozhu* [64: 1167]).

[24] For the underlying notion of "using people" see Kaufmann 2010. Compare Ma 2021 for a recent study of the practice of human resource management in the early empire.

daily wander about in large cities and market towns. By taking advantage of the superior's sense of urgency, whatever they sell is bound to be doubled [in price]. Therefore, men [of the merchant families] neither plow [nor] weed, and their women neither tend silkworms [nor] weave; yet what they wear must be embroidered and variegated, and what they eat must be fine grain and meat. They are without the bitter [toil] of the farmer; yet they are receiving tenfold up to hundredfold [profits]. Taking advantage of their great riches they associate with titular kings and marquises. Their influence exceeds the power of magistrates, and by making use of their profits they ruin each other. They wander idly around roaming [as far as] a thousand *li*; their caps and cart covers [fill the roads] in sight of one another; they ride in well-built [carts] and whip up fat [horses]; they wear shoes of silk and trail white silk [behind them]. This is why tradespeople engross [the lands of] farmers, and farmers therefore are drifting from place to place. (translation modified from Swann 1950: 164–65)

Chao Cuo's arguments bear some resemblance to those of Shang Yang (see Sect. 2 above), but overall display much deeper understanding of the merchants' sociopolitical impact than is observable from *Shangjunshu*. For instance, merchants add to the geographic mobility of peasants not by setting a bad example but by dispossessing small landholders. Moreover, Chao Cuo implies that super-rich business magnates, with the help of the immense wealth they have amassed and their entanglements with local government, will end up joining forces with the titular kings, opposing the central government, escaping from its control and instigating separatist movements in the periphery. Chao Cuo's proposals are based on two beliefs: the ideological conviction that private commerce is detrimental to the central government's authority and the economic conviction that a flourishing primary sector of the economy, i.e. agriculture, is the foundation of the state's economic success. Moreover, he quotes "the teachings of Shennong" 神農之教 from an unknown source to argue that a thriving agricultural economy is also a precondition for being able to defend oneself against foreign invaders like the Xiongnu:[25]

神農之教曰:「有石城十仞,湯池百步,帶甲百萬,而亡粟,弗能守也。」以是觀之,粟者,王者大用,政之本務。(*Hanshu* 24A: 1133–34)
    According to the teachings of Shennong, it is said: "If a city has a stone wall that is more than fifty feet high, [is surrounded by] a moat of boiling water one hundred paces [wide, and is guarded by] a million armored [soldiers] but is without grain, it cannot be defended." Looking at it from this point of view [it is clear that] grain is the most useful thing for the [true] ruler, and [its cultivation] is a fundamental function of government. (translation modified from Swann 1950: 168–69)

Again, similar to the authors of *Shangjunshu*, Chao Cuo claims that not only inner stability but also military strength accrues from a thriving agriculture. The crux of the problem is to have sufficient supplies for the armies. Compare the relevant explanation in *Shangjunshu*:

故兵出,糧給而財有餘;兵休,民作而畜長足。此所謂任地待役之律也。(*Shangjunshu jiaoshu* 6.2: 89)

---

[25] For the lost agricultural text *Shennong* 神農 and Shang Yang's alleged association with it and co-authorship of it see Pines (2021: 78, n. 2). For Chao Cuo's views on border defense and his famous Xiongnu memorial see above.

Hence, when an army is dispatched, provisions are ample, and resources are abundant; when the army is at rest, the people are working, and the accumulated [surplus] suffices for a long time. This is what is called the standard of utilizing territory and being ready for battle. (Pines 2017: 159)

Both Chao Cuo's first and second memorial, which was submitted in 168 BCE (Swann 1950: 170), indicate that grain supplies were first accumulated at the frontiers for the use of the frontier guards (*Hanshu* 24A: 1134–35; Swann 1950: 169, 170–71). In his memorial of 178 BCE, Chao Cuo had proposed to increase demand for grain and price of grain by selling ranks of merit to peasants and pardoning their crimes in exchange for grain. As secondary effects, he envisioned a rise of the price of grain, a bigger grain supply in the capital region for financing central government expenses, and a reduction of taxes to support the rural population and encourage farming:

方今之務，莫若使民務農而已矣。欲民務農，在於貴粟；貴粟之道，在於使民以粟為賞罰。今募天下入粟縣官，得以拜爵，得以除罪。如此，富人有爵，農民有錢，粟有所渫。夫能入粟以受爵，皆有餘者也；取於有餘，以供上用，則貧民之賦可損，所謂損有餘補不足，令出而民利者也。順於民心，所補者三：一曰主用足，二曰民賦少，三曰勸農功。(*Hanshu* 24A: 1133)

At the moment nothing is more urgent than to make the people devote themselves to farming. That is all! If one desires to make the people devote themselves to farming, it is necessary to enhance the value of grain. The way of enhancing the value of grain lies in causing the people to [be able to] use grain for [obtaining] rewards and for [commuting] penalties. Let now there be a general call to All-under-Heaven that whosoever sends grain to the central government shall be bestowed a rank [of merit], and/or pardon for crimes. In this way wealthy individuals will have honorary rank, peasants will have money, and grain will have that by which it can be distributed (that is, an outlet). Now those able to submit grain in order to receive rank are those who live in abundance. Should [these surpluses] be obtained from those who live in abundance to be used for the leadership, then poll taxes of the poor people could be taken away (i.e. reduced). This is the so-called [policy of] "taking away where there is abundance and supplementing what is not enough" [which] as soon as ordered will benefit the people. In accordance with the heart's desire of the people [this policy] will supply three things: (i) the sovereign will have a sufficiency for [governmental] expenses; (ii) the people will pay a lower poll tax; and (iii) [meritorious] service in agricultural [production] will be encouraged. (translation modified from Swann 1950: 166–68)

The idea of encouraging farming through bestowal of ranks is derived from the *Shangjunshu*.[26] So is the underlying strategy to manipulate people by appealing to their greed, namely their desire to obtain high rank or pardon for crimes (*Hanshu* 24A: 1134; Swann 1950: 169). According to the chapter "Qu qiang" 去彊 (Eliminating the Strong) of the *Shangjunshu*, ranks should be bestowed both for military and agricultural achievements, for example, sold in exchange for grain.[27] This is exactly what Chao Cuo proposes. Moreover, he takes precautions not to weaken military defense by unspecifiedly conferring higher ranks that included exemption from military service. He stipulates that peasants who offer grain shall

---

[26] See note 21 above and *Shangjunshu jiaoshu* (3.1–3.2: 39–40) ("Nong zhan"); compare *Shangjunshu zhuizhi* (1996: 3: 20).

[27] *Shangjunshu jiaoshu* (4.11: 72); *Shangjunshu zhuizhi* (4: 34); Pines 2017: 155.

obtain ranks "up to and above the grade of *wudafu*" 令民入粟受爵至五大夫以上 (*Hanshu* 1962: 24A: 1134; Swann 1950: 169). *Wudafu* 五大夫 was the ninth grade in the Han system of ranks of merit, and it allowed for exemption from military service (Swann 1950: 169, n. 199). However, according to the memorial, those who obtained this rank could have "exemption from military service for one man only out of each of their families" 乃復一人耳 (*Hanshu* 1962: 24A: 1134; Swann 1950: 169).

Ten years after Emperor Wen had adopted his proposals, apparently in a modified form, Chao Cuo submitted his second memorial on economic reform. To a certain degree, it mirrors the consequences of the measures previously taken. Of course, it is written from the subjective point of view of its composer, who initially tries to present the reforms as a success:

> 陛下幸使天下入粟塞下以拜爵，甚大惠也。竊恐塞卒之食不足用大漢天下粟。邊食足以支五歲，可令入粟郡縣矣；足支一歲以上，可時赦，勿收農民租。如此，德澤加於萬民，民俞勤農。時有軍役，若遭水旱，民不困乏，天下安寧；歲孰且美，則民大富樂矣。(*Hanshu* 24A: 1134–35)
>
> Your Majesty has fortunately allowed All-under-Heaven to offer grain sent up [to the frontier] near the border fortifications for the grant of rank: this is indeed a great [act of] grace. [Formerly], in private [I] was worried that the insufficiency of food supplies for [use by] frontier guards [would cause] a great drainage all over the empire. Now when food supplies at the frontiers are enough for maintenance for five years, let it be ordered that grain be concentrated in the commanderies and counties. Where enough [has been offered] for maintenance for one year, or more, let there be at appropriate times [local] amnesty, and exemption of farmers' field taxes. By doing so [your] virtue and mercy will fall upon the myriad people; and the people will be increasingly encouraged to commit themselves to farming. [Thus] in case at appropriate times there should be military or labor service, or there should be flood or drought, [then] the people will be neither straitened nor destitute. When the empire is tranquil and quiet, and the year's harvest is ripened and, moreover, excellent, then are the people abundantly rich and happy. (translation modified from Swann 1950: 170–71)

Again, we see that the *primary* goal of Chao Cuo's variety of so-called welfarism is not the welfare of the common people but the well-being of the emperor and his house, which can only prolong and reproduce its dynastic rule as long as its subjects are "tranquil and quiet" (*an ning* 安寧). What is even more interesting, though, is that this memorial of 168 BCE, read within its context and against the historical background, seems to indicate that the measures that had been taken ten years earlier as a consequence of Chao Cuo's first memorial, might in fact have aggravated the situation of the peasants in the central regions of the empire. Why else should its author first have mentioned his former fear that provision of grain supplies on the frontiers might greatly drain the empire's resources and then have asked to allow grain accumulation in the commanderies and counties to relieve the farmers there?

4 Conclusion: Economic Expertise versus Ideological Convictions

The memorial cited in the end of the previous section indicates that the economic reforms proposed by Chao Cuo in 178 BCE did not work as well as he had hoped for. Probably this was also due to a certain lack of economic expertise on his part. As far as one can tell from his biography (see introduction and Sect. 1 above), he was an advocate and practitioner of *Realpolitik* (political realism), but had little experience in matters of economy. His diatribes against rich merchants who, feeding on the toil of the farmers, live in superabundance and threaten the authority of the central government (see Sect. 3 above), show that he mixed up economic arguments with ideological convictions and indicate that he may have misunderstood the new conditions of the highly commercialized Han economy, applying to it the economic advice of Shang Yang and his followers who lived and worked in the far less commercialized state of Qin of the fourth and third centuries BCE. This is also demonstrable from the fact that he does not even shy away from resorting to the crudest recipes of the *Shangjunshu*, parts of which have been characterized as a provocative and even frightening invective by Yuri Pines (Pines 2012), in order to solve the financial plight of the early Han.

As has been shown above (Sect. 3), Chao Cuo's economic thought was not only guided by the moderate chapters of *Shangjunshu*, but seems to have been influenced in places by radical ones such as chapter 4, "Eliminating the Strong" ("Qu qiang"), which Yuri Pines (2017: 141) has rightly dubbed "the richest depository of appalling statements" within the entire corpus of *Shangjunshu*. This is also evident from Chao Cuo's discussion of currency issues, which suggests that he intended to replace the various currencies in circulation with grain and textiles meant to be used as commodity monies in order to promote agriculture. Consider the following passage where he criticizes the use of pearls, jade, gold, and silver as currencies:

夫珠玉金銀，飢不可食，寒不可衣，然而衆貴之者，以上用之故也。其為物輕微易藏，在於把握，可以周海內而亡飢寒之患。此令臣輕背其主，而民易去其鄉，盜賊有所勸，亡逃者得輕資也。粟米布帛生於地，長於時，聚於力，非可一日成也；數石之重，中人弗勝，不為姦邪所利，一日弗得而飢寒至。是故明君貴五穀而賤金玉。(*Hanshu* 24A: 1131–32)

Now pearls, jade, gold, and silver can neither be eaten when food lacking, nor used as garments when one is cold. Nevertheless, they are precious to a great many because they are used by the leadership. They are light, small articles, and are easy to hide. Having them in one's grasp one can travel all around within the seas without the hardships of hunger or cold. This causes ministers lightly to turn their backs upon their sovereigns; this causes people indifferently to go away from their native townships; this gives thieves and robbers the incentive [to commit crimes]; and this makes fugitives able to get lightweight capital.

Grains, unhusked and husked, and textiles, fibrous and silken, are produced from the land; grown according to the seasons; and gathered by manpower, and it is not [a work that] can be accomplished in one day. Several piculs [of grain or rolls of textiles] are too heavy for an ordinary man to carry [in one load], so that no profits are made from them by crime and depravity. [Yet if grains and textiles] are not obtained for a single day, one will suffer hunger and cold. For this reason, a clear-sighted ruler esteems the five grains and despises gold and jade. (translation modified from Swann 1950: 161–62)

This passage has a striking verbal parallel with the penultimate section of the chapter "Guo xu" 國蓄 (The State's Store of Grain) in *Guanzi*, where the circulation of jade, gold and pearls as well as bronze coinage as forms of money is criticized in a similar way: holding on to these monies does not help against hunger and cold, and they served the former kings only as an instrument for the distribution of goods and the administration of their realms.[28] But Chao Cuo seems to go one step further. In doing so, he is probably once again under the influence of a crude economic notion advocated by the author of the chapter "Eliminating the Strong" of *Shangjunshu*, which emphasized the primacy of agriculture over trade in the following terms:

粟生而金死，粟死而金生。本物賤，事者眾，買者少，農困而姦勸，其兵弱，國必削至亡。金一兩生於境內，粟十二石死於境外。粟十二石生於境內，金一兩死於境外。國好生金於境內，則金粟兩死，倉府兩虛，國弱；國好生粟於境內，則金粟兩生，倉府兩實，國強。(*Shangjunshu jiaoshu* 4.9: 69–70)

When grain is born, gold is dead; when grain is dead, gold is born. When basic commodities are cheap, yet producers are many while consumers are few, then farmers will face difficulties, and deceitful [undertakings] will be encouraged; the army will be weak, and the state will surely be dismembered to the point of final collapse. When a *liang* (ounce) of gold is born within the borders, twelve *shi* (piculs) of grain are dead outside the borders. When twelve *shi* of grain are born within the borders, one *liang* of gold is dead outside the borders. When the state is fond of giving birth to gold within the borders, then both gold and grain are dead, both granaries and treasury are empty. When the state is fond of giving birth to grain within the borders, then both gold and grain are born, both granaries and treasury are full, and the state is strong. (translation slightly modified from Pines 2017: 154)

Note that the author of "Eliminating the Strong" does not point to a perceived "fundamental contradiction between commercial and agricultural pursuits" (Pines 2017: 280, n. 75) in order to argue for the abolition of a metal currency in favor of a commodity money in the form of grain. Rather, he is concerned with keeping grain prices high to make farming attractive, and with both boosting grain production so as not to have to buy grain from abroad and filling the treasury with gold so as to be able to arm the military (Pines 2017: 280, n. 76 and 78). But it appears that Chao Cuo may have taken the initial slogan "When grain is born, gold is dead; when grain is dead, gold is born" literally to advocate the abolition, or at least curtailment, of metal currencies in favor of commodity monies such as grain and textiles.

As Yohei Kakinuma has shown, commodity monies in the form of grain and bolts of textiles were used alongside bronze coins and gold as currencies from the Warring States (Zhanguo 戰國 453–221 BCE) through the Eastern Han 東漢 (25–220 CE) periods (Kakinuma 2011: 139–307 and Kakinuma 2021: 361–70). Based on the ample evidence collected by Kakinuma, and assuming that one can take Chao Cuo at his above-quoted word that "a clear-sighted ruler esteems the five

[28] See *Guanzi jiaozhu* (73: 1279), compare Rickett (1998: 386), who dates the chapter to the late second century BCE (Rickett 1998: 377). According to van Ess (2021: 126), its authors do not intend to eliminate the chaos of multiple currencies but rather hold that "money is only a means to control what is really important and should not be thought of as the primary object of one's desires." For the discussion of the disorder resulting from the lack of a standard currency see Sabattini 2021.

grains and despises gold and jade" 明君貴五穀而賤金玉, one may conclude that he wants to dissuade the ruler from using the latter as currencies. He acknowledges that these items are light (*qing* 輕), small, easy to hide and that they allow for mobility: "Having them in one's grasp one can travel all around within the seas without the hardships of hunger or cold." However, as shown above, this is exactly the kind of mobility to which Chao Cuo opposes. Therefore, he suggests to resort to the "five grains" as a "heavy" 重 currency both to prevent theft and robbery and to tie the peasants to the land that they are tilling. Farmers who buy ranks of merit for grain in fact use grain as a currency. Apparently, Chao Cuo employs the concept of "light and heavy" (*qing zhong*輕重) to argue for an introduction of grain (*sumi* 粟米) and textiles (*bubo* 布帛) as commodity monies.[29]

From today's perspective, it seems to be unrealistic and naive to propose to use grain and bolts of textiles as commodity monies in a situation when coinage, that is, standardized metal currency such as the *banliang* 半兩, "half-tael" coin, has been in circulation for at least two hundred years (Sabattini 2021: 323). Was Chao Cuo heeded? Overall, many of his proposals were put in the practice, most notably the establishment of permanent *Wehrbauern* colonies. Speaking of Chao's economic proposals, recall that as early as 177 BCE Emperor Wen issued a decree that echoed the wording of Chao Cuo's first memorial and ordered to reduce the land tax by half (*Hanshu* 4:118). In 168 BCE, i.e. in the year when Chao Cuo submitted his second memorial, Emperor Wen again decreed the reduction of the land tax by half (*Hanshu* 4:124). Only one year later, in 167 BCE, he finally decreed the complete remission of the land tax (*Hanshu* 1962: 4:125). And as late as 141 BCE, Emperor Jing still quoted Chao Cuo in a decree that encouraged agriculture and criticized the use of gold, pearls and jade as currencies (*Hanshu* 5: 152–53). However, the economically suicidal step to abolish these currencies was never attempted to the best of our knowledge.

How should Chao Cuo's ideas and practices be interpreted with regard to the research question posed at the beginning of this chapter? First, it is clear that the pre-imperial *fa* tradition exerted a much stronger influence on statist thought in the early Han period than is commonly assumed. It could be shown that Chao Cuo followed the guidelines of the *Shangjunshu* in his proposals for economic reform over much of his memorials. Some of these proposals such as his demand for the reduction of land tax were even put into practice, but interestingly, not necessarily those that were influenced by the ideology of the *fa* tradition. Apparently, the addressees of Chao Cuo's memorials – Emperor Wen and his ministers – came to the conclusion that many of his ideas were either impractical or too radical. As Emperor Jing's above-mentioned edict shows, Chao Cuo's suggestions were deemed good enough to be quoted, but not always good enough to be put into practice.

Notwithstanding this practical attitude, which apparently was critical of at least some of the ideological overkill, there seems to have been a marked lack of

---

[29] For a recent study of the history of this central concept of early Chinese economic thought see van Ess 2021.

economic expertise at the imperial court. As excavated sources indicate, there may have been much more of that knowledge in the periphery.[30] However, neither the competence of local magistrates nor their experience with grassroot-level reforms seem to have impacted the reformist discussions at the center. Otherwise, Chao Cuo's ideas would not have been in vogue at the court for several decades, including well after his execution in 154 BCE. To put it in the words of Yuri Pines, he seems to have been more of a social engineer and a visionary than an economist.[31] Apparently, he was ready to sacrifice wealth for a mirage of social stability in which he believed under the influence of long-faded pre-imperial statist thinkers.

To return to the beginning of our reflections: Could it be that this is what Yang Xiong had in mind when he called Chao Cuo a fool? This is doubtful; after all, Yang Xiong himself was not an economic specialist, and it was during his lifetime that the ideologically-motivated experiments of Wang Mang 王莽 (45 BCE–23 CE) had derailed the economy altogether. In any case, and going back to Chao Cuo, when reading his memorials one cannot but suspect that for him, as well as for many other top officials, ideological convictions were as important as expertise. This is not at all surprising. Alas, it reminds us of our own age. And it suggests that the innovative ideas of the first generations of *fa* thinkers, who came on the scene in the fourth century BCE and devised groundbreaking social and economic reforms in their day, had already fossilized by the second century BCE to an extent that would have brought tears to the eyes of the pioneers. After all, maintaining flexibility and adapting government to the specific needs of the time had been one of their key demands.

References

Boshu Laozi jiaozhu 帛書老子校注 (Silk Document *Laozi*, Collated and Annotated). 2004. Edited by Gao, Ming 高明. Beijing: Zhonghua shuju.

Emmerich, Reinhard. 2002. "Die Rebellion der Sieben Könige, 154 v. Chr." In: *Und folge nun dem, was mein Herz begehrt. Festschrift für Ulrich Unger zum 70. Geburtstag*, ed. Reinhard Emmerich and Hans Stumpfeldt, 2 vols., vol. 2, 397–497. Hamburg: Ostasien Verlag. (a comprehensive study of the Rebellion of the Seven Kings in 154 BCE)

Fayan yishu 法言義疏 (*Exemplary Sayings* with Glosses and Sub-Commentary). 1987. With the commentary by Wang, Rongbao 汪榮寶. Beijing: Zhonghua shuju.

Gong, Liuzhu 龔留柱. 2014. "Chao Cuo ji Xi Han fajia de chaoqi-chaoluo" 晁錯及西漢法家的潮起潮落 (Chao Cuo and the Rise and Fall of the School of *fa* during the Western Han Dynasty). *Zhongyuan wenhua yanjiu* 中原文化研究 2.3: 39–44.

———— 龔留柱. 2016. "Lun Chao Cuo ji Han chu 'xin fajia'" 論晁錯及漢初"新法家" (On Chao Cao and the 'New School of *fa*' of the Early Han Dynasty). *Zhongguo shi yanjiu* 中國史研究 23.1: 63–90. (a comprehensive study of the influence of the School of *fa* on Chao Cuo)

Guanzi jiaozhu 管子校注 (*Master Guan*, Collated and Annotated). 2004. Edited by Li, Xiangfeng 黎翔鳳. Beijing: Zhonghua shuju.

---

[30] See Maxim Korolkov's (2021) and Robin D.S. Yates' (2021) recent studies of credit, labor and accounting in the Qin empire and the economic activities of its local administrations.

[31] Compare Pines 2016 and Pines (2021: 106–109) on *Shangjunshu*.

Hanshu 漢書 (Documents of the Han). 1962. Compiled by Ban, Gu 班固 et al. Beijing: Zhonghua shuju.

Huangdi Suwen Lingshu jing 黃帝素問靈樞經 (*Basic Questions* and *Canon of the Spiritual Pivot* of the *[Inner Canon] of the Yellow Emperor*). 1966. Rpt. in *Sibu congkan chubian* 四部叢刊初編. Taipei: Shangwu Yinshuguan.

Hulsewé, Anthony F.P. 1987. "Han China – A Proto 'Welfare State'?" *T'oung Pao* 73: 265–285.

Kakinuma, Yohei 柿沼 陽平. 2011. *Chūgoku kodai kahei keizaishi kenkyū* 中国古代貨幣経済史研究 (Historical Studies of the Monetary Economy in Ancient China). Tokyo: Kyūko Shoin.

———. 2021. "The First Chinese Economic Impact on Asia: Distribution and Usage of Monies in Early China in Synchronic and Diachronic Perspective." In *Between Command and Market: Economic Thought and Practice in Early China*, ed. Elisa Levi Sabattini and Christian Schwermann, 358–391. Leiden: Brill.

Kaufmann, Paulus. 2010. *Using People – Scope, Role and Justification of a Common Sense Concept*. Ph.D. dissertation, University of Zurich, Faculty of Arts.

Korolkov, Maxim. 2021. "Between Command and Market: Credit, Labour, and Accounting in the Qin Empire (221–207 BCE)." In *Between Command and Market: Economic Thought and Practice in Early China*, ed. Elisa Levi Sabattini and Christian Schwermann, 162–243. Leiden: Brill.

Kroll, Jurij L. 1978–1979. "Toward a Study of the Economic Views of Sang Hung-yang." *Early China* 4: 11–18.

Liu, Guanghua 劉光華. 1988. *Han dai xibei tuntian yanjiu* 漢代西北屯田研究 (Studies of the Northwestern *tuntian* in the Han Dynasty). Lanzhou: Lanzhou daxue chubanshe.

Loewe, Michael. 2000. *Biographical Dictionary of the Qin, Former Han and Xin Periods (221 BC – AD 24)*. Leiden: Brill.

Ma, Tsang Wing. 2021. "Categorizing Laborers: Glimpses of Qin Management of Human Resources from an Administrative Document from Liye, Hunan Province." *Early China* 44: 351–391. (a contribution on labor mobilization in the Qin dynasty with a sidelight on its possible relation to the statist thought of the School of *fa*).

McLeod, Alexus. 2022. "Philosophy in Han Dynasty China." In *The Stanford Encyclopedia of Philosophy* (https://plato.stanford.edu/archives/spr2022/entries/han-dynasty/), ed. Edward N. Zalta. Accessed 6 Sept 2023.

Nishijima, Sadao. 1986. "The Economic and Social History of Former Han." In Denis Twitchett and John K. Fairbank, eds., *The Cambridge History of China*, vol. 1: *The Ch'in and Han Empires, 221 B.C.–A.D. 220*, ed. Denis Twitchett and Michael Loewe, 545–648. Cambridge: Cambridge University Press.

Nürnberger, Marc. 2008. "Memoir of Yüan Ang and Ch'ao Ts'o, Number 41." In *The Grand Scribe's Records*, ed. William H. Nienhauser, vol. 8, 323–356. Bloomington, Indiana: Indiana University Press.

Nylan, Michael. 2013. *Exemplary Figures / Fayan*. Seattle: University of Washington Press.

Pines, Yuri. 2012. "Alienating Rhetoric in the *Book of Lord Shang* and its Moderation." *Extrême-Orient, Extrême-Occident* 34: 79–110.

———. 2016. "Social Engineering in Early China: The Ideology of the *Shangjun shu* (Book of Lord Shang) Revisited." *Oriens Extremus* 55: 1–37. (a comprehensive study of the institutional thought of early *fa* thinkers and their socio-reformist approach).

———. 2017. *The Book of Lord Shang: Apologetics of State Power in Early China*. New York: Columbia University Press.

———. 2021. "Agriculturalism and Beyond: Economic Thought of *The Book of Lord Shang*." In *Between Command and Market: Economic Thought and Practice in Early China*, ed. Elisa Levi Sabattini and Christian Schwermann, 78–113. Leiden and Boston: Brill.

Qian Hanji 前漢記 (Annals of the Former Han). 1966. Rpt. in *Sibu congkan chubian* 四部叢刊初編. Taipei: Shangwu Yinshuguan.

Rickett, W. Allyn. 1985/1998. *Guanzi: Political, Economic, and Philosophical Essays from Early China*. 2 vols. Princeton: Princeton University Press.

198

C. Schwermann

Sabattini, Elisa Levi. 2012. "'People as Root' (*min ben*) Rhetoric in the *New Writings* by Jia Yi (200–168)." *Extrême-Orient, Extrême-Occident* 34: 167–193.

———. 2021. "To Ban or Not to Ban: Jia Yi on Copper Distribution and Minting Coins." In *Between Command and Market: Economic Thought and Practice in Early China*, ed. Elisa Levi Sabattini and Christian Schwermann, 318–357. Leiden and Boston: Brill.

Schwermann, Christian. 2014. "Composite Authorship in Western Zhōu Bronze Inscriptions: The Case of the 'Tiānwáng *guǐ*' 天亡簋 Inscription." In *That Wonderful Composite Called Author: Authorship in East Asian Literatures from the Beginnings to the Seventeenth Century*, ed. Christian Schwermann and Raji C. Steineck, 30–57. Leiden and Boston: Brill.

———. 2017a. "Anecdote Collections as Argumentative Texts: The Composition of the *Shuoyuan*." In *Between History and Philosophy: Anecdotes in Early China*, ed. Paul van Els and Sarah A. Queen, 147–192. Albany, NY: State University of New York Press.

———. 2017b. "Ökonomische Gerechtigkeit im antiken China? Einige verteilungspolitische Denkansätze. Economic Justice in Ancient China? A Few Thoughts on Distribution Policy." In *Rooted in Hope: China – Religion – Christianity. In der Hoffnung verwurzelt: China – Religion – Christentum. Festschrift in Honour of Roman Malek S.V.D. on the Occasion of His 65th Birthday*, ed. Barbara Hoster, Dirk Kuhlmann, and Zbigniew Wesołowski (2 vols.), vol. 1, 63–73. Abingdon (Oxon): Routledge.

———. 2018. "Von der Sparsamkeit zur Nachhaltigkeit. Zukunftsdenken in der antiken chinesischen Wirtschaftstheorie." *Bochumer Jahrbuch zur Ostasienforschung* 41: 69–98.

Shangjunshu jiaoshu 商君書校疏 (Collated Glosses on the *Documents Pertaining to the Lord of Shang*). 2012. Ed. Zhang Jue 張覺. Beijing: Zhishi chanquan chubanshe.

Shangjunshu zhuizhi 商君書錐指 (Pointing with an Awl at the *Documents Pertaining to the Lord of Shang*). 1996. Ed. Jiang, Lihong 蔣禮鴻. Beijing: Zhonghua shuju.

Shiji 史記 (Records of the Scribes). 1959. By Sima, Qian 司馬遷 et al. With the commentaries by Pei, Yin 裴駰, Sima, Zhen 司馬貞 and Zhang, Shoujie 張守節. Beijing: Zhonghua shuju.

Shuoyuan jiaozheng 說苑校證 (*Garden of Illustrative Examples*, Collated and Corroborated). 1987. Edited by Xiang, Zonglu 向宗魯. Beijing: Zhonghua shuju.

Suishu 隋書 (Documents of the Sui). 1973. Beijing: Zhonghua shuju.

Swann, Nancy Lee. 1950. *Food and Money in Ancient China*. Princeton: Princeton University Press.

TLS 2020ff. *Thesaurus Linguae Sericae*. 漢學文典. *An Historical and Comparative Encyclopaedia of Chinese Conceptual Schemes*. https://hxwd.org/index.html. Edited by Christoph Harbsmeier, Christian Schwermann and Christian Wittern. Accessed 23 Sept 2022.

Van Ess, Hans. 2021. "Situating the 'Qingzhong' 輕重 Chapters of the *Guanzi* 管子." In *Between Command and Market: Economic Thought and Practice in Early China*, ed. Elisa Levi Sabattini and Christian Schwermann, 114–144. Leiden: Brill.

Vogelsang, Kai. 2017. *Shangjun shu: Schriften des Fürsten von Shang*. Stuttgart: Alfred Kröner Verlag.

Yantielun jiaozhu 鹽鐵論校注 (*Debates on Salt and Iron*, Collated and Annotated). 1992. Ed. Wang, Liqi 王利器. Beijing: Zhonghua shuju.

Yates, Robin D.S. 2021. "The Economic Activities of a Qin Local Administration: Qianling County, Modern Liye, Hunan Province, 222–209 BCE." In *Between Command and Market: Economic Thought and Practice in Early China*, ed. Elisa Levi Sabattini and Christian Schwermann, 244–317. Leiden: Brill.

Zhu, Shaohou 朱紹侯. 2012. "Liang Han tuntianzhi yanjiu" 兩漢屯田制研究 (Studies on the *tuntian* System of the Two Han Dynasties). *Shixue yuekan* 史學月刊 46.10: 26–37. (a survey of the establishment and early history of defense farming colonies in the northwest of the Han empire)

Part II
Major Ideas of the *fa* Traditions

Chapter 7
Rule by Impersonal Standards in the Early Empires: Ideas and Realities

Maxim Korolkov

1 Introduction: Standardization and Governance in the Early Empires

Were the early Sinitic empires of Qin 秦 (221–207 BCE) and Han 漢 (202 BCE – 220 CE) ever to choose a motto for their style of governance, it might well be "standardization." Standardization marked the birth moment of the empire, when in 221 BCE the First Emperor of Qin proclaimed the unified system of weights and measures, cart axle length, and a uniform writing system (*Shiji* 2006: 6: 239). Apart from its utilitarian purposes, this measure had strong ideological undertones: the decree was distributed throughout the empire to create common knowledge of the new regime (Sanft 2014: 57–76). Yet the imperial standardization ran deeper than the ideology of universal world-ordering and the crude attempts to impose superficial "legibility" on the society (Scott 1998; Yoffee 2004; Wang 2014). It lay at the heart of what may have been the most ambitious pre-modern project of centralized socio-political transformation.

The bureaucratic organization of government is perhaps the most emphasized facet of rule by impersonal standards in the early empires. Objective standards of competence for appointment, promotion, and dismissal of personnel are part of the definition of modern Western bureaucracy (Mann 2012: 444–45), and the administration of Warring States (453–221 BCE) polities and Qin and Han empires have been on many occasions described as the most fully developed pre-modern bureaucracies (Creel 1970: 3; Bielenstein 1980: 157; Hui 2005: 1–7; Li 2013: 282; but see Grafflin 1990 for criticism). This assumption is not without problems, especially when applied indiscriminately to the five centuries between the Shang Yang 商鞅 (d. 338 BCE) reforms and the disintegration of Eastern Han 東漢 empire (25–220 CE),

M. Korolkov (✉)
Heidelberg University, Heidelberg, Germany

© The Author(s), under exclusive license to Springer Nature Switzerland AG 2024
Y. Pines (ed.), *Dao Companion to China's* fa *Tradition*, Dao Companions
to Chinese Philosophy 19, https://doi.org/10.1007/978-3-031-53630-4_8

a period that witnessed considerable administrative changes. Throughout the period, personal guarantees by senior officials played a crucial role in the appointment and dismissal of their staff. Well into the Western Han 西漢 (202 BCE – 9 CE), clerical personnel and other low-ranking functionaries were conscripted on a full- or part-time basis from among the hereditary professional groups and general populace: they were part of the broader systems of state-dependent labor, not the salaried, career bureaucrats. When impersonal quantitative standards were indeed used to select or promote officials, these criteria could have little to do with the actual quali-fications or performance. Rather, they focused on the parameters most suitable for measurement.

At the same time, in the late Warring States polities and in the early empires, impersonal standards were not limited to the improvement of government apparatus *per se*. Rather, they were an integral part of a comprehensive social reform that enacted core precepts such as meritocracy, centralization of authority, and totality of monarchical power. Unlike the ideologies of bureaucratizing state reform in early modern Europe, standardization policies as they were developed by Warring States period statesmen and carried out in the early empires were aimed at the entire soci-ety, not just its government.[1]

The remainder of this introduction traces the development of the ideas and prac-tices of rule by impersonal standards against the background of the organizational challenges faced by Sinitic polities after ca. 500 BCE, and the responses to these challenges by thinkers of the time, especially those associated with the *fa* tradition. The introduction is followed by two sections that discuss the application of stan-dards in the administration of the early empires. The final section outlines the alter-native approaches to administration that, during the latter Western Han and especially the Eastern Han period, came to challenge the "rule by impersonal standards."

1.1   Impersonal Standards and the Reorganization of Governance in the Warring States Period

During the Warring States period, the rulers of the leading Sinitic polities radically expanded the spatial reach and functional capacity of their governments.[2] Centralized territorial administration was probably pioneered in the states of Chu 楚, Jin 晋, and Qi 齊 (Creel 1964: 155–83; Li 1998: 148–68), but in the middle of the fourth cen-tury BCE, the state of Qin in the west took the lead by reorganizing its core region of Guanzhong into thirty-one counties (*xian* 縣) that encompassed the entire coun-tryside (*Shiji* 68: 2232; Sun 2020: 348–51). Administrative centralization was

---

[1] For the ideological movements behind state reform in early modern Europe, see Tribe 1984: 263–84; Mann 2012: 447–57.

[2] For a general account on the Warring States administrative reforms, see Lewis 1999b.

accompanied by state-organized resettlement and the reclamation of fertile alluvial soils in river plains, facilitated by the spread of iron metallurgy and ox-drawn iron plows.[3] By distributing these newly opened fields to farmer colonists, state governments enhanced their fiscal base.

Revolution in warfare was the major driving force behind the consolidation of centralized state power. Unlike the polities of the Spring and Autumn period (770–453 BCE), whose relatively small armies were organized around aristocratic chariotry as the principal fighting force, the Warring States recruited hundreds of thousands of peasants into mass infantry armies that fought prolonged wars of attrition (Lewis 1990: 54–67; Yang 2003: 303–17; Galvany 2020). Besides the levying, concentration, and leadership of troops, such warfare required enormous logistical effort and the centralization of much greater economic resources than available to the earlier polities that were the loose confederations of aristocratic clans. Military buildup precipitated fiscal innovation, such as the introduction of universal land taxation, which, in turn, required the expansion of the state administration into the countryside.[4]

Urbanization and the growth of trade during the Warring States period created additional sources of state revenue that required a specialized administration (Chen 2003: 290–310; von Falkenhausen 2018: 161–69). As commercial taxes became an important part of the fiscal toolkit, states established offices to manage urban marketplaces, collect tolls, and cast bronze coins (von Glahn 2016: 60–74). Governments also benefited from commercial growth by directly engaging in market transactions. By the end of the Warring States period, state-managed workshops in Qin were selling a wide range of goods to private buyers (Korolkov 2021a: 221–24). Supplying the booming urban centers, such as the Qin capital Xianyang, involved long-distance transportation, storage, and distribution of grain and other supplies, all of which required considerable organizational input by the government: levying labor, constructing and maintaining facilities, and managing the distribution process (Cai 2009).

The Warring States period regimes of compulsory labor, which are particularly well-documented in the state of Qin, prompted some scholars to define Qin as "the state of convicts" (Tomiya 2006: 107). Besides convicted criminals, who by imperial times numbered in the hundreds of thousands at the major construction sites such as the First Emperor's mausoleum (*Shiji* 6: 256), these laborers included farmers conscripted for a fixed period of time every year, as well as debtors working off their obligations to the state (Korolkov 2021b: 160–241). By mobilizing the labor of their subjects for state projects, such as the building of canals, roads, cities, and frontier fortifications, the Warring States rulers transformed natural landscapes to facilitate the extraction, transfer, and amassment of manpower and resources.

---

[3] For state-organized resettlement, see Korolkov and Hein 2021. For the spread of iron metallurgy, see Liu 2017: 29–39.

[4] For a recent discussion of taxation in the state of Qin during the Warring States and imperial periods, see Korolkov 2021a.

By the third century BCE, the rulers of the major Warring States presided over extensive state economies: farms and workshops, transportation and storage infra-structures, and a dependent workforce deployed in agriculture, manufacturing, con-struction, and logistics. Revenues generated by the state sector and raised from the general populace through taxation had to be coordinated with mounting state expen-ditures. Such coordination required increasingly complex planning based on the fixed norms of harvest yields, productivity in various labor processes, speed of travel and transportation, and the efficiency of the administrative apparatus, which swelled with the expansion of the military and economic operations of central governments.

1.2 Ideologies of Standardization in the Warring States Period

Many political thinkers of the Warring States era, including those who later came to be associated with the *fa* tradition, saw the delegation of power by rulers as the central problem in the emerging centralized, bureaucratic monarchies. They were also looking back at the aristocratic polities of the earlier age, with their weak rulers and all-powerful ministerial lineages, and were committed to preventing such an outcome at all costs (Pines 2012: 46–50). What are the appropriate criteria for appointing, promoting, and dismissing administrative functionaries? Is it possible for a ruler to delegate his powers without compromising monarchical authority? How can the behavior of state officials be efficiently monitored? Warring States authors emphasized, cultivated, and propagated the memories of recent revolts, coups, and usurpations that had toppled long-established thrones as the conse-quences of inadequate responses to these challenges. For many text-based currents that were retrospectively identified in the Han period as the *fa*, *Ru*, and *Dao* tradi-tions, the subjectivity of rulers was the principal threat to the survival of their poli-ties. Contrasting solutions to this problem articulated the fault lines between the intellectual traditions.

Impersonal norms, including legal regulations, administrative rules, and perfor-mance standards, were central to the *fa* response to the problem of ruler subjectivity in a centralized monarchical state (cf. Graziani, Chap. 13, this volume). The empha-sis on impersonal standards for controlling officials in the texts of the *fa* tradition contrasts with the *Ru* preoccupation with the moral perfection of individuals aspir-ing to leading positions in society—typically as advisors to rulers—and with the *Dao* ideal of the self-cultivating sage who is capable of spontaneous responses to changing circumstances (Lewis 1999a: 36–38). Whereas the latter two traditions focused on personal improvement, the *fa* texts sought to make the individuality of rulers and ruled irrelevant to the functioning of a polity, just as contemporary mili-tary thinkers required that the commander reduce his subordinates' individuality by obliterating "the senses and minds of his troops so that they would perceive and think only what he directed" (Lewis 1990: 106).

One of the earliest extant *fa* tradition texts, the essay "Within the Borders" ("Jing nei" 境內, dating to roughly 350–300 BCE), which was eventually included in the *Book of Lord Shang* (*Shangjunshu* 商君書), outlines a program of thorough objectification of relations between the state (primarily its military organization) and its subjects (*Shangjunshu jiaoshu* 19: 223–37; Pines 2017: 221–26). This was based on the standardization of private individuals' contributions to the state's projects, conceived primarily as military expansion, and rewards for these contributions. Commoners recruited for military service received one level of social rank (*jue* 爵) for slaying an enemy soldier. Each rank entailed a fixed increase in one's agricultural and residential plots, the right to redeem a criminal punishment, and other privileges (*Shangjunshu jiaoshu* 19: 233–34; Pines 2016: 18–24). The social ranks effectively reflected the balance of payment between the ruler and his subjects, so that standardized and measurable contributions by individuals were offset against standardized and measurable economic, legal, and ritual privileges. Like any other currency, social ranks facilitated transactions by coordinating the values of otherwise incommensurable items.

The rank system was one of the key social innovations that enhanced Qin's military power in the middle and late Warring States period. Excavated texts attest to its role in the functioning of fundamental economic institutions of the Qin and early Western Han empires, such as the state-sponsored distribution of agricultural land.[5]

An emphasis on norms as the main instrument of governance is typical of other late Warring States period texts associated with the *fa* tradition. The essays from the third century BCE that became part of the transmitted collection *Guanzi* 管子 argue that impersonal standards are a more solid foundation of royal administration than relying on individual talent.[6] The assertion that the ruler's task was to establish standards, not to engage in the subjective assessment of his subordinates' personal abilities, is supported by the artisanal analogies that were becoming increasingly popular among late Warring States thinkers: "Even though one may have a clever eye and a skillful hand, these are no match for the correctness of the simple compass and T-square. Therefore, a clever person is able to produce a compass and T-square but is unable to make correct squares and circles without them" 雖有巧目利手，不如拙規矩之正方圓也；故巧者能生規矩，不能廢規矩而正方圓 (*Guanzi jiaozhu* 16: 308; Rickett 1985: 261; see also Graziani, Chap. 13, this volume).[7]

Another *fa* tradition text from the late Warring States period, the *Shenzi* 慎子 (Harris, Chap. 3, this volume), emphasizes the epistemological value of standards

---

[5] The early Western Han legal statutes from tomb 247, Zhangjiashan 張家山 (Hubei Province), provide the most detailed description of the rank-based land distribution system. See Peng et al. 2007: 186–94, slips 239–57; Barbieri-Low and Yates 2015: vol. 2, 692–718.

[6] For the composition and dates of the *Guanzi*, see Rickett 1993: 244–51; see also Sato, Chap. 5, this volume.

[7] A similar metaphor is used in the paramount text of the late Warring States *Ru* tradition, the *Mengzi* 孟子 (*Mencius*), where it serves to admonish the contemporary rulers to adopt the ways of the ancient kings as a standard of benevolent government. See *Mengzi zhengyi* 7.1–2 (4A1–2).

and measurements as the only means to embrace the variety of human and natural phenomena. Equally important, in the view of *Shenzi* authors, was the utility of standards, especially the written law that standardized rewards and punishments, in restraining the negative effects of subjective decisions by the ruler. Such decisions, according to the *Shenzi*, would unavoidably provoke resentment among subjects and undermine monarchical authority (Harris 2016: 110–33).

Impersonal standards of performance were seen as crucial to delegating power to officials, which was one of the central tenets of *fa* tradition. According to the *Han Feizi* 韓非子, a collection of essays from the final decades of the Warring States period, the application of standards allowed rulers to prevent ministers from encroaching on royal prerogatives by delimiting each office's responsibilities and tying promotion and dismissal to the appropriate performance of standardized functions (*Han Feizi jijie* 3: 31–39).[8] These recommendations are encapsulated in early imperial statutes that required each office to have "its own differentiated [responsibilities]. What is not his office's business, the official shall not dare to do" 官各有辨, 非其官事勿敢為 (Peng et al. 2007: 176–77, slip 216).

The collection of essays associated with the late Warring States thinker Xun Kuang 荀況, (Xunzi 荀子, d. after 238 BCE), synthesized the elements of several major intellectual traditions of pre-imperial era, including those of *Ru* and *fa* (Loewe 1993: 178–88; Goldin 2020: 169–200). While critical of unconditional prioritization of standards, including the legal regulations, over moral virtues cultivated by a *Ru* gentleman, the *Xunzi* authors nevertheless endorse the language of impersonal, number-based performance assessment in their exposition of the organization and functional principles of state administration (*Xunzi jijie* 9: 148–74). Obsession with reckoning and relentless imposition of standards to the detriment of leniency and moral governance is condemned (*Xunzi jijie* 10: 192–93), but elsewhere, the application of standards "to each and every one of the myriad things" by the rank-and-file officials is advised as the only alternative to overloading the "Great Gentleman" (*da junzi* 大君子, here probably referring to the ruler or the chief minister) with unnecessary bureaucratic routine (*Xunzi jijie* 11: 221–22; Knoblock 1988, vol. 2: 163).

The incorporation of the central tenet of the Warring States *fa* thinkers – that rulers should rely on laws and other impersonal regulations to manipulate their subjects' behavior towards the desired objectives – in one of the most influential texts of the *Ru* tradition not only manifests syncretic tendencies in late pre-imperial and early imperial political discourse, but also points to the ubiquity of standards and norms as indispensable administrative tools. No credible argument about appropriate governance could be made without reference to this new reality.

---

[8] For a discussion of the administrative theory in the *Han Feizi*, see Lewis 1999a: 32–33; Goldin 2013.

2 The Many Facets of Standardization in Early Empires: The *cheng* 程 Norms

The concept of impersonal standards is amply attested in the excavated official documents from the early imperial period. While in the excavated texts this meaning is conveyed by several terms, the most ubiquitous and general one is *cheng* 程, often translated as "norms" (Hulsewé 1985: 61; Barbieri-Low and Yates 2015: 75). This section, therefore, considers the application of *cheng* norms in the administration of early empires.

The rulers of the Qin and Han empires instituted a range of norms to assess the performance of their subordinates, including officials, soldiers, convict laborers, and various professionals working for the government, such as artisans and couriers. Special productivity norms were applied to revenue-generating material assets, most importantly, agricultural fields. These norms were key to the taxation system in the Qin and early Western Han empires. Their importance subsequently declined as the central government of the Han Empire adopted fixed rates for land taxation and reduced its monitoring of agricultural production (Korolkov 2021a: 237–39).

The *cheng* norms were central to economic administration in the early empires. State-managed construction projects that left behind some of the best-known monuments of early China – such as the First Emperor's mausoleum complex and the burial mounds of the Han emperors, the remains of imperial palaces and early sections of the Great Wall, the Dujiangyan 都江堰 irrigation project in Sichuan and the Lingqu 靈渠 Canal across the Yangzi–Pearl River watershed – involved the distribution of manpower and resources based on official productivity norms. "Individual norms" (*yuan cheng* 員程) are mentioned in the Qin bamboo text titled *The Way of Being a Good Official* (*Wei li zhi dao* 為吏之道, excavated from the burial of a local functionary at Shuihudi 睡虎地), which contains, among other things, a list of technical terms used by the imperial officials (Shuihudi 1990: 170, slip 29).

This section surveys the main areas of governance in the early empires where the *cheng* norms found application: the organization and control of human mobility, including the operation of official communication and delivery systems; state-managed manufacturing; construction projects; military training; and the management of agricultural resources. It also addresses the legal framework for the promulgation of official standards.

2.1 Travel Speed Standards

The early Western Han "Statute on the Forwarding of Documents" (*Xing shu lü* 行書律) prescribed that the foot couriers carrying official documents had to cover two hundred *li* (approx. 83.2 km) in one day and one night. Those who failed to meet this norm faced punishments calibrated to the duration of delay: fifty cane strokes for up to half a day, hundred strokes for up to one day, and a fine of two *liang* (approx. 31 grams) of gold for more than a day (Peng et al. 2007: 203–05, slips 273–75). Similar norms probably existed in Qin legislation, which also included a statute on the forwarding of documents (Chen 2015: 131–33, slips 192–97).

Documents excavated in present-day Inner Mongolia, which used to be the northwestern frontier of the Han Empire, illustrate the use of travel speed norms in the official communication system during the heyday of the early empires, the first century BCE and the first century CE.[9] A typical record of the delivery of an official communication reads as follows: "… In the night, in *hunshi* (17th) time unit, soldier … of Linmu [Section] received [correspondence] from a soldier of Chenghao North watchtower and proceeded to Wuxian [watchtower]. In *yeshi* (19th) time unit, he transferred [the correspondence] to Shou, a soldier of Chengbei [Section]. Seventeen *li* (approx. 7 km), the norms have been met" 已夜昏時臨木卒 受誠勢北 隧卒, 通武武隧, 以夜食七分時付誠北卒壽 十七里中程 (Jiandu 2014, vol. 2: 175, tablet 173.1). In the northwestern frontier region, military watchtowers were also nodes in the official communication system, and servicemen stationed there, apart from their military responsibilities, delivered correspondence and were subject to efficiency controls along with the professional couriers discussed above. The time-reckoning system attested in the northwestern frontier texts divided the day into 32 units, each equivalent to 45 minutes (Hao and Zhang 2008: 68–105). It took soldier Wang one and a half such units to cover the distance of 7 km on foot, which fell within the norm.

Norms for the travel speed applied to other state-ordered or state-authorized movements as well. Of particular importance for the empire was the shipment of tax grain, which fed the imperial court, officials, and armies. The following Table 7.1 summarizes the speed standards for overland transportation of grain in the Qin and Western Han statutes.

The state-organized transportation of tax grain and other materials was carried out by various groups, including convicts, servicemen, and the general population mobilized for labor service.[10] While the travel speed norms probably applied to all

Table 7.1 Travel speed norms for grain transportation corvée (Chen 2015: 150, slip 248; Peng et al. 2007: 248–50, slips 411–15)

Type of transportation	Travel speed norms (per day)	
	Qin	Western Han
Loaded cart	60 *li* = 25 km	50 *li* = 20.8 km
Person with a shouldered burden		
Empty cart	80 *li* = 33.3 km	70 *li* = 29 km
Person without a burden	100 *li* = 41.6 km	80 *li* = 33.3 km

[9] For an English-language introduction to these texts, see Loewe 1967.

[10] The groups of laborers that could be used in the state-organized transportations are carefully listed in the instruction by the Dongting Commandery governor dated March 30, 220 BCE. See Chen et al. 2018: 447–52, tablet 9–2283.

of them, it is unclear whether the penalties for failing to meet these norms were identical for each of these groups. In all likelihood, convicts were penalized more severely than conscripted laborers.

The imperial Qin "Statute on the Checking of Convicts" (*Yu jiao lü* 獄校律) specifies speed norms for yet another category of authorized travelers: exiled criminals and convicts who served their sentences away from home. These people moved in groups escorted by officials. A procedure was in place for enforcing compliance with the speed norms:

> 為質日，署行日，日行六十里，留弗亟遣過五日及留弗傳過二日到十日，貲縣令以下主者各二甲。
>
> Prepare event calendars to record the date of departure and [confirm that the distance of] sixty *li* per day (approx. 25 km) is covered [during the travel]. When [officials] do not immediately dispatch [convicts], so that five days pass, and when [convicts] are delayed on the way by two to ten days, senior [county] officials, including magistrates, should be fined two suits of armor each. (Chen 2015: 145–46, slips 232–36; translation modifies Chen 2018: 460–61)

The "event calendar" (*zhiri* 質日) mentioned in this statute was, in all likelihood, a timeline of official activities, such as inspection tours, sacrificial offerings in the state shrines, and, in the present case, escorting exiles and convicts to their destination (Chen 2018: 446–68). The counterparts of these official event calendars were private calendars that have recently been excavated or looted from several tombs of local officials dated to the Qin and Western Han. According to Chen Wei, such private calendars "could possibly have been used as independent proof of an official's punctuality in performing his duties and provided a degree of protection against potential unjustified prosecution" (Chen 2018: 464–65). Upon the completion of an official mission, these records were used to compile time-efficiency assessments, such as the one that opens a criminal investigation record from 218 BCE: "[The case workers were] traveling for 60 days, traveling by post-horse and boat for 5,146 *li* (approx. 2,139 km), calculating it at 85 *li* (approx. 35 km) per day and not counting the extraneous 46 *li*" 行道六十日，乘恒馬及船行五千一百卌六里，衛(率)之，日行八十五里，畸(奇)卌六里不衛(率) (Peng et al. 2007: 364, slips 147–48; Barbieri-Low and Yates 2015: 1337).

Excavated documents from the early imperial period make it clear that travel speed norms applied to virtually all forms of physical mobility by state personnel: not only in communication and transportation systems but also in the transfers of labor conscripts, soldiers, and convicts from one area to another, as well as in all official tasks that required government functionaries to travel away from their offices.

From the time of Shang Yang's reforms in the mid-fourth century BCE, the central authorities of the Qin and Han empires were gathering information to assess the efficiency of existing routes and to design new ones where greater predictability was possible for travel conditions and speed. This information-gathering is reflected, for example, by excavated maps from the third century BCE, which focused on transportation corridors (Gansu 2009: 73–76, 149–55); by lists that recorded distances between various geographical locations on the routes (Liye 2016: 70, tablet 16–52);

by travel-related event calendars; and by itineraries for traveling personnel with prescriptions regarding the specific sequence of stops where they could enjoy food and lodging.[11] These latter documents, in particular, highlight one of the key rationales for the system of speed standards and the entire apparatus of planning, recording, accounting, and evaluation involved in the official mobility: controlling its costs.

The formation of empire greatly increased the geographical scale of government operations and, consequently, investments in the "state on the move": the resources needed to move people, goods, and materials. Mobile personnel and assets were much more difficult to monitor than fixed ones, yet, when unchecked, the costs of their mobility – for example, the expenses of providing security, accommodation, and sustenance to officials, soldiers, and labor conscripts temporarily deployed outside their offices, garrisons, and villages – were potentially ruinous (Hou 2016). Standards of time efficiency helped to transform this unpredictable world of mobility and contingency into an enormous accounting machine permitting the authorities to establish the location of each person at any point in time.

2.2 Productivity and Material Expenditure Norms in State-Managed Manufacturing

When Emperor Xuan of the Western Han 漢宣帝 (r. 74–48 BCE) appointed Yin Wenggui 尹翁歸 (d. 62 BCE) as governor of one of the three metropolitan circuits of the Han empire, Yin wasted no time in introducing new measures to suppress crime, particularly targeting the powerful local families who, by the first century BCE, had started to challenge imperial authorities. Whenever members of such families were found guilty of a crime, they were required to chop straw for the state-owned cattle farms, which was a form of penal labor. They were not allowed to hire substitutes, and were beaten with sticks if they did not meet individual productivity norms (*yuan cheng*). This punishment proved so severe that, according to the official history of the Western Han Empire, many of the sentenced committed suicide out of despair (*Hanshu* 76: 3208).

"Individual norms" in the *Hanshu* biography of Yin Wenggui is the same term as in the Qin manuscript from Shuihudi mentioned at the beginning of this section. Separated by almost two hundred years, these two texts attest to the imperial government's continuing use of *cheng* norms to evaluate the efficiency of various state-managed production facilities.

The collection of legal statutes excavated from the Qin tomb at Shuihudi contains a section titled "Norms for Artisans" (*gong ren cheng* 工人程), which deals with production standards for convicts in state-managed workshops. One article, for example, correlates the output norms for female convicts, who probably

---

[11] For the documents mentioning such itineraries, which were known as "lists of counties passed on the route" (*guo suo xian* 過所縣), see, for example, Chen et al. 2012: 344–45, tablet 8–1517.

manufactured textiles, to those for professional artisans. When working on a permanent basis, two convicts were expected to match one artisan. This ratio was reduced to four-to-one for convicts working in turns of duty, and five-to-one for underage female convicts (Shuihudi 1990: 45–46, slip 109). The amount of work per day varied from season to season, in accordance with differences in daylight time: three workdays in the winter were equivalent to two in the summer (Shuihudi 1990: 45, slip 108).

The Qin documents from Qianling 遷陵 County mention "Ordinances on Norms" (*cheng ling* 程令), which probably established the amount of tribute in local goods that the county had to deliver to the imperial court (Chen et al. 2012: 259, tablet 8–997; Chen et al. 2018: 109, tablet 9–718). It is also possible that some production quotas were decided at the local level, e.g., by the county authorities or officials in charge of individual workshops. Further discoveries and publication of official documents will shed light on the process by which productivity norms for artisans were elaborated, disseminated, and possibly customized at the local level.

A manual of mathematics from the early second century BCE, excavated in the tomb of a local official, illustrates how these norms were applied in various areas of production.[12] One of the problems deals with arrow manufacturing: "The norm: 1 man in 1 day makes 30 arrows; he feathers 20 arrows. Now it is desired to instruct the same man to make arrows and feather them. In one day, how many does he make? Reply: he makes 12" 程:一人一日為矢卅，羽矢廿。今欲令一人為矢且羽之，一日為幾何?曰:為十二 (Zhangjiashan 2006: 149, slip 131; Cullen 2004: 79). Another task in the same manual considers the production of bamboo tubes. Again, the authors assume a daily output norm for each step in the process (Zhangjiashan 2006: 149, slips 129–30). It is clear that the norms were applied in the context of relatively large-scale production divided into distinct stages in an assembly line.[13]

Arrow manufacturing and, more generally, weapon production, was one of the central occupations of government-operated industry in the early empires. During the fifteen years of Qin imperial administration south of the Yangzi River, the workshops of Qianling County churned out enormous volume of arrows, some of which were exported to other regions of the empire for use by the military.[14] The Qianling archival documents show that the standardization of artisanal production was not limited to per-day and per-person output norms, but also involved material expenditure. One excavated document specifies various types of arrows, whose production required different numbers of feathers (Chen et al. 2012: 332, tablet 8–1457+8–1458).

Qianling officials followed the letter of Qin law when they listed separately items produced under different norms of material expenditure (Shuihudi 1990: 43, slip

---

[12] For an introduction to this and other mathematical manuscripts and transmitted texts from the Qin and Han periods, see Chemla 2018: 473–92.

[13] For the organization of production processes in the Han imperial workshops similar to modern assembly line manufacturing, see Barbieri-Low 2001.

[14] For the large number of arrows stored at the county arsenal, see Chen et al. 2012: 154, tablet 8–458; Chen et al. 2018: 71, tablet 9–124.

99). These norms also guided storehouse officials when they issued materials to artisans in government workshops (Shuihudi 1990: 76, slips 58–60; Peng et al. 2007: 229–30, slip 352). The production process required considerable coordination among the various offices: on receiving a government order for a certain number of objects, workshop officials calculated the necessary volume of raw materials based on the expenditure norms and submitted requests to the storage authorities, who checked the numbers and issued the needed materials. The workshop managers also had to estimate the time needed to fill the order. To do so, they used productivity norms for various categories of labor at their disposal: professional artisans as well as convicts of various age groups. As in the case of travel speed standards, the use of norms greatly facilitated centralized planning and control of the state economy.

2.3   Construction Projects

Next to military campaigns, construction works were by far the largest and most complex state projects in the early empires. Seven hundred thousand convicts are said to have been simultaneously working to erect the Epang Palace and the burial complex of the First Emperor in the vicinity of his capital, Xianyang (*Shiji* 2006: 6: 256). Another three hundred thousand men were needed to build the long walls along the northern frontier of the Qin Empire (Shelach 2014). The Han historiographical tradition condemned these mammoth undertakings for their waste of human resources (*Hanshu* 24A: 1137, 51: 2327). Despite this criticism, imperial construction projects continued unabated into the Han period. The mid-second century BCE mausoleum of the Western Han Emperor Jing 漢景帝 (r. 157–141 BCE) cost the lives of at least ten thousand convicts over the seven years that it took to build (Campbell 2014).

The fact that so many hard labor convicts met their death constructing walls, digging canals, and piling up soil for their emperors' burial mounds does not mean that these projects were not carefully planned, rather that little concern was usually given to the wellbeing of those at the bottom of the social hierarchy. Anthony Barbieri-Low has reconstructed the economic logic of labor mobilizations for the construction of the city walls of the new imperial capital, Chang'an, in 194–190 BCE (Barbieri-Low 2007: 220–23). One of the critical decisions concerned the conscription of statute labor. Calling too many farmers away from their fields potentially threatened economic and social stability. This is probably why general labor levies took place during the off-season, within a relatively limited (ca. 250 km) radius from the capital, and then only for one month at a time. Unlike the labor of convicted criminals, statute labor was a resource that had to be earmarked with discretion.

While we do not have a direct account of the planning process in any of the great construction projects in the early empires, regulations for works at the local level can be found in the Qin "Statute on Labor Services" (*Yao lü* 繇律) from Shuihudi. As in artisanal production, individual output norms were at the center of the planning process:

縣為恒事及灟有為殿(也), 吏程攻(功), 贏員及減員自二日以上, 為不察。上之所興, 其程攻(功)而不當者, 如縣然。度攻(功)必令司空与匠度之, 毋独令匠。其不審, 以律論度者, 而以其實為繇(徭)徒計。

> When the county undertakes routine work as well when it has requested [permission] to undertake work, the officials apply the norms to work. If [the estimate proves to be wrong by] an excess of the [labor force], or a shortage, of two days or more, this is considered 'lack of perspicacity…' When estimating the work, it is imperative to have the Controller of Works estimate it together with the Builder… In case of carelessness, the persons who made the estimate are to be adjudicated according to the Statutes, whereas the actual amount is to be accounted as statute labor for the conscripts. (Shuihudi 1990: 47, slips 122–24; translation modifies Hulsewé 1985: 64)

Of the two officials involved in project planning, the Builder (*jiang* 匠) was the architect who designed the buildings (Shuihudi 1990: 48, comm. 21), the Controller of Works (*sikong* 司空) a county-level official in charge of organizing and supervising the labor force (Miyake 2016: 188–243). The former assessed the amount of work in terms of labor time, or, as the text puts it, "[applied] the norms to the [total amount of] work" (*cheng gong* 程功). The latter assigned necessary workers, taking into account the available human resources, the timing of the project, and the government's declared commitment to minimizing conscriptions of the general populace (Chen et al. 2018: 447–52, tablet 9–2283).

The statute does not specify the productivity norms that the two officials used in their planning. These norms almost certainly varied, depending on the nature of task. By far the most labor-consuming stage in construction projects involved moving earth, for example, excavation and trenching. Arithmetic manuals provide a sense of what these norms may have been. According to *The Nine Chapters on the Mathematical Art* (*Jiu zhang suan shu* 九章算術), a collection of 246 mathematical problems with accompanying solutions probably compiled during the Eastern Han period, each worker was expected to excavate, transport, and construct 7.55 m^3 per month (*Jiuzhang Suanshu jiaozheng* 5:279–81; Shen et al. 1999: 258–59). This norm probably dates to the beginning of the Western Han period (Barbieri-Low 2007: 223).

2.4 Military Training

Universal military service and the mass production of standard-issue weapons in the late Warring States, imperial Qin, and the Western Han Empire set in motion the standardization of military training and assessment.[15] The mass infantry armies of the Warring States necessitated both the provision of minimal general training to peasant conscripts and a set of standardized practices for selecting and training specialized troops (Lewis 1999b: 621). According to one account from the third century BCE, the rulers of the state of Wei 魏 "employ fixed standards in selecting

---

[15] For the military institutions in the Qin and Western Han empires and the abolition of universal military service at the beginning of the Eastern Han period, see Lewis 2000: 33–76.

martial soldiers. They must be able to wear the three types of personal armor, wield the twelve-stone crossbow, carry a quiver with fifty arrows on their back with a halberd placed on top of them, wear a helmet, suspend a sword from their girdle, and carry three days' provisions on a forced march of a hundred *li* by noon. If they succeed in all these tests, then their family is given an exemption from certain taxes and special benefits for farmland and buildings" 魏氏之武卒，以度取之，衣三屬之甲，操十二石之弩，負服矢五十個，置戈其上，冠胄帶劍，贏三日之糧，日中而趨百里，中試則復其戶，利其田宅 (*Xunzi jijie* 15: 272–73; translation modifies Knoblock 1988, vol. 2: 222–23).

One of the critical innovations of the Warring States period was the introduction of the crossbow as a commonly used infantry weapon (Lewis 1999b: 622; Pines 2002: 696–97). Crossbows (and their parts) are the most frequently mentioned weapons in the written records of the Qin county of Qianling (Chen et al. 2012: 154–55, tablet 8–458; 264–65, tablet 8–1028; 460, tablet 8–2345; Chen et al. 2018: 561, tablet 9–599; 180–81, tablet 9–702; 275, tablet 9–1199; 330, tablet 9–1571). The Qin legal texts from Shuihudi refer to shooting tests for crossbow archers, whose officers were penalized when their subordinates failed to meet the requirements (Shuihudi 1990: 79–80, slips 1–4). At the beginning of the Western Han period, officials selected some of the military recruits as "county crossbowmen" (*xian nu* 縣弩), who were obliged to participate in shooting exercises for fifteen days in the spring and autumn every year until they reached the age of retirement. In return, they were exempted from the annual one-month-long labor service (Peng et al. 2007: 248–50, slips 411–15).

That the archery tests involved numerical standards for assessing individual performance becomes clear from the records of the Han military administration of the northwestern frontier. These documents contain accounts of marksmanship tests. According to a document excavated at the headquarters of Jiaqu Company (Jiaqu houguan 甲渠候官) in the Ejin River basin (in the present-day Inner Mongolia Autonomous Region), "when shooting a crossbow, the norm (*cheng*) is that six arrows of twelve should hit the target. If more than six or fewer than six [arrows hit the target], add or subtract fifteen days of service for each arrow" 弩發矢十二中帑矢六為程過六若不帑六矢賜奪勞各十五日 (Gansu et al. 1990: 330, E.P.T56:337). Archery tests, typically carried out in the autumn (Gansu et al. 1990: 210, E.P.T51:461; 234, E.P.T52:95; 282, E.P.T53:34), were obligatory for officers assigned to the frontier (Loewe 1967, vol. 1: 82–83). Superior performance in archery test could advance an officer's career by accelerating the accumulation of service time (*lao* 勞, see Sect. 3.2).

2.5 Agricultural Production and Land Taxation

During the Qin and early Western Han periods, officials applied *cheng* norms to assess agricultural output per unit of land for different kinds of crops under varying farming conditions. The tasks discussed in the Qin and Han arithmetic manuals require the calculation of output in terms of dried grain (*gan* 乾), given the productivity for grain in the field (*he* 禾) and the volume conversion rate between the two (Xiao 2015: 28, slip 0537; Zhangjiashan 2006: 143, slip 83). One can imagine such calculations carried out when the state project planners were deciding on the land area necessary to provide grain for a given number of personnel.[16]

The evaluation of agricultural productivity was dictated by the needs of taxation. A bumper harvest, for example, entailed an increase in the tax rate and permitted the collection of the required amount of grain from a smaller area of land (Xiao 2015: 42–43, slips 0813, 0785). The Qin legal texts indicate that the central government required local officials to report favorable and adverse weather conditions, floods, plagues of locusts, and other factors affecting crops (Shuihudi 1990: 19–20, slips 1–3). This information was used to modify the annual tax quotas passed down to the local authorities and ultimately broken down into individual quotas assigned to farming households.[17]

While the excavated documents provide some scattered evidence on the use of *cheng* norms in land taxation, more detailed information is available in the manuals of arithmetic, where a special category of tasks dealt with incorrect tax assessments (Xiao 2015: 32, slip 0939; Zhangjiashan 2006: 145, slips 93–97). This is an example from the Zhangjiashan 張家山 collection:

租誤(誤)券。田一畝租之十步一斗,凡租二石四斗。今誤券二石五斗,欲益瞏其步數。問益瞏幾何。曰:九步五分步三而一斗。术(術)曰:以誤券為法,以與田為實。

> Taxation: error in ticketing. A field of 1 *mu*: tax it at 1 *dou* for 10 *bu*. The overall tax is 2 *shi* 4 *dou*. Now it is wrongly ticketed at 2 *shi* 5 *dou*; it is desired to increase or cut down the number of *bu*. Question: how much should the increase or decrease be? Reply: 9 *bu* and 3/5 *bu* for 1 *dou*. Method: take the mistaken ticketing as the divisor; take the given (?) field as the dividend. (Zhangjiashan 2006: 145, slips 96–97; Cullen 2004: 70; Chemla and Ma 2015: 50)

The task uses the Qin and Han metric system with its basic unit of area, *mu* 畝 (ca. 461 sq. meters), which consisted of 240 square *bu* 步 ("paces"): a tax norm of 2 *shi* 4 *dou* (or 24 *dou*) of grain collected from 1 *mu* (240 *bu*) means that 1 *dou* was collected from every 10 *bu* of land. Repeated calculation is made necessary by a mistake in what the text refers to as *quan* 券, a "ticket," which sets up a new tax amount per unit of land. The text does not explain the origins of the ticket, but it is clear that whoever was in charge of assessing the new norm was in no position to make changes to the ticket. Instead, he had to act on the basis of the ticket and reassess the land productivity required to match this figure.

Regular adjustments of the land productivity estimates and the amount of tax to be collected from an area of fields explain the large number of "ticketing" problems in the Qin and early Western Han manuals. Rather than collecting a fixed volume of grain per unit of arable land, as was done later in the Han era, local officials in Qin

---

[16] For the close relationship between the excavated mathematical manuals and the administrative practice of the early empires, see Chemla and Ma 2015: 1–53.

[17] For the study of agricultural taxation in the Qin and Western Han empires, see Yamada 1993: 32–59; Yang 2008, 2015: 119–41; Korolkov 2021a.

had to routinely reassess the tax quotas within their jurisdiction on the basis of expected harvest yields. The very small amounts of tax grain considered in the "error in ticketing" tasks suggest these tasks refer to individual household tax quotas assessed on the basis of an area of land under cultivation and expected agricultural output. According to the fragmentary legal texts from the Qin imperial period excavated at Longgang 龍崗 (Hubei), on the arrival of fiscal tallies to the district (*xiang* 鄉), a sub-county administrative unit, the local functionaries had to make the quota known to each taxpayer (Zhongguo and Hubei 2001: 122, slip 150), and probably also to collect and deliver tax grain to the county granary.[18]

The requirement that officials inform taxpayers of their annual quota, and probably also issue receipts,[19] effectively reduced opportunities for embezzlement and manipulation. A partly preserved document record from the Qianling archive refers to an attempt by one of the county's district heads to collect a certain tax, which was against the law and aroused resistance from the population, which refused to pay (Chen et al. 2012: 331–32, tablet 8–1454+8–1629). The details are unclear, so we do not know which tax this document is dealing with. Yet the fact that the matter was brought to the attention of the county authorities and probably entailed an investigation suggests that commoner taxpayers were to a certain degree aware of tax-collecting procedures and could be used as a check on the predatory behavior of local officials.

The first century of the Western Han period was a time of momentous transformations in the imperial fiscal system. The Han founding emperor, Gao 漢高帝 (r. 206/202–195 BCE), experimented with a new land tax based on a fixed rate applied to the nominal average harvest (Korolkov 2021a: 237). By the mid-second century BCE, the tax rate was fixed at one-thirtieth of an average harvest (*Hanshu* 24A: 1135), reducing the need for the annual reassessments of land tax quotas. While the Qin and early Western Han manuals contain many tasks dealing with productivity norms for agricultural crops and tax norms based on the land productivity, such tasks are absent in the major mathematical collection of the Eastern Han period, the *Nine Chapters* (Yang 2015: 139–40). The transition to the low-rate, fixed-rate regime of land taxation considerably reduced the volume of fiscal administration.

Numerical standards and norms permeated the governance of the early empires. In this section, I have focused on their application in some crucial areas of state administration, such as the training of military personnel and tax-collection. In reality, this form of regulation was even more widespread than this discussion suggests.

---

[18] For the reconstruction of the collection process and discussion of government agencies involved, see Yamada 1993: 49–50.

[19] This is suggested by the Qin regulations of labor services, which prescribed the issuing of a special tally to each laborer in acknowledgement of completion of obligations, measured in workdays. See Chen 2015: 149, slips 244–46. Insofar as the procedure for labor mobilizations paralleled that for the assignment of land tax quotas, and the legal texts from Longgang highlight the government's willingness to employ the heads of farming communities and even common taxpayers as a check on local officials, it seems possible that some kind of tax receipts were also issued in land taxation. For a discussion, see Yang 2015: 126–63; and Korolkov 2020: 690–95.

In the Qin Empire, special norms existed for exotic tribute products submitted to the imperial court by the southern commanderies (Chen et al. 2012: 237, tablet 8–855); wooden stationery used by the government offices (Chen 2017: 107–8, slips 120–22); various items delivered to the official storehouses (Chen 2020: 62–63, slips 46–47); and the number of prison inmates who were allowed to die in detention (Chen et al. 2012: 282–83, tablet 8–1139). These norms were promulgated through special legislation, such as the "Norms for Artisans" in the Shuihudi collection of legal statutes, as well as in administrative circulars targeting specific commanderies (Chen et al. 2012: 96–97, tablet 8–159).

3 Impersonal Standards and Official Service

Warring States political thinkers continuously emphasized that impersonal standards were necessary to curb the ruler's subjectivity in distributing rewards, punishments, and official promotions. By the beginning of the common era, the central and provincial governments of the Western Han Empire employed 130,285 officials, while the Eastern Han Empire at its height had over 150,000 officials (Bielenstein 1980: 156; Loewe 2004: 70–71). Standardized evaluation of their performance and clearly defined criteria of promotion and demotion were crucial to the smooth functioning of what was probably the largest and most sophisticated civilian administration in the ancient world.[20]

3.1 Appointment and Performance Evaluation

Scribes (*shi* 史) were one of the most numerous groups in the early imperial bureaucracy.[21] By the beginning of the Western Han period, their appointment was based on examinations. A successful candidate was supposed to be capable of reciting and writing 5,000 graphs or more, and to master eight different fonts. The best performers (*zui* 最) would become county scribes, while the worst performers (*dian* 殿) were dismissed and charged a hefty fine, along with their hapless mentors (Peng et al. 2007: 296–99, slips 474–76; 301–02, slip 480). Similar criteria of eligibility existed for state-employed diviners, who had to be capable of reciting and writing 3,000 graphs, citing 3,000 words from the *Diviner's Book* (*Bushu* 卜書), and making one or more accurate divinations out of six tries; and invocators, who were expected to be able to chant 7,000 words or more from a special book of prayers (Peng et al. 2007: 299–301, slips 477–79; Barbieri-Low and Yates 2015: 1094–95).

---

[20] For a comparison between the civilian administration of the Han and Roman empires, see Scheidel 2015.

[21] 28 of 103 officials on the Qianling County roster were scribes. See Chen et al. 2018: 167–68, tablet 9–633.

The *zui-dian* evaluation system did not end with appointment to office. Functionaries entrusted with the management of state-owned assets were annually assessed for the conditions of the property under their supervision. The great evaluation (*da ke* 大課) of livestock, for example, took place in the first month of the Qin calendar and entailed rewards for good results (*zui*) and reprimands, fines, and corporal punishment for poor performance. Criteria, again, were numerical: for oxen used in agricultural works, decrease in girth by one *cun* (ca. 2.3 cm) warranted ten strokes with a stick (Shuihudi 1990: 22–23, slips 13–14). Annual assessments were also applied to the overseers of state-managed workshops, lac tree orchards, and mines (Shuihudi 1990: 83–85, slips 17–23). A document from the Qianling county archive illustrates the effects of a county's unsatisfactory results at the annual evaluation on an official's career:

廿六年十二月癸丑朔庚申，遷陵守祿敢言之:沮守瘳言:課廿四年畜息子得錢殿。沮守周主。為新地吏，令縣論言史(事)。•問之，周不在遷陵。敢言之。

Twenty-sixth year [of King Zheng, i.e. the First Emperor], in the twelfth month, *guichou* being the first day of the month, on the day *gengshen* (January 5, 221 BCE). Lu, the provisional magistrate of Qianling County, dares to report the following: Liao, the provisional magistrate of Ju County, reports: "[Our county was] the worst performer at the evaluation of cash earnings [for the sale of] livestock offspring in the twenty-fourth year (223 BCE). Zhou, the provisional magistrate of Ju County, was in charge of that, so he was made an official in the new territories. [Your county] is ordered to pronounce a judgment on this matter." We inquired, Zhou is not in Qianling. Dare to report this. (Chen et al. 2012: 343–44, tablet 8–1516)

"New territories" were lands recently conquered by the Qin armies, and service there was considered a kind of exile, perilous and disgraceful for an official.[22] As a county magistrate, Zhou was responsible for its economic performance, including cash earnings through the sale of government-owned livestock. It is unknown how much money the county was expected to make, but it is clear that he failed to meet the norm.

The biography of a famed classical scholar turned high-ranked official, Ni Kuan 兒寬 (d. 103 BCE), is another example of an official career dramatically affected by official evaluation. When appointed to the governorship of one of the metropolitan circuits, Ni, known for his leniency toward subordinates, did not rigorously collect taxes for many years, and his administrative unit accumulated arrears. This situation came to light when war broke out, and the central government undertook an evaluation of each province's financial performance. As a poor performer (*dian* 殿), Ni was about to be dismissed, when the common people became aware of their beloved governor's misfortunes, and flocked to the capital carrying outstanding tax payments (probably grain as well as cash) on their backs. Not only did Ni Kuan end up the top performer (*zui* 最), he also earned the emperor's special attention (*Hanshu* 58: 2630). While the story illustrates the endurance of time-honored Qin practices into the Han period, at the same time, it implies that, at the end of the second century

---

[22] For a recent discussion of the "new territories" in the Qin Empire, see Korolkov 2022: 92–97.

BCE, evaluations became associated with the urgent mobilization of resources, as in the case of war, rather than being part of the administrative routine.

3.2 Quantifiable Criteria of Official Promotion

Streamlining the process of official promotion was critical to the smooth function-ing of the huge (by ancient standards) and centralized administrative apparatus of the early Chinese empires. The regime of "merits and service time" (*gonglao* 功勞) was one of the most sophisticated elements of the government's effort to make this process efficient and transparent, ensuring the compliance of state functionaries involved. One of the earliest records of the "merits and service time" system comes from the official archive of the Qin-period Qianling County in western Hunan:

□□
□□(第一欄)
凡□□□□
為官佐六歲。
為縣令佐一歲十二日。
為縣斗食四歲五月廿四日。
為縣司空有秩乘車三歲【八】月廿二日。
守遷陵丞六月廿七日。
凡【十】五歲九月廿五日。【凡】功三，三歲九月廿五日。(第二欄)
□□□鄉廿二年□□
□功二
□勞四，三【歲】九月廿五【日】
年□凡功六，三歲九月廿五日。
□□遷陵六月廿七日，定□□八月廿日。
□□可□屬洞庭。
□五十歲居內史七歲□□(第三欄)
Register 1
(Illegible)
Register 2
Total…
Served for six years as an Office Assistant.
Served for one year and twelve days as an Assistant to the County Magistrate.
Served for four years, five months, and twenty-four days as a county official fed by the *dou*.
Served for three years, [eight] months, and twenty-two days as the county Controller of Works, salaried and [with the privilege to] ride in an [official] carriage.
Temporarily held [the position of the] Vice-Magistrate of Qianling [County] for six months and twenty-seven days.
The total of fifteen years, nine months, and twenty-five days. [The total of] three merits, three years, nine months, and twenty-five days.
Register 3
…district, twenty-five years…
…two merits.
…four [units of] service time, three years, nine months, and twenty-five days.
…the total of six merits, three years, nine months, and twenty-five days.

…Qianling [County], six months, and twenty-seven days, confirmed… eight months and twenty days.

…belongs to Dongting [Commandery]

…fifteen years, resided in the Capital Region for seven years… (Liye 2016: 196, tablet 10–15)

The wooden tablet was broken in the middle, and the upper part of the third register is no longer legible (Liye 2016: 128). Some scholars doubt that the second and the third registers are related (Zhang 2019: 102), but the identical periods of time mentioned in the two registers ("three years, nine months, and twenty-five days") make it unlikely that they deal with two different persons. The document is the service record of a certain official, who started his career as an office assistant, the lowest step in the Qin and Han bureaucratic ladder, which he climbed over the following fifteen years, to become a vice-magistrate, one of the top-ranking county officials.

The fifteen years, nine months, and twenty-five days of official service translated into three "merits" (gong 功) and a leftover of three years, nine months, and twenty-five days. This suggests that each "merit" was equivalent to four years of service. In fact, this equivalency has long been noted for the Han documents from the northwestern frontier, which contain many records of "merits" and "service time" (lao) accumulated by various local officials (Hu 1995: 51–55; Chen and Xiong 2018: 69–70). These documents also make it clear that lao could be granted as an award, for example, when an officer successfully performed in an archery test (see Sect. 2.4). That the same applied to "merits" is suggested by the fact that the official in the above-quoted Qianling document ended up having six merits, not just three that he accumulated over the duration of service. Two merits mentioned in the second line of the third register may well have been such an award.

In 1986, archaeologists excavating the early Western Han tomb no. 336 at Zhangjiashan (Hubei) discovered a large group of manuscripts, including one titled "Ordinances on Merit" (gongling 功令). This collection of 184 inscribed bamboo slips is by far the most detailed account of the "merits and service time" regime (Jingzhou 2022: 93–125). The following article lays down the rules for acquiring merits and units of service time:

吏自佐史以上，各以定視事日自占勞，勞盈歲為中勞，中勞四歲為一功。從軍勞二歲亦為一功。身斬首二級若捕虜二人，各為一功。軍論之爵二級為半功。

[All] officials from Assistants and Scribes upward each self-reports their service time according to the confirmed [number of] days [they have spent] performing their duties. A full year of service constitutes a "qualifying service," four years of "qualifying service" constitute one merit. Two years of service in an army [on a campaign] also constitute one merit. Cutting off two [enemy] heads or capturing two prisoners constitute one merit. Two levels of social rank conferred in the army constitute half-merit. (Jingzhou 2022: 97, slips 12–13)

This ordinance provides several previously unknown details of the gonglao system. First, active military service not only expedited but also provided an alternative track for earning merits, which were awarded for killing and capturing enemies. This opportunity was open not only to the military officers but also to the civil officials, who were occasionally conscripted into the troops, particularly during the conflict-rich decades around the time of Qin unification (Shuihudi 1990: 7, slips 20, 22; Chen et al. 2018: 221–22, tablet 9–897+9–939).

The meaning of the final sentence concerning the "levels of social rank conferred in the army" remains debated. In the military context, army commanders conferred social ranks to soldiers who distinguished themselves by killing enemies in battle (see Sect. 1.2), which also brought about the granting of merits. This created a situation when an individual could be awarded twice for the same achievement, something that the lawgivers sought to prevent by reducing the amount of merit received by someone who had already had his social rank increased. As we will see shortly, the system of "merits and service duration" was central to the official promotion, which made officials, including military officers, interested in gaining merits and, under certain circumstances, prioritizing them over social ranks. However, I find it unlikely that individuals had a choice as to the form of award. Rather, it was probably defined by the official protocols, e.g., whether or not a person in question was entitled to a certain level of social rank.

Second, we learn about the process of reporting the service time, which was done by officials themselves (*zizhan* 自占). Service time included only the days when one was actually attending to official matters (*shishi* 視事), but not the days of absence due to health conditions, family affairs, temporary conscription for labor services, and so on. In their private event calendars, Qin and Han officials specially marked the days when they were on leave and when they resumed their duties (Chen 2018: 446–68). Such records facilitated self-reporting of service time, as explicitly indicated in one event calendar (Cai, Chen and Xiong 2018: 56, slip 37). The government was keeping its own record of officials' service (Chen 2018: 454–64), which could be used to verify ("confirm," *ding* 定) the self-reports.

Based on their merits and duration of services, officials were listed for potential promotion (Jingzhou 2022: 96, slips 3–4; 99, slip 20). Archaeologists recovered several such lists from the Han-period sites, including four wooden tablets dated to 165–161 BCE and excavated from tomb no. 77 at Shuihudi. The following specimen lists office assistants (*guanzuo* 官佐) of Anlu 安陸 County in the present-day Hubei Province:

二年官佐功次
定邑功二、勞三月一日
任成功二、勞三月
救嬰功二、勞二月
亡臣功二、勞一月六日
申功二、勞十一日
何成功二、勞七日
最功一、勞三歲七月十八日
鄧豕功一、勞三歲四月十五【日】

Sequence of merits of Office Assistants in the second year [of the Latter Period of Emperor Wen (162 BCE)]

Ding Yi, two merits, three months and one day of service.
Ren Cheng, two merits, three months of service.
Jiu Ying, two merits, two months of service.
Wang Chen, two merits, one month and six days of service.
Shen, two merits, eleven days of service.

He Cheng, two merits, seven days of service.

Zui, one merit, three years, seven months, and eighteen days of service.

Deng Shi, one merit, three years, four months, and fifteen [days] of service. (Chen and Xiong 2018: 66)

Since all individuals in the list were office assistants, Ding Yi, on top of the list, would be the first to get promotion when a vacancy became available. Similar lists have been excavated at the northwestern frontier sites, attesting to the ubiquity of the *gonglao* promotion practice throughout the empire (Yao 2021: 368–70, tablets 73EJT30:29, 73EJT30:30).[23] Transmitted texts from the Han era also mention many prominent officials whose career progressed as they accumulated merits and service time (*Shiji* 103: 2768; *Hanshu* 2002: 58: 2628; 59: 2648; 71: 3048).

3.3 Standardization of Official Language and Writing

Recent excavations of Qin and Han official texts have revealed a high degree of formalization in the layout of documents and the standardization of official language. A wooden tablet from the archive of the Qin county of Qianling bears a lengthy list of new terms introduced for the use in official communication soon after the completion of Qin conquests in 221 BCE: "Frontier fortifications should be called 'old fortifications'; when there is no fortification, it should be called 'old frontier'; the royal progress should be called 'imperial progress'; the royal hunt should be called 'imperial hunt'; royal dogs should be called 'imperial dogs'" 邊塞為故塞，毋塞者為故徼，王游曰皇帝游，王獵曰皇帝獵，王犬曰皇帝犬 (Chen et al. 2012: 155–60, tablet 8–461). One of these vocabulary updates, the substitution of "black-headed [people]" (*qianshou* 黔首) for "commoners" (*min* 民), was even noticed in transmitted historical texts (*Shiji* 6: 239).

Standardization involved not only the vocabulary but also the form of official documents. A collection of such forms, or "models" (*shi* 式), was excavated from the tomb of a Qin scribe at Shuihudi, who probably used them to record actual legal cases (Shuihudi 1990: 147–64; McLeod and Yates 1981; Hulsewé 1985: 183–207). Unlike the formulaically simple inventory lists, food ration receipts, and travel passports, all of which were subject to thorough standardization during the Qin and Han periods (Xing 2011: 450–72), judicial proceedings contained a variety of specific information, including arguments by parties in the case, which was difficult to force into the Procrustean bed of an official template. In early imperial court practice, this was achieved not only through minute regulation of the process, which was divided into distinct phases (Barbieri-Low and Yates 2015: 111–86), but also through the

---

[23] It should be pointed out that the sequence of officials in these two lists from Jinguan ("Golden Pass" in the present-day Gansu Province) is not always defined by the number of merits and duration of service. This is probably because the officials had different positions, which affected their place in the list. A higher-ranked official could be placed first, even if his merits and/or duration of service were inferior to his lower-ranked colleague.

rules of legal relevance, whereby scribes recorded only those parts of an argument or investigation that were considered relevant to resolving the case (Korolkov 2011). By enabling the production of standardized case records, such an approach greatly contributed to the development of bureaucratic administration of justice in the early empires (Barbieri-Low 2011: 125–56).

4 Re-discovering the Individual in Governance

Looking back on his twenty-five-year-long reign, Emperor Xuan of Western Han (r. 74–48 BCE) lamented his failure to reestablish order and prosperity in the realm. He laid part of the blame on governmental malfeasance when "accounts submitted to superiors were mere words" 上計簿，具文而已 and officials "engaged in fraud in order to pass the evaluation" 務為欺謾，以避其課 (*Hanshu* 8: 273). The emperor complained about the breakdown of some of the key institutions of the early empires. The official accounting represented society and economy as an inventory of human and material assets. Evaluations tied the official careers to the dynamics of these inventories. Population growth and the expansion of agricultural fields within a county resulted in its magistrate's promotion to a more important and better paid position, while decline entailed fines, punishments, or dismissal. Both systems were fundamentally impersonal. Population registers reduced imperial subjects to a limited number of traits relevant to taxation and legal accountability (Sanft 2015: 249–69). The identity and moral qualities of officials did not matter for the evaluation of their performance.

Emperor Xuan was an eager reader of the *fa* texts who believed in the centrality of law to governance. In his administrative appointments, he applied the *xing ming* ("performance and title") procedures elaborated in the *Han Feizi*, whereby an official's performance was compared to his "title," that is, the tasks that this official declared himself able to perform at the beginning of his tenure (*Hanshu* 89: 3624).[24] Yet, towards the end of his life, even this emperor was forced to recognize that the system of rule by impersonal standards pioneered in the Qin was in disarray.

The late first century BCE official statistics of Donghai Commandery, a populous and rich province in the eastern part of the Han Empire, illustrates what Emperor Xuan was complaining about. These documents were excavated from a local official's tomb (Lianyungang et al. 1997; Loewe 2004: 38–88). The analysis of age distribution in the commandery's population revealed enormous skews, which are best explained by misreporting. By declaring an extraordinarily high proportion of elderly and infants in the subordinate population, provincial officials not only concealed part of the poll tax incomes from the central authorities – the young and old were exempt from tax payments and labor obligations – but also earned

---

[24] For the *xing ming* procedures, see Lewis 1999a: 32–33; Goldin 2013: 8–10; Goldin 2020: 213–14. For Emperor Xuan's penchant for the *fa* teachings and administrative practices, see Cai 2014: 162–75.

themselves a reputation as benevolent administrators (Gao 1998: 110–23; Hsing 2014: 183–84).

Another two wooden tablets from the same tomb bear the reports of the promotion of 122 officials in Donghai Commandery (Lianyungang er al. 1997: 85–95, tablets 3 and 4; Loewe 2004: 71–74). 73 of them (60%) were promoted according to their "merits and service time" (see Sect. 3.2), suggesting that this system was still functional at the end of the Western Han period. At the same time, 20 officials (16%) were appointed by virtue of their exceptional moral qualities, such as "integrity" (*lian* 廉), "righteousness" (*fangzheng* 方正), and "filial piety" (*xiao* 孝). Starting in the reign of Emperor Wen 漢文帝 (181–157 BCE), the Han monarchs required commandery governors to recommend to the court their subjects who distinguished themselves by their virtues (*Hanshu* 4: 116). At the beginning of his reign, Emperor Wu 漢武帝 (r. 141–87 BCE) institutionalized such recommendations by ordering the governors and other high-ranking officials to annually submit the names of two "filial and upright" (*xiaolian* 孝廉) persons, who, after a trial period, were appointed to official positions (*Hanshu* 6:160, 166; Loewe 2004: 123–24). In 106 BCE, another edict called for regular recommendations of "flourishing talents" (*xiucai* 秀材, later written as *maocai* 茂材 to avoid using the tabooed graph in the name of the founder of the Eastern Han Empire, Liu Xiu 劉 秀) from among the officials and general population of the commanderies (*Hanshu* 6: 197).

Although individuals promoted for their virtues were occasionally subjected to the poorly understood procedure of "integrity assessment" (*chalian* 察廉) (Loewe 2004: 130–31), such appointments were a substantial departure from the still predominant regime of standardized "merits and service duration." Most of personalized promotions concentrated at the imperial court and capital, but the Donghai Commandery records indicate that by the turn of the common era, a not insignificant proportion of local officials were also appointed based on the new criteria.

It is tempting to draw a connection between the decline of rule by impersonal standards and the rise of the *Ru* officials during the last decades of the Western Han period. The leading *Ru* figure of the Western Han period, Dong Zhongshu 董仲舒 (179–104 BCE), was also an ardent supporter of promotions of "flourishing talents, pious sons, and the upright" (*Hanshu* 56: 2525). A successful career, especially at the top of bureaucratic hierarchy, was also increasingly defined by one's knowledge of classical texts and participation in master-disciple networks rather than by administrative experience.[25] Writing in the first century CE, Wang Chong 王充 (27–97 CE) overtly contrasted the lower-order technical skills of petty civil officials (*wen li* 文 吏), who knew how to draft formally correct documents, and the superior moral education of the *Ru* statesmen, with its focus on the ancient classics, which provided an orientation for ordering human society according to the principles of the moral universe (*Lunheng jiaoshi* 35: 552).

---

[25] For the historical background of the ascension of *Ru* officials beginning in the reign of Emperor Xuan, see Cai 2014: 113–186.

Historical anecdotes from the Eastern Han period illustrate the new ideals of official performance. When, in response to continuing tribal uprisings in the south-western commanderies, Emperor Ling 漢靈帝 (168–189 CE) ordered a general mobilization, he required the account clerks (*ji li* 計吏) in Yizhou 益州 Province to submit plans for the forthcoming campaign. The fact that the emperor specifically addressed the officials in charge of preparing annual accounts suggests that he expected detailed numerical information central to the military logistics, such as the volume of grain reserves and number of available recruits. Instead, a certain Cheng Bao 程包, an otherwise unknown clerk from Hanzhong 漢中 Commandery, deliv-ered a verbose diatribe against the oppressive provincial administrators and recom-mended the appointment of "enlightened and capable" officials, which would "by itself" (*ziran* 自然) pacify the rebels (*Hou Hanshu* 86: 2843). While the advice, in this case, turned out to be appropriate, it is symptomatic that an account clerk, a specialist *par excellence* in numeracy-based administrative methods, found no bet-ter way to prove his worth than engaging in moral admonition.

Liang Cai has recently, and convincingly argued that the rise of the *Ru* officials in the first century BCE was an outcome of the violent infighting at the imperial court at the end of Emperor Wu's reign, which wiped out many members of the former elite (Cai 2014). However, the transition to the new style of governance, which prioritized individual morality over impersonal standards, was also rooted in a longer-term transformation of economic and administrative institutions that took place throughout the formative period of China's early empires in the late third and second centuries BCE (Korolkov 2021a). The collapse of the Qin Empire not only led to the temporary contraction of the centralized administration, but also acceler-ated the transition from a state-operated command economy and social engineering to indirect forms of socio-economic regulation, which included monetary policy, taxation of wealth, and periodic market interventions.[26]

This transition was accompanied by the central government's withdrawal from the intensive monitoring of administration, economy, and society beyond the capital region. By the end of the Western Han era, powerful magnates controlled resources, commanded the allegiance of the population in the provinces, and cooperated with local officials to form patronage networks that extended all the way to the imperial capital (Ebrey 1986: 608–48; Cui 2004; Lewis 2007: 115–27; von Glahn 2016: 134–42). Provincial elites mobilized these resources, allegiances, and networks to overthrow the short-lived Xin 新 Dynasty (9–23 CE) by the usurper Wang Mang 王莽 (45 BCE – 23 CE) (Bielenstein 1986: 223–90). After the Han restoration, the central government's attempts to conduct the land census and re-establish some degree of economic control in provinces encountered stiff resistance from the "great families," which, on some occasions, reached the point of rebellion (*Hou Hanshu* 1B.66–67; Pines 2012: 110–11).

---

[26] Economic historian Richard Von Glahn describes these changes as a transition from military-physiocratic to mercantilist fiscal regime (von Glahn 2016: 113–20).

The rediscovery of the moral individual in governance not only provided local elites with a conduit for introducing their members to the imperial bureaucracy through the system of provincial recommendations, which emphasized moral traits such as "filiality and integrity" and "virtue and goodness" (*xian liang* 賢良), but also justified their autonomy vis-à-vis the imperial center. As the provincial recommendations and patronage networks became crucial both to the confirmation of social status and to official promotion, the *fa* ideal of rulers in single-handed control of the government apparatus was increasingly detached from the political reality of declining early empire.

References

Barbieri-Low, Anthony. 2001. *The Organization of Imperial Workshops During the Han Dynasty.* Ph.D. Dissertation, Princeton University.
———. 2007. *Artisans in Early Imperial China.* Seattle and London: University of Washington Press.
———. 2011. Model Legal and Administrative Forms from the Qin, Han, and Tang and Their Role in the Facilitation of Bureaucracy and Literacy. *Oriens Extremus* 50: 125–156.
Barbieri-Low, Anthony, and Robin D.S. Yates. 2015. *Law, State, and Society in Early Imperial China: A Study with Critical Edition and Translation of the Legal Texts from Zhangjiashan Tomb No. 247.* Vols. 1, 2. Leiden and Boston: Brill.
Bielenstein, Hans. 1980. *The Bureaucracy of Han Times.* Cambridge: Cambridge University Press.
———. 1986. Wang Mang, the Restoration of the Han Dynasty, and Later Han. In *The Cambridge History of China. Vol. 1: The Ch'in and Han Empires, 221 B.C. – A.D. 220*, ed. Denis Twitchett and Michael Loewe, 223–290. Cambridge: Cambridge University Press.
Cai, Wanjin 蔡萬進. 2009. *A Study of the Grain Economy in the State of Qin* 秦國糧食經濟研究. Zhengzhou: Daxiang.
Cai, Liang. 2014. *Witchcraft and the Rise of the First Confucian Empire.* Albany: State University of New York Press.
Cai, Dan 蔡丹, Chen, Wei 陳偉, and Xiong, Beisheng 熊北生. 2018. Event Calendar Manuscripts from the Shuihudi Collection of Han Bamboo Slips 睡虎地漢簡中的質日簡冊. *Cultural Relics* 文物 3: 54–64.
Campbell, Roderick. 2014. Transformation of Violence: On Humanity and Inhumanity in Early China. In *Violence and Civilization: Studies on Social Violence in History and Prehistory*, ed. Roderick Campbell, 96–104. Oxford and Oakville: Oxbow Books.
Chemla, Karine. 2018. Mathematics. In *Routledge Handbook of Early Chinese History*, ed. Paul R. Goldin, 473–492. London and New York: Routledge.
Chemla, Karine, and Biao Ma. 2015. How Do the Earliest Known Mathematical Writings Highlight the State's Management of Grains in Early Imperial China? *Archive for History of Exact Sciences* 69 (1): 1–53.
Chen, Shen. 2003. Compromises and Conflicts: Production and Commerce in the Royal Cities of Eastern Zhou, China. In *The Social Construction of Ancient Cities*, ed. Monica Smith, 290–310. Washington and London: Smithsonian Books.
Chen, Songchang 陳松長. 2015. *Qin Bamboo Slips from the Yuelu Academy Collection* 嶽麓書院藏秦簡. Vol. 4. Shanghai: Shanghai Cishu.
———. 2017. *Qin Bamboo Slips from the Yuelu Academy Collection* 嶽麓書院藏秦簡. Vol. 5. Shanghai: Shanghai Cishu.
Chen, Wei. 2018. 'Event Calendars' in the Early Imperial Era: A Re-Assessment. *Bamboo and Silk* 1: 446–468.

Chen, Songchang. 2020. *Qin Bamboo Slips from the Yuelu Academy Collection* 嶽麓書院藏秦簡. Vol. 6. Shanghai: Shanghai Cishu.

Chen, Wei, and Xiong, Beisheng. 2018. Documents on the Sequence of Merits in the Han Slips from Shuihudi 睡虎地漢簡中的功次文書. *Cultural Relics* 文物 3: 65–70.

Chen, Wei, et al. 2012. *Qin Documents from Liye, Edited and Annotated* 里耶秦簡牘校釋. Vol. 1. Wuhan: Wuhan Daxue.

———. 2018. *Qin Documents from Liye, Edited and Annotated* 里耶秦簡牘校釋. Vol. 2. Wuhan: Wuhan Daxue.

Creel, Herrlee G. 1964. The Beginnings of Bureaucracy in China: The Origin of the *Hsien. Journal of Asian Studies* 22: 155–183.

———. 1970. *The Origins of Statecraft in China*. Chicago: University of Chicago Press.

Cui, Xiangdong 崔向東. 2004. *Study of Powerful Clans in the Han Period* 漢代豪族研究. Wuhan: Chongwen shuju.

Cullen, Christopher. 2004. *The* Suan shu shu 筭數書 *'Writings on Reckoning': A Translation of a Chinese Mathematical Collection of the Second Century BC, with Explanatory Commentary*. Needham Research Institute Working Papers: 1. Cambridge: Needham Research Institute.

Ebrey, Patricia. 1986. The Economic and Social History of Later Han. In *The Cambridge History of China. Vol. 1: The Ch'in and Han Empires, 221 B.C. – A.D. 220*, ed. Denis Twitchett and Michael Loewe, 608–648. Cambridge: Cambridge University Press.

Galvany, Albert. 2020. The Army, Wars, and Military Arts during the Warring States Period. In *The Oxford Handbook of Early China*, ed. Elizabeth Childs-Johnson, 637–656. Oxford: Oxford University Press.

Gansu sheng wenwu kaogu yanjiusuo 甘肅省文物考古研究所 (Gansu Provincial Institute of Cultural Relics and Archaeology) et al. 1990. *New Documents from Juyan* 居延新簡. Beijing: Wenwu.

Gansu sheng wenwu kaogu yanjiusuo 甘肅省文物考古研究所 (Gansu Provincial Institute of Cultural Relics and Archaeology). 2009. *Qin Documents from Fangmatan, Tiahsui* 天水放馬灘秦簡. Beijing: Zhonghua shuju.

Gao, Dalun 高大倫. 1998. "A Study of the Population Statistics Materials in the "Collected Accounts" on a Wooden Tablet from the Han Tomb at Yinwan" 尹灣漢墓木牘"集簿"中戶口統計資料研究, *Historical Research* 歷史研究 5: 110–123.

Goldin, Paul R. 2013. Introduction: Han Fei and the *Han Feizi*. In *Dao Companion to the Philosophy of Han Fei*, ed. Paul R. Goldin, 1–21. New York: Springer.

———. 2020. *The Art of Chinese Philosophy: Eight Classical Texts and How to Read Them*. Princeton and Oxford: Princeton University Press.

Grafflin, Dennis. 1990. Reinventing China: Pseudobureaucracy in the Early Southern Dynasties. In *State and Society in Early Medieval China*, ed. Albert Dien, 139–170. Stanford: Stanford University Press.

Guanzi jiaozhu 管子校注 (*Guanzi*, collated and annotated). 2004. Ed. Li Xiangfeng 黎翔鳳. Beijing: Zhonghua shuju.

Han Feizi jijie 韓非子集解 (*Han Feizi* with collected commentaries). 2003. Ed. Wang Xianshen 王先慎. Beijing: Zhonghua shuju.

Hanshu 漢書 (*The Book of Han*). 2002. By Ban Gu 班固 (32–92 CE). Beijing: Zhonghua shuju.

Hao, Shusheng 郝樹聲, and Zhang, Defang 張德芳. 2008. *A Study of Han Documents from Xuanquan* 懸泉漢簡研究. Lanzhou: Gansu wenhua.

Harris, Eirik Lang. 2016. *The Shenzi Fragments*. New York: Columbia University Press.

Hou, Xudong. 2016. The Helpless Emperor: The Expenditure on Official Hostel System and Its Institutional Change in the Late Former Han China. *World History Studies* 3 (2): 1–23.

Hou Hanshu 後漢書 (*The Book of Latter Han*). 1965. By Fan Ye 范曄 (398–445/46). Beijing: Zhonghua shuju.

Hsing, I-tien. 2014. Qin-Han Census and Tax and Corvée Administration: Notes on Newly Discovered Materials. In *Birth of an Empire: The State of Qin Revisited*, ed. Yuri Pines, Lothar von Falkenhausen, Gideon Shelach, and Robin D.S. Yates, 155–186. Berkeley: University of California Press.

Hu, Pingsheng 胡平生. 1995. "'Gong' and 'Lao' in the Han Slips from Juyan" 居延漢簡中的"功" 與"勞". *Cultural Relics* 文物 4: 51–55.

Hui, Victoria Tin-bor. 2005. *War and State Formation in Ancient China and Early Modern Europe*. Cambridge: Cambridge University Press.

Hulsewé, A.F.P. 1985. *Remnants of Ch'in Law: An Annotated Translation of the Ch'in Legal and Administrative Rules of the 3rd Century B.C. Discovered in Yün-meng Prefecture, Hu-pei Province, in 1975*. Leiden: Brill.

Jiandu zhengli xiaozu 簡牘整理小組 (Research Group for Ordering the Documents on Wooden and Bamboo Slips). 2014. *The Documents of the Han Dynasty on Wooden Slips from Edsen-gol* 居延漢簡. Vols. 1–4. Taipei: Zhongyang Yanjiuyuan.

Jingzhou bowuguan 荊州博物館 (Jingzhou Museum). 2022. *Han Bamboo Slips from Zhangjishan: Tomb No. 336* 張家山漢墓竹簡:三三六號墓. Beijing: Wenwu.

Jiuzhang Suanshu jiaozheng 九章算術校證 (The Nine Chapters on Mathematical Procedures, Critical Collation). 1993. Ed. Li Jimin 李繼閔. Xi'an: Shaanxi Kexue Jishu.

Knoblock, John. 1988. *Xunzi: A Translation and Study of the Complete Works*. Vol. 1–3. Stanford: Stanford University Press.

Korolkov, Maxim. 2011. Arguing About Law: Interrogation Procedure Under the Qin and Former Han Dynasties. *Études Chinoises* 30: 37–71.

———. 2020. "Empire-Building and Market-Making at the Qin Frontier: Imperial Expansion and Economic Change, 221–207 BCE." Ph.D. Dissertation, Columbia University.

———. 2021a. Fiscal Transformation during the Formative Period of Ancient Chinese Empire (Late Fourth to First Century BCE). In *Ancient Taxation: The Mechanics of Extraction in Comparative Perspective*, ed. Jonathan Valk and Irene Soto Marín, 203–261. New York: New York University Press.

———. 2021b. Between Command and Market: Credit, Labor and Accounting in the Qin Empire (221–207 B.C.E.). In *Between Command and Market: Economic Thought and Practice in Early China*, ed. Elisa Levi Sabattini and Christian Schwermann, 162–243. Leiden: Brill.

———. 2022. *The Imperial Network in Ancient China: The Foundation of Sinitic Empire in Southern East Asia*. London and New York: Routledge.

Korolkov, Maxim, and Anke Hein. 2021. State-Induced Migration and the Creation of State Spaces in Early Chinese Empire: Perspectives from History and Archaeology. *Journal of Chinese History* 5: 203–225.

Lewis, Mark. 1990. *Sanctioned Violence in Early China*. Albany: State University of New York Press.

———. 1999a. *Writing and Authority in Early China*. Albany: State University of New York Press.

———. 1999b. Warring States Political History. In *The Cambridge History of Ancient China*, ed. Michael Loewe and Edward Shaughnessy, 587–650. Cambridge: Cambridge University Press.

———. 2000. The Han Abolition of Universal Military Service. In *Warfare in Chinese History*, ed. Hans van de Ven, 33–76. Leiden and Boston: Brill.

———. 2007. *The Early Chinese Empires: Qin and Han*. Cambridge and London: Harvard University Press.

Li, Ling 李零. 1998. "The Two Systems of Settlement Organization in Ancient China, and Their Diverse Origins" 中國古代居民組織的兩大類型及其不同來源. In Li Ling, *Self-Selected Works by Li Ling* 李零自選集, 148–168. Guilin: Guangxi Shifan Daxue.

Li, Feng. 2013. *Early China: A Social and Cultural History*. Cambridge: Cambridge University Press.

Lianyungang shi bowuguan 連雲港市博物館 (Lianyungang Municipal Museum) et al. 1997. *Documents on Bamboo and Wood from the Han Tomb at Yinwan* 尹灣漢墓簡牘. Beijing: Zhonghua shuju.

Liu, Xinglin 劉興林. 2017. *Archaeological Study of Pre-Qin and Han Agriculture and Rural Settlement* 先秦兩漢農業與鄉村聚落的考古學研究. Beijing: Wenwu.

Liye Qin jian bowuguan 里耶秦簡博物館. 2016. *Qin Documents Stored at the Liye Museum of Qin Documents* 里耶秦簡博物館藏秦簡. Shanghai: Zhongxi.

Loewe, Michael. 1967. *Records of Han Administration*. Vol. 1, 2. Cambridge: Cambridge University Press.

———. 1993. Hsün-tzu 荀子. In *Early Chinese Texts: A Bibliographical Guide*, ed. Michael Loewe, 178–188. Berkeley: The Society for the Study of Early China.

———. 2004. *The Men Who Governed Han China: Companion to A Bibliographical Dictionary of the Qin, Former Han and Xin Periods*. Leiden and Boston: Brill.

Lunheng jiaoshi 論衡校釋 (*Balanced Discussions*, collated and annotated). 1990. Ed. Huang Hui 黃暉. Beijing: Zhonghua shuju.

Mann, Michael. 2012 *The Sources of Social Power*. Volume 2: *The Rise of Classes and Nation-States, 1760–1914. New Edition*. Cambridge: Cambridge University Press.

McLeod, Katrina, and Robin D.S. Yates. 1981. Forms of Ch'in Law: An Annotated Translation of the *Feng-chen shih*. *Harvard Journal of Asiatic Studies* 41 (1): 111–163.

Mengzi zhengyi 孟子正義 (The Correct Meaning of *Mengzi*). 1987. Ed. Jiao Xun 焦循. Beijing: Zhonghua Shuju.

Miyake, Kiyoshi 宮宅潔. 2016. *Studies in the History of Ancient China's Penal System* 中國古代刑制史研究. Guilin: Guangxi Shifan Daxue.

Peng, Hao 彭浩, et al. 2007. *The Statutes and Ordinances of the Second Year and the Collected Cases Submitted for Revision: Annotated Legal Manuscripts Excavated from the Han Tomb No. 247 at Zhangjiashan* 二年律令與奏讞書:張家山二四七號漢墓出土法律文獻釋讀. Shanghai: Shanghai guji chubanshe.

Pines, Yuri. 2002. Lexical Changes in Zhanguo Texts. *Journal of the American Oriental Society* 122 (4): 691–705.

———. 2012. *The Everlasting Empire: The Political Culture of Ancient China and Its Imperial Legacy*. Princeton and Oxford: Princeton University Press.

———. 2016. Social Engineering in Early China: The Ideology of the *Shangjun Shu* (Book of Lord Shang) Revisited. *Oriens Extremus* 55: 1–38.

———, trans. and ed. 2017. *The Book of Lord Shang: Apologetics of State Power in Early China*. New York: Columbia University Press.

Rickett, Allyn. 1985. *Guanzi: Political, Economic, and Philosophical Essays from Early China. A Study and Translation*. Vol. 1. Princeton: Princeton University Press.

———. 1993. Kuan-tzu 管子. In *Early Chinese Texts: A Bibliographical Guide*, ed. Michael Loewe, 244–251. Berkeley: The Society for the Study of Early China.

Sanft, Charles. 2014. *Communication and Cooperation in Early Imperial China: Publicizing the Qin Dynasty*. Albany: State University of New York Press.

———. 2015. Population Records from Liye: Ideology in Practice. In *Ideology of Power and Power of Ideology in Early China*, ed. Yuri Pines, Paul R. Goldin, and Martin Kern, 249–269. Leiden and Boston: Brill.

Scheidel, Walter. 2015. State Revenue and Expenditure in the Han and Roman Empires. In *State Power in Ancient China and Rome*, ed. Walter Scheidel, 150–180. Oxford: Oxford University Press.

Scott, James. 1998. *Seeing Like a State: How Certain Schemes to Improve the Human Conditions Have Failed*. New Haven: Yale University Press.

Shangjunshu jiaoshu 商君書校疏 (*The Book of Lord Shang*, collated with subcommentaries). 2012. Comp. Zhang Jue 張覺. Beijing: Zhishi chanquan.

Shelach, Gideon. 2014. Collapse or Transformation? Anthropological and Archaeological Perspectives on the Fall of Qin. In *Birth of an Empire: The State of Qin Revisited*, ed. Yuri Pines, Lothar von Falkenhausen, Gideon Shelach, and Robin D.S. Yates, 113–138. Berkeley: University of California Press.

Shen, Kangshen, et al. 1999. *The Nine Chapters on the Mathematical Art: Companion and Commentary*. Oxford: Oxford University Press.

Shiji 史記 (*Records of the Historian*). 2006. By Sima Qian 司馬遷 (ca. 145–86 BCE). Beijing: Zhonghua shuju.

Shuihudi Qin mu zhujian zhengli xiaozu 睡虎地秦墓竹簡整理小組 (Research Group for Ordering the Bamboo Slips from the Qin Tomb at Shuihudi). 1990. *Bamboo Slips from the Qin Tomb at Shuihudi* 睡虎地秦墓竹簡. Beijing: Wenwu.

Sun, Wenbo. 2020. Shang Yang's Promotion of the County System and the County-Canton Relations: An Analysis Based on Official Titles, Salary Grades and the Size of the Employed Personnel. *Bamboo and Silk* 3: 344–388.

Tomiya, Itaru 冨谷至. 2006. *A Study of the Qin and Han Penal System* 秦漢刑罰制度研究. Guilin: Guangxi Shifan Daxue.

Tribe, Keith. 1984. Cameralism and the Science of Government. *Journal of Modern History* 56: 263–284.

von Falkenhausen, Lothar. 2018. The Economic Role of Cities in Eastern Zhou China. *Archaeological Research in Asia* 14: 161–169.

von Glahn, Richard. 2016. *The Economic History of China: From Antiquity to the Nineteenth Century*. Cambridge: Cambridge University Press.

Wang, Haicheng. 2014. *Writing and the Ancient State: Early China in Comparative Perspective*. Cambridge: Cambridge University Press.

Xiao, Can 蕭燦. 2015. *A Study of the "Manual of Mathematics" in the Yuelu Academy Collection of Qin Documents* 岳麓書院藏秦簡《數》研究. Beijing: Zhongguo Shehui Kexue.

Xing, Yitian 邢義田. 2011. *Governing the State, Pacifying the Realm: Legal Regime, Administration, and Warfare* 治國安邦:法制、行政與軍事. Beijing: Zhonghua Shuju.

Xunzi jijie 荀子集解 (*Xunzi* with collected commentaries). 1988. Ed. Wang Xianqian 王先謙. Beijing: Zhonghua shuju.

Yamada, Katsuyoshi 山田勝芳. 1993. *Study of the Qin and Han Financial Revenues* 秦漢財政收入の研究. Tokyo: Kyūko Shoin.

Yang, Kuan 楊寬. 2003. *Warring States History* 戰國史. Shanghai: Shanghai renmin chubanshe.

Yang, Zhenhong 楊振紅. 2008. "Collection of Land Tax during the Qin and Han periods as Seen from the Newly Excavated Documents on Bamboo and Wood" 從新出簡牘看秦漢時期的田租徵收. *Bamboo and Silk* 簡帛 3: 331–342.

———. 2015. *Excavated Documents on Bamboo and Wood and the Qin-Han Society (Part Two)* 出土簡牘與秦漢社會(續編). Guilin: Guangxi Shifan Daxue.

Yao, Lei 姚磊. 2021. *Han Documents from Jianshui Jinguan, an Edition with Collected Annotations* 肩水金關漢簡釋文合校. Beijing: Zhongguo Shehui Kexueyuan.

Yoffee, Norman. 2004. *Myths of the Archaic State: Evolution of the Earliest Cities, States, and Civilizations*. Cambridge: Cambridge University Press.

Zhang, Zhongwei 張忠煒. 2019. "A Remark on the Qin Tablet 10–15 from Liye and the Document on the Sequence of Merits from the Han Tomb No. 77 at Shuihudi" 里耶秦簡10–15補論——兼論睡虎地77號漢墓功次文書. *Studies in Ancient Chinese Legal Texts* 中國古代法律文獻研究 13: 97–118.

Zhangjiashan ersiqi hao Han mu zhujian zhengli xiaozu 張家山二四七號漢墓竹簡整理小組 (Research Group for Ordering the Bamboo Slips from the Han Tomb No. 247 at Zhangjiashan). 2006. *Bamboo Slips from the Han Tomb at Zhangjiashan (Tomb No. 247)* 張家山漢墓竹簡(二四七號墓). Beijing: Wenwu.

Zhongguo wenwu yanjiusuo 中國文物研究所 (Chinese Institute of Cultural Relics) and Hubei sheng kaogu wenwu yanjiusuo 湖北省考古文物研究所 (Hubei Provincial Institute of Archaeology and Cultural Relics). 2001. *Qin Documents from Longgang* 龍崗秦簡. Beijing: Zhonghua shuju.

Chapter 8
Fa and the Early Legal System

Ulrich Lau and Michael Lüdke

In the legal system of the Qin and Han periods, *fa* 灋/法[1] is a central term. It refers to legal rules (including to those rules codified in the statutes and edicts), both in the sense of the rules applicable to a specific offence or case and in the sense of the entirety of the legal rules, that is, the legal system as a whole. In this latter sense, the usage of *fa* in early Chinese legal language is very similar to the expression "the law" in English. *Fa* has been understood in this sense for a long time in Chinese studies (Bodde 1981: 175; Vandermeersch 1965: 5 "la loi"). In contrast, recent attempts to understand *fa* as "legal category" (Brown and Sanft 2011) or "categorical principle" (Barbieri-Low and Yates 2015) are misleading. A discussion of the nuances of the concept *fa* in early Chinese philosophical discourse falls to the other contributions in this volume and therefore is beyond the scope of this particular article. However, it is important to note that the term *fa* is closely linked to early Chinese conceptions of the universality and equity of the law that are reflected in legal sources of the time.

---

[1] 灋 is the original form of the character writing *fa*, while 法 is a later, abbreviated form of this character. See section 3 below for a detailed discussion of the usage of these character forms. In block quotations of source texts, we will give the long form 灋 when used in the source and add the abbreviated form 法 (which is also the current form) in parentheses, in line with standard editorial practice. In the main text (except when discussing character forms), we will use the current form 法, including in phrases quoted from epigraphic texts, irrespective of whether the full or abbreviated character form is used in the original. The same applies for 辠 and 罪, the early and the later character used to write *zui*.

U. Lau
University of Hamburg, Hamburg, Germany
e-mail: ulrich.lau@web.de

M. Lüdke (✉)
Saarbrücken, Germany
e-mail: michael.luedke@posteo.de

© The Author(s), under exclusive license to Springer Nature Switzerland AG 2024
Y. Pines (ed.), *Dao Companion to China's* fa *Tradition*, Dao Companions to Chinese Philosophy 19, https://doi.org/10.1007/978-3-031-53630-4_9

This contribution discusses the use of *fa* in the legal system of the Qin and early Han periods. It will mainly draw on the excavated legal sources, which, since the 1970s, have provided a new picture of the law in early China and how it was applied in practice. These sources include, among others, the texts found in Tomb 11, Shuihudi, Yunmeng 雲夢睡虎地 (Hubei), the tomb of a Qin legal official; in Tomb 247, Zhangjiashan, Jiangling 江陵張家山 (Hubei), the tomb of a Han legal official; and the texts looted from an unknown tomb and acquired by the Yuelu Academy 嶽麓書院 on the Hong Kong antiques market. There has been some discussion about the nature of these texts as burial objects and possible implications for their reliability as historical sources.[2] We believe that there is strong evidence that these texts were not specially produced burial goods but were related to the deceased's life. The copies found in the tombs might not in all cases have been a current official fair copy of the texts (which probably would have been too costly or time-consuming to reproduce) but earlier versions or personal copies.[3] Some features of these manuscripts can be interpreted as the results of collation (*chou* 讎),[4] indicating that the copies found in the tombs had been checked against authoritative versions, a step hardly necessary if the texts did not have official character. It is also likely that the texts represent selections or, in some cases, excerpts of those parts relevant to the deceased person's responsibilities.[5] The manuscript texts are to a large extent consistent with each other and with the received historical records, confirming their reliability as historical sources. In evaluating these texts as historical sources, it must be considered that they were found in tombs of officials who almost certainly had been employed at the county level (Lüdke 2004: 194–96; Lau and Staack 2016:

---

[2] For example, Barbieri-Low and Yates believe that the Zhangjiashan legal texts are not actual working documents used by the tomb owner in his career, but "were copied hastily or unsystematically by scribes with only a moderate level of literacy or familiarity with the subject matter of the texts" and "either were produced in a scriptorium as practice texts and later sold as funerary products or were copied in a funerary workshop specifically for inclusion in a burial" (Barbieri-Low and Yates 2015: 106–07, 458–60). However, many of the seemingly hap-hazard features pointed out by Barbieri-Low and Yates can be better explained with physical processes that occurred after interment or with present-day problems of reconstruction, while incorrect graphs, copy errors and multiple scribal hands, to the extent that these are not characteristic of early manuscript texts in general, may be more appropriately understood as features of working and other non-authoritative copies or as the result of the compilatory nature of texts in routine legal use.

[3] See Morgan and Chemla 2018 on the Zhangjiashan *Suanshushu*; see Staack 2016: 17, as well as Fölster and Staack 2021: 900, 904, on legal texts.

[4] Fölster and Staack 2021: 897–901.

[5] For example, the availability of the "Jinguan ling" 津關令 (Edicts for fords and passes) among the Zhangjiashan texts reflects the location of the Han-period commandery Nanjun, in which the tomb owner was buried: One of the fortified passes (Yuguan 扜關 or Jiangguan 江關, see *Ernian lüling* 492 and Barbieri-Low and Yates 2015: 1124n12 and 1149n28) that controlled access to the strategically critical "Area within the passes" (Guanzhong 關中), in which the capital was located and which formed the basis of imperial power, was located at the border of Nanjun commandery (east of present-day Fengjie 奉節, see Tan 1982–1987, 2:29–30 grid ③/6). Therefore, the "Jinguan ling," which regulated the movement of people and goods across the border, would have been of special importance for Nanjun and its officials, making it more likely that it would be included among the burial goods of a local official (for details see Lau and Lüdke Forthcoming).

14) and therefore reflect, especially in their selection, the outlook and responsibilities of local functionaries. At the same time, the excavated compilations of statutes and edicts were part of the body of law promulgated by the central government, while other texts, such as collections of legal cases, legal instructions in question-and-answer-format, or procedural guidelines, most likely originated with the central government and reflect its concern for the uniform administration of justice.[6]

1 *Fa, lü,* and *ling*

To understand how the term *fa* was used in the legal sources, it is crucial to distinguish it from related terms, in particular from *lü* 律 "statutes" and *ling* 令 "edicts", which were the material, embodied form of law. Both *lü* and *ling* contained a wide array of rules regulating administrative and penal matters.[7] An important part of the

---

[6] For the *Zouyanshu*, see Lüdke 2004: 43–48, 63–71; Lau and Lüdke 2012: 19–20, 27, 36–39. Chinese and Japanese scholarship coming to the same conclusion is listed in Barbieri-Low and Yates 2015: 98–99. In contrast, Barbieri-Low and Yates have argued that the *Zouyanshu* from Zhangjiashan "was compiled from the bottom up … by a network of legal scribes from different places," resulting in the "earliest extant example of 'court-case literature' (*gōng'àn xiǎoshuō* 公案小說)" (Barbieri-Low and Yates 2015: 98–99).

[7] The recently discovered sources allow new insights into the distinction of *lü* "statutes" and *ling* "edicts" with regard to legislative procedures, period of validity, and content. Evidence of their legislative formation is provided by the paratextual framing, in particular the introductory formula, of individual edicts (such as 制詔御史… "imperial decision instructing the chief prosecutor …"; e.g. in *Yuelu Lüling* 5.59, 66, 93; *Ernian lüling* 492, 493). The different variants of this introductory formula point to a legislative process in which the initiative for new *ling* came either directly from the ruler himself; or from the chancellor (*chengxiang* 丞相) or chief prosecutor (*yushi* 御史), when they submitted proposals to the emperor; or from other senior (often commandery) officials, when their proposals were forwarded to the emperor by the chancellor. Largely identical forms of paratextual framing found in the "Jinguan ling" 津關令 (Edicts for fords and passes) dating to the very beginning of the Han indicate that the procedures for introducing edicts established in Qin were adopted by Qin's successors after the dynastic change. With regard to the period of validity, the sources indicate that longer-term validity was associated with *lü*, either because they had been inherited from the previous rulers (*Yushu* 1–2; *Shiji* 122: 3153) or because they were intended to remain in force beyond the current ruler. The long-term validity of the *lü* is also corroborated by the large number of identical statutes in collections dating to different points in time in the Qin and Han periods (see the Qin collection found in Shuihudi Tomb 11; the Qin collection held by the Yuelu Academy; the Han collections from Zhangjiashan Tombs 247 and 336, from Hujia caochang 胡家草場 Tomb 12, and from Shuihudi Tomb 77; and the Han list of statute titles found in Tuzishan 兔子山 Well 7). In contrast, *ling*, by default, seem to have been in force only during the reign of the ruler who had issued them, at least in Qin. For example, the sources indicate that during the reign of King Zheng of Qin, the future First Emperor 始皇帝 (king 247–221 BCE; emp. 221–210 BCE), *ling* of former rulers of Qin were no longer in force, with the exception of those explicitly designated *fu yong* 復用 "to be reused" by imperial decision (*Yuelu Lüling* 4.331, 345; see Chen Wei 2017a: 82–104 for this form of designating the previous ruler's edicts as currently). In an edict issued by the Second Emperor 二世皇帝 (emp. 210–207 BCE) on his accession to the throne, the new ruler assured his subjects that the task of abolishing and confirming statutes and edicts had already been completed, in accordance with the instructions bequeathed by the deceased emperor

fa, that is, of the legal rules and thus of the law as a whole, was written down in the *lü* and *ling*; thus, both *lü* and *ling* contained legal rules as their content, but to the best of our knowledge, the law was not exhausted in the *lü* and *ling*. For example, decisions in precedents, especially if made by the ruler, often also had the force of law. *Fa*, referring to the content of the legal rules, and *lü* or *ling*, as their written embodiment, were not the same. However, due to the semantic relationship between them, they could be used interchangeably in some contexts (see below, p. 240, for *wang fa* 枉法 and *wang lüling* 枉律令 as two names for the same offence).

A late tradition claims that *lü* replaced *fa* as the term for written law in the fourth century BCE. According to the *Jinshu* 晉書 (History of the Jin dynasty), Li Kui 李 悝 (ca. 455–395 BCE), employed by Marquis Wen of Wei 魏文侯 (r. 445–396 BCE),[8] compiled a law code from the laws of all the states which was called *Fajing* 法經 (Canon of law) and which in turn was used later by Shang Yang 商鞅 (d. 338 BCE) in his own reforms in Qin (*Jinshu* 30: 922 ["Xingfa zhi" 刑法志]). The *Weishu* 魏書 (History of the [Northern] Wei dynasty) also briefly mentions that Shang Yang based his policy proposals to Qin on a *Fajing* in six chapters (*Weishu* 111: 2872 ["Xingfa zhi" 刑罰志]). The *Tanglü shuyi* 唐律疏議 (The Tang code with commentary and explanations) adds that the chapters in the *Fajing* were titled *fa*, such as "Daofa" (Laws on stealing), but that Shang Yang replaced *fa* with *lü*, resulting in chapters called "Daolü" (Statutes on stealing) etc., the terminology used from Qin to Tang all the way up to the Qing (*Tanglü shuyi* 1:2 [preface to the commentary for "Mingli" 名例]). However, the *Weishu* was compiled in the middle of the sixth century CE, the *Jinshu* and *Tanglü shuyi* not earlier than in the middle of the seventh century CE. Even when assuming that the outlines of the "Xingfa zhi" (Treatise on criminal law) in the *Jinshu* date back to the fifth century CE, all of these

---

(朕奉遺詔，今…律令當除定者畢矣) (Yiyang Tuzishan slip J9.3:1, published in Hunan sheng wenwu kaogu yanjiusuo and Yiyang shi wenwuchu 2016: 43 and ill. 40 on p. 40, transcribed according to Chen Wei 2017b: 124–26; see also Emmerich 2017: 53–87). With regard to differences in content, criminal case records found in the early Han collection *Zouyanshu*, in which edicts are cited together with the applicable statutes as the legal basis for deciding the case (*Zouyanshu* 157–58, 72–73), indicate that *ling* often clarified the application of the statutes in specific situations, added exceptions from statutory rules for special circumstances, or stipulated how a statute should be implemented in a particular case constellation. An analysis of the large collection of Qin edicts published by the Yuelu Academy confirms these and other functions of the *ling* (supplementing and clarifying existing regulations, repealing regulations, applying an existing regulation to a comparable situation, etc.). In essence, the collection of edicts preserved in different offices resembled an open file that was flexible with regard to further expansion and emendation. Some individual provisions of edicts were later incorporated into the statutes, but, based on the currently available sources, this was not the case for the vast majority of the edicts known from Qin and early Han.

[8] The reign periods of pre-Qin rulers are given as the Western years that to the most extent overlap with the first and last year of the respective ruler's official Chinese reign count, irrespective of the Western year in which accession actually took place and in which the first reign year in the official count actually began. For Qin and Han rulers, the actual dates of accession and of the start of the official reign count are given in the notes (relying on Xu Xiqi 1997 for the conversion of Chinese to Western dates).

three sources, which are the earliest that mention the *Fajing*, are far too removed from the time in question to treat them as reliable (Hulsewé 1955: 29–30; Pokora 1959). The tradition is also not supported by what is probably the earliest evidence of actual written law from the late Zhanguo 戰國 (Warring States, 453–221 BCE) period state of Wei: appended to one of the Qin manuscript texts from Tomb 11, Shuihuidi, are two laws that are titled "Wei hu lü" 魏戶律 (Wei household statutes) and "Wei ben ming lü" 魏奔命律 (Wei statutes on rapid-deployment forces), respectively (*Wei li zhi dao* 16–28, 5th register). Even if these laws, which give the date of February 2, 251 BCE, are much later than the apocryphal *Fajing*, the fact that they are designated *lü*, not *fa*, does indicate that *lü* was a term that was not only used in Qin.[9] Furthermore, the earliest surviving material evidence of Chinese written law, a Qin manuscript on a wooden board dated to 309 BCE that has been excavated from Tomb 50, Haojiaping, Qingchuan 青川郝家坪 (Sichuan), also uses the term *lü* to refer to itself as written law:

二年十一月己酉朔朔日，王命丞相戊、内史匽民臂更脩為田律 (*Sanjian* 604)[10]

　　In the second year, eleventh month with the *jiyou* as the first day, on the first day [October 2, 309 BCE],[11] the King ordered Chancellor (Gan) Wu and Minister of Agriculture Yan …[12] to amend and revise the Statute(s) on Creating Fields.

---

[9] In two cases, the *Zouyanshu* uses *fa* 法 (written in its palaeographic form 灋) to refer to purported Chunqiu-period (春秋, 770–453 BCE) laws of the states of Wei 衛 and Lu 魯 (*Zouyanshu* 162, 174). However, these cases are clearly Han-period retellings of historical anecdotes which were included in the *Zouyanshu* to illustrate certain points about investigation and adjudication. Their different format, which does not rely on the formal structure of legal documents, as well as the use of Han terminology, makes clear that they do not claim to present documentary evidence. The use of *fa* (instead of *lü*) here indicates that no claim is made that the legal rules mentioned were part of a written code of law.

[10] For a translation, see also Hulsewé 1985: 211–15 (*RCL* G); for references to further literature and a discussion of similarities to rules in the *Ernian lüling*, see Barbieri-Low and Yates 2015: 710–11.

[11] The date conversion follows Xu Xiqi 1997: 1066.

[12] The meaning of *min bi* 民臂 in this passage is obscure. Korolkov translates as follows: "… [в связи со] <зловредностью народа> внести изменения и исправить статут об устройстве полей" (… [in relation to] the <people's depravity> submit changes and correct the statute on the arrangement of fields) (Korolkov 2017: 77; interpolation in brackets by Korolkov). Korolkov here follows Li Xueqin, who has proposed interpreting *min bi* 民臂 as "the people's depravity" (Li Xueqin 1982: 69), taking *bi* 臂 as writing *pi* 僻 with reference to the *Yushu* 語書 from Shuihuidi, which contains the passages 是以聖王作為法度，以矯端民心，去其邪避(僻)，除其惡俗 (therefore the sagacious kings made legal rules to rectify the people's minds, to eradicate their depravity and eliminate their evil customs) (*Yushu* 1) and 養匿邪避(僻)之民 (foster and shelter depraved people) (*Yushu* 6) (see Korolkov 2017: 78–79). One might also adduce the *Shijing* verse 民之多辟，無自立辟, which Karlgren translates "now when the people have many depravities, do not yourself start depravities" (*Shijing* ode 254:6), taking *bi* 辟 in both instances as writing *pi* 僻 based on Zhu Xi's 朱熹 (1130–1200) *Shi jizhuan* 詩集傳 (Collected commentaries on the Odes) (Karlgren 1944: 97 gloss no. 567). However, the writing of *bi* 臂 (rather than its cognate characters) for *pi* 僻, while phonetically certainly possible, is not attested elsewhere; also, the lack of *yi* 以 (or a functionally equivalent particle) before *min bi* poses syntactical difficulties. It is equally possible that *min bi* is a verb-object phrase or a name. We are grateful to Yuri Pines for pointing us to Korolkov's article.

2 *Fa* in Legal Texts

The following will discuss different usages of *fa* in technical legal texts, where the term is mainly found in the following contexts:

(a) referring to legal rules, often to a set of specific rules;
(b) in the sense of "the law" to refer to the entirety of legal rules, for example in admonitions to apply the law equally and consistently;
(c) as part of the official designation of legal officials;
(d) as a noun modifier in the sense "legal," to distinguish the following noun from uses in non-legal senses; and,
(e) rarely, in the verbal sense "to apply the law."

2.1 Fa *Referring to Specific Rules*

Most often in legal sources, *fa* refers to legal rules, often a set of specific rules applicable to a case or an offense. Instructive for understanding how *fa* is used in the early legal system is the formula A *yu* [B] *tong fa* A與[B]同法 "for A, the same legal rules [as for B] apply," which is found in numerous instances in the Qin and Han legal manuscripts. In this formula, A refers to a specific fact (such as an offence) and B (which is optional if it can be understood from the text) to another fact or person. The formula indicates that "to fact A, the same legal rules [as to B] apply." Within statutes and edicts, the formula is typically used when not a single rule is referred to, but a set of complex rules. In this important respect, A *yu* [B] *tong fa* is distinct from A *yu* [B] *tong zui* "to A, the same punishment [as for B] applies," which is typically used when the code stipulates a single, specific punishment for A rather than a complex set of rules for determining punishment.

The formula is most often found with *dao* 盜 "to steal," that is, in the formula *yu dao tong fa* 與盜同法.[13] See the following example:

> 賊殺傷人畜產，與盜同灋(法)。 (*Ernian lüling* 49)
> For killing or injuring another person's livestock with malice, the same legal rules as for stealing apply.

Or in:

> 殺傷馬牛，與盜同灋(法)。 (*Ernian lüling* 251)
> For killing or injuring a horse or ox, the same legal rules as for stealing apply.

The punishment for stealing was graded (in Qin and Han in five degrees) according to the value of misappropriated goods (*zang* 贓). In this example, the use of *tong fa*

---

[13] *Yuelu Lüling* 4.18, 60, 66, 67, 69; 5.3–5, 40–41, 92, 230–244, 291; 6.2, 6, 9, 18, 47, 50–51, 161–68; *Qinlü shiba zhong* 174–75=*RCL* A 87; *Xiaolü* 35=*RCL* B12; *Falü dawen* 20, 32=*RCL* D 18, 26; *Longgang* 124, 133, 148; *Liye* 9-1874v; *Ernian lüling* 20, 49, 57, 74–75, 77, 180; 261.

indicates that in a case of killing or injuring livestock, the loss in value to the owner was calculated and the perpetrator punished as if he/she had stolen something of the same value, with the punishment graded according to the value. The use of *yu dao tong zui* (for which there are no known examples in legal texts) would have been ambiguous in this case, as there was no single definite punishment for stealing; rather, the calculation of the loss in value was an indispensable part of calculating the punishment. This contrasts with the use of *yu tong zui* in cases such as the following:

> 智人略賣人而與賈，與同罪。 (*Ernian lüling* 67)
> For buying a person from another person with the knowledge that [the seller] has abducted the person in order to sell him/her, the same punishment [as for the seller] applies.

The single punishment of *zhe* 磔 (execution by dismemberment) applied to *lüe mai ren* "abducting and selling another person" (*Ernian lüling* 66). Therefore, it was sufficient to reference the punishment by itself, rather than a set of legal rules.

In neither of these cases would it have been possible to replace *fa* and *zui*, respectively, by *lü*. The offence of *zei sha shang ren xuchan* 賊殺傷人畜產 (with malice killing or injuring another person's livestock) was dealt with in a different *lü*[14] than the offence of stealing. Different offences, with the different elements defining them, were regulated in different *lü*. However, the use of *tong fa* or *tong zui* signaled that for these different offences the same punishment (*tong zui*) or the same legal rules altogether (*tong fa*) applied; that is, while the offences were different, the legal consequences were the same.

This interpretation of *yu A tong fa* is confirmed by its use in the Qin and Han statutes. In the *Ernian lüling* (Statutes and edicts of the second year), in particular, *yu tong fa* always refers to a set of rules, meaning that it would have been insufficient to reference a single punishment or cite a single rule, as evidenced in the following examples.

- All instances of *yu dao tong fa* reference the complex calculation rules for determining punishment for property offences, as discussed above. In essence, *yu dao tong fa* was the formula used to indicate punishment for property offences. In all property offences, punishment was graded in relation to the misappropriated value, so that it was necessary to reference the rules for punishment of theft. It is therefore not surprising that *dao* is probably the offence most frequently found with the formula *yu tong fa*.
- 謀賊殺、傷人，與賊同灋(法)。 (*Ernian lüling* 26)

- For conspiring to kill or injure another person with malice, the same legal rules as for an [actual] malefactor apply.

This rule determines that conspiracy (*mou*) to kill or injure another person with malice (*zei* 賊, as opposed to *dou* 鬥 "in a fight", *xi* 戲 "as a result of play", or

---

[14] The rules for each offence constituted a different *lü*. When *lü* is used in a chapter title, such as in the "Dao lü" of the *Ernian lüling*, it should be understood in a plural sense, that is, in this example, "Statutes regarding stealing."

guoshi 過失 "by inadvertence")[15] is punished in the same way as committing the actual offence by oneself. However, as the punishment for *zei sha* and *zei shang*, respectively, depends on a number of factors, in particular whether the victim had died, *yu zei tong fa* refers to a set of rules (*Ernian lüling* 21–25).

This interpretation of *tong fa* is supported by the following explanation of the difference between *tong fa* and *tong zui* 與同罪 in the Qin period manuscript titled by the present-day editors *Falü dawen* (Answers to questions on legal statutes):[16]

律曰「與盜同灋(法)」，有(又)曰「與同辠(罪)」。此二物。【云「與同灋(法)」
者，】其同居、典、伍當坐之。云「與同辠(罪)」、云「反其辠(罪)」者，弗當
坐。 (*Falü dawen* 20=*RCL* D 18)[17]

---

[15] *Zei* 賊 "with malice," *dou* 鬥 "in a fight," *xi* 戲 "as a result of play," and *guoshi* 過失 "by inadvertence" are technical terms used to qualify the offences of *sha ren* 殺人 "killing another person" and *shang ren* 傷人 "injuring another person," with *zei* indicating the most and *guoshi* the least severe form of committing the offence (*Ernian lüling* 21, 25, 27; the offence of *fan* 燔 "to set fire" was qualified either as *zei fan* 賊燔 or *shi huo yan fan* 失火延燔, see *Ernian lüling* 4–5). In relation to homicide, the distinctions made by these terms fulfil a similar function as those made by terms like "murder," "voluntary manslaughter," or "involuntary manslaughter" in modern legal systems (even though the distinctions are by no means congruent).

[16] The following *Falü dawen* passage addresses a specific problem in prosecution: within the Qin system of collective liability, household members and others in the offender's social orbit (see note 17) were given a (lesser) punishment as a deterrence to the perpetrator and an incentive to report him (as those who did so were exempted from any collective punishment). Collective punishment was tied to the punishment for the main offence. A special problem arose when the legal rules did not directly spell out the punishment for an offence, but referred to other rules, using one of the formulas *yu tong fa, yu tong zui,* or *fan qi zui.* In these cases, where the law referred to the punishment of another offence, the question arose whether the collective punishment for that other offence also applied.

[17] This passage poses problems for interpretation and translation, as the first formula quoted at the beginning from the statutes (與盜同法), is not explicitly taken up again in what follows, unlike the second (與同罪). Hulsewé's solution is to subordinate 其同居典伍當坐之 to 云與同罪 and thus to translate "when his (i.e. the culprit's) household members, the (village) chief and the (members of his) group of five are warranted to be adjudicated for his (crime), this is called 'the same punishment as'." However, this not only reverses the structure of the following sentence (where 云... is clearly subordinated to 弗當坐, not the other way around) but also assumes that the formula 與盜同法, which introduces the passage, is not addressed at all, not even implicitly, and thus left unexplained. It is more plausible to conclude that both formulas quoted in the beginning, 與盜同法 and 與同罪, are addressed in the following, at least implicitly. The solution proposed here suggests that 其同居典、伍當坐之 must be understood to refer to the first formula (與盜同法), which was either sufficiently understood from the context or not repeated due to a copyist's mistake. Another option would be to understand 此二物，其同居、典、伍當坐之? as an implict question in the sense "With regard to these two provisions, are the members of the household … also to be prosecuted for the offence?" (even though in the *Falü dawen* questions appear to be routinely marked as such, e.g., by adding the negated repetition *bu dang,* as in *Falü dawen* 42, 44=*RCL* D 33, 36). While the answer would then explicitly only address the formulas 與同罪 and 反其罪, it would be implicitly understood that the opposite (當坐之) would apply to 與盜同法. The resulting meaning would be the same.

The statutes use the formula "the same legal rules as for stealing apply," and also use the formula "liable to the same punishment." These are two [different] provisions:[18] [Only when the statutes use the formula "the same legal rules apply"] are the members of the [offender's] household, his ward chief, and the members of his neighborhood group[19] also to be prosecuted for the offence. But when [the statutes] use the formula "liable to the same punishment" or the formula "inverse [the original offenders] punishment," [the respective persons] are not to be prosecuted for the offence.

This passage makes clear that, when the statutes use *tong zui*, only the actual punishment is applied to the offender, while the use of *tong fa* requires that the full gamut of rules, including secondary rules, are to be applied, which might include collective punishment, as stipulated for the offence of stealing. This explanation, first of all, accords to the literal meaning of the terms, distinguishing *fa* as the applicable legal rules from *zui*, the specific punishment. The explanation also makes sense from a systematic point of view: The formula *tong fa* makes the same legal rules applicable for different offences that share certain aspects (e.g., belonging to the broad category of property offences in the case of *yu dao tong fa*) but are still not related. One person committing the offence of *dao* "stealing" and another person committing an offence classified as *yu dao tongfa* would still commit two different offences. Consequently, both offenders have to bear the same legal consequences, including collective punishment for their household members etc. In contrast, the formula *yu tong zui* usually was employed to stipulate punishment for an accessory to an offence (for example, somebody who knowingly shared in the illegal profit or gave shelter to the offender). In this constellation, only the household members etc. of the principal offender were liable to collective punishment, but not those of the accessory who was punished due to a *tong zui* rule.

---

[18] *Wu* 物 is attested in the sense of "individual provision within an edict (*ling* 令)" (it is not known whether *wu* also referred to provisions of a statute). See 去苛令三十九物 "[At around 295 BCE, Duke Wei of Zhou] abolished 39 provisions of oppressive edicts" (*Lüshi chunqiu* 16.1: 946 ["Xian shi" 先識]); *zuo ci wu* 坐此物 "to be prosecuted according to these provisions" (*Yuelu Lüling* 5.10–11; 7.51/52; cf. *Yuelu Lüling* 7.87; 6.237); 復禹之績，祀夏配天，不失舊物 "He revived the legacy of Yu, sacrificed to the rules of Xia, and was a partner for Heaven; he did not let lapse the old provisions." (*Zuozhuan*, Ai 1.2).

[19] In Qin and Han, neighboring households were organized into small units called *wu* 伍, literally "group of five," in a system of collective liability. The text in which the present rule is found, the *Falü dawen* from Shuihudi tomb 11, equates *wu*, as the current legal term, with *si lin* 四鄰 "four neighbors," probably an older legal term (*Falü dawen* 99=*RCL* D 83). According to the *Shiji*, Qin first organized households in groups of five by means of the household registration system in 375 BCE under Lord Xian 獻公 (*Shiji* 6: 289). Around 350 BCE, Shang Yang, ordered the population to be organized in groups of five and ten for mutual control, holding them liable for each other's offences (*Shiji* 68: 2230). The Han followed this practice: The "Hu lü" 戶律 (Statutes on households) in the *Ernian lüling* requires that adjoining households are organized in groups of five, which are to surveil each other and to report offences (*Ernian lüling* 305).

2.2   Fa *in the Sense "Legal Rules" or "(The Legal Rules as a Whole:) The Law"*

The technical use of *fa* as referring to a set of specific legal rules is a special use case of the broader legal meaning of *fa*, in which *fa* refers to unspecified legal rules or to the legal rules in their entirety, that is, to "the law." Characteristic for this use are expressions such as *fan fa* 犯法 "offend against the law/the legal rules";[20] *jin feng fa yi zhi* 謹奉法以治 "sincerely upholding the law in governing" (*Zouyanshu* 86; 149 [here written 奏 *zou* due to a scribal error]); *fa bu ming* 法不名 "the legal provisions do not designate (the specific sentence of the person to be sentenced with penal labor of the *nai* category)" (*Ernian lüling* 90); *zhi fa* 致法 "to apply the legal rules, to apply the law" (*Wei yu deng zhuang* 244); *shi fa* 釋法 "to set aside the legal rules, to set aside the law" (*Zouyanshu* 149–150, with *shi* written 擇); and *dang fa* 當法 "to conform to/be adequate to the legal rules/to the law" (*Wei yu deng zhuang* 013).

In the meaning "legal rules; (the legal rules as a whole:) the law," *fa* is widely used in both technical and non-technical sources at least since the Zhangguo period, as discussed below. In this meaning, it also appears in the proclamatory stele inscriptions of the First Emperor of Qin 秦始皇帝 (emp. 221–210 BCE)[21] at Mount Tai 泰山 and Mount Langye 瑯邪山. Kern, in his seminal work on the stele inscriptions, distinguishes between *fa* as meaning "rules"[22] and *fa* as meaning "the law."[23] However, this distinction is unnecessary because here, as in the technical texts, *fa* already means "legal rules" and can be understood as either referring to (a set of) specific rules or to "the law" in the sense of the legal rules as a whole.

As part of the term for the offence *xing shou qiu wang fa* 行受賕枉法 "giving or receiving bribes to bend the law" (*Ernian lüling* 60; *Zouyanshu* 52, with 狂 writing *wang* 枉), *fa* clearly refers to legal rules or even the law in its entirety, as the corrupt bending of specific rules threatens the integrity of the law and thus the legal order as a whole. The Qin text *Wei yu deng zhuang* refers to this offence as *shou ren huo cai yi wang lü ling* 受人貨材(財)以枉律令 "accepting someone else's goods and chattels to bend statutes and edicts" (*Wei yu deng zhuang* 29). These two expressions for the same offence indicate that *fa* in this context is a synonym of *lüling* 律令 "statutes and edicts," in that *fa* refers to the specific contents that are materially embodied in the *lü* and *ling*.

---

[20] *Liye* 8-746+8-1588; *Wei yu deng zhuang* 102–03; *Yuelu Lüling* 6.64; *Yushu* 5; *Hanlü shiliu zhang* 217; *Han Feizi* 34: 324 ("Waichushuo you shang" 外儲說右上).

[21] The future First Emperor acceded to the throne of Qin as King Zheng 秦王政 immediately after the death of his father, King Zhuangxiang of Qin 秦庄襄王, on 6 July 247 BCE (*Shiji* 5: 220); the first year of his reign in the official count began on 6 November 247 BCE. The First Emperor was succeeded by his son Hu Hai 胡亥, who acceded to the throne as the Second Emperor of Qin 秦二世 not later than in September 210 BCE (*Shiji* 6: 265). The first year of the Second Emperor's reign in the official count began on 17 November 210 BCE.

[22] Kern 2000: text 2, p. 17, l. 2 and note 19; p. 20, l. 15.

[23] E.g., *ding fa* 定法 "fixes the law" in Kern 2000: text 3, p. 29, l. 31 with note 59.

On the other hand, while *fan fa* 犯法 "to offend against the law" is found in non-technical sources at least as often as in technical ones,[24] the expressions *fan lü* 犯律[25] "to offend against a statute" and *fan ling* 犯令[26] "to offend against an edict; to offend against a specific statutory provision" are far more common in technical texts. *Fan fa* usually connotes that the legal order has been harmed, it stresses the transgression as such. In contrast, *fan ling* and *fan lü* are used in technical contexts to spell out the legal consequences if a specific rule has been broken, their function typically consists in pointing out a specific rule. Compare, for example the following passages:

> 法者，治之正也，所以禁暴而率善人也。今犯法已論，而使毋罪之父母妻子同產坐之，及為收帑，朕甚不取。(*Shiji* 110: 418)
> [Proclamation by Emperor Wen of Han 漢文帝 (r. 180–157 BCE):[27]] The law is the standard of governance, the means of restraining violence and guiding good people. But presently, even though judgment has been passed after the law has been offended against, to still cause innocent parents, wives, children, and siblings born to the same father to be held liable for [the offence] and to make them confiscated government slaves is something I certainly cannot accept.

> 有不從律令者...吏三問之而不以請(情)實占吏者，行其所犯律令辠(罪)，有(又)駕(加)其辠(罪)一等。(*Yuelu Lüling* 5.168–69)
> If there are any who do not obey the statutes and edicts ... and who, having been asked three times by the authorities, do not according to the truth and the facts make a declaration to the authorities for recording, then execute the punishment stipulated in the statute or edict that they have offended against and, in addition, increase their punishment by one degree.

> 令曰:守以下行縣，縣以傳馬、吏乘給不足，毋賃黔首馬。犯令及乘者，貲二甲，癈。(*Yuelu Lüling* 5.136)
> Edict: When a governor or lower official goes on a tour of inspection through a county and the county does not sufficiently provide him with horses for official conveyances or mounts for officials, then no horses are to be rented from the subjects. Those who offend against this edict as well as those who have mounted [a subject's horse or conveyance drawn by a subject's horse] are to be fined two suits of armor and to be removed from office.

Emperor Wen's proclamation opens with a general statement about the role of the law in the sense of the legal order as a whole; accordingly, *fan fa* 犯法 "offending against the law" here refers to a violation of the legal order in general, not of a specific rule. The excerpt from a Qin edict in the second quote, in contrast, uses *suo fan lü ling zui* 所犯律令罪 "the punishment provided in the statute or edict that has been offended against" to refer with technical precision to the specific applicable

---

[24] See, for example, *Shiji* 68: 2231, translated below (Sect. 2.6).

[25] *Yuelu Lüling* 4.93, 5.198 with fragments C10.3-1-5+C10.1-8-4, 6.196; *fan lüling* 犯律令 in *Yuelu Lüling* 5.169.

[26] *Qinlü shiba zhong* 57, 191=*RCL* A 16, 101; *Qinlü zachao* 28=*RCL* C 17; *Falü dawen* 142, 144=*RCL* D 120, 122; *Wei yu deng zhuang* 105; *Yuelu Lüling* 4.82, 128, 194, 377; 5.1, 3, 36, 42, 91, 136, 165, 206, 213, 310, 311, 312, 333; 6.32, 40, 90, 204, 209; 257; 7.254; *Longgang* 138; *Ernian lüling* 492.

[27] Emperor Wen acceded to the throne on 14 November 180 BCE (*Shiji* 9: 411). The first year of his reign in the official count began on 15 November 180 BCE.

rule in a case. In the third example, *fan ling* 犯令 is used to refer back specifically to that edict's stipulations. In neither of the last two examples, it would have been possible to replace *fan lü ling* or *fan ling* with *fan fa*. In the first example, *fan lü ling* (instead of *fan fa*) would have had the narrower meaning of "offending against a specific statute or edict."

2.3   Feng fa *"Upholding the Law"*

"The law" in the sense of the totality of the legal rules, and thus the legal order, is also the meaning that underpins a use that points to concepts closely linked with this term that go beyond its technical functions. Representative of this use are examples found in the *Zouyanshu* (Documents [on legal cases] submitted for higher-level decision that have been memorialized to the ruler), a manuscript containing a collection of legal cases dating to the early Han (and including a number of pre-Han cases).

In one example, dating to 210 BCE, a county magistrate named Xin is found to have ordered the murder of one of his subordinates. During the formal inquest, he is confronted as follows by the investigating officials:

信，長吏，臨一縣，上所信恃，不謹奉灋(法)以治。 (*Zouyanshu* 86)
> Xin, as a senior official you oversee a county and thus are trusted and relied upon by the ruler. Nevertheless, you did not conscientiously uphold the law in order to govern according to it.

Another example is from Qin and dates to 220 BCE, the second year after the First Emperor had founded the empire. Again, the case concerns a county magistrate, though this time the magistrate is accused of applying, in order to pacify the population in newly conquered territories, sentences more lenient than required by the law to deserters from a battle against rebels:

人臣當謹奏〈奉〉灋(法)以治。 (*Zouyanshu* 149)
> [His Majesty's] subjects[28] have to conscientiously uphold[29] the law in order to govern according to it.

Both passages indicate the importance attached in Qin and Han to a reliable application of the laws. Officials were expected to deviate from the law neither in favor nor to the detriment of the people in their area of responsibility. The whole *Zouyanshu*

---

[28] *Renchen* 人臣, literally "somebody else's [privately owned] slave/servitor" is here used as a reference to the emperor's subjects, reinforcing the notion of obedience owed to the imperial law, in particular by officials.

[29] *Jin feng fa yi zhi* 謹奉法以治 (法 here written in its palaeographic form 灋). The text on the bamboo strip clearly has *zou* 奏 as the second character of this phrase; in view of the same wording in *Zouyanshu* 86, this character is a writing mistake und should be emended to the graphically similar *feng* 奉 (Lau and Lüdke 2012: 210 n. 1030 and 261 n. 1305; Zhang Jianguo 1999: 281; Peng et al. 2007: 369 n. 36 to *Zouyanshu* 149; Barbieri-Low and Yates 2015: 1344 n. 33).

collection can be understood as an attempt by the imperial court to remind them of their duties in upholding the law. The emphasis placed in the legal documents on a reliable administration of justice is echoed in the received sources, where *feng fa* is found in several instances.[30]

2.4 Fa *as Part of Official Designations*

The meanings "law" and "legal provisions" of *fa* as a noun are also found in *zhifa* 執法, a generic designation of an official function. *Zhifa* literally means "(one who maintains the law:) guardian of the law, enforcer of the law," but is more appropriately rendered as "holder of jurisdiction." *Zhifa* is the Qin equivalent of the Han term[31] *erqian shi guan* 二千石官 (literally: the holder of an office with a salary rank of two thousand bushels), a term that refers to officials whose offices were differently named but who shared the salary rank of 2000 bushels and a position at the upper level of the administration, above the local level but below the *yushi* (chief prosecutor) and *chengxiang* (chief minister) (*Ernian lüling* 430). The generic designation *erqian shi guan* (which replaced *zhifa* in Han) was used in stipulations outlining the official chain of bureaucratic hierarchy, for example in phrases such as 縣道官令、長、丞…上屬所二千石官 "the magistrate or vice magistrate of a county or march [...] submit to the two-thousand-bushel official to which they are subordinated" (*Ernian lüling* 116). The general designations *zhifa* and *erqian shi guan* were a shorthand that avoided listing several, potentially confusing individual official titles. Importantly, the use of the collective term *zhifa* (and later *erqian shi guan*) in the text of the statutes ensured consistency, especially if the exact setup of the group of officials qualifying for this status was changed. Without such a term, it would have been necessary to update numerous statutory rules if a single official title was changed or if officials of a certain category were newly given the powers encompassed by the term. The terms *zhifa* (and its Han equivalent *erqian shi guan*) served a similar function as, on a lower level, the term (*guan*) *sefu* (官)嗇夫 "overseer (of an office)," which in legal text referred to the official in charge of a particular (lower-level) office, whatever the office's and the official's actual designation. Thus, *Qian sefu* 汧嗇夫, "overseer of Qian county," refers to the Qian magistrate (or, in the

---

[30] For example, *Shiji* 60: 2119; 111: 2946; 118: 3076; 119: 3101; *Hanshu* 8: 255; 44: 2136; 66: 2878; *jin feng faling* 謹奉法令 "conscientiously uphold the laws and edicts" in *Shiji* 87: 2561 and *feng fa bu jin* 奉法不謹 "not conscientious in upholding the law" in *Shiji* 106: 2835=*Hanshu* 35: 1917 and *Hanshu* 36: 1932.

[31] The term *erqian shi guan* also appears in the *Yuelu Lüling*, mostly in the form "(Ting) Neishi jun erqian shi guan gong ling ..." (廷)內史郡二千石官共令... as the title of specific edicts (*Yuelu Lüling* 4.307, 312, 320, 327, 328, 333, 340, 343, 353, 375, 390; 5.62, 98). When the term appears within a rule (*Yuelu Lüling* 4.192), it refers strictly to the salary rank and not to the role as the topmost official of a government agency. It is likely that the Han replacement of the Qin term *zhifa* in its functional role was based on these earlier uses. Tying the functional designation to the salary rank might have avoided ambiguity.

latter's absence, the vice magistrate) (*Zouyanshu* 122). The Shuihudi *Xiaolü*, Qin "Statutes on Checking," applied to all kind of government offices and therefore use the general term *guan sefu*, rather than the myriad titles of the officials in charge of particular offices, to stipulate that the official in charge must be fined, for example, if the actual stocks did not match the accounts. The term *zhifa* served a similar role in that it avoided enumerating the various officials who at the court and in the commanderies were in charge of the highest-level government agencies. These held the ultimate jurisdiction for their respective agencies and were directly responsible to the ruler.

In the territorial administration, the terms *zhifa* and *erqian shi guan* encompassed the *junshou* 郡守 (commandery governor) and *neishi* 內史 (governor of the capital area), who each were the superiors of county-level units of territorial administration. This also suggested by eight edicts found under the title "Neishi jun erqian shi guan gong ling" 內史郡二千石官共令 (Shared edicts regarding the two-thousand-bushel officials in the capital area and in the commanderies) in the collection of Qin manuscripts held by the Yuelu Academy,[32] of which at least some mention the term *zhifa* explicitly. It is likely that the terms *zhifa* and *erqian shi guan* also included two-thousand-bushel officials in the central government who were responsible for the various offices under central control (*duguan* 都官) and had the jurisdiction over the people employed in these offices. Apart from systematic considerations, this is also implied by the title of some edicts in the Yuelu Academy collection "**Ting** neishi jun erqian shi guan gong ling" 廷內史郡二千石官共令 (Shared edicts regarding the two-thousand-bushel officials at the **imperial court**, in the capital area, and in the commanderies).[33]

The equivalence of *zhifa* and *erqian shi guan* is evident in the parallel structures and matching contents of passages in Qin normative texts on the one hand and Han statutes on the other, such as the following:[34]

> ●治辠(罪)及諸有告劾而不當論者，皆具傳[35]告劾辤(辭)論夬(決)，上屬所執灋(法)，與計偕。•執灋(法)案掾其論… (*Yuelu Lüling* 5.335)

---

[32] *Yuelu Lüling* 4.307, 312, 320, 327, 328, 333, 340, 343.

[33] *Yuelu Lüling* 4.353, 375, 390 (emphasis added by the authors).

[34] Another example are the parallels between *Yuelu Lüling* 4.346-49 and *Ernian lüling* 430.

[35] The character identified by the editors as *chuan* 傳 is to be read *fu* 傅 *b(r)a-s, which is frequently used as a loangraph for *fu* 附 *b(r)o-s "to attach" (*Yuelu Lüling* 4.249; 5.66, 94, 114, 185, 222, 335; 6.65; 7.224) not only in the Qin and Han manuscripts (see Bai 2012, 183 with examples from the *Yinshu* found in Zhangjiashan Tomb 247 and from the *Sun Bin bingfa* 孫臏兵法 and the *Shou fa shou ling* 守法守令 found in Yinqueshan Tomb 1), but also in the received classical literature (see Feng and Deng 2006: 83 with examples from the *Zhouli*, *Zuozhuan*, *Shiji*, and *Hanshu*). For the identification of the character as *fu* 傅, compare the character forms of *fu* in *Yuelu Lüling* 5.185 and 5.66. See also the combination of *ju* 具 and *fu* 傅 in *Yuelu Lüling* 5.66, 114 and the use of the two terms in the edict quoted in *Hanshu* 1997: 23: 1106: 廷尉所不能決，謹具爲奏，傅所當比律令以聞. See also the character forms of *chuan* and *fu* in *Qin jiandu wenzibian*, pages 214 and 245, and in *Zhangjiashan Hanjian wenzibian*, pages 221 and 224.

When trying a case that results in punishment and in all cases where there is a criminal complaint or an ex-officio charge but by law no judgement is to be passed, always fully record and attach the wording of the criminal complaint or the ex-officio charge, the statement and the [proposed] judgement and decision and submit these to the holder of jurisdiction to which [the respective judicial authority] is subordinated, together with the [annual] accounts.—The holder of jurisdiction carefully investigates and examines the respective judgements [...]

縣道官所治死罪及過失、戲而殺人，獄已具，勿庸論，上獄屬所二千石官。二千石官令毋害都吏復案，問(聞)。二千石官、二千石官丞謹掾當，論，乃告縣道官以從事。(*Ernian lüling* 396–97)

In all cases tried by a county or march office that would result in the death penalty or that involve killing another person inadvertently or as a result of play, no judgement shall be passed after the case has been fully recorded; instead, the case is to be submitted to the two-thousand-bushel official to which [the respective county or march] is subordinated. The two-thousand-bushel official orders faultless commandery investigators to investigate the case by way of review and to bring [the results] to the attention [of the two-thousand-bushel official]. The two-thousand-bushel official or his deputy carefully examines the proposed judgement, passes judgement, and then notifies the county or march offices, these proceed in the case accordingly.

Both rules concern the supervision of the administration of justice that was conducted at the lowest level, that is, counties and marches. The *Yuelu Lüling* (Statutes and edicts held by the Yuelu Academy) rule from Qin concerns all criminal cases and requires reporting only as part of the yearly reporting duties, while the *Ernian lüling* rule from Han applies to potential death penalty cases. Both rules apply to cases that did (or would) result in punishment as well as to those that might, but did (or would) not. Both rules require that the case records are to be submitted to the official in charge of the official in charge of the top-level government agency (the governor in the case of territorial administration), who is referred to as *zhifa* in Qin and as *erqian shi guan* in the Han terminology, and who has to examine each case. The structural and terminological similarities are evidence that in Han, the term *erqian shi guan* had replaced *zhifa* in its functional role as a collective designation of the officials in charge of top-level government agencies.[36] Nonetheless, the Qin term

---

[36] The interpretation of the term *zhifa* as the Qin-period predecessor of the term *erqian shi guan* goes beyond previously available scholarship. The editors of volume 4 of the edition of the Yuelu strips seem to assume that *zhifa* designates a hitherto unknown office, stating that *zhifa* referred to officials who held judicial authority on the imperial or commandery level, with responsibilities for the deciding and submitting of cases, the forwarding of accounts, or the transfer of convict laborers (*Yuelu Lüling* vol. 4, p. 78 n. 77). Peng Hao surmises that *zhifa* were related to the *faguan* 法官 (law office) mentioned in the *Shangjun shu* (26.4) and that the office was abolished in the Han period and substituted by the *yushi zhongcheng* 御史中丞 (palace prosecutor) (Peng 2017; cf. Jin Zhuo's 晉灼 commentary on *zhong zhifa* 中執法, *Hanshu* 1B: 72n10). Zhou Haifeng concludes that there was, along with the *chengxiang* and *yushi*, a *zhifa* at the imperial court, who fulfilled judicial duties, as well as a *zhifa* at commandery and county level responsible for bringing charges in penal cases (Zhou 2018: 248). Cao Lüning infers from rules requiring the *zhifa* to handle personnel matters concerning county-level officials with a salary rank of 500 bushels or less that a *zhifa* himself had a salary rank of "at most" 600 bushels and concludes that *zhifa* should be a general term for officials dispatched by central government officials like the *chengxiang*, *yushi*, or *tingwei*, suggesting to understand expressions such as *yushi chengxiang zhifa* 御史丞相執法 as "*zhifa* of the *yushi* and *chengxiang*" rather than as "*yushi, chengxiang*, and *zhifa*" (Cao 2019).

is instructive for understanding the connotations of the term *fa*, as it is the legal jurisdiction over an agency that is the defining criterion for the official in charge.

The designation *zhifa* is mentioned together with two of the three *san gong* 三公, that is, the *yushi dafu* 御史大夫 "chief prosecutor" and the *chengxiang* 丞相 "chief minister" in *Yuelu Lüling* 5.102, 5.128, and 5.157, and, as subordinated to these two senior officials, in *Yuelu Lüling* 4.309–11, 4.348–49, 5.60–61, 6.237–38. Other passages also confirm that, within the context of territorial administration, *zhifa* is the generic term for the senior official at the level of the commandery (*jun* 郡): In *Yuelu Lüling* 4.287 and 5.24, the *zhifa* and *zhifa cheng* 執法丞 are mentioned together with *zushi* 卒史, which are only known as commandery-level officials subordinated to the governor and vice governor; *Yuelu Lüling* 5.24 also stipulates for *zhifa*, *zhifa cheng*, and *zushi* a sentence reduced by one degree, as opposed to the unreduced sentence for senior county officials, for failure to apprehend fugitive offenders, almost certainly because the commandery-level *zhifa* and vice *zhifa* were more removed from the situation and therefore considered less immediately responsible.[37] *Yuelu Lüling* 6.228–29 makes the hierarchy explicit by stating 縣官…各言屬所執法 "the county offices […] each report to the holder of jurisdiction [*zhifa*] to whom they are subordinated."[38]

2.5   Fa *as a Noun Modifier and as a Verb Modifier*

In addition to its use as a noun, *fa* is also attested adverbially in the meaning "according to the law."[39]

When used before a noun, *fa* usually is used attributively as a modifier in the sense "legal" to distinguish the noun that follows it from uses in non-legal senses. This applies in particular to nouns that refer to the written manifestation of legal rules, such as:

– *Falü* 法律 "legal statutes, statutes of law,"[40] as opposed to *yinlü* 音律,[41] where *lü* is used in its musical meaning "musical pitch; pitch-pipe."

---

[37] It was a general principle that supervising officials received lower sentences (for their failure in oversight) than the lower-level officials who were immediately responsible for a contravention of the rules (e.g., *Xiaolü* 51=*RCL* B 25; *Ernian lüling* 144, 147).

[38] See also *Yuelu Lüling* 4.57, 156, 346, 5.78, 216–17, 262, 335; 6.33–34, 52; as well as *Liye* 9–26.

[39] *Qinlü shiba zhong* 153–54 =*RCL* A 90; *Longgang* 147; *Yuelu Lüling* 4.82; *Shiji* 88: 2566; *yi fa* 以灋(法) in *Wei yu deng zhuang* 236; *Zouyanshu* 78, 146; *Yuelu Lüling* 5.79–78, 6.24.

[40] *Qinghua Zichan* 20; *Yuelu Lüling* 5.328; *Qinlü shiba zhong* 200=*RCL* A 109; *Yushu* 2.

[41] *Zhuangzi* 24: 158 ("Xu wugui" 徐無鬼); *Hanshu* 6: 199.

- *Faling* 法令 "legal edicts, edicts of law,"[42] as opposed to other uses of *ling* such as "command" or "order" and, in particular, the *yueling* 月令 "monthly ordinances."[43]
- Both terms combined: *fa lüling* 法律令 "legal statutes and edicts."[44]

A translation of *falü* as "laws and statutes" or of *faling* as "laws and edicts" would be misleading, at least in technical contexts, as the terms are on different conceptual levels: *Fa* refers, as an abstract term, to legal rules as conveyors of specific stipulations, while *lü* and *ling* refer to their written manifestation, that is, legal rules in their codified form. The *lü* contain *fa* "laws/legal rules" as their content but are not identical with them.

2.6   Verbal Usage of **fa**

In legal contexts, *fa* sometimes occurs verbally in the received literature in the sense of "applying the law against someone," as seen in the following examples:

初，繆公亡善馬。岐下野人共得而食之者三百餘人。吏逐得，欲法之。(*Shiji* 5: 189)
　　Some time earlier, Lord Mu [of Qin, r. 659–621 BCE] had lost a good horse. There were more than three hundred people from the countryside below Mount Qi who together caught and eat it. The authorities pursued and caught them and intended to apply the law against them.

於是太子犯法。衛鞅曰：「法之不行，自上犯之。」將法太子。太子，君嗣也，不可施刑，刑其傅公子虔，黥其師公孫賈。(*Shiji* 68: 2231)
　　Then, the heir-designate offended against the law. Wei Yang [Shang Yang 商鞅, d. 338 BCE] said: "The laws not taking effect owes to His Highness offending against them." He intended to apply the law against the heir-designate. But the heir-designate, being the sovereign's successor, could not be subjected to mutilating punishment; instead, [Wei Yang] had the [heir-designate's] tutor, Gongzi Qian, be mutilated and his preceptor, Gongsun Jia, be tattooed.

2.7   Discussion of Other Interpretations of **fa**

The interpretation, favored by some scholars, of *fa* as a "legal category" (Brown and Sanft 2011) or "categorical principle" (Barbieri-Low and Yates 2015, based on Tomiya 2004, see Barbieri-Low and Yates 2015, 431 footnote 102; 436 footnote

---

[42] *Wei yu deng zhuang* 102-3; *Shangjun shu* 26 ("Ding fen" 定分); *Laozi* 57: 35: 法令滋彰，盜賊多有。"The more obvious the legal provisions, the more robbers and murderers there are;" cf. *Guodian Laozi A* 31 and *Mawangdui Laozi B* 193, where *wu* 物 "section/individual provision within an edict" is used instead of *ling* 令.

[43] See "Yueling" 月令 as chapter title in *Liji* 6, *juan* 15; also *Xuanquan* 272: *sishi yueling wushi tiao* 四時月令五十條; see also *Hanshu* 27.B2: 1417.

[44] *Yushu* 2, 3, 4, 5.

119) leads to translations of *A yu dao tong fa* such as "the action A is in the same category as *dao*" or "the criminals share the same categorical principle with robbers." These translations not only ignore the explanation of the distinction between *yu tong fa* and *yu tong zui* quoted above, but also fail to explain what the specific consequences of "being in the same category" or "sharing the same categorical principle" would be. They implausibly construe the statutes as making, in essence, an ontological statement, rather than as stipulating legal consequences. Importantly, these interpretations also do not fit the specific context in which *fa* occurs in other compounds in legal manuscripts, and lead to implausible and inconsistent results.[45]

Of course, not all instances of *fa* in the legal sources mean "law, legal rules." For example, it is sometimes found in the *Ernian lüling* in its established non-technical sense "method" (*Ernian lüling* 478, 484). In these cases, it is clear from the context which meaning is intended.

---

[45] For example, Barbieri-Low and Yates translate the title of Li Kui's apocryphal early law code *Fajing* 法經 as "Canon of legal principles" and its supposed chapter "Bu fa" 捕法 as "Legal principles on Arrest" (Barbieri-Low and Yates 2015: 558), notwithstanding the fact that the seventh-century sources that first mention Li Kui's supposed *Fajing* claim that it was a precursor of Shang Yang's Qin statutes, that is, as containing specific legal rules, not abstract general principles (see above, p. 240). Elsewhere, divergent translations of *fa* are indicative of the problems associated with the interpretation of *fa* as "category" or "principle": Barbieri-Low and Yates translate *shou xing qiu yi wang fa* as "receive and offer bribes in order to warp the law" (Barbieri-Low and Yates 2015: 465, 1237), *Wei fa* 衛(衛)法 as "the laws of [the state of] Wei" (Barbieri-Low and Yates 2015: 1363) and *Lu fa* 魯法 as "the laws of [the state of] Lu" (Barbieri-Low and Yates 2015: 1371), without explaining why they prefer the translation "law" in these cases to their usual translation. Entirely inconsistent is the translation of the expression *feng fa* 奉法, which occurs twice in an identical context in the *Zouyanshu*: In one instance, Barbieri-Low and Yates (correctly) translate *feng fa* as "upholding the law" (Barbieri-Low and Yates 2015: 1295), in the other (implausibly) as "uphold the categorical principles." Similarly, *yi fa lun* 以法論 is in one case translated as to "sentence according to the law" (Barbieri-Low and Yates 2015: 1291), in another as to "sentence according to the categorical principles" (Barbieri-Low and Yates 2015: 1343). No reason for these diverging translations is given, even though a consistent translation would be called for when *fa* is understood as a technical term. The problems associated with translating *fa* as "category" or "principle" also become evident when Barbieri-Low and Yates translate 有罪當耐，其法不名耐者 as "for one who is guilty of a crime that matches undergoing shaving, but its categorical principle does not name [the penalty of] undergoing shaving […]" and explain: "That the categorical principle under which the criminal is to be charged 'does not name shaving' […] means that undergoing shaving is not mentioned in the pertinent statutes as a penalty" (Barbieri-Low and Yates 2015: 501, 519 note 35). The authors here, in identifying "categorical principle" with the content of the statutes, fully conflate "principle" with "statutory legal rule."

3 Etymology and Conceptual History of the Term *fa*

3.1 Xu Shen's Explanation of the Character **fa** 灋 in the Shuowen jiezi

灋, as the original form of the character writing *fa* (*Jinwenbian* 1611), has been classified by Xu Shen 許慎 in his *Shuowen jiezi* 說文解字 as a syssemantic[46] compound (Xu Shen's *huiyi* 會意 category), being composed of the components 水 *shui* "water"; 廌 *zhi*, explained by Xu Shen as "unicorn;" and *qu* "to remove." According to Xu Shen, the component 水 *shui* signifies that *fa* "levels like water" (*ping zhi ru shui* 平之如水), alluding to notions about the law as ensuring both equality in justice (*ping* in the sense of "level, equal") and a peaceful society (*ping* in the sense of "tranquil, peaceful"), while the component *zhi* refers to the mythical unicorn Xiezhi 解廌, which, according to legend, the ancients called upon to decide lawsuits by butting the one who is not in the right with its horn (*zhi, suoyi chu buzhizhe* 廌, 所以 觸不直者).[47] The third component, 去 *qu*, is understood by Xu Shen in the verbal sense "to remove" (*qu zhi* 去之), maybe with the preceding *buzhizhe* 不直者 as implied object and thus setting out the function of the law as getting rid of what is not right (*Shuowen* 10A, 470a).

3.2 Actual Composition of the Character 灋 and Etymological Relationships of the Words for Which It Was Devised

However, Xu Shen's explanations have more to do with Han period ideas than with the actual composition of the graph. In fact, based on its early writing forms in the oracle bones and bronze inscriptions, the graphical element 廌 within the character 灋 depicts a quadruped with two curved horns and a long tail and does not resemble anything that could be identified as a unicorn. Therefore, against Xu Shen, it is more plausible to interpret the original character form 灋 as a phonosemantic compound (Xu Shen's *xingsheng* 形聲 category), in which the two graphical elements 水 "watercourse" and 廌 "wild animal" form a character that was invented to write the word *pei* (now known in its writing 沛) *GSR* 1957: 501f OC *p$^{h?}$at-s <**p$^{h?}$ap-s "swamp with an abundance of wild game" (*Mengzi* 6.9) and then came to serve as the phonophoric element in 灋, while 去 *qu* "eliminate" functions as the semantic determinative.[48] This character, 灋, was probably originally devised to write a verb with the meaning "to cut down trees, to clear rank growth," a verb most likely

---

[46] Boltz's term for *huiyi* (Boltz 1994: 147–49); Mattos and Norman in their translation of Qiu Xigui's *Chinese Writing* use the term syssemantograph (Qiu Xigui 2000: 15).

[47] See also *Shuowen* 10A, 469b s.v. 廌.

[48] *Bushou* 部首 no. 172 of the *Shuowen jiezi* according to Serruys 1984: 691.

etymologically related to the words *pei* 沛 *GSR* 501f OC *pʔat-s "to topple over, to be uprooted", *fa* 伐 *GSR* 307a OC *bat "to cut down, to fell", *bi* 斃 *GSR* 341f OC *bat-s "to topple (said of a tree); to bring down", and *fei* 廢 *GSR* 257f OC *pat-s "to drop, to abandon, to discard." These etymological relationships are also supported by the Tibetan verbs *phap* "to fall down" (related to Chinese *pei* 沛, see Starostin 2005a) and *bab-pa* "to move downwards, to fall down" (Schuessler 2007: 234, s.v. *fei* 廢), as well as by the Proto-Tibeto-Burman *m-bab* "to fall over" (Matisoff 2003: 336).

In the early bronze inscriptions, the character 灋 was almost exclusively used to write the verb *fei* 廢 OC *pat-s<**pap-s "to drop, to abandon, to discard", for example in the expression *wu fei zhen ming* "you shall not disregard my mandate," written 勿廢朕命 in the *Shijing*[49] (Book of songs) and 勿灋朕令 in the bronze inscriptions.[50] Placed before the expression *bao xian wang* 保先王 "to protect the preceding kings", 灋 was probably used adverbially, as evidenced in *Jinwen* 2.2837; however, in this latter inscription, the meaning of 灋 is disputed. Based on an analysis of the context, the two best options probably are "constantly"[51] and "to a great extent."[52]

In both the paleographic and received sources of the Western Zhou 西周 (ca. 1046–771 BCE) and Chunqiu 春秋 (Spring and Autumn, 770–453 BCE) periods, *fa* 灋 does not occur in a legal sense. In particular, *fa* is not found in the *Shijing*, *Yijing* (Book of changes), or those chapters of the *Shangshu* (Venerated documents) that can be reliable dated to before the Zhanguo period. Significantly, *fa* does also not occur (with only one possible exception in the "Da gao" chapter of the *Shangshu*, see below) in its more general meanings of "model, standard, norm, plan" in these early sources. The implications of this finding for the potential derivation of the legal term are discussed below.

---

[49] *Shijing* ode 261:1 ("Han yi" 韓奕).

[50] *Jinwen* 1.60; 5.2816, 2836, 2837; 8.4199, 4288, 4324, 4340, 4343, 4467. Compare also *Jinwen* 1.272, 285; 5.2826; as well as *Jinchu jinwen* 1.29: 余弗假灋其顯光 "I dare not disregard his illustrious fame"; and *Jinchu jinwen* 2.486: 柞白 (柞伯) 十(稱)弓，無灋矢 "The Count of Zuo raised his bow ten times [to shoot], and there were no arrows [dropped:] missing the target."

[51] As in *Shangshu* "Zi cai" 梓材 § 8: 惟王子子孫孫永保民 "may the king's children and children's children constantly guard the people."

[52] 灋 writing 廢 according to Guo Moruo (cited according to Chen Chusheng 1987: 897) in this singular meaning with reference to ode 204, 4: 廢為殘賊 "but greatly they destroy and damage (the trees)"; cf. *Shangshu* "Luo gao" 洛誥, § 20: 誕保文武受民 "grandly protect the people received by Wen and Wu"; § 30: 惟周公誕保文武受命 "Zhou Gong had grandly preserved the mandate, received by Wen and Wu."

3.3   The Appearance of the Legal Term **fa** *in Zhanguo Sources and Other Zhanguo Uses of the Character* 灋

In the sense of "law, legal rules," *fa* first appears in received and epigraphic sources dating to not earlier than the Eastern Zhou period (770–255 BCE), if not to Zhanguo period and later.

In the epigraphic sources, some of the earliest passages[53] in which the character 灋 writes *fa* in its legal meaning are found in the bamboo manuscripts unearthed from Tomb 1, Guodian, Jingmen 荊門郭店 (Hubei), which can be dated to the late 4th century BCE:

> 呂型(刑)員(云):…折(制)以型(刑)，隹(惟)乍(作)五瘧(虐)之型(刑)曰灋 (*Guodian Ziyi* 26–27, citing *Shangshu* "Lü xing" 呂刑 § 3)[54]
> "The *Lü xing* states: […] [The Miao people] regulated by means of punishments; it is they who created the five oppressive punishments and called them 'the law.'"

> 灋勿(物)慈(滋)章 (*Guodian Laozi A* 31)
> "the clearer the legal provisions […]"

> 折(制)垄(刑)灋 (*Guodian Liude* 2)
> "regulate the laws concerning punishments"

As for the received sources, the "Lü xing" 呂刑 (The punishments [introduced] by the prince of Lü) chapter of the *Shangshu* is probably the earliest received text in which *fa* is used in a legal context (*Shangshu* "Lü xing" § 3). The "Lü xing" was most likely not written before the Eastern Zhou period, but not later than in the fourth century BCE.[55] The use of *fa* as a legal term in the "Lü xing" fits together with the fact that one of the earliest occurences of the term in epigraphic sources is a quote of this "Lü xing" passage in the *Guodian Ziyi*, as cited above. Since the Eastern Zhou, *fa* has been attested in the meaning "legal rules" also in other received and epigraphic texts, often in the context of *xing* 刑 (physical punishments) in the sense of "legal rules for [regulating the application of] physical punishments," leaving no doubt that *fa* is used as a legal term.[56]

In the epigraphic Zhanguo sources, the legal term *fa* is consistently written with the character 灋 or, though rarely at first, with its abbreviated form 法. It is therefore

---

[53] Another text that contains *fa* in its legal sense is *Cheng ren* from the Qinghua collection of Chu bamboo scripts, which is roughly contemporary with the Guodian texts and in which the use of *gu* 辜 "punishable offence" in the same context as *fa* confirms the legal meaning (*Qinghua Cheng ren* 19–20).

[54] A variant of this passage is found in the *Shanghai Ziyi* (slip 14), which instead of 灋 writes 佥; according to the *Shuowen jiezi*, 佥 is the *guwen* 古文 form of 灋/法 (*Shuowen* 10A, 470a).

[55] Creel places the "Lü xing" in the Zhanguo period (Creel 1970: 463), Bodde and Morris suggest a date some centuries after 950 BCE, though not later than the fourth century BCE (Bodde and Morris 1967: 495, 560), while Shaughnessy considers an origin early in the Chunqiu period most likely (Shaughnessy 1993: 380).

[56] *Zuozhuan*, Zhao 7.2; *Zuozhuan*, Zhao 29.5; *Guoyu* 14.5: 425 ("Jin 晉 8"); *Qin Yin yuban* (see Pines 2004); cf. *Zouyanshu* 174.

most likely that no separate character had been created for the legal term *fa*, but that the nearly homophonous 灋 , which had been devised to write other words as discussed above, was used as a loan character for it. The abbreviated written form 法 already appears in seals of the Zhanguo period (He Linyi 1998, 1426) as well as in Qin manuscripts[57] and is used alternately alongside the old character form in manuscripts of the early Han period.[58] However, in the manuscripts the abbreviated form became established as the main form of the character to write *fa* only in the course of the second century BCE (*Yinqueshan Hanjian wenzibian*, 324–25). The legal manuscripts of the Qin and early Han periods recovered from Tomb 11, Shuihudi; from Tomb 6, Longgang, Yunmeng 雲夢龍崗 (Hubei); from Tomb 247, Zhangjiashan; and from Tomb 336, Zhangjiashan; as well as the legal manuscripts acquired by the Yuelu Academy continue to use the older character form 灋 to write the legal term, which is also listed in the manuscript of the character dictionary and synonymicon *Cang Jie pian* 蒼頡篇 that has been discovered in Tomb 1, Shuanggudui, Fuyang 阜陽雙古堆 (Anhui), and that is dated to the reign of Emperor Wen (*Fuyang Cang Jie* pian C 002). In view of the epigraphic evidence, the use of the abbreviated form 法 in received texts dating to before the second century BCE almost certainly reflects later orthographic conventions and not the original appearance of these texts.

Zhanguo and preimperial Qin epigraphical sources, including the legal manuscripts, continue to use the character 灋 to write *fei* 廢 "to drop, to discard, to dismiss" in a number of specific senses and contexts,[59] as had already been the case in pre-Zhanguo sources, before *fa* in the senses "law, legal rule" and "model, standard, plan" had come into use and the character 灋 was employed as a loan character for it. In preimperial Qin sources, the character 灋 was also used to write the place name Feiqiu 廢丘 (*Fengzhenshi* 47, 49=*RCL* E 17). To distinguish *fei* from *fa* in the written language, various character forms that include the phonophoric *fa* 發 OC *pat began to be used to write *fei* in the meaning "to drop, to discard" since as early as the Zhanguo period (He Linyi 1998, 952). In the late Zhanguo period, *fa* 乏 *GSR* 641a OC *bap sometimes appears as still another alternative writing of *fei* 廢 "to drop, to discard"[60] but occasionally also served to write *fa* 法 in the sense "plan" (*Zhongshan Zhao yu tuban*).

Of particular interest is the use of 灋 to write *fei* 廢 in the specific sense of "to dismiss from office; removal from office," as it gives insights into the evolution of

---

[57] *Fangmatan Rishu B* 281; *Wei li zhi guan ji qianshou* 83r[3]; *Yuelu Shu* 1r.

[58] *Zhangjiashan Hanjian wenzibian*, 267: *Suanshushu* 6; *Mawangdui jianbo wenzibian* 396: *Wuxing bian* 346, *Jingfa* 20, and *Yao* 23.

[59] *Falü dawen* 142, 143=*RCL* D120, 121; *Yushu* 3–4; *Guodian Ziyi* 9; *Chuxi jianbo wenzibian*, 860: *Shanghai Xizhe jun lao* 3; "Qinghua zhujian wenzibian," 1250: *Qinghua Fengxu* 8; *Qinghua Bangdao* 2, 11; cf. Bai 2012: 598.

[60] Compare 乏其先王之祭祀 in *Jinwen* 15.9735, c. 18, with 廢其祀 in *Liji* 4.2, juan 11: 297 ("Tan Gong xia" 檀弓下), and 無廢祀 in *Zuozhuan*, Zhao 27.2; also compare 無乏吾事 in *Zhuangzi* 12:75 ("Tian di" 天地) and 無乏事 in *Zhanguo ce* 19.2: 953 ("Zhao 趙 2") with 無廢事 in *Zuozhuan* Xiang 31.6, and *Hanshu* 10: 317.

orthographic rules and the role of imperial decree. In preimperial Qin sources, *fei* in the sense "to dismiss from office; removal from office" is consistently written as 灋.[61] However, when the First Emperor, immediately after the establishment of the empire, changed the ruler's title and other important terms (*Shiji* 6: 236), he decreed that the character 廢 (one of the forms sometimes used earlier to distinguish *fei* from *fa*) was to be the official writing form to be used in *fei guan* 廢官 "to dismiss from office" (*Liye* 8–461 AXII; *Yuelu Lüling* 4.215; 5.36). Consequently, in the legal manuscripts acquired by the Yuelu Academy, dating to imperial Qin, no other character than 廢 is used for removal from office.[62] The First Emperor's decree must have been an important step in reserving the character 灋 and its abbreviated form 法 for writing *fa* in both its legal and more general meanings.

In the received literature as well as in the inscriptions and in the non-legal manuscripts of the Eastern Zhou and early Han periods, *fa* is also attested in the meaning "standard, norm, behavioral pattern" (*Zuozhuan*, Cheng 12.4), in particular as a verb in the meaning "to model oneself on."[63] A typical example is the *Sima Mao bianbo* inscription (dating to the late Chunqiu or early Zhanguo period), in which *shuai* 帥, *xing* 型, *fa* 灋, and *ze* 則 are used as synonymous but distinct terms:

朕文考懿叔亦帥刑(型)灋(法)賊(則)祑(先) 公正德 (*Sima Mao bianbo*)
"Our cultured deceased father Yishu also let himself be guided by, emulated, modeled himself on, and took as a guideline the righteous power of the preceding lords."

Scholars have often considered "standard, norm, behavioral pattern" as the primary meaning of *fa* 法, from which the legal meaning in turn evolved (e.g., Bodde and Morris 1967: 11). However, this hypothesis is doubtful, as there is little evidence that *fa* in the sense "standard, norm, behavioral pattern; to model oneself on" appears earlier than *fa* in the legal sense, as both uses are attested only in sources dating to the Eastern Zhou period or later. The only exception might be found in the "Da gao" chapter of the *Shangshu*, which is generally accepted as dating to the early Zhou period (Creel 1970: 1:449; Shaughnessy 1993: 379) and in which the received text contains an instance of *fa* which has been usually understood as "plan (of a house)."[64] However, the evidentiary value of this singular occurrence is limited from the outset by the fact that no palaeographic version of the "Da gao" 大誥 chapter is available, making it impossible to know whether the received version corresponds to early representations of the text. In view of the "Da gao" example, and in spite of the lack of other written evidence, the early existence of a word *fa* meaning

---

[61] *Qinlü zachao* 4, 10, 11, 15, 21, 22=*RCL* C 2, 6, 8, 13, 14; *Falü dawen* 59=*RCL* D 47.

[62] *Yuelu Lüling* 4.212, 222, 238; 5.53, 54, 96, 194, 256, 265, 266, 274, 276, 331; 6.56, 70, 151, 192, 206, 249.

[63] *Jinwen* 15.9735, c. 3; *Guodian Laozi A* 23; *Zhouyi* 7:79a ("Xici shang" 繫辭上); *Zhanguo ce* 14.1: 707 ("Chu 楚 1"); *Shiji* 119: 3100.

[64] *Shangshu*, "Da gao" 大誥 § 11: *Ruo kao zuo shi, ji zhi fa* [...] 若考作室，既底法 "if a father starts to build a house, and when he has (effected =) settled the plan [...]" (Karlgren's translation). Cf. *Fangmatan Rishu B* 281.

"standard, pattern, plan" would also be substantiated if an etymological relationship to Tibetan *babs* "shape, form" (related to *fa* 法 according to Starostin 2005b; see also Schuessler 2007: 229, s.v. *fan* 凡 "general rule") and, in turn, maybe also to Chinese *fan* 範 *GSR* 626d OC *bam? "casting mold"[65] could be established (Tōdō 1978: 725), as this would indicate that *fa* "standard, pattern, plan" belongs to the shared Sino-Tibetan lexicon, thus to an early stratum of the language. However, this latter argument remains tenuous, not the least due to the unsatisfactory state of Sino-Tibetan etymological research. Therefore, based on currently available evidence, it is most likely that both uses of *fa*—in the sense "law, legal rule" and "model, standard, norm, plan"—emerged simultaneously in the Zhanguo period, without one preceding or assuming the other.

4 Conclusions

It is no accident that the term *fa* in its legal sense appears only in the Eastern Zhou, if not the Zhanguo period. Its emergence is connected to the social and intellectual changes characteristic for this period. In particular, *fa* is related to the development of a legal system that came to be characterized, among other aspects, by a division of labor between different levels of judicial administration, by formalized procedures, by technical texts and a technical language, and by specialized officials with expert knowledge. The legal sources indicate that the term *fa* played an important role on multiple technical levels. In its meaning "(specific) legal rule," it served to enable cross-references within the mesh of statutory rules in a way that avoided ambiguity and ensured efficacy. A phrase such as *yu...tong fa* allowed multiple rules, defining multiple offences, to reference a single set of rules defining legal consequences, thereby ensuring consistency in the application of the law. When *fa* was used as part of a generic designation of an official function, *zhifa* "holder of jurisdiction," that applied to different officials at different places in the government structure who shared a specific role, the term embodies an abstraction that served to assign clear roles and responsibilities within a multi-layered system of organization and thus ensured its efficient operation. In its broader sense, referring to the whole of the legal structure, to "the law," the term *fa* is intimately connected to notions of impartial and consistent application of the law throughout society. In all its different roles, the term is part of a social practice that was not only an expression but also a crucial enabling factor of the changes of the Zhanguo period that led to the establishment of the imperial system. It is an open question whether this social practice was made possible by the intellectual innovations of the period, or whether it might not have been the other way around: that the development of more and more

---

[65] In the early Han statutes on cash from Tomb 336, Zhangjiashan, *fa* 灋 was borrowed to write the nearly homophonous word *fan* 范 in the meaning "casting mold", see *Hanlü shiliu zhang* 270: 上所為錢、錢灋(范)及諸其它 "submit the cash and the mold used for the cash [illegally] produced/counterfeited as well as all the other [tools] to the competent authority."

sophisticated and multi-layered practices in different fields were the prerequisite for the new schools of thought.

References

Bai, Yulan 白於藍. 2012. *Compilation of Loan Graphs Used in Warring States, Qin, and Han Period Manuscripts on Bamboo or Silk* 戰國秦漢簡帛古書通假字彙纂. Fuzhou: Fujian renmin.

Barbieri-Low, Anthony J., and Robin Yates. 2015. *Law, State, and Society in Early Imperial China. A Study with Critical Edition and Translation of the Legal Texts from Zhangjiashan Tomb no. 247.* 2 vols. Leiden: Brill.

Bodde, Derk. 1981. Basic Conceptions of Chinese Law: The Genesis and Evolution of Legal Thought in Traditional China. In *Essays on Chinese Civilization*, 171–194. Princeton: Princeton University Press.

Bodde, Derk, and Clarence Morris. 1967. *Law in Imperial China: Exemplified by 190 Ch'ing Dynasty Cases (Translated from the "Hsing-an hui-lan"), With Historical, Social, and Juridical Commentaries.* Cambridge, MA: Harvard University Press.

Boltz, William G. 1994. *The Origin and Early Development of the Chinese Writing System.* New Haven, CT: American Oriental Society.

Brown, Miranda, and Charles Sanft. 2011. Categories and Legal Reasoning in Early Imperial China: The Meaning of *Fa* in Recovered Texts. *Oriens extremus* 50: 283–306.

Cao, Lüning 曹旅寧. 2019. "On the Official *zhifa* Mentioned in Volume 5 of the Qin Manuscripts Held by the Yuelu Academy" 說嶽麓秦簡(伍)中的執法. Bamboo and Silk Manuscripts 簡帛 website, January 1, 2019, http://www.bsm.org.cn/?qinjian/8032.html.

Chen, Chusheng 陳初生. 1987. *Dictionary of Characters Frequently Used in Bronze Inscriptions* 金文常用字典. Xi'an: Shaanxi renmin.

Chen, Wei 陳偉, Wuhan daxue jianbo yanjiu zhongxin 武漢大學簡帛研究中心 [Center for the Research of Manuscripts on Bamboo and Silk at Wuhan University], Hubei sheng bowuguan 湖北省博物館 [Hubei Province Museum], and Hubei sheng wenwu kaogu yanjiu suo 湖北省文物考古研究所 [Cultural Relics and Archeology Institute of Hubei Province], eds. 2014. *Manuscripts on Bamboo and Wood from the Qin Tomb in Shuihudi* 睡虎地秦墓簡牘. Vol. 1 (in 3 continuously paginated books) of *Collection of Qin Manuscripts on Bamboo and Wood* 秦簡牘合集, ed. Chen Wei 陳偉. Wuhan: Wuhan daxue chubanshe. (A new and updated edition of the Qin manuscripts excavated in Tombs 4 and 11, Shuihudi 睡虎地, Tomb 6, Longgang 龍崗, Tomb 50, Haojiaping 郝家坪, Tomb 30, Zhoujiatai 周家臺, Tomb 36, Yueshan 嶽山, and Tomb 1, Fangmatan 放馬灘, published in conjunction with the institutions responsible for the study and preservation of the respective manuscripts and combining the best-quality photographs available with transcriptions and commentary based on the Chinese scholarship that has accumulated since discovery of these texts.)

——— 陳偉. 2017a. *The Collation of Qin Manuscripts on Bamboo and Wood and an Investigation of the Institutions of Which the Manuscripts Give Evidence* 秦簡牘校讀及所見制度考察. Wuhan: Wuhan daxue chubanshe.

——— 陳偉. 2017b. "Comprehensive Explanation of the 'Imperial Instruction of Day *jiawu*, Tenth Month, First Regnal Year of Emperor Ershi of Qin'" 《秦二始元年十月甲午詔書》通釋. *Jiang Han kaogu* 江漢考古 2017 (1): 124–126.

Chuxi jianbo wenzibian 楚系簡帛文字編 [*Compilation of Characters Used in Bamboo and Silk Manuscripts Connected with the State of Chu*]. 2008. Compiled by Teng Rensheng 滕壬生. Revised and enlarged edition. Wuhan: Hubei jiaoyu.

Creel, Herrlee Glessner. 1970. *The Origins of Statecraft in China. Vol. 1, The Western Chou Empire.* Chicago: University of Chicago Press.

Emmerich, Reinhard. 2017. Chinas Zweiter Kaiser in neuem Lichte? In *Über den Alltag hinaus: Festschrift für Thomas O. Höllmann zum 65. Geburtstag*, ed. Shing Müller and Armin Selbitschka, 53–87. Wiesbaden: Harrassowitz.

Ernian lüling 二年律令 [*Statutes and Edicts of the Second Year*]. In Zhangjiashan ersiqi hao Hanmu zhujian zhengli xiaozu 2001: 5–50 (Reproductions 圖版); and in Peng Hao, Chen Wei, and Kudō Motoo 2007: 1–57 (Reproductions 圖版) and 85–328 (Transcription 釋文). [References are to slip number.] (An early Han bamboo manuscript with twenty-seven chapters of statutes, as well as a collection of "Edicts on Fords and Passes" concerned with the regulation of border transit, in a version dating to 186 BC, the second regnal year of Empress Lü, and discovered in Tomb 247, Zhangjiashan, Jiangling, Hubei Province.)

Falü dawen 法律答問 [*Answers to Questions on Legal Statutes*]. In Shuihudi Qinmu zhujian zhengli xiaozu 1990: 47–66 (Reproductions 圖版) and 91–144 (Transcription and Annotation 釋文注釋); and in Chen Wei et al. 2014: 191–281 (Transcription and Annotation) and 1027–88 (Reproductions 圖版 at ratio 2:1). [References are to slip number.] (A Qin period bamboo manuscript containing commentary in question-and-answer form to different penal statutes, discovered in Tomb 11, Shuihudi, Hubei Province.)

Fangmatan Rishu B = Yi hao Qinmu zhujian yi zhong "Rishu" 一號秦墓竹簡乙種《日書》 [*"Daybook" B of Qin Tomb 1*]. 2009. In *Qin Bamboo Manuscripts from Fangmatan, Tianshui* 天水放馬灘秦簡, ed. Gansu sheng wenwu kaogu yanjiusuo 甘肅省文物考古研究所 [Cultural Relics and Archeology Institute of Gansu Province], 15–55 (Reproductions 圖版) and 87–106 (Transcription 釋文). Beijing: Zhonghua shuju. [References are to slip number.] (A Qin-period bamboo manuscript containing the second of two hemerological manuals discovered in Tomb 1, Fangmatan, Gansu Province.)

Feng, Qiyong 馮其庸 and Deng, Ansheng 鄧安生. 2006. *Collected Explanations of Loan Graphs* 通假字彙釋. Beijing: Beijing daxue chubanshe.

Fengzhenshi 封診式 [*Models of Sealing and Judicial Inspection*]. In Shuihudi Qinmu zhujian zhengli xiaozu 1990: 67–78 (Reproductions 圖版) and 145–64 (Transcription and Annotation 釋文注釋); and in Chen Wei et al. 2014: 282–319 (Transcription and Annotation) and 1089–1124 (Reproductions 圖版 at ratio 2:1). [References are to slip number.] (A Qin period bamboo manuscript discovered in Tomb 11, Shuihui, Hubei Province, including model records for sealing the property of suspected offenders, for gathering evidence by judicial inspection, and for investigation and interrogation in the course of criminal proceedings.)

Fölster, Max Jakob, and Thies Staack. 2021. Collation in Early Imperial China: From Administrative Procedure to Philological Tool. In *Exploring Written Artefacts: Objects, Methods, and Concepts*, ed. Jörg B. Quenzer, 889–912. Berlin: De Gruyter.

Fuyang Cang Jie pian = "Fuyang Hanjian Cang Jie pian" 阜陽漢簡《蒼頡篇》 ["The Han-period bamboo manuscript *Cang Jie pian*"]. 1983. By Wenwuju Guwenxian yanjiushi 文物局古文獻研究室 [Ancient Texts Research Office of the Administration of Cultural Heritage], Anhui sheng Fuyang diqu bowuguan 安徽省阜陽地區博物館 [Museum of the Fuyang Region of Anhui Province], and Fuyang Hanjian zhenglizu 阜陽漢簡整理組 [Team for Editing the Han Bamboo Manuscripts from Fuyang]. *Wenwu* 1983.2: 24–34. [References are to slip number.] (A primer for learning characters originally composed in the Qin period found on a bamboo manuscript dating to the Han period and discovered in Tomb 1, Shuanggudui, Fuyang, Anhui Province.)

GSR = "Grammata Serica Recensa". 1957. By Bernhard Karlgren. *Bulletin of the Museum of Far Eastern Antiquities* 29: 1–332. [References are to *xiesheng* series number and index letter for the character.]

Guodian Laozi A = Laozi jia 老子甲 [*Manuscript A of the "Laozi"*]. 1998. In *Bamboo Manuscripts from the Chu Tomb of Guodian* 郭店楚墓竹簡, ed. Jingmen shi bowuguan 荊門市博物館 [Museum of Jingmen City], 3–6 (Reproductions 圖版) and 111–17 (Transcription and Annotation 釋文注釋). Beijing: Wenwu. [References are to slip number.] (A late Warring States bamboo manuscript from Chu containing a fragment of the Daoist classic *Laozi*, discovered in Tomb 1, Guodian, Hubei Province.)

Guodian Liude = *Liude* 六德 [*The Six Virtues*]. 1998. In *Bamboo Manuscripts from the Chu Tomb of Guodian* 郭店楚墓竹簡, ed. Jingmen shi bowuguan 荊門市博物館 [Museum of Jingmen City], 67–73 (Reproductions 圖版) and 185–190 (Transcription and Annotation 釋文注釋). Beijing: Wenwu. [References are to slip number.] (A late Warring States bamboo manuscript from Chu containing a previously unknown philosophical text, discovered in Tomb 1, Guodian, Hubei Province.)

Guodian Ziyi = *Ziyi* 緇衣 [*The "Ziyi"*]. 1998. In *Bamboo Manuscripts from the Chu Tomb of Guodian* 郭店楚墓竹簡, ed. Jingmen shi bowuguan 荊門市博物館 [Museum of Jingmen City], 15–20 (Reproductions 圖版) and 127–37 (Transcription and Annotation 釋文注釋). Beijing: Wenwu. [References are to slip number.] (A late Warring States bamboo manuscript from Chu with a version of the chapter "Ziyi" of the classic *Liji*, discovered in Tomb 1, Guodian, Hubei Province.)

Guoyu = *Guoyu jijie* 國語集解 [*Collected Explanations for the "Speeches of the States"*]. 2002. Annotated by Xu Yuangao 徐元誥 (1878–1955), collated by Wang Shumin 王樹民 and Shen Changyun 沈長雲. Beijing: Zhonghua shuju.

Han Feizi = *Han Feizi jijie* 韓非子集解 [*Collected Explanations for the "Han Feizi"*]. 1998. Compiled by Wang, Xianshen 王先慎 (1859–1922), collated by Zhong, Zhe 鍾哲. Beijing: Zhonghua shuju.

Hanlü shiliu zhang 漢律十六章 [*Sixteen Chapters of Han Statutes*]. In Jingzhou bowuguan and Peng Hao 2022: 39–72 (Reproductions 圖版) and 159–216 (Transcription 釋文). [References are to slip number.] (An early Western Han bamboo manuscript with sixteen chapters of statutes as well as a collection of edicts related to the recognition of merits, discovered in Tomb 336, Zhangjiashan, Jiangling, Hubei Province.)

Hanshu 漢書 [*History of the Han*]. 1997. By Ban, Gu 班固 (32–92) et al. Annotated by Yan, Shigu 顏師古 (581–645). Beijing: Zhonghua shuju.

He, Linyi 何琳儀. 1998. *Dictionary of Ancient Character Forms from the Warring States Period: The Phonological System of the Warring States Characters* 戰國古文字典: 戰國文字聲系. 2 vols. Beijing: Zhonghua shuju.

Hulsewé, A. F. P. 1955. *Remnants of Han Law. Vol. 1, Introductory Studies and an Annotated Translation of Chapters 22 and 23 of the "History of the Former Han Dynasty"*. Leiden: Brill.

———. 1985. *Remnants of Ch'in Law: An Annotated Translation of the Ch'in Legal and Administrative Rules of the 3rd Century B.C. Discovered in Yün-meng Prefecture, Hu-pei Province, in 1975*. Leiden: Brill.

Hunan sheng wenwu kaogu yanjiusuo 湖南省文物考古研究所 [Cultural Relics and Archeology Institute of Hunan Province] and Yiyang shi wenwuchu 益陽市文物處 [Cultural Relics Office of Yiyang City]. 2016. "Brief Report of Finds at the Archaeological Site of Well 9, Tuzishan, Yiyang, Hunan Province" 湖南省益陽兔子山遺址九號井發掘簡報. *Wenwu* 文物 2016.5: 32–48.

Jinchu jinwen = *Jinchu Yin Zhou jinwen jilu* 近出殷周金文集錄 [*Collection of Recently Excavated Shang- and Zhou-Period Bronze Inscriptions*]. 2002. Compiled by Liu, Yu 劉雨 and Lu Yan 盧岩. 4 vols. Beijing: Zhonghua shuju.

Jingzhou bowuguan 荊州博物館 [Museum of Jingzhou] and Peng Hao 彭浩. 2022. *Bamboo Manuscripts from a Han Tomb in Zhangjiashan (Tomb 336)* 張家山漢墓竹簡〔三三六號墓〕. Beijing: Wenwu.

Jinshu 晉書 [*History of the Jin*]. 1974. By Fang, Xuanling 房玄齡 (579–648) et al. Beijing: Zhonghua shuju.

Jinwen = *Yin Zhou jinwen jicheng* 殷周金文集成 [*Comprehensive Collection of Shang- and Zhou-Period Bronze Inscriptions*]. 1984–1994. Compiled by Zhongguo shehui kexueyuan Kaogu yanjiusuo 中國社會科學院考古研究所 [Archeology Institute of the Chinese Academy of Social Sciences]. 18 vols. Beijing: Zhonghua shuju.

Jinwenbian 金文編 [*Compilation of Character Forms in Bronze Inscriptions*]. 1985. Compiled by Rong Geng 容庚. Expanded new edition. Beijing: Zhonghua shuju. [References are to character number.]

Karlgren, Bernhard. 1944. Glosses on the Siao ya Odes. *Bulletin of the Museum of Far Eastern Antiquities* 16: 25–169.

Kern, Martin. 2000. *The Stele Inscriptions of Ch'in Shih-huang: Text and Ritual in Early Chinese Imperial Representation*. New Haven: American Oriental Society.

Korolkov, Maxim [Корольков, Максим Владимирович]. 2017. "Новый источник по земельной реформе в царстве Цинь эпохи Чжаньго: «Указ о полях» 309 г. до н.э. из циньского погребения в Хаоцзяпине" [A new source on the land reform in the state of Qin during the Zhanguo period: The 309 BCE "Ordinance on fields" from the Qin tomb at Haojiaping]. In: *Общество и государство в Китае: XLVII научная конференция* [State and Society in China: 47th Conference], 1: 68–106.

Laozi = *Laozi zhu* 老子注 [*Commentary to the "Laozi"*]. 1954. Commented by Wang Bi. In *Comprehensive Collection of the Masters' Writings* 諸子集成, vol. 3. Beijing: Zhonghua shuju. [References are to section number and page.]

Lau, Ulrich, and Michael Lüdke. 2012. *Exemplarische Rechtsfälle vom Beginn der Han-Dynastie: Eine kommentierte Übersetzung des "Zouyanshu" aus Zhangjiashan/Provinz Hubei*. In *Research Institute for Languages and Cultures of Asia and Africa (ILCAA)*. Tokyo University of Foreign Studies.

———. Forthcoming. "The Craft and Terminology of Early Chinese Law: A Study of the *Zouyanshu* 奏讞書 Case Collection and the *Ernian lüling* 二年律令 Law Code Discovered in an Early Han Tomb in Zhangjiashan, Hubei Province."

Lau, Ulrich, and Thies Staack. 2016. *Legal Practice in the Formative Stages of the Chinese Empire: An Annotated Translation of the Exemplary Qin Criminal Cases from the Yuelu Academy Collection*. Leiden: Brill.

Li, Xueqin 李學勤. 1982. "Research on a Wooden Board from Haojiaping, Qingchuan" 青川郝家坪木牘研究. *Wenwu* 1982.10: 68–72. (Study of a statute on agriculture written on a wooden board dating to preimperial Qin and discovered in Tomb 50, Haojiaping, Qingchuan, Sichuan Province.)

Liji = *Liji jijie* 禮記集解 [*Collected Explanations for the "Record of Rites"*]. 1995. Compiled by Sun, Xidan 孫希旦 (1736–1784), ed. Shen, Xiaohuan 沈嘯寰 and Wang, Xingxian 王星賢. Beijing: Zhonghua shuju.

Liye 8- = *Liye Qin jiandu jiaoshi* 里耶秦簡牘校釋 [*Qin Manuscripts on Bamboo Slips and Wooden Tablets from Liye, Collated and Annotated*], vol. 1. 2012. Ed. Chen Wei 陳偉. Wuhan daxue chubanshe. [References are to slip number.] (First volume of an annotated transcription of Qin-period bamboo slips and wooden tablets with fragments of administrative documents relating to the prefecture of Qianling, discovered in Well 1, Liye, Hunan Province.)

Liye 9- = *Liye Qin jiandu jiaoshi* 里耶秦簡牘校釋 [*Qin Manuscripts on Bamboo Slips and Wooden Tablets from Liye, Collated and Annotated*], vol. 2. 2018. Ed. Chen Wei 陳偉. Wuhan daxue chubanshe. [References are to slip number.] (Second volume of an annotated transcription of Qin-period bamboo slips and wooden tablets with fragments of administrative documents relating to the prefecture of Qianling, discovered in Well 1, Liye, Hunan Province.)

Longgang = *Longgang Qinjian* 龍崗秦簡 [*Qin Bamboo Manuscripts from Longgang*]. 2001. Ed. Zhongguo wenwu yanjiusuo 中國文物研究所 [Chinese Cultural Relics Institute] and Hubei sheng wenwu kaogu yanjiusuo 湖北省文物考古研究所 [Cultural Relics and Archeology Institute of Hubei Province]. Beijing: Zhonghua shuju. [References are to slip or tablet number.] (Fragments of statutes written on bamboo slips and an official record of a judicial decision in a criminal case written on a wooden board, dating to the Qin period and discovered in Tomb 6, Longgang, Hubei Province.)

Lüdke, Michael. 2004. "Professional Practice: Law in Qin and Han China." PhD dissertation, Heidelberg University.

Lüshi chunqiu = *Lüshi chunqiu jiaoshi* 呂氏春秋新校釋 [*The Annals of Lü Buwei, Newly Collated and Annotated*]. 1995. Compiled and annotated by Chen, Qiyou 陳奇猷. Shanghai: Shanghai guji.

Matisoff, James A. 2003. *Handbook of Proto-Tibeto-Burman: System and Philosophy of Sino-Tibetan Reconstruction*. Berkeley: University of California Press.

Mawangdui jianbo wenzibian 馬王堆簡帛文字編 [*Compilation of Character Forms in the Bamboo and Silk Manuscripts from Mawangdui*]. 2001. Compiled by Chen, Songchang 陳松長. Beijing: Wenwu.

Mawangdui Laozi B = Laozi yi ben 老子乙本 [*Manuscript B of the "Laozi"*]. 1980. In Guojia wenwuju Guwenxian yanjiushi 國家文物局古文獻研究室 [Ancient Texts Research Office of the State Administration of Cultural Heritage]. *Silk Manuscripts from the Han Tomb of Mawangui (Vol. 1): Reproductions of Manuscript B of the "Laozi" and of Lost Ancient Texts Found at the Front of the Silk Roll* 馬王堆漢墓帛書(壹):老子乙本及卷前古佚書圖版, unnumbered pages (Reproductions 圖版) and 89–100 (Transcription 釋文). Beijing: Wenwu. [References are to slip number.] (A silk manuscript with one of two versions of the Daoist classic *Laozi* discovered in Tomb 3, Mawangdui, Hunan Province.)

Mengzi = Mengzi yizhu 孟子譯注 [*The "Mengzi", Translated and Annotated*]. 1992. Annotated by Yang, Bojun 楊伯峻. Beijing: Zhonghua shuju.

Morgan, Daniel Patrick, and Karine Chemla. 2018. Writing in Turns: An Analysis of Scribal Hands in the Bamboo Manuscript *Suan shu shu* 算數書 (Writings on Mathematical Procedures) from Zhangjiashan tomb no. 247. *Bamboo and Silk* 1 (1): 152–190.

Peng, Hao 彭浩. 2017. "Discussing the Official *zhifa* Mentioned in Volume Four of the Qin Manuscripts Held by the Yuelu Academy" 談《嶽麓書院藏秦簡(肆)》的執法. *Chutu wenxian yu falüshi yanjiu* 出土文獻與法律史研究 6: 84–94.

Peng, Hao 彭浩, Chen, Wei 陳偉, and Kudō, Motoo 工藤元男, eds. 2007. *The "Statutes and Edicts of the Second Year" and the "Documents on Legal Cases Submitted for Higher-Level Decision that Have Been Memorialized to the Ruler": The Legal Documents from Han Tomb 247, Zhangjiashan, Annotated and Explicated* 二年律令與奏讞書:張家山二四七號漢墓出土法律文獻釋讀. Shanghai: Shanghai guji. (New edition, superseding the original 2001 edition, of the two early Han legal manuscripts *Ernian lüling* and *Zouyanshu*, discovered in Tomb 247, Zhangjiashan, Hubei, Province, with new reproductions based on infrared photographs and a revised annotated transcription.)

Pines, Yuri. 2004. The Question of Interpretation: Qin History in Light of New Epigraphic Sources. *Early China* 29: 1–44.

Pokora, Timoteus. 1959. The Canon of Laws of Li K'uei: A Double Falsification? *Archiv Orientalni* 27: 96–121.

Qin jiandu wenzibian 秦簡牘文字編 [*Compilation of Character Forms in Qin Manuscripts on Bamboo and Wood*]. 2012. Compiled by Fang, Yong 方勇. Fuzhou: Fuzhou renmin.

Qin Yin yuban 秦駰玉版 [*The Qin-Period Jade Tablet of Yin*]. 2000. In Li, Xueqin, "Secrets of a Qin-Period Jade Tablet" 秦玉牘所隱. *Gugong bowuyuan yuankan* 故宮博物院院刊 2000.2: 41–45. (*Moben* 摹本 facsimile and annotated transcription, with further commentary, of a jade tablet dating to preimperial Qin.)

Qinghua Cheng ren = Cheng ren 成人. 2019. In *Warring States-Period Bamboo Manuscripts Held by Tsinghua University* 清華大學藏戰國竹簡, vol. 9, ed. Qinghua daxue chutu wenxian yanjiu yu baohu zhongxin 清華大學出土文獻研究與保護中心 [Center for the Research and Protection of Excavated Texts at Tsinghua University] and Huang, Dekuan 黃德寬, 12–15 (Reproductions in original size 原大圖版) and 153–167 (Transcription and Annotation 釋文注釋). Shanghai: Zhong Xi shuju. [References are to slip number.] (A manuscript in the unprovenanced collection of bamboo slips held by Tsinghua University that are attributed to the Warring States kingdom of Chu.)

"Qinghua zhujian wenzibian" = "Qinghua daxue cang Zhanguo zhujian 1–8 wenzibian" 清華大學藏戰國竹簡 1–8 文字編 [*Compilation of Character Forms in Volumes 1 to 8 of the Warring States-Period Bamboo Manuscripts Held by Tsinghua University*]. 2019. Compiled by Ma, Ji 馬繼. M.A. thesis, Huadong shifan daxue 華東師範大學.

Qinghua Fengxu = Feng xu zhi ming 封許之命. 2015. In *Warring States-Period Bamboo Manuscripts Held by Tsinghua University* 清華大學藏戰國竹簡, vol. 5, ed. Qinghua daxue chutu wenxian yanjiu yu baohu zhongxin 清華大學出土文獻研究與保護中心 and Li, Xueqin 李學勤, 4-5 (Reproductions in original size 原大圖版) and 117-123 (Transcription and Annotation 釋文注釋). Shanghai: Zhong Xi shuju. [References are to slip number.] (A manuscript in the unprovenanced collection of bamboo slips held by Tsinghua University that are attributed to the Warring States kingdom of Chu.)

Qinghua Zichan = Zichan 子產. 2016. In *Warring States-Period Bamboo Manuscripts Held by Tsinghua University* 清華大學藏戰國竹簡, vol. 6, ed. Qinghua daxue chutu wenxian yanjiu yu baohu zhongxin 清華大學出土文獻研究與保護中心 [Center for the Research and Protection of Excavated Texts at Tsinghua University] and Li, Xueqin 李學勤, 83–99 (Reproductions in original size 原大圖版) and 136–45 (Transcription and Annotation 釋文注釋). Shanghai: Shanghai wenyi. [References are to slip number.] (A manuscript in the unprovenanced collection of bamboo slips held by Tsinghua University that are attributed to the Warring States kingdom of Chu.)

Qinghua Bangdao = Zhi bang zhi dao 治邦之道. 2018. In *Warring States-Period Bamboo Manuscripts Held by Tsinghua University* 清華大學藏戰國竹簡, vol. 8, ed. Qinghua daxue chutu wenxian yanjiu yu baohu zhongxin 清華大學出土文獻研究與保護中心 and Li, Xueqin 李學勤, 10-13 (Reproductions in original size 原大圖版) and 69-84 (Transcription and Annotation 釋文注釋). Shanghai: Zhong Xi shuju. [References are to slip number.] (A manuscript in the unprovenanced collection of bamboo slips held by Tsinghua University that are attributed to the Warring States kingdom of Chu.)

Qinlü shiba zhong 秦律十八種 [*Eighteen Qin Statutes*]. In Shuihudi Qinmu zhujian zhengli xiaozu 1990: 13–31 (Reproductions 圖版) and 17–65 (Transcription and Annotation 釋文注釋); and in Chen, Wei et al. 2014: 41–152 (Transcription and Annotation) and 919–87 (Reproductions 圖版 at ratio 2:1). [References are to slip number.] (A bamboo manuscript containing a selection from eighteen administrative Qin statutes, discovered in Tomb 11, Shuihudi, Yunmeng, Hubei Province.)

Qinlü zachao 秦律雜抄 [*Miscellaneous Excerpts of Qin Statutes*]. In Shuihudi Qinmu zhujian zhengli xiaozu 1990: 41–46 (Reproductions 圖版) and 77–90 (Transcription and Annotation 釋文注釋); and in Chen, Wei et al. 2014: 166–90 (Transcription and Annotation) and 1011–26 (Reproductions 圖版 at ratio 2:1). [References are to slip number.] (A bamboo manuscript containing miscellaneous excerpts of Qin statutes, discovered in Tomb 11, Shuihudi, Yunmeng, Hubei Province.)

Qiu, Xigui 裘錫圭. 2000. *Chinese Writing*. Translated by Gilbert L. Mattos and Jerry Norman. Berkeley: Society for the Study of Early China and the Institute of East Asian Studies, University of California.

RCL = Hulsewé 1985. [References are to group and text number.]

Sanjian = Sanjian jiandu heji 散見簡牘合輯 [*Compilation of Bamboo Slips and Wooden Boards Found at Various Places*]. 1990. Ed. Li, Junming 李均明 and He, Shuangquan 何雙全. 1990. Beijing: Wenwu. [References are to slip number.] (A compilation of often fragmentary manuscripts on bamboo slips or wooden boards dating to the Warring States, Qin, and Han periods and discovered at different excavation sites.)

Schuessler, Axel. 2007. *ABC Etymological Dictionary of Old Chinese*. Honolulu: Hawaii University Press.

Serruys, Paul L.-M. 1984. On the System of the Pu Shou (部首) in the *Shuo-wen chieh-tzu* (說文解字). *Bulletin of the Institute of History and Philology, Academia Sinica* 55 (4): 651–754.

Shanghai Ziyi = Ziyi 紂衣 [*The "Ziyi"*]. 2001. In *Writings on Bamboo from Warring States-Period Chu held by the Shanghai Museum* 上海博物館藏戰國楚竹書, ed. Ma, Chengyuan 馬承源, 1: 43–68 (Reproductions 圖版) and 1: 169–214 (Transcription 釋文). Shanghai: Shanghai guji. [References are to slip number.] (A late Warring States bamboo manuscript from Chu, of unknown provenance and held by the Shanghai Museum, with a version of the chapter "Ziyi" of the classic *Liji*.)

Shanghai Xizhe jun lao = Xizhe jun lao 昔者君老. 2002. In *Chu Bamboo manuscripts kept in Shanghai Museum* 上海博物館藏戰國楚竹書, ed. Ma, Chengyuan 馬承源, 2:85-90

(Reproductions 圖版) and 2:239-246 (Transcription 釋文). Shanghai: Shanghai guji chubanshe. [References are to slip number.] (A late Warring States bamboo manuscript from Chu, of unknown provenance and held by the Shanghai Museum.)

Shangjun shu = *Shangjun shu jiaoshu* 商君書校疏 [*The Book of Lord Shang, Collated and Annotated*]. 2012. Compiled and annotated by Zhang Jue 張覺. Beijing: Zhishi chanquan chubanshe. [References are to chapter and section number and chapter name]

Shangshu 尚書 = "The Book of Documents." 1950. Translated by Bernhard Karlgren. *Bulletin of the Museum of Far Eastern Antiquities* 22: 1–81. [References are to chapter name and section.]

Shaughnessy, Edward L. 1993. *Shang shu* 尚書 (*Shu ching* 書經). In *Early Chinese Texts: A Bibliographical Guide*, ed. Michael Loewe, 376–389. Berkeley: Society for the Study of Early China; Institute of East Asian Studies, University of California.

Shiji 史記 [*Records of the Scribe*]. 1997. By Sima, Qian 司馬遷 (ca. 145–90 BCE) et al. Annotated by Zhang, Shoujie 張守節, Sima, Zhen 司馬貞, and Pei, Yin 裴駰. Beijing: Zhonghua shuju.

Shijing 詩經 = *The Book of Odes*. 1950. Translated by Bernhard Karlgren. Stockholm: Museum of Far Eastern Antiquities. [References are to ode and verse.]

Shuihudi Qinmu zhujian zhengli xiaozu 睡虎地秦墓竹簡整理小組 [Team for Editing the Bamboo Manuscripts of the Qin Tomb in Shuihudi], ed. 1990. *Bamboo Manuscripts from the Qin Tomb of Shuihuidi* 睡虎地秦墓竹簡. Beijing: Wenwu. (Edition of the Qin bamboo manuscripts discovered in Tomb 11, Shuihudi, Yunmeng, Hubei Province, with a revised transcription as compared to the original 1977 edition.)

Shuowen = *Shuowen jiezi zhu* 說文解字注 [*Explaining Graphs and Analyzing Characters, with Annotations*]. 1981. Annotated by Duan, Yucai 段玉裁. Shanghai: Guji.

Sima Mao bianbo 司馬楙編鎛 [*The Bronze Chime-Bell of Sima Mao*]. 2007. In *Comprehensive Collection of Bronze Inscriptions from Shandong* 山東金文集成, 2 vols, ed. Li, Daying 李大營, Yu, Qiuwei 于秋偉, and Shandong sheng bowuguan 山東省博物館 [Museum of Shandong Province], 1:104–07. Jinan: Qi Lu shushe. (A bronze chime-bell [*bianbo*] with an inscription dating to the late Chunqiu or early Warring States period.)

Staack, Thies [Shi Da 史達]. 2016. "The Identity of the Owner of the Curriculum Vitae Attached to the *Zhiri Calendar of the Twenty-seventh Year* and of Three *Zhiri Calendars* in the Qin Bamboo Manuscripts Held by the Yuelu Academy" 岳麓秦簡《廿七年質日》所附官吏履歷與三卷《質日》擁有者的身份. *Hunan daxue xuebao* 湖南大學學報 30.4 (July 2016): 10–17.

Starostin, Sergei. 2005a. "Proto-Sino-Tibetan: *wāp." Sino-Tibetan Etymology (database; version of October 9, 2005). The Tower of Babel: An Etymological Database Project (website). https://starlingdb.org/cgi-bin/response.cgi?root=config&basename=\data\sintib\stibet&text_any=%E6%B2%9B&method_any=substring

———. 2005b. "Proto-Sino-Tibetan: *PVp." Sino-Tibetan Etymology (database; version of October 9, 2005). The Tower of Babel: An Etymological Database Project (website). https://starlingdb.org/cgi-bin/response.cgi?root=config&basename=\data\sintib\stibet&text_any=%E6%B3%95&method_any=substring

Suanshushu 算數書 [*Records of Mathematical Procedures*]. In Zhangjiashan ersiqi hao Hanmu zhujian zhengli xiaozu 2001: 81–98 (Reproductions 圖版) and 247–272 (Transcription and Annotation 釋文注釋). [References are to slip number.] (A bamboo manuscript on mathematics discovered in Tomb 247, Zhangjiashan, Hubei Province.)

Tan, Qixiang 譚其驤, ed. 1982–1987. *Historical Atlas of China* 中國歷史地圖集. 8 vols. Beijing: Zhongguo ditu.

Tanglü shuyi 唐律疏議 [*The Statutes of the Tang Dynasty, with Commentary*]. 1983 [652/737]. By Zhangsun Wuji 長孫無忌 (d. 659) et al. Beijing: Zhonghua shuju.

Tōdō, Akiyasu 藤堂明保. 1978. *Gakken Kanwa daijiten* 學研漢和大字典. Tōkyō: Gakushū Kenkyūsha. (Chinese-Japanese dictionary including etymological cognates for each lexeme that is represented by the respective character.)

Tomiya, Itaru 冨谷至. 2004. "*Ninen ritsuryō* ni mieru hōritsu yōgo—sono (ichi)" 二年律令に見える法律用語——その(一) [Legal terms as seen in the *Ernian lüling*, part 1], in: *Tōhō gakuhō* 東方學報 76: 221–255.

Vandermeersch, Léon. 1965. *La Formation du légisme: Recherche sur la constitution d'une philosophie politique caractéristique de la Chine ancienne.* Paris: École française d'Extrême-Orient.

Wei li zhi dao 為吏之道 [*The Proper Way of Serving as an Official*]. In Shuihudi Qinmu zhujian zhengli xiaozu 1990: 79–86 (Reproductions 圖版) and 165–76 (Transcription and Annotation 釋文注釋); and in Chen, Wei et al. 2014: 320–48 (Transcription and Annotation) and 1125–43 (Reproductions 圖版 at ratio 2:1). [References are to slip number.]

Wei li zhi guan ji qianshou 為吏治官及黔首 [*Administering One's Office as well as the People When Serving as an Official*]. 2010. In *Qin Bamboo Manuscripts Held by the Yuelu Academy* 嶽麓書院藏秦簡, vol. 1, ed. Zhu, Hanmin 朱漢民 and Chen, Songzhang 陳松長. Shanghai: Shanghai cishu. [References are to slip number.] (A Qin bamboo manuscript with a textbook for instructing prospective officials in administrative and legal language, part of the bamboo manuscripts of unknown provenance held by the Yuelu Academy.)

Wei yu deng zhuang 為獄等狀 [*Composing the Records for Criminal Cases etc.*]. 2013. In *Qin Bamboo Manuscripts Held by the Yuelu Academy* 嶽麓書院藏秦簡, vol. 3, ed. Zhu, Hanmin 朱漢民 and Chen, Songzhang 陳松長. Shanghai: Shanghai cishu. [References are to slip number.] (A Qin-period bamboo manuscript containing a collection of exemplary criminal cases, part of the bamboo manuscripts of unknown provenance held by the Yuelu Academy.)

Weishu 魏書 [*History of the Wei*]. 1974. By Wei, Shou 魏收 (506–572). Beijing: Zhonghua shuju.

Xiaolü 效律 [*Statutes on Checking*]. In Shuihudi Qinmu zhujian zhengli xiaozu 1990: 33–40 (Reproductions 圖版) and 67–76 (Transcription and Annotation 釋文注釋); and in Chen Wei et al. 2014: 153–65 (Transcription and Annotation) and 989–1010 (Reproductions 圖版 at ratio 2:1). [References are to slip number.] (A Qin manuscript containing a collection of statutes related to the control of state granaries, discovered in Tomb 11, Shuihudi, Hubei province.)

Xu, Xiqi 徐錫祺. 1997. *Calendrical Tables from the Western Zhou (Gonghe interregnum) to the Western Han* 西周(共和)至西漢曆譜. 2 vols. Beijing: Beijing kexue jishu.

Xuanquan = Dunhuang Xuanquan Hanjian shicui 敦煌懸泉漢簡釋粹 [*Selected Explications of Han Bamboo Manuscripts from Xuanquan, Dunhuang*]. 2001. By Hu, Pingsheng 胡平生 and Zhang Defang 張德芳. Shanghai: Shanghai guji.

Yinqueshan Hanjian wenzibian 銀雀山漢簡文字編 [*Compilation of Character Forms in the Han Bamboo Manuscripts from Yinqueshan*]. 2001. Compiled by Pian Yuqian 駢宇騫. Beijing: Wenwu.

Yuelu Lüling 嶽麓律令 [*Statutes and Edicts Held by the Yuelu Academy*] = *Qin Bamboo Manuscripts Held by the Yuelu Academy* 嶽麓書院藏秦簡. 2015–22. Vols. 4–7, ed. Chen, Songzhang 陳松長. Shanghai: Shanghai cishu. [References are to volume number and slip number, separated by a period, slip number, unless otherwise noted.] (The statutes and edicts among the collection of Qin bamboo manuscripts, of unknown provenance, held by the Yuelu Academy.)

Yuelu Shu = Shu 數 [*Mathematics*]. 2011. In *Qin Bamboo Manuscripts Held by the Yuelu Academy* 嶽麓書院藏秦簡, vol. 2, ed. Zhu, Hanmin 朱漢民 and Chen Songzhang 陳松長. Shanghai: Shanghai cishu. [References are to slip number.] (A Qin bamboo manuscript on mathematics, one of the manuscripts of unknown provenance held by the Yuelu Academy.)

Yushu 語書 [*Record of Pronouncements*]. In Shuihudi Qinmu zhujian zhengli xiaozu 1990: 9–12 (Reproductions 圖版) and 11–16 (Transcription and Annotation 釋文注釋); and in Chen Wei et al. 2–14: 29–40 (Transcription and Annotation) and 911–17 (Reproductions 圖版 at ratio 2:1). [References are to slip number.] (A Qin bamboo manuscript, discovered in Tomb 11, Shuihudi, Hubei Province, containing a circular of the governor of the Southern Province [*Nanjun* 南郡] to his subordinates.)

Zhang, Jianguo 張建國. 1999. *Chinese Law in the Imperial Era* 帝制時代的中國法. Beijing: Falü.

Zhangjiashan ersiqi hao Hanmu zhujian zhengli xiaozu 張家山二四七號漢墓竹簡整理小組 [Team for Editing the Bamboo Manuscripts of Han Tomb 247 in Zhangjiashan], ed. 2001. *Bamboo Manuscripts from the Han Tomb of Zhangjiashan (Tomb 247)* 張家山漢墓竹簡〔二四七號墓〕. Beijing: Wenwu.

Zhangjiashan Hanjian wenzibian 張家山漢簡文字編 [*Compilation of Character Forms in the Bamboo Manuscripts from Zhangjiashan*]. 2012. Compiled by Zhang Shouzhong 張守中. Beijing: Wenwu.

Zhanguo ce 戰國策 = *Zhanguo ce jizhu huikao* 戰國策集注彙考 [*Collected Commentaries and Collated Notes for the "Strategies of the Warring States"*]. 1985. Compiled by Zhu Zugeng 諸祖耿. 3 vols. Nanjing: Jiangsu guji.

Zhongshan zhaoyu tuban 中山兆域圖版 [*Plate with a Map of the Burial Ground of Zhongshan*]. 1990. In *Selected Shang and Zhou Bronze Inscriptions* 商周青銅器銘文選, ed. Ma Chengyuan 馬承源, 4:582. Beijing: Wenwu, 1990. (Bronze plate with a map of the burial ground of the royal family of Zhongshan, dating to the Warring States period and discovered in Tomb 1 of the Kings of Zhongshan. Sandi gongshe, Hebei province.)

Zhou, Haifeng. 2018. A Discussion of Qin-Period Laws Relating to Government Officials and the Official Called *zhifa* 秦代官吏法與執法吏考論. Ch. 6 in Cheng Songzhang 陳松長, Zou Shuijie 鄒水傑, Wang Wei 王偉; and Zhou Haifeng 周海鋒, *Studies of Official Institutions of the Qin Period* 秦代官制考論, 245–251. Shanghai: Zhong Xi shuju.

Zhouyi = *Zhouyi zhengyi* 周易正義 [*Correct Meaning of the "Changes" of the Zhou*]. 1980. In *The Thirteen Classics with Commentaries and Appended Collation Notes* 十三經注疏:附校勘記, 2 vols, ed. Ruan Yuan 阮元. Beijing: Zhonghua shuju.

Zhuangzi = *Zhuangzi jijie* 莊子集解 [*Collected Explanations for the "Zhuangzi"*]. 1954. Compiled by Wang Xianqian 王先謙. In Comprehensive Collection of the Masters' Writings 諸子集成, vol. 3. Beijing: Zhonghua shuju.

Zouyanshu 奏讞書 [*Documents on Legal Cases Submitted for Higher-Level Decision that Have Been Memorialized to the Ruler*]. In Zhangjiashan ersiqi hao Hanmu zhujian zhengli xiaozu 2001: 51–72 (Reproductions 圖版); and in Peng Hao, Chen Wei, and Kudō Motoo 2007: 59–83 (Reproductions 圖版) and 329–382 (Transcription and Annotation 釋文). [References are to slip number.]

Zuozhuan 左傳 = *Chunqiu Zuozhuan zhu* 春秋左傳注 [*The "Zuo Tradition" of the "Spring and Autumn Annals", with Commentary*]. 1990. Annotated by Yang Bojun 楊伯峻. Beijing: Zhonghua shuju, rev. ed. [Translation in: Durrant, Stephen W., Li Wai-yee, and David Schaberg. 2016. *Zuo Tradition / Zuozhuan Commentary on the "Spring and Autumn Annals."* Seattle: University of Washington Press.] [References are to ruler of Lu, year of reign and the item's number]

Chapter 9
Two Perspectives on the *Fa* Tradition: Politics Versus the Rule of Impartial Standards

Hongbing Song 宋洪兵

1 Introduction

Modern Chinese scholars, starting with Mai Menghua 麥夢華 (1874–1915) and Liang Qichao 梁啟超 (1873–1929), identified in the ideas of the *fa* tradition, especially the rule of *fa* (*fazhi* 法治) some semblance with the Western concept of the "rule of law" (which, in modern Chinese, is rendered exactly the same, *fazhi*). Yet they were also quick to notice that, in addition to promoting the rule of *fa*, the adherents of China's *fa* tradition were unabashed about the importance of "techniques of rule" (*shu* 術) and "positional power" (*shi* 勢) in governing the state. There is considerable tension between these two orientations. The idea of the "rule of *fa*" emphasizes that impersonal *fa*, as objective standards and laws, possesses supreme authority. Yet "techniques of rule" and "positional power" strongly entail characteristics of person-based rule (*renzhi* 人治, "the rule of/by men"), which is not confined to following objective norms. The crux of the problem is the relationship between *fa* and the ruler. Insofar as *fa* (especially in its meaning as "the law") originates from the ruler, who has the power to legislate, how can it be ensured that the ruler abides by the law? Liang Qichao was the earliest to note this problem. If the ruler has the exclusive power to legislate, he also has the power to abolish laws. This means that legislation and the abolition of laws both depend on the personal will of the ruler, and the ideal of the "rule of *fa*" is ultimately reduced to the personalized

Translated: Ashton Ng

H. Song 宋洪兵 (✉)
School of Guoxue (Chinese Classics), Renmin University of China,
Beijing, China
e-mail: songhongbing@ruc.edu.cn

© The Author(s), under exclusive license to Springer Nature Switzerland AG 2024
Y. Pines (ed.), *Dao Companion to China's fa Tradition*, Dao Companions
to Chinese Philosophy 19, https://doi.org/10.1007/978-3-031-53630-4_10

mode of rule, the "rule of a person" (*renzhi* 人治) (Liang Qichao [1922] 1989b: 148–49).

Later scholars followed Liang Qichao's lead in analyzing tensions in preimperial (pre-221 BCE) *fa* thought. Han Dongyu (1993), for instance, exposed the ostensibly irreconcilable contradiction between the primacy of the laws in theory versus the primacy of the ruler in real society. Jiang Chongyue (2000: 88) further analyzed what he calls "the contradiction" (*maodun* 矛盾) in Han Fei's 韓非 (d. 233 BCE) thought between *fazhi* in its meaning as the "rule of law," which presupposes equality in front of the law, and the ruler-oriented "techniques of rule," and especially "positional power," which is absolute and wielded exclusively by the sovereign.

How can this contradiction be explained and resolved? In his more recent publication, Jiang Chongyue (2019: 93) explains it as a reflection of the unshakable monarchic form of traditional Chinese government: "This contradiction is not a logical error committed by Han Fei, but is a real manifestation of the inherent contradictions within ancient Chinese politics insofar as laws, techniques of rule, and positional power are concerned." Earlier, scholars had pointed out that the solution to the contradictions in *fa* thought lies in modern institutions. Thus, Liang Qichao ([1922] 1989b: 148–49) opined that the real implementation *fazhi* as the rule of law "requires a modern constitutional government to back it up." Han Dongyu (1993) suggested that only when the ruler's position is subordinate to the laws can the principle of the rule of law be truly realized. Their differences aside, all three scholars agree that, first, there is a theoretical conflict between *fazhi* in its meaning as the rule of law on the one hand and the rule by techniques and positional power on the other. Hence, to fully implement the "rule of law," it is necessary to oppose ruling by techniques of rule and positional power. Second, all three views agree that the weaknesses of the *fa* adherents' theories derive from the historical limitations of their outlook, and that these limitations can be overcome only by utilizing the prism of modernity, free of the principle of monarchism. Only in modern political systems can the rule of law constrain political power. Under these circumstances, techniques of rule and positional power lose their importance. The rule of law is then expected to take the lead over any kind of personal political power.

In this chapter, I wish to offer an alternative explanation for the ostensible contradiction between the parallel emphases in *fa* texts on fair and universally applicable standards (*fa* 法) on the one hand, and the means of safeguarding the ruler's authority through applying "techniques of rule" and "positional power" on the other. To do so, I want to highlight an oft-neglected insight of the early *fa* thinkers: their sober realization that human politics contains some harsh and unpleasant aspects that cannot be fully subordinated to impartial *fa*. I shall start by briefly surveying some Western perspectives on politics as encompassing elements of treachery, maneuvering, and harsh power struggles. I shall then shift to the *fa* tradition's texts and expose both conflict and complementarity between the advocacy of the rule of *fa* and rule by techniques and positional power. I shall then expose what I believe was the essential weakness of the *fa* tradition—its overreliance on the ruler's patronage as essential for promoting the rule of *fa*. I hope to show that, their historical limitations aside, *fa* adherents may have exposed—intentionally or unintention-ally—some of the perennial tensions between the rule by impartial standards (or even the "rule of law") and practical politics. These observations may be valid beyond traditional Chinese society.

2   Politics and "the Rule of *fa*"

Scholarly debates in China about the *fa* tradition cannot be separated from the con-cept of *fazhi*. The term *fazhi*, which actually had multiple meanings in China's polit-ical discourse of the twentieth century—from the "rule of law" to the strengthening of centralized authority—still entails a strong emotional value.[1] By contrast, the concept of "politics" is much less value-oriented. In what follows, I take this tension between the concepts of politics and "rule of law" as a starting point in my discus-sion of the complexities of China's early *fa* thought.

As many contributions to this volume clarify, the term *fa* is not identical to the Western "law," and a simplistic equation of *fazhi* with the "rule of law" does not work. This being said, recall that there is also a clear semantic overlap between the two terms. The idea of transparent, fair, and universally applicable standards embed-ded into the concept of *fazhi* (see below) has undeniable parallels with the Western idea of the "rule of law."[2] Confusingly, however, *fazhi* in Chinese may refer not just to the "rule of law" but also to the "rule by law." The precise usage of the term, specifically in the context of *fa* thought, generated lively debates. The dominant view is that the *fazhi* of *fa* thinkers implied purely the "rule by law": "Law was simply a pragmatic tool for obtaining and maintaining political control and social order" (Peerenboom 2004: 114; cf. Fu 1996: 64; Wei Sen 2006: 73–74). By con-trast, the "rule of law" in which the ruler is subordinate to the law is viewed by a vast majority of Chinese scholars as a product of modernity, especially of the democratic political system based on the tripartite separation of powers. As Wang Renbo and Cheng Liaoyuan (1989: 126) put it, "The supreme constraint of the constitution, and the mutual restraint between the departments of power, are the most important requirements of the rule of law."

Insofar as modern democracy is considered the true manifestation of "the rule of law," the logical conclusion is that *fazhi* of the *fa* tradition has nothing to do with it. Since the *fa* tradition had no concepts of democracy, freedom, and human rights, its *fazhi* is often dismissed as nothing more than a tool that allowed autocratic rulers to

---

[1] Recall that the "rule of law" (*fazhi* 法治) is enshrined as one of the twelve "core socialist values" in the current People's Republic of China. For the systematic study of the modern views of rela-tions between the term *fazhi* and the *fa* thought in early China, and for different semantic meanings of *fazhi* in the twentieth-century China, see Hong 2018.

[2] It is not my goal here to address the complexity of Western debates about the rule of law. For a comprehensive discussion on the conceptualizations of the rule of law and key debates surrounding the concept, see Bingham 2010.

control and suppress their subjects. It is not my goal here to challenge this understanding; but I do hope to make it more nuanced. The question remains why *fa* thinkers opted to strengthen the ruler despite the ostensible contradiction between the power of an individual sovereign and the rule by impartial standards? The answer in my eyes lies in the *fa* thinkers' understanding of the deeply unsettling aspects of political life, which I call hereinafter "the treachery of politics" (政治之詭). By this term I refer to a variety of "dirty" means such as deception, trickery, and even violence, used by politicians to obtain positive and even morally laudable ends. I shall argue that the political recipes of *fa* thinkers cannot be reduced to the pure rule of *fa*; rather their valorization of the rule by impartial standards is intrinsically linked with the realization that the treachery of politics cannot be avoided.

Many scholars in China and elsewhere, such as Wang and Cheng cited above, believe—somewhat romantically—that the rule of law within modern democracy has perfected the control of power. Various manifestations of political malpractice—such as conspiracies, power struggles, assassinations, slander, and scapegoating—which originate in the desires of human nature, are allegedly no longer easy to find. It is as though politics has been purified. This imagined purity is contrasted with the harsh authoritarianism of the *fa* thinkers, whose ideas are consequently disparaged. I have no intention to discuss here the advantages and disadvantages of Western democratic systems, but I remain skeptical regarding the possibility that any political system could escape the woes of conspiracy and machinations, and give way to a completely upright rule of law. Can political treachery be eliminated? To answer this, let us briefly look at the ideas of several Western political thinkers.

In the history of Western political thought, Machiavelli (1469–1527) became a watershed figure in determining how to interpret the treachery of politics (for Machiavelli's comparison to the *fa* thinkers, cf. Blahuta, this volume). Before him, whenever political treachery was involved, even if its existence was recognized, it was treated with disapproval. But in Machiavelli's writings, political treachery not only became an important factor of political life; it also became a form of practical political wisdom, to be accepted and even endorsed. As a result, on the question of what politics is, from Machiavelli onwards, a stronger tendency toward realism—by which the "treachery of politics" is recognized—has taken shape. Machiavelli argued that it is an unrealistic fantasy for humanity to expect rulers to abide by the law perfectly and fairly. Good politicians all need to utilize political strategy and even cunning maneuvers:

> Everyone knows how praiseworthy it is for a ruler to keep his promises, and live uprightly and not by trickery. Nevertheless, experience shows that in our times the rulers who have done great things have held the keeping of their word of little account, and have known how, by their cunning, to muddle the brains of men, and in the end have got the better of those who have based themselves on sincerity.

> You should know, then, that there are two ways of contending: one by using laws, the other, force. The first is appropriate for men, the second for animals; but because the former is often insufficient, one must have recourse to the latter. Therefore, a ruler must know well how to imitate beasts as well as employing properly human means… Since a ruler, then, must know how to act like a beast, he should imitate both the fox and the lion, for the lion

is liable to be trapped, whereas the fox cannot ward off wolves. One needs, then, to be a fox
to recognize traps, and a lion to frighten away wolves. (Machiavelli 1988: 59–60)

Followers of Machiavelli have argued that human society's need for order cannot be
separated from politics or any structure of order involving control and subordination. Politics is fundamentally about power as well as the contention over power and
interests. The ebb and flow of the strength of the contenders determine political
outcomes and the direction they take. The contention over power is a complex and
dynamic process, requiring those participating in politics to have sufficient political
wisdom, which includes passion, a sense of responsibility, discernment, and deci-
siveness (Jiang 2019).

Political ethics symbolize humanity's yearning for good order, which is a kind of
"ought," but humanity's politics itself does not completely operate in accordance
with the requirements of political ethics. In the end, all kinds of conspiracies,
maneuvers, deceit, and lies, as well as promises of good values and the desire for
power, accompany humankind like shadows. Politics naturally contains "evil" elements and encompasses political treachery. Human politics—ancient or modern, in
China or elsewhere—is a dynamic process, engaged in an endless contention for
power. As long as humanity continues to lead a communal life characterized by
contention and cooperation, and as long as there exists a structural order of control
and subordination, the abovementioned characteristics of politics will not disappear.

Max Weber (1864–1920) also saw that the essence of politics lies in the contention for power. His definition of politics is as follows: "Hence, what 'politics' means
for us is to strive for a share of power or to influence the distribution of power,
whether between states or between the groups of people contained within a state"
(Weber 2004: 33). Weber was conscious of the fact that politicians must possess
passion, a sense of responsibility, and an appropriate sense of judgment in order to
deal with complex and dynamic political affairs. On the issues of politics and morality, Weber pointed at the tragedy—and the awareness of such tragedy—inherent
within politics:

> No ethic in the world can ignore the fact that in many cases the achievement of 'good' ends
> is inseparable from the use of morally dubious or at least dangerous means and that we can-
> not escape the possibility or even probability of evil side effects. And no ethic in the world
> can say when, and to what extent, the ethically good end can 'justify' the ethically danger-
> ous means and its side effects. (Weber 2004: 84)

This observation by one of the West's most eminent scholars and thinkers is revealing. The need to employ evil means in order to attain "the ethically good end" is a
problem inherent in politics. The dilemma was amplified in Michael Walzer's 1973
famous article about the problem of "dirty hands" in politics. Walzer cited and then
analyzed the conventional wisdom: "No one succeeds in politics without getting his
hands dirty" (Walzer 1973: 164). The "dirty hands" dilemma continues to occupy
thinkers who hope to reconcile morality and politics (cf. Kim 2016; Coady 2023).

In the case of the *fa* thinkers, morality (or, more precisely, the moralizing discourse associated primarily with Confucians and followers of Mozi 墨子) mattered
little. Yet they—especially Han Fei—were well aware of the tension between the

inevitability of political treachery (a term which I prefer to Walzer's "dirty hands") on the one hand, and the rule of *fa* on the other. In what follows, I shall explore how this tension was conceptualized and dealt with; my specific focus will be on the double position of the ruler who was expected to be subordinate to *fa* on the one hand and remain above *fa* on the other. Why did *fa* thinkers opt to safeguard the ruler's authority at all costs? I shall try to answer this question and also highlight the price that the *fa* tradition's adherents paid for this choice.

3   The Rule of *Fa* Versus the Treachery of Politics

3.1   Fa, *Techniques, and Positional Power: A Logical Contradiction?*

At the level of systemic implementation and means of control, political thought of the *fa* tradition is mainly embodied in the trinity of laws (standards), techniques of rule, and positional power. Traditionally, it is thought that Shang Yang 商鞅 (d. 338 BCE) emphasized laws, Shen Buhai 申不害 (d. 337 BCE) emphasized techniques of rule, and Shen Dao 慎到 emphasized positional power, whereas Han Fei synthesized the three.[3] This view correctly identifies the thinkers who prioritized each concept, but one cannot simplistically argue that only Han Fei advocated the combination of laws, techniques of rule, and positional power. Thus, whereas Shang Yang focused on laws, many of the chapters of the *Book of Lord Shang* (*Shangjunshu* 商君書) pay due attention to techniques of rule and positional power.[4] Shen Buhai, according to a *Han Feizi* account, focused on techniques of rule; but the *Shēnzi* 申子 fragments contain primarily references to *fa* (see Yu Zhong, this volume). Shen Dao is associated with the advocacy of positional power, but laws and techniques of rule have an important place in *Shènzi* 慎子 fragments.[5] That the three concepts are well integrated in *Han Feizi* is widely acknowledged.[6] Simultaneous usage of the three is observable in *Guanzi* 管子 as well, notwithstanding differences between this text on the one hand and the *Book of Lord Shang* and *Han Feizi* on the other (Yang 2007: 197–24; see also Sato, this volume).

---

[3] This tripartite division of the *fa* school was proposed by Liang Qichao in Chap. 14 of his *History of Chinese Political Thought* (Liang [1922] 1989b) and was commonly accepted ever since. See, e.g., Feng Youlan [1930] 2000: 237–239; Xiao Gongquan (Hsiao Kung-chuan) [1937] 1998: 213, *et saepe*.

[4] See, e.g., Jiang Lihong 1996: 27; Tong Weimin 2013: 279–87.

[5] Note that contrarily to the common view, *Xunzi* 荀子 associates Shen Dao with *fa* and Shen Buhai with positional power: "Master Shèn [Dao] was blinded by *fa* and did not recognize [the use of] worthy men. Master Shēn [Buhai] was blinded by positional power and did not recognize [the use of] knowledge" (慎子蔽於法而不知賢。申子蔽於埶(→勢)而不知知. *Xunzi* 21: 392 ["Jiebi" 解蔽])

[6] See Jiang Chongyue 2000: 49–88; Song 2010: 17–18; Yusuke 1993; Jia 2018.

Modern scholars, starting with Liang Qichao, tended to approve the concept of "ruling by *fa*" which resonated well with the "rule of law," but denigrated the idea of "ruling by *shu* [techniques of rule]" and "ruling by *shi* [positional power]."[7] This reasoning has deeply influenced the research on the *fa* tradition in Chinese academic circles. Since "ruling by *shu*" is perceived as justification for conspiracies and plotting, whereas "ruling by *shi*" is associated with authoritarianism and the concentration of power in the monarch's hands, both concepts are incompatible with the political stance of modern scholars. The admixture of techniques of rule and positional power led several scholars to conclude that the rule of *fa* as advocated by the *fa* tradition is fundamentally different from the modern concept of the rule of law.[8]

Looking at the development of pre-Qin *fa* tradition, we may notice that even though texts composed before *Han Feizi* routinely invoke *fa*, techniques of rule, and positional power, they do not analyze the nature of interrelations among these three. Han Fei's theoretical contribution lies not in simultaneously emphasizing the importance of all three concepts, but rather in integrating them into a single system of thought, thus forming an organic whole (Jiang Chongyue 2000: 83). Generally speaking, *fa* refers to objective, universal rules (laws, standards); techniques of rule refer to a set of methods and procedures for employing, controlling, and evaluating the administrative personnel; and positional power refers to the ruler's authority and possession of coercive power. The three concepts all reinforce one another: without techniques of rule, the laws by themselves do not suffice to identify treachery and machinations of the underlings; without positional power, there would be no way to ensure that the laws are implemented. Without the laws, techniques of rule alone cannot ensure the stability of policies, and without positional power, the ruler has no authority by which to employ techniques of rule. Without laws, positional power alone cannot ensure that power is fairly exercised, and without techniques of rule, the ruler's authority cannot be protected. Jiang Chongyue suggested this mutually reinforcing relationship between laws, techniques of rule, and positional power; but

---

[7] Liang Qichao exposed the difference between the "rule of *fa*" and "ruling by techniques of rule (*shu*)" as follows: "At the time, the School of *fa* spoke of juxtaposing laws with techniques of rule. The chapter 'Defining standards' (or 'Fixing laws' ['Ding fa' 定法]) of *Han Feizi* states: 'Shen Buhai spoke of techniques of rule, whereas Gongsun Yang dealt with *fa*' (申不害言術，而公孫鞅為法). It also states: 'To practice techniques without *fa*, or practice *fa* without techniques of rule—this is unacceptable' (徒術而無法，徒法而無術——不可). It is clear that *fa* and techniques of rule are not the same thing. *Fa* (laws) are concrete, whereas techniques of rule are abstract. Take Li Si as an example: to call him one who was capable of using techniques of rule would be valid. To call him one who was capable of using laws would be invalid. Thus, he cannot be referred to as a pure *fa* adherent." Liang further pointed out: "The principle of the rule of *fa* (law) 法治主義 perished by the time of Li Si—this would be a valid statement." According to Liang, Li Si pursued not the principle of the rule of *fa*, but "the principle of ruling by *shu*" 術治主義 and "the principle of ruling by *shi*" 勢治主義 (Liang [1904] 1989a: 94).

[8] Guo [1945] 2008: 240; Xiong 1984: 3, 6, 22; Han 1993; Jiang Chongyue 2000 and more in Sect. 2 above.

he also pointed out that there are inherent contradictions between *fa* and the two other concepts that are difficult to reconcile:

> Laws are written and promulgated by the government; they are publicly disclosed and are known to every individual. Techniques of rule are the exact opposite: they are not written down and cannot be publicly disclosed. They can only be hidden within the ruler's mind and must by no means made known to others. Both laws and techniques of rule are the ruler's methods of governance, but one should be made prominent, whereas the other should not be exposed. There is a logical contradiction between the two: they cannot be simultaneously true or false. As such, they violate the norm of non-contradiction.

> Positional power is the ruler's authority. The concept requires the ruler to possess absolute authority. It stands from the ruler's perspective and coerces all individuals to submit. If the ruler above and his ministers below are equal, what positional power is there to speak of? The foundation of laws is fairness and equality, whereas the foundation of positional power is unfairness and inequality. The two of them cannot be simultaneously true or false, and this yet again violates norm law of non-contradiction. (Jiang Chongyue 2000: 87–88)

Jiang argues that the openness of laws and the secrecy of techniques of rule constitute a contradictory pair; and the fairness of laws and the coerciveness and hierarchical nature of positional power constitute another contradictory pair. Thus, an irreconcilable contradiction permeates Han Fei's attempt to integrate the three. Laws (or standards) are public, fair, and open, and are effectively applied to all individuals including the ruler, who cannot violate them (see more in Sect. 3.3 below). Here, laws are logically above the ruler. Techniques of rule and positional power are both individualistic, monopolistic, and secretive, and are exclusively wielded by the ruler. Here, the ruler is above the laws and standards. The contradiction between *fa* on the one hand, and techniques of rule and positional power on the other is essentially the contradiction between the ruler and the laws and standards. By this logic, Han Fei descends into an irresolvable dilemma. If the fairness and openness of laws are to prevail, then the ruler's exclusivity and secrecy must be removed, and vice versa.

However, life does not follow a one-dimensional logic. Political life contains many contradictions and complexities, and is itself mired in deep dilemmas. Attempts at using a single principle to encompass and organize all of humanity's political life are doomed to fail. The most special characteristic of politics is precisely the way in which it succeeds to manage all kinds of conflicting issues with the art of the balancing act. The dilemma of the *fa* tradition concerning the relations between the ruler and impartial standards (laws) not only exemplifies the contradictions in political life of the Warring States period, but is reflective of the broader dilemma between politics and the rule of law in any human society. In other words, the dilemma faced by adherents of the *fa* tradition was not confined to their time. The inherent tension between politics and the rule of law is faced by people today as well.

3.2 Texts of the **Fa** *Tradition: The Contradiction Ignored?*

One of the notable features of early texts of the *fa* tradition is their repeated emphasis on the parallel importance of *fa* and the ruler's authority. For instance, the chapter "Cultivation of Authority" ("Xiuquan" 修權) of the *Book of Lord Shang* states:

國之所以治者三：一曰法；二曰信；三曰權。法者，君臣之所共操也。信者，君臣之所共立也。權者，君之所獨制也。人主失守則危；君臣釋法任私，必亂。

The state is ordered through three [things]: the first is standards, the second is trustworthiness, the third is authority. Standards (*fa*) are what the ruler and ministers jointly uphold; trustworthiness is what the ruler and ministers jointly establish; authority is what the ruler exclusively regulates. When the sovereign loses what he should preserve, he is endangered; when the ruler and the ministers cast away standards and rely on their private [views], turmoil will surely ensue. (*Book of Lord Shang* 14.1; Zhang Jue 2012: 164)[9]

Here, trustworthiness (*xin* 信) is one of the basic properties of laws or standards; both belong to the realm of public knowledge. "Authority" is different, though; it concerns the ruler alone. The same sentiment is expressed in "Seven types of ministers and sovereigns" ("Qi chen qi zhu" 七臣七主) chapter of *Guanzi*: "Laws and ordinances are what the ruler and his ministers establish jointly. Authority and positional power are what the ruler guards alone" 法令者，君臣之所共立也。權勢者，人主之所獨守也 (*Guanzi* 52: 998–99; translation modified from Rickett 1998: 210). Once again, laws and ordinances belong to the realm of public knowledge, or at the very least are shared by the ruler and his ministers, whereas authority and positional power exclusively concern the ruler.

"Objections 3" ("Nan san" 難三) chapter of *Han Feizi* makes a clearer statement:

法者，編著之圖籍，設之於官府，而布之于百姓者也。術者，藏之於胸中，以偶眾端而潛禦群臣者也。故法莫如顯，而術不欲見。

As for the law, it is compiled and written down on charts and documents. It is deposited in the official archives, and disseminated to the hundred clans. As for techniques of rule, they are hidden in the chest. It is that through which you match up all the various ends and from your secret place steer the ministers. Therefore, laws are best when they are clear, whereas techniques should not be seen. (*Han Feizi* 38.8.2; Chen Qiyou 2000: 922–923)[10]

This point is further elaborated in the chapter "Defining standards" (or "Fixing laws" ["Ding fa" 定法]) of *Han Feizi*:

術者，因任而授官，循名而責實，操殺生之柄，課群臣之能者也，此人主之所執也。法者，憲令著於官府，刑罰必于民心，賞存乎慎法，而罰加乎奸令者也，此臣之所師也。君無術則弊於上，臣無法則亂於下，此不可一無，皆帝王之具也。

---

[9] All translations from the *Book of Lord Shang* are from Pines 2017 (including the division into paragraphs).

[10] All translations from Han Feizi are modified from Harbsmeier, forthcoming (including the division into paragraphs, which is borrowed from Zhang Jue 2010).

> As for techniques, this is to bestow office on the basis of concrete responsibilities, to demand performance on the basis of titles, to wield the levers of life and death, and to examine the capacities of the ministers. These are the things the ruler of men is to hold on to.

> As for the law, this is that regulations and ordinances are displayed in the official archives, that punishments and fines appear inevitable to the people's minds, and that rewards are meted on those who are cautious in regard to the laws, and punishments are applied to those who offend against ordinances. This is what the ministers take as their guiding authority. When the ruler is bereft of techniques, there will be harm above. When the subjects are without law, there will be turmoil below. Both are indispensable. These all are the tools of thearchs and monarchs. (*Han Feizi* 43.1.2; Chen Qiyou 2000: 957–958)

Han Fei emphasizes that laws are openly disclosed and made publicly known; ministers and the common people alike must all abide by them. Techniques of rule by contrast remain "hidden in the chest." Note that the techniques of rule as defined in the extract from "Defining standards" have much in common with *fa*, inasmuch as they refer to impartial standards of appointment and dismissal of officials. Nonetheless, even in that context they are related to the ruler's secretive methods; they should be exclusively applied by the sovereign so as to handle power struggles within the ruling stratum. This secrecy may reflect Han Fei's understanding that overall, techniques are used by the ruler to safeguard his authority against the plotters (see more in Sect. 3.4 below). What matters for the current discussion is that neither in *Han Feizi* nor in the passages from other *fa* texts cited above do we discern any awareness of the tension between the openness and fairness of laws and standards and the secretive nature of techniques of rule applied by the ruler alone. The contradiction between the two, outlined by so many modern scholars, seems to escape the authors of the foundational texts of the *fa* tradition.

How do we understand this apparent lack of awareness? A common explanation would be that the authors of the above texts, bound by political circumstances of their time, were forced to revere the ruler and advocate impartial laws and standards simultaneously, thereby falling into an irreconcilable contradiction. Revering the ruler was widely considered the only way to ensure political stability (see, e.g., Liu Zehua 2000), whereas impartial laws and standards were the means of ensuring a fair and functioning sociopolitical order. There is an inherent tension between these two goals, but this tension was never articulated by ancient thinkers. Yet I think their avoidance of dealing with this ostensible contradiction is not only due to the historical limitations of these thinkers' perspectives. I want to propose a new interpretation of their view. The adherents of the *fa* tradition employed a logic that is not often noted by today's observers: namely, they considered the ruler's affairs as belonging only to the ruler (to paraphrase: political affairs belong in the realm of politics), whereas the broader sociopolitical order belonged to the rule of *fa*. Reading through the entire corpus of *fa* texts, we can scarcely see a hint of insistence on constraining the ruler's authority within the framework of "the rule of *fa*." We do see numerous passages requesting that the ruler abides by laws and standards; but this request is never considered as infringing on the ruler's authority. In other words, the *fa* tradition considers the problem of the ruler's power as belonging to the realm of politics, which is separate from the realm of the rule of *fa*. The rule of law (if we adopt this translation of *fazhi*) neither encompasses the realm of politics nor constrains the usage of political techniques. In what follows, I shall explore the point by clarifying the ruler's relation to the realm of *fa* and his relation to the realm of political techniques.

3.3 The Ruler and Laws (fa)

The texts of the *fa* tradition repeatedly emphasize that *fa* in its meaning as "laws" derives from the political realm. Laws are instituted by the ruler in accordance with the trends of the times and the customs and habits of society. The "Reliance on law" ("Ren fa" 任法) chapter of *Guanzi* clearly states that the ruler is the legislator and the ministers should uphold the law, whereas the people should abide by the law. Each of these three entities interacts on the basis of the laws:

> 夫生法者君也，守法者臣也，法於法者民也。君臣上下貴賤皆從法，此謂為大治。The one who generates the law is the ruler; those who safeguard the law are the ministers, those who emulate the law are the people. The ruler and the ministers, superiors and underlings, noble and base—all follow the laws. This is called the great orderly rule. (*Guanzi* 45: 906; translation cf. Rickett 1998: 147)

The ruler is the lawgiver, but he must also follow the laws. This point is clarified in the chapter "Conforming to the law" ("Fa fa" 法法) of *Guanzi*. The chapter emphasizes that having instituted the laws, the ruler (even the sage one) should abide by them:

> 規矩者，方圓之正也，雖有巧目利手，不如拙規矩之正方圓也。故巧者能生規矩，不能廢規矩而正方圓。雖聖人能生法，不能廢法而治國。故雖有明智高行，倍法而治，是廢規矩而正方圓也。
>
> The compass and T-square are the standard of roundness and squareness. Even if one has keen sight and skilled hands, there are no match for the standard roundness and squareness of the compass and T-square. Thus, the skillful can produce a compass and T-square, but cannot discard the compass and T-square when standardizing squareness and roundness. Although the sage can produce the laws, he cannot discard the laws and govern the state well. Hence, even for individuals of enlightened wisdom and high conduct, to turn their backs to the laws and try to govern well is like to discard the compass and T-square and try to standardize roundness and squareness. (*Guanzi* 16: 308; translation cf. Rickett 1985: 261–262).

The ruler's role as legislator is discussed extensively in the *Book of Lord Shang*, most notably in the first chapter, "Revising the laws" ("Geng fa" 更法). There it is emphasized that "Rituals and laws are fixed according to the times" (禮、法以時而定, *Book of Lord Shang* 1.4; Zhang Jue 2012: 11). The one who has the exclusive right to alter the established laws and rituals is the sovereign. It is the task of the ruler—ideally, the sage ruler—to observe the changing political conditions and modify the laws. The "Calculating the land" ("Suan di" 算地) chapter clarifies:

> 故聖人之為國也，觀俗立法則治，察國事本則宜。不觀時俗，不察國本，則其法立而民亂，事劇而功寡。

Hence, in ruling the state, the sage establishes laws after observing customs and then attains orderly rule; he inspects the roots of the state's affairs and then acts appropriately. Without the observation of current customs and without the inspection of the roots of the state, laws can be established, but the people will be in turmoil; undertakings will be numerous, but achievements few. (*Book of Lord Shang* 6.9; Zhang Jue 2012: 100)

Law derives from the demands of the "state's affairs," i.e. from objective political needs. The ruler is the one who establishes the law; he is the one who revises the laws when the newly emerging conditions require this. All this ostensibly places the ruler above the law. And yet the same texts reiterate: once laws are promulgated, they should be made public, open, and clear to everybody; moreover, even the ruler should abide by them.

The insistence that the ruler abides by laws permeates the texts of the *fa* tradition. Any disregard of law by the sovereign will undermine the laws' authority and negatively impact governance as a whole. The texts repeatedly emphasize the ruler's "trustworthiness" (*xin* 信) and the "certainty" (*bi* 必) in observing the laws. The ruler should "lead by example" (*shen xian* 身先) in abiding by the laws—that is, in implementing the rule of law, the ruler should start from himself. Otherwise, the laws will lose their credibility and authority. The "Conforming to the law" chapter of *Guanzi* clarifies:

不法法則事毋常，法不法則令不行，令而不行，則令不法也。……重而不行，則賞罰不信也。信而不行，則不以身先之也。故曰：「禁勝於身，則令行於民矣」。

If [the ruler] does not conform to the law, government affairs will lack a constant [standard]. If he conforms to what is unlawful, his orders will not be carried out. If his orders are not carried out it is because the orders do not conform to the law. ... If [rewards] are generous, but they are not carried out, it is because rewards and penalties are not reliable. If they are reliable but are not carried out, this is because [the ruler] does not lead by an example. Hence it is said: "When prohibitions take precedence over [the ruler] himself, then orders are carried out among the people." (*Guanzi* 16: 293; translation cf. Rickett 1985: 251)

The principle that the ruler is subject to the laws is reiterated in other *fa* texts. Thus, the "Cultivation of authority" chapter of the *Book of Lord Shang* laments: "Rulers of our age frequently cast away standards (laws) and rely on private deliberations: this is why their states are in turmoil" 世之為治者，多釋法而任私議，此國之所以亂也 (*Book of Lord Shang* 14.2; Zhang Jue 2012: 166). The "Eight canons" ("Ba jing" 八經) chapter of *Han Feizi* similarly warns the ruler that casting away standards and laws would result in massive abuse of power by his officials:

官之重也，毋法也；法之息也，上暗也。上暗無度則官擅為。

When officials are powerful, this is because there is no law [imposed on them]. When the law dies out, this is because the superior is benighted. When the superior is benighted and has no norms to go by, then officials will act on their own authority. (Han Feizi 48.7; Chen Qiyou 2000: 1079)

The ruler should abide by the laws that he himself created. This is the most basic concept of the *fa* tradition and it cannot be dismissed as lip service to the principle of fairness. No single text from the corpus of *fa* writings legitimates the ruler's violation of his laws; not a single passage suggests that the ruler is exempt from abiding by the laws he created. To the contrary, any whimsical intervention in regularized laws and standards-based political process is actively discouraged. The final section of "Conforming to the law" chapter states:

明君不為親戚危其社稷，社稷戚於親。不為君欲變其令，令尊於君。

The clear-sighted ruler does not endanger the altars of the state for the sake of his kin, for the altars of the state are closer than the kin. He will not alter his commands for the sake of his own desires, for his commands are more respected than the ruler himself. (*Guanzi* 16: 316; translation cf. Rickett 1985: 266).

The supremacy of law over the ruler is implied also in the concluding passage of the "Ruler and ministers" ("Jun chen" 君臣) section of the *Book of Lord Shang*:

故明主慎法制。言不中法者，不聽也；行不中法者，不高也；事不中法者，不為也。言中法，則聽之；行中法，則高之；事中法，則為之。

Therefore, the clear-sighted sovereign is attentive to laws and regulations. He does not heed words that do not conform to the law; he does not esteem behavior that does not conform to the law; he does not undertake a task that does not conform to the law. If words conform to the law, they are heeded; if behavior conforms to the law, it is esteemed; if a task conforms to the law, it is undertaken. (*Book of Lord Shang* 23.4; Zhang Jue 2012: 260)

Such instances of calling upon the ruler to abide by laws and regulations instead of his personal likes and dislikes recur in *Han Feizi* as well.[11] Politically speaking, this makes perfect sense. Governing the state on the basis of personal preferences and selfish desires would jeopardize the political system; *Han Feizi* clearly summarizes this point in "Signs of ruin" ("Wang zheng" 亡徵) chapter:

辭辯而不法，心智而無術，主多能而不以法度從事者，可亡也。

When his words are eloquent but do not accord with the law, when his mind is erudite but has no techniques of rule, when the ruler has many abilities but does not conduct affairs in accordance with laws and standards, he may perish. (*Han Feizi* 15.1.44; Chen Qiyou 2000: 301)

The laws advocated by the *fa* adherents are inclusive of all social strata. Above (p. 275) we noted the statement from "Reliance on law" chapter of *Guanzi* states: "The ruler, ministers, superiors, subordinates, nobles, and lowly persons all follow the laws. This is called the great order." The laws encompass everybody; they should be clear and well known to all. The "Fixing divisions" ("Ding fen" 定分) chapter of the *Book of Lord Shang* is focused on disseminating legal knowledge among the populace. This knowledge is promulgated by legal officials (*fa guan* 法官), and aims not only to make the people law-abiding, but also to protect the people from abuse at the officials' hands:

吏明知民知法令也，古吏不敢以非法遇民，民不敢犯法以干法官也。

---

[11] See, e.g., "Having the standards" ("You du" 有度) chapter, which cautions the ruler "to cast away his personal abilities and rely on laws and regulations" 舍己能，而因法數 (*Han Feizi* 6.4; Chen Qiyou 2000: 107).

> When the officials clearly know that the people understand the laws and ordinances, they dare not treat the people but in accord with the law, and the people will dare not violate the law and disobey the law officials. (*Book of Lord Shang* 26.4; Zhang Jue 2012: 283).

If an official treats the people unlawfully, they could report him to his superiors in accordance with the laws. Yet the system was predicated not just on the officials' obedience to the law but also on lawful behavior on the part of the ruler himself. The "Biography of Lord Shang" in *Records of the Historian* (*Shiji* 史記) narrates how Shang Yang punished the tutors of the crown prince for the prince's violation of laws. The argument was: "If the laws are not implemented, it is because they are violated from the top" (法之不行，自上犯之) (*Shiji* 68: 2231). The message is clear: laws should be uniformly observed by everybody so as to be truly efficient. However, the story also shows the limitations of this principle. It was impossible to apply mutilating punishments to the crown prince; hence Shang Yang ordered punishing the prince's tutors instead. This story illustrates the gap between the desirable and the attainable. In principle, the ruler should abide by the laws. In practice, there were no acceptable means to impose this abidance on the ruler aside from appealing to his own interest in preserving well-running political system. This point remained an irresolvable weakness in the *fa* tradition.

3.4 Safeguarding the Ruler's Authority

The above subsection demonstrated that in the *fa* tradition the laws' fairness and the ruler's abidance by the laws was a unanimous—even if not necessarily attainable—desideratum. However, this desideratum is dissimilar to the modern concept of using laws to restrain the ruler's power. Nor does this imply that the *fa* tradition wants the ruler to tie his own hands and give up his proactivity and political flexibility. In the political sphere, the ruler's action should be dictated not by impartial and binding laws but by the imperative to preserve his power. This preservation of the ruler's power is deemed in *fa* texts (and elsewhere) as the quintessential precondition for preserving the political stability and a well-functioning state. Thus, the ruler should be first and foremost concerned with safeguarding his authority. In fact, insofar as *fa* is predicated on maintaining well-governed state, the preservation of the ruler's authority is by itself one of its major goals.

Which factors endanger the ruler's power? The *fa* tradition's texts outline two major threats: one emerging from the self and one emerging from others. The former refers to the ruler's own excesses. Imprudent or intemperate behavior would result in personal downfall, or, worse, the loss of a dynasty and a polity. This topic is most conspicuously discussed in *Han Feizi* (e.g., the entire chapter "Ten missteps" ["Shi guo" 十過] deals precisely with the self-defeating missteps of imprudent sovereigns). This problem was the harshest to deal with, as we shall see in the next section. Here, however, we shall focus on the external threat from powerful ministers. To deal with this threat, *fa* texts recommend to the ruler, first, to be aware of and duly protect his positional power, and, second, to employ proper techniques of rule.

The advocacy of positional power (*shi* 勢) as a central political concept is often associated with Shen Dao, but, as noted above, it is shared by a plethora of texts associated with the *fa* tradition. For instance, the chapter "Conforming to the law" of *Guanzi* clarifies:

凡人君之所以為君者，勢也。故人君失勢，則臣制之矣。勢在下，則君制於臣矣；勢在上，則臣制於君矣；故君臣之易位，勢在下也。……故曰:勢非所以予人也。

What makes the ruler a ruler is his positional power. Thus, when the ruler loses his positional power, his ministers will control him. When positional power is with the [ministers] below, the ruler will be controlled by the ministers. When positional power is with [the ruler] above, the ministers will be controlled by the ruler. Thus, the reason why ruler and ministers exchange positions is that positional power is with [the ministers] below.… Hence, it is said, "Positional power is not to be given to others." (*Guanzi* 16: 305; translation cf. Rickett 1985: 259)

The warning that "when majestic positional power is with those below, the ruler will be controlled by his ministers" (威勢在下，則主制於臣) is repeated elsewhere in *Guanzi* (67: 1212 ["Ming fa jie" 明法解]). The *Book of Lord Shang* contains similar pronouncements. For instance, the chapter "Interdicting and encouraging" ("Jin shi" 禁使) states: "All those who understand the Way [rely on] positional power and methods. Hence, the former kings did not rely on strength but relied on positional power; they did not rely on trustworthiness but relied on methods. …. Thus, the former Kings esteemed positional power" 凡知道者，勢、數也。故先王不恃其強而恃其勢，不恃其信而恃其數。……故先王貴勢 (*Book of Lord Shang* 24.2; Zhang Jue 2012: 264). Yet of all the texts of the *fa* tradition, *Han Feizi* is surely the greatest repository of discussions about the importance of positional power. Chapter after chapter reminds the ruler that the loss of positional power will bring about usurpation by a minister or ministerial clique: "when the ruler loses his positional power, his ministers will gain control of the state" (主失勢而臣得國); "Authority and positional power cannot be lent to others. When the ruler loses one bit [of it], the ministers gain a hundredfold" (權勢不可以借人，上失其一，臣以為百).[12]

Han Fei explores the nature of positional power in depth. This topic stands at the center of the chapter "Objections to positional power" ("Nan shi" 難勢), in which Han Fei eloquently defends Shen Dao's insistence on the crucial role of positional power for ensuring the ruler's functioning (see discussion in Pines 2020). The power that derives from the ruler's position is indispensable for maintaining social and political order. It is the major factor that makes people obey: "The people are sure to submit to positional power. Indeed, positional power makes it easy to subjugate others" 民者固服於勢，勢誠易以服人 (*Han Feizi* 49.6; Chen Qiyou 2000: 1096 ["Wu du" 五蠹]). The most important conclusion is that the ruler should always

---

[12] *Han Feizi* 11.6; Chen Qiyou 2000: 251 ("Gu fen" 孤憤) and 31.0.1; Chen Qiyou 2000: 615 ("Nei chu shuo xia" 內儲說下).

keep this power firmly in his hands. The chapter "Favored ministers" ("Ai chen" 爱臣) summarizes:

> 萬物莫如身之至貴也，位之至尊也，主威之重，主勢之隆也。此四美者不求諸外，不請於人，議(→義)之而得之矣。

> Of the myriad things, nothing is better than having your person most esteemed, your position most respected, your sovereign's majesty the weightiest, and your positional power supreme. These four beautiful things can neither be sought from outside nor requested from others. Act appropriately and gain them. (*Han Feizi* 4.1; Chen Qiyou 2000: 59).

Keeping positional power in the ruler's hands is a precondition for controlling the state and stabilizing society. And yet, the ruler cannot rely on himself alone to govern the country. He must also rely on a ruling group, i.e., on his chief bureaucrats. This implies delegating power to underlings: "He who appoints others causes them to gain positional power" 任人者，使有勢也 (*Han Feizi* 47.2; Chen Qiyou 2000: 1024 ["Ba shuo" 八說]). This creates two negative results. First, the ministers below may use the power conferred by the ruler to seek personal gain. Second, and even worse, they may plot to deprive the ruler of his authority altogether and usurp his power.

Fa texts repeatedly warn of the dangers of empowering ministers. *Han Feizi* acknowledges "The difficult matter is that you must rely on others so as to accomplish your positional power, and have to make sure that they do not harm you" 物之所謂難者，必借人成勢而勿使侵害己 (*Han Feizi* 38.3.2; Chen Qiyou 2000: 902 ["Nan san" 難三]). When the ruler loses control of his ministers, the situation of the people below will be particularly gloomy, as outlined in the *Book of Lord Shang*: "great ministers compete for private [interests] and disregard their people" 大臣爭于私而不顧其民, "the underlings of ranked officials obscure [the situation] below so as to plunder the people" 秩官之吏隱下以漁百姓 (*Book of Lord Shang* 14.5; Zhang Jue 2012: 170). *Han Feizi* succinctly summarizes the danger of powerful ministers: they "coerce the sovereign above and oppress the people below" 上逼主而下虐民 (*Han Feizi* 13.3; Chen Qiyou 2000: 275 ["He shi" 和氏]).

How can the ruler deal with these grave threats? The "Cultivation of authority" chapter of the *Book of Lord Shang* optimistically believes that the impartial implementation of rewards and punishments—which are the essence of law or standards (*fa*) advocated in the text—will suffice to ensure the ruler's control:

> 明主不蔽之謂明，不欺之謂察。故賞厚而利，刑重而必，不失疏遠，不私親近。故臣不蔽主，下不欺上。

> The clear-sighted sovereign is called "clear-sighted" because nothing is concealed from him; he is called "scrutinizing" because he cannot be deceived. Thus, his rewards are bountiful and trustworthy, his punishments heavy and ineluctable; [in rewarding] he does not overlook strangers, and [in punishing] he does not avoid relatives and intimates. Thus, the ministers cannot conceal anything from the sovereign, and inferiors cannot deceive superiors. (*Book of Lord Shang* 14.1; Zhang Jue 2012: 165)

Han Fei considered this approach simplistic. In "Fixing the standards" chapter, he famously criticized Shang Yang for paying attention only to laws and lacking understanding of the techniques of rule. Because in the state of Qin "the sovereign had no techniques of rule by which to identify treachery" (主無術以知姦也), the state's power and riches were squeezed by scheming ministers (*Han Feizi* 43.2.3; Chen Qiyou 2000: 959). Curtailing these ministers' power is one of the major imperatives recurring throughout *Han Feizi*. Here, techniques of rule should help. These techniques are outlined with greatest clarity in the chapter "Inner compendium of explanations, A" ("Nei chu shuo shang" 內儲說上):

主之所用也七術……一曰、眾端參觀，二曰、必罰明威，三曰、信賞盡能，四曰、一聽責下，五曰、疑詔詭使，六曰、挾知而問，七曰、倒言反事。此七者，主之所用也。

The techniques that the ruler uses are seven… First: to survey and compare the various views on a matter. Second: to make punishments ineluctable and authority clear. Third: to make rewards reliable and to make people use their abilities to the full. Fourth: to listen to proposals one by one, and to hold subordinates responsible. Fifth: to issue confusing edicts and make wily dispositions. Sixth: to keep your knowledge clasped under your arm and ask [for advice]. Seventh: to say the opposite of what you mean and do the opposite of what you intend. These seven [techniques] are what the ruler uses. (*Han Feizi* 30.0.0; Chen Qiyou 2000: 560)

Han Feizi realized that in the political sphere power struggles and disputes over interests between the ruler and his ministers are intense: "The superior (i.e., the ruler) and his underlings fight a hundred battles a day" 上下一日百戰 (*Han Feizi* 8.8; Chen Qiyou 2000: 170 ["Yang quan" 揚權]). The ministers are hungry tigers ready to devour the ruler,[13] and anything is permissible in the life-or-death struggle against them. Therefore, *Han Feizi* encourages the ruler to use conspiracies and stratagems against his rivals. In the above extract, the first four techniques are acceptable bureaucratic devices; but the latter three are secretive means through which the ruler should combat his ministers and dupe them (cf. Pines, Chap. 4, Sect. 3.2, this volume). The "Eight canons" ("Ba jing" 八經) chapter brazenly adds:

生害事，死傷名，則行飲食；不然，而與其讎；此謂除陰姦也。

If leaving them alive harms your undertakings, yet killing them ruins your reputation, then do it with [poisoned] food and drink. Otherwise, hand them over to their enemies. This is called removing the treacherous. (*Han Feizi* 48.3; Chen Qiyou 2000: 1054)

This is one of the most extreme statements even in *Han Feizi* which does not shun away from provocations. Ministers are enemies who, if needed, should be eliminated. And this ruthlessness is applied not just to those who endanger the ruler directly. Even so-called "worthies" (*xian ren* 賢人), who do not heed the ruler's orders, should be considered the ruler's foes and be mercilessly persecuted. The chapter "External compendium of explanations, right A" ("Wai chu shuo you shang" 外儲說右上) approvingly tells of the sage founder of the state of Qi 齊, Grand Duke Wang 太公望, who ordered the execution of two high-minded recluses. As they were of no use politically and potentially undermined his power, the execution, according to *Han Feizi*, was the only reasonable way to deal with them. In the same

---

[13] *Han Feizi* 8.7; Chen Qiyou 2000: 164 ("Yang quan"); cf. 5.2; Chen Qiyou 2000: 74–75 ("Zhu dao" 主道).

chapter, Han Fei repeatedly advocates the ruthless elimination of potential contenders for power. "When positional power is not enough to transform them, eliminate them" (勢不足以化則除之); "If rewards and praise do not encourage them, if punishment and censure do not overawe them, if, after all four have been applied they do not change their ways—eliminate them" (賞之譽之不勸，罰之毀之不畏，四者加焉不變，則其除之) (*Han Feizi* 34.1.7, 34.0.1, and 34.1.1; Chen Qiyou 2000: 769, 757, and 761).

Han Fei's blatant propositions to eradicate potentially threatening ministers and to eliminate everybody who is not sufficiently compliant are frightening. Any reader with basic moral instincts would immediately reject this approach. Han Fei advocates that the ruler may commit evil in order to maintain his power. However, in allowing the ruler to commit evil, Han Fei does not encourage the ruler to be a morally evil person. Rather, he supports using evil means in order to protect the ruler's authority, thereby achieving his ideal rule of impartial standards. The treacherous character of politics (or Walzer's "dirty hands") is especially clear here.

Without justifying Han Fei's ruthless means, one should recall the backdrop of his gloomy view of the ruler-minister relations. The perennial mistrust and life-or-death struggle between the rulers and their aides were not Han Fei's invention; rather they reflected his internalization of the historical lessons of ministerial usurpations in the past. The partition of the state of Jin 晉 among the leading ministerial lineages, the usurpation of power in the state of Qi 齊 by the Tian 田 (Chen 陳) lineage, and a similar (though by now less known) usurpation in the state of Song 宋 by the Dai 戴 lineage are recurring examples in *Han Feizi*.[14] These lessons made Han Fei aware of the cruelty of power struggles between the ruler and his subjects, as well as the significance of strengthening the ruler's authority. They shaped Han Fei's commitment to preserving and stabilizing political order by all means.

It is somewhat ironic that Han Fei, himself a member of the ruling lineage (whose ancestors were among those who partitioned the state of Jin) was so antagonistic toward the ruling elite. I believe that this antagonism and Han Fei's anti-ministerial stance in general should be understood in the context of his prioritizing of the common (*gong* 公) over "private" (*si* 私) interests. The ruler represented the common interest (note that *gong* also means 'a lord'; it was the designation of territorial rulers prior to the fourth century BCE).[15] Safeguarding his position was the precondition for ensuring viable political order that was the only alternative to dreadful turmoil. As such this was a good thing to do. This is the antinomy of politics; or as Weber has described, good intentions in the political sphere often require evil means to achieve.

---

[14] For details, see such chapters such as "The two handles" ("Er bing 二柄), "Solitary frustration" ("Gu fen" 孤憤), "Loyalty and Filiality" ("Zhong xiao" 忠孝) *et saepe*. See also Yin 1987.

[15] See more in Liu Zehua 2003: 332–73; cf. Goldin 2020: 204–05; Pines, Chap. 4, Sect. 3, this volume.

The *fa* tradition in general, and *Han Feizi* in particular, clarify, even if at times subtly, an unpleasant understanding: the cruelty and darkness of power politics, along with the fairness and uprightness of the rule of *fa*, constitute the two sides of political life. Both are indispensable. This is not something that can be glossed over through appeals to ethical norms. It is the destiny of political affairs.

3.5 Impartial Standards and Political Manipulations: A Synthesis?

The above discussion has demonstrated, I hope, the interrelatedness of the ostensibly contradictory aspects of the *fa* thought: the simultaneous insistence on the rule through fair and universally applicable impartial standards; and the trickery, maneuvering, and cruelty involved in safeguarding the ruler's authority. From the point of view of *fa* adherents, both aspects were not contradictory but mutually reinforcing. The focus of the first was ruling the people; the focus of the second was determining who will rule the state and what its future course will be. The strict enforcement of impartial standards and their comprehensive institutionalization were predicated on political stability. But this stability in turn would not be possible without ensuring stability at the top of the government apparatus. And to ensure the latter, the ruler had to deal with rapidly changing affairs and respond to ferocious contention from his underlings; thus, he must have flexibility. This flexibility could not be achieved through impartial standards alone.

The interdependence between the stability of laws and standards on the one hand and the flexibility of the ruler on the other is hinted at in the chapter "Weakening the people" ("Ruo min" 弱民) of the *Book of Lord Shang*:

法有，民安其次；主變，事能得齊；國守安，主操權利。故主貴多變，國貴少變。

> When there are standards (laws), the people are at peace with hierarchy; when the sovereign makes changes, he employs the able and attains the suitable; when the state preserves peace, while the sovereign holds power, it is beneficial. Therefore, **"the sovereign values multiple changes; the state values minimal changes."**[16] (*Book of Lord Shang* 20.5; Zhang Jue 2012: 242)

In explaining the final sentence of the above passage (which appears first in Chap. 4, Sect. 1), Jiang Lihong (1996: 27) noted: "The ruler prizes adaptability; this is achieved through techniques of rule. The state prizes consistency; this is achieved through *fa*." Jiang's understanding of this passage is convincing. Furthermore, one can well understand why "Objections 3" chapter of the *Han Feizi*, cited above

---

[16] The sentence in bold is citation from Chap. 4.1 ("Eliminating the strong" ["Qu qiang 去強]) of the *Book of Lord Shang* to which Chap. 20, "Weakening the people," serves as exegesis. See more in Pines 143–144 (Editor's note).

(p. 273), emphasizes that "laws are best when they are clear, whereas techniques should not be seen." Laws and standards are announced to the people and need to be universally applicable and transparent. Techniques of rule are used by the ruler to ensure that the ministers abide by the laws, and to prevent power from being usurped. Thus, techniques of rule must be exclusive and secretive. This is the only way to preserve the ruler's power without which the entire sociopolitical order will be endangered.

Fa adherents hoped that the ruler would triumph in the political sphere and lead the state towards wealth and power ("a rich state and a strong army," *fuguo qiangbing* 富國强兵), allowing him to win the contention among the Warring States, unify All under Heaven, and therewith benefit the people. The ruler was the pivot of the system. Not every ruler was expected to act as lawgiver; but every single ruler had the gravest responsibility for implementing the rule of *fa* and for ensuring the proper functioning of the state. And yet, as we shall see below, the ruler was not just the pivot but also the weakest point in the *fa* intellectual construct.

4 The Predicament of the *Fa* Tradition: The Problem of the Ruler

In a recent major study of China's preimperial philosophy, Tao Jiang 蔣韜 offered an insightful reappraisal of habitual denigration of the *fa* tradition as "immoral" or "amoral." Instead, he identified the ideal of impartiality (*gong* 公) as the crucial ethical value in *fa* thought (T. Jiang 2021: 238 ff.). Given the aforementioned identity of the terms "impartiality" and "duke" or "lord," it is often opined (most notably by Paul R. Goldin) that commitment to *gong* refers squarely to safeguarding the ruler's personal interests, "What a ruler needs, then, are instruments of *gong* that will thwart his minions' aspirations of *si* [私]" (Goldin 2020: 205). I beg to disagree. Impartiality, in particular the system in which "everything is determined by *fa*" 一斷於法,[17] was supposed to benefit the polity as a whole. Even if one dismisses the *fa* texts' (admittedly rare) statements that the ultimate goal of their proposals is to "benefit the common people and contribute to the broad masses" 利民萌，便眾庶 or "to implement benevolence and righteousness in All-under-Heaven" 述仁義於天下[18] as mere propaganda, there are plenty of less bombastic pronouncements to convince most skeptics that *fa* thinkers aimed at benefitting the people at large, albeit by employing harsh and oppressive methods. It is true that normally, these thinkers expected that by benefitting the polity and the people they also benefit the

---

[17] This is the bottom line of the *fa* school as identified by Sima Tan 司馬談 (d. 110 BCE) (*Shiji* 130: 3291).

[18] See respectively *Han Feizi* 42.2.1; Chen Qiyou 2000: 955 ("Wen Tian") and *Book of Lord Shang* 13.6; Zhang Jue 2012: 162 ("Jin ling" 靳令).

ruler personally; but clearly their goal was *not* catering to the ruler's whims, as I shall demonstrate below.

The importance of the ruler for *fa* thinkers was twofold. One of its aspects—the common belief of the Warring States thinkers that strict adherence to monarchic rule is the only way to ensure political stability—was noted above (p. 274) and does not require repetition here. The second point is less easily observable but is important nonetheless. The ruler's patronage was the major way in which *fa* thinkers sought to overcome aristocratic opposition to their reforms.

Recall that reforms initiated by *fa* thinkers were predicated at establishing "a feasible policy under which government officials will be selected based on their worth and abilities, so as to satisfy the urgent needs of a new bureaucratically governed state" (Xu Zhuoyun 2006: 212). As such, these reforms were detrimental to the entrenched interests of hereditary ministers and of top aristocracy at large, engendering bitter opposition. Whereas we cannot confirm for sure whether or not the conservative opponents of Shang Yang, the debate with whom is recorded in the first chapter of the *Book of Lord Shang*, were indeed members of Qin's hereditary aristocracy (for this conjecture, see Pines 2017: 268n3), there is no doubt that aristocrats led the opposition to the reforms thereafter. Sima Qian mentions, "After Lord Shang acted as Qin's chancellor for ten years, many among the members of the ruling lineage and the noble consort's families resented him" (商君相秦十年，宗室貴戚多怨望者; *Shiji* 68: 2233). A Chu reformer, Wu Qi 吳起 (d. 381 BCE), who is paired with Shang Yang as a model *fa* reformer in *Han Feizi*,[19] was murdered by "grand ministers from the ruling lineage" 宗室大臣 of Chu (*Shiji* 65: 2168). Later (ca. 235 BCE), Qin's "grand ministers from the ruling lineage" tried to block outsiders from reaching positions in Qin's administration, almost cutting off the career of another major *fa* adherent, Li Si 李斯 (d. 208 BCE) (*Shiji* 87: 2541). This appears to be a constant pattern. For a *fa* minister, overcoming these entrenched interests of older pedigree-based elites was possible only with the support of a powerful ruler. By empowering the sovereign, *fa* thinkers paved the way for the success of the reforms that they sought to initiate.

High hopes for a supportive ruler, however, were in vain. The frustration of *fa* thinkers with the rulers is most clearly visible in several chapters of *Han Feizi*. These chapters, uncharacteristically, focus on worthy ministers, "the possessors of techniques" 有術者 or "men of service who are adept at laws and techniques of rule" 法術之士, with whom Han Fei evidently identified himself. These selfless ministers are a rarity as such; and normally they would be blocked by "political heavyweights" from the ruler's entourage.[20] But even if a committed *fa* adherent

---

[19] See Chap. 14, "Treacherous, Larcenous, Murderous Ministers" ("Jian jie shi chen" 姦劫弒臣); cf. Chap. 42, "Asking Tian" ("Wen Tian").

[20] "Ministers who comply with orders in conducting affairs and stick to the laws when they administer their duties are not the ones I call 'political heavyweights.' As for the political heavyweights: without orders, they act on their own authority, they violate the law to further their private interests, they squander what belongs to the state in order to work for their house, and their power enables them to gain [the support] of the ruler. These are the ones whom I call 'political heavyweights.'" 人臣循令而從事，案法而治官，非謂重人也。重人也者，無令而擅為，虧法以

encounters a supportive sovereign, their symbiosis would not last beyond the patron ruler's death. The chapter "Mr. He" ("He shi" 和氏), for instance, recalls the fate of Shang Yang and Wu Qi, both of whom encountered responsive rulers and contributed greatly to the states of Qin and Chu, respectively. Nonetheless, both were executed or assassinated immediately upon the death of their patrons. Elsewhere, Han Fei's interlocutor mentions that Wu Qi and Shang Yang's "trouble was not meeting the right times and not encountering the right ruler" 不逢世遇主之患也 (*Han Feizi* 42.2.1; Chen Qiyou 2000: 955 ["Wen Tian" 問田]). Needless to say, Han Fei himself was even less successful in encountering a supportive sovereign.

The bitter fate of *fa* reformers was not accidental. When reformers like Wu Qi and Shang Yang enjoyed the rulers' support, they amassed great authority. Would this be tolerated by the successor sovereign? Even if they had no intention of over-stepping their positions, recall the Chinese saying, "A person was innocent, but possessing a precious stone made him a culprit" (匹夫無罪，懷璧其罪). Would the new ruler tolerate extraordinarily powerful ministers inherited from his prede-cessor? Moreover, a reformer had to contend with those who were alienated by the policy of impartial and fair implementation of laws and regulations. "The Biography of Lord Shang" tells of Shang Yang's punishment of the tutors of the crown prince, meted out so as to demonstrate the laws' fairness (see above, p. 278). Yet this was stepping on the toes of the future ruler, and hence was akin to political suicide. Add to this the aristocrats' opposition. Preserving the ruler's support in the face of such opposition was challenging indeed.

To aggravate matters more, *fa* adherents did not endear themselves to the sover-eigns because they demanded of rulers that they remain committed to impartial standards and not give rein to their whims. This topic recurs in *fa* texts, clarifying beyond doubt that the idea of impartiality advocated by *fa* thinkers was not identical to serving the ruler's personal interests. To the contrary, the rulers are repeatedly requested to remain committed to laws and standards that should benefit everybody under Heaven rather than the ruler alone. Take for instance the following passage from the chapter "Cultivating the authority" ("Xiu quan" 修權) of the *Book of Lord Shang*:

> 故堯舜之位天下也，非私天下之利也，為天下位天下也。論賢舉能而傳焉，非疏父子，親越人也，明於治亂之道也。故三王以義親，五霸以法正諸侯，皆非私天下之利也，為天下治天下。

Hence, when Yao and Shun were established in All under Heaven, this was not in order to benefit privately from All under Heaven—they were established for the sake of All under Heaven. They selected the worthy, elevated the able, and transmitted [power] to them not because of alienation between father and son and intimacy with strangers, but because the Way of order and disorder was clear to them. Hence, the Three Kings treated their relatives righteously, and the Five Hegemons used law to rectify regional lords—all this was not in

---

利私，耗國以便家，力能得其君，此所為(謂)重人也。See *Han Feizi* 11.1; Chen Qiyou 2000: 239 ("Gu fen").

order to benefit privately from All under Heaven. They ruled All under Heaven for the sake of All under Heaven. (*Book of Lord Shang* 14.4; Zhang Jue 2012: 168)[21]

The same idea that the ruler-focused political system should benefit everybody is repeated in the "Majestic virtue" ("Wei de" 威德) chapter from the *Shenzi* 慎子 fragments:

> 古者立天子而貴之者，非以利一人也。曰:天下無一貴，則理無由通，通理以為天下也。故立天子以為天下，非立天下以為天子也；立國君以為國，非立國以為君也；立官長以為官，非立官以為長也。

> In antiquity, the Son of Heaven was established and esteemed not in order to benefit the single person. It is said: if All under Heaven lack the single esteemed [person], there is no way to carry out the principles [of orderly government], carrying out the principles is done for the sake of All under Heaven. Hence, the Son of Heaven is established for the sake of All under Heaven, it is not that All under Heaven is established for the sake of the Son of Heaven; a ruler of a state is established for the sake of the state, it is not that the state is established for the sake of the ruler of the state; a head of officials is established for the sake of officials, it is not that officials are established for the sake of the head of officials. (Xu Fuhong 2013: 16; translation cf. Harris 2016: 110, fragments 21–22)

These lofty pronouncements clarify beyond doubt: *fa* thinkers were not senseless tools in the sovereign's hands. Rather, they shared the other intellectual currents' critical view of current rulers and urged the rulers to rein in their whims. But herein lies the problem; committed as they were to the empowerment of the sovereign, *fa* thinkers never proposed any institutional means of correcting or restraining the ruler. In the final account they could rely only on their own moral suasion when facing an uncooperative ruler. And this suasion had obvious limits. It was unrealistic to expect the ruler to act selflessly. Rulers were ordinary human beings with their personal emotions, desires, and biases. These individuals could rarely if at all live up to the lofty expectations expressed in the passages above. Some of the *fa* thinkers, most notably Han Fei, realized this well. In *Han Feizi* we find not just unequivocal understanding that most rulers are mediocrities who cannot be expected to heed lofty advice, but also sober realization that the rulers themselves are too often prone to act intemperately, endangering their polities and their selves.[22]

---

[21] The text refers to Yao and Shun's abdication in favor of meritorious ministers, and to the "Three Kings" (Xia, Shang, and Zhou founders) adopting the system of hereditary succession. Despite the differences between the two, both systems, as well as a more forceful rule by the "Five Hegemons" (powerful regional lords from the Springs and Autumns era)—all supposedly manifest concern for the well-being of "All under Heaven" (Editor's note).

[22] Han Fei's emphatic argument that most of the rulers are just mediocrities (neither sages nor tyrants) is most clearly expressed in Chap. 40, "Objections to positional power" (*Han Feizi* 40.3.2; Chen Qiyou 2000: 945; discussed in Pines 2020). Han Fei's frustration with individual rulers is most strongly evident from the historical anecdotes, scattered throughout *Han Feizi*, which almost invariably depict the rulers as morally and intellectually inferior to their advisors. These rulers are the major reason for their polities' collapse. See, e.g., Graziani 2015; Pines, Chap. 4, Sect. 3.3, this volume.

Tong Shuye (1908–1968) lamented once: "The Han government carried on the policy of 'being overtly Confucian and covertly *fa* adherent' (陽儒陰法). Yet they cast away the true spirit of the *fa* tradition (in fact, in the Qin dynasty, the true spirit of the *fa* tradition had already gradually died out). What remained was primarily the point of 'making the ruler supreme and the ministers lowly' (尊君卑臣)" (Tong 1982: 287). This statement encapsulates the *fa* thinkers' predicament. Whereas the ideal of the ruler who endorses impartial standards and laws remained barely realizable, it was all too easy for the ruler to employ political trickery—which was legitimated by the *fa* adherents in the first place—not just for the sake of securing their position but in the general conduct of government affairs.

The *fa* tradition therefore possessed certain self-defeating features. Once again, the case of *Han Feizi* exemplifies this best. Having convinced the ruler that he is surrounded by plotters, potential usurpers, and bloodthirsty "tigers," Han Fei tried to qualify these statements by introducing a counter-figure of a model minister, adept at "laws and techniques of rule," a person fully devoted to the state's well-being (above, p. 285). But this was of little use. In the bitter contest for power no minister could be trusted forever. The ruler who internalized *Han Feizi*'s ideas would be justified to think that, once his devoted and law-abiding aide assumes high position and wields great power, he will plot usurpation himself. And in that case, all the arsenal of political trickery advocated in *Han Feizi* could be employed against such an aide.

With this understanding in mind, we can conclude that the tragic fate of the *fa* adherents was historically inevitable. It is perhaps not a coincidence that the most prominent thinkers associated with the *fa* tradition met a cruel end, which did not befall adherents of other intellectual currents. Recall that Shang Yang was dismembered by chariots by the order of the son of his benefactor, King Huiwen of Qin 秦惠文王 (r. 337–311 BCE); Han Fei died in Qin's custody; Li Si was cut into two at the waist by the order of the Second Emperor of Qin (r. 209–207 BCE), and Chao Cuo 晁錯 (d. 154 BCE) was executed by Emperor Jing of Han 漢景帝 (r. 157–141 BCE). Their miserable fates were due to the logic of politics and not the result of the "rule of *fa*" ideal.

The tragic fate of the *fa* adherents demonstrates a basic truth: their ideal "men-of-service adept at laws and techniques of rule" remained lonely and weak, unable to promote fundamental political change. These supporters of rule by impartial standards would neither rely on the commoners below (even though the ambitious commoners were the beneficiaries of some of the new laws, which opened more avenues for upward political mobility); nor would they organize themselves in a political faction that would promote institutionalization of the "rule of *fa*." This meant that *fa* adherents remained forever reliant on the ruler alone, whose support was lackluster at best. The lofty goals of universally applicable, fair, and impartial rules of ordering society and the state remained forever dependent on the balance of power in the political sphere, which was dominated by ruthless struggle for survival between the ruler and his underlings. Under these conditions it was impossible to attain anything approximating the real "rule of *fa*." And yet, their failure notwithstanding, *fa* supporters made an important contribution not only on the practical level but also on the level of political ideals. The ideal of the political system that is committed to impartiality and serves the common (*gong* 公) interests of the subjects remains valid well into our days.

5   Afterthought: The *Fa* Tradition's Modern Value

Pre-Qin *fa* tradition contains three types of discourses. The first is the discourse of *fa*, that is the idea of the rule based on impartial standards and laws. This is an idealistic discourse, which contains clear connotation of serving common interests of the subjects. The second, the discourse on techniques of rule and positional power, concerns struggles within the political realm and is predicated on protecting and reinforcing the ruler's authority against powerful ministers and aristocrats. The third is the practical discourse aimed at resolving specific problems of the Warring States-period polity. This discourse—which was not the topic of the current essay but was analyzed in countless studies—focuses on attaining "a rich state and a strong army" 富國强兵, ensuring "a single outlet" (*yikong* 一孔, alternatively 一空) for material and social benefits, rewarding agricultural and military merit, heavily punishing light crimes, promoting collective criminal responsibility, and encouraging individuals to report the crimes of others.[23] The first of these discourses, which is the closest to the concept of the rule of law, contained elements of justice, fairness, and transparency, even if its major impetus came from the need to direct the people towards agriculture and warfare.

The three discourses outlined above formed the organic whole. The *fa*-related discourse was the skeleton, techniques of rule and positional power were one's blood and flesh, whereas practical policies were one's individual abilities. Most scholars who discussed the *fa* tradition paid greater attention to the "individual abilities," confining the relevance of the *fa* ideology to the contemporaneous historical circumstances. By now, many of the specific measures and policies advocated by the *fa* adherents more than two millennia ago became obsolete and largely irrelevant. Thus, whereas agriculture and warfare remain highly important for the state's survival even nowadays, no statesman or thinker in their right mind would demand directing the entire population to these two pursuits, as is repeatedly advocated in the *fa* texts. This results in insufficient scholarly attention to the *fa* ideology in general.

Formed in the Warring States period, the *fa* tradition bore clear signs of its cruel age. This is reflected both on the level of specific laws and on the level of legitimating conspiracy and trickery. Thus, the laws were designed to eradicate the smallest transgressions through merciless punishments inflicted even for minor offences. Speaking of trickery, *fa* adherents did not shy away from eliminating their foes

---

[23] See Sun 2014; Zhang Linxiang 2015; and also Pines 2017: 59–99 for the *Book of Lord Shang* and Song 2010: 297–334 for *Han Feizi*.

either openly with grand justifications, or clandestinely through assassinations. All of these characterized the spirit of "ancient politics" or "ancient monarchic politics." Arguably, modern politics is somewhat more civilized, and bloodshed and violence play an ever-decreasing role, or so we hope. This is especially so in countries where the rule of law concept is matured and where conspiracies and trickery have become subtle. Surely, politics progressed toward establishing the rule of law as its own separate sphere. This progress reflects not just ideological advancement, but, more importantly, is the result of new social constellations that forced the rulers to make concessions and allowed modification of the political system. And yet, we should recall that treachery remains part of politics both ancient and modern.

Following the collapse of the Qin dynasty, the intellectual impact of the *fa* tradition decreased dramatically. Not only its concept of the rule by *fa* was sidelined; so was its understanding of the political sphere. The newly dominant Confucian discourse from the Han dynasty on focused on the "oughts" of politics rather than its unpleasant and cruel realities. Confucians promoted a new form of political ethics, which attempted to blend morality with politics. Laudable as it was, this view impaired the ability of later Chinese thinkers to grasp the shadowy nature of politics. This understanding is not pleasant, but nor can it be simply glossed over. As *The Dictator's Handbook* puts it:

> All of this may be sacrilege to some, but we believe that, in the end, it's the best way to understand the political world—and the only way that we can begin to assess how to use the rules to rule by to rule for the better. (de Mesquita and Smith 2011: 16)

Only by facing political life in its full complexity—including its shadowy aspects, which should not be ignored on account of our value orientations—can one truly see the nature of politics. The *fa* tradition brought these shadowy aspects to light. Was it necessarily bad? Before we answer, recall Zhang Taiyan's 章太炎 (aka Zhang Binglin 章炳麟, 1869–1936) speculative yet brilliant discussion of the *Laozi* 老子. Zhang opined that exposing the clandestine techniques of rule in the *Laozi* is a trick of "fighting the enemy with his own weapons" (入室操戈):

> 老聃所以言術，將以擈前王之隱匿，取之玉版，布之短書，使人人戶知其術則術敗。會前世簡畢重滯，力不遠行，故二三奸人得因自利。及今世有赫蹄雕鏤之技，其書遍行，雖權術亦幾無施矣。

> The reason why Lao Dan spoke of techniques of rule is that he intended to reveal what the former kings had done in secrecy. He took the [secret knowledge enshrined on] jade tablets and disseminated its contents into simple stories, thereby allowing every person to understand these techniques of rule. Then, the techniques of rule ceased to work. Because in the past, the people's knowledge was stagnant and abilities limited, a few treacherous individuals were able to use [the techniques of rule] to profit themselves. But in our generation, although these techniques are written and carved into books that broadly circulate, even if one understands the techniques of rule, one can no longer implement them." (Zhang Taiyan [1910] 1996: 102)

Zhang Taiyan believed that when the *Laozi* popularized the techniques of rule that were hidden away by the former kings, it thereby allowed everybody to understand how treacherous leaders benefit themselves. At this point, the clandestine techniques of rule could no longer be utilized. Adapting this logic, it may be averred that the *fa* texts' elucidation of the tension between politics and "the rule of *fa*" would aid us to recognize the essence of politics and gradually explore ways to achieve progress by reducing its shadowy aspects.

Adherents of the *fa* tradition emphasized both the justness of the rule of *fa* and the flexibility and trickery of practical politics. They advocated that the ruler should be well-versed in plotting and maneuvering. Did they unintentionally highlight the dilemma between *fazhi* in its meaning as the rule of law and practical politics? Or did they intentionally do so? Whether intentional or unintentional, the result is enlightening. The dilemma between the theory of the rule of *fa* and the political recommendations of the *fa* adherents is the irresolvable dilemma of politics. Even the currently dominant ideology that calls upon utilizing the laws to restrain power holders has yet to produce a realistic blueprint that can encompass all of humanity's politics. In this sense, the predicament faced by the *fa* tradition more than two thousand years ago is not only the predicament that they or their age had faced, but is also the predicament facing humanity in our era and beyond. By this logic, in the context of modern thought, the *fa* tradition engages us in intellectual dialogue with the past and provides us with precious wisdom. It is no longer a dead theory buried under the dust of two millennia of indifference, but also a form of wisdom that, even today, continues to discover, explain, and resolve the predicament that faces humanity.

References

Bingham, Tom. 2010. *The Rule of Law*. London/New York: Allen Lane.

Book of Lord Shang. See Pines 2017.

Chen, Qiyou 陳奇猷. 2000. *Han Feizi, With New Collations and Commentary* 韓非子新校注. Shanghai: Shanghai guji chubanshe.

Coady, C.A.J. 2023. The Problem of Dirty Hands. In *Stanford Encyclopedia of Philosophy*, ed. Edward N. Zalta and Uri Nodelman. https://plato.stanford.edu/entries/dirty-hands/.

de Mesquita, Bruce Bueno, and Smith Alastair. 2011. *The Dictator's Handbook: Why Bad Behaviour is Almost Always Good Politics*. New York: Public Affairs.

Feng, Youlan 馮友蘭. [1930] 2000. *History of Chinese Philosophy* 中國哲學史. Rpt. Shanghai: Huadong shifan daxue chubanshe.

Fu, Zhengyuan. 1996. *China's Legalists: The Earliest Totalitarians and Their Art of Ruling*. Armonk NY: M.E. Sharpe.

Goldin, Paul R. 2020. *The Art of Chinese Philosophy: Eight Classical Texts and How to Read Them*. Princeton NJ: Princeton University Press.

Graziani, Romain. 2015. Monarch and Minister: The Problematic Partnership in the Building of Absolute Monarchy in the *Han Feizi* 韓非子. In *Ideology of Power and Power of Ideology in Early China*, ed. Yuri Pines, Paul R. Goldin, and Martin Kern, 155–180. Leiden: Brill.

Guanzi jiaozhu 管子校注 (Guanzi collated and annotated). 2004. Ed. Li, Xiangfeng 黎翔鳳. Beijing: Zhonghua shuju.

Guo, Moruo 郭沫若. [1945] 2008. Criticism of Early *fa* School 前期法家的批判. Reprinted in Guo Moruo, *Ten Critical Studies* 十批判書, 227–249. Beijing: Zhongguo huaqiao chubanshe.

Han, Dongyu 韓東育. 1993. Ruling over Minds, Ruling over Bodies, and the Rule of Law: An Analysis of the Irreconcilable Internal Contradictions in the Political Thought of the *fa* School "心治"、"身治"與"法治":析法家政治思想中不可解的內在矛盾, *Collected Papers in Historiography* 史學集刊 2: 1–5.

Han Feizi. See Harbsmeier, forthcoming.

Harbsmeier, Christoph, trans. Forthcoming. *Han Feizi, A Complete Translation: The Art of Statecraft in Early China*. Ed. Jens Østergaard Petersen and Yuri Pines. Leiden: Brill.

Harris, Eirik Lang. 2016. *The Shenzi Fragments: A Philosophical Analysis and Translation*. New York: Columbia University Press.

Hong, Tao 洪濤. 2018. Studies of the Concept of the 'Rule of Law' (*fazhi*) and the Thought of the School of *fa* in 20th Century China. 20世紀中國的法治概念與法家思想. *History of Political Thought* 政治思想史 9.1: 13–45 and 9.2: 31–58.

Jia, Kunpeng 賈坤鵬. 2018. Rebutting the Theory that Han Fei Simultaneously used Laws, Techniques of Rule, and Positional Power 韓非"法術勢並用說"駁論, in: *Journal of Henan Normal University* 河南師範大學學報 2: 77–84.

Jiang, Lihong 蔣禮鴻. 1996. *Pointing an Awl at the Book of Lord Shang* 商君書錐指. Beijing: Zhonghua shuju.

Jiang, Chongyue 蔣重躍. 2000. *Political Thought of Han Feizi* 韓非子的政治思想. Beijing: Beijing shifan daxue chubanshe.

———— 蔣重躍. 2019. On three Terminological Contradictions in *Han Feizi*: An Example of Critical Study of Traditional Thought 關於《韓非子》中三組概念的矛盾:例說傳統學術思想的批判性研究. *Research in the Traditions of Chinese Culture* 國學學刊 1: 90–103.

Jiang, Tao. 2021. *Origins of Moral-Political Philosophy in Early China: Contestation of Humaneness, Justice, and Personal Freedom*. Oxford: Oxford University Press.

Kim, Sungmoon. 2016. Achieving the Way: Confucian Virtue Politics and the Problem of Dirty Hands. *Philosophy East and West* 66 (1): 152–176.

Liang, Qichao 梁启超. [1904] 1989a. On the History of the Development of Chinese Legal Thought 中國法理學發達史論, rpt. in: Liang, *Collected Works from the Ice Drinker's Studio* 飲冰室合集, vol. 15, 41–94. Beijing: Zhonghua shuju.

———— 梁启超. [1922] 1989b. *History of Pre-Qin Political Thought* 先秦政治思想史, rpt. in: Liang, *Collected Works from the Ice Drinker's Studio* 飲冰室合集, vol. 50, 1–217. Beijing: Zhonghua shuju.

Liu, Zehua 劉澤華. 2000. *China's Monarchism* 中國的王權主義. Shanghai: Renmin chubanshe.

———— 劉澤華. 2003. *Studies from 'Washing the Ears' Studio* 洗耳齋文稿. Beijing: Zhonghua shuju.

Machiavelli, Niccolò. 1988. In *The Prince*, ed. Quentin Skinner and Russell Price. Cambridge: Cambridge University Press.

Peerenboom, Randall. 2004. *Asian Discourses of Rule of Law*. London: Routledge.

Pines, Yuri, trans. 2017. *The Book of Lord Shang: Apologetics of State Power in Early China*. Translations from the Asian Classics. New York: Columbia University Press.

————. 2020. Worth vs. Power: Han Fei's 'Objection to Positional Power' Revisited. *Asiatische Studien/Études Asiatiques* 74 (3): 687–710.

Pound, Roscoe. 1926. *Law and Morals*. Chapel Hill: University of North Carolina Press.

Rickett, W. Allyn, trans. 1985. Guanzi: Political, Economic, and Philosophical Essays from Early China. Vol. 1. Princeton: Princeton University Press.

————, trans. 1998. Guanzi: Political, Economic, and Philosophical Essays from Early China. Vol. 2. Princeton: Princeton University Press.

Shiji 史記 (Records of the Historian). 1997. By Sima, Qian 司馬遷 (ca. 145–90 BCE) et al. Annotated by Zhang, Shoujie 張守節, Sima, Zhen 司馬貞, and Pei, Yin 裴駰. Beijing: Zhonghua shuju.

Song, Hongbing 宋洪兵. 2010. *Re-examining Han Feizi's Political Thought* 韓非子政治思想再研究. Beijing: Zhongguo Renmin Daxue chubanshe.

Sun, Xiaochun 孫曉春. 2014. Contemporary Reflections on the *fa* School Concept of a Rich [State] and a Strong [Army] 先秦法家富強觀念的現代反思. *Journal of Political Science* 政治学研究 5: 3–10.

Tong, Shuye 童書業. 1982. *Research on the Thought of Seven pre-Qin masters* 先秦七子思想研究. Jinan: Qilu.

Tong, Weimin 仝衛敏. 2013. *An Integrative Study of Excavated Documents and the* Book of Lord Shang 出土文獻與《商君書》綜合研究. Taipei: Hua Mulan.

Walzer, Michael. 1973. Political Action: The Problem of Dirty Hands. *Philosophy and Public Affairs* 2 (2): 160–180.

Wang, Renbo 王人博 and Cheng, Liaoyuan 程燎原. 1989. *On the Rule of Law* 法治論. Ji'nan: Shandong renmin chubanshe.

Weber, Max. 2004. In *The Vocation Lectures.*, trans. Rodney Livingstone;, ed. David Owen and Tracy B. Strong. Indianapolis: Hackett.

Wei, Sen 韋森. 2006. *Analytical Economics* 思辨的經濟學. Ji'nan: Shandong youyi chubanshe.

Xiao, Gongquan (Hsiao Kung-chuan) 蕭公權. [1937] 1998. *History of Chinese Political Thought* 中國政治思想史. Shenyang: Liaoning jiaoyu chubanshe.

Xiong, Shili 熊十力. 1984. *Critical Discussion of Han Feizi* 韓非子評論. Taipei: Xuesheng shuju.

Xu, Zhuoyun 許倬雲. 2006. *History of Ancient Chinese Society: Social Mobility in the Spring and Autumn and Warring States periods* 中國古代社會史論:春秋戰國時期的社會流動. Guilin: Guangxi shifan daxue chubanshe.

Xu, Fuhong 許富宏. 2013. *Shenzi, with Collected Collations and Commentary* 慎子集校集注. Beijing: Zhonghua shuju.

Xunzi jijie 荀子集解 (*Xunzi*, with collected explanations). 1992. Ed. Wang, Xianqian 王先謙 (1842–1917), Shen, Xiaohuan 沈嘯寰, and Wang, Xingxian 王星賢. Beijing: Zhonghua shuju.

Yang, Ling 楊玲. 2007. *Balancing and Absolute Confrontation: A Comparative Study of Pre-Qin Legalist Thought* 中和與絕對的抗衡:先秦法家思想比較研究. Beijing: Zhongguo shehui kexue chubanshe.

Yin, Zhenhuan 尹振環. 1987. Using Instances of Royal Succession and Regicide to Analyze the Advance of Authoritarian Dictatorship 從王位繼承和弒君看君主專制理論的逐步形成. *Chinese History* 中國史研究 4: 17–24.

Yu, Keping 俞可平. 2020. *Power and Authority: Several Important Issues in Political Philosophy* 權力與權威:政治哲學若干重要問題. Beijing: Shangwu.

Yusuke, Sakagami 坂冢由树. 1993. The relationship between laws, political maneuvers, and positional power in the *Han Feizi* 《韓非子》中法、術、勢三者的關係, *Journal of the Renmin University of China* 中國人民大學學報 5: 66–71.

Zhang, Taiyan 章太炎 (Zhang Binglin 章炳麟). [1910] 1996. Comprehensive Discourse of the Country's Past: Origins of the Way (I) 國故論衡·原道(上), rpt. in: *Modern Chinese Academic Classics: Zhang Taiyan Volume* 中國現代學術经典·章太炎卷, ed. Liu Mengxi 劉梦溪, 383–87. Shijiazhuang: Hebei jiaoyu chubanshe.

Zhang, Jue 張覺. 2010. *Han Feizi, with Collated Subcommentaries* 韓非子校疏. Shanghai: Shanghai guji chubanshe.

———. 2012. *The Book of Lord Shang, with Collated Subcommentaries* 商君書校疏. Beijing: Zhishi chanquan chubanshe.

Zhang, Linxiang 張林祥. 2015. Criticism of the *fa* School's Concept of a Rich [State] and a Strong [Army]. 法家富强觀批判. *Gansu Theory Research* 甘肅理論學刊 6: 141–146.

Chapter 10
Human Motivation in the *fa* Tradition: Visions from the *Shenzi Fragments*, *Shangjunshu*, and *Han Feizi*

Eirik Lang Harris

One of the first topics any student of Chinese philosophy comes across is that of the various conceptions of human nature in the early texts. Often the discussion focuses on a particular term, *xing* 性, which many scholars take to be roughly analogous to the Western idea of human nature.[1] Another term that often enters discussions of human nature is *qing* 情, which often refers to dispositions, inclinations, or basic tendencies.[2] There is much benefit to be had from digging into these terms, examining how they are used in particular texts and passages, and determining what, if any, overlap there is with Western concepts such as human nature.

However, that will not be the goal of this chapter. Rather than focusing on a particular term, I wish to examine what texts like the *Shenzi Fragments* 慎子逸文, *Shangjunshu* 商君書 (*The Book of Lord Shang*), and *Han Feizi* 韓非子 have to say about what motivates human action, and, in particular, how these motivations are relevant to the task of political organization. To be sure, this will involve discussing terms like *xing* and *qing*, but the fact that the *Shenzi*, for example, never employs the term *xing* need not be taken to imply that it has nothing to say about human motivations.

---

[1] There are those, however, who think that such an understanding of *xing* is problematic. See, for example, Ames 1991 and the response by Bloom 1994. Additionally, as Lau 1953 clearly demonstrates, Mengzi and Xunzi use the term in importantly different ways.

[2] For more on *qing*, see Eifring 2004, particularly the essays by Harbsmeier 2004 and Puett 2004.

I am grateful to Thai Dang, Paul R. Goldin, Philip J. Ivanhoe, and an anonymous reviewer for their insightful criticisms and suggestions on earlier versions of this essay.

E. L. Harris (✉)
Department of Philosophy, Colorado State University, Fort Collins, CO, USA
e-mail: eiriklangharris@gmail.com

© The Author(s), under exclusive license to Springer Nature Switzerland AG 2024
Y. Pines (ed.), *Dao Companion to China's* fa *Tradition*, Dao Companions to Chinese Philosophy 19, https://doi.org/10.1007/978-3-031-53630-4_11

In short, the argument presented here is that these texts contend that, from the perspective of creating and maintaining political order, the most effective method is for the state to employ the already existing motivations of those over whom it rules. Once human motivations are understood, it becomes a relatively simple task to channel those motivations to ensure people act in ways that the state wishes. Implicit in this claim are at least two other commitments: (1) whatever the content of human motivations, this content is sufficiently similar across all human beings that the methods employed to channel them need not vary person by person, and (2) human motivations are fairly stable, and their content does not shift in any appreciable way over time.[3] Whether it is possible to change these motivations, as early Confucians and Daoists endeavor to do, is less clear, though the texts under investigation argue that any attempt to do so at the political level will lead to disaster. Note here that the structure of political argument, as laid out, does not rely upon a particular content to human motivations, and thus the applicability of this methodology as a political tool remains viable even if it were the case that any particular text's conception of human motivation is inaccurate.

1 Human Motivation in the *Shenzi Fragments*

Let us begin by examining how the remaining *Shenzi* fragments attributed to Shen Dao 慎到 (fourth century BCE) conceptualize human motivation. *Shenzi* 28–32[4] notes:

> 28-32. 天道，因則大，化則細；因也者，因人之情也。人莫不自為也；化而使之為我，則莫可得而用矣。是故先王不受祿者不臣，祿不厚者不與入難。人不得其所以自為也，則上不取用焉。故用人之自為，不用人之為我，則莫不可得而用矣。此之謂因。

> The Way of heaven is such that if you "follow" then you will be great, while if you alter then you will be insignificant. To "follow" means to follow the dispositions of people. Among people, no one fails to act for himself. If you [try to] alter them and cause them to act for you, then there will be none whom you can secure and employ. Therefore, the former kings did not use as ministers those who would not accept a salary, and they did not take as partners in difficult endeavors those whose salary was not large. In circumstances where people are not able to act for themselves, those above will not get any use out of them. Therefore, if you make use of people who act for their own benefit rather than those who act for your benefit, then there are none whom you cannot secure and employ. This is what is called following [their dispositions]. (Xu 2013: 24–28)

This advice to the ruler makes two important points. The first is that the only effective means of ensuring that the people of a state act in the way that the ruler wishes is to understand and manipulate the pre-existing motivations that the people have.

---

[3] As noted by a reviewer, this claim does not imply that these texts agreed on the content of human motivations. Their perception of the relative importance of physical, material, and symbolic motivations was not univocal.

[4] The numbering of the *Shenzi* is based on Thompson 1979, which also forms the basis for the numbering in Harris 2016b. The translation of the *Shenzi* throughout is based on Harris 2016b.

Attempting to get the people to act in ways inimical to their pre-existing motivational set will lead to failure.[5] Second, the text makes a claim about the content of this motivational set. No one, the text says, "fails to act for himself." People's fundamental motivation is to act in ways that they believe will benefit themselves. This as well is a bit open, as people could conceivably think that any number of things benefit them. However, the text makes a further claim, that people conceive of what benefits them in material terms; large salaries provide a motivation for engaging in tasks that would not otherwise appeal and, indeed, motivation to engage in tasks that would otherwise be inimical to one's motivational set.

We can look at an additional passage that may shed further light on the subject, *Shenzi* 103:

103. 匠人成棺，不憎人死；利之所在，忘其醜也。

When a craftsman completes a coffin, he does not dislike the fact that people die; where there is profit, odiousness is forgotten. (Xu 2013: 83)

This passage is useful for a couple of reasons. First, it gives further weight to our understanding of the *Shenzi* as claiming that people are motivated by profit. Second, it shows clearly how external circumstances alter how people go about satisfying their motivational sets. In general, humans have an aversion to death and decaying corpses. However, if there is profit to be made by engaging with corpses, as there is for coffin makers, then the original revulsion can be overcome. We can think of it in this way – human motivational sets include, among a wide array to things, both a desire for material profit and an aversion to decaying flesh. Under normal circumstances, when coming close to a decaying corpse, aversion is the strongest, and perhaps only motivation determining how one will act. This is because, in normal circumstances, there is no profit connected to the corpse. If, however, circumstances change and material benefit becomes connected to engaging with the decaying corpse, as is the case when one has a coffin to purvey, then the profit motive will overcome the aversion. It is not that the aversion disappears; rather it is that the coffin maker's desire for profit is stronger than their aversion to decaying corpses.

While the *Shenzi* does not explicitly tie *Fragment* 103 to politics, the relevance should be clear. When conditions are such that one can make a profit from engaging in actions that otherwise one would have no motivation to do, one will be motivated to do those actions. Thus, in order to get people to do what they wish, rulers need simply to alter conditions so that it becomes profitable for people to do as the ruler wishes.

These passages, then, give us a fairly clear understanding of the *Shenzi*'s view of human motivations, but leave unanswered at least two questions: (1) are human motivations solely and necessarily self-interested? and (2) how accurate are people's understanding of what will fulfil their motivational set? Were the *Shenzi* to reply to point (1) in the affirmative, this would be to claim that people are

---

[5] One's motivational set refers to, as described by Williams 1995: 35, "the set of [one's] desires, evaluations, attitudes, projects, and so on."

psychological egoists. While there were those who seem to hold such views in the Western tradition, it is unclear whether anyone in early China clearly holds such a strong position.[6] Furthermore, given strong arguments against such a position – both philosophical and empirical – it behooves us not to assume that this is the position advocated.[7]

Unfortunately, there is little more said in the *Shenzi* to resolve this issue, but the question will return in our later discussion of the *Han Feizi*. The second point remains as well. The *Shenzi* never directly addresses this question, seeming, rather, to assume that people are fairly reliable at means-end reasoning and that there are no fundamental conflicts between, for example, short-term versus long-term goals and desires. This as well is a point on which the *Han Feizi* has more to say. With this understanding of human motivation, and its ambiguities, let us now turn to the *Shangjunshu*.

2   Human Motivation in the *Shangjunshu*

Unlike the *Shenzi Fragments*, which is, as the name suggests, merely a collection of fragments of a much longer and presumably substantially more detailed original text that is now lost to us, the received *Shangjunshu* is a substantive text, consisting of more than 20 chapters on a wide range of philosophical, political, economic, and polemical topics (see more in Chap. 1, this volume).[8] Of these, Chap. 6 "Calculating the Land" is perhaps the most useful for the current endeavor, for it both argues that a well-governed state can arise only when those in power understand and manipulate people's pre-existing motivations and provides a discussion of the content of these motivational sets:

---

[6] In the Western philosophical tradition, Hobbes 1994: 95 and Bentham 1962: 1 are rare psychological egoists. There have been discussions of whether Yang Zhu 楊朱 was a psychological egoist (Van Norden 2011: 70–74). However, all that remains of his ideas comes from a variety of secondary sources. And while some of these sources may be interpreted as implying that Yang Zhu was a psychological egoist, other interpretations remain possible, and, indeed, more plausible.

[7] Butler 2017, and in particular Sermon 11, "Upon the Love of Our Neighbor" is the classic philosophical objection. Empirical arguments against such a position include Batson 2011 and Sober and Wilson 1998.

Note that I am not claiming here that since I find psychological egoism implausible, it should not be attributed to the texts under examination here. This would be to take the "principle of charity" too far. However, it does provide reasons for us to enquire more deeply about what the texts actually say and whether they are committed to such a view.

[8] There are two English language translations of the *Shangjunshu*, Duyvendak 1928 and Pines 2017. As both note, the dating and authorship of the various chapters of the text has long been debated, and both work to resolve these questions to the extent possible in their introductions. Pines's discussion lays out the current state of the field and moves the discussion forward in ways that are useful for those interested in the implications of dating issues for our understanding of the philosophical ideas found within the text.

6.4. 民之性：饑而求食，勞而求佚，苦則索樂，辱則求榮，此民之情也。民之求利，失禮之法；求名，失性之常。奚以論其然也？今夫盜賊，上犯君上之所禁，而下失臣子之禮，故名辱而身危，猶不止者，利也。其上世之士，衣不煖膚，食不滿腸，苦其志意，勞其四肢，傷其五臟，而益裕廣耳，非性之常也，而為之者，名也。故曰：名利之所湊，則民道之。

As for people's natures: when they are hungry, they seek food; when they are tired, they seek rest; when they suffer bitterness, they seek out enjoyment; when they are humiliated, they strive for glory; these are people's dispositions. When people strive for benefits (利), they abandon the models of rituals. When they strive for reputation (or name, 名), they lose what is constant in their nature. How to determine that it is so? Well, take the cases of thieves and bandits. Above, they violate the prohibitions of their rulers and superiors, while below they abandon the rituals of subordinates and sons. Thus, even when their reputations are disgraced and their bodies are endangered, still they do not stop, because of material benefits. [Or take the case of] men of service from past generations. Even though their clothes were insufficient to warm their skin and their food was insufficient to fill their innards, they [persisted in] tempering their determination, exhausting their four limbs, injuring their five internal organs, only increasing the broadmindedness of their actions. This is not because of what is constant in their nature, but rather because of [a desire for] good reputation. Thus, it is said, the people will travel where [the means for achieving] reputation and benefit are gathered. (Zhang 2012: 94)[9]

This is a fascinating discussion that, while in certain ways aligned with what we saw in the *Shenzi*, also moves in an importantly different direction. As with the *Shenzi*, there is an emphasis on people's acting on the basis of what benefits (*li* 利) them. And, as with the *Shenzi*, these benefits are seen in primarily physical terms – food, rest, pleasures. However, unlike the *Shenzi*, we see here the introduction of a separate motivating factor – "name" (*ming* 名). Within this context, the term refers to reputation, fame, and social standing, and the text makes clear that the objects of material benefit on the one hand and reputation or social status on the other are non-identical.[10] Indeed, the pursuit of the former, as in the case of criminals, can lead to the loss of the latter, while, as in the case of certain men of service (or perhaps hermits), the pursuit of the latter can lead to the loss of the former. Hence, for manipulating human behavior, it is necessary for the state to ensure that there are avenues open to people that prize each of these such that the pursuit of either leads them to engage in actions that the state desires.

This passage tells us something important about how the *Shangjunshu* views the motivational sets of the people and brings out a component of these sets not apparent in the *Shenzi*. In a fashion reminiscent of Thomas Hobbes in the *Leviathan*, we see an emphasis on reputation.[11] Human beings, on this account, are not merely

---

[9] All translations of the *Shangjunshu* are my own, but I have consulted both Duyvendak 1928 and Pines 2017. I use the division into sections as in Pines 2017 (which differs slightly from Zhang 2012).

[10] For the most thorough discussion of the term *ming* 名 as reputation and social standing, see Pines 2020.

[11] For more on Hobbes's discussion of what is in our motivational set, see, in particular Chap. 13 of the *Leviathan*, though the discussion of glory can be found throughout. For discussions of Hobbes's conception of glory, see Slomp 2000; Piirimäe 2006. Note as well that while glory is central to Hobbes, it is far from the only motivation he discusses.

motivated by material things; rather, they are also motivated by a desire to be viewed by others in a certain fashion. We might think, as seems to be the case for Hobbes, that a desire for reputation is predicated on its being conducive to self-preservation. However, this does not seem to be the case for the *Shangjunshu*. Rather, the text explicitly acknowledges that some people are motivated by a desire for a good reputation even at the expense of their physical well-being and indeed their life.[12]

This point is important for understanding the *Shangjunshu* and its advice on how rulers can manipulate the motivational sets of their people. People's motivational sets are not unified in the sense of all aiming at one particular goal (say, self-preservation). Rather, they contain a range of potentially conflicting motivations. This is the case even if we were to accept that for the *Shangjunshu* our motivational sets are viewed as either primarily or solely self-interested. Human interests can conflict with one another. And, while the *Shangjunshu* accepts that humans may all have similar components to their motivational sets, the relative strengths of these components vary from individual to individual. Therefore, there are those who are willing to abandon their reputation in pursuit of material goods and those who are equally willing to abandon material goods in pursuit of a good reputation.

This, then, is a simple fact that rulers must take into account if they are to be successful at manipulating the actions of the people under their rule. As passage 6.4 above ends, "Thus, it is said, where reputation and benefit are gathered, the people will travel there." What are the implications for how rulers should act? The text continues, "[What permits] the ruler to control the handles of reputation and benefit and to be able to confer success and good reputation is method" (主操名利之柄而能致功名者，數也。Zhang 2012: 95). Again, this passage implies that a desire for reputation and a desire for material goods can be decoupled. And, if one desire is not reliably stronger than the other, this will lead to unpredictability in the actions of the people. In order to eliminate this unpredictability and ensure that people reliably act as rulers wish, it is necessary to provide avenues for the achievement of material benefit as well as avenues for the achievement of reputation. If external circumstances are such that the various components of people's motivational sets reliably direct them down the avenues that rulers create for them, then, once again, people's actions will be manipulable.

So far, we have focused on the fact that the *Shangjunshu* conceives of the people as having motivational sets that can be manipulated by means of positive reinforcement. By providing avenues for the achievement of material benefits and good reputation, which run along the paths that rulers desire their people to tread, positive incentive is provided for these actions. In the *Shangjunshu* itself, the appropriate paths to be encouraged are farming and warfare:

6.5. 故聖人之為國也，入令民以屬農，出令民以計戰。夫農，民之所苦；而戰，民之所危也。犯其所苦，行其所危者，計也。故民生則計利，死則慮名。名利之所出，不可不審也。利出於地，則民盡力；名出於戰，則民致死。入使民盡力，則草不荒；出使民致死，則勝敵。勝敵而草不荒，富強之功，可坐而致也。

---

[12] Pines 2020 has a particularly insightful discussion of the power that posthumous reputation has as a motivational force in early China.

Therefore, in organizing the state, the sage induces the people to take to agriculture at home and plan for war abroad. Farming is a task that people take to be arduous while war is something that people take to be dangerous. Why do they engage in tasks they take to be arduous and perform tasks that they take to be dangerous? Because they calculate [the resultant material benefit and good reputation]. Thus, while living, the people plan to gain material benefits; when in danger of death, they worry about their reputation. One cannot fail to investigate the sources of good reputation and material benefits. If material benefits arise from the land, then the people will exhaust their strength. If a good reputation arises from warfare, then the people will fight to the death. If at home the people are induced to exhaust their strength, then the fields will not lie deserted. If abroad the people are induced fight to the death, then enemies will be defeated. If enemies are defeated and fields do not lie deserted, then one can sit at ease while the achievements of wealth and strength accrue. (Zhang: 2012: 95)

This passage provides us with a deeper understanding of how the *Shangjunshu* sees a desire for material benefits and reputation to manifest themselves in an ideal polity. As we see throughout the *Shangjunshu*, there are two fundamental roles for the people to play: farmer and soldier. Farming provides the material goods necessary for the survival of those within the state while fighting both protects the state from external attack and provides the state with additional land and people, again helping to expand its strength and territory.

So, the *Shangjunshu*'s sage ruler is one who ensures that, domestically, material benefits accrue only to those who engage in farming. Thus, those who are motivated by material benefits will turn to farming as the only avenue for achieving these benefits. In a similar fashion, the sage ruler ensures that good reputation accrues only to those who serve in the military. Thus, those who are motivated by good reputation will strive to gain military merits as the only avenue for achieving this reputation. In this context, the *Shangjunshu* focuses on rewards as being more effective than punishments in developing the most effective soldiers (Pines 2016a, b).[13]

In terms of our understanding of the conception of human motivations that the *Shangjunshu* is working with, it is unimportant whether the actual goals of the state should be farming and fighting. Rather, what is of central importance is how the text envisions getting people to engage in these two tasks – tasks which, absent external motivation, would be shunned because they are difficult and dangerous. In order to get people to do things that do not satisfy an intrinsic part of their motivational set, it is necessary to somehow tie these actions to desires that do compose an intrinsic part of their motivational set – to activate these desires, as it were.

So, in general, people do not enjoy the hard labor involved in farming. And, while a desire to survive may motivate them to spend a sufficient amount of time farming to meet their own individual needs, they would lack motivation to expend effort beyond this. Therefore, if the state wishes its people to produce a surplus of food, then it must provide its people with material benefits for producing excess. And, importantly, there must be no other avenues for achieving these benefits.

---

[13] While the *Shangjunshu* does not discuss this point, as a reviewer noted, these goals and recommendations were heavily context dependent and suitable for an expansive but underpopulated state such as Qin at that time.

Under these circumstances, farming is tied in to a pre-existing component of people's motivational sets – a desire for material benefits. If people subsequently spend more time farming, it is not because they have gained a desire to farm or that their motivational set has expanded to include farming. Rather, it is merely that now, the only way that they can obtain those things that they have always desired is through tilling the land. And the same goes for warfare. While people may be willing to fight in their own self-defense (as life is a prerequisite for satisfying many of the other components of their motivational set), they have little reason to engage in fighting in scenarios (such as foreign campaigns) where there is no clear link between combat and their own interests. Therefore, if the state wishes its people to fight willingly, it must provide them with motivations to do so, in this case, a good reputation. Again, what is essential is that this be the only avenue for achieving a good reputation and social standing. Under such circumstances, fighting as well is tied to a pre-existing component of people's motivational sets – a desire for a good reputation. Thus, the only way that they can obtain what they have always wanted – a good reputation and social standing – is by joining military campaigns.

Understanding the fundamental motivational sets of the people, then, allows rulers to manipulate people, motivating them to act in the ways that rulers desire. However, as the *Shangjunshu* makes very clear, this is a tool that can be used to instigate a wide variety of behavior on the part of the people, from farming and fighting to studying Classic texts such as the *Book of Odes* and the *Book of History*, long praised by the Confucians, to many others:

> 23.4 臣聞：道民之門，在上所先。故民，可令農戰，可令游宦，可令學問，在上所與。上以功勞與，則民戰；上以詩書與，則民學問。民之於利也，若水於下也，四旁無擇也。民徒可以得利而為之者，上與之也。

> I have heard that the gate through which the people are guided depends on what their superiors take to be of primary importance. So, the people can be induced to take up farming and fighting; they can be induced to be itinerant officials; they can be induced to be scholars – it all depends on the means by which superiors grant [benefits and reputation]. If their superiors grant them for achievement and hard work, then the people will fight; if their superiors grant them for studying the *Book of Odes* and the *Book of History*, then the people will become scholars. People flow toward benefits as water flows downward – without differentiating amongst the four directions. The people merely do what brings them benefit, and benefits are granted by their superiors. (Zhang 2012: 260)

Here we see ideas remarkably similar to a debate in the *Mengzi* 孟子:

> 6A2. 告子曰:「性猶湍水也，決諸東方則東流，決諸西方則西流。人性之無分於善不善也，猶水之無分於東西也。」

> 孟子曰:「水信無分於東西，無分於上下乎？人性之善也，猶水之就下也。人無有不善，水無有不下。

> Gaozi said, "Human nature is like roiling water. Make an opening for it to the east, and it will flow to the east. Make an opening for it to the west, and it will flow to the west. Human nature does not distinguish between good and bad just as water does not distinguish between east and west."

Mengzi replied, "Indeed, water does not distinguish between east and west. But does it not distinguish between upward and downward? The goodness of human nature is like the tendency of water to flow downward. There are no people who lack a tendency toward goodness. There is no water that lacks a tendency to flow downward." (Yang 2003: 254)

There are differences, of course. Gaozi is debating Mengzi on the topic of whether human nature is good, bad, or neutral, while the *Shangjunshu* is uninterested in passing moral judgements or labeling motivations in normative terms. Rather the *Shangjunshu* is concerned with human dispositions and nature for the sole purpose of determining the most effective way for the ruler and state to motivate them to act as desired.[14] That being said, the text draws out a point similar to those made by both Gaozi and Mengzi. Like Gaozi, the *Shangjunshu* notes that people are like water insofar as they can be led to go in any direction. However, like Mengzi, the *Shangjunshu* accepts that there is a tendency in human nature. Unlike Mengzi, however, the *Shangjunshu* does not correlate the tendency of water to go downwards with the tendency of people to pursue goodness. Rather, it is correlated with the tendency of people to pursue benefit. The people can be convinced to go in any direction, so long as they see benefit in doing so, a point that we also see made in the chapters of the *Mozi* 墨子 discussing "Impartial Caring" 兼愛.[15]

So far, we have only focused on the positive – the various ways that human motivational sets make them amenable to acting out of a desire for material benefits or reputation. However, these same motivational sets also lead them not merely to pursue the things they desire but also to avoid the things that they dislike. Aversions, as well as desires, are part of human motivational sets, and thus punishments can be effective tools for guiding human behavior. As we see in Chap. 9 of the *Shangshunju*:

9.3. 人生而有好惡，故民可治也。人君不可以不審好惡。好惡者，賞罰之本也。夫人情好爵祿而惡刑罰，人君設二者以御民之志，而立所欲焉。

People are born with likes and dislikes, and so they can be governed. The ruler cannot fail to examine their likes and dislikes, [for these] likes and dislikes are the roots of rewards and punishments. People's dispositions are such that they like rank and emoluments and dislike punishments and penalties. The ruler implements these two in order to guide the wills of the people and establish what is desired. (Zhang 2012: 131)

Human dispositions are such that they dislike pain and suffering and tend to do what they can to avoid this pain and suffering, unless it would allow them to gain something that they desire even more than they fear the pain and suffering. Therefore, if the ruler implements a scheme that imposes external punishments on activities that the people would generally prefer doing, this will lead them to cease this activity, not because their desires have changed, but rather because they can no longer

---

[14] For analyses that explicitly connect the *Shangjunshu's* discussions of human nature and politics, see Rubin 1976; Zheng 1987, esp. 229–42; Pines 2017, esp. Chap. 3.

[15] In the *Mozi*, people are seen to starve themselves because King Ling of Chu 楚靈王 (r. 540–529 BCE) preferred slender waists and to run onto burning ships because King Goujian of Yue 越王勾踐 (r. 496–464 BCE) was fond of bravery. In both cases, benefit was to be had by doing what these rulers preferred (Sun 2001: 104–05 and 126–27).

continue to satisfy those desires by engaging in that activity without incurring negatives that outweigh the positives. So, let us return to the cases of farming and fighting that are ubiquitous in the *Shangjunshu*. As we saw earlier, human dispositions are such that they have no desire to engage in farming or fighting beyond what is necessary for mere survival. However, if external rewards – in the form of material benefits or good reputation – are on offer for engaging in these tasks (and, in particular, if engaging in these tasks is the only way to obtain these rewards), then this will change people's behavior. In Gaozian terms, an opening has been made in a particular direction, and that is the direction toward which the people will gravitate.

However, given the makeup of human motivational sets, it is also possible to guide them in the direction of farming and fighting by depriving them of the ability to avoid pain and suffering in any other way but engaging in farming and fighting. If refusing to till the land or join the army is met with significant corporal punishments, then the people will turn to farming and fighting as the methods that best allow them to maximize the contents of their motivational set. These punishments work to change behavior by getting the people to focus on minimizing their pain. While this is effective, the *Shangjunshu* at the same time recognizes that positive incentives are also important – the rewards of social standing and reputation encourage people to go beyond merely avoiding punishment to actively excelling in fighting for the state.

As we see, then, the conceptions of human nature, human dispositions, and human motivational sets as elucidated in the *Shangjunshu* have substantial overlap with that which we earlier saw in the *Shenzi*. There are, however, important differences. In addition to material benefits, the *Shangjunshu* recognizes that there is another important, and independent motivation, the desire for a good reputation and social standing.[16] Furthermore, it recognizes that there is a variation in the distribution of these two motivations among people. It is crucial to understand that this motivation is independent of the motivation to pursue material benefits, and thus at times, some people will sacrifice one for the other, and so avenues need to be created so that people are incentivized to act in the ways that the ruler wishes, regardless of what is of greatest importance in their motivational sets.

3 Human Motivation in the *Han Feizi*

The conception of human motivation in the *Han Feizi* is perhaps the most studied of all the conceptions found within the *fa* tradition. However, in part because Sima Qian labelled Han Fei as a student of Xunzi 荀子, many have simply attributed to the *Han*

---

[16] The claim here is not that the *Shenzi* does not recognize this additional source of motivation. Such a source may well be consistent with the vision in the *Shenzi*. It is merely that in the fragments that remain, we see no indication of a role for a desire for good reputation.

Feizi a conception of human nature similar to what is found in the *Xunzi*.[17] There are a range of doubts with this position. First, as Sato (2013) notes, there is no direct evidence that HAN Fei was a student of Xunzi. Second, even if he was, this in and of itself should not lead us to conclude that they have similar conceptions of human nature, particularly given all the other differences in their political theories.[18] Indeed, a range of more recent scholarship has pointed to a fundamental way in which the *Xunzi* and the *HAN Feizi* differ: the *Xunzi* clearly argues that human nature is problematic from a normative standpoint, while the *HAN Feizi* looks at human nature as morally neutral, as being neither good nor bad.[19] Let us, then, begin our investigation of the *HAN Feizi's* conception of human motivation in much the same way as we did with the *Shenzi* and the *Shangjunshu* – by seeing what the text actually says.

In Chap. 17, the *HAN Feizi* discusses a point that we are already familiar with from *Shenzi* 103:

17.2 故輿人成輿則欲人之富貴，匠人成棺則欲人之夭死也，非輿人仁而匠人賊也，
人不貴則輿不售，人不死則棺不買，情非憎人也，利在人之死也。

Therefore, when a cartwright produces chariots, he desires that people be rich and noble. When a craftsman makes coffins, he desires that people die early. It is not that the cartwright is benevolent while the craftsman is villainous. [It is just that] if people are not noble, then chariots will not sell, while if people do not die, then coffins will not be bought. The real disposition [of the craftsman] is not a hatred of people, [it is simply that] his profit lies in people's deaths. (Chen 2000: 322–23)[20]

This passage tells us that we can understand people's actions by understanding what brings them material benefits. And it is important to understand this point, thinks the *HAN Feizi*; otherwise, we are likely to attribute virtues to some and vices to others. To do so, however, is to misunderstand fundamental motivations. On the surface, the cartwright may seem virtuous, as he has a desire for people to be rich and noble, while the craftsman may seem villainous, for he has a desire for people to die early. However, such an attribution of motivations misses the underlying way in which these two are exactly the same – they both desire profit. The cartwright, as a purveyor of a luxury good, is able to make money only if enough people sufficiently rich to buy chariots. The craftsman, as the purveyor of an item used only for funerals, is able to make money only if people die. Neither the cartwright nor the

---

[17] For a discussion of the relationship between the conceptions of human nature found in the *Xunzi* and in the *Han Feizi*, see Bárcenas 2012; Sato 2013.

[18] Aristotle, for example was Plato's student, and yet he advocated very different views on a wide range of issues.

[19] See, for example Shimada 1908; Lin 1990: 97–98n18; Gu 1996: 308–309. For an overview of various interpretations of the *Han Feizi's* conception of human nature, see Yu 2006. Relatedly, the *Xunzi* thinks that a secure, stable, and flourishing state can only be ensured when the ruler and his people are cultivated, while the *Han Feizi* believes that the apex of strength, security, and stability can be achieved without cultivation and, indeed, that cultivation, even if possible, would be inimical to that goal. For more on *Xunzi,* see Harris 2016a; for more on *Han Feizi*, see Harris 2013a.

[20] I cite the *Han Feizi* following the divisions accepted in Harbsmeier, forthcoming (who borrows them from Zhang 2010).

craftsman has any particular concern toward others. They care about others only insofar as these others benefit them. The only difference between the craftsman and the cartwright is what actions of other people (becoming rich or dying) are of benefit.

It is not that the craftsman and the cartwright are unique in their motivations here. Rather, as the *Han Feizi* notes elsewhere,

37.7.2 好利惡害，夫人之所有也。賞厚而信，人輕敵矣；刑重而必，夫人不北矣。長行徇上，數百不一人。喜利畏罪，人莫不然。

Fondness for profit and hatred of harm is something that all humans are alike in having. If rewards are generous and dependable, then people will treat lightly the [dangers of assailing the] enemy. If punishments are heavy and certain, then the people will not be put to flight. As for dying for their superior on an extended march, there is not one among several hundred [who has such a motivation]. [However, to attain] the profit that they are fond of or [to avoid] the punishment that they fear, none would not do so. (Chen 2000: 893).

While this passage is aimed at providing advice to the ruler for how to rule, it does so by pointing to fundamental components of people's motivational sets – components shared by all alike: they are fond of material benefits and they are fearful of being hurt. Therefore, in much the same way as we have seen in the *Shangjunshu*, the *Han Feizi* notes that it is possible to change the behavior of people simply by changing the conditions under which they are able to obtain material benefit and avoid being hurt.

The commonality of human motivational sets and in particular the fact that humans act so as to achieve their desires is also seen when the *Han Feizi* notes that even the great sage kings of the past are similarly motivated:

44.9 察四王之情，貪得之意也；度其行，暴亂之兵也。然四王自廣措也，而天下稱大焉；自顯名也，而天下稱明焉。則威足以臨天下，利足以蓋世，天下從之。

If one investigates the dispositions of the four [sage] kings [Shun, Yu, Tang, and Wu], [one will see that] they focused their attention on gain. If one measures their actions, [it is clear that] they used the military in a violent and rebellious fashion. Nonetheless, these four kings broadened their grasp and all under heaven called them great men. They made their own names prominent, and all under heaven called them enlightened. And so, when one's awe-inspiring majesty is sufficient to overlook all under heaven, and the benefits one metes out are sufficient to cover the generation, all under heaven will follow one. (Chen 2000: 978)

There may well be a rhetorical purpose behind the *Han Feizi's* lack of reverence toward the sage kings of the past.[21] However, there is a philosophical point as well. The sage kings of the past were just like everyone else – they acted so as to achieve their desires. In this way, the *Han Feizi* agrees with the *Xunzi* that anyone can become a sage king. But the reasons are quite different. The *Xunzi* believes that people are able to change and develop their motivational sets until they become like the sage king Yu (Wang 1992: 442–43 [23, "Xing e" 性惡]). The *Han Feizi*, on the

---

[21] For discussions of rhetoric in the *Han Feizi* see Goldin 2008; Lyon 2008; Graziani 2012. For a range of discussions of rhetoric in early China, see also van Els et al.: 2012.

other hand, would say that people already have the same motivational sets as the sage kings. It is just that most (including the Confucians) have made the same mistake in talking about the sage kings as people tend to do when comparing the cartwright and carpenter – not drilling down deep enough to understand the fundamental motivations of each. What is important for the *Han Feizi* is that the desires of the sage kings of the past, and thus their motivational sets, are seen to have had a similar content to the average person. Their military actions were taken to increase their own power and control – to gain material benefits and reputation – the fundamental motivations that we saw arising in the *Shangjunshu*.

There is, however, an important point about human motivational sets in the *Han Feizi* that seems to have no explicit counterpart in either the *Shenzi* nor the *Shangjunshu*. The *Shenzi* seems to imply that people act out of a desire for material benefits. The *Shangjunshu* argues that there are two fundamental sources of motivation – material benefit and reputation. While the *Han Feizi* acknowledges these texts' characterization of motivations for the vast majority of people, it recognizes that not everyone acts on the basis of self-interested motivations. As the *Han Feizi* notes,

> 44.3 若夫許由、續牙、晉伯陽、秦顛頡、衛僑如、狐不稽、重明、董不識、卞隨、務光、伯夷、叔齊，此十二人者，皆上見利不喜，下臨難不恐，或與之天下而不取，有萃辱之名，則不樂食穀之利。夫見利不喜，上雖厚賞無以勸之；臨難不恐，上雖嚴刑無以威之；此之謂不令之民也。此十二人者，或伏死於窟穴，或槁死於草木，或飢餓於山谷，或沉溺於水泉。有民如此，先古聖王皆不能臣，當今之世，將安用之？

> When Xu You… Boyi and Shuqi all saw profits coming from above, they did not celebrate, and when they faced difficulties, they were not fearful. Among them were those who were offered all under heaven but did not accept it. Even at the cost of ruined and humiliated reputations, they refused to enjoy the benefits of eating grain. If they are not pleased when they see profits, then their superiors, even if they offer generous rewards, will be unable to motivate them. If they are not fearful when they face difficulties, then their superiors, even if they impose severe punishments, will be unable to overawe them. These are called people who cannot be commanded.

> Among these twelve, some died while hiding in caves; others shriveled up and died among the bushes and trees; others died of starvation in the mountains and gorges; still others drowned in rivers and springs. When there are people like this, even the sage kings of old would all be incapable of making them serve as ministers. So, in our generation, how could they be employed? (Chen 2000: 969)[22]

Again, the *Han Feizi* discusses these individuals within the context of how to rule. However, the existence of such people demonstrates that there are those, perhaps rare, but real nonetheless, whose motivational sets are substantially different from the norm. Unlike the vast majority, they are not motivated by a desire for material benefit or good reputation. This then, may be seen as a partial retraction of the

---

[22] See also the discussions of the uselessness of Boyi and Shuqi in Chap. 14.5 (Chen 2000: 294) and of Tai Gong's 太公望 execution of the disobedient recluses Kuangju 狂矞 and Huashi 華士 in Chap. 34.1.7 (Chen 2000: 769–70).

strong claim made above in 37.14 that all people are motivated by a desire for profit and a fear of harm. Simply put, there are some who aren't.

What are we to make of this, and what are its implications? One might be tempted to think that the existence of such people, even if rare, indicates that the *Xunzi* may be correct in its contentions that moral cultivation and its accompanying inculcation of new sources of value, is possible.[23] However, the *Han Feizi* is not willing to concede even this, as we see in Chap. 50:

50.9 今或謂人曰："使子必智而壽"，則世必以為狂。夫智、性也，壽、命也，性命者，非所學於人也，而以人之所不能為說人，此世之所以謂之為狂也....以仁義教人，是以智與壽說也，有度之主弗受也。

> Now, if someone says to others, "I can make you wise and long-lived [if you do what I say]," then the world would certainly take him to be deceitful. Wisdom is a matter of one's nature, while long life is a matter of fate. One's nature and fate are not things that can be learned from others; [trying to] tell others [that one can] do something that is not within the realm of human ability, is the reason why the world takes such a person as deceitful.... Persuading someone [to act in a certain way] based on benevolence and proper social norms, [is the same as] persuading someone that one can provide wisdom and long life. Rulers who have a system [of laws] will not accept this. (Chen 2000: 1143)

While this passage can be interpreted in at least two ways, I have argued elsewhere that the *Han Feizi* here seems to be making an argument about human potentials (Harris 2013b: 96). Any particular individual's potential for a long life is substantially beyond that individual's control. One can certainly live a life in which one works to avoid dangerous situations, eats a healthy diet, etc. so as to maximize the chances of reaching one's potential. However, there is still a level at which fate has control – namely what that potential actually is. Some people, no matter how healthy their lifestyle, will die of a heart attack in their 40's, while others, living an identical lifestyle, may well live over twice as long.

In much the same way that one's potential for a long life is substantially beyond one's control, one's potential to be motivated by benevolence (*ren* 仁) and proper social norms (*yi* 義) is also substantially beyond one's control. Just as we would ridicule those who claim that they can alter our potential for wisdom and a long life, so too should we ridicule those who claim that they can alter our potential to be motivated by moral concerns rather than prudential ones. Again, the claim is not that no one is so motivated, just as the claim is not that no one lives to 110. Rather, the claim is that these are circumstances which are not under the control of either the individuals themselves, or other people.[24]

So, yes, there are those like Boyi and Shuqi who are motivated by moral concerns rather than prudential, self-interested ones. However, while this does

---

[23] For a discussion of the *Xunzi's* views on this point, see Goldin 1999: 1–37; Wong 2006: 211–20; Harris 2013b; Hutton 2016; Stalnaker 2016.

[24] Relatedly, this helps to explain why the morally cultivated ruler is irrelevant for the *Han Fezi*. Such rulers, if they exist, do so because of uncontrollable circumstances. Thus, they cannot be reliably developed, and in the political realm, what cannot reliably be obtained should not be depended upon.

demonstrate that there are those whose motivational sets have a content that is very different from the motivational sets of the vast majority of people, it does not demonstrate that it is possible to change one's motivational set. It is merely that Boyi and Shuqi were born with a rare motivational set, just as Pengzu 彭祖 was born with a rare potential for long life.[25] However, just as there is nothing that I can do to live as long as Pengzu, there is nothing I can do to be a moral paragon such as Boyi or Shuqi, for my motivational set, much like that of the vast majority of humanity, according to the *Han Feizi*, lacks the components that motivate these two.

There are two additional, interrelated points about the *Han Feizi's* conception of human motivations that serve to further the text's claim that those like Boyi and Shuqi are rare aberrations. These are the contentions that people act on their *perceived* interests rather than their *actual* interests, and that people are pretty bad at figuring out the latter. As we see in Chap. 18:

18.4 是以愚戇窳墮之民，苦小費而忘大利也。

The people are stupid, dull, corrupt, and lazy, and thus they are bitter over small expenditures and forgetful of great benefits. (Chen 2000: 334)

And, in Chap. 50.11:

民智之不可用，猶嬰兒之心也。夫嬰兒不剔首則復痛，不揖痤則寖益，剔首、揖痤必一人抱之，慈母治之，然猶啼呼不止，嬰兒子不知犯其所小苦致其所大利也。

The wisdom of the people cannot be employed because their minds are like those of babes in arms. If a baby's head is not shaved, then it will be in greater pain, while if a boil is not lanced, then [the infection] will gradually spread. When shaving a baby's head or lancing its boil, it is necessary for someone to hold the baby while its caring mother takes care of it, and still the baby will weep and cry without end. The baby does not understand that enduring this small pain will result in a great benefit. (Chen 2000: 1147)

Children, we all know, are fairly short-sighted. If you put a cookie in front of them, but tell them that you will return 15 min later with a dozen cookies for them, which they can have only if they refrain from eating the cookie in front of them, very few children will not eat that first cookie before the 15 min is up.[26] Similar things happen when one takes children to the dentist to have a tooth filled or to a doctor to get a shot. Simply explaining to them why the pain is both necessary and worth it for their long-term well-being will rarely change their reactions.

What the *Han Feizi* contends, however, is that most people do not really change substantially as they grow and develop. Rather, they continue to be short-sighted, over-valuing short term benefits and under-valuing long term ones. In short, both infants and adults have a tendency to do those things that they think will satisfy their interest sets. However, both groups are quite poor at accurately ascertaining what

---

[25] Pengzu was a legendary figure in early China, said to have lived anywhere from 130 to several hundred years.

[26] There have been numerous psychology studies over the years on this issue, beginning with Mischel et al. 1972.

actions will actually satisfy their interest sets, and thus they cannot be trusted to
reliably pursue the things that will *actually* satisfy their overall interest sets. If this
is the case, and if motivations such as benevolence and proper social norms require,
at the very least, a broader, longer-term understanding of the implications of these
concepts, then it would be rare to see anyone acting from them.

Finally, it is important to note that the *Han Feizi* never claims that our motivational sets are comprised solely of self-interested motivations. It never denies, for
example, the natural feelings of love between mothers and children (子母之性，愛
也; Chen 2000: 1037 [47.6]). Throughout the text, the *Han Feizi* acknowledges that
there are other-regarding feelings and bonds, in particular among family members.
However, the text questions the strength of these bonds, particularly when acting on
the basis of these bonds harms one's own interests. Rarely, if ever, are other regarding feelings as strong as self-regarding ones, and this fact explains (among many
other things) the practice of female infanticide:

46.3   且父母之於子也，產男則相賀，產女則殺之。此俱出父母之懷衽，然男子受
賀，女子殺之者，慮其後便、計之長利也。故父母之於子也，猶用計算之心以相待
也，而況無父子之澤乎!

Furthermore, as for how parents treat their children, when they give birth to a son, they
congratulate each other, while when they give birth to a daughter, they kill her. They consider their future benefits and calculate their long-term profit. Therefore, even when it
comes to how they treat their children, parents use calculating minds in dealing with them,
how much the more so in situations where the [natural] warm feelings between parents and
children are absent! (Chen 2000: 1006)

Female infanticide does not arise because parents lack a natural loving care and
concern for their offspring. All things being equal, they would care for their daughters as they do for their sons. However, within the cultural context of early China,
not all was equal. Given that context, sons had the potential to bring profit to the
family, while daughters were a drain on their resources. This meant that the natural,
other-regarding love and concern that parents have for their daughters was placed in
opposition to the material benefits of the parents themselves. In situations like these,
other-regarding interests are no match for self-regarding ones, unless one happens
to have been born a Boyi or Shuqi.

On such an account, were it the case that daughters brought profit to the family
while sons were a drain on resources, then, we would expect male infanticide.
Importantly, it is not that the fundamental content of people's motivations changes
in different contexts. Actions may well change, but this is because in different contexts or in different time periods, different actions will be necessary for the achievement of fundamental pre-existing motivations. Indeed, this is the *Han Feizi*'s
explanation in Chap. 49 for why rewards and punishments were unnecessary to
prevent conflict in antiquity but are necessary in its time: in the past resources
exceeded demand while in the *Han Feizi*'s time, due to population growth, demand
for resources outstripped supply, leading to conflict that could only be reduced
through the application of the two handles.[27]

---

[27] In Chap. 12 of this volume, Vogelsang's discussion of "The Historiography of Political Realism"
emphasizes that the ways that human motivations are expressed will vary over time because of

4 Conclusion

Herein, we have examined conceptions of human motivations in three important texts from the *fa* tradition: the *Shenzi Fragments*, the *Shangjunshu*, and the HAN *Feizi*. Throughout, we find more similarities than differences. And, when differences arise, they are more often than not differences in focus and detail. The *Shenzi* argues that people are motivated to action based on their own interests, rather than the interests of others, and heavily implies that this attribute cannot be modified. Furthermore, the text focuses on profit and material benefit as being what people see to be in their own interests. The text, perhaps because it has reached us in a fragmentary form, is silent as to whether it thinks that we are motivated for reasons beyond material benefits, as well as the question of how accurate we are at ascertaining our own interests, whatever they may be.

The *Shangjunshu* works with a conception of human motivation that in many ways accords with that of the *Shenzi*. However, it shows a much greater awareness not only that we are motivated by two fundamental and distinct forces – material benefits and good reputation – but that these two do not necessarily pull us in the same direction. As they can diverge, and since some are more motivated by one than the other, some people will tend to follow one to the detriment of the other, while others may do the opposite.

Finally, the HAN *Feizi* provides what is perhaps the most thoroughgoing analysis of human motivations. Again, though, it is not that the text has a fundamentally different conception of human motivations. Rather, it is that the position that can be drawn out is more nuanced than we see in earlier texts. Like both the *Shenzi* and the *Shangjunshu*, the HAN *Feizi* argues that human motivational sets include a healthy dose of self-interest. And, like the *Shangjunshu*, the text acknowledges that both material benefits and reputation are motivators of action. However, the text also acknowledges that there is a small minority who may have radically different motivational sets than the majority, such as Boyi and Shuqi. Furthermore, a concern for others is not limited to a select few. Rather, as the parent-child bond demonstrates, we all have concern for others. However, this concern for others is usually outweighed by concern for self whenever the two come into conflict. Finally, the HAN *Feizi* demonstrates a greater awareness of the fact that we're not particularly good at figuring out what will actually satisfy our interest sets, and thus we may well be motivated to engage in a wide range of self-defeating actions.

---

such differences.

References

Ames, Roger. 1991. The Mencian Conception of *ren xing*: Does it Mean 'Human Nature'? In *Chinese Texts and Philosophical Contexts: Essays Dedicated to Angus C. Graham*, ed. Henry Rosemont Jr., 143–175. La Salle, IL: Open Court.

Bárcenas, Alejandro. 2012. Xunzi and Han Fei on Human Nature. *International Philosophical Quarterly* 52 (2): 135–148.

Batson, C. Daniel. 2011. *Altruism in Humans*. Oxford: Oxford University Press.

Bentham, Jeremy. 1962. *An Introduction to the Principles of Morals and Legislation*. Oxford: Clarendon Press.

Bloom, Irene. 1994. Mencian Arguments on Human Nature (*Jen-hsing*). *Philosophy East and West* 44 (1): 19–53.

Butler, Joseph (1692–1752). 2017. *Fifteen Sermons Preached at the Rolls Chapel and Other Writings on Ethics*. Ed. David McNaughton. Oxford: Oxford University Press.

Chen, Qiyou 陳奇猷. 2000. *Han Feizi, With New Collations and Commentary* 韓非子新校注. Shanghai: Shanghai guji chubanshe. (Excellent modern standard edition of the *Han Feizi* with selected commentaries as well as Chen's own views.)

Duyvendak, J.J.L. 1928. *The Book of Lord Shang: A Classic of the Chinese School of Law*. London: Arthur Probsthain. (Insightful, but dated translation of the *Shangjunshu*).

Eifring, Halvor, ed. 2004. *Love and Emotions in Traditional Chinese Literature*. Leiden: Brill.

Goldin, Paul R. 1999. *Rituals of the Way: The Philosophy of Xunzi*. Chicago: Open Court.

———. 2008. Appeals to History in Early Chinese Philosophy and Rhetoric. *Journal of Chinese Philosophy* 35 (1): 79–96.

Graziani, Romain. 2012. Rhetoric that Kills, Rhetoric that Heals. *Extrême-Orient, Extrême-Occident* 34: 41–78.

Gu, Fang 谷方. 1996. *Han Fei and Chinese Culture* 韓非與中國文化. Guiyang: Guizhou renmin chubanshe.

Harbsmeier, Christoph. 2004. The Semantics of Qíng 情 in Pre-Buddhist Chinese. In *Love and Emotions in Traditional Chinese Literature*, ed. Halvor Eifring, 69–148. Leiden: Brill.

———, trans. forthcoming. *Han Feizi*. Ed. Jens Østergaard Petersen and Yuri Pines. Leiden: Brill.

Harris, Eirik Lang. 2013a. Han Fei on the Problem of Morality. In *Dao Companion to the Philosophy of Han Fei*, ed. Paul R. Goldin, 107–131. New York: Springer.

———. 2013b. The Role of Virtue in Xunzi's 荀子 Political Philosophy. *Dao: A Journal of Comparative Philosophy* 12 (1): 93–110.

———. 2016a. Xunzi's Political Philosophy. In *The Dao Companion to Xunzi*, ed. Eric L. Hutton, 95–138. New York: Springer.

———. 2016b. *The Shenzi Fragments: A Philosophical Analysis and Translation*. New York: Columbia University Press. (Complete, annotated English language translation cum study of the *Shenzi*).

Hobbes, Thomas (1588–1679). 1994. *Leviathan: With Selected Variants from the Latin Edition of 1668*. Ed. Ewin M. Curley. Indianapolis: Hackett Publishing.

Hutton, Eric L. 2016. Xunzi on Moral Psychology. In *Dao Companion to the Philosophy of Xunzi*, ed. Eric L. Hutton, 201–227. New York: Springer.

Lau, D.C. 1953. Theories of Human Nature in *Mencius* (孟子) and *Shyuntzyy* (荀子). *Bulletin of the School of Oriental and African Studies, University of London* 15 (3): 541–565.

Lin, Yizheng 林義正. 1990. A Study of Pre-Qin Legalist Theories of Human Nature 先秦法家人性論之研究. In Taida Philosophy Department 臺大哲學系, ed., *Theories of Human Nature in China* 中國人性論, 75–104. Taibei: Dongda tuishu gonsi.

Lyon, Arabella. 2008. Rhetorical Authority in Athenian Democracy and the Chinese Legalism of Han Fei. *Philosophy and Rhetoric* 41 (1): 51–71.

Mischel, Walter, Ebbe B. Ebbesen, and Antonette Raskoff Zeiss. 1972. Cognitive and Attentional Mechanisms in Delay of Gratification. *Journal of Personality and Social Psychology* 21 (2): 204–218.

Piirimäe, Pärtel. 2006. The Explanation of Conflict in Hobbes's *Leviathan*. *Trames* 10 (1): 3–21.

Pines, Yuri. 2016a. A 'Total War'? Rethinking Military Ideology in the *Book of Lord Shang*. *Journal of Chinese Military History* 5 (2): 97–134.

———. 2016b. Social Engineering in Early China: The Ideology of the *Shangjunshu* (*Book of Lord Shang*) Revisited. *Oriens Extremus* 55: 1–37.

———, ed. & trans. 2017. *The Book of Lord Shang: Apologetics of State Power in Early China*. New York: Columbia University Press. (Most up to date translation of the *Shangjunshu*).

———. 2020. 'To Die for the Sanctity of the Name': Name (*ming* 名) as Prime Mover of Political Action in Early China. In *Keywords in Chinese Culture*, ed. Wai-Yee Li and Yuri Pines, 169–215. Hong Kong: The Chinese University of Hong Kong Press.

Puett, Michael. 2004. The Ethics of Responding Properly: The Notion of *Qing* 情 in Early Chinese Thought. In *Love and Emotions in Traditional Chinese Literature*, ed. Halvor Eifring, 37–68. Leiden: Brill.

Rubin, Vitaly A. 1976. The Theory and Practice of a Totalitarian State: Shang Yang and Legalism. In *Individual and State in Ancient China: Essays on four Chinese Philosophers*. New York: Columbia University Press.

Sato, Masayuki. 2013. Did Xunzi's Theory of Human Nature Provide the Foundation for the Political Thought of HAN Fei? In *Dao Companion to the Philosophy of HAN Fei*, ed. Paul R. Goldin, 147–165. New York: Springer.

Shimada, Kin'ichi 島田鈞一. 1908. A Study of HAN Fei's Theory 韓非の學を論ず. In *Forest of Discourses on Classics and History* 經史說林. Tōkyō: Bunshōkaku.

Slomp, Gabriella. 2000. *Thomas Hobbes and the Political Philosophy of Glory*. New York: Palgrave Macmillan.

Sober, Elliott, and David Sloan Wilson. 1998. *Unto Others: The Evolution and Psychology of Unselfish Behavior*. Cambridge, MA: Harvard University Press.

Stalnaker, Aaron. 2016. Xunzi on Self-Cultivation. In *Dao Companion to the Philosophy of Xunzi*, ed. Eric L. Hutton, 35–66. New York: Springer.

Sun, Yirang 孫詒讓 (1848–1908). 2001. *Leisurely Glosses on the Mozi* 墨子閒詁. Beijing: Zhonghua shuju.

Thompson, P.M. 1979. *The Shen Tzu Fragments*. Oxford: Oxford University Press.

van Els, Paul, Romain Graziani, Yuri Pines, and Elisa Sabattini, eds. 2012. Political Rhetoric in Early China. Special Issue, *Extrême-Orient, Extrême-Occident* 34.

Van Norden, Bryan W. 2011. *Introduction to Classical Chinese Philosophy*. Indianapolis: Hackett Publishing.

Wang, Xianqian 王先謙 (1842–1917). 1992. *Xunzi, with collected explanations* 荀子集解. Ed. Shen Xiaohuan 沈嘯寰, Wang Xingxian 王星賢. Beijing: Zhonghua shuju.

Williams, Bernard. 1995. Internal Reasons and the Obscurity of Blame. In *Making Sense of Humanity, and other Philosophical Papers*, 35–45. Cambridge: Cambridge University Press.

Wong, David B. 2006. *Natural Moralities: A Defense of Pluralistic Relativism*. New York: Oxford University Press.

Xu, Fuhong 許富宏. 2013. *Shenzi, with Collected Collations and Commentary* 慎子集校集注. Beijing: Zhonghua shuju.

Yang, Bojun 楊伯峻. 2003. *Mengzi, with Translation and Commentary* 孟子譯注. Beijing: Zhonghua shuju.

Yu, Xia 于霞. 2006. "A Review of Studies on HAN Fei's Ethical Thought 韓非倫理思想研究述評." *Yanshan University Journal* 燕山大學學報 7.4: 22–27.

Zhang, Jue 張覺, ed. 2010. *Han Feizi, with Collations and Subcommentary* 韓非子校疏. Shanghai: Shanghai guji chubanshe.

———, ed. 2012. *Shangjunshu, with Collations and Subcommentary* 商君書校疏. Beijing: Zhishi chanquan chubanshe. (Excellent modern standard edition of the *Shangjunshu* with selected commentaries as well as Zhang's own views).

Zheng, Liangshu 鄭良樹. 1987. *Shang Yang and his School* 商鞅及其學派. Taibei: Taiwan xuesheng shuju.

Chapter 11
The Ruler in the Polity of Objective Standards

Mark E. Lewis

1 Introduction

In theories of guiding states through objective, impersonal standards and administrative techniques, the ruler was assigned several crucial roles. First, whereas objective standards (primarily written laws) were to constrain all human actions, such standards also had to be adapted to changing material conditions. The power to suspend existing laws and replace them with new ones was assigned by several texts—most notably in the opening chapter of the *Book of Lord Shang* (*Shangjunshu* 商君書)—to the ruler. Second, the ruler was charged with checking or constraining the tendency of officials to abuse both their positions and the laws by forming factions to subvert objective standards. This role, as theorized in detail in the *Han Feizi* 韓非子, was carried out through a combination of self-mastery and administrative techniques. Finally, the ruler was charged with maintaining absolute mastery of the rewards and punishments which were the keys to enforcing the administrative techniques, and for leading all subjects to adhere to the model provided by written laws and other public standards. This article will discuss each of these roles, referring above all to the *Han Feizi* which provided the most elaborate theory of such a government, discuss problems noted by several modern scholars with the ruler's performance of these roles, and finally show how various Warring States texts sought to solve these problems through the idea of the ruler's creation of a supremely potent self through rigorous intellectual self-cultivation.

The emphasis on the ruler as the one who changes the laws, while all others have to obey them, reflects the consensus that had emerged among Warring States thinkers that political institutions and policies must be constantly adapted to fit changing

M. E. Lewis (✉)
Stanford University, Stanford, CA, USA
e-mail: mel1000@stanford.edu

© The Author(s), under exclusive license to Springer Nature Switzerland AG 2024   315
Y. Pines (ed.), *Dao Companion to China's fa Tradition*, Dao Companions
to Chinese Philosophy 19, https://doi.org/10.1007/978-3-031-53630-4_12

times.[1] Moreover, as Yuri Pines has shown, this idea was argued with particular force by those who emphasized rule by objective standards enforced through rewards and punishments, e.g., *The Book of Lord Shang* and the *Han Feizi*. It also emerged in imperial rhetoric in the stele inscriptions of the First Emperor 秦始皇帝 (emp. 221–210 BCE), who proclaimed that his achievements and institutions marked a radical break with all prior political history.[2] To a certain degree, this emphasis on the ruler as the one who changes laws, so that he cannot be restricted by them, anticipates the idea of Carl Schmitt that sovereignty is defined by the power to establish the "state of exception" in which the laws are suspended, and thus to act as the ground from which they emerge and on which they are based.[3]

As for the second role, *The Book of Lord Shang* indicates the crucial role of the ruler in preventing officials from abusing their positions for private gain primarily by expressing suspicion, without elaborating any theory of how to control them.[4]

---

[1] Lewis 1994: 29–39; Lewis 1999: 39–40; Puett 2001; Pines and Shelach 2005: 164–91; Goldin 2005b.

[2] Pines 2013a: 25–45; Pines 2014: 258–79; Kern 2000, esp. pp. 170–74.

[3] Schmitt 1985; Agamben 2005; Kahn 2011. The idea that the ruler's ability to change the law depends on not restricting him is announced at the beginning of *Shangjunshu* 1:16 ("Geng fa" 更法) (hereafter chapter titles in primary texts are provided in the notes only at their first appearance). In the thinking of Schmitt and those elaborating on him, the sovereign is "the point at which law and exception intersect." He rules with and through law in normal times but suspends and modifies the rule of law when "acts of will" are necessary. Such suspensions of law include both such "regular" exceptions as the invocation of equity in cases not covered by written laws and the granting of pardons, and also emergency cases challenging the state's survival such as war and revolution. Thes latter cases, of course, could also enable the creation of new sovereigns.

[4] *Shangjunshu* 23 ("Jun chen" 君臣) and 24 ("Jin shi" 禁使) are devoted to how the illumined ruler can control his officials through laws and methods, as is chapter 25: 179–81 ("Shen fa" 慎法). For discussions of how the ruler controls his officials, see also chapter 2: 19 ("Ken ling" 墾令) (officials, who all seek profit, cannot supervise one another), 2: 20 (the ruler's imposing uniform taxes prevents the officials from deviance), 2: 24 (officials exploit people and waste grain), 2: 26 (officials will devote themselves to intellectual pursuits and travel about between states, which will seduce the peasants into similar behavior), 2: 27–28 (officials will alter regulations and promote clients who support them in such criminality), 2: 30 (officials will act as patrons of criminals to secure their support); 3: 31 ("Nong zhan" 農戰) (officials seek office through glib words), 3: 32 (officials seek posts through literary pursuits), 3: 33 (again denounces officials who seek posts through glibness and debate, or sell promotions to underlings), 3: 35 (officials use glibness and scholarship to wreck the laws), 3: 40 (officials and wandering persuaders form "cliques" who recommend their own members—the promotion of whom leads all people to support private connections and thus undercut the ruler); 5: 53 ("Shuo min" 說民) (officials, claiming to be good, cover up for each other and conceal crimes); chapter 6: 70 ("Suan di" 算地) (officials link up with the powerful and do not punish felons, and only a sage ruler can control such criminality); chapter 7: 73–74 ("Kai se" 開塞) (only sage rulers can establish officials and control them with regulations); chapter 8: 81 ("Yi yan" 壹言) (only the sage ruler can stop cunning speakers and the eminent families from perverting government), 8: 82–83 (the enlightened ruler and the sage prevent officials from blocking the proper functioning of the laws); chapter 11: 96 ("Li ben" 立本) (a ruler must not rely on the reputations of his ministers to guide decisions); chapter 13: 103 ("Jin ling" 靳令) (proper laws prevent depraved officials or villainy in the capital), 13: 107 (when the "six parasites" pervert government, the ruler cannot master his officials); chapter 14: 110 ("Xiu quan" 修權) (only the illumined ruler can see through the schemes of his officials and thereby properly

Indeed, Yuri Pines has shown that *The Book of Lord Shang* says very little about the ruler's functions and that, in contrast with the *Han Feizi*, his person or talents are not normally discussed, thus emphasizing that "the impersonal system of rule should ideally accommodate any sovereign" (Pines 2017: 85–89). However, this must be qualified.

First, the *Book of Lord Shang* constantly repeats that the ruler who can make the system work is either "illumined" (*ming* 明) or a "sage" (*sheng* 聖), and these are not empty formulae, as they are explicitly contrasted with references to "mediocre" (*fan* 凡 or *yong* 庸) rulers or the "conventional rulers of our age" (*shi* 世).[5] Moreover, the ruler is explicitly said to have a "worthiness" or "talent" (*xian* 賢) which resides in him alone, is identified as his "embodied nature" (*ti xing* 體性), and is paralleled to the keen vision of a Li Lou 離婁 or the strength of a Wu Huo 烏獲, i.e., is a personal talent that makes him virtually superhuman.[6] Other passages credit the ruler with a knowledge of the "essentials of all things," or insist that he is "illumined" because he is never "blocked" (*bi* 蔽), a description which matches the *Xunzi*'s 荀子 account of Confucius's sage nature.[7] Yet other passages state that the illumined ruler sees everything (thereby stopping officials' criminality), that his mastery of the world begins with mastering himself (a common formula in Stoic ideals of the philosopher ruler), that like the Daoist sage he knows "the principles of what is inevitably so" (*bi ran zhi li* 必然之理) and "what must be done within the inherent tendencies of the age" (*bi wei zhi shi shi* 必為之時勢).[8] To summarize, while *The*

---

regulate authority), 14: 113 (officials will pander to the ruler's desires in order to manipulate him, so the ruler must desire only proper standards), 14: 114 (only the illumined ruler can stop his officials from selling posts and conniving with their underlings to bully the people); 18: 141 ("Hua ce" 畫策) (only the illumined ruler will exclusively elevate the worthy as officials, so the state will be properly governed, and he will not excessively reward his officials), 18: 143 (only the illumined ruler is all-seeing, so his officials will not behave villainously); 20: 161 ("Ruo min" 弱民) (the illumined ruler controls officials by rewarding them for their merits and labors, and the sage must hold to his nature and not lend power to others); chapter 26: 188–89 ("Ding fen" 定分) (the ruler appoints specialist legal officials who hold written copies of the laws and disseminate these among the people, who thus can challenge any deviance by officials).

[5] *Shangjunshu* 17: 134 ("Shang xing" 賞刑) (contrasts sage with *fan* 凡 ruler); 25: 179 (contrasts the sage king Yu with a *yong* 庸 ruler). For "conventional rulers of our age" as contrasted with the sage or illumined ruler, see 3: 40 (explicitly contrasted with illumined rulers and sages); 6: 61 (2); 8: 84; 20: 161 (again contrasted with illumined rulers and sages).

[6] *Shangjunshu* 9: 90 ("Cuo fa" 錯法); 20: 161.

[7] *Shangjunshu* 13: 109 (the sage ruler, and he alone, knows the essentials of all things, which means that he possesses what is most essential in ruling the people [the same idea, in a negative formulation, appears in chapter 3: 36; chapter 14: 110 (the illumined ruler is illumined because he cannot be "blocked", which makes the officials unable to deceive him). On not being blocked as definitive in the *Xunzi* of the sage rulers and of Confucius, see *Xunzi* 21: 259–60 ("Jie bi" 解蔽) (on how evil rulers were blocked by their obsessions, but the sages were not), 21: 261–62 (on how each master was blocked by his particular obsession, while Confucius escaped this fate), 21: 263 (how sages as a group escape blockage).

[8] *Shangjunshu* 18: 143 (the illumined ruler perceives all things, gains [*de* 得] the world by first gaining himself, and conquers powerful foes by first conquering himself), 18:144 (knowledge of principles and inherent tendencies).

Book of Lord Shang does not provide detailed accounts of the ruler's conduct, in the manner of the *Han Feizi*, it clearly does *not* advocate the idea that once a system of objective standards or laws is created (which itself requires repeated interventions by rulers) it can function with a mediocre ruler on the throne. Just as in confronting the argument that the USA (or any modern democracy) is "a government of laws and not of men," one must note that laws do not create themselves, interpret themselves, administer themselves, nor successfully specify how all agents of a government will behave.

The *Han Feizi*, for its part, develops an elaborate theory of the "techniques" (*shu* 術) by which the ruler can block the officials' constant attempts to form cliques and manipulate (or even ultimately supplant) him for their own private benefits.[9] The most striking technique of control in this text is the manipulation of "performance and title" (*xingming* 形/刑名), in which the ruler keeps himself completely still, ideally becoming effectively invisible, and allows ministers to detail policy suggestions which are then written down so that ultimate performance can be measured against the text.[10] This procedure, which is discussed in several places, emphasizes two major aspects. First, the ruler must have total mastery of his own desires and indeed anything that would define him as a distinct person, so that he offers no aspects of a personality that officials can observe or manipulate in their proposals. Second, the officials must both work out all the details of their own project and perform it, so that all the tasks of governing are distributed among the officials, while the ruler remains still and unmoving.[11] As will be discussed below, the *Han Feizi* articulates this use of techniques as one aspect of a theory of mental self-discipline that is necessary to transform the ruler so that he can perform his functions.

The final defining aspect of the ruler's role is his need to maintain control of the "two handles" of rewards and punishments.[12] In *The Book of Lord Shang* "rewards" refers primarily to the distribution of titles and certain material benefits for excellent military performance, while "punishments" indicates the penalties, often mutilation or death, for disobedience or cowardice in the ranks. These are the primary mechanisms by which the state controls the peasant population, which is the basis of its power. The *Han Feizi* notably extends the use of rewards and punishments to control officials, sometimes as an aspect of the aforementioned *xingming*, in which those who successfully perform the tasks that they have set for themselves are rewarded,

---

[9] The *Shangjunshu* also cites in a few places the ruler's need of *shu* (數 and 術), but it does not explain what these "techniques" are. See chapters 6: 61, 6: 70; 24: 173–74, 24: 176; 25: 181.

[10] Goldin 2013: 8–11, 15–18; Goldin 2020: 213–18, 224–27; Lewis 1999: 33, 35–36; Wang Pei, Chap. 20, this volume. On the necessary invisibility of the monarch in the theories of the *Han Feizi*, see Pines 2013b: 77–82. As examples in the primary source see, for example, *Han Feizi* 5: 66 ("Zhu dao" 主道); 7: 126 ("Er bing" 二柄).

[11] The *Shangjunshu*, while it does not elaborate this theme, *does* warn the ruler that his more brilliant officials will spy out his likes and dislikes to manipulate how he administers his officers. See *Shangjunshu* 3: 35.

[12] Pines 2017: 68–75, 80–84; Goldin 2013: 4–6, 8, 11–12, 17–18; Goldin 2020: 207–09.

while those who fail are punished.[13] Given their centrality to all aspects of the ruler's power, it is not surprising that the theoreticians of rule through objective standards insist that rewards and punishments must be kept under his personal control.[14] This theory of control is also notable in being based on a fairly simplistic psychology in which the desire for rewards and fear of punishments control all human actions. Contempt for material gains or for the threat of pain, celebrated as moral heroism in many contexts, were condemned among the theoreticians of law as a deviant criminality requiring capital punishment, because they placed an individual beyond the state's control (Lewis 2021: 98–100).

As Yuri Pines has noted, the tasks performed by the ruler—creating new laws to respond to an evolving society; controlling legions of scheming ministers, kinspeople, wives, and favorites who were all conspiring to manipulate him (or even seek his death); and securing the correct administration of rewards and punishments throughout the state and court—would "seem to need almost superhuman abilities."[15] Given that, as the *Han Feizi* states in at least one passage, the vast majority of rulers will be of only middling ability, this seems to be a formula for perpetual chaos.[16] Noting the elaborate injunctions for the ruler to suppress all aspects of his personality, and totally discipline his desires and emotions, Pines follows the suggestion of A. C. Graham that the true argument of the text might have been to espouse ministerial rule. However, unable to ignore the mountains of condemnations of ministerial turpitude and selfishness, Pines settles upon a handful of chapters that indicate the existence of a "devoted minority within officialdom" who truly understand the "techniques" and are devoted to the "laws" (and a broader common good). These people, clearly referring to Han Fei and any who followed him, are presented as a means of justifying a supposed "pro-ministerial U-turn in the text." The image of such figures is also supported with the *Han Feizi*'s references to a few historical examples of exemplary reforming ministers—Yi Yin 伊尹, Guan Zhong 管仲 (d.

---

[13] *Han Feizi* 5: 81; 6: 91 ("You du" 有度).

[14] Indeed, Goldin has defined *fa* as "an impersonal administrative technique of determining rewards and punishments in accordance with a subject's true merit." See Goldin 2011: 68.

[15] Pines 2013b: 73–77. In one account of *xingming*, Goldin remarks, "Unable to share his innermost thoughts and feelings with anyone around him, or to love or hate or be motivated by any emotion at all, a ruler is the loneliest of men." This is another way of describing the "superhuman" character of the ruler in this text. See Goldin 2013: 10.

[16] On the middling level of rulers, so that one cannot wait for the arrival of a sage, see *Han Feizi* 40: 945–46 ("Nan shi" 難勢). In fact, what the text says is that rulers as extraordinary as Yao and Shun or as ghastly as Jie and Zhou might not appear for millennia, and that all the rulers in the interim, for whom the text was written, lie "in between" these extremes. The character employed is *zhong* 中, which could mean "middling" or "mediocre," but which the authors specify here means "above they are not as good as Yao and Shun and below they are not as bad as Jie and Zhou." To say that all those who are not as good as the greatest rulers in history nor as bad as the most degenerate are "mediocrities" is doing violence to the English language. The solution offered to this problem is for the ruler to rely on the authority of his position (*shi* 勢) and upon the power of laws (*fa* 法). As touched on above, these both require extraordinary self-discipline and discernment from the ruler.

645 BCE), and Shang Yang 商鞅 (d.338 BCE)—who transformed their rulers into kings or hegemons.[17]

There is no doubt that the *Han Feizi* celebrates this minority of ministers who are committed to serving the ruler through their mastery of techniques and laws (though it has difficulty explaining the existence of such beings who are devoted to a common good outside their own desire for rewards and fear of punishments, nor to justify not calling for their execution because like hermits and some scholars they lie beyond the control of these "two handles"). However, the chapters that discuss such men argue that in the courts of ordinary rulers, invariably dominated by the leading courtiers—who are familiar to the ruler, surrounded by fawning cliques who serve them, and supported by foreign powers—officials devoted to techniques and law will languish in anonymity and ultimately be executed or dismissed.[18]

Pines points out that the single chapter "Treacherous, Larcenous, Murderous Ministers" ("Jian jie shi chen" 姦劫弒臣) begins with an account of sage-like officials who help the ruler control his court and enforce the laws, and presents Guan Zhong, Shang Yang, and Wu Qi 吳起 (d. 381 BCE) as historical precedents (*Han Feizi* 14: 282–83). However, the chapter then argues that a ruler who would employ such men must be able to ignore the intellectual consensus of his age, defy the opposition of his court, and escape from the limits of his bodily senses. Such feats far surpass the capacities of a mediocre ruler. It also states that men of talent will remain unknown, and that virtually all such ministerial sages were ultimately destroyed by the unanimous slanders of courtiers. It specifically *celebrates* Lord Xiao of Qin 秦 孝公 (r. 361–338 BCE) for being able to recognize Shang Yang's value, and for supporting him in the face of universal opposition, but Shang Yang still ended by being torn apart in the market. The other exemplars similarly finished badly. The chapter concludes with an enumeration of rulers who were slain by their kin or officials, and endorses the popular saying that "even a leper would pity a king" (*li lian wang* 厲 憐王) (*Han Feizi* 14: 297).[19]

To summarize, the *Han Feizi* repeatedly rejects the idea that worthy ministers devoted to techniques and law can somehow fill the void left by a mediocre ruler, because they can achieve authority only where the ruler is brilliantly perceptive of talent and heroically determined to pursue its guidance in the face of a negative intellectual consensus and unanimous criticisms. This truth is demonstrated both by

---

[17] Pines 2013b: 78–84; he cites Graham 1989: 291. The argument that the *Han Feizi* can best be explained as a veiled call for ministerial domination is also elaborated in Graziani 2015.

[18] The hopeless situations at court of such men are elaborated in two chapters: chapter 11 ("Gu fen" 孤憤) and chapter 52 ("Ren zhu" 人主). Chapter 13: 271 ("He shi" 和氏) begins with the famous parable of the inability of supposed experts to recognize the true value of Mr. He's jade, cites the examples of Wu Qi and Shang Yang who tried to strengthen their rulers and were executed for their troubles, and concludes that such precedents will prevent any "men of service devoted to law and techniques (*fashu zhi shi* 法術之士)" from proffering their services.

[19] Jean Levi believed that this final statement on the desperate situation of rulers epitomized the message of this chapter, to the extent that he adapted it as the chapter title in his French translation of the *Han Feizi*. See Levi 1999: 147–56.

logical derivation from the basic ideas of the text, and by its historical examples. Consequently, the idea that the *Han Feizi* (or even *The Book of Lord Shang*) reduces the ruler to a cog in a mechanical government of laws must be abandoned. The role of the ruler elaborated in the text requires total devotion to the general interest (as his own private interests made him liable to manipulation), refusing to trust anyone (as even his closest kin were potential assassins), no delegation of authority, the ability to creatively reshape the laws, the skill to guarantee that officials performed their tasks, the percipience to recognize the solitary and hidden men devoted to techniques and law, and the heroism to support them. One might argue that nobody has ever possessed such character and skills, but it certainly is not a case of his being a mediocrity in a self-guiding mechanism or one manipulated by the likes of Han Fei. While the text *does* endorse the possibility of a middling monarch, as part of a polemic against the constant celebration of the ancient sages, the argument cannot be made to work within the context of the entire *Han Feizi*. Moreover, as discussed in note #16, to describe as "mediocre" any ruler who is not as good as a saint or genius who might appear only once every few millennia, or as bad as a monster who would appear with the same infrequency is not an accurate translation.

2   Perfecting the Ruler's Self in the *Han Feizi*

As a preliminary to this discussion, it is important to recognize that the perfecting of the "person" or the "body" through techniques of self-cultivation was a widespread, if not universal, commitment of early philosophy in both the West and in east Asia.[20] The modern academic recognition that these categories were cultural constructs that changed over time and space began with classic essays by Marcel Mauss in the mid-1930s.[21] The essay on the "category of the person/self" argued that this was at its simplest a universal category, as indicated by the possibility in all languages of referring to a self which was distinguished from others. At the next level, the self could be theorized as defined roles, obligations and rights pertaining to those roles, and an ethical character that together defined the nature of a person (*personne*), and which varied among cultures. The article also suggested (without always clearly distinguishing) an interiorized self (*moi*) defined by psychological states, relations to the cosmos, and spiritual relations to other such selves.

Finally, it sketched a triumphalist account of the emergence of a unique Western theory of the person as first a philosophical-religious conception (articulated in Christianity's theory of the soul), and ultimately a fundamental intellectual category

---

[20] This phenomenon is discussed in greater detail in Lewis Forthcoming.

[21] "Une Catégorie de l'esprit humain: La Notion de personne, celle de 'moi'" (1935) and "Les Techniques du corps" (1934) are both in the one-volume collection of his major essays, Mauss 1950: 331–86. A translation of the essay on the person/self, along with essays on its theoretical significance and case studies are published in Carrithers et al. 1985. This volume, pp. 322–23, lists recent (prior to 1985) major studies on the person/self.

(in modern thinking from Descartes's *cogito* through Kant) underlying the emergence of an individualism that treated the self as a discreet monad existing wholly within the mind and detached from the body (Ryle's "ghost in a machine"). This understanding was said to be foundational to the modern world. Several critical essays and case studies written to accompany the English translation of the essay trace the crucial initial step to the philosophy of Plato rather than Christianity. Others reject this evolutionary perspective, arguing instead that the practices and theories that guided both the psychologically defined inner "self" (*moi*) and the exterior "person" (*personne*) shaped by rules and laws should be treated as episodes moving with no clear teleology.

Mauss's essay on "techniques of the body" (written a year earlier and influenced by Marcel Granet's discussions of "bodily techniques" in early China) argued that each society developed distinctive techniques for training the body, techniques which shaped both physical capacities and associated mental mechanisms adapted to their visions of social order. Thus, the body of the Greek citizen trained for the public agon was distinct from that of a monk in his cell, or that of a modern citizen alternating between a home and the site of paid labor. Whereas the purely physical and measurable body of modern science had no history, Mauss's body conceived through its "modes of construction" was "thoroughly historicized and completely problematic."[22]

Numerous modern scholars have studied how in the West, this project of perfecting the self became a fundamental aspect of early philosophy, and was also adapted to the possibility of creating an ideal ruler or rulers through the adaptation of the skills of the philosopher.[23] While Plato's advocacy of making philosophers into rulers is well-known, it constitutes a restricted, text-based program that was not translated into actual government. However, as Erwin Goodenough elaborated in his classic article on "Hellenistic Kingship," the ideal of the king as a figure of Animate Law who embodied the logos of pure reason as the basis of the state was articulated in numerous essays and inscriptions. Moreover, when the Roman empire was converted to Christianity, this idea was applied by Eusebius to Constantine, and thus became an aspect of the theorization of the Christian state.[24] The remaking of men through philosophy also emerged in Roman political thought in the form of stoicism. This theory of mental self-mastery through control of the emotions and desires was introduced into political discourse in Cicero's theory of the rhetorical self-fashioning of "new men" in the late Republic, became central to an elaborate mutual entanglement of self-command and political rule in the ideas that Seneca offered to the Emperor Nero, underlay the Antonine practice of transferring the emperorship to the best official rather than a biological heir, and climaxed in Marcus Aurelius's theory of creating an "inner citadel" from within which he achieved an

---

[22] Feher et al. 1989: "Introduction" (by Michel Feher), p. 11. These volumes provide a useful sketch of many approaches to the body.

[23] On the idea that early philosophy in the West aimed above all at the perfecting of an embodied person, see Hadot 1995, 2002.

[24] Goodenough 1928: 55–102; Drake 1976: 32–34, 84–85, 88, 89–90, 106–11, 115.

immense field of vision that allowed him to act across the great times distances that constituted the empire.[25]

For early China, the most useful elaboration of the interlinked ideas of self, person, and body as cultural constructs is David Hall and Roger Ames's model of the "focus-field self," which is elaborated in several books and essays.[26] This idea—which Ames develops primarily through Confucian and Daoist thinkers—views the self as a focused center embedded within an encompassing field, or rather fields, consisting of other people, places, and, ultimately, the cosmos. This person is defined by a range of roles which he or she enacts relationally with others: son of a father or mother, elder brother of a younger brother, a descendant of deceased ancestors, etc. The person defined by these roles, obligations, and rights (to cite the Maussian idea) exists only within and through these multiple relations, not only those to close kin, but in weakening fashion with more distant kin, fellow villagers, the state's agents, and non-humans. As emphasized more in the Daoist thinkers, any person also exists relationally as the focus of multiple fields formed with the creatures and objects within his or her ambit, and at the highest level with the cosmos viewed with the self as center. Likewise, things in the world can be understood through the multiple fields of which they form the focus/center, e.g., the capital within the state, the court within the capital, the ruler within the court, etc. All these fields created within the society radiate outward around a focus/center with no absolute boundary between the selves and their "outside," a fact that is as true of the body as of the person.[27]

While the Hall/Ames model emphasizes the multiple and evolving relations within which the person emerges, early Chinese thinkers also elaborated a similar image through the idea of *qi* (氣), translated as "energy," "vital breath," "pneuma," or "vapor." This protean concept remains central to Chinese medicine, martial arts, strategy, calligraphy, and any form of dynamism. In the centuries covered in this essay it named a primal "stuff" or "configured energy" that constituted all entities, being common to inanimate matter, plants, animals, and people. This shared substrate meant that not only people and their environment shared common principles, but also that they acted directly upon one another through their *qi*, which thus provided a physical underpinning to the focus-field model. Thus, the outer world could drive the feelings and actions of the embodied self, and that self could radiate outward to control other humans, and even aspects of the physical world. In this way, it led easily into ideas about the creation of an ideal ruler through the perfecting of his embodied self.[28]

---

[25] Dugan 2005; Star 2012; Romm 2014; Wilson 2014; Hadot 2014; Francis 1995. The *Han Feizi*'s argument that perfected government of the self was a necessary step to world government is laid out in Levi 1989: 112–46; Levi 1999: 45–57.

[26] Hall and Ames 1987: 125, 153, 192, 237–47; Hall and Ames 1995: 234–44, 268–78; Hall and Ames 1998: 23–78. See also Ames 1994: 187–212; Ames 2011: 66–79; Ames 2021, chapter 4.

[27] Sommer 2008: 293–324; Sivin 1995: 5–37.

[28] Linck 2012; Hertzer 2006; Kubny 1995; Rappe 1995: ch. 5; Larre 1982; Chen 2009; Li 2009; Kuroda 1977: book 1.

An example in the *Han Feizi* of how philosophy could be adopted to provide a model for the ruler's self-perfection in the world is provided by the handful of chapters arguing that he must pattern himself on the universal Way of the cosmos. As both Paul R. Goldin and Yuri Pines have noted, such invocations of a cosmic model are invariably followed by practical advice.[29] However, they both seem to conclude that the fact that the text is not truly concerned with the workings of the cosmos indicates that the earlier parts of these passages are rhetorical devices, perhaps to please a particular audience or gain prestige within the culture of the period.[30] I would, in contrast, argue that these passages are expressions of an ultimate commitment to a vision of *transforming* the ruler's mind or the self through a distinctive mental regime, patterned at least in part on the workings of the cosmos. This enabled the ruler to attain a total self-mastery that allowed, for example, the disciplining of all his emotions and the ability to endure a total solitude. This in turn made possible his ability to penetrate the prevarications of his courtiers and the illusions of conventional wisdom, and to endure the universal opposition and opprobrium that his policies aroused. As I will discuss below, this vision with variations was adapted from other texts of the period, and passed in turn into further texts.

The idea of a distinctive, mental regime for self-transformation that is essential to the ruler's performance is elaborated throughout the *Han Feizi*. An early example cited by both Goldin and Pines is the discussion at the beginning of "The Way of the Ruler" ("Zhu dao" 主道), which is a lengthy rhyming passage patterned on the *Dao de jing*:

---

[29] Goldin 2005a: 62–65; Goldin 2013: 14–18; Goldin 2020: 226–27; Pines 2013b: 70–71.

[30] Goldin offers four hypotheses to explain these appeals to the model of the Way. First, perhaps the chapters with language adapted from the *Laozi*, or that appear as commentaries (see below), were written by some different author. He rejects this because Sima Qian clearly understood Han Fei as an exemplar of what he called "Huang-Lao" thought, in which political philosophy was based on appeals to the Yellow Emperor and the *Laozi*. I would further argue that all the texts from this period passed through multiple hands, and the fact that later devotees of the *Han Feizi* understood it as closely related to the *Laozi* tells us something about the former text as it was commonly understood. Second, Goldin offers the possibility that Han Fei's thought changed over time, without committing himself to which chapters were earlier and which later. Third, he suggests that as espoused in other chapters, Han Fei was not afraid of contradicting himself, so that he would adopt the *Laozi*'s rhetoric to appeal to a king with a "cultivated appreciation" of such texts. The primary problem with this argument is that it does not explain why the author or authors of the *Han Feizi* would have thought that the only texts which interested the rulers of their day were those related to the *Laozi*. Fourth, he posits that appeals to imitation of the Way might simply have been a way of arguing for practical ideas about being a better ruler, such as keeping your desires hidden. He describes this as a "philosophy of the poker face". This theory, in fact, resembles the model that I will offer, except that, as I will discuss, the *Han Feizi* calls for a transformation of the ruler's self rather than merely surface dissimulation. This could be described as advocating a "poker face" only to the extent that one believed—as in Paul Schrader's movie "The Card Counter"—that a poker face that was held long enough could swallow up the entire person and alter his nature. The ruler described in the *Han Feizi* had to keep himself alone and unreadable to everyone with whom he came into contact, and he had to do this without any relaxation.

道者萬物之始，
是非之紀也。
是以明君守始
以知萬物之源，
治紀以知善敗之端。
故虛靜以待之，
令名自命也，
令事自定也。
虛則知實之情，
靜則知動者正。
有言者自為名，
有事者自為形。
形名叁同，
歸之其情。

故曰:君無見其所欲，臣自將雕琢。君無見其意，君見其意，臣將自表異。故曰:
去好去惡，
臣乃見素。
去智去舊，
臣乃自備。
故有智而不以慮，使萬物知其處。有行而不以賢，觀臣下之所因。有勇而不以怒，
使群臣盡其武。是故去智而有明，去賢而有功，去勇而有強。

The Way is the beginning of all things,
The controlling cord of right and wrong.
The enlightened ruler holds to the beginning
To know the origin of all things,
And regulates the cord to know the origin of success and failure.
Empty and still to await things,
He lets [officials] name themselves,
And those with tasks fix themselves [*xingming*].
Empty, he knows their true sentiments [*qing*];
Still, he knows correctness of their movements.
Those who speak assign their own titles [*ming*], [*C.meŋ]
Those with tasks create their own form [*xing*]. [*[G]'eŋ]
Forms and names are matched and identified,
Tracing it back to [the officials'] true sentiments [*qing*]. [*[dz]eŋ]

The ruler does not show his desires, for if he shows his desires, then the officials will shape themselves accordingly. The ruler does not show his thoughts, for if he shows his thoughts, then the officials will compete [in pandering]. Therefore it is said,

Eliminate loves and hates [*hào wù*], [*'ak-s]
the officials then show their true, simple nature [素 *sù*]." [*s'ak-s]
Eliminate cunning; eliminate deliberate action
The officials will then restrain themselves.
Having intelligence, he does not use it to think,
Causing all things to each know their own place.
Having a worthy character, he does not perform it,
So he can observe the motivations of his officials.
Having courage, he does not become angry,
Causing his officials to use to the full their martial abilities.
By eliminating his intelligence, he is enlightened.

By eliminating his worthiness, he achieves merit.
By eliminating his courage, he becomes strong (*Han Feizi* 5: 66).[31]

This passage echoes stanza 19 of the received version of the *Laozi*, and follows it in arguing that the ruler must eliminate his own personal ideas, sentiments, and desires. Still and empty, he allows things, above all his officials, to take their course.[32] Applied to things, this allows each object to assume its proper place; applied to people, it lets them reveal their true capacities and desires, forcing them to serve the ruler or face elimination. The chapter goes on to note that his calmness and lack of emotion mean that he has no fixed position, so none can know his location. Thus, he remains hidden and unmoving, while his ministers "tremble in fear beneath him."

Remaining hidden and mysterious, the ruler causes his subordinates to exert themselves to the full in proposing and carrying out ideas. Consequently, as they compete in presenting ideas to him, he sees with all the eyes in the empire, hears with its ears, and thinks with the minds of the sages without himself being a sage. Not himself a worthy, he is the master of worthies; without cunning or intelligence, he is the standard for all intelligence.[33] The theme of the hidden ruler, which became fundamental to the spatial order of Chinese politics, is emphasized throughout this and subsequent discussions.[34]

In contrast, the ruler becomes blocked off whenever officials control access to his person, administer the treasury, issue edicts, adjudicate legal cases, or decide promotions. Only by keeping hidden can he control all these elements of his power, and only by stilling personal intellect and desires can he remain hidden. This means that the ruler must eliminate any actions in pursuit of personal desires in order that the laws can act as the sole standard. Thus, he forces his ministers to imitate him in abandoning the pursuit of personal interests in the name of the common interest as embodied in the law.[35]

Later chapters reiterate many themes from the "Way of the Ruler," while adding new emphases. "Brandishing Authority" ("Yang quan" 揚權) which again is largely in verse like the *Laozi*, precedes its discussion of the ruler's invisibility and stillness

---

[31] These two passages are translated as poetry in Graham 1989: 288–89. The chapter continues to elaborate these ideas through p. 81. The proposition that if the ruler eliminates his own hates and loves, the officials revert to simplicity also appears in chapter 7:132. The old Chinese pronunciations, whose transcriptions I cannot exactly reproduce, are from "Baxter-Sagart Old Chinese reconstruction, version 1.1 (20 September 2014)" at http://ocbaxtersagart.lsait.lsa.umich.edu.

[32] *Laozi*, stanza 19. Subsequent sections of this chapter of the *Han Feizi* echo, in the order that they appear, stanza 52; stanzas 20, 21, 25; stanza 67; stanza 73; stanza 27. Three of these seven stanzas appear in the Guodian material related to the *Laozi*. See Guo 2001: 50, 106, 112.

[33] In contrast, were the ruler to try to use his own vision, hearing, and cogitation to supervise his ministers, this would allow them to manipulate him. See *Han Feizi* 6: 107.

[34] On hiding away the ruler to generate power, see Lewis 2006: 114–18, which cites several Warring States texts which make this point. On the ruler remaining hidden, and keeping his ideas and emotions secret, see also *Han Feizi* 5:74, in a passage that begins by saying, "The Way lies in being invisible."

[35] *Han Feizi* 6: 92; 7: 120–21, 126, 130–31; 35: 811–12 ("Wai chu shuo you xia" 外儲說右下).

by describing the sensual and emotional attractions from which he must free himself:

夫香美脆味，厚酒肥肉，甘口而疾形。曼理皓齒，說情而損精。故去甚去泰，身乃無害。權不欲見，素無為也。事在四方，要在中央。聖人執要，四方來效。

Fragrant scents, crisply cooked meats, strong wine, and fatty flesh; these are sweet to the mouth but cause the body [*xing* *[G]‘eŋ] to fall ill. Exquisite beauties with gleaming teeth, these delight the emotions [*qing* *[dz]eŋ] but damage the body's energies [*jing* *tseŋ, often identified with semen]. Eliminate excess, eliminate joy [泰 *tai* *l‘a[t]-s], the body then will not be harmed [*hai* *N-k‘at-s]. Power must not be revealed; its nature lies in non-action. Tasks are in the four directions [*si fang* *C-paŋ]; but the essential control is in the center [*zhong yang* *ʔaŋ]. The sage holds the essential control [*yao* *[q]ew-s]; the four directions come to follow him [*lai xiao* *m-k‘raw-s]. (*Han Feizi* 8: 137)[36]

Here conquering sensual desires and thus keeping the body's energies intact is the first step to establishing the empty and undisturbed interior of the ruler at the center of all things. This echoes not only the *Laozi* (as emphasized later in the *Han Feizi*'s commentary on that text), but also the texts related to "Inner Training" (*nei ye* 內業, which will be discussed below), which emphasize establishing a still center from which the ruler's influence radiates out to the edges of the world.

This theme of mental tranquility based on the absence of conscious reflection and desire, leading to physical completeness and culminating in political power, is given its clearest expression in the *Han Feizi*'s chapter "Explaining Lao" ("Jie Lao 解老):

德者內也。得者外也。"上德不德"言其神不淫於外也。神不淫於外則身全，身全之謂德。德者得身也。凡德者以無為集，以無欲成，以不思安，以不用固。為之欲之，則德無舍。

"Virtuous power [*de* 德 *t‘ək]" is on the inside. "Obtaining [*de* 得 *t‘ək]" is on the outside. [When the *Laozi* says] "the highest virtue is not treated as virtue," this means that his spirit [*shen*] does not overflow [*yin* 淫] outward. If the spirit does not overflow outward, then the embodied self is complete. The embodied self being complete is called "virtuous power." "Virtuous power" means to "obtain" the [entire] body. Virtuous power is always collected through being without conscious action [*wu wei*], and made complete through having no desires [*wu yu*]. It attains peace through not pondering and becomes firm through not being used. If you act or desire, then the virtuous power has no place to lodge [舍*she*, the term referring to the cleansed mind in the "Inner Training"] (*Han Feizi* 20: 370).[37]

---

[36] This link of the mastery of sensual experience with the establishment of the ruler at the center of things also appears in "Illustrating Laozi". See *Han Feizi* 21: 449 ("Yu Lao" 喻老): "The orifices of the senses are the door and windows of spirit illumination [*jing shen*]. When ears and eyes are exhausted through sounds and colors, the quintessential energies will be exhausted by external attractions, and the center will have no ruler. If the center has no ruler, then even if calamities or good fortune are as big as hills or mountains, you will be unable to recognize them." For a detailed study and translation of the two chapters in the *Han Feizi* that comment on the *Laozi*, see Queen 2013.

[37] For *she* in "Inner Training" see *Guanzi* 49: 938 ("Nei ye" 內業). As Harold Roth has noted, this same usage was carried forward in one of the political elaborations of "Inner Training". See Roth 1999: 222, note 64.

Only through purging all mental activity, both emotional and intellectual, can the ruler preserve his body's energetic resources, which in turn form the charismatic power that allows him to command the world from his own center. The theme of eliminating the emotions, or of reducing them to a state of natural spontaneity, which constitutes the ruler's unique ability to keep body and spirit intact and thereby to command all, recurs throughout this chapter. This is contrasted with the common people, who are dominated by desires and feelings that waste away their bodily energies.[38]

This chapter concludes with a lengthy passage on appropriate responses to objects, emotional mastery, and political power:

> 人無愚智，莫不有趨舍。恬淡平安，莫不知禍福之所由來。得於好惡，怵於淫物，而後變亂。所欲然者，引於外物，亂於玩好也。……至聖人不然，一建其趨舍，雖見所好之物不能引，不能引之謂"不拔"。一於其情，雖有可欲之類，神不為動，身不為動之謂"不脫"。……身以積精為德，家以資財為德，鄉國天下皆以民為德。今治身而外物不能亂其精神，故曰："修之身，其德乃真。"治家，無用之物不能動其計，則資有餘。……治邦者行此節，則鄉之有德者益眾，故曰"修之邦，其德乃豐。"莅天下者行此節，則民之生莫不受其澤，故曰"修之天下，其德乃普。"

> Whether stupid or clever, all people have inclinations and aversions. When contented and at peace, they all know the sources of calamity or good fortune. But when seized by loves and hates, shaken by luxury objects [*yin wu* 淫物], they are thrown into turmoil. The reason for this is that they are dragged astray by external objects, and plunged into disorder by their likings and pleasures. …

> The sage is different. Having once settled his inclinations or aversions, when he sees some object that he loves, it cannot drag him. Since he cannot be dragged astray, this is called [in the *Laozi*] "not pulled out." Being entirely unified in his emotions, even when he sees something desirable, his spirit is not disturbed. The fact that his spirit cannot be unsettled is called "not removed." …

> The individual body/self thereby accumulates refined energies that become virtuous power. The household thereby turns wealth into resources that become virtuous power. The village, state, and world all use their people to become virtuous power.

> Now if you regulate the body/self, then external objects cannot throw your refined, spirit energies into disorder. So [the *Laozi*] says, "Cultivating the body/self, the virtuous power is then perfected." If you thus regulate the household, then useless objects cannot disturb calculations, and resources will be in abundance. … If those who regulate a state practice this discipline, this will increase the number of villages that have virtuous power, so [the *Laozi*] says, "Cultivating it in the state, its virtuous power will be plentiful." If the ruler of a world empire practices this discipline, then all people will flourish from his influence, so

---

[38] *Han Feizi* 20: 374, 376, 380 (contrasts the ruler's relation to ritual, which expresses his "uncarved heart/mind," with that of commoners, who use ritual to secure gains, and become either "happy" or "resentful" depending on the result), pp. 387, 388 (ordinary people desire wealth, fame, and long life, but due to this longing they wind up with the opposite), p. 390 (the sage ruler, unlike commoners, obtains a "complete embodied self" and consequently "long life"), pp. 394, 395 (the emotional agitation of ordinary people wastes their spirit), p. 396 (keeping the senses clear through lack of desires accumulates harmonious energies [*qi*], thus creating virtuous power), p. 397 (links preserving the state with preserving the body), pp. 398–99, 402–403, 405, 407 (only the sage ruler avoids the desire for sensual pleasures and lascivious enjoyments that produce disorder and calamity), pp. 416–17 (the sage ruler alone does not waste his spirit energies and so remains safe and healthy), p. 421 (people expend themselves on what they love, while the ruler keeps his energies replete), p. 423.

[the *Laozi*] says, "Cultivating it in the world [*tianxia*天下] its virtuous power will be universal." (*Han Feizi* 20: 428)[39]

This moves from the sage's ability to escape emotional responses to objects, to the physical perfection that this allows and the charismatic power that radiates from his perfected self. This mental regime is then extended to the heads of sequentially larger social groups—household, village, state, and world—and in all cases the perfection of virtuous power through mental discipline leads to order and abundance.

One final argument in the *Han Feizi* that elaborates the ruler's unique mental capacities as the basis for effective laws and techniques appears in "Brandishing Authority":

夫道者宏大而無形。德者覈理而普至，至於群生，斟酌用之，萬物皆盛，而不與其寧。道者下周欲事，因稽而命，與時生死，叁名異事，通一同情。故曰:"道不同於萬物，德不同於陰陽，衡不同於輕重，繩不同於出入，和不同於燥溼，君不同於群臣。"凡此六者，道之出也。道無雙，故曰一。是故明君貴獨道之容。君臣不同道，下以名禱，君操其名，臣效其形，形名叁同，上下和調也。

The Way is vast and formless; its Power, searching through the structuring principles of things, reaches everywhere.

Reaching to living things (*sren),
Judiciously applied,
The myriad things are all completed (*[d]len-s),
but [the Power] does not share their ease (*n'en).

The Way permeates all affairs; its Mandate [*ming* *m-rin-s] accords with their character, so they live and die with the seasons. Matching names and distinguishing tasks, it penetrates through the One and joins all feelings. So it is said, "The Way is distinct from the myriad things; its Power is distinct from *yin* and *yang*; the balance is distinct from the light or heavy [that it measures]; the [straight-edge] cord is distinct from the ins and outs [that it corrects]; the pitchpipe is distinct from the dryness and dampness [of its tones].[40] The ruler likewise is distinct from his myriad officials."

These six things are all manifestations of the Way. The Way has no peer, so it is called "the One." Therefore, the enlightened ruler exalts the all-encompassing character of the unique, solitary Way. The ruler and ministers have distinct Ways. The officials use their titles [*ming* *C.men] to make reports and petitions, while the ruler controls these titles. The ministers then render up their results/achievements [*xing* *[G] 'en]. Achievements and titles are matched, and ruler and ruled thus attain harmony. (*Han Feizi* 8: 152)

Here the ruler is the human equivalent of the unitary Way that pervades all things without itself being one thing among the others. He is like the objective standards of measure that correct all things, remaining distinct from what they measure. Set apart in the solitude created by his position and his unique mental discipline, he guides the state so that every person, like the myriad objects guided by the Way, has his or her proper place and acts appropriately to that place. Eliminating sentiments is

---

[39] Some of these ideas are also discussed in the "Yu Lao" ("Illustrating Lao") chapter. On the control of desire sequentially leading to the health of the body and the survival of the state see 21: 434. The same link, including an unending continuity of sacrifices appears on p. 435. On the link between emotional mastery, sagehood, and recognizing calamities or good fortune, see p. 453.

[40] The idea that musical tones are distinguished by their dryness or dampness is articulated in a story that appears in two Han anthologies of anecdotes. See *Shuo yuan* 12: 293 ("Feng shi" 奉使); *Hanshi waizhuan* 7: 238.

central to the ruler's performance of this function, enabling him to act on the pattern of Heaven, which covers, and Earth, which carries, all things without discrimination. It also distinguishes him from the officials and the people, who resemble the objects to which their emotions tie them. These ideas are elaborated in subsequent passages of the same chapter, and figure in the texts from Guodian 郭店 related to the *Laozi*.[41]

These injunctions that the ruler should completely master his desires and emotions also take the practical form of pointing out that officials will avail themselves of any loves or hates that he reveals by pandering to these feelings:

故君見惡則群臣匿端，君見好則群臣誣能。人主欲見，則群臣之情態得其資矣。……人臣之情非必能愛其君也，為重利之故也。今人主不掩其情，不匿其端，而使人臣有緣以侵其上，則人臣為子之，田常不難矣。

Therefore, if the ruler shows what he hates, then all the officials will hide such tendencies. If he shows what he loves, then all the officials will falsely display such capacities. When the ruler's desires become visible, these become resources that the officials use to make a display of their supposed sentiments. ...

As for the sentiments of the ministers, they do not necessarily love their prince; [they] serve him] for great profit. Now if the ruler does not hide his sentiments and cover up the "beginnings" [*duan*, as in Mencius's 'four beginnings'], and lets his ministers seek these out to encroach on him, then it will not be hard for the ministers to become usurpers Zizhi and Tian Chang (*Han Feizi* 7: 130–31). [42]

The chapter thus concludes that if the ruler does not hide his feelings and inclinations, then he allows his ministers to encroach on his powers and, ultimately, take his position.

After being announced in "The Way of the Ruler" and "Brandishing Authority," the need for the ruler to hide his likes and dislikes, to prevent anyone in the court from spying them out and thus being able to manipulate him, became a topic of anecdotes and persuasions throughout the text.[43] The most extensive discussion is in "Signs of Perishing" ("Wang zheng" 亡徵), which lists factors indicating that a ruler was going to fall or his state perish. Many of these are based on the ruler being guided by his emotions, rather than by laws or administrative methods, or allowing officials to discern his loves and hates, and then to manipulate these to improve their own positions at the expense of the common interest. Thus, if the ruler evinces a passion for palaces, towers, ponds, chariots, fine clothing, and other luxuries, then officials exhaust the people to feed these desires, and transfer needed money from the army. The list of such factors goes on and on, demonstrating that any ruler who cannot keep his thoughts and desires a secret will perish (*Han Feizi* 15: 300–03). The same theme informs much of the chapter "The Difficulties of Persuasion"

---

[41] *Han Feizi* 8: 156, 163–64; Guo 2001: 60, 64, 71.

[42] For historical examples of ministers who ruined their rulers by pandering to their desires, see *Han Feizi* 35: 822–25; 39: 937 ("Nan si" 難四); 44: 967 ("Shuo yi" 説疑). The *Book of Lord Shang* also points out this problem. See *Shangjunshu* 3: 35–36.

[43] *Han Feizi* 17: 321, 323 ("Bei nei" 備內); 18: 330, 331 ("Nan mian" 南面); 24: 522 ("Guan xing" 觀行); 31: 622–23 ("Nei chu shuo xia" 內儲說下); 34: 773, 775 (2), 776 ("Wai chu shuo you shang" 外儲說右上); 35: 803, 832–33; 38: 921–22 ("Nan san" 難三); 48: 1072 ("Ba jing" 八經).

("Shui nan" 說難), which warns those in the court how they could ruin himself through divulging matters, notably being unable to keep the ruler's desires and plans secret from other officials (*Han Feizi* 12: 256–57, 261, 266–67, 268–69). Here the insistence that the ruler should hide his feelings and desires becomes entangled in any political discussion in the court, making any proposition grounds for dismissal because of the possibility that it is a veiled reference to some hidden feeling or plan.

While the ruler had to fear all his officials, the greatest danger came from those of whom he was fond, whether favorite officials, beloved concubines, or even his closest kin, including his mother. In such cases the ruler's emotions again posed serious dangers if he let them be known or guide his decisions. The threat posed by favorites was in part the most extreme version of that posed by any official, since rulers were more likely to reveal their desires and thoughts to those with whom they were most intimate. The longest discussion of the danger posed by favorites and kin is "Eight Kinds of Treachery" ("Ba jian" 八姦), which enumerates eight methods of treachery employed against the ruler. These are listed in order of increasing distance from the ruler, from those who share the same bed, to those who stand at his side, to elder kin, to "encouraged calamities [pandering by officials in the court]," to "sprouts among the people [officials buying popular support by distributing the state's wealth as if it were their own generosity]," to being manipulated by persuaders from foreign courts, to being bullied by the threat of private armies into pandering to the desires of one's own officials, to finally being forced to serve the demands of foreign powers (*Han Feizi* 9: 181–83).

These people, whose sole qualifications were their physical and emotional ties to the ruler, were the extreme form of spying out the ruler's sentiments to manipulate him. They translated familiarity with the ruler, and his comfort with them, into controlling appointments and deciding which proposals were adopted. They are sometimes paired with palace women, but enjoy the advantage of not relying on physical appearance, and of more freely consorting with officials to form factions. His relations to his women and children are further elaborated in "Precautions Against the Entourage" ("Bei nei" 備內), and anecdotes about or discussions of the need for the ruler to totally control his emotions and avoid all exposure of his desires recur throughout the text.[44]

Rulers who allowed themselves to be guided by their feelings opened illicit routes to office and honor other than performance in office or conduct in battle. Such deviations included honoring moral worthies, appointing skilled speakers or eminent scholars, rewarding hermits, or distinguishing any "virtues" or

---

[44] *Han Feizi* 6: 84, 91–2, 99–100; 9: 181–83, 190, 194, 196 ("Ba jian" 八姦); 15: 301–302 (4); 16:318 ("San shou" 三守); 17: 321–23; 19: 366–67 ("Shi xie" 飾邪); 20: 407–08, 421; 30: 577–78 ("Nei chu shuo shang" 內儲說上); 31: 617, 634, 635, 636, 643 (2), 646, 647 (2); 32: 683–84 ("Wai chu shuo zuo shang" 外儲說左上); 34: 780, 800–01; 38: 922–23; chapter 45: 992 ("Gui shi" 詭使); 46: 1006–07 ("Liu fan" 六反); 48: 1053–54 ("Ba jing" 八經); 49: 1120 ("Wu du" 五蠹); 52: 1164. The danger of being emotionally close (*qin*) to morally base people (*xiao ren*) is also cited in the military treatise *Wei Liaozi* 尉繚子. See *Wei Liaozi* 7: 35a ("Shier ling" 十二陵).

achievements that were honored by people, but of no use to the state. The two most frequently cited chapters in the *Han Feizi*—"The Five Vermin" ("Wu du" 五蠹) and "Eminent Teachings" ("Xian xue" 顯學)—are devoted to this theme, and ot examples are scattered through the text.[45] These actions are as destructive as rewarding officials or pardoning crimes due to sentimental weakness.

The opposition between emotion, which binds people to particularist commitments, and the objective standards of the shared, common good is also read into the cosmic patterns for proper government in "Great Principles" (大體 *da ti*). First invoking Heaven, Earth, the four seasons, and natural phenomena, it then enumerates the necessity of law, techniques of administration, rewards and punishments, and objective standards. It continues:

不逆天裡，不傷情性。不吹毛而求小疵，不洗垢而察難知。不引繩之外，不推繩之內，不急法之外，不緩法之內。守成理，因自然。禍福生於道法而不出乎愛惡。……故至安之世，法如朝露，純樸不散。心無結怨，口無煩言。

Do not go against the principles of Heaven, nor harm human nature [*qing xing* 情性]. Do not seek out petty flaws or investigate what is difficult to know. Do not deviate in any way from the standard of the straight-edge cord or that of the laws. Hold to established principles and follow what is natural. Calamity or blessing emerge from the Way and the law, not from loves and hates. ... In times of peace, the law is like the morning dew, pure and simple, without mingling or disorder. [The people's] heart/minds have no congealed resentments [*jie yuan* 結怨] and their mouths no excess words. (*Han Feizi* 29: 555)

Here the highest principles of order, the Way and law, are set against the ruler's loves and hates as standards of actions, and achieving order culminates in the absence of resentment in the people's hearts. (Such "congealed resentment" became the routine explanation for natural calamities in Eastern Han memorials, although that idea is not operant here.[46]) The chapter concludes with the argument that Mt. Tai becomes tallest because it has no "loves and hates [*hào wù*]," just as the ocean is abundant because it does not choose among the petty streams that flow into it, and continues:

故大人寄形於天地而萬物備。歷心於山海而國家富。上無忿怒之毒，下無伏怨之患。上下交樸，以道為舍。

Therefore the "Great Man" lodges his body between Heaven and Earth, and the world's objects are complete. He passes his heart/mind through the mountains and seas [Mt. Tai and the ocean], and the state is rich. The ruler has no poison of anger, and the subjects no calamity of submerged resentment, so ruler and ruled join in unspoiled simplicity, and take the Way as their lodging. (*Han Feizi* 29: 559)[47]

---

[45] *Han Feizi* 6: 99–100; 7: 130–31; 8: 156–57; 9: 181–82; 11: 251–52; 13: 275; 14: 287, 289–90, 293; 15: 300–02; 19: 344–45, 362–63; 32: 662–63, 700; 33: 734 ("Wai chu shuo zuo xia" 外儲說左下); 34: 769–70; 36: 861, 862 ("Nan yi" 難一); 44: 965, 967; 45: 987–88, 991–92, 997–98; 46: 1000–01, 1006–07; 47: 1023 ("Ba shuo" 八說); 51: 1154–55, 1159 ("Zhong xiao" 忠孝).

[46] For a discussion of the people's congealed resentment as the source of disasters in Eastern Han memorials, see Lewis 2017.

[47] The vision of the ideal ruler as defined in part by a mental mastery that enables the imposition of objective standards is also announced at the beginning of "Measures of the Heart/Mind" ("Xin du" 心度). See *Han Feizi* 54: 1176: "As for the sage's control of the people, he measures against the fundamental and does not follow his desires, fixed on benefitting the people and that is all."

Thus the ruler is ultimately modeled on the "Great Man" as described in detail in the *Zhuangzi*, (although in this text he was not identified with the ruler), suppressing his personal sentiments and concerns in imitating Heaven and implementing a pure, objective law that applies to all things.[48] This provides another cosmic version of the fusion of the Way and law-based administration in the perfected person of the ideal ruler.

The notion that law, an objective and impersonal standard, necessarily conflicts with any subjective and particular manifestations of the ruler's personal tastes, appears throughout the text:

愛多者則法不立，威寡者則下侵上。

Where love is great, then the law is not established; where majesty [*wei*] is lacking, then subordinates encroach on their superiors (*Han Feizi* 30: 563 ["Nei chu shuo shang" 內儲說上]).

Elsewhere the tension between laws and personal desires is described in terms of punishments "not avoiding those one cherishes [*qin*] and honors, and imposing laws upon those one loves [*ai*];" opposition between laws that produce good order and strength, and sycophancy that produces chaos and weakness; the supremely well-governed state where "there will be rewards and punishments, but not delight or anger;" fining peasants for expressing their love (*ai*) for the ruler through sacrifices for his health, which would incline him to alter the law; and so on.[49] In all these cases personal sentiments lead people to bend or modify the law's functions, and thus undercut the basis of the ruler's power and the state's prosperity.

Before proceeding, it is important to note that in much of the preceding discussion, the exposition of what makes the ideal ruler—invisibility, refusal of all human attachments, gathering of energies, and suppression of all emotions and desires—are not limited to those chapters that invoke the Way, copy the *Laozi*'s style and rhetoric, or offer commentaries on the *Laozi*. The ideas and language of the *Laozi*

---

[48] On the "Great Man" in the *Zhuangzi*, see Graham 1989: 204–11. On the later evolution of this idealized figure, see Holzman 1976, chapter 10.

[49] *Han Feizi* 27: 549 ("Yong ren" 用人): "In the supremely well-governed state there are rewards and punishments, but no delight and anger"; 34: 797–98; 35: 803, 815; 39: 937: "To employ as worthy those that one thinks are worthy but are not really so, is the same as employing those one loves [*ai*]"; 46:1006–07, 1016–17; 47: 1037–38: "So what preserves a state is not humaneness and duty. The humane are compassionate and generous, regarding material wealth as unimportant. The violent have resolute heart/minds and find it easy to execute people. If you are compassionate and generous, then you cannot bear to punish, and if you regard material wealth as unimportant then you love [*hào*] to give things away. If your heart/mind is resolute, then your hating [*zeng*] heart will be displayed to your subordinates, and if you find it easy to execute people, your subjects will be recklessly killed"; 48: 1075: "The Way of the enlightened ruler is that when someone is presented to him when he is pleased [*xi*], or when a project is offered when he is angry [*nu*], only after his mood has changed does he judge it, in order to verify what is slander or unmerited praise, what is in the common interest and what in the private"; 49: 1096: "If punishments are carried out according to the law, and the ruler weeps on account of it [described earlier as proving 'universal love' (*jian ai*)], this is to display his benevolence, but it is not the means of regulating the state. To weep and desire not to punish is humaneness, but the necessity of punishment is the law"; pp. 1099–1100; 50: 1141–42, 1147 ("Xian xue" 顯學); 52:1164.

are only one among many textual resources employed by the authors/ compilers of the *Han Feizi*. In this increasing construction of their own text through adapting or arguing against the other texts circulating through the intellectual realm, these men are another example of the late Warring States development of articulating one's ideas through confronting the many texts that circulated in the period. Thus, the *Han Feizi*'s use of the *Laozi* could be compared with the way in which parts of the *Zhuangzi* elaborated its critique of language through adapting the later Mohist discussions of logical argument, or how the *Lüshi chunqiu* 呂氏春秋 constructed arguments and sought intellectual authority by incorporating ideas and language from the full range of intellectual traditions that had emerged by the end of the Warring States period.[50]

One should also note the possible objection that the *Han Feizi*, while insisting on the necessity of the ruler's identifying himself with the Dao (through eliminating emotions, desires, and active planning, thereby allowing the collection and circulation of proper *qi* energies), it does not dictate any methods by which this could be attained. However, as will be shown below, none of the master's texts that call for the self-perfection of the ruler describe the actual procedure by which this is to be achieved. Even the "Inner Training," which provides the most detailed account of any such text of the perfection of the embodied self, does not actually prescribe any specific, detailed means of proceeding. Thus, while calling on the reader to "align" or "correct" the body, it says nothing about actual postures or exercises. Similarly, it advocates stilling the mind, eliminating emotions and desires, and thereby preventing external objects from impinging, but how any of this would be achieved is left to the reader. This is significant, because the texts on self-cultivation or nourishing life from Mawangdui 馬王堆 and Zhangjiashan 張家山, circulating among the elite only a generation or two after the *Han Feizi*, give detailed accounts of exactly such procedures—stipulating times of day and bodily poses for meditative exercises, enumerating the specific muscles and limbs to be worked in bodily drills, offering precise accounts of shared sexual routines, and even giving illustrated and step-by-step instructions for animal imitation routines—for transforming the embodied self into a superior being. The master's texts refusal to do this probably reflects the idea that such detailed accounts of procedures reflect the concerns of a lower form of "technical" literature, rather than the generalizing intellect of the philosopher, an idea that later structured much of the bibliographic catalogue of the imperial library.[51] Thus the *Han Feizi*'s failure to provide such detailed instructions

---

[50] On this feature of the *Zhuangzi*, see Graham 1989: 183–91, 199–202. On the *Lüshi chunqiu*, see Lewis 1999: 289–97, 302–08.

[51] Harper 1998: 110–48; Lewis Forthcoming: "Nourishing the Embodied Self through Hygienic Culture".

does not reflect any idea that the goal is not significant, but simply the generic exclusion of such focused, step-by-step accounts of working towards it.[52]

Finally, one should note that while late Warring States accounts of the ruler as a Sage or embodiment of the Way are part of a broader range of ideas about perfecting the human self, the *Han Feizi* differs from other texts of its period in that it restricts its ideal of self-perfection to the ruler. This probably is because the ruler alone is placed in circumstances that make objectively possible the universalization of his self as the natural embodiment of a political order containing the entire world.[53] While other individuals might discipline and improve their embodied conditions, their positions as particular selves restricted to being part of a broader whole, make objectively impossible their full participation in the all-encompassing Way.

3   Perfecting the Self in Other Warring States Masters' Texts

Above we have sketched the theory in the *Han Feizi* of how the ruler can only totally master himself and his officials through a program of absolute correction of the body-self and its relations to the people around him. This was one version of a set of similar theories that were articulated in diverse texts during the late Warring States period (fourth and third centuries BCE). In these texts, as Harold Roth has described, self-cultivation (often based on meditative and breathing practices) and politics were fused into "one coherent system based on the cosmology of the Tao" (Roth 1991: 649).

The earliest and most influential elaboration of such a model of purifying the embodied self as a center for projecting cultivated energies that might ultimately extend one's power through the cosmos was the fourth-century BCE poem "Inner Training" ("Nei ye" 內業).[54] This presents a holistic transformation of the entire person, beginning with correctly placing the physical body, working through the sense organs to the mind, and culminating in gathering refined energies that trans-

---

[52] Another example among late Warring States texts of repeatedly invoking an idealized mental state that borders on the divine, without indicating how such a state was to be achieved, is the *Sunzi bingfa* 孫子兵法. This text repeatedly describes the general's capacities as "numinous" or "divine" (*shen*), inexhaustibly inventive, speaks of him as a form of god or the embodiment of Heaven and Earth, assimilates his endless fecundity of stratagems to the generative power of Heaven, and invokes his powers as "subtle, reaching to formlessness" 微乎至于無形, "divine, reaching to soundlessness" 神乎至于無聲, insisting that they cannot be put into language. However, it offers not a single word on any self-perfecting exercises to achieve such capacities, and indeed insists that any such "prior transmission" is impossible. See *Sunzi* 1: 18 ("Ji" 計); 3: 68 ("Mou gong" 謀攻); 4: 80, 86, 94 ("Xing" 形); 5: 101, 104, 111, 117 ("Shi" 勢); 6: 133, 139, 149, 150, 152 ("Xu shi" 虛實); 7: 169, 177 ("Jun zheng" 軍爭); 13: 329, 340 ("Yong jian" 用間).

[53] This idea is expressed in some of the text's appeals to the "power of circumstances" (*shi* 勢) as an essential third element of the ruler's power, along with the force of "objective standards" to guide the state, and the use of "techniques" to control his officials.

[54] Roth 1999; Graham 1989: 100–05; Lewis 2006: 20–29.

formed the body and radiated outward to the limits of the cosmos. The primary dangers that must be mastered were the sense organs, emotions, desires, and worries which disturbed the tranquility of the heart/mind. The text *does* make a few references to political attainments such as ruling the myriad things, imposing orderly tasks upon others, putting the whole world in order, and making the whole world submit and obey not through punishments and rewards but through the unified flow of bodily energies and a completely stabilized mind. However, such considerations remain marginal to the text, which is largely devoted to self-perfection.[55]

However, the text was influential, as demonstrated by allusions to it or related writings in other texts, including the *Mencius*'s discussion of "flood-like *qi*".[56] Most importantly, passages from the "Inner Training" were adapted into extensive political discussions in the two chapters "Techniques of the Heart/Mind" ("Xin shu" 心 術 A 上 and B 下) that were collected along with the poem in the *Guanzi* 管子. Thus the latter of these chapters, sometimes described as a commentary on the "Inner Training," follows quotations from the poem with accounts of how the sage can rule all things, how the ordering (*zhi* 治) and peace of his heart/mind produces order and peace in the state, that the people are restrained and the peasants made orderly not through his anger and punishments but because he follows the Way from its ultimate beginnings, how his transformed body can carry Heaven and embody the Earth, and how his completed heart/mind cannot be blocked so it illumines and comprehends the entire world. It even narrates how things present to him their names (like the officials in the *Han Feizi*'s *xingming*) so that he can decide about them and thereby put the world in order.[57]

"Techniques of the Heart/Mind A" is not so totally mapped onto the "Inner Training" as the second chapter, but it still adopts passages from it, and it begins with the argument that if the ruler strays from the Way, due to being possessed by emotions or sense impressions, then his subordinates will all fail in their tasks. It also argues that the ruler will hold to his position if he attains total self-control through quiescence, that the Great Way will achieve peace although it cannot be spoken, and that the sage rules through letting things name and order themselves (again suggesting *xingming*). It also makes the argument, which also appeared in the Mawangdui corpus associated with the Yellow Emperor 黃帝 (see below), that laws (or "objective standards") emerged from the Way.[58] Even more significant is the fact

---

[55] *Guanzi* 49: 937, 939, 943. In arguing that the ruler commands through the charismatic power of his perfected self, rather than rewards and punishment, the "Inner Training" differs from the later *Han Feizi* which, as shown in notes 47 and 49, argued self-transformation culminated in the ability to punish and reward according to purely objective standards without the interference of personal sentiments.

[56] On the relation of the discussions of "flood-like *qi*" in the "Inner Training" and the *Mencius*, and the probability that the latter is adopting the idea from the former, see Lewis 2006: 20–27.

[57] *Guanzi* 37: 778–779, 780, 781–782, 783 ("Xin shu xia" 心術下).

[58] *Guanzi* 36: 759–760 (3), 764, 767 (2), 770 (2), 771 (on *xingming*, which it refers to as a "technique"), 776 (2) ("Xin shu shang" 心術上). On the "Inner Training" and the related chapters in the *Guanzi*, see also Graziani 2001.

that the "Inner Training" was quite close to the *Laozi*, except that the latter was considerably more interested in political matters, and it is precisely this political shift of contemplative self-perfecting that is highlighted in the chapters of the *Han Feizi* that were discussed above.[59]

Nor was the idea that mental self-cultivation was essential to becoming a true ruler limited to texts directly linked to the "Inner Training." Thus the *Xunzi* 荀子, while showing no evidence of any derivation, argued at length in its later chapters that disturbances aroused by emotions and desires had to be mastered in order that the ruler could perform his roles. Notably, the method of attaining such mastery is also referred to as the "technique of the heart/mind." This appears, for example, in the discussion of the centrality of mental mastery in the chapter "Eliminating Blockage" ("Jie bi" 解蔽):

胡為蔽?欲為蔽，惡為蔽，始為蔽，終為蔽，遠為蔽，近為蔽，博為蔽，淺為蔽，古為蔽，今為蔽。凡萬物異則莫不相為蔽。此心術之公患。

What creates blockage? Desires [*yu*] create blockage, aversion [*wu*] creates blockage, beginnings create blockage, endings create blockage, distance creates blockage, closeness creates blockage, breadth creates blockage, shallowness creates blockage, antiquity creates blockage, and modernity creates blockage. In all cases where objects differ, they can mutually create blockage, one for the other. This is the universal calamity for the "technique of the heart/mind." (*Xunzi* 21: 259)[60]

This is followed by a list of the failed rulers of the past who were unable to perform their roles because some obsession blocked their ability to perceive and respond to the actual situation. In this chapter the "technique of the heart/mind" refers to a mental control that eliminates all desires and dislikes, removing the distinctions that create objects of fixation. Only the sage can escape such blockages:

聖人知心術之患，見蔽塞之禍。故無欲無惡，無始無終，無近無遠，無博無淺，無古無今。兼陳萬物而中縣衡焉。

The sage recognizes the calamities that befall the "technique of the heart/mind" and perceives the disaster of being blocked. Therefore, he has no desires or loathing, treats nothing as a beginning or an end, nothing as near or far, nothing as broad or shallow, nothing as ancient or modern. He lays out everything and precisely sets it in the balance (*Xunzi* 21: 263; Knoblock 1994: 103).

Through controlling his mental responses, and through transcending all the petty oppositions by which ordinary people carve up the world before falling into preferences for one side, the sage invariably makes correct judgments. Thus the *Xunzi* overlaps with the "Inner Training" and the "Techniques of the Heart/Mind" texts, and anticipates the Daoist turn of the *Han Feizi*. Like the *Han Feizi* it also makes the ideal ruler and minister crucial within its exposition, although it ultimately centers on the philosophical sage exemplified by Confucius. It is also notable that this text

---

[59] Roth 1999: 186–90. Pages 190–203 are also relevant, although less directly so.

[60] Page 258 in the same chapter states, "When the mind is not employed in this [avoiding blockage], then when black and white are in front of the eyes, they will not see them, and when thunder strikes right by the ears they will not hear it." This echoes or anticipates passages in "Techniques of the Heart/Mind A". For a published translation of this passage, see Knoblock 1994: 100.

celebrates Confucius by arguing that he equaled the great rulers of the past, and that it parallels "sageliness" with "true kingship", and calls on students to take the "sage king" as their teacher and his regulations as their model/law (*fa*).[61]

Elsewhere the *Xunzi* offers another version of a technique of the heart/mind. It begins with what seems to be a rubric: "the technique of regulating the vital breath and nourishing the heart/mind" (治氣養心之術), which echoes the chapters in the *Guanzi* cited above. After listing therapies for defects of temperament and thought—most associated with intemperate or violent responses, or guile in calculations—it concludes:

> 凡治氣養心之術，莫徑由禮，莫要得師，莫神一好。
>
> For all techniques employed to regulate one's vital breath/energy and nourish the heart/mind, nothing is more direct or rapid than ritual, nothing is more important than obtaining a teacher, and nothing is more miraculously transformative [*shen*] than totally unifying your likes [一好 *yi hào*]. (*Xunzi* 2: 16 ["Xiu shen" 修身]; Knoblock 1988: 154)

Here the technique of "nourishing" the heart/mind culminates in mastery of one's likes (and presumably dislikes), but it takes a Confucian turn by insisting that these are based on guidance provided by ritual and a good teacher. Another passage links nourishing the heart/mind with total concentration and sincerity, as identified by the term *cheng* 誠. This perfected inner state, which is the central virtue in the "Zhongyong" 中庸, in this passage of the *Xunzi* leads to self-mastery where the true gentleman matches Heaven: silent but understood, never giving but regarded as generous, and never angry but held in awe.[62] This mental state also gives him the ability to "carefully preserve his solitude/concentration" (*shen qi du* 慎其獨), a crucial capacity discussed in the "Chapter on the Five Virtuous Forms of Conduct" ("Wu xing pian" 五行篇) found at Mawangdui and Guodian, where it indicates an ability to escape the dominance of sense impressions through a complete focus of the mind and thereby create an internal virtuous power that makes one a match for Heaven.[63]

The theme of a mental technique [*shu*] linked with total concentration, the mastery of which allowed one to attain sagehood, also figures in *Xunzi*'s chapter "Man's Nature is Evil (Xing e" 性惡)"

> 今使塗之人伏術為學，專心一志，思索孰察，加日縣九，稽善而不息，則通於神明，叁於天地矣。
>
> Now if a man in the street were to submit to this technique [*shu*] in conducting his studies, concentrate his heart/mind and unite his resolve [*zhuan xin yi zhi* 專心一志, also translatable as "focus his heart/mind on a single resolve"], contemplating and carefully examining, continuing this over a long period of time, unceasingly accumulating goodness

---

[61] *Xunzi* 21: 262, 271. Knoblock 1994: 103, 111. The merging of the philosophical sage and the political ruler recurs repeatedly throughout the *Xunzi*.

[62] On *cheng* in the "Zhongyong," see Ames and Hall 2001: 30–38, 61–63; Tu 1989: 3–4, 16–17, 70–93.

[63] *Xunzi* 3: 28–29 ("Bu gou" 不苟). On the relevant passages in both versions of the "Chapter on the Five Forms of Virtuous Conduct," see Csikszentmihalyi 2004: 287–88, 321–23. On the sense of "*shen qi du*" in the *Xunzi*, see Knoblock 1988: 170, 178. On the sense of the same phrase in the *Zhongyong*, see Ames and Hall 2001: 89, 118–19.

without respite, then he would penetrate through to "spirit brilliance" [*shen ming* 神明] and become a "third to Heaven and Earth." (*Xunzi* 23: 296; Knoblock 1994: 159)[64]

This again describes a mental technique that through total concentration eliminates distractions and desires, culminating in a perfected mental brilliance that takes on cosmic attributes.

This linkage of a technique of the mind with sagehood and authority, and the echoes of the "Inner Training," are even clearer in another passage in the *Xunzi*:

水至平，端不傾。心術如此象聖人。……必叄天。

> Water is supremely level [*ping*]; its correctness [*duan* 端] cannot be tipped [i.e., made biased]. When the "technique of the heart/mind" is like this, it resembles the sage. ... certain to become a third with Heaven {and Earth} (*Xunzi* 25:306–07 ["Cheng xiang" 成相]; Knoblock 1994: 176).[65]

The "Inner Training" describes the trained mind, which in its commentaries is the foundation of supreme political authority, as "level and correct [*ping zheng*]."[66] While the term used for "correct" in the *Xunzi* passage is different, the two are synonymous. Moreover, although the ideal of mental mastery that leads to perfected personhood in "Inner Training" and the "Techniques of the Heart/Mind" chapters is not Confucian, it shares considerable ground with works in that tradition, just as the "Inner Training" did with the *Mencius*'s discussion of the "flood-like *qi*." Mastery that leads to an undisturbed mind had thus become an ideal common to many intellectual traditions of the late Warring States period, although some texts focused specifically on political authorities, while others extended it more generally to philosophical masters or even (at least in theory) the man in the streets.

The theme of water also figures in an important account in the *Xunzi* of mental tranquility that leads to becoming a "Great Man," which we saw above was a characterization of the ideal ruler in the *Han Feizi*, and of the perfected person in the *Zhuangzi*. The passage stipulates that the Way can be known only through the mind which has become empty, unified, and still. Only such a mind can avoid blockage and thereby correctly respond to all objects and regulate all of space and time. The text then delivers a poetic rhapsody on one who achieves such a mind, describing him as the "Great Man" who has attained a comprehensive view of the cosmos, free from partiality and prejudice.[67]

---

[64] Of course, this argument that an ordinary man could achieve a self-perfection sufficient to make him a "third to Heaven and Earth" marks a clear difference between the late Warring States Confucian ideal of perfected personhood, and that of the *Han Feizi* with its exclusive focus on the ruler.

[65] The "and Earth" is omitted in the Chinese to achieve a rhyme of *ren* 人 (*ni[n]) and *tian* 天 (*l̥i[n]), but the idea of "being a third to…" necessitates its inclusion.

[66] Roth translates the term *zheng* throughout the text as "aligned," which perhaps suggests a technical sense in text, but the more conventional translation as "correct" works reasonably well. See Roth 1999: 56, 58, 60, 66, 70, 76, 82, 88. On his discussions of the term in this and other texts, see the index entry on p. 254.

[67] *Xunzi* 21: 263–64; this discussion resumes later in the chapter, in the image of the mind as a pan of water that must remain still. See p. 267.

In addition to these discussions of the "technique of the heart/mind," other passages in the *Xunzi* also develop the idea that the ruler's mental mastery leads to comprehensive knowledge of the world, while his falling prey to the senses and emotions leads to catastrophe, but place this under the aegis of Heaven. By not allowing the world's objects to delude his senses and thereby his mind, the sage ruler becomes a replica of Heaven, who makes the whole world his realm and brings it to perfect order. He also makes it so that his own life suffers no harm, thus linking the argument back to those in texts on "nourishing life."[68] However, unlike the texts derived from meditative practices, the *Xunzi* did not emphasize the accumulation of refined energies as the key to creating a refined body and perfected mind, but instead focused on adhering to an all-encompassing, moral Way (*Xunzi* 21: 263).

We noted above how both the *Han Feizi* and the *Xunzi* celebrated their self-transformed, ideal ruler by invoking the image of the Great Man, who is most closely identified with the *Zhuangzi* (where it does not describe the ideal ruler, but the perfected person). While some people might be surprised by this, given the *Zhuangzi*'s reputation as a text that denounces political service and conventional values, it resembles the chapters from the *Guanzi* described above, in that while some chapters deal with individual transformation through inner cultivation, others develop these in a cosmological and sometimes a political direction (Roth 1994: 5–7).

These *Zhuangzi* chapters' invocation of self-transformation to create a true ruler also discuss a "technique of the heart/mind" like those in the *Guanzi* and *Xunzi*, while citing rewards, punishments, and other aspects of ruling through objective standards:

本在於上，末在於下，　要在於主，詳在於臣。三軍五兵之運，德之末也。賞罰利害，五刑之辟，教之末也。禮法度數形名比詳，治之末。鐘鼓之音，羽　旄之容，樂之末也。哭泣衰絰，隆殺之服，哀之末也。此五末者，須精神之運，心術之動，然後從之者。

The root is in the ruler, and the branch tip in the subordinates; the essential is in the ruler, and the details in the subordinates. The use of armies and weapons is the branch tip of innate power [*de*]. Rewards and punishments, benefitting and harming, the laws of the five mutilating punishments, these are the branch tips of teaching. Rituals, laws, measures, numbers, administrative terminology [*xingming*], and matching of details, these are the branch tips of governance. The sounds of bells and drums, the look of feathers and banners [in dances], these are the branch tips of music. Weeping and graded degrees of mourning costume, these are the branch tips of grieving. As for these five types of branch tips, only when [the ruler] uses his refined spirit energies [*jing shen* 精神] and sets into motion his "technique of the heart/mind" can they be pursued. (*Zhuangzi* 13: 209 ["Tian dao" 天道])[69]

The passage is built around an opposition between the true ruler, who is the root of social order, and the details of government activity, on the one hand, and ritual and

---

[68] See *Xunzi* 17: 206 ("Tian lun" 天論); 22: 274–75, 284 ("Zheng ming" 正名).

[69] For a published translation of this passage, see Graham 1986: 261. Just before this the text argues: "The one who harmonizes with Heaven, bestows blessings on the whole world, and helps shape all things will enjoy 'Heavenly joy;' being without 'Heavenly resentment [*yuan*]' he can fix his heart/mind and is king of the whole world, possessing the mind of the sage, to whom all things submit." See pp. 206–07. Graham 1986: 260.

musical performance, on the other. This first category (political procedures) functions as a synecdoche for the theorists of statecraft, while ritual and music indicate
the Confucians. Thus, the *Zhuangzi* here portrays contemporary political and social
practices as properly functioning only when grounded in the rule of a perfected
person. This idealized ruler, through his mastery of the "techniques of the heart/
mind" accumulates mental energies which are necessary for ruling through the
administrative procedures of objective standards, or the social arts of music
and ritual.

As Harold Roth has argued, it is primarily chapters 12–15 of the *Zhuangzi* that
identify the true ruler as the one who through inner cultivation can identify himself
with Heaven and Earth, or with the Way, and thereby accumulate inner power that
allows him to command his officials and perfect his administration. Thus, the chapter "Heaven and Earth" describes how every aspect of the ruler and his relation to
his government is transformed and corrected by viewing it through the Way. It then
discusses how all the specialist arts of administration are combined under the Way
that runs through all things, and by the virtuous potency that permeates the cosmos.
For the ruler who thus completes all things by holding to the One, even "the ghosts
and spirits will submit" (*Zhuangzi* 12: 181–82 ["Tian di" 天地]).[70] This account
could be a variation of the Daoist vision articulated in the *Han Feizi*.

Similarly, the next chapter begins with a discussion of the mind of the sage ruler
as being still so that like water or a mirror it can properly reflect all things. In the
person of a king it shapes a Yao, and in the person of a commoner it creates a "king
without attributes" (*su wang* 素王) (*Zhuangzi* 13: 204–05 ["Tian dao"]; Graham
1986: 259).[71] It goes on to describe the ruler who matches perfectly with Heaven
and Earth:

一心定而王天下。其鬼不崇，其魂不疲。一心定而萬物服。言以虛靜，　　推於天
地，通於萬物。此之謂天樂。天樂者，聖人之心以畜天下也。夫帝王之德以天地為
宗，以道德為主，以無為為常。無為也，則用天下而有餘。……上必無為而用天
下，下必有為，為天下用。

> With his united mind, he is king of the world. His spirit (*gui* 鬼) is not afflicted and his
> soul (*hun* 魂) not wearied. With his united mind, all things submit—which means that
> through emptiness and stillness he reaches throughout the cosmos and penetrates all things.
> This is called Heavenly joy, through which the sage's mind shepherds the entire world.
>
> The virtuous power of kings and thearchs [*di wang zhi de* 帝王之德] takes Heaven and
> Earth as its ancestor, the Way and its Virtuous Power as its guiding principle, and inaction
> as its constant rule. With inaction you put the whole world to work for you and have leisure

---

[70] The chapter subsequently discusses who could succeed Yao as king, and uses the ability to
"match Heaven" (*pei tian* 配天) as the standard of measure. See pp. 186–87 (2). It also discusses
the "virtuous potency of the true ruler" (*di wang zhi de* 帝王之德) which allows the sage ruler to
get the people to rule themselves according to their natures. See pp. 192–193. On sage government
through the man of virtuous power, see also p. 197. The vision of "sage rulership" here is clearly
at odds with the Confucian model, and even with that of the *Han Feizi*, but it does argue for the idea
that the person of the ruler must be transformed and perfected to achieve efficacious rule.

[71] Again, one should note that the "king without attributes" has different meanings in other contexts, as in the Confucian use of this term to describe Confucius who assumed the role of the king
in writing the *Spring and Autumn Annals* (*Chunqiu* 春秋), while not actually being a king.

to spare. … Superiors must adopt inaction and make the world work for them, while inferiors must adopt action and work for the world (*Zhuangzi* 13:207–08; Graham 1986: 260–61).

Here once again the ruler's assimilation of himself to the cosmos or the Way becomes the background condition to effective government. While, unlike the previous passage, it does not specify that all the conventional methods of government are assimilated under the powers of the Way, many forms of administration and work are to be drawn together under the ruler's aegis. This, and the next two chapters of the *Zhuangzi*, sketch other visions of ruling through mastery of the cosmic Way, including citing the vitality of the ruler's "technique of the heart/mind" that brings life to all the rules and regulations that define government and ritual performances.[72]

Another, later passage also elaborates a model of the man who becomes ruler of the world by achieving mental self-mastery:

宇泰定者發乎天光。發乎天光者，人見其人。人有脩者，乃今有恆。有恆者，人舍之，天助之。人之所舍，謂之天民。天之所助，謂之天子。

The one who fixes [within] the Great Serenity emits a Heavenly light. Though he emits a Heavenly light, people see him as a human. When he has cultivated this, he achieves constancy. Because he is constant, people will lodge [*she* 舍, the word applied to the "spirits" in the "Inner Training"] with him, and Heaven will help him. Those people who are lodged are called "Heaven's People," and the man Heaven helps is called the "Son of Heaven" (*Zhuangzi* 23: 344 ["Gengsang Chu" 庚桑楚]).[73]

Here the traditional epithet of the Zhou king, which later came to refer to the emperor, indicates a unique relation to Heaven achieved through perfecting internal serenity. As in the *Mencius*, this perfect emotional state of the ruler causes people to flock to him, but here the resulting community looks as much like a theocratic association ("Heaven's People") as a state.

A final body of texts from the late Warring States (or the early Han) that enmesh the true ruler and his use of law with the cosmic Way are the four silk texts, some of

---

[72] *Zhuangzi* 13:208 ("Nothing is more numinous than Heaven, richer than Earth, or greater than the ruler. Thus, it is said that the ruler's Virtuous Power matches Heaven and Earth. This is the Way of riding upon Heaven and Earth, making all things gallop, and employing the mass of men."), 209 (the "technique of the heart/mind" that vitalizes all the rules of government and ritual), 210 (the men of antiquity first illumined the Great Way, then Heaven, then the Way and its Virtuous Power, then goodness and duty, then observance of duties, then *xingming*, then government posts, then inspections, then judgment of right and wrong, then rewards and punishments, then the rankings of intelligence and of social status, which all culminate in the Great Peace), 216 (on the "Perfect Man" [*zhi ren* 至人] ruling the world, causing the mechanism to function without personally working the handles); chapter 14: 219–220 ("Tian yun" 天運) (rulers bring order to the world by following the six directions and five constants of Heaven), and pp. 222–225.

[73] Pages 353–54 also describe these "Heavenly people [*tian ren*]" who "become identical with Heaven's harmony." P. 351 describes a process in which the elimination of emotions and of errors induced by sensory experience will make the ruler enlightened and empty, and thus able to control all things without deliberate action.

which speak of the Yellow Emperor, that were discovered at a Mawangdui.[74] These texts begin:

道生法。法者，引得失以繩，而明曲直者也。故執道者，生法而弗敢犯也。法立而弗敢廢也。口 能自引以繩，然後見知天下而不惑矣。

The Way produces law, which stretches out the objective standard of success and failure, and makes clear the curved and straight. Thus, he who holds to the Way produces laws and does not violate them, so that laws are established and not set aside. Able to align himself with this measure, he can perceive the whole world without confusion.[75]

The text continues with a description of the formless, empty Way from which all things come, how the ruler must master his emotions and desires so that he can properly know all things, and only by imitating the formlessness and stillness of the Way can he cause things to spontaneously present their tasks and names (*xingming*), which make it impossible for anything to escape his regulations. The rest of the texts elaborate the nature of the Way of Heaven and Earth, how the ruler imitates it (emphasizing the calendrical model of government based on the Way of Heaven), the reliance on objective standards in order to attain "spirit brilliance" (*shen ming* 神明), the need to eliminate all personal concerns (*si* 私) in order to devote oneself to the common interest, the correct ways of fighting wars, the uses of rewards and punishments, and numerous other detailed aspects of government. It also resembles the *Han Feizi* by listing those close to the ruler—sons, ministers, favorites, wives, concubines—who endanger the state, and the techniques (*shu* 術) by which he can ward off these threats. [76]

The second essay, entitled "Canon" ("Jing" 經), is devoted to the Yellow Emperor and his officials, and he appears as a model of the ruler who follows the celestial patterns, using them to introduce both correct warfare and legal punishments.[77] The conduct attributed to these mythic exemplars evokes many of the same points as those sketched above. The final essay, "On the Origins of the Dao" ("Yuan dao" 原道) provides an elaborate cosmogony which turns into an outline of the conduct of the ideal ruler (*Huangdi shu* 3: 237–45). It is also noteworthy that these texts were buried in a tomb along with two copies of the *Laozi*. Many scholars have debated the links of this combination of texts about the Yellow Emperor with the *Laozi* to Sima Qian's 司馬遷 (ca. 145–90 BCE) references to "Huang-Lao" as a type of philosophy.

---

[74] For introductions that sketch earlier scholarship, and complete translations along with the original texts, see Yates 1997, or Chang and Yu 1998.

[75] *Huangdi shu* 黃帝書 1.1: 1 ("Dao fa" 道法). A later passage on the ruler's ability to perceive the whole world specifies that through his "mysterious Virtuous Power" (*xuan de* 玄德) he alone can see what he sees and know what he knows. See 1.4: 38 ("Da fen" 大分); 1.6: 55 ("Lun" 論); 3: 241, 244–45 ("Dao yuan" 道原). The theme of laws as a device or standard for measurement also recurs, as in 1.1: 7; 2.5: 49 ("Si du" 四度); 3: 191 ("Cheng" 稱), and this metaphor is also provided by the sun, moon, and stars, as on 1.6: 57 (3).

[76] *Huangdi shu* 1.1: 8–9, 10; 1.2: 14, 16 ("Guo ci" 國次); 1.3 22, 24, 25, 27 ("Jun zheng" 君正); 1.4: 35; 1.5: 42, 43, 45, 51; 1.6: 55, 57, 63; 1.8: 78, 80 ("Lun yue" 論約); 2: 191–194. For lists of those who imperil the ruler and the state, and the techniques of guarding against them, see, for example, 1.4: 30–31, 32, 36; 1.7: 73 ("Wang lun" 亡論).

[77] *Huangdi shu* 2: 95–189. On the Yellow Emperor as the mythic inventor of using violence (both war and punishments) in government, see Lewis 1990: ch. 5.

However, this combination of detailed discussions of law, tools of measure as a figure of objective standards, the Way, and the *Laozi* also shows a correspondence between the contents of this tomb and the intellectual program of the *Han Feizi*. It is also noteworthy here that Sima Qian identified Han Fei as a follower of Huang-Lao.[78]

This widespread practice in late Warring States and early Han literature of insisting that the ruler must transform himself through mental discipline to become capable of the immense tasks incumbent upon him indicates that the *Han Feizi*'s appeal to a Daoist model for rulership was not a rhetorical gesture to a certain audience, an extraneous addition by later compilers, or a means of smuggling in a hidden advocacy of ministerial authority. Instead, this program of self-transformation as the basis of effective political authority is a central element of scholars' practice of using their own educational programs to provide methods for imagining a new type of person who could fulfill the ever-expanding role by which the ruler made himself the exalted center of the emergent territorial state. The "men-of-service of law and techniques" (*fa shu zhi shi* 法術之士) cited in the *Han Feizi* functioned not as over-ambitious claimants to de facto royal authority, but as veiled models for the king's transformation through self-mastery. Moreover, while one might dispute whether this program for the ruler had any real, practical referent, it *does* pervade the stone inscriptions in which the First Emperor was declared to be a sage whose cosmic governance stretched across all of space, and whose reign marked a pivot in human history where endless wars were ended, and a regime of peace and lawful order established that would last through the rest of time (Kern 2000; Pines 2014).

4 Epilogue

While this chapter focused on the *Han Feizi*'s ideal of perfecting the monarch through self-cultivation, it has situated that ideal within broader ideas in the Warring States about creating a higher form of person (or embodied self) through similar efforts. Specifically, it examined the text of the *Han Feizi* as part of the early history

---

[78] For a discussion of Huang-Lao thought, see Peerenboom 1993. Chapter 5 of this book is devoted to proving that the *Han Feizi* is clearly distinct in its basic assumptions from Huang-Lao thought. The same conclusion, based on Peerenboom's characterization of Huang-Lao, is argued in Goldin 2020: 223–27. Peerenboom argues (1) that the Mawangdui texts represent a tradition of thought known as Huang-Lao, (2) that this tradition advocates a "foundational naturalism" which closely resembles certain Western versions of "natural law", and (3) that the *Han Feizi* does not share this foundational naturalism. While the first two points are contestable, the last one is almost certainly true (see also Wang Pei, Chap. 20, this volume). The *Han Feizi* advocates holding to the Way not because it is normative or law-like but because it is supremely efficacious. The program laid out in its so-called Daoist chapters, as discussed above, is presented as a step in making possible effective rule through law, techniques, and the power of position. The Yellow Emperor also figures in medical or "nourishing life" texts found in the tomb, which are quite distinct from the later Yellow Emperor medical texts gathered in the "Internal Canon" ("Nei jing" 內經). See Harper 1998: 29, 56, 60–65, 122, 135–136, 280, 299–300, 384–99, 425.

of programs to fashion superior persons both in the West and in East Asia, and the links of such programs to ideas about perfecting a ruler. The *Han Feizi* borrowed ideas from other texts of the period—most notably, but not exclusively the *Laozi*—to suggest how the ruler could transform himself to effectively carry out the full program—essential to the functioning of a Warring States polity—of decreeing and enforcing laws, managing officials, and preserving his own life. It also participated in a pattern of influence flowing in the opposite direction, where the perfected ruler provided a model for the ideal person, or more narrowly the ideal teacher and scholar. The clearest evidence of this was how the categories of "sage," "king," and "sage-king" came to form a single, grand ideal of the highest person that was celebrated in the *Xunzi*, later chapters of the *Zhuangzi*, and the Mawangdui texts focused on the Yellow Emperor. More narrowly, it can be seen in the politicizing of Confucius, who grew from a sage and an ideal teacher into a "king without qualities" or an author who acted as a king in writing the *Spring and Autumn Annals*.[79]

This mutual patterning in inventing the person and the ruler, or political power, was previously theorized in Lewis Mumford's *The City in History*. He argued that the city, with its high degree of the division of labor and the leisure that could be devoted to self-cultivation, allowed for the emergence of role-playing to create a new type of person. At the same time, the king, who had formed the nexus around which the city emerged, provided the ideal type of the freedom, autonomy, choice, and effective power which allowed for the re-invention of the person as a *personality*. "Thus the city," as he argued, "became a special environment not just for supporting kings but for making persons: beings who were more fully open to the realities of the cosmos, more ready to transcend the claims of tribal society and custom, more capable of assimilating old values and creating new ones, of making decision and taking new directions, than their fellows in more limited situations" (Mumford 1961: 110).

Nor is this simply an imaginative myth of origins made possible by the scarcity of early documentation, as Mumford extends the argument for the mutual shaping of ideals of personhood and political power to the Greek *polis*, where the free citizen in his devotion to the agonistic ideals of self-cultivation through competition provided a new model of personhood (In this way Mumford echoed a central step of the argument in Mauss's essay cited in this article, without necessarily having read it). Moreover, studying a much later period in history Peter Haidu has examined how the revival of royal power and state administration under the Capetians in twelfth-century France led to the elaboration of new ideals of human subjectivity in *The Song of Roland* and the later works of Chrétien de Troyes.[80] This recurring

---

[79] This "politicization" of Confucius also figures in the myths that grew up around his life and first appear in his biography written by Sima Qian (*Shiji* 47). See Lewis 1999: 218–38.

[80] Mumford 1961: 109–10. See also p. 116, where he quotes Robert Redfield's assertion that "the remaking of man was the work of the city." On the *polis* and its new model of personhood, see pp. 153–57, 165–71. On the re-assertion of royal power and emergence of new models of the person in Capetian France and the later Middle Ages, see Haidu 1993, 2004. See also Greenblatt 1980: ch. 1, 6; Jackson 1982. While the theme of individualism and the revolutionary restructuring of power in the modern world (the climax of Mauss's essay) figures throughout a massive body of scholarship, one could cite Wahrman 2004: Part 2; and Izenberg 1992.

interplay between the elaboration of new forms of rulership and new models of personhood can be understood as a reflection of the range of ideas embraced in the term "power", from the capacity for effective action in the world (necessary to creating person or self) to the essence of political organization, as embodied in the monarch.[81] The interaction of new ideals of the person and new models for the ruler in Warring States China can be viewed as an example of this phenomenon.

References

Agamben, Giorgio. 2005. *State of Exception*. Trans. Kevin Attell. Chicago: University of Chicago Press.

Ames, Roger. 1994. The Focus-Field Self in Classical Confucianism. In *Self as Person in Asian Theory and Practice*, ed. Roger T. Ames, Wimal Dissanayake, and Thomas P. Kasulis, 187–212. Albany: State University of New York Press.

———. 2011. *Confucian Role Ethics: A Vocabulary*. Honolulu: University of Hawai'i Press.

———. 2021. *Human Becomings: Theorizing Persons for Confucian Role Ethics*. Albany: State University of New York Press.

Ames, Roger, and David L. Hall. 2001. *Focusing the Familiar: A Translation and Philosophical Interpretation of the Zhongyong*. Honolulu: University of Hawai'i Press.

Carrithers, Michael, Steven Collins, and Steven Lukes. 1985. *The Category of the Person: Anthropology, Philosophy, History*. Cambridge: Cambridge University Press.

Chang, Leo S., and Yu, Feng. 1998. *The Four Political Treatises of the Yellow Emperor: Original Mawangdui Texts with Complete English Translations and an Introduction*. Honolulu: University of Hawai'i Press.

Chen, Qiyou 陳奇猷. 2000. *Han Feizi, with new collations and commentary* 韓非子新校注. Shanghai: Guji.

Chen, Dexing 陳德興. 2009. *Philosophy of the Body Based on Using the Qi Discourse to Explain Matter: Yin/Yang, the Five Phases, and the Structure of the Body in the Theory of Qi* 氣論釋物的身體哲學:陰陽, 五行, 景氣理論的身體形構. Taipei: Wunan Tushu Chuban.

Csikszentmihalyi, Mark. 2004. *Material Virtue: Ethics and the Body in Early China*. Leiden: E. J. Brill.

Drake, Harold Allen. 1976. *In Praise of Constantine: a Historical Study and New Translation of Eusebius' Tricennnial Orations*. Berkeley: University of California Press.

Dugan, John. 2005. *Making a New Man: Ciceronian Self-Fashioning in the Rhetorical World*. Oxford: Oxford University Press.

Feher, Michel, Ramona Naddaff, and Nadia Tazi, eds. 1989. *Fragments for a History of the Human Body*, 3 vols. New York: Zone.

Francis, James A. 1995. *Subversive Virtue : Asceticism and Authority in the Second-Century Pagan World*. University Park, Pennsylvania: Penn State University Press.

Gao, Heng 高亨. 1974. *The Book of Lord Shang, with commentary and translation* 商君書注譯. Beijing: Zhonghua.

Goldin, Paul R. 2005a. *After Confucius: Studies in Early Chinese Philosophy*. Honolulu: University of Hawai'i Press.

———. 2005b. The Theme of the Primacy of the Situation in Classical Chinese Philosophy and Rhetoric. *Asia Major (Third Series)* 18 (2): 1–25.

---

[81] For philosophical and sociological studies of the links between the creation of persons and political power, see Peckham 1979; Wrong 1979.

———. 2011. Persistent Misconceptions about Chinese 'Legalism'. *Journal of Chinese Philosophy* 38 (1): 64–80.

———. 2013. Introduction: Han Fei and the *Han Feizi*. In *Dao Companion to the Philosophy of Han Fei*, ed. Paul R. Goldin, 1–21. Dordrecht: Springer.

———. 2020. *The Art of Chinese Philosophy: Eight Classical Texts and How to Read Them*. Princeton NJ: Princeton University Press.

Goodenough, Erwin R. 1928. The Political Philosophy of Hellenistic Kingship. *Yale Classical Studies* 1: 55–102.

Graham, Angus C. 1986. *Chuang-tzu: The Inner Chapters*. London: Unwin Paperbacks.

———. 1989. *Disputers of the Tao: Philosophical Argument in Ancient China*. La Salle IL: Open Court.

Graziani, Romain. 2001. "De la régence du monde à la souveraineté intérieure : Une étude des quatre chapitres de 'L'art de l'esprit' du *Guanzi*." Ph. D. dissertation. Université Paris VII.

———. 2015. Monarch and Minister: The Problematic Partnership in the Building of Absolute Monarchy in the *Han Feizi* 韓非子. In *Ideology of Power and Power of Ideology in Early China*, ed. Yuri Pines, Paul R. Goldin, and Martin Kern, 156–180. Boston and Leiden: Brill.

Greenblatt, Stephen. 1980. *Renaissance Self-Fashioning: From More to Shakespeare*. Chicago: University of Chicago Press.

Guanzi 管子. See Li Xiangfeng.

Guo, Qingfan 郭慶蕃. 1974. *Zhuangzi, with collected explanations* 莊子集釋. Commentaries by Guo Xiang 郭象 (CE 252–312) and Lu Deming 陸德明 (CE 556–627). In *Xin bian zhuzi ji cheng*. Vol. 3. Taipei: Shijie.

Guo, Yi 郭沂. 2001. *The Bamboo Strips of Guodian and Pre-Qin Intellectual Thought* 郭店竹簡 與先秦學術思想. Shanghai: Shanghai jiaoyu chubanshe.

Hadot, Pierre. 1995. *Philosophy as a Way of Life*. Trans. Michael Chase. Oxford: Blackwell.

———. 2002. *What is Ancient Philosophy?* Trans. Michael Chase, Cambridge, Mass.: Harvard University Press.

———. 2014. *La Citadelle Intérieure: Introduction aux Pensées de Marc Aurèle*. Paris: Fayard.

Haidu, Peter. 1993. *The Subject of Violence: The Song of Roland and the Birth of the State*. Bloomington: Indiana University Press.

———. 2004. *The Subject Medieval/Modern: Text and Governance in the Middle Ages*. Stanford: Stanford University Press.

Hall, David, and Roger Ames. 1987. *Thinking through Confucius*. Albany: State University of New York Press.

———. 1995. *Anticipating China: Thinking through the Narratives of Chinese and Western Culture*. Albany: State University of New York Press.

———. 1998. *Thinking from the Han: Self, Truth, and Transcendence in Chinese and Western Culture*. Albany: State University of New York Press.

Han Feizi 韓非子. See Chen Qiyou 2000.

Hanshi waizhuan 韓氏外傳. See Xu Weiyu 1980.

Harper, Donald. 1998. *Early Chinese Medical Literature: The Mawangdui Medical Manuscripts*. London: Kegan Paul International.

Hertzer, Dominique. 2006. *Das Leuchten des Geistes und die Erkenntnis der Seele: Die medizinische Vorstellung vom Seelischen als Ausdruck philosophischen Denkens—China und das Abendland*. VAS: Bad Homburg.

Holzman, Donald. 1976. *Poetry and Politics: The Life and Works of Juan Chi (A.D. 210–263)*. Cambridge: Cambridge University Press.

Huangdi shu 黃帝書. See Wei Qipeng 2004.

Izenberg, Gerald N. 1992. *Impossible Individuality: Romanticism, Revolution, and the Origins of Modern Selfhood, 1787–1802*. Princeton: Princeton University Press.

Jackson, W.T.H. 1982. *The Hero and the King: An Epic Theme*. New York: Columbia University Press.

Kahn, Paul W. 2011. *Political Theology: Four New Chapters on the Concept of Sovereignty*. New York: Columbia University Press.

Kern, Martin. 2000. *The Stele Inscriptions of Ch'in Shih-huang: Text and Ritual in Early Chinese Imperial Representation*. New Haven: American Oriental Society.

Knoblock, John. 1988. *Xunzi: A Translation and Study of the Complete Works*, Volume I, *Books 1–6*. Stanford: Stanford University Press.

———, trans. 1994. Xunzi: A Translation and a Study of the Complete Works, Volume III, *Books 17–32*. Stanford: Stanford University Press.

Kubny, Manfred. 1995. *Qi Lebenskraftkonzepte in China: Definitionen, Theorien und Grundlagen*. Heidelberg: Haug Verlag.

Kuroda, Genji 黑田源次. 1977. *The Study of Qi 氣の研究*. Tokyo: Tokyo Bijutsu.

Laozi 老子. See Wang Bi 1974.

Larre, Claude. 1982. *Le Traité VII du Houai Mam Tseu*. Taipei: Institut Ricci.

Lewis, Mark Edward. 1990. *Sanctioned Violence in Early China*. Albany: State University of New York Press.

———. 1994. Les rites comme trame de l'histoire. In *Notions et Perceptions du Changement en Chine*, ed. Viviane Alleton and Alexeï Volkov, 29–39. Paris: Collège de France Institut des Hautes Études Chinoises.

———. 1999. *Writing and Authority in Early China*. Albany State University of New York Press.

———. 2006. *The Construction of Space in Early China*. Albany: State University of New York Press.

———. 2017. Emotions and Rumors in Early China. *Studies in Chinese History* 26: 1–24.

———. 2021. *Honor and Shame in Early China*. Cambridge: Cambridge University Press.

———. Forthcoming. *On the Self and Body in Early East Asian Thought*, Elements Series. Cambridge: Cambridge University Press.

Li, Xiangfeng 黎翔鳳. 2004. *Guanzi, with collations and commentary 管子校正*. Beijing: Zhonghua Shuju.

Li, Cunshan 李存山. 2009. *The Discourse of Qi and the Study of Humaneness氣論與仁學*. Zhengzhou: Zhongzhou Guji Chubanshe.

Linck, Gudula. 2012. *Leib oder Körper: Mensch, Welt und Leben in der chineschischen Philosophie*. Munich: Verlag Karl Alber.

Liu, Yin 劉寅 (*jinshi* 1371). 1972. *Correct Commentary on the Wei Liaozi 尉繚子直解*. In *Correct commentaries on the Ming edition of the seven military (examination) classics 明本武經七書*. Taibei: Shi Di Jiaoyu Chubanshe.

Mauss, Marcel. 1950. In *Sociologie et anthropologie*, ed. Claude Lévi-Strauss. Paris: Presses Universitaires de France.

Mumford, Lewis. 1961. *The City in History: Its Origins, Its Transformations, and Its Prospects*. New York: MJF Books.

Peckham, Morse. 1979. *Explanation and Power: The Control of Human Behavior*. New York: Seabury Press.

Peerenboom, R.P. 1993. *Law and Morality in Ancient China: The Silk Manuscripts of Huang-Lao*. Albany: State University of New York Press.

Pines, Yuri. 2013a. From Historical Evolution to the End of History: Past, Present and Future from Shang Yang to the First Emperor. In *Dao Companion to the Philosophy of Han Fei*, ed. Paul R. Goldin, 25–45. Dordrecht: Springer.

———. 2013b. Submerged by Absolute Power: The Ruler's Predicament in the *Han Feizi*. In *Dao Companion to the Philosophy of Han Fei*, ed. Paul R. Goldin, 67–86. Dordrecht: Springer.

———. 2014. The Messianic Emperor: A New Look at Qin's Place in China's History. In *Birth of an Empire: The State of Qin Revisited*, ed. Yuri Pines, Gideon Shelach, Lothar von Falkenhausen, and Robin D.S. Yates, 258–279. Berkeley: University of California Press.

———. 2017. Editor and trans. *The Book of Lord Shang: Apologetics of State Power in Early China*. New York: Columbia University Press.

Pines, Yuri, and Gideon Shelach. 2005. Using the Past to Serve the Present: Comparative Perspectives on Chinese and Western Theories of the Origins of the State. In *Genesis and Regeneration: Essays on Conceptions of Origins*, ed. Shaul Shaked, 164–191. Jerusalem: The Israel Academy of Science and Humanites.

Puett, Michael J. 2001. *The Ambivalence of Creation: Debates Concerning Innovation and Artifice in Early China*. Stanford: Stanford University Press.

Queen, Sarah A. 2013. "*Han Feizi* and the Old Master:A Comparative Analysis and Translation of *Han Feizi* Chapter 20, 'Jie Lao,' and Chapter 21, 'Yu Lao.'" In *Dao Companion to the Philosophy of Han Fei*. Ed. Paul R. Goldin. 197-256. Dordrecht: Springer.

Rappe, Guido. 1995. *Archaische Leiberfahrung: Der Leib in der frühgriechischen Philosophie und in aussereuropäischen Kulturen*. Berlin: Akademie Verlag.

Romm, James. 2014. *Dying Every Day: Seneca at the Court of Nero*. New York: Vintage Books.

Roth, Harold. 1991. Psychology and Self-Cultivation in Early Taoistic Thought. *Harvard Journal of Asiatic Studies*. 51 (2): 559–650.

———. 1994. Redaction Criticism and the Early History of Taoism. *Early China* 19: 1–46.

———. 1999. *Original Tao: Inward Training (Nei-yeh) and the Foundations of Taoist Mysticism*. New York: Columbia University Press.

Schmitt, Carl. 1985. *Political Theology: Four Chapters on the Concept of Sovereignty*. Trans. George Schwab. Chicago: University of Chicago Press.

Shangjunshu 商君書. See Gao Heng 1974.

Shiyi jia zhu Sunzi 十一家注孫子. 1978. Shanghai: Shanghai guji chubanshe.

Shuo yuan 說苑. See Xiang Zonglu 1987.

Sivin, Nathan. 1995. State, Cosmos, and Body in the Last Three Centuries B.C. *Harvard Journal of Asiatic Studies* 55 (1): 5–37.

Sommer, Deborah. 2008. Boundaries of the *Ti* Body. *Asia Major (Third Series)* 21 (1): 293–324.

Star, Christopher. 2012. *The Empire of the Self: Self-Command and Political Speech in Seneca and Petronius*. Baltimore: Johns Hopkins University Press.

Sunzi 孫子. See *Shiyi jia zhu Sunzi*

Tu, Wei-ming. 1989. *Centrality and Commonality: An Essay on Confucian Religiousness: A Revised and Enlarged Edition of Centrality and Commonality, an Essay on the Chung-Yung*. Albany: State University of New York Press.

Wahrman, Dror. 2004. *The Making of the Modern Self: Identity and Culture in Eighteenth-Century England*. New Haven: Yale University Press.

Wang, Bi 王弼 (CE 226–249). 1974a. *Laozi's Canon of the Way and Its Power* 老子道德經. Commentary by Lu Deming 陸德明 (CE 556–627). In *Xin bian zhuzi ji cheng*. Vol. 3. Taipei: Shijie Shuju.

Wang, Xianqian 王先謙 (1842–1918). 1974b. *Xunzi, with collected explanations* 荀子集解. In *Xin bian zhuzi ji cheng*. Vol. 2. Taipei: Shijie Shuju.

Wei, Qipeng 魏啟鵬. 2004. *The Book of the Yellow Emperor, a Silk Text from a Han Tomb at Mawangdui, with Commentary* 馬王堆漢墓帛書"黃帝書"箋證. Beijing: Zhonghua Shuju.

Wei Liaozi 尉繚子. See Liu Yin 1972.

Wilson, Emily. 2014. *The Greatest Empire: A Life of Seneca*. Oxford: Oxford University Press.

Wrong, Dennis H. 1979. *Power: Its Forms, Bases, and Uses*. Oxford: Basil Blackwell Publishers.

Wu, Zeyu 吳則虞. 1962. *The Springs and Autumns of Master Yan, with collected explanations* 晏子春秋集釋. Beijing: Zhonghua.

Xiang, Zonglu 向宗魯. 1987. *The Garden of Persuasions, with collations and verifications* 說苑校證 *Shuo yuan jiaozheng*. Compiled by Liu Xiang 劉向 (77–6 BCE). Beijing: Zhonghua Shuju.

Xunzi 荀子. See Wang Xianqian 1974.

Yanzi chunqiu 晏子春秋. See Wu Zeyu 1962.

Yates, Robin D.S. 1997. *Five Lost Classics: Tao, Huanglao, and Yin-yang in Han China: Translated, with and Introduction and Commentary*. New York: Ballantine Books.

Zhuangzi 莊子. See Guo Qingfan 1974.

Chapter 12
The Historiography of Political Realism

Kai Vogelsang

There seems to be an intrinsic relationship between political and historical thought. There is a "Whig interpretation of history" (Butterfield 1951), Marxism goes hand in hand with historical materialism, and every nationalist movement will create its own specific view of history. Ancient Chinese Political Realism (which is dubbed elsewhere in this volume as *fa* tradition) is no exception.[1] While clearly focused on politics, it comes with a distinct view of history, which differs significantly from those found in other texts. Especially the prevalent mode of "exemplary history," which draws lessons from historical events, is discredited by Political Realists. Ridiculing all backward orientation, they insist that "times change": hence, history cannot serve as a teacher for the present. Since its successive epochs differ substantially, so they argue, no guiding principle can be derived from them.

In this essay, I will first discuss the importance of history for Political Realism, then illustrate how its basic tenet that "times change" invalidates exemplary history and how the latter is ridiculed by Realist authors, then discuss some elaborate historical narratives that seem to be closely linked to Political Realism and, finally, outline the limits of this mode of historical thought.

---

[1] For the term "Political Realism," which is used here instead of the misleading "Legalism" or other direct translations of *fajia*, see Vogelsang 2016: 39–45, and Vogelsang 2017, as well as fn. 5, below.

K. Vogelsang (✉)
Hamburg University, Hamburg, Germany
e-mail: kai.vogelsang@uni-hamburg.de

© The Author(s), under exclusive license to Springer Nature Switzerland AG 2024
Y. Pines (ed.), *Dao Companion to China's* fa *Tradition*, Dao Companions
to Chinese Philosophy 19, https://doi.org/10.1007/978-3-031-53630-4_13

351

1 Politics and Historical Change

Arguably, all "schools" of ancient Chinese thought were concerned with politics. But none was as "single-mindedly concerned with how to preserve and strengthen the state"[2] as the tradition of Political Realism embodied in texts like *Shangjun shu* 商君書 and *Han Feizi* 韓非子, as well as parts of *Guanzi* 管子 and *Lüshi chunqiu* 呂氏春秋.[3] These latter were not just concerned with politics, they were *all about* politics. Especially the *Shangjun shu* is representative of an "amoral science of statecraft,"[4] which has discovered the political sphere as an "autonomous sphere of action" that follows only its own logic.[5] There is no concern whatsoever with religion, ritual, aesthetics, scholarship, or morals in this text.[6] It is strictly about the *ratio politica*: about the mechanisms of reaching and implementing political decisions.

It is no accident that the tradition of Political Realism has for more than 2000 years been called *fajia*: after all, *fa*—meaning rules, laws, standards, methods, principles, etc.—are the principal means by which politics are enacted. *Fa* are the results of political decisions. This is the clincher: they are man-made—positive law, as it were—not fixed by tradition but laid down by rulers and thus subject to *change*. Arguably, the introduction of positive law "marks a threshold in the development of society at which the new autonomy of the political system rose to consciousness and its increased capacity for decision-making had to be organized."[7]

It is precisely this crucial moment that is captivated in the first paragraphs of the *Shangjun shu* which describe a scene at the court of Lord Xiao of Qin (秦孝公, r. 361–338 BCE). "Now I want to govern by changing the rules, alter the rites and instruct the hundred lineages – but I am afraid that all under heaven will criticize me" (今吾欲變法以治，更禮以教百姓，恐天下之議我也), the lord says. Thereupon Gongsun Yang 公孫鞅 (i.e. Shang Yang 商鞅), the proponent of Political Realism, reassures him that he is doing the right thing:

君亟定變法之慮，殆無顧天下之議之也。⋯⋯ 郭偃之法曰：「論至德者不和於俗。成大功者不謀於眾。」法者所以愛民也。禮者所以便事也。是以聖人苟可以強國，不法其故；苟可以利民，不循其禮。

---

[2] Hui 2005: 18.

[3] For the fragments attributed to Shen Buhai 申不害 (d. 337 BCE) and Shen Dao 慎到, which are also associated with Political Realism, see Creel 1974 and Thompson 1979 as well as Harris 2016, respectively. For the composite nature of all these texts, cf. fn. 39.

[4] Graham 1989: 267.

[5] This is the reason why I choose the term "Political Realism" (instead of "Legalism") for this tradition. Political Realism, as defined by Hans Morgenthau, "sets politics as an autonomous sphere of action and understanding apart from other spheres, such as economics, ethics, aesthetics, or religion" (Morgenthau 1978: 5): this is precisely what texts like *Han Feizi* and *Shangjun shu* postulate.

[6] This, of course, has always been held against Political Realism. Ancient and imperial China, like all pre-modern societies, could not tolerate the pure logic of functionally differentiated systems. Only in 20th-century China did Political Realism regain some measure of recognition.

[7] Luhmann 2013: 93, n. 113.

> You, my lord, have already made up your mind about changing the rules, so you should not care about whether all under heaven criticizes it. ... A rule by Guo Yan says: "He who discourses on the highest virtue does not harmonize with the vulgar, and he who achieves great success does not consult with the masses." Laws are a means to care for the people; rites are a means to facilitate endeavors. Therefore a wise man, if only he can strengthen the state, does not take old customs as a model, and if only he can benefit the people, does not follow the rites.[8]

But then two advisers object to the duke's plans: "Now, if you change the rules without adhering to the old customs of the Qin state, and alter the rites in order to instruct the people, I am afraid that all under heaven will criticize you, my lord" (今 若變法，不循秦國之故，更禮以教民，臣恐天下之議君), says the first, and the second adds "that unless the advantage is a hundredfold, one should not change the rules, and unless the achievements are tenfold, one should not alter the devices. I have heard that taking tradition as a rule keeps from mistakes, and that following the rites keeps from evil" (利不百，不變法；功不十，不易器。臣聞:法古無 過，循禮無邪).[9]

Evidently, the debate is not about changing specific rules, but about whether one should change rules *at all*. For Lord Xiao's conservative advisers it seems unthinkable not to adhere "to the old customs"; the traditional rules are their timeless guidelines. But Shang Yang, rankled by these conservative claims, counters the protest with a decisive argument:

前世不同教，何古之法?何禮之循?伏羲、神農教而不誅。黃帝、堯、 舜誅而不怒。及至文、武，各當時而立法，因事而制禮。禮法以時而定。制令各順 其宜。兵甲器備，各便其用。臣故曰:治世不一道。便國不必古。湯、武之王也， 不循古而興。商、夏之滅也，不易禮而亡。然則反古者未可非，循禮者未足多 是也。君無疑矣。

Former ages did not have the same teachings, so which tradition should one take as a rule? Thearchs and kings did not refer to one another, so which rites should one follow? Fuxi and Shennong instructed without punishing; Huangdi, Yao and Shun punished without wrath. Finally, [kings] Wen and Wu each established laws according to their times and instituted rites according to their endeavors. Rites and laws are determined according to the times; institutions and orders each conform to what is appropriate; weapons, armors, tools and devices each suited their function. Therefore I say: There is no sole principle for ordering the age, and one does not need tradition for benefitting the state. When Tang and Wu reigned as kings, they flourished without following ancient practice; and when the Shang and Xia perished, they fell without having changed the rites. Therefore, opposing ancient practice is not necessarily wrong, and following the rites is not always right. You, my lord, should no longer hesitate![10]

Shang Yang's point, illustrated by a succinct historical sketch, is as simple as it is striking: traditions are subject to *change*, there are no timeless rules appropriate to

---

[8] *Shangjun shu* 1.1: 7. In quotes from *Shangjun shu*, I have adopted the division into sections from Zhang Jue 2012; I have also consulted – and often followed – the translation by Pines 2017 (were division into sections slightly differs from that of Zhang).

[9] *Shangjun shu* 1.1: 10–11.

[10] *Shangjun shu* 1.1: 6–7. For a discussion of the philological issues involved, cf. the notes by Zhang Jue, ibid.

all ages. "Times change" (時變也) as it says in another part of the *Shangjun shu*.[11] This simple observation, so commonplace in modern times, seems to have been groundbreaking in the Warring States (Zhanguo 戰國, 453–221 BCE) times. It discredited appeals to tradition and orders based on customary rules.[12] Instead it provided a justification for "changing the rules" – in modern terminology: for positive law[13] – and a rationale for a genuinely *political* sphere in which rules were not simply inherited but decided. The scene at the beginning of the *Shangjun shu* thus marks the birth of *politics*,[14] and it is no mere coincidence that it does so with reference to *history*: the insight that "times change" also encapsulates a radically new concept of history.

2 Exemplary History and Its Discontents

Of course, the origins of historical thought in China are much older than Shang Yang and his times. The discovery of historical change may be traced back as far as Western Zhou times. Bronze inscriptions from the 9th century BCE testify to the fact that a more distant – and potentially: different – past came into view.[15] Some inscriptions even directly express that things were *different* – meaning: better – in the past, testifying to an awareness of change over time.[16] Such inscriptions may be the first evidence of *historical consciousness* in Chinese history: the awareness that the past is different from the present.

Things have changed, these inscriptions tell us, and not for the better. From the very beginning, historical change seemed to appear as a disturbing problem: it was

---

[11] *Shangjun shu* 18.1: 208 ("Hua ce" 畫策).

[12] In other words, it discredited the time-honored lineage rules of the old aristocracy, which "were the society's fundamental law" (Chang 1983: 35). For Qin, just like for any other ancient polity, the foremost task of state-building lay in the subjection of the powerful regional lineages. Just like central rule had to replace fragmented lineage rule, so centralized law had to supersede lineage rules, which applied to particular lineages only (cf. Liu Yongping 1998: 12).

[13] It is precisely the fact that laws are no longer eternal but may be changed that defines positive law: it is effective *because* it can be changed; cf. Luhmann 1993: 533.

[14] For a discussion of this aspect, see Vogelsang 2016.

[15] Significantly, new words for the distant past—*zai* 載 and *zhou* 繇—appear in some of these inscriptions (e.g. Shi Hu-*gui* 師虎簋, YZJC 4316, Lu Bo Dong-*gui* 彔伯冬簋, YZJC 4302, Shi Ke-*xu* 師克盨, YZJC 4467, Lai-*pan* 逨盤, discussed in Shaanxisheng kaogu yanjiusuo 2003). These words are frequently used when referring to a time that dates back more than a generation: to "ancestors" and "former kings." By contrast, the word *xi* 昔, which already appears on many earlier inscriptions, only refers back to events within the present generation (cf. the contrasting use in Lai-*ding* 逨鼎, Shaanxisheng kaogu yanjiusuo 2003: 16–17, and Mao-*gui* 卯簋, YZJC 2001: 4327). For a full discussion, cf. Vogelsang 2007, 110–18.

[16] Cf. Shi Huan-*gui* 師袁簋 (YZJC 2001: 4313), where the king laments: "Shi Huan … The Huaiyi *once* were our tributary vassals. *Now* they dare to force their people into indolence, resisting our intendant of works [?] and not supplying our eastern regions"; also Mu-*gui* 牧簋 (YZJC 2001: 4343) and Shi Hong-*gui* 師訇簋 (YZJC 2001: 4342).

not conceived as progress – this concept did not exist – but as decline. All the more important it must have seemed to claim elements of the past that did *not* change: "Don't you dare not to follow the former kings and take them as a shining model!" (女毋敢[弗] [帥]先王作明型用), the Mu *gui* inscription urges.[17]

In fact, this became the premise of Chinese historiography in the following centuries: that despite historical change there were things that remained unchanged.[18] "Arguably, the basic function of historiography is to compensate for this perceived discontinuity by constructing new continuities."[19]

No matter how history was narrated in ancient China, it was always rested on an *ahistorical* core which guaranteed permanence in change. In genealogical writings, which are attested since late Western Zhou times, it was the unbroken family line that provided continuity, bridging the gap between past and present. The narrations of "traditional history," which are attributed to so many ministers and rulers in *Zuozhuan* 左傳 and *Guoyu* 國語, refer to origins of social order and binding commitment that remain valid until the present day.[20] Finally, and most importantly, the mode of "exemplary history," apparent in countless historical episodes of Zhanguo literature, is based on the assumption that despite the difference between past and present there remains a fundamental correspondence between them. This is most clearly stated in the *Lüshi chunqiu*:

今之於古也，猶古之於後世也。今之於後世，[亦猶古之於今也]。 故審知今則可知古，知古則可知後，古今前後一也。故聖人上知千歲下知千歲也。

The relation between the present and the past resembles that between the past and later ages. The relation between present and later ages [also resembles that between the past and the present]. Therefore, by examining the present, one can know the past; and knowing the past, one can know what follows: therefore past and present, before and after, are one. Therefore the sages know the past thousand years and the coming thousand years.[21]

By "knowing the past, one can know what follows": the idea underlying this concept of history is that general rules of conduct and basic patterns of cause and effect are timeless, they always follow the same logic. Despite historical change, similar actions will lead to similar results. This is why history remains a guide for the

---

[17] Mu *gui* 牧簋 (YZJC 4343). For the meaning of 明, which may go well beyond "shining," cf. Vogelsang, forthcoming.

[18] Cf., for example, *Xunzi* 15: 290 ("Yi bing" 議兵): "He who unites men by virtue will be king; he who unites men by force will be weak; he who unites men by riches will be poor: this has been the same in in antiquity and the present." (以德兼人者王，以力兼人者弱，以富兼人者貧，古今一也。) Cf. also, for similar statements, *Xunzi* 5: 82 ("Fei xiang" 非相), and 8: 138 ("Ru xiao" 儒效). I thank Yuri Pines for reminding me of these passages.

[19] Vogelsang 2014: 580. It was the philosopher Odo Marquardt who observed that the sense of history is primarily a sense of continuities and slowness (Marquardt 2003: 228). So history is all about constructing continuities that bridge the disturbing chasm between past and present, which became apparent with the rise of historical consciousness. History is the problem for which history is the solution.

[20] For a fuller discussion, cf. Vogelsang 2014: 582–91, and Vogelsang 2007: 188–222.

[21] *Lüshi chunqiu* 11.5: 604: The emendation in brackets has been proposed by Chen Qiyou (ibid., 606, n. 3).

present. The scenes and anecdotes it offers are "exemplary" of human affairs in general. One can learn from historical precedents and take them as a guide for present action.[22]

References to historical precedents are ubiquitous in Zhanguo texts, so one example, taken from *Mengzi* 孟子, may suffice:

齊人伐燕，勝之。宣王問曰：「或謂寡人勿取，或謂寡人取之。以萬乘之國伐萬乘之國，五旬而舉之，人力不至於此，不取必有天殃，取之何如?」孟子對曰：「取之而燕民悅，則取之。古之人有行之者，武王是也。取之而燕民不悅，則勿取。古之人有行之者，文王是也。以萬乘之國伐萬乘之國，簞食壺漿，以迎王師，豈有他哉，避水火也。如水益深，如火益熱，亦運而已矣。」

The people of Qi attacked Yan and defeated it. King Xuan asked: "Some people tell me not to annex it, and some tell me to annex it. For a state of 10,000 chariots, to attack a state of 1000 chariots and take it within 50 days is something that human strength [alone] cannot achieve. If I do not annex it, this will certainly cause Heavenly disasters, so what if I annex it?"

Master Meng replied: "If the people are happy if you annex it, then do so. Among the ancients, it was king Wu who acted like this. If the people are not happy if you annex it, then do not. Among the ancients, it was king Wen who acted like this. [...]"[23]

The ancients, especially the sage kings of early Zhou, are the models to follow. This seems to have been common sense among political advisers of Zhanguo times, and it is precisely the position of Lord Xiao's conservative advisers: "taking tradition as a rule keeps from mistakes."

Given this background, it becomes clear how revolutionary Shang Yang's statement that "opposing tradition is not necessarily wrong, and following the rites is not always right" must have been in his times. His criticism of traditional thought pinpoints a weakness that is evident even in *Mengzi*'s argument, above. King Wu annexed, but king Wen did not: "so which tradition should one take as a rule?" There are *different* traditions, epochs of the past were unlike one another, and, by the same token, these epochs were also different from the present. Whereas the exemplary mode of history reckoned with change *in* time but insisted on certain principles that remained unchanged, Political Realism recognized a change *of* time which left nothing unaltered.[24] There is no more permanence in change. Even the cherished institutions of the ancient sages lost their validity over time.

Thus only "ordinary people are content with long-established habits, and students are steeped in what they have heard" (常人安於故習，學者溺於所聞).[25]

---

[22] This had important consequences for historiography. Since "what mattered for their authors was not how things happened in the past but how they should have happened and which moral lessons should be gleaned from these events" (Pines 2020: 27), historical anecdotes could simply be made up. There is no indication that such inventions were considered dishonest. We must reckon with the fact that many—perhaps most—exemplary anecdotes in ancient Chinese texts are fiction. Cf. van Els and Queen 2017, esp. the introduction and the chapter by van Els.

[23] *Mengzi* 1B10: 150–51.

[24] Cf. *Shangjun shu* 18.1, quoted above, and also *Lüshi chunqiu* 15.8: 936 ("Cha jin" 察今): "time has changed" (時已徙矣).

[25] *Shangjun shu* 1.3: 10.

Such "students," *Han Feizi* informs us, are complete fools because they "act out the hazy truths of the former kings which quite possibly do not fit the present age. Under these circumstances these scholars have no ability to modify [the ancient ways]"   (請許學者而行宛曼於先王，或者不宜今乎。如是，不能更也。).[26] This realization not only debunked the belief in time-honored rules, it also refuted the premise of exemplary history. The author of the *Lüshi chunqiu* was wrong: past and present are *not* one; by examining the present, one *cannot* know the past. It is no coincidence that the *Shangjun shu* is almost entirely devoid of historical anecdotes, which are so characteristic of exemplary history.[27] Its authors were not interested in individual deeds at all but in general rules, not in timeless wisdom but in practical measures that were adjusted to historical circumstances.

The authors of the *Han Feizi*, while largely agreeing with the *Shangjun shu*, are less clear on the matter. They are much less averse to historical anecdotes, adducing individual rulers, prehistoric sages like Yao 堯 and Shun 舜, and "former kings" in many places. The *Han Feizi* approvingly cites the "rules of the former kings" (先王 之法), and praises the fact that "In ancient times the people who were well governed for generations upheld the impartial law" (古者世治之民，奉公法).[28] These "impartial laws," of course, were just the kind of man-made, changeable law that Shang Yang contrasted with customary rules. So the *Han Feizi* takes the ancient kings as timeless models for not taking any timeless models (I shall return to this paradox below). Conversely, adherence to eternal truths without consideration of historical change is ridiculed in the *Han Feizi*:

> 鄭縣人卜子，使其妻為袴。其妻問曰:「今袴何如?」夫曰:「象吾故袴。」妻 因毀新令如故袴。
>
> Buzi, a man from a Zheng [Han 韓] county, told his wife to make trousers. His wife asked him: "How would you like the new trousers to be?" The husband said: "Like my old trousers." So the wife went ahead and ruined the new trousers and saw to it that they looked like old trousers.[29]

The point is: torn old trousers are just as useless as old traditions, and Buzi's wife is just as foolish as those that cling to ancient ideals. The famous anecdote about the farmer and the hare conveys the same message:

> 宋人有耕者，田中有株，兔走觸株，折頸而死；因釋其耒而守株，冀復得兔，兔不 可復得，而身為宋國笑。今欲以先王之政，治當世之民，皆守株之類也。

---

[26] *Han Feizi* 32.0.3: 263 ("Wai chu shuo zuo shang" 外儲說左上); translations from *Han Feizi* are borrowed (and modified) from Harbsmeier, Forthcoming, whose division into chapter's sections I adopt throughout.

[27] Notable exceptions are found in *Shangjun shu* 17.2–3: 191–92, and 196 ("Shang xing" 賞刑), as well as 20.11: 247–48 ("Ruo min" 弱民), the latter likely being an interpolation. Incidentally, this distinguishes the *Shangjun shu* from Machiavelli' *Principe*, with which it is often compared, since the latter holds "knowledge of the deeds of great men" in high esteem and makes liberal use of historical anecdotes.

[28] *Han Feizi* 6.3: 35–36 ("You du" 有度).

[29] *Han Feizi* 32.3.9: 277–78 ("Wai chu shuo zuo shang"外儲說左上).

A man from Song was working his field and in his field there was a tree-stump. A hare came running along and rammed his head against the tree stump, breaking his neck and dying. So the man from Song abandoned his plough and kept guard at the tree-stump, hoping he would get more hares, he could not get another one, and he became the laughing stock of the state of Song. Now, those who use the administrative methods of the former kings and wish to govern the people of our time, are all of the same kind as he who kept guard at the tree-stump.[30]

The old tree stump is the fitting metaphor for history itself, which is not a source of timeless wisdom but the remnant of singular events that belong to a past writ large. Like the hare, the olden times were gone, and they will not recur. In a similar vein, the *Lüshi chunqiu* 呂氏春秋 also makes a mockery of traditional orientation:

楚人有涉江者，其劍自舟中墜於水，遽契其舟曰:「是吾劍之所從墜。」舟止，從其所契者入水求之。舟已行矣，而劍不行，求劍若此，不亦惑乎?以此故法為其國與此同。時已徙矣，而法不徙，以此為治，豈不難哉?

When a man from Chu was fording a river, his sword fell from the boat into the water. He immediately made a notch in the boat and declared, "This is where my sword went in." When the boat stopped, he went into the water to search for his sword in the spot indicated by the notch he had made. The boat had moved, but his sword had not. Was it not sheer delusion to search for a sword this way? Using ancient laws to govern the state is no different. Since the time has changed but the laws have not followed suit, will it not be difficult to bring about order using them?[31]

Whereas the above anecdotes seem to have been made up in order to ridicule any sort of backward orientation, the following purports to be based on a real event. This makes it structurally similar to exemplary history. But despite this similarity, its message is quite the opposite of *historia magistra vitae*:

荊人欲襲宋，使人先表澭水。澭水暴益，荊人弗知，循表而夜涉，溺死者千有餘人，軍驚而壞都舍。嚮其先表之時可導也，今水已變而益多矣，荊人尚猶循表而導之，此其所以敗也。今世之主，法先王之法也，有似於此。

The army of Chu, wanting to make a surprise attack on Song, first sent a man to go and mark the fording place across the Yong River. But the Yong River was subject to violent floods. The Chu army did not know this, so when they tried to ford the river at night, following the markers that had been set, more than a thousand of their men drowned. The army panicked and destroyed their whole encampment. When the markers had first been placed, they could have been followed. But the river had changed and deepened considerably. Because the Chu army still followed the markers it was defeated. When the rulers of the present age adopt the laws of the Former Kings, it is rather similar to this.[32]

Times change, just like the tides of the Yong River. And just like the obsolete markers, history cannot serve as a guide: the only thing to be learned from history is that there is nothing to be learned from history.

---

[30] *Han Feizi* 49.1: 442–43 ("Wu du" 五蠹).

[31] *Lüshi chunqiu* 15.8: 936; tr. Knoblock and Riegel 2000, 371. There follows another anecdote about a man who wanted to throw a child into the water because its father was a good swimmer: the lesson is the same.

[32] *Lüshi chunqiu* 15.8: 935 ("Cha jin"); tr. Knoblock and Riegel 2000: 369.

3 Sequential History

If ancient Chinese Political Realists ridiculed or ignored the exemplary mode of history, this does not mean that they rejected history altogether. Quite the opposite: the realization that history does not repeat itself, that even the most cherished principles and social rules change over time leads to an even more consistent and compelling view of history. Whereas exemplary history was paradoxically based on a non-historical residue—the timeless principles—Political Realism potentially subjects *everything* to change. Obviously, this does not imply a devaluation of history but rather a heightened sense of history, the expansion of historical thought into realms heretofore excluded from history. The history of Political Realism is relentless: nothing is exempt from the corrosive effect of time.

This elaboration of historical thought led to entirely new forms of historiography. As mentioned above, the *Shangjun shu* contains almost no historical anecdotes: they simply do not make sense within its view of history. But instead, it contains some historical narratives that go far beyond anything exemplary history has to offer. These narratives are not limited to single events but present the course of history in unprecedented scope.[33] The most striking example of these appears in *Shangjun shu* 7 ("Kai sai" 開塞):

> 天地設而民生之。當此之時也，民知其母而不知其父，其道親親而愛私。　親親則別，愛私則險。民眾，而以別、險為務，則有亂。當此時也，民務勝而力征。務勝則爭，力征　則訟，訟而無正，則莫得其性也。故賢者立中正，設無私，而民說仁。當此時也，親親廢，上賢立矣。凡仁者以愛利為務，而賢者以相出為道。民眾而無制，久而相出為道，則有亂。故聖人承之，作為土地、貨財、男女之分。分定而無制，不可，故立禁；禁立而莫之司，不可，故立官；官設而莫之一，　不可，故立君。既立君，則上賢廢而貴貴立矣。然則上世親親而愛私，中世上賢而說仁，下世貴貴而尊官。上賢者以道相出也，而立君者使賢無用也。親親者以私為道也，而中正者使私無行也。此三者非事相反也，民道弊而所重易也，世事變而行道異也。

> When Heaven and Earth were formed, the people were born. At that time, the people knew their mothers but not their fathers; their way was one of attachment to relatives and of selfishness. Attachment to relatives results in particularity; selfishness results in malignity. The people multiplied, and as they were engaged in particularity and malignity, there was turmoil. At that time, the people began seeking victories and forcefully seizing [each other's property]. Seeking victories results in struggles; forceful seizure results in quarrels. When there are quarrels but no proper [norms], no one attains his natural life span. Therefore, the worthies established impartiality and propriety and instituted selflessness; the people began rejoicing in benevolence. At that time, attachment to relatives declined, and elevation of the worthy was established.

> In general, the benevolent are devoted to the love of benefit, whereas the worthy view overcoming one another as the [proper] Way. The people multiplied yet lacked regulations; for a long time they viewed overcoming one another as the [proper] Way, and hence there again was turmoil. Therefore, the sages took responsibility. They created distinctions among lands, property, men, and women. When distinctions were fixed but regulations were

---

[33] Note that even the massive *Zuozhuan* 左傳, which probably predates the *Shangjun shu* by well over a century, does not narrate a continuous, integrated history but a collection of discrete, albeit often quite long stories.

still lacking, this was unacceptable; hence, they established prohibitions. When prohibitions were established but none supervised [their implementation], this was unacceptable; hence they established officials. When officials were instituted but not unified, this was unacceptable; hence they established the ruler. When the ruler was established, the elevation of the worthy declined, and the esteem of nobility was established.

Thus, in the early ages, [the people] were attached to relatives and were devoted to themselves; in the middle ages, they elevated the worthy and rejoiced in benevolence; in the recent age, they esteem nobility and respect officials. When they elevated the worthy, they used the Way to overcome each other; but the establishment of the ruler caused the worthies to become useless. Being attached to relatives, they considered selfishness as the Way; but the establishment of impartiality and propriety caused selfishness no longer to be practiced. In these three cases, it is not that their affairs are opposite; it is that the Way of the people is base and what they value changes. When the affairs of the age change, one should implement a different Way.[34]

This narrative displays an unprecedented level of abstraction. It does not cite examples in order to illustrate a general rule of history, but it recounts general history itself. It does not focus on events, but on *processes*. It is not restricted to the deeds of exemplary individuals – not a single name appears in the passage – but with *social* history. The passage recounts the succession of segmentary society ("attachment to relatives," "particularity"), hierarchical elite society ("elevation of the worthy"), and centralized bureaucratic society ("they established officials," "they established the ruler"). Transcending the ages, the narrative creates something entirely new: a scheme of historical epochs, which it calls "early ages," "middle ages," and "recent age."

This mode of history, which describes a sequence of historical ages, may aptly be called "sequential history." It describes history as a succession of epochs which logically lead to one another ("Therefore, the worthies established impartiality"; "hence they established officials"), but nonetheless fundamentally differ from one another: "in the early ages, [the people] were attached to relatives and were devoted to themselves; in the middle ages, they elevated the worthy and rejoiced in benevolence; in the recent age, they esteem nobility and respect officials." The epochs appear in a sequence, but they share no structural similarities or common principle. Rather, their basic social structures are vastly dissimilar. Indeed, this is the entire point of the narrative: instead of illustrating unchanging rules, its emphasis is precisely on change. The bottom line is: "When the affairs of the age change, one should implement a different Way."

Another historical narrative, which appears in chapter 18 ("Hua ce" 畫策) of the *Shangjun shu*, puts it even more succinctly. Its explanation for historical change is: "because times changed":

昔者昊英之世，以伐木殺獸，人民少而木獸多。黃帝之世，不麛不卵，官無供備之民，死不得用槨。事不同，皆王者，時異也。神農之世，男耕而食，婦織而衣；刑

---

[34] *Shangjun shu* 7.1: 107 ("Kai sai" 開塞); tr. Pines 2017: 167–68. For appraisals and discussions of this passage, cf. Vogelsang 2007: 281–84; Pines 2013; Vogelsang 2017: 23–24 as well as 152–55; and Rogacz 2020: 51–52.

政不用而治，甲兵不起而王。神農既沒，以強勝弱，以眾暴寡。故黃帝作為君臣上下之義、父子兄弟之禮、夫婦妃匹之合，內行刀鋸，外用甲兵，故時變也。

Formerly, in the age of Hao Ying, the people cut trees and slaughtered animals [for food]; the people were few, whereas trees and animals plenty. In the age of the Human Thearch the people consumed neither fawns nor eggs; officials had no servants to support them, and at death they could not obtain outer coffins. Undertakings [of Hao Ying and the Human Thearch] were not the same, but they all were Monarchs: this is because the times were different. In the age of Shennong, men plowed to obtain food, women wove to obtain clothing; he used neither punishments nor regulations, yet there was order; armor and weapons were not set up, but [Shennong] became a Monarch.

After Shennong, the strong overpowered the weak, the many lorded over the few. Hence, the Yellow Thearch created the duties of rulers and ministers and of superiors and inferiors, rituals of fathers and sons and elder and younger brothers, and harmony between husband and wife and between spouses. At home, he applied knife and saw, abroad he used armored soldiers: this was because times changed.[35]

The fundamental difference of these narratives to those of exemplary history is that they offer no lesson. Since "times change," the historical experiences they recount cannot be applied to the present. There is no *moral* to these stories. Again, this tallies well with the statecraft of Political Realism: just like the latter brooks no moral considerations, so its historical narratives contain no moral principles. The *Shangjun shu* takes the change of time just as seriously as the interest of the state: its historical logic is just as consistent as its political logic.

The insight that "times changed" bears equally on politics and history. It implies that politics needs to adapt and that history needs to be rewritten. This structural parallel is evident in the narratives themselves. It is probably no pure coincidence that many examples of sequential history focus on the origins of *the state*. The emergence of inequality, hierarchical social order, and political institutions are its main themes.[36] This also becomes evident in another passage from *Shangjun shu* 23 ("Jun chen" 君臣):

古者未有君臣上下之時，民亂而不治。是以聖人列貴賤，制爵位，立名號，以別君臣上下之義。地廣，民眾，萬物多，故分五官而守之。民眾而姦邪生，故立法制為度量以禁之。是故有君臣之義，五官之分，法制之禁，不可不慎也。

In ancient times, when there were no princes and ministers or superiors and inferiors, the people were chaotic and disorderly. Therefore, the sages ranked the noble and the ignoble, instituted ranks and posts, established names and appellations in order to distinguish the responsibilities of princes and ministers, superiors and inferiors. The land was vast, the people numerous, and the creatures many, so they assigned five offices in order to take care of them. The people were numerous, deceit and depravity appeared, so they established laws, created weights and measures in order to prevent that. Therefore, the responsibilities of princes and ministers, the assignments of the five offices, and the prohibitions of laws and regulations must be attended to.[37]

---

[35] *Shangjun shu* 18.1: 207–8 ("Hua ce" 畫策); tr. Pines 2017: 214–15; cf. the discussion in Vogelsang 2017: 348–50.

[36] For another example, cf. *Lüshi chunqiu* 20.1: 1321 ("Shi jun" 恃君), which starts by stating that "Long ago, in great antiquity, there were no rulers, but people lived together in herds …" (昔太古嘗無君矣，其民聚生群處; tr. Knoblock and Riegel 2000: 511).

[37] *Shangjun shu* 23.1: 258 ("Jun chen" 君臣).

Hierarchies, offices, and laws: this is Political Realism in a nutshell, supported by a historical narrative. Unlike most other examples of sequential history, this passage ends with an explicit exhortation derived from history. It is precisely because of historical change that one needs clear hierarchies, offices, and laws. Interestingly, this passage has a close parallel in a *Guanzi* chapter bearing the same title, "Jun chen" (君臣):

> 古者未有君臣上下之別，未有夫婦妃匹之合，獸處群居，以力相征。於是智者詐愚，強者凌弱，老幼孤獨，不得其所。故智者假眾力以禁強虐，而暴人止。為民興利除害，正民之德，而民師之。是故道術德行出於賢人。其從義理，兆形於民心，則民反道矣。

> In ancient times there were no distinctions between princes and ministers or superiors and inferiors, nor did there exist the union of husband and wife or man and mate. People lived like beasts and dwelt together in herds, using their strength to attack one another. Consequently, the clever cheated the stupid, and the strong maltreated the weak. The old and young, orphaned and alone were thus unable to obtain the means to subsist. Therefore, the wise took advantage of the strength of the masses to restrain the cruelty of the strong, and violence against people was brought to an end. On behalf of the people, they promoted [policies] that were beneficial and eliminated those that were harmful. They established correct standards of virtue for the people so the people took them as their teachers. It was because of this that political methods of the Way and virtuous conduct emanated from worthies, and, as adherence to righteousness and proper order took shape in the minds of the people, they turned to the moral way.[38]

This narrative, while beginning with the same observation as that of the *Shangjun shu*, takes quite a different turn. Instead of hierarchies, offices, and laws, it stresses "virtuous conduct." In fact, it does not offer much support at all for the amoral positions of Political Realism, culminating instead in "righteousness and proper order" and the "moral way." Evidently, the mode of sequential history may accommodate quite different political messages. While it is typical for Political Realism, it is not unique to it.[39] Some texts from other traditions contain quite similar narratives.[40] Their focus and details as well as reasons for historical change may differ, the story may be one of increasing or declining order – but the basic mode of sequential history remains the same. One particularly elaborate example of sequential history

---

[38] *Guanzi* 31: 259 ("Jun chen xia" 君臣下). Cf. Rickett 1985: 412–13.

[39] That is, if one follows the traditional scheme of classification, which assigns texts to certain "schools." Apart from the misleading concept of "schools," which certainly does not apply to Political Realism, it rests on the dubious assumption that texts were, more or less, theoretically coherent. They surely were not. Compilations like the *Lüshi chunqiu* were overtly eclectic, often presenting multiple – even contradictory – views and versions of events; but even seemingly homogeneous works, upon closer inspection, turn out to be of "composite nature" (Boltz 2005). So instead of labelling the *Xunzi* as "Confucian," the *Laozi* as "Daoist," or the *Han Feizi* as "Legalist," it would seem more fruitful to disentangle the diverse strands of thought in ancient Chinese texts: to discover the Political Realist elements in *Xunzi* and *Laozi*, and the Confucian elements in *Han Feizi*. Not even the *Shangjun shu* is free of Confucian intrusions (cf. 13.5: 162, with its talk of "benevolence and righteousness").

[40] Cf., in addition to the passages quoted below, *Mozi* 21: 168 ("Jie yong" 節用 2); *Xunzi* 19: 346 ("Li lun" 禮論); *Zhouyi* 周易 9: 630–32 ("Xici zhuan" 繫辭傳 2); *Zhouyi* 11: 724 ("Xu gua" 序卦); *Liji* 禮記 9: 587 ("Liyun" 禮運).

appears in *Mozi*. It unspools from a lawless antiquity, in which people lived like beasts, to the establishment of bureaucracy and orderly life in later times.

子墨子言曰:「古者民始生,未有刑政之時,蓋其語『人異義』。是以一人則一義,二人則二義,十人則十義,其人茲眾,其所謂義者亦茲眾。是以人是其義,以非人之義,故文相非也。是以內者父子兄弟作怨惡,離散不能相和合。天下之百姓,皆以水火毒藥相虧害,至有餘力不能以相勞,腐臭餘財不以相分,隱匿良道不以相教,天下之亂,若禽獸然。夫明虖天下之所以亂者,生於無政長。是故選天下之賢可者,立以為天子。天子立,以其力為未足,又選擇天下之賢可者,置立之以為三公。天子三公既以立,以天下為博大,遠國異土之民,是非利害之辯,不可一二而明知,故畫分萬國,立諸侯國君,諸侯國君既已立,以其力為未足,又選擇其國之賢可者,置立之以為正長。

Master Mozi spoke, saying: "Ancient times, when people first came into being, were times when there were as yet no laws or government, so it was said that people had differing principles. This meant that, if there was one person, there was one principle; if there were two people, there were two principles; and if there were ten people, there were ten principles. The more people there were, the more things there were that were spoken of as principles. This was a case of people affirming their own principles and condemning those of other people. The consequence of this was mutual condemnation. In this way, within a household, fathers and sons, and older and younger brothers were resentful and hostile, separated and dispersed, and unable to reach agreement and accord with each other. Throughout the world, people all used water and fire, and poisons and potions to injure and harm one another. As a result, those with strength to spare did not use it to help each other in their work, surplus goods rotted and decayed and were not used for mutual distribution, and good doctrines were hidden and obscured and not used for mutual teaching. So the world was in a state of disorder comparable to that amongst birds and beasts.

It is quite clear that what is taken as disorder in the world arises from lack of effective rule. Therefore, the one who was the most worthy and able in the world was selected and established as the Son of Heaven. When the Son of Heaven was established, because his strength alone was not sufficient, there was also selection and choice of the worthy and able of the world who were set up and established as the 'Three Dukes.' When the Son of Heaven and the 'Three Dukes' were already established, because the world was vast and wide and there were people of distant countries and different lands, the distinctions between right and wrong, and between benefit and harm could not be clearly understood by one or two people. There was, therefore, division into ten thousand states with the establishment of regional lords and rulers of states. When regional lords and rulers of states were already established, because their strength alone was not sufficient, there was also the choice and selection of the worthy and able of the states and their establishment as government leaders."[41]

This, too, is a story about the origins of the state. Just like the *Shangjun shu*, *Mozi* recounts how after a period of "differing principles" (compare "particularity" in *Shangjun shu*) first "the most worthy and able in the world was selected" and established as "Son of Heaven"; and subsequently, how a quasi-feudal, decentralized form of government was established. Obviously, this narrative is meant to justify the "elevation of the worthy" (*shang xian* 尚賢), which was a core tenet of the Mohists. It does so by emphasizing the decisive caesura between the "Ancient times" and those in which state institutions emerged. Just like those of the *Shangjun shu*, this is

---

[41] *Mozi* 墨子 11: 74–75 ("Shang tong" 尚同 1); tr. Johnston 2010: 91–93. Compare the parallel narratives in *Mozi* 12: 78 and 13: 91 ("Shang tong" 尚同 2–3). For a discussion of this passage in comparison to *Shangjun shu* 7, cf. Pines and Shelach 2005: 131–36.

not a story of continuity but of *discontinuity*. Although the *Mozi* neither distinguishes historical ages by name nor continues the narrative with the establishment of bureaucracies, the way in which history is presented is familiar: as a sequence of epochs that are quite distinct in their social orders.

Even the "Daoist" classic *Zhuangzi* 莊子 contains several specimen of sequential history, the most remarkable of which appears in chapter 29 ("Dao Zhi" 盜跖):

> 古者禽獸多而人少，於是民皆巢居以避之，晝拾橡栗，暮栖木上，故命之　曰有巢
> 氏之民。古者民不知衣服，夏多積薪，冬則煬之，故命之曰知生之民。神農之世，
> 臥則居居，起則于于，民知其母，不知其父，與麋鹿共處，耕而食，織而衣，无有
> 相害之心，此至德之隆也。

> In ancient times the birds and beasts were many and the people few. Therefore the people all nested in the trees in order to escape danger, during the day gathering acorns and chestnuts, at sundown climbing back up to sleep in their trees. Hence they were called the people of the Nest Builder.

> In ancient times the people knew nothing about wearing clothes. In summer they heaped up great piles of firewood; in winter they burned them to keep warm. Hence they were called 'the people who know how to stay alive.'

> In the age of Shennong, the people lay down peaceful and easy, woke up wide-eyed and blank. They knew their mothers but not their fathers and lived side by side with the elk and the deer. They plowed for their food, wove for their clothing, and had no thought in their hearts of harming one another. This was Perfect Virtue at its height![42]

This is perfect sequential history. Although it does not convey the message of Political Realism—quite the opposite—it presents history in the same way: as a sequence of distinct epochs that are entirely unconnected. Every generation "is in immediate relation to God," as Leopold von Ranke put it, "its value lies in its own existence."[43]

The other characteristic that this *Zhuangzi* narrative shares with others of its kind, however, is not Rankean at all: its total lack of references to sources. Whereas traditional history is often backed up by archival or other documents,[44] and exemplary history is regularly supported by quotes from the *Documents* or the *Odes* (not for factual evidence, to be sure, but for the lesson it conveys), sequential history is purely conjectural.[45] *Zhuangzi* does not need to present any evidence, its narrative lays claim to a self-evident logic, as it were.

---

[42] *Zhuangzi* 29: 994–95 ("Dao Zhi" 盜跖); tr. Watson 2013: 255–56. For other examples, cf. *Zhuangzi* 9: 336 ("Ma ti" 馬蹄), and 16: 551–52 ("Shan xing" 繕性).

[43] Ranke 1975, 260: "jede [Generation] steht zu Gott in einem unmittelbaren Verhältnis: ihr Wert liegt in ihrer eigenen Existenz."

[44] There are telltale signs for such sources in several anecdotes. Thus Prince Zhao 王子朝 of Zhou, who "fled to Chu, carrying with him Zhou canonical documents," thereupon delivered an impeccable example of traditional history (*Chunqiu Zuozhuan zhu*, Zhao 26.9: 1475–79; tr. Durrant et al. 2016: 1663–67); other specimen of traditional history explicitly quote from covenant texts (Xi 26.3: 439–40; Xiang 10: 983; tr. Durrant et al. 2016: 397 and 981) or investiture documents (Ding 4.1: 1537–42; tr. Durrant et al. 2016: 1751).

[45] It may, however, have had models for its conjectures. Pines and Shelach 2005: 145–46, and Vogelsang 2023, have suggested that the observation of foreign peoples may have supplied the template for the description of ancient Chinese history.

The same is true for the following passage from *Han Feizi*, which presents details about everyday life in antiquity that are remarkably similar to those of *Zhuangzi*:

> 上古之世，人民少而禽獸眾，人民不勝禽獸蟲蛇；有聖人作，搆木為巢，　以避群害，而民悅之，使王天下，號曰有巢氏。民食果蓏蚌蛤，腥臊惡臭而傷害腹胃，民多疾病；有聖人作，鑽燧取火，以化腥臊，而民說之，使王天下，號之曰燧人氏。中古之世，天下大水，而鯀、禹決瀆。近古之世，桀、紂暴亂，而湯、武征伐。

> In high antiquity the people were few and wild beasts were many, and the people could not overcome the birds and beasts, the insects and the snakes. Then a sage appeared; he arranged pieces of wood to make nests, so the people could escape from all sorts of harm, and the people felt pleased with this and set him to rule as king over the world. They gave him the byname "Nest Builder." The people ate fruits, berries, mussels and clams. These turned rank and putrid and gave off nasty smells harmful to people's stomachs, and the people were often sick. Then a sage appeared; he drilled firewood and brought forth fire in order to get rid of the rank and putrid, and the people felt pleased and set him to rule as king over the world. They gave him the name "Fire-driller."

> In middle antiquity, there was a great flood in the world and Gun and Yu dug drainage canals.

> In recent antiquity, Jie and Zhou were violent and chaotic, and Tang and Wu launched a punitive expedition against them.[46]

Han Feizi presents the past as radically different from the present (which, in Zhanguo times was characterized by rapid population growth), and this in itself may have sufficed to lend credibility to his narrative: it underscored the credo of sequential history that "times changed." Like the "ages" of the *Shangjun shu*, the epochs called "high," "middle," and "recent antiquity" mark stages in an historical evolution that are genuinely new and different from all others. "In middle antiquity there was a great flood," and "In recent antiquity Jie and Zhou were violent and chaotic rulers": they are independent epochs, one cannot serve as an example for another.

Compared to this basic premise, the specific factors that lead from one epoch are a secondary consideration. It may be noted that in the above narrative *technological* advances – carpentry and fire-making – are presented as main drivers of historical change whereas in the *Shangjun shu* 7 social structure was the decisive factor.[47] In another *Han Feizi* account, demographic development is stressed:

> 古者丈夫不耕，草木之實足食也；婦人不織，禽獸之皮足衣也。不事力而　養足，人民少而財有餘，故民不爭。是以厚賞不行，重罰不用，而民自治。今人有五子不為多，子又有五子，大父未死而有二十五孫。是以人民眾而貨財寡，事力勞而供養薄，故民爭，雖倍賞累罰而不免於亂。

> In ancient times adult males did not till—the fruits of bushes and trees were enough to live on; women did not weave—the hides of wild animals were enough to make clothes with. They did not exert their strength, but there was enough to sustain them, the population was small, but the resources plentiful, so the people did not compete with each other. Therefore bountiful rewards were not dealt out and severe punishments were not employed, but the people were well-governed of themselves. Nowadays, for a person to have five sons is not regarded as many, the sons in turn have five sons, so before the grandfather is dead there are twenty five grandsons. As a result the population is large and the resources scarce,

---

[46] *Han Feizi* 49.1: 442 ("Wu du" 五蠹).

[47] But compare *Shangjun shu* 18.1, which also emphasizes agriculture and weaving. For these arguments, cf. Pines and Shelach 2005: 138–39.

one exerts all his strength but barely has enough to sustain himself. Hence, the people compete with each other, and although you multiply rewards and pile up punishments, you cannot avoid turmoil.[48]

Even clearer than in the above episodes, the difference between historical stages is attributed not to some benevolent or malevolent personality, but to the anonymous forces of social change. But whatever the logic that leads from one epoch to another, all accounts agree on one main point: the process of historical change is *unidirectional*. There is no indication that it could be reversed. The wild animals did not return, the inventions of fire and drainage canals are there to stay, the demographic trend is unbroken. In a word: the past is bygone, there is no way back. Indeed, there is no looking back: the past cannot serve as a guide for the present.

今有搆木鑽燧於夏后氏之世者，必為鯀、禹笑矣；有決瀆於殷、周之世者，必為湯、武笑矣。然則今有美堯、舜、湯、武、禹之道於當今之世者，必為新聖笑矣。是以聖人不期脩古，不法常可，論世之事，因為之備。

    Now, suppose that there had been someone who had made nests of wood or drilled firewood during the times of the Xia —they would certainly have been laughed at by Gun and Yu. Suppose that there had been someone who dug drainage canals during the times of the Yin (Shang) and Zhou —they would certainly be just laughed at by Tang and Wu. So, if people praise the Way of Yao, Shun, Tang, Wu and Yu in our own time, then they will certainly be laughed at by the new sages. Thus the sages are not committed to cultivating antiquity and do not take something constantly acceptable as their standard.[49]

It would seem that there could be no way back for this view of history, either. However, the heyday of sequential history was soon over. Instead of taking root in Chinese historiography, perhaps evolving into more elaborate forms, it was once again overshadowed by exemplary history. The following section will discuss why sequential history so soon reached its limits.

4 The Limits of Sequential History

The history of Political Realism seems strikingly modern. In fact, quite a few historical narratives of modern Europe bear close resemblances to the above-quoted examples of sequential history. Compare *Shangjun shu*'s assertion that when the people "were engaged in particularity and malignity, there was turmoil," that "the people began seeking victories and forcefully seizing [each other's property]," so that "no one attains his natural life span" with Thomas Hobbes pre-state condition "where every man is enemy to every man," where there is "continual fear, and

---

[48] *Han Feizi* 49.2: 443. Compare, in a similar vein, *Han Feizi* 47.4: 426 ("Ba shuo" 八說): "In ancient times men were few and they were close to each other, things were abundant and the people considered material benefits lightly and were willingly yielded to each other, and as a result there were those who bowed politely and yielded all under Heaven." 古者人寡而相親，物多而輕利易讓，故有揖讓而傳天下者.

[49] *Han Feizi* 49.1: 442 ("Wu du").

danger of violent death; and the life of man, solitary, poor, nasty, brutish, and short."[50] And in both accounts, the emergence of the state provides the solution for turmoil, fear, and violent death.

Or take Jean-Jacques Rousseau's famous *Discours sur l'origine et les fondements de l'inégalité parmi les hommes* (1755), in which he describes how humans, thanks to their "faculty of self-improvement" and the invention of language developed from "the savage, living among the animals … solitary, idle, and always close to danger," into sociable hunter-gatherers that "generated the sweetest sentiments known to man, conjugal love and paternal love."[51] This sounds like an echo of *Han Feizi*'s description of "high antiquity," when "people were in a minority compared to birds and beasts, insects and snakes," living unsheltered until a sage "tied pieces of wood together to make nests in order to protect the people from all sorts of harm." *Han Feizi*'s description of social evolution is strikingly similar to Rousseau's history, the stages of which were also marked by innovations in technology and social structure:

> Soon, ceasing to doze under the first tree, or to withdraw into caves, men discovered that various sorts of hard sharp stones could serve as hatchets to cut wood, dig the soil, and make huts out of branches, which they learned to cover with clay and mud. This was the epoch of a first revolution, which established and differentiated families, and which introduced property of a sort from which perhaps even then many quarrels and fights were born.[52]

Although *Han Feizi* does not recount the birth of civil society,[53] its account, just like that of Rousseau is about the origins of *inequality*: "they set him to rule as king over all under Heaven" and raised him above all other human beings.

Finally, consider Schiller's inaugural lecture at the university of Jena on the subject of "What Is, and to What End Do We Study, Universal History?", in which he describes

> savages … without any knowledge of the most indispensable skills, without iron, without the plow, some even without the possession of fire. Some still wrestled with wild beasts for food and dwelling, among many language had been scarcely elevated from animal sounds to understandable signs. In some places, there was not even the simple bond of marriage, as yet no knowledge of property …[54]

This lecture combines several elements that are also found in Ancient Chinese narratives of sequential history: When in "high antiquity there were fewer people than wild beasts," people certainly "wrestled with wild beasts for food and dwelling" like Schiller speculates; just like among the "savages" there was "not even the simple bond of marriage," so in Chinese antiquity "the people knew their mothers but not

---

[50] Hobbes 1651: 78.

[51] Rousseau 1985 [1755]: 351, 369, and 499.

[52] Rousseau 1985 [1755]: 497–98.

[53] Which begins with the famous sentence: "The first man who, having enclosed a piece of land, thought of saying 'This is mine' and found people simple enough to believe him, was the true founder of civil society" (Rousseau 1985 [1755]: 480).

[54] Schiller 1988 [1789]: 258; cf. Schiller 1980, vol. IV: 754.

their fathers"; and just like Schiller's primitive people were "without iron, without the plow, some even without the possession of fire," so in Chinese lore "adult males did not work the fields" and had to wait for the "Flint Man" to bring forth "fire in order to cook the things that were getting rank and putrid."

Most importantly, the histories outlined by Hobbes, Rousseau, Schiller, and other European thinkers[55] follow the same logic as ancient Chinese sequential history: breaking with the paradigm of *historia magistra vitae*,[56] they describe a series of discrete historical stages that follow one another in a process that cannot be reversed. In Europe, these narratives laid the ground for the discovery of "history" as such, a new concept of "genetic" history, a sophisticated philosophy of history, and for the emergence of history as an academic discipline.[57] They led the way to modern history.

The history of Political Realism, too, was on the threshold of a modern understanding of history. But this threshold was not crossed. The vogue of sequential history turned out to be ephemeral. It never displaced the didactic, moralistic view of exemplary history, which remained dominant throughout imperial times. It took another two millennia for a modern concept of history to be introduced in China. What happened? Why did Chinese historical thought fail to develop a modern, "genetic" history from the basis laid by Political Realists?

The simple answer would be that the history propagated by Political Realism was discredited just like the political doctrine itself. After the fall of the Qin, Political Realism was rejected in theory – if not in practice – by most scholars, and in Western Han times the Confucian school gradually rose to new prominence.[58] With its veneration of ancient Zhou models, the exemplary mode of history, which rests precisely on the model function of historical figures, all but obliterated the sequential mode.

However, there may be more to the story. Perhaps the demise of sequential history was not only due to external but also to internal factors. For all the similarities to early modern European histories described above, there are some significant differences. The first observation to be made is that the narratives of sequential history – with the possible exception of *Shangjun shu* 7 – never lead up to the present. Whereas Rousseau describes the emergence of his own society and Schiller relates historical events to "this epoch in which we are now living," their Chinese conterparts end long before their own times. *Shangjun shu* 18 dwells on the ages of Shennong and the "Yellow Thearch"; *Mozi*'s account ends before the spread of bureaucracy; and even *Han Feizi*'s last stage, called "recent antiquity," lies almost a millennium before the "new sages" of its own times. This is no mere trifle. Arguably, it was precisely the fact that their narratives led to the present that made Schiller and

---

[55] For further comparisons with Hobbes, Rousseau, Henry Maine, Lewis Henry Morgan, and others, cf. Pines and Shelach 2005: 147–58.

[56] Cf. the classic analysis by Koselleck 1989.

[57] For the mode of "genetic" history, cf. Rüsen 1989: 52–55.

[58] For Han Confucianism, cf. the classic article by Dubs 1938, and Loewe 2012.

other European thinkers – Hegel being the prime example – believe that history *culminated* in their own times. This is what gave history a *telos* and an inner logic, indeed, it made history *as such* conceivable. Now it seemed plausible that to think of history as a *collective singular* instead of a multitude of discrete histories: as history "above the [hi]stories," as Droysen put it, that gave a purposeful direction to the course of events.[59]

Despite their keen sense of history, ancient Chinese Political Realists never developed any of these notions. There is no *telos* to their social histories: they do not lead anywhere, in fact, they are not meant to lead anywhere.[60] The focus of sequential history is on the *difference* of historical epochs, on what separates them, not on what leads from one to the other:

周不法商，夏不法虞，三代異勢，而皆可以王。故興王有道，而持之異理。
> The Zhou did not take the Shang as a model, and the Xia did not take the Yu as a model: the three dynasties existed under different circumstances, yet they all achieved kingly rule. Thus there is a way of establishing kingly rule, but the principles to preserve it are different.[61]

In this view of history, there was "only change *without* progress or evolution."[62] In extreme cases, historical epochs are simply juxtaposed. Thus *Han Feizi* lists the stages of "high antiquity," "middle antiquity," and "recent antiquity" with no logical connection between them, and *Shangjun shu* 1 simply states: "Fuxi and Shennong instructed without punishing; Huangdi, Yao and Shun punished without wrath. Finally, [kings] Wen and Wu each established laws …" In the case of *Shangjun shu* 7, logical reasons for each historical transformation are given, but there is no overarching teleology, no "grand narrative" that makes sense of history as such. In fact, precisely for this reason, there was no ancient Chinese concept of "history" as such: history "above the [hi]stories" could not come into view as long as discrete epochs were described as distinct and not as connected by some higher logic.

By the same token, Political Realists never developed a philosophy of history. Absent a concept of "history" as such, there could be no reflection on its purposeful development. Nor could "history" become the object of scholarly inquiry in its own right. In Europe, by contrast, the insight that every generation "is in immediate relation to God" led scholars to conclude that history cannot simply be inferred from pre-conceived principles or propositions. Instead, historians had to base their narratives on *sources*, which needed to be attended to in a systematic way: in this way, history became a scholarly discipline. This did not happen in ancient China. Although sequential history described distinctive epochs, it never relied on sources

---

[59] Droysen 1960, 354: "Aber über den Geschichten ist die Geschichte." For the emergence of "history" as a collective singular, cf. also Koselleck et al. 1975, esp. 647–53.

[60] Unsurprisingly, they did not lead into the *future*, either. Just like there was no concept of "history," so there was none of the "future." While the ancient Chinese certainly had a notion of "coming" or imminent events, they knew no "future" in the sense of as collective singular: no concept of a coming age which the historical process as a whole will reach. For different opinions, cf. Schwermann 2018, esp. 87, and Pines 2013: 35.

[61] *Shangjun shu* 7.3: 111 ("Kai sai").

[62] Ames 1994, 13 (original italics).

in order to support its narratives. Sequential history, just like exemplary history, was *deductive*: it was not based on evidence but on the principle that "times changed". And its purpose was not to recount the past "as it actually was" but to elucidate this principle. Just like exemplary history, it amounted to a Q.E.D.

In fact, for all its specific features, sequential history still retained an affinity to exemplary history. Despite its logical premise that history will teach us nothing, it paradoxically uses history to convey this lesson. The *Han Feizi* takes the ancient kings as timeless models for not taking any timeless models; *Shangjun shu* 23 ends with the explicit conclusion that "Therefore, the responsibilities of princes and ministers, the assignments of the five offices, and the prohibitions of laws and regulations must be attended to"; and all Realist texts also contain historical anecdotes that plainly represent exemplary history. And although they theoretically subject everything to historical change, Realist thinkers fail to apply this logic throughout. When the *Shangjun shu* claims that "shame and disgrace are what the people hate, fame and glory are what the people strive for," or *Han Feizi* makes the sweeping statement that "Ministers are afraid of punishments and fines, and covet praise and rewards," they seem to regard these inborn and ineradicable human traits as ahistorical.[63] Arguably, no mode of historical thinking – not even modern academic history – can do without some ahistorical residue, or else it would forsake its potential to provide orientation. If "the sense of history is primarily a sense of continuities" (cf. fn 19), a history in which *everything* changes would lose its sense. Sequential history is no exception: despite its claim to the contrary, it nonetheless rested on an ahistorical core, which guaranteed permanence in change.

Such inconsistencies may also be explained by the fact that, despite its sophisticated inner logic, sequential history was never fully emancipated from politics. Just like traditional and exemplary history it was not narrated as an end it itself but in order to underscore arguments in court debates. It did not function to establish historical truth but served political ends. Political Realism was all about politics, and its historiography was no exception. By recounting the emergence of the state it justified the program of Political Realism, and therein lay its purpose. That is why it was so readily discarded once Political Realism fell into disrepute, and why it was so easily replaced by another mode of history that supported another political program.

References

Ames, Roger. 1994. *The Art of Rulership: A Study of Ancient Chinese Political Thought*. Albany: State University of New York Press.

Boltz, William G. 2005. The Composite Nature of Early Chinese Texts. In *Text and Ritual in Early China*, ed. Martin Kern, 50–78. Seattle: University of Washington Press.

Butterfield, Herbert. 1951. *The Whig Interpretation of History*. London: Bell.

---

[63] *Shangjun shu* 6.9: 102–3 ("Suan di" 算地): 羞辱勞苦者，民之所惡也；顯榮佚樂者，民之所務也; *Han Feizi* 7.1: 39 ("Er bing" 二柄): 為人臣者畏誅罰而利慶賞.

Chang, Kwang-chih. 1983. *Art, Myth, and Ritual: The Path to Political Authority in Ancient China.* Cambridge, MA: Harvard University Press.

Chunqiu Zuozhuan zhu 春秋左傳注 (*Chunqiu* and *Zuozhuan*, annotated). 1981. Ed. Yang, Bojun 楊伯峻. Beijing: Zhonghua shuju.

Creel, Herrlee G. 1974. *Shen Pu-hai: A Chinese Political Philosopher of the Fourth Century B.C.* Chicago: University of Chicago Press.

Droysen, Johann Gustav. 1960. In *Historik: Vorlesungen über Enzyklopädie und Methodologie der Geschichte*, ed. Rudolf Hübner. Darmstadt: Wissenschaftliche Buchgesellschaft.

Dubs, Homer H. 1938. The Victory of Han Confucianism. *Journal of the American Oriental Society* 58 (3): 435–449.

Durrant, Stephen, Wai-yee Li, and David Schaberg. 2016. *Zuo Tradition/ Zuozhuan* 左傳: Commentary on the "Spring and Autumn Annals". 3 vols. Seattle: University of Washington Press.

Graham, Angus C. 1989. *Disputers of the Tao: Philosophical Argument in Ancient China.* Chicago and LaSalle: Open Court.

Guanzi jiaoshi 管子校釋. (*Guanzi, Collated and Explained*). 1996. Ed. Yan Changyao 顏昌嶢. Changsha: Yuelu shushe.

Han Feizi jijie 韓非子集解. (*Han Feizi*, with collected explanations). 1998. Ed. Wang, Xianshen 王先慎. Beijing: Zhonghua shuju.

Harbsmeier, Christoph, trans. Forthcoming. *Han Feizi, A Complete Translation: The Art of Statecraft in Early China.* Ed. Jens Østergaard Petersen and Yuri Pines. Leiden: Brill.

Harris, Eirik Lang. 2016. *The Shenzi Fragments: A Philosophical Analysis and Translation.* New York: Columbia University Press.

Hobbes, Thomas. 1651. *Leviathan or the Matter, Forme, & Power of a Common-wealth Ecclesiasticall and Civill.* London: Andrew Crooke.

Hui, Victoria Tin-Bor. 2005. *War and State Formation in Ancient China and Early Modern Europe.* Cambridge: Cambridge University Press.

Johnston, Ian. 2010. *The Mozi: A Complete Translation.* Hongkong: The Chinese University Press.

Knoblock, John, and Jeffrey Riegel. 2000. *The Annals of Lü Buwei: A Complete Translation and Study.* 2 vols. Stanford University Press.

Koselleck, Reinhart. 1989. Historia Magistra Vitae: Über die Auflösung des Topos im Horizont neuzeitlich bewegter Geschichte. In *idem, Vergangene Zukunft: Zur Semantik geschichtlicher Zeiten*, 38–66. Suhrkamp: Frankfurt/M.

Koselleck, Reinhart, et al. 1975. Geschichte, Historie. In *Geschichtliche Grundbegriffe: Historisches Lexikon zur politisch-sozialen Sprache in Deutschland*, ed. Reinhart Koselleck, Otto Brunner, and Werner Conze, vol. 2, 593–717. Stuttgart: Ernst Klett Verlag.

Liji jijie 禮記集解. (*Record of Rites*, with collected explanations). 1998. Ed. Sun, Xidan 孫希旦. Beijing: Zhonghua shuju.

Liu, Yongping. 1998. *Origins of Chinese Law: Penal and Administrative Law in Its Early Development.* Hong Kong: Oxford University Press.

Loewe, Michael. 2012. 'Confucian' Values and Practices in Han China. *T'oung Pao* 98: 1–30.

Luhmann, Niklas. 1993. *Das Recht der Gesellschaft.* Frankfurt/M.: Suhrkamp.

Luhmann, Niklas. 2013. In *Macht im System*, ed. André Kieserling. Frankfurt/M: Suhrkamp Verlag.

Lüshi chunqiu jiaoshi 呂氏春秋校釋. (*Springs and Autumns of Mr. Lü*, collated and explained). 1984. Annotated by Chen, Qiyou 陳奇猷. Shanghai: Xuelin.

Marquardt, Odo. 2003. Zeit und Endlichkeit. In *idem, Zukunft braucht Herkunft: Philosophische Essays*, 220–233, Stuttgart: Reclam.

Mengzi zhengyi 孟子正義. (*Mengzi*, The correct meaning). 1998. Annotated by Jiao, Xun 焦循. Beijing: Zhonghua shuju.

Morgenthau, Hans Joachim. 1978. *Politics among Nations: The Struggle for Power and Peace.* New York: Knopf.

Mozi xiangu 墨子閒詁. (*Mozi*, free interpretation). 2001. Ed. Sun, Yirang 孫詒讓. Beijing: Zhonghua shuju.

Pines, Yuri. 2013. From Historical Evolution to the End of History: Past, Present and Future from Shang Yang to the First Emperor. In *Dao Companion to the Philosophy of Han Fei*, ed. Paul R. Goldin, 25–46. Dordrecht: Springer.

———, ed. and trans. 2017. *The Book of Lord Shang: Apologetics of State Power in Early China*. New York: Columbia University Press.

———, ed. and trans. 2020. *Zhou History Unearthed: The Bamboo Manuscript Xinian and Early Chinese Historiography*. New York: Columbia University Press.

Pines, Yuri, and Gideon Shelach. 2005. 'Using the Past to Serve the Present': Comparative Perspectives on Chinese and Western Theories of the Origins of the State. In *Genesis and Regeneration: Essays on Conceptions of Origins*, ed. Shaul Shaked, 127–163. Jerusalem: The Israel Academy of Science and Humanities.

Ranke, Leopold von. 1975. *Vorlesungseinleitungen*. Ed. by Volker Dotterweich and Walther Peter Fuchs. München/Wien: Oldenbourg Verlag.

Rickett, W. Allyn (trans.). 1985 and 1998. *Guanzi*. 2 vols., Princeton: Princeton University Press.

Rogacz, Dawid. 2020. *Chinese Philosophy of History: From Ancient Confucianism to the End of the Eighteenth Century*. London/New York: Bloomsbury.

Rousseau, Jean-Jacques. 1985 [1755]. *A Discourse on Inequality*. Tr. by Maurice Cranston. E-book. London: Penguin.

Rüsen, Jörn. 1989. *Lebendige Geschichte: Formen und Funktionen des historischen Wissens*. Göttingen: Vandenhoeck & Ruprecht.

Schiller, Friedrich. 1980. *Sämtliche Werke*. 5 vols. Darmstadt: Wissenschaftliche Buchgesellschaft.

———. 1988 [1789]. *What Is, and to What End Do We Study, Universal History?* Tr. by Caroline Stephan and Robert Trout. Washington, D.C.: Schiller Institute.

Schwermann, Christian. 2018. Von der Sparsamkeit zur Nachhaltigkeit. Zukunftsdenken in der antiken chinesischen Wirtschaftstheorie. *Bochumer Jahrbuch zur Ostasien forschung* 41, 79–98.

Shaanxisheng kaogu yanjiusuo 陝西省考古研究所 [Shaanxi Province Archaeological Research Institute] et al. 2003. Brief Report on the Excavation of a Hoard of Western Zhou Bronze Vessels in Yangjia Village, Mei County, Shaanxi 陝西眉县杨家村西周青铜器窖藏发掘简报, *Cultural Relics*文物6: 4–42.

Shangjun shu jiaoshu 商君書校疏. (*Book of the Lord of Shang*, collated with subcommentaries). 2012. Ed. Zhang Jue 張覺. Beijing: Zhishi chanquan chubanshe.

Thompson, P.M., ed. 1979. *The Shen Tzu Fragments*. Oxford: Oxford University Press.

van Els, Paul, and Sarah H. Queen, eds. 2017. *Between History and Philosophy: Anecdotes in Early China*. Albany: State University of New York Press.

Vogelsang, Kai. 2007. *Geschichte als Problem. Entstehung, Formen und Funktionen von Geschichtsschreibung im Alten China*. Wiesbaden: Harrassowitz.

———. 2014. The Shape of History: On Reading Li Wai-Yee. *Early China* 37, 579–599.

———. 2016. Getting the Terms Right: Political Realism, Politics, and the State in Ancient China. *Oriens Extremus* 55: 39–72.

———. 2017. *Shangjun shu: Schriften des Fürsten von Shang*. Stuttgart: Kröner.

———. 2023. 'Times have Changed': History beyond the *Zuozhuan*. In *Zuozhuan and Early Chinese Historiography,* 289–324. Ed. by Yuri Pines, Martin Kern, and Nino Luraghi. Leiden: Brill.

———. Forthcoming (2024). Rulership in the Discourse of Political Realism: The Concept of *mingzhu* 明主. *Bochumer Jahrbuch zur Ostasienforschung* 46.

Watson, Burton. 2013. (Tr.) *The Complete Works of Zhuangzi*. New York: Columbia University Press.

Xunzi jijie 荀子集解. (*Xunzi*, with collected explanations). 1996. Ed. Wang Xianqian 王先謙. Beijing: Zhonghua shuju.

YZJC = *Yin Zhou jinwen jicheng shiwen* 殷周金文集成釋文. (*Transcriptions of Yin and Zhou Bronze Inscriptions*). 2001. Ed. Institute of Archeology of China's Academy of Social Sciences 中國社會科學院考古研究所. 6 vols., Hong Kong: Chinese University Press.

Zhouyi jijie zuanshu 周易集解纂疏. (*The Zhou Changes*, with collected explanations and assembled subcommentaries). 1994. Ed. Li, Daoping 李道平. Beijing: Zhonghua shuju.

Zhuangzi jishi 莊子集釋. (*Zhuangzi*, with collected explanations). 1997. Ed. Guo, Qingfan 郭慶藩. Beijing: Zhonghua shuju.

Chapter 13
The Ruler's New Tools: *Fa* 法 and the Political Paradigm of Measure in Early China

Romain Graziani

1   Introduction: The Long Search for a Political Panacea

The political promotion of the notion of *fa* 法 over the course of the Warring States period can be examined against the backdrop of a widely shared rejection of major traits of the old Zhou culture. Its gradual dominance in political theories can also be situated in the dynamics of an emerging vision of statecraft that profoundly redefined ties between knowledge, violence and sovereignty. Reflections on *fa* flourished in a period of new experimentations during which the state was redefined as a set of institutions, laws, measures and contracts shaped after the paradigm of impersonal rule. Instead of letting ministerial families or hereditary officers govern with discretional power, the devisers of *fa* contend that the state should be run by a closely-supervised and technically-trained managerial elite. This elite must be equipped with objective standards and common methods to organize social production, develop a mass-scale cooperation, ensure political stability, and calculate everyone's faults and merits. *Fa* is the brainchild of thinkers and statesmen who set in motion this gigantic undertaking of standardization of society through uniform rules and procedures.[1]

Before becoming the linchpin of the grand chariot of the state, *fa* was initially associated with patterns, measures, models and geometric figures.[2] Taken as a set of

---

[1] For a full appreciation of the actual magnitude of this process of quantitative uniformization in early Chinese society, I refer the reader to Korolkov, Chap. 7, this volume.

[2] See, e.g., Goldin 2013: 4 and the discussion of *Mozi* in section 1 of this chapter. For the early usages of the word *fa*, see Creel 1974: 144–45 (and up to p. 149 for the Warring States-period evolution of this term).

R. Graziani (✉)
École Normale Supérieure de Lyon, Lyon, France

© The Author(s), under exclusive license to Springer Nature Switzerland AG 2024
Y. Pines (ed.), *Dao Companion to China's* fa *Tradition*, Dao Companions to Chinese Philosophy 19, https://doi.org/10.1007/978-3-031-53630-4_14

norms of conduct issued by the ruler, *fa* had four main characteristics: it had to be uniform across the whole kingdom, legible and clear for all, impartial (leaving no room for personal sentiments), and incontrovertible (binding for everyone). These features of norms and laws leave in a state of relative indetermination their specific content, as *fa* thinkers are not concerned with the question of establishing fundamental laws or translate into legal codes a set of values held as natural or divine.[3] Specific laws, ordinances and statutes (*lü* 律, *zhang* 章, or *ling* 令) were not their primary focus. *Fa* rather describes the formal properties of all the various articles, ordinances and statutes forming a legal code.[4] What mattered above all was to impose the primacy of *fa* per se.

In what ways was the role and status of the ruler altered, or even antagonized, by this change of paradigm? How did this new political recipe recombine the basic components of sovereign authority? And, finally, how did *fa* thinkers anticipate the limits and shortcomings of the system they promoted? Leaving aside the question of a proper translation of the term *fa*, I will begin by examining how and why this notion was devised, what kind of difficulties it was supposed to remove, what kind of methods it imported in the sphere of the state, and, finally, what obstacles remained along its conceptual trajectory from craftsmanship to rulership. I will concentrate on what can be considered the main textual sources that introduced *fa* into the political vocabulary: *Shangjunshu* 商君書, associated with Shang Yang 商鞅 (d. 338 BCE), *Shènzi* 慎子, associated with Shen Dao 慎到 (fourth century BCE), *Guanzi* 管子 (anonymous collection of texts mostly originating from Qi 齊 and written roughly between the fourth and the second centuries BCE), and *Han Feizi* 韓非子 (ascribed to Han Fei, d. 233 BCE) (for these texts, see Chaps. 1, 2, 3, 4, and 5, this volume). I shall also adduce passages from *Shēnzi* 申子 fragments, attributed to Shen Buhai 申不害 (d. 337 BCE).

In order to explain the function and value of *fa*, the textual sources quoted above, ranging from the mid-fourth century to the end of the third century BCE, resort to a small set of didactic comparisons between *fa* and precision tools or measurement devices. Objects theretofore unrelated to the art of ruling surface in political discourse—weighing scales, compasses, T-squares, spirit level, plumb lines, and other such instruments—served as core images that helped redefine the proper way of governance based on *techniques*, in an explicit opposition to the cognitive sagacity and intellectual acumen of the ruler (*zhi* 智), and to the ideal of kingship based on ritual norms (*li* 禮), spiritual potency and moral virtue (*de* 德).[5]

---

[3] On the differences between Chinese and Western conceptions of law (from the ancient Greek to the Enlightenment) and the original metaphor of "laws of nature" that proved critical in the terminology of modern science, see Needham 2005, chapter 8; Peerenboom 1993: 80–83; Wang Pei, Chap. 20, this volume.

[4] See Lau and Lüdke, Chap. 8, this volume.

[5] For an in-depth analysis of the debate between *de* 德 and *fa* 法, persuasion and coercion, ritual education and punishments, in the light of the Guodian manuscripts, see Cook 2019, *passim,* and in particular pp. 290 and 296.

The present essay examines the ambivalent ties between discourses of *fa* and early self-cultivation texts and how the set of oppositions between the way of the mind and the way of tools is worked out. The comparison of these two trends of thought offers a distinct perspective on the paradigm of tools, enabling us to examine the competition between "techniques of the self" relying on the innate tools of eyes, ears and heart-mind (*ermu* 耳目 and *xin* 心), along with the inner resources of vital energy, essence and spirit (*qi* 氣, *jing* 精, *shen* 神), and, on the other hand, the rule of *fa* drawing on external instruments and impersonal procedures.

Didactic tropes and rhetorical devices conjuring up various tools and instruments in *fa* discourses do not only introduce the value of objectivity in the handling of state affairs through the ideas of exact measure and strict adequation. They also show through this shared terminology how rulers can exploit and extend the ability to scare and hurt. In fact, comparisons with *fa* oscillate between standard images of precision tools and scenes of aggression. In later textual sources, the *fa*-equipped ruler is sometimes likened to the figure of a Master Measurer holding a compass and a T-square, sometimes equated with that of a warrior and a hunter, availing of his nets, axes, saws and swords in order to control, trim and tame, subdue and threaten. In this web of violent metaphors and analogies unspooling throughout chapters of the *Han Feizi* and the *Guanzi*, we can observe, unresolved, the fundamental ambivalence of *fa*, as a tool and a weapon.

2 The Geometry of Politics

In the *Mozi*, the opening lines of chapter 4, "Fa yi" 法儀, present the word *fa* and the expression *fayi* as norms of conduct and patterns of behavior: it is the yardstick we have in mind when acting and without which one cannot do anything properly in a technical context or in the moral realm. When the author asks whom one should take as a model for one's behavior, the term *fa* is used in its verbal function (to take as a model, to imitate, or emulate) and is associated with parents (父母), teachers (學), rulers (君), and Heaven (天), with only the latter deserving to be constantly emulated (cf. Tao, this volume). The core analogy in this chapter is drawn from the milieu of artisans (*bai gong* 百工), who all use a *fa* to carry out their various tasks. Using *fa* is not a substitute for a lack of skills, on the opposite, it is indispensable to bring out one's talent.

> 雖至百工從事者，亦皆有法。百工為方以矩，為圓以規，直以繩，正以縣。無巧工不巧工，皆以此五者為法。
>
> Even when it comes to artisans who carry out their tasks, all of them also have their *fa*. Any artisan will use a carpenter's square to make a square, a pair of compasses for a circle, a carpenter's line marker for a straight line, and a wire weight for a right angle. Regardless their skills or lack of skills, they all must employ these five tools to obtain a perfect figure (*fa*). (*Mozi jiaozhu* 4: 20–21 ["Fayi"]).

Fa is both the adequate tool and the exemplary figure obtained by dint of this tool; *fa* ensures the proper way of proceeding, and nothing can be as accurate and as reliable. Dispensing with these devices and obtaining perfect geometrical figures remains theoretically possible, but the result would be either good fortune, or the expression of an exceptional skill that cannot be passed down to others. Even a mediocre worker with a shaky sense of dimensions will obtain more reliable measures than an exceptionally sharp-eyed artisan if he resorts to tools that the latter ignores. [6] The analogy is transparent with the art of ruling: it is sheer madness to count on one's natural abilities; the ruler must be well equipped and tooled up to design his state and shape his people As chapter 6, "You du" 有度, of the *Han Feizi* reminds us: "A skilled carpenter may intuitively find with his naked eye the size indicated by a measuring rope, yet he must still beforehand resort to a T-square in order to establish the standard measure" (巧匠目意中繩，然必先以規矩為度) (*Han Feizi* 6: 111). *Fa* is the only thing that enables the perfect geometric standard to be reproduced at will and by anyone. The skill lies not any longer in the hands of the worker but in the device he resorts to.

In the chapter "Tian zhi, shang" 天志上, Mozi draws an audacious analogy between craftsmen's tools and the *fa* of Heaven. He claims that he has attained the will of Heaven that he now possesses in the same way a wheelwright has a compass, or a carpenter a T-square (*Mozi* 26: 197). And just as these two artisans measure rectangular and circular shapes with their tools and see what fits and what does not, Mozi can evaluate the writings and sayings of the scholars thanks to the clear standard that applies to all-under-Heaven, and thereby dismiss wrong assumptions and falsehood. What this passage confirms is that *fa* takes on the meaning of a *cognitive tool*: it is what enables one to tease out what is right and true among a confusing array of rival assumptions, discourses and theories.[7] It is as if tools used by artisans were just specific instances of a more general idea of *fa*, which, as a concept, stands out as the ultimate touchstone that one needs when speaking, judging or working. To trace the influence of the idea of *fa* as a cognitive tool, a good case in point can be found in a passage of *Han Feizi*'s chapter 20, "Jie Lao" 解老, about T-squares and compasses (*gui ju* 規矩). After explaining that every creature has a shape, a size, a degree of solidity, a weight and a color, and that such properties enable to determine them, the author introduces the idea that every affair in this world can be measured and evaluated by appropriate compasses and squares. This whole section in the chapter makes the transition from geometry to politics and concludes: "There is none amid the myriad things that does not have its T-square and compass" 萬物莫不有規矩 (*Han Feizi* 20: 422).

---

[6] The memorable story of Wheelwright Bian in the *Zhuangzi* undermines the assumption that the possession of a tool like a pair of compasses suffices to carve out perfect circles such as wheels. Tools are one thing, acquired competence, body-embedded know-how and personal experience another one; see *Zhuangzi* 13: 358 ("Tian Dao" 天道). It is also one of many tales in the *Zhuangzi* that saps the idea that proper tools render human qualities redundant; on the contrary, the paradigm of compasses and squares tend to destroy natural drives and agility. For a comment on Wheelwright Bian's story from the perspective of artisans in early China, see Barbieri-Low 2007: 51.

[7] For an engaging comparison of views of standards (*fa*) and Heaven in the "Tian zhi" triplet and the "Fa yi" chapter, see Standaert 2013.

The two extracts of the *Mozi* quoted above (from chapters "Fayi" and "Tianzhi, shang) that stressed the need to rely on fixed standards may well have been a launching pad propelling *fa* toward the political sphere (cf. Jiang 2021: 142–47). They make an unprecedented advocacy of *measure*, held as a paradigm of a precise, efficacious, rational and unsurpassable way of working. And, by judging from its long legacy in the history of Chinese political thought, these two extracts could be regarded as the birth certificate of technocracy.[8] Over the course of the fourth century BCE, a terminology developed around the term *fa* to designate fixed and objective references (*fadu* 法度: measure; *fashi* 法式: model, standard); even today "compasses and squares" (*guiju* 規矩) still designate norms and rules. Such devices are conducive to an apprehension of reality in terms of figures, numbers and quantities. The geometrical reference of *fa* became a paragon of adequation, a pattern unfiltered by the biases and distortions of human subjectivity.[9] Around the same time, the political measures that were taken in Qin in order to obtain the standardization of units of length, weight, and volume used in the kingdom were plowing the same furrow (see more in Korolkov, Chap. 7, this volume).

In the wake of the Mohist conceptual thrust, the *Shēnzi, Shangjunshu, Shènzi* and *Han Feizi* all took up the geometrical imagery of circles and squares and, on the basis of these analogies, shaped a vision of laws and statutes defined as objective *measures*. Norms associated to numbers apply to officials (quantifying their endeavors and achievements), to merits and offenses, and to deeds and words (measuring if performance matches the task undertaken, and if the task matches the initial statement). The idea of applying to the government apparatus yardsticks, figures and numbers was already hinted at in the *Mozi*.

> 故當是時，以德就列，以官服事，以勞殿賞，量功而分祿，故官無常貴，而民無終賤。
>
> In the present age, ranks must be granted in consideration of one's virtue, assignments must be given according to the office, rewards must be bestowed in function of the efforts one has expended. Measure achievements and then distribute emoluments. Thus, office holders will not be constantly esteemed, and commoners will not be forever debased. (*Mozi* 8: 46 ["Shang xian, shang" 尚賢上])

In keeping with this orientation, Shen Buhai may be the earliest author to introduce didactic similes of tools in order to explain statecraft as a construction work (see

---

[8] Note that the very idea, taken from the *Mozi*, of a proper way of governing by dint of instruments taking measures or tracing figures offered other possibilities than the ideal of an amoral objectivity: one of this possibility is visible in the *Mencius*, which reminds keen eyes still need a pair of compasses or a T-square to trace perfect circles and right-angled figures, just like benevolent people still need to learn about the way of the ancient wise kings (see *Mengzi* 7.1: 162) The *Mencius* subverts the meaning of the tool analogy that develops in *fa*-centered discourses: far from relying on tools to demonstrate the superiority of a neutral and non-subjective way of governing, he moralizes the very meaning of measuring instruments by introducing the universal standard of ancient morality.

[9] In chapter "You du," the *Han Feizi* also uses as an expressive analogy with *fa* the *sinan* 司南, a compass that indicates the axes of time and space and prevents one from straying (不遊意於法之外, *Han Feizi* 6: 111).

also Yu Zhong, Chap. 2, this volume). He combines the lexical field of weighing tools, measurement devices and mechanisms (*ji* 筴→機 and *shu* 樞) with the semantics of political authority (cf. Creel 1974 : 354 n.2). The figure of the ruler is not that of a cultural hero or a charismatic chief, no mention of exploits whatsoever appears in his credit. The ruler is simply likened to someone (like a trader or a merchant) equipped with a weighing balance whose fixed system of reference automatically reveals the exact weight of something without any action on his part. This new terminology stands at the core of the mechanistic horizon of statecraft.

> 君必有明法正義若懸權衡以稱輕重，所以一群臣也。
>
> The ruler must have clear standards and straight principles, just like someone suspending the plates of a balances in order to gauge the weight of something. Therewith he unifies his ministers. (Creel 1974: 352–53)

Shen Buhai imagines the governing apparatus like a montage, the result of an assemblage of various mechanisms that produce automatic reactions, predictable effects and reliable results.[10] The ruler himself, likened to a scale, is also envisioned as a mirror (objectively reflecting what stands before him), a pivot, or a door hinge (*ji* 機) preserving the state with the simple twist of a short metal piece.

In keeping with the *Mozi* and the *Shēnzi, the Shangjunshu* develops notions heretofore unrelated to the art of ruling, centered on the ideal of accurate measures and objective references that cannot be questioned. Chapter 14 "Xiu quan" 修權 is a good example of the major concern for exactitude and objectivity. It deploys a lexicon that contains all the key terms that were to gradually structure the new political imagination. The main notions used in this chapter to account for the necessity of objective references with which no one can tamper refer to the act of weighing,[11] to the act of measuring the size or the length of an object.[12] Such concrete and trivial actions become under the author's brush a series of strokes that delineate what is expected from a ruler and his men: by dint of recurring and didactic analogies, measuring, counting and weighing become a paradigm of political action, in contrast to teaching, morally transforming or carrying out ritual actions. The merchant's and the artisan's way of working (paradoxically two social roles held in contempt and suspicion elsewhere in the *Shangjunshu*) [13] serve as templates to explain what is a *fa*

---

[10] See for instance the passages on tallies (*fu* 符) in *Shēnzi* 1(4), (Creel 1974: 330 and 346–47), or the one on the use of names, compared to the main cord of the net (*gang* 綱), which enables to retrieve in an effortless motion everything that can be caught between heaven and earth (*ibid.*)

[11] Among other terms repeatedly employed in the *Shangjunshu*, we find *xuan* 縣: suspend by a thread, a scale or a balance); 衡 *heng*: a weighing apparel, or the graduated arm of a steelyard; 程 *cheng*: to gauge, or weigh up.

[12] *Chicun* 尺寸 and *changduan* 長短.

[13] Shang Yang mentions in this chapter how merchants and traders (*shanggu* 商賈) proceed, as a didactic analogy for the ruler who should trust his tools and not his own inclinations. This of course stands in stark contrast to the strong anti-mercantile skew permeating the *Shangjunshu*, especially palpable in chapter 2 "Ken ling" 墾令. On the anti-merchant ideology in the *Shangjunshu*, see Pines 2021.

and how *fa* should become the rule to assess everything, from routine administrative tasks to annual tax payments.

夫釋權衡而斷輕重，廢尺寸而意長短，雖察，商賈不用，為其不必也。故法者，國之權衡也，夫倍[背] 法度而任私議，皆不知類者也。不以法論知能賢不肖者，惟堯，而世不盡為堯，是故先王知自議譽私之不可任也，故立法明分。[14]

> Determining what is the right weight while dispensing with scales and balance beams, or fixing the exact length while disregarding standard units of measure, that is what traders and merchants would never do, no matter how perceptive they may be, because such a method is not based on anything certain (*bi*). Now, *fa* is the scale and the balance beam of the state. If you reject standards and measures and solely rely on your personal judgement, it becomes impossible to classify anything. Only a [ruler of the magnitude of] Yao was able to tell without resorting to *fa* who were the competent and the worthy and who the worthless. Now, the world does not exactly reduce itself to a collection of Yaos, and that is why the wise rulers of the past, who knew they could not rely on personal judgement, reputation or individual interest, established models of reference and made clear divisions.

Fa is the objective counterpart of subjective dispositions, it is the impersonal operator that secures the exercise of authority regardless of the mindset or the abilities of the person in charge. In keeping with the rhetoric of *fa* based on the tool metaphor, qualities and actions should all be weighed and measured just like material objects. As we shall see below, instead of expecting good will or acquired loyalty, *fa* must make impossible acting in a malevolent, treacherous or negligent way. The rewards and punishments that automatically ensue from the examination of what is said and done in the light of what norms prescribe or proscribe are therefore not the expression of affective or moral reactions (such as gratitude for a loyal servant or anger against a wrongdoer), they are the objective tariffs determined by an unvarying standard.

3 Two Ways of Transcending Humanity and Controlling the World (Techniques of the Mind 心術 vs. Techniques of *fa* 法術)

Around the end of the fourth century BCE, a powerful answer to the faults and failures of human perception had crystallized in one the many trends of self-cultivation developed in early China.[15] The foundational texts of this tradition—most notably

---

[14] *Shangjunshu* 14: 83–84 ("Xiu quan " 修權). The comparison of *fa* with scales also appears in *Shènzi* (fragment 102; see Harris 2016: 129).

[15] On the diversity of cosmological visions and ways to attain a spirit-like or divine condition in early China, see Puett 2002. For a synoptic description of self-cultivation traditions, see Weingarten 2015. The fourth century BCE dating of this phenomenon is based on the dates for the "Nei ye 業 chapter of *Guanzi* between the end of the fourth century and the middle of the third century (see Kanaya 1987; Rickett 1998).

represented in a set of four treatises collected in the *Guanzi*[16]—imparted a set of mental techniques (*xinshu* 心術) based on the storage and regulation of the vital flow (*qi* 氣 and *jingqi* 精氣) and ultimately on its transformation through a physiological askesis into a Spirit-like condition (*shen* 神).[17] This orientation leading to the appropriation of divine abilities found within the self, appeared as a *personal* way of overcoming the disturbances created by anger and sadness, restlessness and lust.

In spite of, or because of, the structural opposition between this "personal way" and the paradigm of impersonality favored by *fa* thinkers, the *xinshu* trend of self-cultivation is particularly interesting to analyze in the light of the *fa* project of control of society, for the following reasons:

1) Chapters "Xinshu, shang" 心術上, "Xinshu, xia" 心術下 and "Baixin" 白心 stretch ideas conveyed in the earlier chapter "Nei ye" 內業 towards the perspective of domination and control and, among other terminological innovations, introduce the notion of *fa*.[18]

2) "Xinshu, shang" and "Xinshu, xia" reveal a host of formulae and ideas than can be found in an identical or similar form in the *Shēnzi* fragments. These fragments impart advice for the ruler that resonate with the *Guanzi* "techniques of the mind." Proper techniques of administration and control of information combine with a self-effacing attitude and a sense of secrecy on the part of the ruler and these advice and injunctions are couched in the same terminology we find in the *xinshu* chapters. Mental techniques and *fa* techniques converge at some stage in the ideal of a supremely impersonal and perfectly effective way of acting, transcending the flaws and laws of ordinary human conduct (cf. Lewis, Chap. 11, this volume).

3) Many similarities can also be spotted between these chapters and the *Shènzi*, to such an extent that many scholars have concluded that "Xinshu, shang" was written by Shen Dao and his alleged disciple Tian Pian 田駢.[19]

4) *Han Feizi*'s chapters 20 and 21 ("Jie Lao" 解老 and "Yu Lao" 喻老) link the ruler's method of domination with a personal ascetic discipline that finds many echoes in the "Xinshu" chapters, and not only in the *Laozi*, the latter being prob-

---

[16] This trend of thought seems to have exerted a strong traction among scholars and philosophers of the time, chiefly Mengzi and, later, Xunzi, who sojourned at the so-called Jixia 稷下 academy of Qi in Linzi 臨淄. On the impact of the *Guanzi*'s cluster of "Xinshu" chapters and the extent of the repository of early Jixia-oriented self-cultivation texts, among which many chapters of the *Huainanzi*, see Roth 1999, and Graziani 2009.

[17] On the significations, uses and transformations of *qi* 氣 in self-cultivation practices, see Gu 1987, Ma 1988, Li 1989, Qiu 1992, Le 1996, Zhou and Wang 1983, Roth 1999, Graziani 2009, and Graziani 2011.

[18] On the relationship between "Nei ye", "Xinshu, shang", "Xinshu, xia" and "Bai xin" from the perspective of this political swerve, see Rickett 1998; Roth 1994 and 1996; Graziani 2011.

[19] Qiu 1980, Wu 1986, Meng 1987. Sima Qian mentions the presence of Shen Dao among a group of scholars at the Jixia academy (*Shiji*: 74: 2346). Hu Jiacong rightly objects that if Shen Dao were the author of "Xinshu, shang," Liu Xiang would have had no reason to include this text in the *Guanzi*, at a time when copies of the Shènzi were still in circulation. I concur on this point with Hu Jiacong (Hu 2003: 307).

ably a common source of inspiration. The ruler is therein entreated to build up his inner potency (*de*), generate in himself a state of deep calm, keep his apertures empty and open himself to the outflow of cosmic energies. [20]

Let us now turn to the main divergence between these two competing paths toward absolute sovereignty, namely the personal way drawing on the inner resources of the self (heart-mind, vital breath, vital essence, organs) and the impersonal way of external tools (*fa* and *shu*).

Breathing practices, as repeatedly explained in the *Guanzi*'s "Xinshu" 心術 chapters, most notably chapter 49, "Inner training" ("Nei ye" 內業) help nurture, channel and refine the *qi*, while stillness, inaction and silence enable to ground or "center" oneself (*zhong* 中). The form of spiritual apex that is referred to by the obtainment of the Dao or the manifestation of *shen* is repeatedly celebrated, endowing the practitioner with an unsurpassed sharpness of sight and hearing and a quasi-divine capacity of gently subduing people and ordering the world.[21] But to enjoy this optimal state of authority and control, the beclouded vision or the jaundiced perspective on human affairs created by the influence of desires and emotions must first be transcended by a radical cleansing of the mind and an emotional askesis.[22] External tools (such as milfoil stalks used for divination) are no longer needed in order to enjoy clarity of vision;[23] laws, punishments and executions are insufficient to obtain order, and in the best case only peripheral when the ruler manages to produce a *jing*-suffused (精) or *shen*-replete mind, endowing him with authority, sagacity and charisma.[24] In chapter "Xinshu, shang," *fa* is defined as that which unifies executions, prohibitions and punishments. This unity is obtained by political authority (*quan* 權), which it itself the expression of the Way (*Guanzi* 36: 329). [25]

---

[20] See in particular *Han Feizi* 20: 396 ("Jie Lao"). The place and meaning of these two Laozi-based chapters in the corpus of the *Han Feizi* is not clear. This question is explored in Queen 2013.

[21] For instance: "When inner potency is perfected, sagacity emerges, and all things are fully grasped" 德成而智出，萬物畢得 (*Guanzi* 49: 397). For a similar idea in "Xinshu, xia" see *Guanzi* 37: 332. On the political resonance of the "Nei ye" see Pines 2009: 39–41.

[22] "If you can get rid of sadness and joy, pleasure and anger, desire and profit, the mind will revert to its original balance" 能去憂樂喜怒欲利，心奈反 (濟) [齊] (*Guanzi* 49: 397); "When the intact mind stands at the center, there is no way it can be muddled or obfuscated" 全心在中，不可蔽匿 (*Guanzi* 49: 404); on the regulation of emotions through poetry, music and ritual, see also *Guanzi* 49: 406. On the metaphor of the inn that must be fully cleansed so that a noble man can dwell therein, just like the spirit will materialize in the corporeal abode, see chapter "Xinshu, shang" (*Guanzi* 36: 327 and 330).

[23] See *Guanzi* 49: 405 ("Nei ye") and *Guanzi* 37: 332 ("Xinshu, xia").

[24] "Rewards are not enough to exhort to goodness, and punishments are not enough to reprimand wrongdoings" 賞不足以勸善，刑不足以懲過 (*Guanzi* 49: 404 ["Nei ye"]) The "Xinshu, xia" chapter also says that it is not with punishments that one can have the high hand on people (*Guanzi* 37: 333). About the insufficiency of rewards and punishments to make people love goodness and hate evil, see also *Guanzi* 37: 334. The "Xinshu, xia" further reminds that the key to social order is the ruler's capacity to still (*an* 安) his mind and order (*zhi* 治) his thoughts (*Guanzi* 37: 333).

[25] On the importance of patterns of the natural world in the social and political realm according to the *Shènzi*, see Harris 2016: 17–25.

The Way can be attained by the enlightened ruler who manages to reach through proper practice a perfect state of stillness and mental acuity. The proper technique for ruling people is therefore within the self and depends on one's personal efforts and discipline;[26] one has first to work on oneself in order to sharpen one's inner tools, as is eloquently asserted in the "Nei ye" 內業 chapter in the *Guanzi*.[27] If the ruler's mind and body are properly administered from the inside, if the inner work is brought to fruition, there should naturally ensue a state of order secured by *fa* in the outside world (Li 1994).

> 治心在中，治言出於口，治事加於人，然則天下治矣。一言得而天下服，一言定而天下聽，公之謂也。
> When the mind is well ordered inside, the mouth issues well-ordered words, and people deal with well-ordered affairs; then, everything in the world is well ordered. One word suffices to have the whole world submit; fix things in one word, and the whole world will listen: such is the meaning of an impartial authority (*gong* 公). (*Guanzi* 49: 401).

If the ruler understands the necessity to replicate within himself the monarchical structure of society by letting his mind take absolute control of his organs (*guan*) and apertures (Li 1994), he can reach universal rulership thanks to the almighty cognitive apparatus refined from within. Authority, unity and order are ensured thanks to the ruler's self-reformation process through practices of emotional cleansing and mental concentration. Chaos and violence are not suppressed by impersonal tools of command such as *fa*, but by the self-initiated production of a divine self, endowed with the potency of *shen*.

In the self-cultivation texts examined above, the solution devised in order to transcend ordinary human condition buffeted by surges of emotions and muddled by defective perceptions lies within the self and not in external techniques of command. As we shall see now, thinkers promoting *fa* endeavored to demonstrate the weakness of this reasoning and seek an institutional solution to the problem posed by the human factor. Against the option of a superior man, they opted for a purely objective way of restoring order and strengthening political power.

4 The End of Charisma? The Contingency of the Human Factor

In spite of common features sketched out in the previous section, the conceptual promotion of *fa* entails the redundancy of the outstanding human skills traditionally singled out as markers of superior rulership. The prevalence of *fa* over the way of

---

[26] On the idea that a noble man can find anything within himself to govern and need not seek external means, see Cook's analysis of the Guodian text *Cheng zhi wen zhi* 成之聞之 (Cook 2012: 602–03, 606–07, 614–16 and Cook 2019: 295–96).

[27] "If [the sage ruler] holds onto Unity and does not lose it, then he can lord it over everything" 執一不失，能君萬物 (*Guanzi* 49: 401); "When a still mind occupies the center, when eyes and ears are sharp and clear, when the four members are steady and solid, then you can become an abode for the essence" 定心在中，耳目聰明，四肢堅固，可以為精舍 (*Guanzi* 49: 400).

the human mind is mainly based on five arguments, each of which will be detailed hereafter: the system of hereditary succession, which is bound to produce less than perfect individuals on the throne; the frailty and finitude of human perception; the amount of information to be processed by a single source of authority; the stability of the state and its institutions; and, finally, the problem of human arbitrariness and the need to dissociate public command from subjective decisions.

In a political system of hereditary succession, rulers do no sit on the throne owing to their individual merit or past achievements. As they are never properly selected, one should expect them to be, statistically speaking, unredeemable mediocrities, definitely not cut out to undertake an ascetic program of self-cultivation, requiring moral strength, maturity and discipline. The political system must work around this initial and incontrovertible situation by devising a way to function by itself, thanks to its inner mechanisms.

There is however here in *fa*-thinkers' writings a discernible tension. The importance for the ruler to unconditionally submit to *fa* without putting into play his personal qualities is time and again challenged by the necessity of changing laws when new contexts demand realistic adaptation (evolution of demography, competition for resources, general conformity to orders, etc.) The way of governing men and organizing the state must keep pace with ever-changing circumstances; now these reforms are incumbent upon the ruler,[28] who is suddenly expected to be sufficiently clear-sighted to carry out adequate reforms and remain unswayed by conservative opposition. The unresolved discrepancy between modest expectations concerning average rulers and the high ambitions put in law-changing monarchs permeates *fa* texts.[29] Tensions aside, the default expectation of the *fa* thinkers was that most rulers remain mediocrities. The valorization of techniques, methods and savoir-faire in the art of ruling was evidently in the interest of court advisers and ministers who had to persuade the ruler not to intervene in the practical business of daily affairs (cf. Pines 2009: 102–06). The promotion of *fa* was a means to ensure that a good tool will be effective even when the artisan proves incompetent or unreliable. In the "ruler-centered" state (Lewis 1999: 597), which the *fa* thinkers eagerly accepted, the insistence on the objective approach in the art of ruling was a reasonable solution to the ruler's expected inadequacy. The stability of the state must depend on the objective properties of the system and not on the subjective qualities of the present incumbent.

The possibility of transmitting *fa* as opposed to a personal style of government allows for the longevity of the state and its resilience across generations of good, middling and bad rulers. Objective norms can be written down, copied, circulated

---

[28] See for instance *Han Feizi* 18: 334 ("Nan mian" 南面) ; *Shènzi*, fragments 78–79; Harris 2016: 124 and *Shangjunshu* 7:53 ("Kai sai" 開塞) "As situations change, current methods must vary accordingly" 世事變而行道異也; *Shangjunshu* 8:62 ("Yi yan" 壹言) and 18: 107 ("Hua ce" 畫 策). See more in Vogelsang, Chap. 12, this volume.

[29] See e.g. Pines, Chap. 1, Sect. 6 and Chap. 4, Sect. 3.3; Lewis, Chap. 11, and Song, Chap. 9, this volume.

and preserved by scribes and officials.[30] They can be shown, read, explained and verified in the presence of the people, thereby protecting both the laws and the people from unfair treatment by officials. *Fa* thus guarantees the possibility of handing over a solid political savoir-faire across generations, and averts the risk of having the whole state see its fate depend uniquely on the personal qualities of the heir accessing the throne.

> 夫離朱見秋豪百步之外，而不能以明目易人；烏獲舉千鈞之重，而不能以多力易人。夫聖人之存體性，不可以易人；然而功可得者，法之謂也。
>
> Li Zhu could spot a tiny hair from a hundred paces away, but he could not hand over his sharp vision to others; Wu Huo was able to lift a ton of weight,[31] but he could not pass on his formidable strength to others. Sages likewise cannot transfer to others their inherent nature. And yet, successes can be attained – such is the meaning of *fa*. (*Shangjunshu* 10: 66 ["Cuo *fa*" 錯法]).

For the authors of the *Shēnzi* and *Shènzi* fragments, as well as the *Shangjunshu* and *Han Feizi*, it is always too hazardous, if not foolish, to rely on the information provided by one's senses, however clear they may be. An exceptional mental sharpness can even prove detrimental in the end, as it may delude a ruler into thinking he can solve and sort out anything, without resorting to his informants or to administrative devices, while a mediocre man will more likely from the outset rely on tools and mechanisms that enable him to control his subjects, just as a man equipped with a sword and a shield will have more chance to stay alive than a man fighting with no other defense than his uncanny ability to dodge blows.[32] Precisely because some rulers are blessed with a unique clarity of mind, they might be tempted to impose a certain style of rulership and overstep their natural limits by meddling in every possible affair. As a general cautionary rule, it would be safe and wise to refuse to rely on the acuity of one's senses under any circumstances. The brighter the ruler, the greater the peril (see, e.g., *Shēnzi* warning in Creel 1974: 370). In the *Shènzi*, the ruler is entreated to shut off his senses, lest he should lend a complacent ear to individual opinions:

> 為人君者不多聽；據法倚數以觀得失。無法之言，不聽於耳。無法之勞，不圖於功。

---

[30] On the copying, storing and dispatching of written laws, see *Shangjunshu* 26: 142–44 ("Ding fen" 定分).

[31] Literally: a thousand *jun* 鈞, roughly thirty thousand pounds (*jin* 斤). The figure being here a hyperbole, it is more sensible to translate with an idiomatic equivalent.

[32] On the analogy of relying confidently on one's innate capacities with the ability to dodge blow and arrows, and face the enemy with bare hands, see the anecdote of the presumptuous monkey in the *Zhuangzi*: "When the pack of monkeys saw [the king of Wu], they dropped what they were doing in terror and scampered off to hide in the deep brush. But there was one monkey who, lounging about nonchalantly, picking at things, scratching, decided to display his skill to the king. When the king shot at him, he snatched hold of the flying arrows with the greatest nimbleness and speed. The king thereupon ordered his attendants to hurry forward and join in the shooting, and the monkey was soon captured and killed" (*Zhuangzi* 24: 645 ["Xu Wugui" 徐無鬼], transl. Watson 1968: 270).

He who is in charge of ruling men should not listen to everything around him. He relies on standards (*fa*) and sticks to quantitative data (*shu* 數) in order to apprehend success and failure. He should not lend his ear to speeches that are without norms (*fa*). He should not list among achievements undertakings that ignore standards (*fa*). (*Shènzi*, fragments 66–67; Harris 2016: 121).

The conclusion to be drawn from the repeated observations of the patent limitations of human cognitive abilities is expressed in a typical *Laozi*-style rhetoric: the clear-sighted ruler must make himself blind, the sharp-eared king must deafen himself.[33] Inspired by this provoking paradox, Shen Dao captures this idea in a rhyming formula:

諺云:不聽不明, 不能為王; 不瞽不聾, 不能為公。

A saying has it that without keen ears and sharp eyes, you cannot become the True Monarch, but if you can't make yourself deaf and blind, you cannot be impartial. (*Shènzi*, fragment 100; Harris 2016: 128–29).

The sheer volume of information makes it impossible for one single person to supervise and verify everything.[34] One should always bear in mind that ears cannot even grasp what is being whispered ten yards away, eyes cannot discern what takes place behind a thin curtain, and a lord cannot remain cognizant of all the scheming and plotting hatched in a middle-sized palace.[35] Instead of hoping to find in the ruler an exceptional mind innately graced with unsurpassed cognitive and sensory capacities, or rather than expecting a ruler to develop such capacities through a program of self-cultivation and then pattern the system of governance on such an ideal human type, it appears much more sensible to develop cognitive instruments that do not require a miracle, and that anyone can use. The *Shènzi* is one of the earliest sources to assert that a proper tool used by a mediocre intelligence obtains results superior to that attained by an exceptional mind only counting on itself (e.g., fragment 120; Harris 2016: 133). *Han Feizi* elaborates further:

大為人主而身察百官,則日不足,力不給。且上用目則下飾觀。上用耳則下飾聲。上用慮則下繁辭。先王以三者為不足,故舍己能而因法術,審賞罰。

If the ruler of men were to inspect in person all his officials, he could spend all his days and that would still not be enough, as his strength would not suffice. Moreover, when the sovereign uses his own eyes, his subjects will embellish what he is given to see; if he wants to listen by himself, his subjects will embellish what he is given to hear. And when the ruler uses his own mind, they will complicate the matter by speaking profusely. The ancient kings deemed these three methods inadequate, and therefore they dispensed with their personal abilities and instead followed objective norms and techniques of government, focusing on rewards and punishments. (*Han Feizi* 6: 107 ["You du"]).

---

[33] See, for instance, the Shen Buhai-related section of the *Lüshi chunqiu* 呂氏春秋 (17.3 ["Ren shu" 任數]), in which the author sets out to prove that a ruler who does away with his own senses is in a better position to stay informed. Control of information should not be done by personal inspection but by means of such instruments as reports and statistics (Creel 1974: 69 and Yu Zhong, Chap. 2, this volume).

[34] *Shènzi*, fragment 42–43; Harris 2016: 128–29, and p. 59 for Harris's take on this passage. See also *Han Feizi* 6:107 ("You du").

[35] See *Shēnzi* fragment in Creel 1974: 373.

The concept of *fa* enables to bypass the problem of individual limitations by endowing a ruler with techniques of command that draw their strength neither from his virtue and charisma (*de* 德),[36] nor his vital force (*qi* 氣 and *jing* 精), nor his spiritual acumen (*shen* 神), but from unchanging things: the structural vulnerabilities of his subjects and the efficacy of his tools. The discrepancy between the body politic and the body of the ruler calls for a technology of an unsurpassed scale in order to obtain that kind of universal coverage. Pro-*fa* texts thus favor the total abdication of personal abilities in the exercise of authority. Rather than endeavoring to hone his eyesight and sharpen his ears, a ruler would be better inspired to control the eyesight and hearing of all his subjects, complemented by an arsenal of far-reaching instruments.[37] The tool trumps the agent, a compass surpasses any skilled hand; the middling ruler with the right toolbox supersedes the meddling ruler who exclusively relies on his personal talent or his spiritual acumen.

> 釋法術而心治，堯不能正一國。去規矩而妄意度，奚仲不能成一輪。廢尺寸而差短長，王爾不能半中。使中主守法術，拙匠守規矩尺寸，則萬不失矣。
>
> Even a Yao could not order a single country if he did away with *fa* and techniques of control and relied on his own mind to govern. If [paragon wheelwright] Xi Zhong had discarded his square and compass and randomly followed any thought that crossed his mind when taking measures, he wouldn't have been able to complete a single wheel. Without a measuring rod to mark differences (*ci* 差) between objects of various length, the [paragon carpenter] Wang Er would not even have succeeded every other time. Even average rulers and mediocre artisans can never fail, provided the former preserve their standards and techniques and the latter their measuring tools (lit.: their compasses and squares, *chicun guiju* 尺寸規矩). (*Han Feizi* 27: 542 ["Yong ren" 用人]).

Among the three major features that characterize figures of rulership—charisma, cunning and ruthlessness—theories of *fa* dispense with the former, and combine the other two in order to sculpt the new face of power.[38] Indeed, and paradoxically perhaps, the enlightened ruler chooses not to use, and much less to display, his own sagacity[39] or his personal opinions. If he can be said to be enlightened or clear-

---

[36] On the notion of *de* 德 as charisma or *mana*-like influence producing compliance and obedience, see for instance Kryukov 1995 and Van Norden 2013: 135. On the charismatic authority and the power of *de* to inspire the people, see Cook 2019: 291–93.

[37] Shen Dao argues: "If you relinquish proper methods and techniques of government, if you dispense with instruments of measure and weight and seek in one man only the comprehension of everything that takes place in the world, then who on earth will ever be up to the task?" 棄道術，舍度量，以求一人之識識天下，誰子之識能足焉 (*Shènzi* fragments 52 and 107, Harris 2016: 117 and 130). See also *Han Feizi* 14: 283 ("Jian jie shi chen" 姦劫弒臣); 21: 458 ("Yu Lao"); 24: 520 ("Guan xing" 觀行).

[38] On these three elementary forms of social domination, see Graeber and Wengrow 2021: 362–70.

[39] We find one nuance in *Shènzi*: "A discerning ruler never initiates tasks or apportions duties by any criterion other than intelligence" 明君動事分職，必由慧 (fragment 25; Harris 2016: 111); this seems to be the only instance where a standard procedure such as *fa* does not replace personal judgement. On this difference with Han Fei, who claims that in order to hire and assess officials, *fa* suffices, see *Han Feizi* 6: 92 ("You du") and, as a good description of the *xingming* 刑名 ("title and performance") process, see *Han Feizi* 5: 81 ("Zhu dao" 主道) and 7: 126 ("Er bing" 二柄); see also Yang 2013: 60–61.

sighted (*ming* 明), it is only because he is wise enough to remain at rest in the shade while espying others toiling under his multiplying eyes.[40] Domination is much rather characterized by the exclusive alliance of two forms of control, the control of violence (to wit the monopoly of coercive force),[41] encapsulated in the closely related terms *fa* and *xing* 刑, and, secondly, the control of knowledge, associated with a certain sense of secrecy, assured by techniques of information and surveillance, and summarized in the term *shu* 術 (on which see more in Song, Chap. 9, this volume).

The coercive force of properly defined norms of behavior and methods of management (*fa* and *shu*) can endow the ruler with enhanced sensory organs that can spread everywhere without the risk of vital exhaustion. Foreshadowing the today pervasive technology of global observation and surveillance (face-recognition cameras, phone tapping, computer surveillance, covert listening devices, GPS tracking, DNA sensors, etc.), the *Han Feizi* calls for the development of techniques of inspection of the deeds and words of everyone in the kingdom, forcing every subject to become a relay point and an extension of the ruler's personal body. The discrepancy between what a ruler can do when he relies on his sole resources and what he is able to achieve when he brings into play the instruments of *fa* and *shu* can be aptly compared to the difference between what an archer is able to catch with his arrows and what he can effortlessly capture with a hunting net spread across a whole valley.[42]

Finally, *fa* is supposed to erase all impressions of human arbitrariness in decisions, judgments and verdicts. By granting a universal validity to norms defined as *fa*, thereby depersonalizing the voice of authority, sovereign power remains protected and does not betray the all too human condition of those who exercise political or judicial authority. *Fa* ensures the triumph of universal subjection over individual subjectivity. The strength of a state lies in the necessity of its statements. If a same crime is punished according to different standards and two different penalties are meted out, or if the same meritorious deed is gratified with two different rewards, the contingency of its statements contradicts the political necessity to appear as absolutely incontrovertible, making everyone feel nothing can be changed about decisions and judgements.[43]

---

[40] See also *Han Feizi* 15: 300 ("Wang zheng" 亡徵) where the author warns about the fatal threats awaiting those who count on their intelligence and stratagems instead of relying on laws and strictures. For Han Fei, the law as a tool of government is systematically opposed to intelligence and human penetration; on the position of shady retreat from where the ruler observes, see chapter 8: 156 ("Yang quan" 揚權). See also chapter 24 "Guan xing" (*passim*) on the necessity of tools and instruments to accomplish what the natural instruments of the human body (the *guan*) are unable to achieve by themselves, and also *Han Feizi* 6: 111 ("You du").

[41] With the reservation that, for Shen Buhai, legal violence is not advocated, in contradistinction to the *Shangjunshu* and the *Han Feizi*. On this moderation in favor of persuasion see Creel 1974: 91.

[42] On the technology of the hunting-net (*luo* 羅) to catch everything, see *Han Feizi* 38: 914 ("Nan san" 難三).

[43] See *Shènzi* fragments 61–65 (Harris 2016: 120 and for a commentary of the passage 32–35).

Through constant analogies with measuring instruments, *fa* ingrains the idea of an undisputed authoritative reference that is delivered not by one law-maker deemed wiser or superior, but by an external instrument whose verdict cannot be challenged. Only the homogeneity of decisions taken through impersonal devices can ensure the proper administration of human society.

5   The Redundancy of Social Virtues

No more necessary than the ruler's spiritual acumen are the virtuous dispositions of the people. As long as order is secured by the deterrent impact exerted by heavy punishments, the obligation to denounce crimes, and the collective character of penal liability (*lianzuo* 連坐), practically they will have no other choice than to act in conformity with public norms and laws.

The ideological crusade for *fa* comes from the observation that expecting people to behave in a loyal and honest way is a dangerous, if not irrational, postulate. Not that both things are impossible but, statistically speaking, it would be foolish to count on it, and one cannot let the chasm widen between the number of needed officials and the number of morally suitable persons.[44] Shen Dao may be the first to contend that the ideal of the ruler's moral and intellectual influence must give way to institutional devices in order to secure political authority and social order (Yang 2013: 60). Coming after centuries of failed attempts to restore order and security through ritual observance or the cultivation of virtues, Shen Dao pushes to its logical conclusion the idea that an external device forcing people to behave as is required for the security of the collective and the reinforcement of state power is the most effective method.[45] Only *fa* understood as a set of mechanisms can achieve in a perennial way what a scarcity of rulers and a minority of subjects has managed to achieve for a short period of time. Qualities that may be prized among the Ru 儒 such as kindness to others, solidarity with one's kin, unconditional affection for parents, compassion for the people, an aesthetic sense of manners and decorum, or a vast textual knowledge of the past, are deliberately left out of the picture. It is not only that they are hard to produce in people: most of the time such virtues appear

---

[44] *Han Feizi* 49: 1109 ("Wu du" 五蠹): "Today, there may be at most ten upright and trustworthy men-of-service within the state, whereas hundreds of offices need filling in. If you make it mandatory to appoint only honest and faithful men-of-service, there will never be enough personnel to staff these official positions. ... Hence, the method of the clear-sighted ruler is not to seek wise men but to unify *fa*, not to revere trustworthiness but to firm up his ruling techniques." 今貞信之士不盈於十，而境內之官以百數，必任貞信之士，則人不足官......故明主之道，一法而不求智，固術而不慕信。

[45] On the use of external devices prevailing on inner qualities, see Harris's commentary about *Shènzi*'s fragments 7–9 and 119 in Harris 2016: 55 and 58.

detrimental to political stability; they undermine the awe-inspiring authority of the state and favor a slack interpretation of laws.[46]

Fa is not only the institutional rival of virtue. It must also be understood as a device to detect offenders. The key properties of *fa* (unremittable laws, universal obligations, uniform measures) modify the psychology of subjects in a way that renders impossible or overly dangerous their endeavors to further their own private ends at the expense of the state.

是故有法度之制者，不可巧以軸偽［詐偽］。

For this reason, when there is a system of laws and procedures, clever ruses based on deceit become impossible. (*Guanzi* 46: 386 ["Ming fa" 明法]; trans. Rickett 1998: 160)

Fa supposedly avoids the risk of having to rely on the loyalty of servants by instituting an objective form of trust and efficiency, regardless of the inner dispositions and ambitions of those who are at the service of the monarch. According to the logic of *fa*, "when a wise man rules the kingdom, he does not expect people to be good out of consideration for him, but he uses the means to prevent them from doing him wrong" 聖人之治國，不恃人治為吾善也，而用其不得為吾非也 (*Han Feizi* 50: 1141 ["Xian xue" 顯學]). There may be indeed a few people who will be spontaneously good, but a ruler must act according to the lot of common men, and discount the tiny virtuous minority that does not need the coercive frame of a punitive legislation:

夫必恃自直之箭，百世無矢；恃自圜之木，千世無輪矣。自直之箭，自圜之木，百世無
有一，　然而世皆乘車射禽者何也?隱栝之道用也。雖有不恃隱栝而有自直之箭，自
圜之木，良工弗貴也。　何則?乘者非一人，射者非一發也。不恃賞罰而恃自善之民，
明主弗貴也。何則?國法不可失，　而所治非一人也。故有術之君，不隨適然之善，
而行必然之道。

If one had to depend on bamboo sticks that are naturally straight to make shafts, one could wait a thousand years and still not get a proper arrow. Similarly, if, to make wheels, one counted on perfectly circular boles in nature, one could let eons pass by and still not obtain a single wheel. And yet, in every generation, people do shoot birds and ride carts: how come? It is because artisans use tools that can rectify the natural shape of things. Though one may find bamboo shafts that are straight by nature or tree boles that are of themselves perfectly round, a seasoned artisan will not regard them as highly valuable. Why is that? Because the activity of riding carts is not limited to one single man and the action of shooting is not limited to one single arrow. Likewise, a clear-sighted ruler shall not excessively value people who, because they show themselves spontaneously good, needn't be held in check by the system of rewards or punishments. And why is that? The reason is that the *fa* of a kingdom should never be relinquished, since those who must be ruled are not limited to a single individual. A sovereign endowed with proper techniques will not pursue the contingent nature of moral excellence, but will proceed according to necessity. (*Han Feizi* 50: 1142 ["Xian xue"])

The lesson is clear enough for the fine-eared ruler: if it befalls upon you to manage the multitude, do not take moral exceptions as a yardstick, do not set out to find

---

[46] See for instance *Han Feizi* 30: 563 ("Nei chu shuo shang" 內儲說上) "With an excess of love and care, laws cannot be maintained. If they are not overawed, inferiors will encroach upon the ruling sphere's authority." 愛多者則法不立，威寡者則下侵上。

providential men, abandon all hope to rule a nation of sages, just act as if you had to bridle a pack of thugs. *Fa* refers to the punitive mechanisms of compliance and obedience that are set up to curb people into docile subjection. Collective penal responsibility among the population or mandatory reports of one's activities reinforce the fear of being caught in the nets of laws,[47] while the deliberate physical heaviness of punishments (Pines 2016: 12) deters people from flouting publicly issued norms of conduct. In this perspective, *fa* is clearly a synonym of penal law (*xing* 刑):

> 恃人之為吾善也，境內不什數，用人不得〔為〕非，一國可使齊。為治者用眾而舍寡，故不務德而務法。
>
> Were the ruler to count on others to behave in a good way, he may only find in the whole country a paltry handful of people, whereas if he manipulates them so that they cannot act in the opposite way, the whole country can be put in order. To rule a country, one should thus use what suits the great majority and ignore what is only good for a tiny minority. Consequently, he does not devote his efforts to virtue, but only devotes to *fa*. (*Han Feizi* 50: 1141–42 ["Xian xue"])

Dissuasion is safer than discussion. The ruler can be spared the vagaries of virtue. The author observes that the majority of people do not readily assent to moral norms and infers (very arguably though) that the only way to ensure order is to resort to deterrents and coercive force for everybody. *Fa* has to take over, just like a stern master replaces an indulgent mother doting on her children (*Han Feizi* 50: 1141 ["Xian xue"]).[48] *Fa* is not supposed to produce good people, it is only devised to stop people from behaving badly or boldly. It is held and hailed as the only proper method to achieve peace and prosperity because it neutralizes the harmful potential of individual dispositions and extracts the pure force of energies and ambitions toward common goals.

The parallel between precision instruments foiling fraud and public norms dictating right conducts is developed in *Shènzi* in order to show that virtue can find its counterpart in objective mechanisms.

> 有權衡者，不可欺以輕重；有尺寸者，不可差以長短；有法度者，不可巧以詐偽。
>
> He who holds a beam balance with pans cannot be tricked about weight. He who uses measures such as inches and feet cannot be cheated about length. And he who uses norms (*fa*) and measures (*du*) cannot be hoodwinked by any craft or cunning. (*Shènzi* fragment 102; Harris 2016: 129)

Instead of relying on people's loyalty, it is wiser to establish an objective form of trust through a legal apparatus that compels the honoring of contracts and the fulfillment of obligations (*Shènzi* fragment 73; Harris 2016: 123), just like it is safer to rely on standardized measurements to assess a volume or a weight of a merchandise and not put too much trust in the seller's saying. Loyalty is not the strict observance of moral norms, on the contrary it is publicly proclaimed norms that define loyalty by rendering treason or treachery impossible. This vision is shared by the author(s)

---

[47] See *Shangjunshu* chapter 17 ("Shang xing" 賞刑) and Pines 2016: 11.

[48] Do note that, in a perplexing contrast with this passage, the good ruler is likened to a loving and caring mother in *Han Feizi* 20: 412 ("Jie Lao").

of the *Guanzi* chapter "Ming fa" 明法 and its exegetical sequel "Ming fa jie" 明法解, both very close to the spirit and the phraseology of *Han Feizi*'s chapter 6, "You du": "If you use a steelyard with a graduated arm and a sliding weight to weigh something, there is no way you can be cheated about the right weight" 有權衡之稱者，不可欺以輕重 (*Guanzi* 46: 386 ["Ming fa"]).

6   The Coordination of Public and Private Interests through *fa*

In a similar reasoning with that of Adam Smith in *The Wealth of Nations* (Smith 1976), Han Fei contends that, for the sake of the common good, it is more sensible to rely on egoistic instincts rather than on generosity.[49] A wise ruler is able to control the complex dynamics of individual interests, and exploit their constant clash by manoeuvring the primeval instincts of fear and greed. "The (nature of the) link between the state's interest and private interests determines if a state will survive or perish" 故公私之交，存亡之本也 (*Shangjunshu* 14: 85 ["Xiu quan"]). The legal institution is rooted in this almost universal tendency of human nature to hunger for enjoyment and honours, and to abhor danger and pain.[50] So much so that if human venality is the original source of conflict and chaos, it eventually becomes, by dint of *fa*, the only means of establishing order and security.

A sound and steady political machinery must therefore rely on the instrumental handling of men's private passions and the shared sense of self-preservation.[51] Against all expectations of a sovereign morally educating his people and endeavoring to suppress in them egoistic and self-serving instincts, the discerning head of state must be able to do without virtue and morals,[52] and draw his strength from the people's cravings for fame and wealth, as well as from their visceral fright of suffer-

---

[49] Jean Levi was the first to draw this parallel in a study dealing with market economy and democratic despotism; see Levi 1992/93. On a comparison between Adam Smith and Shen Dao's reasonings on individual interest, see Harris 2016: 27–28.

[50] See *Shangjunshu* 9.3 translated and commented in Pines 2016: 9 : "Likes and dislikes are the root of rewards and penalties. The disposition of the people is to like ranks and emoluments and to dislike punishments and penalties. The rulers sets up the two in order to guide the people's will and to establish whatever he desires." And Pines adds: "To properly motivate the people, the ruler should employ a combination of positive (ranks, rewards, emoluments) and negative (punishments, penalties) incentives. A clear, fair and unequivocal implementation of these two will direct the people to the pursuits desired by the ruler (…)" (*ibid.*)

[51] On the ruler's need to employ people by orchestrating their private interests, and the dangers of emulating virtue, see Harris 2016: 41–43.

[52] For a purely moral view of rulership, see the position held by Mencius in his conversation with Gongsun Chou 公孫丑 (*Mengzi* 12.13: 296): the love of goodness (*hao shan* 好善) suffices to qualify a man to rule even if he is not perspicacious (*zhi lü* 知慮) nor knowledgeable (*wen shi* 聞識). Do note that this view is fairly nuanced in *Mengzi* 7.1: 162 "Goodness alone is not sufficient to govern" 徒善不足以為政.

ing and perishing. Selfish dispositions can be exploited once they are made compatible with the ruler's own objectives. People may have many desires but strictures and statutes ensure that there are only two ways of achieving them, by merits won in war and agriculture.[53] *Fa* redefines the things one wants to pursue and the things one will shun from as the only means to satisfy fundamental and universal inclinations. What accrues the ruler's wealth or strength must thus be firmly tied to the fundamental drives of humans by promotions and penalties, so that purely private preferences can only be congruent with public norms. That is how the state's interest and people's private profit are brought in tune with one another. It is in the light of the duality of *si* 私 and *gong* 公, along with the attempt to transcend this original contradiction, that we should read the following lines of the *Shènzi*:

> 故蓍龜，所以立公識也；權衡，所以立公正也；書契，所以 立公 信也；度量，所以立公審也；法制禮籍，所以立公義也。凡立公，所以棄私也。
>
> Therefore, milfoil and tortoise shell divination are how decisions are recorded publicly. Balance weights and beams are how true weight is established publicly. Documents and contracts are how trust is established publicly. Standardized measurements are how length and volume are determined publicly. Laws, institutions, rituals, and documents are how norms are set up publicly. In all these cases, establishing public standards is the means by which private interests are eliminated. (*Shènzi*, fragment 73; Harris 2016: 123)

In this passage, the author explains that tools, balance weights and beams, documents and contracts, laws, institutions and rituals must all be *li gong* 立公,[54] in other words established as a public principle (or "publicly established" as translated by Eirik Lang Harris), but also, at least ideally, instituted in all impartiality, in consideration of the public good.[55] Only private desires that run afoul of to the demands of the state must be discouraged and banned.

> 法之功，莫大使私不行；君之功，莫大於使民不爭。今立法而行私，是私與法爭，其亂甚於無法。立君而尊賢，是賢與君爭，其亂甚於無君。故有道之國，法立則私善不行，君立則賢者不尊，民一於君，事斷於法，國之大道也。
>
> The greatest merit of *fa* is to prevent people from pursuing their private interests. Just as the greatest achievement of a ruler is to put a stop to quarrels among the people. Now, if you establish laws (*fa*) but give way to private interests, it comes down to putting them in conflict. The chaos that results thereof is even worse than the absence of *fa*. Similarly, if you

---

[53] The topic of positive incentives with the fruitful exploitation of egoistic interests in *Shangjunshu* is carefully explained and analyzed in Pines 2016. "It had to be an exclusive system of social, economic and political advancement" based on three principles, "clarity, fairness, and exclusivity" (Pines 2016: 25).

[54] Cf. *Shènzi* fragment 23; Harris 2016: 110.

[55] De facto, nothing precludes the ruler from issuing ordinances and prohibitions that exclusively favor his own individual interest at the expense of the common weal. *Li gong* 立公 indicates before all that what the ruler stipulates must be universally applied and publicly acknowledged. *Gong* does not refer to universal patterns organizing the natural world nor to a common good defined by *vox populi*, it just designates the mandatory character of deeds and decisions that favor the interest of the ruler and his administration, based on a mechanism taking advantage of anthropological constants (greed and fear). I translate *gong* as 'public' in such a perspective: it is public because it can be advertised, proclaimed, and circulated. For a different view of *gong*, see Goldin 2013: 10–11; cf. Pines, Chap. 4, Sect. 3, this volume.

install a lord as a ruler and simultaneously honor his servants as worthy men, you just pit them one against the other, and the ensuing chaos is worse than if there were no ruler at all. The proper way to run a state consists in instituting *fa* so that privately pursuing one's own good becomes impossible; it consists in establishing a ruler so that no one else can be revered as worthy. When the ruler brings together the people into a single entity, when affairs are sorted out by *fa* and nothing else, then the state has found the true Way. (*Shènzi*, fragments 75–77; Harris 2016: 123)

Fa is introduced here as a way of binding together individual actions and the supreme principle of order ("the true Way" or "the great Way" 大道). By constantly exploiting the distressing possibility for any subject of enduring pain or a dishonorable and violent death, by luring people into a realm of wealth and fame through strictly defined meritorious deeds,[56] *fa* achieves the convergence of private interest and public norms, the coincidence of individual drives and state priorities. It does not suppress inborn tendencies and biased conducts, but prevents them from leading the game of human interactions.

Fa comprises then all the methods, standards, regulations and procedures that prevent an individual put in a position of public responsibility from carrying out a course of action or take a decision in the light of his own interest, or rather, to be more accurate, of his own benefit at the detriment of the ruler's good. It forces every subject to establish a distinction between his instinctive unmediated appetites and his rational interest as a person subjected to laws and liable for his actions. This second-degree interest produced by the clear knowledge of legal statutes is a form of benefit that prompts people to integrate in their plans the interest of the state and to never ignore or antagonize it. For instance, recoiling from or refusing to engage in combat out of the fear of being maimed, of suffering or of losing life is the kind of behavior dictated by one's primal instinct of self-preservation; but from the moment *fa* stipulates that warriors who prove themselves brave in combat will be rich and famous, and cowardly soldiers will be shamed and executed, with punishments extending to their relatives,[57] there arises a state-reshaped form of personal interest.

夫農，民之所苦；而戰，民之所危也。　犯其所苦，行其所危者，計也。故民生則計利，死則慮名。

Farming is a thing that people regard as repulsive; as to war, they find it perilous. If they (nonetheless) commit to what they dislike and set out to do what they find perilous, it is due to the calculation they make (about the potential profit). That is the reason why when people (want to secure) their life, they calculate their own interest, and if they (accept) to die, it is in expectation of the fame (to be gained from losing life on the battlefield). (*Shangjunshu* 6: 46 ["Suan di" 算地]).

The pressure induced by *fa* on basic human characteristics (fear of suffering, lust for wealth, fame and rank) redefines at the ruler's will the objects one will endeavor to obtain and the behaviors one will prudently abstain from. When backed up by the sovereign power to hurt, *fa* appears in this context as an administrative tool that

---

[56] On the importance of *ming* as "name" and "fame" see Pines 2016, in particular 7–8.

[57] See *Shangjunshu*, in particular chapter 18; for the most relevant passages, see Pines 2016: 13–14 and Pines 2017: 216 (18.3).

imprints a publicly defined and controlled form to the raw energies loosely circulating in the social body; it is the levers (*er bing* 二柄) forcing conflicting interests to converge in public unity.

We can thus tease out three external sources of *fa* :

1) The force of deterrence exerted by laws stem from the psycho-biological structure of human beings. Regardless of the specific content of desires and fears in every individual, inbuilt tendencies in humans take the form of a structural polarity: they love gratification and loathe violence, they seek pleasure and shun pain (aside from the problematic exception of sages and criminals). This duality, when properly maneuvered, institutionally translates into the dual aspects of *fa*, rewards and punishments, which in turn allow for the blending of public benefits and individual preferences. It enables the ruler to dispense with the task of eliminating the plagues of selfishness, treachery and greed through tireless efforts of public education.

2) The core values that *fa* seeks to preserve are not moral principles or personal virtues, but rather functional features of the state: public order and security, strength and authority. Such qualities do not dictate any specific content[58] regarding the empirical multiplicity of statutes and ordinances: it is incumbent upon the ruler to prescribe what favors the state's best interest in a given situation, provided he does not violate the fundamental nature of the human heart and remains abreast of the realities of his time.[59]

3) A persistent inspiration for devising *fa* is a human-made reality, as opposed to something observed or provided by nature, yet exempt from any trace of personality or subjectivity: an impersonal measuring device, repeatedly featured by analogies, metaphors and parallels with the daily working instruments of artisans and merchants. With the imposition of this new paradigm, the supreme value in the political realm becomes that of *measure*. The major change of paradigm takes place here precisely: from the guiding value of moral exemplarity incarnated by certain individual figures located in a remote past, to that of all-embracing and constantly present impersonal standards. Moral codes of conduct give way to objective figures, numbers and indications, all provided by the test of instruments and the verdict of reality itself. Prior to any translation into laws and statutes, the task of *fa* is to *measure*, with all its semantic nuances: to demarcate and delimit people's tasks, offices and statutes; to weigh, size up and appraise people's sayings and actual deeds, or calculate their faults and merits; finally, in the sense of taking measures: to deal out or administer punishments and rewards by referring to written documents indicating the sanction corresponding to the pending case.

These three external sources of *fa*, that were credited to remain impervious to the toxic influence of human subjectivity, may have nonetheless profoundly reshaped

---

[58] A concurring observation is made in Harris 2016: 47.

[59] On the question of the content of *fa*, see Harris 2016: 48–49 and 53–54.

the psychology of subjects, whom we can easily picture as constantly anxious to remain in conformity with the measures indicated by the balance beam or the sliding weight of *fa* when about to deliver its incontrovertible verdict and unquestionable tariff. If we take into account the subjective impact of the model of measurement devices, we can intuit how the very image of a simple instrument can have seamlessly become, in the political imagination of the time, an object of apprehension as powerful as a weapon wielded by the ruler above the head of his servants and people.

7   When the Tool Takes its Toll: The Ambivalence of *fa* Analogies

As the *Han Feizi* repeatedly explains, if legal measures seem to fail to secure order, it is only owing to the human handling of penal laws and the lack of diligence in the administration of the state. When laws are systematically applied and heavy punishments relentlessly meted out, the temptation to flout norms or contravene orders is nipped in the bud. Therefore, if disorder persists in a state equipped with clear and relentless *fa*, it is not because of the harshness of penal laws or the indifference of people facing sanctions, it can only be due to the fact that these sanctions are not rigorously applied by people in charge.[60] In other words, *fa* has no flaws per se, it is the occasional human failures in the enforcement of public norms and the necessarily limited competence (or good will) of magistrates that are accountable for the disorders and crimes that may subsist in the state. The human capacity to track down offenders and subject them to the official order defined by *fa* is limited and will always remain so. As the *Shangjunshu* explains:

> 國之亂也，非其法亂也，非[61]法不用也。國皆有法，而無使法必行之法。國皆有禁姦邪刑盜賊之法，而無使姦邪盜賊必得之法。為姦邪盜賊者，死刑，而姦邪盜賊不止者，不必得也。必得，而尚有姦邪盜賊者，刑輕也。
>
> If a state is thrown into turmoil, it is not because laws (*fa*) are in complete disarray or because they are useless. All states have laws, but there are no laws that can guarantee that laws will be indeed implemented. All states have laws that prohibit crimes and wickedness,

---

[60] On this aspect of *fa*, see the well-crafted analogy in *Han Feizi* 17: 323 ("Bei nei" 備內): "Laws are like water that extinguishes the fire of violence and chaos, but if water is not in contact with fire and stays contained within a cauldron heated by flames, it loses its power to defeat fire and just resolves itself into thin vapors." Neither compulsory denunciation of crimes, nor collective penal responsibility can guarantee laws will be enforced if a cauldron of frustrations and slackness inverts the chemical process between the fire of human violence and the water poured out in order to quell fiery ardors.

[61] I do not follow here the indication in Jiang Lihong's edition of the *Shangjunshu* according to which the second *fei*非 is an erroneous interpolation (*Shangjunshu* 18: 109) but base my reading on Zhang Jue's version (Zhang 2012: 214). Most scholars and translators (Duyvendak 2003; Levi 2005) eliminate the negation and have the sentence mean that the real problem is that laws are not (properly) implemented, as if this were the gist of the argument. In fact, this passage says something else: the law cannot guarantee that all offenders will be caught. I follow here Pines' understanding (Pines 2017: 216 [18.4]).

that chastise thieves and robbers, but there are no laws that can absolutely guarantee that criminals and wicked people, thieves and robbers, will be caught. If those who are guilty of crime and wickedness, theft and robbery, were to be all executed and yet crime and wickedness, theft and robbery did not cease, then it would simply mean that the offenders cannot systematically be caught. Now, if they were systematically caught, and if nonetheless there still remained criminals, wicked people, thieves and robbers, then it would simply mean that punishments are too light. (*Shangjunshu* 18: 109 ["Hua ce"])

The elaboration of *fa*, aiming at the suppression of the human factor, only solves the question of the inner necessity of laws. There remained for *Shangjunshu* authors a major problem to be solved, a problem we may call the external necessity of *fa*. Indeed, there is no perfectly efficient device that can secure the automatic application of punishments, as opposed to what can be metaphorically called "laws of nature," whose necessity, universality and regularity are not hinged on anyone's knowledge, decision or judgement. If the elaboration of *fa* signifies a substantial improvement in the quest for universality and impartiality, by getting rid of discretionary justice and preference-based decisions, the problem shifts to the superior level, that of the automatic implementation of the legal tools referred to by the notion of *fa*.

Fa theorists laid the ground for controlling the desires and actions of the people and reducing the wide variety of human types to an army of docile and productive farmers and fighters; they developed with *fa* a formidably efficacious political weapon capable of removing troubles and disorder, but this weapon had to be timely implemented. Once the problem of cognitive limitations and individual qualities is theoretically solved by the imposition of impersonal precision tools, the human factor resurfaces in the handling of these tools. You cannot leave human agency out of the sphere of *fa*, or the person away from governance: the degree of depersonalization of the administrative apparatus finds here its inherent limits.[62]

Perhaps it is bearing in mind this difficulty that the main architects of a *fa*-centered state were not entirely content with the pervasive analogy with measuring tools and precision instruments, as the role of *fa* was not only to weigh and count, but also to catch and trap in a systematic and relentless way, as do hunting-nets or pitfall traps. Whilst scales and compasses remain inert tools in the hands of administrative agents, another type of metaphors in *fa*-centered texts sketch out the ideal vision of a self-automated device, unleashing a frightening violence as soon as transgression occurs.

We are touching here upon another significant aspect of the central set of analogies between instruments and *fa*. The initial comparison of norms and laws with geometric tools resumed by thinkers of *fa* in order to explain how to obtain well-defined standards and neat patterns of human behavior undergoes a change somewhere around the third century BCE that is worth retracing. The web of comparisons with tools that enable to measure length, draw figures, calculate weight or find the right direction[63] with precision is gradually overshadowed by the invasion of images

---

[62] Note also the need in human touch whenever the rules are to be changed (as discussed above).

[63] See the analogy with the compass (*sinan* 司南) in *Han Feizi* 6: 111.

of another kind of tools, associated with explicit violence: bills and blades, whips, axes and saws, all used to fell, cut, trim, chisel or reshape; and also snares, nets and glue, made for trapping and catching. While there is no clear and neat divide yet between textual sources of *fa*, the imagery of precision tools is pervasive in the *Mozi*, the *Shènzi* or the *Shangjunshu*; in addition to this, many chapters of the *Han Feizi* and the *Guanzi* teem with images of "ominous instruments" (*bu xiang zhi qi* 不祥之器 as the *Laozi* 31 coins it) that imprint a violent action on the body in order to correct and castigate the warped nature and the biases of common men, and to hunt down those who venture beyond legal boundaries.

Short of these hunting tools, the people—as *Shangjunshu* states—would be like birds flying away or feral beasts on the prowl.[64] This strand of violent imagery tends to grow and flourish in later texts. In *Guanzi*'s chapter 53, laws and regulations are aptly compared to snares and nets (*wei gang* 維綱) or to fishing nets (*wang gu* 網罟),[65] sustaining the underlying analogy of the people with packs of beasts or shoals of fish to catch automatically.

What could simply appear as an extension of the gamut of tools and instruments adduced for a didactic purpose is in fact quite a significant change. The transition from the analogy with tools that measure but leave the measured objects intact (weighing scale, measuring knots, T-square, compass, spirit level, etc.) to the recurring parallels with tools altering the shape, form and texture of the object they apply to (as do forges and hammers, chisels, axes and blades),[66] makes it clear that *fa* is not exclusively the objective norm of human actions: it is a weapon in the hands of the ruler that is wielded in the context of a constant and large-scale campaign in which autonomous decisions have no room.

In a similar vein, in *Han Feizi*'s chapter 26, "Shou dao" 守道, *fa* and contracts (*fu* 符) in the hands of the rulers are equated to cages (*xia* 柙) to entrap tigers (*Han Feizi* 26: 536). In chapter 8, "Yang quan" 揚權, we find throughout the text long-sustained metaphors revolving around the basic idea of cutting and trimming the raw wood of human nature with the sharp blades of laws and punishments. In chapter 34, "Wai chushuo you shang" 外儲說右上, violent corrective actions are not simply meted

---

[64] For instance: "Thus, the key element when subduing the people lies in having them under your sway, just like iron that you smelt or clay that you knead. If your grasp on this basic capacity remains shaky, then the people will be like birds fluttering around or like wild animals prawling about" 故勝民之本在制民，若冶於金，陶於土也。本不堅，則民如飛鳥走獸，其孰能制之?民本，法也 (*Shangjunshu* 18: 107 ["Hua ce"]). These analogies are resumed in *Guanzi* 53: 442 ("Jin cang" 禁藏); for a translation see Rickett 1998: 223.

[65] "Laws and orders should be treated as anchoring cords, and civil functionaries as an overlying net" 法令為維綱，吏為網罟 (*Guanzi* 53: 439 ["Jin cang"]; trans. Rickett 1998, 220).

[66] See for instance *Han Feizi* 50: 1142 ("Xian xue"); for a comparison between *fa* and hammers, forges, sticks and poles, see *Han Feizi* 35: 832 ("Wai chu shuo you xia" 外儲說右下): "Hammers and forges serve to level (*ping*) what is not even; sticks and straighteners serve to make regular (*ping*) what is not upright. And the *fa* created by the sages is that by which things that are not regular are made uniform (*ping*) and things that are not upright are straightened out" 椎鍛者所以平不夷也，榜檠者所以矯不直也，聖人之為法也，所以平不夷 矯不直也。

out to people who violate common norms, as the author encourages the ruler to put all his ministers in a position of weakness and vulnerability:

> 夫馴烏者斷其下翎焉。斷其下翎則必恃人而食，焉得不馴乎?夫明主畜臣亦然。
>
> To tame birds you must trim their tail feathers. If you do so, they will necessarily depend on you to feed. How then could you not succeed? The clear-minded ruler must do the same when he tends to his ministers and servants. (*Han Feizi* 34: 773)

The security of the bird breeder lies in the mutilation of his livestock.[67] Chapter 35 ties in quite fittingly with these views about the importance for the ruler to avail himself of instruments of aggression in order to preserve *fa*. He must use his agents, his orders and what leverage he has as a net (*gang* 綱), as a lash (*bian* 鞭), a bridle (*pei* 轡), a rod (jia 笧), a hammer (*zhui* 錐) or a bow-straightening frame (*qing* 檠) to tame, subdue, rectify, and hurt (*Han Feizi* 35: 805–06 and 829 ["Wai chushuo you xia" 外儲說右下]). In the first chapter of the *Guanzi*, the ruler is not depicted with a balance and a square but with reins (*pei* 轡)[68] in order to bridle his people. In chapter 32 "Xiao cheng" 小稱, the good ruler is paralleled to a craftsman who knows "how to use his axe and adze" *jin zhu* 斤欘, to the archer Yi who excels at using his bow and arrows, to the charioteer Zao Fu who "had an intuitive grasp of how to use reins and whip."[69]

The central paradigm of objective measure and quantitative data foreshadowed in the *Mozi*, fully developed in the *Shènzi*, the *Shangjunshu* and some parts of the *Han Feizi*, gives way in the purely narrative chapters of the *Han Feizi* and in the *Guanzi* to an invasion of aggressive metaphors explaining how a ruler should proceed with his people. Two new features of *fa* appear in this second web of analogies departing from the initial paradigm of measuring tools: the aggressive nature of the tools implemented, establishing a direct equivalence of *fa* with physical punishments, and, secondly, the automaticity of the sanction, which, once set up as a trap which is set off without any possibility of hesitation, delay or moderation.

8   Conclusion: Measure for Measure

The notion of *fa* was promoted as a solution to three main issues: it reinforced the ruler's sovereign power by mustering resources compensating for his personal shortcomings; it prevented incompetence and mistrust among the ruling elite; and,

---

[67] The ruler's isolated position and consequently his being constantly outnumbered by his subjects require a system of norms that enables him to compensate for these structural deficiencies and protect himself: on this topic see Galvany-Larrouquere 2017.

[68] *Guanzi* 1.6 ("Mu min" 牧民). That the author speaks about the law is confirmed by the recurrence of the analogy between letting the reins loose and granting pardon in chapter "Fa fa" 法法 (*Guanzi* 16: 143; trans. Rickett 2001: 256).

[69] *Guanzi* 32: 272 ("Xiao cheng"); trans. Rickett 2001: 429. On the parallel between Yi's shooting arrows and the ruler's harmonizing *fa*, see also *Guanzi* 64: 493 ("Xing shi jie" 形勢解), trans. Rickett 2001: 71.

finally, it warranted obedience and productivity among the populace. With the promotion of *fa*, two paradigms of governance were facing each other, to wit individual sovereignty vs. impersonal rulership. The latter paradigm expresses the quest of a spontaneous self-regulating order free of the quirks and biases of subjectivity, ranging from bureaucratic habits to cognitive limitations. It results from the fruitful convergence of two phenomena: the consecration of practices typical of artisans and merchants acquainted with tools and measurement devices whose didactic images became part of the semantic vocabulary of political power, and, secondly, the discipline of warfare applied to the whole body politic, through positive incentives and deterrent measures: ranks of merit to climb up the degrees of social and political hierarchy, and, on the other side the harshly punitive aspect of legislation. Hence the ambivalence of analogies with tools, that gradually pass from simple measurement devices to instruments of correction and aggression.

Along with the attempt to relegate the ruler to a symbolical position, *fa* is undoubtedly the most powerful and consistent attempt at rationalizing the state and redefining on a sound and clear basis relationships between the ruler, his agents and the people. At that early stage of political reflection, the elaboration of *fa* already reveals an unparalleled effort to experiment a more objective and efficacious method of administering the human community by factoring out individual biases, personal interests and purely subjective intuitions. The centralization of power in the newly emerging bureaucratic state, described as a range of routine mechanisms, homogenous norms and standardized procedures enabled the ruler's power to extend far beyond where he can dwell, observe or transport himself, and curb the power of hereditary aristocracy. The introduction of *fa* in the new political architecture sidelines the vision of the state as a family and replaces it with the image of a complex administrative machine that extends uniformly across the territory. In this territory, no personality is indispensable in itself, including that of the sovereign, whose power and authority lie exclusively in his shrewd use of tools, techniques and methods to control his agents and his people. *Fa* is to ritual rules and judicial authority held by aristocrats what administrative units such as commanderies (*jun* 郡) and counties (*xian* 縣) are to private allotments, that were the major means of territorial control in the aristocratic age. We could even argue that the same change is at work in the replacement of hereditary officials and ministerial families by a class of *shi* 士 selected on the base of their abilities, expertise and merits, regardless of regional provenance, family ties or personal sympathies.[70] Lastly, the spread of money in the economy between the fourth and third century BCE can be paralleled to the introduction of *fa* in the administrative system. Like *fa*, it is based on the principle of uniformity and sameness.[71] The development of all these new institutions over the course of the Warring States period (legal, bureaucratic, territorial, economic) seems

---

[70] The process of bureaucratization and centralization of power in the Warring States period is depicted in numerous studies; see, e.g., Lewis 1999; Yang 2003. For the rise of *shi*, see also Pines 2009: 115–31.

[71] On the ascent of money and administrative reforms in the pre-imperial period, see Von Glahn 2016, chapters 2–3.

to follow a common pattern of impersonal standardization and rational management. The vision of rulership that can be drawn from the *Han Feizi* or the *Shēnzi* fragments even suggest a "cult of impersonality" tailored for the monarch.[72]

The necessity of devising a steady and dependable government apparatus implied for the ruler not to rely any longer on his personal cognitive abilities, not to trust his "natural tools," not to count on his moral qualities, nor on his subjects' moral conduct. In discourses on *fa*, the elimination of subjectivity when it comes to the figure of the ruler is accomplished only very partially through "techniques of the mind" leading to a still, silent and de-individualized self, as evinced for instance in the *Shēnzi* fragments, the *Guanzi*'s chapter "Bai xin" and the exegesis of the *Laozi* in the *Han Feizi*. While governance through the charismatic suasion of a heroic ruler was pushed out of the sphere of daily human affairs, the role of *fa* and its coercive apparatus combines impersonal sovereignty and bureaucratic expertise in an unprecedented way.

If the dividing line remains blurry between absolute monarchy and unrestrained tyranny in spite of the institution of a system of public norms and standards, it may be due to the fact that the central institution of hereditary kingship bequeathed by the Zhou political order remains fundamentally unaltered by the political promotion of *fa*. *Fa* thinkers no doubt saw the advantages of a system in which the ruler would comply to *fa*, as is clearly and repeatedly recommended. But they were at the same time adamant they would not let the monarch's supreme power be restricted in any way, since the constant reinforcement of monarchical power stood at the core of their political project. This major reservation prevented them from developing institutional means of subordinating the ruler to *fa*. In the *Han Feizi*, the *Laozi*-inspired doctrine of non-action could only require a monarch wise enough and disciplined enough to hide or to suppress the faintest manifestation of his own subjectivity. In sum, nothing can protect the state from its head if the latter refuses to accept the supremacy of *fa*. The legal order remains subordinated to the regal order.[73]

As to the paradigm of objectivity associated to *fa,* it is not without shortcomings. This paradigm implies indeed that the only alternative to objectivity is a pure and deleterious subjectivism, associated to all the negative connotations borne by the term *si* 私 (selfish interest, individual biases, personal quirks, cognitive limitations, all arousing dissent and disorder). In *fa* theories, there is no acknowledgment of a

---

[72] Harris, from another perspective, hints at the great advantage for a ruler to disappear behind the system: "By making rules and regulations fixed and unalterable, there is no one individual toward whom to feel resentment. In essence, the political system Shen Dao envisions attempts to deprive individuals of a clear target toward which to aim their resentment" (Harris 2016: 36).

[73] The regime of absolute monarchy does not mean naturally that each ruler was *de facto* a strong one. Actually, rulers may have been weak and easily swayed (that is precisely one of Han Fei's main concern). As Graeber and Wengrow observe: "Ancient kings were rarely able to enforce this power systematically (often, as we've seen, their supposedly absolute power really just meant they were the only people who could mete out arbitrary violence within about 100 yards of where they were standing or sitting at any given time)" (Graeber and Wengrow 2021: 366). Naturally, the development of a central bureaucracy must have greatly enhanced a ruler's reach across his kingdom.

grey zone between civil discussion and sterile disputation, there is no recognition that it might indeed be possible without imperiling the state to let sensible people discuss, and even disagree.[74] Now, one is tempted to raise a concern about the implications of this dual vision, that may account for the pervasiveness of the rudimentary analogy between *fa* and instruments marked in standard units that enable to assess the size, the volume or the weight of an object. Theorists of *fa* and lawmakers were obsessively concerned with quantification, with data, numbers and degrees to guide legal procedures such as fines or rewards.[75] Yet, such markers of objectivity in the handling of public affairs cannot hide the fact that, in the end, there is always a subject who has to "do the math," and sometimes the equation is not obvious. The recurring opposition between the fallibility of subjective representations and the objective character of laws remained at this early stage of political reflection too rigid and too plain. Words and actions in the field of politics are not objects like beams to measure or bags of millet to be weighed, they are manifestations of the human mind tied to intentionality, and involve exchange relationships. Deciding on the guilt of someone for instance requires more complex operations than a simple addition or a geometrical operation. There is no measuring tap to indicate the extent of one's offense, there is no scale to weigh the exact merits of an individual in his service to the state: every decision requires a part of personal judgement, an operation of contextualization and interpretation, and here the key analogy with precision instruments finds its objective limit. In the end, one can never entirely extract the person out of *fa*.

We should not forget that the real tools *fa* thinkers resort to are not geometric instruments or measurement tools, but rhetorical tropes, a skein of analogies and similes unspooled in a discourse that purports to impose a universally valid interpretation of political reality. Without the awareness of the imaginative foundation of this new political dispensation, the arithmetical conception of laws may run the risk of degrading itself into a blind and meaningless exercise of justice. It is only with the reflection of legal thinkers of later dynasties (the Tang in particular) on other factors (social status, family context, state of mind of the defendant at the time) that the notions of exact measure and proportion between actions and sanctions will be nuanced and mitigated in order to absorb more variables and lend justice to the complexities of social behavior.

---

[74] See for instance *Shangjunshu* 3: 22 ("Nong zhan" 農戰): "The outstanding ruler appoints his officials by observing a norm that is clear (for all), and therefore does not depend on knowledge or deliberations" 善為國者，官法明，故不任知慮. See also Pines 2016: 26.

[75] See Chap. 7 in this volume Korolkov's description of how the scrupulous implementation of quantitative standards and impersonal norms (*cheng* 程) during the Qin and the Western Han empires organized times, space, mobility, work and merit. Quantitative norms permeated all aspects of social life, such as military training, agricultural quotas, travel speed, ranks in society, taxes to levy, evaluation of bureaucratic personnel, or productivity in state-monitored workshops to quote just a few examples.

References

Barbieri-Low, Anthony J. 2007. *Artisans in Early Imperial China*. Seattle: University of Washington Press.

Cook, Scott. 2012. *The Bamboo Texts of Guodian: A Study and Complete Translation*. 2 vols. Ithaca, N.Y.: Cornell East Asia Series.

———. 2019. The Debate over Coercive Rulership and the 'Human Way' in Light of Recently Excavated Warring States Texts. In *Dao Companion to the Excavated Guodian Bamboo Manuscripts*, ed. Shirley Chan, 285–318. Dordrecht: Springer.

Creel, Herrlee Glessner. 1974. *Shen Pu-hai: A Chinese Political Philosopher of the Fourth Century B.C.* Chicago and London: University of Chicago Press.

Duyvendak, J.J.L., tr. 2003(1928). *The Book of Lord Shang: A Classic of the Chinese School of Law*. Rpt., Clark, N.J.: Lawbook Exchange.

Galvany-Larrouquere, Albert. 2017. The Court as a Battlefield: The Art of War and the Art of Politics in the *Han Feizi*. *Bulletin of the School of Oriental and African Studies* 80 (1): 73–96.

Goldin, Paul Rakita. 2013. Han Fei and the *Han Feizi*. In *Dao Companion to the Philosophy of Han Fei*, ed. Paul R. Goldin, 1–21. Dordrecht: Springer.

Graeber, David, and David Wengrow. 2021. *The Dawn of Everything. A New History of Humanity*. New York: Farrar, Straus & Giroux.

Graziani, Romain. 2009. The Subject and the Sovereign: Exploring the Self in Early Chinese Self-Cultivation. In *Early Chinese Religion, Part One: Shang through Han (1250 BC–220 AD)*, ed. Lagerwey John and Marc Kalinowski, 459–517. Leiden: Brill.

———, trans. 2011. *Écrits de Maître Guan: Les Quatre traités de l'Art de l'esprit*. Bibliothèque chinoise. Paris: Les Belles Lettres.

Gu, Baotian 顧寶田. 1987. The Nature of the 'Vital Essence' theory in the *Guanzi* 試論《管子》精氣說的性質. In *Studies of Guanzi* 管子研究, ed. Zhao Shouzheng 趙守正 and Wang Demin 王德敏, 114–122. Jinan: Shandong Renmin.

Harris, Eirik Lang. 2016. *The Shenzi Fragments. A Philosophical Analysis and Translation*. New York: Columbia University Press.

Hu, Jiacong 胡家聰. 2003. *New Investigations into the* Guanzi 管子新探. Beijing: Sheke xue-shu wenku.

Jiang, Tao. 2021. *Origins of Moral-Political Philosophy in Early China: Contestation of Humaneness, Justice, and Personal Freedom*. Oxford: Oxford University Press.

Kanaya, Osamu 金谷治. 1987. *Research on the Guanzi: One perspective on Early Chinese Intellectual History* 管子の研究 : 中國古代思想史の一面. Tokyo: Iwanami shoten.

Kryukov, Vassili. 1995. Symbols of Power and Communication in Pre-Confucian China (on the Anthropology of *de*): Preliminary Assumptions. *Bulletin of the School of Oriental and African Studies* 58 (2): 314–333.

Le, Aiguo 樂愛國.1996. The dialectic of 'Vital essence' in the *Guanzi* 《管子》的精氣說辨正. *Journal of Guanzi Studies*管子學刊 1: 3–6.

Levi, Jean. 1992/93. "Gouvernement naturel, économie de marché et despotisme démocratique" in *Le Genre Humain* 26: 141–161.

———, trans. 2005. *Shang Yang: Le Livre du Prince Shang*. Paris: Flammarion, 2nd ed.

Lewis, Mark Edward. 1999. Warring States Political History. In *The Cambridge History of Ancient China*, ed. Edward L. Shaughnessy and Michael Loewe, 587–650. Cambridge: Cambridge University Press.

Li, Jinglin 李景林. 1989. On the Monistic theory of the Way (*dao*), the One (*yi*), and vital breath (*qi*) in the four "Xinshu" chapters of the *Guanzi* 論《管子》四篇的"道—氣"一元論. *Journal of Guanzi Studies*管子學刊4: 3–9.

Li, Dongsheng 栗冬生. 1994. A brief discussion of the relationship between objective and subjective forms of knowledge in the *Guanzi* 略論《管子》認識論的主客體關係. *Journal of Guanzi Studies*管子學刊 4: 3–6.

Ma, Feibai 馬非百. 1988. On the doctrine of 'Essence and Spirit' "(*jingshen*)" in the *Guanzi* chapter "Nei ye" and other considerations 《管子·內業》篇之精神學說及其它. *Journal of Guanzi Studies* 管子學刊 (4): 4–7.

Meng, Wentong 蒙文通. 1987. 楊朱學派考 (Examining the school of Yang Zhu) in *Meng Wentong wenji 1, guxue zhenwei* 蒙文通文集·第一卷·古學甄微. Chengdu: Bashu.

Needham, Joseph. *The Grand Titration.* 2005 (1969). *Science and Society in East and West.* London: Routledge.

Peerenboom, Randall P. 1993. *Law and Morality in Ancient China: The Silk Manuscripts of Huang-Lao.* Albany (NY): SUNY Series in Chinese Philosophy and Culture.

Pines, Yuri. 2009. *Envisioning Eternal Empire: Chinese Political Thought of the Warring States Era.* Honolulu: University of Hawai'i Press.

———. 2016. Social Engineering in Early China: The Ideology of the *Shangjun shu* (Book of Lord Shang) Revisited. *Oriens Extremus* 55: 1–37.

———, trans and ed. 2017. *The Book of Lord Shang: Apologetics of State Power in Early China.* Translations from the Asian Classics. New York: Columbia University Press.

———. 2021. Agriculturalism and Beyond: Economic Thought of the *Book of Lord Shang*. In *Between Command and Market: Economic Thought and Practice in Early China*, ed. Elisa Sabattini and Christian Schwermann, 76–111. Leiden: Brill.

Puett, Michael J. 2002. *To Become a God: Cosmology, Sacrifice, and Self-Divinization in Early China.* Cambridge MA: Harvard University Press.

Qiu, Xigui 裘錫圭. 1980. "Lost Texts Attached to the two Mawangdui versions of the *Laozi* and the Dao-Fa School", 馬王堆老子甲乙本卷前後逸書與道法家, *Chinese Philosophy* 中國哲學, 68–84. Beijing: Sanlian.

——— 裘錫圭. 1992. "Research on the Jixia Taoist theory of Essence (*jing*) and Energy (*qi*)" 稷下道家精氣說的研究. *Studies in Daoist Culture* 道家文化研究 2: 167–192. Shanghai: Shanghai guji.

Queen, Sarah A. 2013. *Han Feizi* and the Old Master: A Comparative Analysis and Translation of *Han Feizi* Chapter 20, 'Jie Lao,' and Chapter 21, 'Yu Lao'. In *Dao Companion to the Philosophy of Han Fei*, ed. Paul R. Goldin, 197–256. Dordrecht: Springer.

Rickett, W. Allyn. trans. 1998. *Guanzi: Political, Economic, and Philosophical Essays from Early China.* Vol. 2, Princeton: Princeton University Press, 1998.

———. trans. 2001. *Guanzi: Political, Economic, and Philosophical Essays from Early China.* Vol. 1, rev.ed. Boston: Cheng and Tsui.

Roth, Harold D. 1994. Redaction Criticism and the Early History of Taoism. *Early China* 19: 1–37.

———. 1996. "The Inner Cultivation Tradition of Early Daoism." In *Religions of China in Practice*, ed. Donald Lopez, Jr., 123–148. Princeton: Princeton University Press.

———. 1999. *Original Tao: Inward Training and the Foundations of Taoist Mysticism.* Translations from the Asian Classics. New York: Columbia University Press.

Smith, Adam. 1976. *An Inquiry into the Nature and Causes of the Wealth of Nations.* In *The Glasgow edition of the Works and Correspondences of Adam Smith*, ed. R.H. Campbell and A.S. Skinner, vol. 2. Oxford: Oxford University Press.

Standaert, Nicholas. 2013. Heaven as a Standard. In *The Mozi as an Evolving Text*, ed. Carine Defoort and Nicholas Standaert, 237–269. Leiden: Brill.

Van Norden, Bryan W. 2013. Han Fei and Confucianism: Toward a Synthesis. In *Dao Companion to the Philosophy of Han Fei*, ed. Paul R. Goldin, 135–145. Dordrecht: Springer.

Von Glahn, Richard. 2016. *The Economic History of China: From Antiquity to the Nineteenth Century.* Cambridge: Cambridge University Press.

Watson, Burton, trans. 1968. *The Complete Work of Chuang-tzu.* New York: Columbia University Press.

Weingarten, Oliver. 2015. Self-Cultivation' (*xiu shen* 修身) in the Early Edited Literature: Uses and Contexts. *Oriens Extremus* 54: 163–208.

Wu, Guang 吳光. 1986. "An analytic comparison of the four "Xinshu" chapters of the *Guanzi* with the school of Song Xing and Yin Wen" 管子四篇與宋尹學派辨析. *Studies in the History of Chinese Philosophy* 中國哲學史研究 4: 37–42.

Yang, Kuan 楊寬. 2003. *Warring States History*戰國史. Shanghai: Renmin chubanshe, rev. ed.

Yang, Soon-ja. 2013. Shen Dao's Theory of *fa* and His Influence on Han Fei. In *Dao Companion to the Philosophy of Han Fei*, ed. Paul R. Goldin, 47–63. Dordrecht: Springer.

Zhang, Jue 張覺. 2012. *The Book of Lord Shang, Collated with Subcommentaries* 商君書校疏. Beijing: Zhishi chanquan chubanshe.

Zhou, Lisheng 周立升 and Wang, Demin 王德敏. 1983. The Theory of Essence and Energy in the *Guanzi* and its contribution to [Chinese intellectual] history 《管子》中的精氣說及其歷史貢獻. *Historical Research*歷史研究 5: 73–78.

Chapter 14
Philosophy of Language in the fǎ 法 Tradition

Lisa Indraccolo

Philosophy of and about language might not immediately come to mind as being a primary concern when discussing the *fǎ* tradition and *fǎ*-related writings, as has often been assumed, somewhat erroneously. This is an aspect of *fǎ* thinking that is still largely understudied, besides the analysis of the most eloquent chapter 12, "Shuìnán" 說難 ("The Difficulties of Persuasion"), of *Hán Fēizǐ* 韓非子 (Hunter 2013; Graziani 2012; and Indraccolo 2021b). However, the discourse about the more or less deliberate mis-use of language and the dangers it entails – not only posing a potential life-threatening risk to an advisor or minister at court, but endangering the stability of the whole government, and even the organic functioning of the state at large – plays a cardinal role in *fǎ* thinking. In particular, the polysemy and the ensuing problematic nature of language, determined by its constitutive ambiguity and malleability, is at the heart of a broader intellectual reflection in writings associated with this trend of thought. The rhetorical use of language is notoriously acknowledged as being a "double-edged sword," as Matthias L. Richter (2014) has defined it, as it can be used as an "instrument of both persuasion and deception," a definition that will be especially fitting in the third part of the present analysis. Hence, the need arises to apply a similar approach to language and "names" (*míng* 名)[1] as to government praxis, as part of the pool of phenomenological objects that need to be subjected to and consistently normalized by "objective norms and standards" (precisely, *fǎ*). These objective standards are necessary and sufficient

---

[1] "Names" is a neutral overgeneralization used here for the sake of simplicity. For a preliminary discussion of the polysemy of *míng* see p. 5 below (cf. Pines 2020: 170–71); for a thorough analysis of its different connotations in the *fǎ* context, see pp. 417–420.

L. Indraccolo (✉)
Tallinn University, Tallinn, Estonia
e-mail: lisa.indraccolo@tlu.ee

© The Author(s), under exclusive license to Springer Nature Switzerland AG 2024
Y. Pines (ed.), *Dao Companion to China's* fa *Tradition*, Dao Companions to Chinese Philosophy 19, https://doi.org/10.1007/978-3-031-53630-4_15

405

preconditions for the establishment of a functioning society that further ensure its stability and long-term survival.

There are three main aspects to be considered in the approach to the problem in *fǎ* thinking, which we might tentatively divide into and organize under two main categories **(a) philosophy of and about language** as a meta-discourse on the role, value and characteristics of language in general, and the use of "names" (*míng*) in particular; and **(b) language philosophy**, loosely meant as a code of appropriate conduct in language use, where 'appropriate' needs to be understood in *fǎ* terms, i.e. what is the most suitable, desirable and effective course of action to be performed or behaviour to be assumed contextually, with the aim to achieve the intended communication or suasive goal, without the interference of any moral judgement or consideration. Hence, a) philosophy of language has a theoretical approach to language and is primarily concerned with the correct use of "names," while b) language philosophy focuses on the boundaries of the pragmatic use of language, meant as "speech" (*yán* 言), as will be discussed in more detail below. The present chapter addresses these cardinal issues, providing relevant illustrative examples drawn from main received texts associated with the *fǎ* tradition, namely *Hán Fēizǐ* 韓非子 and *Shāngjūnshū* 商君書, but when appropriate also considers and integrates pertinent quotations taken from the fragmentary *Shēnzǐ* 申子 (attributed to Shēn Búhài 申不害, d. 337 BCE) and from the composite collection *Guǎnzǐ* 管子.

In accordance with primarily goal-oriented *fǎ* thinking, as might be expected, some of the principles predicated according to (a) need to be twisted, subverted, and even openly contravened – and, somewhat paradoxically, rightfully so – when engaging in activities that pertain to the area of (b) or are subjected to its rules. This seeming contradiction creates a normative tension that is reconciled within the underlying principle that the end justifies the means, but at the same time that objective standards must be invariably applied without any exception or hesitation, and need to regulate all aspects of life. This apparently "adaptive"[2] attitude does not jeopardize the foundational *fǎ* principle of the inflexibility of rules, i.e., that rules must not at any time be bent or adjusted to meet the specific situation, and even less so to the particular individual. Rather, one must understand that under different circumstances people find themselves assuming different roles; hence, different rules apply. It is by walking this very fine line and progressively achieving a thorough understanding and mastery of all the facets of *fǎ* that a true *fǎ* thinker and administrator can eventually emerge victorious. These are the means by which he can successfully advantage the state and preserve its stability against all odds, even under the most adverse circumstances, whatever the cost in terms of ethics or integrity.

Before we proceed to address the main aspects of the philosophy of language and language philosophy of *fǎ* thinking, a short digression must be made to disambiguate what "names" actually mean within this context. The term *míng* 名 does mean "names," strictly speaking (Cáo 2017; Pines 2020), referring to the man-made denominations that human beings have elaborated and developed over time, and

---

[2] On the strategy of "adaptation" and "adaptive agency" in early Chinese philosophy, see Valmisa 2021.

agreed upon to communicate with each other as conventions within a community. From an ideal point of view, such denominations are meant to denote the set of characteristics that their corresponding objects – whether concrete or abstract – embody. They supposedly constitute objective standards of reference, and it is adamantly held that objective standards must regulate the application and the use of said names.

However, in the *fǎ* context, the term should often – though not consistently – be understood rather as meaning "(names of) ranks and titles," "names of punishments," or "self-proclamations about one's worth," as "reputation" (Pines 2020; Harris, Chap. 10, this volume), as well as "names" in the integrative sense of "making a name for oneself and earning status – by gaining official ranks and titles, as a result of and in strict connection with the outcomes of one's performance." The polysemy of *míng* is especially important and needs to be considered in its relationship to *xíng* 刑 ("punishments") / *xíng* 形 ("achievements, deeds")[3] that will be discussed below as one of the two main aspects addressed by the philosophy of language in the *fǎ* tradition.[4]

1 Philosophy of and About Language

When addressing the philosophy of language in *fǎ* texts, there are two main aspects, or more precisely, two cardinal mutual relationships that need to be analyzed and disentangled: (1) the relationship between "names" and their corresponding "actualities" (*shí* 實) (Makeham 1994), and the correlated theory or principle of the "rectification of names" (*zhèngmíng* 正名, or better *míngzhèng* 名正, the typical formulation in *fǎ* texts); and (2) the relationship between "punishments" (*xíng* 刑) or "(outer) form or achievements, deeds" (*xíng* 形) and "official title, name of an office or position, name of a punishment," or "self-proclamations about one's worth" (*míng* 名), as will be illustrated in detail below.

1.1 Names and Actualities: The Rectification of Names

The principle at the basis of the "rectification of names"[5] claims the necessity to restore a univocal, mutual correspondence between "names" and their corresponding "actualities" (reified, concretized things or living beings existing in the world

---

[3] The accomplishment of a task carried out to completion and the results thereof, to be considered altogether as the actual performance to be evaluated by the sovereign.

[4] For the latter aspect, see Creel 1970: 79–91; Lau 1973; Makeham 1990–91 and 1994; Wang Pei, Chap. 20, this volume.

[5] See MacCormack 1986; Gassmann 1988; Yáng 1999 and 2002; Defoort 2001 and 2021; Loy 2003 and 2014; Cáo 2008, 2016; Dīng 2008.

that are knowledgeable and can be objects of human thought), and is most often associated with and considered a genuine tenet of the Confucian tradition, despite textual evidence that suggests otherwise. Leaving aside the somewhat later *Xúnzǐ* 荀子, which features a whole chapter dedicated to the rectification of names (chapter 22, "Zhèngmíng" 正名), the binomial expression *zhèngmíng* is absent from *Mèngzǐ* 孟子, and is cited and addressed explicitly only once in *Lúnyǔ* 論語[6] embedded in a case of anadiplosic staircase parallelism (Berlin 1995):

> 子路曰：「衛君待子而為政，子將奚先?」子曰：「必也正名乎!」子路曰：「有是哉，子之迂也!奚其正?」子曰：「……名不正，則言不順；言不順，則事不成；事不成，則禮樂不興；禮樂不興，則刑罰不中；刑罰不中，則民無所措手足。故君子名之必可言也，言之必可行也。君子於其言，無所苟而已矣。」
>
> Zǐlù asked: "The Lord of Wèi has been waiting for you to take the reins of the government, what are you going to prioritize?" The Master answered: "What is necessary is to rectify names (*zhèngmíng* 正名)!" Zǐlù replied: "Is that so? Then you are missing the point. Why rectifying?" The Master said: "[…] if names are not rectified, then words do not match; if words do not match, then official tasks are not brought to completion; if official tasks are not brought to completion, then rituals and music do not flourish; when rituals and music do not flourish, then punishments and fines are not equitable; when punishments and fines are not equitable, then the people do not know how to move their hands and feet [what to do with themselves]. Therefore, when it comes to the *jūnzǐ* 君子 [i.e. the morally and intellectually superior person], he is aware of the need for names to be utterable, and the need for utterances to be enactable. When it comes to his utterances, the *jūnzǐ* does not allow any ambiguity whatsoever, and that is all."[7] (*Lúnyǔ* 13.3: 517–23 ["Zǐlù" 子路])

In this passage, the primary importance of rectifying names is articulated by Confucius as the first act of government he himself would undertake, so as to ensure that words match one's deeds, but also, most interestingly, that tasks are fulfilled and punishments are commensurate, which are also the two main concerns of *fǎ* texts when it comes to discussing the practice of *zhèngmíng*, as will be discussed in more detail below. It is noteworthy that the figure of the Master here is already expressing a major concern about the appropriate use of denominations, and the necessity of establishing univocal correspondences by drawing a close connection between "names" and their corresponding "punishments and fines." The passage further underlies the disastrous consequences that the disruption of this correspondence might have for the people who would not know anymore what is licit, hinting also at the imbalance between faults and punishments that might ensue, and the inevitable consequent misapplication of the law.

Besides this passage, the theory of the "rectification of names" is supposed to have found its most complete formulation in the famous sentence, allegedly uttered by Confucius, "let a ruler be a ruler, let a minister be a minister, let a father be a father, let a son be a son" (「君君，臣臣，父父，子子。」 *Lúnyǔ* 12.11). This sentence embodies the principle that all individuals should behave according to and fully embody their "names" (or "titles," "denominations") by fulfilling the related

---

[6] On the contested authenticity of this passage, see Goldin 2020: 256 n. 60; see also Waley 1938: 21–22, and 172 n. 1; and Creel 1960: 321 n. 13.

[7] Translations are mine unless otherwise stated.

set of duties and tasks in both their public (political and social) and private (lineage and family) life without overstepping their boundaries in their performance of said duties and tasks, thereby matching not only the expectations of their superior and society, but also "names" with their corresponding "actualities" (or "realities," *shí* 實). This goal can be accomplished by embracing and embodying the social roles identified by such "names," thereby performatively imbuing these otherwise empty and artificial "names" with actual meaning. Thus, far from being some abstract, auto-referential theory about language use, the rectification of names is the only way to make sure that the words by which we define the boundaries of our world match their corresponding actualities. The urge to disambiguate appellations is prompted by the need to ensure that roles in society are all clearly defined and respected. Rectifying names is crucial in order to avoid not only any source of confusion or misunderstanding in communication, but also any deliberate manipulation of language and consequent distortion of reality that might eventually devolve into the disruption of the socio-political order.

Despite the traditional association with Confucianism, the theory of the rectification of names is by no means exclusive to it. The rectification of names represents, rather, a cardinal principle at the centre of an ongoing discourse about the inexorable process of corruption of the meaning of certain terms that was animating the intellectual landscape during the Warring States (453–221 BCE) and early Hàn 漢 (206/202 BCE–220 CE) periods (Defoort 2001). This discussion emerges in particular as a consequence of the moralistic reconceptualization of the figure of the *jūnzǐ* 君子, from "prince" or "lord" to "nobleman," meant as a morally and intellectually superior person (Pines 2017b); and in reaction to the progressive appropriation of the sacred term "*wáng*" 王 – originally an exclusive designation of the Zhōu 周 king, with its cultural, religious, and political set of connotations, by local rulers that gradually divested the ruling dynasty of its political and religious power, but also of its cultural supremacy in the area of the Central Plains.[8]

The theory of the rectification of names plays a major role and is central to *fǎ* texts, where it is closely entangled with the following main concerns of *fǎ* thought: a) government practice and the performance of one's official duties; b) the potential punishments one might incur when one falls short or oversteps the boundaries of one's position and the related fixed set of tasks and duties; c) the recruitment of suitable professionals as members of the bureaucracy, necessary for the successful running of the state administration and government (MacCormack 1986, esp. p. 384). Just as Confucius remarked in the passage from *Lúnyǔ* 13.3 above, *Hán Fēizǐ* states explicitly that the path towards the achievement and maintenance of political stability starts precisely from the task of rectifying names.[9] Once names are univocally

---

[8] On the appropriation of the title of *wáng*, see Yáng 1998: 341–352; Lewis 1999: 354–360.

[9] On the rectification of names as central in Hán Fēi's thought, see Martinich 2014, esp. 381–384 (despite some disputable claims, such as that Hán Fēi would not be especially interested in language [383], or that he would be confusing "meaning and criteria" [see paragraph 4 "The Confusion of Meaning and Criteria," 384–88]).

and unequivocally associated with their corresponding actualities and regularly so employed, all matters will spontaneously fall into place:

用一之道，以名為首。名正物定，名倚物徙。故聖人執一以靜，使名自命，令事自定。

> Pursue the way of unified control by prioritizing names. When names are rectified, matters will be fixed and settled; when names are partial and ambiguous, matters go astray. Therefore, the Sage holds on to unity in still quietude, so that names determine themselves and commands and tasks settle themselves. (*Hán Fēizǐ* 8.3; Chén 2000: 145 ["Yáng quán" 揚權]) [10]

And again, in chapter 45, "Guǐshǐ" 詭使 ("Absurd Encouragements"), expertise on the correct use of names is acknowledged as one of the three fundamental methods of the governmental practice of a sage:

聖人之所以為治道者三：一曰利，二曰威，三曰名。夫利者所以得民也，威者所以行令也，名者上下之所同道也。非此三者，雖有不急矣。

> The way in which a Sage rules comprises three tools: the first is said to be profit, the second is said to be authority, the third is said to be names. Profit is the means by which he wins people over; authority is the means by which he ensures that his commands are enforced; names are the means by which superior and inferior can follow the same path. Any other [technique] that is not one of these three [tools], even if it is available, it is by no means as urgent. (*Hán Fēizǐ* 45.1; Chén 2000: 986–87)

However, in general *Hán Fēizǐ* is primarily concerned with the attunement of names to the corresponding punishments – *xíng* 刑 ("capitol or corporal punishment") or *fá* 罰 ("fines," "pecuniary penalties"), rather than delving into a more comprehensive discussion of the necessity of rectifying names per se (see more in Sect. 1.2 below). Another prominent *fǎ* text, *Shāngjūnshū*, seems to talk predominantly of *míng* 名 in terms of "fame," "reputation," "honor and glory," and "making a name for oneself" (Pines 2020: 195–98),[11] with the exception of a few passages in the last chapter, 26, "Dìngfēn" 定分 ("Fixing Divisions"). This chapter praises the clear-sightedness of the ancient sages, who grasped the importance of defining names unequivocally and fixing their meanings to avoid social and political turmoil:

今先聖人為書，而傳之後世，必師受之，乃知所謂之名；不師受之，而人以其心意議之，至死不能知其名與其意。故聖人必為法令置官也，置吏也，為天下師，所以定名分也。名分定，則大詐貞信，民皆愿愨，而各自治也。故夫名分定，勢治之道也；名分不定，勢亂之道也。

> Now, the former sages created writings and transmitted them to later generations, and there should be teachers to transmit them: only then can we understand the names (terms) [in these writings]. If they are not transmitted by teachers, and everyone discusses them according to his own mind, then until the end of his life he will not comprehend the names and the meaning of these writings. Hence, the sages must establish officials for the laws and establish clerks, making them the teachers of All-under-Heaven. Names and divisions will

---

[10] All translations from *Hán Fēizǐ* refer to the division of the text into paragraphs adopted in Harbsmeier Forthcoming (based on Zhāng 2010) and pages from Chén's 2000 edition. All translations are mine unless indicated otherwise. Cf. translations in Liao 1939: 53, Harbsmeier, Forthcoming; Geaney 2018: 191.

[11] Also, as "people's registration" in official registries, but this meaning does not concern the present discussion.

thereby be fixed. When names and divisions are fixed, great deceivers become trustworthy, great thieves become cautious and sincere, and each governs himself. Therefore, fixing names and divisions is the way of positioning oneself in orderly rule; not fixing names and divisions is the way of positioning oneself in turmoil. (Modified from Pines 2017a: 247–48, *Shāngjūnshū* 26.5; Zhāng 2012: 286)[12]

Once again, we are reminded from the example set by the sages that rectifying names is the key to solid governance, and the only reliable way to avoid social and political turmoil. Similarly, in *Guǎnzǐ*, *míng* mostly means "(achieve) fame," "reputation," "make a name for oneself," but we do find a few scattered references to the necessity of "understanding the distinction among names" *míng míngfēn* 明名分 and "understanding names and regulating actualities" (*míng míng zhāng shí* 明名章 實).[13] Moreover, we learn that "if names are rectified and duties are clear, then people will not be confused about the way" 名正分明，則民不惑於道 (*Guǎnzǐ* 2004: 30: 551 ["Jūnchén shàng" 君臣上, "Ruler and Ministers I"]). Three passages from *Guǎnzǐ* that are most relevant to the present discussion and help contextualize the relationship between names and things, and especially the necessity to prioritize the rectification of names as a prerequisite for establishing a stable and effective governance are the following, from chapter 16, "Fǎfǎ" 法法 ("Standardizing Regulations"); chapter 36, "Xīnshù shàng" 心術上 ("Techniques of the Heart I"); and chapter 55, "Jiǔshǒu" 九守 ("The Nine Things to Be Preserved").

The first passage (coming from the chapter that is among those most clearly aligned to *fǎ* thought in the entire *Guǎnzǐ*; see Sato, Chap. 5, this volume) is particularly relevant, as it clearly states that the act of rectification, and in particular the rectification of names, is at the core of governmental practice, and establishes a direct connection between the lack of rectification and unlawful behavior. Also, this passage introduces a topic that will be dealt with in detail in the second part of my inquiry, which is dedicated to language philosophy, namely the pernicious nature and effects of argumentation (*biàn* 辯).

政者，正也；正也者，所以正定萬物之命也。是故聖人精德立中以生正，明正以治國，故正者所以止過而逮不及也。過與不及也，皆非正也。非正，則傷國一也。[… …] 仁而不法，傷正。[… …] 法之侵也，生於不正，故言有辯而非務者，行有難而非善者。故言必中務，不苟為辯。行必思善，不苟為難。

To govern means to rectify. To rectify is the process through which the names[14] of the myriad things are rectified and fixed. Therefore, the sage refines his virtue and positions himself at equilibrium in order to bring about rectification. He makes rectification intelligible [to the mass of people] to bring order to the state, thus rectification is the means by which one is capable of curbing excesses and overtaking shortcomings. Both excesses and

---

[12] Hereafter all divisions of *Shāngjūnshū* are based on those adopted in Pines 2017a (from whose translations I borrow, with minor changes); references are also made to Zhāng's 2012 edition.

[13] Both expressions appear once in two chapters of *Guǎnzǐ*, 8 "Yòuguān" 幼官 (Dark Palace) and 9 "Yòuguāntú" 幼官圖 (Blueprint of the Dark Palace). *Guǎnzǐ* 8: 153; 9: 187. On the title of these two chapters, see Rickett 2001: 148–49.

[14] The original Chinese text uses 命 *mìng* (OC *m-riŋ-s), which however is commonly used in place of 名 *míng* (OC *C.meŋ) from which it seemingly derives, assuming also the meaning of "assigning a name (to a certain thing)."

shortcomings are incorrect. If they are not rectified, they become the first source of harm for a country. Humaneness without conformity to normative standards is harmful to rectification. The transgression of normative standards (fǎ) springs from the lack of rectification. As a consequence, speech is argumentative but unfocused, and actions deal with difficulties but are not considerate of what is good. Therefore, one's speech must be focused and not argumentative. Actions must be considerate of what is good, and not carelessly deal with difficulties.[15] (*Guǎnzǐ* 16: 307–08 ["Fǎfǎ" 法法])

The passage preserved in chapter 36, "Xīnshù shàng," instead has a decidedly cosmological tone. It focuses on the supernatural abilities of the sage, including his capacity to discern how the inner workings of the Dao play out in the world, and especially the superior knowledge of the two necessary skills of non-speech and non-action. These two skills are combined in him with the ability to assign things the most appropriate name that is respectful and expressive of their intrinsic nature and characteristics – an almost epiphanous moment in which the sage is able to detect their still unspoken proper name and reveal it to the world.

物固有形，形固有名，名當謂之聖人。故必知不言無為之事，然後知道之紀。
　　Things intrinsically have a shape, shapes intrinsically have a name; he who can match names is called a sage. Therefore, one must understand non-speech and non-action, and afterwards one understands the regulations of the Way.[16] (*Guǎnzǐ* 36: 764)

It is especially the last passage, in chapter 55, "Jiǔshǒu," that is relevant in the context of the discussion about the need for titles and official positions earned through appointments to match (*dāng* 當) the actual results achieved:[17]

修名而督實，按實而定名。名實相生。[... ...] 名實當則治，不當則亂。
　　Revise [office] titles by monitoring their actual results, assign [office] titles accordingly (lit. on the basis of their actual results). Titles and results are mutually dependent and engender one another. [...] If titles and results match, then there is order; if they do not match, then there is disorder.[18] (*Guǎnzǐ* 55: 1046)

A passage similar to the previously cited quotation from *Hán Fēizǐ*, chapter 8, "Yáng quán" is found in *Shēnzǐ* 申子, a text attributed to the Warring State thinker Shēn Búhài, a chancellor of Marquis Zhāo of Hán 韓昭侯 (r. 362–333 BCE).[19] In chapter 1, "Dàtǐ" 大體 ("The Main Principle"), we find the following passage:

為人君者，操契以責其名。名者，天地之綱，聖人之符。......名自正也，事自定也。是以有道者自名而正之，隨事而定之也。......昔者堯之治天下也以名。其名

---

[15] Cf. Rickett 2001: 261. See also MacCormack 1986: 384.

[16] Cf. Waring 2020: 139–40.

[17] The idea that names and actualization should match (*míngshí dāng* 名實當) is mentioned in *Hán Fēizǐ* 48.3 ("Bājīng" 八經) (Chén 2000: 1054), which shows a general concern with the correct use of names.

[18] Cf. Roth 2012–13: 161–62.

[19] Only a few fragments of *Shēnzǐ* have been preserved, primarily in political compendia such as *Qúnshū zhìyào* 群書治要 (*Compilation of Writings on the Cardinal Principles of Governance*), compiled in 631 by the famous historian Wèi Zhēng 魏徵 (581–643), and *Yìlín* 意林 (*Forest of Ideas*) compiled around 786 by Mǎ Zǒng 馬總 (d. 823). The text has undergone several attempts of reconstruction during the Qīng 清 Dynasty (1636/1644–1912); see more in Creel 1974a, b; Louton 1979; Yu Zhong, Chap. 2, this volume.

正，則天下治。桀之治天下也，亦以名，其名倚，而天下亂。是以
聖人貴名之正也。

> The one who acts as ruler holds on to (his part of) the tally in order to honor his obligations and thereby take responsibility for his name.[20] Names are the guiding principle of Heaven and Earth, the matching tally of the sages. [...] Names rectify themselves, tasks settle themselves. Therefore, those who have mastered the way, employ names to rectify them, and comply with their tasks to settle them. In antiquity, Yáo ordered All-under-Heaven through (the use of) names. His (use of) names was correct, and then All-under-Heaven was ordered. Jié ordered All-under-Heaven also through (the use of) names. His (use of) names was ambiguous, and, as a consequence, All-under-Heaven fell into chaos. Therefore, the sages take into the utmost consideration the correctness of names. (Qúnshū zhìyào vol. 4, juàn 36: 949–50; cf. Creel 1974a: 346–51)

Here, the correct use of names is not only elevated to cardinal guiding principle of government practice in the human dimension of existence. According to Shēnzǐ, the rectification of names also regulates the workings of the whole cosmos through the coordinated action of Heaven and Earth, and thereby extends its influence on everything that exists in the world. Thus, it is a principle that only a sage – a fully accomplished human being who has reached a higher level of consciousness and wisdom – can know how to apply correctly, as witnessed in the consequences of the actions of two epitomes of positive and negative leadership, Yáo and Jié. The sage has the ability to intuitively perceive the proper name to be assigned to things, but also the duty to rectify any denominations in use so that the whole world is ordered. Once names are correctly assigned, everything else will spontaneously fall into place.

1.2 Punishments/Achievements, Deeds and Names

Let us now proceed to disentangle and analyse the relationship between "punishments" (xíng1 刑) or "(outer) form or achievements, deeds" (xíng2 形) on one side, and "official title," "name of an office or position," "name of a punishment," or "self-proclamations about one's worth," (míng 名) on the other side. The first issue that needs to be addressed is whether the two graphs 刑 and 形 are actually two different words, namely if they refer to different concepts or theories, since it is well attested since ancient times that xíng1 and xíng2 are common graphic variants that were used interchangeably at least until well into the Hàn, when their meaning and use started to diverge in a more consistent manner. Xíng1 is seemingly the oldest graph and was largely used to mean "form, pattern" in place of xíng2, before the latter gradually imposed itself towards the end of the Hàn period, eventually replacing xíng1 completely in this meaning (Makeham 1990–91: 102–4 and 1994). This can be further clarified through the analysis of the compounds xíng (1 or 2) + míng.

Between the two binomial expressions, xíng1míng 刑名, "punishments" and "names (of said punishments)," is the one that initially raised scholars' attention the most. At a first look, this expression would indeed seem the most appropriate to

---

[20] Modified from Goldin 2005: 64.

express and embody *fǎ* philosophy at best. It would comply with the underlying logic that regulates the state, and especially the predominant role assigned to and played by a system of unfailingly applied, objective punitive prescriptions, as promoted by *fǎ* political discourse. However, as will be shown, *fǎ* received textual sources tell us otherwise.

According to Sīmǎ Qīan's 司馬遷 (c. 145–c. 86 BCE) *Shǐjì* 史記 (*Records of the Grand Historian*), three of the key figures of the *fǎ* tradition –Shēn Búhài 申不害, Shāng Yāng 商鞅 (d. 338 BCE), and Hán Fēi 韓非 (d. 233 BCE) – are all explicitly associated with the practice of the doctrine of *xíng1míng*. While Shāng Yāng and Hán Fēi are both reported to have been interested but only tangentially involved in the theorization and practice of this teaching,[21] Shēn Búhài is the one that is most closely associated with, and even attributed, the theory of *xíng1míng*. However, despite what is stated in *Shǐjì*,[22] as Herrlee G. Creel (1905–1994) has shown, in the surviving fragments of the currently identifiable *Shēnzǐ* 申子 there is no mention at all of such a theory.[23]

Creel explored the issue in depth, attracting quite some criticism with his interpretation, as he attributed this binomial expression a meaning that would actually be a more fitting description for *xíng2míng*, as will be shown. Creel's much-debated interpretation of the meaning of *xíng1míng* in his famous short essay "The Meaning of Hsing-Ming"[24] associates this binomial expression closely with personnel control, and especially with the performance of scholar-officials. Creel harshly criticizes the hypothesis that *xíng1míng* would simply be just another way of writing *xíng2míng*, although, as has been mentioned, the two graphs could be used interchangeably. He rather proposes to understand 刑名 as "performance and title," and in particular 刑 as "to perform a function" (Creel 1970: 84–5). This assumption leads him to the following, somewhat disputable statement that "*Hsing-ming*, then, is equivalent to *ming-shih* 名實." Shortcomings of Creel's theory are clear. Its

---

[21] *Shǐjì* mentions that Shāng Yāng: "When he was young, he was fond of the teaching of *xíng1míng*" 少好刑名之學 (*Shǐjì* 68: 2707 ["Shāngjūn lièzhuàn" 史商君列傳]). About Hán Fēi, the text claims that he "was fond of the teachings of *xíng1míng*, and of methods and techniques, but his own (teaching) is originally rooted in Huáng-Lǎo thought 喜刑名法術之學，而其歸本於黃老 (*Shǐjì* 63: 2612 ["Lǎozi Hán Fēi lièzhuàn" 老子韓非列傳]).

[22] *Shǐjì* mentions: "Shēnzǐ's teachings are rooted in Huáng-Lǎo thought, but prioritize *xíng1míng*. […] Shēnzǐ put considerable effort in applying it to the pursuit of a correspondence between names and actualities" 申子之學本於黃老而主刑名 […] 申子卑卑，施之於名實 (*Shǐjì* 63: 2611 ["Lǎozi Hán Fēi lièzhuàn"]). A similar assessment of Shēnzǐ is provided by Liú Xiàng 劉向 (77–6 BCE), both in his catalogue, *Biélù* 別錄 (*Separate Records*) and in the lost segment of his *Xīnxù* 新序 (*New Prefaces*). See Sīmǎ Zhēn's 司馬貞 (679–732) and Pei Yin's 裴駰 (420–478) glosses to *Shǐjì* (63: 2612) and Yán Shīgǔ's 顏師古 (581–645) gloss in *Hànshū* 漢書 (*History of the [Former] Hàn Dynasty*) (*Hánshū* 9: 278 ["Yuándì jì" 元帝紀]); see also Makeham 1990–91: 91).

[23] Creel 1974a: 119–24; see also Caldwell 2018: 88, n. 24.

[24] The short study was first published in the Festschrift *Studia Serica Bernhard Karlgren Dedicata*, edited by Egerod and Glahn (1959), and subsequently reprinted and included in the collection of essays *What is Taoism? And Other Studies in Chinese Cultural History* (1970: 79–91); see also Creel 1974a: 119–24.

weakness is in large part due the fact that it is based on a debatable and eventually unfounded interpretation of *xíng*1 刑 in a very small number of textual occurrences, the relevance of which is eventually far too limited to provide any solid, convincing evidence to support his claim about the alleged performativity of *xíng*1.[25] Despite the evident limits of this theory, somewhat surprisingly his translation of *xíng*1*míng* as "performance and title" has been extremely successful. It has managed to impose itself among the scholarly community and has stuck across the decades, to the point that it is still popular today and is often cited uncritically as a standard translation for *xíng*1*míng* (including in several chapters of this volume).

The most complete account on *xíng*1*míng* to date has been provided by John Makeham, who also delves into the paleographic evidence, integrating data drawn from unearthed manuscripts dating back to the third and second centuries BCE. He gathers substantial evidence to show that the graph for 刑 was originally polysemic, and that, besides the meanings it is more commonly associated with, it was already used interchangeably with 形 to mean "'form', 'to take on a definite form', 'to give form to', and 'pattern, standard'" (Makeham 1990–91: 88). He also closely associates the theory (or "doctrine," as he himself defines it) of *xíng*1*míng* with language theory in the *fǎ* tradition, and in particular with the concept of *míngshí* 名實, the necessary mutual relationship between names and their corresponding realities. Makeham claims that, despite the scant available textual sources associated with the thought and teachings of Shēn Búhài and their potentially corrupted nature, there is enough information to acknowledge him as the possible originator of a "Legalist doctrine of names" (Makeham 1990–91: 89 and 1994: 68), in accordance with what early imperial sources assess. While I would not go as far, considering the corrupted and fragmentary nature of surviving materials related to and associated with Shēn Búhài, I do agree that (1) there evidently was a "doctrine of names" and a philosophy of language and about language in the *fǎ* tradition; (2) seemingly, Shēn Búhài was one of its main promoters; and (3) the concept of *míngshí* and hence the principle of *xíngmíng* 刑(=形)名 were closely connected with personnel recruitment, as long as *xíng*1*míng* 刑名 actually occurs as a textual variant for *xíng*2*míng* 形名, with the meaning of "achievements and names/titles."

However, Makeham does not seem to build a very strong argument regarding the inappropriateness of "performance" as a suitable translation for *xíng* 刑/形. It must be remarked that the difference between "achievements" and "performance" is very subtle, if we consider "performance" as related not to the ongoing process of performing a certain assigned task, but rather to the *ex post* evaluation or assessment of

---

[25] This point had been made by D.C. Lau (1921–2010) in his criticism of Creel (Lau 1973: 122–23). Lau underlined that Creel's argument was based on a far too limited number of occurrences of *xíng*1*míng* (namely, two occurrences in *Lìjì* 禮記 [*Records of the Rites*]; one in the "Yáodiǎn" 堯 典 ["The Canon of Yao"] chapter of *Shūjīng* 書經 [*Classic of Documents*]; and one in *Mòzǐ* 墨子), and these do not provide sufficient evidence to support Creel's theory. Makeham also provides a detailed and thorough criticism of Creel's interpretation of *xíng*1*míng* as "performance and title," starting from and integrating the analysis by D.C. Lau as well as the critical comments expressed by A.C. Graham in that regard (Makeham 1990–91: 94–99; see also 1994: 70–72).

the outcome of the executed task after its fulfillment, i.e. in the sense of "performance review" (Goldin 2011: 92–93) of a minister or official. While this is a fine distinction, it might still be productive to preserve it in the interpretation of *xíng*1*míng*, and to opt for "achievements and names/titles" to provide a more fine-grained focus.

Actually, the binomial expression *xíng*1*míng* is quite rare in pre-imperial texts. There are only five occurrences in the extant corpus of *fǎ* writings, all of them in *Hán Fēizi*.[26] Leaving aside the examples preserved in "Difficulties II" ("Nán èr" 難 二) which, being a cluster of anecdotal material, has a substantially different internal structure, nature and scope in respect to the other chapters, it can be noticed that in the first three cases the compound term *xíng*1*míng* appears embedded in four-character expressions such as "assimilate, bring together and harmonize *xíng*1 and *míng*" (同合刑名) or "carefully investigate and harmonize *xíng*1 and *míng*" (審 合刑名). The occurrence in chapter 7, "Èr bǐng," is particularly significant when we try to disambiguate the meaning and the use of the composite expression *xíng*1*míng* in *Hán Fēizi*. The passage addresses the principle of the necessary adequacy of the breadth and scope of one's accomplishments, as a result of the actions performed, to one's own assigned tasks and actual official role played in government and in the administrative structure. It underlines the risks and inevitable punishments connected with overstepping the boundaries of one's position by over- or underperforming, which, as previously mentioned, are considered equally dangerous to the stability of the established social and political order and the delicate internal balance of the state machine (Indraccolo 2021b).

人主將欲禁姦，則審合刑名者。刑名者，言異事也。為人臣者陳而言，君以其言授之事，專以其事責其功。功當其事，事當其言，則賞；功不當其事，事不當其言，則罰。故群臣其言大而功小者則罰，非罰小功也，罰功不當名也。群臣其言小而功大者亦罰，非不說於大功也，以為不當名也害甚於有大功，故罰。

When the ruler of men wishes to curb illicit behaviour, he carefully examines and harmonizes achievements and claims (*xíng*1*míng*). "Achievements and claims" refers to the difference between words and tasks. Those who serve as ministers utter their words (to elucidate their skills), and the sovereign confers them a task based on their words. The sovereign relies exclusively on their assigned tasks to assess their accomplishments. If accomplishments match the tasks conferred to them, and tasks match their words, then they are rewarded. If accomplishments do not match the tasks conferred to them, and tasks do not match their words, then they are punished. Therefore, when it comes to the body of ministers, if their words are lofty but their accomplishments are meager, then they are punished. They are not punished because the accomplishment is meager, but because their accomplishment does not match the title (of their position).[27] When it comes to the body of ministers, if their words are humble but their accomplishments are substantial, then they are punished. It is not because he (the sovereign) does not rejoice at their substantial accomplishments, it is because he believes that the harm produced by the fact that these do not

---

[26] See *Hán Fēizi* 5.2 ("Zhǔdào" 主道); 7.2 ("Èr bǐng," twice); 8.7 ("Yáng quán" 揚權); 37.5.2 ("Nán èr" 難二, twice) (Chén 2000: 74, 126, 163, 882).

[27] Cf. Caldwell 2018: 53.

match the title (of their position) is much greater than their having achieved a substantial accomplishment, therefore they are punished.[28] (*Hán Fēizǐ* 7.2; Chén 2000: 126)

As is illustrated in this passage, to ensure that the personnel recruitment process is transparent and efficient, and that the most talented people are chosen to be assigned to the most suitable government and administrative positions, the ruler should first listen to what prospective officials claim to be their alleged strong points and abilities. The sovereign must rely exclusively on their words to assign them the most fitting tasks without indulging in any other considerations. Finally, the accomplishments of officials must be rigorously scrutinized by the ruler, with particular attention to the correspondence between the duties entailed by the assigned task and the outcome of the officials' performance. Under- or over-performance are both punished, as there is no higher priority than ensuring that accomplishments meet expectations and that these are neither deluded nor exceeded, and that one's words match one's deeds at all times.

The passage, however, reconfirms that the meaning of the expression should not be interpreted as "punishments and names" – with reference to the necessity of strictly adhering to correct naming standards of different types of punishments, so that what is meant by these names is accurate and corresponds to reality; their execution and implications are unmistakably fixed; and ensuing fines and chastisements are adequate and commensurate to the crimes committed. It clearly does not refer to the necessary correspondence between "names" and "punishments" that ministers guilty of such a crime would have had to undergo. Rather, as Makeham has also underlined, "*ming* means 'word, speech, declaration, or claim', and on the basis of his claim a candidate is appointed to office or allotted a task" (Makeham 1994: 73). It evidently refers to the achievements or deeds of a minister or official, suggesting that there should be a univocal correspondence between "accomplished tasks and results thereof, achievements" on one side, and "claims about one's skills and capabilities" as a preliminary self-assessment of one's own abilities and a self-promotional discourse made to advertise oneself, on the other side. Such correspondence implies that one's successfully accomplished tasks have to be evaluated against the set of duties and obligations proper to one's official position, or more simply put, it defines the mutual relationship between "deeds" and "words" (Makeham 1994: 78–80). Makeham also makes a compelling argument to prove that *xíng* 刑 (= 形) would actually still entail and express at the same time also the underlying intrinsic nuance of meaning contributed by its graphic variant 型, which would turn the most complete rendering of the expression into "accomplishment as per standards."[29]

---

[28] Cf. Makeham 1990–91: 96, see esp. 96–98 on this topic.

[29] Or, as Makeham says, "outcome cum standard" (Makeham 1990–91: 106). See also pp. 100–01; 104–07. Makeham (1994, appendix D) suggests that 刑 would have been used to express the connotation of 型 as "mould, pattern, model." I am more inclined to think that the two graphs are co-existing graphic variants that share a common semantic field, and that most probably 刑 already entailed also the connotation of "(abiding by, embodying) standards," which seems to be also the direction in which his reasoning is going towards the end of his argument: "Of course the semantic niceties of this distinction should not lead one to overlook the essential unity of form and standard, because the realization of a job and the achievement thereby affected are really two sides of the same coin," (Makeham 1990–91: 107; see also 1994: 75–76).

Interestingly, there are almost no occurrences of *xíng2míng* in the whole corpus of *fǎ* writings (Cáo 2015). There are only three occurrences, all in *Hán Fēizǐ*: once in chapter 5.1, "Zhǔdào," and twice in chapter 8.2–8.3, "Yáng quán" (Chén 2000: 66–67 and 141–45). In all three cases the expression *xíng2míng* is embedded in a four-character sentence: *xíng2míng cāntóng* 形名參同 "achievements and claims match" (Sun 2015: 31). In chapter 5, "Zhǔdào," we first find a passage in which 形名 appears, in the sense of matching one's deeds with one's words, i.e. assessing and evaluating whether and insofar the final achievement of a duty has been successfully accomplished, and whether it fulfils the expectations of one's official title, in other words whether an official has fulfilled his function in full:

道者、萬物之始，是非之紀也。是以明君守始以知萬物之源，治紀以知善敗之端。故虛靜以待令，令名自命也，令事自定也。虛則知實之情，靜則知動者正。有言者自為名，有事者自為形，形名參同，君乃無事焉。

The Dao is the beginning of the myriad things and the regulative principle of right and wrong. Therefore, the discerning ruler[30] observes the beginning to understand the origin of the myriad things. He regulates the principle to learn about the source of success and defeat. Therefore, he stays empty-minded and tranquil waiting for someone's words to determine their official assignment, and for someone's deeds to settle (their evaluation). Being empty-minded, he discerns the intrinsic nature of matters. Being tranquil, he discerns whether those who are acting are upright. There are claims that in themselves stand for a title, and actions that in themselves stand for the achievement thereof. If achievements and titles support each other and are in harmony with one another, then the ruler has no concerns over it [...]. (*Hán Fēizǐ* 5.1, Chén 2000: 66–67)

This passage is of utmost importance, since making a claim about one's abilities was considered already as a sort of binding contract: "[i]n the *hsing-ming* context then, the claim that an official makes can be understood to be a *declaration*. And as a binding declaration it functions like a legal contract" (Makeham 1990–91: 100; 1994: 74, see also pp. 79–80). These claims represent the ultimate criteria by which official positions are assigned by the ruler. The ruler must not let any external factor influence his final decision regarding assignments: by detaching himself from any disturbance and keeping his mind in a state of perfect stillness and imperturbability, he is capable of making the most appropriate choice. Most importantly, the ruler assumes a primary role in this scenario, as he is the only one who has the necessary power and the authority – and the right to exercise them – to assess his ministers' and officials' achievements, and evaluate whether said achievements do indeed match the original claims they had made about their own skills and abilities (Makeham 1994: 80–81). This passage also brings the discussion one step further, underlying how officials are useful and represent a fundamental component of the government machine, but at the same time they are eventually just pawns that can be easily replaced should their performance diverge from expectations. The ruler exploits them for their ideas and useful skills, sparing his own energies and preserving his reputation from being tarnished in case of mistakes.

---

[30] Kai Vogelsang (Forthcoming) has recently pointed out and problematized the issue of the inadequacy of the well established translation of *míngzhǔ* 明主 as "enlightened" or "clairvoyant" ruler, especially in the context of texts of the *fǎ* tradition.

The pre-eminence of inferiors' "claims" (*míng* 名) and the performative role they play are made very clear in chapter 8, "Yáng quán":

物者有所宜，材者有所施，各處其宜，故上下無為。[...] 因而任之，使自事之。因而予之，彼將自舉之。正與處之，使皆自定之。上以名舉之，不知其名，復脩其形。形名參同，用其所生。[...] 形名參同，上下和調也。

Things have their ideal collocation, talents have their use. When everyone occupies the suitable position, as a consequence superiors and inferiors do not need to act [proactively]. [...] He [i.e. the sage ruler] appoints them to office on this basis, and lets them handle tasks by themselves. He confers responsibilities upon them on this basis, and lets them advance in rank by themselves. He verifies their claims and appoints them, he lets everybody decide for themselves. Superiors promote them on the basis of their claims, if they are not aware of their claims, they scrutinize once again their achievements. When achievements and claims match, they put to good use what results therefrom. [...] When accomplishments and claims match, then relationships between superiors and inferiors are harmonious and perfectly attuned. (Modified from Liao 1939: 55–56; *Hán Fēizǐ* 8.2–8.3; Chén 2000: 141–145)

The passage underlines the individual responsibility of making claims about one's skills that are truthful, as these are of utmost importance for the proper functioning of the recruitment system and of the whole government machine at large. Assignments to official posts are made on the basis of such claims, and superiors evaluate someone's performance by verifying that their claims match accomplishments achieved during service. Lying about one's abilities not only endangers one's position at court and jeopardizes possibilities of being promoted in the future, but also negatively affects the relationship between superiors and inferiors.

Ernest Caldwell (2018: 84) also considers *xíng2míng* as "to adequately perform or meet the quality expectations." He circumscribes its scope and area of application to government practice and administration, and specifically to the evaluation of officials, ministers and bureaucrats. *Xíng2míng* is an effective principle providing a reliable standard of reference that can be used to assess and evaluate their performance adequately, so that the sovereign and the government at large can select the best available persons, and promote them to the most suitable positions based on their skills and personal characteristics. Caldwell further interprets it as meaning the necessary correspondence that should be in place between the outcome of the performance of one's tasks and duties, always to be carried out to full extent and to the best of one's ability (but at the same time remaining within the limits imposed by the boundaries that define the duties prescribed by one's position or official title), and the actual name of the rank and title (Caldwell 2018: 71, 82). While according to him, *xíng2* 形 per se is not connected to the idea of "punishment" nor does it have any related underlying meaning, "failure to adequately perform or meet the quality expectation (*xing* 形) leads to a punishment."[31] This principle is illustrated nicely by the concept of "accountability" that Makeham (1990–91: 90; 1994: 68–69)

---

[31] Caldwell 2018: 84. Caldwell briefly mentions *xíng1míng* as well (53 and the related footnote n. 26, 88) when discussing how Shāng Yāng is introduced in *Shǐjì* as a promoter of such theory, see note 21 above. He suggests two hypotheses, that 刑 might indeed be used as a variant of 形, or that in this context it might actually mean "punishments" and refer to the necessary correspondence between punishments and the name of the crime committed. On the basis of the present analysis, I am inclined to think that the former is more likely to be the correct interpretation.

introduces in this context, and was first proposed by Wang Hsiao-po and Leo S. Chang (Wang and Chang 1986: 57–68; see also Ames 1994: 47).

Based on the present analysis, and in agreement with Caldwell's considerations, we can conclude that punishments seems to play no direct role in *fǎ* philosophy of language – according to *Hán Fēizǐ* they are, in fact, one of the "two handles" (*èrbǐng* 二柄)[32] of government that belong to pragmatic governance and management "techniques" (*shù* 術), a fairly different area of concern.

In the *xíngmíng* context instead, 刑 consistently assumes a connotation that belongs to the semantic domain of 形, hence it should be interpreted accordingly, as meeting expectations by producing results and reaching accomplishments that match claims someone makes about one's skills and capabilities. Hence, the main focus of interest in *fǎ* philosophy of language within the discourse of *xíngmíng* is performative speech, and the performative use of language made by prospective officials in order to be promoted to a certain position and entrusted with a set of related tasks and duties.

2 Language Philosophy

2.1 Language as Argument Technique

Distrust of the spoken word and a condemnation of the resort to the rhetorical arts in general, and to artful, cunning speech in particular – exemplified by the techniques of argumentation (*biàn* 辯/辨) and persuasion (*shuì* 說) – is a broadly shared concern in early Chinese philosophy.[33] It is a hotly-debated topic that is addressed by different intellectual currents, and the *fǎ* tradition is no exception. Two texts in particular, *Hán Fēizǐ* and *Shāngjūnshū*, show a deep concern for the misuse of these rhetorical techniques and the potentially devastating effects they can exert in the long run on the sovereign's psyche, and, through him, on the government and the state at large. As we are told, words can be deceitful, meaning can be deliberately twisted and exploited to pursue any goal, hence people whose deeds match one's

[32] Namely, "rewards and punishments" (*shǎngfá* 賞罰), as the eponymous chapter 7, "Èrbǐng," discusses in detail. It is interesting to note that the term *Hán Fēizǐ* uses to indicate "punishments" is *fá* 罰 ("fines," "penalties," "punishments") and not *xíng* 刑, which, as already noted, does however appear in the same chapter in the four-character expression "to scrutinize and harmonize achievements and claims" (*shěnhé xíngmíng* 審合刑名) – precisely with the different meaning of "achievements" with which it has been treated in the present paragraph. In *Shāngjūnshū* instead we do find a whole chapter entitled "Shǎngxíng" 賞刑 ("Rewards and Punishments"), in which case 刑 unmistakeably means "punishments." This further reinforces the assumption according to which 刑 in connection with 名 does not typically mean "punishments" in *fǎ* texts, but is rather related to a discourse on the performative use of language. See pp. 414–420 above; see also Indraccolo 2021b.

[33] On the rhetorical techniques of argumentation and persuasion, see for instance Crump 1964; Reding 1985; Kroll 1985–86; Levi 1992; Garrett 1993; Lu 1998; Harbsmeier 1998; Goldin 2005; van Els et al. 2012; Hunter 2013; Indraccolo 2020, 2021a, 2021b.

words (*dāng qí yán* 當其言,[34] *dāng yán* 當言[35]) are the most precious and hard-to-find allies. This is yet another point that, quite interestingly, texts of the *fǎ* tradition seems to share with *Lúnyǔ*.

Both *Hán Fēizǐ* and *Shāngjūnshū* warn the reader/user of the text (Richter 2013) against sycophants infesting the court who make use of the rhetorical arts to climb the social ladder, a motley bunch of pettifoggers, shrewd persuaders and "smooth talkers" – literally, "those who are fond of arguments" (*hào biàn* 好辯,[36] *hàobiànzhě* 好辯者[37]), a term that appears in both texts, or "those who are fond of argumentation and persuasion" (*hào biànshuì* 好辯說), employed in *Hán Fēizǐ*.[38] These are most often – or aspire to become – members of the ruler's entourage, retainers at court or cunning ministers exerting their suasive arts to influence a ruler's decisions and gain power and titles for themselves.[39] Sovereigns are particularly receptive to their ideas, shrouded in a cloud of seductive words, and seem to be oblivious of the influence these persuaders are exerting upon them, to the point that smooth and skilled talkers are listed by *Hán Fēizǐ* as the sixth of the offensive "eight villainies" (from the eponymous chapter 9, "Bā jiān" 八姦):

> 六曰流行。何謂流行?曰:人主者,固壅其言談,希於聽論議,易移以辯說。為人臣者求諸侯之辯士、養國中之能說者,使之以語其私,為巧文之言,流行之辭,示之以利勢,懼之以患害,施屬虛辭以壞其主,此之謂流行。
>
> The sixth (villainy) is called "smooth and persuasive talk." What is meant by "smooth and persuasive talk"? I say: when it comes to the ruler of men, he is kept away and prevented from engaging in regular conversation, and rarely has the opportunity to hear different theories and opinions, so he is easily induced to change his mind through argumentation and persuasion. Ministers look for debaters (*biànshì* 辯士) from the regional lords' courts and support skilled persuaders from their own state, and let them plead on their behalf their selfish interests, employing refined and polished words (*qiǎowén zhī yán* 巧文之言) and smooth, persuasive phrases; instructing him [i.e. the ruler] about (personal) profit (*lì* 利) and positional power (*shì* 勢); instilling fear of disasters and calamities in him; spreading false sayings to undermine his authority. This is what is called "smooth and persuasive talk." (*Hán Fēizǐ* 9.1.6, Chén 2000: 182; cf. Watson 1964: 45; Liao 1939: 64–65.)

These persuaders are called out by both texts for their use of a crafty speech that disguises a concealed goal or twists the truth, and are thus deliberately employed to deceive and manipulate the addressee. *Hán Fēizǐ* uses terms such as *qiǎoshuō* 巧說, *qiǎowén zhī yán* 巧文之言, and *yínshuō* 淫說, while the most common *qiǎoyán* 巧言 appears in both *Hán Fēizǐ* and *Shāngjūnshū*. The latter binomial expression

---

[34] *Hán Fēizǐ* 5.3 ("Zhǔdào," twice); 7.2 ("Èrbǐng," twice); 37.5.2 ("Nán èr") (Chén 2000: 81, 126, 882).

[35] *Guǎnzǐ* 22: 452 ("Bàxíng" 霸形).

[36] *Hán Fēizǐ* 15.1.3 ("Wáng zhēng") (Chén 2000: 300); *Shāngjūnshū* 3.6 ("Nóngzhàn" 農戰) (Zhāng 2012: 49).

[37] *Shāngjūnshū* 3.5 ("Nóngzhàn") (Zhāng 2012: 47).

[38] *Hán Fēizǐ* 15.1.10 ("Wáng zhēng") (Chén 2000: 300).

[39] On Warring States politics, and especially the relationship between rulers and ministers, see for instance Pines 2009: 163–80. On the subversion of the categories of private and public interest, see Pines 2022.

invariably assumes a negative connotation and is typically embedded in four-character structures where it is juxtaposed to equally negative expressions, such as "sharp words" (*qiǎoyán lìcí* 巧言利辭);[40] "empty teachings" (*qiǎoyán xūdào* 巧言虛道) and "argumentation and persuasion" (*qiǎoyán biànshuì* 巧言辯說);[41] and a "compelling countenance" (*qiǎoyán lìngsè* 巧言令色).[42]

These cunning debaters, variously called *biànshì* 辯士,[43] *biànzhě* 辯者,[44] but also *biànzhì zhī shì* 辯智之士[45] and *biànzhī/zhìzhě* 辯知/智者,[46] master the rhetorical arts and employ "artful words" that are embellished ad hoc and tailored to suit the addressees in order to exploit their vulnerabilities and soft spots, their likes and dislikes; the debaters use this information to their advantage in order to entrap their interlocutor in an alluring web of words.[47] The latter two terms for "debater," which appear respectively in *Hán Fēizǐ* and *Shāngjūnshū*, build a meaningful conceptual connection between the two texts by calling out as potentially dangerous for the state both officials or retainers endowed with rhetorical prowess, as well as wit and intelligence.[48] As will be shown below, the association between rhetorical ability and wisdom, and the negative opinion of those intellectuals that possess these characteristics or have developed such abilities is typical of *Shāngjūnshū*, which prefers the binomial *biànhuì* 辯慧.[49]

These ruthless, shady personages are described as engaging in endless discussions ("men of service that engage in remonstrances, persuasions, discussions and disquisitions" *jiànshuì tánlùn zhī shì* 諫說談論之士[50]) and scheming behind closed doors. In particular, they resort to the rhetorical arts to deceive and manipulate their

---

[40] *Hán Fēizǐ* 45.5 ("Guǐshǐ" 詭使) (Chén 2000: 991).

[41] *Shāngjūnshū* 3.1 and 3.3 ("Nóngzhàn") (Zhāng 2012: 39 and 42).

[42] *Guǎnzǐ* 45: 911 ("Rèn fǎ" 任法).

[43] *Hán Fēizǐ* 9.1.6 ("Bā jiān") and 32.2.4 ("Wài chǔshuō zuǒ shàng" 外儲說左上) (Chén 2000: 182 and 675); and *Guǎnzǐ* 2004: 53: 1027 ("Jìncáng" 禁藏).

[44] *Hán Fēizǐ* 32.2.3 ("Wài chǔshuō zuǒ shàng," twice) and 48 ("Bā jīng" 八經) (Chén 2000: 674 and 1074).

[45] *Hán Fēizǐ* 46.1 ("Liù fǎn" 六反) (Chén 2000: 1000).

[46] *Shāngjūnshū* 22.1 ("Wàinèi" 外內, twice) (Zhāng 2012: 253–54).

[47] The psychology of the addressee plays a fundamental role in persuasion, see Galvany 2012 and Schaberg 2016; on the psychology of the ruler in particular, and especially the potential threat posed by persuaders exploiting his likes and dislikes to their advantage in persuading him, see Graziani 2012 and 2015, and Goldin 2005.

[48] On the systematic ideological attack against intellectuals perpetrated by *fǎ* thinkers, see Pines 2022 and Chap.18, this volume.

[49] There are altogether six occurrences of this binomial expression in *Shāngjūnshū* in the following chapters: *Shāngjūnshū* 3.4 and 3.5 ("Nóngzhàn," twice) (Zhāng 2012: 46 and 47), in one of the two however the text is not referring specifically to orators, but simply juxtaposes the two terms in a list of ten nefarious sources of disgrace for a state's stability and survival; 5.1 ("Shuōmín" 說民, once); 17.4 ("Shǎngxíng"); 25.4 ("Shènfǎ" 慎法); and 26.4 ("Dìngfēn") (Zhāng 2012: 74, 202, 275, and 283).

[50] *Hán Fēizǐ* 12.7 ("Shuìnán") (Chén 2000: 269).

opponents and political adversaries at court, but, first and foremost, the ruler. Their primary goal is to win his favor, thereby gaining personal advantages in terms of emoluments, career advancements and honors, and to persuade him to pursue policies that would favor their lineage and affiliates. Deprived of any moral scruples or sense of decency, their only goal is to benefit themselves by gaining political influence, and honors and titles, thereby improving their status at court and concomitantly increasing their wealth. Criticism is directed in particular at two categories of persuaders: a) persuaders who enjoy arguing for the sake of arguing and engage in pointless, absurd discussions of no practical use. These debates typically revolve around paradoxical statements or short stories that were part of a shared cultural repertoire of the time, such as the most famous "white horse (is not horse)" argument (*báimǎ fēi mǎ* 白馬非馬), or the "bramble thorn" story (*jícì* 棘刺);[51] and b) parasites who make strategic use of these undignified stratagems to climb the social ladder and make a significant advancement in their career, especially in terms of economic gain, "peripatetic moochers" (*yóushí* 游食, as the text disparagingly calls "wandering persuaders" (or "peripatetic eaters," as in Pines 2017a). As will be discussed in more detail in Sect. 2.2, this practice is widely criticized in *Shāngjūnshū*, as their behaviour and their promotion through the ranks of the administrative system is detrimental to other social strata that instead are deemed worthy because of their service to the state, i.e. tillers and soldiers, and eventually disrupts the carefully constructed social system based on meritocracy promoted by the text.[52]

While warning against the potentially devastating effects of deliberately deceptive, misleading language, *Hán Fēizǐ* assumes an ambiguous stance towards argumentation and persuasion, like most contemporaneous texts. It is no secret that intellectuals of the time *nolens volens* were employing the rhetorical arts themselves in order to make their words more alluring and convincing, and to gain the ruler's, i.e. their patron's attention, so as to persuade him to enact their political agenda. At the same time, the harsh criticism expressed against adversaries at court or in the political arena is a typical example of a staged performance, and has to be considered accordingly as a sophisticated rhetorical tactic in itself, a form of "rhetoric of anti-rhetoric" (Valesio 1980: 41–60, esp. 41–42) rather than a heartfelt, sincere criticism and a stance taken against the abuse of rhetoric in politics.

Effective or persuasive speech as a form of rhetorical prowess is indeed a "double-edged sword" (Richter 2014), a powerful but also dangerous communication tool that should be employed carefully. It is one of the "techniques" (*shù*

---

[51] These two arguments are both mentioned together in *Hán Fēizǐ* 32.0.2 ("Wài chǔshuō zuǒ shàng") (Chén 2000: 658) and embedded into short narrative anecdotes used as illustrations, respectively in *Hán Fēizǐ* 30.0.7 and 30.7.4 ("Nèi chǔshuō shàng" 內儲說上) and 32.2.3 ("Wài chǔshuō zuǒ shàng") in the case of the "white horse" (Chén 2000: 570, 613, and 674); and 32.0.2 ("Wài chǔshuō zuǒ shàng") in the case of the "bramble thorn" (Chén 2000: 671–73). See Liao 1939 vol. 2: 35–38. On paradoxes in early Chinese texts, see for instance Reding 1985; Stevenson 1991; Raphals 1998; De Reu 2006; Chen 2014; Indraccolo 2016; and Fraser 2020.

[52] Pines 2016: 27–29; 2017a: 85–95; 2022; Chap. 18, this volume.

術) – and one of the most vital ones – that the smug advisor and courtier need to master at its finest to pursue their political goals, while at the same time defending themselves from adversaries' attacks (Galvany 2012 and 2017). But rhetorical ability does come with both great responsibility – insofar as one's intentions are good – and danger in dealing with a potentially quick-tempered and irrational ruler. A good example of the conundrum regarding the ambiguity and intrinsic *problématique* of language is provided by the long, autobiographical cri de coeur in which Hán Fēi himself engages, pouring out all his frustration with being constantly attacked, in chapter 3, "Nányán" 難言 ("On the Difficulty of Speaking"):

臣非非難言也，所以難言者:言順比滑澤，洋洋纚纚然，則見以為華而不實。敦祇恭厚，鯁固慎完，則見以為掘而不倫。多言繁稱，連類比物，則見以為虛而無用。總微說約，徑省而不飾，則見以為劌而不辯。激急親近，探知人情，則見以為譖而不讓。閎大廣博，妙遠不測，則見以為夸而無用。家計小談，以具數言，則見以為陋。言而近世，辭不悖逆，則見以為貪生而諛上。言而遠俗，詭躁人間，則見以為誕。捷敏辯給，繁於文采，則見以為史。殊釋文學，以質信言，則見以為鄙。時稱詩書，道法往古，則見以為誦。此臣非之所以難言而重患也。

It is not that your subject, Fēi, finds speaking hard, and therefore is embarrassed to speak: if his speech comes along fluently, smooth and suave, then it is considered pretentious and without substance. If it is sincere and deferential, straightforward yet cautious, then it is considered crooked and unsystematic. If it is profuse and makes wide use of citations, and establishes analogical connections to compare things, then it is considered shallow and useless. If it generalizes on the basis of details or talks approximately, being direct and concise and not overly embellished, then it is considered plain and ineloquent. If it is vehement and talks urgently about close relationships and personal matters, and inquires deeply into human inclinations, then it is considered slanderous and disrespectful. If it is extensive and broadly learned, subtle and farsighted and yet not speculative, then it is considered boastful and useless. If it touches upon management of household affairs and talks about concrete figures, then it is considered tasteless. If it discusses contemporary times, but its words are not critical, then it is considered cowardly and flattering. If it is detached from common life, yet vehemently blames society, then it is considered unrealistic. If it is sharp and witty, endowed with argumentative prowess, and rich in refinement and talent, then it is considered convoluted. If it dispenses with any literary refinement and form of erudition to focus on the bare facts, then it is considered vulgar. If it cites at the appropriate time the *Odes* and the *Documents*, and speaks about the methods used in ancient times, then it is considered a dirge. These are the reasons why your humble servant, Fēi, is embarrassed to speak and seriously dismayed about it. (*Hán Fēizǐ* 3.1; Chén 2000: 47–48)

In this beautifully constructed, emotional monologue, Hán Fēi chooses to express himself in the first person and to address the ruler directly in a heartfelt appeal, in which he denounces the toxicity of the court environment. Exasperated by the constant skirmishing with other members of the court, he gives vent to all the bitterness and frustration of having his intentions constantly misunderstood, and most often deliberately misrepresented by his peers in order to present him in a bad light. No matter how carefully he chooses his words, formulates his argument or picks his topics, or even how genuine his actual concern for the wellbeing of the sovereign and the state might be, he still ends up being mocked, slandered and criticised by envious adversaries. In this way, his words cannot make their way through this curtain of lies and reach the ruler. The obsessiveness of the rhythm of the text, built of couplets of more or less parallel sentences, addressing complementary opposite types of speech and the equally negative reception they invariably receive, contributes to building a crescendo of frustration, conveying a sense of unease.

Overall, *Hán Fēizǐ* shows a more pronounced concern about the consequences of persuasion than *Shāngjūnshū*, as the most famous chapter 12, "Shuìnán," testifies, though the former also dedicates a whole chapter to *biàn*, chapter 41, "Wèn biàn" 問辯 ("Inquiring about argumentation").[53] *Hán Fēizǐ* assumes either the perspective of a high-ranking minister or official at court, or that of the ruler in almost equal proportion. Chapter 12, "Shuìnán," in particular could have also been addressed to the sovereign in order to make him aware of and warn him against the deceptiveness of the techniques employed by his own ministers, rather than providing advice to an audience or readership of peers engaging in persuasion (Goldin 2013: 1–21; Indraccolo 2021b).

Shāngjūnshū instead has more of a bird-eye perspective, and seemingly assumes the point of view of someone in power and already well-established – a minister, or in any case someone who occupies a position of high responsibility at court and within the government – who has to keep the state running and the population under control. The text provides pragmatic advice about how to ensure that inferiors stay willingly within their ranks, hence why it appears to identify a major source of concern in the display of a refined intellect as manifested in the ability to engage in sophisticated debates (*biàn* 辯), due to its subversive potential. This aspect will be addressed in the following paragraph.

2.2 Language for Social Climbing

The criticism that *Shāngjūnshū* directs against "peripatetic moochers" or "peripatetic eaters" (*yóushí*), is threefold, as we are told explicitly in chapter 3, "Nóngzhàn" 農戰 ("Agriculture and Warfare"). In part, it resembles the critiques expressed also in *Hán Fēizǐ*, but at the same time advances a distinct viewpoint: a) the bizarre and overly elaborate discussions in which persuaders indulge are pointless, and eventually of no practical use; b) by indulging in these pointless discussions, they however manage to entice the ruler, gain his attention, and thereby advance their career and gain wealth; c) by doing so, they set a bad example for the common people, as their behavior embodies an easy shortcut to improve one's economic and social conditions that disrupts the rigid social order that *Shāngjūnshū* promotes and tries to realize on the basis of a strict assessment of merit gained on the battlefield or in agricultural production (Pines 2022). The text lucidly summarizes the steps leading to the inevitable social disruption generated by the pernicious influence of

---

[53] On criticism against *biàn* in *Hán Fēizǐ*, see Conde 2016a: 53–58, as well as the corresponding section in the Italian translation of this article in 2016b: 29–34.

"peripatetic moochers" or "peripatetic eaters" and the emulation of their behaviour by the population:

今世主皆憂其國之危而兵之弱也，而強聽說者。說者成伍，煩言飾辭，而無實用。主好其辯，不求其實。說者得意，道路曲辯，輩輩成群。民見其可以取王公大人也，而皆學之。夫人聚黨與說議於國，紛紛焉。小民樂之，大人說之。故其民農者寡，而游食者眾；眾則農者怠，農者怠則土地荒。學者成俗，則民舍農，從事於談說，高言偽議，舍農游食，而以言相高也。故民離上而不臣者成群。此貧國弱兵之教也。

Nowadays all the rulers of our age are worried that their states are endangered and their soldiers are weak, so they strive to heed the persuaders. Persuaders form legions; they multiply words and adorn sayings but are of no real use. The sovereign is fond of their arguments and does not seek their substance. The persuaders are satisfied; the roads are full of skillful talkers, and from generation to generation they go on and multiply. The people see that this is the way to reach kings, lords, and grandees, and all learn from them. They form cliques and associations, debate state affairs, and proliferate. Lower people are fond of them; grandees are delighted by them. Therefore, among the people few are engaged in agriculture, whereas "peripatetic eaters" are plenty; as they are plenty, the farmers are indolent; as the farmers are indolent, the land becomes wasteland. If learning becomes habitual, the people turn their backs on farming: they follow talkers and persuaders, speak grand words, and [engage in] false debates. They turn their backs on farming and travel to get food, trying to exceed each other in words. Hence, the people abandon their superiors, and those who do not behave as subjects become more and more numerous. This is the teaching that impoverishes the state and weakens the army. (Modified from Pines 2017a: 139–40, *Shāngjūnshū* 3.10; Zhāng 2012: 55)

Even more worrying, the chapter further warns us, is that it only takes a few such people to encourage the populace to slack off, abandon its duties and follow their lead instead:

農戰之民千人，而有《詩》、《書》、辯慧者一人焉，千人者皆怠於農戰矣

When one thousand people are engaged in agriculture and warfare, yet there is a single man among them engaged in *Poems*, *Documents*, argumentativeness, and cleverness, one thousand people will all become remiss in agriculture and warfare. (*Shāngjūnshū* 3.4; Zhāng 2012: 42)

Intellectuals seem to be a main target of *Shāngjūnshū*, as they are considered to be dangerous both to sociopolitical stability and to policy implementation. While *Shāngjūnshū* is far less critical of the apparently idle, useless content of the debates in which persuaders indulge than *Hán Fēizǐ*, the text seems to be particularly concerned about another aspect: the predictable unpredictability of savvy people, who have the intellectual and cognitive skills to disclose any hidden goals of the government and to unravel the mechanisms and workings of the state.[54] This knowledge would potentially allow them to oppose and even counteract government policies with which they might disagree, thereby undermining the foundations of the state. Whether they be imposters who pose as persuaders and dabble in the rhetorical arts or actually clever, refined debaters with a serious political agenda, intellectuals pose a major threat to the experiment of social engineering prompted by *Shāngjūnshū*.

---

[54] Pines 2002 and 2022; see also Galvany 2012; Indraccolo 2021b.

3 Concluding Remarks

In this chapter I tried to show that, understudied as it is, philosophy of language does play a cardinal role in *fǎ* thinking. Most of the texts traditionally associated with or acknowledged as embodying the principles of the *fǎ* intellectual tradition – in particular *Hán Fēizǐ*, and to a somewhat lesser though still significant extent *Shāngjūnshū*, *Shēnzǐ*, and *Guǎnzǐ* –show a rather pervasive interest in and an evident concern about the use, and especially the deliberate mis-use, of language. *Hán Fēizǐ*, in particular, problematizes the power that the spoken word can exercise on the psyche of the ruler and, through him, on government practice, but also in diplomacy and in the political realm at large.

All these texts seemingly assume an ambivalent attitude toward the rhetorical arts – and in particular the two complementary techniques of argumentation (*biàn*) and persuasion (*shuì*) – and the resort to these and other similar allegedly undignified, malicious linguistic stratagems. These techniques are often singled out for criticism by *fǎ* texts, as is the case also for more or less contemporary works that are representative of other competing trends of thought. Criticism aside, some of the texts associated with the *fǎ* tradition, most notably *Hán Fēizi*, make undisguised use of these very techniques, and consistently rely on their refined polemical skills to pursue their goals. They also openly promote them in an a-moral, detached way as a viable and perfectly acceptable means to reach one's communicative goal, regardless of one's intentions, and even instructing a potential audience on how to perform them effectively. On the one hand, it is clear that mastering these techniques is fundamental for intellectuals who aspire to succeed in politics and hold office, and to progressively advance in their career so as to exercise influence on government policies by promoting their own political agenda. To excel in these techniques also means to stand out among the crowd and have the opportunity to be noticed by the ruler, and possibly to be offered the chance to make a difference in the state administration.

On the other hand, it is also an ability of vital importance to navigate and survive – quite literally – court life, as it can make the difference between life and death. Rhetorical prowess as much as intellectual and political acumen represent the most effective weapons to fend off attacks and vicious slanders coming from competitors in the political arena at court, as well as to spare an advisor or minister from the ruler's wrath: addressing the mediocre sovereigns of the time and having to deal with their tantrums, paranoia, and egotistic "will to power" is no mean feat. As *Hán Fēizǐ* tells us in chapter 12, "Shuìnán," engaging the ruler in conversation is as dangerous and potentially deadly as caressing a dragon's throat where sharp scales grow that should not be stroked in the wrong way (Indraccolo 2021b; Hunter 2013). Hence, when approaching the ruler, learning how to strategically progress in the discussion by carefully attuning one's speech to the sovereign's reactions, personal inclinations, wishes and innermost desires, is crucial (Olberding 2013; Graziani 2015).

All these texts take into account both advantages and disadvantages that the use of rhetorical techniques might entail. Even if the supreme goal of a *fǎ* thinker is to contribute to a stable, efficient, and ultimately orderly state, regardless of the cost in terms of personal sacrifice and loss of humanity, it is obvious that these techniques could also be efficiently used by ill-minded retainers and ministers who pursue exclusively selfish interests to the detriment of the superior good, which, in the *fǎ* political project, is represented by the social and political stability of the state.[55] These sycophants represent a danger to both civil society and the government, inasmuch as, by exerting influence over the sovereign, they can persuade him to enact a certain policy, or favor them over honest, devoted officials, further undermining the power and authority of the government.

The performative and prescriptive power of the spoken word is also at the center of a complex, articulated discourse that is born within and develops from the ongoing contemporary debate concerning the urgent necessity to "rectify names" (*zhèngmíng*), i.e. to re-establish clear, univocal correspondences between names (of titles, official positions, but in *fǎ* texts also occasionally punishments and legal forms of action) and their corresponding realities. This aims to ensure that phenomena, particularized things, as well as – most importantly in this case – social and political actors fully embody the characteristics and values, but also embrace the duties, that are intrinsically entrenched within a certain name or title that is bestowed upon them, either by social conventions in the private dimension of community and family life, or by the government and the state in the performance of their public, official commitment to society.

Finally, from this analysis it emerges that the *fǎ* tradition has indeed developed a well-articulated philosophical discourse on language that invests different aspects of, and is well-inserted within, the ongoing philosophical debates of its time, sharing the same concerns about the unreliability and intrinsic ambiguity of the spoken word, but also proposing an original, distinctive perspective that not only rehabilitates, but also actively promotes the resort to the dreaded rhetorical arts. These are considered part of the necessary compromises and adjustments required to achieve the final superior goal of the establishment of an orderly, and hence eventually peaceful, government and society.

---

[55] It must be noted here that the *fǎ* tradition does not condemn the private interest or personal profit (*sī* 私, *sīlì* 私利) of the individual per se. The problem arises only when and if such private interests or profit clash against and come in the way of the realization of the superior good (i.e. what is beneficial for the state, or the community as a whole, considered as an organized socio-political organism, *gōnglì* 公利). On the contrary, what other intellectual traditions would define "selfish" desires, according to *fǎ* thinkers can be smugly exploited to bring the people to willingly collaborate and work towards the goal of the establishment of the envisioned political ideal – a pacified, orderly state ruled by a functioning government that ensures stability and continuity of rule (Harris, Chap. 10, this volume). On the concept of self interest in *Hán Fēizǐ*, see Goldin 2005: 58–65).

References

Ames, Roger T. 1994. *The Art of Rulership: A Study of Ancient Chinese Political Thought*. Albany, NY: State University of New York Press.

Berlin, Adele. 1995. *The Dynamics of Biblical Parallelism*. Bloomington, IN: Indiana University Press.

Chen, Bo. 2014. Six Groups of Paradoxes in Ancient China from the Perspective of Comparative Philosophy. *Asian Philosophy* 24 (4): 363–392.

Caldwell, Ernest. 2018. *Writing Chinese Laws – The Form and Function of Legal Statutes Found in the Qin Shuihudi Corpus*. London/New York: Routledge.

Cáo, Fēng 曹峰. 2008. "A New Discussion of 'Rectification of Names' in *Xúnzǐ*"《荀子 • 正名》篇新論. In *Forest of Scholars* 儒林, vol. 4, ed. Páng Pǔ 龐樸, 268–82. Jǐnán: Shāndōng Dàxué chūbǎnshè.

——— 曹峰. 2015. "The Theories of Forms and Names', 'Rectification of Names', and 'Names and Reality' as a Kind of Political Thought" 作為一種政治思想的'形名'論、'正名'論、'名實'論. *Social Science* 社會科學 12: 109–120.

——— 曹峰. 2016. "A New Examination of Confucius' Rectification of Names." *Journal of Chinese Humanities* 2: 147–171.

——— 曹峰. 2017. *A Study of the Political Thought of* '*Míng*' *in Ancient China* 國古代"名"的政治思想研究. Shànghǎi. Shànghǎi gǔjí chūbǎnshè.

Chén, Qíyóu 陳奇猷 (1917–2006). 2000. *Hán Fēizǐ, With New Collations and Commentary* 韓非子新校注. Shànghǎi: Shànghǎi gǔjí chūbǎnshè.

Conde, Juan Luis. 2016a. "La discreta y sorprendente vigencia del ideólogo del despotismo chino: Han Feizi" (The Discreet and Surprisingly Ongoing Influence of Han Feizi, Ideologue of Chinese Despotism). *ISEGORÍA. Revista de Filosofía Moral y Política* 54: 51–74.

———. 2016b. Come frecce senza bersaglio: retorica e ideologia in Han Feizi e nel discorso neo-liberale. *Rivista Italiana di Filosofia del Linguaggio* 1–3: 28–42.

Creel, Herrlee G. 1960. *Confucius and The Chinese Way*. New York: Harper and Row.

———. 1970. *What is Taoism? And Other Studies in Chinese Cultural History*. Chicago/London: University of Chicago Press.

———. 1974a. *Shen Pu-hai – A Chinese Political Philosopher of the Fourth Century B.C.* Chicago/London: University of Chicago Press.

———. 1974b. Shen Pu-hai: A Secular Philosopher of Administration. *Journal of Chinese Philosophy* 1 (2): 119–136.

Crump, James I., Jr. 1964. 戰國策 *Intrigues: Studies of the Chan-kuo Ts'e*. Ann Arbor, MI: The University of Michigan Press.

De Reu, Wim. 2006. Right Words Seem Wrong: Neglected Paradoxes in Early Chinese Philosophical Texts. *Philosophy East and West* 56 (2): 281–300.

Defoort, Carine. 2001. Ruling the World with Words: The Idea of *Zhengming* in the *Shizi*. *Bulletin of the Museum of Far Eastern Antiquities* 73: 217–242.

———. 2021. Confucius and the 'Rectification of Names': Hu Shi and the Modern Discourse on *Zhengming*. *Dao* 20: 613–633.

Dīng, Liàng 丁亮. 2008. "No Names" and "Correct Names" – About the Cultural Use and Development of China's Early and Middle Ancient Issue of Names Versus Realities "無名" 與 "正名" – 論中國上中古名實問題的文化作用與發展. Táiběi: Huā Mùlán wénhuà chūbǎnshè.

Egerod, Søren, and Else Glahn, eds. 1959. *Studia Serica Bernhard Karlgren Dedicata – Sinological Studies Dedicated to Bernhard Karlgren on His Seventieth Birthday, October Fifth, 1959*. Copenhagen: Ejnar Munksgaard.

van Els, Paul, Romain Graziani, Yuri Pines and Elisa Sabattini, eds. 2012. *Political Rhetoric in Early China/ Rhétorique et politique en Chine ancienne*, Special Issue, *Extrême-Orient Extrême-Occident* 34. Paris: Presses Universitaires de Vincennes.

Fraser, Chris. 2020. Paradoxes in the School of Names. In *Dao Companion to Chinese Philosophy of Logic*, ed. Fung Yiu-ming, 285–307. Dordrecht: Springer.

Galvany, Albert. 2012. Sly Mouths and Silver Tongues: The Dynamics of Psychological Persuasion in Ancient China. In *Political Rhetoric in Early China/ Rhétorique et politique en Chine ancienne*, Special Issue, *Extrême-Orient Extrême-Occident* 34, ed. Paul van Els, Romain Graziani, Yuri Pines, and Elisa Sabattini, 15–40. Paris: Presses Universitaires de Vincennes.

———. 2017. The Court as a Battlefield: The Art of War and the Art of Politics in the *Han Feizi*. *Bulletin of the School of Oriental and African Studies* 80 (1): 73–96.

Garrett, Mary M. 1993. Classical Chinese Conceptions of Argumentation and Persuasion. *Argumentation and Advocacy* 29 (3): 105–115.

Gassmann, Robert H. 1988. *Cheng Ming. Richtigstellung der Bezeichnungen – Zu den Quellen eines Philosophems im antiken China: ein Beitrag zur Konfuzius-Forschung*. Schweizerische Asiengesellschaft. Berne/Frankfurt am Main/New York/Paris: Peter Lang.

Geaney, Jane. 2018. *Language as Bodily Practice in Early China – A Chinese Grammatology*. Albany, NY: State University of New York Press.

Goldin, Paul R. 2005. *After Confucius: Studies in Early Chinese Philosophy*. Honolulu: University of Hawai'i Press.

———. 2011. Persistent Misconceptions about Chinese 'Legalism'. *Journal of Chinese Philosophy* 38 (1): 88–104.

———., ed. 2013. *Dao Companion to the Philosophy of Han Fei*. Dordrecht: Springer.

———. 2020. *The Art of Chinese Philosophy – Eight Classical Texts and How to Read Them*. Princeton/Oxford: Princeton University Press.

Graziani, Romain. 2012. Rhetoric that Kills, Rhetoric that Heals. In *Political Rhetoric in Early China/ Rhétorique et politique en Chine ancienne*, Special Issue, *Extrême-Orient Extrême-Occident* 34, ed. Paul van Els, Romain Graziani, Yuri Pines, and Elisa Sabattini, 41–78. Paris: Presses Universitaires de Vincennes.

———. 2015. Monarch and Minister: The Problematic Partnership in the Building of Absolute Monarchy in the *Han Feizi* 韓非子. In *Ideology of Power and Power of Ideology in Early China*, ed. Yuri Pines, Paul R. Goldin, and Martin Kern, 155–180. Leiden/Boston: E.J. Brill.

Guǎnzǐ jiàozhù 管子校注 (*Guǎnzǐ, With Collations and Commentary*). 2004. Annotated by Lí Xiángfēng 黎翔鳳 (1901–1979). Běijīng: Zhōnghuá shūjú.

Hànshū 漢書 (History of the [Former] Hàn Dynasty). 1964. By Bān Gù 班固 (32–92). Běijīng: Zhōnghuá shūjú.

Harbsmeier, Christoph. 1998. *Language and Logic vol. 7*. In *Science and Civilization in China*, ed. Joseph Needham. Cambridge: Cambridge University Press.

———, trans. Forthcoming. *Han Feizi, A Complete Translation: The Art of Statecraft in Early China*. Ed. Jens Østergaard Petersen and Yuri Pines. Leiden/Boston: E.J. Brill.

Hunter, Michael. 2013. The Difficulty with the 'Difficulties of Persuasion' ("Shuinan" 說難). In *Dao Companion to the Philosophy of Han Fei*, ed. Paul R. Goldin, 169–195. Dordrecht: Springer.

Indraccolo, Lisa. 2016. The 'White Horse,' the 'Three-Legged Chicken' and Other Paradoxes in Classical Chinese Literature. *Antiquorum Philosophia* 10: 67–88.

———. 2020. Argumentation (*bian* 辯). In *Dao Companion to Chinese Philosophy of Logic*, ed. Fung Yiu-ming, 171–180. Dordrecht: Springer.

———. 2021a. Argumentation and Persuasion in Classical Chinese Literature. In *Essays on Argumentation in Antiquity*, ed. Joseph A. Bjelde, David Merry, and Christopher Roser, 21–48. Dordrecht: Springer.

———. 2021b. Political Rhetoric in the *Hán Fēizǐ* – A structural analysis of Ch. 12 'Shuìnán' 說難. *Asiatische Studien/Études asiatiques* 74 (3): 655–686.

Kroll, Jurij L. 1985–86. Disputation in Ancient Chinese Culture. *Early China* 11–12: 119–145.

Lau, Dim Cheuk. 1973. Herrlee G. Creel, *What is Taoism and other Studies in Chinese Cultural History*, viii + 192 pp. Chicago and London, The University of Chicago Press, 1970. *Asia Major* 18: 121–123.

Levi, Jean. 1992. L'art de la persuasion à l'epoque des Royaumes Combattants (V^e–IIIe Siècles a.v. J.C.). *Extrême-Orient Extrême-Occident* 14: 49–89.

Lewis, Mark Edward. 1999. *Writing and Authority in Early China*. Albany, NY: State University of New York Press.

Liao, Wen-Kuei, trans. 1939. *The Complete Works of Han Fei Tzǔ* 韓非子 – *a Classic of Chinese Legalism*. 2 vols. London: Arthur Probsthain.

Louton, John. 1979. She Pu-hai: A Misunderstood and Wrongly Neglected Thinker? Reviewed Work: *Shen Pu-hai: A Chinese Political Philosopher of the Fourth Century B.C.* by Herrlee G. Creel. *Journal of the American Oriental Society* 99 (3): 440–449.

Loy, Hui Chieh. 2003. Analects 13.3 and the Doctrine of 'Correcting Names'. *Monumenta Serica* 58: 19–36.

———. 2014. Language and Ethics in the *Analects*. In *Dao Companion to the Analects*, ed. Amy Olberding, 137–158. Dordrecht: Springer.

Lu, Xing. 1998. *Rhetoric in Ancient China, Fifth to Third Century B.C.E. – A Comparison with Classical Greek Rhetoric*. Columbia, SC: University of South Carolina Press.

Lúnyǔ zhèngyì 論語正義 (The Correct Interpretation of the Analects). 1990. Annotated by Liú Bǎonán 劉寶楠 (1791–1855). Běijīng: Zhōnghuá shūjú.

MacCormack, Geoffrey. 1986. Rectification of Names in Early Chinese Legal and Political Thought. *Archiv für Rechts- und Sozialphilosophie / Archives for Philosophy of Law and Social Philosophy* 72 (3): 378–390.

Makeham, John. 1990–91. The Legalist Concept of Hsing-Ming: An Example of the Contribution of Archaeological Evidence to the Re-Interpretation of Transmitted Texts. *Monumenta Serica* 39: 87–114.

———. 1994. *Name and Actuality in Early Chinese Thought*. Albany, NY: State University of New York Press.

Martinich, Aloysius P. 2014. Political Theory and Linguistic Criteria in HAN FEIZI's Philosophy. *Dao* 13: 379–393.

Olberding, Garret P., ed. 2013. *Facing the Monarch – Modes of Advice in the Early Chinese Court*. Cambridge, MA: Harvard University Press.

Pines, Yuri. 2002. Friends or Foes: Changing Concepts of Ruler-Minister Relations and the Notion of Loyalty in Pre-Imperial China. *Monumenta Serica* 50: 35–74.

———. 2009. *Envisioning Eternal Empire – Chinese Political Thought of the Warring States Era*. Honolulu: University of Hawai'i Press.

———. 2016. Social Engineering in Early China: The Ideology of the *Shangjunshu* (*Book of Lord Shang*) Revisited. *Oriens Extremus* 55: 1–37.

———, ed. and trans. 2017a. *The Book of Lord Shang: Apologetics of State Power in Early China*. Princeton: Princeton University Press.

———. 2017b. Confucius' Elitism: The Concepts of *junzi* and *xiaoren* Revisited. In *A Concise Companion to Confucius*, ed. Paul R. Goldin, 164–184. Oxford: Wiley-Blackwell.

———. 2020. 'To Die for the Sanctity of the Name': Name (*ming* 名) As Prime Mover of Political Action in Early China. In *Keywords in Chinese Culture*, ed. Wai-yee Li and Yuri Pines, 169–215. Hong Kong: The Chinese University of Hong Kong Press.

———. 2022. Class Traitors? The Assault on the Intellectuals' Power in the *Book of Lord Shang* and *Han Feizi*. Presented at the workshop "Chinese Political Thought: A Global Dialogue beyond 'Orientalism.'" January 20th, on-line.

Qúnshū zhìyào 群書治要 (Compilation of Writings on the Cardinal Principles of Governance). 2011. Compiled by Wèi Zhēng 魏徵 (581–643). Táiběi: Shìjiè shūjú.

Raphals, Lisa. 1998. On Hui Shi. In *Wandering at Ease in the Zhuangzi*, ed. Roger T. Ames, 143–161. Albany, NY: State University of New York Press.

Reding, Jean-Paul. 1985. *Les fondements philosophiques de la réthorique chez les sophistes grecs et chez les sophistes chinois*. Berne/Frankfurt/New York: Peter Lang.

Richter, Matthias L. 2013. *The Embodied Text – Establishing Textual Identity in Early Chinese Manuscripts*. Leiden/Boston: E. J. Brill.

Richter, Matthias L. 2014. Handling a double-edged sword: Controlling rhetoric in Early China. In *Masters of Disguise? Conceptions and Misconceptions of 'Rhetoric' in Chinese Antiquity*,

Special Issue, *Asiatische Studien/Études asiatiques* 68: 4, ed. Wolfgang Behr and Lisa Indraccolo, 1021–1068.

Rickett, W. Allyn, ed. and trans. 2001. *Guanzi – Political, Economic, and Philosophical Essays from Early China: A Study and Translation. Vol. 1, Chapters I, 1–XI, 34 and XX, 64–XXI, 65–66, Revised Edition*. Princeton: Princeton University Press.

Roth, Harold D. 2012–13. The Daoist Concept of *Li* 理 (Pattern) and Early Chinese Comsology. *Early China* 35–36: 157–183.

Schaberg, David. 2016. The Ruling Mind. Persuasion and the Origins of Chinese Psychology. In *The Rhetoric of Hiddenness in Traditional Chinese Culture*, ed. Paula M. Varsano, 33–51. Albany, NY: State University of New York Press.

Shǐjì 史記 (*Records of the Grand Historian*). Compiled by Sīmǎ Qiān 司馬遷 (ca.145–86 BCE). 2014. Běijīng: Zhōnguá shūjú.

Stevenson, Frank W. 1991. South Has (No) Limits: Relative and Absolute Meaning in Hui Shih's Ten Points. *Tamkang Review* 21 (4): 325–346.

Sun, Zhenbin. 2015. *Language, Discourse, and Practice in Ancient China*. Dordrecht: Springer.

Valesio, Paolo. 1980. *Novantiqua – Rhetorics as a contemporary theory*. Bloomington, IN: Indiana University Press.

Valmisa, Mercedes. 2021. *Adapting – A Chinese Philosophy of Action*. New York: Oxford University Press.

Vogelsang, Kai. Forthcoming. Rulership in the Discourse of Political Realism – The Concept of *mingzhu* 明主. *Bochumer Jahrbuch zur Ostasienforschung* 46(2023).

Waley, Arthur D., trans. 1938. *The Analects of Confucius*. London: George Allen and Unwin.

Wang, Hsiao-po, and Leo S. Chang. 1986. *The Philosophical Foundations of Han Fei's Political Theory*. Honolulu: University of Hawai'i Press.

Waring, Luke. 2020. Introducing the *Wu Ze You Xing Tu Manuscript from Mawangdui. *Early China* 43: 123–160.

Watson, Burton, ed. and trans. 1964. *Han Fei Tzu – Basic Writings*. New York/London: Columbia University Press.

Yáng, Kuān 楊寬. 1998. *History of the Warring States* 戰國史. Shànghǎi: Shànghǎi Rénmín chūbǎnshè, rev. ed.

Yáng, Xiùgōng 楊秀宮. 1999. A Comparison of Confucius' and Xúnzǐ's "Theory of the Rectification of Names" 孔子與荀子「正名論」之比較. *Tunghai Journal* 東海學報 40.1: 243–278.

——— 楊秀宮. 2002. The Feasability of Developing Xúnzǐ's Thought on the Rectification of Names into a Philosophy of Language 荀子正名思想朝語言哲學向度發展的可行性. *Journal of Shu-Te University* 樹德科技大學學報 4.2: 321–335.

Zhāng, Jué 張覺, ed. 2010. *Hán Fēizǐ, With Collations and Annotations* 韓非子校疏. Shànghǎi: Shànghǎi gǔjí chūbǎnshè.

——— 張覺, ed. 2012. *The Book of Lord Shāng, With Collations and Annotations* 商君書校疏. Běijīng: Zhīshi chǎnquán chūbǎnshè.

Chapter 15
The *Fa* Tradition and Morality

Alexus McLeod

1 Introduction

The *fa* tradition, associated with political thinkers of the late Warring States period (453–221 BCE), such as Shen Dao 慎到, Shen Buhai 申不害 (d. 337 BCE), Shang Yang 商鞅(d. 338 BCE), Han Fei 韓非 (d. 233 BCE), Li Si 李斯 (d. 208 BCE), and others, is often presented as an amoralistic tradition.[1] I argue in this paper that *fa* tradition thinkers generally accepted morality as valuable, even while they rejected it as playing a role in political strategy (at least in their own time). The view of *fa* tradition thinkers as amoralist overlooks the ways in which moral concerns were worked into *fa* tradition texts, as well as the ways in which *fa* tradition thinkers took morality to be a necessary and useful component of human life (and even, in certain rare conditions, of the ruler's political toolkit), even if they did not take it to play the same role Confucians argued it should.

I argue that the *fa* tradition response to Confucian morality largely has to do with their rejection of the Confucian view of *morality as strategy*. I distinguish between the views of morality as strategy and morality as end or general value. I then look at the accounts of virtue in two specific *fa* tradition texts, the *Han Feizi* 韓非子and the

---

[1] Graham 1989: 267; Kim 2012: 192. For contrary views, see Bárcenas 2013; Goldin 2011. While my view here echoes that of Goldin in rejecting the "amoralist" characterization of the *fa* tradition in general, Goldin seems to concede that the *Han Feizi* might be read as amoralist (even if the rest of the *fa* tradition cannot). I build my case here primarily on the *Han Feizi*—I think we have evidence to reject the characterization of that text as amoralist as well.

A. McLeod (✉)
Indiana University, Bloomington, IN, USA
e-mail: almcleo@indiana.edu

© The Author(s), under exclusive license to Springer Nature Switzerland AG 2024   433
Y. Pines (ed.), *Dao Companion to China's fa Tradition*, Dao Companions
to Chinese Philosophy 19, https://doi.org/10.1007/978-3-031-53630-4_16

Shangjunshu 商君書 (Book of Lord Shang).[2] I argue that ultimately these texts should be read not specifically as challenges to Confucian (or any other) morality, but instead as criticizing the Confucian focus on moral self-cultivation as a key response to social disorder, and the idea of the efficacy of the ruler's focus on self-cultivation to bring about virtue in society. The *Han Feizi* and *Shangjunshu* do not reject the value of Confucian virtue as end, and when they do discuss this value, they actually seem to give a positive evaluation. This is particularly pronounced in *Shangjunshu*. In essence, the *fa* tradition largely (but as we will see, not universally) rejects morality as strategy, while for the most part embracing morality as end or value.

In this way, we might see the *fa* tradition's stance on morality as in line with that found in texts such as the *Laozi* 老子, on which we find commentary in the *Han Feizi* (some of which I discuss below). Yuri Pines writes, for example, that "Shang Yang's writings resemble the *Laozi* in dissociating political practice from moralizing discourse" (Pines 2017: 15). In discussions of politics, as we see in stanzas 17, 37, 39, and others of the *Laozi*, we see things reminiscent of *fa* tradition views. A ruler achieves political order not through cultivation of morality, but through emptying oneself of such concerns, and achieving *wu-wei* 無為 (non-forced action). *Laozi* 37, for example, reads:

> 侯王若能守之，萬物將自化。
>
> If the nobles and rulers can guard this [the possession of *wu-wei*], then the myriad things will transform themselves on their own.

The similarity between *fa* tradition texts and the *Laozi* here is in the focus on *strategy* rather than ends. Unlike Confucian and Mohist texts that are largely concerned with ends and how to bring about certain desired ends (such as virtue for the Confucians and benefit, *li* 利, for the Mohists[3]), the *Laozi* is less concerned in general with the kinds of ends we achieve than with the best ways to achieve these ends—or at least no such clear statement of ends can be found in the *Laozi*. But whereas texts such as the *Laozi* focus on general strategy, including political strategy among other topics, *fa* tradition texts such as the *Han Feizi* and *Shangjunshu* focus on political strategy exclusively. They also offer a somewhat different approach than that of the *Laozi* to the maintenance of political order, even though there is much from the *Laozi* concerning political strategy that *fa* tradition thinkers would accept.[4]

---

[2] The issue of virtue in the Shenzi 慎子 fragments is covered in Eirik Harris' contribution to this volume (Chap. 3).

[3] Although both the Confucians and the Mohists ultimately aim to generate social order, their views of how such harmony is attained leads to these differences in the ends they pursue. (He 2021; Park 2021).

[4] A good example of this is *Laozi* 17, which claims that the best kind of ruler is one of whom the people know nothing more than that he is there (太上，下知有之). The loved and the feared rulers are not as good as this ruler, because the best ruler is able to manipulate the people to follow the ruler's desires (to become ordered) of their own volition, and thinking that it is their own will.

Similarities and differences between the *fa* texts and the *Laozi* can be observed from several examples. Thus, Han Feizi's view of using *fa* 法 (laws, standards) to mask the desires of the ruler[5] has strong echoes with the recommendations of the *Laozi* that being without desire leads to effective action (par. 37 for example—不欲 以靜，天下將自定 "lacking desire and with stillness, all in the world achieve a determinate position on their own"). But the key component of the ruler's desire that is problematic in the case of Han Feizi is its capacity to be used by others for manipulative purposes, whereas in the *Laozi* (similar to texts such as "Neiye" 內業 chapter of *Guanzi* 管子)[6], the problem with desire seems to be its tendency to disturb or preoccupy one who possesses it. Although this difference may lead to the possibility of different strategies concerning desire—in *Han Feizi*, desire needs to at least be masked, while in *Laozi*, desire must be lessened or quieted—both texts are similar in their marking features of desire as problematic in obtaining political order (or any other aim).[7] Another parallel with the *Laozi* is in the *Shangjunshu* claim that when *fa* are properly applied, the people will become "self-ordering" (*zi zhi* 自治). This argument echoes the political language and views of the *Laozi* (*Shangjunshu* 2017: 26.6; Zhang 2012: 288).[8] The *fa* texts and the *Laozi* also share the view that focus on morality is not an ultimately effective political strategy.

Despite the *fa* tradition's rejection of morality as political strategy in most cases, their rejection of it is neither complete nor unqualified. As I show below, both the *Han Feizi* and the *Shangjunshu* seem to accept morality not only as an end and value, but in certain circumstances also as political strategy. Where they reject morality is in cases of contemporary political strategy. Both texts insist that morality will be ineffective at best and disastrous at worst in the political situation of their time. This does not exclude the possibility that morality might *become* effective as a strategy at some point in the future, however. Both texts also concede that there were periods in the ancient past in which morality *was* an effective political strategy, which leaves open the possibility that this may happen again with crucial changes

---

[5] *Han Feizi* forthcoming: 5.1 (Chen 2000: 66) ("Zhu dao" 主道).

[6] See Roth 2004; Rickett 1998: 15–55.

[7] While the way the *Han Feizi* suggests to deal with this problematic aspect of desire in some chapters is to mask or conceal desires, in the "Jie Lao" chapter, achieving a state of non-desire is recommended. Notice that these two positions are by no means inconsistent, as surely the most effective way to conceal desires would be not to have them at all. Thus, this discrepancy does not give us evidence that "Jie Lao" is not by Han Feizi. See Denecke 2010: 288–89. It is quite possible that Han Feizi held that elimination of desire is most effective, but if this is not possible (as would be expected in the case of rulers accustomed to indulging desires), then one should at least mask desires. And given his practical focus in chapters such as "Zhu dao" (see the above note), this is exactly what one would expect. Ivanhoe 2011: 37 claims that Han Feizi rejects the view that desire can be eliminated because he thinks this is impossible, but provides no textual evidence or argument for this claim.

[8] All citations from *Shangjunshu* hereafter refer to the divisions into paragraphs adopted in Pines 2017 and the page from Zhang 2012 edition.

to the political situation.[9] Yuri Pines discusses the view of the possibility of morality as political strategy in an ideal future in the *Shangjunshu,* in the introduction to his translation of the text. He points out that in Chapter 13 of the text, which includes perhaps its most incisive criticism of morality as strategy, the closing passage shift gears dramatically and presents morality as the ultimate end at which political order aims. Pines writes: "[the chapter] does not deny the importance of coercion, and it rejects application of moral means of rule under the current condition of bitter competition among rival states, but it also clearly promises a future of 'benevolence and righteousness' under the future sage's rule. This finale gives us a hint of a barely noticed utopian strand in the *Book of Lord Shang*" (Pines 2017: 99).

Below, I look more closely at the views concerning morality as strategy and morality as value or end in the *Han Feizi* and *Shangjunshu,* developing the view that in these texts, as representative of *fa* tradition, we find a general (though not absolute) rejection of morality as strategy alongside an acceptance of morality as value or end.

2   Morality as Strategy vs. Morality as End/Value

The issue of morality is discussed by Confucians and other authors in terms of self-cultivation, strategy for political order, aim of political order, source of individual and communal thriving, and a number of other ways. For the Confucians, morality is clearly the primary concern. An important distinction between Confucian and *fa* tradition texts is what these texts are ultimately *about.* Much of what appears to be disagreement can be understood as simply difference of subject matter. Confucian texts are largely about morality, while *fa* tradition texts are primarily about political order. Insofar as Confucian texts discuss political order or *fa* tradition texts discuss morality, they do so to make points about their chief subject matter, to which other issues are subordinated.[10]

In Confucian texts, morality is generally taken as a necessary part of an effective strategy of maintaining political order, even if the generation of such order is not in itself sufficient to achieve the level of moral development at which Confucians argue we should aim. *Analects* 15.5 (Cheng 1990: 1062), for example, discusses the sage Shun's ability to bring about political order without having to do anything more than simply sitting in his throne facing south (due to the moral potency or virtue that influenced those around him). In a number of famous passages in the first

---

[9] Or the possibility that situations might obtain in contemporary states elsewhere in the world that make morality effective as a strategy. This is generally not the case in the Warring States, due to the political and social situation.

[10] This "traditional" view is challenged by Loubna El Amine, who argues that political discussion in Confucian texts is independent of consideration of virtue and grounded in realpolitik. (El Amine 2015). Yutang Jin argues against this position, defending the traditional account offered here (Jin 2022).

chapter of the *Mengzi* 孟子, Mengzi (d. ca. 304 BCE) explains to King Hui of Liang 梁惠王 (r. 370–319 BCE),[11] and later his son and heir, King Xiang of Wei 魏襄王 (r. 318–296 BCE), and King Xuan of Qi 齊宣王 (r. 319–301 BCE), that political order and various political gains can be attained primarily through a focus on moral cultivation (*Mengzi* 1992: 1.1–1.7). Mengzi's explanation to King Xuan of how he can overcome the surrounding states, gain supremacy, and bring about order shows us how early Confucians think about the political power of morality and morality as strategy:

> 小固不可以敵大，寡固不可以敵眾，弱固不可以敵彊。海內之地方千里者九，齊集有其一。以一服八，何以異於鄒敵楚哉?蓋亦反其本矣。今王發政施仁，使天下仕者皆欲立於王之朝，耕者皆欲耕於王之野，商賈皆欲藏於王之市，行旅皆欲出於王之塗，天下之欲疾其君者皆欲赴愬於王。其若是，孰能禦之?
>
> The small cannot contend with the large, as the few cannot contend with the many, and the weak cannot contend with the strong. The territory within the seas consists of nine states of one thousand li square in size—of which Qi is one. If you use one to oppose eight, how is this different from [the statelet of] Zou's clashing with [the great power] Chu? Instead, you should protect yourself and return to the essentials. Now, if you put forth your government through benevolence, this will make all the men-of-service in the world desire to come serve in your court, all the farmers in the world desire to come cultivate your fields, all the merchants in the world desire to store their wares in your markets, all the travelers from other states desire to go forth on your roads, and everyone in the world who dislikes the rulers of their states desire to come take their complaints to you. In a case like this, how could any state resist you? (*Mengzi* 1992: 1.7).

We see here a statement that the aims of political and military operation, in this case overcoming rival states and gaining control over the world, are best achieved through cultivation or morality, rather than through military strength or political intrigue. This cultivation of morality can do what other techniques cannot, enabling even relatively small and weak states to overcome their neighbors.

Mengzi makes an even more direct claim about benevolence as a political strategy:

> 地不改辟矣，民不改聚矣，行仁政而王，莫之能禦也。
>
> One's territory does not have to become larger, and one's population does not have to become more plentiful—if you practice benevolence, you will become the True Monarch—there will be no one able to resist you. (*Mengzi* 1992: 3.1)

This all relies on a view of human motivation that is disputed by *fa* tradition thinkers. These thinkers agreed with the Confucians that human motivational considerations ultimately make the difference in the power of a state, but they disagreed on the strategy to generate the proper actions based on these motivations. Notice in the *Mengzi* passages above that the primary motivator is *self-interest*, just as it is for *fa* tradition thinkers. King Xuan has self-interested reasons to cultivate morality, just as the people who would be drawn to King Xuan's state would be so for self-interested reasons. Men-of-service would rather serve in a court more likely to hear

---

[11] Liang was identical to the state of Wei, which was referred to during this time by the name of its capital, Liang 梁 (modern Kaifeng), after King Hui moved the capital there from the Western city of Anyi in 361 BCE.

their concerns, farmers would rather cultivate fields when they are more likely to keep their yield of crops because of less onerous taxation demands from the state, travelers from other states would rather travel on roads where they are less likely to be attacked and robbed, etc. What facilitates this attainment of what is in people's self-interest is virtuous rule, as the virtuous ruler has a benevolence (*ren* 仁) such that he is concerned for others and aims to help them collectively achieve their aims of attaining what is in their self-interest.

Only the benevolent ruler, according to Mengzi, will reliably assist his people in attaining what is in their self-interest, because only the benevolent ruler ultimately *cares* about the people's attainment of what is in their self-interest.[12] This is why "the benevolent person has no rivals" 仁者無敵 (*Mengzi* 1992: 1.5). The benevolent ruler's concern for his people, in order to work in the way Mengzi suggests, has to be *seen* and understood by the people of his state and other states. That is, it must be accessible by the people. It will not be sufficient for the ruler to have a kind of "hidden" virtue.

There is also an important issue here concerning the cultivability of virtue for Mengzi and other Confucians. Mengzi's view of the benevolent ruler relies on the position that it is possible to cultivate oneself so as to reliably be motivated by virtue and not by self-interest or circumstances. The benevolent ruler, like the benevolent person more generally, has stable motivations and has cultivated global character traits operative across situations. While certain situations must obtain in order to fully cultivate virtue (thus *Analects* 1990: 1.8 enjoins "not to befriend those not equal to oneself [in virtue]"), once virtuous character is established, this character is for the most part stable (although it could be ruined given bad enough situations). For *fa* tradition thinkers, on the other hand, situations have far more influence over behavior, and while these situations may lead one to act virtuously, they can also lead to very different behavior. Ultimately virtuous activity depends on situational features rather than character, thus employing morality as general strategy for maintaining order is unreliable at best and foolish and disastrous at worst.[13]

To understand further the Confucian view of morality as strategy that *fa* tradition thinkers ultimately reject, we have to briefly turn to the concept of *fa* 法 (law, standard), which in Confucian texts is connected to the issue of morality as strategy. The Confucian philosopher Xunzi 荀子 (d. after 238 BCE), in particular, used the concept of *fa* to facilitate morality as strategy, making codifiable the moral actions of sages.

---

[12] Thus Mengzi discusses King Xuan of Qi, in his benevolent rule, having concern above all for four categories of people among the most disadvantaged of society. This kind of thing leads the people to love a ruler and be devoted to him, which practically manifests itself in their willingness to die for him: 君行仁政，斯民親其上，死其長矣。*Mengzi* 1992: 2.12.

[13] *Han Feizi* 49.1 ("Wu du" 五蠹).

3   Xunzi's Conception of *Fa* and the *Fa* Tradition Alternative

One of the key features of *fa* for Xunzi 荀子 (d. after 238 BCE) as well as other early thinkers such as Shen Dao is the concreteness and objectivity of *fa*. It is something clearly action-guiding on which we can rely.[14] It can also be a substitute for deliberation, motivated action, and a host of other things that could lead us astray. The concept of *fa* is central to the determination of morality as strategy, as the morally cultivated ruler skillfully creates and employs *fa* for the purpose of bringing about order.[15]

Xunzi, as a thoroughgoing Confucian, accepted the general ideas of Confucianism focusing on *ren* 仁 (humanity) and *li* 禮 (ritual) as central to both individual and collective social thriving. Cultivating the various Confucian virtues, was taken as necessary to develop the self, and also to play an essential role in ordering of society. As do other Confucian texts, the *Xunzi* focuses on the key role of the ruler in ordering society through virtue. Organization and order were associated with the ruler's ability to govern through virtue (*Xunzi* 1992: 12: 230 ["Jun dao" 君道]). The Confucian ideal ruler was one whose outward activities were few because he relied on the power of his virtue and his moral example to influence those below him, who would then influence those below them, and so on throughout the world.

Xunzi responded to a number of practical political problems with the earlier Confucian approach, including that of how the ruler makes clear for society the proper actions. Part of the process of self-cultivation is the imitation of virtuous exemplars. These exemplars, in particular virtuous rulers, originate the *fa* that others then follow to develop themselves.[16]

For Xunzi, while *fa* can serve as the basis for generating order, *fa* alone is not sufficient, and we still require virtuous rulers and other exemplars for this task.[17] This is at least in part because the flexibility of the virtuous person is required to guide situations at times when good *fa* would not otherwise lead to good outcomes.[18] Xunzi discusses the possibility of this kind of defect of even well-constructed *fa*, in arguing for the necessity of the exemplary person (*junzi*):

---

[14] For Shen Dao, see Yang 2013: 50–51; Harris 2016a: 46–50. On Xunzi's views on *fa*, see Hagen 2007: 146, Harris 2016b: 120–23. Xunzi criticizes Shen Dao on what he takes to be the latter's overreliance on *fa* alone. (Harris 2016a: 74–75).

[15] Xunzi connects *fa* directly to order in terms of maintaining the state (*Xunzi* 1992: 11: 219 ["Wang ba" 王霸]). He talks particularly about the ordering *fa* (*zhi fa* 治法). In *Xunzi* 1992: 12: 230 ["Jun dao" 君道], Xunzi calls *fa* "the sprout (*duan* 端) of order"—the idea being that the *fa* is necessary but not sufficient to bring about order—the cultivation of the people is also needed. Loubna El Amine argues that there are two senses of *fa* at work in the *Xunzi*, one of which requires the development of virtue to properly use (El Amine 2015: 138–39).

[16] Neville 2014: 73; *Xunzi* 1992: 23: 437 ("Xing e" 性惡).

[17] Xunzi ties order to the "way of the ruler" in the chapter of the same name (*Xunzi* 1992: 12: 230).

[18] Roger Ames maintains that Xunzi's view here is "typical of the Confucian position on penal law and government." Ames 1994: 124.

君子也者，道法之摠要也，不可少頃曠也。得之則治，失之則亂；得之則安，失之
則危；得之則存，失之則亡，故有良法而亂者有之矣，有君子而亂者，自
古及今，未嘗聞也

    The exemplary person is crucial for models (*fa*) of the Way (*dao*), and one cannot lack him for even a moment. If one loses him, there will be chaos. If one obtains him, there will be security. If one loses him, there will be danger. If one obtains him, there will be preservation. If one loses him, there will be destruction. Thus, there have been instances of chaos even where there are good models (*fa*), but from ancient times to the present it is unheard of to have chaos where the exemplary person is in charge. (*Xunzi* 1992: 14: 261 ["Zhi shi" 致士])

One of the innovations of the *Han Feizi* and the *fa* tradition texts more generally is the way in which *fa* is de-linked from sagehood, morality, or the exemplary person. *Fa* are instead rules adopted by the ruler to ensure order, rather than standards to bring about the moral development of society. While the *Han Feizi* does away with the need of the sage or morally excellent ruler, however, *fa* alone is not sufficient to maintain an orderly society. There must also be a skilled ruler to employ *fa* in the most effective ways. The *Han Feizi* mentions the need for "skillfulness" or "technique" (*shu* 術) in addition to *fa*. Skillfulness in this context has to do with understanding context and the motivations of others. *Fa* can be followed while villainous ministers fail to be ferreted out due to the ruler's lack of techniques. One can also fail to skillfully apply *fa* by insufficiently considering the implications of a given set of *fa* and failing to modify them as needed. The *Han Feizi* includes two interesting examples of this in Chapter 43, "Defining standards" ("Ding fa" 定法). He discusses Shen Buhai, who was purported to be a master and exemplar of technique, and Shang Yang, who was purported to be a master and exemplar of the use of *fa*. Even though these two figures understood important aspects of the proper way to maintain the state, neither was perfect, and each failed to completely hit the mark concerning artfulness or the use of *fa*.[19] Han Feizi gives examples from each of them (for this comparison, see Yu Zhong, Chap. 2, this volume; for the tension between *fa* and *shu*, see Song, Chap. 9, this volume).

    Shen Buhai said that officials should not violate certain injunctions to speak out of place, so that even if they have knowledge, they should not speak. Han Feizi criticizes this, saying that the ruler will lack crucial resources if officials follow this. The ruler cannot see and hear everything, and his knowledge is limited. If the ruler's knowledgeable ministers hold back from speaking even when they have the knowledge the ruler lacks, how can the ruler possibly remedy the gaps in his knowledge? Shang Yang, on the other hand, created a *fa* such that cutting off the head of an enemy in battle was rewarded with a promotion in rank and appointment to office.

---

[19] This discussion serves the purpose of endorsing the views of Shen Buhai and Shang Yang while at the same time avoiding commitment to taking their words as guides or exemplars. Han Feizi is in general opposed to using the views of the past or the works of past sages as guides, and thus is being thoroughgoing of his rejection of following past standards in criticizing even these *fa* tradition figures who approach his own views most closely. We should not take even their views as guides to follow, rather we should understand how to employ *fa* and become artful based on current and real-world situations before us.

Such a *fa* is ill-conceived, according to Han Feizi, because in the result is/will be that those who are experts in one area will take up positions in other areas where they lack expertise. Being skilled in warfare doesn't translate to being skilled in politics—so such a *fa* will ultimately cause political offices to be filled by people who are not suited to the task of politics and don't possess the requisite skills (*Han Feizi* forthcoming: 43.3; Chen 2000: 962).[20]

This focus on *fa* as stripped of moral content and concern shows us that, unlike Confucians such as Xunzi, the *fa* tradition thinkers in general (though as we will see not absolutely!) rejected the idea of morality as strategy. Morality as strategy, however, is only one aspect of the moral view of the early Confucians and others. It is far from clear that *fa* tradition thinkers reject morality as end and value, and indeed there is some evidence from numerous texts that these thinkers agree with the Confucians and others about the independent value of morality. Below, I look at two important *fa* tradition texts, the *Han Feizi* and *Shangjunshu*, to show that the rejection of morality as strategy accompanies the acceptance of morality as value and end, to varying extents. The *fa* tradition thinkers do not reject morality as such; they simply wish to relegate it to a different area of human life than the Confucians and others. They think that morality has no role to play in politics, at least during their own time. While morality may have value and may even have its own uses, generation and maintenance of political order are not among those uses. In addition, *fa* tradition thinkers are skeptical concerning moral discourse due to its use by scholars to ingratiate themselves with rulers to obtain position, which then undermines the ruler's commitment to upholding *fa*. Han Feizi writes of this situation:

學者則稱先王之道，以籍仁義，盛容服而飾辯說，以疑當世之法而貳人主之心。

Scholars then promote the way of the former kings in order to maintain benevolence and righteousness. They put on airs through their appearance and flowery speech, which throws into doubt the laws of society and divides the mind of the ruler. (*Han Feizi* forthcoming: 49.18; Chen 2000: 1122 ["Wu du"])

As we will see below, for *fa* tradition thinkers, the injunction against morality as strategy cannot be taken as universal or absolute. Indeed, to take *any* position concerning strategy as universal or absolute would be a violation of key *fa* tradition principles. As Han Feizi writes in the "Five Vermin" chapter:

聖人不期脩古，不法常可，論世之事，因為之備。

...the sage doesn't try to follow the ways of the ancients, and doesn't establish *fa* that are meant to endure forever. Instead, he reflects on the matters of his own generation, and for this reason is prepared for things. (*Han Feizi* forthcoming: 49.1; Chen 2000: 1085 ["Wu du"])

If morality is stable, universal, and endures in the same way through time, as the Confucians hold, or at least Han Feizi believes that they hold, then it cannot serve as the basis for *fa* that will be effective. *Fa* that serve the purpose of ordering the

---

[20] All citations from *Han Feizi* follow the division into paragraphs adopted by Christoph Harbsmeier in his forthcoming translation of the text; in addition, the reference to the page in Chen 2000 edition is provided.

state must be responsive to the circumstances of one's time and place, while the dictates of morality in its Confucian interpretation are independent of such local features—which is why it is possible, for example, for the Confucians to take ancient sages as models for action.

4   Morality in *Han Feizi*

As we have seen, a central concern in Han Feizi's thought is maintenance of order (*zhi* 治) in the state. The ways to achieve this are through employing *fa*, being skillful or having technique (*shu* 術), and utilizing rewards and punishments. Han Feizi removes moral considerations from the picture, as he thinks these are ineffective at best in bringing about order, and harmful at worst.

Han Feizi's critique of morality and moralists is harsh in much of the text, even extreme in its forcefulness. In Chapter 44, Han Feizi writes that those who are concerned with "benevolence, righteousness, and wisdom (*ren* 仁, *yi* 義, *zhi* 智) hobble the ruler and endanger the state (卑主危國)" (*Han Feizi* forthcoming: 44.1; Chen 2000: 965 ["Shuo yi" 說疑]). In chapter 32 Han Feizi goes so far as to call the desire to cultivate *ren* and *yi* weak (*ruo* 弱), disastrous (*luan* 亂), and a mistake (*guo* 過) (*Han Feizi* forthcoming: 32.2.14 and 32.5.5; Chen 2000: 683 and 704 ["Waichushuo zuo shang" 外儲說左上). In the first of these examples, Han Feizi contrasts the "three Jins" 三晉, referring to the state of Jin, which through internal conflict collapsed and was separated into the three states of Zhao, Wei, and Han, and the state of Qin, which retained its territorial integrity and became dominant in the region (eventually, shortly after Han Feizi's death defeating all of its rivals to create the first unified empire in East Asia in 221 BCE). Following the desire to become benevolent and righteous is to be like Jin, while turning away from concern with benevolence and righteousness and instead becoming orderly and strong is to be like Qin.[21] In chapter 47, Han Feizi even claims that benevolence stands beside violence in its ability to destroy the state (*Han Feizi* forthcoming: 47.6; Chen 2000: 1037 ["Ba shuo"]).

As numerous scholars point out, however, even for its strength and vehemence, Han Feizi's criticism of Confucian morality need not be seen as an anti-moralist critique.[22] Han Feizi does not object to morality as such. Rather, what Han Feizi objects to is the idea that morality can ultimately be effective in ensuring social order—that is, he rejects the Confucian idea of morality as strategy. Confucian claims like those of Xunzi (with whom Han Feizi is most directly connected) rely on the position that political order can be ensured by the cultivation of virtue by the

---

[21] Han Feizi writes presciently here, saying that Qin "has not yet become emperor, because its order is not yet perfected" 然而未帝者，治未畢也 (*Han Feizi* forthcoming: 32.2.14; Chen 2000: 683).

[22] See for example Winston 2005; King 2020. Not all agree on this—Eirik Harris, for example, argues that Han Feizi thoroughly rejects morality. See Harris 2013.

ruler and those surrounding him. Han Feizi and other *fa* tradition thinkers reject this view as naïve and out of step with what they take to be facts about human nature.[23]

There is an open question as to whether Han Feizi's views of human nature are informed by those of Xunzi. Masayuki Sato argues that, against the traditional view, Han Feizi's conception of human nature does not appear to be linked to Xunzi's.[24] The conception we find of human inclinations in the *Han Feizi* (not often flagged by the term *xing* as is the case in the *Xunzi*) is that humans are fundamentally self-interested, where we can think of interest in terms of satisfaction of desires and avoidance of harm. While this may appear to be a difference between Han Feizi and Confucians such as Xunzi, Xunzi's moral system involves an account of desire satisfaction linked to limiting desires via ritual. Sato (2013: 164) argues that Han Feizi's view of humans as fundamentally self-interested has a stronger connection to texts such as the *Shangjunshu* and *Guanzi* than to the *Xunzi*, but such a picture only emerges if we look solely at Han Feizi's views on human nature and inclinations, and of order (*zhi*) and how it is maintained.

Han Feizi seems to accept a conception of order in line with what we find in Confucian texts such as *Xunzi*. Wealth and military strength of the state are signs of order for Han Feizi, as they are for Xunzi. Han Feizi's contention concerns how this order is brought about and maintained. The *Han Feizi*, like other *fa* tradition texts, is concerned primarily with political *strategy*, rather than with appraisal of specific ends. The goal of political order is taken as a given and its value is not debated in the text. The key to strategy is to take the most effective and efficient means to the desired end. The question of *why* morality does not work as a strategy to ensure political order can be answered in part by appeal to facts about human nature and in part by understanding of current circumstances.

Han Feizi points out in Chapter 54 that people are by nature opposed to order, as their perceived self-interest cuts against that of the ruler or the ordered state (and indeed against their own *actual* interest). He writes:

夫民之性，喜其亂而不親其法。
The nature of the people is to delight in disorder and not to follow the laws. (*Han Feizi* 54.1; Chen 2000: 1176 ["Xin du" 心度])

夫民之性，惡勞而樂佚，佚則荒，荒則不治。

---

[23] "Human nature" here translates *xing* 性. There has been a great deal of debate in the literature on this concept in early China (see for example Chan 2019; Robins 2011), and I have tended to translate it myself as something like "inborn characteristics" in some texts (Harris, Chap. 10, this volume, prefers to speak of "human motivation"). I stay with "human nature" here because this translation is most commonly used to render *xing* in the early Confucian texts Han Feizi criticizes.

[24] Masayuki Sato also challenges the traditional view, based on claims in the *Shiji*, that Han Feizi was a student of Xunzi. See Sato 2013: 148–49. There seems to me little evidence on which to question the *Shiji*'s claim. As Bertil Lundahl points out, a failure to mention Xunzi in the *Han Feizi* could imply a rejection of Xunzi's thought (Lundahl 1992). Or it could simply be that Han Feizi did not want to associate his specific items of critique to his old teacher, even though he rejected his views. There are so many possibilities that speculation seems of limited value here.

> The nature of the people is to abhor labor and take joy in leisure. Engaging in leisure leads to wastefulness, and wastefulness undermines order. (*Han Feizi* 54.2; Chen 2000: 1178)

Interestingly, Han Feizi's proposed solution to this is not to endorse a universal, specific, unchangeable injunction, but instead to turn to *fa*, which he sees as variable based on time, place, and other relevant situational features, and established by the ruler. On *fa* as a response to the disorder of the people, Han Feizi writes in Chapter 54:

> 故治民無常，唯治為法。法與時轉則治，治與世宜則有功。
>
> Thus there is no constant [universal] way to order the people—only through laws can they be ordered. Laws constructed according to the changing features of the times lead to order, and an order that is fitting to the current generation leads to success. (*Han Feizi* 54.2; Chen 2000: 1178)

In the "Five Vermin" ("Wu du" 五蠹) chapter, Han Feizi begins by using a host of examples of ineffective methods—of relying on the standards and methods of the past or in unique situations to guide action in periods with their own unique features. Such reliance on the past is ultimately a mistake. However, despite this view that morality is not effective in his own time to bring about order, Han Feizi admits that given different circumstances, morality may indeed be effective as political strategy. He discusses Yao's abdication of rulership and the stress laid on morality in ancient times, and how this was (at least in certain cases) appropriate in the past. Han Feizi attributes this difference between the effectiveness of morality in some cases in antiquity and its ineffectiveness in his own time to a difference in level of resources. Natural resources and goods were abundant in antiquity, according to Han Feizi, which is why the people of that time had the luxury to be unconcerned with wealth or titles. In his own day, on the other hand, resources are more limited, creating concern with wealth and titles (*Han Feizi* 49.3; Chen 2000: 1088–89). Han Feizi here seems to reduce morality to concern with material gain, or at least claim that it is possible to engage in moral considerations without undermining one's survival only in times of abundance.

It was because of this abundance in resources that morality *did* (at least sometimes) work as a political strategy in the past, according to Han Feizi, as mentioned in the "Five Vermin" in the case of King Wen.[25] Even in the past, however, morality was not a universally or generally effective strategy for the maintenance of order. Han Feizi contrasts the story of King Wen, who pacified his region through his possession of virtue and practice of morally positive actions, and that of King Yan of Xu 徐偃王, who practiced moral action and virtue, and was rewarded for it by elimination of his state by a rival king who was worried about the influence King Yan was building over states in the region. Interestingly and perhaps surprisingly, Han Feizi

---

[25] He also considers this directly in the chapter, attributing the lack of conflict among people in the past (following virtue) to abundance of resources undermining the need to fight over them. "Without exerting strength, there was enough to nourish one, for people were few and supplies were abundant, and thus people did not contend" 不事力而養足，人民少而財有餘，故民不爭. (*Han Feizi* forthcoming: 49.3, Chen 2000: 1088; Harris 2013: 113).

seems to take from this that morality *was* successfully applied as strategy at one point in the past, but can no longer be so applied. A critical passage reads:

> 文王行仁義而王天下，偃王行仁義而喪其國，是仁義用於古不用於今也。
>
> King Wen practiced humanity and righteousness and it made him king throughout the world, while King Yan [of Xu] practiced humanity and righteousness and it resulted in the loss of his state. Just like this, humanity and righteousness were useful in ancient times, but are not useful today. (*Han Feizi* 49.4; Chen 2000: 1092)

This of course raises the possibility that morality might be properly used again at some point in the future. Han Feizi, we see, rejects morality as a strategy in his own political milieu, but does not universally reject morality even as a strategy. Indeed, a blanket rejection of morality as a strategy in the future would seem to violate Han Feizi's own guiding principle concerning action, that proper action is determined by circumstances and the times.[26] What we lack here is any indication as to whether Han Feizi thinks that the material conditions that made morality effective as a strategy in the past can ever be obtained again. Is abundance of resources limited to the ancient times, such that it can never recur? Whether it can, of course, will have to do with issues such as population, skillful production and maintenance, and other factors which may be outside of human control. There is however no obvious reason that a situation of abundance similar to what the ancients had could not obtain again, and thus no obvious reason that morality as strategy could not become effective again in the future. And as we will see below in the *Shangjunshu*, there are passages in *fa* tradition texts claiming that regaining such a state where morality can work as political strategy is indeed the *goal* of rule based on punishment and reward rather than morality in the current age.

Indeed, Han Feizi's view here is actually not far off from even that of Mengzi, who claims that the common people cannot maintain a *heng xin* 恆心 (constant heart/mind) unless they have sufficient resources (*Mengzi* 1.7). While scholars can maintain this constant heart even in the absence of sufficient resources, most people cannot, and thus it is necessary to ensure that the people have sufficient resources. Having a constant heart is essential because lacking it is what leads to disorder. As Mengzi says:

> 苟無恆心，放辟，邪侈，無不為已。
>
> If they are without a constant heart, they turn away from the laws, take part in evil and transgressive activity, and there is nothing they won't do. (*Mengzi* 1992: 1.7)

We already see developed here the idea that political order cannot happen unless there are sufficient resources. That is, even for Mengzi, having sufficient resources in the state is a necessary condition for political order, and morality can only do its work when such a condition is met. This much is perfectly consistent with what we find in the *Han Feizi*.[27] The seeming disagreement here is that Han Feizi thinks that

---

[26] 事因於世，而備適於事. (*Han Feizi* forthcoming: 49.3).

[27] Although in the case of Confucians such as Mengzi material resources are a precondition for virtue, but once virtue obtains it is not undermined by changing material circumstances, while this is not the case for Han Fei, as he denies the role of virtue in behavior, taking a more situational approach as shown above.

in the current day the requisite situation for morality to be effective does not (and cannot?) obtain. One of the main points of the "Five Vermin" chapter (like others in Han Feizi) is not that morality is either effective or ineffective, but that what is effective in bringing about order will change with circumstances. If one wishes to create political order it is of vital importance to understand the circumstances of one's time and place, including the inclinations of the people, the resources of the state, the military situation with respect to other states, and other key features that do not remain stable across time, place, individual, and state. This is why it is fruitless at best and dangerous at worst to rely on the teachings of the ancient sages as guidance.

Despite this general rejection of morality as strategy, Han Feizi seems to have a somewhat positive view of virtue or moral potency (*de* 德) as general value or end, as Eric Hutton points out, given the discussion of the topic in Chapter 20, "Explaining *Laozi*" ("Jie Lao" 解老) (Hutton 2008: 429). If we focus on the concepts of *fa* and social order (*zhi*), and the implications of Confucian morality for the formation of these standards, we can see why Han Feizi and other *fa* tradition thinkers would have thought of morality as dangerous, without necessarily rejecting it altogether. This distinction between morality as strategy and morality as value or end is consistent with the differential way Han Feizi thinks about other ostensibly moral concepts, such as that of *yi* (righteousness). Han Feizi uses *yi* in two different senses, one having to do with individual and private interests, and the other having to do with what is "right" in terms of benefit to the state (Harris 2013: 127; Schneider 2014: 26). Individual interests often conflict with those of the state, and thus what may be of value from the individual perspective (and following *yi* as such) can be dangerous as a tool for governing the state.

In "Explaining *Laozi*," we find what seems to be a positive evaluation of morality, in connection with discussion of passages from the *Laozi*.[28] The opening passage of the chapter is a commentary on *Laozi* 38, which is a discussion of *de* 德 (virtue, moral potency). One of the difficulties here, of course, is that the concept of *de* is understood differently in parts of the *Laozi* than it is in early Confucian texts such as the *Analects, Mengzi,* and *Xunzi*. In the context of the *Laozi*, it is much less clear that *de* refers to something like virtue, as it does in Confucian texts. In *Laozi* 38, however, there seems to be an implicit criticism of certain views of *de* found in early Confucian texts, so it may be more justified to read *de* here as a moral concept. The passage links *de*, for example, with the clearly Confucian concepts of *ren* and *li* 禮, in its discussion of insufficient conceptions of *de*. The passage in general reads as a criticism of Confucian conceptions of *de*, and the proposal of an alternative, in

---

[28] There is disagreement among scholars concerning whether this chapter is consistent with the rest of the *Han Feizi* or even whether it is a later addition to the text unrelated to the other chapters. I treat the chapter here as continuous with the rest of the *Han Feizi*, as the only evidence we have to think that it isn't is its seeming inconsistency with the rest of the text. I explain in this section how this seeming inconsistency can be resolved, thus undercutting the main reason for rejecting the chapter. See the discussion in the final paragraph of this section.

which there is less stress on concepts such as *li*.[29] In Han Feizi's commentary on the passage, we find much that does not seem at all consistent with Han Feizi's attacks on morality in other parts of the text.

聖人之復恭敬盡手足之禮也不衰

    The sage remains respectful and reverent to the utmost and in neither hand nor foot ever weakens from observing ritual. (*Han Feizi* forthcoming: 20.1.5; Chen 2000: 376)

But we also find implicit criticism of Confucian views of virtue, offering an alternative, more in line with the accounts of *de* we find in the *Laozi*. That is, Han Feizi seems to accept the value of morality, but not the kind of morality advocated by the Confucians, or at least not *exactly* that kind. The opening of "Explaining Laozi" reads:

德者，內也。得者，外也。上德不德，言其神不淫於外也。神不淫於外則身全，身全之謂德。德者，得身也。凡德者，以無為集，以無欲成，以不思安，以不用固。為之欲之，則德無舍，德無舍則不全。用之思之則不固，不固則無功，無功則生於德。德則無德，不德則在有德。故曰：「上德不德，是以有德。」

    Virtue is internal. Obtaining is external. To say "the highest virtue is not virtue" [as in *Laozi* 38] is to say that one's spirit is not dissolute in connection with the external. If the spirit is not dissolute in connection with the external, then the self remains intact. If the self remains intact, this can be called virtue. Virtue is to obtain the self. Generally, virtue arises with non-action, is completed with non-desire, is pacified with non-thought, and is solidified with non-use. If one desires it, then virtue has nowhere to dwell. If virtue has nowhere to dwell, then it cannot remain intact. If one uses it and thinks about it, then it is not solidified. If it is not solidified, then it cannot be achieved, and non-achievement gives rise to virtue. If there is virtue, then there is non-virtue, and if there is not virtue then there is virtue. Thus it is said [in *Laozi* 38], "The highest virtue is not virtue—and this is why it is virtuous." (*Han Feizi* forthcoming: 20.1.1; Chen 2000: 370)

It becomes clear as one works through the passage that Han Feizi's intention here is to criticize certain conceptions of ritual and benevolence, in a manner consistent with the original *Laozi* passage. The virtue that is explicit, external, and connected to the kinds of desires to become virtuous that one finds in Confucian texts is not true virtue. Desiring virtue, using it (presumably in terms of political strategy), thinking about and in terms of it—all of this is the way to non-virtue, according to Han Feizi (and *Laozi* 38, on his reading). Thus to bring about the end of virtue, if this is something of value (which this chapter suggests that it is), we have to focus on something other than virtue. This might be seen as an argument for the political approach of *fa* tradition thinkers focusing on laws and enforcement, rather than morality, as a way to ensure political order. Once political order is maintained, virtue may result from this.

    A passage in Chapter 14, "Treacherous, Larcenous, Murderous Ministers" ("Jian jie shi chen" 姦劫弒臣), is also revealing for its seemingly positive evaluation of morality. Eirik Harris also discusses this passage in his "Han Fei on the Problem of Morality," although he offers a somewhat different interpretation than the one I offer here. I think we should read this passage as concerning the distinction between

---

[29] The passage is clearly a criticism of some aspect of those who take such things as *ren* and *li* to be necessary components of "virtue," whether or not the passage ultimately endorses moral virtue or some alternative.

morality as strategy and morality as effect, and demonstrating an acceptance of the latter alongside a rejection of the former.

世主美仁義之名而不察其實，是以大者國亡身死，小者地削主卑。何以明之?夫施與貧困者，此世之所謂仁義；哀憐百姓不忍誅罰者，此世之所謂惠愛也。夫有施與貧困，則無功者得賞；不忍誅罰，則暴亂者不止。國有無功得賞者，則民不外務當敵斬首，內不急力田疾作，皆欲行貨財、事富貴、為私善、立名譽以取尊官厚俸。故姦私之臣愈眾，而暴亂之徒愈勝，不亡何待?

The rulers of our generation prize having a name for benevolence and righteousness, but they don't investigate the reality of these things, and so at worst they lose their states or their lives, and at best their territory is reduced and their status is lowered. How can I clarify this? Now, to give to the needy and those in difficulty is what this generation calls benevolent and righteous. To sympathize with the people and be unable to endure enforcing executions and punishments is what this generation calls kindness and compassion. Now, when you give to the needy and those in difficulty, this is to reward people even though they haven't accomplished anything. When you're unable to endure enforcing executions and punishments, then those who engage in violence and disorder are not stopped. If in the state those without accomplishment are rewarded, then the people will not be motivated outside to fight enemies and cut off heads in battle, or at home to work hard to cultivate their fields. Everyone will desire to gain goods and riches, to serve the wealthy and famous, and to attend to those who bestow on them personal favors, and to attain name and reputation so as to become honored officials with fat emoluments. This leads to a proliferation of wicked and self centered ministers, and victory after victory of those who follow violence and disorder. How can one but lose the state? (*Han Feizi* forthcoming: 14.5; Chen 2000: 290)

Investigating the reality of benevolence and righteousness would entail, if we connect this to the consideration above from "Explaining *Laozi*," that benevolence and righteousness (or virtue more generally) are obtained not through seeking a name or even thinking in terms of benevolence and righteousness, but through non-action, non-desire. A focus on order of the state might *bring about* virtue, but we can never hope to attain virtue through concentration on virtue.[30] The Chapter 14 passage can be seen as an explanation of *why* the way of attending to virtue cannot itself yield virtue, as Chapter 20 argues.

Harris is surely correct that Han Feizi aimed to undermine the idea that "the ultimate justification for the political state is not (and perhaps cannot be) simply derived from morality" (Harris 2013: 108). The central concern of the *Han Feizi* is with ordering the state, and morality is then mainly understood in terms of its relationship to such order. As we have seen, Han Feizi not only rejects the Confucian

[30] While neither of these positions can be definitively demonstrated based on the text, we do have evidence that Han Feizi thought that virtue was possible, particularly given that he mentioned that not only was it followed, but it also worked in the time of the ancients (*Han Feizi* forthcoming: 49.4 ["Wu du"]). The passage from Chapter 14 above also claims that disorder in the state can create vice. So what reason is there to think that the orderly state cannot create virtue, unless Han Feizi thinks that virtue is not possible, but vice is. Such a position conflicts with numerous passages of the text such as 49.4, which would have to be explained away by arguing that when Han Feizi talks about virtue such as *ren* and *yi*, he doesn't mean actual *ren* and *yi*, but only the semblance or imitation of these. Such readings are forced for a number of reasons, including that if Han Feizi believed that people could have only semblances of virtue and not actual virtues, he could have said this and made it clear, which would have been necessary for his intended audience, surely quite familiar with contemporary views concerning virtue.

idea that moral cultivation plays a necessary role in bringing about political order, but he also goes so far as to say that concern with morality undermines political order. However, as pointed out above, we do not find in Han Feizi's discussions a view that morality did not have an effect in the past. Harris argues, on the basis of Han Feizi's claims about the sufficiency of resources in the past, that his assessment that morality "worked" at that time "was not because virtue had the power of laws and regulations, but rather because the strength of laws and regulations (and their attendant punishments) was not necessary, as contention over resources was not a large problem" (Harris 2013: 113). This is one possible way to understand Han Feizi's position that the abundant resources of ancient times made a difference in which kinds of actions effectively led to order, but it is by no means the only possible way, or the way most consistent with the text. A focus on morality can work when the situation is such that resources are plentiful—we know at least this much from Han Feizi's discussion in the *Five Vermin* chapter. What he does not tell us and we have to surmise is *why* morality works in such a situation. If Harris' reading is correct, then it turns out that morality is not "working" in such a case at all. But this directly conflicts with Han Feizi's own claim in the chapter about its usefulness (*yong* 用) in the past. Perhaps the claim is only a rhetorical one, but to determine that we would have to have some reason to think that the straightforward reading that Han Feizi actually believes that focus on morality "worked" in the past cannot be or is unlikely to be correct. But do we have such reason?

An equally reasonable reading of Han Feizi's statements in the "Five Vermin" are that morality worked in the ancient situation in which there were sufficient resources because the conditions under which it is possible to reliably develop virtue obtained. If one has a view that virtue is only possible when material needs are met,[31] then the fact that virtue only works when there are sufficient resources does not show that morality has little power. It may well have been the case by Han Feizi's lights that virtue still played an important role in the ancient case, but that this virtue was only possible due to possession of sufficient material resources. And this reading of the text has the virtue of allowing us to make sense of the seemingly straightforward claim 是仁義用於古不用於今也 ("humanity and righteousness were useful in ancient times, but are not useful today")[32] in a way that takes it at face value, rather than requiring us to give a non-literal meaning of the sentence, such as the view that Han Feizi intended to say that morality *appeared* to be useful in the past. In addition, if Han Feizi accepted the view Hutton attributes to him, it's unclear why he would maintain that morality was useful *at all* in the past. If order was maintained on the basis of lack of contention and thus need for laws, it's unclear how morality would add anything at all to this. It would go from having *little* effect, as Hutton claims Han Feizi held, to having *no* effect. And this would require an even more strained reading of the sentence from the "Five Vermin" chapter above.

---

[31] A view that has some contemporary support in psychology. See for an overview Vansteenkiste et al. 2020.

[32] *Han Feizi* 49.4

According to Eric Hutton, Han Fei's primary argument against Confucian morality is that there is something intrinsic to the strategy of virtue itself that leads one astray and leads to disaster for a ruler (Hutton 2008: 432–41). This may be part of what's going on in the *Han Feizi*, but there is another point. Namely, that the focus on moral self-cultivation is inconsistent with the focus on the development of skills necessary for the maintenance of order and a powerful state. This latter objection is not an objection to morality as such; rather it is an objection to the focus on moral self-cultivation. And, as we see in the *Shangjunshu*, morality is still possible without Confucian moral self-cultivation. In fact, in an attempt to undermine the Confucian position by its own lights, it turns out that virtue itself is more reliably created when one focuses on the necessities of state power, rather than directly on virtue itself as a beginning point. The objection, that is, seems to be not so much to Confucian virtue itself, but to its level on the hierarchy of needs, its role in the generation and maintenance of order, and its causes. This reading also makes the rejection of morality as strategy consistent with the acceptance of morality as strategy in particular cases as well as the seeming positive evaluation of morality as end in numerous parts of the text.

Some have argued that instead of trying to unify portions of the text that seem to negatively and positively evaluate morality, we ought to take the passages that seem to positively evaluate morality from chapters such as "Explaining *Laozi*" (or the entirety of chapters such as "Explaining *Laozi*" and "Illustrating *Laozi*" ["Yu Lao" 喻老]) as inauthentic additions to the *Han Feizi*.[33] But what definitive reason do we have for thinking that the "Explaining *Laozi*" chapter or passages like those from "Treacherous, Larcenous, Murderous Ministers" are not the work of Han Feizi, beside their seeming inconsistency with what Han Fei says elsewhere in the text or common ways of interpreting what he says elsewhere? There is little textual or other evidence to demonstrate this. And the view that "Explaining *Laozi*" represents something at odds with other sections of the *Han Feizi* is difficult to maintain, as all of the *Laozi* passages selected for discussion after the first on *Laozi* 38 are passages directly relevant to rulership and order—topics on which there is a clear focus

---

[33] See Queen 2013: 198–99. Queen argues on the basis of her analysis of the language of the "Jie Lao" and "Yu Lao" chapters that the former was written later than the latter, but that this cannot show that either text was written by someone other than Han Feizi or outside of the lifetime of Han Feizi. Bertil Lundahl, on the basis of works by Kimura Eiichi (Kimura 1944) and Rong Zhaozu (Rong 1972), rejects the association of the chapter with Han Feizi. In all cases, however, this rejection is on the basis of the association of the chapter with Daoist ideas. Lundahl writes: "The Daoist ideas in this chapter led many earlier scholars, including Rong and Kimura, to deny Han Fei's authorship of it." (Lundahl 1992: 219). Lundahl's own argument relies on the supposed inconsistency of the views of "Jie Lao" with other chapters of the *Han Feizi* he determined to be "authentic". As I point out below, however, rejecting the authenticity of the chapter on that basis is straightforwardly question begging, as it assumes the view one is presumably trying to demonstrate, that Han Feizi's work is free of Daoist ideas. And it is also the case that we find inconsistent views across the group of chapters Lundahl determines to be "authentic" as well. See Durica 2014: 69–76. My own position echoes that of Zhang Jue, who argued that the presumption should be to accept all of the *Han Feizi* chapters as authentic unless we have sufficient evidence to reject any of them (Zhang 2006: 12–19).

throughout the text of *Han Feizi*. In addition, the position taken on those issues in "Explaining *Laozi*" is basically the same as the positions taken on them in other parts of the text. The only reason for thinking that "Explaining *Laozi*" is an anomaly is the first passage on *Laozi* 38 in which Han Feizi seems to praise "virtue." But as I show here, the views expressed in "Explaining *Laozi*" and other praising of moral ideas are not at all inconsistent with what we find elsewhere in the text, if we understand those views as about morality as a strategy (or standard) rather than morality as end or effect. And given the focus of Han Feizi (and *fa* tradition thinkers in general) on strategy and standard (thus the centrality of *fa*), we should expect it to be the case that most of the discussion surrounding morality would concern the issue of morality as a strategy—the very idea Han Feizi is responding to, as developed most fully by Xunzi. Ironically perhaps, what seemingly gave Xunzi's system an advantage over its competitors such as Mengzian Confucianism or Mohism— namely its heavily externalist view of moral strategy—also left it vulnerable to the criticisms of Han Feizi and other *fa* tradition thinkers. This may have had something to do with the popularity of later Confucian moves back toward Mengzian internalism.[34]

5   Morality in *Shangjunshu*

Numerous *fa* tradition texts disparage moral concepts in numerous ways. In the *Shangjunshu*, we find harsh words about the morality prized by the Confucians and Mohists, including *ren* (humanity) and *yi* (righteousness). These two terms are often used together, to signify ethical concern in general and the numerous concepts associated with it. As in the *Han Feizi*, a key problem with moral virtue according to the *Shangjunshu* is its ineffectiveness in changing behavior. A key component of early Confucian moral theory is the idea of the reformative power of the morally exemplary person (*junzi* 君子) or sage. This power is associated with the concept of *de* 德 (moral potency). For the Confucians, moral excellence has an intrinsically attractive and motivational quality. It draws people toward it, and encourages people (via shame through comparison) to rectify themselves morally. The *Shangjunshu*, like other *fa* tradition texts, rejects this position. Whatever morality might do for the individual, it simply does not have the effect on the behavior of others that the Confucians contend. The *Shangjunshu*, while accepting the possibility that there may be individuals who are humane and righteous, rejects the idea that these traits can have any effect on the behavior of others. A passage from chapter 18 reads:

> 仁者能仁於人，而不能使人仁；義者能愛於人，而不能使人愛。是以知仁義之不足以治天下也。
>
> Those who are humane are able to have humane feelings toward people, but they are unable to make other people humane. Those who are righteous are able to care about peo-

---

[34] The view that morality depends primarily on motivational and emotional states of the individual moral agent rather than features of the environment and community. See Liu 2002.

ple, but they are unable to make others care about people. This is how we can know that humanity and righteousness are insufficient to order the world. (*Shangjunshu* 2017: 18.8; Zhang 2012: 220 ["Hua ce" 畫策])

The *Shangjunshu* goes so far as to refer to the Confucian virtues as 'pests,' 'lice,' or 'parasites' (*shi* 蝨). These are to be rejected, according to the author(s), because they not only are ineffective at motivating the kind of behavior that leads to a strong state, but they actively *interfere* with such behavior. A passage from Chapter 13 ("Making Orders Strict") reads:

六蝨:曰禮樂，曰詩書，曰修善，曰孝弟，曰誠信，曰貞廉，曰仁義，曰非兵，曰羞戰。國有十二者，上無使農戰，必貧至削。

The six parasites are these: ritual and music, the *Odes* and *Documents*, moral cultivation and goodness, filial its and brotherliness, sincerity and honesty, integrity and uprightness, humanity and righteousness, rejection of military, and being ashamed of warfare. If a state possesses these twelve,[35] the ruler will be unable to make the people commit to farming or warfare, which will surely result in poverty culminating in the dismemberment of the state. (*Shangjunshu* 2017: 13.4; Zhang 2012: 180 ["Jin ling" 靳令])

Given this, we might expect virtue and morality in general to be thoroughly rejected, but later in the same chapter, we find something very different. In the final passage of the chapter, the author discusses the activity of the sage ruler (*sheng jun* 聖君). The author explains what the reliance on force enables:

聖君知物之要，故其治民有至要。[…] 聖君之治人也，必得其心，故能用力。力生強，強生威，威生德，德生於力。聖君獨有之，故能述仁義於天下。

The sage ruler understands what is essential in things, thus in his ordering of the people, he possesses what is essential. ... The sage ruler, in ordering the people, must (first) win over their hearts, and hence can then use force. Force gives birth to strength, strength gives birth to majesty, majesty gives birth to virtue. Virtue, then has its birth in force. The sage king alone has it, and is thus able to transmit humanity and righteousness throughout the world. (*Shangjunshu* 2017: 13.6; Zhang 2012: 162)

This might seem to be a bizarre conclusion to a chapter in which humanity and righteousness were earlier disparaged as "parasites." Some suggest that there are additions and corruptions in this part of the chapter, but the idea expressed in the above paragraph is consistent with what we see throughout the *Shangjunshu* (as well as the *Han Feizi*, as discussed in the previous section), namely, that the problem with Confucian virtues is primarily a *practical* problem—that focusing on the cultivation of these virtues gets in the way of the kinds of commitments, abilities, and attitudes that are necessary to ensure the order and strength of the state. What *Shangjunshu* straightforwardly rejects is morality as strategy (although like the *Han Feizi*, it admits that there were times in which morality was useful as political strategy),[36] but where it is even clearer than *Han Feizi* is in its acceptance of moral-

---

[35] The text here is inconsistent—the "twelve" referred to seem to amount to sixteen. It is unclear whether this is due to addition to the text, scribal error, etc. See Pines 2017: 191, 290; Zhang 2012: 159–60.

[36] See particularly *Shangjunshu* 2017: 7.1 ("Kai sai") and the discussion in Pines, Chap. 1, Sect. 4, this volume.

ity as desirable end. Morality cannot help us gain order, but order can help us gain virtue.

Where the *Shangjunshu* criticizes the standard Confucian virtues, it is always on these practical grounds, and never on the grounds that there is some sort of deeper theoretical problem with morality as end or as general value. The problem with Confucian morality, according to the text, is that it is not only ineffective at bringing about and maintaining order, but it actively undermines the project of ordering society. As discussed in Chapter 7 of *Shangjunshu*, those who are ruled with virtue become licentious, prone to transgressions, and unwilling to farm or fight (similar to the message we see in Chapter 54 of the *Han Feizi*) (*Shangjunshu* 2017: 7.4; Zhang 2012: 113 ["Kai sai" 開塞]). Part of what is going on here may be that the true target of criticisms of Confucian morality is the class of *ru* scholars who endorsed such morality (compare Pines, Chap. 18, this volume). Spending time and effort in self-cultivation takes time and effort away from cultivating the land and training for warfare. Thus, insofar as a ruler makes moral self-cultivation a focus of society or prizes it in his people, the crucial activities of farming, warfare, and other central activities of the state will go unmet. The *Shangjunshu* and other *fa* tradition text seem to be primarily advocating a hierarchy of needs, where wealth and strength are most essential, and virtue can come only after these are attained. Notice that this does not, however, show that virtue and morality do not have a value, only that they can or have the tendency to get in the way of the activity that leads to the generation of more central needs. Indeed, even if we care about generating virtue in society, we still have reason to care primarily about and promote things like farming and warfare, because it is only when these are established that the state becomes strong and achieves a position in which it is possible to spread virtue.

There are numerous additional passages from the *Shangjunshu* that demonstrate a positive evaluation of virtue and morality in general, though of as end rather than strategy.[37] We can see the basis for this in passages like that of Chapter 13 above, which clearly take the development of virtue to be an overall aim of the political project, in terms of the results produced when the orderly state is achieved. The view expressed in the *Shangjunshu* is reminiscent in this way of the famous quote from John Adams (in a letter to his wife Abigail): "I must study politics and war that my sons may have liberty to study mathematics and philosophy. My sons ought to study mathematics and philosophy, geography, natural history, naval architecture, navigation, commerce, and agriculture, in order to give their children a right to study painting, poetry, music, architecture, statuary, tapestry, and porcelain."[38] Adams here is not rejecting the value of things such as painting and poetry, on the contrary, it is for the ultimate benefit of painting and poetry that he sees himself as needing to focus on war. Nonetheless, for Adams to focus on painting and poetry would be a disastrous strategy in his position, as his times called for something dif-

---

[37] In the introduction to his translation of the *Shangjunshu*, Yuri Pines argues that the text should not be taken as endorsing a kind of amoralistic view. Pines 2017: 95–99.

[38] John Adams to Abigail Adams, post May 12, 1780. *Massachusetts Historical Society Archives*.

ferent. Earlier in the letter he described how he enjoyed things like painting and poetry, but that engaging in them would cause him to neglect his duty, which was binding on his based on his commitment to securing the values of things such as the enjoyment of painting and poetry for his descendants. There is an important passage in Chapter 18 of *Shangjunshu* that echoes almost exactly Adams' sentiment, which is very much one of expedient means thinking, in which the ends justify the means:

> 故以戰去戰，雖戰可也；以殺去殺，雖殺可也；以刑去刑，雖重刑可也。
>
> In order to eradicate war with war, even waging war is permissible; to eradicate murder with murder, even murdering is permissible; to eradicate punishments with punishments, even making punishments heavy is permissible. (*Shangjunshu* 2017: 18.1; Zhang 2012: 208 ["Hua ce"])

Like Adams, Shang Yang advocates war and political realism not for their own sake, but for the sake of ultimately attaining a situation in which these are not necessary. While for Adams, the aim is enjoyment of painting and poetry, for Shang Yang, the aim is *morality*—the attainment of virtue. He must study politics and war that his sons may study benevolence and righteousness. As Pines writes, "the harsh means that are currently inevitable [in Shang Yang's time] actually serve moral ends: when the goal of subjugating domestic and foreign rivals is attained, peace and tranquility will be possible" (Pines 2017: 96–97).

The seemingly positive evaluation of morality in a number of parts of the *Han Feizi* can be understood in this way as well. That is, if we separate the issue of morality as strategy from that of morality as end, the various *fa* tradition thinkers seem to have a very consistent view concerning the desirability of the latter combined with the foolishness of the former. The *Shangjunshu*'s statement of the value of morality as end is far more forceful and explicit than that of the *Han Feizi*, but if we take it to be a position shared in the *Han Feizi*, this helps us make sense of the seeming conflict between negative and positive evaluations of morality in that text. A shared *fa* tradition view seems to emerge here, one that holds that in order to ensure political order, we cannot rely on morality, even if (and even though) morality is what we ultimately seek to bring about in our quest for political order.

6   Conclusion

Ultimately what we see in the *Han Feizi*, *Shangjunshu*, and other *fa* tradition texts is not a rejection of morality, but an insistence on making a distinction between politics and morality, and a severing of the necessary link between the two that the Confucians insist on. This position would have struck the Confucians as an attack on morality, which colors our readings of *fa* tradition texts to this day. From a modern perspective, however, the *fa* tradition views here are quite standard, and would strike many as intuitive, if we were able to read these texts outside of the Confucian framework in which we often do. They offer a vision of politics completely in line with the organizational principles underlying governance in almost all contemporary institutions, from corporations to governments. Not many CEOs or presidents would declare themselves unconcerned with morality or think of it as something to be rejected. Any successful one would, however, see it as unhelpful at best and disastrous at worst as a strategy or standard to guide their operation of their business or state. This separation of organizational/political strategy and morality as effect is something we today assume and take for granted. In the early Chinese intellectual context, this was a radical idea.

References

Ames, Roger. 1994. *The Art of Rulership: A Study of Ancient Chinese Political Thought*. Albany: State University of New York Press.

Analects. See Cheng Shude 1990.

Bárcenas, Alejandro. 2013. Han Fei's Enlightened Ruler. *Asian Philosophy* 23 (3): 236–259.

Chan, Shirley. 2019. *Xing* 性 and *Qing* 情: Human Nature and Moral Cultivation in the Guodian Text *Xing zi ming chu* (Nature Derives from Endowment). In *Dao Companion to the Excavated Guodian Manuscripts*, ed. Shirley Chan, 213–237. Dordrecht: Springer.

Chen, Qiyou 陳奇猷. 2000. *HAN Feizi, With New Collations and Commentary* 韓非子新校注. Shanghai: Shanghai guji chubanshe.

Cheng, Shude 程樹德. 1990. *Collected Explanations of the Analects* 論語集釋. Beijing: Zhonghua shuju.

Denecke, Wiebke. 2010. *The Dynamics of Masters Literature: Early Chinese Thought from Confucius to Han Feizi*. Cambridge: Harvard University Press.

Durica, Jan. 2014. Han Fei: His Thought and Work and the Problem of Inconsistencies. *Studia Orientalia Slovaca* 13 (1): 55–76.

El Amine, Loubna. 2015. *Classical Confucian Political Thought: A New Interpretation*. Princeton: Princeton University Press.

Goldin, Paul R. 2011. Persistent Misconceptions About Chinese 'Legalism'. *Journal of Chinese Philosophy* 38 (1): 88–104.

Graham, Angus C. 1989. *Disputers of the Tao: Philosophical Argument in Ancient China*. La Salle, Ill.: Open Court.

Hagen, Kurtis. 2007. *The Philosophy of Xunzi: A Reconstruction*. Chicago and La Salle, Ill.: Open Court.

Han Feizi. See Harbsmeier. Forthcoming.

Harbsmeier, Christoph, trans. Forthcoming. *Han Feizi, A Complete Translation: The Art of Statecraft in Early China*. Ed. Jens Østergaard Petersen and Yuri Pines. Leiden: Brill.

Harris, Eirik L. 2013. Han Fei on the Problem of Morality. In *Dao Companion to the Philosophy of Han Fei*, ed. Paul R. Goldin, 107–131. Dordrecht: Springer.

———. 2016a. *The Shenzi Fragments: A Philosophical Analysis and Translation*. New York: Columbia University Press.

———. 2016b. Xunzi's Political Philosophy. In *Dao Companion to the Philosophy of Xunzi*, ed. Erik Hutton, 95–138. Dordrecht: Springer.

He, Fan. 2021. *Tong*: A Mohist Response to the Confucian Harmony. In *Harmony in Chinese Thought: A Philosophical Introduction*, ed. Chenyang Li, Sai Hong Kwok, and Dascha Düring. Lanham: Rowman and Littlefield.

Hutton, Eric. 2008. Han Feizi's Criticism of Confucianism and Its Implications for Virtue Ethics. *Journal of Moral Philosophy* 5 (3): 423–453.

Ivanhoe, Philip. 2011. Hanfeizi and Moral Self-Cultivation. *Journal of Chinese Philosophy* 38 (1): 31–45.

Jin, Yutang. 2022. Confucian Political Order and the Ethics/Politics Distinction: A Reassessment. *Dao* 21: 389–405.

Kim, Sungmoon. 2012. Virtue Politics and Political Leadership: A Confucian Rejoinder to Hanfeizi. *Asian Philosophy* 22 (2): 177–197.

Kimura, Eiichi 木村英一. 1944. *Research on Legalist Thought* 法家思想の研究. Tokyo: Kobundo.

King, Brandon. 2020. Moral Concern in the Legalist State. *Dao* 19 (3): 391–407.

Liu, Xiusheng. 2002. Mengzian Internalism. In *Essays on the Moral Philosophy of Mengzi*, ed. Liu Xiusheng and Philip J. Ivanhoe, 101–131. Indianapolis: Hackett.

Lundahl, Bertil. 1992. *Han Fei Zi: The Man and the Work*. Stockholm: Institute of Oriental Languages.

Mengzi yizhu 孟子譯注 (*Mengzi*, Translated and Annotated). 1992. Annotated by Yang Bojun 楊伯峻. Beijing: Zhonghua shuju.

Neville, Robert. 2014. Ritual and Religion: A Lesson From Xunzi for Today. In *Ritual and Religion in the Xunzi*, ed. T.C. Kline and Justin Tiwald. Albany: SUNY Press.

Park, So Jeong. 2021. *He* (和), The Concept Cluster of Harmony in Early China. In *Harmony in Chinese Thought: A Philosophical Introduction*, ed. Chenyang Li, Sai Hong Kwok, and Dascha Düring, 3–22. Lanham: Rowman and Littlefield.

Pines, Yuri, trans. and ed. 2017. *The Book of Lord Shang: Apologetics of State Power in Early China*. New York: Columbia University Press.

Queen, Sarah. 2013. Han Feizi and the Old Master: A Comparative Analysis and Translation of Han Feizi Chapter 20, 'Jie Lao', and Chapter 21, 'Yu Lao'. In *Dao Companion to the Philosophy of Han Fei*, ed. Paul R. Goldin, 197–256. Dordrecht: Springer.

Rickett, W. Allyn. 1998. *Guanzi: Political, Economic, and Philosophical Essays from Early China*. Princeton: Princeton University Press.

Robins, Dan. 2011. The Warring States Concept of *Xing*. *Dao* 10 (1): 31–51.

Rong, Zhaozu 容肇祖. 1972. *Textual Research on the Han Feizi* 韓非子的考證. Taibei: Tailian guofeng chubanshe.

Roth, Harold. 2004. *Original Tao: Inward Training (Nei-yeh) and the Foundations of Taoist Mysticism*. New York: Columbia University Press.

Sato, Masayuki. 2013. Did Xunzi's Theory of Human Nature Provide the Foundation for the Political Thought of Han Fei? In *Dao Companion to the Philosophy of Han Fei*, ed. Paul R. Goldin, 147–165. Dordrecht: Springer.

Schneider, Henrique. 2014. Han Fei and Justice. *Cambridge Journal of China Studies* 9 (4): 20–37.

Shangjunshu. See Pines 2017.

Vansteenkiste, Maarten, Richard Ryan, and Bart Soenens. 2020. Basic Psychological Need Theory: Advancements, Critical Themes, and Future Directions. *Motivation and Emotion* 44: 1–31.

Winston, Kenneth. 2005. The Internal Morality of Chinese Legalism. *Singapore Journal of Legal Studies* (December): 313–347.

Xunzi jijie 荀子集解 (*Xunzi* with Combined Glosses). 1992. Ed. Wang Xianqian 王先謙 (1842–1917), Shen Xiaohuan 沈嘯寰 and Wang Xingxian 王星賢. Beijing: Zhonghua shuju.

Yang, Soon-ja. 2013. Shen Dao's Theory of *Fa* and His Influence on Han Fei. In *Dao Companion to the Philosophy of Han Fei*, ed. Paul R. Goldin, 47–63. Dordrecht: Springer.

Zhang, Jue 張覺. 2006. *Han Feizi with Collations and Annotations* 韓非子校注. Changsha: Yuelu shushe.

———張覺. 2012. *The Book of Lord Shang Collated with Sub-commentary* 商君書校疏. Beijing: Zhishi chanquan chubanshe.

Part III
Fa Traditions in History

Chapter 16
The Historical Reputation of the *Fa* Tradition in Imperial China

Hongbing Song 宋洪兵

The *fa* tradition was an important intellectual current in preimperial China. The difference between this tradition and Confucianism or Mohism is that among the masters of the *fa* tradition there was neither a distinct student-master relationship, nor common intellectual origins. Furthermore, the *fa* tradition never emerged as a scholarly community on a par with Confucians and Mohists. The main reason why they were regarded as a distinct "school" by later generations is a high degree of similarity of their ideas and political practices. This tradition had a clear political orientation, it emphasized utility and practicality, and opposed empty moral preaching. *Fa* adherents esteemed strength; they promoted the strengthening of centralized power, advocated harsh punishments and strict laws, cracked down on the aristocracy, directed the people toward agriculture and warfare, and supported a strong interventionist state so as to realize the ideal of "a rich state and a strong army" (*fuguo qiangbing* 富國强兵). Liu Shao 劉劭 (186–245) summarized the essentials of this tradition in his *Records of Personalities* (*Renwuzhi* 人物志), in which he identified Guan Zhong 管仲 (d. 645 BCE) and Shang Yang 商鞅 (d. 338 BCE) as the *fa* tradition's representatives:

> 建法立制，強國富人，是謂法家，管仲、商鞅是也.
>
> To establish laws and set up institutions, to strengthen the state and enrich the people— this is what is called the *fa* school. Guan Zhong and Shang Yang are its representatives. (*Renwuzhi* 3:64 ["Liu ye" 流業])

Guanzi, attributed to Guan Zhong, actually reflects the ideas of the thinkers of the Warring States-period (Zhanguo 戰國, 453–221 BCE) Jixia 稷下 Academy. Whereas it may have some connection to the historical Guan Zhong, it is overall more reflective of Warring States-period thinking (Sato, Chap. 5, this volume). In the "Treatise on Arts and Letters" ("Yiwenzhi" 藝文志) of the *Hanshu* 漢書

H. Song 宋洪兵 (✉)
School of Guoxue(Chinese Classics), Renmin University of China, Beijing, China
e-mail: songhongbing@ruc.edu.cn

© The Author(s), under exclusive license to Springer Nature Switzerland AG 2024
Y. Pines (ed.), *Dao Companion to China's fa Tradition*, Dao Companions to Chinese Philosophy 19, https://doi.org/10.1007/978-3-031-53630-4_17

(*History of the Former Han Dynasty*), *Guanzi* is classified as a "Daoist" work, but the "Treatise on Classics and Other Texts" ("Jingjizhi" 經籍志) of *Suishu* 隋書 (*History of the Sui Dynasty*) lists it under the *fa* school. As a result, later generations also regarded *Guanzi* and Guan Zhong as belonging to the *fa* tradition. Other major surviving texts of the *fa* tradition are those identified as such in the "Treatise on Arts and Letters" of the *Hanshu*: *Lord Shang* 商君 (better known as the *Book of Lord Shang* 商君書) in 29 chapters (*pian* 篇); *Shēnzi* 申子 in six chapters; *Shènzi* 慎子 in 42 chapters, and *Hanzi* 韓子 (i.e., *Han Feizi* 韓非子) in 55 chapters. The corresponding thinkers are Shang Yang, Shen Buhai 申不害 (d. 337 BCE), Shen Dao 慎到 (fl. ca. 300 BCE), and Han Fei 韓非 (d. 233 BCE). My discussion of the historical reputation of the *fa* tradition will focus mainly on the attitudes toward the above thinkers. Note that these thinkers were often grouped together not under the rubric of "the school of *fa*" 法家, but rather under the combination of their names, i.e. "Guan [Zhong] and Shang [Yang]" 管商, "Shen [Buhai] and Han [Fei]" 申韓, "Shang [Yang] and Han [Fei]" 商韓, "Guan, Shang, Shen, Han" 管商申韓, and so forth.[1]

There has been ample attention in scholarly circles to the historical reputation of the *fa* tradition and its theories.[2] So why ought we discuss these further? The reason is that whereas most scholars have noted that the *fa* tradition has historically had a very poor reputation, they also generally realize that, despite having declined as a powerful intellectual current since the Han 漢 dynasty (206/202 BCE–220 CE) to the point of having withdrawn from the ideological stage, the *fa* tradition has always had an impact in Chinese history. How ought such an ideological phenomenon be explained? What role has the *fa* tradition played in imperial China since the Han dynasty? How are we to evaluate it? Most previous studies have described the changing reputation of the *fa* tradition from the perspective of intellectual history, but there is still much room for in-depth historical research on the ostensible paradox: how, despite its bad reputation, did the *fa* tradition continue to influence Chinese history? This requires new insights and perspectives in order to further examine and analyze this phenomenon. This question is what my chapter addresses.

---

[1] The question of whether or not "the school of *fa*" (*fajia* 法家) can be considered a school of thought has been discussed by many scholars; e.g., most recently Goldin 2011; Pines 2014; Qiao 2018. In Chinese, the compound *fajia* is used so broadly nowadays that it is not feasible to replace it with alternatives. In English, following the volume's convention, I accept the advantages of "the *fa* tradition," except when I refer to the text that clearly speaks of the "school of *fa*" (e.g., when I cite Sima Tan 司馬談).

[2] For general discussions, see Wu 1976; Wu 2017; for Guan Zhong's image, see Geng 2018; for Shang Yang, see Li 1977; Zeng 2003 [2016]; Zhang 2011; Zhang 2012: 352–415; Pines and Defoort 2016; Pines 2017: 100–114; for *Han Feizi*, see Chen Qianjun 1936a and 1936b; Chen 1945; Zhang 2010: 1463–1571; Song 2017; for Shen Buhai, see Creel 1974: 233–293; for Shen Dao, see Harris 2016: 96–103.

1   Bad Reputation

The *fa* tradition has enjoyed both good and bad reputation in Chinese history, but overall, the negative has far outweighed the positive. The mainstream attitude toward the *fa* tradition was negative, and this attitude was based on three main arguments. First, the *fa* thinkers were assumed to have serious moral flaws; generally, they were associated with cruelty and harshness. Second, these personal defects of *fa* thinkers were viewed as related to their ideological propositions, characterized by cruelty and vitriol, such as the advocacy of severe punishments and harsh laws, belittling morality and educational transformation (*jiaohua* 教化), and ignoring sympathy and human sentiments. Thirdly, the doctrine of the *fa* thinkers was viewed as related to oppressive rule, which by no means could bring lasting peace. That the Imperial Qin (221–207 BCE) perished after just two generations was the disastrous consequence of the *fa* doctrine. These three arguments are organically connected: cruel and harsh personalities promoted cruel and harsh ideas, and the practical effects of these ideas led to Qin's swift collapse. The seeds of these criticisms are discernible already in the works of preimperial Confucians; and they were advanced by the Han Confucians who nailed the *fa* tradition to the pillar of historical shame. The historical infamy of the *fa* tradition has greatly influenced general opinion in imperial China for more than two millennia.

Among the *fa* thinkers, Guan Zhong enjoyed the best historical reputation. But even so, as Liang Qichao 梁啟超 (1873–1929) noted, Guan Zhong's reputation in Chinese history is still "as much defamed as praised" (Liang 2014: 5). Guan Zhong was often viewed as the predecessor to the Warring States-period *fa* thinkers, and the text that borrows his name, *Guanzi*, was seen by many as a *fa* text. When Ban Gu 班固 (32–92) categorized historical personalities in the *Hanshu* "Table of ancient and recent personalities" ("Gujin ren biao" 古今人表), he listed Guan Zhong under the "middle upper" 上中 rank as "a benevolent person" 仁人, second only to the "sages" 聖人 of the "upper upper" 上上 rank and above the "wise people" 智人 of the "lower upper" 上下 rank. The identification of Guan Zhong as a "benevolent person" is based on the judgment attributed to Confucius himself. In the *Analects*, Confucius praised Guan Zhong as a "benevolent person" due to Guan Zhong's practical achievements in assisting Lord Huan of Qi 齊桓公 (r. 685–643 BCE) in "ordering All-under-Heaven" and protecting it against the "barbarians" ("if it were not for Guan Zhong, we would all be wearing our hair loose and fastening our garments on the left" 微管仲，吾其被髮左衽矣) (*Lunyu* 14.16–14.17). Elsewhere in the *Analects*, however, Confucius is also cited as criticizing Guan Zhong's "being a small vessel" 器小, assaulting his "lack of frugality" 不儉, "lack of understanding of ritual" 不知禮, and so forth (*Lunyu* 3.22). These conflicting evaluations of Guan Zhong in the *Analects* foreshadowed the basic stances and criteria for judging *fa* thinkers by later scholars, who either focused their criticisms on these thinkers' personal flaws or took a broader view of their historical achievements in order to put forward limited approval. What needs to be pointed out is that judgement on the basis of morality was the mainstream form of evaluation, so by and large the *fa* thinkers have had a bad reputation throughout history.

Though Guan Zhong had a relatively good historical reputation compared to other preimperial *fa* thinkers,[3] his *fa* affiliations still made him the target of bitter criticism. Geng (2018) believes that the two most ferocious critics of Guan Zhong in the history of imperial China were Gao Sisun 高似孫 (1158–1231), and Wu Hai 吳海 (fl. 1340). Gao Sisun echoed *Records of Personalities*, identifying Guan Zhong and Shang Yang as representatives of the *fa* tradition. He argued that Guan Zhong had corrupted the "system of the former monarchs" 先王之制, allegedly in place since the Western Zhou 西周 dynasty (ca. 1046–771 BCE): "He caused All-under-Heaven to unite in military engagements and forget about agriculture; to unite in pursuit of benefit and forget about righteousness" 使天下一於兵而忘其為農，天下一於利而忘其為義. "Was Guan Zhong the first to corrupt the standards of the Three Dynasties?" 壞三代之法，其一出於管仲乎. "Wuhu! Guan Zhong is *not* benevolent" 嗚呼，仲之不仁也 (*Zilüe* 1: 27–28). Gao Sisun equated the thought of *Guanzi* with Guan Zhong, and Geng Zhendong commented on this approach: "Because he did not acknowledge that *Guanzi* reflects ideas from the time of Shang Yang, and because he rejected the ideas of *Guanzi*, he had to reject Guan Zhong as an individual… Naturally, this is a wrong approach" (Geng 2018: 307–08). Gao Sisun's criticisms of Guan Zhong were focused primarily on the *fa* utilitarian thought of "enriching the country and strengthening the army" 富國強兵.

Wu Hai said: "The books of Guan [Zhong], Shang [Yang], Shen [Buhai] and Han [Fei]—are all criminals against the Way of orderly rule" 管商申韓諸書，治道之賊也 (*Wenguozhai ji* 8: 4). He severely criticized Guan Zhong's character in an essay "Reading *Guanzi*" 讀《管子》：

> 蓋其才雖富而心則狹，故識甚淺而功可羞。然其不仁亦甚矣!後世申商晁錯之倫，無非宗管仲者，孔明自擬，豈謂其才邪?
>
> Perhaps, although Guan Zhong's skills were rich, his heart was narrow; hence his knowledge was shallow and his achievements were shameful. Ah, how unbenevolent he was! The theories of Shen [Buhai], Shang [Yang] and Chao Cuo 晁錯 (d. 154 BCE) of the later generations—all originated from Guan Zhong. Kongming 孔明 (i.e., Zhuge Liang 諸葛亮, 181–234) compared himself to Guan Zhong—what does it tell us of [Zhuge's] abilities? (*Wenguozhai ji* 8: 8)

Clearly, Wu Hai was calling into question Guan Zhong's character. Guan Zhong's historical achievements of "honoring the king and repelling the aliens" 尊王攘夷 and of "preserving the ruined [states] and continuing interrupted [sacrifices]" 存亡

---

[3] Guan Zhong's personal achievements aside, his relatively good reputation derived also from his association with *Guanzi*, several chapters of which were hailed because they espoused ideas and values more aligned with mainstream Confucian thought. For instance, "Shepherding the people" ("Mu min" 牧民) chapter advocates the four cardinal virtues 四維 of ritual 禮, righteousness 義, incorruptibility 廉, and a sense of shame 恥, for each it was much praised. Also, the economic chapters on "Light and Heavy" 輕重 of *Guanzi* were endorsed by supporters of the state's intervention into commercial economy, specifically supporters of monopolies on salt and iron. See more in Geng 2018.

繼絕,[4] are not sufficient to gloss over Guan's selfishness. Guan Zhong's thought was designed to entice the monarch with profit, which wreaked endless disasters on future generations. Shen Buhai, Shang Yang, and Chao Cuo were all influenced by him. Wu Hai essentially rejected Guan Zhong and his thought in its entirety, linking it with later main representatives of the *fa* tradition.

Compared with Guan Zhong's historical reputation, Shang Yang, Shen Buhai, Han Fei, and others were not so fortunate. Although the "Table of Ancient and Recent Personalities" ranks Shang Yang, Han Fei, Shen Buhai, Shen Dao, and others among the "upper-middle" 中上 category, and relegates Li Si 李斯 (d. 208 BCE) and the First Emperor of Qin 秦始皇 (emp. 221–210 BCE) to the "lower-middle" 中下 rank, their place in historical public opinion on the whole would perhaps be "lower-lower" 下下 rank. At the very least, these thinkers were all considered to have moral flaws. For example, Sima Qian 司馬遷 (ca. 145–90 BCE) comments on Shang Yang "Heaven endowed him with a harsh and relentless nature" 其天資刻薄人 (*Shiji* 68: 2237); and on Han Fei: "He carried cruelty and harshness to the extreme and had little kindness" 極慘礉少恩 (*Shiji* 63: 2156). Sima Qian's evaluation of Guan Zhong also focused on Confucius' criticism of him "being a small vessel," summarizing that "although the generation calls Guan Zhong a worthy minister, Confucius belittled him" 管仲世所謂賢臣，然孔子小之 (*Shiji* 62: 2136). This ad hominem criticism was a useful means of denigrating the *fa* ideology in general.

The character flaws of the *fa* thinkers were perceived to be reflected in the brutality of and cruelness of their thought. Sima Qian's father, Sima Tan 司馬談 (d. 110 BCE) summarized the *fa* school as being "strict and having little kindness" 嚴而少恩 (*Shiji* 130: 3289). In the "Treatise on Arts and Letters" of the *Hanshu*, this school is defined as "being cruel even to the relatives, damaging kindness and diminishing generosity" 殘害至親，傷恩薄厚 (*Hanshu* 30: 1736). The *fa* tradition's strict impartiality and incorruptibility, its idea of "not differentiating between noble and base: everything is determined by *fa*" (*Shiji* 130: 3291) can be said to be incompatible with the Confucian doctrine of gradualism between kin and strangers, of the rule by virtue and benevolence. In the eyes of Confucians, the *fa* tradition was regarded as a despised tool of oppressive rule. Yang Xiong 揚雄 (53 BCE–18 CE) succinctly summarized this point: "The techniques of Shen [Buhai] and Han [Fei] are the apex of being non-benevolent. Why treat people as oxen and sheep?" 申、韓之術，不仁之至矣，若何牛羊之用人也? (*Fayan* 4.22 ["Wen Dao" 問道]). Yang Xiong focuses on preserving human dignity; for him, Shen Buhai and Han Fei's techniques were "inhumane" because they eliminated the difference between humans (the state's subjects) and the beasts. Being treated like oxen and sheep, humans subjected to ruthless techniques of Shen Buhai and Han Fei would be reduced to tools and lose their dignity.

---

[4] The first of these achievements of Guan Zhong's partner, Lord Huan, is hailed in *Gongyang zhuan* 公羊傳 (Xi 4: 203); the second—in *Guliang zhuan* 穀梁傳 (Xi 17; *Chunqiu Guliang jingzhuan buzhu* 10: 305).

The collapse of the Qin dynasty marked the great setback for the *fa* tradition. Gradually, the Han intellectual atmosphere changed, and the *fa* tradition was identified as the major culprit behind Qin's rapid collapse. The seeds of the negative view of the *fa* thought are observable already in the writings of Lu Jia 陸賈 (ca. 228–140 BCE), who, shortly after the Qin downfall singled out the excessive reliance on punishments by the *fa* adherents as the reason for the Qin collapse

> 事逾煩，天下逾亂，法逾滋而奸逾熾，兵馬益設而敵人逾多，秦非不欲為治，然失之者，乃舉措暴眾，而用刑太極故也。
>
> The more oppressive their undertakings became, the more the world was disordered; the more the laws multiplied, the more treachery spread like wildfire; the more troops were deployed, the more the enemies increased. It is not that the Qin did not desire order, but its failure was that its mobilizations were too profuse, its use of corporal punishments excessive." (*Xinyu* 4: 62; ["Wu wei" 無爲]; trans. Goldin and Sabattini 2020: 51)

Lu Jia was relatively mild in his criticism, and so was Jia Yi 賈誼 (ca. 200–168 BCE), who emphasized the negative impact of Shang Yang's reforms on the people's customs in Qin: "Shang Yang deviated from ritual and propriety, cast away norms and principles, focused on advancement and seizure. After practicing this for two years, Qin's customs became daily corrupted" 商君違禮義，棄倫理，並心於進取，行之二歲，秦俗日敗 (*Xinshu* 3: 97 ["Shi bian" 時變]). This spoilage of Qin's customs was, in Jia Yi's eyes, the root of the swift collapse of Imperial Qin as famously exposed in his treatise "Faulting the Qin" ("Guo Qin lun" 過秦論; *Xinshu* 1: 1–25). In the slightly later *Huainanzi* 淮南子, we encounter yet harsher evaluation of the *fa* thinkers. Whereas some of the *Huainanzi* chapters, most notably "The Ruler's Techniques" ("Zhushu" 主術) bear the clear imprint of *fa* thought (Ames 1994), the text as a whole is overtly critical of Shang Yang, Shen Buhai, and Han Fei for discarding benevolence and righteousness:

> 今若夫申、韓、商鞅之為治也，挬拔其根，蕪棄其本，而不窮究其所由生，何以至此也？鑿五刑，為刻削，乃背道德之本，而爭於錐刀之末，斬艾百姓，殫盡太半，而忻忻然常自以為治，是猶抱薪而救火，鑿竇而出水。
>
> Now, take for example, the methods of government [proposed by] Shen [Buhai], Han [Fei], and Shang Yang. They proposed to pluck out the stems [of disorder] and weed out the roots [of disobedience], without fully investigating where they come from. How did things get to this point? They forcibly imposed the five punishments, employed slicing and amputations, and turned their back on the fundamentals of the Way and Virtue, while fighting over the point of an awl. They moved the common people like hay and exterminated more than half of them. Thus filled with self-admiration, they constantly took themselves as [representing] orderly rule; but this was just like adding fuel to put out a fire or boring holes to stop water [from leaking]. (*Huainanzi* 6.9: 215 ["Lanming xun" 覽冥訓]; translation modified from Major et al. 2010: 230–31).

Huainanzi represents clear escalation of anti-*fa* thinkers' sentiments during the Han dynasty. Back in the first generations of the Han rulers, these sentiments were not uniformly negative though. Sometimes, criticism was coupled with approval of certain aspects of the *fa* ideas. Thus, Sima Tan in his famous treatise "On the Essentials of the Six Schools of Thought" ("Lun liujia yaozhi" 論六家要旨) summarizes:

法家不別親疏，不殊貴賤，一斷於法，則親親尊尊之恩絕矣。可以行一時之計，而
不可長用也，故曰"嚴而少恩"。若尊主卑臣，明分職不得相逾越，
雖百家弗能改也。

    The *fa* school does not distinguish between kin and stranger, nor differentiate between
noble and base: everything is determined by the standard (or law, *fa*); hence the kindness of
treating the kin as kin and respecting the respectable is severed. It is a one-time policy that
could not be constantly applied, hence it is said, they are "strict and having little kindness."
As for honouring rulers and derogating subjects, clearly distinguishing offices so that no
one can overstep [his responsibilities]—even the Hundred Schools cannot change it. (*Shiji*
1997: 130: 3291)

Sima Tan acknowledged the strengths of the *fa* school, viz. safeguarding of political
and ethical order in which the ruler is respected and the ministers remain subordinate. Yet he criticized the *fa* school's denigration of kin affection, its being "strict
and having little kindness," and its total commitment to *fa*. As such this was "a one-
time policy that could not be constantly applied." This judgment was tantamount to
depriving the *fa* tradition of long-term legitimacy. This view is reflected throughout
the *Shiji* 史記 (Records of the Historian), which was started by Sima Tan and completed by his son, Sima Qian. Whereas *Shiji* records the deeds of the *fa* thinkers and
likeminded statesmen such as Wu Qi 吳起 (d. 381 BCE), Shang Yang, Han Fei, and
Li Si, and recognizes their achievements, it repeatedly criticizes their harshness. In
particular, the biographies of Shang Yang and Li Si merit negative summary by
Sima Qian, which is very rare in the "Arrayed biographies" 列傳 section (*Shiji* 68:
2237 and 87: 2563; see also Jiang 2021). Insofar as *Shiji* was a must-read for scholars in later generations, its impact throughout the ages was quite exceptional. Its
association of the leading *fa* figures such as Shang Yang and Han Fei as "harsh and
relentless" 刻薄 and having "little kindness" 少恩 (see above) became the stock
evaluation of the *fa* tradition in later history. As such, *Shiji* contributed much to the
poor reputation of the *fa* tradition well throughout the entire imperial period.

    Whereas *Shiji* presents a negative but still relatively balanced view of the *fa* tradi-
tion, some of Sima Tan and Sima Qian's contemporaries—most notably Dong
Zhongshu 董仲舒 (ca. 195–115 BCE)—were incomparably harsher in anti-*fa* and
anti-Qin philippics. Dong stated:

至秦則不然。師申商之法，行韓非之說，憎帝王之道，以貪狼為俗，非有文德
以教訓於天下也。

    When it came to the Qin, however, it was not so (as Zhou). Guided by the standards of
Shen [Buhai] and Shang [Yang], and implementing the theories of Han Fei, it loathed the
Way of the Thearchs and Monarchs and instead made greed and avarice customary. It
lacked the refined virtue with which to instruct and teach All-under-Heaven. (*Hanshu* 56:
2511; translation modified from Queen and Major 2016: 632)

The above attack on Qin continues with a list of its malpractices in which Qin's
harshness and suppression of the people figure prominently. Yet once we read Dong
Zhongshu's memorial further, we discover its major goal—to let Emperor Wu 漢武
帝 (r. 141–87 BCE) dispel the "poisonous" legacy of Qin and start "nurturing men
of service" 養士. It is with this regard that Qin—notorious for its book burning of
213 BCE—provided an especially negative example. Qin's biblioclasm was directly
related to Han Fei invectives again the "scholars" 學者, whom he derided as one of

the "five vermin" 五蠹 (*Han Feizi* 49.18; Chen 2000: 1122).[5] As such, Qin, Han Fei, and the *fa* tradition in general became the focus of immense hatred of the imperial literati. Whereas this topic usually figures less prominently in anti-*fa* and anti-Qin invectives, one may be sure that the *fa* thinkers' assault on the intellectuals, what Pines (2023) dubs as their "class betrayal," generated even harsher anti-*fa* sentiments than the *fa* tradition's perceived oppressiveness.

Rather than piling examples of negative remarks about the *fa* thinkers throughout the centuries, I prefer to focus on one representative case, that of one of China's most illustrious literati, Su Shi 蘇軾 (1037–1101). His detailed comments on Shang Yang, Shen Buhai, Han Fei, Li Si, and the First Emperor may be considered a microcosm of the historical reputation of the *fa* tradition.[6] Su Shi combined criticism of Han Fei, Shang Yang, and Shen Buhai with that of Laozi 老子 and Zhuang Zhou 莊周 (i.e., Zhuangzi 莊子). His reasoning is as follows: *Laozi* and *Zhuangzi* criticized Confucian virtues of benevolence, righteousness, ritual, and music, undermining social distinctions and "wanting to place All-under-Heaven in nothingness" 欲置天下於無有. Whereas their ideas as such were of little damage to All-under-Heaven, their legacy of "treating All-under-Heaven lightly" 輕天下 was inherited by Shang Yang, Shen Buhai, and Han Fei, who complemented it with the severe punishments and strict laws of the *fa* tradition, and thereby gave rise to great disaster:

> 自老聃之死百餘年，有商鞅、韓非著書，言治天下無若刑名之賢，及秦用之，終於勝、廣之亂，教化不足而法有餘，秦以不祀，而天下被其毒。後世之學者，知申、韓之罪，而不知老聃、莊周之使然。
>
> More than a century after Lao Dan's (Laozi's) death, there were books written by Shang Yang and Han Fei. They argued that nothing can order All-under-Heaven better than the worth of *xingming* (performance and titles) theory. As Qin had used these methods, it ended with the turmoil of [Chen] Sheng [i.e. Chen She 陳涉, d. 208 BCE] and [Wu] Guang 吳廣 [d. 208 BCE]. Its educational transformation was lacking, whereas its laws were superfluous.
>
> Qin's ancestral sacrifices were discontinued, but All-under-Heaven was covered by its poison. Scholars of later generations understood the crime of Shen [Buhai] and Han [Fei], but did not understand that this was caused by Lao Dan and Zhuang Zhou. (*Su Shi wenji*, pp. 102–03 ["Han Fei lun" 韓非論]).

Su Shi's lines of argumentation were later echoed by Wang Fuzhi 王夫之 (1619–1692) who added Buddha to the list of negative personages who undermined political morality. Wang argued: "From the days of old to the present there were

---

[5] The references to *Han Feizi* are to the divisions into chapters and paragraphs adopted in the forthcoming translation by Christoph Harbsmeier (who borrows it from Zhang 2010).

[6] Among thinkers associated with the *fa* tradition, Su Shi holds only Guan Zhong in high regard. Su does criticize Guan Zhong for "having not learned the Way, and having not sincerely rectifying himself to provide a model for his state" 不學道，不自誠意正身以刑其國, as well as for "having the malady of 'three returns'" 三歸之病 and having "the disaster of six female favorites" 六嬖之禍 (these latter accusations refer to alleged immorality of Guan Zhong hinted at in *Lunyu* 3.22 [see Yang Bojun's gloss there, pp. 31–32]); Su also criticizes Lord Huan's excessive number of favored concubines, which eventually brought about a severe succession crisis after his death. These criticisms aside, Su Shi, following Confucius's praise, admired Guan Zhong's assistance to Lord Huan of Qi as being "an undertaking of utmost virtue" 盛德之事. See *Su Shi wenji*, p. 146 ("Lun Guan Zhong" 論管仲).

three sources of damage: Laozi and Zhuangzi, the Buddha, and Shen [Buhai] and Han [Fei]. The ways that these three brought about disasters differ, but they inherited each other in generating these [disasters], and in the end they should be discussed as one" 古今之大害者有三：老莊也，浮屠也，申韓也。三者之致禍異，而相沿以生者，其歸必合於一. He then added that despite their ostensible difference, the ideas of these thinkers are actually the same: "Their teaching is that of Buddha and Laozi, but their *fa* must be that of Shen [Buhai] and Han [Fei]" 其教佛老者，其法必申韓. "Above is Shen [Buhai] and Han [Fei]; below it must be Buddha and Laozi" 其上申韓者，其下必佛老 (*Du Tongjian lun* 17: 500–01).[7] Indeed from the vantage point of Confucian thinkers, the assault on Confucian values from the proponents of inaction and nothingness and from proponents of extreme empowerment of the state could be considered equally damaging.

Going back to Su Shi, we should notice his exceptionally fierce criticism of Shang Yang. Su Shi censured Sima Qian for making a serious mistake in praising the merits of Shang Yang and Sang Hongyang 桑弘羊 (152–80 BCE).[8] Su Shi argued that "from the Han dynasty on, scholars have been ashamed to talk about Shang Yang and Sang Hongyang" 自漢以來，學者恥言商鞅、桑弘羊. Su Shi denied Shang Yang's contribution to the success of Lord Xiao of Qin 秦孝公 (r. 361–338 BCE). According to Su, even without Shang Yang, Lord Xiao could have made Qin prosperous and strong. Shang Yang actually caused only damage to Qin, as his unpopular policies made Qin the object of the people's hate. Su argued that the techniques of Shang Yang and Sang Hongyang would inevitably result in "destroying the state and losing one's ancestors" 破國亡宗 (*Su Shi wenji*, pp. 155–57 ["Shang Yang lun" 商鞅論]).

Why was Su Shi so vehement in denying Shang Yang even his most evident practical achievements? Why did he argue that even speaking about Shang Yang is shameful? The reasons should be explored in the context of the political cleavages of the Northern Song 北宋 (960–1127) era. As noted by Xiao Gongquan 蕭公權 (1897–1981), the attacks on the *fa* thinkers back then were used to criticize the state activism associated with Wang Anshi 王安石 (1021–1086). Su Shi was not concerned much with the ideas of the *fa* thinkers as such. What mattered to him was that the attack on the much maligned intellectual tradition was a convenient tool for undermining Wang Anshi's activism (of which see more below) (Xiao 1996: 424–25). Demonization of Shang Yang and his like—the notable state activists of the past—was used to denigrate Wang Anshi and his reforms.

---

[7] Buddha figures prominently in Wang's discussion because it is made in the context of his criticism of Emperor Wu of Liang 梁武帝 (r. 502–549), who was renowned for his Buddhist inclinations.

[8] Sang Hongyang was in charge of economic policies adopted under Emperor Wu of Han; he is paired with Shang Yang not only because of Sang's praise of Shang Yang (see Sect. 2 below), but because his policies were direct antecedent to Wang Anshi's 王安石 economic activism, which Su Shi detested.

Su Shi's criticism epitomizes one of the major reasons for the opposition to the *fa* thinkers throughout the centuries. All those who opposed activist and interventionist state apparatus found it expedient to identify it with the *fa* legacy, coming through the much-hated Qin. Insofar as the *fa* thinkers were repeatedly maligned for being harsh, having little kindness, or being "without virtue" 無德[9]—any association with them sufficed to sully political activists such as Wang Anshi and his ilk. For the mainstream imperial political tradition, the *fa* thinkers became a negative example to be studied only so as to avoid their deeds. This understanding was conveniently summarized by the Qing 清 (1636/1644–1912) scholars in charge of composing the "Complete Books from the Four Treasuries" (*siku quanshu* 四庫全書), who argued:

> 觀於商鞅、韓非諸家，可以知刻薄寡恩之非。鑒彼前車，即所以克端治本。
> When we observe thinkers such as Shang Yang and Han Fei, we can know the negative impact of being "harsh and relentless" and "having little kindness." Learning from their experience is the means of overcoming heterodoxies and ordering the roots [of good government]. (*Siku quanshu zongmu* 141: 847)

The negative views of the *fa* thinkers' morality, of their excessively interventionist policies, and of their assault on fellow intellectuals—all turned them into potent negative symbols, which could be used in a great variety of contexts, not always directly related to the *fa* legacy. Above we have seen how the implied association with the *fa* tradition was used against Wang Anshi's reforms. Elsewhere, the names of Shang Yang, Shen Buhai, or Han Fei could be used as handy tools with which to attack one's opponents, even when the association was dubious. Take, for instance, Wang Fuzhi's opposition to Song Confucianism. In Wang's view, Shen Buhai and Han Fei represented "defective personalities and a sick culture" (Zhao 2015b: 465). Wang criticized Song Confucians for being fake Confucians: "From the Song dynasty on, those who pretend to be the 'noble men Confucians,' spoke the words of the Sage [Confucius], but acted according to Shen [Buhai] and Han [Fei]" 自宋以來，為君子儒者，言則聖人而行則申韓也. Wang derisively called these people "Shen and Han Confucians" 申韓之儒.[10] Here, "Shen and Han" are used as a synonym for "extremely negative" without much concern for actual resemblance between Song Confucianism and the ideas of Shen Buhai and Han Fei. What Wang Fuzhi really hints at was the notorious harshness of the Ming 明 (1368–1644) laws, which were bitterly criticized by the thinkers writing in the aftermath of Ming's downfall.

Let us summarize the discussion heretofore. Imperial Confucian scholars by and large accepted the Confucian doctrine of the rule of virtue and benevolence as a self-evident concept. This was a sincere acceptance. Their criticisms of the brutality and harshness of the *fa* tradition were also sincere. It is precisely because of this

---

[9] The identification of the *fa* tradition as "lacking virtue" (with *de* 德 here referring both to moral qualities and to mild, non-coercive means of rule) is epitomized in Wang Chong's 王充 (27–ca. 97 CE) *Lunheng* 論衡 (Balanced discussions). Wang criticizes Han Fei: "The techniques of Master Han do not nourish virtue" 韓子之術不養德; "I know that Master Han for sure will have the trouble of lacking virtue" 知韓子必有無德之患 (*Lunheng* 10: 438 ["Fei Han" 非韓]).

[10] *Wang Chuanshan shi wen ji*, pp. 6–7 ("Lao Zhuang Shen Han lun" 老莊申韓論).

sincerity that the *fa* tradition could be made into a symbol for all things negative to be used in political struggles. Yet resentment against the tradition that "lacked virtue" 無德 and epitomized "brutality" 殘暴 aside, two powerful factors fueled negative views of the *fa* tradition. The first was a widespread (even if by no means unanimous) opposition to an assertive and interventionist state which was routinely associated with the Qin legacy and through it with the *fa* thinkers. The second was a less visible but no less potent view of the *fa* thinkers as responsible for the persecution of fellow intellectuals. Deep in their hearts, the imperial literati could not possibly forgive those who dubbed their preimperial ancestors as part of the "five vermin."

2   Good Reputation

Its predominantly negative image notwithstanding, the *fa* tradition has received sporadic endorsements throughout the centuries. Compared to its historical notoriety, positive reception of the *fa* tradition has been very faint. The one notable exception is the early Han period, when the *fa* tradition had not yet been fully stigmatized. In the later historical periods, open endorsement of the *fa* thinkers was extremely rare, even if not entirely non-existent. In this section, I shall focus on the open endorsement of the *fa* tradition; in the next—I shall discuss its practical impact which was often left far from the limelight.

Xiao Gongquan was among those who discussed at length the ongoing impact of the *fa* tradition in the Han dynasty. Although after the fall of Qin "there never again was one who attempted to carry into practice a purely *fa* government, and likewise the learning of Lord Shang and Han Fei marked the end of all further advances in the realm of theory," there were quite a few "immediate followers and more distant disciples" of the *fa* thinkers throughout the early Han (Xiao 1996: 252–53; translation modified from Hsiao 1979: 446–47). Indeed, historical analyses attest to a number of early Han thinkers and statesmen who studied the theories of Shen Buhai and Shang Yang, or of Shen Buhai and Han Fei. Among the most notable examples are the aforementioned Jia Yi and his contemporary Chao Cuo 晁錯 (d. 154 BCE; of Chao, see more in Schwermann, Chap. 6, this volume).[11] The Imperial Counsellor Han Anguo 韓安國 (d. 127 BCE) is also said to have studied *Han Feizi* (*Shiji* 108: 2857). The *fa* tradition was attractive enough to merit specific proposals of the Chancellor Wei Wan 衛綰 (d. 133 BCE) to prohibit adherents of Shen Buhai, Shang Yang, and Han Fei from being promoted from among the "worthy and good" 賢良 category of candidates for the positions in bureaucracy (*Hanshu* 6: 156). This recommendation, made early during the reign of Emperor Wu, was of lasting impact on the legitimacy of the engagement in *fa* studies. Yet even it did not mean immediate cessation of the interest in the *fa* legacy.

---

[11] See, e.g., *Shiji* 101: 2745 (for Chao Cuo); *Shiji* 130: 3319 (for Jia Yi and Chao Cuo).

The major testimony of the ongoing legitimacy of the *fa* tradition are the Salt and Iron Debates of 81 BCE recorded in Huan Kuan's 桓寬 (fl. ca. 50 BCE) eponymous *Yantielun* 鹽鐵論. During the meeting, the Imperial Counsellor Sang Hongyang and other representatives of the imperial government faced the opposition of the "worthy and the good" and the "literati" (*wenxue* 文學). The latter squarely represented the Confucian (Ru 儒) opposition to the government's activism, especially in the economic sphere (the introduction of the monopolies on salt, iron, and other products). In their defence of the government policies, Sang Hongyang and his fellow officials were not shy to openly endorse the *fa* thinkers, most notably Shang Yang. The bitter exchange between the opponents is presented in chapters 7 ("Rejecting [Shang] Yang" 非鞅) and 56 ("Shen [Buhai] and Han [Fei]" 申韓) of the *Yantielun*. The debate, in which the literati accuse Shang Yang of being the reason for the Qin dynasty's swift downfall, whereas Sang Hongyang praises Shang Yang's achievements, is among a few instances in the imperial-era literature in which the legacy of Shang Yang could be openly and unequivocally defended at great length.[12] From this point, until Zhang Taiyan's 章太炎 (aka Zhang Binglin 章炳麟, 1869–1936) endorsement of Shang Yang at the very end of the imperial era (for which see below), public endorsement of the *fa* tradition was extremely rare, and systematic ideological defense of it was almost non-existent.

The weakening of centralized power since the second half of the Latter Han dynasty (25–220) created a powerful countertrend of calling for renewed centralization and for the promulgation of "a rich country and a powerful army" policies. Not a few scholars such as Zhang Taiyan and Lü Simian 呂思勉 (1884–1957) identified this period as an age of resurrection in the interest in the *fa* tradition (Zhang 1996: 228–29; Lü 1982: 866). It is certainly true that contemporaneous thinkers, such as Wang Fu 王符 (ca. 85–163), Zhongchang Tong 仲長統 (180–220), Cui Shi 崔寔 (d. 170), Liu Yu 劉廙 (180–221), Huan Fan 桓範 (d. 249), and others incorporated many *fa* tradition elements into their thought. Nonetheless, they were not the successors of the *fa* tradition in an ideological sense, nor did they systematically defend the *fa* tradition like Sang Hongyang. By this stage, the *fa* tradition had already become a symbol for all things negative. Even if thinkers wanted to learn from some of its ideological propositions, they had to handle it carefully and properly, and none would have dared to defend it publicly.[13] The same situation continued during the subsequent age of political fragmentation, dubbed the age of Wei, Jin, and Southern, and Northern Dynasties 魏晉南北朝 (220–589) Whereas certain thinkers and statesmen were applying elements of the *fa* tradition in political practice (see the next section), there were fewer and fewer voices recognizing and evaluating them positively at the level of theoretical discussion. Ge Hong's 葛洪 (283–343) *Baopuzi*

---

[12] The ideological cleavages in *Yantie lun* had been studied by Guo 1985. For a recent attempt to defend the reliability of the text as rooted in real debates (rather than being Huan Kuan's invention), see Polnarov 2018.

[13] For a discussion on the *fa* elements in the thought of Wang Fu, Zhong Changtong, Cui Shi, Liu Yu, and Huan Fan, see Song 2017: 137–216.

抱樸子 is a rare instance of those who criticized the people for failing to understand the usefulness of studying Shen Buhai and Han Feizi for political governance:

> 世人薄申韓之實事，嘉老莊之誕談。然而為政莫能錯刑，殺人者原其死，傷人者赦其罪，所謂土木半瓦菽，無救朝饑者也。
>
> The people of our generation look down upon the practical affairs exposed by Shen [Buhai] and Han [Fei], and praise the absurd talks of Lao[zi] and Zhuang[zi]. Yet he who in governance is unable to implement punishments, who pardons the murderer and annuls punishment of the one who injured others, is like one who uses mud as gruel and wooden planks as meat[14]—this will not save the starving. (*Baopuzi* 14: 361 ["Yong xing" 用刑])

Voices like that of Ge Hong who openly acknowledged the practical advantages of *fa* thought were extremely uncommon. Most notable among them was that of Wang Anshi. Wang's complex relation to the *fa* tradition will be discussed in the next section; here it suffices to remind ourselves of his poem with the provocative title "Acclaiming Shang Yang" 詠商鞅:

> 自古驅民在信誠，一言為重百金輕。今人未可非商鞅，商鞅能使令必行。
>
> From the old days, driving the people depended on trust and sincerity.
> One word was heavy, whereas a hundred [catties] of gold—light.
> People today should not fault Shang Yang;
> Shang Yang was able to let his orders be inevitably implemented. (*Wang Wengong ji* 73: 777)

This poem alludes to an anecdote in *Shiji*'s "The Arrayed Biography of Lord Shang," which tells of Shang Yang promising lavish reward for anybody who would move a three-yard pole; once the promise was implemented he acquired the people's trust (*Shiji* 68: 2231). It is worth thinking about why Wang was willing to disadvantage himself with this political incorrectness at a time when Shang Yang and the *fa* tradition were stigmatized.[15] I shall discuss Wang's possible ideological affiliation with Shang Yang in the next section. Here suffice it to say that Wang's rare endorsement of Shang Yang may well be the reason behind Su Shi's anti-Shang Yang's invectives cited in the previous section.

In the mid- to late- Ming Dynasty, the study of the Masters' 子 texts gained more prominence; occasionally it generated positive comments about the *fa* tradition. Particularly of note among them are those of a brilliant, provocative and unorthodox thinker, Li Zhi 李贄 (1527–1602). Li Zhi argued, "The learning of Master Shang [Yang] esteems *fa* (law); the learning of Master Shen [Buhai] esteems *shu* (techniques), the learning of Master Han Fei esteems both *fa* and *shu*. Although the world considered them cruel and harsh, they were unabashed" 商子之學術貴法，申子之學術貴術，韓非子之學術兼貴法術，雖天下以我為殘忍刻薄不恤也. Li expressed his appreciation of the practical value of the three masters' learning and summarized: "one whose achievements are great should not concern themselves with future troubles. Hence, those

---

[14] An allusion to *Han Feizi* 32.2.14 ("Wai chu shuo zuo shang" 外儲說左上; Chen 2000: 683).

[15] See more about Wang's provocative poems in Yang Xiaoshan 2007.

who achieved all that they sought are Lord Shang in Qin and Wu Qi[16] in Chu" 成大功者 必不顧後患，故功無不成，商君之於秦，吳起之於楚是矣 (*Fenshu* 5: 224–25). Li Zhi for sure was not a follower of the *fa* tradition. His positive comments on the *fa* Masters were primarily designed to attack the mainstream opinion of his contemporaries and prove Li's credentials as an unorthodox and provocative thinker (see more in Handler-Spitz 2017). To a certain extent it can be opined that his praise of the *fa* Masters buttresses the ubiquity of their negative image in late imperial China.

To be sure, even in the late imperial period we encounter scholars who admired the *fa* thinkers. For instance, Li Zhi's contemporary, who published an edition of *Han Feizi* under the penname Men Wuzi 門無子, expressed great appreciation of the practical value of *Han Feizi*.[17] It may not be a coincidence that Men Wuzi's edition of *Han Feizi* (*Hanzi yuping* 韓子迂評) with a rare laudation of this thinker was published in 1578, i.e., during the heyday of Zhang Juzheng's 張居正 (1527–1582) reforms, when *fa* ideas appeared more relevant than ever (see the next section). Yet overall, such voices remained a rarity.

Things started changing at the very end of the imperial period. In the second half of the nineteenth century, when the Qing dynasty faced an existential threat from domestic and foreign foes, and imperial China had to yield its position as the center of All-under-Heaven and start accommodating the new world order of competing nation-states (not unlike the Warring States era), the *fa* legacy of seeking "a rich state and a strong army" seemed more relevant than ever. It is then that we hear new voices of clear admiration of the *fa* tradition. One of the notable examples is a man of letters Wang Shiduo 汪士鐸 (1802–1889). In 1861, he told his friend Xiao Mu 蕭穆 (1835–1902):

管商申韓孫吳，後人所唾罵，而儒者尤不屑置齒頰。要而論之，百世不能廢，儒者亦陰用其術，而陽斥其人耳。蓋二叔之時已不能純用道德，而謂方今之世，欲以儒林道學兩傳中人遂能登三鹹五，撥亂世而返之治也，不亦夢寐之囈言乎?

Guan [Zhong], Shang [Yang], Shen [Buhai], Han [Fei], Sun[zi], and Wu [Qi] are all cursed by posterity, especially through the mouths of Confucians. Yet if we discuss their essentials, they cannot be dismissed even after a hundred generations. Even the Confucians clandestinely use their techniques while overtly castigating these men. Even in the age of the [rebellious] brothers [of the Duke of Zhou] one could not purely rely on the Way and its virtue.[18] In our generation some want to use the Confucian teaching of the True Way and its two traditions to be able to exceed the Three [Sovereigns] and to equal the Five [Thearchs]

---

[16] Wu Qi, a military leader and a renowned reformer is often associated with the *fa* thinkers; in *Han Feizi*, in particular, he is paired with Shang Yang as a model state-strengthening minister (see, e.g., *Han Feizi* 13.3 ["He shi" 和氏; Chen 2000: 275]. Wu Qi is more often identified as a military thinker though, as he is an alleged author of the treatise *Wuzi* 吳子.

[17] Men Wuzi, "Ke *Hanzi yu ping* xu" 刻韓子迂評序, cited in Chen 2000: 1231–1232. Men Wuzi's identity is known only from Chen Shen's 陳深 preface to his edition of *Han Feizi*, published in 1578; there it is said that Men Wuzi was a Suzhou "noble man" of seventy years old, whose surname was Yu 俞 (Chen 2000: 1231).

[18] The Duke of Zhou 周公 (d. ca. 1035 BCE) quelled in ca. 1042 BCE the pro-Shang rebellion to which two (or three) of his brothers joined; subsequently he had to execute one of them and banish another.

[of antiquity], to pacify the calamitous age and reverse to orderly rule—but is not this just sleep-talking? [19]

As noted by Yu Yingshi 余英時 (1930–2021), Wang was an exceptional personality, the first Qing intellectual to openly oppose the Neo-Confucian Teaching of the True Way (Daoxue 道學). Although Wang himself received a conventional Neo-Confucian education, he realized that the new age of Western encroachment and domestic crisis epitomized by the Taiping 太平 War (1851–1864) required radical altering of the state's fate and intense search for renewed enrichment and empowerment (Yu 2004: 48). Wang did not hesitate to elevate *fa* thinkers and military thinkers and practitioners of the past above the Confucian paragons. He provocatively averred that "[The Duke of] Zhou and Confucius are twice worthier than Yao and Shun; Shen [Buhai] and Han Fei are ten times worthier; and [the military leaders] Han [Xin 韓信, 231–196 BCE] and Bai [Qi 白起, d. 257 BCE]) are a hundred times worthier" 周孔賢於堯舜一倍，申韓賢於十倍，韓白賢於百倍 (*Wang Huiweng Yibing riji*, pp. 94–95). The new era demanded new paragons, whose advantages were not in the world of moral discourse but in that of administrative and military skills.

In the final decades of the Qing dynasty, not a few scholars started expressing positive views of the *fa* thinkers. For instance, the famous philologist Yu Yue 俞樾 (1821–1907) dismissed Su Shi's criticism of Han Fei and approvingly discussed the political activism of Shen Buhai and Han Fei.[20] Another famous personality who emphasized the importance of studying Shen Buhai and Han Fei's thought was Yan Fu 嚴複 (1851–1924), one of the first thinkers to open China to Western ideas. Yan Fu explained the importance of the *fa* thinkers as follows:

居今而言救亡學，惟申韓庶幾可用，除卻綜名核實，豈有他途可行？　賢者試觀歷史，無論中外古今，其稍獲強效，何一非任法者耶？管商尚矣；他若趙奢、吳起。王猛、諸葛、漢宣、唐太，皆略知法意而效亦隨之；至其他亡弱之君，大抵皆良懦者。

Of those who speak today of the teaching that can save [China]—it is Shen [Buhai] and Han [Fei] who are likely to be usable. Nothing but a comprehensive investigation of the name and actuality—is there any other path that can be taken? When the worthies explore history, they do not focus on whether or not the matter is Chinese or foreign, ancient or novel; what matters only is its effectiveness. How then can one dismiss the *fa* [teaching]? There is also Guan [Zhong] and Shang [Yang] and other such as Zhao She[21] and Wu Qi. [Such statesmen] as Wang Meng, Zhuge [Liang], Emperor Xuan [of Han] and Tang Taizong[22]—all understood something about the *fa* tradition and the effects soon transpired.

[19] *Jingfu leigao*, p. 330 ("Wang Meicun xiansheng biezhuan" 汪梅村先生別傳).

[20] Yu Yue, "Shen Han lun" 申韓論 cited from Chen 1945: 144–145.

[21] Zhao She 趙奢 (third century BCE) was a renowned general from the state of Zhao.

[22] Wang Meng 王猛 (325–375) was the chief minister at the court of Fu Jian 符堅, a Former Qin 前秦 emperor who helped his master to reunify northern China. Zhuge Liang is China's most renowned strategist, whose interest in the *fa* thought is discussed in the next section. For the views of Emperor Xuan of Han 漢宣帝, see note 25 below. Tang Taizong's 唐太宗 (r. 626–649) interest in the *fa* tradition requires further discussion.

As for the weakling rulers—most of them were good only at being timid. (*Yan Fu ji*, p. 620 ["A letter to Xiong Chunru" 與熊純如書])

Yan Fu, just as Yu Yue and others, such as Xu Tongxin 許同莘 (1878–?) (for whose positive appraisal of *fa* thinkers, see Liu 2004: 257) were all influenced by the atmosphere of their times, which required reorientation from easy-going Confucian ideals (Yan Fu's "timidity") toward practical methods associated with the *fa* tradition and with the military masters such as Sunzi 孫子 and Wu Qi. The voices advocating reorientation toward political activism and the state's empowerment increased in tandem with a new wave of disasters that erupted at the end of the nineteenth century, when the Qing suffered a series of humiliations, starting with the failure in the war with Japan (1894–1895), through the "Scramble for Concessions" (1897–1899), to the disastrous defeat in the Boxer War (1900). It is then that we hear entirely new voices, such as that of Zhang Taiyan, whose essay "Shang Yang," published in 1900, marked a radical departure from the two millennia of that thinker's demonization. Zhang vehemently defended Shang Yang as not just a successful reformer but as a champion of the masses, who was by no means responsible for the authoritarian usage of his system by later imperial sycophants. Actually, according to Zhang, Shang Yang had not turned to democracy only because the people of Qin were too primitive at that time.[23]

Throughout more than two millennia of imperial China's history, voices approving the *fa* tradition were weak, but they never ceased to exist. The *fa* tradition's advocacy of impartiality, its pragmatic character, and its historical achievements were the major reasons for its positive reputation. Although the intellectual development of the *fa* tradition stopped in the beginning of the imperial era, and despite its stigmatization since the latter half of the Former Han dynasty, it was not entirely put into oblivion. The resurrection of interest in the *fa* tradition in the waning years of the imperial China's history could not occur without subtle but ongoing engagement with this tradition throughout the imperial era. This engagement was often covert, however. Whereas on the practical level, as we shall see below, the impact of the *fa* tradition remained palpable in the imperial-era political life, the open recognition of its importance was a rarity. Zhang Taiyan's explicit endorsement of Shang Yang was a departure from the predominantly clandestine interest in the *fa* thinkers in the past. By itself, this open endorsement marked China's culture stepping into a new era.

3   The Usages of the *fa* Tradition in Imperial China

Traditional China is routinely viewed as a Confucian state; yet many scholars have noted the lasting impact of the *fa* tradition on its institutions and its functioning. Thus, Zhao (2006, 2015a) has recently called it a "Confucian-Legalist" state. Other scholars proposed that Chinese imperial state was "Confucian from without but *fa*

[23] For Zhang's views, see Zhang 2014: 79; see more in Zeng 2003 [2016] and Song 2021.

from within" 外儒内法 (Hou 1957: 63; Qin 2004: 171), or "overtly Confucian but covertly *fa*" (陽儒陰法) (Chen 1990: 2 ["Preface" 前言]). That the Qin legacy of centralized bureaucratic state, rooted as it was in the ideas of the *fa* thinkers had a lasting profound impact on imperial China is undeniable, indeed. Nor can it be denied that in times of internal weaknesses or aggravating external threats, the resolute proposals of the *fa* thinkers could have considerable appeal for imperial statesmen, as we have seen in the previous section and shall see more below. But the question is—given the poor reputation of the *fa* tradition as discussed above, how much of the policies of the state's empowerment can be attributed to its direct impact? After all, within the broadly defined Confucian tradition one can also identify ideas and texts that were conducive to the state's and the ruler's empowerment (Xunzi 荀子 is a good example).[24] The question is, to which extent what Zhao Dingxin dubs a "Legalist" state was "Legalist" indeed?

To answer this question, I shall focus on a few selected examples from different periods in the imperial history when not just the rulers pursued the policies of centralization and empowerment but also when these policies could be meaningfully associated with the *fa* impact—e.g., through direct invocation of the *fa* texts. I shall skip the Western Han dynasty, during much of which the *fa* tradition's impact was still relatively overt.[25] I have selected four cases from both early and later imperial periods to demonstrate the ongoing relevance of the *fa* tradition on the practical level.

The first instance is the deathbed instructions by Liu Bei 劉備 (161–223), the founder of the Shu-Han 蜀漢 kingdom to his heir Liu Shan 劉禪 (207–271). Pei Songzhi's 裴松之 (372–451) commentary in "The Biography of the Former Sovereign" in the *Book of Shu* section of the *Records of the Three Kingdoms* (三國志•蜀書•先主傳) cites Liu Bei's valedictory edict recorded in the *Collected Works of Zhuge Liang* 諸葛亮集. There Liu Bei recommends that his son read the *History of the [Former] Han* 漢書, *Records of the Rites* 禮記, and, if time allowed, the books of different Masters, as well as the military text *Liu tao* (六韜, Six Secret Teachings), attributed to Taigong Wang 太公望, the *Book of Lord Shang*, and Zhuge Liang's own comments on *Shen[zi]* 申, *Han [Feizi]* 韓, *Guanzi* and *Liu tao* (*Sanguozhi* 32: 891). The prominent position of the *Book of Lord Shang*, *Shenzi*, *Han Feizi*, and *Guanzi* among the recommended texts and Liu Bei's remark that these works, particularly the *Book of Lord Shang* "strengthen one's will" 益人意志 suggest that Liu Bei (and his chancellor, Zhuge Liang) realized the importance of these texts notwithstanding the predominantly negative image of the *fa* tradition in

---

[24] Note, for instance, that Zhang Taiyan, before he turned to Shang Yang, identified Xunzi and Han Fei as the only thinkers whose views are "indispensable" for the state (Zhang 1977: 734).

[25] Recall that Confucianization of the Han dynasty was a long process which by no means ended with the endorsement of the Confucian classics by Emperor Wu. Suffice it to cite Emperor Xuan's 漢宣帝 (r. 74–48 BCE) statement: "The Han house has its own system, which is rooted in the joint usage of the Way of [the True] Monarch and that of the Hegemon. How can we purely resort to the moral teaching and use the Zhou governance? 漢家自有制度，本霸王道雜之，奈何純任德教，用周政乎!" (*Hanshu* 9: 277).

the eyes of their contemporaries. Perhaps, facing the difficult task of creating a viable state in their relatively remote territory, Liu Bei and Zhuge Liang came to value anew the practical contribution of the *fa* texts.

The second instance comes from the Northern Wei 北魏 (386–534) dynasty established by the Tuoba 拓跋 clan of Xianbei 鮮卑. The "Biography of Gongsun Biao" 公孫表傳 in the *History of [Northern] Wei* 魏書 records:

初，太祖以慕容垂諸子分據勢要，權柄推移，遂至亡滅；且國俗敦樸，嗜欲寡少，不可啟其機心，而導其巧利，深非之。表承指上《韓非書》二十卷，太祖稱善。

> Earlier, Taizu (i.e., Tuoba Gui 拓跋珪 or Emperor Daowu 道武帝 of Northern Wei, r. 386–409) observed that the sons of [the Latter Yan 後燕 emperor], Murong Chui 慕容垂 (r. 384–296) divided power among themselves, and, as the levers of authority shifted from one to another, this brought about the demise [of their state]. He also considered his statesmen's customs as simple and sincere, with little engagement in self-indulgence; opening their heart to trickery would be unacceptable. So he deeply rejected guiding them toward trickery. [Gongsun] Biao submitted him *Han Feizi* in 20 *juan*, which Taizu commended. (*Weishu* 33: 782)

Murong Chui was the emperor of the short-lived Latter Yan 後燕 dynasty (384–407) established by another Xianbei clan; after his death, his sons were engaged in fratricidal struggle, which was aggravated by repeated ministerial coups; the state was soon extinguished by the Tuoba (Wang 2003: 274–75). Gongsun Biao 公孫表 (360–423), originally a servant of the Murong and later a court erudite (*boshi* 博士) in Northern Wei, realized that *Han Feizi* with its intrinsic fear of coups and of any dispersal of the ruler's authority could offer suitable lessons to the internal turmoil that plagued the Murong state. Tuoba Gui duly approved of this book. Slightly later we learn that Tuoba Gui's son, Emperor Taizong 北魏太宗 (r. 409–423) extolled his advisor, Li Xian 李先 (335–429) because the latter excelled in expounding the ideas of *The String of Pearls of Hanzi* 韓子連珠 in 22 chapters (probably another edition of *Han Feizi*) and of *Taigong's Methods of War* 太公兵法 (i.e., the aforementioned *Liu tao*). Taizong was especially glad to learn that his advisor understood "the great affairs of the army and the state 軍國大事 (*Weishu* 33: 790). Clearly, *Han Feizi* retained its popularity during the struggles of the Northern Wei's consolidation.

In the waning years of the Northern Wei, we learn once again about the renewed importance of *Han Feizi*. The Northern Wei was divided into two rival dynasties—the Western and Eastern Wei. The former, ruled by the Yuwen 宇文 clan eventually transformed into the Northern Zhou dynasty 北周 (557–581). The dynasty's de facto founder, Yuwen Tai 宇文泰 (505–556) employed an eminent scholar Su Chuo 蘇綽 (498–546). Su Chuo's biography in the *Zhoushu* 周書 (History of [Northern] Zhou) narrates:

綽於是指陳帝王之道，兼述申、韓之要。太祖乃起，整衣危坐，不覺膝之前席。

> [Su] Chuo then exposed the Way of Thearchs and Monarchs, and also explained the essentials of Shen [Buhai] and Han [Fei's ideas]. Taizu (i.e., Yuwen Tai) then rose, arranged his garments, sat uprightly and "before he knew it he was kneeling on the very edge of his mat." (*Zhoushu* 23: 382)

The latter sentence in the above extract is a verbatim quotation from *Shiji*'s depiction of the meeting between Lord Xiao of Qin and Shang Yang (*Shiji* 68: 2228). The parallels were clear to the *Zhoushu* authors. Much like Lord Xiao beforehand, Yuwen Tai (ruling from the old Qin heartland) had to find ways to consolidate and strengthen his state engaged as it was in life-to-death competition with the eastern regime of the Gao 高 lineage, the Northern Qi 北齊 (550–577). In both cases practical advice of the *fa* tradition was crucial for reinvigorating the polity.

Our third example comes from the Northern Song dynasty. Above, we have noted already a rare poem of laudation written by Wang Anshi to commend Shang Yang. Wang's employer, Emperor Shenzong 宋神宗 (r. 1067–1085) was also fond of *fa* thinkers. *Songshi* 宋史 (History of the Song dynasty) tells that early in his life, when still the Prince of Ying 穎王, the future Shenzong took a recently published copy of *Han Feizi* and wanted the palace servants to proofread it. The prince's attendant Sun Yong 孫永 (1019–1086) protested: "Fei is treacherous and mean, harsh and cruel. His book goes contrary to the essentials of the *Six Classics*; I ask you to pay no attention to it" 非險薄刻核，其書背《六經》之旨，願勿留意. The prince was embarrassed and claimed that he was just interested in *Han Feizi* as a bibliophile and was not attracted to its content (*Songshi* 342: 10900). However, it seems that reading *Han Feizi* was a more meaningful exercise for Shenzong, who eventually became fully committed to Wang Anshi's reforms. Whether or not these reforms can be directly connected to the *fa* legacy is a matter of considerable discussion, which cannot be fully engaged in the context of the present essay.[26] What is clear that Shenzong's and Wang's commitment to the goal of "a rich state and a strong army" made them more receptive to the *fa* ideas than was common in China's imperial history.

The fourth example of interest in the *fa* tradition comes from another major reformer, Zhang Juzheng 張居正 (1525–1582). Much like Wang Anshi beforehand, Zhang sought to reinvigorate the Ming dynasty in order to combat domestic decline and foreign threats. In 1568, he presented to the Longqing 隆慶 Emperor (r. 1567–1572) the "Memorandum on six affairs" ("Chen liushi shu" 陳六事疏), which can be said to be the programmatic document of Zhang's later reforms. The memorandum puts forward reform measures that covered six aspects: "reducing deliberations" 省議論, "reinvigorating legal foundations" 振紀綱, "adding weight to edicts" 重詔令, "verifying names and substance" 核名實, "strengthening the state's foundations" 固邦本, and "ordering military preparations" 飭武備. These are imbued with a strong *fa* sentiment. For example:

欲用舍賞罰之當，在於綜核名實而已。……臣願皇上慎重名器，愛惜爵賞，用人必考其終，授任必求其當，有功於國家，即千金之賞，　通侯之印，亦不宜吝，無功於國家，雖鑾睨之微，敝袴之賤，亦勿輕予。

The appropriateness of rewards and punishments is based on thorough investigation of the name and actuality and that is all… I want your majesty to be careful about titles and [ritual] vessels, to sparingly mete out ranks and rewards. When you employ anybody, you must investigate how he finished [his task]; when you appoint somebody, you must demand

---

[26] For a variety of views, see, e.g., Deng 2000: 95; Zhao 2021; Qiao 2021.

the appropriateness [of the appointment]. One who has merits for the state—do not be stingy in granting him even the rewards of a thousand [catties] of gold and the seals of a regional lord; when one has no merits for the state—then do not grant him easily even as petty a thing as a frown or a brief glance, nor even as base a thing as worn-out trousers.[27]

The point of making rewards and punishments fit one's real achievements is of course one of the essential points in *Han Feizi*; but the above passage hints at the *Han Feizi* connection more clearly with the mention of "a frown" and "worn-out trousers." That these should be used sparingly and not meted out to underserving servants is a topic discussed in *Han Feizi* anecdote about Marquis Zhao of Han 韓昭侯 (r. 362–333 BCE), the employer and avid student of Shen Buhai.[28] The principle of "thorough investigation of the name and actuality" was demonstrated by Zhang Juzheng in his enactment of the standard of the officials' attestation 考成法 adopted in 1573:

> 蓋天下之事，不難於立法，而難於法之必行，不難於聽言，而難於言之必效，若詢事而不考其終，興事而不加屢省，上無綜核之明，人懷苟且之念，雖使堯舜為君，禹皋為佐，恐難以底績而有成也。
>
> Among the affairs of All-under-Heaven, perhaps nothing is more difficult that establishing laws, and the difficulty is in making laws that will inevitably be carried out. It is not difficult to heed one's proposal, but it is difficult to make the proposal inevitably effective. If one contemplates an undertaking but does not investigate how it will end, if one starts an undertaking but does not add to this constant supervision then the superior has no clarity of thorough investigation and the inferiors hope to continue with perfunctory [performance]. Then, even if you have a ruler as Yao and Shun assisted by the like of Yu and Gao Yao, I am afraid that it would be very difficult to succeed.[29]

The principles here of supervision of one's performance and clearly matching a minister's proposal and its results are clearly related to the ideas of *Han Feizi*, as shown for instance in the chapter "The Way of the Sovereign" ("Zhu Dao" 主道; *Han Feizi* 5.3; Chen 2000: 81). The close relation between Zhang's practices and the teachings of Han Fei and Shen Buhai was noted by Ming historians. For instance, Tan Qian 談遷 (1594–1648) unequivocally stated that "Jiangling [i.e. Zhang Juzheng] was rooted in the learning of Shen [Buhai] and Han [Fei]" 江陵本申韓之學. Tan Qian had lamented the discontinuation of Zhang's policies after his death. Zhang's opponents accused him of being "the scholar of punishments and laws 刑法家, which in their eyes was a negative yardstick, whereas in Tan's opinion it referred primarily to Zhang Juzheng's fairness and impartiality.[30]

It is noteworthy in light of the above discussion, that despite his clear indebtedness to the *fa* thinkers—indebtedness fully recognized by posterity—Zhang Juzheng himself refrained from openly invoking *Han Feizi* or other *fa* works as authoritative

---

[27] *Zhang Wenzhonggong quanji* 1: 4–5 ("Chen liushi shu" 陳六事疏).

[28] *Han Feizi* 30.3.8 ("Nei chu shuo shang" 內儲說上); Chen 2000: 600.

[29] *Zhang Wenzhonggong quanji* 1: 40 ("Qing jicha zhangzou suishi kaocheng yi xiu shizheng shu" 請稽查章奏隨事考成以修實政疏).

[30] *Guoque* 69: 4252–53 [Year 1573; 神宗萬曆二年]. On the links between *fa* thought and Zhang Juzheng's reforms, see more in Han 2019.

texts. This was not an accidental omission. Given the overwhelmingly negative reputation of the *fa* tradition, open invocation of its texts and thinkers would be self-defeating. It is against this backdrop that we can understand frequent complaints of Confucian critics against emperors and their advisors who openly distance themselves from the *fa* legacy but clandestinely employ *fa* methods and ideas. Thus, when Su Shi argued, as cited above, that "scholars are ashamed to talk about Shang Yang and Sang Hongyang" he added: "However, the rulers of each generation alone willingly embrace them. All overtly curse their names, but covertly employ their actual [teachings] 而世主獨甘心焉，皆陽諱其名，而陰用其實" (*Su Shi wenji*, p. 155 ["Lun Shang Yang"]). Similar observations were made also by endorsers of *fa* thinkers. For instance, Zhao Yongxian 趙用賢 (1535–1596) averred: "After the Three Dynasties [Xia, Shang, and Zhou], the theories of Shen [Buhai] and Han [Fei] were constantly victorious. The people of every generation, when speaking of orderly rule, employ their techniques but always eschew their footprints" 三代而後，申韓之說常勝。世之言治者，操其術而恒諱其跡.[31] The pattern is clear. Their ideological differences aside, many imperial scholars agreed that the practical impact of the *fa* thinkers was much stronger than their overt appeal. Stigmatization of the *fa* tradition did not mean its abandonment; it was just put out of the limelight. The reasons of this tradition's lasting, if covert, appeal were neatly summarized by the Southern Song man of letters, Chen Liang 陳亮 (1143–1194):

> 自孟荀在時，商鞅假帝王之道以堅其富強之說，秦用是以並天下，而始皇不能傳之二世，此其說蓋伯道之靡也。而漢唐願治有為之君亦或采之，乘時趨利之士亦或用之，儒者能言其非而不能廢其用。
>
> From the time of Meng[zi] and Xun[zi], Shang Yang borrowed the Way of Thearchs and Monarchs to strengthen his theory of "a rich [state] and a strong [army]." Qin utilized it to annex All-under-Heaven, but the First Emperor was unable to transmit his rule for more than two generations. This theory probably is just the refining of the Way of the Hegemon.[32] However, from Han to Tang, those rulers who aspired for order were often borrowing it, and the scholar-officials who wanted to seize an opportunity and attain benefits were often utilizing it. The Confucians could speak about it negatively, but could not dismiss its usefulness. (*Chen Liang ji*, pp. 172–173 ["Wen huangdi, wang, ba zhi Dao" 問皇帝王霸之道]).

Chen Liang, whom Hoyt Tillman (1982, 1994) dubbed a "utilitarian Confucianist" was not a committed follower of the *fa* tradition, nor was he blind to its failure in ensuring the lasting rule of the Qin. However, he could not ignore its practical appeal, which was strong enough to overcome the Confucians' distaste for the *fa* methods. On the level of practical policies, of promoting state activism and pursuing "a rich state and a strong army," the *fa* ideas remained indispensable. Even though they were denounced as "criminals against the Way of orderly rule," the *fa* thinkers'

---

[31] Zhao Yongxian, "*Han Feizi* shu xu" 《韓非子》書序, cited in Chen 2000: 1226.

[32] The references to the Way of Thearchs and Monarchs and the Way of the Hegemon hint at the *Shiji* story (68: 2228), according to which Shang Yang first espoused to Lord Xiao of Qin the Way of the Thearch 帝道, then the Way of the Monarch 王道, then the Way of the Hegemon 霸道, and only after failing to impress him with all these, shifted to the "techniques of strengthening the state" 強國之術, which finally met with Lord Xiao's approval.

views could not be glossed over. This can be considered a wonder of China's imperial political culture.

Let me end the above discussion with one observation. The "overtly Confucian but covertly *fa*" model, through which the *fa* tradition—however maligned—exercised profound impact on China's political practice and political culture may reflect the logic of Chinese—and not just Chinese—political life. The tension between the laudable moral qualities of political actors that should be overtly promulgated and the cruel dictates of political practice that demand at times abandonment of lofty ideals was not unique to China. Consider the following observation by Niccolò Machiavelli:

> And I know that every one will confess that it would be most praiseworthy in a prince to exhibit all the above qualities that are considered good, but … they can neither be entirely possessed nor observed, for human conditions do not permit it. … Therefore, it is unnecessary for a prince to have all the good qualities I have enumerated, but it is very necessary to appear to have them. And I shall dare to say this also, that to have them and always to observe them is injurious, and that to appear to have them is useful: to appear merciful, faithful, humane, religious, upright, and to be so, but with a mind so framed that should you require not to be so, you may be able and know how to change to the opposite. (Machiavelli 2008: 110 and 123).

Machiavelli's astute observation may serve a convenient summary to the above discussion. In politics, which concerns fierce struggle for benefits, full observation of moral requirements is at times impossible and even "injurious." This explains the reasons behind the "covertly *fa*" nature of traditional Chinese political system (see also my discussion in Chap. 9, this volume). This being said, the political actors, and especially the ruler, would benefit much from overt commitment to moral principles, even if those principles are not fully exercised in practice. Any overt dismissal of morality would be as harmful for the ruler as inability to depart from the lofty ideals in practice. This explains the "overt Confucian" nature of traditional Chinese politics. Inadvertently, it seems that the majority of traditional China's political leaders, followed Machiavelli's advice.

4   Concluding Remarks

The above discussion outlined the ostensible paradox of the overt dismissal of the *fa* tradition amid its lasting, even if covert, appeal. The reasons for the millennia-long stigmatization of the *fa* tradition are clear. Its notorious derision of the moralizing discourse and abundance of appalling statements in the *fa* texts, its association with excessively intrusive and oppressive state, and its thinkers' "class betrayal" of the fellow intellectuals—all explain why the *fa* tradition was denigrated repeatedly from the Han to the end of the Qing dynasty. Dissenting voices were few and far between, and even these were often raised—as in the case of Li Zhi—primarily as a protest against the suffocating discourse of Confucian hypocritic moralizers rather than out of genuine interest in the *fa* legacy.

This overwhelmingly negative reputation could not, however, bring about cessation of the interest in the *fa* tradition. The appeal of this tradition can be summarized in four points. First, texts such as *Han Feizi* and the *Shenzi* fragments taught rulers the art of self-preservation. Confucian discourse which emphasized morality and the ruler's self-cultivation was often insufficient to safeguard the sovereign against malicious plotters from within his family or his entourage. Here, the methods of Shen Buhai and Han Fei were much more efficient, as is demonstrated from the above example of Tuoba Gui's interest in their teachings.

Second, during the periods of domestic turmoil and military weakness, rulers of China could not but pay attention to the imperative of restoring "a rich state and a powerful army." On this front, Confucian ideas could not match the practical appeal of Shang Yang and Han Fei's legacy. Although the Warring States-period model of "tillers and soldiers" was abandoned early in the Han dynasty, which weakened the relevance of Shang Yang's system, the concept of the state's active intervention in social and economic life so as to maximize its material and human resources could not be abandoned in its entirety. The policies adopted by political activists such as Sang Hongyang, Wang Anshi, or Zhang Juzheng were not a mere restoration of Shang Yang's and Han Fei's ideas; but the activists' indebtedness to early *fa* thinkers is undeniable. In times of crisis, the *fa* methods worked and resultantly the appeal of the *fa* tradition increased, as we have seen from the resurrection in the final years of the Qing rule.

Third, the *fa* tradition provided a set of convenient means of controlling the bureaucracy. Confucian preoccupation with the officials' morality was surely appealing to many rulers (and to the vast majority of the literati), but it could not come at the expense of such more practical means as performance control, usage of rewards and punishments, close monitoring of the officials' conduct, and the like. As we have seen from the case of Zhang Juzheng and his adoption of the new standards of the officials' attestation, the legacy of *Han Feizi* remained highly relevant in this respect, moralizers' protests notwithstanding.[33]

Fourth, throughout its history, China faced the challenging question of how to synthesize the old and the new, how to justify reforms and departure from the long-entrenched methods of rule, which could become obsolete under new circumstances. Here, the unequivocal endorsement of reforms and change by the early adherents of the *fa* tradition vis-à-vis a much more conservative and traditional-minded Confucian way, made the ideas of the *fa* thinkers particularly attractive to radical reformers. At new historical junctures, whenever social and political reality demanded urgent change, *fa* thought provided much stronger justification for new departures than any other intellectual tradition. This may explain its attractiveness for such reformers as Wang Anshi and Zhang Juzheng.

In the final account, whatever its shortcomings, the *fa* tradition contributed toward the empowerment of the state and the monarch, toward solidifying

---

[33] Ray Huang in his immortal *1587: A Year of No Significance* (1981) vividly depicts how Zhang Juzheng's methods, inspired as they were by Han Fei's ideas, generated deep resentment among the Ming literati.

centralized control, and toward more efficient mobilization and utilization of the country's resources. These contributions laid the foundation for the exceptional power (not always actual, but almost always potential) of the Chinese imperial state. This phenomenon of a powerful state is viewed by many as one of the most notable features of China's political history (see, e.g., Fukuyama 2014: 136–37). This state would be unthinkable without the *fa* tradition. Whether or not Sima Tan's observation that the *fa* tradition "is a one-time policy that could not be constantly applied" is correct deserves another discussion. What is clear that even if this policy could not be constantly applied, nor could it be permanently dismissed. This point is relevant in China past and present.

References

Ames, Roger T. 1994. *The Art of Rulership: A Study of Ancient Chinese Political Thought*. Albany: State University of New York Press.

Baopuzi waipian jiaojian 抱樸子外篇校箋 (*The Master who Embraces Simplicity*, Collated and Annotated). 1996. Ed. Yang Mingzhao 楊明照. Beijing: Zhonghua shuju.

Chen, Qianjun 陳千鈞. 1936a. "Review of *Han Feizi* Studies Throughout History" 歷代韓學述評. *Scholarly world* 學術世界 1.11: 81–91.

——— 陳千鈞. 1936b. "Continuing the Review of *Han Feizi* Studies Throughout History" 歷代韓學述評續. *Scholarly world* 學術世界 1.12: 68–75.

Chen, Qitian 陳啟天. 1945. *Summary of Reference Texts to Han Feizi* 韓非子參考書輯要. Beijing: Zhonghua shuju.

Chen, Qiyou 陳奇猷. 1990. *The Book of Lord Shang and Han Feizi* 商君書•韓非子. Changsha: Yuelu shushe.

——— 陳奇猷, ed. 2000. *Han Feizi, With New Collation and Annotation* 韓非子新校注. Shanghai: Shanghai guji chubanshe.

Chen Liang ji 陳亮集 (Collected writings of Chen Liang). 1987. By Chen, Liang 陳亮 (1143–1194). Beijing: Zhonghua shuju (rev. ed.).

Chunqiu Gongyang zhuan yizhu 春秋公羊傳譯注 (*The* Gongyang Commentary *on the* Springs-and-Autumns Annals, *Translated and Annotated*). 2011. Ed. Liu, Shangci 劉尚慈. Beijing: Zhonghua shuju.

Chunqiu Guliang jingzhuan buzhu 春秋穀梁經傳補注 (*The* Guliang Commentary *on the* Springs-and-Autumns Annals, *Translated and Annotated*). 2009. Ed. Zhong, Wenzheng 鍾文烝 (1818–1877), Pian, Yuqian 駢宇騫 and He, Shuhui 郝淑慧. Beijing: Zhonghua shuju.

Creel, Herrlee G. 1974. *Shen Pu-hai: A Chinese Political Philosopher of the Fourth Century B.C.* Chicago: University of Chicago Press.

Deng, Guangming 鄧廣銘. 2000. *Northern Song Political Reformer Wang Anshi* 北宋政治改革家王安石. Hebei: Jiaoyu chubanshe.

Du Tongjian lun 讀通鑑論 (Discussion based on reading the *Comprehensive Mirror*). 1975. By Wang, Fuzhi 王夫之 (1619–1692). Beijing: Zhonghua shuju.

Fayan zhu 法言注 (*Model Sayings,* Annotated). 1992. By Yang, Xiong 揚雄 (53 BCE–18 CE), ed. Han Jing 韓敬. Beijing: Zhonghua shuju.

Fukuyama, Francis 法蘭西斯·福山. 2014. *The Origins of Political Order: From Prehuman Times to the French Revolution* 政治秩序的起源: 從前人類時代到法國大革命. Trans. Mao Junjie 毛俊傑. Guilin: Guangxi Normal University Press.

Geng, Zhendong 耿振東. 2018. *History of Guanzi Studies* 管子學史. Beijing: Shangwu.

Goldin, Paul R. 2011. Persistent Misconceptions about Chinese 'Legalism'. *Journal of Chinese Philosophy* 38 (1): 64–80.

Goldin, Paul R. and Sabattini, Elisa Levi, trans. 2020. *Lu Jia's* New Discourses. *A Political Manifesto from the Early Han Dynasty*. Leiden: Brill.

Gongyang zhuan. See *Chunqiu Gongyang zhuan*

Guo, Moruo 郭沫若. 1985. *Textbook for Salt and Iron Debates* 鹽鐵論讀本. Rpt. in *The Complete Works of Guo Moruo: History* 郭沫若全集·歷史編, Vol. 8. Beijing: Renmin chubanshe.

Guoque 國榷 (Discussion about the [Ming] Dynasty). 1958. By Tan, Qian 談遷 (1594–1658). Beijing: Zhonghua shuju.

Han, Jing 韓靖. 2019. "Political Praxis of *fa* Thought: An Example of Zhang Juzheng" 法家思想學說的政治實踐: 以張居正變法為例. MA Thesis. Renmin University of China.

Handler-Spitz, Rebecca. 2017. *Symptoms of an Unruly Age Li Zhi and Cultures of Early Modernity*. Seattle: University of Washington Press.

Hanshu 漢書 (*History of the [Former] Han Dynasty*). 1997. By Ban, Gu 班固 (32–92) et al. Annotated by Yan, Shigu 顏師古 (581–645). Beijing: Zhonghua shuju.

Harbsmeier, Christoph, trans. Forthcoming. *Han Feizi, A Complete Translation: The Art of Statecraft in Early China*. Ed. Jens Østergaard Petersen and Yuri Pines. Leiden: Brill.

Harris, Eirik Lang. 2016. *The Shenzi Fragments: A Philosophical Analysis and Translation*. New York: Columbia University Press.

Hou, Wailu 侯外盧 et al. 1957. *Comprehensive History of Chinese Thought* 中國思想通史, Vol. 2. Beijing: Renmin chubanshe.

Hsiao, Kung-Chuan (Xiao Gongquan 蕭公權). 1979. *A History of Chinese Political Thought. Volume One: From the Beginnings to the Sixth Century A.D.*, translated by Frederick W. Mote. Princeton NJ: Princeton University Press.

Huainanzi 淮南子 = *Collected Glosses to the Grand Illumination from Huainan* 淮南鴻烈集解. 1997. Ed. by Liu, Wendian 劉文典, Feng, Yi 馮逸, and Qiao, Hua 喬華. Beijing: Zhonghua shuju.

Huang, Ray. 1981. *1587: A Year of No Significance*. New Haven, CT: Yale University Press.

Jiang, Chongyue 蔣重躍. 2021. "Chongdu Shang Yang he *Shangjunshu*" Re-reading Shang Yang and the *Book of Lord Shang* 重讀商鞅和《商君書》. *Journal of Bohai University* 渤海大學學報 3: 1–13.

Jingfu leigao 敬孚類稿 (Classified Draft of Xiao Mu's Writings). 1992. By Xiao, Mu 蕭穆 (1835–1904); ed. Xiang, Chunwen 項純文. Hefei: Huangshan shushe.

Fenshu 焚書 (Book for Burning). 1975. By Li, Zhi 李贄 (1527–1602). Beijing: Zhonghua shuju.

Li, Yu-ning. 1977. Introduction. In *Shang Yang's Reforms and State Control in China*, ed. Li Yu-ning, xiii–cxx. White Plains, N.Y: M. E. Sharpe.

Liang, Qichao 梁啟超 (1873–1929) et al. 2014. *China's Six Great Statesmen* 中國六大政治家. Vol. 1, *Guanzi* 管子. Beijing: Zhonghua shuju.

Liu, Zhonghua 劉仲華. 2004. *Research on the Masters's Studies during the Qing Dynasty* 清代諸子學研究. Beijing: Zhongguo renmin daxue chubanshe.

Lü, Simian 呂思勉. 1982. "The Teaching of *fa* and *shu* During the Wei and Jin Dynasties (Part 2)" 魏晉法術之學(中). Rpt. In Lü Simian, *Reading Notes* 讀史札記, 866–867. Shanghai: Guji chubanshe.

Lunheng jiaoshi 論衡校釋 (*Balanced Discourses,* Collated and Explicated). 1990. Ed. Huang, Hui 黃暉. Beijing: Zhonghua shuju.

Lunyu yizhu 論語譯注 (*Analects,* Translated and Annotated). 1992. Ed. Yang Bojun 楊伯峻. Beijing: Zhonghua shuju.

Machiavelli, Niccolò (1469–1527). (1908) 2008. *The Prince*, trans. W.K. Marriott. The Floating Press (electronic edition).

Major, John S., Sarah A. Queen, Andrew Seth Meyer and Harold D. Roth, trans. and ed. 2010. *The Huainanzi: A Guide to the Theory and Practice of Government in Early China*. New York: Columbia University Press.

Pines, Yuri. 2014. "Legalism in Chinese Philosophy." In: *Stanford Encyclopedia of Philosophy*, ed. Edward N. Zalta et al. http://plato.stanford.edu/entries/chinese-legalism/ (*First published Dec 10, 2014*).

———, trans. and ed. 2017. *The Book of Lord Shang: Apologetics of State Power in Early China*. New York: Columbia University Press.

———. 2023. "Class traitors? Revisiting 'anti-intellectualism' of the *Book of Lord Shang* and *Han Feizi*" 階級背叛者? ——再論《商君書》和《韓非子》中的"反智論". *Zhuzi xuekan* 諸子學刊 27: 161–82.

Pines, Yuri, and Carine Defoort, eds. 2016. Chinese Academic Views on Shang Yang Since the Open-up-and-Reform Era. *Contemporary Chinese Thought* 47 (2): 59–68.

Polnarov, Anatoly. 2018. Looking Beyond Dichotomies: Hidden Diversity of Voices in the *Yantielun* 鹽鐵論. *T'oung Pao* 104: 465–495.

Qiao, Songlin 喬松林. 2018. "Looking for the *fajia* Concept's Reality to Correspond its Name: Synopsis of the Conference on the Correct Name of *fajia*" "法家"概念的循名責實: 為"法家"正名學術研討會紀要, *Guangming Daily* (National Studies edition) 光明日報 (國學版) Sept. 11.

Qiao, Jiyan. 2021. *Human Nature and Governance: Soulcraft and Statecraft in Eleventh Century China*. PhD Diss.: Leiden University.

Qin, Hui 秦暉. 2004. "Amalgamation of the West and Confucianism; Deconstructing '*Dao* and *fa* are Complementary" 西儒會融,解构 "道法互補". Rpt. in idem, *Ten Discussions of Tradition* 傳統十論. Shanghai: Fundan daxue chubanshe.

Queen, Sarah A. and John S. Major, trans. and ed. 2016. *Luxuriant Gems of the Spring and Autumn, Attributed to Dong Zhongshu*. New York: Columbia University Press.

Renwuzhi jiaojian 人物志校箋 (*Records of Personalities*, Collated and Annotated). 2001. By Liu, Shao 劉劭 (186–245); annotated by Li Chongzhi 李崇智. Bashu shushe.

Sanguozhi 三國志 (*Records of the Three Kingdoms*). 1997. By Chen, Shou 陳壽 (233–297); ed. Pei, Songzhi 裴松之 (372–451) and Chen, Naiqian 陳乃乾. Beijing: Zhonghua shuju.

Shiji 史記 (*Records of the Historian*). 1997. By Sima, Qian 司馬遷 (ca. 145–90 BCE) *et al.* Ed. Zhang, Shoujie 張守節, Sima, Zhen 司馬貞, and Pei, Yin 裴駰. Beijing: Zhonghua shuju.

Siku quanshu zongmu 四庫全書總目 (Catalogue of the *Complete Books in Four Storehouses*). 1965. Ed. Yong Rong 永瑢 (1744-1790) et al. Beijing: Zhonghua shuju.

Song, Hongbing 宋洪兵. 2017. *Origins and Evolution of Han Feizi Studies* 韓學源流. Beijing: Falü chubanshe.

——— 宋洪兵. 2021. "Zhang Taiyan's View of the *fa* Tradition, and the *fa* Tradition's Impact on his Political Thought" 章太炎的法家觀及其政治思想的法家因素. *Political Studies* 政治學研究 6: 109–118.

Songshi 宋史 (History of the Song Dynasty). 1997. By Toqto'a (Tuotuo 脫脫, 1314-1356) *et al.* Beijing: Zhonghua shuju.

Su Shi wenji 蘇軾文集 (*Collected Writings of Su Shi*). 1986. By Su Shi 蘇軾 (1037–1101). Beijing: Zhonghua shuju.

Tillman, Hoyt C. 1982. Utilitarian Confucianism: Chen Liang's Challenge to Chu Hsi. Cambridge MA: Harvard University Press.

———. 1994. *Ch'en Liang on Public Interest and the Law*. Honolulu: University of Hawaii Press.

Wang, Zhongluo 王仲犖. 2003. *History of Wei, Jin, and Southern and Northern Dynasties* 魏晉南北朝史. Shanghai: Renmin chubanshe.

Wang Chuanshan shi wen ji 王船山詩文集 (*Collected Writings and Poems of Wang Fuzhi*). 1962. By Wang, Fuzhi 王夫之 (1619–1682). Beijing: Zhonghua shuju.

Wang Huiweng Yibing riji 汪悔翁乙丙日記 (Wang Huiweng's Diary from 1855–1856). 1967. By Wang, Shiduo 汪士鐸 (1802–1889), ed. Deng, Zhicheng 鄧之誠. Rpt. In: *Collection of Historical Materials on Modern History* 近代中國史料叢刊, vol. 13. Taibei: Wenhai chubanshe.

Wang Wengong ji 王文公文集 (*Collected Writings of Wang Anshi*). 1974. By Wang, Anshi 王安石 (1021–1076). Shanghai: Shanghai renmin chubanshe.

Weishu 魏書 (History of the [Northern] Wei dynasty). 1997. By Wei, Shou 魏收 (506–572). Beijing: Zhonghua shuju.

Wenguozhai ji 聞過齋集 (Collection from the Studio of 'Hearing about Transgressions'). By Wu, Hai 吳海 (fl. 1340). E-*Siku quanshu* edition

Wu, Jiang 吳江. 1976. "Historical Evolution of the *fa* Tradition's Theory" 法家學說的歷史演變. *Historical Research* 歷史研究 6: 50–71.

Wu, Shuchen. 2017. *General Survey of the Legal Culture of the fa Tradition*法家法律文化通論. Beijing: Shangwu.

Xiao, Gongquan 蕭公權. 1996. *History of China's Political Thought* 中國政治思想史. Liaoning: Jiaoyu chubanshe.

Xinshu jiaozhu 新書校注 (*New Book*, Collated and Annotated). 2000. By Jia, Yi 賈誼 (ca. 200–168 BCE); ed. Yan, Zhenyi 閻振益 and Zhong, Xia 鍾夏. Beijing: Zhonghua shuju.

Xinyu jiaozhu 新語校注 (*New Sayings*, Collated and Annotated). 1996. Ed. by Wang Liqi 王利器. Beijing: Zhonghua shuju.

Yan Fu ji 嚴複集 (*Collected Writings by Yan Fu*). 1986. By Yan, Fu 嚴複 (1854–1921), ed. Wang, Shi 王栻. Beijing: Zhonghua shuju.

Yang, Xiaoshan. 2007. "Wang Anshi's 'Mingfei qu' and the Poetics of Disagreement," *Chinese Literature: Essays, Articles, Reviews* 29: 55–84.

Yantielun jiaozhu 鹽鐵論校注 (*Salt and Iron Debates*, Collated and Annotated). 1996. Compiled by Huan, Kuan 桓寬 (first century BCE). Ed. Wang, Liqi 王利器. Beijing: Zhonghua shuju.

Yu, Yingshi 余英時. 2004. "Changes in Contemporary China's Value Outlook" 中國現代價值觀念的變遷. Rpt. in Yu, Yingshi, *China's Intellectual Tradition and its Contemporary Changes* 中國思想傳統及其現代變遷, 58–96. Guilin: Guangxi shifan daxue chubanshe.

Zeng, Zhenyu 曾振宇. 2003. "Shang Yang as a Historical Personality and as a Symbol" 歷史的商鞅與符號化的商鞅. *Qilu Journal* 齊魯學刊 6:115–120. Translation by Yuri Pines published in *Contemporary Chinese Thought* 47.2 (2016): 69–89.

Zhang, Taiyan 章太炎 (1869–1936). 1977. *Selected Political Commentaries by Zhang Taiyan* 章太炎政論選集, ed. Tang Zhijun 湯志鈞. Beijing: Zhonghua shuju.

——— 章太炎 (1869–1936). 1996. *Zhang Taiyan's Volume* 章太炎卷, ed. Chen Pingyuan 陳平原. Shijiazhuang: Hebei jiaoyu chubanshe.

Zhang, Jue 張覺, ed. 2010. *Han Feizi, Collated with Subcommentary* 韓非子校疏. Shanghai: Shanghai guji chubanshe.

Zhang, Ning 張寧. 2011. "Rejecting [Shang] Yang? Respecting [Shang] Yang? Investigating Shang Yang's Image in Political Thought from Pre-Qin to Two Han Dynasties" 非鞅? 尊鞅? ——先秦到兩漢時期政治思想史中的商鞅形象探究. MA Thesis, China Zhengfa Daxue.

Zhang, Jue 張覺, ed. 2012. *The Book of Lord Shang, Collated with Subcommentary* 商君書校疏. Beijing: Zhihui caichanquan chubanshe.

Zhang, Taiyan. 2014 (1869–1936). *Forceful Book* 訄書. Rpt. in *Complete Writings by Zhang Taiyan* 章太炎全集, Vol 3. Shanghai: Renmin chubanshe.

Zhang Wenzhonggong quanji 張文忠公全集 (Complete Writings by Zhang Juzheng). 1935. By Zhang, Juzheng 張居正 (1525–1582). Shanghai: Shangwu yinshuguan.

Zhao, Dingxin 趙鼎新. 2006. *Eastern Zhou Wars and the Birth of Confucian-Legalist State*東周戰爭與儒法國家的誕生, trans. Xia Jiangqi 夏江旗. Shanghai: Huadong shifan daxue chubanshe.

———. 2015a. *The Confucian-Legalist State: A New Theory of Chinese History*. Oxford: Oxford University Press.

Zhao, Yuan 趙園. 2015b. *Political System, Discourse, Mentality: Continuation of "Studies of Scholar-Officials During the Ming-Qing Interregnum"* 制度·言論·心態:《明清之際士大夫研究》續編. Beijing: Beijing daxue chubanshe.

Zhao, Dongmei 趙冬梅. 2021. "The Crux of Wang Anshi's Reform is the Transformation of Northern Song Politics from Benevolence and Righteousness to the *fa* Tradition" 王安石變法是北宋政治由仁義轉向法家的關鍵所在, presented at the International Consensus Forum 共識國際講壇 conference, June 29 (online).

Zhoushu 周書 (History of the [Northern] Zhou Dynasty). 1997. By Linghu, Defen 令狐德棻 (583–666) et al. Beijing: Zhonghua shuju.

Zilüe 子略 (Resume of the Masters). 1935. By Gao, Sisun 高似孫 (1158–1231). Rpt. in *Complete Collection of Books from [Various] Collectanea* 叢書集成初編 Vol. 19. Shanghai: Shangwu.

Chapter 17
The *fa* Tradition and Its Modern Fate: The Case of the *Book of Lord Shang*

Yuri Pines

1 Introduction: The *fa* Tradition's Comeback?

In the previous chapter, Song Hongbing demonstrated how, at the very end of the imperial era (221 BCE–1912 CE), seeds of a more positive attitude toward the *fa* tradition were sown. After two millennia of predominantly pejorative views of the ideology that focused too narrowly on empowering the state and derided moralizing discourse, the practical value of the *fa* tradition became attractive again. This nascent reevaluation of long-maligned thought accelerated in the aftermath of the events that demonstrated woeful inadequacy of traditional values in coping with a plethora of foreign and domestic challenges. A series of debacles at the end of the Qing 清 dynasty (1636/1644–1912)—starting with the defeat in the Sino-Japanese war of 1894–95, through the "scramble for concessions" of 1896–98, and culminating with the disastrous Boxer War of 1900—caused many of the educated elite to lose faith in the revered tradition. Nothing was sacrosanct any longer—neither the principle of monarchic rule, nor the venerated "Three Bonds" (*san gang* 三綱), nor the superiority of Confucian teachings. So rapid was the change that some of the most audacious radicals of the 1898 Reform Movement were perceived a few years later as diehard conservatives (an example is discussed below, p. 496).

The retreat of Confucian orthodoxy created an intellectual void that was filled primarily by ideas borrowed from the West (mostly via Japan). Simultaneously, however, long marginalized native traditions were rediscovered by some as a new source of inspiration, especially when they were deemed advantageous for adding a

This research was supported by the Israel Science Foundation (grant No. 568/19) and by the Michael William Lipson Chair in Chinese Studies.

Y. Pines (✉)
Hebrew University of Jerusalem, Jerusalem, Israel
e-mail: yuri.pines@mail.huji.ac.il

© The Author(s), under exclusive license to Springer Nature Switzerland AG 2024
Y. Pines (ed.), *Dao Companion to China's* fa *Tradition*, Dao Companions
to Chinese Philosophy 19, https://doi.org/10.1007/978-3-031-53630-4_18

native flavor to Western ideas.[1] This facilitated renewed engagement with the *fa* tradition. There were at least three reasons for its attractiveness in the eyes of many. First and foremost, the *fa* thinkers were renowned for their commitment to the ideal of "a rich state and a strong army" (*fuguo qianbing* 富國强兵)—i.e., precisely what the battered China needed most. Second, their principle that "everything is determined by *fa*" 一斷於法 (*Shiji* 130: 3291) appeared to many observers as related to or even coterminous with the Western notion of the "rule of law" (*fazhi* 法治).[2] This suddenly made *fa* ideas more acceptable than was possible in traditional China. Third, the historical outlook of the *fa* texts, particularly their advocacy of "sequential history," which resembled modern Western ideas of historical progress (Vogelsang, Chap. 12, this volume), made their ideology appear more "scientific" and "progressive" than Confucianism and other schools. This, in addition to the *fa* tradition's vehement anti-conservatism, increased its appeal to such an extent that even a leading liberal thinker, Hu Shi 胡適 (1891–1962), was willing to forgive the *fa* thinkers for their notorious harshness and oppressiveness. Hu even hailed what is usually considered the major *fa*-inspired atrocity, namely Qin's book burning of 213 BCE:

> Political dictatorship is surely frightening, but the dictatorship of adoring the past is even more frightening. … After two thousand years, fed up with two millennia of "narrating the past to harm the present and adorning empty words to harm the substance," we cannot but admit that Han Fei and Li Si were the greatest statesmen in Chinese history. Although we cannot completely endorse their methods, we should never let fall into oblivion their brave spirit of opposing those who "do not make the present into their teacher but learn from the past"—it deserves our utmost adoration! (Hu Shi [1930] 1998: 6.480–81)

This outburst of pro-*fa* enthusiasm from a thinker whose ideas were normally far removed from the *fa* thought is revealing. It suffices to demonstrate a deep shift in the attitudes toward *fa* ideology in modern China. The renewed acceptability of this ideology prompted deeper scholarly engagement, with numerous studies of *fa* texts, publication of new critical editions, and increasing attention to the *fa* tradition in educational curriculum ensuing. Politically speaking, this enthusiasm peaked during the bizarre anti-Confucian campaign of 1973–1975, when thinkers such as Shang Yang 商鞅 (d. 338 BCE) were lionized as progressive representatives of the correct ideological line, almost the direct precursors of Mao Zedong 毛澤東 (1893–1976; see below, Sect. 5). Overall, one can easily identify the *fa* tradition's comeback as an example of China's profound reevaluation of its past and correction of earlier historical verdicts.

---

[1] This point was made by Liang Qichao 梁啟超 (1873–1929) in his 1904 essay "Mozi's theory" 子墨子學説; but seeds of this search for domestic parallels with the newly imported Western ideas can be traced to Liang's 1896 writings. See Hong Tao 2018a: 23–24. See also a case study of "the discovery of Chinese logic" in Kurtz 2011: 277–337.

[2] For the debates about the connection between the idea of *fazhi* (which could mean very different things in different contexts in modern China—from the rule of law to centralized control over localities) and the *fa* tradition, see Hong Tao 2018a, b.

This comeback has attracted considerable scholarly attention. In light of the abundance of earlier publications,[3] my goal here will be not to summarize previous studies but to ask a different question. Why, more than a century after the rediscovery of the value of *fa* thought, does the topic remain sensitive in China and elsewhere? What hindered and continues to hinder systematic engagement with *fa* thought in the Chinese academy and elsewhere? To answer this question, I shall focus on the fate of the *Book of Lord Shang* (*Shangjunshu* 商君書)—one of the two best preserved *fa* texts. I shall try to demonstrate that despite periodic outbursts of enthusiasm toward the text's putative author, Shang Yang, the text itself has remained understudied and undervalued.

My decision to focus on the *Book of Lord Shang* reflects its somewhat exceptional status in modern China. Whereas in studies of the *fa* philosophy the *Book of Lord Shang* is usually overshadowed by the much longer and more sophisticated *Han Feizi* 韓非子, in the twentieth century the political importance of the *Book of Lord Shang* was arguably greater. Unlike *Han Feizi*, which is primarily concerned with ruler-minister tensions and safeguarding the monarch's power, the *Book of Lord Shang* is more focused on state-society relations, which was by far a more important issue for China's modernizers. In particular, the text became highly relevant because it addressed the problems of universal conscription and the need to motivate peasant conscripts (Pines, Chap. 1, this volume)—an issue of high importance for China in the first half of the twentieth century (see Sect. 4 below). This relevance was duly noted by some, but, as we shall see, it was overwhelmingly glossed over even by the scholars who remained sympathetic to Shang Yang and his reforms. Paradoxically, the interest in Shang Yang as a statesman (duly analyzed by Li Yu-ning 1977) did not entail a parallel rise in the interest in Shang Yang as a thinker. By analyzing the ebbs and flows in academic and political engagement with the *Book of Lord Shang*, I hope to explore the reasons why the *fa* comeback remained abortive.

2   The Background: Between Oblivion and Philological Interest

Shang Yang and Han Fei are often paired as major representatives of the *fa* tradition, and the similarities in how these thinkers were viewed throughout the imperial millennia are undeniable (Song, Chap. 16, this volume). Yet there was also one

---

[3] Reevaluations of Shang Yang and the *Book of Lord Shang* are summarized in Li Yu-ning 1977 and the follow-up in Pines and Defoort 2016. For *Han Feizi*, see Song 2013 (for the Republican period only) and Sato 2013 (slightly updated in Sato 2018). There are no parallel studies of modern interest in the texts associated with Shen Buhai 申不害 (d. 337 BCE; but see Creel 1974: 285–89) and Shen Dao 慎到. For the modern views of *Guanzi* 管子, see Geng 2018 (but recall that *Guanzi*'s *fa* affiliations are disputable; see Sato, Chap. 5, this volume). For a general survey of modern studies of the *fa* thinkers, see Li Haisheng 1997. Note that all the above studies are focused on the work of mainland scholars only, except for Sato, who also addresses studies in Japan and Taiwan (but not Hong Kong).

important difference. The text of *Han Feizi* was prized for its literary brilliance, wit, and humor; hence it was sometimes praised even by the imperial literati who disliked Han Fei's ideas.[4] By contrast, the *Book of Lord Shang* was considered disappointing from the literary point of view. It continued to circulate, but did not attract much attention of imperial literati. By the Song dynasty 宋 (960–1279) a few chapters were lost; of others, only badly corrupted fragments survived. The book was never divided into paragraphs and sentences (*zhangju* 章句); it merited almost no glosses; and we know of no serious scholarly work on it before the very end of the eighteenth century. This neglect made the text notoriously difficult to understand. Most literati seem to have followed the advice of Zhou Duanchao 周端朝 (1172–1234), who plainly recommended learning about Shang Yang's legacy from "The Biography of Lord Shang" in Sima Qian's 司馬遷 *Records of the Historian* (*Shiji* 史記).[5] Through much of the late imperial period, only a few thinkers who spoke about Shang Yang referred to the *Book of Lord Shang*.[6] For majority, Sima Qian's opus remained the major source of knowledge about Qin's statesman.

Then came philologists. In 1793, an eminent man of letters, Yan Wanli 嚴萬里, better known by his later name, Yan Kejun 嚴可均 (1762–1843), prepared the first collated edition of the *Book of Lord Shang* using five Yuan 元 (1261–1368) and Ming 明 (1368–1644) recensions. Soon enough (1803), another collation by Sun Xingyan 孫星衍 (1753–1818) and Sun Fengyi 孫馮翼 (fl. 1800) was published, prompting Yan Wanli (now under the name of Yan Kejun) to prepare a second improved edition of the text (1811). These publications, in addition to another critical edition by Qian Xizuo 錢熙祚 (1839) generated renewed philological interest in the *Book of Lord Shang*. By the late nineteenth century, the book had benefited from efforts of such eminent scholars as Sun Xingyan, Yu Yue 俞樾 (1821–1907), and Sun Yirang 孫詒讓 (1848–1908), whose glosses became indispensable for all the subsequent publications of the text through the twentieth century and beyond.[7]

Notably, philological interest was not immediately accompanied by parallel interest in Shang Yang's ideas. To the contrary, even the editors of the new editions of the *Book of Lord Shang* retained their predecessors' derisive view of Shang Yang. Yan Wanli openly stated that his efforts in reconstructing the *Book of Lord Shang* are aimed at providing the literati with a warning against this "criminal of thearchs and monarchs" 帝王之罪人. Sun Xingyan was interested in the text just as a provider of a few pieces of historical information but not as a source of political

---

[4] For instance, Huang Zhen 黃震 (1213–1280), who derided the low literary quality of the *Book of Lord Shang* (and therefore doubted its authenticity), was full of praise for *Han Feizi*'s elegance, despite distancing himself from Han Fei's ideology; see *Huangshi richao* 55: 30–32.

[5] Cited from Ma Duanlin's 馬端臨 (1254–1332) compilation *Wenxian tongkao* 212: 7.

[6] Zhang Jue (2012: 352–415) has conveniently assembled hundreds of references to Shang Yang and the *Book of Lord Shang* from the Warring States period to the Republican era (1911–1949). Those from the last imperial millennium are almost invariably short and, with a very few exceptions, do not display knowledge of the *Book of Lord Shang*.

[7] All the studies of the Qing and Republican-era scholars of the *Book of Lord Shang* are collected nowadays in Fang Yong 2015.

inspiration. Sun Yirang's introduction to his annotated edition focused exclusively on the issues concerning the book's textual history, glossing over its content altogether.[8] This seems to be the norm well into the end of the nineteenth century. Overall, the philologists prepared a fine ground for in-depth engagement with the *Book of Lord Shang*, but the field waited for political thinkers to come in.

3 Late Qing Rediscovery of Shang Yang

In the late nineteenth century, as the calls for comprehensive reforms became louder in China, the time appeared to be ripe for rediscovery of Shang Yang as one of the country's most successful reformers. This however, did not happen immediately. When the major late Qing reformer, Kang Youwei 康有爲 (1859–1927) sought inspiration from the country's cultural tradition, it came exclusively from his iconoclastic reinterpretation of Confucius's 孔子 (551–479 BCE) legacy. In Kang's major work, *On Confucius's Reforms* 孔子改制考 (1898), Shang Yang merits barely a few phrases.[9] It was—perhaps not surprisingly—Kang's major ideological rival, Zhang Binglin 章炳麟 (a.k.a. Zhang Taiyan 章太炎, 1869–1936), who rediscovered Shang Yang and noted Shang's potential relevance for China's current predicament. Zhang's essay "Shang Yang," published in 1900, is full of polemical zeal. The essay starts by asserting Zhang's revolutionary stance with regard to Shang Yang:

> Shang Yang was vilified for two millennia, particularly in recent times. The charge is that since the Han dynasty suppression and deprivation of the people's power [*minquan* 民權] and unrestrained indulgence of the rulers—all originated from the theories of Shang Yang and other *fa* thinkers. Alas! People have been deeply deceived by specious arguments.[10]

Zhang Binglin argues that twisting the laws so as to empower the ruler and weaken the people is the fault of Han statesmen, such as Xiao He 蕭何 (d. 193 BCE), Gongsun Hong 公孫弘 (200–121 BCE) and Dong Zhongshu 董仲舒 (ca. 195–115 BCE). Unlike these sycophants, Shang Yang was a "political thinker" (*zhengzhijia* 政治家),[11] a new term introduced under the clear impact of Western ideas. Shang Yang's goal was to benefit the people, not to suppress them:

> [Shang Yang's] heart was strengthened by [commitment to] achievements; he directed the people of Qin to agriculture and husbandry, he caused indolent, unemployed and constantly

---

[8] Most introductions to early publications of the *Book of Lord Shang* are collected by Zhang Jue (2012: 318–28). For Sun Yirang, see Sun 2014.

[9] See Kang [1898] 2007: 27–28 (note that Kang never addresses the *Book of Lord Shang*). For Kang's ideology, see, for example, Chang Hao 1987; compare Zarrow 2012: 24–88. Li Yu-ning briefly considers Shang Yang's possible influence on Kang's thought (1977: l–li), but all of the examples she gives come from Kang's favorite book, *Gongyang zhuan* 公羊傳, and its commentaries.

[10] Zhang Binglin [1900] 2000, 35: 565; translation cited with minor modifications from Li Yu-ning 1977: lxv.

[11] Note that the term *zhengzhijia* in Zhang's writings differs from its current usage as "politician."

drifting people to be registered as farmers.[12] Hence there were plenty of commodities, and the taxes and levies were not missed. At the start, [the people] were impoverished; by the end, they had more than enough: is it not different from the way of oppressing the people, whipping and flogging them just to fill the ruler's granaries? (Zhang Binglin [1900] 2000, 35: 568)

Zhang Binglin then launches a strong criticism against oppressive laws promoted by Confucian sycophants under the Han dynasty. By contrast, Shang Yang was a true champion of the people's power (*minquan* 民權, then a common term for "democracy"), who did not turn to democracy only because the people of Qin were too primitive at that time. Zhang conceded moral flaws in Shang Yang's thought, most notably his rejection of filial piety, but hailed his ability to revitalize Qin and concluded that Shang Yang's achievements outweigh his flaws. It is only because he had punished the tutor of the crown prince that Shang Yang was smeared in the Qin and in later generations. Actually, however, this punishment was a rightful act that demonstrated Shang Yang's impartiality (Zhang Binglin [1900] 2000, 35: 575–80).

Zhang Binglin's essay, published in his *Forceful Book* (*Qiu shu* 訄書), did not enjoy broad circulation at the time of its publication, but it is the earliest testimony to a shift in interest in Shang Yang from the philological to the political realm, and the first attempt to discuss this thinker from the point of view informed by modern (Occidental) political theories. Intriguingly, though, the essay never discusses the content of the *Book of Lord Shang*. Zhang analyzes Shang Yang's views primarily on the basis of Sima Qian's biography, infrequently utilizing other sources, such as Jia Yi's 賈誼 (200–168 BCE) criticism of Shang Yang's attack on family values (cited from *Hanshu* 48: 2244). Zhang Binglin seems much less interested in discussing Shang Yang's ideas than in using his name as a symbol of a suppressed political modernizer from China's remote past. Hence Zhang can portray Shang Yang as a champion of democracy, disregarding such statements in the *Book of Lord Shang* as "When the people are weak, the state is strong; when the people are strong, the state is weak. Hence the state that possesses the Way devotes itself to weakening the people" 民弱國強，民強國弱，故有道之國，務在弱民 (*Book of Lord Shang* 20.1; Zhang Jue 2012: 238).[13] That a highly educated man of letters such as Zhang Binglin did not bother to strengthen his claims with references to the *Book of Lord Shang* is perhaps attributable to his expectation that readers would not be well-read in the latter text; like himself, they would recognize Shang Yang primarily from the portrait in *Records of the Historian*.

One of Zhang Binglin's invectives against the Han sycophants focused on those—like Gongsun Hong and Dong Zhongshu—who utilized the *Springs-and-Autumns Annals* (*Chunqiu* 春秋) "to let the ruler indulge himself and suppress the ministers." This may be read as a hint against Kang Youwei, who—much like the aforementioned Han sycophants—considered the *Annals* (in their *Gongyang zhuan* 公羊傳 interpretation) as the most important repository of Confucius's political

---

[12] Hinting at the policies advocated in Chap. 2 of the *Book of Lord Shang*.

[13] All the citations from the *Book of Lord Shang* follow the divisions into sections adopted in Pines 2017. I provide Chinese characters only to the sections that were not cited in Chap. 1, this volume.

wisdom, a text that could remedy the country's ills (for the rivalry between Zhang and Kang, see Wong 2010). However, it was Kang's associate, Mai Menghua 麥夢華 (1874–1915), who eventually contributed more than anybody else toward the revival of interest in Shang Yang and his thought.

Mai published his *Biography of Lord Shang* 商君傳 in 1903, and this work became a milestone in Shang Yang studies.[14] Unlike Zhang Binglin's essay, Mai's was based on a thorough reading of the *Book of Lord Shang* and on systematic attempts to correlate the book's content with the biography of Shang Yang from *Records of the Historian*. More notably, Mai's study also demonstrated good knowledge of Western history, philosophy, and political theories, to which he explicitly tried to connect Shang Yang. Starting with the assertion that the absence of the rule of law is one of the sources of China's weakness vis-à-vis the Western powers, Mai proclaims Shang Yang both the Great Master of legal thought and the supreme political thinker (法學之鋸子而政治家之雄) (Mai [1903] 1986: 1). He then explores Shang Yang's legal philosophy, his historical outlook, his economic, military, and administrative policies—and in all finds multiple parallels with Occidental theories and practices.

Shang Yang's ideas are related to those of imperialism, nationalism, statism (*guojiazhuyi* 國家主義), and historical evolution. His promulgation of legal officials is tantamount to the endorsement of an independent judiciary, and his ideas of the law's transparency and of equality of all before the law have clear parallels in Western thought and practices as well. Mai is not oblivious to weaknesses in Shang Yang's thought, but these are related to the specific circumstances of Shang Yang's age. For instance, echoing Zhang Binglin, Mai assumes that Shang Yang could not further promote the people's power (*minquan* 民權) because of the underdeveloped nature of contemporaneous Qin society. Besides, Mai reminds his readers that Shang's promulgation of the unified authority (*daquan zhengzhi* 大權政治) parallels current political trends in many Western countries: without a strong executive power, implementing laws is simply impossible. Shang Yang's somewhat parochial insistence on the absolute primacy of agriculture at the expense of commerce is explained again by the contemporaneous economic conditions in the state of Qin, which precluded the economy's commercialization. Overall, Mai reasserts the greatness of Shang Yang, whom he deems China's Bismarck (Mai [1903] 1986: 21).

Mai Menghua's essay is one of the finest studies of Shang Yang's thought, and many of his perceptive observations are valid even today. Especially commendable is his effort to prove every single point with extensive citations from the *Book of Lord Shang* and not just from references to later works. Naturally, however, Mai's analysis suffers from certain weaknesses, the most important of which is his attempt to relate Shang Yang's ideas too neatly to their Western parallels. Two examples

---

[14] All the subsequent discussion of Mai Menghua is based on the revised edition of his essay, named *Critical Biography of Lord Shang* 商君評傳, reprinted in Volume 5 of the *Grand Compendium of the Masters* (*Zhuzi jicheng* 諸子集成). See Mai [1903] 1986; Li Yu-ning 1977: lv–lxiv. For Mai's broad intellectual outlook, see a somewhat apologetic study by Zhang Xiqin 2004; for an outline of Mai's biography, see Wang Mingde 2008.

suffice to illustrate the problem of this approach. One is the desire to present Shang Yang as a champion of the rule of law. The topic of whether or not *fa* thinkers promote anything akin to the Occidental "rule of law" is enormously complex and cannot be adequately dealt with here. What is clear that the simplistic equation of *fa* in the *Book of Lord Shang* and "law" does not work, at least not in many of the book's chapters.[15] By glossing over this obvious difference, Mai Menghua (and his countless followers) presented a grossly misleading view of the *Book of Lord Shang*.

An attempt to "Westernize" Shang Yang backfires again when Mai discusses Shang Yang's military ideas. The discussion is perceptive overall: Mai notes the importance of the promulgation of universal military service under Shang Yang, and also mentions, even if briefly, the novelty of Shang Yang's ranks of merit—the major means employed by historical Shang Yang and advocated throughout the *Book of Lord Shang* to motivate the conscripts (see more in Pines, Chap. 1, this volume). Yet it is precisely when dealing with how to motivate soldiers that Mai seems to misinterpret the text. To illustrate this point, I shall reproduce two excerpts from the *Book of Lord Shang* analyzed by Mai Menghua, and then propose an alternative analysis:

> Thus, the gates of riches and nobility are exclusively in the field of war. He who is able to [distinguish himself at] war will pass through the gates of riches and nobility; he who is stubborn and tenacious will meet with constant punishments and will not be pardoned. Therefore, fathers and elder brothers, minor brothers, acquaintances, relatives by marriage, and colleagues all say: "What we should be devoted to is only war and that is all." Hence, the able-bodied are devoted to war, the elderly and infirm are devoted to defense; the dead have nothing to regret; the living are ever more devoted and encouraged. This is what I, your minister, call the "unification of teaching."
>
> The people's desire for riches and nobility stops only when their coffin is sealed. And [entering] the gates of riches and nobility must be through military [service]. Therefore, when they hear about war, the people congratulate each other; whenever they move or rest, drink or eat, they sing and chant only about war. This is why I, your minister, say: "Clarifying teaching is like arriving at no teaching." (*Book of Lord Shang* 17.4; Zhang Jue 2012: 202–03 ["Shang xing" 賞刑])

The second excerpt says:

> When the people are brave, war ends in victory; when the people are not brave, war ends in defeat. He who is able to unify the people in war, his people are brave; he who is unable to unify the people in war, his people are not brave. … When you enter a state and observe its governance, you know that he whose people are usable is powerful. How can I know that the people are usable? When the people look at war as a hungry wolf looks at meat, the people are usable.
>
> As for war: it is something the people hate. He who is able to make the people delight in war is the [True] Monarch. Among the people of a powerful state, fathers send off their sons, elder brothers send off their younger brothers, wives send off their husbands, and all say: "Do not come back without achievements!" They also say: "If you violate the [mili-

---

tary] law and disobey orders, you will die, and I shall die. Under the canton's control, there is no place to flee from the army ranks, and migrants can find no refuge."

To order the army ranks: link them into five-men squads, distinguish them with badges, and bind them with orders. Then there will be no place to flee, and defeat will never ensue. Thus, the multitudes of the three armies will follow orders as [water] flows [downward], and even facing death they will not turn back. (*Book of Lord Shang* 18.3; Zhang Jue 2012: 211–12 ["Hua ce" 畫策])

Both passages are rightly identified by Mai as the crux of Shang Yang's concept of military indoctrination. The picture of the entire population looking at war "as a hungry wolf looks at meat," "congratulating each other" when hearing about war, "singing and chanting only about war," and sending off sons, younger brothers, and husbands, saying "Do not come back without achievements!"—rare for a Chinese thinker—unmistakably recalls the militaristic spirit of the West. Mai Menghua immediately connects them to Sparta, proclaims Shang Yang as coequal to Lycurgus (eight century BCE), and laments that we do not know enough about the system of military education promulgated by Shang Yang. Ostensibly, the parallel seems to work; on closer inspection, however, we may discern a fundamental flaw.

Both passages cited above indeed speak of what appears to be military indoctrination; the first of these even employs the term *jiao* 教 ("teaching," "indoctrination," and, in certain contexts, "military training"). However, let us look at how this internalization of military ethos is achieved. The answer is given in the first excerpt: "The gates of riches and nobility are exclusively in the field of war." It is out of purely selfish desire for riches and nobility (a desire that "stops only when their coffin is sealed") that the people will commit themselves fully to war. The second passage clarifies a negative incentive: the ineluctable punishment of deserters who will face execution along with their family members, and who will not be able to escape because of the universal registration of the populace and the bonds of mutual responsibility with one's neighbors and fellow squad members. It is out of the fear of inevitable punishment coupled with the desire for riches and glory granted to meritorious soldiers that the people—who, it is frankly admitted, "hate war"—will fully commit themselves to warfare. There is no need for brainwashing, no need to imbue the people with martial spirit, no need to develop a Lycurgus-style sense of commitment to the common polity. The people will kill and risk being killed out of pure self-interest. This point is repeated in many other chapters of the *Book of Lord Shang* (Pines 2016b, c, and more in Chap. 1, this volume).

Shang Yang's system of channeling humans' selfishness toward desired ends (in this case engaging in war) is less glorious from the point of view of the early twentieth century than Lycurgus's upbringing of Spartan "Homoioi" (the "Equals"). Some of Shang Yang's recommendations—such as conferring the ranks of merit in exchange for the severed heads of the enemy combatants—are surely deplorable in the eyes of most modern and traditional observers. This, however, should not obscure the effectiveness of Shang Yang's system, which was acknowledged even by staunch critics of Qin, such as Xunzi 荀子 (d. after 238 BCE) (*Xunzi* 1992: 16: 303–04 ["Qiang guo" 強國]). That Mai Menghua preferred to gloss over the grisly details of Shang Yang's success is understandable, but the result is unfortunate.

After all, what Mai and his associates were seeking was not a full resurrection of Shang Yang's system but inspiration from that thinker in China's search for effective responses to its current predicament. By skewing the picture of the real Shang Yang and overemphasizing commonalities between Shang Yang and Western thinkers and statesmen, Mai missed important peculiarities of Shang Yang's thought that could have been relevant to a country that was in search of military modernization, including expanding conscription. As we shall see, this insufficient attention to the peculiarities of Shang Yang's approach remained common in the works of most of Mai's successors.

4 Shang Yang and the *Book of Lord Shang* in the Republican Era

Mai Menghua's essay, which was eventually included in the prestigious publication *Grand Compendium of the Masters* (*Zhuzi jicheng* 諸子集成), could have had a considerable impact on Shang Yang-related studies, but this did not happen. In my survey of major discussions of Shang Yang by Republican-era authors, I found that only a small proportion refer to Mai. Whether or not this relative neglect is related to Mai's somewhat stained political stance—as a constitutional monarchist and supporter of Kang Youwei's "Protecting the Emperor" party (*Baohuang dang* 保皇黨), he was inadvertently shifted from the radical to the conservative wing of China's rapidly changing political landscape—is difficult to say. What is clear is that, in at least one respect, Mai exercised a lasting impact on studies of Shang Yang and the *fa* thinkers in general. This was an indirect impact, though, exercised through Mai's influence on his close collaborator, and a much more famous member of Kang Youwei's circle, Liang Qichao 梁啟超 (1873–1929).

Liang incorporated Mai's biography of Shang Yang into his study of *China's Six Great Statesmen* (中國六大政治家, 1911). Mai's insights influenced Liang's other publications, such as his earlier *On the History of the Development of Legal Theory in China* (中國法理學發達史論, 1906) and the later *History of Pre-Qin Political Thought* (先秦政治思想史, 1919).[16] Liang shared Mai's fascination with Shang Yang's evolutionary historical worldview, with his "statist" ideology, and most notably, with his role as an alleged proponent of the rule of law, i.e., a promoter of progressive Western ideas that were lacking in Confucian China (see more in Hong Tao 2018a: 19–39). Given the exceptional impact of Liang Qichao on the intellectual life of his time, the proliferation of positive views of Shang Yang after the first decade of the twentieth century comes as no surprise. Shang Yang became the country's long-forgotten and now rediscovered intellectual asset.

---

[16] Liang [1911] 2014; [1906] 2003, esp. pp. 342–45. For Liang's later views of Shang Yang, see Liang [1919] 1996: 78–80 and 167–97; see also Li Yu-ning 1977: li–lv.

The resurrection of interest in Shang Yang can be demonstrated from manifold parameters. For instance, Shang Yang's legacy became a topic to be taught in some of the "New Schools" established as part of the late Qing educational reforms, as well as in newly established universities[17]; incidentally, the earliest known essay by a secondary school student named Mao Zedong was dedicated to Shang Yang.[18] Numerous annotated editions of the *Book of Lord Shang* were published, the most influential ones being those by Wang Shirun 王時潤 (1879–ca. 1937) (1915), Yin Tongyang 尹桐陽 (1882–1950) (1918), Zhu Shizhe 朱師轍 (1878–1969) (1921, revised in 1948), Jian Shu 簡書 (1886–1937) (1931), and Chen Qitian 陳啓天 (1893–1984) (1935) (for all, see Fang Yong 2015). Notably, some of these authors were important officials and politicians. Wang Shirun, a graduate of the School of Law at Hōsei University 法政大學, Tokyo, pursued a legal career, culminating in the position of judge in China's supreme criminal court (1933). Jian Shu was a member of the Central Committee of the Guomindang (GMD or KMT, "Party of the Nation"), and a head of the secretariat of the ninth field army during the Northern Expedition of 1926–1928. Chen Qitian was a leader of China's Youth Party (one of the "Third Way" parties that tried to navigate between the GMD and the Communist Party of China [CPC]). Among endorsers of their studies we find even higher-ranking officials, most notably one of the GMD leaders, Hu Hanmin 胡漢民 (1879–1936), who wrote a preface to Jian Shu's edition.[19]

This outburst of interest in Shang Yang appears to be impressive at the first glance. However, the reading of relevant publications—whether specific studies focused on Shang Yang and his thought or prefaces to manifold editions of the *Book of Lord Shang*—leaves one disappointed. Take, for instance, the prefaces, which were written either by the editors themselves or by their friends and mentors. Often a preface to the book is used to emphasize the importance of the book's content. Indeed, authors of the prefaces time and again express their regret for the insufficient attention paid to Shang Yang and his legacy; in at least one case (that of Wang Shirun), the publication of the new edition was directly related to the author's desire to prepare a textbook for future schoolchildren who would study "law and politics" 法政 from the *Book of Lord Shang* and *Han Feizi* (cited from Zhang Jue 2012: 333). But what are the lessons that could be studied from this book? Here the authors confined themselves primarily to the advantages of the "rule of law" associated with Shang Yang; some briefly mentioned the thinker's interest in military affairs and agriculture, but never expanded on these subjects. Hu Hanmin, whose energetic preface stands apart from the much drier style of most other authors, hails Shang

---

[17] See Zhu Shizhe's 朱師轍 (1878–1969) reminiscences in his introduction to the 1948 edition of his annotated *Book of Lord Shang* (Zhu [1948] 1956, 1).

[18] Published in Schram 1992–2004, 1: 5–6.

[19] To these one may add endorsers of Chen Lie's 陳烈 study of the *fa* political philosophy: these include important GMD judicial figures, Wu Jingxiong 吳經熊 (John C.H. Wu, 1899–1986) and Wang Chonghui 王寵惠 (1881–1958, a Minister of Justice and later Foreign Minister in GMD government), as well as a leading GMD general, He Yingqin 何應欽 (1890–1987). See Chen 1929 and Li Yu-ning 1977: lxxii–lxxiiv.

Yang's perceptive analysis of laws as an essential social necessity and the thinker's insistence on the laws' transparency; but he does not go further in investigating Shang Yang's ideas as potentially fitting the country's current needs.[20]

Since the authors of prefaces aimed at promoting interest in Shang Yang and his legacy remained reluctant to explore in depth the *Book of Lord Shang*'s ideas, it is less surprising that the same reluctance characterizes the vast majority of other publications on Shang Yang. The engagement of leading scholars with the *Book of Lord Shang* throughout the Republican period remained minuscule. The immediate reason was the widespread conviction that the text is a later forgery unworthy of further study. At the heyday of the atmosphere of "doubting antiquity" (*yigu* 疑古), the dominant tendency was to point out obvious or perceived anachronisms in the *Book of Lord Shang* (such as references to events that happened after Shang Yang's death) and dismiss the book in its entirety as unrelated to Shang Yang. Scholars could remain quite positive toward Shang Yang's historical achievements, but having dismissed the authenticity of the text associated with him, they concluded—echoing Hu Shi—that Shang Yang was an important reformer but not a thinker whose views deserve attention.[21]

To be sure, not everybody shared the dismissive view of Hu Shi and his associates. Liang Qichao, for instance, observed that even though the *Book of Lord Shang* was not written by Shang Yang, it still retains much importance; Hu Hanmin emphatically emphasized the same point.[22] A few authors of less influential publications, such as Chen Lie 陳烈 (1929: 6–38) and Lü Zhenyu 呂振羽 (1900–1980) (1937: 137–44), did attempt to address the ideas of the *Book of Lord Shang* more systematically. However, throughout the Republican period scholars retained the habit of assessing Shang Yang solely on the basis of his biography in *Records of the Historian*. For instance, Qi Sihe 齊思和 (1907–1980) dedicated a serious and overall sympathetic study to Shang Yang's reforms, but cautioned at the beginning of his study against Mai Menghua's uncritical acceptance of the authenticity of the *Book of Lord Shang*; accordingly, he omitted any consideration of this book from his research (Qi [1947] 2001: 250n3).

The only major exception is the study by Chen Qitian. Chen, who combined staunch statism with democratic ideas, is considered the major representative of the so-called "New *Fa* Thinkers" (*xin fajia* 新法家) of the Republican period. His

[20] Most prefaces to the Republican period editions of the *Book of Lord Shang* are conveniently assembled by Zhang Jue 2012: 328–46. In addition to these, I consulted prefaces to Zhu Shizhe [1948] 1956 and to Jian Shu [1931] 1975.

[21] See Hu Shi [1919] 1996: 322–23; this view is echoed in Hsiao Kung-Chuan 1979: 373 (Chinese original written in 1940 and published in 1945). Both Hu Shi and Hsiao Kung-Chuan for all practical reasons ignore Shang Yang's thought, and so does Fung Yu-lan (Feng Youlan 馮友蘭, 1895–1990) (1952; original published in 1931–1934). For more about Republican-period discussion of the *Book of Lord Shang*'s dates and methodological weaknesses of these discussions, see Pines 2016a, especially pp. 156–57.

[22] Liang Qichao [1919] 1996: 80; Hu Hanmin [1931] 1975: 5–6.

contribution to research on both the *Book of Lord Shang* and *Han Feizi* is outstanding.[23] He followed the lead of Mai Menghua (whom he consciously emulated, calling his own new study of Shang Yang and his legacy *The Critical Biography of Shang Yang* 商鞅評傳, 1935), but also sought to correct some of Mai's weaker points. Chen dismissed the cavalier attitude of contemporaneous scholars who would use just a single instance of a real or perceived anachronism to invalidate the entire *Book of Lord Shang*; instead, he proposed to date each chapter separately (Chen 1935: 113–21; this view is widely endorsed nowadays; see Pines 2016a). Most importantly, in contrast to most of his contemporaries, Chen based his analysis of Shang Yang's thought on the *Book of Lord Shang* rather than on Sima Qian's "Biography of Lord Shang." This allowed him to present a novel analysis of Shang Yang's ideas and practices.

Chen Qitian identifies "the principle of the rule of law" 法治主義 as the major means employed by Shang Yang to attain his two goals: "militarism" 軍國主義 and "agriculturalism" 重農主義; these three, in addition to administrative centralization, are the core of Chen's discussion. On many topics, most notably the "rule of law," he echoes his predecessors; but some of his observations, especially with regard to Shang Yang's "militarism," are highly original, and I shall focus on these in what follows. Chen starts his discussion with the reference to the evolutionary theory of Edward Jenks (1861–1939), according to which society evolves from a totemistic to a kinship-based stage, and then to a society based on military organization (Chen 1935: 44).[24] The transformation from a kinship-based to a military-based society was a crucial step in human history; in China, it was accomplished precisely through Shang Yang's reforms, which Chen identifies as having a revolutionary impact on Qin's society. Shang Yang's determination to overthrow the moribund kinship-based order explains, in Chen's eyes, his vehement assault on traditional culture and moral values; it stands at the backdrop of his radical overhaul of Qin's social system (namely, the introduction of ranks of merit, intrinsically linked to military achievements) and of his political and administrative reforms. Shang Yang's profound militarization of Qin's political and social system and of the country's culture and customs laid the foundations for Qin's ultimate success in unifying the Chinese world a century after Shang Yang's death (Chen 1935: 44–62).

Chen Qitian provided the most systematic and, in my eyes, the most accurate discussion of Shang Yang's military thought and of the exceptional role of "militarism" in Shang Yang's ideology and practice. Surprisingly, however, this analysis was not much noticed either during the time of Chen's publication of his *Critical Biography of Shang Yang* or thereafter. I do not know whether or not Chen's political stance as both a fierce anti-Communist and a bitter critic of the Guomindang regime made his views less popular than they deserved to be, or there were other

---

[23] For the "New *Fa* Thinkers," see Yu Zhong 2018; for Chen Qitian's role in this group, see Liu Xinjie 2020. For Chen's ideology, see Fung 1991. For Chen's "epoch-making" work on *Han Feizi*, see Sato 2013: 59.

[24] Chen refers to Jenks's *A History of Politics* (1900), which was translated by Yan Fu 嚴復 (1854–1921).

reasons for the neglect of his contribution, but it is clear that his impact on subsequent Shang Yang-related studies remained negligent. Not only did later scholars—from Qi Sihe, mentioned above, to Guo Moruo, discussed below—ignore Chen's study, but the very core idea of Chen, namely utilizing Shang Yang's insights to deal with the country's current maladies, remained unheeded.

Take, for instance, Shang Yang's "militarism." Shang Yang's ideas and practices—from endorsing mass conscription to creating a system of incentives so as to direct the entire society toward warfare—were of great relevance to the Republican regime which fought domestic (CPC) and foreign (Japan) enemies.[25] In particular, the idea of mass mobilization was entertained by a variety of thinkers and statesmen, from Jiang Baili 將百里 (1882–1938), whom Arthur Waldron dubs "the most important military thinker of twentieth-century China," to He Yingqin 何應欽 (1890–1987), one of the top military figures in GMD military.[26] Yet none of the discussants whose works I have consulted seems to be aware of Shang Yang's ideas on mass mobilization. Even Lei Haizong 雷海宗 (1902–1962), the prominent member of the so-called *Stratagems of the Warring States* Clique (*Zhanguoce pai* 戰國策派), paid scant attention to Shang Yang in his historical survey of views of military in China, in comparison to his much more detailed discussion of the entirely mythical system of military conscription attributed to Guan Zhong 管仲 (d. 645 BCE).[27] Shang Yang's potential relevance to these debates—just like his potential relevance to China's other needs during the bitter period of domestic disintegration and coping with the foreign aggression—remained largely unnoticed. Chen Qitian's insights were a voice calling in the desert.

5   Shang Yang and the *Book of Lord Shang* Under Mao

Among the Republican-period scholars who discussed Shang Yang and his ideas, Guo Moruo 郭沫若 (1892–1978) is exceptionally important for his impact on Chinese historical circles during the first decade and a half of Mao Zedong's era (1949–1976). When Guo wrote on Shang Yang back in 1945, he could not conceal his negative view of the Qin thinker. He blamed Shang Yang for lacking scruples, dismissed the entire *Book of Lord Shang* (except for a badly corrupted Chap. 19) as unrelated to the historical Shang Yang, largely ignored the book's content, and confined his discussion of Shang Yang's thought in the context of "early *fa* school" to

---

[25] For the pivotal importance of military issues under the GMD regime, see Van de Ven 2003.

[26] For Jiang Baili, see Waldron 2003: 200. Note that Jiang's credentials as "the most important military thinker" appear quite questionable in retrospect; see Setzekorn 2015. For He Yingqin's ideas, see Van de Ven 2003: 144–45.

[27] See Lei Haizong [1940] 2001: 3–5 (for discussing "Guan Zhong's" system of conscription). For the *Stratagems of the Warring States* Clique, see Jiang Pei 2001.

an absolute minimum. Guo Moruo's study appears as a direct inversion of Chen Qitian's approach.[28]

Given Guo Moruo's impact on China's historical studies under Mao, one should not be surprised that other mainland scholars remained reluctant to deal with the ideological contents of the *Book of Lord Shang*. Shang Yang's reforms were discussed primarily in the context of debates over the periodization of Chinese history according to the Marxist five-stage historical scheme, namely whether or not they marked the end of the slave society or just a modification of this historical stage. These debates have been aptly summarized by Li Yu-ning (1977: lxxxi–lxxxxvi), and will not be addressed here anew. Suffice it to say that the lion's share of these debates revolved around Shang Yang's biography in *Records of the Historian*, rarely augmented with additional information from elsewhere. The *Book of Lord Shang* was mentioned only whenever some of its chapters could be immediately related to Sima Qian's narrative. The major contemporaneous study of China's intellectual history—*A Comprehensive History of Chinese Thought* 中國思想通史 (1957–1963), by Hou Wailu 侯外廬 (1903–1987) et al.—paid even less attention to the *Book of Lord Shang* than was the case with Guo Moruo (Hou et al. 1957–1963, 1: 595–96). The habitual eschewing of the *Book of Lord Shang* is evident also in another major post-1949 publication, Yang Kuan's 楊寬 (1914–2005) *Shang Yang's Reforms* 商鞅變法 (1955). Yang Kuan kept references to the *Book of Lord Shang* to an absolute minimum, and even when referring to it, he felt it necessary to apologize for invoking the "late Warring States-period product" to discuss the historical Shang Yang (Yang 1955: 36–37n3). Subsequently, Yang eschewed discussion of the book's ideological content.

It is against this backdrop of overwhelming scholarly indifference toward Shang Yang as a thinker that we can evaluate fully the magnitude of "Shang Yang's fervor" drama that unfolded in 1973–1975. The campaign "Reappraise the *fa* thinkers, criticize Confucians" 評法批儒 (otherwise known as "Criticize Lin [Biao 林彪, 1907–1971], criticize Confucius 批林批孔) started with a major article by Yang Rongguo 楊榮國 (1907–1978), "The Struggle between the Two Lines in the Field of Thought during the Springs-and-Autumns and the Warring States Periods" (春秋戰國時期思想領域內兩條路綫的鬥爭) published in December 1972 (Li Yu-ning 1977: lxxxvi–cii).[29] The article augured the beginning of one of the most bizarre outbursts of intellectual activism in China's long history. The struggle between the two lines was viewed as perennial, starting with the contest between *fa* thinkers, most notably Shang Yang, and reactionary Confucians, and going well into Mao's days, when his correct line was challenged by various deviationists (for the peak of this propaganda campaign, see Liu Zehua 2019: 148–52). All the party, government, military, cultural, and educational units were required to organize their staff for active participation in this pro-*fa* and anti-Confucian struggle (Hong Tao 2018a:

---

[28] Guo Moruo [1945] 2008: 234–40; remark on the *Book*'s lack of authenticity on p. 236. See also Li Yu-ning 1977: lxxvii–lxxx.

[29] The original text can be read on https://zhuanlan.zhihu.com/p/478388813 (accessed Sept 9, 2022).

14n2). As a result, "everybody—from scholars and cadres to toilers in the work-shops and peasants amid their fields—all became able to speak with righteous indignation, to punish with words and attack with brush. All criticized Confucius and extolled Shang Yang" (Zeng 2016: 83).

Limitations of space prevent me from analyzing the campaign's political back-ground and the reason for singling out Confucius as the major culprit.[30] What mat-ters for the current discussion is that for the first time under the People's Republic of China, Shang Yang's credentials as a thinker were recognized. Thus, at the start of the anti-Confucian campaign, Yang Kuan had to revise his essay on Shang Yang. This revised essay became arguably the single most influential study of the Qin's reformer (according to Li Yu-ning [1977: xiv], the three editions of 1973–74 amounted to an unbelievable 1,750,000 copies!).[31] The new version moderated a few critical comments on Shang Yang and added a section called "The Continued Struggle of the Shang Yang School of Legalists," which briefly summarized a few ideas from the *Book of Lord Shang*. A few more references to the book were added to the main body of Yang Kuan's essay. However, even in the revised version, the *Book of Lord Shang* remained of relatively negligible importance in comparison to the ongoing focus on Sima Qian's "Biography of Lord Shang." This was to change, though.

In 1974, at the heyday of "Reappraise the *fa* thinkers, criticize Confucians" cam-paign, the *Book of Lord Shang* came finally into the full limelight, attracting the attention of Chairman Mao himself.[32] It was then that a new annotated edition, translated into colloquial language, was prepared by Gao Heng 高亨 (1900–1986), who also provided a useful analysis of the individual chapters' dating, distinguish-ing between those penned during and after Shang Yang's time.[33] Gao, however, eschewed in-depth discussion of the book's ideological content (Gao 1974). This latter task was undertaken by the "Great Criticism Group of Peking University and Tsinghua University" under the pen name Liang Xiao 梁效 (a pun for "Two

---

[30] For more details about the campaign's ideology (especially its anti-Confucian content), see e.g., Louie 1980: 97–136; Perelomov 1993b: 362–386. For its political background, see MacFarquhar and Schoenhals 2006: 366–373.

[31] The 1973 essay is translated in full in Li Yu-ning 1977: 3–99 (all subsequent references are to this edition). For comparing the two versions, see Li Yu-ning 1977: lxxxiv–lxxxvi.

[32] Between October 1972 and June 1975, Mao Zedong, who suffered from worsening eyesight, ordered a group of scholars to prepare him a series of texts he wanted to read, annotated and writ-ten in especially large characters. This allows us to trace Mao's foci of interest in historical, philo-sophical, and literary texts during the last years of his life. In March–July 1974, Mao's interest was clearly dominated by the texts associated with the *fa* tradition: he ordered preparing three chapters of the *Book of Lord Shang*, five of *Han Feizi*, and several texts of imperial-era thinkers who were back then identified as carrying on the "*fa* line." See details in *Mao Zedong wannian* 2013 (see especially the editors' preface on pp. 1–6 and Liu Xiuming's introduction [Liu 2013: 16–18]).

[33] For a comprehensive study of Shang Yang-related publications during the anti-Confucian campaign, see Chen Chuang 2019: 75–92.

Schools" [*liang xiao* 兩校]). Their "On Shang Yang" 論商鞅 became the hallmark of "Shang Yang fervor" in the People's Republic of China.[34]

Reading "Liang Xiao's" essay as a serious scholarly product is not easy. The text is full of Cultural Revolution-period jargon. Its derision of "Second Brother Kong" (Kong Laoer 孔老二, i.e., Confucius), praise for Shang Yang's alleged mass murder of dissidents as "sweepingly carrying out dictatorship over the restorationist forces of the slaveowners and revolutionary suppression of the old social forces," or equation of the famous poet (and Shang Yang-basher) Su Shi 蘇軾 (1037–1101) with "Soviet revisionists of social-imperialism"—all create an image of a worthless propaganda piece. Yet beneath the abusive language employed by the authors, one can discern serious scholarly work and one of the most penetrating analyses of Shang Yang's ideology on a par with Mai Menghua and Chen Qitian.

The "Liang Xiao" authors avoided the common pitfall of discussing Shang Yang's ideas on the basis of *Records of the Historian*; rather, they synthesized the biography with the information from the *Book of Lord Shang* that received their primary attention. They hailed many ideas of the *Book of Lord Shang* that had been noted by previous scholars, such as its evolutionary historical view and its insistence on the rule of law (which in the Cultural Revolution parlance referred to the effective centralized control—see Hong Tao 2018a:15), but their focus lay elsewhere. The authors identified the *Book of Lord Shang* as a revolutionary text that was intended to comprehensively "dig out the old foundation … [of the] slave-owning society … from its economic base to the superstructure and in the political, economic, ideological, cultural and other fields" (Li 1977: 193). The new system of ranks of merits was duly identified as the crux of Shang Yang's innovations. The authors noted the exceptionality of Shang Yang's assault on the entire spectrum of old elites (dubbed "villains" 姦民 in *The Book of Lord Shang* 18.6) and correctly identified this assault as reflective of the social revolution envisioned by Shang Yang. Echoing Chen Qitian but radicalizing his terminology, the authors lauded Shang Yang's attack on traditional culture and moral values as a manifestation of his resolve to remove "the cancer" of "the parasitic slave-owning class and its decadent ideology" (Li 1977: 184–85). Needless to say, the thinker's insistence on heavy punishments was hailed as giving "full play to the revolutionary role of violence" (Li 1977: 189).

"Liang Xiao's" imposition of Marxist and Maoist paradigms on Shang Yang and his legacy may distract the reader from their otherwise accurate analysis of Shang Yang's thought. More than previous scholars, the authors paid due attention to the totality of Shang Yang's vision, its internal logic, and the close relations between Shang Yang's reforms and the ideas expressed in the *Book of Lord Shang*. Much like Chen Qitian, the authors admired Shang Yang's non-conformism and his "revolutionary" stance. They did acknowledge from time to time that Shang Yang belonged

---

[34] "Liang Xiao's" essay is fully translated by Li Yu-ning 1977: 180–95, to which translation I refer hereafter. The original was published in *Hongqi* 紅旗 6 (June 1, 1974). For the composition of "Liang Xiao" group and its activities, see http://baike.baidu.com/item/%E6%A2%81%E6%95%88 (accessed Sept. 1, 2022).

to "exploitive classes," but their admiration of this "revolutionary" thinker caused them to gloss over some of the problematic statements in the book. For instance, the pronouncements about the need to overpower the people, as well as the book's assault on filiality and fraternal obligations (*Book of Lord Shang* 4.3, 13.4), were not mentioned. Moreover, although the authors did note aspects of the total state ideology promulgated in the *Book of Lord Shang* they seem to stop short from exploring potential parallels between that total state and the one imposed under the current "proletarian dictatorship."

This glossing over of similarities between Shang Yang's vision and the practice of Mao's China is not incidental. On the one hand, the parallels are obvious: in both cases, the ideal was to make the state the sole provider of material, social, and political benefits; in both cases, autonomous elites were not tolerated. On the other hand, however, there was a major difference between Mao's emphasis on ideology and Shang Yang's lack of interest in it. In contrast to Mao (and other twentieth-century thinkers and leaders), Shang Yang never intended to create a new man, free of selfishness and full of moral commitment to the sociopolitical order. Instead, he (and the followers who contributed to "his" book) sought a less impressive but a workable order in which every member of society retains his or her selfish desires, but is able to fulfill them exclusively through the means deemed appropriate by the state (Pines, Chap. 1, this volume). Unwilling to change humans for the better, Shang Yang did not envision any serious ideological work aside from a negative one: stemming ideas that allowed talkative intellectuals to ascend the social ladder at the expense of tillers and fighters (Pines 2017: 89–99). The difference with Mao's extreme concern with proper thought and proper values of the masses could not be greater (see also Bai, Chap. 23, this volume). In all likelihood, this difference was noted by the "Liang Xiao" group members, who as a result decided to downplay the parallels between theirs and Shang Yang's vision of a total state.

6 Shang Yang Studies After Mao: A Global Perspective

The abrupt end of ideological radicalism in the aftermath of Mao's death proved to be detrimental to research on the *Book of Lord Shang* in China. The "Shang Yang fervor" ended as rapidly as it unfolded. Eager to turn the page on the dramas of ten years of madness, scholars opted to eschew not just the abusive and bizarre language of the Cultural Revolution-era pro-Shang Yang pamphlets, but also glossed over good studies of the text. The "Liang Xiao" discussion was all but forgotten. Even Gao Heng's fine edition of the *Book of Lord Shang* was sidelined; when the Zhonghua shuju 中華書局 publishers had to select the best edition for the *New Grand Compendium of the Masters* 新編諸子集成, they oddly opted for a much weaker edition prepared back in 1944 by Jiang Lihong 蔣禮鴻 (1916–1995), rather than Gao's version (Jiang 1986). Overall the number of publications dedicated to the *Book of Lord Shang* shrank dramatically.

Meanwhile, outside mainland China, the short-lived endorsement of the *fa* thinkers under Mao created a considerable backlash. Naturally, Taiwanese scholars published immensely on the topic, opposing the "rehabilitation" of the *fa* thinkers (Sato 2013: 263–64; 2018: 168–69). A more interesting development is visible in Soviet scholarship. Whereas in the early 1960s, the view of Shang Yang and the *Book of Lord Shang* was very positive, as expressed in Leonard S. Perelomov's (1928–2018) major translation-cum-study (1968), once Shang Yang was endorsed by Mao, the attitude toward him changed dramatically. It was precisely then that a dissident Soviet scholar, Vitaly Rubin (1923–1981), penned his major study of Chinese political philosophy, one-quarter of which was dedicated to Shang Yang, whom Rubin vehemently attacked as a despised totalitarian. The study was eventually published outside the Soviet Union (Rubin 1976: 55–88; republished in Russian in Rubin 1999: 8–76), but in the USSR itself the attitude toward Shang Yang also became negative. Not accidentally, when Perelomov published a renewed version of his translation cum study of the *Book of Lord Shang* shortly after the USSR collapse (1993a), he added an afterword which was incomparably more Confucian-leaning than his earlier publications.

The relaxation of the political atmosphere in China in the 1980s and thereafter allowed—for the first time in the twentieth century—considerable depoliticization of Shang Yang. However, interest in the *Book of Lord Shang* remained lackluster. Periodic campaigns about the need to enhance the "rule of law" (*fazhi* 法治) were met with due increase in publications on the notion of *fazhi* in the *Book of Lord Shang* (Pines and Defoort 2016: 64–65), but overall the scope of scholarly production remained small in comparison with the enthusiastic rise of interest in other political philosophers of the Warring States era. It is perhaps no coincidence that the two major studies of the *Book of Lord Shang* published in the last quarter of the twentieth century were produced by non-mainland scholars—Zheng Liangshu (a.k.a. Tay Lian Soo, Malaysian Sinologist) (1989, original published in 1987), and Yoshinami Takashi (1992). The latter also became—to the best of my knowledge—the first Japanese monograph fully dedicated to the *Book of Lord Shang*. In Japan, much as in Taiwan, Shang Yang remained primarily an object of interest of political, social, or administrative historians, but not of scholars of Chinese political thought.[35]

In Western Sinology outside the USSR, the *Book of Lord Shang* remained for generations terra incognita. After the publication of an excellent translation and study of the text by Jan J.L. Duyvendak (1889–1954) in 1928 (Duyvendak [1928] 1963), generations passed with just a handful of articles and one translation into French by Jean Lévi (1981, 2005)—not a very rigorous work, but successful at making the text accessible to broader public. The situation started changing only very recently with two new translations-cum-studies (Vogelsang 2017; Pines 2017), and

---

[35] For important exceptions, see, e.g. Shibata 1996; Huang Shaomei 2010. For a sample of historical studies in Japan and on Taiwan that address Shang Yang's reforms, see, e.g., Yoshimoto 2005; Du Zhengsheng 1985. Note that the situation in Japan regarding the *Book of Lord Shang* and *Han Feizi* differs dramatically: the latter text had been an object of intense study ever since the late seventeenth century (Sato 2013 and 2018).

several articles, including some penned by the present author.[36] An extensive treatment of Shang Yang and the *Book of Lord Shang* in general studies of early Chinese thought is still a rarity, but Tao Jiang's recent publication (2021: 243–67) is an excellent exception to this rule. It may be hoped that more comparatists, especially scholars of political thought, will engage the *Book of Lord Shang* in earnest.

Going back to China, one can discern a gradual increase in Shang Yang-related publications in the twenty first century. Among most notable developments was the publication of a very good (even if not flawless) critical edition of the text by Zhang Jue (2012), a study of the *Book of Lord Shang* in the context of unearthed documents (Tong 2013; Tong is a mainland scholar whose study was published in Taiwan), as well as a few monographs focusing on the ideology of the *Book of Lord Shang* (e.g., Zhang Linxiang 2008; Ouyang 2011). In addition, several translations into modern Chinese or annotated editions of the text have been published, not all of which are of good quality. Among these the most notable is the recent annotated edition and study by Jiang Chongyue (2022). To these one should add dozens of articles, which cannot be adequately summarized here. Suffice it to say that some of them (such as Hu Tieqiu 2016; Jiang Chongyue 2021) display very astute understanding of the text's content.

One of the most notable features of post-Mao engagement with the *Book of Lord Shang* is its emancipation from immediate political supervision. There is currently (2023) no observable Party line with regard to studies of the *fa* thinkers in general and Shang Yang in particular. Whereas Shang Yang's vehement assault on traditional moral and cultural values can no longer be welcome in a country that tries to reconnect with its Confucian past, his achievements cannot be denigrated, either. After all, the first of the twelve Core Socialist Values, adopted at the Eighteenth Congress of the Communist Party of China in 2012, is "rich and strong" (*fuqiang* 富強)—a clear nod to the *fa* ideology with which this value is associated.[37] Another one of the Core Socialist Values—"the rule of law" (*fazhi* 法治)—also resonates with the *fa* tradition, enhancing its legitimacy. Thus, Shang Yang can be studied

---

[36] For a brief summary of earlier Western language publications focused on Shang Yang and the *Book of Lord Shang*, see Pines 2017: 251–52nn3–5. In an earlier study (Pines 2009: 225n18), I lamented the odd situation in which articles dedicated to the so-called "nominalist" (*mingjia* 名家), Gongsun Long 公孫龍 exceeded those dedicated to Shang Yang four or fivefold, despite the fact that surviving Gongsun Long fragments are tiny in comparison with the *Book of Lord Shang*. Actually, this state of the field was one of the reasons that prompted my own engagement with the *Book of Lord Shang*. As an example of recent change, consider a series of articles on the *Book of Lord Shang* that are due to be published in *Bochumer Jahrbuch zur Ostasienforschung* 46 (2023).

[37] This abbreviation of "a rich state and a strong army" slogan is now conveniently glossed as "a rich state and a strong people" (which is not a purely modern reinterpretation; the "people" are substituted for the "army" as early as in the account about the Salt and Iron Debates of 81 BCE; see *Yantielun* 7: 93 ["Fei yang" 非鞅]). Notably, during the author's travel to Lhasa (Tibet Autonomous Region) in 2018, I observed there the slogan being reverted back to "a rich state and a strong army" (*fuguo qiangjun* 富國強軍) reflecting the importance of the People's Liberation Army (PLA) presence in the area.

relatively freely of the Party interference—as an object of neither admiration nor defamation.

This said, the emotional involvement of scholars in studies of the *fa* tradition and of Shang Yang in particular is easily observable. Whereas some try to improve Shang Zhang's image, for instance, by reaffirming that "in the depth of his heart, Shang Yang was still an ethical thinker" (Zeng 2016: 76), others vehemently disagree. Zhang Linxiang concluded his study of Shang Yang's historical outlook with the claim that Shang Yang's "ideal society is just a society in which the cessation of punishments and the quelling the military result exclusively from the people's total submission to the tyranny and abuses of the dictatorship; although stable and unified, this society is merciless and unrelenting" (Zhang 2016: 107). Zhang further emphasized:

> Based on Shang Yang's theories, the state of Qin established a military state organization, which was able to use stern laws so as to direct the people to agriculture and warfare, to comprehensively mobilize the state's power so as to engage in unprecedented wars of expansion and annexation and to eradicate the rival six states. It is true that putting an end to prolonged military turmoil and attaining unification reflected the general course of social development and accorded with the people's expectations. Yet the fact that unification was attained by Qin and not by another state and that it was attained in this and not in an alternative manner means the victory of savagery over civilization. It is a hugely unfortunate event in the history of our nation. (Zhang Linxiang 2016: 106)

This strong emotional outburst in an academic article (recently reiterated in Zhang Linxiang's new publication 2022) reminds us of the exceptional position of Shang Yang in Chinese intellectual history. A millennium after Su Shi's verdict that "from the Han onward, scholars have been ashamed to speak about Shang Yang" 自漢以來學者恥言商鞅 (*Dongpo quanji* 105: 14), the figure of the Qin thinker remains as divisive as ever.

7 Epilogue: Methodological Reflections and Future Perspectives

The intense emotions that hinder the studies of the *Book of Lord Shang* are understandable. This is a frightening text. Its "alienating rhetoric," including a vehement assault on a variety of most cherished moral values (Pines 2012), its derision of intellectuals (who are pejoratively dubbed "peripatetic eaters" 游食者), its advocacy of total control over society achieved in part through merciless punishments—all these irritate modern readers as much as they irritated traditional Chinese literati. This explains why so many colleagues would eagerly relegate the *Book of Lord Shang* to the dustbin of history. Indeed, in China scholars engaged in studies of the *Book of Lord Shang* are sometimes considered by their peers as shameless supporters of totalitarianism. Even in the Western academy, I have been accused twice of quasi-Nazi inclinations merely because of my presentation of Shang Yang's ideas. It is difficult to find another Chinese (or non-Chinese) early thinker the mere study of whose thought can arouse similar emotions.

Negative emotions aside, one cannot ignore the appeal of certain aspects of Shang Yang's ideology. Think of the advantages of the rule by impersonal standards, that is, the existence of clear, transparent and uniform game rules that aim to create a level playing field for everybody. Moreover, Shang Yang soberly allows subjects to remain selfish (i.e. pursue their material and social aspirations) insofar as this selfishness serves rather than infringes upon the interests of society and the state. One need not endorse Shang Yang's experiment in social engineering (Pines 2016c and Chap. 1, Sect. 5, this volume) to acknowledge that this experiment is more viable and reasonable than the ideological brainwashing of twentieth-century regimes that tried to create an ideal selfless citizen, only to be frustrated by bitter reality. And think of the slogan "a rich state and a strong army"—is not it a reasonable goal for policymakers? In light of all this, it is clear that glossing over Shang Yang's and his followers' acumen and their practical success is imprudent and self-defeating.

The *Book of Lord Shang* (or any other early text) should not be studied as a foil to current political regimes in China and elsewhere but on its own terms and within its own sociopolitical and intellectual context. Luckily, the recent explosive increase in archeological and paleographic discoveries that revolutionized our knowledge of the Warring States-period and early imperial China allows us to engage this text anew. What is needed for a "thicker" (Goldin 2005: 1–18) engagement with it is not just a better understanding of its historical setting. We need also to overcome generations of scholarly inertia, which, no less than political and ideological factors, hindered the studies of the *Book of Lord Shang* in the past. Once the text is studied neither through the prism of *Han Feizi*, nor through that of Sima Qian's "Biography of Lord Shang," once we go beyond the habitual reduction of its messages to the sole focus on "the rule of *fa*" and its relations to the "rule of law," we shall be able to assess fully its intellectual richness.

Once the text is understood within its own context, we may ask which—if any—of its aspects are relevant for the present. To paraphrase Brian Van Norden (1996: 226), should the *Book of Lord Shang* remain just of high "notional" interest (expanding our horizons but not influencing our lives), or can it become a "real" option (that the modern audience can learn something useful from)? An almost intuitive answer makes the former choice. After all, few, if any, of us would seriously contemplate living under Shang Yang's regime of a total state that directs everybody to agriculture and warfare through rewards and punishments, a state that declares its will to weaken and overpower its people and to diminish spiritual culture to the love of war. This being said, the text's relevance in certain circumstances—especially for countries in crisis, seeking the ways to mobilize their material and human resources for the sake of survival—is undeniable. The fact that, among its twentieth century admirers in China, we find figures as diverse as a constitutional monarchist, Mai Menghua, a democratic statist, Chen Qitian, and the radical revolutionaries of the "Liang Xiao" group bespeaks the lasting appeal of the *Book of Lord Shang* and its potential relevance to China's twentieth-century challenges. Is it still relevant in the twenty-first century? Probably less than in the past, yet some of its ideas may remain of interest in the present, both in China and outside it (cf. Bai, Chap. 23, this volume). One should, however, also be reminded of Sima Tan's 司馬談 (d. 110 BCE) insight: Shang Yang and the *fa* thinkers in general propose only "a one-time policy that could not be constantly applied" 可以行一時之計，而不可長用也 (*Shiji* 130: 3291).

References

Book of Lord Shang. See Pines 2017.

Chang, Hao. 1987. *Chinese Intellectuals in Crisis: Search for Order and Meaning (1890–1911)*. Berkeley: University of California Press.

Chen, Lie 陳烈. 1929. *Political Philosophy of the fa School* 法家政治哲學. Shanghai: Huatong shuju.

Chen, Qitian 陳啓天. 1935. *Critical Biography of Shang Yang* 商鞅評傳. Shanghai: Shangwu. (One of the finest studies of Shang Yang's ideology).

Chen, Chuang 陳闖. 2019. "Studies of Ancient Texts during the Movement 'Reappraise the *fa* Thinkers, Criticize Confucians'" "評法批儒"運動時期的古典學術研究. PhD. Dissertation, Shandong University. (Systematic analysis of the new editions of the *fa* texts published in 1972–76).

Cheng, Liaoyuan 程燎原. 2011. Reinterpreting the Concept of the 'Rule of *fa*' before the Qin 先秦"法治"概念再釋. *Tribune of Political Science and Law* 政法論壇 29.2: 3–13.

Creel, Herrlee G. 1974. *Shen Pu-hai, A Chinese Philosopher of the Fourth Century B. C.* Chicago IL: The University of Chicago Press.

Dongpo quanji 東坡全集 (Collected writings of [Su] Dongpo). n.d. By Su, Shi 蘇軾 (1036–1101). E-*Siku quanshu* edition.

Du, Zhengsheng 杜正勝. 1985. "Analyzing Society Formed by Shang Yang's Reforms Through the Prism of the System of Ranks" 從爵制論商鞅變法所形成的社會. *Bulletin of the Institute of History and Philology, Academia Sinica* 中央研究院歷史語言研究所集刊 56. 3: 485–544.

Duyvendak, Jan J.-L., trans. [1928] 1963. *The Book of Lord Shang: A Classic of the Chinese School of Law*. Rpt. Chicago: University of Chicago Press.

Fang, Yong 方勇, ed. 2015. *The Masters' Collection, The fa School Section: The Book of Lord Shang Volumes* 子藏.法家部.商君書卷. 9 vols. Beijing: Guojia tushuguan chubanshe. (Reprint of major pre-1949 editions of the *Book of Lord Shang*).

Fung, Edmund S.K. 1991. The Alternative of Loyal Opposition: The Chinese Youth Party and Chinese Democracy, 1937-1949. *Modern China* 17 (2): 260–289.

Fung, Yu-lan (Feng Youlan 馮友蘭, 1895–1990). 1952. *History of Chinese Philosophy*. Trans. Derk Bodde. 2 vols. Princeton: Princeton University Press.

Gao, Heng 高亨. 1974. *The Book of Lord Shang, with Commentaries and Translation* 商君書注譯. Beijing: Zhonghua shuju. (A very good study and annotations of the text despite being produced under the duress of the Cultural Revolution).

Geng, Zhendong 耿振東. 2018. *History of the Studies of Guanzi* 管子學史. Beijing: Shangwu yinshuguan.

Goldin, Paul R. 2005. *After Confucius: Studies in Early Chinese Philosophy*. Honolulu: University of Hawai'i Press.

———. 2011. Persistent Misconceptions about Chinese 'Legalism'. *Journal of Chinese Philosophy* 38 (1): 88–104.

Guo, Moruo 郭沫若 [1945] 2008. "Criticism of the Early *fa* School" 前期法家的批判. Rpt. in Guo Moruo, *Ten Critical Tractates* 十批判書, 227–249. Beijing: Zhongguo huaqiao chubanshe.

Hanshu 漢書 (*History of the [Former] Han Dynasty*). 1997. By Ban, Gu 班固 (32–92) *et al.* Annotated by Yan, Shigu 顏師古 (581–645). Beijing: Zhonghua shuju.

Hong, Tao 洪濤. 2018a. "The Concept of the Rule of *fa* and the *fa* Tradition's Thought in the 20th Century" (A) 20世紀中國的法治概念與法家思想(上). *History of Political Thought*政治思想史 9.1: 13–45. (A systematic study of the concept of *fazhi* and its different conceptualizations throughout the twentieth century).

——— 洪濤. 2018b. "The Concept of the Rule of *fa* and the *fa* Tradition's Thought in the 20th Century" (B) 20世紀中國的法治概念與法家思想(下). *History of Political Thought*政治思想史 9.2: 31–58.

Hou, Wailu 侯外廬 et al. 1957–1963. *Comprehensive History of Chinese Thought* 中國思想通史, 5 vols. Beijing: Renmin chubanshe.

Hsiao, Kung-Chuan (Xiao Gongquan 蕭公權, 1897–1981). 1979. A History of Chinese Political Thought. Vol. 1, From the Beginnings to the Sixth Century A.D.., trans. Frederick W. Mote. Princeton: Princeton University Press.

Hu, Hanmin 胡漢民. [1931] 1975. "Preface" 序. In *Glosses and Corrections on the Book of Lord Shang* 商君書箋正, ed. Jian Shu 簡書, 1–7. Rpt. Taipei: Guangwen shuju.

Hu, Shi 胡適. [1919] 1996. *Synopsis of the History of Chinese Philosophy* 中國哲學史大綱. Rpt. Beijing: Dongfang.

——— 胡適. [1930] 1998. *A Lengthy Discussion of the History of Thought During China's Middle Ages*中國中古思想史長篇. Rpt. in *Collected Writings of Hu Shi* 胡適文集. Ed. Ouyang Zhesheng 歐陽哲生, vol. 6. Beijing: Beijing Daxue chubanshe.

Hu, Tieqiu 胡鐵球. 2016. "The Rationale Behind Shang Yang's Construction of the Agriculture cum Warfare State, and its Impact: The Discussion on the Basis of the *Book of Lord Shang*" 商鞅構建農戰之國的理念及其影響———以《商君書》為中心討論. *Social Sciences* 社會科學1: 135–152.

Huang, Shaomei 黃紹梅. 2010. *Study of Shang Yang's Anti-Humanism*商鞅反人文觀研究. Yonghe (Taipei County): Hua Mulan chubanshe.

Huangshi richao 黃氏日抄 (*Mr. Huang's Daily Transcriptions*). n.d. By Huang, Zhen 黃震 (1213–1280). E-*Siku quanshu* edition.

Jenks, Edward. 1900. *A History of Politics*. London: Dent.

Jian, Shu 簡書. [1931] 1975. *Glosses and Corrections on the Book of Lord Shang*商君書箋正. Rpt. Taipei: Guangwen shuju.

Jiang, Chongyue 蔣重躍. 2022. *The Book of Lord Shang* 商君書. (Series "A Hundred Classics in China's Traditional Culture" 中華傳統文化百部經典). Beijing: Guojia tushuguan chubanshe. (A useful introductory-level edition).

Jiang, Lihong 蔣禮鴻, ed. 1986. *Pointing an Awl at the Book of Lord Shang* 商君書錐指. Beijing: Zhonghua shuju.

Jiang, Pei 江沛. 2001. *Study of the Thought of "The Stratagems of the Warring States" School* 戰國策派思想研究. Tianjin: Tianjin renmin chubanshe.

Jiang, Tao. 2021. *Origins of Moral-Political Philosophy in Early China: Contestation of Humaneness, Justice, and Personal Freedom*. Oxford: Oxford University Press.

Kang, Youwei 康有爲. [1898] 2007. *On Confucius's Reforms* 孔子改制考. Rpt. in *The Collected Works of Kang Youwei* 康有爲全集, ed. Jiang Yihua 姜義華 and Zhang Ronghua 張榮華, Vol. 3, 1–260. Beijing: Zhongguo renmin daxue chubanshe.

Kurtz, Joachim. 2011. *The Discovery of Chinese Logic*. Leiden: Brill.

Lei, Haizong 雷海宗. [1940] 2001. *China's Culture and China's Armies* 中國文化與中國的兵. Rpt. Beijing: Shangwu yinshuguan.

Lévi, Jean, trans. 1981. *Le livre du prince Shang*. Paris: Flammarion.

———, trans. 2005. *Le livre du prince Shang*. 2nd ed., with an updated introduction. Paris: Flammarion.

Li, Haisheng 李海生. 1997. *The Dignity of the Image of* fa: *Modern and Contemporary Studies of the pre-Qin School of* fa 法相尊嚴:近現代的先秦法家研究. Shenyang: Liaoning Jiaoyu.

Li, Yu-ning, ed. 1977. *Shang Yang's Reforms and State Control in China*. White Plains, N.Y.: M. E. Sharpe. (An excellent summary of the twentieth-century changing views of Shang Yang in China).

Liang, Qichao 梁啟超. [1906] 2003. "History of the Evolution of China's Judicial Thought" 中國法理學發達史論. Rpt. in Liang Qichao, *Complete Works from the 'Ice Drinking' Room, Collated* 飲冰室文集點校, 6 vols., ed. Wu Song 吳松, Lu Yunkun 盧雲崐, Wang Wenguang 王文光, and Duan Bingchang 段炳昌, Vol. 1, 340–75. Kunming: Yunnan jiaoyu chubanshe.

———— 梁啟超. [1911] 2014. *China's Six Great Statesmen* 中國六大政治家. Rpt. Beijing: Zhonghua shuju.

———— 梁啟超. [1919] 1996. *History of Pre-Qin Political Thought* 先秦政治思想史. Rpt. Beijing: Dongfang.

Liu, Xinjie 劉昕傑. 2020. "When Law Changes According to the Times, There is Orderly Rule: Analyzing Chen Qitian's 'New School of *fa*' Thought" 法與時轉則治:陳啓天"新法家"思想析論 *Journal of 'Tracing the Way to its Origins'* 原道 39: 164–176.

Liu, Xiuming 劉修明. 2013. "Preface" 前言. In *Records of Poems and Texts Read by Mao Zedong in his Final Years* 毛澤東晚年過眼詩文錄. 2013. Ed. Wang Shoujia 王守稼 *et al*, booklet 1, pp. 1–33. Shijiazhuang: Huashan wenyi chubanshe (2nd edition).

Liu, Zehua 劉澤華. 2019. *Autobiography at the Age of Eighty* 八十自述, ed. Institute of History, Nankai University 南開大學歷史學院. Tianjin: Tianjin renmin chubanshe.

Louie, Kam. 1980. *Critiques of Confucius in Contemporary China*. New York: St. Martin's Press.

Lü, Zhenyu 呂振羽. 1937. *History of Chinese Political Thought* 中國政治思想史. Shanghai: Liming shuju.

MacFarquhar, Roderick, and Michael Schoenhals. 2006. *Mao's Last Revolution*. Cambridge, MA: Belknap Press of Harvard University Press.

Mai, Menghua 麥孟華. 1903[1986]. *Critical Biography of Lord Shang* 商君評傳. Rpt. in *Grand Compendium of the Masters* 諸子集成. Shanghai: Shanghai shudian. (The first modern systematic study of the *Book of Lord Shang*).

Mao Zedong wannian guoyan shiwenlu 毛澤東晚年過眼詩文錄 (*Records of Poems and Texts Read by Mao Zedong in his Final Years*). 2013. 2nd ed., ed. Wang, Shoujia 王守稼 et al. Shijiazhuang: Huashan wenyi chubanshe.

Ouyang, Fenglian 歐陽鳳蓮. 2011. *Study of the Thought of the Book of Lord Shang* 商君書思想研究. Nanning: Guangxi renmin chubanshe.

Perelomov, Leonard S. (Переломов, Леонард С.). 1968. *Книга правителя области Шан (Шан цзюнь шу) (The Book of Lord Shang)*. Moscow: Nauka.

————. (Переломов, Леонард С.). 1993a. *Книга правителя области Шан (Шан цзюнь шу) (The Book of Lord Shang)*. *With a new afterword*. Moscow: Ladomir.

———— (Переломов, Леонард С.). 1993b. *Конфуций: жизнь, учение, судьба* (Confucius: Life, teaching, destiny). Moscow: Nauka.

Pines, Yuri. 2009. *Envisioning Eternal Empire: Chinese Political Thought of the Warring States Era*. Honolulu: University of Hawai'i Press.

————. 2012. Alienating Rhetoric in the *Book of Lord Shang* and its Moderation. *Extrême-Orient, Extrême-Occident* 34: 79–110.

————. 2016a. Dating a Pre-imperial Text: The Case Study of the *Book of Lord Shang*. *Early China* 39: 145–184.

————. 2016b. A 'Total War'? Rethinking Military Ideology in the *Book of Lord Shang*. *Journal of Chinese Military History* 5 (2): 97–134.

————. 2016c. Social Engineering in Early China: The Ideology of the *Shangjunshu* (*Book of Lord Shang*) Revisited. *Oriens Extremus* 55: 1–37.

————, trans. and ed. 2017. *The Book of Lord Shang: Apologetics of State Power in Early China*. New York: Columbia University Press.

Pines, Yuri, and Carine Defoort. 2016. Chinese Academic Views on Shang Yang Since the Open-up-and-Reform Era. *Contemporary Chinese Thought* 47 (2): 59–68.

Rubin, Vitaly. 1976. *Individual and State in Ancient China*. New York: Columbia University Press.

———— (Рубин, Виталий). 1999. *Личность и власть в древнем Китае: собрание трудов*. Moscow: "Vostochnaia literatura" RAN.

Qi, Sihe 齊思和. [1947] 2001. "On Shang Yang' Reforms" 商鞅變法考. Reprinted in Qi Sihe, *Discussions of China's History* 中國史探研, 247–278. Shijiazhuang: Hebei jiaoyu chubanshe.

Sato, Masayuki. 2013. Studies of *Han Feizi* in China, Taiwan, and Japan. In *Dao Companion to the Philosophy of Han Fei*, ed. Paul R. Goldin, 257–281. Dordrecht: Springer.

———— 佐藤將之. 2018. "Studies of *Han Feizi* in Mainland China, Taiwan, and Japan" 中國大陸、臺灣、日本的《韓非子》研究. *Journal of Sinological Studies* 漢學研究集刊 26: 157–198.

Schram, Stuart R., ed. 1992–2004. *Mao's Road to Power: Revolutionary Writings 1912–1949*. Vol. 7 vols. Armonk, NY: M. E. Sharpe.

Setzekorn, Eric. 2015. Jiang Baili: Frustrated Military Intellectual in Republican China. *Journal of Chinese Military History* 4 (2): 142–161.

Shibata, Noboru 柴田昇. 1996. "The Historical Position of the *Book of Lord Shang*" 『商君書』の歴史的位置. *Journal of History* 史林 79.1: 95–123.

Shiji 史記 (Records of the Historian). 1997. By Sima, Qian 司馬遷 (ca. 145–90 BCE) et al. Annotated by Zhang, Shoujie 張守節, Sima, Zhen 司馬貞, and Pei, Yin 裴駰. Beijing: Zhonghua shuju.

Song, Hongbing 宋洪兵. 2013. "Studies of *Han Feizi* during the Republican Period" 民國時期之"韓非學"研究. *National Studies Journal* 國學學刊 4: 91–103.

Sun, Yirang 孫詒讓 (1848–1908). 2014. *Collated Text of Shangzi* (i.e. *The Book of Lord Shang*) 商子校本, ed. Xu, Jialu 許嘉璐, Zhu, Honglie 祝鴻杰. Beijing: Zhonghua shuju.

Tong, Weimin 仝衛敏. 2013. *Integrative Study of the* Book of Lord Shang *and Unearthed Documents*出土文獻與《商君書》綜合研究. Vols. 16–17 of *Series of Studies of Classical Texts* 古典文獻研究輯刊, ed. Pan Meiyue 潘美月 and Du Jiexiang 杜潔祥. New Taipei City: Hua Mulan chubanshe. (A good study of the *Book of Lord Shang* in the context of recently unearthed paleographic documents).

Van de Ven, Hans J. 2003. *War and Nationalism in China, 1925–1945*. New York: Routledge.

Van Norden, Bryan W. 1996. What Should Western Philosophy Learn from Chinese Philosophy? In *Chinese Language, Thought, and Culture: Nivison and His Critics*, ed. Philip J. Ivanhoe, 224–249. La Salle, Ill: Open Court.

Vogelsang, Kai, trans. 2017. *Shangjun shu: Schriften des Fürsten von Shang*. Stuttgart: Alfred Kröner.

Waldron, Arthur. 2003. From Jaurès to Mao: The *Levée en masse* in China. In *The People in Arms: Military Myth and National Mobilization since the French Revolution*, ed. Daniel Moran and Arthur Wadron, 189–207. Cambridge: Cambridge University Press.

Wang, Mingde 王明德. 2008. "On Mai Menghua" 論麥孟華. *Journal of Wuyi University (Social Sciences)* 五邑大學學報(社會科學版)10(1): 22–33.

Wenxian tongkao 文獻通考 (Comprehensive Examination of Authoritative Sources and Later Interpretations). n.d. By Ma, Duanlin 馬端臨 (1254–1332). E-*Siku quanshu* edition.

Wong, Young-tsu. 2010. *Beyond Confucian China: The Rival Discourses of Kang Youwei and Zhang Binglin*. London and New York: Routledge.

Wu, Baoping 吳保平 and Lin, Cunguang 林存光. 2016. "Reflections on the Concept of 'Law' of Shang Yang from the Perspective of Political Philosophy: Function, Value, and Spirit of the 'Rule of Law.'" *Contemporary Chinese Thought* 47.2: 125–137.

Xunzi jijie 荀子集解 (*Xunzi*, with Collected Explanations). 1992. Annotated by Wang Xianqian 王先謙 (1842–1917). ed. Shen Xiaohuan 沈嘯寰 and Wang Xingxian 王星賢. Beijing: Zhonghua shuju.

Yang, Kuan 楊寬. 1955. *Shang Yang's Reform* 商鞅變法. Shanghai: Renmin chubanshe.

Yantielun jiaozhu 鹽鐵論校注 (*Salt and Iron Debates*, Collated and Annotated). 1996. Compiled by Huan, Kuan 桓寬 (first century BCE). ed. Wang, Liqi 王利器. Beijing: Zhonghua shuju.

Yoshimoto, Michimasa 吉本道雅. 2005. *Study of China's Pre-Qin History* 中國先秦史の研究. Kyōto: Kyōto University Press.

Yoshinami, Takashi 好并隆司. 1992. *Study of the Book of Lord Shang* 商君書研究. Hiroshima: Keisuisha. (The best study of the *Book of Lord Shang* in Japan).

Yu, Zhong 喻中. 2018. "On the New 'School of *fa*' in East Asia" 論東亞新法家. *Politics and Law Tribune* 政法論壇 36.3: 28–40.

Zarrow, Peter. 2012. *After Empire: The Conceptual Transformation of the Chinese State, 1885–1924*. Stanford: Stanford University Press.

Zeng, Zhenyu 曾振宇. 2016. "Shang Yang as a Historical Personality and as a Symbol." Trans. Yuri Pines. *Contemporary Chinese Thought* 47.2: 69–89.

Zhang, Binglin 章炳麟. [1900] 2000. *Forceful Book with Detailed Glosses* 訄書詳注. ed. Xu Fu 徐復. Shanghai: Shanghai guji chubanshe.

Zhang, Jue 張覺. 2012. *The Book of Lord Shang, Collated with Subcommentaries* 商君書校疏. Beijing: Zhishi chanquan chubanshe. (The most systematic textual study of the *Book of Lord Shang*).

Zhang, Linxiang 張林祥. 2008. *Study of Composition and Thought of the* Book of Lord Shang 《商君書》的成書與思想研究. Beijing: Renmin chubanshe.

———— 張林祥. 2016. Progress or Change? Rethinking the Historical Outlook of the *Book of Lord Shang*. Trans. Yuri Pines. *Contemporary Chinese Thought* 47.2: 90–111.

———— 張林祥. 2022. "Re-reading the *Book of Lord Shang* from a Humanist Point of View" 從人道的立場重讀《商君書》. *Pre-Qin Literature and Culture* 先秦文學與文化 10: 135–142.

Zhang, Xiqin 張錫勤. 2004. "A Brief Discussion of Mai Menghua's Thought" 麥孟華思想簡論. *Seeking Truth Journal* 求是學刊 31.1: 39–44.

Zheng, Liangshu 鄭良樹. 1989. *Shang Yang and his School* 商鞅及其學派. Shanghai: Shanghai guji chubanshe. (An engaging attempt to trace intellectual evolution of "Shang Yang's school" through the chapters of the *Book of Lord Shang*).

Zhu, Shizhe 朱師轍. [1948] 1956. *The Fixed and Commented Upon Text of the Book of Lord Shang* 商君書解詁定本. Rpt. Beijing: Beijing guji chubanshe.

Part IV
Comparative Perspectives

Chapter 18
The *fa* Tradition Versus Confucianism: Intellectuals, the State, and Meritocracy

Yuri Pines

Contrasting Confucians (Ru 儒) with the *fa* tradition is among the most common tropes in studies of China's intellectual history.[1] Mutual enmity between the two currents has been observable ever since the fourth century BCE. Take, for instance, the *Book of Lord Shang*'s (*Shangjunshu* 商君書) invectives against cultural and moral values associated with Confucians, or *Mengzi*'s 孟子 identification of wars and land reclamation (two major emphases of Shang Yang's 商鞅 [d. 338 BCE] policies) as crimes, the first severe enough that even death was considered too light a punishment.[2]

---

[1] As demonstrated by Michael Nylan (1999), *Ru* and "Confucians" were not coterminous definitions. I use both terms interchangeably, though, borrowing from the chapter "Eminent Teachings" ("Xian xue" 顯學) of *Han Feizi*. For the *fa* tradition, in this chapter I focus on the *Book of Lord Shang* and *Han Feizi* only.

[2] The *Book of Lord Shang* proclaims: "*Poems, Documents*, rites, music, goodness, self-cultivation, benevolence, uprightness, argumentativeness, cleverness: when the state has these ten, superiors cannot induce [the people] to [engage in] defense and fighting" 詩、書、禮、樂、善、修、仁、廉、辯、慧，國有十者，上無使守戰 (*Book of Lord Shang* 3.5; cf. 4.3 and 13.4; Zhang Jue 2012: 47, 62, 158 [in citing the *Book of Lord Shang*, I refer to divisions adopted in Pines 2017a, which differ slightly from those in Zhang Jue 2012]). Compare to *Mengzi* 7:14: "In wars to gain land, the dead fill the plains; in wars to gain cities, the dead fill the cities. This is known as leading the land to devour human flesh. Death is too light a punishment for such a crime. Hence those are fond of war should suffer the most severe punishments; those who secure alliances with regional lords come next; and then come those who open up wasteland and manage the soil" 爭地以戰，殺人盈野；爭城以戰，殺人盈城，此所謂率土地而食人肉，罪不容於死。故善戰者服上刑，連諸侯者次之，辟草萊、任土地者次之 (translation modified from Lau 1970: 124).

This research was supported by the Israel Science Foundation (grant No. 568/19) and by the Michael William Lipson Chair in Chinese Studies.

Y. Pines (✉)
Hebrew University of Jerusalem, Jerusalem, Israel
e-mail: yuri.pines@mail.huji.ac.il

© The Author(s), under exclusive license to Springer Nature Switzerland AG 2024   517
Y. Pines (ed.), *Dao Companion to China's* fa *Tradition*, Dao Companions
to Chinese Philosophy 19, https://doi.org/10.1007/978-3-031-53630-4_19

Move forward to acerbic remarks against useless Confucians in *Han Feizi* 韓非子, to the endorser of Shang Yang trading barbs with Confucians during the "Salt and Iron" debates of 81 BCE, to countless anti-*fa* tirades by the imperial-era Confucians—and the picture becomes overwhelming.[3] One can easily conclude that the two ideological currents were full antipodes.

It is indeed easy to think of Confucianism versus the *fa* tradition dichotomously. Confucians prioritized moral self-cultivation; the *fa* adherents prioritized impartial standards. Confucians were staunch traditionalists; the *fa* supporters were ready to dismiss the past models and innovate. Confucians were fully committed to moral values; the *fa* texts dispense with moralizing discourse altogether. Yet beyond these dichotomies we also discover similarities and even complementarities between the two major ideological currents. The quest for political stability which both traditions associated with political unification under the aegis of a single omnipotent monarch; the support for meritocratic principle of rule; the paternalistic view of the people, whose interests should be of utmost concern for the rulers but who should not normally participate in decision-making—all these were common foundations of Chinese political thought shared by the vast majority of competing "schools of thought," Confucians and *fa* supporters in particular (Liu Zehua 1991, 1996, 2000; Pines 2009; Song 2010: 104–90). It is the persistent tension between the common political objectives and the radically different means to attain these objectives that makes the comparison between the Confucian and *fa* traditions so fascinating.

In what follows, I shall focus on a single aspect of comparison—the two traditions' views of the proper relation between the educated elite and the state. Whereas both traditions broadly agreed that skilled and ambitious men should be employed in the government, they disagreed dramatically about the conditions for entering government service. In a nutshell, Confucians wanted to join the ruler-centered political order on their own terms, retaining a considerable degree of intellectual and moral autonomy. The educated elite itself should define who is eligible to join its ranks as a "noble man" (*junzi* 君子). Even when serving the ruler, the noble man should maintain his dignity, independent mind, and commitment to the moral Way (Dao 道). For the *fa* thinkers, these views were a direct threat to the political order, first, because they opened the way for manipulative und unscrupulous fake "noble men" to enter government service, and second because the elite empowerment undermined the cherished principles of impartiality and orderly monarchic rule. The debate between the two currents had profound ramifications on traditional

---

[3] For *Han Feizi*'s attack, see e.g., Chap. 50, "Eminent Teachings" *et saepe*. The "Salt and Iron" debates (the content of which is reproduced in eponymous *Yantielun* 鹽鐵論) was the last court event in which one side (the Imperial Counsellor, Sang Hongyang 桑弘羊 [152–80 BCE]) openly defended the *fa* thinkers (see *Yantielun* chapters 7, "Rejecting [Shang] Yang" 非鞅, and 56, "Shen [Buhai] and Han [Fei]" 申韓). Sang's view was bitterly contested by the die-hard government opponents, the Literati (*wenxue* 文學; see more in Polnarov 2018). For anti-*fa* criticism by the Han and later Confucians, see, e.g., Song, Chap. 16, this volume.

Chinese political culture in general, and on the complex pattern of China's meritocratic government in particular.[4] Some of its aspects may still be relevant today.

1   Background: The Rise of the *shi*

Much of the Warring States-period (Zhanguo 戰國, 453–221 BCE) ideological
dynamics, arguably the very intellectual flowering of that age, should be understood
against the backdrop of the phenomenal rise of *shi* 士 to the forefront of political,
social, and intellectual life.[5] *Shi* is a notoriously polysemic term that can refer in
different contexts to a male, a warrior, a retainer, a petty official, an acting or aspir-
ing elite member, and the like (Pines 2009: 116–17). In many cases the translation
"men of service" works well; and insofar as intellectually active members of this
stratum are concerned, the translation "intellectuals" is entirely valid (Yu Yingshi
2003: 3–4). Yet this polysemy is primarily a Warring States-period phenomenon.
Before the fifth century BCE, the *shi* were a marginal stratum of low nobility. Then,
as hereditary aristocrats were weakened by internecine struggles among ministerial
lineages and between these lineages and the rulers, *shi* began filling in the vacuum
created by the aristocrats' retreat. The corresponding expansion of the government
apparatus offered *shi* ample additional opportunities for employment. Finally, proliferation of meritocratic discourse, which emphasized the government servant's
qualities as more important than pedigree, sealed the fate of the hereditary aristocracy. By the fourth century BCE, this stratum had been swallowed by the new broad
shi elite.

It is significant in this context that the principle of meritocracy was endorsed
unanimously across the spectrum of competing ideologies. Ever since Mozi 墨子
(ca. 460–390 BCE) put forward the idea of "elevating the worthy and employing the
able" 尚賢使能, we hear no significant voices that support pedigree as the determinant of one's position (Pines 2013a). This situation was particularly favorable
toward the formation of an ideal of service (*shi* 仕) as the most appropriate self-
realization for a *shi*. Whereas what made a man eligible to government service was
a bitterly contested issue, and not a few dissenting voices criticized the unwavering
commitment of *shi* to political career, generally most thinkers—including in particular Confucians and the *fa* adherents—agreed that a skilled and ambitious man
should find himself in service of the government. It is within this common conviction that further Confucian-*fa* debates unfolded.

---

[4] The concept of meritocracy as the major feature of China's political culture was promulgated
primarily by Daniel Bell (Bell and Li 2013; Bell 2015), and rapidly became the focus of scholarly
interest. Among recent publications, see particularly Harris 2020 who compares Han Fei's and
Confucian views of meritocracy.

[5] This topic has been studied extensively; see, e.g., Yu Yingshi 2003: 3–76; Liu Zehua 2004; Pines
2009: 116–31.

Parallel to their political advancement, *shi* secured an equally important asset—the position of society's moral and intellectual leaders, the possessors of the Way ("Dao" 道). This success of political outsiders to attain intellectual dominance is one of the most curious phenomena of the Warring States era. Judging from our (admittedly limited) sources, early in the Zhou era the ideological authority was firmly in the hands of kings and their chief advisors, whose speeches are (re)produced in the canonical *Classic of Documents* (*Shujing* 書經). In the subsequent Springs-and-Autumns period (Chunqiu 春秋, 770–453 BCE), the seeds of change are observable. Among many dozens of ideologically important speeches cited in *Zuozhuan* 左傳 (*Zuo Tradition*), only a tiny proportion are attributed to the rulers. However, ideological authority at this time still remained largely at the rulers' courts. Most of the speakers are courtiers (i.e., members of the upper to middle nobility), whereas outsiders, such as *shi*, largely remain silent. This changes once we enter the Warring States period. The feeling is that all of a sudden, the courts had lost their ideological prestige. Judging by a variety of existent sources (written overwhelmingly by the *shi* for the *shi*), it seems that everyone acquiesced to the idea that the true locus of intellectual authority is neither the rulers nor their chief advisors, but the *shi* Masters (*zi* 子) and their disciples (Pines 2009: 123–31).

The ease with which *shi* attained both political and ideological superiority is somewhat surprising. It is not at all clear, for instance, why the hereditary aristocracy gave up its political privileges with only minimal resistance. The ideological success of *shi* intellectuals is even more astounding. How did it happen that during the Warring States period, which was otherwise marked by the centralization of power in major polities and the formation of what Mark E. Lewis (1999: 597) aptly names the "ruler-centered state," the realm of ideology appears to have been fully emancipated from political control? Is it possible that we are simply misled by the nature of our sources? Without ruling out this possibility, one can provide an indirect supporting evidence to the phenomenon of *shi* intellectual hegemony—specifically the texts associated with the *fa* tradition.

As amply demonstrated in the contributions to this volume, *fa* adherents were fully committed to strengthening and perfecting the ruler-centered polity. By contrast, nowhere did they endorse the notion of the ruler's superiority in the ideological realm. To the contrary, both the *Book of Lord Shang* and *Han Feizi* frequently lament the inadequacy of current sovereigns (*shizhu* 世主) who fail to understand the ways of empowering their states.[6] Clearly, it is the thinkers—whatever political position they occupy—who have the correct understanding of political tasks, whereas the sovereigns should heed their advice. In neither of these texts do we encounter a ruler who makes authoritative pronouncements. In the *Book of Lord Shang*, Shang Yang's employer, Lord Xiao of Qin 秦孝公 (r. 361–338 BCE), makes

---

[6] See, e.g., *Book of Lord Shang* 3.10, 6.1, 6.3, 6.6, 8.3 (Zhang Jue 2012: 55, 88, 92, 97, 124); *Han Feizi* 14.7, 19.5, 46.1, 46.9, 50.2 (Chen Qiyou 2000: 293–94, 355, 1000, 1021, 1129), *et saepe*. In citing *Han Feizi*, I refer to divisions of Zhang Jue 2010, adopted by Harbsmeier, forthcoming; I often borrow Harbsmeier's translations.

a single meaningful appearance in the first chapter, where he outlines his plans to alter the existent laws, then listens to the advisors' opinions, and finally approves Shang Yang's proposal to institute radical reforms. Henceforth, the lord disappears from the text. In *Han Feizi* we do not encounter even this minimal appearance of a law-changing ruler; when, in manifold anecdotes, the rulers talk, they are almost invariably wrong (see, e.g., Graziani 2015: 167; see more in Pines, Chap. 1, Sect. 6 and Chap. 4, Sect. 3.3, this volume).

These two points—that *shi* are supposed to be engaged in government service (which, recall, implied subjugation to the ruler-centered order) and that they are morally and/or intellectually superior to the sovereigns—were shared by Ru and *fa* adherents. The thinkers of both currents were well aware of the inevitable tension between the simultaneous subordination to the ruler and commitment to the Way (see more in Liu Zehua 2004: 161–267). They diverged sharply, however, about the how to deal with this tension. In a nutshell, Confucians proposed a bottom-up vision of meritocracy in which the intellectuals should play a leading role. The *fa* thinkers opted for a radically different top-down model in which intellectuals should be fully subordinate to the ruler-led political apparatus. Below we shall survey the advantages and disadvantages of both models.

2   Confucius and Mengzi: Elite's Pride

Confucius (Kongzi 孔子, 551–479 BCE), to start with, was not a die-hard promoter of meritocracy. He lived at the end of China's aristocratic age, during the period when one's social status still depended primarily on one's pedigree. Confucius never openly challenged the pedigree-based social order, but some of his ideas contained the seeds of social revolution. In particular, Confucius's ethical interpretation of the term "noble man" is of profound importance. As we can judge from *Zuozhuan*, prior to Confucius, the term *junzi* had both ethical and pedigree-based connotations, but it was exclusively applied to the members of middle and high-rank nobility. Confucius, conversely, turned this designation into an overwhelmingly ethical term, to which his fellow members of low nobility, to wit, the *shi* were henceforth eligible. In due time, this "semantic revolution" allowed the *shi* to claim not just the noble men's qualities but also the noble men's status, that is the right to ascend to the top of sociopolitical ladder (Pines 2017b; cf. Gassman 2007).

Confucius redefined not only the term *junzi*, but also the term *shi* itself, which he imbued with moral value. In the *Analects* (*Lunyu* 論語), neither *junzi* nor *shi* refer to one's ascribed status. It is only through self-cultivation that a man can become an exemplary person. As a result, *shi* is no longer a neutral designation; rather it is a valorized term, a model personality. Thus, one of Confucius's disciples, Zizhang (子張, 503–? BCE), defines a *shi* as a person who "sacrifices his life when facing danger, thinks of righteousness when facing [possible] gains" 士見危致命，見得思義 (*Lunyu* 19.1). Zengzi (曾子, 502–435 BCE) speaks even more assertively: "A *shi* cannot but be strong and resolute, as his task is heavy and his way is long. He

considers benevolence as his task—is not it heavy? He stops only after death—is
not [his way] long?" 士不可以不弘毅，任重而道遠。仁以為己任，不亦重乎?
死而後已，不亦遠乎 (*Lunyu* 8.7). Both statements reflect the immense self-
respect among the members of the newly rising stratum, who accepted their mission
to improve governance above and public mores below, and who considered themselves spiritual leaders of society.

Self-cultivation and moral conduct were essential for becoming a noble man or a
shi; but the goal was higher—it was influencing society. Confucius explains to a
disciple that whereas the starting goal of self-cultivation is to behave reverently
(*jing* 敬, which implies being in a relatively low position), it then moves to "bringing peace to others" (*an ren* 安人), with the ultimate goal being "bringing peace to
the hundred clans" (*an baixing* 安百姓). Whereas the latter lofty goal may be unattainable—"even Yao and Shun considered that difficult" 堯舜其猶病諸 (*Lunyu*
14.42)—the second implies attaining a position of influence, perhaps as a mid-rank
official. This is the true epitome of one's self-realization. Confucius himself
searched—with limited success—for a position in the state apparatus, and he
expected his disciples to realize themselves accordingly. Government service was
attractive not only in terms of the accompanying economic and social benefits, but
as a lofty moral mission. It was the means through which a noble man could disseminate morality downwards to the people (see, for example, *Lunyu* 8.2,
19.21, 12.19).

Here comes the first catch. Confucius encourages the noble men to serve not as
the ruler's servitors but rather as servitors of the Way—the one, "hearing of which
in the morning one can die [without regret] in the evening" 朝聞道，夕死可矣
(*Lunyu* 4.8). Adherence to one's moral Way is the criterion according to which the
political service should be judged.[7] Confucius reiterates: "When the Way prevails
under Heaven, show yourself; when there is no Way, hide yourself. When the Way
prevails in the state, it is shameful to be poor and base there; when the state lacks the
Way, it is shameful to be rich and noble there" 天下有道則見，無道則隱。邦有
道，貧且賤焉，恥也；邦無道，富且貴焉，恥也 (*Lunyu* 8.13). One should
always check whether or not one's service conforms to the norms of the Way and
disengage from the government once it "lacks the Way." Thus, "What is called 'the
great minister' is the one who serves the ruler according to the Way and stops when
it is impossible" 所謂大臣者:以道事君，不可則止 (*Lunyu* 11.24).

One can admire the lofty commitment to the Way which Confucius endorsed and
which he bequeathed to his followers. But think of the ruler's side of the equation.
Insofar as the nature of the "Way" was determined by the minister, the self-cultivated
"noble man," the ruler had very little leverage over his proud aide. Worse, the ruler
was also powerless to determine who deserves the designation of a "noble man."
The *Analects* is full of Confucius's discussions of this topic, and it is very clear that

---

[7] It is not my intention here to discuss whether or not Confucius speaks of an objective discoverable
Way or of a subjective one. Politically speaking, insofar as the Way is determined by a noble man
and not by the ruler, the Way remains an employee's (or a potential employee's) asset.

the nature of the "noble man" status should be determined by the Master and his disciples (e.g., *Lunyu* 2.13, 12.4, 14.42). Similarly, when Confucius discusses the importance of renown or repute ("a name," *ming* 名), it refers primarily to one's renown among peers (*Lunyu* 15.2, 9.23, 9.2).[8] It should be the members of the newly formed elite, bonded by the ties of friendship[9] who will define the elite belonging for newcomers. The rulers have very little, if anything, to contribute to this process.

It can be summarized that Confucius empowered his fellow *shi* in three ways. First, he made them eligible to *junzi* status. Second, he provided them with the seeds of group identity, which henceforth allowed them to determine who is qualified to join the new elite. And third, by postulating superiority of the Way over the ruler, Confucius provided *shi* with excellent leverage against employers. In due time, this triple power became a huge asset of men of service.

How effective this empowerment worked can be observed from the case of Mengzi (孟子, d. ca. 304 BCE). Mengzi represents the apex of *shi* self-confidence. In the text that bears his name nobody asks the master "Who is *shi*?" or "Who is *junzi*?" (a common question in the *Analects*). Instead, there are plenty of pronouncements that hail *shi* as lofty individuals who share common values. Mengzi states: "Only a *shi* is able to preserve a stable heart without stable livelihood" 無恒產而有恒心者，惟士為能 (*Mengzi* 1.7); elsewhere he cites a saying: "A *shi* with high aspirations will never forget [that he may end] in a ditch, a brave *shi* will never forget [that he may] lose his head" 志士不忘在溝壑，勇士不忘喪其元 (*Mengzi* 6.1). One of Mengzi's disciples cites another saying: "[As for] *shi* with abundant virtue, rulers were unable to treat them as subjects, fathers were unable to treat them as sons" 盛德之士，君不得而臣，父不得而子 (*Mengzi* 9.4). All these statements, while containing an element of bravado, create the sense of a proud community, united by common behavioral norms, a community whose members do not feel inferiority even vis-à-vis the rulers. The pride of belonging to this exclusive group peaks in Mengzi's panegyric to the Great Man, an ideal personality used as a foil to those contemporaries who compromised their integrity for the sake of career:

> 以順為正者，妾婦之道也。居天下之廣居，立天下之正位，行天下之大道；得志與民由之，不得志，獨行其道；富貴不能淫，貧賤不能移，威武不能屈——此之謂大丈夫。
>
> To consider compliance as correctness is the way of wives and concubines. [The Great Man] resides in the broad lodging of All-under-Heaven, occupies a proper position in All-under-Heaven, follows the great Way of All-under-Heaven. When his aspirations are fulfilled—he follows [the Way] together with the people; when they are not—he realizes his Way alone. Wealth and high status cannot tempt him, poverty and low status cannot move

---

[8] The question of whether or not Confucius approved of seeking a name was subject for significant controversies ever since the Han dynasty. See Makeham 1993; see also Roetz 1993: 181–83; Pines 2020: 175–77.

[9] As Zha Changguo ([1998] 2006: 109–11) demonstrates, the ties of friendship were used to characterize also the master-disciples relations in the *Analects*.

him, majestic awe and military might cannot subdue him—this is called the "Great Man."[10] (*Mengzi* 6.2)

Mengzi presents the Great Man as an entirely self-sufficient person, a proud counterpart of the ruler above and the people below. Being internally empowered by firm attachment to the Way, he is able to defy whatever external challenges are presented by those who want either to entice or overawe him. The Great Man is almost superhuman: he is not a minor actor on the sociopolitical scene, but a creator of his own moral universe, to which he can retreat from the inadequate outside world. This moral universe, as Mengzi clarifies elsewhere, is not desolate, but rather is inhabited by aspiring Great Men—the *shi*:

> 孟子謂萬章曰:「一鄉之善士, 斯友一鄉之善士; 一國之善士, 斯友一國之善士; 天下之善士, 斯友天下之善士。以友天下之善士為未足, 又尚論古之人。頌其詩, 讀其書, 不知其人, 可乎?是以論其世也。是尚友也。」
>
> Mengzi told to Wan Zhang: "Good *shi* of a village should befriend good *shi* of the village; good *shi* of a state should befriend good *shi* of the state; good *shi* of All-under-Heaven should befriend good *shi* of All-under-Heaven. If befriending good *shi* of All-under-Heaven is still insufficient, then you still can debate with the ancients. Recite their *Poems*, read their *Documents*: is it possible that then you will not understand these people? Thus when you discuss their generation, this is as if you befriend them." (*Mengzi* 10.8)

The picture of a community of friends who share aspirations and educational background (which allows them also to debate canonical works with "the ancients") supplements logically the notion of a self-sufficient Great Man. This synchronic and diachronic community, being apparently independent of the state and its hierarchy, may have been particularly appealing to critically minded people like Mengzi's interlocutor in the above passage, his disciple Wan Zhang 萬章, who once defined the lords of his time as "robbers" (*Mengzi* 10.4). Upright *shi* may have found relief in such a self-sufficient community, probably even an escape from the predicament of serving morally inferior rulers.

Mengzi's insistence on *shi* autonomy from state power comes hand in hand with a more politically potent concept of coexistence of parallel hierarchies—social, political, and moral. As the thinker clarifies, "There are three matters that command respect under Heaven: first is rank, second is age; third is virtue. At court, rank is supreme; in the village community, age; but in supporting the generation and prolonging the people's [life], nothing is comparable to virtue" 天下有達尊三:爵一, 齒一, 德一。朝廷莫如爵, 鄉黨莫如齒, 輔世長民莫如德 (*Mengzi* 4.2). Mengzi positions himself and like-minded lofty *shi* at the apex of moral hierarchy, which implies a parity with the ruler. At times he goes even further. In one of the text's most provocative statements, Mengzi explains why he dismisses the notion of ruler-minister friendship, which gained much popularity among lofty *shi*:

---

[10] Note that in this passage Mengzi defines the "Great Man" in strong gender-specific terms as *da zhangfu* 大丈夫, whereas elsewhere he uses more common *da ren* 大人. This may be prompted by the usage of a rare *da zhangfu* by Mengzi's interlocutor, but it is also possible that Mengzi wants to contrast the masculine independence with the feminine ("wives and concubines") subservience as he sees it.

以位，則子君也，我臣也，何敢與君友也?以德，則子事我者也，奚可以與我友?
Judging by position, you are the ruler, and I am the minister—how dare I befriend a ruler?
Judging by virtue (*de* 德), you serve me—how can you befriend me? (*Mengzi* 10.7)

This statement is outright subversive. Whereas Mengzi recognizes the ruler's political superiority, his insistence on the inadequacy of the ruler's *de*, creates a potentially explosive situation. As Mengzi and his disciples knew perfectly, the term *de* meant not only moral virtue but also referred to charismatic power, or, in other words, to the very right to rule.[11] Thus, if a minister had superior *de*, and the ruler was supposed to "serve" (*shi* 事) him, this effectively meant that the sovereign and his underling should shift their positions.

This haughtiness created an irresolvable predicament for Mengzi and like-minded thinkers. Recall that Mengzi was fully committed to the ruler-centered political order. Actually, he proudly proclaimed that "only the Great Man is able to rectify the wrongs in the ruler's heart. When the ruler is benevolent—everybody is benevolent; when the ruler is righteous—everybody is righteous; when the ruler is correct—everybody is correct. Just rectify the ruler and the state will be stabilized" 惟大人為能格君心之非。君仁莫不仁，君義莫不義，君正莫不正，一正君而國定矣 (*Mengzi* 7.20). Namely, only under an ideal monarch could Mengzi's aspirations of a moral universe be fulfilled (Pines 2023). This in turn implied unwavering commitment to serving (and guiding) the sovereign; and *Mengzi* duly records many putative meetings between the thinker and the rulers whom he tried to direct toward good moral ends—alas, with limited success.[12] And this success was limited precisely because Mengzi's haughty stance and his frequent affronts to the sovereigns (Pines 2013b: 80–89) could not endear him to the rulers. Mengzi's career was as frustrating as that of Confucius. Time and again, Mengzi had to resign—either because the ruler was not attentive enough to his advice, or because the ruler did not treat him with sufficient politeness, or both.[13] The results were gloomy. Bolstering one's pride as a moral leader of the *shi* came at the expense of Mengzi's ability to realize his program.

This understanding demonstrates both the power and the weakness of the bottom-up meritocratic ideal promulgated by Confucius, Mengzi, and their disciples and followers. Their achievement in fostering the *esprit de corps* of the *shi* is undeniable; and the notion of parallel—political and moral—hierarchies is also laudable from the intellectuals' point of view. But the elite pride fostered by these thinkers was a double-edged sword. Not only did it alienate potential employers (the rulers), but, worse, it could easily be hijacked by unscrupulous men of service for whom lofty discourse was just a veneer to hide uninhibited quest for riches and social

---

[11] See more in Kominami 1992; Martynov 1998; Kryukov 1995; Nivison 1996; Wang Huaiyu 2015.

[12] The accounts about these meetings dominate the first two chapters of *Mengzi*, implying perhaps that for the editors of the book they were of key importance for understanding the Master's thought and deeds.

[13] It is symptomatic that when discussing the conditions of serving the ruler, Mengzi immediately feels it necessary to outline the conditions for resignation (*Mengzi* 12.14). See more in Pines 2009: 147–50.

status. Indeed, this is precisely what ensued in the Warring States period, igniting the ire of the *fa* thinkers.

3   The Inflation of Self-Esteem

The Warring States period was the golden age for men of service. They were sought after both because of their administrative skills and because of the intellectual prestige of their stratum. Rulers and nobles vied to extend patronage to outstanding *shi*, raising private think tanks staffed by hundreds (or even thousands) of *shi* retainers.[14] As *shi* enjoyed freedom of movement across state boundaries, they could benefit from a huge inter-state market of talent, which ensured a favorable ratio of demand versus supply for their services (Goldin 2022). All this put *shi* in an excellent bargaining position vis-à-vis the rulers. Add to this strong collective identity of the *shi*, fostered by Confucius and his followers, and their sense of moral and intellectual superiority over the rest of the population—the rulers included—and you have a potent mixture that explains the explosion of haughty pro-*shi* discourse in Mengzi's generation and especially thereafter.

The excessive self-confidence of the *shi* was directly related to the Confucian bottom-up model of meritocracy, even if not necessarily to Confucian moral vision. Recall that peer recognition was essential for being identified as a worthy *shi*; without this renown, an aspiring man of service had little chance of coming into the sight of a ruler. This prompted intense competition among the *shi* for attaining "a name" (Pines 2020). Curiously, whereas the objective of attaining a name was to enter the ruler's service, the immediate goal was to impress fellow *shi* rather than the rulers. Hence, the stories that circulated about outstanding *shi* normally emphasized their moral excellence rather than their administrative skills. Hundreds of these stories are scattered throughout contemporaneous or slightly latter collections, such as *Lüshi chunqiu* 呂氏春秋 (Springs and Autumns of Sire Lü), the *Stratagems of the Warring States* (*Zhanguoce* 戰國策), and multiple Master's texts. The heroes are hailed primarily for their eloquence, wit, forthrightness, courage, and so forth; their practical (economic, military, or administrative) contribution to the employer is only rarely addressed. We encounter lofty recluses whose adherence to the Way causes them to abandon filthy courts and refuse appointments—which, of course, makes them singularly deserving of appointment in the first place![15] We encounter paragons of loyalty, such as assassin-retainers who were willing to repay an

---

[14] The most famous of these think tanks or patronage communities was the so-called Jixia 稷下 academy in the state of Qi (fourth–third centuries BCE) (for which see Weingarten 2015) and the team of scholars assembled by the Qin prime-minister Lü Buwei 呂不韋 (d. 235 BCE) (Knoblock and Riegel 2000: 12–20). Yet fostering *shi* retainers was a much more widespread phenomenon as is testified by the patronage of *shi* by four major political leaders of the third century BCE, whose biographies are assembled in chapters 75–79 of *Shiji*.

[15] See Vervoorn 1990; Berkovitz 2000; Pines 2009: 152–61.

employer's lavish patronage by sacrificing themselves in his service ("a *shi* dies for the sake of the one who profoundly understands him" 士為知己者死).[16] We encounter skillful persuaders, whose rhetorical skills are hailed even if practical results of their advice matter little.[17] All these exemplars cater to the needs of peer opinion rather than to that of the rulers.

This prioritization of the *shi* public opinion over that of the rulers is most evident in the proliferation of the notion of *shi*'s parity with or even superiority over the rulers. We have encountered this *topos* in *Mengzi*; elsewhere it is expressed more blatantly. For instance, not a few texts present the ruler-minister ties as those of friends: to ensure the employee's loyalty the ruler should display utmost respect to a *shi* and even attain deeper spiritual affinity with him, as epitomized by the term *zhi ji* 知己 (literally, to understand other as deep as you understand yourself).[18] Yet for some *shi* even friendship was not enough: they boldly demanded the position of the ruler's teachers, i.e., de facto superiors, rather than mere friends.[19] Not a few anecdotes (including those in the *Mengzi*) demonstrate *shi*'s condescending attitude toward rulers, who, if we are to believe the anecdotes, seemed to tolerate this attitude. In one of the most ridiculous stories from that lore, we learn of an otherwise unknown high-minded recluse, Yan Chu 顏斶, who first infuriated the Qi king by claiming that a *shi* by definition is more important than the ruler, then made a long speech hailing *shi*, and then was offered most lavish patronage by the humiliated king, whose offer Yan Chu duly dismissed.[20] It seems that for some of the *shi* affronting the ruler was considered the best way of getting an appointment!

To exemplify the power of pro-*shi* discourse, let us turn to *Lüshi chunqiu*, a multi-authored compilation composed ca. 240 BCE under the aegis of the Qin prime minister Lü Buwei 呂不韋 (d. 235 BCE). So brazen is the approbation of *shi* in this

---

[16] *Zhanguoce* 18.4: 617 ("Zhao 趙 1"); for the *topos* of assassin-retainers and their "dying for the name," see Pines 2020: 183–89.

[17] This is most clear from a variety of *Zhanguoce* anecdotes, which often dispense with factual setting of the cited speech; what matters is the speaker's eloquence rather than his impact on real life affairs. See Schaberg 2023.

[18] For *zhi ji*, see *Zhanguoce* 18.4: 617 ("Zhao 1"); 27.22: 1035 ("Han 韓 2"); *Yanzi chunqiu* 5.24: 265–66. For the clearest statement interpreting the ruler-minister relations as those of friends, see, e.g., "Thicket of Sayings" 語叢 1 manuscript, from Tomb 1, Guodian 郭店 (Hubei): "Ruler and minister are [like] friends; [they] select [each other]" 君臣，朋友；其擇者也 (slip 87; cf. translation in Cook 2012: 826). See more in Zha [1998] 2006; Pines 2002.

[19] See for instance an argument from the "Cheng" 稱 manuscript from Tomb 3, Mawangdui 馬王堆 (Hunan): "The Thearch's minister is named minister, but in fact he is a teacher. The True Monarch's minister is named minister, but in fact he is a friend. The hegemon's minister is named minister, but in fact [he is a guest. The imperiled ruler's] minister is named minister, but in fact he is a servant. The due-to-perish ruler's minister is named minister, but in fact he is a slave." 帝者臣，名臣，其實師也。王者臣，名臣，其實友也。霸者臣，名臣，其實【賓也。危者】臣，名臣，其實庸也。亡者臣，名臣，其實虜也。*Mawangdui Hanmu boshu* 3: 191; cf. *Zhanguoce* 29.12: 1110–11 ("Yan 燕 1"); *Heguanzi* 1:7 ("Bo xuan" 博選).

[20] See *Zhanguoce* 11.5: 395–96 ("Qi 齊 4") and discussion in Pines 2009: 131–33. It is possible that the story was invented as a parody on the "lofty *shi*" lore. For more about irony in the *Stratagems of the Warring States*, see Pines 2018.

text that I have suggested elsewhere to treat it as a promotion campaign by Lü Buwei's "guests" (Pines 2009: 133). The text abounds with stories of wise rulers who attracted *shi* and benefited enormously from their service and those who failed to do so, bringing disaster on themselves.[21] Frequent references to "*shi* who possess the Way" (有道之士) convey a feeling that the authors considered the Way (viz. the guiding moral, sociopolitical, and cosmic principles, essential to the well-being of the state and a single person) as a kind of a common possession of the worthy members of their stratum. Repeatedly hailing impoverished, but upright, "plain-clothed" (*bu yi* 布衣) *shi*, the authors proclaim their membership in a morally dignified and incorruptible elite. The following passage illustrates their views:

士之為人，當理不避其難，臨患忘利，遺生行義，視死如歸。有如此者，國君不得而友，天子不得而臣。大者定天下，其次定一國，必由如此人者也。故人主之欲大立功名者，不可不務求此人也。賢主勞於求人，而佚於治事。

    Shi are those men who, when acting in accord with [proper] patterns, do not avoid difficulties; when facing troubles, forget about profit; they cast aside life to follow righteousness, and consider death as a homecoming. If there are such men, the ruler of a state will not be able to befriend them, the Son of Heaven will not be able to make them servants. At best, stabilization of All-under-Heaven, or, second to it, stabilization of a single state must come from these men. Hence a ruler who wants to greatly establish achievements and the name cannot but devote himself to searching for these men. A worthy sovereign works hard looking for [proper] men and rests maintaining affairs. (*Lüshi chunqiu* 12.2 ["Shi jie" 士節])

This passage is plain and unsophisticated, as are many similar ones scattered throughout the *Lüshi chunqiu*. First, it hails the high morality of the *shi*, who prefer righteousness to gains and even to life. Second, it hails their loftiness: the mere ruler of a state would be unable to befriend them and the Son of Heaven would fail to turn them into servants. Then the authors go to the most important part of their message: they advise the ruler to acquire the services of these lofty *shi* as the one necessary precondition for overall success. With these servants, the ruler will rest—presumably because the worthy aides will maintain affairs in his stead.

    Those of us who cherish the intellectuals' pride and self-esteem may be fond of *Lüshi chunqiu* and related pronouncements, but from the rulers' perspective the above passage epitomizes all that went wrong with the *shi* self-glorifying discourse. The authors provide no clue about how one may distinguish between worthy from unworthy *shi*. Eager to propagate their stratum as a whole, they create an impression that any *shi* (士之為人) may fulfil the lofty goal of stabilizing a state or even All-under-Heaven. Nor do the authors explain how this stabilization will be achieved. What we are left with is just unbearable haughtiness: the ruler's sole task should be to "devote himself to searching for these men," whose hallmark attitude is contempt to power holders. That such a hollow PR campaign aroused resentment not just among the rulers but also among some of the intellectuals comes as no surprise.

---

[21] See, for example, *Lüshi chunqiu* 8.5 ("Ai shi" 愛士); 9.3 ("Zhi shi" 知士); 12.2 ("Shi jie" 士節) *et saepe*. One of the chapters (12.3 ["Jie li" 介立]) plainly proclaims that the only reason why Lord Wen of Jin 晉文公 (r. 636–628 BCE) failed to become the True Monarch was the maltreatment of his devoted aide, Jie Zitui 介子推.

4   Xunzi Between the Ruler and the Elite

Xunzi was arguably the first of Confucius's major followers to realize the danger of unabashed pro-*shi* discourse. His unwavering commitment to the principle of monarchism (Pines 2009: 82–97) made him more averse to pro-*shi* hype than either Confucius or Mengzi. This being said, Xunzi's portrait as a thinker totally committed to the ruler's interest is misleading.[22] Xunzi's viewpoint remains that of a Confucian "noble man" rather than that of a ruler-oriented chief administrator; and his views of political order are decidedly influenced by the bottom-up perspective. Time and again Xunzi reiterates that staffing the government with morally cultivated "noble men" is an essential precondition for the state's and society's wellbeing—what matters is the quality of the employees rather than institutional (*fa* 法) solutions.[23] He argues that an intellectual in serving the ruler should prioritize the Way ("follow the Way, do not follow the ruler" 從道不從君 [*Xunzi* 13: 250 {"Chen dao" 臣道}]). He also pays utmost attention to elite opinion; actually, in *Xunzi* attaining a good "name" (meaning peer recognition) becomes a singularly important asset of the noble man, the compensation for his failure in fulfilling political aspirations (see *Xunzi* 8: 117–18 ["Ru xiao" 儒效], 4:61 ["Rong ru" 榮辱]; and more in Pines 2020: 179–82). On all these essential points, Xunzi appears as a determined follower of Confucius and Mengzi.

Nonetheless, Xunzi realized that Mengzi's pro-*shi* radicalism is a non-starter. Not incidentally, the only encounter between the Master and a ruler recorded in *Xunzi* starts with a provocative question by King Zhaoxiang of Qin 秦昭襄王 (r. 306–251 BCE), "Are Ru useless for the state?" 儒無益於人之國 (*Xunzi* 8:117 ["Ru xiao"]). In response, Xunzi dispenses with Mengzi's arrogance; instead, he politely emphasizes the Ru's usefulness to the ruler and society. This usefulness has clear practical dimensions: the Ru are hailed because they are able to "maintain ritual norms at the court; order laws, models, gauges, and measures among the officials; manifest loyalty, trustworthiness, care, and benefit among the inferiors" 禮節脩乎朝，法則度量正乎官，忠信愛利形乎下 (*Xunzi* 8: 120). This exchange between Xunzi and King Zhaoxiang is highly significant. The text's editors clearly want to distinguish Xunzi's deportment from Mengzi's habitual affronts to the rulers (Pines 2013b: 89–94). Besides, the emphasis on the Ru practical usefulness may be a conscious attempt to distinguish Confucians from the talkative and good for nothing *shi* such as those who contributed to *Lüshi chunqiu*.

---

[22] Xunzi's accusation as the one who "granted the ruler greatest and limitless power, allowing him to coerce Confucius's teaching so as to control the world" 荀子……授君主以莫大無限之權，使得挾持孔教以制天下 was made on the eve of China's entrance into the modern era by a radical reformer, Tan Sitong 譚嗣同 (1865–1898) (*Renxue* 29: 95 and 30: 99); it is echoed in not a few later studies (e.g., Jia Haitao 1997). For more nuanced analyses of *Xunzi*'s political philosophy, see Sato 2003; Harris 2016; Goldin 2020: 169–200.

[23] "Thus, it happens that having good *fa* still results in turmoil; but from antiquity until now, having a noble man and resulting in turmoil is unheard of" 故有良法而亂者，有之矣，有君子而亂者，自古及今，未嘗聞也 (*Xunzi* 9: 151 ["Wang zhi" 王制]; cf. 12: 230 ["Jun dao" 君道]).

This subtle differentiation of Confucians from the rest of *shi* and further differentiation of worthy from unworthy Confucians recur throughout the *Xunzi*. Xunzi qualifies his predecessors' comprehensive valorization of the term *shi*; instead, he tries to grade the men of service according to their mental and moral abilities. Xunzi distinguishes between "all-penetrating" *shi* 通士, *shi* committed to common good 公士, upright *shi* 直士, and honest *shi* 愨士; whereas their qualities are not identical, all are clearly distinguishable from "petty men" (*Xunzi* 3: 49–51 ["Bu gou" 不苟]). Elsewhere, Xunzi grades his ideological affiliates, the Ru, into "vulgar Ru" 俗儒, "refined Ru" 雅儒, and the truly capable "great Ru" 大儒; below all these he places the "vulgar men" 俗人 (*Xunzi* 8: 129–34 ["Ru xiao"]). Clearly, not every *shi* and not every Ru deserved automatic employment and the ruler's endorsement. Only the truly outstanding ones should ascend the top of the political ladder.

Xunzi dislikes much of contemporaneous pro-*shi* discourse. He notably avoids any mention of the ruler-minister friendship or of parity in the ruler-minister relations; whereas defying the ruler's orders is justifiable, adopting a condescending attitude toward the sovereign is not (Pines 2002: 68–71). Xunzi dismisses the lofty recluses as brazen hypocrites (*Xunzi* 6: 101 ["Fei shier zi" 非十二子]) and accuses them of "stealing a name" which is even worse than stealing property 盜名不如盜貨 (*Xunzi* 3: 52 ["Bu gou" 不苟]). He despises moral radicals, such as supporters of the abdication discourse, which was popular among some of pro-*shi* thinkers (*Xunzi* 18: 331–36 ["Zheng lun" 正論]; Pines 2005: 289–91). Xunzi is dismissive of glib talkers and useless sophistry. He derides proponents of "strange arguments" 怪說 and "bizarre words" 奇辭 (*Xunzi* 21: 408 ["Jie bi" 解蔽]). Elsewhere he cautions that sophistry may impact negatively sociopolitical order: these are "seditious words" 姦言 and "deviant theories" 邪說 that should be eradicated (*Xunzi* 22: 420–22 ["Zheng ming" 正名]; Fraser 2016: 294).

This latter point brings us to another important departure of Xunzi from earlier Confucians—namely the readiness to curb the intellectual autonomy of fellow *shi*. A whole chapter "Contra Twelve Masters" ("Fei shier zi") is dedicated to bitter polemics against deviant doctrines, which, despite their fallacy, employ sophisticated arguments that "suffice to deceive and confuse the stupid masses" 足以欺惑愚眾. Xunzi leaves no doubt that these deviant doctrines should be suppressed. But who will do it? Here Xunzi hesitates. On the one hand, he prefers to settle ideological cleavages among the intellectuals alone, much as Mengzi did when he attacked the heterodox doctrines of Mozi and Yang Zhu 楊朱 (*Mengzi* 6.9, 13.26, 14.26; Andreini 2014). But Xunzi is aware that coping with deviant ideologies cannot be done exclusively through polemics. Administrative means are needed. In the chapter "Efficacy of the Ru" ("Ru xiao"), one of the achievements of the noble man's government that he praises is that "Shen [Dao] and Mo[zi] cannot advance their talks; Hui Shi and Deng Xi dare not to smuggle in their investigations" 慎、墨不得進其談，惠施、鄧析不敢竄其察 (*Xunzi* 8: 123; trans. Hutton 2014: 56). Elsewhere Xunzi goes one step further and proposes that ideological cleansing should be performed not by the noble man but by the Sage Monarchs:

故勞力而不當民務，謂之姦事，勞知而不律先王，謂之姦心；辯說譬諭，齊給便
利，而不順禮義，謂之姦說。此三姦者，聖王之所禁也。

    Thus, to exert one's strength in a way that does not fit with the tasks of the people is called vile undertakings. To exert one's understanding in a way that does not match with the former kings is called a vile heart. When one's arguments, persuasions, and explanations are hasty, opportunistic, and not in conformity with ritual and propriety, this is called vile theories. These three vile matters are what the sage monarchs prohibited. (*Xunzi* 1992: 6: 98 ["Fei shier zi"]; translation modified from Hutton 2014: 43).

If so, prohibiting "vile speech" that does not conform to ritual and propriety is after all the task of power holders, is it not? Xunzi, however, remains cautious. This task should be legitimately performed only by the sage monarchs—exceptional human beings who combine the utmost political and moral authority (Pines 2009: 83–86). Unless a new sage monarch—that is, the future unifier of All-under-Heaven—appears, the realm of ideology should remain in the intellectuals' hands. Xunzi clarifies:

今聖王沒，天下亂，姦言起，君子無埶以臨之，無刑以禁之，故辨說也。

    Now, as the sage monarchs have passed away, All-under-Heaven is in turmoil, and vile speech is arising. A noble man has neither positional power to control it, nor punitive means to prohibit it, hence he uses argumentative persuasions [to confront it]. (*Xunzi* 22: 422 ["Zheng ming" 正名]; cf. Hutton 2014: 240)

Xunzi fluctuates between his commitment to the intellectuals' autonomy and the fear that this autonomy, if unchecked, will jeopardize sociopolitical order. His views are closer to those of *fa* thinkers than ideas expressed in the *Analects* and *Mengzi*. Xunzi evidently realized that the empowerment of the elite went too far, endangering the ruler-centered political order. But he never crossed the line into the pro-state and anti-elite camp. It was up to the *fa* thinkers to promote without any hesitation an alternative top-down vision of meritocracy and of intellectual order.

5   Shang Yang: Top-Down Meritocracy

In light of the above discussion, we may assert that promotion of the top-down meritocratic system was one of the greatest revolutions of the *fa* thinkers. Whereas the seeds of this model can be traced to the "father of China's meritocracy," Mozi,[24] it was only with Shang Yang's reforms that the new vision of meritocratic order crystallized fully. Recall that Shang Yang's major novelty was the replacement of the erstwhile aristocratic order with the new system of the ranks of merit. The ranks were granted for concrete achievements (most notably decapitation of enemy soldiers, but also high grain contribution). The new system, which granted rank holders a variety of economic, social, legal, and even sumptuary privileges, eventually encompassed

---

[24] Recall that Mozi was the first to promulgate "elevating the worthy" idea making it into one of the cornerstones of his political program. Mozi clearly envisioned a top-down process of selecting the worthy (see, e.g., *Mozi* 8: 67 ["Shang xian shang" 尚賢上]), but he did not put forward any mechanism of identifying and promoting the worthies.

much of Qin's society. It was arguably the world's boldest experiment not just in "social engineering" but also in imposing uniform, quantifiable, and transparent means of determining an individual's socioeconomic and political position.[25]

Shang Yang's system had manifold flaws, to be sure. Putting aside the moral problem of turning head-cutting into the major means of social advancement, one should acknowledge the system's other weaknesses. One was noted by Han Fei, who ridiculed the idea that good head-cutters will become adequate officials (*Han Feizi* 43.3.2; Chen Qiyou 2000: 962 ["Ding fen" 定分]). Another was the difficulty of introducing quantifiable standards for high grain yields on a par with head cutting. A further weakness was the system's long-term unsustainability: in due time Qin would inevitably run out of resources to reward each rank holder with land and slave allocations (Korolkov 2010: 99–138). But these flaws notwithstanding, one cannot ignore the boldness of Shang Yang's experiment. To the best of my knowledge nowhere in human history was a comparable attempt made to make the entire society into meritocratic and to base the meritocracy on purely impartial standards. Nor can we deny the experiment's immediate success. In particular, Shang Yang's reform not only curbed dramatically the power of Qin's aristocracy but even hindered the formation of a new powerful hereditary elite that could challenge the throne in the future. Insofar as ranks of merit were not fully inheritable, and insofar as granting the ranks (at least on the lower levels) was independent of the superiors' personal interference, the system inhibited the formation of a new self-perpetuating social elite.[26] This was a triumph (even if short-lived) of the principle of absolute impartiality.

Shang Yang's dislike of elite power was intrinsically related to his program of promoting fair, transparent, and universally applicable rules of promotion and demotion. A cohesive elite group endangered the system of the ranks of merit in a variety of ways. Think of an ostensibly minor issue such as the importance that Confucians attached to peer recognition. For Shang Yang, this was a direct threat to what should be one of the state's major assets—its monopoly on the subjects' renown. Recall that in the *Book of Lord Shang*, the ubiquitous quest for a "name" (*ming* 名) (referring both to reputation and enhanced social status) plays an equally important role with the quest for material benefits as a major lever that enables the state to maintain its program of social engineering (Pines, Chap. 1, Sect. 4, this volume):

名利之所湊，則民道之。……名出於戰，則民致死

---

[25] For details, see Pines 2016 and Chap. 1, Sect. 1, this volume, q.v. for further references.

[26] For the rules of appointing heirs as reflected in the early Han code from Tomb 247, Jiangling 江陵張家山 (Hubei), see Barbieri-Low and Yates 2015: 850–63. Note that in the Han code the reduction of the rank was dramatic for holders of ranks 10–18, but the holders of two upper ranks could bequeath the rank in full on their heir. It seems that the Han was predicated on maintaining a small hereditary aristocracy at the top of a broad meritocratic elite. Whether or not a similar idea was present already in Shang Yang's reform is currently unverifiable.

> Wherever the name and benefit meet, the people will go in this direction. ... When the name comes from war, the people are ready to die. (*Book of Lord Shang* 6.4–5; Zhang Jue 2012: 94–95 ["Suan di" 算地])

Insofar as a "name" is the major means through which the people can be turned into valiant soldiers, it is clear that it should be firmly controlled by the state. Privately gained reputation undermines the state's monopoly on "names" and erodes the efficiency of Shang Yang's system. Hence, the *Book of Lord Shang* reiterates: when "those who have privately established a name are deemed illustrious" (私名顯之), this is "a licentious way" (淫道). The text recommends the unification of "the gates of prominence and glory" (顯榮之門) and preventing anybody outside the state-mandate system of ranks to enter these gates. Those "who do not fight but attain glory, who have no rank but are respected" (不戰而榮，無爵而尊) are called "villains" (姦民) (*Book of Lord Shang* 22.1 ["Wai nei" 外內], 6.10 ["Suan di"], and 18.6 ["Hua ce" 畫策]; Zhang Jue 2012: 254, 103, 216). Glory, respect, renown—all should be inseparable from the ranks of merit bestowed by the state.

Intellectuals endangered Shang Yang's system not only because of their interference with the formation of one's "name," but, more directly, because their sociopolitical success undermined the exclusivity of the system of the ranks of merit. To be able to direct the population toward the "dangerous" and "bitter" tasks of fighting the enemy and tilling the soil, the leaders had to ensure that no alternative means of socioeconomic and political advancement existed. Appointments based on one's eloquence, morality, or forthrightness—namely the features most readily associated with the *shi*-oriented discourse outlined in Sects. 2 and 3 above—would corrode a system based on rewarding meritorious tillers and soldiers and annul its effectiveness. This explains the *Book of Lord Shang*'s immense dislike of the intellectuals' self-serving moralizing discourse, of their useless learning, and of their despicable glibness:

> 今夫螟螣蚼蠋春生秋死，一出而民數年乏食。今一人耕，而百人食之，此其為螟螣蚼蠋亦大矣。雖有詩書，鄉一束，家一員，獨無益於治也，非所以反之之術也。
>
> Now: various sorts of caterpillars are born in spring and die in autumn, but once they appear, the people lack food for several years. And now: when a single person tills, but one hundred are eating what he produces, it is much worse than all the caterpillars! Hence, even if in every rural canton there is a bundle of *Poems* and *Documents*, and in every household one scroll, it is still of no use for orderly rule. It is not the technique to reverse [poverty and danger]. (*Book of Lord Shang* 3.6; Zhang Jue 2012: 49 ["Nong zhan" 農戰])

Studies of the *Classic of Poems* and *Classic of Documents* are of no use for orderly rule; and worse, they distract the people from agriculture and warfare. Consequently, these studies—and intellectual pursuits as a whole—become as damaging as caterpillars. They foster the despicable social group of travelling persuaders—derisively designated in the *Book of Lord Shang* as "peripatetic eaters" (*youshizhe* 游食者)[27]—who vie for the ruler's patronage and bring about grave social and political consequences for the state. The chapter's author clarifies the point elsewhere:

---

[27] *Book of Lord Shang* 3.6, 3.10 ("Nong zhan" 農戰), 22.2 ("Wai nei"), 23.3 ("Jun chen" 君臣); Zhang Jue 2012: 49, 55, 255, 259.

今世主皆憂其國之危而兵之弱也，而強聽說者。說者成伍，煩言飾辭，而無實用。主好其辯，不求其實。說者得意，道路曲辯，輩輩成群。民見其可以取王公大人也，而皆學之。夫人聚黨與說議於國，紛紛焉。小民樂之，大人說之。故其民農者寡，而游食者眾；眾則農者怠，農者怠則土地荒。學者成俗，則民舍農，從事於談說，高言偽議，舍農游食，而以言相高也。故民離上而不臣者成群。此貧國弱兵之教也。

Nowadays all the rulers of our age are worried that their states are endangered and their soldiers are weak, so they strive to heed persuaders. Persuaders form legions; they multiply words and adorn sayings but are of no real use. The sovereign is fond of their arguments and does not seek their substance. The persuaders are satisfied; the roads are full of skillful talkers, and from generation to generation they go on and multiply. The people see that this is the way to reach kings, lords, and grandees, and all learn from them. They form cliques and associations, debate state affairs, and come in profusion. Lower people are fond of them; grandees like them. Therefore, among the people few are engaged in agriculture, whereas "peripatetic eaters" are plenty; as they are plenty, the farmers are indolent; as the farmers are indolent, the land becomes wasteland.

If learning becomes habitual, the people turn their backs on farming: they follow talkers and persuaders, speak grand words, and [engage in] false debates. They turn their backs on farming and travel to get food, trying to exceed each other in words. Hence, the people abandon their superiors, and those who do not behave as subjects become more and more numerous. This is the teaching that impoverishes the state and weakens the army. (*Book of Lord Shang* 3.10; Zhang Jue 2012: 55 ["Nong zhan" 農戰])

The damage of peripatetic persuaders is twofold. First, and most significant, is social damage—distracting the people from agriculture and warfare by outlining alternative routes of enhancing one's sociopolitical and economic status. Second, talkative intellectuals exercise a corrosive impact on political mores. The very attractiveness of their careers and the ease with which they receive patronage cause the people to "abandon their superiors." The problem is not necessarily the subversive content of the persuaders' "false debates" but rather their intrinsic unruliness. As the author of another chapter clarifies, unlike the peasants, who are easily controllable, intellectuals (as well as artisans, merchants, and peddlers) are prone to escape the state's control: "For them, All-under-Heaven is just one home, and they move across it with their bodies as their capital. ... they can empower themselves anywhere abroad; carrying their accumulated capital, they flock to any place as if to their home" (故天下一宅，而圓身資民。……偏託勢於外，挾重資，歸偏家; *Book of Lord Shang* 6.6; Zhang Jue 2012: 97 ["Suan di"]). It is this ease with which they escape control rather than the intellectuals' critical mindset that makes this stratum as a whole politically and not just socially unwelcome.

Anti-intellectuals' tirades in the *Book of Lord Shang* focus primarily on their corrosive influence on the system of ranks of merit and more broadly on the state-society relations. By contrast, their role in the top echelons of the government is rarely addressed. Only once do we encounter the author's dissatisfaction with the common discourse of "elevating the worthy," prone as it is to political manipulations:

夫舉賢能，世之所以治也；而治之所以亂。世之所謂賢者，言正也；所以為言正者，黨也。聽其言，則以為能；問其黨，以為然。故貴之，不待其有功；誅之，不待其有罪也。

Elevation of the worthy and the able is what the world considers orderly rule: that is why orderly rule is in turmoil. What the world calls a "worthy" is one who is defined as upright;

but those who define him as good and upright are his clique. When you hear his words, you consider him able; when you ask his associates, they approve it. Hence, one is ennobled before one has any merits; one is punished before one has committed a crime. (*Book of Lord Shang* 25.1; Zhang Jue 2012: 271; ["Shen fa" 慎法])

This short statement is unusually perceptive. It is almost tempting to say that it anticipates our age in which mass media has become the major determinant of one's worth or one's guilt. The author identifies the problem of PR campaigns in which the appointee's ability and worth are determined by his reputation, which, in turn, is manufactured by his partisans (a "clique," *dang* 黨). The result is proliferation of fake worthies. In due time, this point was to be addressed with greater clarity by Han Fei, who had further strengthened the top-down meritocracy model.

6 Han Fei: Combatting Subversive Discourse

Han Fei accepted the essentials of Shang Yang's meritocratic system, but he shifted the focus from the system's broad aspects (how to direct the entire population to agriculture and warfare) to its narrower aspects, to wit, staffing the upper echelons of bureaucracy. This point had not been systematically addressed in the *Book of Lord Shang*; and it is here, as Han Fei duly noted, that Shang Yang's system blundered. Thus, after Shang Yang's death, even though Qin armies remained victorious, it was Qin's selfish ministers who benefitted at the expense of the ruler and the state (*Han Feizi* 43.2.3; Chen Qiyou 2000: 959 ["Ding fen"]).

This hijacking of the state's interests by its ministers was not an accident. As Han Fei reminds his audience repeatedly, an absolute majority of ministers are self-interested petty men. The reliance on "noble men" in staffing the government apparatus is a dangerous delusion: "Today, there are no more than ten honest and trustworthy men of service, but there are hundreds of offices within the boundaries. If you insist on exclusively appointing honest and trustworthy men of service, then there will be not enough people for the official positions 今貞信之士不盈於十，而境內之官以百數，必任貞信之士，則人不足官 (*Han Feizi* 49.11; Chen Qiyou 2000: 1109 ["Wu du" 五蠹]). The Confucian solution simply does not work. A bottom-up system will result in the proliferation of fake noble man who will subvert the state's and the ruler's interests. And the real danger is their impact on the ruler himself:

人主有二患：任賢，則臣將乘於賢以劫其君；妄舉，則事沮不勝。故人主好賢，則群臣飾行以要君欲，則是群臣之情不效；群臣之情不效，則人主無以異其臣矣。

The sovereign has two worries: when he appoints the worthy, ministers will utilize "worthiness" in order to rob [the state] from their ruler; when he makes wanton promotions, undertakings will be irreparably destroyed. Thus, when a ruler is fond of the worthy, multiple ministers adorn their actions to satisfy the ruler's expectations; hence, the real situation of the ministers cannot be verified. When the real situation of the ministers cannot be verified, the ruler cannot distinguish between [qualified and unqualified] ministers. (*Han Feizi* 7.3; Chen Qiyou 2000: 130; ["Er bing" 二柄])

Han Fei does not attack here the meritocratic principle as such—this principle is reasserted repeatedly throughout the text[28]—but rather the ruler's succumbing to meritocratic discourse which can be manipulated by scheming ministers to advance their sinister goals. This manipulation is performed on two levels. First, the proliferation of Confucian discourse prioritizing morally upright intellectuals results in the advancement of useless and talkative individuals at the expense of tillers and fighters who really contribute to the state.[29] The latter observation was made in the *Book of Lord Shang*, whose ideas *Han Feizi* borrows (e.g., *Han Feizi* 49.10 ["Wu du"] and 50.4 ["Xian xue"]; Chen Qiyou 2000: 1105 and 1135). But the problem is much deeper than the existence of superfluous upward routes open to intellectuals. What threatens the political order even more is the intellectual autonomy of the elite. This autonomy results in proliferation of values that benefit selfish intellectuals rather than rulers. The moralizers' hijacking of political discourse is a major source of concern for Han Fei.

Several chapters of *Han Feizi* (especially 46–51) are focused on polemics with moralizers who try to impose their agenda on rulers and subjugate the state to their selfish interests. Page after page, the author discloses his opponents' tricks and demonstrates the fallacy of their premises. Take, for instance, manipulative designations of lofty men of service:

以公財分施謂之 "仁人" …… 輕祿重身謂之 "君子" ……

Taking common (or ruler's) resources and doling them out is called "being a benevolent person"... regarding emoluments unimportant and one's own person as important is called "being a noble man." (*Han Feizi* 47.1; Chen Qiyou 2000: 1023; ["Ba shuo" 八說])

遊居厚養，牟食之民也，而世尊之曰 "有能之士"。語曲牟知，偽詐之民也，而世尊之曰 "辯智之士" ……

Those who are always on the move and get lavishly patronized are the kinds of people who always look for a free meal, but our generation honors them and names them "capable men of service." Those whose speech is all twisted and who pretend to knowledge are fraudulent and deceitful people, but our generation honors them and names them "argumentative and intelligent men of service." (*Han Feizi* 46.1; Chen Qiyou 1000 ["Liu fan" 六反]).

The exalted designations serve to promote selfish men who do not benefit the state. Alternatively, those who serve the state faithfully are maligned. Han Fei calls this situation "six contrarieties" 六反 (*Han Feizi* 46.1; Chen Qiyou 2000: 1000; ["Liu fan"]) and summarizes elsewhere:

匹夫有私便，人主有公利。不作而養足，不仕而名顯，此私便也；息文學而明法度，塞私便而一功勞，此公利也。

---

[28] See, e.g., Chap. 46, "Six Contrarieties" ("Liu fan" 六反), which advocates the importance of impartial promotion of the able (*neng* 能) as the means to ensure the success of the system of ranks of merit, which in turn will encourage the "men of service and the people" 士民 to commit themselves to the ruler (*Han Feizi* 46.4; Chen Qiyou 2000: 1006).

[29] Note that Confucians themselves were fully aware of the danger that their lofty values will be hijacked by unscrupulous individuals. Distinguishing between true and fake "noble men" is among the crucial issues in Confucian thought (see, e.g., Richter 2017). The problem was that the Confucian "bottom-up" model did not provide an adequate means of screening out fake worthies.

Ordinary men have their private interests, whereas the sovereign is concerned with common benefit. Not to work but to have enough to sustain oneself, not to serve but to have one's name illustrious—these are private interests. Stopping textual studies and publishing the laws and measures, blocking private interests and unifying merit and toil [on agriculture and warfare]—that is the common benefit. (*Han Feizi* 47.3; Chen Qiyou 2000: 1027 ["Ba shuo"])

Adherents of "textual studies" are determined to avoid bitter toil or government service and yet enjoy material and social benefits. To advance this selfish goal, they create a favorable reputation for their peers as an alternative to the state-sponsored system of the ranks of merit. This amounts to the formation of a parallel hierarchy of values, which, as Han Fei is quick to observe, erodes the foundations of the sociopolitical order:

民之重名與其重賞也均。賞者有誹焉，不足以勸；罰者有譽焉，不足以禁。……明主之道，賞必出乎公利，名必在乎為上。

The people attach the same importance to reputation and rewards. If some of those who are rewarded are also blamed, then [the rewards] will not suffice to encourage them; if some of those who are punished are also praised, then [the punishments] will not suffice to prohibit [transgressions]. ... The Way of the clear-sighted sovereign is such that rewards inevitably derive from benefitting the common interest, and reputation inevitably comes from acting in behalf of superiors. (*Han Feizi* 48.7; Chen Qiyou 2000: 1079 ["Ba jing" 八經])

That the intellectuals trick the ruler to respect them even though their practical value to the state is minuscule is bad enough. Yet aside from the influx of useless individuals to bureaucracy, the problem with their discourse is deeper. This discourse lauds forthright ministers, denigrates the rulers, and hails lofty *shi*, who, like Mengzi's Great Man, "depart from the masses and practice [their ideas] alone" 離眾獨行 (*Han Feizi* 51.5; Chen Qiyou 2000: 1154 ["Zhong xiao" 忠孝]). This discourse, designed as it is to acquire peer recognition for moral radicals, undermines the ruler's (common) interests. Hence it must be outlawed. "Stopping textual studies" and "blocking private interests" are the only ways to ensure "common benefits" (see the citation on p. 535 above and more in Pines, Chap. 4, Sect. 4, this volume).

Aside from the intellectuals' subversive discourse, Han Fei identifies a second, equally dangerous problem posed by the bottom-up meritocratic system. This is the problem of empowering ministers, especially the notorious political heavyweights (*zhongren* 重人), the influential members of the ruler's entourage. Those heavyweights will block any worthy individual who, against all the odds, remains committed to the rulers' interests and wants to serve the sovereign. This blockage is clarified in Chap. 11, "Solitary Outrage" ("Gu fen" 孤憤):

人主之左右不必智也，人主於人有所智而聽之，因與左右論其言，是與愚人論智也。人主之左右不必賢也，人主於人有所賢而禮之，因與左右論其行，是與不肖論賢也。

Those in the entourage of a ruler are not necessarily wise; if the ruler considers somebody wise and listens to him, and then discusses this man's proposals with his entourage, this is to discuss wisdom with the foolish. Those in the ruler's entourage are not necessarily worthy; if the ruler considers somebody worthy and treats him with ritual propriety, and then discusses this man's behavior with his entourage, this is to discuss worth with the unworthy. (*Han Feizi* 11.5; Chen Qiyou 2000: 248)

Han Fei's frustration with his failed career made him understand the mechanism of mediocracy which exists beneath the veneer of meritocracy. Whenever the system allows elite members to select their peers, the results will be gloomy. A brilliant newcomer will be blocked; instead, political heavyweights will staff the court with their cronies. This, as Han Fei warns, will be the first step toward the planned usurpation. To avoid the trap, the ruler should liberate himself twice—from the preeminent morality-oriented meritocratic discourse promoted by selfish intellectuals, and from the dominance of his own entourage. The solution, expectedly, is turning to Han Fei's panacea—impartial standards.

> 明主之國，有貴臣，無重臣。貴臣者，爵尊而官大也；重臣者，言聽而力多者也。明主之國，遷官襲級，官爵受功，故有貴臣。言不度行而有偽，必誅，故無重臣也。
>
> The state of a clear-sighted sovereign has noble ministers, but not heavyweight ministers. Noble ministers hold a distinguished rank and high office; heavyweight ministers are those whose proposals are heard and power is great. In the state of a clear-sighted sovereign, promotion in office proceeds step by step, office and rank are in accordance with merit, and therefore there are noble ministers. When proposals are not measured by deeds and pretense reigns, then the person concerned is bound to be punished. That is why there are no heavyweight ministers. (*Han Feizi* 47.12; Chen Qiyou 2000: 1044)

To avoid being duped, the ruler should promote the able exclusively in accord with strict and uniform rules based not on verifying their morality but rather on assessing their performance. "Judge them according to their tasks, check them according to their performance, assess them according to their merits." 論之於任，試之於事，課之於功 (*Han Feizi* 38.8.4.2; Chen Qiyou 2000: 908 ["Nan san" 難三]). This will eliminate the personal input from the entourage members and create fair play, which will eventually put the state apparatus as a whole in order. Elsewhere, Han Fei reiterates that promotions should be based neither on one's eloquence, nor on reputation, nor on the immediate impression one makes on the ruler; after all, even such a knowledgeable person as Confucius could not avoid mistakes when making subjective judgments. The solution is, again, reliance on impartial norms:

> 故明主之吏，宰相必起於州部，猛將必發於卒伍。夫有功者必賞，則爵祿厚而愈勸；遷官襲級，則官職大而愈治。夫爵祿大而官職治，王之道也。
>
> Thus, as for the officials of an enlightened ruler: chief ministers and chancellors must rise from among local officials; valiant generals must rise from among the ranks. One who has merit must be rewarded—then ranks and emoluments are bountiful and they are ever more encouraging. One who is promoted and ascends to higher positions, his official responsibilities increase, and he performs his tasks ever more orderly. When ranks and emoluments are great and official tasks are well ordered, this is the Way of the [True] Monarch. (*Han Feizi* 50.5; Chen Qiyou 2000: 1137 ["Xian xue"])

Han Fei proposes a meritocratic system that would not depend on the vague notion of "worthiness" but will function according to objective criteria of merit. Administrative and military officials will be promoted from the lower ranks of the bureaucracy and the army; they will be judged according to their performance, and, if successful, given ever more important offices. While the system is far from perfect (it does not explain how the people will join the administrative apparatus in the first place), it is much more sophisticated than anything proposed in other Warring

States-period texts. It bears clear resemblance to the rules of promotion in such modern meritocratic systems as the army or academia. And it is the system most readily associated with the current state of affairs in the People's Republic of China, even though the fairness of its implementation is questioned by many.[30]

Han Fei's top-down meritocratic system run by the ruler according to impartial standards deals with inadequacies of Shang Yang's model and solves the inherent weaknesses of the Confucian bottom-up alternative. It was surely a major step toward making meritocracy viable. But Han Fei's model is also far from perfect. In the final section, I want to summarize the pluses and minuses of the competing systems and argue that each had clear advantages and equally clear disadvantages. The cleavage between two models stands behind the Confucian-*fa* controversy that persisted throughout the imperial millennia.

7 Epilogue: Two Meritocratic Models Compared

The essay "On the Essentials of the Six Schools of Thought" 六家之要指, by Sima Tan 司馬談 (d. 110 BCE), starts with the following assertion:

> 易大傳:「天下一致而百慮，同歸而殊涂。」夫陰陽、儒、墨、名、法、道德，此務為治者也，直所從言之異路，有省不省耳。
>
> According to the "Great Commentary" to the *Book of Changes*, "All-under-Heaven shares one thought, but [uses] a hundred deliberations; they return to the same [destination], but use different paths." As for *yin-yang*, Ru, Mo[hist], nominalist, *fa*, and the Way and its Virtue [schools]—all are committed to orderly rule. It is just that the words they follow advance along different routes; some are more perceptive and some are not; that is all. (*Shiji* 130: 3289; cf. translation in de Bary and Bloom 1999: 279)

Sima Tan's conclusion—that, divergences aside, all the competing schools of thought pursued the common goal of orderly rule—is, overall, convincing. It surely fits both the Confucians and the "*fa* school." Both sought political stability; both agreed on fundamental principles of the ideal regime (universal, meritocratic, and paternalistic monarchy). Their differences about the proper mode of the elite-state relations and about the proper model of meritocracy exemplify "different paths" that should have led to the same destination insofar as political goals were concerned.

The advantages of the Confucian bottom-up model are clear. This model was predicated on forming a proud and self-confident elite that would comprise cultivated, moral, and intelligent "noble men." The noble men would serve the ruler out of commitment to the common good; they would be loyal but not subservient; and they would exercise a positive moral impact on the ruler above and the populace

---

[30] Han Fei's statement above was approvingly cited by China's president, Xi Jinping (during an interview on March 19, 2013) as reflecting the mechanism of selecting officials in current China. Xi gave an example of his own ascendancy from the Party secretary in a rural production brigade, through "county, municipal [i.e. prefecture-level], provincial and central levels" (Xi 2018: 457). For more about China's current meritocratic system, see Bell 2015. The flaws of China's current employment system and its achievements are beyond the scope of current discussion.

below. Even a partial fulfillment of these noble goals cannot but be lauded today as in the past.

The problem with these noble goals was the difficulty of realizing them. First, it was difficult to prevent the self-selecting elite from gradual ossification. Second, insofar as morality was the major criterion for joining the elite, it was impossible to prevent fake noble men from using moralizing discourse to disguise their selfishness and covetousness. And third, a powerful elite whose members often adopted a condescending attitude toward the rulers endangered the ruler-centered political order to which everybody—including Confucians—was committed. As we have seen, Xunzi was already aware of these problems (and seeds of understanding are clearly present in a variety of other Confucian texts, including the *Analects* and *Mengzi*), but the hopes for the elite's self-policing simply could not work well.

The *fa* thinkers' top-down model based on impartial standards of promotion and demotion had clear advantages in terms of enhancing fairness and transparency of competition, broadening the elite's base, and limiting the potential for mediocracy and cronyism at the top. However, these solutions created a new set of problems. First, establishing commonly accepted and easily quantifiable criteria for promotion and demotion was a daunting task. Whereas Shang Yang's use of head cutting as the primary means to get the ranks of merit was indeed fair and transparent, its inadequacy for staffing bureaucracy was espoused fully by Han Fei (not to speak of its dubious moral nature). Han Fei's solution—to evaluate the performance of low-level officials and determine their career accordingly—fit the bureaucracy's needs better, but still left many questions unanswered. Given the multiplicity of tasks facing a magistrate, the creation of uniform rules of performance evaluation was not easy (for some rudimentary attempts, see Korolkov, Chap. 7, this volume). This problem hinders the applicability of impartial standards in governance well into present.[31]

The second problem was that the top-down model of meritocracy required an adequate ruler at the top—one astute enough to assess the officials' performance, perspicacious enough to avoid being duped by his underlings, self-confident enough to withstand the power of elite public opinion, and disciplined enough to prevent his personal sentiments from interfering in promotions and demotions at the expense of impartial standards. As Han Fei himself would readily admit, such expectations of a ruler were unrealistic (cf. Pines, Chap. 4, and Lewis, Chap. 11, this volume). In this respect, the Confucian bottom-up model, in which the locus of gravity shifted toward cultivated elite members with proven intellectual abilities, appears more implementable.

The third flaw of the *fa* model of meritocracy was its tendency to advance obedient servants at the expense of outstanding individuals. Whereas Han Fei clearly envisioned the top tier staffed by intelligent and dynamic ministers (as embedded in his "performance and titles" principle [Goldin 2020: 214; Pines, Chap. 4, Sect. 3.2, this volume]), he paid little attention to the fact that the system he promoted would

---

[31] For advantages and difficulties of performance evaluation in current China, cf. Burns and Zhou 2010; Jing et al. 2015; Wu and Chang 2020; Wu Bin 2020.

not foster such ministers in the first place. Low to midlevel functionaries in the system ruled by impartial standards had primarily to fulfill the tasks imposed on them from above, rather than think independently and creatively. Ironically, neither Shang Yang nor Han Fei would succeed much personally in the system that required step by step advancement and discouraged any deviation from existing norms. This weakness was well grasped by Xunzi, who explained the advantage of the Confucian emphasis on "noble men" in government:

故法而不議，則法之所不至者必廢。職而不通，則職之所不及者必隊。故法而議，職而通，無隱謀，無遺善，而百事無過，非君子莫能。

    Thus, one who follows *fa* (models, laws, standards) without debating [their content], is bound to fail once he encounters [a problem] that the *fa* does not reach. One who holds a position but does not penetrate [its underlying tasks], is bound to blunder once he encounters [matters] that the position does not cover. Therefore, to have *fa* and yet to debate it, to have a position and yet to penetrate [its tasks], to have no secret plotting, to leave nobody's goodness behind, to never err in a hundred undertakings—nobody but the noble man is able to do it. (*Xunzi* 9: 151, cf. Hutton 2014: 69 ["Wang zhi" 王制])

We can understand now the predicament of *fa* thinkers. Their contempt of fake noble men and self-serving intellectuals was understandable; but their proposed alternative of a totally depersonalized civil service was equally a dead end. The Confucian system could be easily abused (and was abused through much of Chinese history), but it also allowed outstanding individuals to contribute from time to time to the empire's success (cf. Van Norden 2013). The *fa* thinkers' idea of depersonalizing the civil service was detrimental to the emergence of such individuals. In addition, their hatred of partisanship left the *fa* thinkers devoid of supporters from below. The success of their program ultimately relied on its endorsement by the ruler, allying with whom was intrinsically precarious (Song, Chap. 9, this volume). In the long term, complete depersonalization of the civil service was not possible. Impartiality could not overcome partisanship.

    One final observation may suggest how the Confucian-*fa* debates retain their current relevance. To avoid sensitive political issues, let us exemplify this relevance from the angle of promotion procedures in academic institutions. The "Confucian" bottom-up promotion would mean that the candidate is selected by the member of her/his prospective department, i.e., persons with deep knowledge of the field. Presumably they can select the best candidate. And yet, as is well known, the system may well give rise to mediocracy and cronyism. The candidate will focus on flattering the senior colleagues; and a brilliant outsider will be vetoed by mediocre professors fearful of competition with a more promising colleague. Besides, there is a danger of inbreeding, in which only the former students of senior colleagues have a chance of being appointed.

    A *fa* system of top-down appointments would give the final say to an outsider (e.g., the Provost). It would favor objective criteria (the number of publications, students' surveys, and the like). Ideally, under such a system there would be no need even for personal interviews—the quality of any candidate will be easily observable even for an outsider of the field (the Provost). The system will be much fairer, but, as is again well known, it may result in mistaken appointments. For instance, the quantity of publications does not necessarily match their quality (which, despite the usage of citation indices, can often be judged only by the field's insiders). An emphasis on objective criteria may result in paying little attention to the candidate's mental characteristics, which are often no less important than pure academic brilliance for an appointee's success. And many colleagues will be frustrated once a new appointee is imposed on them by the Provost, whose understanding of the field is often minuscule.

The search for hybrid models and creative solution continues in many academic institutions. The same search continued throughout China's long history and is still ongoing. Learning from the solutions proposed by Confucians and *fa* adherents, from their advantages and pitfalls, and from the debates between the two currents may be relevant not just for understanding the complex pattern of China's meritocratic experiments but also for considering the strengths and weaknesses of meritocracy worldwide.

References

Andreini, Attilio. 2014. The Yang Mo 楊墨 Dualism and the Rhetorical Construction of Heterodoxy. *Asiatische Studien–Études Asiatiques* 68 (4): 1115–1174.

Barbieri-Low, Anthony J., and Robin D.S. Yates. 2015. *Law, State, and Society in Early Imperial China: A Study with Critical Edition and Translation of the Legal Texts from Zhangjiashan Tomb No. 247*. Leiden: Brill.

de Bary, Wm. Theodore, and Irene Bloom. 1999. *Sources of Chinese Tradition*. New York: Columbia University Press.

Bell, Daniel. 2015. *The China Model: Political Meritocracy and the Limits of Democracy*. Princeton: Princeton University Press.

Bell, Daniel, and Li, Chenyang, eds. 2013. *The East Asian Challenge for Democracy: Political Meritocracy in Comparative Perspective*. Cambridge: Cambridge University Press.

Berkowitz, Alan. 2000. *Patterns of Disengagement: The Practice and Portrayal of Reclusion in Early Medieval China*. Stanford: Stanford University Press.

Book of Lord Shang. See Pines 2017.

Burns, John P., and Zhou, Zhiren. 2010. Performance Management in the Government of the People's Republic of China: Accountability and Control in the Implementation of Public Policy. *OECD Journal on Budgeting* 2: 1–28.

Chen, Qiyou 陳奇猷 (1917–2006). 2000. *Han Feizi, Newly Collated and Annotated* 韓非子新校注. Shanghai: Shanghai guji chubanshe.

Cook, Scott. 2012. *The Bamboo Texts of Guodian: A Study and Complete Translation*. Vol. 1–2. Ithaca, NY: Cornell University East Asia Program.

Fraser, Chris. 2016. Language and Logic in the *Xunzi*. In *Dao Companion to the Philosophy of Xunzi*, ed. Eric L. Hutton, 291–321. Dordrecht: Springer.

Gassmann, Robert H. 2007. Die Bezeichnung *jun-zi*: Ansätze zur Chun-qiu-zeitlichen Kontextualisierung und zur Bedeutungsbestimmung im *Lun Yu*. In *Zurück zur Freude: Studien zur chinesischen Literatur und Lebenswelt und ihrer Rezeption in Ost und West: Festschrift für Wolfgang Kubin*, ed. Marc Hermann and Christian Schwermann, 411–436. Sankt Augustin: Institut Monumenta Serica.

Goldin, Paul R. 2020. *The Art of Chinese Philosophy: Eight Classical Texts and How to Read Them*. Princeton NJ: Princeton University Press.

————. 2022. Pre-Qin and Han Philosophical and Historical Prose: Self-Interest, Manipulation, and the Philosophical Marketplace. In *How to Read Chinese Prose: A Guided Anthology*, ed. Cai Zong-qi, 112–125. New York: Columbia University Press.

Graziani, Romain. 2015. Monarch and Minister: The Problematic Partnership in the Building of Absolute Monarchy in the *Han Feizi* 韓非子. In *Ideology of Power and Power of Ideology in Early China*, ed. Yuri Pines, Paul R. Goldin, and Martin Kern, 155–180. Leiden: Brill.

Harbsmeier, Christoph, trans. Forthcoming. *Han Feizi, A Complete Translation: The Art of Statecraft in Early China*. ed. Jens Østergaard Petersen and Yuri Pines. Leiden: Brill.

Harris, Eirik Lang. 2016. Xunzi's Political Philosophy. In *Dao Companion to the Philosophy of Xunzi*, ed. Eric L. Hutton, 67–94. Dordrecht: Springer.

————. 2020. A Han Feizian Worry with Confucian Meritocracy—And a Non-Moral Alternative. *Culture and Dialogue* 8 (2): 342–362.

Heguanzi jiaozhu 鶡冠子校注 (*Heguanzi*, collated and annotated). 2004. ed. Huang, Huaixin 黃懷信. Beijing: Zhonghua shuju.

Hutton, Eric L., and trans. 2014. *Xunzi: The Complete Text*. Princeton NJ: Princeton University Press.

Jia, Haitao 賈海濤. 1997. "My Brief Analysis of Xunzi's Arguments that Rationalized the System of the Ruler's Dictatorship" 簡析荀子對君主獨裁專制政治"合理性"的論證. *Journal of Fuyang Normal University (Social Sciences)* 阜陽師院學報(社科版) 2: 19–24.

Jing, Yijia, Yangyang Cui, and Danyao Li. 2015. The Politics of Performance Measurement in China. *Policy and Society* 34 (1): 49–61.

Knoblock, John, and Jeffrey Riegel, trans. 2000. *The Annals of Lü Buwei*. Stanford: Stanford University Press.

Kominami, Ichirō 小南一郎. 1992. "Heaven's Mandate and Virtue" 天命と德. *Journal of Oriental Studies* 東方學報 64: 1–59.

Korolkov, Maxim [Корольков, Максим В.]. 2010. "Земельное законодательство и контроль над землей в эпоху Чжаньго и в начале раннеимперской эпохи (по данным обнаруженных законодательных текстов" [Land Law and Land Control in the Zhanguo Era and Early Imperial Era (According to Discovered Legalist Texts)]. Ph.D. thesis. Russian Academy of Sciences, Institute of Oriental Studies.

Kryukov, Vassili. 1995. Symbols of Power and Communication in Pre-Confucian China (On the Anthropology of *De*). *Bulletin of the School of Oriental and African Studies* 58: 314–333.

Lau, Dim-cheuk. 1970. *Mencius*. Harmondsworth: Penguin.

Lewis, Mark E. 1999. Warring States: Political History. In *The Cambridge History of Ancient China: From the Origins of Civilization to 221 B.C*, ed. Michael Loewe and Edward L. Shaughnessy, 587–650. Cambridge: Cambridge University Press.

Liu, Zehua 劉澤華. 1991. *Traditional Chinese Political Thinking* 中國傳統政治思維. Changchun: Jilin jiaoyu chubanshe.

———— 劉澤華, ed. 1996. *History of Chinese Political Thought* 中國政治思想史. 3 vols. Hangzhou: Zhejiang renmin chubanshe.

———— 劉澤華. 2000. *China's Monarchism* 中國的王權主義. Shanghai: Renmin chubanshe.

———— 劉澤華. 2004. *Shi and Society before the Qin* 先秦士人與社會. Tianjin: Tianjin renmin chubanshe, rev. ed.

Lunyu yizhu 論語譯注 (*Analects*, translated and annotated). 1992. Ed. Yang, Bojun 楊伯峻. Beijing: Zhonghua shuju.

Lüshi chunqiu jiaoshi 呂氏春秋校釋 (*Lüshi chunqiu*, collated with explanations). 1995. Ed. Chen, Qiyou 陳奇猷. Shanghai: Xuelin.

Makeham, John. 1993. The *Analects* and Reputation: A Note on *Analects* 15.18 and 15.19. *Bulletin of the School of Oriental and African Studies* 56 (3): 582–586.

Martynov, Aleksandr S. [Мартынов, Александр С.] 1998. "Категория дэ – синтез «порядка» и «жизни»" [The Category *de*: Synthesis of "Order" and "Life"]. In *От Магической силы к моральному императиву: категория дэ в китайской культуре*, ed. L.N. Borokh (Л. Н. Борох) and A.I. Kobzev (А. И. Кобзев), 36–75. Moscow: Izdatel'skaia firma 'Vostochnaia Literatura' RAN.

Mawangdui Han mu boshu Huang Di shu *jianzheng* 馬王堆漢墓帛書《黃帝書》箋證 (*The Book of the Yellow Thearch, a Silk Text from a Han Tomb at Mawangdui, with Commentary*). 2004. ed. Wei, Qipeng 魏啓鵬. Beijing: Zhonghua shuju.

Mengzi yizhu 孟子譯注 (*Mengzi*, translated and annotated). 1992. ed. Yang, Bojun 楊伯峻. Beijing: Zhonghua shuju.

Mozi jiaozhu 墨子校注 (*Mozi*, collated and annotated). 1994. ed. Wu, Yujiang 吳毓江 (1898–1977). Beijing: Zhonghua shuju.

Nivison, David S. 1996. 'Virtue' in Bone and Bronze. In David S. Nivison, *The Ways of Confucianism*, ed. Brian Van Norden, 17–30. Chicago/La Salle: Open Court.

Nylan, Michael. 1999. A Problematic Model: The Han 'Orthodox Synthesis' Then and Now. In *Imagining Boundaries: Changing Confucian Doctrines, Texts and Hermeneutics*, ed. Kai-Wing Chow, On-cho Ng, and John B. Henderson, 17–56. Albany: State University of New York Press.

Pines, Yuri. 2002. Friends or Foes: Changing Concepts of Ruler-Minister Relations and the Notion of Loyalty in Pre-Imperial China. *Monumenta Serica* 50: 35–74.

———. 2005. Disputers of Abdication: Zhanguo Egalitarianism and the Sovereign's Power. *T'oung Pao* 91 (4–5): 243–300.

———. 2009. *Envisioning Eternal Empire: Chinese Political Thought of the Warring States Era*. Honolulu: University of Hawai'i Press.

———. 2013a. Between Merit and Pedigree: Evolution of the Concept of 'Elevating the Worthy' in Pre-imperial China. In *The Idea of Political Meritocracy: Confucian Politics in Contemporary Context*, ed. Daniel Bell and Li Chenyang, 161–202. Cambridge: Cambridge University Press.

———. 2013b. From Teachers to Subjects: Ministers Speaking to the Rulers from Yan Ying 晏嬰 to Li Si 李斯. In *Facing the Monarch: Modes of Advice in the Early Chinese Court*, ed. Garret Olberding, 69–99. Cambridge, MA: Harvard University Asia Center.

———. 2016. Social Engineering in Early China: The Ideology of the *Shangjunshu* (*Book of Lord Shang*) Revisited. *Oriens Extremus* 55: 1–37.

———, trans. and ed. 2017a. *The Book of Lord Shang: Apologetics of State Power in Early China*. New York: Columbia University Press.

———. 2017b. Confucius's Elitism: The Concepts of *junzi* and *xiaoren* Revisited. In *A Concise Companion to Confucius*, ed. Paul R. Goldin, 164–184. Newark: Wiley Blackwell.

———. 2018. Irony, Political Philosophy, and Historiography: Cai Ze's Anecdote in *Zhanguo ce* Revisited. *Studia Orientalia Slovaca* 17 (2): 87–113.

———. 2020. 'To Die for the Sanctity of the Name': Name (*ming* 名) as Prime-mover of Political Action in Early China. In *Keywords in Chinese Culture*, ed. Li Wai-yee and Yuri Pines, 169–218. Hong Kong: The Chinese University Press.

———. 2023. Mencius and Early Chinese Political Thought. In *Dao Companion to the Philosophy of Mencius*, ed. Yang Xiao and Kim-chong Chong, 259–280. Dordrecht: Springer.

Polnarov, Anatoly. 2018. Looking Beyond Dichotomies: Hidden Diversity of Voices in the *Yantielun* 鹽鐵論. *T'oung Pao* 104: 465–495.

Renxue 仁學 (Study of benevolence). 2002. By Tan, Sitong 譚嗣同 (1865–1898); annotated by Wu Hailan 吳海藍. Beijing: Huaxia chubanshe.

Richter, Matthias L. 2017. Roots of Ru 儒 Ethics in *shi* 士 Status Anxiety. *Journal of the American Oriental Society* 137 (3): 449–471.

Roetz, Heiner. 1993. *Confucian Ethics of the Axial Age*. Albany: State University of New York Press.

Sato, Masayuki. 2003. *The Confucian Quest for Order: The Origin and Formation of the Political Thought of Xun Zi*. Leiden: Brill.

Schaberg, David. 2023. On Quoted Speech in Anecdotal History: *Zhanguoce* as Foil to *Zuozhuan*. In *Early Chinese Historiography: Zuozhuan in Comparative Perspective*, ed. Yuri Pines, Martin Kern, and Nino Luraghi, 209–243. Leiden: Brill.

Shiji 史記 (Records of the Historian). 1997. By Sima, Qian 司馬遷 (ca. 145–90 BCE) et al. Annotated by Zhang, Shoujie 張守節, Sima, Zhen 司馬貞, and Pei, Yin 裴駰. Beijing: Zhonghua shuju.

Song, Hongbing 宋洪兵. 2010. *A New Study of Han Feizi's Political Thought* 韓非子政治思想再研究. Beijing: Zhongguo renmin daxue chubanshe.

Van Norden, Bryan W. 2013. Han Fei and Confucianism: Toward a Synthesis. In *Dao Companion to the Philosophy of Han Fei*, ed. Paul R. Goldin, 135–146. Dordrecht: Springer.

Vervoorn, Aat. 1990. *Men of the Cliffs and Caves: The Development of the Chinese Eremitic Tradition to the End of the Han Dynasty*. Hong Kong: Chinese University Press.

Wang, Huaiyu. 2015. A Genealogical Study of *De*: Poetical Correspondence of Sky, Earth, and Humankind in the Early Chinese Virtuous Rule of Benefaction. *Philosophy East and West* 65 (1): 81–124.

Weingarten, Oliver. 2015. Debates around Jixia: Argument and Intertextuality in Warring States Writings Associated with Qi. *Journal of the American Oriental Society* 135 (2): 283–307.

Wu, Bin. 2020. *Government Performance Management in China: Theory and Practice*. Singapore: Springer.

Wu, Jing, and I-Shin Chang. 2020. Target Responsibility System of Environmental Protection and Performance Evaluation System. In *Environmental Management in China*. Singapore: Springer. https://doi.org/10.1007/978-981-15-4894-9_7.

Xi, Jinping. 2018. *The Governance of China*. Vol. 1. 2nd ed. Beijing: Foreign Languages Press.

Xunzi jijie 荀子集解 (*Xunzi*, with collected explanations). 1992. ed. Wang, Xianqian 王先謙 (1842–1917), Shen, Xiaohuan 沈嘯寰, and Wang, Xingxian 王星賢. Beijing: Zhonghua shuju.

Yantielun jiaozhu 鹽鐵論校注 (*Salt and Iron Debates*, collated and annotated). 1996. Compiled by Huan, Kuan 桓寬 (first century BCE). ed. Wang, Liqi 王利器. Beijing: Zhonghua shuju.

Yanzi chunqiu jiaozhu 晏子春秋校注 (*Yanzi chunqiu*, collated and annotated). 2014. ed. Zhang, Chunyi 張純一 (1871–1955). Collated by Liang, Yunhua 梁雲華. Beijing: Zhonghua shuju.

Yu, Yingshi 余英時. 2003. *Shi and Chinese Culture* 士與中國文化. Shanghai: Shanghai renmin chubanshe.

Zha, Changguo 查昌國. [1998] 2006. "Friendship and the Change in Ruler-Minister Relations Throughout the Zhou Dynasty" 友與兩周君臣關係的演變. Rpt. in Zha Changguo, *Study of Pre-Qin "Filiality" and "Friendship"* 先秦[孝]、[友]觀念研究, 98–125. Hefei: Anhui daxue chubanshe.

Zhang, Jue 張覺, ed. 2010. *Han Feizi, Collated with Subcommentary* 韓非子校疏.Shanghai: Shanghai guji chubanshe.

———. 2012. The Book of Lord Shang, Collated with Subcommentaries 商君書校疏. Beijing: Zhishi chanquan chubanshe.

Zhanguoce zhushi 戰國策注釋 (*Stratagems of the Warring States*, with glosses and explanations). 1991. ed. He, Jianzhang 何建章. Beijing: Zhonghua shuju.

Chapter 19
Fajia and the Mohists

Tao Jiang

In Chinese intellectual history as well as in contemporary scholarship, Mohist philosophy and *fajia* 法家[1] thought (translated in this volume as the *fa* tradition) have not received the kind of attention they deserve, especially given their extraordinary importance in Chinese history. The understudy of Mohism and *fajia* thought has had the unfortunate consequence of underappreciation of the genealogy of critical ideas in the early China period as well as their central roles in shaping subsequent Chinese intellectual and political history. Many studies of Mohist philosophy tend to be colored by the Mencian perspective that dismisses the normative Mohist ideal of impartial care as inhuman; on the other hand, most of the studies (or honorable mentions) of *fajia* thought focus on its practical as well as its cynical and brutal aspects while ignoring its normative dimensions (or dismissing it as immoral/amoral).[2]

---

[1] *Fajia* thinkers in this essay refer to Shen Buhai 申不害 (d. 337 BCE), Shang Yang 商鞅 (d. 338 BCE), Shen Dao 慎到 (fourth century BCE), and Han Fei 韓非 (d. 233 BCE), even though only Shang Yang and Han Fei are discussed in this chapter. For a more comprehensive coverage of all four *fajia* thinkers as well as the problematic category of *fajia*/Legalism, see Jiang 2021, Chaps. 4 and 7.

[2] For example, Angus Graham calls *fajia* (Legalism) "an amoral science of statecraft" (Graham 1989: 267). Wing-tsit Chan observes that the *fajia* thinkers "rejected the moral standards of the Confucianists and the religious sanction of the Moists in favor of power" (Chan 1963: 251). Michael Hunter notes that Yang Xiong (53 BCE – 18 CE) in the Han Dynasty already observed that Han Feizi was someone who "cared about being persuasive to the exclusion of morality" (Hunter 2013: 181).

This essay is based on my book, *Origins of Moral-Political Philosophy in Early China: Contestation of Humaneness, Justice, and Personal Freedom* (Jiang 2021).

T. Jiang (✉)
Rutgers University, New Brunswick, NJ, USA

© The Author(s), under exclusive license to Springer Nature Switzerland AG 2024
Y. Pines (ed.), *Dao Companion to China's* fa *Tradition*, Dao Companions
to Chinese Philosophy 19, https://doi.org/10.1007/978-3-031-53630-4_20

Furthermore, the relationship between Mohist philosophy and *fajia* thought has been largely ignored. As a result, there is a lack of recognition of the fact that *fajia* thinkers were indebted to the Mohists for the moral-political norm of impartiality as well as the central notion of *fa* 法 (law, standard) in the *fajia* theories. Recognizing such a genealogy can help us appreciate the fact that there is indeed a normative dimension in the *fajia* political philosophy, namely the norm of impartiality in its deliberation on political governance, instead of seeing *fajia* teaching as just a set of practical (and sinister) techniques of political control. That is, between the two dominant groups of thinkers in early China, the Confucians and the Mohists, the *fajia* thinkers were much more aligned with the Mohists than the Confucians in their respective moral-political deliberations. The *fajia* philosophy was by no means an intellectual aberration in the landscape of early Chinese philosophical discourse, but rather a major participant.

In this essay, I focus on the connection between Mohist and *fajia* thoughts. I argue that the Mohists championed the ideal of universal justice in their teachings of impartial care (*jian ai* 兼愛) and objective standards (*fa* 法) and that the *fajia* thinkers appropriated the impartialist element in the Mohist ideal of universal justice by adopting the idea of objective standards in their design of an impartialist and impersonal state bureaucracy.

1   Impartial Care and Objective Standards in Mohist Philosophy

To some contemporary scholars of Chinese philosophy, it was Mozi (墨子 c. 470–390 BCE) who represented the true beginning of Chinese philosophical reasoning. Indeed, it was Mozi and his followers, the Mohists, who laid the foundation for adjudicating whether an argument or idea is right or wrong. Their separation of the quality of an idea from the person who formulates it, making them independent of each other, was indeed revolutionary in the development of logic and reasoning in classical Chinese philosophy.[3] This would lead to the Mohist commitment to the independence of standards when adjudicating policies and practices.

The idea of *jian ai* is the most fundamental moral teaching of Mozi and the Mohists. *Jian ai* has been translated as universal love, universal care, concern for everybody, inclusive care, and impartial care, etc. While universal love was a

---

[3] As Graham observes, the Mohism represented the beginning of systematic debate in China: "It is in *Mozi* that we first meet the word *bian* 辯 'argue out alternatives,' cognate with *bian* 辨 'distinguish', which was to become the established term for rational discourse. It is the distinguishing of the right alternative, the one which 'is this' (*shi* 是) from the wrong alternative, the one which 'is not' (*fei* 非). We find also in *Mozi* a recognition that the soundness of a thought has nothing to do with who thinks it." (Graham 1989: 36, updating the transliteration to *Hanyu pinyin*)

popular translation early on, it has been largely shunned by scholars in recent years.[4] I adopt impartial care as the translation for this essay as it best captures the Mohist ideal of universal justice. Justice is defined in this essay as the impartialist conception of moral obligation, namely our exercise of impartial judgment on the merits of persons and states of affairs, especially in lieu of articulated and publicized standards and codes, irrespective of their relations to us. By contrast, humaneness is understood here as the partialist conception of moral obligation, namely our natural inclination to be partial toward those who are close to us, especially our family/kin members.[5] Mohists were the champions of universal justice whereas Confucians were the advocates of humaneness. As an ideal of universal justice *jian ai* by itself is inadequate. There need to be uniform and objective standards and criteria that are universally applied in order to accomplish the ideal of *jian ai*. Therefore, discussion on objective moral standards, *fa*, is also critical in the Mohist philosophical discourse.

1.1 Impartial Care

The point of departure for the Mohist project is the idea of benefits (*li* 利). Coming primarily from the lower strata of society, the Mohists were mostly worried about basic human needs. In Van Norden's words, "early Mohism identifies benefit (*lì* 利) with having particular concrete goods, and harm (*hài* 害) with lacking these goods: wealth (*fù* 富), populousness (*zhòng* 眾), and good order (*zhì* 治)" (Van Norden 2007: 145). Therefore, proper adjudication and distribution of benefits lie at the heart of the Mohist project. That is, the Mohists advocated bringing benefits to all as the way to bring about welfare in the world. It is in this connection that we find the signature Mohist moral teaching, impartial care, which underlies the Mohist commitment to universal justice and whose radical nature within the context of early Chinese philosophy is hard to overestimate.

The term "care" (*ai* 愛), appears in the *Analects* in connection with Confucius's iterations of the consummate virtue of *ren* 仁. However, *ai* makes only an occasional appearance in Confucius's thought. By contrast, *ai* is a much more central concept in the Mohist moral system, especially as part of *jian ai*. Developmentally, *jian ai* builds on *ai* by adding a critical component of impartiality (*jian*) to the expression and articulation of care. That is, despite *jian ai*'s radicality within the context of classical Chinese thought, there is actually a clear conceptual connection

---

[4] As Graham points out, "The Mohists were dour people whose ears were open to the demands of justice rather than to the appeal of love" (Graham 1989: 41). Carine Defoort, in tracing the evolution of the idea of *jian ai* in the *Mozi*, makes a good case for flexibly translating it as "inclusive care" and "impartial care" (Defoort 2013: 36).

[5] For a more detailed discussion of partialist humaneness versus impartialist justice as the fundamental philosophical dialect in the mainstream early Chinese moral-political projects, see Jiang 2021: 35–42.

with the notion of care in the *Analects*. Mozi is believed to have studied Confucius's teachings early on. It is conceivable that Mozi might have seen himself as someone who developed certain aspects of Confucius's teachings.

In this connection, we should note that Mozi and his followers inherited and developed a critical component of Confucius's teaching, (negative) Golden Rule (*shu* 恕), i.e., "Do not impose upon others what you yourself do not desire" (*Analects* 12.2, trans. Slingerland 2003: 126).[6] Interestingly, *shu* was practically ignored by the self-professed followers of Confucius during the Warring States period (Jiang 2021: 153–54). The Mohists took the Golden Rule much more seriously than the Confucians after Confucius and pushed it to its logical conclusion, namely impartial care. In fact, it was Mozi and the Mohists who vigorously applied the Golden Rule to care and pushed Confucius's idea of caring for people to its logical conclusion of caring for *all*, often to the exasperation of later Confucians like Mencius who accused the Mohists of being unfilial (無父, *Mencius* 3B/9).

For example, in "Jian Ai" I 兼愛上, Mozi uses the idea of the Golden Rule to explain impartial care:

若使天下兼相愛，愛人若愛其身，猶有不孝者乎？視父兄與君若其身，惡施不孝？猶有不慈者乎？視弟子與臣若其身，惡施不慈？故不孝不慈亡有。猶有盜賊乎？故視人之室若其室，誰竊？視人身若其身，誰賊？故盜賊亡有。猶有大夫之相亂家、諸侯之相攻國者乎？視人家若其家，誰亂？視人國若其國，誰攻？故大夫之相亂家、諸侯之相攻國者亡有。若使天下兼相愛，國與國不相攻，家與家不相亂，盜賊無有，君臣父子皆能孝慈，若此則天下治。

If we could induce everyone in the world to love others impartially, so that each person loved others just as he loved himself, would there be any person who failed to be obedient to superiors? If each person regarded his father and elder brothers as well as his lord just as he did himself, how could he do anything that was disobedient? And would there be any person who failed to be affectionate to inferiors? If each person regarded his younger brothers and sons as well as ministers just as he did himself, how could he do anything that was unaffectionate? Thus disobedient and unaffectionate conduct would cease to exist. And would there be robbery and murder? If each person regarded the families of other men just as he regards his own family, from whom would he steal? And if he regarded other men's bodies just as he regards his own, on whom would he inflict injury? Thus robbers and murderers would cease to exist. And would there be grand officers who bring disorder to each other's houses and lords of the various states who attack each other's states? If a grand officer regarded other men's houses just as he regards his own, to whom would he bring disorder? If the lord of a state regarded another lord's state just as he regards his own, whom would he attack? Thus grand officers who bring disorder to each other's houses and the lords of the various states who attack each other's states would both cease to exist. If we could induce everyone in the world to love others impartially, states wouldn't attack each other, houses would not bring disorder to each other, there would be neither robbers nor murderers, and every lord and minister, father and son, would be capable of behaving obediently and affectionately. If the world were like this, then it would be well ordered. (*Mozi* 14.3; Sun 2001: 100–1)[7]

---

[6] For a more detailed discussion of the Golden Rule in the *Analects*, see Jiang 2021: 89–93.

[7] All translations of the *Mozi* in this essay are by Knoblock et al. 2013; the Chinese version is from Sun 2001.

In this passage, Mozi uses the idea of the Golden Rule to make the case that if we could care about others the way we care about ourselves, there would be no unfilial son, no unloving parent, no theft, no attack on another's house, and no aggression among states, etc. In formulating the idea of *jian ai*, the Mohists advocated according equal moral status to people regardless of their relationships to the adjudicating agent, heralding the ideal of universal justice in Chinese history. Indeed, the Mohists were radicals, aiming at remaking Chinese society by putting forward universally applicable objective standards that can be deployed impartially to adjudicate policies and practices based on the benefits they bring about. Such a standard is the Mohist formulation of *fa* 法.

1.2 Objective Standards

The Mohists insisted on formulating and applying standards and criteria for moral judgment that were objective, public, and reliable. This was revolutionary in the history of Chinese philosophy, according to which practices and policies that had a distinguished pedigree should still be subject to the test of objective criteria. The legitimacy of particular practices and arguments should have more to do with desirable consequences they brought about, not just their pedigree as such, since their pedigree itself was or should have been the product of their initial effectiveness in promoting order and well-being in the world. This implies that there must have been some objective standards when those practices were instituted in the first place that could evaluate their results. The Mohist project was precisely a systematic and methodic attempt to articulate such underlying standards and criteria.

In this connection, the Mohists formulated three gnomons (*biao* 表) or standards (*fa* 法) when adjudicating the validity of an argument (Chapters 35–37; "Against Fatalism" ["Fei ming" 非命]). The three gnomons or standards are similarly worded in the three chapters, namely, "Testing whether the doctrine has a proper basis (*ben* 本), a proper origin (*yuan* 原), and can be put to proper use (*yong* 用)" 有本之者，有原之者，有用之者 (*Mozi* 36.1; Sun 2001: 266).

The fact that the Mohists formulated standards/models to adjudicate a moral argument does not mean there was no tension or conflict among those standards/ models. Still, the Mohists made a critical step in the history of Chinese philosophy in that very attempt to formulate standards and models, moving the criteria to adjudicate moral argument away from contestations of moral agents' intuitions, which tends to characterize the Confucian moral reasoning.[8] Indeed, one of the greatest contributions of the Mohists to Chinese philosophy lies in their remarkable endeavor to move the gravity of philosophical reasoning from a debate focusing on personal intuitions or inclinations to one emphasizing objective criteria that are publicly

---

[8] Bryan Van Norden calls the Confucians "ethical connoisseurs" who adopt an intuitionist approach to moral arguments (Van Norden 2007: 54–58).

accessible and defendable. As such, the Mohists were much more clear-eyed and skeptical about the limitations of moral intuitions by self-proclaimed moral experts.

How did the Mohists get to such objective and publicly accessible standards and criteria? For this, the Mohists turned to Heaven's intent, which they saw as representing the clearest standard to measure the world:

> 子墨子言曰:我有天志,譬若輪人之有規,匠人之有矩。輪匠執其規矩,以度天下之方圜,曰:「中者是也,不中者非也。」今天下之士君子之書不可勝載,言語不可盡計,上說諸侯,下說列士,其於仁義則大相遠也。何以知之?曰:我得天下之明法以度之。
>
> The teachings of our Master Mozi say: "My possessing the will of Heaven is, to use an analogy, like a wheelwright owning a compass or a carpenter, his square." The wheelwright and carpenter wield their compass and square in order to measure how round or square the things of the world are, saying, "What exactly coincides with this tool is right, and what does not is wrong." Now the documents of the scholars and gentlemen of the world today are so numerous that they cannot be listed, and their doctrines and sayings are too numerous to be examined in full. They offer persuasions to the lords of the various states above and to the distinguished gentlemen below. Yet their conceptions of what constitute humaneness and propriety are far from the truth. How do I know this? I say because I possess the clearest standard in the world by which I measure them. (*Mozi* 26.7; Sun 2001: 197)

The Mohists turned to supernatural moral agents as a way to overcome the apparent deficiencies of human moral agents. Such a deeply religious worldview would provide the ultimate ground for their overall moral project. Here Mozi compares Heaven's intent to a compass or a square to measure the moral qualities of people's actions and government policies. Fraser summarizes:

> The Mohists thus mounted a search for objective moral criteria, or as they saw it, reliable, easily applicable "models" or "standards" (*fǎ* 法) by which to guide judgment and action. These would guide everyone to distinguish right from wrong correctly, just as a straight-edged tool guides a carpenter in sawing a straight line. The models would provide the content of the unified moral norms. (Fraser 2016: 16)

Fa within the Mohist context can usually be understood in terms of objective standards. As Chad Hansen observes,

> Mozi's discussion of *fa* makes it more theory laden than mere 'standards.' *Fa*[standards] are publicly, objectively and naturally accessible, measurement-like standards. The prototype is a pair of contrasting terms. They are not, that is, rules—not universal sentential prescriptions. Mozi's appeal to *fa*[standards] contrasts explicitly with the elite intuition standard that is implicit in the Confucian theory of traditional codes and their practical interpretation. Tradition is not a *fa*, because all traditional language is equally permissible and traditional codes are subject to interpretative dispute.
>
> *Fa*[objective standards] should be reliably projectable standards for selecting some language and rejecting other language. Other paradigm *fa*[standards] were measurements (plumb line, sunrise gnomons, carpenter's square). Therefore, a code that is clear and openly published would fall *in the range of denotation of fa*[measurement standards]. Mozi advocated applying the *fa*[standards] to the language used in *xing*[punishment] and in *zheng*[administration]. This is not because *fa* means *law*, but because we should have codes that qualify as objective, measurable, public standards of behavior. (Hansen 1994: 464, original italics)

This means that the primary meaning of *fa* is not law in the Mohist framework, even though law can be one of its derivative meanings. That is, to the extent that laws, as publicly promulgated codes, represent objective standards that are reliably and fairly enforced in a polity, it is a case of *fa*. All law is or should be *fa*, but not all *fa* is law.

In many ways, *fa* can be viewed as the instrument of the Mohist moral ideal of *jian ai*, advocating the establishment of objective measures and models *morally and institutionally* against which what is right and wrong can be properly and systematically (as opposed to haphazardly) adjudicated. More specifically, *fa* is the institutionalization of *jian ai*. Such an idea was especially appealing during a time of extraordinary chaos when everything was thrown into doubt. This has serious consequences for the model of political governance:

> 當皆法其父母奚若?天下之為父母者眾, 而仁者寡, 若皆法其父母, 此法不仁也。法不仁, 不可以為法。當皆法其學奚若?天下之為學者眾, 而仁者寡, 若皆法其學, 此法不仁也。法不仁, 不可以為法。當皆法其君奚若?天下之為君者眾, 而仁者寡, 若皆法其君, 此法不仁也。法不仁, 不可以為法。故父母、學、君三者, 莫可以為治法。
>
> Supposing everyone were to model themselves (*fa* 法) on their parents, what would that be like? There are many parents in the world, but very few of them are *ren* 仁. If we were to model ourselves on our parents, the model we chose would not be one of *ren*. A model that is not *ren* cannot serve as a model. Supposing everyone were to model themselves on their teachers, what would that be like? There are many teachers in the world, but very few of them are *ren*. If we were to model ourselves on our teachers, the model would not be one of *ren*. A model that is not *ren* cannot serve as a model. Supposing everyone were to model themselves on their rulers, what would that be like? There are many rulers in the world, but very few of them are *ren*. If we were to model ourselves on our rulers, then the model would not be one of *ren*. A model that is not *ren* cannot serve as a true model. Therefore of the three—parents, teachers, and rulers—not one can be regarded as the model for governing. (*Mozi* 4.2, with modifications; Sun 2001: 21-22)

In this passage, Mozi deals with the problem of standard/criterion/model (*fa* 法) in governance by refuting parents, scholars, and rulers as possible candidates of model and standard-bearer. His reasoning is simple and straightforward, namely given the plurality and heterogeneity of parents, teachers, and rulers in the world, following any of them would entail setting up standards, criteria, or models that are not *ren*. It makes sense to translate *ren* here as justice, meaning that the law/standard/model cannot be just if it is inconsistent as they would lead to differential treatments of people, which is unjust. The idea of *ren* in the *Mozi* is a much more justice-oriented concept than it is in the *Analects*.[9] By linking *ren* directly with *fa*, Mozi makes an explicit point that a good *fa* is one that is just.

Consequently, the Mohist teaching calls for a robust sense of communal and reciprocal commitment among its members. This is how we should interpret the Mohist teaching in the "Conforming upward" ("Shang tong" 尚同) chapters, wherein Mozi touts the leader of a community, whether hamlet (*li* 里), district

---

[9] I have translated *ren* in the *Analects* as "humaneness-cum-justice" which blends partialist humaneness and impartialist justice (Jiang 2021: 74) and have argued that in the hands of the Mohists and the Mencians the meaning of *ren* would diverge, orienting more toward justice and humaneness respectively, signifying critical developments of philosophical arguments in early China after Confucius (Jiang 2021: 115 *ff*).

(*xiang* 鄉) or regional state (*guo* 國), as a person of *ren* (*ren ren* 仁人) and advocates the idea that everybody in a given community conform him/herself to the leader by taking his ideas, speech, and actions as the sole criterion in that community. This might appear to contradict Mozi's idea that rulers cannot serve as models as we just saw previously, but the key difference is the singularity of model within a community in "Conforming upward" chapters versus multiplicity of models in the above passage. In another passage, the text makes it clear that eventually it is Heaven that all should conform to:

天下之百姓皆上同於天子，而不上同於天，則菑猶未去也。

If the common people of the world all upwardly conform with the Son of Heaven but do not upwardly conform with Heaven itself, then the calamities sent down by Heaven will never cease. (*Mozi* 11.3; Sun 2001: 77).

The Mohist concern is how a robust community can be constituted with uniform standards and models so that *jian ai* can be put into practice within such a vigorously disciplined community. We can also see the potentially dark side of the single-perspective approach to justice that takes the person at the top of the pecking order as the only model for an entire community for the sake of impartiality. The potential perils of upward conformity would become more apparent within the *fajia* political theories that operationalize this essentially Mohist ideal of justice and impartiality within a statist framework.

Normatively Mohist philosophy can be understood as a form of consequentialism,[10] "the view that normative properties depend only on consequences" (Sinnott-Armstrong 2021). The primary object of concern for the Mohist consequentialism is the collective, rather than the personal, regarding the personal welfare as derivative of the collective welfare, but not the other way around. The *Mozi* refers to the state as the place where Mohist ideals are implemented, but the Mohist ideals, especially *jian ai*, are not constrained by the boundary of a regional state (or any territorial state by implication). Rather, the Mohist ideals apply to all people under the Heaven (*tianxia* 天下). Therefore, the ideal state in the Mohist philosophy is a universal state, which, as a global community, encompasses all people. This universal state is the correlative of the Heaven that covers all under-the-Heaven.

Let us call this form of consequentialism "universal state consequentialism."[11] Framing the Mohist philosophy this way will help us see more clearly its connection with the *fajia* project. Indeed, one of the most significant impacts exerted by the Mohists was on the development of the *fajia* thought, a connection that has been largely ignored. As we will see in the following, the *fajia* thinkers would appropriate the Mohist idea of *fa*, the elements of impartiality, uniformity, upward conformity, and the statist approach to politics to build a theoretical and bureaucratic model with the most profound and far-reaching consequence in Chinese political history.

---

[10] For an alternative interpretation to the Mohist project as a Divine Command theory, see Jiang 2021: 128–31.

[11] Philip J. Ivanhoe first characterizes the Mohists as state consequentialists in his *Confucian Moral Self-Cultivation* (Ivanhoe 2000: 15). For a more detailed discussion of what I call the Mohist "universal state consequentialism," see Jiang 2021: 132–33.

2 Impartiality and *Fa* in *Fajia* Thought

One of the most consequential political developments in the Warring States period was the increasing concentration of power in the monarchy and the accelerating bureaucratization of the state.[12] Such a development was reflected most directly in the writings of what came to be known as the *fajia* 法家 thinkers. In this section, I will look into the writings by two prominent *fajia* representatives, Shang Yang 商鞅 (d. 338 BCE) and Han Fei 韓非 (d. 233 BCE). I argue that it was in the hands of the *fajia* thinkers that classical Chinese political philosophy took a decidedly bureaucratic turn, away from the paradigmatic norm that saw politics as derivative of the moral virtues of the political actors, which characterized the Confucian approach to politics. The *fajia* thinkers saw the institution of the state as a domain that required its own operating norm, irreducible to other domains. In these *fajia* thinkers, we see that impartiality, first formulated and defended by the Mohists, became the most important institutional norm.

Moreover, the *fajia* thinkers' effort to formulate an impartial political order for the sake of all people points to the critical value of justice in their political thought. These *fajia* thinkers operationalized universal state consequentialism that characterized the Mohist moral-political norm and advocated implementing the Mohist ideal of impartiality in the state bureaucracy such that the state apparatus could function by itself, just like Heaven or nature,[13] without constant intervention from the ruler. Furthermore, many of the *fajia* thinkers problematized personal virtues they considered to be at odds with the interest of the state and instead touted professional virtues of specialization and impersonal application of standards when an official was acting on behalf of the state.

For all its imperfections (Goldin 2011), the traditional nomenclature of *fajia* does capture certain key features that can justify grouping those thinkers under one category, namely their problematization of the assumed connection between personal virtues and political authority and their singular focus on the institutionalization of political power. Most other philosophers of the classical period did not separate the two and often regarded the political as derivative of the moral. For the *fajia* thinkers, such a way of conceptualization vastly underappreciated the uniqueness and independence of the political domain, especially the nature of political power, that is irreducible to personal virtues. The *fajia* thinkers were the most clear-eyed about this unique and *sui generis* nature of political power.

---

[12] For an informative discussion of this development, see Lewis 1999.

[13] As Yuri Pines points out in his review of the *fajia* sections of my book (Pines 2023: 453–54), this view is much more prominently featured in the so-called "Huang-Lao" texts than the *fajia* texts. While agreeing with the general point, I take the position that the *fajia* thinkers were operating within the broad context of the naturalization of Heaven during the Warring States period such that some of them, especially Shen Dao, took Heaven to be the ultimate model to build an ideal state bureaucracy. See Jiang 2021: 267–82.

2.1 *Shang Yang and His Indebtedness to the Mohists*

Shang Yang was the pivotal figure who set in motion dramatic political transformations of the state of Qin that would make Qin the ultimate unifier of warring states. A great deal of *fajia* thought can be traced to Shang Yang's ideas and formulations. He was put in a powerful position by a trusting ruler, Lord Xiao of Qin 秦孝公 (r. 361–338 BCE), so that he could implement his ideas in changing the polity under his supervision. *The Book of Lord Shang* (*Shangjunshu* 商君書) has traditionally been attributed to Shang Yang. As is the case with most classical texts, the authorship and the dating of the text have been called into question. Yuri Pines places the bulk of the text in the fourth century BCE (Pines 2017: 51).

Shang Yang's Political Project

Shang Yang was an impartial institutionalist whose effort to bureaucratize the state (and the military) was unprecedented in Chinese (and perhaps even world) history, laying a powerful material and ideological foundation for the eventual unification of China under the state of Qin he worked for. Narrowly speaking, Shang Yang's political project was "enriching the state and strengthening the military" (*fuguo qiangbing* 富國强兵). To this end, Shang Yang proposed a set of measures that singularly focused on encouraging agricultural production and participation in the military, to the exclusion of other possible venues of promotion and reward. For him, agriculture was the means to enrich the state, and warfare the way to expand and strengthen the state.

More broadly, especially from the vantage point of historical hindsight, it is fair to characterize Shang Yang's political project as a pioneering effort in bureaucratizing the state such that it could function largely on its own, ideally without constant interference from external factors, including the monarch. Many contemporary scholars have characterized the Chinese state as precocious, largely due to its extraordinary maturity at such an early stage of China's political history, especially when compared with other early polities around the world.[14] The precociousness of the Chinese state was the result of efforts initiated by Shang Yang, who was singularly important in bureaucratizing the state apparatus.

In contrast with the Confucians, Shang Yang was skeptical about the political system that was based on a promissory note of moral education aiming at transforming the problematic aspects of human nature, selfishness (*si* 私) being one of the most prominently featured flaws in the classical discourse. Shang Yang did not think that moral education was or should be the solution to the problem of human selfishness. Rather, the problem of human selfishness required a political solution. The

---

[14] For example, Francis Fukuyama argues that "It is safe to say that the Chinese invented modern bureaucracy, that is, a permanent administrative cadre selected on the basis of ability rather than kinship or patrimonial connection" (Fukuyama 2011: 113).

ingenuity of his political project lay in the idea that the selfishness of people should and could be redirected as a source for political order, through the mechanisms of reward and punishment, given people's penchant for wealth and status and aversion to poverty and pain. In Shang Yang's eyes, people's thirst for name and benefit could be exploited since people would do anything in order to achieve those. This portrait of human nature appears rather dark or cynical, *if and only if* our concern is moral. But if the concern is primarily political, such an understanding of human nature can actually provide a solid ground for enhancing the interest of the state. The key is how to construct a political system in such a way that can channel people's desires to endeavors that benefit the state. This was precisely Shang Yang's political project, namely, to build a robust political system that could align people's desires with the interest of the state (see also Pines, Chap. 1, this volume).

Shang Yang proposed a highly centralized political system to establish and safeguard a new political order wherein impartial and impersonal laws of reward and punishment were reliably enforced.

> 國之所以治者三:一曰法，二曰信，三曰權。法者，君臣之所共操也；信者，君臣之所共立也；權者，君之所獨制也。人主失守，則危；君臣釋法任私，必亂。故立法明分，而不以私害法，則治；權制獨斷於君，則威；民信其賞則事功成，信其刑則姦無端。
>
> The state is ordered through three [things]: the first is standards 法, the second is credibility 信, the third is authority 權. Standards are what the ruler and ministers jointly uphold; credibility is what the ruler and ministers jointly establish; authority is what the ruler exclusively regulates. When the sovereign loses what he should preserve, he is endangered; when the ruler and the ministers cast away standards and rely on their private [views], turmoil will surely ensue. Hence, when standards are established, divisions are clarified, and when standards are not violated for private reasons, then there is orderly rule. When authority and regulations are decided exclusively by the ruler, [he inspires] awe; when the people trust his rewards, success is accomplished; and when they trust his punishments, wickedness has no starting point. (*Book of Lord Shang* 14.1, modified; Zhang 2012: 164)[15]

Here Shang Yang explicitly advocates the use of standards, credibility, and authority as the tools of governance and, in so doing, implicitly excludes personal virtues, so exulted by the Confucians, as politically irrelevant or worse. In Shang Yang's formulation, standards (*fa*) were regulations issued by the state that were in accordance with people's dispositions and customs; credibility referred to the reliable, predictable, and impartial enforcement of those regulations; and authority was what made regulations and enforcement possible. While standards and credibility were established and maintained by the ruler and his officials, authority should be wielded by the ruler alone and exercised in his name only.

At the heart of Shang Yang's political project was his theorization of *fa*, whereas credibility and authority can be understood as the requirements for enforcing *fa* in a sustainable fashion, credibly and authoritatively. *Fa* has two primary meanings in the text: (a) punitive laws, and (b) standards of promotion and demotion. Shang Yang sought to institute a highly centralized and autonomously functioning

---

[15] All translations from the *Book of Lord Shang* are by Yuri Pines 2017 (whose divisions into section numbers I adopt); the Chinese version follows Zhang 2012.

bureaucratic system to impersonally enforce standardized criteria in rewards and punishments that were aligned with the interest of the state.

故君子操權一正以立術，立官貴爵以稱之，論勞舉功以任之，則是上下之稱平。上下之稱平，則臣得盡其力，而主得專其柄。

Hence, when the superior man holds authority, he establishes techniques of rule by rectifying [everything]; he establishes offices and makes rank esteemed so as to correspond [to office]; he investigates one's labor, elevates the meritorious, and then makes the appointments. Then superior and inferior are balanced. When superior and inferior are balanced, then ministers are able to fully commit their strength, and the sovereign is able to monopolize the handles of authority. (*Book of Lord Shang* 6.11; Zhang 2012: 103)

As a result, a sophisticated and efficient state bureaucracy was established to define an official's role in terms of his position alone and evaluate his performance on that basis. This system removed elements of unpredictability and chaos in the officialdom and protected the interest of the state (as well as the ruler) by impartially enforcing the established standards.

Shang Yang's unequivocal advocacy of standardizing rewards and punishments was clear: "Rulers of our age frequently cast away standards and rely on private deliberations: this is why the state is in turmoil" 世之為治者，多釋法而任私議，此國之所以亂也 (*Book of Lord Shang* 14.2; Zhang 2012: 166). The imperative to rely on standards had to do with the fact that most rulers were not sages like Yao (*Book of Lord Shang* 14.2), a crucial point Shang Yang and other *fajia* thinkers took to heart in their political thinking. In so doing, they challenged the Confucians, who insisted on building their model of political governance on the premise of sage-rulers.

Using *fa* to standardize reward/punishment and promotion/demotion constitutes a sharp contrast with doing so on the ruler's favors, a common practice Shang Yang adamantly opposed. In Shang Yang's eyes, such a practice undermined the ruler's authority, instead of enhancing it, since that practice encouraged currying the ruler's personal favors instead of performing tasks that were in the interest of the state (and the ruler by implication). A ruler was the custodian of the state, but at times the interest of the state could diverge from the private interest of that ruler, even though the two often overlapped as the ruler clearly benefited from the strong state he ruled over. "Only a clear-sighted sovereign cares for his authority, takes trustworthiness seriously, and does not damage law through his private [interests]" 惟明主愛權重信，而不以私害法 (*Book of Lord Shang* 14.1; Zhang 2012: 164).

As Shang Yang argued, relying on *fa* would promote coherence within the political order and prevent the festering of resentment among those who were not rewarded for their achievements:

是故先王知自議譽私之不可任也，故立法明分，中程者賞之，毀公者誅之。賞誅之法，不失其議，故民不爭。不以爵祿便近親，則勞臣不怨；不以刑罰隱疏遠，則下親上。

Therefore, the former kings knew that they could not rely on their own deliberations and private appointments; hence, they established standards and clarified divisions so that those who were within the norms were rewarded, and those who damaged the common [interests] were prosecuted. The standards of rewards and prosecutions did not lose their appropriateness; hence, the people did not struggle. If one does not use ranks and appointments to benefit intimates and kin, hard-working ministers are not resentful. If one does not use punishments and penalties to obstruct strangers and outsiders, inferiors are close to superiors. (*Book of Lord Shang* 14.2; Zhang 2012: 166)

It is rather interesting that Shang Yang was touting the virtue of humility, exemplified by former kings who recognized their own limitations and established standards to deal with those limitations such that rewards and punishments were handled fairly without incurring resentment. This means that the establishment and promotion of explicit and transparent standards of reward and punishment required a ruler who recognized his own inadequacy. Instead of indulging in his own glorified virtuosity when ruling over a state, an ideal *fajia* ruler would rather put his faith in the system that was carefully set up and let it operate as designed on its own without unnecessary and constant interference.

Shang Yang elaborated the *fa*-centered tools of governance in Chap. 17, "Rewards and Punishments" ("Shang xing" 賞刑):

> 聖人之為國也：壹賞，壹刑，壹教。壹賞則兵無敵，壹刑則令行，壹教則下聽
> 上。 When the sage rules the state, he unifies rewards, unifies punishments, and unifies teaching. When rewards are unified, the army has no rivals. When punishments are unified, orders are implemented. When teaching is unified, inferiors heed superiors. (Book of Lord Shang 17.1; Zhang 2012: 190)

Clearly Shang Yang saw consistency and reliability in enforcing the uniform standards for rewards (*yi shang* 壹賞) and punishments (*yi xing* 壹刑) as the most critical element of a sustainable political order. In enforcing such standards and exercising the will of the state, the principle of impartiality had to be applied:

> 所謂壹刑者，刑無等級。自卿相將軍以至大夫庶人，有不從王令，犯國禁，亂上制
> 者，罪死不赦。有功於前，有敗於後，不為損刑。有善於前，有過於後，不為虧
> 法。忠臣孝子有過，必以其數斷。
>
>   What is called unifying punishments means imposing punishments without regard for one's status. From chief ministers, chancellors, and generals down to nobles and commoners, whoever disobeys the king's orders, violates the state's prohibitions, or wreaks havoc on the regulations of one's superior should be executed without pardon. If he had merits before but failed thereafter, this should not reduce the punishment. When one was good previously but transgressed thereafter, this should not diminish the law. When loyal ministers and filial sons transgress, their cases should be decided according to the rules. (*Book of Lord Shang* 17.3; Zhang 2012: 196)

The principle of equal treatment without regard for status was revolutionary and antithetical to the ritual order advocated by the Confucians wherein one's status and relationships within that order were essential considerations. This prompted the accusation of inhumaneness and cruelty against Shang Yang, especially by those who would lose their privilege under the new political norm. Of course, it would be rather naïve to believe that privileged treatment of the elite would disappear under the regime proposed by Shang Yang. Still, even though his clear advocacy of equal treatment without consideration of status should not be taken as an accurate description of the actual Qin practice since there were plenty of ways the powerful could leverage their status for more lenient treatment (Pines 2017: 207), the principle of equal treatment before the law—even as a desideratum—was a significant development in the Chinese political and legal systems, which were not separate institutions in Chinese history.

Shang Yang's Indebtedness to the Mohists

As we have seen previously, *fa* is also a central concept in the Mohist moral-political philosophy. It represents the Mohist advocacy of the establishment of objective measures and models, *morally and institutionally*, which can be employed to adjudicate what is right and wrong properly and systematically. That is, *fa* is the institutionalization of impartial care (*jian ai*), the highest moral ideal in Mohism. In Shang Yang's thought *fa* becomes the kernel of a political system to impersonally enforce a set of rules about rewards and punishments. The connection between the Mohist *fa* and Shang Yang's *fa* is unmistakable in that they both valorized establishing universal standards of adjudication and impersonal enforcement without considerations of relationships (Mohists) or status/rank (Shang Yang). Such traits make Shang Yang's philosophy much more aligned with the value of impartiality championed by the Mohists. In the case of Shang Yang, impartiality is an institutional norm that impersonally enforces standardized rules of reward and punishment without considerations of the status or rank, at least in principle.

As Shang Yang's political project was to establish a *fa*-based bureaucratic machine that could impartially enforce standards of reward and punishment instituted by the state, he was clearly cognizant of the threat posed to such a system. In fact, a critical component of Shang Yang's political philosophy was his clear-eyed analysis of the conflict of interest between the private (*si* 私) and the public (*gong* 公) domains.[16] Prior to the mid-Warring States period, the prevailing sense of *si* and *gong* were more neutral, without the moral and evaluative overlay. This was the case with the *Analects* (Brindley 2013: 9) and much of the *Mencius* (Brindley 2013: 10). Erica Brindley credits the Mohists as one of the earliest voices in articulating clusters of positive and negative values that would eventually coalesce around *gong* and *si* (Brindley 2013: 16). But the big shift from neutral to moral in describing *gong* and *si* took place in mid-fourth century BCE, with the *Book of Lord Shang* as critical evidence in such a change (Brindley 2013: 12–13).[17]

---

[16] Paul Goldin has argued that "*Gong* is derived from the old word meaning 'patriarch' or 'duke,' and by Han Fei's time it had come to refer more broadly to the interests of the ruler" (Goldin 2020: 204) and cautions against interpreting it as something like something like "the general interests of the state as opposed to the private interests of its ministers…, because the interests of a particular ruler—even long-term, prudential interests—are not necessarily identical to those of the abstract state" (Goldin 2020: 204–5). However, according to Liu Zehua, during the Spring and Autumn period and the Warring States period the meaning of *gong* expanded from social status to affairs of the state and the court, public matters, and, most importantly, to social values and moral concepts having to do with the public (Liu 2003a: 64). Liu's essay has listed many examples of *gong* that refer to the public.

[17] Liu Zehua's article on the concept of "establishing the common, eradicating the private" 立公滅私 (Liu 2003a, b), provides a comprehensive coverage of the *si* and *gong* debate during the Spring and Autumn period and the Warring States period, but his discussion is less clearly delineated than Brindley's. Interested readers can refer to both Liu's and Brindley's essays to get a comprehensive and clear picture of the evolution of the values concerning *si* and *gong* during this critical period of Chinese intellectual history.

Significantly, Shang Yang built on the Mohist deliberations on *gong* and *si* in his own political project. Indeed, the juxtaposition of *gong* and *si* and the normative values attached to them are so pervasive in the *Book of Lord Shang* that the conceptual pair must have become a critical preoccupation in Shang Yang's political project. While most, if not all, classical philosophers recognized the conflict between the private and the public, what distinguished Shang Yang from many others was that he sought solution to such a conflict in the political domain, rather than in the domain of moral virtues as most other thinkers did. This means that Shang Yang saw the conflict between the private and the public as primarily a political problem that required a political solution instead of a moral one. Shang Yang's genius was to look for a solution in the way a political system could be set up such that people's selfishness would be redirected toward activities conducive to the public interest of political order.

Still, Shang Yang, as well as other *fajia* thinkers, put too much faith in a bureaucrat's willingness to follow the rules, to such an extent that he was almost blind to the nearly endless opportunities for officials to abuse power in the name of following the rules (even though Shang Yang was trying to limit the power of those very officials). Indeed, one of the major flaws in Shang Yang's political philosophy and the political project embedded in such a philosophy was the dilemma of power, namely, how to make sure that those in positions of power follow the rules. To some extent, Shang Yang was aware of the challenge (e.g., *Book of Lord Shang* 24.2), but he did not seem to be able to solve such a central problem, other than appealing to the power of position (*shi* 勢) and methods (*shu* 數) without offering any detail. It is unclear whether such a flaw could be effectively dealt with at all in the system designed by Shang Yang or even tolerated by the powers that be. And the subsequent history of Chinese politics was a testimony to such a challenge, both practical and theoretical, to monitor those in power within the political system.

2.2 Han Fei and the Mohists

Han Fei has been regarded as *the* representative of *fajia* thinkers who has received more attention than Shang Yang in contemporary scholarship.[18] It is important to recognize that Han Fei positioned himself as Shang Yang's heir and improver.[19] Similar to Shang Yang, Han Fei's conception of a sustainable political order centered on the standardization of the state bureaucracy. Such an order was rule-based, regulating the state through clearly established standards for reward and punishment that were publicly promulgated, and enforced impartially, uniformly, and

---

[18] For example, Bryan Van Norden's *Introduction to Classical Chinese Philosophy* (Van Norden 2011) and Paul Goldin's *The Art of Chinese Philosophy: Eight Classical Texts and How to Read Them* (Goldin 2020) only cover Han Fei.

[19] In Chapter 43 (*Ding fa* 定法), Han Fei defends and integrates Shang Yang's and Shen Buhai's ideas.

reliably. Indeed, standardization, clarity, transparency, impartiality, uniformity, and reliability characterized Han Fei's *fajia* political order.

Han Fei's Political Project

Like Shang Yang, Han Fei's *fajia* project can also be understood as the operationalization of state consequentialism in carrying out essentially the Mohist project of universal justice, especially the aspect of impartiality, within an exclusively statist framework. Much of Han Fei's effort was devoted to perfecting the mechanism and the method in order to ensure the execution of impartiality in political governance and to safeguard the monarchy against being hijacked by powerful private interests. He mocked the normative Confucian political paradigm that links the political order to personal virtues of the ruler, ostensibly placing their hope for a fulfilling moral-political life on the ideal of sage-kings (for a different view, see Lewis, Chap. 11, this volume). For Han Fei, the orderly governance under sage-kings and the disorderly rule under tyrants were accidents of history that should not serve as the norm of governance.[20] For a more sustained political order, a source had to be located elsewhere than the personal qualities of those individual rulers.

Han Fei challenged building an entire political system on the ideal of sage-kings in two ways: scarcity of sages and the source of political authority. First, there were very few sages in Chinese history, a point not even the Confucians could really disagree with. Therefore, if we were to wait for the arrival of a sage-king once every several hundred years, the world would be condemned to an almost constant state of hopelessness, perhaps punctuated by some bright spots occasionally. Han Fei did not theorize from the perspective of either a sage or a tyrant, but an average/mediocre ruler, which was the most common kind of ruler. His reason for not obsessing over sage-kings was that political order should be largely independent of moral virtues of a ruler so that it could operate on its own without interference from the ruler. As such, Han Fei thought that the political domain had a high degree of

---

[20] For example, in the "Nan shi" 難勢 ("Critique of the Power of Position") chapter, Han Fei defends his model of governance based on the power of position this way: "Even if a Yao, Shun, Jie, or Zhou only emerged once in every thousand generations, it would still seem like they were born bumping shoulders and treading on each other's heels. But those who actually govern each age are typically somewhere in the middle between these two extremes. The reason why I discuss the power of position is for the sake of these mediocre rulers. These mediocre rulers, at best they do not reach the level of a Yao or Shun, and at worst they do not behave like a Jie or Zhou. If they hold to the law and depend on the power of their position, there will be order; but if they abandon the power of their position and turn their backs on the law, there will be disorder." 且夫堯、舜、桀、紂千世而一出，是比肩隨踵而生也，世之治者不絕於中。吾所以為言勢者，中也。中者，上不及堯、舜，而下亦不為桀、紂。抱法處勢則治，背法去勢則亂。 (*Han Feizi* 40.3; Chen 2000: 945; trans. Sahleen [Ivanhoe and Van Norden 2001: 330–31]; see also Pines, Sect. 3.3, this volume). The numeration of *Han Feizi* passages follows the one adopted by Christoph Harbsmeier in his forthcoming translation. The Chinese version follows Chen Qiyou's 2000 edition.

autonomy, decoupling it from personal qualities of individual rulers which vacillated from one to the next.

Second, Han Fei rejected the premise that political authority was derived from moral virtues of a ruler.[21] From Han Fei's perspective, if political authority were built upon moral virtues, we would be in the constant state of mismatch between political authority and moral virtues of the ruler, with the consequence of disorder prevailing throughout history. Han Fei conceptualized the foundation for political order rather differently from the Confucians in that he saw the cycle of order and chaos as the failure of a theoretical model that linked the political order with the moral virtues of a particular ruler which was notoriously unpredictable. If, however, the state was set up properly, political order would follow from such a setup and moral virtues of its ruler would be irrelevant. Indeed, according to Han Fei, a political order should not be built on the ideal of a morally perfect sage because the source of political authority *should* not derive from moral virtues of a ruler at all. The more irrelevant the ruler's moral virtues are to the political authority, the more sustainable and durable the political order would become. For Han Fei, political authority was itself the creation of political order alone.

Without constant personal interference from the ruler, the state bureaucracy could operate impersonally on its own. Moreover, those who staffed the state bureaucracy should not be expected to be personally virtuous since that would render the ranks completely empty, as few would measure up.[22] What should be demanded of the officeholders would be their expertise and professional virtue of faithful execution of their official charge. An officeholder's authority within the state bureaucracy was derived from the position he occupied instead of from the moral virtues he might or might not possess. This also means that a new kind of virtue should be inculcated in order to be more aligned with the interest of bureaucracy, i.e., professional virtues dictated by one's position in the bureaucracy and professional performance evaluated by the assessment about whether the performance matches the mandate of the position. This was called *xing ming* 刑名 (performance and title), which dictated the professional obligations of office holders in a bureaucratic state (see more in Wang Pei, Chap. 20, this volume).

Han Fei considered it the main challenge to the rulers when their ministers became independent sources of political authority, depriving the rulers of their

---

[21] Han Fei is following Shen Dao here, e.g., *Shenzi* 10–14. For a more detailed discussion of Shan Dao on political authority and moral virtues, see Jiang 2021: 274–76 and Harris, Chap. 3, this volume.

[22] "Now, there are no more than ten officers in the whole world who are virtuous and honest, and yet the officials within the borders of a single state number in the hundreds. So if one insists on employing only officials who are virtuous and honest, there will not be enough men to fill the offices of the state. … Therefore, the Way of an enlightened ruler is to unify *fa* and not seek after wisdom, to establish the proper techniques of rule and not yearn for honesty. In this way, *fa* will not be violated and the offices will all be free of treachery and deceit." 今貞信之士不盈於十，而境內之官以百數，必任貞信之士，則人不足官。……故明主之道，一法而不求智，固術而不慕信，故法不敗，而群官無姦詐矣。 (*Han Feizi* 49.11; Chen 2000: 1109 ["Wu du"]; trans. Sahleen [Ivanhoe and Van Norden 2001: 346, revised])

authority and power. In order to deal with such a danger posed to the rulers, Han Fei proposed instituting standards in selecting and evaluating officials. In the Chap. 6, "On Having Standards" ("You du" 有度), he argued, "If those who uphold the law are strong, the state will be strong; if they are weak, the state will be weak" 奉法者 強則國強，奉法者弱則國弱 (*Han Feizi* 6.1; Chen 2000: 84; trans. Watson 2003: 21). In Han Fei's eyes, a person's ability to uphold the law should be the standard for their appointment in the state bureaucracy. He condemned the ministers who disregarded the law and sought personal gains at the expense of their ruler and the state and called such people "hefty persons" or "political heavyweights" (*zhongren* 重人). It was in the interest of the state as well as that of the ruler to select officials who could uphold the law and shun private scheming.

故當今之時，能去私曲就公法者，民安而國治；能去私行行公法者，則兵強而敵 弱。In our present age he who can put an end to private scheming and make men uphold the public law will see his people secure and his state well ordered; he who can block selfish pursuits and enforce the public law will see his armies growing stronger and his enemies weakening. (*Han Feizi* 6.2; Chen 2000: 91; trans. Watson 2003: 22)

Here Han Fei emphasized the nature of the law as public and impartial (*gong fa* 公 法) and contrasted it with scheming activities that were against the law, the state, and the ruler, characterizing the latter as private and partial (*si qu* 私曲). The conflict between the public and the private was clearly highlighted in Han Fei's and other *fajia* thought, whereas the tension between the two domains tended to be smoothed over by the Confucians, not infrequently at the expense of the state and to the private benefits of powerful people and their families.[23]

Han Fei made it clear that in selecting high officials, their understanding of the interest of the state was the most important consideration:

故審得失有法度之制者加以群臣之上，則主不可欺以詐偽；審得失有權衡之稱者以 聽遠事，則主不可欺以天下之輕重。

Find men who have a clear understanding of what is of gains and losses and a feeling for the system of laws and regulations, and place them in charge of the lesser officials; then the ruler can never be deceived by lies and falsehoods. Find men who have a clear understanding of what is of gains and losses and the judgment to weigh issues properly, and put them in charge of foreign affairs; then the ruler can never be deceived in his relations with the other powers of the world. (*Han Feizi* 6.2; Chen 2000: 91; trans. Watson 2003: 22, modified)

Han Fei implored the ruler that it was in his interest to align his activities with laws and standards, especially in appointing officials. To ensure this, the ruler should put in place some mechanism for selection. What is interesting in this connection is that, as a solution to the problem posed by the private scheming against the ruler,

---

[23] For example, in Chapter 43 (*Ding fa* 定法) Han Fei lists many cases wherein, after the death of Shang Yang and his patron Lord Xiao of Qin, due to the lax in enforcing the *fa* used to be championed by Shang Yang many powerful people took advantage of the state power to enrich themselves and to enlarge their landholdings at the expense of the Qin state. On the other hand, Mencius famously says, "Governing is not difficult. Do not commit any offenses against the great houses of one's state. He to whom the great houses defer, the whole state will defer. He to whom the whole state defers, the world will defer" (*Mengzi* 4A6, trans. Van Norden 2008: 91).

Han Fei advocated using clearly stipulated laws and standards to select, promote, and punish officials, instead of doing it by the ruler himself:

> 故明主使法擇人，不自舉也；使法量功，不自度也。能者不可弊，敗者不可飾，譽者不能進，非者弗能退，則君臣之間明辨而易治，故主讎法則可也。
>
> A truly enlightened ruler uses the law (*fa*) to select men for him; he does not choose them himself. He uses the law to weigh their merits; he does not attempt to judge them for himself. Hence men of true worth will not be able to hide their talents, nor spoilers to gloss over their faults. Men cannot advance on the basis of praise alone, nor be driven from court by calumny. Then there will be a clear understanding of values between the ruler and his ministers, and the state can be easily governed. But only if the ruler makes use of law can he hope to achieve this. (*Han Feizi* 6.2; Chen 2000: 92; trans. Watson 2003: 24)

In making use of law as the standard to select officials instead of relying on his personal opinions or preferences, the ruler would be directing office-seekers' calculations and talents to the benefit of the monarchy itself, inhabited by the ruler. As such there would be no divergence between the monarch and the monarchy, a tension that was clearly on Han Fei's mind.

The standardization of state bureaucracy through *fa*, with standards including legal code and criteria of the selection and evaluation of officials, required that such standards be instituted and enforced. In Han Fei's *fajia* system, the standards for reward and punishment should be clear, publicly promulgated, and executed impartially, uniformly, and reliably. First, *fa* should be clear, easy to understand, and does not cause confusion.[24] Second, in order for *fa* to work as designed, it should be publicly promulgated in a way anybody on the street should be able to understand.[25] Third, once *fa* was put in place and publicly pronounced, it should be properly implemented and enforced. In this connection, Han Fei steadfastly upheld the ideal of impartiality when it came to reward and punishment, regardless of the person's status or relationship.[26] Another important aspect of the *fajia* political order regulated by standard, according to Han Fei, was its uniformity and reliability, for which

---

[24] "Now in administering your rule and dealing with the people, if you do not speak in terms that any man and woman can plainly understand, but long to apply the doctrines of the wise men, then you will defeat your own efforts at rule. Subtle and mysterious words are no business of the people" 今所治之政，民間之事，夫婦所明知者不用，而慕上知之論，則其於治反矣。故微妙之言，非民務也 (*Han Feizi* 49.11 ["Wu du"]; Chen 2000: 1109; trans. Watson 2003: 109).

[25] "Government through law exists when the ruler's edicts and decrees are promulgated among the various departments and bureaus, when the certitude of punishments and penalties is understood in the hearts of the people, when rewards are given to those who respect the law, and when penalties are imposed on those who violate the ruler's decrees" 法者，憲令著於官府，刑罰必於民心，賞存乎慎法，而罰加乎奸令者也 (*Han Feizi* 43.1.2 ["Ding fa"]; Chen 2000: 957; trans. Sahleen [Ivanhoe and Van Norden 2001: 320]).

[26] "Thus if a man has truly won merit, no matter how humble and far removed he may be, he must be rewarded; and if he has truly committed error, no matter how close and dear to the ruler he may be, he must be punished. If those who are humble and far removed can be sure of reward, and those close and dear to the ruler can be sure of punishment, then the former will not stint in their efforts and the latter will not grow proud" 是故誠有功，則雖疏賤必賞；誠有過，則雖近愛必誅。疏賤必賞，近愛必誅，則疏賤者不怠，而近愛者不驕也 (*Han Feizi* 5.3 ["Zhu dao" 主道]; Chen 2000: 81; trans. Watson 2003: 19).

he was willing to sacrifice discretion in the exercise of law so as to root out confusion caused by discretions.

In a word, Han Fei's conception of political order, much of which was built on earlier *fajia* thought as well as elements of the Mohist ideas, centered on standardization of the legal code and the criteria for selecting and evaluating officials. He argued that the standards should be clear and transparent, and should be executed impartially, uniformly, and reliably. Han Fei was clearly a statist, theorizing from the perspective of a strong state or monarchy in the context of early Chinese history. He was advancing the politics of impartiality pioneered by the Mohists and further developed by the earlier *fajia* thinkers, advocating the well-regulated state as the sole agent to bring about impartiality.

However, it is also important to recognize the element of justice in Han Fei's political project:

上古之傳言，春秋所記，犯法為逆以成大姦者，未嘗不從尊貴之臣也。然而法令之所以備，刑罰之所以誅，常於卑賤，是以其民絕望，無所告愬。大臣比周，蔽上為一。

Judging from the stories handed down from high antiquity and the incidents recorded in the *Spring and Autumn Annals*, those men who violated the laws, committed treason, and carried out major acts of evil always worked through some eminent and highly placed minister. And yet the laws and regulations are customarily designed to prevent evil among the humble and lowly people, and it is upon them alone that penalties and punishments fall. Hence the common people lose hope and are left with no place to air their grievances. Meanwhile the high ministers band together and work as one man to cloud the vision of the ruler. (*Han Feizi* 17.3 ["Bei nei" 備內]; Chen 2000: 323; trans. Watson 2003: 89, slight revision)

This is one of Han Fei's most powerful condemnations of the gross injustice suffered by the commoners. It clearly points to the moral dimension in his vision of the political order. There was a heightened recognition in Han Fei and other *fajia* thinkers with regard to the tension between the norms of partialist humaneness and impartialist justice in the political domain. This means that when enforcing the law, if various relationships and status were taken into consideration, it would inevitably result in inconsistencies and confusions. Whereas the Confucians saw the imperative of humaneness at stake in those discretionary exercise of power that take in to considerations relationships and status, Han Fei discerned something far more cynical or even nefarious at play, namely the bending of the legal code issued by the state to the advantages of powerful officials and their family interests while subjugating ordinary people to the full weight of the punitive measures. Such a dynamic is famously captured in the *Liji* 禮記 (*Records of the Rites*), an important early Confucian canon, that penal laws should not be applied to high officials (刑不上大夫; *Liji jijie* 4.82 ["Qu li shang" 曲禮上]). Han Fei was adamant that such blatant subversion of law to the detriment of the state and the ruler should never be tolerated. Instead, Han Fei describes his law-governed ideal world this way:

故至安之世，法如朝露，純樸不散，心無結怨，口無煩言。故車馬不疲弊於遠路，旌旗不亂乎大澤，萬民不失命於寇戎，雄駿不創壽於旗幢；豪傑不著名於圖書不錄功於盤盂，記年之牒空虛。故曰：利莫長乎簡，福莫久于安。

In the age of ultimate peace, laws are like morning dew, pure and simple but not yet scattered. People's heart-minds harbor no resentment and their mouths utter no confusing words. Therefore, wagons and horses are not exhausted on the long roads; flags and banners are not littered across big swamps; people do not lose their lives to bandits and military affairs; [those who ride on] strong horses do not cut short their years following military banners; brave heroes do not write their names on maps and books; nor are their deeds recorded on plates and vessels; and the wooden boards of the annals are left empty.[27] As a saying goes: "No benefit is more lasting than simplicity, no blessing is more enduring than peace." (*Han Feizi* 29.1 ["Da ti" 大體]; Chen 2000: 555, my translation)

This passage paints a rather idyllic picture of a peaceful world as the ultimate goal of law.[28] The contrast with the Confucian ideal cannot be sharper. Even though it is unclear how much normative weight we can give to this political ideal in Han Fei's thought, given its rather unusual nature in the corpus, this passage would at least complicate the conventional understanding of Han Fei's political thinking. It is worth pondering what entailments can be extrapolated or imagined if we give it more normative weight within the broader *fajia* political framework.

Han Fei's Engagement with the Mohists

Compared with Shang Yang, Han Fei's engagement with the Confucians and the Mohists was more explicit. Even though he often critiqued the Confucians and the Mohists together, e.g., in the chapter "Eminent teachings" ("Xian xue" 顯學), he reserved most of his firing prowess for the Confucians. His attitude toward the Mohists was more complicated. His criticism of the Mohists often had little to do with the substantive aspects of the Mohist teaching per se. Rather, it had more to do with the confusion the Mohist teachings supposedly caused due to the internal divisions of the Mohist movement as well as the fact of their disputations with the Confucians. On the other hand, in terms of substance Han Fei appropriated a great deal of important elements from the Mohist system, especially the centrality of *fa* and the statist ideology.

Zhou Fumei 周富美, one of the few contemporary scholars who have addressed the relationship between Mozi and Han Fei in some length, summarizes three aspects in Han Fei's critique of the Mohists, primarily in Chapter 50, "Eminent teachings": first, the Mohists split into three groups after the death of their grand master Mozi (墨離為三) (Zhou 2008: 583); second, their teachings were those of fools and charlatans (愚誣之學) (Zhou 2008: 586); and third, they advocated inconsistent and contradictory codes of conduct (雜反之行) (Zhou 2008: 596). The first point of Han Fei's critique has to do with the internal divisions among the Mohists (as well as the Confucians) which, from Han Fei's perspective, indicates the futility

---

[27] Empty year records refer to the chronicles of the type of the canonical *Springs-and-Autumns Annals*: when no events of significance (such as wars and diplomatic meetings) occurred, the season was left blank with a single record, e.g. "Summer. Fourth month" (see Chen 2023).

[28] For a more detailed discussion of Han Fei's ideal world governed by *fa*, see Jiang 2021: 407–10.

and self-defeating nature of the mainstream discourse. That is, if the Mohists (and the Confucians) could not even agree among themselves the correct way of interpreting their own master's teachings, what were the odds that the rest of the world could figure them out? Here Han Fei's critique had to do with the organizational divisions among the Mohists which resulted in inconsistency and contradiction within the Mohist teachings, making them unfit for an enlightened ruler to adopt as his governing philosophy.

The second point in Han Fei's critique of the Mohist (and other eminent) teachings is that they were the teachings of fools or charlatans, or both. This had to do with the practice by the Mohists (and even more so by the Confucians) who based their teachings on the words and conducts of ancient sages and former kings who lived hundreds or even thousands of years ago. Due to the long passage of time, the veracity of those sagely teachings could not possibly be verified.

> 無參驗而必之者、愚也，弗能必而據之者、誣也。故明據先王，必定堯、舜者，非愚則誣也。
>
> Someone who is sure about something without supporting evidence is a fool. Someone who bases their views on something they cannot be sure about is a charlatan. Thus, those who depend on the teachings of the former kings and are absolutely sure about the Way of Yao and Shun are either fools or charlatans. (*Han Feizi* 50.1; Chen 2000: 1125; trans. Sahleen [Ivanhoe and Van Norden 2001: 352])

Put differently, Han Fei's second critique had to do with the historical foundation of the Mohist (and the Confucian) teachings that appealed to claims whose veracity could not be verified.

Zhou elaborates this point by delving into Han Fei's view on historical evolution (歷史進化論) (Zhou 2008, 588) and his method of verification (參驗之法) (Zhou 2008: 592) when it comes to the efficacy of laws, policies, and practices. Han Fei's view of history is similar to that of Shang Yang who proposed a rather sophisticated and materialist view of historical change that treated material conditions as the primary mover of historical changes (see more in Vogelsang, Chap. 12, this volume). In the "Five vermin" ("Wu du" 五蠹) chapter, Han Fei echoes Shang Yang's view and explicitly argues that "the sage does not expect to follow the ways of the ancients or model his behavior on an unchanging standard of what is acceptable. He examines the affairs of the age and then makes his preparations accordingly" 是以聖人不期脩古，不法常可，論世之事，因為之備 (*Han Feizi* 49.1; Chen 2000: 1085; trans. Sahleen [Ivanhoe and Van Norden 2001: 340]). Since history is not a reliable guide for adopting the kind of particular policies and practices that would suit the present age, either because the world has changed or because there is no way to ascertain what really transpired in history anyway, Han Fei appealed to more reliable and verifiable methods to make sure that laws, policies, and practices could yield the desired results.

The third point in Han Fei's critique of the Mohists had to do with inconsistencies and contradictions between the Mohist and the Confucian teachings. Han Fei used the example of different funeral arrangements advocated by the Mohists and the Confucians and the example of different approaches to adversities between the two groups to illustrate the danger to a ruler, when trying to accommodate these differences, implementing inconsistent and contradictory policies. That is, for Han Fei, if a ruler honored these inconsistent and even contradictory practices advocated by different schools, the state under his rule would be confused and doomed.

> 故明主之國，無書簡之文，以法為教；無先王之語，以吏為師；無私劍之捍，以斬首為勇。
>
>   Therefore, in the state of an enlightened ruler there are no books written on bamboo slips; law supplies the only instruction. There are no sermons on the former kings; the officials serve as the only teachers. There are no fierce feuds of private swordsmen; cutting off the heads of the enemy is the only deed of valor. (*Han Feizi* 49.13; Chen 2000: 1112; trans. Watson 2003: 112)

However, Han Fei's apprehension about the inconsistencies and contradictions in laws and policies was very much shared by the Mohists. In fact, Han Fei's understanding of *fa* and his valorization of the public and the state over the private and the family were very much aligned with the Mohist approach, some differences notwithstanding.

I have been making the case in this essay that Han Fei's (and other *fajia*) thought can be considered the development of the Mohist political philosophy, operating on a version of state consequentialism and pushing the statist orientation of the Mohist project to its logical conclusion. It was the *fajia* thinkers who sought to transform the state apparatus in order to carry out a statist vision of impartiality whereas the Mohists were not quite as focused as the *fajia* thinkers on developing the state apparatus to promote the kind of institutional changes required to bring about their pioneering vision of universal justice.

Zhou Fumei addresses Han Fei's appropriation of the Mohist thought in three aspects, namely the centrality of *fa* (law, model, standard), the priority of the public over the private, and the idea of upward conformity. We have seen that *fa* represents objective standards in the Mohist philosophy against the Confucian, especially Mencian, intuitionist approach to morality. Han Fei (and other *fajia* thinkers) took the objectivist *fa* to the next level, institutionalizing it as the central mechanism of state bureaucracy with as little interference from the ruler as possible since the interference would inevitably inject personal biases into the impersonal operations of *fa*, favoring those close to power. Han Fei's *fa* is a major constraint on the potential for corruption and favoritism within the *fajia* political system.

Han Fei also shared the Mohist prioritization of the public over the private in his approach to politics. In fact, Han Fei was so wary of the hijacking of state interests by powerful private interests that he categorically separated the two domains and vehemently attacked any expression of private interests that could encroach the operation of the state.[29] For him and other *fajia* thinkers, the public/political domain is governed by the standardized norm of impartiality that does not take into

---

[29] For example, in the 備内 ("Vigilance inside the Palace") chapter Han Fei observes, "Judging from the stories handed down from high antiquity and the incidents recorded in the *Spring and Autumn Annals*, those men who violated the laws, committed treason, and carried out major acts of evil always worked through some eminent and highly placed minister" (*Han Feizi* 17.3; Chen 2000: 323; trans. Watson 2003: 89, slight revision).

consideration people's status or relationships when adjudicating cases involving them or evaluating their performances. Within the public realm there is no room for expressions of personal sentiments that would invariably favor those in or close to power. While the Mohists separated the private from the public and focused on the norms governing the public domain, Han Fei's discussion of the private domain focused almost exclusively on its potential detriment to the impartialist norm of the state.

Lastly, the Mohists advocated upward conformity (*shang tong* 尚同) and honoring the talented and meritorious people (*shang xian* 尚賢) to achieve two goals: to avoid confusion of standards by promoting uniform criteria set by those at the top of the Mohist order and to promote those who are talented and virtuous to the top of that order. However, Han Fei would reformulate the two ideas within the *fajia* framework such that upward conformity became absolute obedience to the monarchy irrespective of the personal qualities of any particular monarch. Han Fei sought to render the personal qualities of the monarch irrelevant to the impersonal operation of the impartial state. Ideally the conformity advocated by Han Fei is fulfilling one's roles within the political apparatus in conformity to the state, the institution of monarchy, although he often equivocated between monarchy and monarch.

3   Conclusion

I have characterized Mohism as a form of universal state consequentialism that promotes a statist approach to maximize wealth, order, and population. It is useful to view the *fajia* project as a way to operationalize the Mohist project, attempting to work out in granular details how to institute the Mohist principle of impartiality through state bureaucracy and enforcement of a uniform standard, i.e., legal and administrative codes. The *fajia* political theories can be considered to operate on universal state consequentialism in positing a universal state or "cosmic imperium" as "an idealized, universally-encompassing state" (Brindley 2013: 29) that "takes everyone's interests into account in an objective and impartial manner" (Brindley 2013: 29). This means that in Shang Yang's and Han Fei's *fajia* visions the idea of a universal state and the ideal of universal justice became concomitant in that the former was the agent for achieving the latter. However, in order for such a conception of political order to work as designed, the private interests of the monarch and the public interests of the monarchy needed to be strictly separated, and that was precisely where the *fajia* thinkers failed.

Fajia thinkers' singular focus on institutional and bureaucratic aspect of the state apparatus distinguishes the *fajia* project from the Mohist one. In this respect, the *fajia* thinkers were much more of a statist than the Mohists when comparing their theoretical outlooks and their practical advice. For the *fajia* thinkers, the state should be engineered in such a way that it could abide by the principle of impartiality and become a lasting, wealthy, and powerful universal state. The *fajia* thinkers pushed the Mohist project to its statist conclusion, irrevocably reshaping the trajectory of Chinese political history. Our study of the connection between *fajia* thinkers and the Mohists is a testimony that Mohist ideas did not really disappear from Chinese history. Rather, they were incorporated by the *fajia* thinkers into the very way state apparatus was set up. It is perhaps not an accident that Confucians regarded both the Mohists and *fajia* thinkers as inhumane, which points to the Confucian monopoly of the moral discourse in pre-modern China, even though Confucians would appropriate ideas from both the Mohists and the *fajia* thinkers.

Another important difference between the Mohists and the *fajia* thinkers was that the Mohists built their moral philosophy on an understanding of human nature that is malleable and can be trained toward the good, whereas the *fajia* thinkers were not interested in the moral potentials of human nature at all. Rather, the latter's interest in human nature was exclusively its political implications, namely, given the fact that the humans are selfish, how a political system can be built to channel such destructive potentials toward goals and objectives favored by the state. The distinctly *political* approach to human nature is a striking aspect of the *fajia* thinkers, especially Shang Yang and Han Fei.

The form of government theorized in the *fajia* thought can be characterized as totalitarian in nature, in the sense that it did not allow any moral-political authority outside the state, at least according to one popular definition of totalitarianism as a "form of government that theoretically permits no individual freedom and that seeks to subordinate all aspects of individual life to the authority of the state."[30] *Fajia* thinkers', especially Han Fei's, rejection of any political actors and agents independent of the state was so total and complete that totalitarianism is a fitting characterization of this particular aspect of the *fajia* political project.[31]

Fajia thinkers put all their faith in the political system they designed, which was supposed to operate on its own, vastly underestimating the intractable variations of problems and situations in the human world beyond the inevitably limited imagination of the designers and the engineers of that system. Left to its own device, the impartialist state, conceived of by *fajia* thinkers, was totalitarian in its monopoly of values under Heaven since no alternative source of values was allowed under such a system. This totalitarian orientation toward impartiality, already implicit in Mohism, articulated and defended by *fajia* thinkers exposed a dark side to a single-perspective, monistic notion of justice, especially when it is enforced by an all-powerful state, if justice is untampered or unbalanced by other norms like humaneness or personal freedom.

---

[30] This is from the *Encyclopedia Britannica* (https://www.britannica.com/topic/totalitarianism), accessed online on February 2, 2020.

[31] For a detailed exploration of the *Han Feizi* as a potential resource for the ideal of rule of law, see Jiang 2021: 447–51.

References

Brindley, Erica. 2013. The Polarization of the Concepts *Si* (Private Interest) and *Gong* (Public Interest) in Early Chinese Thought. *Asia Major (Third Series)* 26 (2): 1–31. (an important discussion of the critical development of 私 and 公 in early Chinese texts; can be usefully read together with Liu 2003a&b).

Chan, Wing-tsit, trans. and comp. 1963. *A Source Book in Chinese Philosophy*. Princeton: Princeton University Press. (comprehensive, but a bit dated).

Chen, Minzhen. 2023. How to Understand 'Empty' Records: On the Format and Compilation of *Chunqiu* from the Perspective of Bamboo Manuscripts. In *Zuozhuan and early Chinese historiography*, ed. Yuri Pines, Martin Kern, and Nino Luraghi, 63–88. Leiden: Brill.

Chen, Qiyou 陳奇猷 (1917–2006). 2000. *Han Feizi with New Collated Glosses* 韓非子新校注. Shanghai: Shanghai guji chubanshe. (the most widely-used contemporary edition of the *Han Feizi*).

Defoort, Carine. 2013. Are the Three "Jian Ai" Chapters about Universal Love? In *The Mozi as an Evolving Text: Different Voices in Early Chinese Thought*, ed. Carine Defoort and Nicolas Standaert, 35–68. Leiden: Brill.

Fraser, Chris. 2016. *The Philosophy of the Mòzǐ: The First Consequentialists*. New York: Columbia University Press. (a comprehensive study and a spirited defense of the Mohist consequentialism, the first of its kind in English).

Fukuyama, Francis. 2011. *Origins of Political Order: From Prehuman Times to the French Revolution*. New York: Farrar, Straus and Giroux.

Goldin, Paul. 2011. Persistent Misconceptions about Chinese 'Legalism'. *Journal of Chinese Philosophy* 38 (1): 64–80. (a useful discussion on peril of anachronism in the discussion of early Chinese philosophy).

———. 2020. *The Art of Chinese Philosophy: Eight Classical Texts and How to Read Them*. Princeton, NJ: Princeton University Press. (a comprehensive study of early Chinese philosophical texts, emphasizing the primary texts and some salient interpretative issues).

Graham, A. C. 1989. *Disputers of the Tao: Philosophical Argument in Ancient China*. LaSalle, IL: Open Court. (long considered the best and most influential study of early Chinese philosophy and its historical context in English, even though some of its scholarly claims are based on scholarship and materials that are a bit dated now).

Hansen, Chad. 1994. *Fa* (Standards: Laws) and Meaning Changes in Chinese Philosophy. *Philosophy East and West* 44 (3): 435–488.

Hunter, Michael. 2013. The Difficulty with 'The Difficulties of Persuasion' ('Shuinan' 說難). In *Dao Companions to the Philosophy of Han Fei*, ed. Paul Goldin, 169–195. New York: Springer.

Ivanhoe, Philip J. 2000. *Confucian Moral Self-Cultivation*. Indianapolis: Hackett.

Ivanhoe, Philip J., and Bryan Van Norden, eds. 2001. *Readings in Classical Chinese Philosophy*. New York: Seven Bridges Press.

Jiang, Tao. 2021. *Origins of Moral-Political Philosophy in Early China: Contestation of Humaneness, Justice, and Personal Freedom*. New York: Oxford University Press. (a new narrative about early Chinese philosophy, emphasizing the normative dimensions of the philosophical discourse while incorporating a good deal of secondary literature on textual history).

Knoblock, John, Jeffrey Riegel, and trans. 2013. *Mozi: A Study and Translation of the Ethical and Political Writings*. Berkeley: Institute of East Asian Studies, University of California Berkeley.

Lewis, Mark Edward. 1999. Warring States: Political History. In *The Cambridge History of Ancient China: From the Origins of Civilization to 221 B.C*, ed. Michael Loewe and Edward L. Shaughnessy, 587–650. New York: Cambridge University Press.

Liji jijie 禮記集解 (*Records of the Rites with Combined Glosses*). 1995. Compiled by Sun Xidan 孫希旦 (1736–1784). Ed. Shen Xiaohuan 沈嘯寰 and Wang Xingxian 王星賢. Beijing: Zhonghua shuju.

Liu, Zehua 劉澤華. 2003a. "The Springs-and-Autumns and the Warring States Periods' Concept of 'Establishing the Common and Eradicating the Private' and Social Integration (A)" 春秋

戰國的"立公滅私" 觀念與社會整合(上). *Nankai Journal (Philosophy and Social Sciences Edition)* 南開學報(哲學社會科學版) 4: 63–95.

———— 劉澤華. 2003b. . "The Springs-and-Autumns and the Warring States Periods' Concept of 'Establishing the Common and Eradicating the Private' and Social Integration (A)" 春秋戰國的"立公滅私" 觀念與社會整合(下) *"Chunqiu Zhanguo de 'ligong miesi' guannian yu shehui zhenghe"* (II). *Nankai Journal (Philosophy and Social Sciences Edition)* 南開學報(哲學社會科學版)5: 87–94.

Pines, Yuri, trans. and ed. 2017. *The Book of Lord Shang: Apologetics of State Power in Early China*. New York: Columbia University Press. (the best translation and interpretation of *The Book of Lord Shang* in English).

————. 2023. Tao Jiang on the *Fa* Tradition 法家. *Philosophy East and West* 73 (2): 449–458.

Sinnott-Armstrong, Walter. 2021. Consequentialism. In *The Stanford Encyclopedia of Philosophy*, ed. Edward N. Zalta; https://plato.stanford.edu/archives/fall2021/entries/consequentialism/. Accessed 16 July 2022.

Slingerland, Edward G., trans. 2003. *Confucius Analects*. Indianapolis, IN: Hackett.

Sun, Yirang 孫詒讓 (1848–1908). 2001. *Free Interpretation of the* Mozi 墨子閒詁. Beijing: Zhonghua shuju. (the most widely used edition of the *Mozi*).

Van Norden, Bryan. 2007. *Virtue Ethics and Consequentialism in Early Chinese Philosophy*. New York: Cambridge University Press.

————, trans. 2008. *Mengzi: With Selections from Traditional Commentaries*. Indianapolis: Hackett.

————. 2011. *Introduction to Classical Chinese Philosophy*. Indianapolis: Hackett.

Watson, Burton, trans. 2003. *Han Feizi: Basic Writings*. New York: Columbia University Press.

Zhang, Jue 張覺. 2012. *Book of Lord Shang Collated with Sub-commentary* 商君書校疏. Beijing: Zhishi chanquan chubanshe.

Zhou, Fumei 周富美. 2008. *Collected Essays on Mozi and Han Fei* 墨子韓非論集. Taipei: Guojia chubanshe. (one of the few contemporary studies that focus on the connections between Mozi and Han Fei).

Chapter 20
Laozi, Huang-Lao and the *fa* Tradition: Thinking Through the Term *xingming* 刑名

Pei Wang 王沛

1 Introduction

The Warring States period (Zhanguo 戰國, 453–221 BCE) was an age of vigorous debates among different schools of thought, which continue to fascinate scholars well into our days. Of the many interesting questions related to these debates, the relationship between what is usually dubbed Daoism (*daojia* 道家) and the *fa* tradition (*fajia* 法家) is particularly intriguing. The fundamental works of Daoism, such as *Laozi* 老子 and *Zhuangzi* 莊子, hold a negative view of *fa* 法 (law) and of state activism in general, whereas the *fa* texts, by contrast, firmly uphold it. For instance, *Laozi* insists, "the more illustrious laws and ordinances are made, the more widespread theft and robbery will be" 法令滋彰，盜賊有多 (*Laozi* 57).[1] *Fa* texts, by contrast, repeatedly emphasize the need for clear laws (see below). However, many of these texts clearly display indebtedness to *Laozi*, as was recognized long ago. For example, when Sima Qian 司馬遷 (ca. 145–90 BCE) composed the *Shiji* 史記 (Records of the Historian), he not only incorporated Laozi and several *fa* thinkers into the same collective biography, but also offered the following observation:

---

[1] All the references to the *Laozi* are to *Boshu Laozi* edition, using the stanza division in the received text annotated by Wang Bi 王弼 (226–249).

Translated by Cao Yan; Revisions by Avital Rom
This paper was supported by the National Social Science Foundation of China project 20&ZD180 "Legal history compilation and database construction on the basis of oracle bones, bronze inscriptions, and bamboo and wooden manuscripts."

P. Wang 王沛 (✉)
Eastern China University of Political Science and Law, Shanghai, China

© The Author(s), under exclusive license to Springer Nature Switzerland AG 2024   575
Y. Pines (ed.), *Dao Companion to China's fa Tradition*, Dao Companions
to Chinese Philosophy 19, https://doi.org/10.1007/978-3-031-53630-4_21

老子所貴道，虛無，因應變化於無為，故著書辭稱微妙難識。莊子散道德，放論，
要亦歸之自然。申子卑卑，施之於名實。韓子引繩墨，切事情，明是非，其極慘礉
少恩。皆原於道德之意，而老子深遠矣。

The Way that Laozi esteemed was [based on] emptiness; thus, he reacted to changes
through non-action. Hence the words of his book are profound and subtle and are difficult
to comprehend. Zhuangzi was unfettered by the Way and virtue and set loose his discussions; yet his essentials also go back to spontaneity. Master Shen [Shen Buhai 申不害, d.
237 BCE] treated the lowly as lowly, applying to it the principle of "names and substance."
Master Han [Han Fei 韓非, d. 233 BCE] drew on ink line, penetrated the nature of the matters, and was clear about right and wrong. He was extremely cruel and had little compassion. All these ideas originated from the meaning of the Way and its virtue, but Laozi was
the most profound of them. (*Shiji* 63: 2156)

How can we explain this paradoxical pairing of two ostensibly contradictory traditions? The answer possibly lies in the terms "Huang-Lao" 黄老 and *xingming* 刑
名.[2] Sima Qian notes that Shen Buhai's teachings "were rooted in Huang-Lao and
prioritized *xingming*" 本於黄老而主刑名 and that Han Fei "enjoyed the teachings
of *xingming*, *fa*, and *shu*, but his roots can be traced back to Huang-Lao" 喜刑名法
術之學而歸本於黄老 (*Shiji* 63: 2146). The so-called Huang-Lao tradition (or
Huang-Lao school) is the common designation of texts that are based on the sayings
attributed to the Yellow Thearch (Huangdi 黄帝) and Laozi, and are focused on
providing cosmological stipulations for sociopolitical order. Needless to say, this
designation, as any other "school" classifier, is nothing but a heuristic device and
will be used hereinafter for heuristic convenience only.

The Huang-Lao tradition differs significantly from that of *Laozi* and *Zhuangzi*
inasmuch as it attaches great importance to the law (*fa*), and elaborates the *xingming*
theory. This is the key difference between *Laozi* and the Huang-Lao tradition.
However, we should note that there is also a fundamental terminological divergence
between the Huang-Lao and the *fa* traditions insofar as the concept of *xingming* is
concerned. It can be said that *xingming* is the central term that distinguishes between
the legal-administrative thought of *Laozi*, Huang-Lao and the *fa* tradition. This
paper will take the theory of *xingming* as the starting point to discuss the relations
between these intellectual currents.

2 The Novelty of Dao and *xingming*

The theory of Dao (the Way) that rose during the Eastern Zhou period (770–255 BCE)
transformed the traditional view of legislation, offering an entirely new way of
thinking. The earlier view of legislation, current under the Western Zhou (ca.
1046–771 BCE) was closely related to the theory of the Mandate of Heaven (*tian*

---

[2] Throughout most of this paper we opted to transliterate the term *xingming* (刑名 or 形名) rather
than to translate. Only in the last parts of the essay, especially when it comes to the texts of the *fa*
tradition we use the established English translation as "performance and titles." For the origin of
this translation, see Creel 1974: 119–24, for a different view, see Makeham 1990.

ming 天命). This theory held that the Lord-on-High (Shangdi 上帝) transferred the power to rule All-under-Heaven from the last king of the Shang 商 dynasty (ca. 1600–1046 BCE) to the founder of the Zhou dynasty, King Wen 周文王 (d. ca. 1047 BCE).[3] The descendants of King Wen inherited this power to govern All-under-Heaven. The reason for which the Lord-on-High granted King Wen the power to rule All-under-Heaven was that King Wen possessed "virtue" (*de* 德), whereas the last Shang king, Zhòu 紂, had lost it.

De (virtue) as the term promulgated in Western Zhou texts and bronze inscriptions, had multiple connotations, such as benefitting others, respecting elders, being friendly and caring toward peers, acting with caution when offering sacrifices, not cheating, and even maintaining marital harmony.[4] However, to judge what is virtue in the context of this theory, we must ultimately rely on King Wen's actions. After all, it was King Wen who is said to have gained recognition from the Lord-on-High as being in line with virtue. It is due to these actions that the Lord-on-High granted his Mandate to King Wen. The descendants of King Wen should be careful to uphold virtue so as to maintain their hereditary rule and avoid losing the Mandate. To do so they should pattern themselves after King Wen. This idea is reflected in Western Zhou-period texts and inscriptions, which emphasize the term *xing* 刑 as the foundation of the rules. In bronze inscriptions, *xing* is written as *jing* 井. As a verb it means "to imitate"; as a noun it refers to "model" or "regulation." The meanings of *xing* as a verb and a noun are connected, as is seen, for instance, from the Da Yu-*ding* 大盂鼎 inscription, which says "Now I have already reached the stage when I have modeled myself upon and stored up the corrective virtue of King Wen" 今我隹即井(刑)禀于文王正德.[5] Here, *jing* (*xing*) refers to modeling oneself after or imitating the virtue of the former kings represented by King Wen. Their norms of conduct should be the basis for handling government affairs and dealing with lawsuits (Wang 2013). This is precisely the meaning of the saying that recurs in the bronze inscriptions: "[I] do not have the temerity to not follow the luminous rules created by the former kings" (毋敢弗帥先王作明井(刑)用).[6]

By the Springs and Autumns period (Chunqiu 春秋, 770–453 BCE), the authority of the Zhou kings had collapsed, and the rulers of regional states started claiming that they were the holders of the Mandate of Heaven, which also implied them having legislative power. This phenomenon is fully reflected in recently published

---

[3] In the early Western Zhou documents, the person who received the Mandate of Heaven was King Wen, whereas after the middle Western Zhou, King Wen's son, King Wu, also became identified as the recipient of the Mandate of Heaven (Li 2010: 297).

[4] The term *de* is a multi-faceted term, which in the early Zhou texts and bronze inscriptions may refer to royal charisma, and, arguably, *mana* rather than the moral virtue per se. I use the translation "virtue" primarily for heuristic convenience. There are many discussions of *de* in Western Zhou texts; see, for instance, Kominami 1992; Kryukov 1995; Nivison 1996; Wang 2015. For the more mature concept of virtue in the middle to late Western Zhou, see the inscription on Bin Gong-*xu* 豳公盨 (Wu 2012, #5677); and the discussion in Wang 2012.

[5] See *Yin Zhou jinwen jicheng* # 2837; translation borrowed from Cook and Goldin 2020: 33.

[6] Cited from the Mu-*gui* inscription, *Yin Zhou jinwen jicheng* # 4343.

paleographic materials. For instance, the inscription on the Jin Gong-*pan* 晉公盤, which was cast in the middle of the Springs and Autumns period and published in 2016, says that the Lord of Tang 唐公 (better known as Tangshu Yu 唐叔虞), the founder of the state of Jin 晉, had received the Mandate of Heaven early in the Western Zhou age.[7] The lengthy Zeng Hou Yu-*bianzhong* 曾侯與編鐘 inscription, cast on the bells of Marquis Yu of Zeng 曾侯與 from the late Springs and Autumns period, unearthed in 2009 from Tomb No. 1, Wenfengta 文峰塔 cemetery, Suizhou Municipality 隨州 (Hubei), says that Kings Wen and Wu of the Zhou had originally received the Mandate of Heaven, but now as the "Zhou house has already declined" 周室之既卑, the Mandate is possessed by the southern state of Chu 楚. The inscription also mentions that due to the attack by the newly rising southeastern state of Wu 吳, Chu had almost lost the Mandate.[8]

The above invocations of Heaven's Mandate as being possessed by regional lords rather than by the Zhou Son of Heaven are quite common in the Springs and Autumns period inscriptions.[9] They allow us to re-examine the inscription on the bell of the lord of Qin (Qin gong-*bo* 秦公鎛), which was known from the Northern Song record in *Kaogu tu* 考古圖 (Lü 2003; Fig. 20.1). In that inscription, a Qin ruler (whose identity is contested) claims that not only had his ancestors received the Mandate of Heaven long ago, but also that "I respectfully obey and adhere to the bright virtue and wisely spread the bright punishments" (穆穆帥秉明德, 叡敷明刑).[10] It should be noted that whereas the lord of Qin echoes the Zhou legal theory, he makes a subtle change. For the Zhou speakers, the laws (referred to here as

Fig. 20.1 Excerpt from the Qin Gong Bo (秦公鎛) Inscription (after Lü 2003: 409–10; *Yin Zhou jinwen jicheng* # 270)

---

[7] For study of this inscription (and its earlier parallel on Jin Gong-*pen* 晉公盆), see Wu 2014; Deng 2019: 75–125; see also Luo and Pines 2023.

[8] Hubeisheng and Suizhoushi 2014; see also Luo and Pines 2023: 11–13.

[9] See more examples in Luo 2020 and Luo and Pines 2023: 6–17.

[10] *Yin Zhou jinwen jicheng* # 270; translation modified from Kern 2000: 74.

"bright punishments") were supposedly established by the recipients of Heaven's Mandate, kings Wen and Wu; later kings should respect and emulate these laws, i.e. not deviate from the patterns established by the dynastic founders. By contrast, the lord of Qin who donated the *bo* bell clarified that he himself was a legislator. On the question of whether the law should be inherited from one's predecessor or produced anew, the Qin ruler provided a new answer—the current ruler can act as a legislator.

This shift in the possessors of legislative power from the Zhou kings to regional lords, and the increasing flexibility in adopting new laws, was paralleled by an even more far-reaching development, viz. the evolvement of the concept of the Way (Dao). This concept is first attested in the Springs and Autumns period, although its maturation occurred perhaps in the early Warring States period. Unlike the concept of the Mandate of Heaven, the idea of the Way dissociates political power from the supervision of the Lord-on-High. Texts that focus on the Way no longer consider the law as deriving from the former kings, the Mandate recipients. Since the functioning of Heaven, Earth, and society is regulated by the impartial Way, the law should be the embodiment of that Way. It should be based on the emulation of or being modelled after (*fa* 法) constant patterns of Heaven and Earth. As *Laozi* 1996: 25 explains: "Men models himself on Earth, Earth models itself on Heaven, Heaven models itself on the Way, the Way models on what is so by itself" 人法地，地法天，天法道，道法自然. Eventually, this line of thought will bring about the idea that "the Way generates the law" 道生法 (*Huangdi shu* 1.1:1 ["Dao fa" 道法]) (see more in Sect. 3).

In terms of legal thought, the connection between emulating Heaven and legislation appears in the texts that probably date from the early Warring States period. The sixth volume of the collection of the Warring States-period bamboo slips in possession of the Tsinghua 清華 university contains a manuscript titled *Zichan* 子產. This manuscript provides many previously unknown details on the legislative thought of Zichan (d. 522 BCE), who headed the government of the state of Zheng 鄭 in the late Springs and Autumns period.[11] According to the manuscript, although Zichan established the laws according to the precedents of the Xia, Shang, and Zhou dynasties, the basis of his legislation lay in understanding "Heaven and Earth, disobedience and compliance, harshness and softness" 天地、逆順、強柔. This view resonates with the ideas in the chapter "Discourses of Yue B" 越語下 of *Discourses of the States* (*Guoyu* 國語). The latter recommends, "one must have something through which to know the constant regulations of Heaven and Earth" 必有以知天地之恒制 and "death and life are based on the constant model of Heaven and Earth 死生因天地之刑 (*Guoyu* 21.1: 578 and 580; here *xing* 刑 refers to a model [=型]

---

[11] See Li 2016: 83–99 (plates), 136–45 (transcription). Prior to the publication of the Tsinghua University *Zichan* manuscript, the major source for Zichan's legislation was *Zuozhuan* 左傳 (Zhao 6.3). The *Zichan* manuscript was produced in the Warring States period, perhaps parallel to the composition of *Zuozhuan*. It obviously bears the imprint of the Warring States-period ideology; but it is also plausible that it preserves certain aspects of Zichan's legislative thought.

rather than "punishments"). In both cases, the political system should be based on emulation of or a following of Heaven and Earth, i.e., following the cosmic Way.[12]

Whereas the above examples speak of mere emulation of Heaven and Earth (i.e., the Way), eventually, a more sophisticated concept evolved as an intermediary between the Way and the law. This concept was *xingming* 刑名. The meaning of *xing* 刑 (which is also transcribed as *xing* 形 in the Warring States-period texts) broadly refers to the shape or form of things and undertakings.[13] More narrowly, *xing* refers to the form that everything *should have* (see more below). As such, on the political level *xing* holds the meaning of "rules and regulations" (which is similar to the concept of *xing* 刑 in the Western Zhou texts).[14] As for *ming* 名 (name), it refers to the precise designation of things and undertakings, including rules and laws. Rules and regulations must conform to the Way. Only through precise designation and expression can the Way be successfully translated into laws that society members should follow. As we shall see below, the evolution of the *xingming* theory led to a differentiation between *Laozi* and the Huang-Lao school. Eventually, the reinterpretation of the concept of *xingming* led to the formation of a new theory, that of the *fa* thinkers.

3   *Xingming* in *Laozi* and Huang-Lao School

Traditional views identify Laozi, the founder of Daoism, as a late Springs and Autumns period personality. However, judging from the bamboo manuscript of *Laozi* unearthed in 1993 at Tomb 1, Guodian, Jingmen 荊門郭店 (Hubei), until the middle of the Warring States Period (i.e., until ca. 350–300 BCE), there were still many differences between the proto-*Laozi* and the text of *Laozi* as it was known from the early Han dynasty onward (Wang and Yang 1997; Qiu 2021: 65–80). It may be assumed that the final version of *Laozi* was still then in the process of formation. As for the Huang-Lao tradition, the best source for understanding it are the so-called silk manuscripts *Huangdi shu* 黃帝書 (Yellow Thearch Manuscripts) unearthed in 1973 from the early Han Tomb No.3, Mawangdui, Changsha 長沙馬 王堆 (Hunan). The dating of these texts is disputed, but we can accept the fourth century BCE as a tentative date (Tang 1975: 7–36).

---

[12] See more in Wang 2018. As for the "Discourses of Yue B" chapter, Li (1990) considers it reflective of the early stage in the evolution of Daoist thought.

[13] For more on the interrelations between 形 (form), 型 (model), and the characters 井 and 刑, see Zhang 2009: 2192–2193.

[14] *The Canon: Law* (*Jing fa* 經法) manuscript from Tomb No. 3, Mawangdui cache (discussed below in the text) contains the following passage: "Beauty and ugliness have their names, opposition and compliance have their rules (*xing* 刑), truth and false have their substance. The monarchs and the lords hold X [the one?] and become the rectifiers of All-under-Heaven 美惡有名，逆順有刑，情偽有實，王公執囗以為天下正 (*Huangdi shu* 1.5: 50 ["Si du" 四度]). For the analysis of this text and related questions, see Wang 2013.

The so-called Huang-Lao school borrows the names of Huangdi (Yellow Thearch) and Laozi. Between the mid-Warring States period to the early Han era, its impact rivaled that of *Laozi* itself (Wang 2009: 7–9). Putting aside the speculations about the authorship of *Laozi* and *Huangdi shu*, we can compare these two textual traditions treating them as roughly contemporaneous. From the comparison between the two we can immediately note that their different views of *xingming* generated radically different approaches to law theory. According to *Laozi*, "the Way is forever nameless" 道常無名 (*Laozi* 32); whereas *Huangdi shu* conversely argue that Dao will definitely be transformed into a "name"; thus *The Canon: Law* 經法manuscript from that collection argues, the Way "is bound to possess *xingming*" 必有刑名 (*Huangdi shu* 1.1: 4 ["Dao fa" 道法]). Insofar as the Way is expressed through *ming* (its name, designation, or appropriate terminology), it can become a guideline for society to follow, whereas a nameless Way cannot give way to legal regulations. Herein lies the crucial difference.

According to *Laozi*, "With the beginning of regulations, there came to be names. As soon as there were names, one ought to know when to stop. Knowing when to stop, one can avoid danger. 始制有名，名亦既有，夫亦將知止，知止可以不殆 (*Laozi* 32). Wang Bi's 王弼 (226–249) commentary explains, "With the beginning of regulations, leaders of officials cannot but set up names and divisions so as to fix the honored and the base" 始制，官長不可不立名分以定尊卑.[15] Qing scholar Fu Shan 傅山 (1607–1684) further explained, "'regulations' refers to the political system; the sentence speaks of the initial institution of the legal system by the ruler of All-under-Heaven" 制，即制度之制，謂治天下者初立法制 (*Shuanghongkan ji* 32: 451). "With the beginning of regulations, there came to be names" means the establishment of names (or titles), assignment of duties, and foundation of the social system. But these "names" exist only temporarily; those who consider them constant actually forget their root.[16] Therefore, "one ought to know when to stop." "The names" cannot establish a constant system, because their appearance means the fixation of the perception of things. The function of law is also the fixation of the existing social order. In the *Laozi* interpretation, both "fixations" are incompatible with the Way.

By contrast, the *Huangdi shu* authors assert that through *xingming* the Way can originate the law. The laws derived from the Way are as well-ordered as the movements of the sun, moon and the stars. In the huge network of laws, any social relations, however complicated, can be accommodated. *The Canon: Law* manuscript from *Huangdi shu* explains:

天下有事，必有考驗。事如直木，多如倉粟，斗石已具，尺寸已陳，則無所逃其神。

When there are undertakings in All-under-Heaven, they should inevitably undergo testing and verification. The undertakings are like straightening the timber. Although there are

---

[15] *Wang Bi ji* 82. Compare with the translation in Wagner 2000: 225.

[16] Fu Shan explains: "In later generations those who rely on elevating them, only know that the names have been established; respect [them], and you can constantly possess [them]" 後世之據崇高者，只知其名之既立，尊而可以常有 (*Shuanghongkan ji* 32: 451).

many issues to deal with, if one prepared *dou* and *dan* [measures of volume], *chi* and *cun* [measures of length], then nothing will escape one's spirit-like [investigation] (*Huangdi shu* 1.1: 6 ["Dao fa"]).

The process of establishing laws is the process of implementing the Way through *xingming*. The Way is "empty and formless" 虛無無形 (*Guanzi* 36: 759 ["Xin shu shang" 心術上]); it is only through the wisdom of the sage adept, the one who "upholds the Way" 執道者 (*Huangdi shu* 1.1.2: 4 ["Jing fa" 經法]), that it can be discovered, accurately described, and communicated to ordinary members of society. Only then can human society be properly ordered. This is what *The Canon: Law* means by "As soon as *xingming* is set up and the sounds and designations established, there will be nowhere to escape and hide from correctness 刑名已立，聲號已建，則無所逃跡匿正矣 (*Huangdi shu* 1.1: 4 ["Dao fa"]).

The fundamental reason for the confidence of *Huangdi shu* regarding the establishment of *xingming* lies in the author's belief that the one who "upholds the Way"[17] can accurately express the Way through his language or words (*yan* 言), letting *xingming* appropriately manifest itself as the ideal law. The process through which the adept observes the Way and transforms it into *xingming* is depicted in another silk manuscript from Mawangdui Tomb No. 3., named by the editors *Wu ze you xing tu* 物則有形圖 (Chart on things having forms). The *Wu ze you xing tu* manuscript adopts the same ideas as *Huangdi shu*, and it can be viewed as the illustration to the *Huangdi shu*'s ideas (Fig. 20.2).

The manuscript consists of three parts: an outer square written in red ink (this part of the text is badly damaged), an internal circle written with blue-green characters, and the innermost spiral, which emulates the diviner's board (*shipan* 式盤).[18] The circle represents Heaven, and the square represents Earth. The text depicts how the adept, who comprehends the way of Heaven and Earth, precisely and selflessly presents the nature of *xingming*. The core ideas of the manuscript are presented in its innermost spiral. The characters there are written clockwise from the center outside. The four characters on the outside are "Unstimulated, there is no response" 不淦(→感)无應,[19] which summarizes the meaning of the characters at the center of the spiral. The inscription inside the spiral says:

> 應於淦(→感)，行於誰(→推)，心之李(→理)也。不淦(→感)无應。誰(→推)无不行。
> 淦(→感)至而應和，非有入也；蔡(→察)解而忘，非有外也。
>
> Responding when stimulated, proceeding when pushed, this is the patterning of the heart. Unstimulated, there is no response; when pushed it never fails to proceed. When

---

[17] Note that the one who sticks to the Way in *Huangdi shu*, may refer either to an ordinary sage adept or to the ruler.

[18] *Shipan* was used by diviners and specialists in occult arts (*shushujia* 數術家), and it represented an ancient view of the universe. The currently preserved ancient *shipan* belongs to the "Liu Ren" 六壬 type. It is divided into two plates, symbolizing heaven and earth. The two plates are connected by the axis that can be rotated.

[19] For the original, see Chen 2006. Our translation of the text follows Waring 2020 with minor modifications. The character *bu* 不 is based on Dong Shan's identification (Qiu 2014: 217–220; Waring 2020: 132n35).

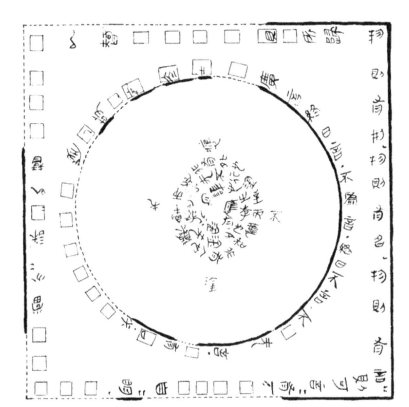

Fig. 20.2 Drawing of *Wu ze you xing tu* manuscript (by Dong Shan; from Qiu 2014: 217)

stimulation arrives and the response harmonizes, it is not a case of letting [things] in. Investigating, understanding, and then forgetting, it is not a case of letting [things] out.[20]

The vocabulary and the ideas of this short passage are deeply connected to those expressed in some of *Guanzi* 管子 chapters, as well as in the *Huangdi shu*. For instance, "being stimulated" (*gan* 感) or "responding when stimulated" 應於感 is reminiscent of such statements as "stimulated and then responding" 感而後應 in *Guanzi*[21] or "when the myriad things arrive together, I will not fail to respond" 萬物群至，我无不能應 in *Huangdi shu*.[22] Through responding to external impacts, the adept moves toward "the patterning of the heart" 心之理, which reminds of *Guanzi*'s "techniques of the heart" (*xin shu* 心術) ideas. The external characters "unstimulated, there is no response" imply that unless the heart is properly stimulated, it cannot generate the right response to the myriad things and myriad affairs. The balance of the external impact and the internal response brings to mind the idea of

---

[20] Translation borrowed from Waring 2020: 134.

[21] *Guanzi* 36: 776 ("Xin shu 心術 shang"); compare translation in Rickett 1998: 80.

[22] *Huangdi shu* 2.15: 186 ("Shi da jing" 十大經).

self-awareness (*zizhi* 自知) promulgated, for example, in the "Five Regulators" ("Wu zheng 五正) chapter of *Huangdi shu* (*Huangdi shu* 2.3: 116–23). The chapter recommends that the adept (the Yellow Thearch) first balances himself from within and grasps the proper measures, and then externalizes them in the political action. In the *Wu ze you xing tu* manuscript, the notion is similar. "Being stimulated" is the logical starting point of "responding," "being pushed" and "proceeding" (i.e., acting, *xing* 行). The pattern of interrelation between the subjective and the objective factors in one's conduct fits the ideas scattered throughout *Huangdi shu*.

The second layer of text that surrounds the spiral at the center of the manuscript reads:

> 終日言·。不為言·。終日不言·，不【為】無言·。□有□·，必□□□□□惰□故
> □□□□□□廣言。[23]
>   Speaking all day is not speaking. Not speaking all day is not being speechless. ... has ...
>   Necessarily ... idleness ... for this reason ... expands speech. (Waring 2020: 136)

The blue-grey circle around which this sentence is written symbolizes Heaven. The characters around the circle depict the process through which the adept, having grasped the Way of Heaven internally, externalizes it and expands its impact to the people. Even though the text is badly damaged and does not allow full reconstruction of its content, one can note the importance of speaking (*yan* 言) and of "expanding the speech" as part of outer impact. This allows us to connect this manuscript with the chapter "Complete laws" ("Cheng fa" 成法) of *Huangdi shu*, which reads:

> 昔天地既成，正若有名，合若有刑(形)，□以守一名。上淦(感)之天，下施之四
> 海。吾聞天下成法，故曰不多，一言而止。循名復一，民无亂紀。
>   In the past, as Heaven and Earth were completed, the names were correct, the forms
>   were harmonized. ... therewith preserve the name of the one. Above, it responds to Heaven;
>   below, it is implemented within the four seas. I have heard, as laws of All-under-Heaven
>   were completed it was said: "they are not many; [use] one word and there it stops." Follow
>   the names and return to the One; then the people's principles will not be in turmoil.
>   (*Huangdi shu* 2.9: 157; translation modified from Yates 1997: 135)

When Heaven and Earth were completed, the names (*ming*) accurately depicted the forms (*xing*); and as the two were harmonized, the Great Way was upheld. Note the resemblance of "responding to Heaven" in the above passage to the idea of "responding" in the internal spiral text in *Wu ze you xing tu* manuscript. The chapter "Complete laws" depicts the sage monarch, who, having internalized the Way of Heaven, completes the laws and then applies them among the four seas. The point in "completing laws" is not making anew many of these laws, but rather adhering to "one word and then stopping" (一言而止). The text recommends: "Follow the names and return to the One—then the people's principles will not be in turmoil" 循名復一，民無亂紀 (the One normally stands for the Way). The chapter further explains: "The hundred words have their root, the thousand words have their essentials, the myriad words have their commonalities. All pass through the single outlet

---

[23] Black dots in-between certain characters are used to divide the text into clauses. □ stands for missing characters.

夫百言有本，千言有要，萬【言】有總，皆閱一空(孔) (*Huangdi shu* 2.9: 159). This focus on multiple words or speeches (*yan*言) that all pass through the "single outlet" (i.e., the Way) brings us back to the statement "speaking all day is not speaking" 終日言，不為言 in *Wu ze you xing tu*. The meaning of that statement is probably that the speech must be aligned with the Way; otherwise it is not considered proper speech. What matters is not how much one speaks but the correctness of the speech's content. Although the textual corruption of the manuscript prevents us from proposing definitive interpretation of its content, in general it seems that the relation between its views of speech and those in the chapter "Complete laws" of *Huangdi shu* can be ascertained.

The outermost red square symbolizes Earth. The text on the inside of the square is about the *xingming* theory which holds that in order for the Way of Heaven to be implemented in the world, it is necessary to match the name with reality. It reads:

物則有刑，物則有名；物則有言，言則可言，言有【所】 【自】(自自)明 當分(分分)誅(謀?) 以智員(實?) 所歸。

> Things have forms (*xing*); things have names (*ming*); things have [ways of being put into] speech. Having [ways of being put into] speech, they can be spoken of. Speech has … illuminating … match allotments, allotments conspire [?] … in order to know … in order to know … to where [substance?] … returns. (Waring 2020: 138–39)

The sentence "Having [ways of being put into] speech, it is possible to speak about them [i.e. things]" in the *Wu ze you xing tu* manuscript emphasizes once more the importance of "speech" (*yan* 言) when implementing *xingming*. In the process of "the Way generates the law" 道生法 (which is the opening sentence of *Huangdi shu*),[24] examining *xingming* is the crucial matter. As is repeatedly emphasized in *Huangdi shu*, *xingming* is expressed through speech. Speech is intrinsically related to the process of formation of proper laws, standards and measures. For instance, "what is placed within the gauges does not speak but is trustworthy. What is observable outside the gauges, cannot be altered even if it speaks" 處於度之【內】者，不言而信。見於度之外者，言而不可易也 (*Huangdi shu* 1.9: 83 ["Ming li" 名理]).[25] In the *Wu ze you xing tu* manuscript, the term "speech" (*yan*言) appears outside the blue-grey circle (Heaven) and inside the red square (Earth), indicating its mediating role between the Way of Heaven and human affairs. The *Wu ze you xing tu* manuscript reveals the deep value of "speaking" in Huang-Lao thought, which deserves our utmost attention.

These observations allow us to contrast some of the Huang-Lao ideas with those expressed in *Laozi* and in some of the *Zhuangzi* chapters. *Laozi* famously starts with the statement, "The Way that can be spoken about is not the constant way, the name that can be named is not the constant name" 道可道，非常道；名可名，非常名

---

[24] *Huangdi shu* 1.1:1 ("Dao fa" 道法).

[25] Note that "what is placed inside the measures" can attain trustworthiness without speaking, which means that the speech is not essential (Qiu 2014: 147).

(*Laozi* 1). Here and throughout the text, it is clear that names and words do not suffice to express the Way. In *Zhuangzi*, in the chapter "Northern voyage of knowledge" ("Zhi bei you" 知北游), we encounter a similar idea: "The Way cannot be
spoken about; once you spoke, you are wrong" 道不可言，言而非也 (*Zhuangzi*
20: 192). This undermining of speech makes the idea of "the Way generates the
law" impossible for *Laozi* and *Zhuangzi*. The opposition to the sages and the laws
that they promulgate is expressed even stronger in the "Rifling trunks" ("Qu qie" 胠
篋) chapter of *Zhuangzi*: "Utterly demolish the laws of the sages in All-under-
Heaven, and for the first time it will be possible to sort out and discuss things with
the people" 殫殘天下之聖法，而民始可與議論 (*Zhuangzi* 10: 353; translation
modified from Graham 2001: 208).

This being said, we should note that certain chapters of *Zhuangzi* reflect a very
different approach toward the possibility of understanding and implementing the
Way. Among Zhuangzi's followers who contributed to the eponymous text, some
seem to have accepted the basic tenets of *xingming* thought and particularly the
importance of "names" (*ming* 名). Among the "outer chapters" of *Zhuangzi*, several—such as "Heaven and Earth" ("Tian di" 天地), "The Way of Heaven" ("Tian
Dao" 天道)and "The Turning of Heaven" ("Tian yun" 天運)— offer a reexamina-
tion of the function of law. Let us look at one extract from "The Way of Heaven":

是故古之明大道者，先明天而道德次之，道德已明而仁義次之，仁義已明而分守次
之，分守已明而形名次之，形名已明而因任次之，因任已明而原省次之，原省已明
而是非次之，是非已明而賞罰次之，賞罰已明而愚知處宜，貴賤履位，仁賢不肖襲
情。必分其能，必由其名。以此事上，以此蓄下，以此治物，以此修身，知謀不
用，必歸其天。此之謂太平，治之至也。
　　故書曰："有形有名。"形名者，古人有之，而非所以先也。古之語大道者，五變
而形名可舉，九變而賞罰可言也。驟而語形名，不知其本也；驟而語賞罰，不知其
始也。倒道而言，迕道而說者，人之所治也，安能治人!驟而語形名賞罰，此有知
治之具，非知治之道；可用於天下，不足以用天下，此之謂辯士，一曲之人也。禮
法數度，形名比詳，古人有之，此下之所以事上，非上之所以畜下也。

Thus, the men of ancient times who clearly understood the Great Way, first clearly
understood Heaven, and the Way and Virtue followed. As the Way and Virtue were clearly
understood, benevolence and righteousness followed. As benevolence and righteousness
were clearly understood, divisions and duties followed. As divisions and duties were clear,
performance (or form) and titles (*xingming* 形名) followed. As performance and titles were
clearly understood, appropriate appointments followed. As appropriate appointments were
clearly understood, inquiry and inspection followed. As inquiry and inspection were clearly
understood, right and wrong followed. As right and wrong were clearly understood, rewards
and penalties followed. As rewards and penalties were clearly understood, ignorant and
clever were properly placed, noble and base were rightly ranked, benevolent and worthy as
well as unworthy showed their true form; invariably, all were allotted tasks according to
their abilities, invariably, [the tasks] derived from their titles. This is how the superiors were
served, inferiors were shepherded, things were ordered and one's person was cultivated.
Cleverness and scheming were unused; invariably each returned to its Heavenly [endowed
nature?]. This was called the Great Peace, the utmost in government.
　　Therefore, the book says, "There is performance (forms?) and there are titles."
Performance and titles are what the men of ancient times possessed, but they did not put
them first. In ancient times, when the great Way was discussed, only at the fifth of the stages
performance and titles deserved a mention, only by the ninth stage one could speak of
rewards and penalties. To be in too much of a hurry to discuss performance and titles is to

be ignorant of their root; to be in too much of a hurry to discuss rewards and penalties is to be ignorant of their origin. Those whose words turn the Way upside down, whose explanations run counter to the Way, should be governed by others, how can they govern others? To rush into discussing performance and titles, rewards and punishments, this is to have the tools for knowing how to govern, it is not the Way of knowing how to govern. Such men are usable in All-under-Heaven, but are inadequate to make use of All-under-Heaven; these are those who are called argumentative men of service, men of one corner [of learning]. The details of rites and laws, methods and measures, performance and titles—the men of old possessed all these. Yet these are the means by which those below serve the one above, not the means by which the one above to shepherds those below. (*Zhuangzi* 13: 116; translation modified from Watson 1968: 146–48 and Graham 2001: 262)

The cited section differs dramatically from many other segments of *Zhuangzi* causing quite a few scholars to ponder whether or not it was misplaced into the text from elsewhere.[26] In the context of the current discussion, this point is less important; suffice to say that the above section reflects aspects of Huang-Lao thought. It straightens up the relationship between "Heaven," "the Way and Virtue," "benevolence and righteousness," "divisions and duties" (*fenshou* 分守), "performance (or forms) and titles" (*xingming* 形(刑)名), "appropriate appointments" (*yinren* 因任), "inquiry and inspection" (*yuanxing* 原省), "judging right and wrong" (*shifei* 是非), and "rewards and penalties" (*shangfa* 賞罰). There are nine stages from Heaven to "rewards and penalties," and *xingming* is in the pivotal fifth stage. In the stages before *xingming*, the Great Way gradually evolves from Heaven above into rules and norms that can be followed below. In the stages after *xingming*, the text shifts attention to specific administrative measures that should be carried out according to the rules derived from Heaven and the Way, ending with meting out rewards and penalties. *Xingming* is aligned with the Way, and so are rewards and penalties. *Xingming* and rewards and penalties are the branches, whereas the Way is their root or trunk. The moment these relationships between the Way and Heaven, *xingming* and rewards and penalties are established, the dividing line between theories of *Laozi* and *Zhuangzi* on the one hand and the Huang-Lao school on the other, becomes blurred. Thanks to *xingming*, the Way and law can be connected. The adherents of *fa* used this connection to establish a new theory by altering the meaning of *xingming*.

4   *Fa* Texts and the Transformation of Huang-Lao's *xingming*

The *fa* tradition, the "roots" of which "can be traced back to Huang-Lao" is fundamentally different from Huang-Lao theory. Its theory of *xingming* emphasizes the practical function of serving the monarch, and is not devoted to discovering laws that are in line with the Way. Instead, the core idea is that people should obey the law as they would be obeying the Way. The monarch should emulate the hidden and

---

[26] See the summary of different views in Chen 1994: 342–343. Chen himself considers this section an unrelated interpolation.

omnipresent power of the Way to control the people. Parallel to that, the notion of *xingming* itself is also fundamentally different from the one we encountered in Huang-Lao texts. These differences are clearly visible in the texts associated with Shang Yang 商鞅 (d. 338 BCE) and Han Fei 韓非 (d. 233 BCE).

China's traditional legal system is based on Shang Yang's legislation adopted by the state of Qin in the middle of the Warring States period. Shang Yang, who, reportedly, "in his youth was fond of *xingming* theory" 少好刑名之學 (*Shiji* 68: 2227) was an early representative of the *fa* tradition. However, he did not seek to use the Way as a blueprint for the laws. Rather, it is commonly asserted that Shang Yang's legal ideas were inspired by the *Canon of Law* (*Fajing* 法經) in six chapters composed by the Wei 魏 minister, Li Kui 李悝 (fl. 400 BCE). Putting aside the issue of the latter text's authenticity (for which see Hirose 2010: 41–69), it is clear that both Li Kui's and Shang Yang's legal systems were focused on solving practical problems and were essentially pragmatic. Li Kui's *Canon of Law* opens with items dealing with "Thieves" (盜) and "Robbers" (賊), which recalls the saying "In the governance of the True Monarch, no matters are more urgent than dealing with thieves and robbers" 王者之政，莫急於盜賊 (*Xin jiben Xin lun* 2: 5). Its subsequent chapters also focus on dealing with the problems of theft and robbery. This type of legislation is predicated on addressing society's urgent needs rather than seeking deep theoretical constructs. Therefore, the legal ideas promoted by Li Kui, Shang Yang, and their followers were primarily concerned with clarifying the content of the laws promulgated by the ruler, so that officials and the people at large could understand the laws and duly observe them. This concept of legal transparency is most vivid in the "Fixing divisions" ("Ding fen" 定分) chapter of the *Book of Lord Shang*:

> 夫微妙意志之言，上知之所難也。夫不待法令繩墨而無不正者，千萬之一也。故聖人以千萬治天下。故夫知者而後能知之，不可以為法，民不盡知。賢者而後知之，不可以為法，民不盡賢。故聖人為法，必使之明白易知，名正，愚知徧能知之；為置法官，置主法之吏以為天下師，令萬民無陷於險危。
>
> The subtle and mysterious words that should be pondered over are difficult to grasp even by a man of superior knowledge. Only one in a myriad will be able to rectify everything without resorting to laws and ordinances, rules and regulations. Hence, the sages rule All-under-Heaven as appropriate to the myriad [and not to a single person]. Thus, if only a knowledgeable [man] can understand something, it cannot become law because not all the people are knowledgeable. If only a worthy can understand something, it cannot become law because not all the people are worthy. Therefore, when the sage makes a law, he must make it clear and easily understandable. When the names are correct, both the ignorant and the knowledgeable can understand them. Law officials and clerks in charge of laws are established as teachers of All-under-Heaven to let the people avoid sinking into a perilous situation. (*Shangjunshu* 26: 146, trans. *Book of Lord Shang* 26.6)

As the above extract clarifies, the ruler should neither expect his people to understand the legal principles of order expressed in subtle language, nor should he expect the subjects to be exceptionally worthy and gifted. Rather, the chapter explains, "When the people are ignorant, it is easy to rule them" 民愚則易治也.[27] The key is to let the subjects have a clear understanding of what to do and what not to do. The

---

[27] *Shangjunshu* 26: 144; *Book of Lord Shang* 26.4; note that the sentence maybe an accidental interpolation into that chapter (Pines 2017: 307n19).

formulation of laws and the establishment of law enforcement agencies shall be based on this principle. "When the names are correct, both the ignorant and the knowledgeable can understand them" is the core of Shang Yang's theory of *xingming*. As for whether this set of laws conforms to the Way of Heaven or is integrated into a harmonic whole, it is not the matter of concern for Shang Yang and his school's theory of *xingming*. The chapter "Revising the laws" ("Geng fa" 更法) of the *Book of Lord Shang* explains: "Rituals and laws are fixed according to the times; regulations and orders are all expedient" 禮法以時而定，制令各順其宜 (*Shangjunshu* 1:4; *Book of Lord Shang* 1.4). This approach liberates legislative work from the Western Zhou principle of "clearly emulating" the legacy of former kings. But the new legislation lacks a stable and reasonable basis. The reason why the people should obey the law lies in their fear of the monarchic power. As expressed in the chapter "Making orders strict" ("Jin ling" 靳令): "Force gives birth to strength; strength gives birth to majestic awe; majestic awe gives birth to virtue; virtue is born of force. The sage ruler alone possesses it; hence, he is able to implement benevolence and righteousness in All-under-Heaven" 力生強，強生威，威生德，德生於力。聖君獨有之，故能述仁義於天下 (*Shangjunshu* 13: 82; *Book of Lord Shang* 13.6). The ultimate decisive power is the ruler's force.[28]

The idea that laws should deal with practical matters alone and should not necessarily be grounded in Heaven and the Way was at the heart of the Qin legal system. Li Si 李斯 says in the Kuaiji 會稽 stele inscription (211 BCE): "The Qin (or great?) sage looks down at his state. In the beginning, he fixed performance and titles (*xingming*); manifested and displayed old statutes, started levelling laws and models, meticulously distinguished duties and tasks, so as to establish constancy and permanence" 秦(泰?)聖臨國，始定刑名，顯陳舊章，初平法式，審別任職，以立恒常.[29] Both "performance and titles" and "laws and models" refer to the legal system. However, this kind of legal system, which reflects the will of the ruler and forces the people to follow, is quite different from the Huang-Lao theory of *xingming*. It is not concerned with internal reasonableness of the laws, nor with the Way of Heaven. The focus is purely on helping the rulers control the people by means of law. Therefore, the notion of *xingming* in the *fa* tradition is very different from that of Huang-Lao. This difference can be exemplified in the thought of the *fa* thinker who paid utmost attention to *xingming*, namely Han Fei.

The *xingming* theory in *Han Feizi* departs from the Huang-Lao theory in two important respects. First, when it speaks of the Way, it refers to "the Way of the sovereign" (*zhu Dao* 主道, the title of chapter 5 in *Han Feizi*), rather than the Way of Heaven or some other ineffable superior Way. Second, *xingming* is no longer

---

[28] This said, the *Book of Lord Shang* also cautions that laws cannot be whimsically established. The text explains: "[the sage] evaluates customs and makes them into law. Thus, when a law is established without investigating the people's disposition, it will not succeed" 度俗而為之法。故法不察民之情而立之，則不成 (*Shangjunshu* 8: 63; *Book of Lord Shang* 8.3).

[29] *Shiji* 63: 2227; for translation cf. Kern 2000: 45–46 (and n.136 there for the possible replacement of Qin 秦 with "great" [*tai* 泰]).

related to legislation, but rather focuses on supervising the ministers' words and deeds.

Let us start with the Way. *Han Feizi* devotes much space to describing the elevated status of the Way, but it skillfully interprets the Way as intrinsically related to the authority and governance techniques of the ruler. It is commonly believed that Han Fei's major contribution to the *fa* tradition was the amalgamation of the "law" (or standards, *fa* 法), "techniques" (*shu* 術), and "positional power" (*shi* 勢) into an organic whole. Yet, of high importance is Han Fei's reinterpretation of the Way as deeply enmeshed with the ruler's governance techniques, and the resultant "profanation" of the Way. This is expressed in the chapter "The Way of the sovereign" ("Zhu dao" 主道):

> 道者，萬物之始，是非之紀也。是以明君守始以知萬物之源，治紀以知善敗之端。
>
> The Way is the origin of the myriad things, the guideline of right and wrong. Therefore, the enlightened ruler holds unto the beginning and thereby understands the source of the myriad things. He examines the guideline and thereby understands the beginnings of success and failure. (*Han Feizi* 5.1; Chen 2000: 66)[30]

The chapter starts with the reaffirmation of the Way's superiority and the recommendation that the ruler grasps and follows the Way. These ideas resemble those of Huang-Lao texts. Yet the chapter continues in a different way:

> 道在不可見，用在不可知；虛靜無事，以暗見疵。見而不見，聞而不聞，知而不知。知其言以往，勿變勿更，以參合閱焉。
>
> The Way lies in being invisible; [its] utilization lies in being unknowable. Empty and still, unoccupied by any affairs, [the ruler] observes the faults of others from the shadows. He sees but is not seen; he hears but is not heard; he knows but is not known. Having understood the proposal after it was made, do not allow any changes or alterations. Check words against deeds and observe the performance. (*Han Feizi* 5.2; Chen 2000: 74)

The so-called Way of the sovereign is to prevent the ministers from observing their ruler. The ruler is still and inactive; he observes his ministers' performance and judges them accordingly. He checks their words against their deeds and then decides on rewards or punishments. The Way of this ruler—which at the beginning of the chapter is identified in a very "Daoist" manner as the "origin of the myriad things"—is for all practical matters the Way through which the ruler manipulates and controls his ministers. It is the Way of operating power. The concept of *xingming,* which in Huang-Lao thought mediated between the Way and the law, becomes here a tool of the law, the means of monitoring the ministers. This point is further clarified in the chapter "Two handles" ("Er bing" 二柄) of *Han Feizi*:

> 人主將欲禁姦，則審合刑名，刑名者，言與事也。為人臣者陳而言，君以其言授之事，專以其事責其功。功當其事，事當其言，則賞；功不當其事，事不當其言，則罰。
>
> If a ruler wishes to prohibit treachery, he should examine things and compare performance and titles (*xingming*). "Performance and titles" refer to whether one's proposals differ from one's tasks. When a minister has laid out a proposal, the ruler, on the basis of

---

[30] Here and throughout the chapter, the translation of *Han Feizi* borrows from Harbsmeier Forthcoming. The numeration of passages in Harbsmeier's translation follows Zhang 2010.

this proposal, assigns him a task, and solely on the basis of this task, demands achievements of him. When the achievements match the task, and the task matches the proposal, he is rewarded; when the achievements do not match the task, and the task does not match the proposal, he is penalized. (*Han Feizi* 7.2; Chen 2000: 126)

Here the term *xingming* is elucidated with utmost clarity. *Ming* refers to the ministers' proposals; *xing* refers to their performance. The tasks are assigned on the basis of the proposals, and the practical achievements are checked against these tasks. If the minister fails to complete the task, and his deeds did not match his proposal, he is penalized. "The Way of the sovereign" chapter further clarifies,

> 有言者自為名，有事者自為形，形名參同，君乃無事焉。
>
> Those who have proposals produce their own titles, and those who have assignments produce their own performance. When performance and title match each other, the ruler does not need to be involved. (*Han Feizi* 5.1; Chen 2000: 66)

The "speech" or "proposals" (*yan* 言) in this context is confined to the ministers, the ruler's underlings; and their speech is the foundation for applying the *xingming* technique. This differs markedly from the Huang-Lao idea of the speech being pronounced by the adept or the sage monarch, whereas *xingming* expresses the reflection of the Way of Heaven. To summarize, both the subject and the object of *xingming* have changed. *Xingming* is no longer related to legislation. The theory of *xingming* based on the desire to discover the Way of Heaven, has morphed into the technique of supervising the ministers.

5 Summary

The *Laozi* author(s), Huang-Lao thinkers and the *fa* tradition adherents—all revered the Way. *Laozi* considered the Way as ineffable and nameless; as such the Way could not be transformed into a specific law. Huang-Lao adherents, by contrast, insisted that the Way "is bound to possess *xingming*," and as such it can be expressed through "speech" and can become the law. The *fa* tradition was less interested in pursuing laws that conform to the Way. Its goal was to devise laws that could be strictly observed by the people, and that could give answers to the practical needs of the ruler and state. As a result of this reinterpretation of the law, the notion of *xingming* changed as well. It turned into a supervisory technique that could be employed by the rulers against their subordinates.

In terms of their theoretical foundations and their vocabulary, we can discover obvious similarities among *Laozi*, Huang-Lao thinkers and the *fa* tradition adherents. However, their interpretation of the core concepts led them in very different directions. Understanding these differences—in particular understanding the different view of the *xingming* idea in the texts discussed above—is essential for clarifying the gist of the three doctrines. The difference among the three epitomize the dramatic transformation of the political structure of China from the fifth to the third centuries BCE.

References

Book of Lord Shang. See Pines 2017.

Boshu Laozi jiaozhu 帛書老子校注 (Silk manuscript of *Laozi*, collated and annotated). 1996. Ed. Gao, Ming 高明. Beijing: Zhonghua shuju.

Chen, Guying 陳鼓應, ed. and trans. 1994. *Zhuangzi, with Modern Glosses and Modern Translation* 莊子今注今譯. Beijing: Zhonghua shuju.

Chen, Qiyou 陳奇猷, ed. 2000. *Han Feizi, Newly Collated and Annotated* 韓非子新校注. Shanghai: Shanghai guji chubanshe.

Chen, Songchang 陳松長. 2006. Preliminary Study on the Mawangdui Silk Manuscript *Wu ze youxing Diagram* 馬王堆帛書"物則有形圖"初探. *Cultural Relics* 文物 6: 82–97.

Chunqiu Zuozhuan zhu 春秋左傳注 (*Springs-and-Autumns Annals* and the *Zuo Tradition*, annotated). 1990. Ed. Yang, Bojun 楊伯峻. Beijing: Zhonghua shuju, rev. ed.

Cook, Constance A. and Paul R. Goldin. 2020. *A Source Book of Ancient Chinese Bronze Inscriptions*. Berkeley: The Society for Study of Early China, rev. ed.

Creel, Herrlee G. 1974. *Shen Pu-Hai: A Chinese Political Philosopher of the Fourth Century B.C.* Chicago: University of Chicago Press.

Deng, Peiling 鄧佩玲. 2019. *Study of Newly Discovered Bronze Inscriptions and Illustrative Passages* 新出兩周金文及文例研究. Shanghai: Shanghai guji chubanshe.

Durrant, Stephen W., Wai-yee Li, and David Schaberg. 2016. *Zuo Tradition / Zuozhuan Commentary on the "Spring and Autumn Annals"*. Seattle: University of Washington Press.

Graham, Angus C., trans. 2001. *Chuang-tzŭ: The Inner Chapters*. Rpt. Indianapolis: Hackett.

Guanzi jiaozhu 管子校注 (*Guanzi*, collated and annotated). 2004. Ed. Li, Xiangfeng 黎翔鳳. Beijing: Zhonghua shuju.

Guoyu jijie 國語集解 (*Discourses of the States* with combined explanations). 2002. Ed. Xu, Yuangao 徐元誥 (1878–1955), Wang, Shumin 王樹民, and Shen, Changyun 沈長雲. Beijing: Zhonghua shuju.

Han Feizi. See Harbsmeier, forthcoming.

Harbsmeier, Christoph, trans. Forthcoming. *Han Feizi, A Complete Translation: The Art of Statecraft in Early China*. Ed. Jens Østergaard Petersen and Yuri Pines. Leiden: Brill.

Hirose, Kunio 廣瀨熏雄. 2010. *Study of Qin and Han Laws and Ordinances* 秦漢律令研究. Tokyo: Kyuko shoin.

Huangdi shu: Mawangdui Han mu boshu Huang Di shu *jianzheng* 馬王堆漢墓帛書《黃帝書》箋證 (*The Book of the Yellow Thearch, a Silk Text from a Han Tomb at Mawangdui, with Commentary*). 2004. Ed. Wei, Qipeng 魏啓鵬. Beijing: Zhonghua shuju.

Hubeisheng wenwu kaogu yanjiusuo 湖北省文物考古研究所 and Suizhoushi bowuguan 隨州市博物館. 2014. "Excavation Report about Tomb M1 (the Tomb of Marquis Yu of Zeng), and Tomb M2, Suizhou Wenfengta" 隨州文峰塔M1(曾侯與墓地)、M2發掘簡報. *Jianghan Archeology* 江漢考古 4: 3–51.

Kern, Martin. 2000. *The Stele Inscriptions of Ch'in Shih-huang: Text and Ritual in Early Chinese Imperial Representation*. New Haven: American Oriental Society.

Kominami, Ichirō 小南一郎. 1992. Heaven's Mandate and Virtue 天命と德, *Journal of Oriental Studies* 東方學報 64: 1–59.

Kryukov, Vassili. 1995. Symbols of Power and Communication in Pre-Confucian China (On the Anthropology of *De*). *Bulletin of the School of Oriental and African Studies* 58: 314–333.

Laozi. See *Boshu Laozi*

Li, Xueqin 李学勤. 1990. Fan Li's Thought and the Silk Manuscript *The Book of the Yellow Thearch*. 范蠡思想與帛書《黃帝書》. *Zhejiang Periodical* 浙江學刊 1: 97–99.

Li, Feng 李峰. 2010. *Bureaucracy and the State in Early China: Governing the Western Zhou* 西周的政體——中國早期的官僚制度和國家. Shanghai: Sanlian.

Li, Xueqin 李学勤. ed. 2016. *The Tsinghua University Warring States Bamboo Manuscripts (six)* 清華大學藏戰國竹簡(六). Shanghai: Zhongxi shuju.

Lü, Dalin 呂大临 (1042–1090). 2003. *Diagrams of Investigating Antiquity from the Stillness Studio* 泊如斋考古圖. Rpt. Beijing: Beijing tushuguan chubanshe.

Luo, Xinhui 羅新慧. 2020. The Changing Concept of the Mandate of Heaven during the Springs-and-Autumns Period 春秋時期天命觀念的演變. Social Sciences in China 中國社會科學 12: 99–118.

Luo, Xinhui 羅新慧 and Yuri Pines. 2023. "The Elusive Mandate of Heaven: Changing Views of *Tianming* 天命 in the Eastern Zhou period." *T'oung Pao* 109: 1–47.

Makeham, John. 1990. The Legalist Concept of *Hsing-Ming*: An Example of the Contribution of Archaeological Evidence to the Re-Interpretation of Transmitted Texts. *Monumenta Serica* 39: 87–114.

Nivison, David S. 1996. 'Virtue' in Bone and Bronze. In *The Ways of Confucianism*, ed. Brian Van Norden, 17–30. Chicago/La Salle: Open Court.

Pines, Yuri, ed. and trans. 2017. *The Book of Lord Shang: Apologetics of State Power in Early China*. New York: Columbia University Press.

Qiu, Xigui 裘錫圭. 2014. *Collection of Bamboo and Silk Manuscripts from the Han Tomb at Mawangdui, Changsha* 長沙馬王堆漢墓簡帛集成. Beijing: Zhonghua shuju.

———裘錫圭. 2021. *Modern Study of the Laozi* 老子今研. Shanghai: Zhongxi shuju.

Rickett, W. Allyn, ed. and trans. 1998. *Guanzi – Political, Economic, and Philosophical Essays from Early China, A Study and Translation*. Vol. 2. Princeton NJ: Princeton University Press.

Shangjunshu zhuizhi 商君書錐指 (Pointing an awl at the *Book of Lord Shang*). 1986. Ed. Jiang Lihong 蔣禮鴻 (1916–1995). Beijing: Zhonghua shuju.

Shiji 史記 (Records of the Historian). By Sima, Qian 司馬遷 (ca. 145–90 BCE) et al. Annotated by Zhang, Shoujie 張守節, Sima, Zhen 司馬貞, and Pei, Yin 裴駰. Beijing: Zhonghua shuju, 1997.

Shuanghongkan ji 霜紅龕集 (Collection from the Red-Frost Shrine). 2010. By Fu, Shan 傅山 (1607–1684). Rpt. in *Compilation of Qing-Era Poems and Prose* 清代詩文集匯編, vol. 25. Shanghai: Shanghai guji chubanshe.

Tang, Lan 唐蘭. 1975. Study of the Lost Manuscripts Discovered Attached to Two Copies of *Laozi* from Mawangdui: Also Discussing Confucian-*fa* Struggle in the Beginning of the Han Dynasty　馬王堆出土《老子》乙本卷前古佚書的研究——兼論其與漢初儒法鬥爭的關係. Acta *Archaeologica Sinica* 考古學報 1: 7–36.

Wagner, Rudolf G. 2000. *The Craft of a Chinese Commentator: Wang Bi on the Laozi*. Albany: State University of New York Press.

Wang, Pei 王沛. 2009. *Study of the Origin and Development of the Huang-Lao "fa" Theory* 黃老"法"理論源流考. Shanghai: Shanghai Renmin chubanshe.

——— 王沛. 2012. "Revisiting the Concept of *fa* in the *Analects*: A Study Based on Integration of Unearthed Documents" 《論語》法觀念的再認識:結合出土文獻的考察. *Journal of the Eastern University of Political Science and Law* 東政法大學學報 1: 98–106.

——— 王沛. 2013. "*Xingming* Teaching and the Compilation of Ancient Legal Codes: Clues from the Tsinghua Bamboo Slip Collection and the *Book of the Yellow Thearch*" 刑名學與中國古代法典的形成——以清華簡、《黃帝書》資料為線索. *Historical Research* 歷史研究 4: 16–31.

Wang, Huaiyu. 2015. A Genealogical Study of *De*: Poetical Correspondence of Sky, Earth, and Humankind in the Early Chinese Virtuous Rule of Benefaction. *Philosophy East and West* 65 (1): 81–124.

Wang, Pei 王沛. 2018. New Textual Criticism on Zichan's Casting Penal Code: Research Centering around the *Zichan Bamboo* Manuscript from the Tsinghua University Collection 子產鑄刑書新考——以清華簡《子產》為中心的研究. *Tribune of Political Science and Law* 政法論壇 2: 162–170.

Wang Bi ji jiaoshi 王弼集校釋 (Collected works of Wang Bi, collated and explained). 1980. Ed. Lou, Yulie 樓宇烈. Beijing: Zhonghua shuju.

Wang, Chuanfu 王傳富 and Yang, Xuefeng 湯學鋒. 1997. "Jingmen Guodian No.1 Chu Tomb 荊門郭店一號楚墓." *Cultural Relics* 文物 7: 35-48.

Waring, Luke. 2020. Introducing The *Wu Ze You Xing Tu* Manuscript from Mawangdui. *Early China* 43: 123–160.

Watson, Burton, trans. 1968. *Zhuangzi: Basic Writings*. New York: Columbia University Press.

Wu, Zhenfeng 吳鎮烽. 2012. *Compilation of Inscriptions and Images of the Shang and Zhou Bronze Vessels* 商周青銅器暨圖像集成. Shanghai: Shanghai guji chubanshe.

——— 吳鎮烽. 2014. Combined Reading of the Inscriptions on *pan* and *dian* Vessels of the Duke of Jin 晉公盤與晉公𥂴銘文對讀 http://www.fdgwz.org.cn/Web/Show/2297 (downloaded April 5, 2022)

Xin jiben Huan Tan Xin lun 新輯本桓譚新論 (Newly Collated *New Discourses* by Huan Tan). 2009. Ed. Zhu, Qianzhi 朱謙之. Beijing: Zhonghua shuju.

Yates, Robin D.S., trans. 1997. *The Five Lost Classics: Tao, Huang-Lao and Yin-Yang in Han China*. New York: Ballantine Books.

Yin Zhou jinwen jicheng 殷周金文集成 (Compilation of bronze inscriptions from Yin [Shang] and Zhou eras). 2007. Ed. The Institute of Archaeology of China's Academy of Social Sciences 中國社會科學院考古研究所. Beijing: Zhonghua shuju, rev. ed.

Zhang, Shunhui 張舜徽, ed. 2009. *Shuowen jiezi with Brief Glosses* 說文解字約注. Wuhan: Huazhong shifan daxue chubanshe.

Zhang, Jue 張覺, ed. 2010. *Han Feizi, Collated with Subcommentaries* 韓非子校疏. Shanghai: Shanghai guji chubanshe.

Zuozhuan: see *Chunqiu Zuozhuan zhu* and Durrant, Li, Schaberg 2016

Chapter 21
Machiavelli and the *fa* Tradition

Jason P. Blahuta

The comparative literature analyzing Niccolò Machiavelli's philosophy in relation to ancient Chinese philosophy, scant as it is, is invariably drawn to the *fa* tradition. This rash decision to cast Machiavelli (1469–1527) and *fa* thinkers in similar molds is understandable, if regrettable. The *fa* tradition, articulated most fully by Shang Yang (d. 338 BCE) and Han Fei (d. 233 BCE),[1] posits a dim view of human nature necessitating severe penalties and state-controlled rewards to motivate the population, a strong military force, and the need to consolidate all power in a solitary ruler—all of which resonates well with the erroneous but popular interpretation of Machiavelli as a teacher of evil and counsellor of tyrants. Digging past Machiavelli's rhetorical flare as well as considering his other works such as the *Discourses on Livy*, the *History of Florence*, his poetry, and his military treatise *The Art of War* quickly reveals that Machiavelli is a far more nuanced thinker than has traditionally been acknowledged in this literature. Despite the many similarities between Machiavelli and his *fa* tradition counterparts, his conception of history and his more sophisticated reaction to the idea of human nature being self-interested, offers

---

[1] Machiavelli's life, at least from the moment he held his first government post, is well documented and there is no dispute concerning the authorship of his works. The same cannot be said of Shang Yang and Han Fei. Contemporary scholars have less reliable information about their lives (we have to rely overwhelmingly on the biographies prepared by Sima Qian [ca. 145–90 BCE] more than a century after Han Fei's death and two centuries after Shang Yang's death). Besides, the works attributed to them were not composed solely by them, but were in all likelihood—especially in the case of Shang Yang—the product of multiple authors articulating, and at times amending, the ideas associate with the titular figures. Despite this, for the sake of readability I refer to Shang Yang and Han Fei as the authors of these texts. Following Tao Jiang, I treat both as "textual authors," that is "an authorial personality that is primarily the product of a text" (Jiang 2021: 21–22).

J. P. Blahuta (✉)
Lakehead University, Thunder Bay, ON, Canada
e-mail: jason.blahuta@lakeheadu.ca

© The Author(s), under exclusive license to Springer Nature Switzerland AG 2024
Y. Pines (ed.), *Dao Companion to China's* fa *Tradition*, Dao Companions to Chinese Philosophy 19, https://doi.org/10.1007/978-3-031-53630-4_22

a far more viable political science than either Shang Yang or Han Fei do. Much like Jia Yi (200–168 BCE) (cited in Sima Qian 1993: 81), we may surmise that Machiavelli recognized that the methods which enable a ruler to gather his strength and overcome domestic and foreign enemies, are not the same methods which will allow that ruler to successfully govern his people during times of peace.

1 Historical Settings: Warring States China and the Italian Renaissance

The parallel historical situations these writers were born into goes a long way towards explaining why their philosophies share similar views of human nature and call for strong-measures to restore order. The political landscapes of both Warring States China (453–221 BCE) and Renaissance Italy of the late fifteenth and early sixteenth centuries were characterized by significant social and political turmoil as a string of wars were waged between various powers with plans of conquest over each region. Approaching the end of the Warring States period, the major powers consisted of Qin, Chu, Qi, Wei, Zhao, Han, and Yan. The political landscape of the Italian peninsula was similarly fractured, with five major powers—Naples, the Papal States, Venice, Milan, and Florence—all seeking to dominate the others, and all failing militarily to do so because of a reliance on low quality mercenaries and a strategy of shifting alliances that would see fear of one city's success leading to a coalition of the remaining powers against the aggressor. The situation became worse in 1494 when the French invaded Italy, as this introduced non-Italian forces with far better trained standing armies, primarily the French, the Spanish, and the Holy Roman Empire, into the Italian theatre of war. The difference between the internecine wars among the Italian powers and the intervention of foreigners highlights a significant difference between the historical contexts of Machiavelli and his *fa* tradition counterparts. Machiavelli was painfully aware of the difference of scale between the Italian states and their foreign adversaries, as evidenced by his call in the final chapter of *The Prince* for a leader to arise, unify the Italian peninsula, and push out all foreign invaders (Machiavelli 1965: 92–96). What this means for discussions of Machiavelli and the *fa* tradition, is that despite the parallel drive to end war and unite various states, Machiavelli's immediate concern deals with small states akin to city-states, whereas the *fa* theorists are concerned with much larger territorial states. Consequently, how a state is organized, including the need for and role of a bureaucracy, plays a much larger role in the *fa* tradition than it does in Machiavelli's philosophy.

The political problems of the two eras both had their roots in the legacy of preceding centuries. The Warring States period emerged out of the aristocratic Springs and Autumns period (770–453 BCE). That age was marked by the devolution of authority, first from the Zhou Son of Heaven to regional lords and then from the lords to heads of major ministerial lineages in every polity. In due time this resulted in a debilitating political crisis, the remedies to which were sought throughout much of the Warring States era (Pines 2009: 20–24). In the political realm Machiavelli saw around him, the crisis stemmed from the policies enacted by Lorenzo the Magnificent, patriarch of the infamous banking clan, who kept Florence safe for much of the fifteenth century through a strategy of playing the interests of the Italian powers off one another, but at the cost of weakening all of them over time with expensive and pointless military engagements. This became disturbingly evident when Lorenzo's heir, Piero de Medici, inherited a city that was poor and unable to defend itself. When the French invaded Italy less than two years after he took control of Florence, Piero surrendered so quickly and on such generous terms that the Florentines exiled him, and Florence switched from rule by the Medici to a republican constitution overnight. It is in these eras of uncertainty and violence in which Machiavelli, Shang Yang, and Han Fei sought to survive and serve their respective governments.

There are two differences in the cultural and intellectual contexts of these eras which help explain why the *fa* theorists and Machiavelli, despite their affinities, diverge in their conclusions, and why their proposals for how to govern have not been equal in efficacy. The first difference lies in what was considered to be a feasible form of government. Due to the large size of the states in the Warring States period and the lack of alternative political traditions, the only form of government considered viable was strict monarchism (Pines 2009: 13–111). In contrast, the legacy of the ancients provided Machiavelli with a range of government models he could draw upon, most notably republicanism which is the subject of the *Discourses on Livy*, and monarchism which is the subject of *The Prince*. The second difference is the role of the people. As far as Shang Yang and Han Fei are concerned, the monarch represents and pursues the common good, whereas subjects are seen as pursuing only their private interests, and if left unchecked, this pursuit of private interests will weaken the state. The only way to prevent the negative effects resulting from the pursuit of private interests is to put in place a system of state-controlled rewards that constitute the sole path for the people to realize their private interests, reduced to material gain and social advancement, while simultaneously manipulating their interests via a system of harsh punishments. Machiavelli also sees the people as being primarily concerned with their own interests, but the option of state intervention to direct these interests as blatantly as the *fa* theorists do is not acceptable to either him or his fellow citizens. Machiavelli proposes two solutions to the problem of the people's ambitions getting out of hand. For a solitary ruler, the prince is to ensure that the people are convinced that the prince's success and well-being are a necessary condition to their fulfilling their private interests. For a republic, Machiavelli advises organizing the political institutions such that they play the ambitions of the people off of the ambitions of the nobility in order to create conditions that will strengthen the state. In effect, this is a parallel project to Shang Yang's program of social engineering that channels the people's private interests towards the common good through state-monopoly on social and material advancement (Pines 2016: 3–4). However, in neither scenario does Machiavelli resort to state control of all aspects of life, and this allows him to avoid the problems such extreme measures generate.

2   Machiavelli, Han Fei, and Shang Yang

The political upheaval of these ages had immense consequence for all three thinkers. Not only did the existential threats facing their societies help shape their philosophies, but in the end the upheaval would largely determine their personal and
political fates as well. Someone such as Niccolò Machiavelli, talented and equipped
with a rich humanist education, but who was not politically connected to the Medici,
had little hope of participating in Florentine politics. Under the Medici, appointments were ostensibly filled via lottery, but in reality they were all patronage
appointments, not unlike the hereditary appointments that were the norm in the
Chinese world of the Springs and Autumns period. Under a republic however, much
like in the Warring States-period, merit became important, and allowed Machiavelli,
the son of a lawyer in a family that had long lost its influence in aristocratic circles,
to be nominated and appointed to office. Continued political upheaval impacted
Machiavelli many years later when the Medici were reinstated by Pope Julius II as
a punishment for Florence's refusal to join the Holy League of 1510 in the Pope's
quest to push the French out of Italian territory. Known for his republican sympathies, Machiavelli was implicated in an anti-Medici plot and subsequently impris-
oned, tortured, and exiled to his family estate outside of Florence. He was freed due
to a combination of lack of evidence and a papal amnesty. Ever devoted to Florence,
he spent the rest of his life writing about politics (as well as writing comedies for the
stage, poetry, and histories), and trying with limited success to regain a foothold in
Florentine public affairs, hoping to one day again serve the city he loved.

Han Fei had a more elevated birthright than Machiavelli, but this did not save
him; in fact, it doomed him. Like Machiavelli, he enjoyed a robust education, allegedly studying under the Confucian Xunzi (d. after 238 BCE). Whether Han Fei was
a student of Xunzi, and if so what the extent of Xunzi's influence was on Han Fei,
remains a matter of debate. Alejandro Bárcenas, for example, argues not only that
Han Fei was a student of Xunzi, but that his account of human nature is influenced
by his teacher's philosophy, and Erik Lang Harris maintains that Han Fei appropri-
ates terminology from Xunzi only to alter it to suit his own ends, while Masayuki
Sato questions the accuracy of Sima Qian's biographical account of the student-
teacher relationship between Han Fei and Xunzi and argues that Han Fei's account
of human nature could have come from sources other than Xunzi, specifically Shang
Yang, Shen Dao, and Tian Pian of the early *fa* tradition (Bárcenas 2012; Harris
2013: 127; Sato 2013). Regardless of his relationship with Xunzi, the depth of Han
Fei's knowledge of the various philosophies he discusses, his graceful writing style,
and cogent arguments make it clear that he was well-educated. Unfortunately, the
fact that he stuttered (if we trust Sima Qian's account) prevented him from advancing in the court, an arena where eloquent speech was crucial to impressing the ruler.
Han Fei's high birthright also tied him to Han and prevented him from seeking
employment abroad, unlike his fellow student Li Si (d. 208 BCE) who shared Han
Fei's intellectual sympathies and was welcomed into service with the ruler of Qin.
When Qin attacked Han in 233 BCE, the floundering Han government finally, and

far too late, turned to Han Fei for advice. He was sent on a diplomatic mission that was doomed from the start. Upon hearing that Han Fei sought an audience with the ruler of Qin, Li Si, perhaps sincerely concerned for his patron king or perhaps motivated by self-interest and considering Han Fei an intellectual threat to his own position, warned his king that Han Fei could not be trusted because his loyalty—secured by his birthright—would always remain with Han, never with Qin. Before anything came of the investigation, Li Si sent Han Fei poison in prison with instructions to kill himself, and without any hope of a personal audience with the king or of being cleared, Han Fei chose suicide (Nienhauser 1994: 29).

While Machiavelli and Han Fei were tied to their respective states, Machiavelli by patriotic love and Han Fei by birthright, Shang Yang (d. 338 BCE) was not. Shang Yang was also a scion of the ruling house in the tiny polity of Wei 衛 (sometimes transcribed Wey), but he sought employment at the neighboring powerful polity of Wei 魏. When the ruler of Wei failed to make use of Shang Yang's talents, despite the disturbing endorsement of *either make him prime minister or kill him* by his dying supervisor, Shang Yang sought employment with Lord Xiao of Qin (r. 361–338 BCE). Lord Xiao made full use of Shang Yang's ideas regarding *fa*, and Qin was quickly transformed from an aristocratic polity into a meritocracy governed by *fa* (law, standards) and devoted to agriculture and warfare. The radical changes Shang Yang introduced made him hated to the point that he reportedly required an armed escort to go out in public, as noted in the "Facing South" chapter of the *Han Feizi* (*Han Feizi* 18.4; Watson 2003: 95).[2] This pent up hatred was unleashed on Shang Yang after the death of Lord Xiao left him vulnerable, and his enemies conspired to destroy him. In the end, he was hunted down by the Qin military who killed all his family members and tore his body apart by chariots (see Sima Qian 1993: 89–100; Pines 2017: 7–24 for further details of Shang Yang's career).

The impacts of these thinkers vary considerably. Both Han Fei and Machiavelli are credited with leaving political treatises that are masterpieces in their wake, but neither made a significant impact on their immediate political settings, largely because of the ineptitude of their superiors. Had the ruler of Han, King An, listened to Han Fei, perhaps the state of Han would not have fallen so easily to Qin; and if Piero Soderini, the gonfalonier for life of Florence, had listened to Machiavelli's advice to break Florence's treaty with France and join the Holy League of 1510, the Medici may have never been reinstated and the Republic of Florence might have flourished. By contrast, the impact of Shang Yang's reforms on the state of Qin and beyond cannot be overstated and outstrip Machiavelli's impact on Florentine politics. While Machiavelli, like Shang Yang, was a philosopher and a practitioner, his efforts to make Florence strong and respected were largely thwarted by the short-sightedness of Florence's leaders and its poverty. Machiavelli excelled as a diplomat, but on one occasion was denied an important diplomatic mission because the

---

[2] Hereafter all references to the *Han Feizi* are to the division into paragraphs adopted in the forthcoming translation by Harbsmeier. Whenever relevant, I refer to Watson's 2003 translation as well.

aristocratic elements of the Florentine republic felt his heritage too lowly (Viroli 2000: 97–9). It was on another mission to the court of the French king where Machiavelli famously lamented that no other European power took Florence (or any other Italian state) seriously because they possessed weak armies and empty coffers. Even his attempts at military projects—creating a Florentine militia and diverting the river Arno to deny Pisa access to vital trade routes—ended in failure, largely because of underfunding from the Florentine government (Masters 1998). In contrast, Shang Yang was embraced by Lord Xiao and was given all the resources, both political and financial, that were necessary to enact his ideas. Consequently, Shang Yang succeeded not only in small, individual endeavours such as twice defeating the army of Wei, but also in the monumental task of transforming the state of Qin from an aristocratic polity in which heredity was the primary principle of social structure into a new type of polity in which the social structure was based on a very specific conception of merit as defined by *fa*. This system laid the foundation to Qin's success, and it was largely employed across the empire once Qin eliminated the rival states in 221 BCE.

While Machiavelli pales in comparison to Shang Yang in terms of his impact of the social-political context of his day, he exceeds his *fa* tradition counterparts in the longevity his ideas deliver. Whereas Shang Yang's system was largely discontinued shortly after the fall of Qin's empire in 207 BCE, the vast majority of states organized on the basis of Machiavelli's philosophy have lasted far longer. This lends credence to Machiavelli's claim in *Discourses on Livy* 1.2 that a state organized with sufficient prudence, viz. according to his ideas, has the potential to remain strong and independent indefinitely (Machiavelli 1965: 199).

3   The Role of History in the Philosophies of Machiavelli and the *fa* Tradition

History is central to the political philosophies of Machiavelli and his *fa* tradition counterparts, and in the end, the difference in how they conceive of history, specifically whether it is cyclic or linear, determines the viability of their advice to rulers. The idea that the *fa* tradition is grounded in an account of history may seem counterintuitive, for both Shang Yang and Han Fei make a point of disparaging habitual resort to history by their opponents, most notably the Confucians. The Confucians endorse what Kai Vogelsang (Chap. 12, this volume) dubs exemplary history, namely a view that there is an ahistorical set of principles that can apply with equal efficacy to all eras. It is not a claim that what worked in the past will work in the present, but an insistence that certain principles will hold true regardless of historical context. The *fa* tradition rejects the existence of ahistorical principles; even the *fa* itself was not eternal but was created on a certain stage of human society's evolution (*Book of Lord Shang* 7.1[3]; *Han Feizi* 49.1). For Confucians righteousness and benevolence are timeless principles. Shang Yang vehemently opposes this supposition. He admits that benevolence could be useful in the past (the middle ages), but it is irrelevant in the present when what matters is force only (*Book of Lord Shang* 7.1; 7.3). Han Fei agrees: from a series of historical examples he reminds his audience: "This can demonstrate that benevolence and righteousness had its use in antiquity but is not useful in our times" (*Han Feizi* 49.4; Watson 2003: 100). Moreover, Han Fei develops a detailed critique of history arguing that the past is an unreliable and even contradictory guide to ruling. He voices epistemological concerns about the authenticity of the teachings of the past, citing the differing interpretations of Confucians and Mohists as evidence that the true legacy of the paragon kings of the past or even of Confucius (551–479 BCE) and Mozi (ca. 460–390 BCE) are unverifiable, and hence are useless to the ruler. This skeptical logic is then applied in the "Illustrious Teachings" chapter to all attempts to find answers in the past, condemning them as the products of either fools who believe without evidence or imposters who believe what can never be substantiated (*Han Feizi* 50.1; Watson 2003: 119–20). As Vogelsang observes, even when Han Fei does praise former kings, he does so only insofar as these kings rejected following previous modes of government (Chap. 12, this volume). In short, the purpose of the *fa* theorists' critique of history, especially as it appears in the *Han Feizi*, is to undermine the value of historical knowledge as a normative guide to ruling, or as Henrique Schneider puts it, to establish that "history is a source of knowledge, not wisdom" (Schneider 2018: 45).

Like Han Fei, Machiavelli acknowledges that there are problems with historical accounts. Historical records are always incomplete, historians may whitewash the deeds of ancestors of powerful contemporaries to avoid angering the descendants of these historical figures, and even when sincere and honest, Machiavelli is aware that historians are often inconsistent in their appraisal of a subject (Machiavelli 1965: 340, 1031–32, and 63). None of this, however, is enough to cause Machiavelli to ignore the past as Rowe claims (Rowe 1982: 47). Machiavelli saw great value in history as a pedagogical tool for leaders to inform their own rule. For the solitary leader, Machiavelli counsels in Chap. 14 of *The Prince* to study military history in order to learn what to do and what not to do when they themselves must engage in warfare, and generalizes this advice to all political activity in Chap. 6 of *The Prince*, arguing that a prudent ruler looks to the conduct of legendary rulers in the past and tries to imitate them, even if he can only approximate their greatness. And in the case of a republic, Machiavelli finds value in history claiming in the Preface to the *Discourses on Livy* that the opinions of ancient jurists are the basis of current civil laws and teach present jurists how to judge (Machiavelli 1965: 56–57, 24–25, and 191).

Vogelsang argues that the *fa* tradition rejects exemplary history, adopting instead what he calls sequential history. Sequential history is not concerned with details or

---

[3] All references to the *Book of Lord Shang* are to the translation by Yuri Pines (2017).

truth per se, but provides a narrative explaining the evolution of society. These narratives lack a "common principle" and are unidirectional (Vogelsang, Chap. 12, this volume). Hence, Han Fei's sequential history manifests in his decrying references to golden ages of the past in "The Five Vermin" chapter, arguing instead that if there was more peace and less conflict in earlier ages, this was due to there being less people to compete for a finite amount of resources (*Han Feizi* 49.2; Watson 2003: 97–99). It was not the case that people were more benevolent or righteous, or even better governed, there was simply less cause for conflict. To some extent, Han Fei inherited this view of history from Shang Yang, who provides three separate accounts of the origin of society and the state as explanations for why the past was more peaceful than his own day. The first claims humans originated in female-led families (not knowing the identities of their fathers) and enjoyed relative peace until population pressure necessitated adjusting the entire sociopolitical system. The second account, which Han Fei echoes, explains the possibility of harmonious life in pre-state society because the people were few and resources were abundant. The third account deviates from the first two and portrays the primeval past as chaotic until good governance through *fa* was introduced by the sages (*Book of Lord Shang* 7.1, 18.1, and 23.1). These accounts (or at least the first two) are all unified by one idea for Shang Yang: the past cannot guide the present, because the times have changed, and what is appropriate in one era is inappropriate in another. In a manner compatible with Vogelsang's assessment, Vincent S. Leung characterizes the *fa* conception of history as a series of "irrevocable ruptures," stressing that what worked in previous ages will not work in the present age, and opening the door to the possibility that the *fa* tradition itself is only appropriate to a particular age, and will not work indefinitely (Leung 2019: 111, 117).

Machiavelli presents an account of the formation of society which parallels the origin story Shang Yang and Han Fei share. He claims in *Discourses on Livy* 1.2 that the origins of the world saw few inhabitants which were scattered and lived like beasts. Conflicts were sparse because resources were plentiful given the small and dispersed population. However, as the population grew, resources became harder to acquire, and people gathered together under the banner of the strongest among them and made that person their leader—thus, the first prince was created (Machiavelli 1965: 197). Despite the similar accounts of the origins of society, Machiavelli posits a very different conception of history than the unidirectional sequential narrative espoused by his *fa* tradition counterparts. Appearing at the beginning of Book 5 of *The History of Florence,* Machiavelli sketches out a cyclical conception of history that fluctuates broadly between states of order and disorder, with the full cycle being: "ability brings forth quiet; quiet, laziness; laziness, disorder; disorder, ruin; and likewise from ruin comes order; from order, ability; from the last, glory and good fortune" (Machiavelli 1965: 1232).[4] The consequence, for Machiavelli, is that the circumstances make the history, and thus history is subject to change according

---

[4] This view, curiously, is reminiscent of Mencius's claim that history revolves between periods of order and disorder (*Mencius* 3B9).

to the general model of this cycle, unless actions are taken by the prince to reset or prolong the cycle (Machiavelli 1965: 419–423). This quote also speaks to the relation between Machiavelli's princely and republican writings, where republics enjoy relative peace through the rule of law, while the prince appears only in times of corruption and chaos.

Both the *Book of Lord Shang* and the *Han Feizi* contain passages which resonate with, but fall short of, Machiavelli's cyclical account of history. In 4.8, Shang Yang states that "Punishments give birth to force; force gives birth to strength; strength gives birth to awesomeness; awesomeness gives birth to kindness: kindness is borne of force" (*Book of Lord Shang* 4.8). However, this claim is both unidirectional and is part of a justification of harsh punishments on the grounds that they result in kindness, for severe punishments will establish sufficient order such that no rules are broken and therefore no further punishments will be necessary. In 7.4, Shang Yang comes even closer to Machiavelli's cyclical conception of history:

> When the people worry, they become thoughtful; when they are thoughtful, they generate [proper] measures. When the people are happy, they are licentious; when they are licentious, they give birth to laxity. Hence, if you order them through punishments, the people are overawed; when they are overawed, there is no depravity; when there is no depravity, the people reside in peace, doing what they like. If you instruct them through righteousness, the people indulge themselves; when the people indulge, there is turmoil, the people will be hurt by what they detest. (*Book of Lord Shang* 7.4)

Despite the similarities, 7.4 also fails to exhibit the full cycle of historical movement present in Machiavelli's philosophy, as it maps out that (a) force (because of social disorder) creates peace, and (b) peace creates social disorder—but the two movements are not connected into a cycle, rather, they are juxtaposed to illustrate the difference between Confucian and *fa* styles of government.

Han Fei's more nuanced philosophy approaches Machiavelli's cyclical account of history at times. In "Explaining Laozi," his commentary on Chap. 58 of the *Daodejing*, Han Fei traces the interconnected origins of good and bad fortune to the point of anticipating Machiavelli's thought on this issue. He begins by locating the source of good fortune in misfortune, which gives rise to fear, causing a person's actions to be "upright and straight," which in turn leads to their reflections and plans maturing and their apprehending the "principles of things," culminating in avoiding harm, living a long life, achieving meritorious works, and enjoying wealth and nobility. Thus, Han Fei proclaims: "Bad fortune is what good fortune depends on" (*Han Feizi* 20.2.1). No sooner does Han Fei write these words, then he completes the circuit by discerning the source of disaster in good fortune, arguing that wealth and nobility make a person vain and arrogant, causing his conduct to become wicked and without "Principle," resulting in the disaster of dying before having accomplished anything. Thus, Han Fei concludes "Good fortune is where bad fortune hides" (*Han Feizi* 20.2.2). It can be said that Han Fei discerns the cyclical process, but only on a small scale—he never applies it to the level of states and history writ large.

Machiavelli, Shang Yang, and Han Fei all agree that successful rule requires one's actions being in accord with the circumstances, but for Machiavelli this means the prince must always keep up with the unpredictable Roman goddess Fortuna. In the *Tercets on Fortune*, Machiavelli describes Fortune's palace as being filled with numerous wheels turning in different directions, at varying speeds, powered by Laziness and Necessity, subject to change speed or direction without warning, and upon which the relative good and ill fortune of all persons are tied. He depicts the prince's plight as one of trying to remain on the rim of an ascending wheel, and so the prince must jump from wheel to wheel, always anticipating Fortune's whims, or risk falling to his ruin when the wheel he clings to passes its apex or changes its direction. This applies not only to the micro level of specific situations, but also to the rise and fall of states and the macro level of historical epochs (Machiavelli 1965: 747–48, 90–91). Specifically, times of chaos call for different styles of ruling than do times of peace. In contrast, for the *fa* tradition, history is unidirectional: what worked in the past is useless in the present. In the terms Han Fei uses: history has proceeded from good fortune to bad, and a return to good fortune is impossible, despite the fact that good fortune has its origins in misfortune. As a result, Shang Yang and Han Fei suffer from a blind spot that prevents them from seeing that the peace the *fa* tradition promises to establish merely sets the stage for the return of corruption and chaos. This conceptual lacuna can be explained by the fact that thoughts of the distant future were not a priority for Shang Yang and Han Fei; their energies were directed at designing a state that could survive the Warring States. It is only the First Emperor, who emerged victorious from the Warring States, but who lacked the intellectual prowess of the *fa* theorists, that rashly declared that the Qin state would rule for 10,000 generations (Leung 2019: 124–25).

4   Human Nature in Machiavelli and the *fa* Tradition

The reason history repeats itself according to Machiavelli—why rulers of different cultures and ages make the same mistakes and meet the same fates, and why the people react predictably to increased taxes, conscription, and corrupt leaders—is that human nature is constant (Machiavelli 1965: 278). Commenting on the *fa* tradition, Harris finds the most basic formulation of human nature in the *Shenzi Fragments*, which states that persons are motivated by attraction and aversion to objects and activities. This is further refined in the *Book of Lord Shang* 9.3 with social standing and material rewards being identified as what persons are attracted to, while dangerous and onerous activities are identified as what they seek to avoid. Both Shen Dao and Shang Yang assume this account of human nature and motivation to be universal, although as Harris notes, Han Fei acknowledges in "Explaining Suspicious Behavior" that there will always be exceptions (*Han Feizi* 44.3; Harris, Chap. 10, this volume). This consistency must be dealt with on two levels: motivating the people and the effectiveness of the ruler.

In terms of the people, human nature poses a serious problem for the ruler. Machiavelli and his *fa* tradition counterparts all maintain that human beings, while capable of acts of benevolence and altruism, are primarily self-interested beings.

Han Fei illustrates this in "Precautions Within the Palace" with the simple but poignant example of the carpenter who profits from making coffins; he harbours no malice toward others, but will happily benefit from their deaths (*Han Feizi* 17.2; Watson 2003: 87). This assertion forms the basis of the *fa* political doctrine that human beings are self-interested. This self-interest is the foundation of the idea that a uniform code of laws which rewards compliance and severely punishes transgressions is the most effective form of government. In particular, Shang Yang maintains this self-interest needs to be manipulated in order to motivate people to engage in activities to which they have an aversion, such as tilling and going to war. By making rewards that are valued—material benefits and social rank—available only through behavior the ruler wants to see, such as agriculture and warfare, the people will willingly partake in these activities. Coupling these rewards with severe penalties for dereliction of duty will further ensure that the people take these tasks seriously (*Book of Lord Shang* 6.5).

Machiavelli shares the same basic understanding of human nature, although he dresses it up with his characteristic flair. He states that in general men are ungrateful, inconsistent, prone to lying, and courageous in the absence of danger but cowardly when threats approach (Machiavelli 1965: 62). In judging others, he acknowledges ambition as part of human nature and observes that "it is a very natural and normal to wish to conquer, and when men do it who can, they always will be praised, or not blamed. But when they cannot and try to do so all the same, herein lies their error and their blame" (Machiavelli 1965: 18). Han Fei makes a similar prognosis, claiming that while all persons "desire to be rich and noble and to have sound health and a long life, but no one can ever be sure to avoid poverty, turpitude, and early death" (*Han Feizi* forthcoming: 20.2.4). Some commentators, such as Wu, have been swayed by Machiavelli's rhetoric and maintain his account of human nature is wicked (Wu 1970: 72–3). Yet in actuality, Machiavelli says nothing divergent from Han Fei, and offers a far more optimistic view of human nature than other Western figures such as St. Augustine or Thomas Hobbes. People are not malicious beings, but they are primarily self-interested ones. Machiavelli laments the fact that human nature is such a mixed bag, as this is what causes political problems; for if people were completely bad, the prince would be perfectly ruthless and not make so many mistakes, and if people were completely good, governing them would be easy (Machiavelli 1965: 254–5). It is the failure of humans to be consistently good or bad that complicates matters.

In "Precautions Within the Palace" the inference Han Fei draws from human nature being predominantly self-interested, is that no one can ever be trusted by the ruler (*Han Feizi* 17.1). Even under the best of circumstances, with a loyal and competent minister devoted to his ruler, Song Hongbing observes that any trust between ruler and minister is necessarily short-lived, because a ruler who takes Han Fei's advice seriously will view a successful minister as a threat which needs to be eliminated (Song, Chap. 9, this volume). While agreeing that persons are primarily self-interested, Machiavelli stops short of Han Fei's conclusion, and maintains that one can secure the trust and loyalty of others by linking them to their self-interest. Here, Machiavelli is closer to the *Book of Lord Shang* than he is to the *Han Feizi*, favoring manipulation over paranoia. Thus in *The Prince,* Machiavelli counsels that the prudent ruler commands the loyalty of his people by ensuring the people always realize that they need him regardless of the situation (Machiavelli 1965: 42). Machiavelli goes so far as to advise that the support of the people is the surest defence a prince can have against scheming ministers and aristocrats, because none of them will risk moving against a prince if it means making an enemy of large swaths of the population (Machiavelli 1965: 80, 444). This is also a corollary to one of Machiavelli's more infamous pieces of advice: it is safer to be feared than loved (Machiavelli 1965: 62). Machiavelli's rationale goes back to the prince's contest with Fortune, for the prince cannot control the people's affections, but he can control their fear, and so whereas relying on the former leaves him vulnerable to Fortune, relying on the latter does not. Similarly, Shang Yang maintains that in controlling all avenues of material benefit and social advancement, while simultaneously possessing the ability to inflict harsh penalties for the smallest infractions of the law, the ruler can manipulate the people into acting as he desires.

Even if the ruler can sufficiently manipulate the people into doing what he wants, the ruler is not exempt from human nature, and in fact, represents a special case of the problem which human nature poses, as the ruler will possess his own biases and failings, and everyone seeks to manipulate the ruler for their own gain. The stakes here are high, as Pines points out that should the ruler be manipulated and forsake enforcing the *fa* which is directed toward the common good (*gong*) in favor of his own preferences (*si*), the entire system of rewards and punishments is undermined as a new avenue of social and material advancement, namely the favor of the ruler, will become open to some (Pines 2016: 26). Machiavelli shares this concern about the ruler being manipulated by his ministers, although for him such wayward influences only effect the ruler's judgement, not the social structure itself. His primary concern regarding human nature and the ruler is that the prince's success is threatened by his inability to continually adapt to Fortune's changes due to the rigidity of his personality and the laziness of his intellect, and worse, the ever present temptation to abuse his power and become a tyrant (Machiavelli 1965: 25, 91, and 747). Han Fei also sees human nature as rendering the ruler vulnerable to manipulation and error in judgement, which is why he urges the ruler to rely on *fa* to guide him. *Fa* is the ruler's primary means of protecting himself from his human nature. Yet there is no check on the ruler to compel him to adhere to *fa* or to refrain from meddling with *fa* to suit his own personal interests (see more in Song, Chap. 9, this volume). Schneider argues against this claim, maintaining that *fa* ultimately diminishes the power of the ruler by subjecting all activities to *fa*, but as Leung aptly notes, in a state organized according to the tenets of Shang Yang and Han Fei, the ruler is an "extralegal entity" which in its singular ability to change *fa* can either ensure the adaptability of *fa* or ruin it (Schneider 2018: 47; Leung 2019: 119). Schneider is forced to concede this point, acknowledging that even in a well-organized *fa* state, at some point the ruler will need to act (Schneider 2018: 62). Human nature, it would appear, is the ruler's undoing according to both thinkers. Unfortunately, neither Shang Yang, Han Fei, nor Machiavelli offer a meaningful solution to the problem. The *fa* tradition encourages the ruler to let *fa* replace his faulty and vulnerable judgment, while Machiavelli resorts to cunning and guile for the prince, and if he succeeds in establishing a strong state, he urges him to transform his principality into a republic which will be run by political institutions and laws more than variable and fallible political actors. Yet neither Shang Yang, nor Han Fei, nor Machiavelli can force the ruler to do anything, and can only hope that the ruler will show personal restraint and act prudently when the time comes.

5   The Art of Ruling and the Science of Law

It is this realistic account of human nature that determines how a ruler must govern for Machiavelli and the *fa* tradition, but the differences in their approaches can be seen in how they respond to the role of the ruler vis-à-vis *fa*, techniques of rule (*shu*) such as the tallying of names and the two handles of government, and abuse of the system.

5.1   *Virtù* Verses **fa**

The question of the ruler's personal qualities is one of the thorniest for the adherents of the *fa* tradition (see more in Lewis, Chap. 11, this volume). In the *Book of Lord Shang* it is never addressed in earnest. Han Fei often speaks of a "clear-sighted ruler"; but overall the thinker accepts the situation that such clearsighted rulers are a rarity. In one of the text's most sophisticated chapters ("Objection to Positional Power," Han Fei plainly recognizes that his theory is based on the expectation that average rulers will be mediocrities (*Han Feizi* 40.3.2; Pines 2020). Overall, according to Shang Yang and Han Fei, the ruler is just as human as his subjects, and hence just as susceptible to manipulation, perhaps even more than the average person, because all want to manipulate the ruler. Distraction, vice, and error also plague the ruler more than most, because his position endows him with excessive means and places his every action and decision on display. Both Shang Yang and Han Fei offer the supremacy of *fa* or law as a remedy for such failings, for laws prevent error and act as a bulwark against manipulation because the ruler relies on the law instead of his own judgement in governing (*Han Feizi* 6.2; Watson 2003: 26–27; *Book of Lord Shang* 14.5). In order for the law to serve as an objective and reliable substitute for the ruler's subjective, capricious, and error-prone judgment, the law must be clearly articulated and simple in nature, and applied universally regardless of social standing or political connections (*Han Feizi* 18.1 and 49.11; Watson 2003: 91 and 109; *Book of Lord Shang* 17.2 and 26.6). Han Fei goes further and devotes significant attention to the role of positional power (*shi*) and techniques of ruling (*shu*) as means of preserving the ruler's authority and preventing him from falling prey to the manipulations of his ministers (*Han Feizi* 40.3.2, 43.1.2).

Machiavelli agrees that a well-ordered state, free of corruption, will not make exceptions to the law. In the *Discourses on Livy* 1.24 he cites Horatius' being brought up on charges of having killed his sister, despite his exemplary service to Rome, as a good thing, arguing that a well-organized republic will never allow a citizen's good deeds to excuse a violation of the law, but will mete out punishments for transgressions based on the law and not the citizen's other actions. Failure to do so opens the door to tyranny, Machiavelli argues that once a citizen knows that his reputation for good deeds has placed him above the law, he (and others like him) have no cause to fear the law. Once such arrogance takes root in a state, free government wanes (Machiavelli 1965: 251).

Despite Machiavelli's insistence on upholding the law, a significant discrepancy between Machiavelli and his *fa* tradition counterparts is clear, for Machiavelli maintains the prince must succeed not just through law, but through his virtù as well. Virtù is an ambiguous term which Machiavelli uses to refer to a range of qualities, most prominent of which are the cunning of the fox and the strength of the lion. An affinity with the techniques of ruling (*shu*) advocated by Han Fei is obvious. Of the techniques Han Fei cites in "Inner Congeries of Explanations, Part I: The Seven Techniques," the last three—issuing confusing edicts and making wily dispositions, keeping knowledge to one's self and asking advice, and saying the opposite of what one means and doing the opposite of what one intends—resonate with the cunning of the fox (*Han Feizi* 30.0.0; Machiavelli 1965: 65). The similarity is superficial, however, as Machiavelli condemns Maximilian I, a leader renowned for acting along similar lines, as being impossible to serve because none of his ministers could tell what he expected of them. For Machiavelli, the cunning of the fox is a way to anticipate traps and outmanoeuvre one's adversaries, not a technique of ruling (Machiavelli 1965: 87).

The term virtù becomes more problematic because Machiavelli often uses it in two distinct ways, the virtù of the prince and the virtù appropriate to the citizenry (Plamenatz 1972: 158). The latter, for Machiavelli, can be inculcated via laws and prudent social planning. The former, however, cannot and is ultimately the gift of Fortune. That princely virtù cannot be recreated at will in the same manner as civic virtù may be what prompts Schwartz to hold the position that Machiavelli offers a political art as opposed to a political science (Schwartz 1985: 348). However, it is inaccurate to say that Machiavelli is not offering a political science. True, he is extremely sensitive to the fact that success in politics often depends on the specific skills and personality traits—the virtù—of a prince, but Machiavelli is also concerned with establishing a well-ordered society that will retain its strength over time, and he asserts the only way to do this is through prudent social organization and law, for the prince's virtù dies with him. Thus, in Chap. 18 of *The Prince* Machiavelli claims the ancients knew of his teachings and taught them allegorically through the stories that Achilles and other princes had their upbringings entrusted to Chiron the Centaur. Commentators often make much of the animal traits of this image—the cunning of the fox and the strength of the lion—which Machiavelli focuses on, but this ignores two significant points Machiavelli makes. First, Machiavelli claims the mode of fighting appropriate to the human half of the centaur is fighting through laws, and it is only when laws are insufficient due to crisis or severe corruption that fighting like an animal becomes necessary. Second, Machiavelli argues that both modes of fighting are necessary: "a prince needs to know how to adopt the nature of either animal or man, for one without the other does not secure him permanence" (Machiavelli 1965: 64–65).

Machiavelli goes on to stress in Chap. 12 of *The Prince* that the foundation of all stable states are "good laws and good armies," a claim that Shang Yang and Han Fei would surely applaud, and in the *Discourses on Livy* 1.11 Machiavelli insists the longevity of the state depends on the prince transforming his state into a republic and organizing its social institutions so that they mimic the effects of his virtù, to the end of fostering civic virtù throughout the population (Machiavelli 1965: 47 and 226). The republican option, if properly implemented, is what enables a state structured according to Machiavellian principles to endure much longer than states structured according to the doctrines of the *fa* tradition, for states based on monarchical principles are more vulnerable to corruption and are unlikely to be the beneficiary of a consistent series of skillful rulers.

5.2 The Tallying of Names and the Two Handles of Government

A second glaring point of contention between Han Fei and Machiavelli is their respective approaches to the tallying of names (*xingming*) and wielding the two handles of government: rewards and punishments. Both are part of the techniques of rule (*shu*) Han Fei advises the ruler to employ. Whereas the previously examined techniques are secretive, to be known and employed only by the ruler, the remaining techniques must be public so that ministers and others can alter their behavior accordingly. In order to discern when rewards and punishments are merited, at least for ministers, Han Fei encourages the tallying of names (*xingming*), a strategy in which the ruler remains silent and empty, and waits for ministers to make proposals. When the minister's actions and accomplishments match the proposal, rewards are deserved. If there is a discrepancy between the proposal and the result—either excess or deficiency—then the ministers either overstated their abilities or failed in their task, and deserve to be punished. Goldin aptly characterizes this as a strategy to turn the self-interest of the ministers against them, getting maximum performance out of their abilities by encouraging them to promise the most ambitious results they can safely deliver, while simultaneously dissuading them from deceiving the ruler by promising too much (Goldin 2020: 213–15).[5]

Once it has been established that names have been tallied, Han Fei insists in "The Two Handles" that the ruler jealously guard the authority to dispense rewards or punishments, and never allow any of his ministers to exercise this authority. If

---

[5] For further discussion of the term *xingming* and its meanings, cf. Indracollo, Chap. 14, and Wang, Chap. 20, this volume.

he does so, then the people will recognize the minister as the true seat of power, and not the ruler, and the ruler will end up intimidated by his minister's growing power (*Han Feizi* forthcoming: 7.1; Watson 2003: 30–31). Despite devoting a full chapter to the topic of faithfully and effectively serving one's ruler, in which the ideal relationship between minister and ruler is characterized as one in which they "aid and sustain each other," Han Fei doubts in "The Difficulties of Persuasion" that such a relationship will last because of the self-interest of the minister and the paranoia and personal failings of the ruler (*Han Feizi* 12; Watson 2003: 77). While rulers without accountability are liable to be fickle, Han Fei devotes his critique to the ministers, itemizing in "The Eight Villainies" the various strategies in which ministers will try to use anything at their disposal to advance by either usurping the ruler's power or rendering him ineffective in particular situations (*Han Feizi* 9.1; Watson 2003: 43–48). Han Fei sums up the dangers ministers pose with the simple image of a kettle. He argues in "Precautions Within the Palace": "It is obvious that, under normal conditions, water will overcome fire. But if a kettle comes between them, the water will bubble and boil itself completely dry on top, while the fire goes on burning merrily away underneath, the water having been deprived of the means by which it customarily overcomes fire" (*Han Feizi* 17.3; Watson 2003: 89). This image illustrates how a ruler can be contained and undermined by his ministers, for if there are problems among the people, the ruler's only way to extinguish these problems is through the law and the two handles of government. If, however, ministers are allowed to assume the authority of the two handles of government, either doling out punishments or rewards, or if they are permitted to make exceptions or changes to the law, they render the ruler impotent. The fact that water—the Daoist ideal of efficacy—can be contained and made useless is a strong indictment for Han Fei to make, and one that shows that while some of the roots of his philosophy may be Daoist, he clearly rejects Daoism as a practical guide to ruling in favor of rule by law (Blahuta 2015: 147–75). Shang Yang also views the possibility of ministers blocking the law as so dangerous to the ruler, that he insists on the death penalty for even low-level administrators who abuse their power by altering the law, even by one character, through addition or omission (*Book of Lord Shang* 26.3).

Machiavelli generally agrees, claiming in Chap. 3 of *The Prince* that making others, even ministers, powerful is a bad idea likely to cause serious problems for the prince, but he disagrees with the claim that one should never divest himself of certain powers (Machiavelli 1965: 20). Instead, in Chap. 19 Machiavelli offers the prince a strategy premised on a more nuanced view of human emotions than Shang Yang or Han Fei possess: the prince should retain the authority to mete out rewards and punishments, however whenever punishments are severe, the prince should delegate their distribution to an underling (Machiavelli 1965: 70). Han Fei considers and rejects this option in "The Two Handles," citing the case of the ruler of the state of Song, who delegated this ability to the chief minister Zihan, only to lose influence and eventually the throne to Zihan (*Han Feizi* 7.1; Watson 2003: 30). However, Han Fei, not to mention the ruler of Song, never fully did what Machiavelli advises, for the Florentine continues: once the extreme punishments have been administered, and the people resent and hate the underling and his usefulness is over, the prince should exterminate this minister. As a result, the people will be grateful to the prince for having killed someone who terrorized them, and will be in awe of the prince because he killed someone they feared. As evidence of this policy's effectiveness, Machiavelli points in Chap. 7 of *The Prince* to the example of Cesare Borgia, who tasked Remirro de Orco with subduing the lawless Papal States by whatever cruelties were necessary, and afterwards cut him in half and left his body in the public square (Machiavelli 1965: 31). Had the ruler of Song executed Zihan after he meted out a series of punishments, he would have never become intimidated by the growing power of his minister.

The difference between this approach and the one advocated for by the *fa* tradition is significant. *Fa* thinkers maintain that only fear will keep ministers and subjects obedient, and therefore only the ruler can be allowed to command the fear of others through the use of punishments. However, both Shang Yang and Han Fei are oblivious to the fact that fear can become hatred if fear or state sanctioned violence becomes extreme or is prolonged over a long period of time. Machiavelli was well aware of this possibility and so in addition to the strategic use of expendable underlings, he advises in Chap. 8 of *The Prince* that violence is to be done all at once, with surgical scope and precision, so as to avoid generating hatred (Machiavelli 1965: 38). Machiavelli's sensitivity to the full range of human emotions and his reliance on political artistry enables him to skirt around the deficiencies of his *fa* tradition counterparts in this respect and offer a more open society, one in which citizens can lead full and rich personal lives but in which the prince can still command the people's obedience.

5.3   Abuse of the System

A third significant difference between Machiavelli and the *fa* tradition is how violations of the law are handled. This is a crucial issue, for such violations can be devastating to the legitimacy of a system if they are seen to go unpunished. In the *fa* tradition, such abuse of the system is best illustrated by the Crown Prince of Qin who broke the law (Wilkinson 1998: 137). The story is narrated in the "Biography of Lord Shang" (Sima Qian 1993: 93). According to the *fa* principles, the crown prince had to be punished, as no one was exempt from the law. Since the mutilating punishment could not be applied to the crown prince, however, a literal application of the law was perverted to the point where the prince's tutor (also a senior member of the ruling lineage) was punished in his stead as the one responsible for forming the crown prince's character. This logic quickly leads to a problematic conclusion: if breaking the law is a result of bad character, and it is the one who formed the character that is truly responsible and deserves to be punished, then it is the ruler who should be punished when any law is broken. After all, the ruler makes the laws, and the laws are the sole source of education in the state envisaged by Shang Yang and Han Fei, hence the ruler is ultimately the one who forms the character of each and every subject. Clearly, this would be unacceptable to any *fa* thinker. As Victoria Tin-bor Hui aptly observes, while it is generally assumed that a body of impersonal laws will mitigate arbitrary rule, in the absence of constitutional democracy, customs possess the inertia of tradition, and are thus more stable than any set of positive laws, even if universally binding, which ultimately reflect the mercurial will of the ruler. Thus, Hui concludes that under such circumstances "there could be only the rule *by* law (with rulers above the law), not the rule *of* law (with rulers subject to the law)" (Hui 2005: 181).

The difference between Han Fei and Machiavelli on this point is telling—in a state based on *fa*, the ruler will always be beyond the law for the simple reason that he is the sovereign, whereas the prince will preserve the illusion of his law-abidingness by using craft and guile to avoid being seen as breaking the law, by having others violate the law for him, and then, if necessary, holding them accountable. In the *Discourses on Livy* 1.34 Machiavelli is clear that for the ruler to openly break the laws, even for good reasons, sets a dangerous precedent and will quickly lead to the law being broken for bad reasons (Machiavelli 1965: 268).

The problem is there will be times, such as states of emergencies and times of severe corruption, when the prince will need to flout the law and discard conventional morality so openly and so often that he will be unable to blame these transgressions on others. In the case of a republic, Machiavelli offers a solution that resonates with the *fa* tradition: the legal office of dictator. Machiavelli vehemently defends the office used effectively during Rome's republican phase, arguing it allows for swift action unencumbered by the ambitions and factionalism of committees, and if properly organized, will never do harm to a state. The similarity with the *fa* tradition quickly breaks down, however, when what Machiavelli means by *properly organized* is considered, for the office of dictator, unlike the political structures of monarchism in Warring States China is entirely subject to the law. The dictator is chosen by the Consuls, the term of dictator is not open ended, but is set by the crisis at hand and cannot exceed the resolution of the crisis, and the power of the dictator is circumscribed to only dealing with the crisis at hand and meting out punishments without the possibility of appeal—no authority can be taken from the people or the Senate, no institutions can be abolished and none created, thus neither the people nor the structure of the government can be perverted (Machiavelli 1965: 267–69). The most important aspect of these restrictions for Machiavelli is that they make the office of dictator a constitutionally sanctioned phenomenon. That legality be observed is of the utmost importance for Machiavelli, for any public violation of the laws undermines the credibility of the system of government, and this is why Machiavelli holds Cincinnatus in such high regard. Lucius Quinctius Cincinnatus (d. ca. 430 BCE) was plowing his small farm when he was called upon by the Roman Senate to assume the office of dictator and save the Consul Minutius and his army from certain ruin at the hands of the Aequi. Cincinnatus raised an army of his own, rescued Minutius and his army, demoted Minutius for his incompetence, forbid the troops to keep any plunder, and then promptly vacated the post of dictator so as to return to tilling his meagre lands (Machiavelli 1965: 487). The focus of Machiavelli's comments are on the modest economy which satisfied Cincinnatus, and on the effect this had on the troops who followed his example. Part of this, and even more important, is that Cincinnatus' honoring of poverty extended to the possession of power too—the relinquishing of power when the situation calls for it is the truest sign of greatness in Machiavelli's philosophy and is often what distinguishes legendary princes from tyrants.

6   Nothing Lasts Forever: Corruption and the Need for Renewal

Machiavelli's worldview, heavily influenced by the Roman philosopher-poet Lucretius, maintains that the world is constantly changing and thus no state of affairs can last indefinitely. This idea of constant change underlies his cyclical conception of history. Even if no states of emergency arise, corruption of even the most well-ordered state is inevitable according to Machiavelli, for the simple reason that unless the people experience something themselves, the impact of dramatic events fades and is quickly forgotten. This renewal, Machiavelli claims in *Discourses on Livy* 3.1, is a cyclical returning to the state's roots, specifically the general conditions of their origin and early years: "The way to renew them, as I have said, is to carry them back to their beginnings; because all the beginnings of religions and of republics and of kingdoms must possess some goodness by means of which they gain their first reputation and their first growth" (Machiavelli 1965: 419). This is a crucial difference between Machiavelli and his *fa* tradition counterparts, because while Shang Yang and Han Fei accept the inevitability of occasional bad rulers, neither anticipates or directly addresses the possibility that a state structured faithfully according to their philosophies could ever become so corrupt that it would require a reset.

If the renewal Machiavelli envisages is the result of internal factors, these will either be the laws of the state or the actions of good citizens. The legal path to renewal requires laws which combat the ambitions and pride of citizens, a proposition with which Shang Yang fully agrees if such ambitions operate outside of *fa*, and further, that these laws be brutally enforced at least once every decade as the Florentine government did from 1434 through 1494. The other internal option for renewal is the appearance of an exceptional citizen who will act as a nexus that will become the center of such a rejuvenation. This option relies less upon the wisdom of those who govern and more on the whims of Fortune—in this sense it is no better than the necessity imposed from without, for it is entirely beyond the control of the government. The qualities of this individual are described vaguely by Machiavelli, and it is clear that this person is princely material in that they possess virtù in such abundance and their reputation is so renowned, that good citizens want to imitate them, and bad citizens become ashamed to be seen as failing to be like them (Machiavelli 1965: 421).

The external route is the least preferable means of rejuvenation because it is delivered entirely unto a state by Fortune. Machiavelli discusses Rome's loss to Gaul as such an occurrence that finally brought the Roman people back to their beginnings, so that they were able to rise to the occasion, clamp down on corruption, and renew their religious institutions and commitment to justice. Despite Rome's eventual resurgence and victory, it is clear from Machiavelli's attitude that a victory like this, one that is given by Fortune, is a second rate victory. Far better would it have been for the Romans to have reformed themselves without the need of Fortune's prompting, for Fortune is fickle and could just as easily have abandoned Rome to the Gauls.

Like his *fa* tradition counterparts, Machiavelli's preference is clearly for laws, but there are two times when the extraordinary citizen is the only recourse. The first is the founding of a state, which always requires swift action and some form of violence in Machiavelli's estimation due to the precarious and vulnerable conditions into which new states are born. The second is when the state has let itself go too far and suffers from widespread corruption, both in the sense of the behavior of the populace as well as the legal structures that form the government. In such a case, the enforcements of the law necessary to restore order would not occur due to influence peddling, or if such extreme punishments did occur, they would be the result of partisan politics and be directed towards the ambitions of factions within the state, not the good of the state. Machiavelli reaffirms this point, albeit in a slightly different context, when he judges that introducing a republic into the Kingdom of Naples, Rome, or the Papal states would be a venture doomed to failure because of the widespread corruption of the people, for "where the matter is so corrupt that the laws are not restraint enough, along with them some greater force must of necessity be established, namely, a kingly hand that with absolute and surpassing power puts a check on the over-great ambition and corruption of the powerful" (Machiavelli 1965: 309). This resonates strongly with Shang Yang and Han Fei: the reform of a weak and corrupt state cannot be accomplished without harsh measures. This focus on the good of the state, even if the prince is clearly the primary beneficiary of it, parallels Han Fei's portrayal of the rule as devoted to the common good (*gong*) as opposed to partisanship (Pines 2009: 105).

Thus, in a manner echoing the *fa* tradition, Machiavelli counsels that when reforming a state that has grown corrupt, one ought to gather all authority unto oneself and act alone. Reforming a corrupt state will require sacrifices; if not of blood, certainly of the interests of many partisans, and the only way to ensure that these sacrifices are made is to be free of those factions. A senate or other ruling body simply has too many persons to be effective, and will instead be a septic pond of divided loyalties and conflicting ambitions. A single individual has a better ability to be focused on a vision of the health of the state, and if they do so sincerely, without any thought of their own personal self-interests (beyond historical glory, which is the only personal interest a great leader is permitted by Machiavelli), he deems them praiseworthy no matter their actions, arguing in *Discourses on Livy* 1.9 that a prudent intellect would never "censure anyone for any unlawful action used in organizing a kingdom or setting up a republic. It is at any rate fitting that though the deed accuses him, the result should excuse him; and when it is good, like that of Romulus, it will always excuse him, because he who is violent to destroy, not he who is violent to restore, ought to be censured" (Machiavelli 1965: 218).

Machiavelli also acknowledges that the renewal of a republic done by one individual must be the exception to the rule, otherwise tyranny is likely if not inevitable. The authority the individual claims for himself must be returned to the republic when the time of crisis is over, or if not then, at the end of the individual's life, for the odds of multiple lone rulers who are equally talented and devoted to the public good ruling a state in succession are not favorable. Abuses will happen, and corruption will occur all the more rapidly because of the centralized authority. A well-ordered state under the control of one person can survive the incompetence of a leader for a limited time, as many examples from recent history demonstrate, but Machiavelli is pessimistic about the long-term prospects of such a state. Han Fei dismisses fears of an incompetent or tyrannical ruler in "Objection to Positional Power," arguing that while oppressive rulers such as Jie and Zhòu are possible, just as morally enlightened rulers such as Yao and Shun, they are all exceptions to the rule. The point of unassailable centralized power, or positional power (*shi*) in Han Fei's terms, is to allow for the mediocre ruler, of which there are plenty, to rule effectively. Han Fei concedes that every once in a thousand generations positional power will allow for a sadistic tyrant to ascend the throne, but he maintains that such an isolated incident is better than suffering through the chaos of a poorly organized state with no positional power for a thousand generations waiting for the appearance of morally exemplary rulers like Shun and Yao to appear and set things right (*Han Feizi* 40.3.2). Han Fei concludes that the individual qualities of the ruler are irrelevant, if positional power is in place, a mediocre ruler is sufficient to run the state and there is no need to wait for a ruler of elevated moral worth (Pines 2020: 702–03).

The logic of Han Fei appears solid, except that he underestimates the damage an exception can do. Cruel, short-sighted leaders such as Jie and Zhòu, can make life hard for a generation, but a ruler who is intelligent and malicious, or weak-minded but surrounded by astute ministers, can undermine the entire system (possibly even rejecting the *fa* system in favor of a competing philosophy) and create a lasting chaos that threatens the very existence of the state. This may not justify the call for leaders to be "worthies," which is the view Han Fei seeks to refute, but the fact that the ruler is capable of bringing the entire system down does expose the fatal flaw in the *fa* system of governance. Times will change, crises will occur, and given enough time, corruption will take root and grow. The short and dramatic history of the Qin empire—the only imperial dynasty that had openly endorsed the *fa* tradition, and which was ruined, if we are to believe Sima Qian (ca. 145–90 BCE) because of the notorious ineptitude of the Second Emperor (r. 209–207 BCE)—can prove this point. On this count, Machiavelli is more realistic than his *fa* tradition counterparts.

7 The Failure of the *fa* Tradition: The Descent from Order to Tyranny

The *fa* tradition is shockingly effective in times of crisis. It can take a weak, impoverished and unproductive state and transform it into a financial and military force to be respected, if not outright feared. The methods Shang Yang and Han Fei recommend are severe, but given the alternative of living with constant internecine warfare of the Warring States period, life in a *fa*-based state may have been preferable for most subjects. The question is: can the *fa* tradition serve as a viable form of government once peace, viz. military supremacy, has been achieved? Without the chaotic suffering of the Warring States period looming as a threat, the *fa* tradition has little to offer the populace and becomes a pointless tyranny which can only be borne for so long. This explains, at least partially, why the state of Qin could overcome all other states and bring an end to the Warring States period where other states failed to do so, but could not survive under the weight of its own system of governance for more than a couple of decades as Jia Yi (above, p. 596) observed.

Part of the wisdom of Machiavelli is the intelligent and strategic application of violence so as to make it known that such consequences can and will be visited upon anyone who transgresses the law in a significant manner, while stopping short of traumatizing the general population or becoming ineffective. The goal is to make people fear violating the law, not to terrorize them, but despite Shang Yang's claims to the contrary (*Book of Lord Shang* 17.3), this is exactly what the constant threat of harsh punishments and collective responsibility do. Far from the *fa* tradition which holds everyone under the ruler's microscope, Machiavelli's prescription is simply to make an episodic example of someone who has violated the law, and if no such person can be found, to trump up charges against an individual. Rather than make the entire population suffer, all that is needed is a high-profile enforcement of the law roughly every ten years, for when the memory of such spectacle and punishment fades, individuals will become arrogant and "take courage to attempt innovations and to speak evil" (Machiavelli 1965: 421). Periodic violence is enough to stress respect for the law, but is rare enough not to bully people and elicit their hatred. Violence can be kept to a minimum, Machiavelli insists, if a state can be rejuvenated before descending into widespread chaos or has made legal preparations for dealing with crises.

Shang Yang and Han Fei reduce the richness of life, including morality, to mere adherence to *fa*. The regime sponsored by the *fa* tradition allows no citizen to have a personal space; collective spying (which Han Fei inherits from *The Book of Lord Shang*) and the need to tally names leaves no room for privacy, basic freedoms, or error. Everything must be exact and controlled, subject to *fa*, and directed towards the ruler. In short, the *fa* tradition sponsors a vision of society that goes beyond authoritarianism and is disturbingly close to some aspects of Hannah Arendt's analysis of totalitarianism. Arendt equates totalitarianism with an "iron band" which "presses people together" to such an extent that there is no space, no freedom of movement, no freedom of thought, neither in public life nor in private life (Arendt

1994: 466). The control over society which Han Fei advocates is so extreme that he advocates killing anyone who does not submit to the state-sponsored system of rewards and punishments, such as the two recluses (*Han Feizi* 34.1.7). In short, anyone whose existence is not controlled by the state apparatus and who therefore does not exist for the ruler, is a threat to the ruler and must be eliminated. People may be beaten into submission in this manner, but it pushes them too far and robs them of their humanity too much for such a political system to endure for very long. As Machiavelli observed, it is better to be feared than loved, however one can never allow oneself to become hated. Ultimately, the *fa* tradition is a political systems that provokes hatred from its subjects, and all the more quickly if the *fa* tradition is abused or becomes corrupt. As Tao Jiang comments:

> The *fajia* thinkers put all their faith in the political system they designed, which was supposed to operate on its own, vastly underestimating the intractable variations of problems and situations in the human world beyond the (inevitably) limited imagination of the designers and the engineers of that system. Left to its own device, the impartialist state, conceived of by Han Feizi and other *fajia* thinkers, was totalitarian in its monopoly of values under Heaven since no alternative source of values was allowed under such a system. ... This totalitarian orientation toward impartiality articulated and defended in the *fajia* project exposed a dark side to a single-perspective, monistic notion of justice, especially when it is enforced by an all-powerful state, if that idea is untampered or unbalanced by other norms like humaneness or personal freedom (Jiang 2021: 457).

In contrast, Machiavelli clearly believes that while rule of law is important, even if it can and should be violated when necessary, morality was not simply adherence to the law as it is for Shang Yang and Han Fei. In *The Prince* he argues that power at any price cannot be justified, claiming that "[i]t cannot... be called virtue to kill one's fellow-citizens, to betray friends, to be without fidelity, without mercy, without religion" and advises the prince to be moral when possible, but to be willing and capable of being immoral when necessary (Machiavelli 1965: 36 and 66). Clearly there is a standard of morality which may be reflected in the law, but which is not exhausted by the law, and this is indicative of Machiavelli's approach to political philosophy in general. He offers a vision of the state, be it a princedom or a republic, that allows for significantly more freedom than Shang Yang and Han Fei can tolerate; there is space in Machiavelli's advice to the ruler for people to have privacy, professions, and personal relations that are not intruded upon by the state and are not geared towards the ruler. Even his infamous claim that it is better to be feared than loved is benign in comparison to the attitude of *fa* thinkers, for Machiavelli advises this only because one cannot be simultaneously feared and loved for a long period of time. Instead of controlling everyone through the use of spies, collective responsibility, and the tallying of names, Machiavelli's advice to the prince is much more humane—the prince is to ensure that everyone at all times needs him, and if this is done well, he will have no fear of anyone moving against him or of the people not being there to serve him faithfully when he requires it. This is seen in Chap. 20 of *The Prince* where Machiavelli cites the fearful support of the people as the best defense against assassination, and again in Chaps. 12 and 13 from a different perspective in his analysis of the different kinds of armies, where his advice is that the prudent ruler will rely on a militia as opposed to an ally's army or mercenary soldiers because, among other considerations, a militia is bound to the ruler more strongly than these other types of troops (Machiavelli 1965: 80–21 and 46–55).

The only time that Machiavelli approaches the uncompromising, heavy-handedness of his *fa* counterparts is in relation to the political aspirations of others. Otherwise, citizens, beyond fulfilling their civic duties, are free to have personal lives and to participate in the private and social goods that make persons full-fledged human beings. The schism between Machiavelli and the *fa* tradition on this point undoubtedly is influenced by the difference in size between the states they were dealing with (large territorial states as opposed to city-based regional powers) as well as the precedents for political organization available in each context. Rome's republican legacy allows Machiavelli to see the people as citizens capable of participating not just in bureaucracy, but in governing themselves; whereas in the Warring States era, with monarchism as the only viable system of government, the *fa* tradition can see the people only as subjects in need of a ruler.

Admittedly, there are times when the prince will have to contravene the law due to a crisis or extreme corruption. In such instances Machiavelli still maintains that the law must appear to be sacrosanct; violations of the law are to be delegated to disposable underlings who can take the fall and be made examples of afterwards. Thus Cesare Borgia's use of Remirro de Orco to pacify the lawless papal states via bloodshed and cruelty followed by the well-advertised execution of this monstrous lieutenant would have a greater effect on the public's respect for the law than punishing the Crown Prince of Qin's tutor for his charge's breaking of the law, for Cesare's actions stressed not just the importance of respect for the law, but through his guile showed no exception in holding those of high rank directly accountable.

If the prince transforms his kingdom into a well-organized republic, as Machiavelli advises, corruption should be minimal and kept at bay by periodic examples of what happens to those who violate the law, and therefore the need to take actions that would contravene the law should be rare and prompted only by cases of supreme emergency. Even in such isolated situations, Machiavelli still insists on the rule of law, which is why he endorses the constitutional legality of the office of dictator to grant a chosen individual the sweeping powers necessary to deal with the crisis.

Machiavelli's republic has checks and balances within it, but the state Shang Yang and Han Fei envisage has only *fa*, which an inept ruler can change in an unwise fashion, or easily circumvent to the detriment of all. Further, *fa* is unlikely ever to apply to the ruler himself, which undermines the entire basis of a *fa*-based state: the impartial application of law to all persons. More importantly, Machiavelli understands that in the bigger picture, not everything is a crisis. As Fabrizio declares in Book 1 of *The Art of War*: "I have never practiced war as my profession, because my profession is to govern my subjects and to defend them, and, in order to be able to defend them, to love peace and to know how to make war" (Machiavelli 1965: 580). Thus, in Machiavelli's experience, war is simply part and parcel of politics in a world where others are not going to be consistently good. But for the *fa* tradition almost everything is—or threatens to become—an existential threat that requires the total mobilization of human and material resources of the state to combat it. The leader takes Machiavelli's assertion in Chap. 14 of *The Prince* that war be the sole occupation of the prince and applies it to all situations. This, in effect, distorts Machiavelli's advice, for the idea that the prince must devote himself entirely to the art of war is appropriate guidance only because the prince's very presence is made possible and necessary by the extreme, widespread corruption from which the state suffers. In short, times of corruption and crises require the art of war, and the crises the prince faces require him to be constantly engaged in warfare or planning for it. The well-ordered republic, however, will have peace as its norm and corruption or crisis as the exception to the rule, and hence Fabrizio's wisdom of the need for knowing how to govern under both conditions. Even if the prince never transforms his state into a republic as Machiavelli encourages, Machiavelli makes it clear throughout his writings that attaining power and ruling are two different things, and require different methods on the part of the prince.

The *fa* theorists do not generally make such distinctions. This was the point noted by Jia Yi who viewed this lack of differentiation as the major reason for Qin's swift collapse: "[I]t [Qin] failed to rule with humanity and righteousness, and did not realize that the power to attack, and the power to retain what one has thereby won, are not the same" (Sima Qian 1993: 80). Dawid Rogacz characterizes Han Fei's comments on the future as utopian, but notes that Shang Yang is somewhat silent on what an established *fa* state, a fourth dynasty, would look like, refraining from providing "a direct form to this vision as any kind of description of an epoch" akin to the epochs he discusses in Chaps. 7 and 18 (Rogacz 2020: 52, 54; *Han Feizi* 28.7; *The Book of Lord Shang* 7.1, 18.1). Pines is more charitable to the *fa* tradition, noting that while Han Fei is vague on what a *fa*-based state would look and function like during times of peace, the *Book of Lord Shang* offers a reference to what such rule *might* look like, arguing that only the sage ruler is capable of "implementing benevolence and righteousness in All-under-Heaven" (*Book of Lord Shang* 13.6; Pines 2013: 34). However, this is only one passage, possibly the addition of a later contributor as Pines suggests, between the two most renowned treatises of the *fa* tradition. And while it can be interpreted as an admission that once order and security have been achieved, something different from, or in addition to *fa*, will be appropriate, it says nothing specific as to what this form of rule would actually look like. Further, when viewed against passages such as 18.8, where "[real] righteousness" is equated with the results of structuring society according to *fa* as opposed to Confucian principles, the "benevolence and righteousness" referred to in 13.6 may be nothing more than the lack of punishments which result from social stability and unwavering adherence to *fa* (*Book of Lord Shang* 18.8). As a result, this passage, even if charitably interpreted, is drowned out by the rest of the *fa* tradition, which does not merely use times of peace as opportunities to prepare for future conflicts, but treats peace as a mere lull in the battle, and views the people as a constant threat. In short, the *fa* thinker sees the ruler as always being at war—with other states, with his ministers, and with his subjects—and makes no attempt to characterize politics as anything else.

References

Arendt, Hannah. 1994. *The Origins of Totalitarianism*. New York: Harcourt.

Bárcenas, Alejandro. 2012. Xunzi and Han Fei on Human Nature. *International Philosophical Quarterly*. 52 (2): 135–148. (A thorough examination of the aspects of Han Fei's account of human nature which can plausibly be attributed to Xunzi's influence.).

Blahuta, Jason P. 2015. *Fortune and the Dao: A Comparative Study of Machiavelli, the Daodejing, and the Han Feizi*. Lanham MD: Lexington Books.

The Book of Lord Shang: Apologetics of State Power in Early China. 2017 (abridged and rev. ed., 2019). Trans. and ed. Yuri Pines. New York: Columbia University Press.

Goldin, Paul R. 2020. *The Art of Chinese Philosophy: Eight Classical Texts and How to Read Them*. Princeton NJ: Princeton University Press.

Han, Feizi. forthcoming. Trans. Christoph Harbsmeier, ed. Jens Østergaard Petersen and Yuri Pines. Leiden: Brill.

Harris, Erik Lang. 2013. Han Fei on the Problem of Morality. In *Dao Companion to the Philosophy of Han Fei*, ed. Paul R. Goldin, 107–130. Dordrecht: Springer.

Hui, Victoria Tin-bor. 2005. *War and State Formation in Ancient China and Early Modern Europe*. New York: Cambridge University Press.

Jiang, Tao. 2021. *Origins of Political-Moral Philosophy in Early China: Contestation of Humaneness, Justice, and Personal Freedom*. Oxford: Oxford University Press.

Leung, Vincent S. 2019. *The Politics of the Past in Early China*. New York: Cambridge University Press. (An insightful analysis of the various conceptions of the past and how they were used in different ancient Chinese philosophies.).

Machiavelli, Niccolò. 1965. *Machiavelli: The Chief Works and Others*, vol. 3. ed. Allan Gilbert. Trans. Allan Gilbert. Durham [NC]: Duke University Press.

Masters, Roger D. 1998. *Fortune is a River: Leonardo da Vinci and Niccolò Machiavelli's Magnificent Dream to Change the Course of Florentine History*. New York: The Free Press.

Nienhauser, William H., Jr., ed. 1994. *The Grand Scribe's Records. Volume VII. The Memoirs of Pre-Han China, by Ssu-ma Ch'ien*. Bloomington: Indiana University Press.

Pines, Yuri. 2009. *Envisioning Eternal Empire: Chinese Political Thought of the Warring States Era*. Honolulu: University of Hawai'i Press.

———. 2013. From Historical Evolution to the End of History: Past, Present, and Future from Shang Yang to the First Emperor. In *Dao Companion to the Philosophy of Han Fei*, ed. Paul R. Goldin, 25–45. Dordrecht: Springer. (An insightful look at Shang Yang and Han Fei's philosophy of history, including the implications for a state run according to *fa* principles.).

———. 2016. Social Engineering in Early China: The Ideology of the *Shangjunshu* (*Book of Lord Shang*) Revisited. *Oriens Extremus* 55: 1–37.

———. 2020. Worth Vs. Power: Han Fei's "Objection to Positional Power" Revisited. *Asiatische Studien—Études Asiatiques* 74 (3): 687–710.

Plamenatz, John. 1972. In Search of Machiavellian Virtù. In *The Political Calculus: Essays on Machiavelli's Philosophy*, ed. Anthony Parel, 157–178. Toronto ON: University of Toronto Press.

Rogacz, Dawid. 2020. *Chinese Philosophy of History: From Ancient Confucianism to the Eighteenth Century*. New York: Bloomsbury Academic.

Rowe, Robert T. 1982. Han Fei Tzu and Niccolo Machiavelli. *Chinese Culture* 23 (3): 29–55.

Sato, Masayuki. 2013. Did Xunzi's Theory of Human Nature Provide the Foundation for the Political Thought of Han Fei? In *Dao Companion to the Philosophy of Han Fei*, ed. Paul R. Goldin, 147–165. Dordrecht: Springer. (A rejection of the standard view that Han Fei was a student of Xunzi and influenced by him, combined with an argument that Han Fei's account of human nature could have been derived from early *fa* sources.).

Schneider, Henrique. 2018. *An Introduction to Hanfei's Political Philosophy: The Way of the Ruler*. Newcastle upon Tyne: Cambridge Scholars.

Schwartz, Benjamin I. 1985. *The World of Thought in Ancient China*. Cambridge MA: Belknap Press.

Sima, Qian. (ca. 145–90 BCE) 1993. *Records of the Grand Historian: Qin Dynasty*. Trans. Burton Watson. New York: Columbia University Press.

Viroli, Maurizio. 2000. *Niccolò's Smile: A Biography of Machiavelli*. Trans. Antony Shuggar. New York: Farrar, Staruss, and Giroux.

Watson, Burton. 2003. *Han Feizi: Basic Writings*. New York: Columbia University Press.

Wilkinson, Robert. 1998. Introduction to *The Book of Lord Shang*, 135–45. Trans. J.J.L. Duyvendak. Hertfordshire [UK]: Wordsworth.

Wu, John C.H. 1970. Machiavelli and the Legalists of Ancient China. *Review of National Literatures* 1: 63–77.

Chapter 22
The *Book of Lord Shang* and Totalitarianism's Intellectual Precursors Compared

Alexandre Schiele

> *[…] legal stability and a totalitarian movement could not be reconciled.*
> Hannah Arendt ([1963] 2006: 186)
>
> *In this period, after liberation, it is secret work that is fundamental. We no longer use the terms 'legal' and 'illegal'; we use the terms 'secret' and 'open'.*
> Nuon Chea, Deputy Secretary, Communist Party of Democratic Kampuchea (1978)
>
> *Sage kings did not esteem 'righteousness' but esteemed the law: laws must be clear; orders must be implemented–and that is all.*
> Book of Lord Shang (18.8)

This chapter proposes a comparative analysis of the political projects embodied by the *Book of Lord Shang*[1] and of those which accompanied the rise of totalitarianism during the twentieth century. It presents the context in which the two intellectual traditions emerged, with a focus on Italy and Germany, where the intellectual precursors of totalitarianism were the strongest. The three quotations above perfectly encapsulate the two main ideas in this chapter: (1) governance by impartial standards and totalitarianism are antithetical, and (2) if governance by impartial standards can be abstracted to a Weberian ideal type, totalitarianism, which by virtue of its very dynamism is perpetually propelled and compelled to constantly reinvent itself, can be described only in concrete situations. This chapter argues that the main

---

[1] This chapter focuses on the *Book of Lord Shang*, as it is one of the main textual evidence for the political changes that took place in the Qin polity in the late fourth century BCE. All translations from the *Book of Lord Shang* and the numeration of its paragraphs are borrowed from Pines 2017.

A. Schiele (✉)
Hebrew University of Jerusalem, Jerusalem, Israel
e-mail: alexandre.schiele@mail.huji.ac.il

© The Author(s), under exclusive license to Springer Nature Switzerland AG 2024
Y. Pines (ed.), *Dao Companion to China's fa Tradition*, Dao Companions to Chinese Philosophy 19, https://doi.org/10.1007/978-3-031-53630-4_23

difference between the political project embodied by the *Book of Lord Shang* and totalitarianism resides not in the vast period of time that separates them, but in their relation to the benchmark of rational-legal authority—the defining feature of the modern state.

Rational-legal authority, as a Weberian ideal type, truly emerged in the West over the course of the nineteenth century. It is characterized by an indivisible sovereignty, the depersonalization of power, and a hierarchy of rules and functions, and therefore stands in contrast to both traditional and charismatic authorities. Totalitarianism, including its intellectual precursors, is both a reaction to and an attempt to transcend the limitations of rational-legal authority, which were made apparent during the Great War, and the degeneration of that authority during the interwar years, which was more visible in Italy and Germany than anywhere else. In contrast, the *fa* tradition not only emerged in the context of the incessant and ever larger and longer wars of the Warring States period. It verbalized the ongoing dynamic towards political, legal, and administrative centralization, thus anticipating the rational-legal state.

The argument is organized in four main parts. First, it reminds the reader that for most of the latter half of the twentieth century, the *fa* tradition was mainly discussed through the prism of totalitarianism, stirring up nightmarish images of the past century, although for specialists of totalitarianism from Hannah Arendt to Enzo Traverso, it is almost exclusively a twentieth-century phenomenon, largely confined to Europe—even if the shadows of Maoist China and Khmer Rouge Cambodia loom large. The second part discusses the origin of the term, how it originated as a rhetorical device directed against Mussolini's regime, before being embraced by the fascists themselves. The third part compares the intellectual reflections on war and the state which preceded the establishment of the post-Shang Yang Qin state and totalitarian regimes. I shall try to demonstrate that although they share unmistakable similarities, significant differences emerge. The fourth and final part highlights the close parallels between the ideas laid down in the *Book of Lord Shang Yang* and the ideal-type of the rational-legal state as described by Max Weber.

1   The Thorny Legacy of *"Legalism"* as Totalitarianism

For most of the second half of the twentieth century, scholars in the West looked at the *fa* tradition, which they overwhelmingly still referred to as "Legalism," through the lens of twentieth-century totalitarianism, or more generally of tyranny, which they conceptualized largely interchangeably. When tackling this thorny issue, many respected scholars appear to have merely repeated a label, which freed them from analyzing a tradition that conventional wisdom had long dismissed as not merely dated and pointless, but as truly dangerous. The main representatives are Derk Bodde ("A Totalitarian Form of Government in Ancient China," 1942), Herrlee G. Creel ("The Totalitarianism of the Legalists," in *Chinese Thought from Confucius to Mao Tse-Tung*, 1953), Vitaly A. Rubin ("Theory and Practice of a Totalitarian

State" in *Individual and State in Ancient China*, 1976), Lanny B. Fields ("The Legalists and the Fall of Ch'in: Humanism and Tyranny," 1983), and Fu Zhengyuan (*China's Legalists: The Earliest Totalitarians and their Art of Ruling*, 1996).

Although totalitarianism was not the main preoccupation of his 1965 thesis on the formation of the *fa* tradition, Léon Vandermeersch nonetheless wrote: "The first aspect comes from the antique despotism, converted through legalism into a totalitarian statism" (Vandermeersch 1965: 174). The view is still dominant among French scholars. In his entry on China in the *Dictionnaire de Philosophie Politique*, François Jullien (2003) asserted most categorically: "... China, regardless of the school of thought, has focused on the issue of power and not of Law; and, far from defending the individual, the 'legalists' are on the contrary the theorists of the most extreme of despotism; ending in totalitarianism" (Jullien 2003: 82). As recently as 2015, in a new edition of her *Histoire de la pensée chinoise*, Anne Cheng presents the *fa* tradition as "a totalitarian thought of power in its purest form" (Cheng 2015: 311).

The consensus was that, although the *fa* tradition birthed the Empire, it culminated in the "burning of books and the burying of scholars" (*fenshu kengru* 焚書坑儒), with the Qin dynasty quickly crumbling under the weight of its own tyranny, utterly discrediting itself. Finally, its caricatural centrality in the Anti-Confucius, Anti-Lin Biao Campaign in the early 1970s, which today is seen as the most totalitarian phase of China's Cultural Revolution (MacFarquhar and Schoenhals 2006: 366–73), was and remains for most, with the notable exceptions of Schwartz (1985) and Graham (1989), the final nail in the coffin of the legitimacy of the *fa* tradition.

It is only with the turn of the new millennium that the *fa* tradition truly began to be consistently researched as a legitimate object in its own right. And this volume is proof of the dynamism of this area of scholarship. Yet, the association of the *fa* tradition with totalitarianism nevertheless lingers (see Blahuta, Chap. 21, this volume). As this chapter argues, that reading is not warranted.

2   Totalitarianism: A Label of Questionable Value

Although largely forgotten today, Bodde's 1942 article is probably the first to establish an equivalence between the *fa* tradition as exemplified by the Qin Empire and totalitarianism. And yet, it merely reads as an updated version of the traditional indictment, since he held that, just as the tyrannical Qin dynasty was doomed to be overthrown by the moral forces of the Han, so were the totalitarianisms of the twentieth century quickly doomed to be overthrown by the moral forces of the free world. In fact, Bodde's article is less an honest discussion of the Qin dynasty and the *fa* tradition than a patriotic outburst in the weeks that followed the December 7th, 1941, attack on Pearl Harbor—"A day that will live in infamy" (Roosevelt 1941a).

In parallel, and without any reference to Bodde, Étienne Balazs was the first to genuinely make use of the concept of totalitarianism from a scholarly perspective. And he argued in his *China as a Permanently Bureaucratic Society* (1964) that it was only with the rise of the totalitarianisms in the 1930s and 1940s that the Chinese Empire as a political regime could start to make sense to foreign observers, because there had been no equivalent in Western history with which to compare it. Of course, the takeaway was that the Empire, and traditional China overall, were "totalitarian." Thus, three key hypernyms are constantly reified in discussions of the *fa* tradition—the state, statism, and totalitarianism—and yet they remain undefined, as authors and readers alike still fall back on conventional wisdom and their own individual and fluid impressions.

2.1 The Polemics of Totalitarianism

The past century will long be remembered for its failed radical, not to say millenarian, attempts at political, economic, social and cultural transformation, the raw passions they aroused and the tragedies, sorrows and broken dreams they left in their wake. Very early on, a label for those attempts was coined: totalitarianism. And yet, the concept is still no more clearly defined than when it was originally proposed. In fact, it was long polemical precisely because it was polysemic and, beyond that, because it referred both to an analytical concept and to a rhetorical device. In the wake of the end of the Cold War, the word imposed itself despite its polysemic nature because alternatives to liberal democracies seemed condemned to the dustbin of history (Fukuyama 1992). At the extreme, Nazism—the variant of fascism that overshadowed fascism as a whole—was equated with communism, regardless of communism's particular iteration. And yet, even in the free world during the Cold War, the concept had mixed fortunes: from being a dominant paradigm in the 1950s and 1960s, it was all but forgotten in the 1970s, and largely non-existent on the other side of the Iron Curtain (Traverso 2001: 71–75)

2.2 Interwar Anti-Fascist Concept

The creation of the label was contemporaneous with the earliest triumph of fascism: Mussolini marched on Rome in 1922, and from the following year his regime was already condemned as "totalitarian" by anti-fascist intellectuals and activists. However, "totalitarian" was just that: a derogatory label. Anti-fascists were united only in their opposition to fascism, and the diversity of their political persuasions was reflected in the diversity of their positions on fascism. How to reconcile the heterogeneous and often contradictory conceptions of ideocratic autocracy (Tillich 1934); technocratic autocracy (Ortega y Gasset 1930); police, if not terrorist, state (Salvemini 1935); ideocratic and terrorist castocracy (Serge 1933); a party enthralled by the cult of personality (Sturzo 1938); unstable bureaucratic state (Trotsky 1939); or polycratic regime in a precarious equilibrium (Neumann 1942)? Was it born out of a will to dominate or was it the reaction of capitalism threatened by the revolution

(Marcuse 1934)? Globally, the dominant impression was that fascism was merely tyranny by another name. Yet, it was felt that the accusation of tyranny could not comprehensively reflect the modernity and urgency of the threat posed by fascism, which Mussolini himself notoriously defined in a 1927 boast as "Everything in the state, nothing outside the state, nothing against the state."

2.3   Core Fascist Creed

In a deliberate attempt to muddy the waters even more, Mussolini made the label his in 1925. But he was notorious for his provocative rhetoric, so can he be taken at his word? Nevertheless, fascists increasingly embraced the pejorative label (Gentile 1928; Jünger 1930; Schmitt 1933a, b), and, in 1932, in the *Doctrine of Fascism*, Mussolini and Giovanni Gentile—the "Philosopher of Fascism" (Gregor 2004)—attempted to theoretically ground the equivalency of fascism and totalitarianism: "Thus, for the fascist, everything is in the state, and nothing human or spiritual existing, or even having any value, outside the state. In this sense, fascism is totalitarian, and the fascist state, [the] synthesis of the unity of every value, interprets, develops and strengthens all the life of the people" ([Gentile] Mussolini [1932] 1935). In short: the total identification of the nation with the state. In contrast, the Nazis strongly identified with the *Volksgemeinschaft*—the unified and hierarchized racial community (Hitler [1925–1927] 1943: 49), which was transnational, while the state and the nation were infiltrated by race enemies and race traitors (p. 80), and for that reason saw both the state and the nation as constraints upon it.

2.4   Cold War Catch-All Label

Regardless, when the first shots of the Second World War rang out, the world fell neatly into two camps: the regimes that wished to subjugate it, and those that fought for "freedom" (Roosevelt 1941b). After the defeat of fascism in the smoldering ruins of Berlin and Tokyo in 1945, the template of the life-and-death-struggle between the free world and fascism could readily be superimposed on the coming rivalry of the two superpowers that would define the next 45 years. However, because the anti-fascism of communists was beyond dispute, the term "totalitarianism" not only supplanted "fascism" in the discourse but became interchangeable with "communism," overshadowing "fascism and Nazism" in the process. In 1954, Hannah Arendt condensed the dominant mood into a simple, some would say simplistic, definition: "Totalitarianism is the most radical denial of freedom" (Arendt [1954] 1994: 328). The use of the term was most common when the Cold War rivalry, and by extension anti-communism, was strongest, and waned in the wake of the US–Soviet détente. Thus, "totalitarian" has always been more of a pejorative label than an analytical concept, and even as such it remains tainted by the legacy of the term as a derogatory label.

2.5   Towards a Conceptual Tool

The first true attempt at a typology is found in Friedrich and Brzezinski's 1956 "The General Characteristics of Totalitarian Dictatorship" (1956): "The 'syndrome', or pattern of interrelated traits, of the totalitarian dictatorship consists of an ideology, a single party typically led by one man, a terroristic police, a communications monopoly, a weapons monopoly, and a centrally directed economy." That remains to this day more or less the standard scholarly definition of totalitarianism. However, as the authors themselves acknowledged in their very next sentence, the last two features ("weapons monopoly" and "centrally directed economy") could also be found in "constitutional systems" (Friedrich and Brzezinski [1956] 1965: 21): welfare states with mixed economies were then becoming the norm among democracies (Hobsbawm 2003). Another patent issue with this definition, on the very eve of destalinization, which largely put an end to the totalitarian phase of the Soviet Union, is that it held totalitarianism to be both monolithic and immutable.

Obviously, it would be anachronistic to apply Friedrich and Brzezinski's 1956 definition to the Qin Empire. And the consensus of specialists of totalitarianism, in the footsteps of Hannah Arendt's groundbreaking *The Origins of Totalitarianism* (1951), remains that totalitarianism was not only a novel regime grown from seeds planted no earlier than the late nineteenth century, but truly an avatar of the "short twentieth century" (Hobsbawm 2003), rising under the unique conditions of interwar Europe before foundering in the wake of the Second World War. Therefore, how can this definitive judgment be reconciled with the judgment, long dominant in Chinese studies, that the *fa* tradition was both totalitarian and a political philosophy characteristic of ancient China (Vandermeersch 1965)? And yet, the question remains: can ideologies and regimes twenty-two centuries removed from one another and separated by the whole of the Eurasian landmass be legitimately compared? Balazs most certainly thought so, and so did Bodde in his own way. The most evident starting point is the Qin and Nazi onslaughts upon their own respective worlds, although our knowledge of the latter is far greater.

3   Forged in the Crucible of War and Political Instability

However, the question of those wars will not be tackled from a historical perspective but from a theoretical one: how did the Warring States scholars and twentieth-century interwar theorists, although separated by time and space, anticipate the coming wars, and propose to prosecute them? From the onset, it is clear that war, and the imperative to prepare for a coming war they deemed inevitable, were central to representatives of both the *fa* tradition and the conservative revolution. And, just as clear, is that war was formative for both. However, they had significant differences. The representatives of the conservative revolution had lived through the Great War, which was 'great' not only because it had involved the total mobilization of the resources and industrial capacities of many of the belligerent states, but also because it was without precedent in living memory: the romantic idealization of war, which had stirred the imagination of generations in peacetime, burst in the pure ugliness and savagery of trench warfare. By contrast, the representatives of the *fa* tradition lived at a time when war among the great powers of their age not only increasingly mobilized all the resources available within a predominantly agrarian economy, but was endemic (Pines 2016). As the next section shows, this fundamental difference in experience is clearly manifest in and distinguishes the reflections of both groups of intellectuals.

3.1   From Total War …

Two of the most important intellectual links between "total war" and totalitarianism were Ernst Jünger (1895–1997), who had been a German junior officer at the front, and Erich Ludendorff (1865–1937), who had been the First Quartermaster General and the German co-Commander-in-Chief alongside Field Marshal Paul von Hindenburg (1847–1934). Jünger, one of the most renowned interwar representatives of the conservative revolution,[2] is most famous for the 1920 publication of his war memoirs, *In Stahlgewittern* (Storms of Steel), which was controversial for its aestheticization of carnage and its celebration of the violence of warfare as the moment of the regeneration of the best qualities of man, and for his increasingly critical stance towards liberalism and democracy the more the failure of the Weimar Republic became apparent.

In contrast, while Hindenburg remained a celebrated hero, Ludendorff was left to carry the full weight of the defeat on his shoulders. And, unable to accept responsibility, he laid the blame on the Jews, capitalists, pacifists, Catholics, liberals, and socialists—the internal enemy (Ludendorff 1935: 13)—and was one of the first to actively spread the *Dolchstosslegende* (the stab-in-the-back myth). He considered the liberalism and democracy of the Weimar Republic to be illegitimate from the start and conspired to overthrow it, joining the Kapp Putsch in 1920 and the Beerhall Putsch of 1923 (the Hitler–Ludendorff Putsch). He was the very symbol of the violent opposition (Lemay 2010: 10–11), before Adolf Hitler—the corporal—sidelined him and outshone him as Führer.

Nevertheless, Jünger's 1930 *Die totale Mobilmachung* (Total Mobilization) and Ludendorff's 1935 *Der totale Krieg* (Total War) converged on three main points. First, the Great War was unprecedented to the point that Clausewitz[3] had become a

---

[2] When Walter Benjamin attempted in 1930 to circumscribe the essence of German fascism, he looked not to the rising threat posed by fascist-inspired German parties, but to Jünger and his cult of war and of the warrior, thus clearly identifying the conservative revolution as the German avatar of intellectual fascism (Benjamin 1930).

[3] Carl von Clausewitz (1780–1831), who wrote *Vom Kriege* (On War, published posthumously in 1832), was the dominant military theorist of the 19th century.

relic of the past and that it was no longer sufficient to throw masses of men at the enemy in order to overcome him. In fact, the major mistakes committed in the Great War were directly attributable to the continued dominance of the nineteenth-century mindset in the context of twentieth-century warfare and therefore to a lack of adequate preparation for twentieth-century war. Thus, Jünger unequivocally asserted that "the last war—our war—[was] the greatest and most influential event of our age. [It differed] from other wars whose history has been handed down to us" (Jünger [1930], trans. Golb and Wolin 1993) because "the relation of each individual contestant to progress was bound to play a decisive role": alongside "the armies meeting on the battlefields, the modern armies of commerce and transport, foodstuffs, the manufacture of armaments," including "the homeworker at her sewing machine"—that is, "the army of labor in general" (Jünger [1930] 1993). In other words, "the image of war as armed combat merges into the more extended image of a gigantic labor process" (Jünger [1930] 1993).

Ludendorff went even further when he asserted that the Great War irreversibly replaced Clausewitz's nineteenth-century ideal of a war freed from all constraints in the pursuit of the total annihilation of the enemy's armed forces—*absoluter Krieg* (Absolute War)—with the twentieth-century reality of war that "not only concerns the armed forces, but also and directly the life and soul of every member of the belligerent races" and therefore "not only targets the army, but directly the races" with all available means, and not solely physical means of destruction—*totaler Krieg* (Total War) (Ludendorff 1935: 5–6) In short: the full incorporation of civilian populations into the war effort makes them legitimate military targets. This conclusion should not be mistaken for the mass executions of prisoners of war and the wanton massacres of whole cities in pre-industrial warfare which, if revenge and cruelty are set aside, largely derived from the victors' inability to house and feed such large numbers (Gelb 1973; Wickham 2014: 22–28).

In contrast, the *Book of Lord Shang* was composed in the Warring States period, which, as its name implies, was not characterized by a single war of unprecedented proportions but by endemic warfare: "every state of ten thousand chariots [major power] is engaged in war, and every state of one thousand chariots [minor power] is engaged in defense" (*Book of Lord Shang*, 7.3). How different was Europe on the eve of the Great War, which ended a long century of peace guaranteed by the balance of power of the Concert of Nations, great powers that recognized each other as equals. Yet, a balance of power which paradoxically was enforced by an arms race, national conscription, and national myths—the very factors that, after a century of peace, made the Great War *great*. For the sovereigns of the Warring States, the pressing issue was how to constantly mobilize a fighting force and the supplies to sustain it, especially as, in the words of the *Book of Lord Shang*: "Farming is what the people consider bitter; war is what the people consider dangerous" (*Book of Lord Shang*, 6.5).

Thus, the question was how to entice the people to go against two of their basic instincts, and no text was more devoted to the issue of "[directing] the people in agriculture [, and focusing] the people on waging war" (*Book of Lord Shang*, 6.8) than the *Book of Lord Shang*. According to its authors, the most basic instinct is the pursuit of what is in one's interest: "Yet, they brave what they consider bitter and perform what they consider dangerous because of calculation" (*Book of Lord Shang*, 6.5), and it was therefore the task of the rulers to entice the people to farm and fight by stimulating their thirst for reward: "When benefits come from land, the people fully utilize their strengths; when name [that is, renown, title, rank] comes from war, the people are ready to die" (*Book of Lord Shang*, 6.5); and fear of punishments: "When penalties are heavy and rewards are light, then superiors love the people, and the people are [ready] to die for their superiors" (*Book of Lord Shang*, 4.4).

That warfare was essential for the *Book of Lord Shang*, on a par with agriculture, to the point of military merit being advocated as the main avenue for social promotion is beyond dispute. That the Warring States were an age of mass mobilization (Lewis 1990: 54–67), and that the *Book of Lord Shang* expressed as much as it contributed to the then ongoing rationalization of mass mobilization is also beyond dispute. It is nowhere more evident than in Chapter 12 which specifically focuses on "Military defense":

> The way of defending a fortress is by accumulating power. When there is an invader, put military registers in order and divide the multitudes of the three armies according to the number of the invader's observation chariots. The three armies are: first, the army of adult men; second, the army of adult women; third, the army of the elderly and the infirm: these are called "the three armies." (*Book of Lord Shang* 12.3)

Of course, the mobilization of women and of the elderly and the infirm is a last-ditch measure, but one which unfortunately occurred all too often in times of endemic warfare. And on this question, the military chapters of the *Mozi* are far more detailed (Yates 1979). Yet, there is no talk of symbolic incentives, of a culture of honor, of something akin to patriotism or nationalism: the people, and by extension, individuals, are simply to be instrumentalized, if not reduced to "automatons" (Lévi 1985).

General mobilization was not an issue for the belligerents of nineteenth and early twentieth-century Europe. Yet, because it remained "based upon a fixed calculation of armaments and costs, which made war seem like an exceptional, but not limitless, expenditure of available force and supplies," Jünger asserted that "even general mobilization had the character of a partial measure" (Jünger [1930] 1993). In contrast, total war, for Jünger, not only calls for the total mobilization of human, material and technical resources but is truly a transcendent, if not mystical, experience[4]—language that would have seemed wholly alien to the authors of the *Book of Lord Shang*. That is why Jünger's and Ludendorff's conception of total war was not purely a pragmatist rationalization of the experience of the Great War, but as much, if not more so, an ideological construct: "We can now pursue the process by which the growing conversion of life into energy, the increasingly fleeting

---

[4] Under the pen of Julius Evola (1898–1974; *Rivolta contro il mondo moderno*, 1934), Savitri Devi (1905–1982; *The Lightning and the Sun*, 1958), Miguel Serrano (1917–2009; *El Cordón Dorado: Hitlerismo Esoterico*, 1978) and others, the transcendent dimension turned into a full-blown *esotericism*, which had a major influence upon postwar neo-fascism and neo-Nazism, although they themselves had little to no influence upon postwar politics.

content of all binding ties in deference to mobility, gives an ever-more radical character to the act of mobilization" (Jünger [1930] 1993). Again, Ludendorff proves the more radical: "By its very spirit, the total war can only be fought when the very existence of the whole race is threatened and if it is determined to fight for it" (Ludendorff 1935: 6).

For Jünger, the coming inevitable war required "a new form of armament": the "mobilization of the German—nothing else" (Jünger [1930] 1993), and for Ludendorff "the race will have to extend its psychical, physical and material strength in full," as "the army [was now fully] dependen[t] upon the race and especially its psychical unity" (Ludendorff 1935: 9). According to Jünger, fascist Italy and the Five-Year Plan in Stalin's Soviet Union, first launched two years before Jünger wrote his essay, were prime illustrations of his own vision of "total mobilization" (Jünger [1930] 1993): i.e., the distinction between fascism and Stalinism is one of aims, not means[5]—total war implies "total politics." And, in the words of Ludendorff: "[T]otal politics must already in peacetime prepare for this racial life-and-death struggle, and strengthen the foundation of this life-and-death struggle so that no wartime attempt by the enemy to displace, weaken or destroy it will succeed" (Ludendorff 1935: 10). Thus, the essence of total war inverts Clausewitz's founding principle of "war [as] an instrument of politics" to, in Ludendorff's words, "Politics serve war" (Ludendorff 1935: 10). The contrast with the *Book of Lord Shang* could not be starker: although the product of an age of endemic wars, with war increasingly crucial to the state (and state-building), its authors never conceived of war as the sole finality of the state.

3.2   ... To Totalitarianism

In 1932, Giovanni Gentile and Benito Mussolini, after 10 years of effective fascist rule, rejected the very distinction of war and politics:

> The Fascist State is an embodied will to power and to command. [...] Within the Fascist doctrine, the Empire is not only a territorial, or military or mercantile expansion, but also spiritual and moral. [...] For Fascism, the tendency to the Empire, i.e. the expansion of nations, is a manifestation of vitality [.] However, the Empire implies discipline, the coordination of efforts, duties and sacrifice: this explains numerous practical aspects of the regime and the necessary severity against those who oppose the spontaneous and fatal movement of twentieth century Italy by agitating for obsolete nineteenth century ideologies [.] ([Gentile] Mussolini [1932] 1935)

And, while the Italian fascist state in its most accomplished form emerged over the course of a decade or so of trials and errors that began with street fighting, Carl Schmitt, one of the most notorious jurists and constitutionalists of the twentieth

---

[5] Karl Kautsky, the major anti-Leninist Marxist of the time, drawing parallels between Mussolini's and Lenin's new regimes, went so far as to assert in the same year that "Fascism is nothing but the counterpart of Bolshevism, Mussolini only Lenin's monkey" (Kautsky 1930: 102).

century and the foremost of Nazi Germany, attempted to lay down the constitutional and legal principles of the total state, which, by drawing upon the Italian fascist precedent without any longing for the collapsed Wilhelmine Empire, would have none of the fundamental flaws of the parliamentary Weimar Republic.

To his credit, Schmitt (1933a) did not fault the nineteenth-century ideas that informed the Weimar Republic, but rather its failure to harness the rapid and continuous progress of technologies, and notably telecommunication technologies. According to him, it was technology that gave contemporary "partisan agitation" (Schmitt 1933a, *passim*) much of its strength and reach, and caused deleterious effects upon a state that, more than any other, or so he held, rejected politics—a paradox, if, as he contends, the barest definition of the state is the enforcement and expansion of political domination. And that avowed withdrawal from politics, combined with modern partisan agitation, had for effect the "politicization of every domain of human existence—economic, cultural, religious, etc." and the weakening of the state (Schmitt 1933a: 185). Thus, to his eyes, the crisis of the Weimar Republic could be solved only if the state fully embraced politics and made use of all the modern instruments and techniques to enforce its political domination, starting with the takeover of the modern means of mass communication that are radio and cinema, stressing the fact that virtually all liberal states did so to varying degrees.

However, in a sharp departure from the liberal model dominant at the turn of the century, Schmitt asserted that no "real" state would allow anything hostile, obstructing or dividing, holding fast to his understanding that the very essence of politics resides in the clear distinction between "friend" and "foe."[6] And yet, he warned strongly against the wanton intervention of the state into every conceivable domain. In essence, he was stating the core values of the conservative revolution—a positive totalism.

Schmitt despaired nonetheless that, although weak, the Weimar state continuously extended its reach under the pressure of the "five" or so mass parties espousing irreconcilable ideologies and vying for power. They "totally" dominated their members "from the cradle to the grave" and continuously vied for "total" dominance not only over the state but over all domains of life, short-circuiting traditional political communication and parliamentary politics with the effect of splitting Germany into as many competing "total" systems (Schmitt 1933a, *passim*)—a negative totalism. This issue dominated most of his intellectual life (*Die Diktatur*, 1921; *Politische Theologie*, 1922; *Verfassungslehre*, 1928). In the final instance, he held that only the function of the presidency, far removed from partisan infighting, had until then prevented the Weimar Republic from descending into chaos, making it the only viable starting point from which to rebuild the state from the top down.[7]

---

[6]A caveat: only in the heat of battle is the distinction the clearest. Thus, politics remains dysfunctional until it is reduced to a war of every day. And yet, a war of every day—a *civil war mentality*—is the clearest sign of dysfunctional politics. The 1929 statutes of the National Fascist Party (*Partito Nazionale Fascista*) state that, from its very creation, it was "in a permanent state of war".

[7]However, considering that Hindenburg—the victor of Tannenberg—was President (1925–1934), it is arguable that *who* occupied the function was at least as important as the function itself.

Schmitt grew overtly preoccupied with strengthening the executive power of the state and specifically the office of President—a non-partisan office constitutionally mandated to not only symbolize the state but to enforce it if need be—in order to enforce the very existence of the German state. In fact, for him, sovereignty resided in the power to declare the *Ausnahmezustand*, commonly translated as "state of exception" (Schmitt 1922).[8]

On a surface level, Schmitt's "state of exception" seems to resonate with the idea in the *Book of Lord Shang* that, under certain circumstances, when convinced that his actions "benefit the people" (1.2), the ruler is allowed to dispel with extant laws and rituals and adopt something substantially new. However, the state of exception is both conceptually contrasted with the rule of law and the means of its enforcement in situations in which its normal functioning would undermine it; that is, exceptional situations. Its proclamation aims to ensure the continuity of the state by temporarily suspending the entirety of the constitutional–legal order, even if it implies the creation of a new one. Thus, by its very definition, the state of exception cannot be subjected to legal norms, while remaining distinct from anarchy or chaos.[9] Nevertheless, for Schmitt (1921), the Leninist dictatorship of the proletariat (in practice, the dictatorship of the Communist Party, born out of a revolutionary act), is a prime example of the state of exception in practice.

Schmitt's "state of exception" should not be confused with the total state: it is only a potentiality, although it is that very potentiality which grounds the existence of the *state*. Under his influence, the Weimar Republic grew authoritarian at the turn of the 1930s (Möller 2021: 232), yet, the turn failed to restore order. It is only then that Schmitt first advocated for the *total state*, a constitutional presidential statist authoritarianism with the power to transcend the constitutional-legal order when it is at risk. And it is here that Schmitt and the *Book of Lord Shang* come the closest to one another. Yet the Nazis, through the voice of Alfred Rosenberg (1933), one of their main ideologues, immediately and forcefully attacked the very concept of the total state.

After they seized power in early 1933, suspending *de facto* the Constitution, Germany quickly nazified, and Schmitt came to define Nazi Germany as a "triadic structure" (Dreigliederung): a regime composed of the "state" (Staat), "movement" (Bewegung) and "people" (Volk) (Schmitt 1933b).[10] A year later, upon Hindenburg's death and without significant opposition, Hitler fused the functions of Chancellor

---

[8] "Is sovereign who decides on the state of exception" is the first line of *Politische Theologie* (1922) and one of the most (in)famous aphorisms in all of political science.

[9] Second caveat: the *state of exception* can thus theoretically be indefinitely extended, in effect becoming *permanent*. That is, the exception can become the norm.

[10] Schmitt sought to ingratiate himself with the new regime. He became its greatest jurist, albeit one without much influence, before becoming a personal target of the SS, leading him to opt for obscurity well before the end of the decade. And yet, his ideas would continue to have a major impact, both for future dictatorships and, strangely enough, for postwar democracies, not least of all on the strongly presidential constitution of the French Fifth Republic (1958–present)—the longest and most stable to date (Le Brazidec 1998).

and President into the new informal status of Führer, which was a title he already held within the Nazi Party, transcending the limits of all three functions. Schmitt further amended his definition: a triadic structure unified and led by the Führer (Schmitt 1934). The infamous Nazi slogan: "Ein Volk, Ein Reich, Ein Führer"—the three organic components of the *Volksgemeinschaft*—not merely expresses that fact, but does away with the very concepts of the Law, the state and the party.[11] The two core concepts here are truly that of the *movement*, dynamic and formless yet sustained by its very dynamism, and the *leader*, who, bound by neither rules nor conventions, animates, invigorates, and guides the movement with his vision and charisma; movement and leader thus constituting an organic whole (Arendt [1951] 1979: 305–315). In other words, state, party, and ideology are always, at best, but aspects of a totalitarian regime, and transitory ones at that.

This is the fundamental difference between the *Book of Lord Shang* and totalitarians: the former is predicated on establishing a stable and predictable order that the latter utterly reject. According to the *Book of Lord Shang*, once a new legal framework is instituted, legal stability is expected:

> Whenever a state is established, one must understand regulations and measures, be cautious in governance and law, be diligent in [pursuing] the state's commitments, and consolidate essential occupations. When regulations and measures are timely, the customs of the state can be transformed, and the people will follow regulations. When governance and law are clear, there are no deviations among officials. When the state is committed to the One (viz. agriculture and warfare), the people can be used. When essential occupations are consolidated, the people are glad to farm and enjoy war. (*Book of Lord Shang*, 8.1)

In the growing instability of the *Warring* States, this passage clearly expresses the aspiration to establish the conditions of a stable and predictable order, of a lasting order characterized by the return to the "essential occupations," and the conviction that such an order can only rest upon laws and regulations. However, it also recommends timeliness and moderation in governing because its authors have grown keenly aware that governing may itself be a cause of disorder.[12] And for all these reasons, totalitarianism might not be the best basis for the comparison, but the regime which preceded it and which it sought to transcend.

---

[11] The *Reich* was not only the formal name of Germany between 1871 and 1945, but also referred to the congruence of territory and the ethnocultural *Volk*, which spread beyond what were then the official borders of Germany. The Weimar Constitution contradictorily drew upon both (see *Die Verfassung des Deutschen Reichs* 1919). Although the *Führerprinzip* has become somewhat controversial, *Volk* (internally diverse European) and *Reich* (post-, trans- or supranational and post-state European) remain core concepts of the contemporary European New Right (see de Benoist 1993–1994, the first true attempt by one of its main figures to theoretically articulate the concept).

[12] Whether the objective of establishing a perfectly predictable order amidst the unpredictability of endemic wars is achievable is beyond the scope of this chapter.

4 Rational-Legal Authority and the Rise of the Modern State

The divergence between governance by impartial standards as expressed in the *Book of Lord Shang* and totalitarianism becomes even clearer in the light of the ideal type of *rational-legal authority*, the defining feature of the modern state. Rational-legal authority was first conceptualized by Max Weber in *The Three Types of Legitimate Rule* (Weber [1922] 1958), now considered one of the foundational texts of political science. For clarity's sake, this descriptive ideal type, born out of careful observation, will be broken down in its four main components: (1) structure, (2) specialization, (3) professionalization, and (4) neutrality. In fact, although lacking its level of abstraction, the prescriptions contained in the *Book of Lord Shang*, the implementation of which is well attested in the paleographic record (see, e.g., Sun Wenbo 2020 and Korolkov, Chap. 7, this volume), appear to closely anticipate Weber's ideal type.

Structure. The system is characterized by a hierarchy of offices ("best represented by bureaucracy" (Weber [1922] 1958: 2) in which "lower offices are subordinated to higher ones" (Weber [1922] 1958: 2). This bureaucracy not merely represents sovereignty, it enacts its decisions as expressed in laws ("changed at pleasure by formally correct procedure" (Weber [1922] 1958: 2), and enacts them according to legal procedures, even "when giving an order" (Weber [1922] 1958: 2), and "'functional' considerations of expediency" (Weber [1922] 1958: 2) when such procedures prove lacking. The *Book of Lord Shang* has long been recognized as one of the first works to endorse the idea of a bureaucracy governed by law and procedure: "This is the orderly rule of the state: when [affairs are] determined by officials, you will be strong. [...] The well-ordered state values decisions made below" (*Book of Lord Shang*, 5.9), emphasizing that "[w]hen governance and law are clear, there are no deviations among officials". (*Book of Lord Shang*, 8.1) And although composed on the eve of the imperial unification (Pines 2017: 243–44), chapter 26 goes into the detail of this hierarchy:

> The Son of Heaven establishes three law officials. In the palace, one law official is established. The chief prosecutor establishes one law official and one clerk. The prime minister establishes one law official. All regional lords and heads of commanderies and counties establish one law official and one clerk. All these should provide for one law official. Heads of commanderies and counties and regional lords, once they receive the laws and ordinances dispatched to them, should study their content. (*Book of Lord Shang*, 26.4)

Specialization. This hierarchy of offices is staffed by "officials appointed by the ruler" (Weber [1922] 1958: 2): offices are neither inherited nor bought nor can be alienated, as they derive their authority from a single point of sovereignty (nation, monarch or other). Officials are not appointed as individuals but to fill a specific task for which they have a specific expertise ("The typical official is a trained specialist" (Weber [1922] 1958: 2). This specialization of offices aims to ensure efficiency, avoid overlap of their areas of action, but also "sets limits with regard to the functional purpose and required skill of the office incumbent" (Weber [1922] 1958: 2). The centrality of appointment on the basis merit is constantly reaffirmed in the

Book of Lord Shang, notably: "[The superior man] investigates one's labor, elevates the meritorious, and then makes the appointment. Then superior and inferior are balanced." (*Book of Lord Shang*, 6.11) And so is the importance of "regulat[ing]" offices and of assigning to them "constant tasks" (*Book of Lord Shang*, 23.1).

Professionalization. The hierarchy of offices doubles as a fixed salary scale based on administrative rank, and not on the individual, the amount of work or the specialized task, with promotions to higher offices similarly governed by "fixed rules of advancement" (Weber [1922] 1958: 2). This is one of the conditions for the creation of a professional body of administrators. The *Book of Lord Shang* espouses strikingly similar languages when it says that "[the superior man] establishes and makes rank esteemed so as to correspond [to office]" (*Book of Lord Shang*, 6.11) and "rewards [...] reflect the full exertion of their labor" (20.11), with "methods of appointing officials [made] clear" (*Book of Lord Shang*, 3.4).

Neutrality. This hierarchy of offices contrasts with a hierarchy of persons because "[o]bedience is not owed to anybody personally but to enacted rules and regulations which specify to whom and to what rule people owe obedience" (Weber [1922] 1958: 2). Officials "ideally [proceed] *sine ira et studio*, not allowing personal motive or temper to influence conduct, free of arbitrariness and unpredictability; especially he proceeds 'without regard to person', following rational rules with strict formality." (Weber [1922] 1958: 2) This idea is expressed in the negative in the *Book of Lord Shang*, through the denunciation of specific habits, behaviors, and values which impede the proper discharge of their functions, to potentially catastrophic effects:

> *Poems, Documents*, rites, music, goodness, self-cultivation, benevolence, uprightness, argumentativeness, cleverness: when the state has these ten, superiors cannot induce [the people] to [engage in] defense and fighting. If the state is ruled according to these ten, then if the enemy arrives, it will be dismembered, and even if the enemy does not arrive, the state will be impoverished. If the state eradicates these ten, then the enemy will not dare arrive, and even if he arrives, he will be repelled; when an army is raised and sent on a campaign, it will seize [the enemy's land]; whereas if the army is restrained and does not attack, the state will be rich. (*Book of Lord Shang*, 3.5)

However, the *Book of Lord Shang* never discusses the political regime for which it advocates in terms of "authority", the idea that officials will carry out a command without persuasion or constraint, or of "legitimacy", the idea that officials will not only accept the established order but internalize it (Weber [1922] 1958: 1), but only of constraints: "When governance and law are clear, there are no deviations among officials" (*Book of Lord Shang*, 8.1). "When orders are strict, there is no procrastination in governing; when laws are fair, there are no depraved officials" (*Book of Lord Shang*, 13.1).

Rational-legal authority has been dominant since the late nineteenth century, and not only in the political sphere, because it proved far more efficient than preceding and competing forms of authority, all the while enforcing stability and predictability. No student of pre-imperial China, and especially of the *fa* tradition, would fail to recognize the parallels. However, rational-legal authority is not without its limitations, becoming the subject of attacks in the crisis-prone interwar years. And if totalitarianism cannot be understood without rational-legal authority, if only because it could not have existed without it, it cannot be confused with it. Since the late 1970s, "governance"—"the various institutionalized modes of social coordination to produce and implement collectively binding rules, and/or to provide collective goods" (Börzel et al. 2018: 9)—has in many respects displaced rational-legal authority (Boltanski and Chiapello 2011).

5 Conclusion

Ever since the Second World War and the immediate threat posed by totalitarian Germany and later Soviet Union, the *fa* tradition became associated with totalitarianism, to the point that totalitarianism became the main paradigm for analyzing this philosophical tradition, in effect dismissing any value it could hold. To a large extent, that was simply an actualized version of the opprobrium that this tradition has encountered ever since the fall of the Qin dynasty, which had embraced it against Confucianism (Song, Chap. 16, this volume). Although the turn of the new millennium has brought much welcome renewed interest in the *fa* tradition, and more open-minded approaches, the tradition is still instinctively described as totalitarian, even by its most sympathetic scholars (e.g., Jiang 2021: 457).

This chapter has attempted to clarify the distinction between both in relation to the core concept of rational-legal authority that has defined the modern state since the nineteenth century. This concept is fundamental because, for specialists of totalitarianism, the phenomenon is largely specific to twentieth-century Europe, and especially the second quarter of the century, and they would balk at the idea of projecting such a model onto historical regimes, especially outside the West. The problem, to restate it, lies in the fact that totalitarianism is both an analytical model and a rhetorical device. In fact, the need to develop an analytical concept of totalitarianism postdates the emergence of totalitarianism as a rhetorical device. And, whether for opponents or proponents, the totalitarian threat was a specificity of their own modernity; and the analytical models reflect that by incorporating features that would have been impossible before the emergence of the bureaucratic state, industrial society, mass communication, mass politics and total war.

China of the Warring States period was far removed from the realities of twentieth-century Europe, where fascist intellectuals, but not only, were becoming painfully aware of the limitations of the rational-legal state (impersonal, hierarchical, rules-based) in dealing with the increasing complexity of their world—a feeling that was even more acute in countries that had lost the Great War (Germany) or felt that they had been robbed of the spoils of victory (Italy), and which the Great Depression made more pressing. They expressed a rejection of rationality for irrationality, or rather an attempt to merge rationality with irrationality with calls for "total war," a "total state," and "total mobilization." "Total" is contrasted with "general" because it is not the mere addition of all available human and material resources, but an organic vision in which the whole is more than the sum of its parts, dynamized by the mobilization of all symbolic resources. Rules, regulations, and organizations remain important but not absolute: when they become limits to the goal that they serve to achieve, they must be suspended or changed, necessity itself granting legitimacy to all extraconstitutional and extrajudicial measures deemed necessary to achieve the goal at hand.

How different from that is the *fa* tradition, which explicitly sought to impose a rules-based order in which duties, obligations, procedures, rewards, and punishments were minutely prescribed and transparent, banishing uncertainty; in which authority resided not in the individual but in the office, and from which none, not even the ruler (at least desirably), could derogate, banishing arbitrariness. In essence, the *Book of Lord Shang* called for greater centralization and rationalization of state power as much as it expressed the then-ongoing movement towards it. And in so doing, it closely anticipated Weber's rational-legal state. And for this reason, it cannot be assimilated with totalitarianism, although, as an attempt to transcend the rational-legal state, totalitarianism inevitably shares commonalities with it as it does with the liberal democracies of its age.

References

Arendt, Hannah. [1951] 1979. *The Origins of Totalitarianism*. San Diego/New York/London: Arthur Brace & Company. (A foundational analysis of the origin and practice of totalitarianism)
———. [1954] 1994. On the Nature of Totalitarianism: An Essay in Understanding. In Arendt, *Essays in Understanding 1930–1954: Formation, Exile and Totalitarianism*. New York: Harcourt, pp. 328–360.
———. [1963] 2006. *Eichmann in Jerusalem: A Report on the Banality of Evil*. London: Penguin.
Balazs, Étienne. 1964. China as a Permanently Bureaucratic Society. *Chinese Civilization and Bureaucracy*. New Haven: Yale University Press. (A dated though still relevant analysis of the bureaucratic logic and structure of the Chinese empire)
Benjamin, Walter. [1930] 1991. Theorien des Deutschen Faschismus. Zu der Sammelschrift 'Krieg und Krieger'. Herausgegeben von Ernst Jünger. In Benjamin, *Gesammelte Schriften III. Herausgegeben von Hella Tiedemann-Bartels*. Berlin: Suhrkamp, pp. 238–250.
Bodde, Derk. 1942. A Totalitarian Form of Government in Ancient China. *Far Eastern Leaflets, Washington* 1 (6): 23–25. (The first text to explicitly associate the *fa* tradition with totalitarianism).
Boltanski, Luc, and Chiapello, Ève. [1999] 2011. *Le Nouvel Esprit du Capitalisme*. Paris: Gallimard.
Börzel, Tanja A., Risse, Thomas, and Draude, Anke. 2018. Governance in Areas of Limited Statehood: Conceptual Clarifications and Major Contributions of the Handbook. In Risse, Thomas, Börzel, Tanja A., and Draude, Anke (Eds), *The Oxford Handbook of Governance and Limited Statehood*. Oxford: Oxford University Press, pp. 3–25.
Chea, Nuon. 1978, *Statement of the Communist Party of Kampuchea [CPK] to the Communist Workers' Party of Denmark*, July https://www.marxists.org/history/erol/denmark/kr.pdf. Accessed 1 Jan 2022.
Cheng, Anne. 2015. *Histoire de la pensée chinoise*. Paris: Seuil.
Creel, Heerlee G. [1953] 1971. *Chinese Thought from Confucius to Mao Zedong Tsê-tung*. Chicago: University of Chicago Press.
de Benoist, Alain, 1993–1994. The Idea of Empire. *Telos* 98–99: 81–98.

"Die Verfassung des Deutschen Reiches vom 11 August 1919. " *Reichsgesetzblatt*, 1919, S. 1383.

Fields, Lanny B. 1983. The Legalists and the Fall of Ch'in: Humanism and Tyranny. *Journal of Asian History* 17: 1–39.

Friedrich, Carl J., and Zbigniew Brzezinski. [1956] 1965. "The General Characteristics of Totalitarian Dictatorship." In idem, *Totalitarian Dictatorship and Autocracy.* Cambridge MA: Harvard University Press, 15–27.

Fu, Zhengyuan. 1996. *China's Legalists: The Earliest Totalitarians and their Art of Ruling.* Armonk: New Studies in Asian Culture.

Fukuyama, Francis. 1992. *The End of History and the Last Man.* New York: Free Press.

Gelb, Ignace J. 1973. Prisoners of War in Early Mesopotamia. *Journal of Near Eastern Studies* 32 (1/2): 70–98.

Gentile, Giovanni. 1928. The Philosophic Basis of Fascism. *Foreign Affairs* 6 (2): 290–304.

Graham, Angus C. 1989. *"Legalism: an Amoral Science of Statecraft" in Disputers of the Tao: Philosophical Argument in Ancient China.* Chicago: Open Court.

Gregor, A. James. 2004. *Giovanni Gentile: Philosopher of Fascism.* London/New York: Routledge.

Hitler, Adolf. [1925–1927] 1943. *Mein Kampf.* Munich: Franz Eher Nachfolger GmbH.

Hobsbawm, Eric. 2003. *The Age of Extremes 1914–1991.* London: Abacus.

Jiang, Tao. 2021. *Origins of Moral-Political Philosophy in Early China: Contestation of Humaneness, Justice, and Personal Freedom.* Oxford: Oxford University Press.

Jullien, François. 2003. Chine. In *Dictionnaire de philosophie politique*, ed. Philippe Raynaud and Stéphane Rials. Paris: PUF.

Jünger, Ernst. [1930] 1993. Total Mobilization. Trans. Joel Golb and Richard Wolin. In *The Heidegger Controversy: A Critical Reader*, ed. Richard Wolin, 119–139. Cambridge, Mass: MIT Press.

Kautsky, Karl. 1930. *Der Bolschewismus in der Sackgasse.* Berlin: J. H. W. Dietz Nachfolger.

Le Brazidec, Gwénaël. 1998. *René Capitant, Carl Schmitt: Crise et Réforme du Parlementarisme. De Weimar à la Cinquième République.* Paris: L'Harmattan.

Lemay, Benoit. 2010. Préface. In *La guerre totale by Erich Ludendorff*, 7–48. Paris: Perrin.

Lévi, Jean. 1985. *Le Grand empereur et ses automates.* Paris: Albin Michel.

Lewis, Mark E. 1990. *Sanctioned Violence in Early China.* Albany: State University of New York Press.

Ludendorff, Erich. 1935. *Der totale Krieg.* Munich: Ludendorffs Verlag.

MacFarquhar, Roderick, and Michael Schoenhals. 2006. *Mao's Last Revolution.* Cambridge, Mass: The Belknap Press of Harvard University Press.

Marcuse, Herbert. 1934. Der Kampf gegen den Liberalismus in der totalitären Staatsauffassung. *Zeitschrift für Sozialforschung* 3: 161–195.

Möller, Horst. 2021. *La République de Weimar.* Trans. Claude Porcell. Paris: Texto.

Mussolini, Benito. 1927. *Discorso dell'Asensione: Il regime fascist per la grandezza d'Italia. Pronunciato il 26 maggio 1927 alla Camera dei Deputati.* Rome: Libreria del Littorio.

——— (Giovanni Gentile). [1932] 1935. *La dottrina del Fascismo.* Florence: Vallechi Editore.

Neumann, Franz. 1942. *Behemoth: The Structure and Practice of National Socialism, 1933–1944.* New York: Harper and Row.

Ortega y Gasset, José. [1930] 1995. *La Rebelión de las Masas.* Madrid: Alianza Editorial.

Pines, Yuri. 2016. A 'Total War'? Rethinking Military Ideology in the *Book of Lord Shang. Journal of Chinese Military History* 5: 97–134.

———, trans. and ed. 2017. *The Book of Lord Shang: Apologetics of State Power in Early China.* New York: Columbia University Press.

Roosevelt, Franklin Delano. 1941a. *Speech by Franklin D. Roosevelt.* New York (transcript), 8 December, https://www.loc.gov/item/afccal000483/.

———. 1941b. *Roosevelt's Annual Message to Congress (Four Freedoms).* 6 January. Records of the United States Senate; SEN 77A-H1; Record Group 46; National Archives.

Rosenberg, Alfred. 1933. "Totaler Staat?" *Völkischer Beobachter*, 9 January.

Rubin, Vitaly A. 1976. *Individual and State in Ancient China: Essays on Four Chinese Philosophers*. New York: Columbia University Press.

Salvemini, Gaetano. 1935. Pour la liberté de l'esprit. *Les Humbles* 7: 5–9.

Schmitt, Carl. 1921. *Die Diktatur: Von den Anfängen des modernen Souveränitätsgedankens bis zum proletarischen Klassemkampf*. Berlin: Duncker & Humblot. (This text and the following two were highly influential in the 1920s and early 1930s on the reform of constitutional regimes, and remain so today)

———. 1922. *Politische Theologie. Vier Kapitel zur Lehre von Souveränität*. Berlin: Duncker & Humblot.

———. 1928. *Verfassungslehre*. Berlin: Duncker & Humblot.

———. [1933a] 1988. Weiterentwicklung des totalen Staat in Deutschland. In Scmitt, *Positionen und Begriffe im Kampf mit Weimar-Genf-Versailles 1923–1939*, 185–190. Berlin: Duncker & Humblot.

———. 1933b. *Staat, Bewegung, Volk: Die Dreigliederung der politischen Einheit*. Hamburg: Hanseatisch Verlagsantalt.

———. [1934] 1988. Der Führer schützt das Recht: Zu Reichstagsrede Adolf Hitler vom 13 juli 1934. In Schmitt, *Positionen und Begriffe im Kampf mit Weimar-Genf-Versailles 1923–1939*, 199–203. Berlin: Duncker & Humblot.

Schwartz, Benjamin I. 1985. *The World of Thought in Ancient China*. Cambridge, Mass: Belknap Press.

Serge, Victor. [1933] 1978. Lettre sur le totalitarisme stalinien. In *Mémoires d'un révolutionnaire 1901–1946*. Paris: Point.

Sturzo, Luigi. 1938. L'État totalitaire. In *Sturzo, Morale et Politique: Orientations et expérience*, 19–33. Paris: Bloud & Gay.

Sun, Wenbo. 2020. Shang Yang's promotion of the county system and the county-canton relations: an analysis based on official titles, salary grades and the size of the employed personnel. Trans. Yuri Pines. *Bamboo and Silk* 3 (2): 344–388.

Tillich, Paul. 1934. The Totalitarian State and the Claims of the Church. *Social Research* 1: 405–433.

Traverso, Enzo. 2001. Introduction. In *Traverso, Le Totalitarisme: le XXe siècle en débat*, 9–110. Paris: Seuil.

Trotsky, Leon. 1939. *The USSR in War*, 325–332. November: *The New International*.

Vandermeersch, Léon. 1965. *La formation du Légisme: Recherche sur la constitution d'une philosophie politique caractéristique de la Chine ancienne*. Paris: Presse de l'École Française d'Extrême Orient. (The first French-language in-depth study of the *fa* tradition).

von Clausewitz, Carl. 1832. *Vom Kriege*. Berlin: Ferdinand Dümmler.

Weber, Max. [1922] 1958. The Three Types of Legitimate Rule. Trans. Hans Gerth. *Berkeley Publications in Society and Institutions* 4 (1): 1–11. (Foundational text describing rational-legal authority – modern authority – and contrasting it with the two other main forms of authorities – traditional and charismatic).

Wickham, Jason Paul. 2014. *The Enslavement of War Captives by the Romans to 146 BC*. Ph.D. thesis, University of Liverpool.

Yates, Robin D. S. 1979. The Mohists on Warfare: Technology, Technique, and Justification. In Studies in Classical Chinese Thought, ed. Henry Rosemont Jr. and Benjamin I. Schwartz, thematic issue of *Journal of the American Academy of Religion* 47 (3): 549–603.

Part V
Epilogue

Chapter 23
The *Han Feizi* and Its Contemporary Relevance

Tongdong Bai

There was an *open* revival of Legalism in China in the early twentieth century,[1] after it was "in the closet" (at best) in traditional China since the Han Dynasty on (cf. Song and Pines, Chaps. 16 and 17, this volume). This revival peaked under Mao Zedong's rule (1949–1976). For example, Mao repeatedly made approving comments on the First Emperor of Qin, who carried the image of a Legalist practitioner, jokingly commenting that the only reservation he has is that the latter didn't go far enough in that he only buried alive 460 Confucians, whereas Mao's government buried alive 46,000, a hundred times of the former figure.[2] In another place, Mao said that in governing, there should be a combination of Marx with the First Emperor.[3] During the Cultural Revolution, there was the movement of "(re-)evaluating Legalism and criticizing Confucianism" (評法批儒), in which Legalism was portrayed positively (see, e.g. Liu 2012). After Mao died, Legalism quickly fell out of favor. It has been often used as a target of criticism for the past and present despotisms, although it has a comeback in some circles when China becomes a

---

[1] "Legalism" is a conventional translation of the Chinese term *fajia* 法家. Whether the Chinese term describes a group of thinkers, and whether the translation is a proper translation are highly controversial (see the introduction to this volume). To use "*fa* tradition" may be a better rendering of the Chinese term in English, as most contributors to this volume have done. But I will stick to "Legalism" or "Legalist" in this chapter purely out of heuristic convenience. For the meaning of "*fa*" and reasons why "Legalism" is not a very good translation, see my discussion at the beginning of Section 4.

[2] See Mao's speech on May 8, 1958. https://www.marxists.org/chinese/maozedong/1968/4-029.htm

[3] See his speech on August 19, 1958. https://www.marxists.org/chinese/maozedong/1968/4-050.htm

---

T. Bai (✉)
Fudan University, Shanghai, China

© The Author(s), under exclusive license to Springer Nature Switzerland AG 2024   645
Y. Pines (ed.), *Dao Companion to China's fa Tradition*, Dao Companions
to Chinese Philosophy 19, https://doi.org/10.1007/978-3-031-53630-4_24

powerful country and the "Legalist" Qin Dynasty is also viewed in a more positive light by some.[4]

In this chapter, I will focus on one specific and important Legalist text, the *Han Feizi* 韓非子—addressing, when relevant, its antecedent texts, such as the *Book of Lord Shang* (*Shangjunshu* 商君書, hereafter SJS)—and see whether its ideas are relevant to post-traditional China (from 1911 on), especially the New China (from 1949 on). More importantly, I will show how its ideas can be relevant in a universal manner and to the theory and practice in today's world.[5] In order to show the contemporary relevance of the *Han Feizi* (hereafter HFZ), I will also review some of its key ideas that have been discussed in other chapters of this volume. But my survey is not comprehensive, and I will focus on the ideas that I consider to have clear contemporary and comparative relevance.

1 The Unchanging: Han Feizi's View of Human Nature

Arguably, Han Fei 韓非 (d. 233 BCE) is a political theorist, even a political philosopher. But more than two thousand years have passed since his times, and so why should we pay attention to his views of politics? In fact, he himself was known to be unusually critical of those who paid undue attention to things from the past. It is true that many things have changed, for better or for worse. But a great political theorist such as Han Fei is still worth reading today because he grasped something unchanging, for example, human nature. His account of human nature can be challenged: for example, maybe there is no such a thing as a universal human nature to begin with, or his account fails to pay adequate attention to certain aspects of human nature. But his observations are worth reckoning with because they reveal something profound, if one-sided, about human beings.[6]

A widely shared view of HFZ is that he believed that the primary driving force of human actions is the pursuit of material profit and the avoidance of harm. This view of human nature seems to be in line with the view of his alleged teacher Xunzi 荀子 (d. after 238 BCE), and Western thinkers such as Machiavelli and Hobbes. Moreover, for HFZ, the above description is a *fact* of human beings, and instead of changing it, as some Confucians (including Xunzi) would like to do, we should follow it, the idea of "following" (*yin*因 or *shun*順) what is natural and factual being a

---

[4] See Barbieri-Low 2022. For a critical review of this book, see Pines 2023.

[5] To be clear, some of the ideas discussed in this chapter may have been introduced first in other Legalist texts, such as SJS, *Shenzi* 慎子, and so forth. But to draw from different texts will encounter the problem of consistency among them. To be sure, the coherence of the *Han Feizi* can also be questioned, and some parts of it are clearly not written by Han Fei. But the problem of consistency or coherence is less serious if we mainly use *Han Feizi* than if we draw from a variety Legalist texts.

[6] For a detailed discussion, see Bai 2021a. See also discussions in Sato 2013; Harris, Chap. 10, Sect. 3; Pines, Chap. 4, Sect. 2.3, this volume.

prominent idea in the so-called Huang-Lao黄老 tradition.[7] This view is shared by many of the Legalist thinkers, especially the authors of the SJS, and is the basis for their state-building, although HFZ may have been the most explicit and elaborate about how the state-building is rooted in the fact of human beings.

A closer look, however, reveals something subtler. For Han Fei seems to believe that in the age of plenty, human beings are not driven by the pursuit of profit anymore, but can be nice to each other, such as offering a stranger free food and living peacefully with one another with no need of morality or rewards and punishments (*Han Feizi* 49.2; Chen 2000: 1088 ["Wu du" 五蠹]), which is in sharp contrast to Xunzi's and Hobbes's view that, without external constraint, human beings will always fight against each other.[8] In Chapter 20 ("Jie Lao" 解老), HFZ even suggested that the good will is inborn (*Han Feizi* 20.3; Chen 2000: 374). The beauty of this apparently minor correction is that this view of human nature can resist the challenge from thinkers such as Mencius 孟子 (d. ca. 304 BCE) better than the view that denies the inborn goodness of human beings. In the famous "thought-experiment" in *Mencius* 2A6, Mencius tried to show the universality of our inborn goodness by asking if we could feel a sense of alarm and distress if we suddenly see a small child who is failing into a well (i.e., about to be killed)?[9] It is really hard for anyone to say no. Though not going that far, Han Fei would have no problem with what this story revealed. His response, which is also a key criticism of the Confucian ideal of virtuous rule, is that this good will is too fragile to resist challenges in slightly more trying times, which are most of the times we human beings live in. Indeed, in the age of scarcity, we wouldn't feed our younger brother even if he starved to death (*Han Feizi* 49.3; Chen 2000: 1088 ["Wu du"]).

Han Fei's view could also accommodate the most updated empirical studies better than the Hobbesian one. Frans de Waal, a primatologist, argues that there is inborn goodness in human beings, even in chimpanzees. He believes that this discovery challenges the Hobbesian view of human nature, which is widely shared by modern Western thinkers, and according to which our moral appearance is a "veneer" at best (de Waal 2006: 6–8). In contrast, HFZ could easily acknowledge this inborn goodness, although his belief in the fragility of it damps down the upbeat tone of de Waal about human morality.

Despite his concession to the inborn goodness of human beings, in most of the times, humans are merely rational animals—"rational" in the sense that people are able to calculate the benefits and harms of an action, although, to be clear, to be able to calculate does not mean being able to do it correctly and well. Indeed, for Han

---

[7] See, for example, the opening paragraph of Chapter 48 of the *Han Feizi* (*Han Feizi* 48.1; Chen 2000: 1045 ["Ba jing" 八經]). In referring to *Han Feizi*, I employ divisions into paragraphs adopted by Zhang 2010. For Huang-Lao's idea of *yin*, see Wang 2018: 225–26.

[8] My references to *Han Feizi* follow Zhang 2010 divisions, adopted by Harbsmeier in his forthcoming translation. But otherwise I rely only on Chen 2000.

[9] The translations of the *Mencius* as well as the *Analects* (*Lunyu* 論語) and the *Laozi* 老子 in this chapter are all mine. For different translations, see, e.g., Lau 2003 (*Mencius*), Lau 2000 (*Analects*), and Lau 1963 (*Laozi*).

Fei, the masses are like babies, and they are only slightly better than beasts by being able to calculate short-term material interests. Enlightened rulers such as the Great Yu 大禹 or the Zheng 鄭 chief minister Zichan 子產 (d. 522 BCE), in contrast, could do long-term policy making, but the masses maligned and slandered them and even threw stones at Great Yu (*Han Feizi* 50.11; Chen 2000: 1147 ["Xian xue" 顯學]).

In addition to the pursuit of material benefits, Han Fei (as Shang Yang before him) seems to appreciate a secondary driving force, which, in addition to rationality, distinguishes humans from animals: vanity, or, in his own terms, the pursuit of glory (*rong* 榮) and the avoidance of shame (*ru* 辱), or as is more commonly defined, the quest for a good name (*ming* 名, a term that can refer to reputation, fame, and also enhanced social status).[10] An ideal state should, through its institutions of rational bureaucracy, make these two kinds of driving forces in lockstep to promote the good of the state—the good of the state being economic prosperity and military strength (*fuguo qiangbing* 富國强兵). That is, the state should reward and glorify actions that are good for the state, and punish and stigmatize actions that are bad for it. This way, the interest of the state and that of the individual are in line with each other, and by following the fact of human beings, the state ends up being orderly and strong. This understanding stands at the foundations of Shang Yang's 商鞅 (d. 338 BCE) program of "social engineering," especially the system of the ranks of merit, which granted their owner a variety of economic, social, legal, political, and even sumptuary benefits (Pines 2016 and Pines, Chap. 1, this volume). This idea was fully inherited and further developed by Han Fei.

If a ruler doesn't understand this Dao of politics, and uses state machines to promote Confucian or other kinds of virtues, people will behave morally, but this is not because they are moral, but because morality pays. For the state, however, morality is not profitable. An enlightened ruler should reject this approach, and virtuous people will be replaced by law-abiding and hard-working subjects. People will behave morally when the state becomes so militarily powerful and economically prosperous through following Han Fei's proposal that people's innate but fragile goodness kicks in, which would be *Han Feizi*'s utopia (for a rare instance of utopian vision in *Han Feizi*, see, e.g., *Han Feizi* 14.5; Chen 2000: 287 ["Jian jie shi chen" 姦劫弑臣]).

In a few places, however, Han Fei seems to acknowledge that there are certain human beings, such as the legendary Boyi 伯夷 and Shuqi 叔齊, who pursue virtues for virtues' sake, and cannot be swayed by profit and glory. For Confucians, they are laudable paragons. But for Han Fei, since the order of the state is maintained through rewards and punishments (and to a lesser extent, glorifications and stigmatizations), these people would be unruly and un-governable disruptors. They should not be employed by the state. Indeed, they should be eliminated, by force if necessary.[11]

---

[10] For the importance of *ming* in early China, see Pines 2020, especially pp. 195–198 for Shang Yang's idea of utilizing the people's perennial quest for "a name" as a major tool of policymakers.

[11] See the discussion of how to treat the aforementioned two legendary figures in Chapters 14.7 and 44.3 ("Shuo yi" 說疑); Chen 2000: 294 and 969; see also Harris, Chap. 10, Sect. 3, this volume.

Han Fei's view of human nature, then, is more complicated than the Xunzian, Hobbesian, or the utilitarian view. Pleasure and pain are indeed the main driving force for most people, but there is a secondary driving force, which is vanity. All of us also have the innate goodness or innocence, but it is too fragile to have an effect in most circumstances.[12] Although all of us are rational, only the few can plan long-term, and they should be political leaders. There are also the few who can ignore the calculation of utility and the allure of vanity, and they should be eliminated from an orderly state.

With Han Fei's views of human nature and the ideal state that follows such a nature clarified, we should immediately see that the comparison between Mao and Legalism is apparently misguided. Mao wished to re-educate the masses and turn them into good communists, whereas Han Fei asked the state-builders to follow the natural dispositions of human beings. A good representation of Mao's ideal product is LEI Feng 雷鋒 (1940–1962), who is said to be "not concerned with benefiting himself, but only concerned with benefiting others" (毫不利己，專門利人). He is a Maoist version of Boyi and Shuqi, which means that the people like him, according to HFZ, should be executed! In contrast, a good subject for HFZ is one who tries to get rich by following laws of the state. There is nothing wrong to be self-interested and to pursuit wealth. Indeed, to be rich is (and should be sanctioned by the state as) glorious, which recalls a famous slogan in DENG Xiaoping's 鄧小平 (1904–1997) era "to become rich is glorious" (致富光榮).

2 The Change: Antiquity vs. (Han Fei's) Modernity

In contrast to the fact or nature of human beings that remains a constant, the world we live in can be and is indeed changing. To Han Fei, then, historical precedents are not normative ideals to be followed, as some pre Qin Confucians and other thinkers suggested, but are contingencies that can be explained by the constants in politics, such as the fact of human beings (see Vogelsang, Chap. 12, this volume). This view of Han Fei distinguishes him from many of his contemporaries, and makes him rather "modern," and a proper political *scientist*.[13]

It was a "fad" among thinkers in the Warring States China to bolster the prestige of their own ideals by putting words in the mouths of legendary figures from the past. Xunzi questioned the reliability of the words and actions of the sage rulers from the distant past (*Xunzi* 1992: 5:79 ["Fei xiang" 非相]). Han Fei went one step further by questioning the eternity and universality of the Confucian Dao that was

---

[12] Han Fei's view of human nature is actually more comparable with that of Jean-Jacques Rousseau, for the latter believes all human beings have *amour de soi* (self-love) and are rational, and we also have *amour-propre* (vanity) and pity (some kind of innate goodness) (Rousseau 1964: 221–22). But there are also important differences between the two.

[13] For comparing Han Fei to modern social scientists, see Graham 1989: 267; Schwartz 1985: 347–48.

derived from the former paragons' words and actions. Circumstances have changed, and thus the sages' way of doing things is not applicable to today's world anymore.[14] The key to the change from antiquity to HFZ's times is about the few vs. the many. According to *Han Feizi* 49.2 (Chen 2000: 1087 ["Wu du"]), in the time of sage rulers Yao 堯 and Shun 舜, people were few, whereas goods were many. If we recall HFZ's view of human nature, in this age of plenty, human beings could be very kind to each other, even without external moral and legal restraints. Thus, the ideal world of Yao and Shun was not the result of their moral leadership, as Confucians claim. HFZ explained away and deconstructed the Confucian advocacy for the good old days as irrelevant.

What changed, then? The simple answer is population growth:

> 今人有五子不為多，子又有五子，大父未死而有二十五孫，是以人民眾而貨財寡，事力勞而供養薄，故民爭，雖倍賞累罰而不免於亂。
>
> Nowadays, five children are not considered too many, and each child also has five children; the grandfather is still alive, and he already has twenty-five grandchildren. Therefore, the people are plenty while commodities and goods are few; people work laboriously, but provisions are scanty; hence the people compete. Even if [the ruler] multiplies rewards and piles on punishments, he will not avoid calamity. (*Han Feizi* 49.2; Chen 2000: 1087 ["Wu du"])

The dramatic population increase makes the competition for goods incomparably fiercer than in the good old days. The far more "solid" part of our nature kicks in, and we end up with a Hobbesian jungle if no external force is applied.

There was another profound social change in Warring States China, the collapse of hereditary aristocracy. During the Springs and Autumns period (Chunqiu 春秋, 770–453 BCE), the political, military, social, and economic power was concentrated in the hands of ministerial lineages, who managed to prevent outsiders from ascending the top of the political ladder. By the Warring States period, this system was dramatically altered with the appearance of a highly centralized territorial state ruled by the bureaucrats most of whom owed their position to merit rather than pedigree.[15] The so-called Legalist thinkers—especially Han Fei's predecessor, Shang Yang—were the theoretical and practical builders of this state, especially of its centralized and rational bureaucracy. This dramatic change is not explicitly addressed in *Han Feizi* but it underlies much of ideological debates of the Warring States era.

Facing this change, the Confucians offered their own solution: replace the nobility of blood with nobility of virtue—i.e., create a new elite of morally cultivated "noble men" (*junzi* 君子). This meritocracy, or nobility by virtues (which resembles the original sense of the term aristocracy, i.e., rule of the excellent, those with "arête") appeals to many scholars (including myself) who wish to revive some form of Confucian virtue politics as a remedy to the troubles of democracy (and

---

[14] See Bai 2020a for a detailed discussion of Han Fei's view of history and of the change from antiquity to (his) modernity (古今之變). For a general discussion of the use of history in pre-Qin China, see Pines 2005 and Roetz 2005 (the former is far more detailed than the latter). See also Pines, Chap. 4, Sect. 2.2 and Vogelsang, Chap. 12, this volume.

[15] See details in Tian and Zang 1996; Yang 1998; Lewis 1999.

non-democracy).[16] We should, however, respond to HFZ's criticisms of the Confucian proposal. I have reconstructed Han Fei's criticisms elsewhere (Bai 2020b), and let me give only an outline here, which is a reconstruction of arguments in chapters 49, "Five vermin" ("Wu du") and 50, "Illustrious teachings" ("Xian xue") of HFZ. Confucians—even Mencius—admit that the universal seed of compassion may be too fragile to resist challenges in reality (see, for example, *Mencius* 6A7 and 7A23), but they (including Mencius's rival Xunzi) optimistically insist that the "noble men" would be able to cultivate morality and make it strong enough to survive in trying times. To this, Han Fei has two responses: the moral cultivation is not as reliable as the use of rewards and punishments to regulate people's behaviors, and even if it succeeds, what is cultivated from the family setting is in conflict with what the state needs. A filial son is not a good subject when his father's interests and the state's interests are in conflict (or, more blatantly, "a filial son to a father is an absconding subject to the ruler" 夫父之孝子，君之背臣也 [*Han Feizi* 49.9; Chen 2000: 1104]).

The Confucians could bite the bullet and say that there are still the few successful results of moral cultivation who can also navigate through the conflict between family and state, and we can use them as political leaders. To this, HFZ has a four-layer response. First, virtues are relied on by the common people in their daily dealings because they have nothing else to resort to.[17] The ruler of a state has all the wealth and power, and can use them to reward and punish people, which, according to HFZ's view of human nature, is far more effective than any other means (*Han Feizi* 49.11; Chen 2000: 1109). Therefore, morality is not needed in state affairs. Second, there are not enough virtuous people around to fill the [bureaucratic] posts created by the emergence of large and populous state. Here we see again HFZ's portrait of the contrast between antiquity and modernity as one between the few and the many. Third, the Confucians hope that their virtuous leaders win the hearts and minds of the masses. But according to HFZ, the masses cannot even do long-term rational planning, let alone appreciating virtues (see above, p. 648). Fourth, even if we let virtuous people rule, what virtues are they? The "subtle and mysterious words even the most intelligent find hard to understand" 微妙之言，上智之所難知也 (*Han Feizi* 49.11; Chen 2000: 1109). Actually the intellectuals themselves cannot agree about which virtues are required; hence after Confucius died, "the Confucians were divided into eight," whereas after Mozi's 墨子 (ca. 460–390 BCE) death, "the Mohists were split into three" (*Han Feizi* 50.1; Chen 2000: 1124). Besides, even

---

[16] For a Confucianism-inspired meritocracy, see Bell 2006 and 2015; Chan 2013; Bell and Li 2013; Bai 2019. For a proposal of virtue politics that draws its inspiration from the humanists in Renaissance Italy, see Hankins 2019.

[17] Curiously enough, the virtue HFZ discussed was trustworthiness (貞信), which is not a typical Confucian virtue, but something that is necessary for a large society to function and is thus political.

Confucius himself couldn't identify people of virtues successfully (*Han Feizi* 50.5; Chen 2000: 1137).[18]

Here Han Fei introduced perhaps one of the earliest arguments for the inevitable plurality of values. This plurality seems to be again a result of numbers: when there are too many people, it is just impossible to unify their thoughts or value systems. The proliferation of different ideologies and values was duly noted by other Warring States-period thinkers, such as Xunzi and Mozi, who openly worried about it and wished to unify opinions for the good of the state.[19] By contrast, Han Fei *explained* why there were different values and why this plurality is *inevitable*. Only in *Zhuangzi* we find an argument to a similar effect.[20] If opinions cannot be unified, the unity should be found somewhere else.

Then, facing the change from antiquity to modernity, from the world of the few to world of the many, what is Han Fei's or the Legalist proposal? To Han Fei, recall, the goal of the state is to become strong economically and militarily (*fuguo qiang-bing*). State institutions should use rewards and punishments to align individual's self-interests with those of the state. Institutions and laws cannot run by themselves, and it has to be humans who run them. These officials should be selected on the basis of whether they deliver the expected results. Put it in another way, Han Fei and many other pre-Qin Chinese thinkers actually agree on the idea that we need an equality-based (equal-opportunities-based) meritocracy, but they differ on what is counted as merits.[21] For Han Fei, merits have to be verifiable with universal and objective criteria, and they are constitutive to the end of the state (cf. Pines, Chap. 18, Sect. 6, this volume). Put it in today's terminology, Han Fei and the Legalists were perhaps the first practical and theoretical builders of rational bureaucracy.

Han Fei's ideal political regime (and modern bureaucracy) may be criticized as a big machine, in which people are reduced to faceless and mindless parts. Indeed, those who consider traditional Chinese regimes to be legalistic and despotic denounce the machine as oppressive, a tool for the ruler to manipulate people any way he likes. But we need to see that in this ideal regime, everyone is making his or her own rational choice. It is just that the state institutions are designed in such a way that only actions that are good for the strength of the state will be rewarded, and the bad actions will be punished. People are indeed controlled by the so-called "two handles" (of rewards and punishments), but these handles are effective because people are rational decision-makers. The ruler of a state cannot be regulated by anyone higher anymore, but even he will be guided by his self-interests, which

---

[18] To be clear, although to Han Fei, he clearly won the debate with the Confucians, it is not necessarily the case in the eyes of other observers. Recall that some of his representations of the Confucian position, especially with regard to the family-state tensions, are caricatures and distortions of it, and the Confucians could respond to his criticisms. See more in Bai 2020b.

[19] In *Mozi*, the unity of opinions is considered the precondition of orderly rule as explained in "Conforming upwards" (or "Elevating uniformity" ["Shang tong" 尚同]) chapters. For *Xunzi*'s views, see chapter 6, "Against twelve philosophers" ("Fei shier zi" 非十二子).

[20] See chapter 33, "The world" ("Tianxia" 天下) of the *Zhuangzi*.

[21] Cf. Ivanhoe 2011 and Pines 2013 for the introduction of meritocracy in Warring States China.

dictate that he should be a faceless guarantor of the smoothing running of the state machine. If he fails to do this but takes actions into his own hands, his own state will become weak, meaning that his own self-interests will be harmed (*Han Feizi* 6.1; Chen 2000: 84 ["You du" 有度]). This way, Han Fei's ideal state can be described in a beautifully elegant manner: the ruler is the ultimate guarantor of the state institutions, which employ rewards and punishments to guide people to make "free" rational choices that are good not only for them, but also for the state. The Dao (or in today's terms, the law of politics) guides the ruler to be this guarantor through Dao's rewards (making the ruler's state strong if he follows Dao) and punishments. If we understand the idea of non-action (*wu wei* 無爲)—which is often described as a characteristic of the philosophy of the *Laozi*—as avoiding unnatural and un-Dao-like actions, Han Fei's ideal regime is a regime where everyone, including the ruler, takes no action beyond what Dao dictates, through its "invisible hands." Yes, it is like a machine. But a more accurate analogy is that it is not a simple machine (cf. Graham 1989: 291), but a computer. People other than the ruler are parts of the computer whose actions are controlled by the CPU, that is, the ruler. But the CPU or the ruler doesn't control the parts with its own will, but by following the Dao of computer or political science.

A few general lessons can be drawn from the discussion in this section. The first is about the nature of modernity. Francis Fukuyama argues that if we follow Max Weber on his idea that rational bureaucracy is the essential feature of modernity, the allegedly Legalist Qin empire was the first politically modern state in human history (Fukuyama 2011: 125–26; cf. Schiele Chap. 22, Sect. 4, this volume). By implication, Han Fei and the Legalists were the first modern political thinkers. If we reject the above claims, we will have to argue that either there is a subtle difference between the Legalists and the Legalistic Qin and Weber's understanding, or Weber was wrong about the nature of modernity. To study *Han Feizi*, then, will help us to understand the nature of modernity and rational bureaucracy.

The second lesson is about Han Fei's argument for the inevitable plurality of values, which was a key element of pluralism. Unlike modern liberals, Han Fei was not concerned with tolerating different values. Rather, he wished to show through this argument that values cannot unite a state. We need to resort to something "lower" or "more base," which is universally shared by all human beings. This is why Han Fei appealed to the pursuit of material profit and "a name." Not only did he anticipate utilitarianism, but he explained why we had to resort utility at the risk of being accused of advancing "a doctrine worthy only of swine":[22] only on the level of the swine can human beings act in unison. Moreover, although Han Fei didn't care about tolerance, he actually posed in advance a challenge to today's liberal pluralism: tolerate as you like, but something else is needed to bond the state together. Without addressing the issue of bonding, the liberal pluralistic state would disintegrate. It is not HFZ, but the liberal pluralist who owes us an explanation.

---

[22] This is an accusation John Stuart Mill the utilitarian tried to address (2001: 7).

Third, *Han Feizi* had arguments that would challenge democracy as well. Clearly, he was no democrat, and he would reject many democratic ideas and principles (most fundamentally, the rationale behind allowing the people—who have "the mind of a little child" 嬰兒之心 [*Han Feizi* 50.11; Chen 2000: 1147]—to participate in politics). What I wish to point out here, however, is not the obvious objections. As we have seen, his ideal regime is a rational bureaucracy that is aimed at increasing the strength of the state. Bureaucrats are chosen on the basis of their effectiveness of accomplishing their institutional tasks, no less and *no more*.[23] Bureaucrats on the higher level all the way to the supreme ruler should not use their own personal and subjective criteria to evaluate lower-level officials. In particular, Han Fei warned against using reputation to evaluate officials. The reputation can come from "influencers" (he called them *neng ren* 能人 in Chapter 6.2 [Chen 2000: 91, "You du"]), from the peers, or from the people (see #5 of the eight villainous acts in Chapter 9.1 [Chen 2000: 182, "Ba jian" 八姦]). But actions that are good for cultivating reputation are not necessarily good for the state, and they may even lead to factions and treasonous conspiracies. In today's democracies, there are also influencers (lobbyists, celebrities, and so on), and legislators in American congress often support the so-called pork-barrel projects that are good for their constituencies (and their reelection) but not for the wellbeing of the nation as a whole. Despite being an "ancient" thinker with a reputation of autocracy-lover, HFZ actually raised some *internal* challenges to modernity and modern liberal democracy.

3 Focusing on the Truly Productive Sector: HFZ's Political Economics

As we have seen, pre-Qin Confucians were "vermin" to the state because they were defending a wrong kind of meritocracy. Moreover, their very existence is bad for the morale of the working people. For if an unenlightened ruler rewards them for being able to read and write, profit-driven and rational people are faced with two choices: either work hard day in and day out in the field to make living, or read and write in the comfort of one's own home to make an equal or higher income. Obviously, they will choose the latter. But if a state is full of book worms, and no one tills the soil, in an agrarian society when economy is based on agricultural output, the state will become poorer and poorer. Therefore, put their poisonous values aside, to value book-reading and book-writing Confucians is also bad for the state.

This reasoning actually applies to all literati (文學之士). This will then include Han Fei himself and those who read and write "Legalist" books. He bravely bit the

---

[23] The "no more" part is actually very counterintuitive. See the discussion in Chapter 7 ("Er bing" 二柄), especially the puzzling story about Marquis Zhao of Han 韓昭侯, who punished not just the Supervisor of the Jacket (who forgot to cover him with a jacket) but also the Supervisor of the Crown who did cover him, overstepping therewith his office's prerogatives (*Han Feizi* 7.2; Chen 2000: 126).

bullet and openly denounced the valuing of all of the "scholars" 學者 in the famous
"Five Vermin" chapter (*Han Feizi* 49.10; Chen 2000: 1111–12). Han Fei read and
wrote to denounce those who read and write, making him a member of the literati
who is against the literati. He is brave and stays true to his logic and reasoning.

To be clear, for Han Fei there is no need for scholars supporting his own—
correct —ideology.[24] Indeed, if we understand his teachings, we should stop reading and arguing for them, but roll up our sleeves and start working in the
field or killing enemies in the (battle) field. Confucians, in contrast, are bad on two
fronts, both in terms of their teachings and in terms of their very existence.
This is why they (and not the literati in general) are the Number One vermin among
the five vermin (*Han Feizi* 49.13; Chen 2000: 1122). They are a kind of vermin because they are not only useless to the "host" (the state and its ruler), but are
actively harming it. If we apply Han Fei's analogy through, other scholars
should be called parasites, not vermin.

The hostility to the literati is a theoretical endorsement of the notorious policy by
the First Emperor: burning books and—allegedly—burying Confucians/literati (Ru
儒) alive.[25] This may have reminded readers of the Nazi book burnings and other
totalitarian policies. But we need to see a key difference. The Nazis wished to purify
the German thought, but HFZ was not interested in thought-control—perhaps more
accurately, "positive thought control"[26]—because thoughts or values are too weak
as a driver for human actions. It is just that if the literati have a good life, it will
discourage people from working hard in the truly productive sectors. It is true that
Confucians were also spreading dangerous ideas, but the key is that rulers should be
so enlightened as not to listen to them—thus what is needed is only a "negative
thought control," making booking-learning not prominent and not highly rewarding.
In a perverse way, the Nazis are more egalitarian and spiritual than HFZ in that they
believe in *positively* "enlightening" all Aryans, including the common folks, with
the "right" spiritual teachings.

Following a similar logic that the state should promote the truly productive sector, we can see why Han Fei was against the merchants and the artisans. The opposition to these two groups is most vividly present in SJS, the text most fully committed
to the promulgation of pure agriculturalism and suppression of commercial and

---

[24] Elsewhere (*Han Feizi* 49.12; Chen 2000: 1111), Han Fei laments that although many families
posses "the laws of Shang [Yang] and Guan [Zhong]" 藏商、管之法者家有之 (here probably
referring to the early versions of SJS and *Guanzi* 管子), the state becomes ever poorer. Clearly,
even possession of the texts the ideas of which Han Fei normally endorses is of no good.

[25] The story of book burning in 213 BCE is indeed historically reliable. The story of burying the Ru,
by contrast, is a later invention. In 212 BCE, unrelated to the book burning, the First Emperor
executed "scholars" (*sheng* 生) who promised him the pill of immortality and failed to deliver. Two
centuries later this barbarous, albeit not entirely unprecedented act, was reinterpreted as another
ideological assault on the Ru. See more in Zhang 1988; Zhang 1991; cf. Neininger 1983; Barbieri-
Low 2022: 127–30). Nevertheless, it is indisputable that scholars, their teaching activities and even
their personal libraries that were not part of the imperial system were indeed suppressed, just as
Han Fei would prefer.

[26] I thank Yuri Pines for coining this term and the term "negative thought control" for me.

other distracting activities (Sterckx 2015; Pines 2021). In HFZ, the assault on the merchants is less prominent, but in the ending paragraphs of the "Five vermin" chapter, merchants and craftsmen who "cultivate the production of shoddy objects and accumulate extravagant wealth" 脩治苦窳之器，聚弗靡之財 (*Han Feizi* 49.13; Chen 2000: 1122) are identified as the fifth and last vermin. The reason for this identification is clear (and echoes the SJS): the easy enrichment of these two groups distracts the farmers from tilling the soil and weakens the country economically. Obviously, merchants are needed for the functioning of the state machine, and artisans are needed to produce tools for war, just as the country needs some who can read and write. Despite the occasional inflammatory rhetoric, Han Fei would allow a very limited number of these people to exist in his ideal state. It is just that they should not be too visible and "flashy" to ruin the morale of the working people.

Traditional China was often criticized for belittling commerce, but this was not necessarily the case in the Warring States period (Sterckx 2015). Suffice it to recall Han Fei's alleged teacher, Xunzi, who dedicated a panegyric to the merchants whose contribution to the common prosperity he called "greatly divine" 大神 (*Xunzi* 1992: 9: 162 ["Wang zhi" 王制]). In later Chinese empire, commerce prospered despite periodic restrictions; and sometimes commercial activism could even compensate the state for its weakness as was the case with the Southern Song Dynasty 南宋 (1127–1279). Among the Warring States-period texts, *Laozi* does express serious concern with commerce, especially in luxury goods, which would drive people's desires to run wild, causing strife and even war among people (*Laozi* 3). Han Fei seems to inherit and develop *Laozi*'s message. Therefore, if there was anticommerce sentiment and, related to this, the sentiment of the attachment to the land and not migrating casually (安土重遷)[27] in traditional Chinese culture, we should better look at *Laozi* and HFZ for theoretical foundation for these sentiments.

At the same time, let us not hasten and dismiss Han Fei's dislike of merchants as entirely wrong. Not only does it reflect the logic of the Warring States period economy, when possession of ample agricultural supplies was essential for providing for the armies; more generally, the desire to link individual income to the contribution to the "real economy" is at the very least very intuitive and persuasive.

In fact, two thousand years after HFZ, the French physiocrats, the most famous of whom is François Quesnay (1694–1774), also argued that agriculture was the true productive sector of the economy, and merchants are of the "barren" or "sterile" class that doesn't contribute to the real economy (Quesnay 2004). It is also interesting to note that the name of this school means "the rule of nature," and this resonates with the Huang-Lao and Han Fei's idea that we should follow what is natural. Indeed, the physiocrats' idea of following nature is said to be influenced by the Chinese idea of non-action, and the term "laissez-faire" is a translation of or is inspired by non-action (Clarke 1997: 50; McCabe 2008: 171; Mungello 2013: 120). It should be recalled also that physiocrats may have influenced among others Adam

---

[27] The earliest appearance of this stock phrase postdates Han Fei. It comes from a Han imperial edict (*Hanshu* 9: 292).

Smith and his notion of laissez-faire, a key idea in modern market economy (Clarke 1997: 50 and Bodde 1948: 8). Smith believed that the physiocrats came closest to the truth of political economy, and "they are generally acknowledged as the first to have developed a coherent economic theory" (Charbit 2002: 856). If so, and the European ideas that parallel those of HFZ could be adapted and developed into modern market economy, then would it be possible for Han Fei's own thought to be so adapted?

It may sound strange to many to make a connection between Han Fei and market economy, for he and the Legalists give many people the impression of being pro-state-control. But as we have seen, the state controls the people through two handles, and the two handles are effective because people can make their own rational choices. This interesting combination of state control and free market reflects the reality of Qin economic structure which was based not on suppression of the merchants but on complex modes of cooperation between merchants and officials (Korolkov 2021). In today's world, many market economies are successful precisely because of the active state control and promotion of market forces, or at least their successes are accompanied by active state promotion. One can look at the economical miracles of many East Asian countries and regions as well as the so-called "Miracle of Chile" under the authoritarian Pinochet to see the connection.

Notably, whereas in the earliest chapters of SJS one can discern clear preponderance of command economy, in the later chapters market forces are assigned ever increasing role (Pines 2021). HFZ itself also demonstrates clear "free-market" inclinations. For instance, it opposes the redistribution of land from the opulent to needy peasants, because for him "this amounts to taking from the hard-working and frugal and giving to the wasteful and lazy" 是奪力儉而與侈惰也 (*Han Feizi* 50.3; Chen 2000: 1134 ["Xian xue"]). Clearly, Han Fei would be against the land-reform done by Mao, and he would be against welfare state in general. But we can also see a caveat in his proposal: barring accidental factors, the fact that one could become rich or poor is due to one's efforts. Han Fei would be fine, in similar situations, with levelling the playing field and offering equal opportunities for competition, but after that, and after the establishment of effective institutions, the state should leave the matters to the natural tendencies of the people and let Dao or the invisible hands run things.

Therefore, we can imagine that HFZ—much like SJS—would be able to acknowledge the significance of artisanship (manufacturing sector) and commerce (trade) to the economic strength of the state. But he would still have reservations, rightly or wrongly, about other sterile and unproductive sectors. For example, his argument could be easily applied to the 2008 financial crisis. Finance is a lubricant of economy, but neither the core, nor the real productive sector of economy. Yet if one can make the quickest and easiest money in finance, people, especially the best and the brightest, will be enticed to work in this sector. For a large country, the prosperity built mostly on finance is a house of cards that is doomed to collapse. The Chinese might feel lucky, because China's financial market was not that developed, and China's success in the past four decades is largely due to being the factory of the world. But Han Fei's argument could be applied to China's economy as well. For a lot of the wealth the Chinese people have accumulated in the past two decades comes from the real estate. If a woman buys an apartment in Shanghai, the money she can make after ten years of doing nothing else can be comparable to the earning of the factory her husband owns and runs in the neighboring Zhejiang province. Stories like this abound. If this is the case, people would either invest in real estate or work in industries that are associated with real estate. Other manufacturing sections will be sucked dry by this. Clearly, a country with a lot of empty apartment buildings is also a house of cards, more accurately, empty houses of bricks. The *Han Feizi* argument can be wrong, but it is still pretty powerful and needs to be taken seriously and answered adequately.

4 Between Natural Law and Legal Positivism: HFZ's Thin Version of the Rule of Law

Legalism is often characterized as a defense of authoritarianism and even despotism. An apparent difficulty with this characterization is that the Chinese term for "Legalism," *fajia* 法家, has "*fa*" in it, which could mean "law." But as a few scholars have pointed out, "Legalism" is really a misleading translation because "*fa*" doesn't only mean law (Creel 1970: 93 and 1974: 162; Winston 2005; Goldin 2011: 91–92). On the basis of the meaning of the Chinese character and on these scholars' works, I think that the generic meaning of "*fa*" is "method" or "standards," and given the "Legalists'" focus on politics, it also means in their texts method in politics, or administrative and governing techniques. The use of laws is one of the techniques, and a crucial one for the Legalists. In HFZ, "*fa*" is used on all three levels. But in many cases, it does have the meaning of "law." In this section, we will look at how its understanding of the law should be characterized.

Putting aside the problem of the misleading translation, law does play a central role in Legalist political theory. Those who are critical of Legalism often ignore this, and give uninformed and confused accusations of Legalism as being pro-despotism. There are some more serious scholars who try to assert that the Legalist use of law is really rule by law, and not rule of law (see, for example, Zhang 1999: 124; see also the discussion in Song, Chap. 9, this volume). The former suggests that law is merely a tool of control. If the controlling party is not the state, but a ruler, rule by law degenerates into rule by man, that is, a kind of autocracy or despotism.

To be clear, law is always administered by human beings, as long as we live in a human society. What makes "rule by man" repulsive is the implication that the rule is at the ruler's own personal, subjective, and arbitrary discretion. But if a ruler is ruling over a large group of people, obviously, it is inconvenient and even impossible for this person to judge every case. He or she may then delegate the authority to others to execute his or her will that is written out in the form of laws. But the interpretation of the laws is eventually up to the ruler, and he or she may simply change the laws when they become inconvenient for his or her rule. This is how "rule by law" is usually understood, which Kenneth Winston calls "ad hoc instrumentalism" (2005: 316).

Identical with rule by law is concept of "positive law." According to this concept, laws are posited by human beings out of the convenience to rule. Thomas Hobbes, whose philosophy is often compared with HFZ's, can be considered to be advancing such an understanding of law in the *Leviathan*. John Austin, who followed the Hobbesian spirit and was a main representative of the positive law tradition or legal positivism, said plainly, "every supreme government is legally *despotic*" (Austin 1995: 225).

Opposite to "rule by law" is the "rule of law." The preposition "of" suggests that "law" is an autonomous authority, and it is not subjected to the discretion or the arbitrariness of a person. What is often considered interchangeable with this concept is "natural law," but there is a crucial distinction between them. The "nature" in natural law could mean something impersonal and beyond a particular community of people. Indeed, an origin of the search for an impersonal and universal system of law was the attempt by ancient Greeks and Romans to find something beyond the plurality of laws they experienced in their world (Unger 1976: 76–77 and Hart 2012: 187–88). This kind of natural law doesn't have to have a "Divine Governor or Lawgiver of the universe" (Hart 2012: 187), and is indeed interchangeable with the concept of rule of law. However, the other origin of natural law is rooted in some kind of transcendent religiosity, Christianity in particular (Unger 1976: 76–77 and Hart 2012: 187–88). This kind of natural law has a strong religious or moral undertone, which is well captured by the famous slogan that is attributed to Thomas Aquinas and Augustine: "*Lex iniusta non est lex*" (unjust laws are not laws).[28] For conceptual clarity, I will use the "rule of law" in the amoral or thin-moral sense, and "natural law" with a religious or moral significance.

Many laymen and even legal scholars, however, give a rather thick reading of the rule of law by conflating it with "democracy, justice, equality (before the law or otherwise), human rights of any kind or respect for persons or for the dignity of man." This way, rule of law is turned into "the rule of the good law," and as a result, it loses "a useful function" (Raz 1979: 211). Here the contemporary legal positivist Joseph Raz was commenting on "the promiscuous use" of the concept of the rule of law in general, and it is also quite widespread among contemporary Chinese legal scholars and laymen. For example, an influential contemporary legal theorist XIA Yong 夏勇 offers this promiscuous reading of the rule of law and even defends the necessity and desirability of it (Xia 1999: 134–25). WANG Renbo 王人博 (2003) and ZHANG Qianfan 張千帆 (2006) are critical of this thick reading, and argue that, with the thin reading, what the Legalists advocated is indeed the rule of law.

Therefore, as long as we do not conflate the aforementioned concepts, it is actually quite obvious that HFZ and the Legalist in general could be interpreted as

---

[28] In the *Summa Theologica*, Aquinas said, "As Augustine says (De Lib. Arb. i, 5) 'that which is not just seems to be no law at all': wherefore the force of a law depends on the extent of its justice" (https://www.gutenberg.org/ebooks/17897). For Augustine's original words, see *On the Free Choice of the Will* Chapter 5, Book 1 (Augustine 1993: 8).

advocating a thin concept of the rule of law. But before I go into some details, let me make some further conceptual clarifications. Although I try to distinguish among these concepts, it should be clear that in any real thinker's legal philosophy or in any real-world situations, there can be a sliding scale, and the difference is a difference of degrees, not of kinds, when we apply these concepts. As we have seen, rule by man is a form of rule that is totally up to the discretion or whim of one person or a group of people. But we can observe their rulings and gather some rationales for it ("the ruler really doesn't like someone with a mustache, and such a person is always executed by the ruler"), thus reducing its unpredictability. When ruling over a large number of people, rules and laws are formulated out of the convenience of the ruling party, turning rule by man into rule by law (legal positivism). Although laws can be interpreted, revised, or created for the interests of the rulers, the ruling becomes even less arbitrary. If laws become more and more stable, rule by law can be transformed into the rule of law. Although the law in the rule of law doesn't have to have a thick moral or religious content, it can have certain basic features, which can be understood as a thin morality of law, giving the rule of law some moral content.

For example, as was mentioned, Hobbes was often considered to advocate rule by law or legal positivism. Having the absolute power, the sovereign in the *Leviathan* can dictate whatever laws it wishes. But the sovereign can be the people, which *could* limit the arbitrariness of the legislation. Of course, the people can be as whimsical as a despot—one only need to look at the French Revolution to appreciate this. Moreover, although the sovereign in Hobbes's *Leviathan* can dictate whatever laws it wishes, the subjects can still refuse to obey if these laws violate the Hobbesian laws of nature. That is, the arbitrariness of Hobbes's sovereign and the rule by its law can be reduced through other factors.

Generally, meta-rules can be applied to rule by law and turn its ad hoc instrumentalism into "principled instrumentalism" (Winston 2005: 316). In fact, according to Winston, the legal positivist Austin thought that there are two features that are essential to law: generality and intelligent guidance. The contemporary legal positivist Raz argued that there are eight principles law should follow (1979: 214–18). Interestingly enough, the contemporary natural law theorist John Finnis also proposes eight similar principles (Wang 2003: 18). According to Winston, the contemporary legal theorist Lon Fuller, too, offers eight principles, and he further argues that there is internal moral of the law, thanks to these principles (Winston 2005: 318). But this morality is a rather thin morality, and I believe that it is more in line with the *de*德 in the Huang-Lao and HFZ tradition than in the Confucian tradition.[29]

Zhang Qianfan in his article (2006) shows how the Legalists' legal philosophy is in line with a thin version of the rule of law, which is the proper and non-conflated and non-inflated understanding of the rule of law. Wang's and Winston's works are much more detailed. They analyze how the legal philosophy of the Legalists in general (Wang) and of HFZ in particular (Winston) meets the eight principles Raz (Wang) and Fuller (Winston) have listed. Overall, I am in agreement with their

---

[29] For the Huang-Lao understanding of *de*, see, for example, Wang 2018: 224.

analyses, with a minor reservation with Wang's (and Zhang's) works: I am more comfortable with focusing on one particular text than talking about "Legalism" in general. To save some space, then, I won't repeat their works, and will only mention a few points as examples and offer further points of comparison.

Why do we insist on a thin reading of the rule of law, other than for conceptual clarity with which we can distinguish between the rule of law and the rule of the good law or some kind of Natural Law (the first letters capitalized to indicate some thick moral contents)? In Wang's article, he argues that the thin reading (he calls it the universalist reading) is universal and is good for it to be spread and adopted in non-Western countries. Indeed, if we follow Rawls's later political liberalism, a thick reading that is inevitably associated with a comprehensive doctrine can never become universal without using some oppressive power. Even if this doctrine advocates some metaphysical form of freedom, it will end up forcing people—those people who, with liberty, may reject this peculiar metaphysical reading of liberty—to be free.

To insist on a thin version of the rule of law does not mean the rejection of any moral content. Indeed, a criticism of Rawls's liberalism is that it is too thin, and some kind of moral perfectionism is needed to make liberalism work (Chan 2000). This is perhaps a hidden reason for Fuller to emphasize the internal morality of the law, although the moral content he advocated is still rather thin and is not different from the kind of liberal neutrality implied by Rawls's liberalism. According to Winston's reading, the moral core of the thin theory of the rule of law is impersonal governance (2005: 315). If this is the core of the rule of law, we can clearly see why what Han Fei advocated is also the rule of law. Especially in Chapter 5, "The Way of the Ruler" ("Zhu dao" 主道), he argued that the ideal ruler should be quiet and empty, blocking his own personal preferences, desires, moral sentiments, "wisdoms," and so on. This impersonal governance is not only about executing the law, but about legislation as well. For he said that the ruler should be "empty and inactive, waiting for order" 故虛靜以待令 (*Han Feizi* 5.1; Chen 2000: 66).[30] The ruler is the absolute sovereign of the state, and the only thing higher than him has to be Dao, the universal and impersonal law of politics. In another place, he said the ideal governance is "to follow Dao and to preserve the law" 因道全法 (*Han Feizi* 29.1; Chen 2000: 555 ["Da ti" 大體]). One can question how this impersonal legislation is realized. To this question, Han Fei would have said that he (or another good "Legalist") knew what the law should be like. In contrast, the Rawlsian "veil of ignorance" is a better conceptual tool to reveal the content of the law, although, obviously, the criteria of those who will be put behind this veil, that is, the hidden moral assumptions of using this mechanism, will be different in the case for Han Fei. Nevertheless, it cannot be denied that Han Fei's ideal law is impersonal.

In the thin theory of the rule of law, it is expected that people obey the law voluntarily. As we have seen, Han Fei's ideal regime is built on the recognition and the

---

[30] Some believe that "order" should not be there, and is a result of a mistake in transmission of the text (Chen 2000: 68–69). Even if this is the case, in Chapter 8, Han Fei explicitly said that the ruler should "wait for order from Heaven" 待命於天 (*Han Feizi* 8.3; Chen 2000: 145).

embrace of the rational nature of human beings. But one can question whether one's obedience under the state institutions of rewards and punishments is out of one's own volition or not. This leads to the perennially difficult question of free will. But at least for Hobbes, to obey the law under some duress is still out of one's own volition (Chapter 14 of the *Leviathan*; Hobbes 1985: 189–201), and Austin thought that the voluntariness of Fuller's kind is not necessary (Winston 2005: 327). That is, we can acknowledge the existence of voluntariness in Han Fei's ideal regime if we take a "thin" reading of it, or we can deny it while claiming that voluntariness in a thick sense is not essential to the rule of law.

Among the specific principles for law, there is clarity of the law. This is something HFZ obviously embraced. His concern, like Hobbes's, is the absolute authority of the sovereign. For if the law is vague and up to the interpretations of the magistrates of the law, these people become de facto sovereign in their own jurisdictions, taking authority away from the absolute sovereign. Winston put it well:

> In the English case Re Castioni, Judge Stephen captures something of the spirit of the Han Feizi when he says: "[I]t is not enough to attain to a degree of precision which a person reading [the statute] in good faith can understand; but it is necessary to attain if possible to a degree of precision which a person reading in bad faith cannot misunderstand." (Winston 2005: 336)

This is also related to another principle: congruence. On both principles, HFZ would insist on the literal reading of the law and its strict application, whereas Fuller, according to Winston, would only require the fidelity to the law, leaving some discretion to the judges (Winston 2005: 324). We can discuss which approach is better, but it is clear that HFZ embraced the principles of clarity and congruence, which are considered crucial for a system to be the rule of law.

In general, although the rule of law is not the rule of the good law, it is still better than rule by law or rule by man. For example, Rawls defines formal justice as the "impartial and consistent administration of laws and institutions" (Rawls 1971: 58). But this "justice as regularity" "excludes significant kinds of injustices," such as the personal and monetary influences (ibid.: 59). "Moreover, even where laws and institutions are unjust, it is often better that they should be consistently applied" because those who are subjected to them can protect them by following the rules (ibid.). Indeed, the worst tyranny is not the rule of harsh laws, but arbitrary rule.

One last objection is that in HFZ's system, the ruler has the absolute and unchecked authority, whereas under the rule of law, law should be the highest authority, and everyone, including the ruler, is under the law. Otherwise, it is only rule by law at best. But as I have already shown, according to HFZ, the ruler, being human, is also expected to be rational. The state is his, and his state can only become strong, that is, his interests can only be protected, if he is a faceless executive of the law. One can then argue that it would be better if we could have institutional checks and balances against the ruler. But this idea is actually very counterintuitive, while HFZ's insistence on the absolute authority of the ruler is very intuitive. He offered a very good analogy in Chapter 8, "Brandishing Authority" ("Yang quan" 揚權), where he said that the ruler is different from his subjects just as the scales (*heng* 衡)

are different from lightness and heaviness (*Han Feizi* 8.4; Chen 2000: 152). If we wish to know the weight of something, we use a tool to weigh it. But if we think the tool is not accurate, we find a standard tool or standard weight. Eventually, there is the ultimate standard weight by which the weights of all others depend on, and its own weight cannot be challenged because any challenge presupposes a more reliable standard weight. Similarly, when we have quarrels with each other, we go to authority. If we don't agree with the authority, we can go to the higher authority. To avoid infinite regress or infinite ascent, there has to be the highest authority. We cannot question it anymore, because if we do, there will be no ultimate authority and the world will become chaotic. Therefore, it is quite intuitive to think that in a regime with stability, there should be the highest authority. But laws themselves cannot impose themselves on any human beings, and only human beings can. Therefore, this ultimate authority has to be a human being or a group of human beings. But what if this human entity abuses his or their power? This is really a very difficult question, and the constitutional checks and balances seem to be the answer. Defending Legalism, a twentieth century historian of thought, Lü Simian呂思勉 (1884–1957), challenged the constitutional answer (Lü 2016: 66–67). He asked, what could stop these institutions of checks and balances from abusing the law? Indeed, for there to be stability, there has to be a final authority. If two or three institutions always check and balance one another, how do we settle anything? If we can settle anything, one of the institutions must have had the de facto highest authority.

To be clear, like all my defenses of HFZ in this chapter, I am not saying that he was right. Personally, I wish he was wrong in many of the ideas I tried to defend. For one thing, I really like to live in a constitutional regime with checks and balances. What I am trying to say here is that his idea, even if it were wrong, is rather intuitive and is very difficult to reject. He is a very worthy enemy for those of us who wish to think about politics carefully.

To sum up, HFZ's theory of law is on the same side as legal positivism in their rejection of the (thick?) morality of the law. But he also insisted on the idea that it is not any human being, including the ruler, who makes laws. Dao does. In the impersonal origin of the law, he is on the same side of the natural law tradition. But he is neither. This makes his legal theory rather peculiar and thus interesting.[31]

5   Han Fei's *shu*: Open and Hidden Art of Bureaucratic Governance

Even to many who lauded the idea of *fa*, the concept of *shu* 術 (techniques or art of rule) was often interpreted negatively as related to trickery and unfair play (see more in Song, Chap. 9, this volume). The general meaning of *shu* is method, tactic,

---

[31] For other discussions of the relations between Han Fei and the rule of law, see, for example, Peerenboom 2002; Harris 2011; Schneider 2014; Martinich 2014.

or strategy. Given the Legalists' focus on politics, in their texts it usually means the art of politics (or the political art), or governing techniques (or techniques of governance). But to the critics, this art of politics often means some black art or a form of Machiavellianism (which is negatively perceived, *pace* Blahuta, Chap. 21, this volume). Those who are slightly less critical would argue that it is only the later Legalists such as Shen Buhai申不害 (d. 337 BCE) and Han Fei who are obsessed with this art, and other than Shen's influence, these critics often blame on the influence of the *Laozi* (maybe a distorted version of it) for HFZ's development of his "black art."[32]

To complicate matters, *shu* in *Han Feizi*, can refer to a variety of governing methods. There are several definitions of *shu* in the text, and I shall focus on the lengthiest one, in chapter 30, "Inner congeries of explanations A" ("Neichu shuo shang" 內儲說上)

七術：一曰眾端參觀，二曰必罰明威，三曰信賞盡能，四曰一聽責下，五曰疑詔詭使，六曰挾知而問，七曰倒言反事。此七者，主之所用也。

    The seven techniques are as follows: First: survey and compare all the various views on a matter; second: make punishments inevitable and majestic authority clear; third: make rewards reliable and make people use their abilities to the full; four: listen to proposals one by one, and hold the subordinates responsible [for proposals]; five: issue confusing edicts and make wily dispositions; six: keep your knowledge to yourself and ask for advice; seven: communicate words from one person to another and to say the opposite of what you mean. These seven are what the ruler should use. (*Han Feizi* 30.0.0; Chen 2000: 560)

One can divide these seven techniques into two groups (cf. Pines, Chap. 4, Sect. 3.2, this volume). The first deals with a variety of bureaucratic devices aimed at monitoring the officials' performance. These aspects of *shu* fit other definitions of this term in *Han Feizi*, such as "Technique is bestowing office on the basis of concrete responsibilities, demanding performance on the basis of titles, wielding the levers of life and death, and examining the abilities of the ministers" 術者，因任而授官，循名而責實，操殺生之柄，課群臣之能者也 (*Han Feizi* 43.1; Chen 2000: 957 ["Ding fa"]). These means (many of which apparently derive from Shen Buhai; see Yu Zhong, Chap. 2, this volume) belong to one of the most important aspects of Han Fei's legacy—establishing transparent and impartial norms of monitoring bureaucracy, of assigning tasks to the officials, and of maintaining performance control. Their lasting impact is undeniable (see, e.g., Creel 1974). Many of Han Fei's techniques (which are not uniformly identified as *shu*) retain their relevance well into present.

The above bureaucratic techniques can be considered a publicly known or "sunshine" aspects of the art of rule, *yang shu* 陽術 (Gong 2020: 492). But as sun cannot shine on every corner, the sunshine-line *shu* is not sufficient in running a large state. They must be complemented by the "shadowy techniques" *yin shu* 陰術 (Gong 2020: 492). These can be read as dark arts that are meant to eliminate the stubbornly

---

[32] See, for example, Guo 1982: 353–64; Mou 2005: 134–39; Wang 1994: 172–78; Zhang 1999: 124–27.

dark corners, that is, to control the powerful ministers (Wang 2023). *Han Feizi* openly contrasts them with the transparent *fa* (laws):

術者，藏之於胸中，以偶眾端而潛禦群臣者也。故法莫如顯，而術不欲見。

As for techniques of rule, they are hidden in the chest. It is that through which you match up all the various ends and from your secret place steer the ministers. Therefore, laws are best when they are clear, whereas techniques should not be seen. (*Han Feizi* 38.16; Chen 2000: 922–923 ["Nan san" 難三])

Techniques five to seven from the list presented above belong to these clandestine means of controlling the ministers. Their moral problematique (and the hidden reasons for their promulgation) have been discussed by Song (Chap. 9, Sect. 3.4, this volume). I want to offer an additional angle to that discussion. Let us analyze these techniques, which may appear to be the darkest and the blackest strategies HFZ offered.

The first of these (technique # 5), is called "issue confusing edicts and make wily dispositions" 疑詔詭使. It is about creating an atmosphere where the people whom the "political artist" wishes to scare straight are fearful of what he or she knows and will do, although he or she doesn't really know anything concrete and has no action plan. In a story HFZ told to illustrate this point (*Han Feizi* 30.5.1; Chen 2000: 606), the county magistrate called on a manager of a market, stood with him in public for a while, but didn't really say much or give any order. But other people were convinced that the magistrate did, and stopped trusting the manager. As a result, they wouldn't dare to conspire with him anymore. This indeed looks dark, but this is a strategy that, for example, even the police in today's liberal democratic states can use. They would detain someone from a criminal gang, and quickly let him go without really interrogating him. But other gang members suspect that he must have been a "rat" and stop trusting him. This may lead to further factions and infights, even the demise of the gang.

The second "dark art" (technique #6) is called "keep your knowledge to yourself and ask advice" 挾知而問. The "artist" of the strategy does have some particular fact, and he or she uses it to discover dishonest people or to create an atmosphere where other people think that the "artist" knows everything and thus stops covering up facts in general. In one story (*Han Feizi* 30.6.1; Chen 2000: 609), a ruler pretended to lose a fingernail and asked others to search for it. Many of them gave their own to the ruler, revealing their untrustworthiness.

The final "dark" strategy is called "communicate words from one person to another and to say the opposite of what you mean" 倒言反事. In a story, Zichan, the wise prime minister of Zheng, separated two litigants, so that they couldn't talk to each other. He then told what one person said to the other, so as to discover the truth (*Han Feizi* 30.7.5; Chen 2000: 613). Han Fei didn't give all the details, but anyone with any knowledge of police interrogation can immediately see that this is a strategy the police are still using, sometimes also claiming one party to have said something that party didn't really say. Although it didn't happen in the above story from

Han Feizi, the second half of the strategy is precisely about "saying or doing the opposite."[33]

Now that we understand the three "blackest" strategies, we can again see that they can be understood as strategies that are broadly useful in political matters, and are not merely for some evil rulers.

It is also interesting to note that at some places of the *Guanzi*, it is stated that the way of the ruler should be secretive (*zhou mi* 周密) (*Guanzi* 2004: 11:223 ["Zhou he" 宙合], 16:293 ["Fa fa" 法法]). Xunzi criticized this position, and insisted that the way of the ruler should be manifested and open (*ming* 明 and *xuan* 宣) (*Xunzi* 1992: 18: 321–22 ["Zheng lun" 正論] and 21: 409–10 ["Jie bi" 解蔽]), thus offering role models to the people and attracting the morally exemplary people. For Han Fei, *fa* and some *shu* should be open and manifested, but some other *shu* need to be secretive. It is an interesting synthesis of *Guanzi*, which is sometimes categorized as a Legalist text (Sato, Chap. 5, this volume) and *Xunzi* (the Confucian thinker and the alleged teacher of Han Fei).

6   HFZ's Realpolitik Without Nationalism and Ideology[34]

HFZ lived in the so-called Warring States period, and how to deal with interstate relations was an important issue. These relations between the competing states were very similar to what we call international relations today. Therefore, Han Fei can also be considered an IR (international relations) theorist. Some of his discussions are contingent on historical circumstances of his times, such as his arguments about why the powerful Qin should—or should not—conquer and annex his home state Han, the weakest among the seven strong states (Pines, Chap. 4, Sect. 1, this volume), but some, especially those in the "Five Vermin" chapter (49), can be generalized as theoretical analysis of international relations.

According to HFZ, in his times,

皆曰：“外事，大可以王，小可以安。”

> Everyone claims, "In foreign affairs, at best, you will become the true King [i.e., the unifier of All under Heaven]; at least, you can ensure security." (*Han Feizi* 49.11; Chen 2000: 1114)

The foreign affairs he discussed in this part were about the two grand strategies of his times, the (anti-Qin) Vertical Alliance and the (pro-Qin) Horizontal Alliance. But what he offered is actually a general criticism of relying on inter-state alliances as a strategy of self-preservation and even expansion, because what he analyzed is

---

[33] The stories in this chapter are sometimes not very detailed, and why they are put under this or that strategy can be debated. Whether and why there are mis-categorizations are important issues I cannot go into here.

[34] This section is partly based on Bai 2021b. For a general discussion of the relation between Legalism and IR theories, especially offensive realism, see Lo 2015.

an alliance between a stronger state and a weaker state, without referring to the particularities of the states during his times.

According to those who promote strategic alliances, the stronger one might wish to save the weaker one in order to preserve the balance of power and itself. However, HFZ argued that this action couldn't guarantee the preservation of the smaller state(s) (and the preservation of the world order through maintaining the balance of power), and what is guaranteed is the harm the stronger state would have to endure by going to war with another strong state. To make the matter worse, even if the stronger state saved the weaker one (s), the latter may not come to the former's rescue in the next wave of wars, the expectation of which is a reason of the stronger one's attempt to save the weaker ones.

In such an alliance, the reason for the smaller state to form an alliance with a greater power is the hope for the stronger one to rescue it when being attacked by other strong states. But before it can get any real protection, the smaller state has to give up some national interests (land, or in the contemporary setting, for example, the right to use a harbor as a military base) to the greater power. As a result, what is guaranteed is the harm the small state has to endure, but the protection is not guaranteed.

In both cases, the underlying premise is that states operate only with the principle of realpolitik, and are, like individual persons, driven purely by the calculation of national interests. Promises, treaties, and alliances can be readily broken whenever it is not convenient to keep them. What both sides of an alliance are doing is to give up the present interest in the hope of future rewards, but the fact that international relations are determined by expediency means that the hope is built on quick sand.

To be clear, in the text, HFZ seems to say that to both sides of the alliance, to give up present interests for future gains will necessarily lead to the destruction of the states involved. This may be merely rhetorical because one failed calculation doesn't necessarily lead to the downfall of a state. However, if a state is obsessed with using diplomacy to save itself, after playing this "game" repeatedly, this state is indeed doomed. For although it is not certain that the future reward be not obtained, the odds are against this state. Just like gambling, because the odds favor the house, the gambler will eventually lose.

But in such gambles, the stronger state and the weaker one are not on an equal footing. Han Fei quoted a proverb, "he who has a lot of money will be a good merchant" 多錢善賈 (*Han Feizi* 49.11; Chen 2000: 1115). He then referred to a few historical cases in which smaller states were annihilated after only one failed gamble, while a strong state such as Qin was apparently doing fine despite periodical setbacks. Those who defend the usefulness of international strategies could point to this fact and argue that the apparent failures of other states are due to the ill use of these strategies, and they could even argue that the success of Qin is due to its smart use of these strategies. For Han Fei, the reason for the different fates is clear. In the case of business, one who has a lot of money can withstand the loss of one or even a few failed business adventures easily, while the poor ones can't and may be totally destroyed in one failed business adventure. In the case of international politics, although eventually and statistically, alliance-based gambles will make everyone involved lose in the end, yet the strongest state will survive after all weaker states lose out. In fact, the strongest state would be better off if it didn't adopt alliance-based strategies at all. In particular, the success of the state of Qin was not because of the alliance strategies, but in spite of them. So, although it is not the best possible strategy for the stronger state, there is a chance for it to win, or to appear to win, in the end. But the smaller state is indeed doomed to lose in the most wretched manner.

If the obsession with international strategies is such a useless and even dangerous distraction, why were there so many international strategists, whom Han Fei considered one of the five vermin, in his times? For Han Fei, the answer is simple. For they can satisfy their interests either directly (monetary or other rewards, revenge on personal grievances, and so on) or by promoting the interests of their factions or patrons. They can do so because the ruler fails to see the futility and danger of their strategies and to punish them for the poor results from them. A proper regime of reward and punishment, then, can eliminate these "swindlers."[35]

Within a state, the ruler can use the wealth and violence of the nation to guarantee the trust among individual subjects, but there is no world leader who can do this in the relations among individual states. These states, then, have to rely on their own strength for security and dominance. According to HFZ, the expansion of a strong state relies solely on its power, and the self-preservation of a small state relies solely on domestic order, which is the precondition of self-empowerment. Both power and order come from "internal governance," and not from external (international) policies, however smart. The goal of governance is to improve the strength of the state, which comes from its economic and military might. The state institutions should be so designed that they reward those who contribute to the state's strength, and punish those who don't, making individual interests and the interests of the state in line with each other. In the case of the small state, its ruler should put aside the plans to join an alliance, and focus instead on improving internal strength through the above policies. In the case of war, he should "make the people risk their lives to strengthen the defense of the walls" 致其民死以堅其城守 (*Han Feizi* 49.11; Chen 2000: 1115). As a result, the loss the aggressor has to endure by attacking this small state is great, and the gain is relatively little. Still, a strong state can conquer the small state before it can become completely impregnable: it is just that the former needs to pay a high price, which it may be able to afford. In the Warring States period, or in a state of war of all against all, the time of peaceful development is short, and it is unrealistic for a small state to become so strong as to be impregnable over such a short period of peace and development. According to Han Fei, however, the small state could survive as long as it is able to defend itself against a powerful enemy for a little while, which is a more realistic goal than becoming totally impregnable in a short period of time. For the aggressor, though strong, doesn't dare to wear itself out

---

[35] It should be noted that during Han Fei's times, many ministers were supported—and even at times openly employed—by foreign powers, which added a thick flavor of treachery to their advice. Nowadays there are still lobbyists, foreign agents, and other shadowy figures who promote, even if less overtly, interests of foreign entities.

against such a strong defense over a long period of time: this would invite the attacks on itself by other strong states.

We can easily see the applicability of Han Fei's ideas in our current (2023) world. Take the Ukrainian example. For decades after gaining its independence, the country fluctuated between pro-Russia and pro-EU course (the current version of a "Vertical" and "Horizontal" alliances). These fluctuations weakened the country internally and made it appear to be an easy prey for Russia. Should we think of Han Fei's strategy, Ukraine would never give up its nuclear weapons (which the Ukrainians did in 1994 in exchange for the good-for-nothing assurances of its territorial integrity, the so-called Budapest Memorandum). As such it would be all but impregnable. This gloomy recommendation runs against our hopes for nuclear nonproliferation, but one must work hard to disapprove its clear advantages. Han Fei's realism seems more convincing.[36]

Going back to "making people risk their life to strengthen the defense." It may sound cold-blooded, but it is interesting to note that Han Fei didn't consider resorting to patriotism and other "isms" to increase the people's commitment. Although it is apparently "cheaper" if a state could brainwash its people with these "isms" and make people risk their lives for free, Han Fei refuses to consider this and prefers to rely on the proven means of rewards and punishments. The question, then, is why didn't Han Fei consider a "patriotic" alternative? It is really interesting that despite the resemblances between Warring States China and early modern Europe, nationalism never emerged in the former, and even a negative portrait of the enemy, an apparently convenient tool of war, only emerged toward the very late period of the Warring States.[37] This difference itself is rather striking and worth exploring. As a normative theorist, the question I want to ask is, if the idea of nationalism were available to Han Fei, what would he say about it? It is indeed cheaper than paying the brave soldiers, but as we have seen in his account of human nature, people who are motivated by things other than rewards and punishments are potential disruptors of the state order. For this order is maintained through institutions the effectiveness of which is based on rewards and punishments. Indeed, precisely because "isms" are cheap, everyone can use them to challenge the existent authority. But only a sovereign of the state can use the treasury and the state machine of violence to reward and punish people. Tools such as nationalism, then, are dangerous, and using them is like playing with fire.

---

[36] Plato in the *Republic* and the *Mencius* also discussed the issue of how to defend a small state. It is an interesting project of comparing all three accounts with one another, and such comparisons can help us to see the merits and problems with Han Fei's account. See Bai 2021b for further discussions.

[37] It was Yuri Pines who first brought this issue to my attention in a talk he gave at Fudan University. See also Pines forthcoming.

7   HFZ's Philosophy: Its Problems, and the Historical and Philosophical Significance

I have been trying to defend the soundness and the relevance of Han Fei's philosophy against a comparative background, among schools within the realm of Chinese philosophy, between Chinese and Western philosophy, and between the ancients and moderns. I mentioned some problems with his philosophy earlier in this chapter, and let me briefly list a few general issues in this concluding section.

The first set of problems with Han Fei's political philosophy is about the limits and inadequacy of rewards and punishments, on which his political construction is based. Pushed to the extreme, these two handles will lose their force. At one end, how about an over-achiever who is now only below the ruler? In Chinese history, this person was often persecuted with trumped-up or made-up charges or simply "disappeared," but this would violate and disrupt HFZ's meritocracy. Symmetrically, at the other end, what about a person who is already under the harshest penalty, but still needs to be punished further? As was said in *Laozi* 74, "could you scare people straight with death if they are not afraid to die anymore?" 民不畏死，奈何以死懼之.

Second, rewards and punishments may not be effective, and may even be counterproductive, according to the motivation crowding theory.[38] That is, external and material rewards and punishments may "crowd out" internal motives to follow rules and customs. For example, after a fine is imposed on the parents who are late to pick up their kids in a kindergarten, more parents are late for the pick-up. For before the fine is imposed, a parent may feel guilty for being late. But with the fine, it is just a paid service.[39]

Third, rewards and punishments lack immediacy sometimes, losing their motivating power. This is perhaps why it is so difficult for people not to eat unhealthy food because the bad effect is not immediately present. In the case of the ruler, the delay is even worse, for his mismanagements will be punished by the Dao, but it may only happen after the death of the ruler. The ruler can always comfort himself by thinking "after me, the flood!"

In general, the premise of Han Fei's whole political construction is that human beings are rational. Many economists believe in the idea of the (rational) economic man, and Han Fei believed in the (rational) political man. Both are doomed to fail because human beings are not always rational (as plenty of historical anecdotes scattered in *Han Feizi* itself amply exemplify). In most cases and for most people, we follow what is "hot-wired" in us, our animalistic and emotional responses, or our moral habits as a result of Confucian or Aristotelian moral cultivations. "Cold" rationality is only used in some situations by some people.

---

[38] See, for example, Titmuss 1970; Frey 1997; Gneezy and Rustichini 2000; Gneezy et al. 2011.

[39] An obvious response is to increase the fine. A key argument of Han Fei against the Confucian appeal to virtue is that rewards and punishments are cost-effective. But whether this argument still holds in this case, especially when the fine is increased so much, is highly debatable. On a more detailed discussion of Han Fei's defense of heavy punishments, see Bai 2022.

Therefore, morality can be profitable, sometimes more so than profit-driven rational calculations. As Confucius said,

道之以政，齊之以刑，民免而無恥；道之以德，齊之以禮，有恥且格。

Guide them by edicts, keep them in line with punishments, and the masses will be saved [from getting into trouble] but will have no sense of shame. Guide them by virtue, keep them in line with rites, and they will have a sense of shame and will obey willingly. (*Analects* 2.3)

Morality may even be more needed for the elite class. Indeed, if we followed HFZ's logic through, he should be the first one to be executed in his ideal state. For he was a patriot who really wanted to save his home state. That is, he was driven by something other than self-interest, which makes him a potential disruptor of the state order that is rooted in rewards and punishments. If he was a true Han Feizian, he could find a most profitable position anywhere, probably in the state of Qin, rather than writing "Lonely indignation" (Chapter 11, "Gu fen" 孤憤) and "Difficulty in persuasion" (Chapter 12, "Shui nan" 說難). Lonely indignation seems to be what he deserves, thanks to his own philosophy.

As we have seen, Han Fei has really intuitive and sound arguments for the absolute authority of the ruler. To talk about the legitimacy of the ruler would lead to a path of disorder. But the ruler will be left completely unchecked, other than by his rationality, the effect of which, I just argued a few paragraphs back, can be limited when the punishment doesn't come immediately. To protect this absolute authority, Han Fei's ideal regime has to run perfectly, with little tolerance of errors and free experiments on the local level. But if he were truly a realist, he should know that the society he faced with is extremely complex, meaning that to create our way out is often inevitable. But how do we reconcile stability with flexibility? It is a question Han Fei didn't consider, but it is an important question in politics and political theory. Indeed, it can be argued that the Qin empire collapsed due to the conflict between the rigidity of laws and the complexity on the ground. If Sima Qian's 司馬遷 account can be trusted, the popular rebellion that eventually led to the downfall of the Qin empire got started when the conscripts thought, according to the Qin legal codes, that they would face certain death due to their expected delay to get to some military post, although the delay was caused by unexpected heavy rain (*Shiji* 48: 1950).

A powerful criticism by Han Fei of the Confucians is that they didn't understand the change of historical circumstances, and did not adapt their policies accordingly. In retrospect, this very accusation could be—and was—launched against the *fa* thinkers in general, including of course Han Fei. Indeed, the abandonment of ruler-specific titles and the adoption of a faceless "number" system to name the emperors, "The First Emperor," "The Second Emperor," in the Qin Dynasty are signs of the desire to "freeze" history. More specifically, Qin, a "state organized for war" (Lewis 2007), failed to adapt itself to the new post-Warring States situation. Its ongoing expansion northward and southward, megalomaniac construction projects, suppression of private learning, and unbearable costs of maintaining tight bureaucratic control over hugely expansive realm—all backfired (see, e.g., Shelach 2014). The Han thinker, Jia Yi 賈誼 (ca. 200–168 BCE) pointed out that the Qin's problem was not adapting to new circumstances (*Shiji* 1997: 6: 283). This verdict was widely accepted thereafter. A theoretical problem here is: is adaptation possible within Han Fei'z own political philosophy? He said, "a man who cannot even fill up his belly with the coarsest grain does not plan on having fine meat" 糟糠不飽不務梁肉 (*Han Feizi* 49.9; Chen 2000: 1109), that is, in the time of urgency, we don't plan for the "luxurious" world of abundance and prosperity. He even claimed that the Confucian ideal world, a world of peace, prosperity, and loving relations between fathers and sons, and between rules and subjects, can only be realized through his means (*Han Feizi* 14.3; Chen 2000: 287). But since we never plan for it, how can we know when it comes, and when we can stop doing what we have done through various urgencies? After the reality prompted the abandonment of extra-effective model of centralized control associated with Han Fei and his *fa* predecessors, a search for hybrid models under the guise of Confucian (but in reality, "Confucian-Legalist"; Zhao 2015) state would become inevitable.

This search remains somewhat relative even in the "New China." As noted at the beginning of this chapter, Mao Zedong compared himself with the First Emperor and praised the Legalists, although he understood Legalism very differently from what I presented here. Actually, Mao's successor, Deng Xiaoping, may have been a far better Legalist than Mao was. While Mao was a true revolutionary who was not happy with the bureaucracy he himself helped to build and wished to destroy it through the Cultural Revolution, Deng rebuilt the bureaucracy and resumed the use of college entrance exam—a clear and verifiable measure—to select talents. In the Mao era, a famous slogan is "we'd rather have the Socialist grass than the Capitalist seedlings" 寧要社會主義的草不要資本主義的苗, while one of Deng's famous slogans is "a cat is a good cat if it can catch rats, no matter it is a white or a black cat" 不管黑貓白貓抓到耗子的就是好貓. If we read HFZ carefully, we should see immediately who is the Legalist here.

Throughout this chapter, I have also shown comparisons and contrasts between HFZ's ideas and ideas in Western political theories. Therefore, to examine HFZ's ideas can also help us to understand Western political ideas better, and to have a richer ground on which we build an ideal political theory. In particular, HFZ was trying to build a kind of "skeleton regime" or "a basic good state," a state with all the basic necessities, but without luxuries and complicated morals. Even if we wish to have a more complicated society with Confucian morality or contemporary Western liberal values (justice, dignity, etc.), we still need to have a functioning polity that can bring about minimal peace and prosperity. Maybe in the recent decades (if not longer), we political theorists (especially Western thinkers and those who emulate them) have focused too much on the ideal theory, "a theory of justice" and such, which is really a luxury of developed Western liberal democracies, and is thus completely inadequate to deal with other regimes, states, and peoples who are under duress and with urgent issues to address. After the disgraceful and horrible failures in promoting democracy in Iraq, Afghanistan, and many other countries, maybe we should pay more attention to HFZ and think about how to build a *basically or minimally good* state, a state that is orderly, peaceful, and prosperous, rather than an ideal state. Only after the urgent issues are addressed, can we begin to think about luxuries such as justice as fairness or human dignity.

Acknowledgments This research is supported by China's National Social Sciences Fund (major project, "Investigations of the Contemporary Reconstruction of the Conceptual Systems of Traditional Chinese Political Philosophy," 23&ZD235).

References

Augustine (Saint) (354–430). 1993. *On Free Choice of the Will*. Trans. Thomas Williams. Indianapolis, IN: Hackett.

Austin, John (1790–1859). 1995. *The Province of Jurisprudence Determined*, ed. Wilfrid E. Rumble. Cambridge, UK: Cambridge University Press.

Bai, Tongdong 白彤東. 2019. *Against Political Equality: The Confucian Case*. Princeton, NJ: Princeton University Press.

———. 2020a. Han Fei Zi's Account of the Transition from Antiquity to 'Modernity' 韓非子對古今之變的論說. *Fudan Journal* (Social Sciences Edition) 復旦學報(社會科學版) 5: 47–56.

———. 2020b. Han Fei Zi's Critique of Confucianism: A Reconstruction 韓非子對儒家批評之重構. *History of Chinese Philosophy* 中國哲學史 6: 48–55.

———. 2021a. Han Feizi on Human Nature 韓非人性說探微. *Philosophical Researches* 哲學研究 4: 56–66.

———. 2021b. How to Defend a Small State? – Han Fei Zi, Plato, and Mencius. *Dao: A Journal of Comparative Philosophy* 20 (2): 231–244. https://doi.org/10.1007/s11712-021-09774-z.

———. 2022. Heavy Punishment and Light Reward—On Han Fei Zi's Unequal Reliance on the Two Handles 重罰輕賞——韓非子對二柄的不對等使用詮釋. *Modern Philosophy* 現代哲學 6: 52–62.

Barbieri-Low, Anthony J. 2022. *The Many Lives of the First Emperor of China*. Seattle: University of Washington Press.

Bell, Daniel. 2006. *Beyond Liberal Democracy*. Princeton, NJ: Princeton University Press.

———. 2015. *The China Model*. Princeton, NJ: Princeton University Press.

Bell, Daniel and Li, Chenyang. 2013. *The East Asian Challenge for Democracy: Political Meritocracy in Comparative Perspective*. Cambridge, UK: Cambridge University Press.

Bodde, Derek. 1948. Chinese Ideas in the West. Originally prepared for the Committee on Asiatic Studies in American Education, available on: http://afe.easia.columbia.edu/chinawh/web/s10/ideas.pdf.

Chan, Joseph. 2000. Legitimacy, Unanimity, and Perfectionism. *Philosophy & Public Affairs* 29 (1): 5–42.

——— 2013. Political Meritocracy and Meritorious Rule—A Confucian Perspective. In Bell and Li 2013, 55–87.

Charbit, Yves. 2002. The Political Failure of an Economic Theory: Physiocracy. Trans. Arundhati Virmani. *Population* 57 (6): 855–884.

Chen, Qiyou 陳奇猷. 2000. *Han Feizi, with New Collations and Commentary* 韓非子新校注. Shanghai: Shanghai Guji chubanshe. (A very useful collected commentaries on the Han Feizi.)

Clarke, John J. 1997. *Oriental Enlightenment: The Encounter Between Asian and Western Thought*. New York, NY.: Routledge.

Creel, Herrlee G. 1970. *What is Taoism?* Chicago, IL: The University of Chicago Press.

———. 1974. *Shen Pu-Hai: A Chinese Political Philosopher of the Fourth Century B. C.* Chicago, IL: The University of Chicago Press. (These three books by Creel offer good introduction to early Chinese thoughts, "Legalism" in particular.).

De Waal, Frans. 2006. *Primates and Philosophers: How Morality Evolved*. Princeton, NJ: Princeton University Press.

Frey, Bruno. 1997. *Not Just for the Money*. Cheltenham: Edward Elgar Publishing.

Fukuyama, Francis. 2011. *The Origins of Political Order: From Prehuman Times to the French Revolution*. New York: Farrar, Straus, and Giroux.

Gneezy, Uri, and Aldo Rustichini. 2000. A Fine Is a Price. *Journal of Legal Studies* 29 (1): 1–18.

Gneezy, Uri, Stephan Meier, and Pedro Rey-Biel. 2011. When and Why Incentives (Don't) Work to Modify Behavior. *Journal of Economic Perspectives* 25 (4): 191–210.

Goldin, Paul. 2011. Persistent Misconceptions about Chinese 'Legalism'. *Journal of Chinese Philosophy* 38 (1): 88–104. (This article is part of a special issue on the Han Feizi, and readers can check out other articles in this issue.).

Gong, Liuzhu 龔留柱. 2020. On Chao Cuo and the 'New Legalists' at the Beginning of Early Han 論晁錯及漢初"新法家". In Song 2020, 463–500.

Graham, A.C. 1989. *Disputers of the Tao: Philosophical Argument in Ancient China*. Chicago/La Salle: Open Court. (Another classic on early Chinese philosophy.).

Guanzi jiaozhu 管子校注 (Guanzi, collated and annotated). 2004. Ed. Li, Xiangfeng 黎翔鳳. Beijing: Zhonghua shuju.

Guo, Moruo 郭沫若. 1982. *Ten Criticisms* 十批判書. Beijing: Renmin Press.

Hankins, James. 2019. *Virtue Politics: Soulcraft and Statecraft in Renaissance Italy*. Cambridge, MA: The Belknap Press of Harvard University Press.

Harris, Eirik Lang. 2011. Is the Law in the Way? On the Source of Han Fei's Laws. *Journal of Chinese Philosophy* 38 (1): 73–87.

Hart, H. L. A. 2012. *The Concept of Law* (3rd edition). Oxford, UK: Oxford University Press.

Hobbes, Thomas (1588–1679). 1985. *Leviathan*. Ed. C. B. MacPherson. London: Penguin Books.

Ivanhoe, Philip J. 2011. Han Fei Zi and Moral Self-Cultivation. *Journal of Chinese Philosophy* 38 (1): 31–45.

Korolkov, Maxim. 2021. Between Command and Market: Credit, Labour, and Accounting in the Qin Empire (221–207 BCE). In *Between Command and Market: Economic Thought and Practice in Early China*, ed. Elisa Sabattini and Christian Schwermann, 162–243. Leiden: Brill.

Lau, Dim-Cheuk 劉殿爵. trans. 1963. *Tao Te Ching*. Baltimore, MD: Penguin Books.

——— 2000. *Confucius: the Analects* (first paperback edition). Hong Kong: The Chinese University Press.

——— 2003. *Mencius*, revised and bilingual edition. Hong Kong: The Chinese University Press.

Lewis, Mark E. 1999. Warring States: Political History. In *The Cambridge History of Ancient China: From the Origins of Civilization to 221 B.C*, ed. Michael Loewe and Edward L. Shaughnessy, 587–650. Cambridge: Cambridge University Press.

———. 2007. *The Early Chinese Empires: Qin and Han*. Cambridge, MA: The Belknap Press of Harvard University Press.

Liu, Zehua 劉澤華. 2012. "Closely Following, Disorientation, and the Emergence of the Sense of Autonomy during the Cultural Revolution" "文革"中的緊跟、錯位與自主意識的萌生. *Journal of Historical Science* 史學月刊 11: 97–101.

Lo, Ping-cheung. 2015. "Legalism and Offensive Realism in the Chinese Court Debate on Defending National Security 81 BCE." In: *Chinese Just War Ethics: Origin, Development, and Dissent*, ed. Ping-cheung Lo and Sumner B. Twiss, 249–280. London: Routledge, 2015

Lü, Simian 呂思勉. 2016. *Introduction to Pre-Qin Scholarship* 先秦學術概論. Nanjing: Yilin Press.

Martinich, Aloysius P. 2014. Political Theory and Linguistic Criteria in HAN Feizi's Philosophy. *Dao* 13: 379–393.

McCabe, Ina Baghdiantz. 2008. *Orientalism in Early Modern France: Eurasian Trade Exoticism and the Ancien Regime*. New York, NY: Berg.

Mill, John Stuart (1806–1873). 2001. *Utilitarianism* (2), ed. George Sher. Indianapolis, IN: Hackett.

Mou, Zongsan 牟宗三. 2005. *Nineteen Lectures on Chinese Philosophy* 中國哲學十九講. Shanghai: Shanghai guji chubanshe.

Mungello, Davie Emil. 2013. *The Great Encounter of China and the West, 1500–1800*. 4th ed. Lanham, MD: Rowman and Littlefield.

Neininger, Ulrich. 1983. Burying the Scholars Alive: On the Origin of a Confucian Martyrs' Legend. In *East Asian Civilizations: New Attempts at Understanding Traditions. 2 Nation and Mythology*, ed. Wolfram Eberhard, Krzysztof Galikowski, and Carl-Albrecht Seyschab, 121–137. München: Simon and Magiera.

Peerenboom, Randall. 2002. *China's Long March toward Rule of Law*. Cambridge: Cambridge University Press.

Pines, Yuri. 2005. Speeches and the Question of Authenticity in Ancient Chinese Historical Records. In *Historical Truth, Historical Criticism, and Ideology*, ed. Heiwig Schmidt-Glintzer et al., 197–226. Brill.

———. 2013. *Between Merit and Pedigree: Evolution of the Concept of 'Elevating the Worthy' in the Pre-Imperial China*. In Bell and Li, 2013, 161–202.

———. 2016. A 'Total War'? Rethinking Military Ideology in the Book of Lord Shang, *Journal of Chinese Military History* 5: 97–134.

———. 2020. 'To Die for the Sanctity of the Name': Name (*ming* 名) as Prime Mover of Political Action in Early China. In *Keywords in Chinese Culture: Thought and Literature*, ed. Li Wai-yee and Yuri Pines, 169–215. Hong Kong: The Chinese University of Hong Kong Press.

———. 2021. Agriculturalism and Beyond: Economic Thought and of *The Book of Lord Shang*. In *Between Command and Market: Economic Thought and Practice in Early China*, ed. Elisa Levi Sabattini and Christian Schwermann, 78–113. Leiden: Brill.

———. 2023. Another Life of the First Emperor. *Journal of the American Oriental Society* 143 (3): 687–695.

——— forthcoming. Serving All-under-Heaven: Cosmopolitan Intellectuals of the Warring States Period. *Modern Asian Studies*.

Quesnay, Francois (1694–1774). 2004. *The Economic Table*. Honolulu, HI.: University Press of the Pacific.

Rawls, John. 1971. *A Theory of Justice*. Cambridge, MA: Harvard University Press.

Raz, Joseph. 1979. *The Authority of Law*. Oxford, UK: Oxford University Press.

Roetz, Heiner. 2005. Normativity and History in Warring States Thought. *In: Heiwig Schmidt-Glintzer et al.* 2005: 79–91.

Rousseau, Jean-Jacques (1712–1778). 1964. *The First and Second Discourses*. Trans. Roger D. and Judith R. Masters. New York: St Martin's Press.

Sato, Masayuki. 2013. "Did Xunzi's Theory of Human Nature Provide the Foundation for the Political Thought of Han Fei?" In: *Dao Companion to the Philosophy of Han Fe,i* ed. Paul Goldin, 147–65. Berlin: Springer.

Schmidt-Glintzer, Helwig, et al., eds. 2005. *Historical Truth, Historical Criticism, and Ideology: Chinese Historiography and Historical Culture from a New Comparative Perspective*. Leiden and Boston: Brill.

Schneider, Henrique. 2014. Han Fei and Justice. *Cambridge Journal of China Studies* 9 (4): 20–37.

Schwartz, Benjamin. 1985. *The World of Thought in Ancient China*. Cambridge, MA: The Belknap Press of Harvard University Press. (Yet another classic on early Chinese thoughts. The Legalism section is very insightful.)

Shelach, Gideon. 2014. Collapse or Transformation? Anthropological and Archaeological Perspectives on the Fall of Qin. In *Birth of an Empire: The State of Qin revisited*, ed. Yuri Pines, Lothar von Falkenhausen, Gideon Shelach, and Robin D.S. Yates, 113–140. Berkeley: University of California Press.

Shiji 史記 (*Records of the Historian*). 1997. By Sima, Qian 司馬遷 (ca. 145–90 BCE) et al. Annotated by Zhang, Shoujie 張守節, Sima, Zhen 司馬貞, and Pei, Yin 裴駰. Beijing: Zhonghua shuju.

Song, Hongbing 宋洪兵 (ed.). 2020. *Legalist Theory and Its Historical Impact* 法家學說及其歷史影響. Shanghai: Shanghai Guji chubanshe. (A good collection on recent mainland Chinese scholarship on Legalism.)

Sterckx, Roel. 2015. Ideologies of the Peasant and Merchant in Warring States China. In *Ideology of Power and Power of Ideology in Early China*, ed. Yuri Pines, Paul R. Goldin, and Martin Kern, 211–248. Leiden: Brill.

Tian, Changwu 田昌五 and Zang, Zhifei 臧知非. 1996. *Zhou Qin shehui jiegou yanjiu* 周秦社會結構研究. Xian: Xibei daxue chubanshe.

Titmuss, R.M. 1970. *The Gift Relationship*. London: Allen and Unwin.

Unger, Roberto Mangabeira. 1976. *Law in Modern Society*. New York, NY: The Free Press.

Wang, Yuanhua 王元化. 1994. *Collection of Scholarly Commentaries at Qingyuan*清園論學集. Shanghai: Shanghai Guji chubanshe.

Wang, Renbo 王人博. 2003. A Minimalist Concept of the Rule of Law and a Modern Interpretation of Chinese Legalist Thoughts 一個最低限度地法治觀念——對中國法家思想的現代闡釋. *Legal Forum*法學論壇 1 (18): 13–26.

Wang, Zhongjiang 王中江. 2018. *Origin, Regime, and Order: From Laozi to Huang-Lao*根源、制度和秩序:从老子到黄老. Beijing: Renmin University Press.

Wang, Hongqiang 王宏强. 2023. *A Study of Han Fei Zi's Thought on the Way of Governing*韓非子治道思想研究. Beijing: Zhongguo Shehuikexue chubanshe.

Winston, Kenneth. 2005. The Internal Morality of Chinese Legalism. *Singapore Journal of Legal Studies* (December): 313–347. (A good piece on why the idea of law in Legalism is consistent with the rule of law.)

Xia, Yong夏勇. 1999. What is the Rule of Law 法治是什麼. *Social Sciences in China*中國社會科學 4: 117–143.

Xunzi jijie 荀子集解 (*Xunzi*, with collected glosses). 1992. Ed. Wang Xianqian 王先謙 (1842–1917), Shen Xiaohuan 沈嘯寰, and Wang Xingxian 王星賢. Beijing: Zhonghua shuju.

Yang, Kuan 楊寬. 1998. *History of the Warring States Period* 戰國史. Rev. ed. Shanghai: Shanghai Renmin chubanshe.

Zhang, Shilong 張世龍, 1988. On the First Emperor 'Burning the Books' but not 'Burying the Confucians Alive' 論秦始皇"焚書"未"坑儒". *Journal of China's Renmin University* 中國人民大學學報 3: 114–120.

Zhang, Zixia 張子俠, 1991. Detailed Analysis of 'Burning the Books and Burying Alive Confucians " 焚書坑儒" 辨析. *Journal of the Huaibei Coal Normal University*淮北煤師院學報 2: 41–48, 18.

Zhang, Nie 張涅. 1999. Rule of Law and Rule by *shu* in Pre-Qin China 先秦的法治主義和術治主義. *Zhejiang Social Sciences*浙江社會科學 5: 124–129.

Zhang, Qianfan 張千帆. 2006. The Inadequacy of the Concept of the Rule of Law 法治概念的不足. *Study and Exploration*學習與探索 6: 89–93.

Zhang, Jue 張覺. 2010. *Han Feizi with new Collation and Sub-glosses* 韓非子校疏. Shanghai: Shanghai guji chubanshe.

Zhao, Dingxin. 2015. *The Confucian-Legalist State: A New Theory of Chinese History*. New York, NY: Oxford University Press.

Index, cumulative

A

abdication, 113, 130, 287, 386, 444, 530

abilities, 41, 44, 59, 60, 63, 64, 72, 76, 77, 80, 90, 107, 116–121, 123, 125, 126, 151, 152, 174, 175, 187, 205, 277, 281, 285, 289, 290, 304, 308, 316, 319, 321, 324, 325, 328, 329, 336–338, 341, 343, 375, 376, 379, 380, 384–386, 399, 400, 412, 413, 417–419, 422, 424, 425, 427, 436, 439, 442, 452, 462, 492, 525, 530, 535, 540, 556, 564, 586, 602, 606, 609, 610, 614, 664

absolute war, 630

agriculture (*nong* 農), 1, 25, 30, 31, 36, 40–42, 44, 46, 47, 51, 52, 107, 120, 133, 153, 161, 184, 188, 190, 193–195, 204, 289, 301, 365, 392, 426, 453, 459, 462, 491, 493, 497, 507, 508, 533–535, 537, 556, 599, 605, 630, 631, 635, 656

  See also farming; tilling

agro-managerial state, 30

All-under-Heaven (*tianxia* 天下), 23, 28, 29, 39, 48, 51, 52, 70, 72–75, 77, 101, 113, 124, 125, 128, 130, 131, 151, 154, 156, 161, 173–176, 187, 191, 192, 284, 286, 287, 306, 307, 329, 352, 353, 366, 367, 376, 410, 413, 461, 462, 465, 466, 472, 478, 479, 523, 524, 528, 531, 534, 539, 554, 577, 580, 581, 584, 586–589, 619, 652, 666

allusions, 57, 336, 471

Analects, see Lunyu

anecdotes, 76–79, 100, 112, 114, 126, 134, 141, 225, 235, 287, 329–331, 356–359, 364, 370, 384, 423, 471, 478, 521, 527, 670

arbitrariness, 383, 387, 637, 639, 659, 660

Arendt, Hannah (1906–1975), 13, 616, 624, 627, 628, 635

argumentation, argumentativeness (*bian* 辯), 6, 8, 28, 99, 102, 105, 107, 112, 124, 125, 129, 154, 162, 167, 172, 173, 175, 411, 420–427, 466, 517, 548, 637

artisans, 11, 42, 46, 47, 187, 207, 211, 212, 217, 375, 376, 378, 383, 386, 389, 394, 399, 534, 655, 656

Austin, John (1790–1859), 659, 660, 662

authority, political, 118, 126, 175, 339, 344, 378, 381, 388, 555, 562, 563, 571

authoritarianism, 8, 124, 268, 271, 616, 634, 658

B

bai gong 百工, *see* artisans

Balazs, Étienne (1905–1963), 625, 628

Ban Gu 班固 (32–92), 3, 143, 461

banliang 半兩, "half-tael" coin, 195

benefit (profit) (*li* 利), 34–37, 39, 42–44, 88, 94, 111, 114, 115, 123, 127, 129, 132–134, 185–189, 191, 193, 214, 284, 286, 287, 289, 295, 297, 299–307, 309, 366, 434, 446, 462, 480, 526, 529, 536, 537, 605, 634

benevolence (*ren* 仁), 29, 32, 52, 111, 129, 175, 176, 284, 308, 310, 333, 359, 360, 362, 436–439, 441, 442, 447, 448, 454, 463, 464, 466, 468, 517, 522, 549, 553, 586, 587, 589, 601, 604, 619, 637

  See also humaneness

biblioclasm, *see* book burning

© The Editor(s) (if applicable) and The Author(s), under exclusive license to Springer Nature Switzerland AG 2024

Y. Pines (ed.), *Dao Companion to China's fa Tradition*, Dao Companions to Chinese Philosophy 19, https://doi.org/10.1007/978-3-031-53630-4

Printed in the USA
CPSIA information can be obtained
at www.ICGtesting.com
CBHW071402211124
17801CB00003B/166